HAWAII

11

10

ALASKA

TIME-LIFE BOOKS

# COMPLETE GUIDE TO GARDENING AND LANDSCAPING

TIME-LIFE BOOKS

# COMPLETE GUIDE TO GARDENING AND LANDSCAPING

by the Editors of the Time-Life
Gardener's Guide Series

PRENTICE
HALL
PRESS

NEW YORK • LONDON • TORONTO • SYDNEY • TOKYO • SINGAPORE

Time-Life Books Inc.
is a wholly owned subsidiary of
**THE TIME INC. BOOK COMPANY**

*President and Chief Executive Officer* Kelso F. Sutton
*President, Time Inc. Books Direct* Christopher T. Linen

## TIME-LIFE BOOKS INC.

*Managing Editor* Thomas H. Flaherty
*Director of Editorial Resources* Elise D. Ritter-Clough
*Director of Photography and Research* John Conrad Weiser
*Editorial Board* Dale M. Brown, Roberta Conlan, Laura Foreman, Lee Hassig, Jim Hicks, Blaine Marshall, Rita Thievon Mullin, Henry Woodhead
*Production Manager* Prudence G. Harris

*PUBLISHER* Joseph J. Ward
*Associate Publisher* Susan J. Maruyama

*Time-Life Books Complete Guide to Gardening and Landscaping* was produced by **ST. REMY PRESS**

*PUBLISHER* Kenneth Winchester
*PRESIDENT* Pierre Léveillé

*Senior Editor* Dianne Stine Thomas
*Editor* Marc Cassini
*Senior Art Director* Francine Lemieux
*Designer* Shirley Grynspan
*Contributing Research Editor* Naomi Fukuyama
*Contributing Editorial Assistants* Sari Berger, Jennifer Meltzer
*Index* Shirley J. Manley

*Administrator* Natalie Watanabe
*Production Manager* Michelle Turbide
*Coordinator* Dominique Gagné
*Systems Coordinator* Jean-Luc Roy
*Proofreader* Judy Yelon

## THE CONSULTANTS

**Maureen Heffernan,** a horticulturist at the American Horticultural Society, has worked for the New York Botanical Garden, Blooms of Bressingham in England and various other gardens and nurseries in North America and abroad.

**Dale Leggett** represents Jack Vincelli Inc., a garden-supply center specializing in turf and landscape maintenance and construction in the Montreal area since 1909.

**Rosalind Stubenberg,** consulting editor, served as senior editor at *Time-Life Books.*

 Prentice Hall Press
15 Columbus Circle
New York, New York 10023

Copyright © 1991 by Time-Life Books

All rights reserved,
including the right of reproduction
in whole or in part in any form.

PRENTICE HALL PRESS and
colophons are registered trademarks
of Simon & Schuster Inc.

LC No. 91-053108

ISBN 0-13-028614-1

Manufactured in the United States of America

10 9 8 7 6 5 4 3 2 1

First Edition

# CONTENTS

*Refer to the second page of each chapter
for a detailed Chapter Contents listing.*

# HOW TO USE THIS BOOK

**Time-Life Books Complete Guide to Gardening and Landscaping** is designed to give you all the information you are likely to need about gardening, no matter what size your garden is or how much experience you have. For easy use, the book is divided into ten chapters.

The first two chapters explain how to plan your yard and garden, and the techniques necessary for successful gardening. The subsequent eight chapters offer step-by-step information on the raising and enjoyment of various types of plants, from trees to annuals, from perennials to vegetables and—for indoor gardeners—houseplants. Each of these eight chapters concludes with an illustrated dictionary, in which you will find descriptions of selected species and varieties, the soil and climatic conditions they need, and—for plants that must survive winter in your garden—the zones in which they are most likely to thrive. Where plants are listed by botanical names, common names are cross-referenced. When shopping for a plant, refer to its botanical name to be sure that you get the plant you want.

It pays, both economically and in subtler satisfactions, to choose your plants with forethought, plant (or transplant) them with care and maintain them faithfully. To help you choose plants that will flourish in your garden, refer to the Zone Map *(inside front cover):* Identify your zone, then consult the dictionaries for the plants suited to where you live. The Frost-Date Map *(inside back cover)* indicates when annuals and vegetables can be safely planted, depending on where you live. In seven chapters, you'll also find a seasonal maintenance checklist; chapter 9 gives a schedule of planting dates for vegetables. Once the plants are safely in the ground, Troubleshooting Guides will help you diagnose and combat diseases and pests.

The plants covered in this book are enormously varied. They are adaptable enough for the amateur to plant and care for, and diverse enough for the hobbyist to experiment with. With proper planning and gardening techniques, these plants can boost the value of your home and add to your quality of life. The following pages show you how.

## INTRODUCTORY TEXT
Gives an informative overview of the subject plus tips and techniques for success with various types of plants and procedures.

## STEP-BY-STEP INSTRUCTIONS
Follow the numbered sequence. Depending on the result of each step, you may be directed to a later step or to another part of the book for supplementary information.

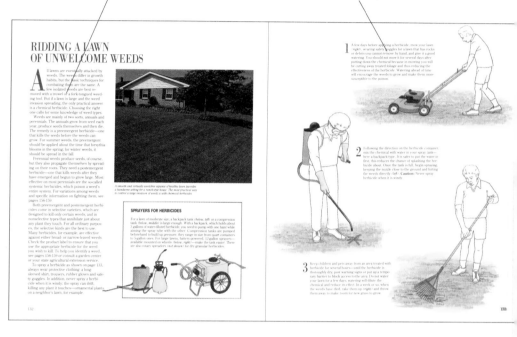

## SPECIAL FEATURES
Practical tips to make everyday gardening more effective, more fun and less work.

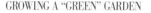

## CROSS-REFERENCES
Direct you to important relevant information elsewhere in the book.

# TROUBLESHOOTING GUIDES
Problem, cause and solution help identify pests, diseases and other problems. Organized for quick action.

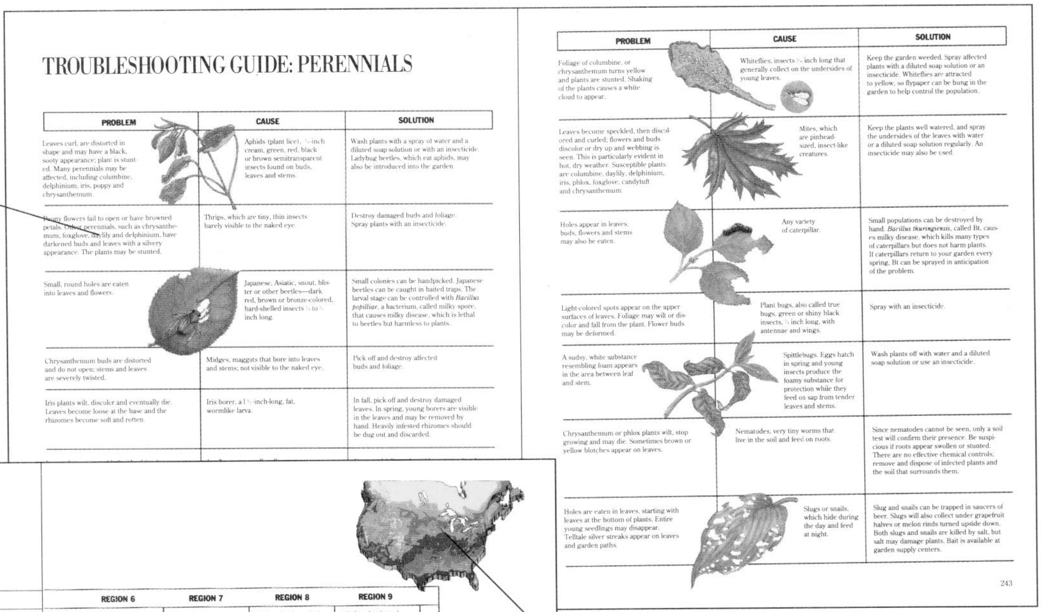

# MAINTENANCE CHECKLISTS
Month-by-month or season-by-season maintenance tasks for every category of plant.

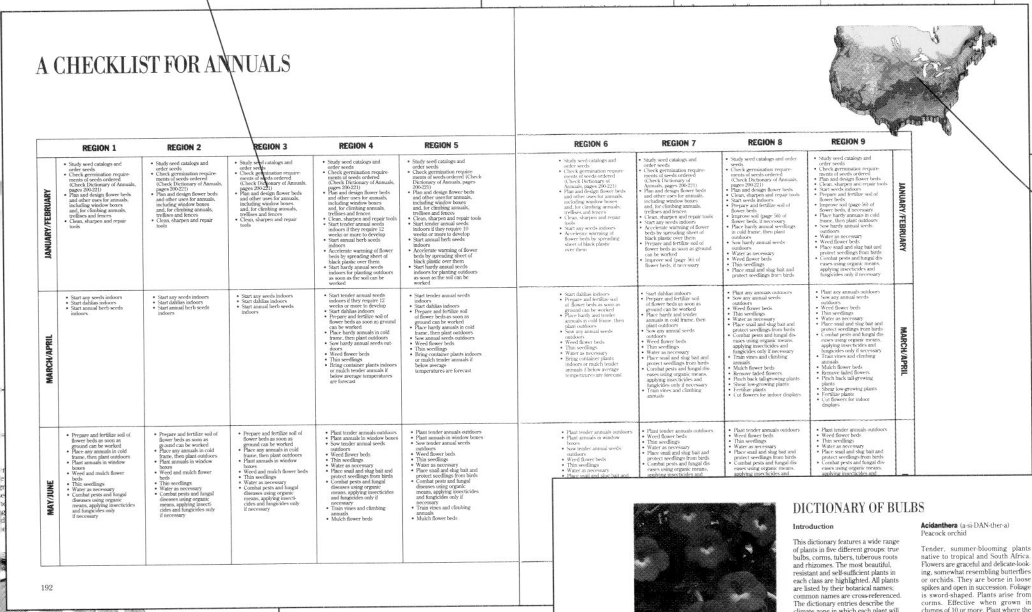

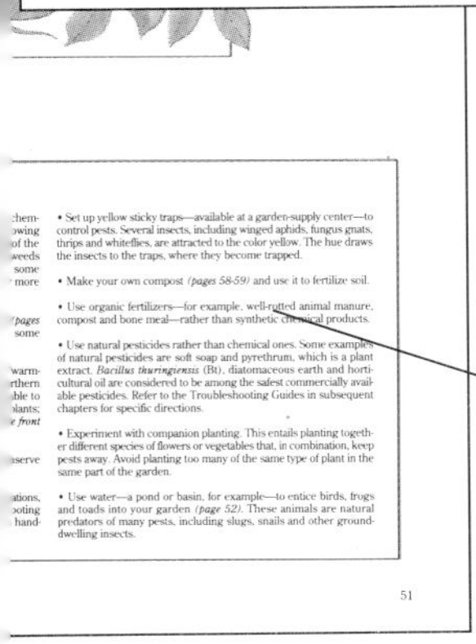

# ENVIRONMENT-FRIENDLY TIPS
Informative facts for organic gardeners.

# FULL-COLOR MAPS
Information essential to planting and plant care—North American zones and frost dates.

# DICTIONARY ENTRIES
Illustrated entries for grasses, trees, shrubs, ground covers, flowers, vegetables and houseplants include detailed descriptions and valuable information about growing conditions.

---

## TROUBLESHOOTING GUIDE: PERENNIALS

| PROBLEM | CAUSE | SOLUTION |
|---|---|---|
| Leaves curl, are distorted in shape and may have a black, sooty appearance; plant is stunted. Many perennials may be affected, including columbine, delphinium, iris, poppy and chrysanthemum. | Aphids (plant lice), ⅛-inch cream, green, red, black or brown semitransparent insects found on buds, leaves and stems. | Wash plants with a spray of water and a diluted soap solution or with an insecticide. Ladybug beetles, which eat aphids, may also be introduced into the garden. |
| Young flowers fail to open or have browned petals. Many perennials, such as chrysanthemum, foxglove, daylily and delphinium, have darkened buds and leaves with a silvery appearance. The plants may be stunted. | Thrips, which are tiny, thin insects barely visible to the naked eye. | Destroy damaged buds and foliage. Spray plants with an insecticide. |
| Small, round holes are eaten into leaves and flowers. | Japanese, Asiatic, snout, blister or other beetles—dark red, brown or bronze-colored, hard-shelled insects ¼ to ½ inch long. | Small colonies can be handpicked. Japanese beetles can be caught in baited traps. The larval stage can be controlled with *Bacillus popilliae*, a bacterium, called milky spore, that causes milky disease, which is lethal to beetles but harmless to plants. |
| Chrysanthemum buds are distorted and do not open; stems and leaves are severely twisted. | Midges, maggots that bore into leaves and foliage. | Pick off and destroy affected buds and foliage. |
| Iris plants wilt, discolor and eventually die. Leaves become loose at the base and the rhizomes become soft and rotten. | Iris borer, a 1½-inch-long, fat, wormlike larva. | In fall, pick off and destroy damaged leaves. In spring, young leaves are visible in the leaves and may be removed by hand. Heavily infested rhizomes should be dug out and discarded. |

| PROBLEM | CAUSE | SOLUTION |
|---|---|---|
| Foliage of columbine, or chrysanthemum turns yellow and plants are stunted. Shaking of the plants causes a white cloud to appear. | Whiteflies, insects ⅛ inch long that generally collect on the undersides of young leaves. | Keep the garden weeded. Spray affected plants with a diluted soap solution or an insecticide. Whiteflies are attracted to yellow, so flypaper can be hung in the garden to help control the population. |
| Leaves become speckled, then discolored and curled; flowers and buds discolor or dry up and wedding is seen. This is particularly evident in hot, dry weather. Susceptible plants are columbine, daylily, delphinium, iris, phlox, foxglove, candytuft and chrysanthemum. | Mites, which are pinhead sized, insect-like creatures. | Keep the plants well watered, and spray the undersides of the leaves with water or a diluted soap solution regularly. An insecticide may also be used. |
| Holes appear in leaves, buds, flowers and stems may also be eaten. | Any variety of caterpillar. | Small populations can be destroyed by hand. *Bacillus thuringiensis*, called Bt, causes milky disease, which kills many types of caterpillars but does not harm plants. If caterpillars return to your garden every spring, Bt can be sprayed in anticipation of the problem. |
| Light-colored spots appear on the upper surfaces of leaves. Foliage may wilt or discolor and fall from the plant. Flower buds may be deformed. | Plant bugs, also called true bugs, green or shiny black insects, ¼ inch long, with antennae and wings. | Spray with an insecticide. |
| A sudsy, white substance resembling foam appears in the area between leaf and stem. | Spittlebugs. Eggs hatch in spring and young insects produce the foamy substance for protection while they feed on top from tender leaves and stems. | Wash plants off with water and a diluted soap solution or use an insecticide. |
| Chrysanthemum or phlox plants wilt, stop growing and may die. Sometimes brown or yellow blotches appear on leaves. | Nematodes, very tiny worms that live in the soil and feed on roots. | Since nematodes cannot be seen, only a soil test will confirm their presence. Be suspicious if roots appear swollen or stunted. There are no effective chemical controls; remove and dispose of infected plants and the soil that surrounds them. |
| Holes are eaten in leaves, starting with leaves at the bottom of plants. Entire young seedlings may disappear. Telltale silver streaks appear on leaves and garden paths. | Slugs or snails, which hide during the day and feed at night. | Slug and snails can be trapped in saucers of beer. Slugs will also collect under grapefruit halves or melon rinds turned upside down. Both slugs and snails are killed by salt, but salt may damage plants. Bait is available at garden supply centers. |

243

---

## A CHECKLIST FOR ANNUALS

| | REGION 1 | REGION 2 | REGION 3 | REGION 4 | REGION 5 | REGION 6 | REGION 7 | REGION 8 | REGION 9 | |
|---|---|---|---|---|---|---|---|---|---|---|
| **JANUARY/FEBRUARY** | • Study seed catalogs and order seeds<br>• Check germination requirements of seeds ordered (Check Dictionary of Annuals, pages 196-221)<br>• Plan and design flower beds and other uses for annuals, including window boxes, trellises and fences<br>• Clean, sharpen and repair tools | • Study seed catalogs and order seeds<br>• Check germination requirements of seeds ordered (Check Dictionary of Annuals, pages 196-221)<br>• Plan and design flower beds and other uses for annuals, including window boxes, trellises and fences<br>• Clean, sharpen and repair tools | • Study seed catalogs and order seeds<br>• Check germination requirements of seeds ordered (Check Dictionary of Annuals, pages 196-221)<br>• Plan and design flower beds and other uses for annuals, including window boxes and, for climbing annuals, trellises and fences<br>• Clean, sharpen and repair tools | • Study seed catalogs and order seeds<br>• Check germination requirements of seeds ordered (Check Dictionary of Annuals, pages 196-221)<br>• Plan and design flower beds and other uses for annuals, including window boxes and, for climbing annuals, trellises and fences<br>• Start tender annual seeds indoors if they require 12 weeks or more to develop<br>• Start annual herb seeds indoors | • Study seed catalogs and order seeds<br>• Check germination requirements of seeds ordered (Check Dictionary of Annuals, pages 196-221)<br>• Plan and design flower beds and other uses for annuals, including window boxes and, for climbing annuals, trellises and fences<br>• Clean, sharpen and repair tools<br>• Start tender annual seeds indoors if they require 12 weeks or more to develop<br>• Start annual herb seeds indoors<br>• Accelerate warming of flower beds by spreading sheet of black plastic over them | • Study seed catalogs and order seeds<br>• Check germination requirements of seeds ordered (Check Dictionary of Annuals, pages 196-221)<br>• Plan and design flower beds and other uses for annuals, including window boxes and, for climbing annuals, trellises and fences<br>• Clean, sharpen and repair tools<br>• Start any seeds indoors<br>• Accelerate warming of flower beds by spreading sheet of black plastic over them | • Study seed catalogs and order seeds<br>• Check germination requirements of seeds ordered (Check Dictionary of Annuals, pages 196-221)<br>• Plan and design flower beds and other uses for annuals, including window boxes and, for climbing annuals, trellises and fences<br>• Clean, sharpen and repair tools<br>• Start any seeds indoors<br>• Accelerate warming of flower beds by spreading sheet of black plastic over them<br>• Prepare and fertilize soil of flower beds as soon as ground can be worked | • Study seed catalogs and order seeds<br>• Check germination requirements of seeds ordered (Check Dictionary of Annuals, pages 196-221)<br>• Plan and design flower beds and other uses for annuals, including window boxes<br>• Clean, sharpen and repair tools<br>• Improve soil (page 56) of flower beds, if necessary<br>• Place hardy annuals in cold frame, then plant outdoors<br>• Sow hardy annual seeds outdoors<br>• Water as necessary<br>• Weed flower beds<br>• Place mail and slug bait and protect seedlings from birds | • Study seed catalogs and order seeds<br>• Check germination requirements of seeds ordered (Check Dictionary of Annuals, pages 196-221)<br>• Plan and design flower beds and other uses for annuals, including window boxes<br>• Clean, sharpen and repair tools<br>• Improve soil (page 56) of flower beds, if necessary<br>• Place hardy annuals in cold frame, then plant outdoors<br>• Sow hardy annual seeds outdoors<br>• Water as necessary<br>• Weed flower beds<br>• Thin seedlings<br>• Place mail and slug bait and protect seedlings from birds | **JANUARY/FEBRUARY** |
| **MARCH/APRIL** | • Start any seeds indoors<br>• Start dahlias indoors<br>• Start annual herb seeds indoors | • Start any seeds indoors<br>• Start dahlias indoors<br>• Start annual herb seeds indoors | • Start any seeds indoors<br>• Start dahlias indoors<br>• Start annual herb seeds indoors | • Start tender annual seeds indoors if they require 12 weeks or more to develop<br>• Start dahlias indoors<br>• Prepare and fertilize soil of flower beds as soon as ground can be worked<br>• Place hardy annuals in cold frame, then plant outdoors<br>• Sow annual seeds outdoors<br>• Weed flower beds | • Start tender annual seeds outdoors<br>• Prepare and fertilize soil of flower beds as soon as ground can be worked<br>• Place hardy annuals in cold frame, then plant outdoors<br>• Sow annual seeds outdoors<br>• Weed flower beds<br>• Thin seedlings<br>• Water as necessary<br>• Bring container plants indoors or mulch tender annuals if below average temperatures are forecast | • Plant any annuals outdoors<br>• Sow any annual seeds outdoors<br>• Water as necessary<br>• Weed flower beds<br>• Thin seedlings<br>• Place mail and slug bait and protect seedlings from birds<br>• Combat pests and fungal diseases using organic means, applying insecticides and fungicides only if necessary<br>• Train vines and climbing annuals<br>• Mulch flower beds | • Plant any annuals outdoors<br>• Sow any annual seeds outdoors<br>• Water as necessary<br>• Weed flower beds<br>• Thin seedlings<br>• Place mail and slug bait and protect seedlings from birds<br>• Combat pests and fungal diseases using organic means, applying insecticides and fungicides only if necessary<br>• Train vines and climbing annuals<br>• Mulch flower beds<br>• Remove faded flowers<br>• Pinch back tall-growing plants<br>• Shop low-growing plants<br>• Fertilize plants | • Plant any annuals outdoors<br>• Sow any annual seeds outdoors<br>• Water as necessary<br>• Weed flower beds<br>• Thin seedlings<br>• Place mail and slug bait and protect seedlings from birds<br>• Combat pests and fungal diseases using organic means, applying insecticides and fungicides only if necessary<br>• Train vines and climbing annuals<br>• Mulch flower beds<br>• Remove faded flowers<br>• Pinch back tall-growing plants<br>• Shop low-growing plants<br>• Fertilize plants<br>• Cut flowers for indoor displays | | **MARCH/APRIL** |
| **MAY/JUNE** | • Prepare and fertilize soil of flower beds as soon as ground can be worked<br>• Place any annuals in cold frame, then plant outdoors<br>• Plant annuals in window boxes<br>• Weed and mulch flower beds<br>• Thin seedlings<br>• Water as necessary<br>• Combat pests and fungal diseases using organic means, applying insecticides and fungicides only if necessary | • Prepare and fertilize soil of flower beds as soon as ground can be worked<br>• Place any annuals in cold frame, then plant outdoors<br>• Plant annuals in window boxes<br>• Weed and mulch flower beds<br>• Thin seedlings<br>• Water as necessary<br>• Combat pests and fungal diseases using organic means, applying insecticides and fungicides only if necessary | • Plant tender annuals outdoors<br>• Plant annuals in window boxes<br>• Sow tender annual seeds outdoors<br>• Weed flower beds<br>• Thin seedlings<br>• Water as necessary<br>• Place mail and slug bait and protect seedlings from birds<br>• Combat pests and fungal diseases using organic means, applying insecticides and fungicides only if necessary<br>• They cut and slug bait and | • Plant tender annuals outdoors<br>• Plant annuals in window boxes<br>• Sow tender annual seeds outdoors<br>• Weed flower beds<br>• Thin seedlings<br>• Water as necessary<br>• Place mail and slug bait and protect seedlings from birds<br>• Combat pests and fungal diseases using organic means, applying insecticides and fungicides only if necessary | • Plant tender annuals outdoors<br>• Plant annuals in window boxes<br>• Weed flower beds<br>• Thin seedlings<br>• Water as necessary<br>• Place mail and slug bait and protect seedlings from birds<br>• Combat pests and fungal diseases using organic means, applying insecticides and | • Plant tender annuals outdoors<br>• Plant annuals in window boxes<br>• Weed flower beds<br>• Thin seedlings<br>• Water as necessary<br>• Place mail and slug bait and protect seedlings from birds<br>• Combat pests and fungal diseases using organic means, applying insecticides and | • Plant tender annuals outdoors<br>• Weed flower beds<br>• Thin seedlings<br>• Water as necessary<br>• Place mail and slug bait and protect seedlings from birds<br>• Combat pests and fungal diseases using organic means, applying insecticides and | • Plant tender annuals outdoors<br>• Weed flower beds<br>• Thin seedlings<br>• Water as necessary<br>• Place mail and slug bait and protect seedlings from birds<br>• Combat pests and fungal diseases using organic means, applying insecticides and | | |

192

---

• Set up yellow sticky traps—available at a garden-supply center—to control pests. Several insects, including winged aphids, fungus gnats, thrips and whiteflies, are attracted to the color yellow. The lure draws the insects to the traps, where they become trapped.

• Make your own compost (pages 58-59) and use it to fertilize soil.

• Use organic fertilizers—for example, well-rotted animal manure, compost and bone meal—rather than synthetic chemical products.

• Use natural pesticides rather than chemical ones. Some examples of natural pesticides are soft soap and pyrethrum, which is a plant extract; *Bacillus thuringiensis* (Bt), diatomaceous earth and horticultural oil are considered to be among the safest commercially available pesticides. Refer to the Troubleshooting Guides in subsequent chapters for specific directions.

• Experiment with companion planting. This entails planting together different species of flowers or vegetables that, in combination, keep pests away. Avoid planting too many of the same type of plant in the same part of the garden.

• Use water—a pond or basin, for example—to entice birds, frogs and toads into your garden (page 32). These animals are natural predators of many pests, including slugs, snails and other ground-dwelling insects.

51

---

ACHIMENES LONGIFLORA 'BLAUER PLANET'

## DICTIONARY OF BULBS

### Introduction

This dictionary features a wide range of plants in five different groups: true bulbs, corms, tubers, tuberous roots and rhizomes. The most beautiful, resistant and well-sufficient plants in each class are highlighted. All plants are listed by their botanical names; common names are cross-referenced. The dictionary entries describe the climate zone in which each plant will grow; refer to the Zone Map (inside front cover) to locate your zone.

### Achimenes (a-KIM-e-nez)
Monkey-faced pansy, orchid pansy

A genus of species distributed throughout the American tropics. They are in the gesneriad family and are related to African violets and gloxinias. Plants have fibrous roots with scaly rhizomes and trumpet-shaped with flaring lobes and flat, pansy- or impatiens-like faces. Grow achimenes outdoors in beds or baskets in annuals, indoors as potted plants. Zones 10 and 11.

### Selected species and varieties.
*A. longiflora* has large, red-purple, white-throated flowers that are 1½ inches long and 1½ inches wide. Leaves are hairy and up to 3 inches long and 1½ inches wide. 'Blauer Planet' is more compact than the species. It has 1½- to 3-inch blue-purple flowers with white throats.

### Growing conditions.
Grow achimenes in bright light and not direct sun and in rich, well-drained soil to which organic matter and coarse sand or vermiculite have been added. Keep soil evenly moist after plants begin to grow. Plant the rhizomes in pots or baskets in early spring for summer bloom, three or four rhizomes per 6-inch pot. Place the rhizomes horizontally, ½ to 1 inch below the surface. Rhizomes can also be started in flats filled with moist peat moss and moved to pots or beds when growth is 3 inches high. Achimenes can also be grown from stem cuttings. Plants perform best when temperatures remain above 60° F at night and below 80° F during the day. In fall, gradually withhold water and dry the plants out. Store the rhizomes in a cool, dry place over winter. In spring, resume watering and repot if necessary. For summer bloom, store potted in dry soil at 50° to 60° F for 8 to 12 weeks in winter.

### Acidanthera (a-si-DAN-ther-a)
Peacock orchid

Tender, summer-blooming plants native to tropical and South Africa. Flowers are graceful and delicate-looking, somewhat resembling butterflies or orchids. They are borne in loose spikes and open in succession. Foliage is sword-shaped. Plants arise from corms. Effective when grown in clumps of 10 or more. Plant where the fragrance of the flowers can be appreciated. Zones 9-11.

### Selected species and varieties.
*A. bicolor* (sometimes listed as *A. marvilae*) bears spikes with three or more white flowers with chocolate-brown centers. Plants are 2 to 3 feet tall. Peacock orchid blooms are 3 inches across and very fragrant, and make excellent cut flowers.

### Growing conditions.
Plant peacock orchids in full sun in a location protected from high winds. Space corms about 6 inches apart at a depth of 3 to 4 inches. Enrich the soil with compost and fertilize with 5-10-5 when plants emerge and again one month later. North of Zone 9, start peacock orchids indoors and move them to the garden after danger of frost has passed. (See the Frost Date Map on the inside back cover.) They can be difficult to transplant, so start the plants in peat pots that can go directly into the ground or grow them in tubs. North of Zone 9, peacock orchids should be dug after the first hard frost. Shake off excess soil and allow them to dry for several days in a cool, dry place out of direct sun. Cut back the tops of the plants, discard the remains of the previous season's corms, and separate the cormels. Store the corms and cormels in dry peat moss or vermiculite at a temperature of 55° to 60° F. Peacock orchids require a long growing season to bloom. Propagate plants from the small cormels that are borne around old corms. Small corms take up to two seasons to bloom.

### Agapanthus (ag-a-PAN-thus)

Amaryllis-family members from South Africa with thick rhizomes and fleshy roots. Strap-shaped or linear leaves are borne at the base of the stems and may be deciduous or evergreen. Flowers are tubular and borne in umbels on leafless stalks. They come in blue, purplish blue or white. Zones 9-11.

AGAPANTHUS ORIENTALIS

ACIDANTHERA BICOLOR

292

---

tivar. Zones 7-9. *A. rosenbachianum*, rosenbach onion, white staterms contrast with dark violet flowers on 3- to 4-inch stems; blooms in early summer. Zone 5. *A. schoenoprasum*, chives, is a 12-inch plant with tubular, grasslike leaves. It is widely used as an herb. Flowers appear in spring, are rose-pink and are borne in dense, 1-inch, many-flowered umbels. Zones 4-9. *A. sphaerocephalum*, ball-head onion, produces dense, ball-shaped, 2-inch umbels of reddish-purple flowers in midsummer. Plants reach 2 to 3 feet. Zones 5-9. *A. tuberosum*, Chinese chive, Chinese garlic, is an edible, 1½-foot plant producing small, fragrant, white flowers in summer. Zone 4.

### Allium (AL-ee-um)
Onion

A large genus best known for its edible members: chives, onions, garlic and leeks. Leaves are usually grasslike or cylindrical and hollow. Like the vegetables to which they are related, ornamental onions arise from rhizomes or bulbs and are onion-scented when bruised. Small flowers are borne in few- to many-flowered umbels on leafless stems. Blooms appear in spring and summer and are yellow, white, pink, red, violet and blue. Excellent for beds and borders; smaller species are fine for the rock garden. All make excellent cut flowers, and also can be used for dried arrangements. Zones 2-11.

### Selected species and varieties.
*A. aflatunense* bears 4-inch globes of rose-purple flowers on 2½- to 5-foot stalks. Flowers appear in spring. Zones 5-11. *A. christophii*, star-of-Persia, is a 1-foot plant bearing lacy-looking, 8- to 12-inch umbels of star-shaped flowers that are lilac and have a metallic sheen. Blooms appear in late spring. Zones 4-11. *A. giganteum*, giant onion, produces 4- to 5-inch, ball-shaped umbels of flowers carried on leafless 4-foot stems. Lilac flowers appear in early midsummer. Zones 5-8. *A. moly*, lily leek, golden garlic, bears 3-inch clusters of yellow, star-shaped flowers in June. Zones 3-8. *A. neapolitanum*, daffodil garlic, Naples onion, is a spring-blooming, 1½-foot plant with fragrant, white starlike flowers borne in 2- to 3-inch umbels. 'Grandiflorum' is a large-flowered cul-

ALLIUM APLATUNENSE

### Amaryllis
(am-a-RIL-is)

A one-species South African genus that once contained many species now classified as *Hippeastrum*. Flowers are funnel-shaped and appear in clusters on solid stems. (*Hippeastrum* bears its flowers on hollow stems.) The bulbs produce strap-shaped leaves after the flowers have begun to fade. Amaryllis can be grown in beds and borders in frost-free areas and in greenhouses where not hardy. Zones 9-11.

### Selected species and varieties.
*A. belladonna*, belladonna lily, naked lady, bears fragrant rose, pink or white blooms that are 3½ inches across. Flowers appear atop naked 18-inch stalks; foliage appears after the flowers.

### Growing conditions.
Grow belladonna lilies outdoors in a sunny site with deeply prepared, rich, well-drained soil. Plant the bulbs in spring or early summer, before the leaves develop, at a depth of 4 to 6 inches. Do not disturb the bulbs unless absolutely necessary. Pot-grown plants should be set with the neck of the bulb at the soil surface. Keep the soil moist but not wet. To force for late summer or fall bloom, store potted in dry soil at 50° to 60° F for 8 to 12 weeks in winter.

ALLIUM MOLY

AMARYLLIS BELLADONNA

293

7

# 1

# DESIGNING YOUR YARD AND GARDEN

*Beds of mixed shrubs and flowers seem to disappear in several places behind foliage, giving a sense of spaciousness to this garden plan.*

The design of a yard or garden can be serenely simple, composed of only a few well-chosen types of plants that are artfully arranged. Or it can be exuberant and colorful, punctuated with unexpected combinations of textures and shapes. In most cases much of the design depends on the function of the space.

More than any other garden area, the one at the front of the house reflects the tastes of its owners. Probably this is because in the front yard alone, the garden is purely decorative. It does not have to function as an outdoor family room; its sole purpose is to frame the house and to welcome guests.

Behind the house, away from the street, is the garden that most passersby never see. Often that garden is a constantly changing scene of family activity—a playground, an outdoor dining room, a peaceful, private place for reading, sunbathing or simply watching the bees flit from flower to flower. With all those demands made on it, the garden is likely to pose some special design problems. To keep it looking tidy, the plantings must often function as screens or dividers without actually interrupting the sense of space and movement through the area.

When designing outdoor spaces, professional gardeners routinely rely on several basic plant types. Trees, sometimes even a single tree, will provide a visual point of focus; shrubs, often called the workhorses of the garden, establish line and shape and texture—and are sometimes a source of seasonal color. Azaleas, for instance, are synonymous with spring, and the familiar red berries of the pyracantha can decorate the winter lawn. Rounding out the list are the bulbs and herbaceous annuals and perennials that come and go, enlivening the scene with flashes of color and variety.

# CHAPTER CONTENTS

Of special concern in this outdoor living space is the disposition of sun and shade, conditions that vary in importance with season and personal predilection, and that in turn dictate the choice of plant materials. Refer to pages 10 and 11 for the basics of evaluating your garden's conditions. This chapter also explains how to use the elements of design, from color and texture to shape and form.

Garden design, if it is to be successful and enduring, must make use of plants that adapt themselves to the specific environment and can be kept healthy without herculean caretaking efforts. This means giving thought to such matters as soil composition, length of growing season, temperature extremes, annual rainfall and prevailing winds. Depending on where you live, it may mean dealing with such localized problems as salt air and heavy snowfalls that wreak havoc with brittle limbs. In other areas, rabbits and field mice may pose special problems, or air pollution can be a major concern.

The basics given here will get you started—whether you are gardening in the prairie, by the sea, in an arid region or a small space. The finishing touches are important, too. A brick walkway from street to house, for example, may be an important component of your front yard. A curved, lighted path of stone or wood chips may lend a distinctive casual ambience to your garden.

Finally, to save you from having to correct a gardening mistake, the chapter tells how to plan the design for your yard and garden with paper and pencil—before you set shovel to soil. There is nothing more satisfying to gardeners than designing— or redesigning—their outdoor living space, then making the plan a reality. This chapter gives you guidelines to create a basic plan. The subsequent chapters can help you make it happen.

# TAKING STOCK OF A GARDEN'S ENVIRONMENT

Turning a backyard into a garden with the most suitable plants in all the right places takes some knowledge of the plot's own natural weather, its soil and the other conditions that affect growing things. So before acquiring any plants or putting in a terrace, take time to survey the environment. How much sun will the garden get and precisely where? How hot will it be in August, how windy in spring? The answers to these questions will help determine the garden's design and what plantings should go where.

For a general idea of the climate, refer to the Zone Map *(inside front cover)*. For specifics about the weather in your immediate area, you can consult the people at a local nursery. Then study your garden's special microclimates —spots where the air is warmer than average, or cooler. Place a thermometer in one corner, then another, to see which is best for warmth-loving plants, which for hardy ones.

Wind affects microclimates, of course, so find out whether a chill breeze whistles around the north side of the house. And it is vital to measure what parts of the plot get the most sun. Remember that walls and fences cast long shadows in late summer and fall.
An urban backyard can be bright in the spring when the sun is high—and shaded much of the day later in the year when the lowering sun slips behind a nearby house.

How to assess the soil and improve it is shown on pages 56-57. Also look at existing plants. There may be several you want to dig up, but think twice about taking out a large tree unless it sheds annoying pods or fruit, or has too many surface roots to allow other plants to grow. Buying a mature tree is expensive; getting it to thrive can be difficult.

The illustrated checklist opposite will serve as a reminder of decisions that should be made before a plot is planted, to avoid mistakes that can be annoying and costly later on and to make sure the garden is a relatively trouble-free delight.

*Bright impatiens and hydrangeas bloom near some healthy azaleas in a pleasantly crowded border. The presence of such shade-tolerant plants as impatiens suggests the garden gets a mixture of sun and shade; the flourishing azaleas and blue hydrangeas reveal that the soil is acidic.*

## MAKING USE OF SUNLIGHT AND SHADOW

The farther north you live, the longer the shadows; the farther south, the shorter. You can approximate the length of the shadows in your area by reference to these two extremes and use the information in designing your garden. Walls and hedges can be sited to block or trap the sun's heat; beds and shrubs can be placed so they receive some light each day. Sun-loving annuals like marigolds belong in beds that face south or west, where the sun is strongest. Broad-leaved evergreens like holly and rhododendrons do best in shady northern and eastern exposures because they cannot tolerate too much sun.

## SLOPE AND DRAINAGE

Good drainage is vital because excess water will suffocate the roots of most plants. Note where water collects after rain; if puddles form at the bases of trees and shrubs—or near the foundation of the house—the land in such spots may need to be graded to encourage water to run off. Awkward, unwanted slopes may need to be leveled.

## TEMPERATURE

Find out the dates of the last spring frost, the first killer frost in the fall and the lowest recorded winter temperature in your area. Then keep track of temperature fluctuations—the microclimates—in various parts of your plot. It will be a good deal warmer, for example, near the brick wall of a house—especially one facing south—than in an exposed section of the yard.

## EXISTING VEGETATION

Look at the plants already growing on your site, if any, and decide what to keep. See what is growing well; this can tell you about the environment. For example, if there is a flourishing camellia, it indicates that the soil is probably acidic, since camellias prefer acid rather than alkaline conditions.

## WIND

Evaluate how much wind your plot gets and where the wind is strongest. Outside corners are often windy; so are exposed edges that have neither buildings nor tall plantings nearby. In the worst spots, plan on planting rugged species that can stand cold breezes. You can also build a windbreak. Even a head-high fence such as that shown below will help. So will a tree or two, or a tall-growing hedge.

## SUNLIGHT

Keep track of patterns of sunlight and shade at various times of the day, and assess how they will change from season to season if a tree, a wall or a fence lies in the path of the sun. Keep in mind that an ideally sunny spot in the spring may be too bright and too hot for some plants in the summer. Figuring out where the sunlight remains fairly stable will help you design your plantings.

## WATER

Apart from a general knowledge of rainfall patterns in your area—the local agricultural extension office will have such data—keep an eye on the moisture in your own plot. If you plan on having plants that need a good deal of moisture, you may want to install a water outlet or even a small irrigation system as part of your design.

# ELEMENTS OF GARDEN DESIGN

*Low, clipped boxwood hedges wind around a brick walkway in a garden that neatly combines a variety of textures, colors and forms. The flowering plants in the enclosed beds—some warm yellow blooms played off against cool blues and lavenders—help create a bright yet spacious look.*

arden design is largely a matter of organizing space. Although the same elements of design *(pages 13-17)* apply to both large and small spaces, making the most of small garden areas can be a particular challenge, often calling for some of the thought and imagination that Oriental masters devote to flower arrangements.

As in bouquets, the flowers and foliage in a garden should be varied in color, shape and texture for a maximum of visual interest. Yet they should also harmonize in tone and outline, be in scale with their settings, and create the desired mood or atmosphere. The illustrations opposite and on the following four pages show some typical small garden settings and how they can be planted to produce varied and original effects. Also shown are the wealth of plant types from which you can choose when doing your own landscape planning.

Color is always important. Some areas may demand banks of bright blooms, but most small gardens will seem more spacious and restful if softer colors predominate.

Texture is equally important. Foliage can look rough or smooth, the leaves large and leathery or small and delicate. In most cases a mixture will look best, giving the plot a fascinating variety. Letting certain textures predominate, though, along with some subdued colors, can give the illusion that a small space is larger than it actually is.

Then there are the varying shapes of flowering plants, shrubs and trees. Again, a mixture will usually look best. In fact, plantings of dramatically contrasting shapes can give a small, flat and otherwise uninteresting plot a sense of variety, depth, even mystery.

Ultimately, how you mix and match these various elements is a matter of taste. There are no hard and fast rules. But the combinations shown on these pages can be taken as starting points for your own designs. Analyze the plot first, imagine what will look most striking there and then select the plants that will fit into your overall concept.

## ATTRACTING BIRDS

Birds add color and action to a garden, and there are many ways to attract them. Dense trees and shrubs offer them shelter and sites for their nests. Berries give them food. Evergreen cones provide food for warblers during the spring and winter months; honeysuckle draws hummingbirds in summer. Spring and summer flowers invite birds of all kinds to feed on seeds and nectar.

To make birds feel at home, houses and feeders are essential. So is a year-round supply of drinking and bath water, which can be kept from freezing in winter with special heaters available at hardware stores. Place feeders and birdbaths outside the windows of the kitchen or a living area so that you can watch the activity. Make sure that you select a spot in the sun, away from the wind and beyond the reach of cats and squirrels.

## THE EFFECTS OF COLOR

Hot, intense colors—the reds, yellows, oranges—glow so brightly that they seem to foreshorten space, as in the yard at right with its plantings of marigolds and other warm-hued flowers. By contrast, the same yard, below, with pale blue and purple flowers and blue-green foliage, seems to recede and have more space in front. When thinking of plant color, consider the effects of seasonal change. Azalea bushes have bright blooms in the spring but will be green the rest of the year.

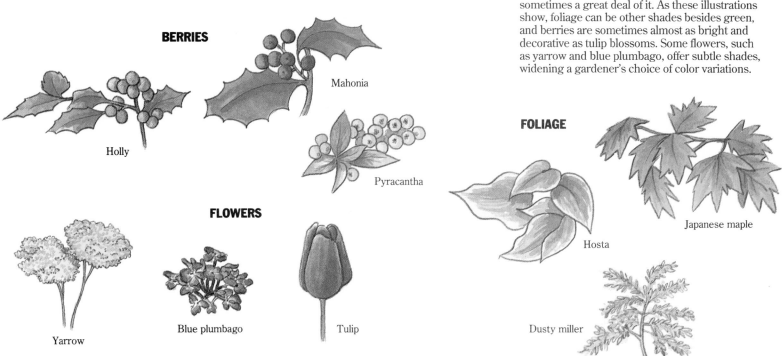

## SOURCES OF COLOR

People think of flowers as the main sources of garden color. But other plants can provide color, sometimes a great deal of it. As these illustrations show, foliage can be other shades besides green, and berries are sometimes almost as bright and decorative as tulip blossoms. Some flowers, such as yarrow and blue plumbago, offer subtle shades, widening a gardener's choice of color variations.

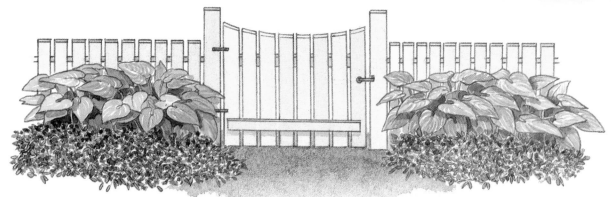

**BERRIES**

Mahonia

Holly

Pyracantha

**FLOWERS**

**FOLIAGE**

Japanese maple

Hosta

Yarrow

Blue plumbago

Tulip

Dusty miller

## TRICKS WITH TEXTURES

The many textures offered by foliage plants—and by flowers and trees as well—make it easy to add variety to the smallest plot. You can put plants that have smooth, waxy foliage next to others with rough-textured leaves. With plants whose small, thin leaves create a lacy effect, you can combine others having broad, fleshy foliage. You can also, by using plants in combination, play tricks with perspective, making a small area look larger. In the picture of a garden wall above, a large-leaved species has been placed in front of another with thin, spiky foliage. This arrangement of textures creates an illusion of depth lacking in the picture below, where the same plantings are reversed.

## LOOKING FOR VARIETY

Foliage plants offer perhaps the widest variety of textures, but flowers have it, too. Their blossoms range from the fragile softness of the clematis to the coarse and spiky structures of astilbe flower heads *(below)*. Trees are also highly varied. Their bark can be mottled or striated, rough or parchment-smooth. Trees are particularly valuable in a winter landscape; the bark provides interest when most other growing things have lost all their summer texture and color.

Bear's-breech

**FOLIAGE**

**FLOWERS**

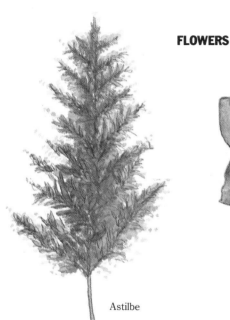

Clematis

Liriope

Astilbe

**TREE BARK**

Paperbark maple

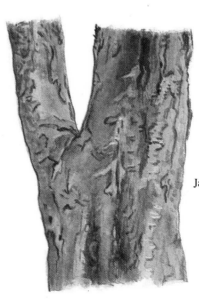

Japanese dogwood

15

## MAKING USE OF SHAPE

You can also create a sense of spaciousness, an illusion of depth, by combining shrubs and trees of various shapes. The densely foliaged shrubs by the garden gate above provide a strong focal point and lend strength to the wall—but make the wall seem close. The tree in the drawing below is open and airy enough to let other plants thrive beneath it. And in leading the eye to these other plants and to the wall behind, it gives the whole arrangement an illusion of extra space.

# A CATALOG OF FORMS

Most trees and shrubs take on one of six basic shapes *(below)*. A vase-shaped crape myrtle might be perfect in the corner of a garden. A few low-growing shrubs can clothe and beautify a house foundation; a columnar juniper can do the same for an exposed corner. For softness, opt for a graceful weeping cherry, not a spiky spruce.

WEEPING
Weeping cherry

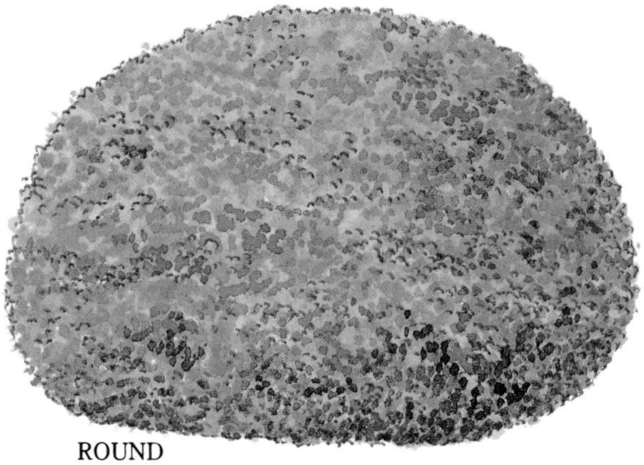

ROUND
Boxwood

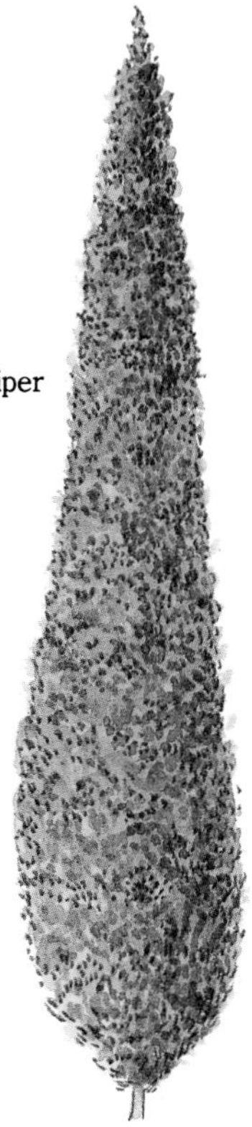

COLUMNAR
Rocky Mountain juniper

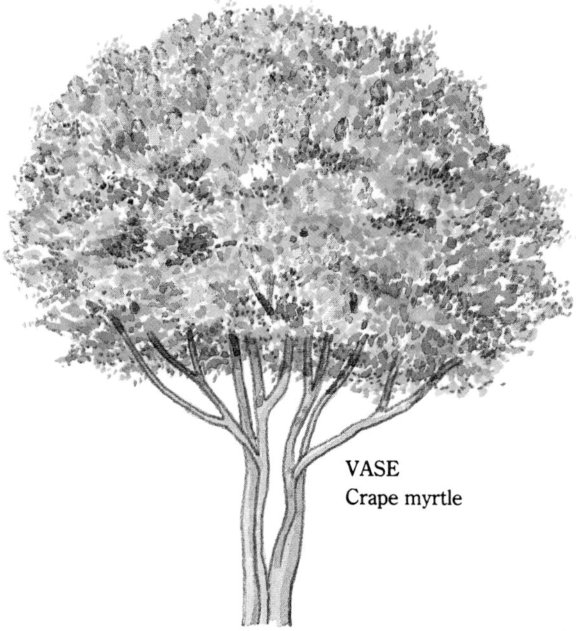

VASE
Crape myrtle

CONICAL
Spruce

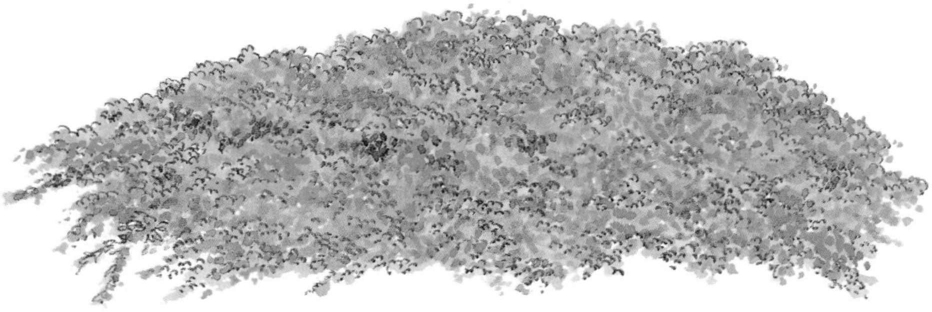

PROSTRATE
Bearberry

# TREES TO GIVE STRUCTURE TO A LANDSCAPE

*Used as a decorative planting in front of a home, a date palm sends out a fountain of rich green swordlike leaves. Date palms, which grow as high as 50 feet, are tropical evergreens that flourish only in the warm sun of Florida and other semitropical parts of the United States.*

Trees are by all odds the most important elements in the landscaping around a house. Handsome plantings of trees add beauty and elegance—and cash value—to any property. They offer cool, inviting shade during the hot months of summer and can deflect the wind when winter comes. Their flowers, buds and berries provide splashes of color. Also used as screens, trees give privacy and block out eyesores. Their leaves even cleanse the air of pollutants.

To grow well and look effective, trees have to be carefully chosen, and planted in the right spots. Even a handsome tree planted in the wrong location may become an unsightly annoyance. Imagine putting a young maple in a small front yard—and finding that the grown tree dwarfs the lot, hides the front door and casts the house in deep gloom during the brightest days of summer. A handy rule: Do not buy a tree and then decide where to put it. Rather, study a spot and match the tree to it. The landscape plan on the opposite page shows some ideal places to plant and suggests some first-rate choices of trees.

Happily, trees come in a vast variety of shapes and sizes, and so they offer a wealth of options. The many deciduous trees have special virtues, providing shade in summer, brilliant color in the fall and bare branches in winter that let in the sun. Tall evergreens make fine windbreaks and screens, keeping their color year round; small ones make neat accents around windows and doors.

There is rich variety as well in the colors and textures of bark, of foliage, of flowers and of fruits and pods. Choosing trees that offer such extra interest can produce not just a handsome setting for a house, but what amounts to a garden in the air, full of contrasts, surprises and unequaled delights.

## BRINGING OUTDOOR FRAGRANCE INDOORS

The fresh scents of the forest can add charm to your yard and to your house. Several broad-leaved evergreens, such as bay laurel and eucalyptus, and many conifers, such as balsam, cedar, fir and pine, have bark and foliage with long-lasting fragrance. To bring these scents indoors, you can make sachets filled with scraps of aromatic bark and foliage, and spread them around your house. Some tree fragrances also repel insects. Aromatic cedar bark placed in closets and drawers will help keep moths away from woolens. Redwood bark used as a mulch can keep many crawling insects, such as caterpillars, out of planting beds in the garden.

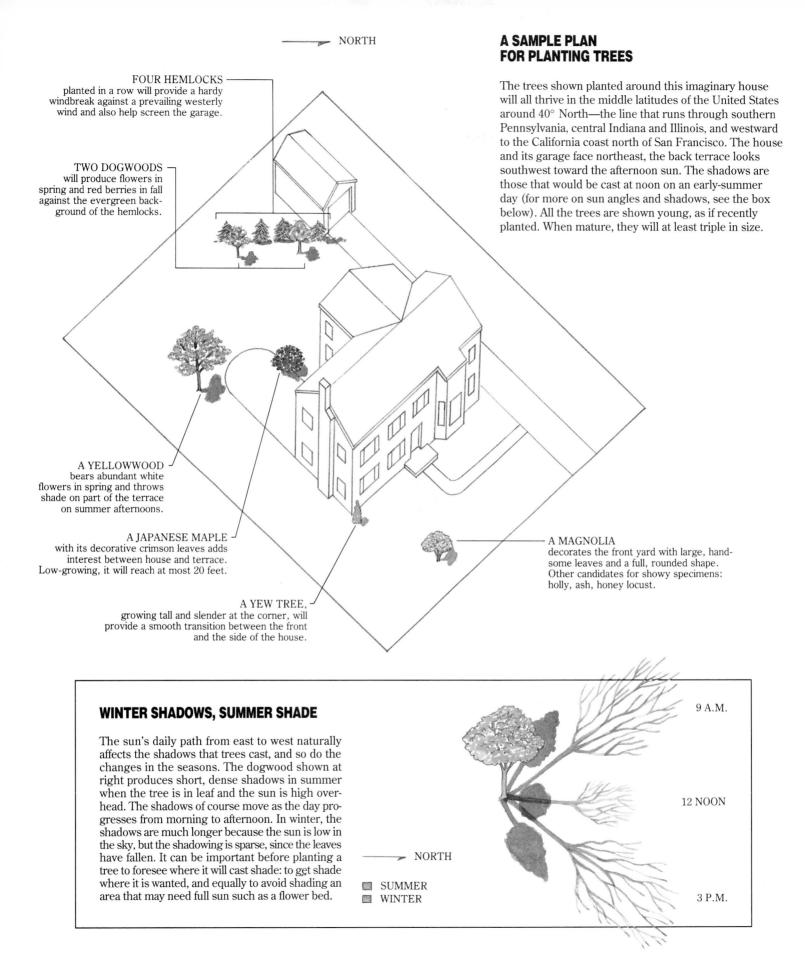

NORTH

FOUR HEMLOCKS
planted in a row will provide a hardy
windbreak against a prevailing westerly
wind and also help screen the garage.

TWO DOGWOODS
will produce flowers in
spring and red berries in fall
against the evergreen background of the hemlocks.

A YELLOWWOOD
bears abundant white
flowers in spring and throws
shade on part of the terrace
on summer afternoons.

A JAPANESE MAPLE
with its decorative crimson leaves adds
interest between house and terrace.
Low-growing, it will reach at most 20 feet.

A YEW TREE,
growing tall and slender at the corner, will
provide a smooth transition between the front
and the side of the house.

A MAGNOLIA
decorates the front yard with large, handsome leaves and a full, rounded shape.
Other candidates for showy specimens:
holly, ash, honey locust.

## A SAMPLE PLAN FOR PLANTING TREES

The trees shown planted around this imaginary house
will all thrive in the middle latitudes of the United States
around 40° North—the line that runs through southern
Pennsylvania, central Indiana and Illinois, and westward
to the California coast north of San Francisco. The house
and its garage face northeast, the back terrace looks
southwest toward the afternoon sun. The shadows are
those that would be cast at noon on an early-summer
day (for more on sun angles and shadows, see the box
below). All the trees are shown young, as if recently
planted. When mature, they will at least triple in size.

## WINTER SHADOWS, SUMMER SHADE

The sun's daily path from east to west naturally
affects the shadows that trees cast, and so do the
changes in the seasons. The dogwood shown at
right produces short, dense shadows in summer
when the tree is in leaf and the sun is high over-
head. The shadows of course move as the day pro-
gresses from morning to afternoon. In winter, the
shadows are much longer because the sun is low in
the sky, but the shadowing is sparse, since the leaves
have fallen. It can be important before planting a
tree to foresee where it will cast shade: to get shade
where it is wanted, and equally to avoid shading an
area that may need full sun such as a flower bed.

9 A.M.

12 NOON

3 P.M.

NORTH

SUMMER
WINTER

19

# SITING SHRUBS TO SUIT YOUR LANDSCAPE

*The bright blossoms and gracefully sweeping foliage of hydrangea make a beautiful boundary marker. These fast-growing shrubs reach up to 25 feet, flower from June to September, tolerate sun or partial shade, and can be used in a freestanding hedge or as a screen against a wall.*

Well-chosen shrubs can do more for the appearance of a house and its landscape than any other plantings. More than flower beds, even more than trees, shrubs help a house blend into its surroundings, and make the surroundings harmonious, varied and inviting.

Shrubs can do a number of vital jobs—often several at once. Hedges can delineate property lines and at the same time provide privacy, block an unattractive view and serve as a windbreak. Groupings of various shrubs are ideal for sheltering a deck or a patio and softening its contours. Banked shrubs are matchless backdrops for beds of annual and perennial flowers. Particularly handsome flowering shrubs, planted singly or in groups, add drama to an expanse of lawn. Perhaps most important, shrubs serve as foundation plantings around a house, framing windows and doors, hiding unsightly foundation walls and helping the house blend into its site. Shrubs are marvelously versatile because they themselves are so varied—in the color and texture of their foliage, in their flowers and fruits, in shape and size.

Before choosing shrubs, it is a good idea to make a checklist *(box, opposite)*, noting all of the factors—soil type, sunlight, wind, rain—that will affect their growth. Consider also the climatic zone; winter-hardy plants may not flourish in Florida, and plants suited to the Gulf Coast may perish if planted in Michigan. Then it is vital to consider the lay of the house and the grounds, and decide where shrubs are needed, and what sorts are required *(opposite)*. Hardy species are clearly best for screening harsh northerly winds. By the same token, a more delicate flowering specimen should go on the sunny, wind-protected southern side of the house. After your planning is done, consult the Dictionary of Shrubs *(pages 449-459)* to select the most appropriate shrubs for various locations in your yard and garden.

## PLANTING SHRUBS TO ATTRACT BIRDS

Mockingbirds and finches like to nest in the security of evergreen shrubs, and wrens, robins and sparrows often take up residence among the dense branches of deciduous hedges and small trees. If you have a wildflower garden well established in an open area, plant some of these shrubs and small trees alongside it to make a home for the birds; they will be more readily attracted to a site that provides shelter and camouflage as well as food. You will be able to watch some of them raise their young, and some—such as the wrens—will return to the same site year after year.

## HOW DOES YOUR GARDEN GROW?

Before choosing shrubs to add to your landscape, it is important to determine what sort of soil you have and how much sun, rain and wind. Many shrubs are hardy and adaptable, but some will flourish only in certain conditions. Fortunately, shrubs have such varied habits that some do well under almost any circumstances.

• **Soil:** Most evergreen shrubs like a slightly acidic growing medium that drains well. Have your soil tested before selecting shrubs to plant in it. If the soil is too clayey or too sandy, adding organic matter will improve its texture and help its drainage.

• **Sun and shade:** Determine where sunlight falls at various seasons and times of day. Some shrubs like direct all-day sun, but others are shade growers and many do well only with a combination of sun and shade.

• **Wind:** Find out where the prevailing wind comes from. There are tough shrubs that shrug off steady wintry blasts, but many more need protection from cold and from the wind's drying effects.

• **Rain:** Note your area's average rainfall. Some shrubs require large amounts of water and are almost impossible to grow in desert areas; others are highly drought-resistant.

## LOOKING AT THE LAY OF THE LAND

The sketch below suggests ways shrubs may be used to beautify a house and its grounds. In planning your own plantings, consider all structures and any trees or other plantings already there, including walkways, patio and spaces that should be left open as play areas. Note where the best view is—and the worst. Think about where privacy is needed, and where you may want a hedge, a windbreak, some ornamentals and other plantings around the house. In the sketch below, an arrow indicates North, to help figure angles of sunlight and wind directions.

NORTH

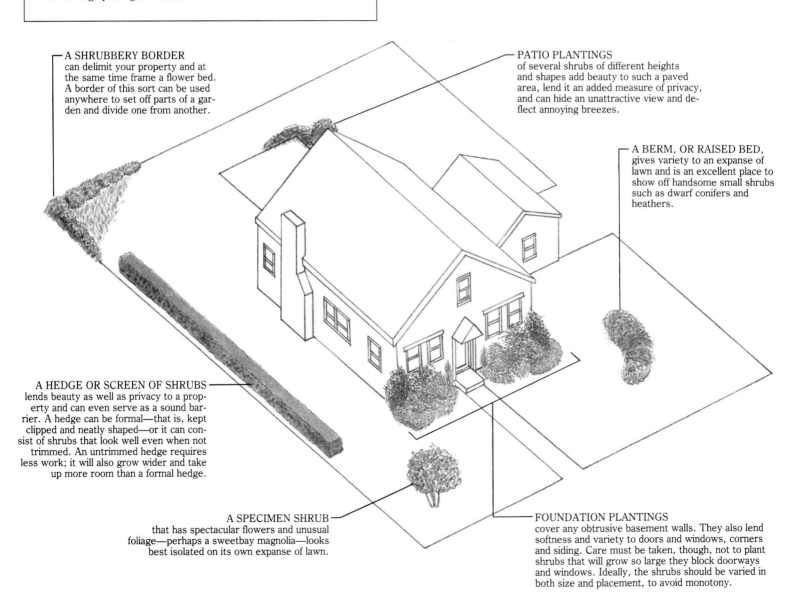

A SHRUBBERY BORDER can delimit your property and at the same time frame a flower bed. A border of this sort can be used anywhere to set off parts of a garden and divide one from another.

PATIO PLANTINGS of several shrubs of different heights and shapes add beauty to such a paved area, lend it an added measure of privacy, and can hide an unattractive view and deflect annoying breezes.

A BERM, OR RAISED BED, gives variety to an expanse of lawn and is an excellent place to show off handsome small shrubs such as dwarf conifers and heathers.

A HEDGE OR SCREEN OF SHRUBS lends beauty as well as privacy to a property and can even serve as a sound barrier. A hedge can be formal—that is, kept clipped and neatly shaped—or it can consist of shrubs that look well even when not trimmed. An untrimmed hedge requires less work; it will also grow wider and take up more room than a formal hedge.

A SPECIMEN SHRUB that has spectacular flowers and unusual foliage—perhaps a sweetbay magnolia—looks best isolated on its own expanse of lawn.

FOUNDATION PLANTINGS cover any obtrusive basement walls. They also lend softness and variety to doors and windows, corners and siding. Care must be taken, though, not to plant shrubs that will grow so large they block doorways and windows. Ideally, the shrubs should be varied in both size and placement, to avoid monotony.

# FLOWERS: USING COLOR

*A broad swath of tulips forms a warm, welcoming curve leading to a front door. The red flowers border a broad expanse of green lawn, creating bold color contrast. The gray-green foliage softens the combination.*

Flowers are the glory of the garden. They provide the color that gives it personality and character. They lift the spirit in spring, after the bleakness of winter; they perk up the dog days of summer and they brighten the lengthening shadows of fall.

You can change color from season to season against an established backdrop. To conduct a successful show, first develop a plan. Use colors singly or in combination to achieve special effects, and maintain color as long as possible by planting with the seasons in mind.

In selecting a color theme, consider some facts of color theory having to do with analogous and complementary colors *(opposite)*. Then plan for the spatial effects you want. Warm colors, such as red and orange, seem to advance, and are useful at the far end of a yard because they are visible from a distance. Cool colors, such as blue and violet, tend to recede and give an open feel to a small area.

White flowers stand out in the dark and are effective in a garden that you use at night. To give a finished look to your overall design, plants with gray-green foliage will unite different elements and soften the hard edges between colors.

Different types of flowering plants can be mixed to provide color throughout the growing season. Spring-blooming bulbs will come to life soon after all danger of freezing is past; other bulbs emerge with the first signs of fall. Annuals started indoors can be transplanted in early spring, and perennials will surface for late-spring and summer color.

To kick off a parade of color in the first rush of spring, create a bed of spring-flowering bulbs. Plant the bulbs in the fall, either singly in individual holes, or if you have a large area to be planted, in trenches, as shown here. Since bulbs provide an inviting feast for rodents, protect your investment by lining the trench with wire mesh. For continuing color when spring yields to summer, see the following pages.

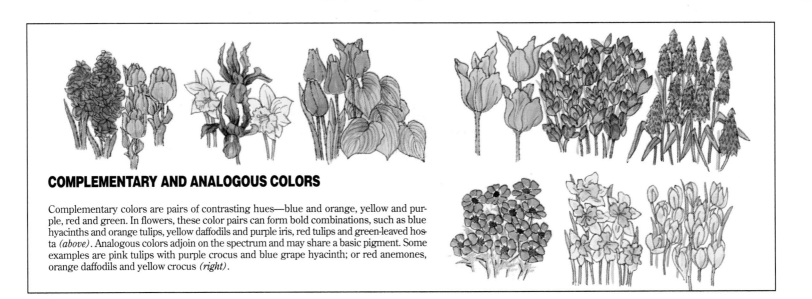

## COMPLEMENTARY AND ANALOGOUS COLORS

Complementary colors are pairs of contrasting hues—blue and orange, yellow and purple, red and green. In flowers, these color pairs can form bold combinations, such as blue hyacinths and orange tulips, yellow daffodils and purple iris, red tulips and green-leaved hosta *(above)*. Analogous colors adjoin on the spectrum and may share a basic pigment. Some examples are pink tulips with purple crocus and blue grape hyacinth; or red anemones, orange daffodils and yellow crocus *(right)*.

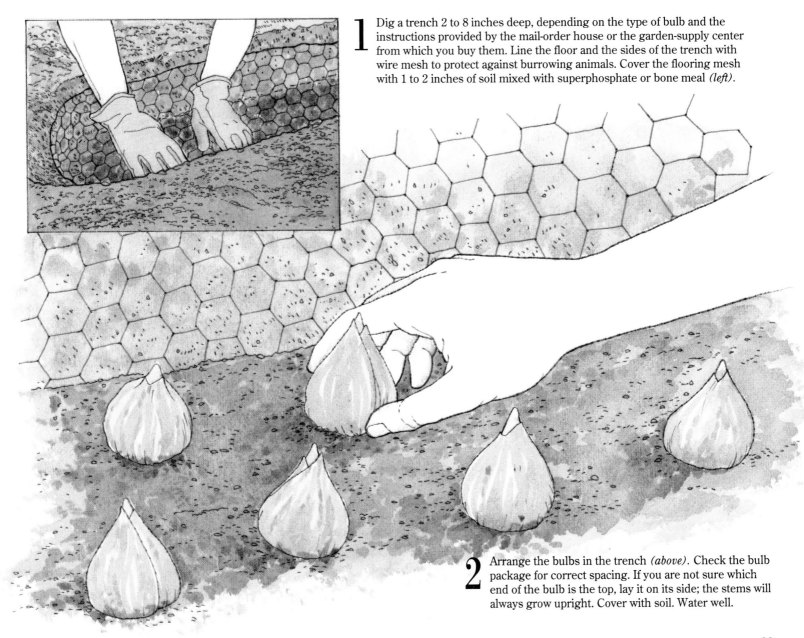

1 Dig a trench 2 to 8 inches deep, depending on the type of bulb and the instructions provided by the mail-order house or the garden-supply center from which you buy them. Line the floor and the sides of the trench with wire mesh to protect against burrowing animals. Cover the flooring mesh with 1 to 2 inches of soil mixed with superphosphate or bone meal *(left)*.

2 Arrange the bulbs in the trench *(above)*. Check the bulb package for correct spacing. If you are not sure which end of the bulb is the top, lay it on its side; the stems will always grow upright. Cover with soil. Water well.

# FLOWERS AND THEIR LIFE CYCLES

## ANNUAL

An annual (like the marigold shown to the right) sprouts from a seed in spring, sending some delicate roots belowground and some tender green shoots above. By early summer the plant has grown fuller and begun to blossom. It then blooms with increasing fullness and vigor, reaching its peak in late summer. In fall its roots, stems and flowers have begun to wither; by winter they will have died.

A seed sown in spring

SPRING

EARLY SUMMER

FIRST YEAR

## BIENNIAL

A biennial (like the sweet William illustrated here) normally divides its life cycle into two distinct periods. After a seed has sprouted in spring, the plant develops roots and foliage throughout the summer, but no flowers. The roots and foliage cease to grow but survive the winter and then have a spurt of new growth early in the second spring. Flowers appear in late spring. In midsummer the plant sets seed and withers; by fall it will have died.

A seed sown in spring

SPRING

SUMMER

FIRST YEAR

SECOND YEAR

## PERENNIAL

A perennial (shown here is a Shasta daisy) goes through a yearly cycle of growth after a seed sprouts in spring, but one cycle does not end with the plant's death as it does in annuals; instead it repeats itself. In the first summer the plant develops roots and foliage, but no flowers. In fall the foliage withers and the roots go dormant underground and survive the winter. In spring the plant reawakens; over the summer and into the fall, its roots and foliage put out new growth, and flowers appear. From now on, the plant will continue to go dormant in winter and to produce new growth and new flowers season after season.

A seed sown in spring

SUMMER

SPRING

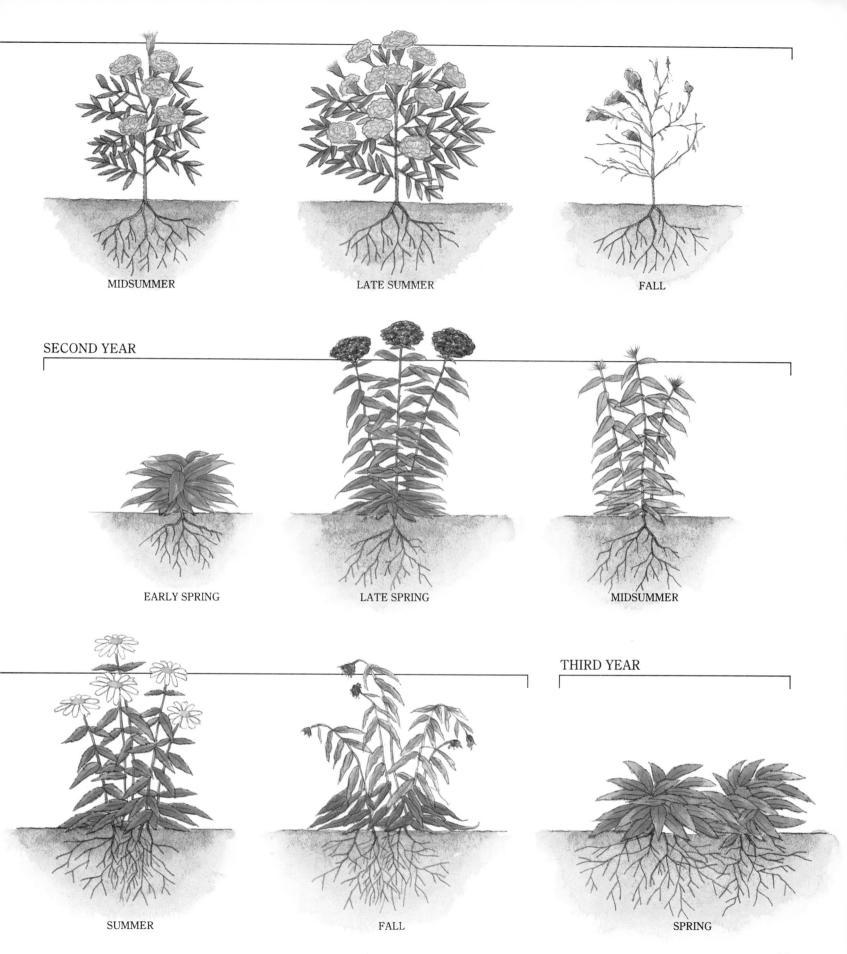

MIDSUMMER

LATE SUMMER

FALL

SECOND YEAR

EARLY SPRING

LATE SPRING

MIDSUMMER

SUMMER

FALL

THIRD YEAR

SPRING

# CHOOSING A STYLE IN DESIGNING YOUR GARDEN

All gardens express a style, whether intentionally or not. The simple act of weeding—rejecting one kind of plant in favor of another—is a statement of personal taste. By thinking carefully about the design of your garden before you plant, you can ensure that the result will accurately—and beautifully—reflect your own style and personality.

The style of a garden is determined by four factors: the plants that grow there, the way they are arranged, the materials that accent them (pathways, walls, patios, pools), and the relationship of the whole to the adjacent house and to the surrounding landscape or cityscape.

All garden designs can be divided into two basic types: formal and informal. Formal designs tend to be strongly geometrical, with features like circular or rectangular beds arranged symmetrically around a clear focal point. Informal gardens imitate the asymmetrical forms of nature, with irregularly shaped beds and less rigid sight lines.

Over the years certain types of gardens have become associated with particular cultures. When gardeners speak of formal gardens, they usually mean the elegant parterres and reflecting pools of Italian villas and French châteaus. Informal gardens bring to mind either the free-form plantings of English country cottages or the minimalist esthetic of the Japanese rock garden.

Before deciding on a style, take a good look at your house and neighborhood. Gardens should harmonize with their surroundings. The same geometric patterns that complement a classic brick Colonial would be jarring alongside a rambling ranch house. You'll also want to consider time and budget restraints: Formal hedges must be kept neatly trimmed; elaborate brick terraces require little maintenance, but they are expensive to install.

Shown on the following pages are three different designs that can be realized on the same 24-by-32-foot site. By applying the illustrated principles creatively, you can come up with a pleasing and practical style that is distinctively all your own.

*Twin geometric beds of low-lying ground covers lend a strong visual rhythm to this formal garden. Gracing the central axis are a dwarf white pine ringed by golden sedum (foreground), a small fountain and (against the far wall) a topiary juniper flanked by Alberta spruces.*

## DESIGNING FOR FRAGRANCE

Of the many aspects of garden design, one that is often overlooked is fragrance. Nothing is more relaxing on a cool summer evening—or more heartening on a warm spring morning—than the aroma of a garden.

If you plant a border along a walk that leads to and from the front door, you can smell the flowers each time you come or go. Fill a shrub border with lilac, viburnum, osmanthus or gardenia. Trim it with hyacinth and lily of the valley in the spring and with sweet alyssum, heliotrope or garden pinks in the summer. Drape wisteria or star jasmine over a trellis near a window, where the scent can drift into the house. Use aromatic plants in containers on a terrace or a patio to enhance outdoor living areas.

# DESIGN FOR A FORMAL GARDEN

The emphasis is on symmetry and geometry; plantings follow the rigid lines imposed by the structural features. Precisely centered on the rear wall is a semicircular pool that defines a clear viewing axis. Attention is drawn to this feature by four upright yew trees planted directly behind it. On either side of this focal point, the garden is laid out in neatly demarcated areas that are virtual mirror images of each other. A large brick patio in the foreground connects to three brick pathways; the one in the center leads directly to the pond; the other two offer access to the plants along the walls. Two solitary trees accent the flat grassy areas between the paths. The three concrete squares set diagonally into the patio emphasize the orderliness and precision of the design, and serve as well to point the eye in the direction of the pond at the rear.

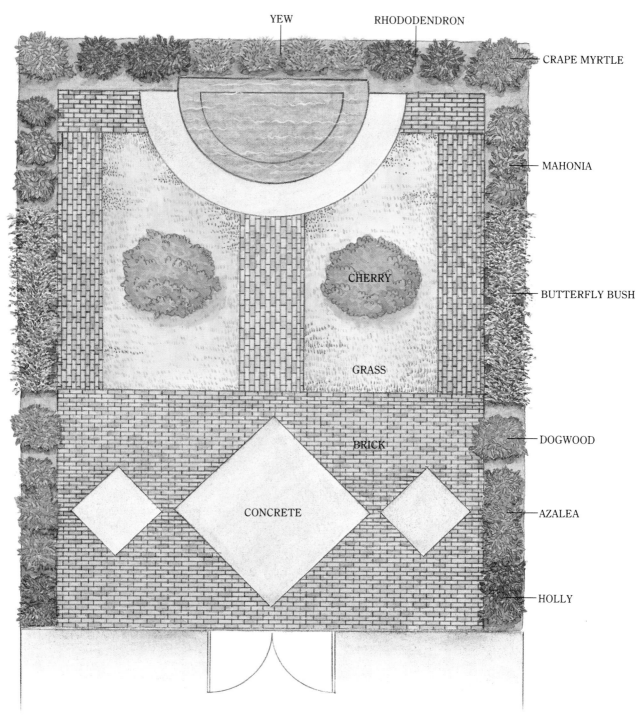

# DESIGN FOR AN INFORMAL GARDEN

Loose and unrestrained in spirit, this design shuns straight lines and right angles in favor of softened edges and gradual transitions. The varied plantings along the perimeter—from evergreen trees to deciduous shrubs to annuals and perennials—offer visual interest throughout the year. Spring brings a burst of intense color to the flanking beds of azaleas and rhododendrons. When these fade in summer's heat, the mixed beds of annuals and perennials come into bloom. And when the rest of the garden lies dormant for the winter, the assorted evergreens emerge from the background to provide color and texture. The area in the center is reserved for casual recreation; it can be either grass or a paved patio.

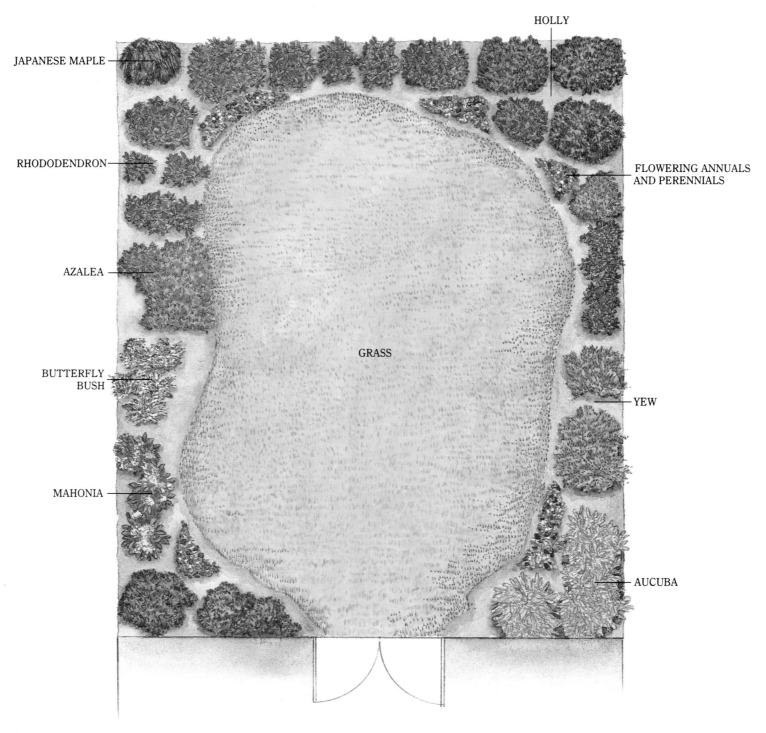

HOLLY

JAPANESE MAPLE

RHODODENDRON

FLOWERING ANNUALS AND PERENNIALS

AZALEA

GRASS

BUTTERFLY BUSH

YEW

MAHONIA

AUCUBA

# DESIGN FOR AN ORIENTAL GARDEN

The simplicity of this design draws inspiration from the gardening traditions of China and Japan. Prominently featured are rough stones whose uneven texture and asymmetrical arrangement suggest the "accidental" beauty of nature. Although many of the plants used here can be found in the other two designs, the overall effect is entirely different. Scattered azalea bushes give a brief show of color in the spring, but during most of the year the garden is subdued and unobtrusive. The flat expanse of loose gravel in the center invites contemplation; the mood is tranquil, a soothing balm for the unquiet spirit.

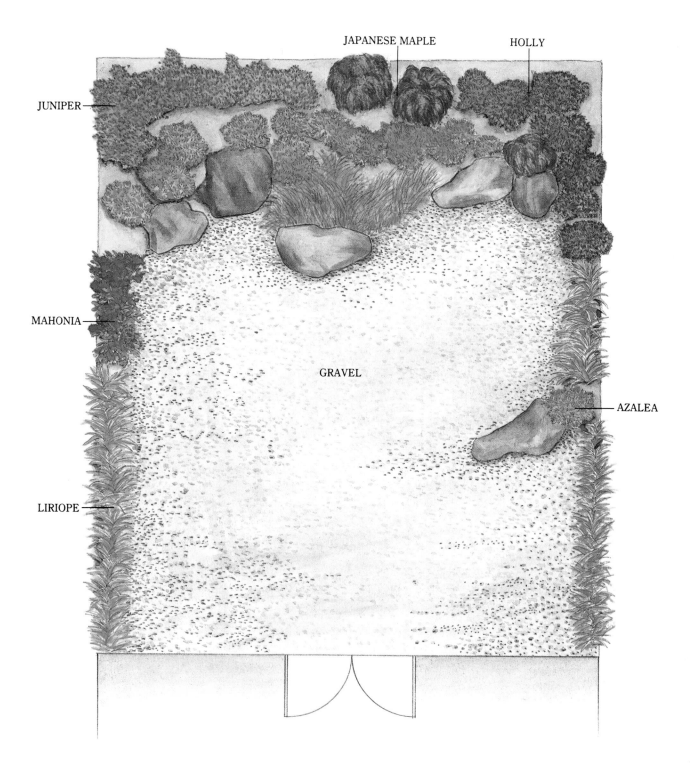

JAPANESE MAPLE

HOLLY

JUNIPER

MAHONIA

GRAVEL

AZALEA

LIRIOPE

# DESIGNING A WILDFLOWER MEADOW AS NATURE WOULD

*Lavender-blossomed moss phlox blankets several large boulders in a dramatic, steeply sloped rock garden. Since it creeps on horizontal stems, this species of phlox is especially appropriate for rock gardens.*

A wildflower meadow is one of the most pleasurable gardens to grow. You use plants native to your area, so you can create a field that seems to have sprung up naturally. It will do almost that. Wildflowers are so hardy and prolific that the gardener need only give the meadow a good start and an annual mowing to control weeds.

Most wildflower seed mixes are designed for specific conditions—for location, for kind of soil, for shade or for sun. The packet label will describe the growing conditions and the type of seeds the mix contains. Avoid mixes containing invasive species that will choke out the flowers you want. To find out what plants are invasive in your region, and to check the reliability of various commercial mixtures, consult a local wildflower society.

Some communities prohibit uncut fields on front lots; check your local ordinances or plant the meadow in your backyard. Do your annual meadow mowing in the fall, after the flowers have produced seed, or in the early spring, before growth starts.

## HOLDING BACK THE FOREST PRIMEVAL

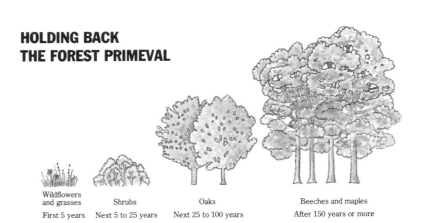

| Wildflowers and grasses | Shrubs | Oaks | Beeches and maples |
|---|---|---|---|
| First 5 years | Next 5 to 25 years | Next 25 to 100 years | After 150 years or more |

Left unmowed, a meadow will revert to wilderness. Land that was once forest will turn back to forest in precise stages. The outcome of this process varies by region. In the northeastern United States *(above),* grasses and wildflowers will yield to shrubs after several years. Soil changes will then permit a succession of evergreen and deciduous trees to flourish. In time, oaks will grow; then maple and beech will dominate what is known as a climax forest, an environment that stays stable unless upset by catastrophe or human intervention.

**1** To prepare for sowing, wet the soil and remove by hand any unwanted plants that can be easily yanked out. Then turn the soil with a rotary tiller  or with a heavy-duty garden fork to a depth of 2 inches.

**2** Water the tilled area thoroughly to encourage all exposed weed seeds to germinate. After one to two weeks, remove weed sprouts with a hoe *(below)*. Remove rocks unearthed by tilling, break up large soil clods and smooth with a steel rake.

**3** Soak the seedbed. Blend coarse sand with seed mix to add volume and aid in even distribution. Then sow by hand *(left)* or by spreader. Go from one end of the field to the other, then make a right-angle turn and walk back and forth again as shown in the diagram. You will need 5 to 6 pounds of seed per acre.

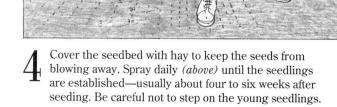

**4** Cover the seedbed with hay to keep the seeds from blowing away. Spray daily *(above)* until the seedlings are established—usually about four to six weeks after seeding. Be careful not to step on the young seedlings.

# TERRACING TO MAKE USE OF AN AWKWARD SLOPE

A little hillock that juts out into a small garden, its sloping sides too steep and erosion-prone to sustain any flowering plants, can seem a discouraging waste of precious space. But in fact a slope offers a fine opportunity to give a garden some welcome multilevel variety. What is needed is some terracing—a few steps carved into the slope to prevent rainy washouts and to provide a series of neatly defined planting areas.

The earth in the terraces or steps will need to be held in place by what amount to miniature retaining walls. They can be made of stones, as in the illustrations opposite and on the following two pages, or of railroad ties or bricks. The idea is to choose the buttressing that goes best with your garden's tone or mood—and perhaps with the walls of your house. Bricks, of course, will harmonize with a brick wall; they also lend a garden a formal air. Railroad crossties are rugged and informal. Stones create the countryish atmosphere of a cottage garden.

The terraces should all be the same size. How many you build and how high and how deep you make them will vary with the height and steepness of the slope—and with what your taste tells you will look pleasing. As a general rule, each terrace should be at least 1 foot deep. In other words, allow at least 1 foot of space from the terrace's front edge to the rise where the next terrace begins in order to accommodate plants. Also, each step should be at least 5 inches high, for visual definition and stability. On the other hand, terraces ought not to be more than 12 inches in height.

Terraces drain so well that if they are too tall they may dry out too fast. The box at right explains how to calculate the dimensions of a slope and how many terraces will fit into it. The sample dimensions—8-inch rises and 2-foot depths—will work well with most slopes, and will also look appropriate in a majority of small garden areas.

*Rows of bluestone rocks, looking neat and orderly with their flat sides up, support a series of terraces cut into an incline. The handsome mixed plantings include some hostas, ferns and other perennial foliage plants; a few herbs such as thyme and oregano; and some colorful annuals— red geraniums, blue ageratum and white impatiens.*

## SIZING THE TERRACES

Figuring out how many terraces a slope will accommodate is a matter of simple arithmetic. Measure the rise and the run of the slope *(right)*. Suppose the rise is 32 inches and you want terraces 8 inches high. Just divide 8 into 32 and you get four steps. Now assume the run is 96 inches. Divide 96 by your four steps and you have 24 inches—the depth of each terrace. In actuality, the numbers seldom work out so neatly, but by adjusting an inch or two this way or that you will come up with some regular, usable dimensions.

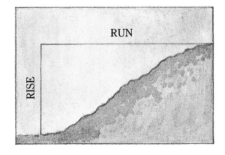

# A GARDEN POOL FOR A TRANQUIL SCENE

*A garden pool—encircled by stones and flowers, freckled with lily pads, stirred by falling water and brightly colored fish—brings a timeless air of peace to this sunny nook between brick wall and patio.*

A garden pool is like an oasis in your backyard. Even the smallest pool reflects objects around it; therefore it lends the illusion of height to a horizontal surface. The easiest pools to install—and the most durable—are made of preformed fiberglass. They have an in-ground life of up to 50 years and require little maintenance.

Once your pool is filled, you will have only to top it off every few days with a garden hose to replace water lost to evaporation. Keep the water level a couple of inches below the rim to allow for heavy rains. The raised lip of the pool, which may be camouflaged beneath decorative stones or bricks, helps prevent soil and mulch from drifting from the surrounding garden into the pool.

If you intend to stock your pool with fish and aquatic plants, add a dechlorinating compound once the water has warmed up to air temperature. Ask your garden-supply center for help in creating a balanced ecosystem in which the fish and plants will supply each other's nutrients.

Both fish and plants can come through even the longest winters in good health in a filled pool—provided the water does not freeze to the bottom. Keep the pool almost full at all times and make sure ice does not form around the bases of the plants. If it does, use a broom handle to knock off the ice.

With a proper ecosystem, the water is not likely to turn cloudy or scummy. But once a year—probably in the spring—you may want to drain, clean and refill the pool. First remove all plants. Catch the fish with a net and put them in a pail of water. To drain the pool, use a suction pump (the kind that attaches to an electric drill) or make a syphon by submerging a coiled hose in the pool until it fills with water. Leaving one end of the hose submerged, tightly cover the other end with your palm and carry it to any place in your garden that is lower than the pool. When you take away your hand, the water will empty out through the hose.

## ENLISTING NATURE'S BALANCING ACT

A healthy balance between animal and plant life will keep a pool clean. Japanese black snails control scum. Plants such as cabomba and sagittaria, which grow entirely underwater, compete with algae for nutrients. The shade provided by water-lily pads also discourages algae growth. All plants should be set in containers of heavy soil. The containers of those to be submerged should stand on the bottom of the pool. The lily pads and any other plants meant to show above the surface may need to be elevated. If so, place freestanding bricks on the floor of the pool to raise them. Fish such as koi, comets, Japanese fan-tails and Chinese moors eat insects and plant debris.

# A RAISED BED
# TO BOOST SOIL QUALITY

Where poor soil or poor drainage is a problem, it may pay to think small. Instead of regrading your entire garden—an expensive and time-consuming task—you can build a raised bed that is both practical and quite attractive.

Because you fill a raised bed with soil you mix yourself, you can customize the growing medium to the plants you intend to grow. By virtue of its elevation, a raised bed has a visual impact that ground-level plantings often lack. You can choose the siding material—brick, stones, railroad ties, treated boards—to harmonize with the surroundings.

Since even a small raised bed is a permanent addition to your garden, choose its location only after a thorough site analysis *(pages 10-11)*. If you are going to place the bed directly against any kind of wall other than stone, be sure to protect the wall surface. Coat a brick wall with a waterproofing solution such as concrete primer. Protect a wooden wall by inserting fiberglass sheeting between the bed and the wall.

A good height for a raised bed is 12 to 18 inches; if you build it any higher, the top layer of soil may drain too quickly and dry out. To make maintenance easy, the bed should be no broader than the reach of your arm.

After constructing the sides, fill the bed with a good soil mix, such as topsoil, compost and coarse sand. Be sure to incorporate some soil from the site into the mix to facilitate drainage; water will not pass easily across a distinct boundary between two entirely different types of soil.

*Surrounded by a picturesque wall of unmortared stone, a mixed planting of annuals and perennials thrives in a raised bed, which makes it easy to amend the soil to suit the flowers.*

1 To prepare for building a raised bed, mark the corners of the proposed area with stakes. Then tie strings to the stakes to indicate the height of the top of the bed. Check with a carpenter's level *(right)* and adjust the strings until they are level.

**2** Dig down inside the marked area and remove at least 2 inches of soil. With a tamper, tamp down the exposed soil until it is firm, especially around the edges *(left)*. This will provide a level surface for rough-cut stones or whatever other siding material you will be laying.

**3** Start laying the bottom row of stones *(right)*. Experiment with different combinations to find a good fit between stones. Use gravel or stone dust (available at stone yards) to raise up smaller stones. When the bottom row is laid, shovel 2 inches of stone dust or gravel in a foot-wide band around the inside perimeter. This will keep stones from heaving during periodic freezings and thawings.

**4** Finish laying stones up to the string marker. If necessary, shore the stones up with some soil to keep them in place as you work. When the siding is completed, dig up the bottom of the bed with a garden fork or a shovel to a depth of 8 to 10 inches; this will speed drainage. Then fill with a good soil mix to within an inch of the top *(left)*. Let the bed settle before you plant anything; add more soil to top it off if necessary.

# DESIGNING A XERISCAPE TO CONSERVE WATER

Gardeners who live in the western United States know how frustrating and costly it can be to fight nature by trying to re-create the moist-climate gardens of England and New England. One solution is xeriscaping. The word comes from the Greek *xeros*, which means "dry." Xeriscaping takes full advantage of plants that have adapted to arid conditions. The result does not have to resemble a cactus ranch; there is a great variety of moisture-thrifty plants. The goal is to create a garden that does not consume much water.

Such a garden is best designed with little or no lawn, since turfgrasses are among the thirstiest of all plants. By making use of a patio paved with brick or flagstone, you can keep grass to a minimum. Where a patch of green is desired, use buffalo grass or some other drought-tolerant species instead of traditional bluegrass. Also avoid using rosebushes and conventional annuals and perennials; instead, choose wildflowers, trees and shrubs that are native to arid habitats.

Lay out your garden with water conservation in mind. The unrelenting sun in south-facing beds is suitable only for drought-tolerant plants; other plants will do better in more protected northerly exposures. Group together plants with similar water needs, so you won't be forced to overwater some plants in order to keep their neighbors happy.

To improve moisture retention, amend the soil with organic matter and keep it well mulched. Deep, infrequent waterings are best because they encourage the growth of root systems that reach deep into the soil for moisture belowground, and thus help plants get through long dry spells. For efficient watering, install a drip irrigation system *(pages 62-63)*.

Since healthy plants are better able than sickly ones to resist the stress of drought, you should weed and prune regularly and give prompt attention to any pests and diseases that may appear.

Snowy white blossoms cluster atop yucca plants' towering stems. Though it grows in a range of climates, yucca prefers hot, dry conditions and is an excellent choice for gardens where conserving water is important.

## SHRUBS FOR THE SEASHORE

Gardening at the seashore is a special challenge. The soil is usually sandy and dry, and there are often drying winds and salt spray to deal with. The gardener can meet this challenge with the right choice of shrubs and a little preparation prior to planting.

Shrubs tolerant of seashore conditions include cotoneaster, elaeagnus, juniper, myrtle, podocarpus and wild lilac. To make the soil moisture-retentive and help the shrubs become established, add organic matter to the soil before planting. To help maintain the shrubs once they are planted, give them an occasional heavy watering to leach out the salt in the soil, and hose down the foliage to wash off the salt spray.

# A PLAN FOR A XERISCAPE

The basic principles of xeriscaping apply to all arid land—whether desert, chaparral, high plains or seashore. The plan below illustrates these principles. Lawn is restricted to small areas where children may play and grownups may stroll and sit. The patio adjacent to the house provides additional outdoor living space. In front of the house and along two sides is a meadow of native wildflowers that takes the place of traditional turfgrass. Ground cover lies alongside the front walk. On the remaining side, beyond a bed of wildflowers bordering the lawn, are groups of native shrubs and trees arranged according to their watering needs. All the beds are served by an efficient drip irrigation system (not visible) and mulched to retain moisture in the soil.

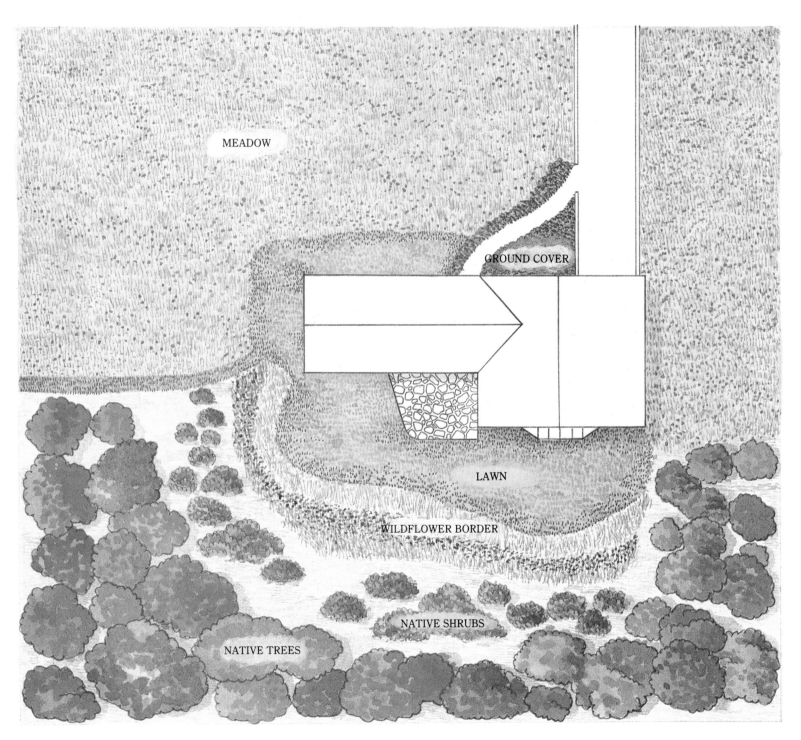

# PAVING THE WAY THROUGH THE YARD

A walkway is far more than a means of getting around the garden; it can create a mood, make a small space appear larger or draw attention to a particular feature. It can also help organize and highlight various parts of the garden by unifying separate elements and leading the eye—and the feet—to a favorite spot or two.

Layout and choice of materials are key factors in making the walkway do what you want it to do. A curved path lends a casual ambience, for example; a straight walk is likely to exert a more formal influence. The paving surface makes a difference, too: Gravel and wood chips are informal; brick and precast concrete tend to be formal. But the surface should accent, echo or at least harmonize with the materials of which the house is constructed—brick, stone or wood.

Although many a walkway is laid in a bed of concrete, stone dust makes a suitable foundation and is easy to install. It allows greater flexibility if adjustments have to be made as the walk is laid. If you choose a loose paving material such as gravel or shredded bark, remember first to build a border of boards, metal strips or brick to keep the material from spreading. If the walkway is to be primarily functional and will receive much foot traffic, it should be at least 5 feet wide, so two people can walk abreast. A backyard path that is meant primarily for design and that will be walked on only occasionally can be narrower—about 3 feet. In general, straight walks are the most functional in small gardens.

No matter what its purpose, the walkway must be constructed so that rainwater will drain off it. It should slope away from the house at a drop of $\frac{1}{8}$ to $\frac{1}{4}$ inch per foot, and along its full length it should lie about $\frac{1}{4}$ inch higher than the surrounding land. In digging out the bed for the walkway, remember to account for the depth of the stone-dust foundation and for the paving material itself.

*Flanked by a bed of ferns, spring bulbs and woodland flowers, a rustic stone path leads the eye through a lush garden that is canopied by flowering dogwoods.*

# A VARIETY OF PAVINGS

Many different paving materials are suited to garden walkways. Before you purchase any, measure the area of the proposed walkway and consult with your supplier, who can help you figure how many units you will need of any particular material, and how to deal with its peculiarities.

### WOOD CHIPS AND SHREDDED BARK
These soft pavings are laid loose, and lend a relaxed and natural feel to the garden. Chips and bark must be edged with boards, metal strips or bricks so they will not scatter, and they need to be replaced regularly. Both are ideal for woodland settings but are very absorbent and become soggy after a rainfall.

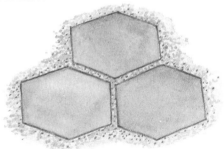

### PRECAST CONCRETE
Available in a wide range of sizes, shapes and colors, precast concrete is useful for many styles of walkways. It is sometimes sold in geometric shapes that can be laid in interlocking patterns, sometimes in pieces resembling bricks or stone slabs.

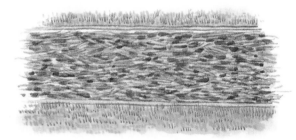

### GRAVEL
Gravel is laid loose and gives a casual tone well suited to wildflower, herb and woodland gardens. It should be laid about 1 inch below ground level or edged on all sides to prevent scattering. Gravel can be difficult to walk on, and needs yearly replenishment and regular raking to keep it smooth.

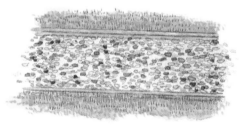

### WOOD
Redwood boards, wood blocks and round cross sections of tree trunks add a rustic feeling in casual settings. Any wood for outdoor use must be pressure-treated so it will not rot in dampness. Wood surfaces also tend to be slick when wet.

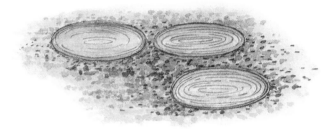

### FLAGSTONE
The varied sizes and shapes of most flagstones give them an informal look. Colors range from blue to gray and tan to brown. When laid on a bed of stone dust, flagstones should be at least 1 inch thick. Because they are heavy and odd-shaped, stones may be difficult to lay out.

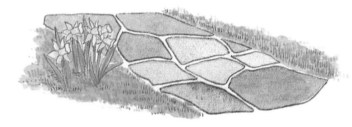

### BRICK
Attractive and versatile, brick goes well with almost any style of garden. It gives a formal look when laid out in straight lines and patterns, but is equally at home in an informal garden. To avoid cracking, buy paving bricks, which are harder and thinner than the bricks used in house construction.

# FOR SUCCESSFUL DESIGN:
# A PLAN ON PAPER

The foundation for a well-designed yard and a beautiful garden is a drawing that you make of your existing property. Such a drawing is called a base plan. One of its most important functions is to give a two-dimensional overview of the space you have to work with. A careful look at the base plan will reveal relationships between large plants and small ones, and also between them and the spaces that you have to fill. It will enable you to try out different arrangements—before you make costly mistakes with real plants.

To begin, draw the base plan on graph paper with eight squares to the inch. Let the length of each square equal 1 foot; if necessary, tape two sheets of paper together. To get the boundary and house measurements, you can use the plot survey of your property, or you can do the measuring yourself with a 50- or 100-foot carpenter's measuring tape.

To try out different designs, lay a piece of tracing paper over the base plan and sketch in the plants you want to add, allowing for their size at maturity. A colorful border will define an area; ground cover will unify several plantings. Give thought to what designers call focal points—places on which the eye focuses. An intersection of two lines (as in a corner) is a ready-made focal point and a good spot for an attractive planting. You can create a new focal point, however, by placing a tree or any other conspicuous planting in the middle of an open expanse of lawn. Consider how various trees, shrubs and flowers will look from different angles—and how they will look in different seasons and at different times of day. Consider wind pattern, too. For example, if cold north winds blow through your yard, think about planting tall evergreens to block them. If one design doesn't work on paper, just take a fresh sheet and try another.

*Purple lobelia are among the flowers edging a curving border of pink and orange impatiens, leafy rhododendron and graceful juniper that combine to draw the eye to an inviting front door.*

## THE MASTER PLAN FOR LAWN AND GARDEN

1 After determining the measurements, draw property boundaries and the outline of your house on graph paper. Draw in the driveway, walkways, and existing trees, shrubs and flower beds. Indicate the direction north and any other pertinent information—an unsightly view to be obscured, the location of a septic tank, a window from which you want to maintain or create a pleasing view, and the prevailing wind direction.

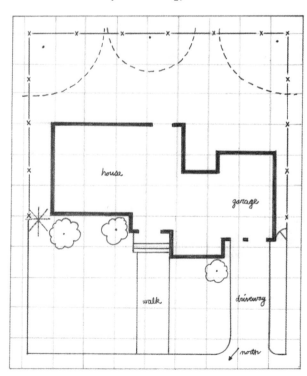

## SKETCHING GARDEN SHAPES

Symbols like these are useful for showing plants and other landscape features. Draw plants and trees as they will appear when fully grown so that you give them enough space. Note the approximate heights of all plants.

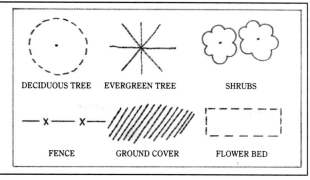

DECIDUOUS TREE    EVERGREEN TREE    SHRUBS

FENCE    GROUND COVER    FLOWER BED

2 Lay a sheet of tracing paper over the base plan and sketch in your ideas. You can use symbols such as those shown in the box at left to represent plants and other features. Two trees, ground cover and a walkway are being added here.

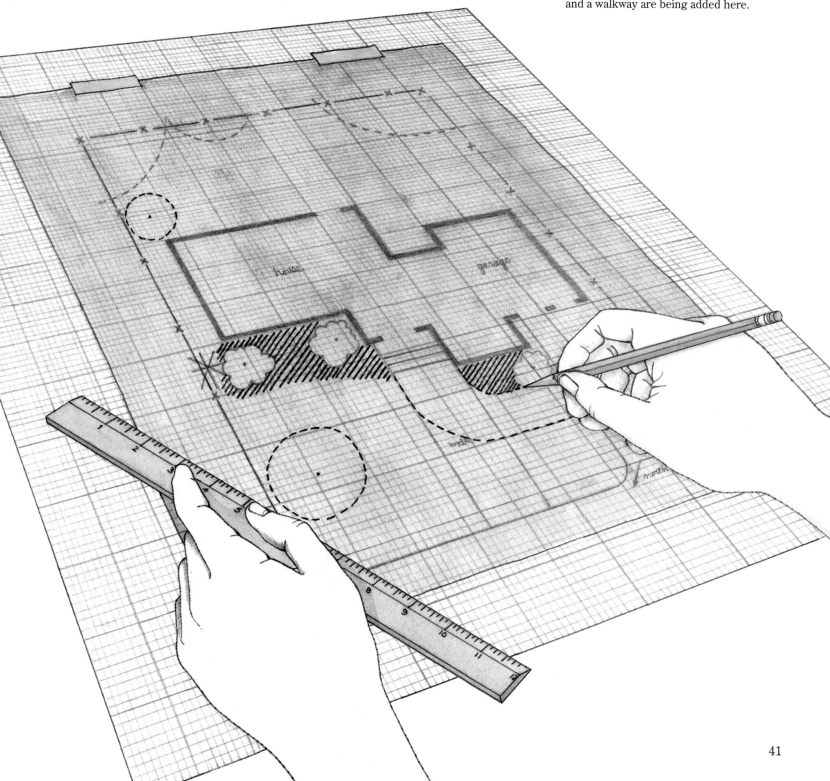

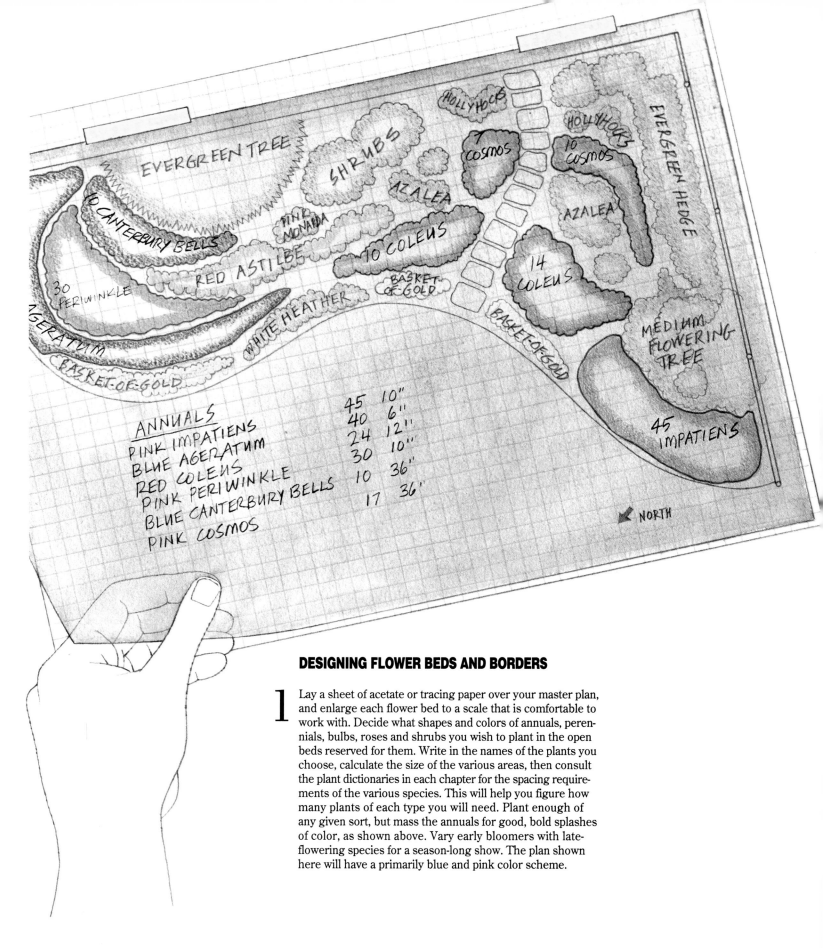

EVERGREEN TREE

SHRUBS

HOLLYHOCKS

HOLLYHOCKS

7 COSMOS

10 COSMOS

EVERGREEN HEDGE

AZALEA

10 CANTERBURY BELLS

PINK MONARDA

10 COLEUS

AZALEA

RED ASTILBE

14 COLEUS

30 PERIWINKLE

BASKET-OF-GOLD

AGERATUM

WHITE HEATHER

BASKET-OF-GOLD

MEDIUM FLOWERING TREE

BASKET-OF-GOLD

45 IMPATIENS

ANNUALS
PINK IMPATIENS              45   10"
BLUE AGERATUM              40   6"
RED COLEUS                 24   12"
PINK PERIWINKLE            30   10"
BLUE CANTERBURY BELLS      10   36"
PINK COSMOS                17   36"

NORTH

## DESIGNING FLOWER BEDS AND BORDERS

1 Lay a sheet of acetate or tracing paper over your master plan, and enlarge each flower bed to a scale that is comfortable to work with. Decide what shapes and colors of annuals, perennials, bulbs, roses and shrubs you wish to plant in the open beds reserved for them. Write in the names of the plants you choose, calculate the size of the various areas, then consult the plant dictionaries in each chapter for the spacing requirements of the various species. This will help you figure how many plants of each type you will need. Plant enough of any given sort, but mass the annuals for good, bold splashes of color, as shown above. Vary early bloomers with late-flowering species for a season-long show. The plan shown here will have a primarily blue and pink color scheme.

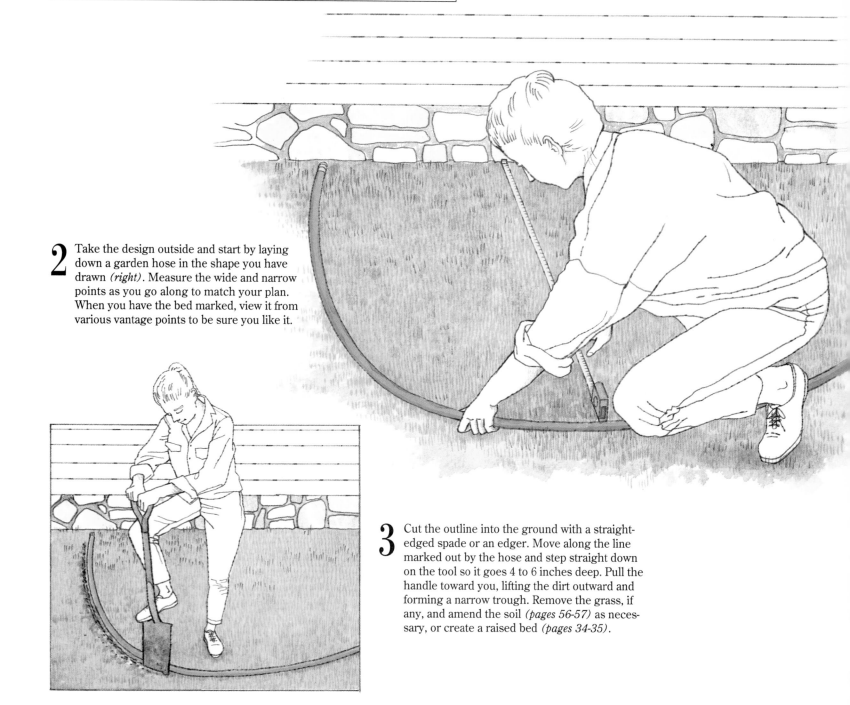

## EDIBLE ANNUALS

Most annuals are not considered to be edible, but there are several that can add color and flavor to various recipes. Nasturtium leaves and flowers add a peppery flavor to garden salads; dianthus flower petals add a taste of clove. Impatiens, pansies and violets are bland in flavor but can be used as a colorful garnish in salads or floating atop cold, creamy soups. Chrysanthemum petals, with their tangy, slightly bitter taste, can be sprinkled over salads, soups and cooked vegetables. Similar in taste to chrysanthemum are the golden petals of calendula and marigold. Sunflower seeds are well known to be edible. Less well known is that the buds of sunflowers can also be cooked and used for flavor accents similar to those of capers.

**2** Take the design outside and start by laying down a garden hose in the shape you have drawn *(right)*. Measure the wide and narrow points as you go along to match your plan. When you have the bed marked, view it from various vantage points to be sure you like it.

**3** Cut the outline into the ground with a straight-edged spade or an edger. Move along the line marked out by the hose and step straight down on the tool so it goes 4 to 6 inches deep. Pull the handle toward you, lifting the dirt outward and forming a narrow trough. Remove the grass, if any, and amend the soil *(pages 56-57)* as necessary, or create a raised bed *(pages 34-35)*.

# TRANSFERRING A PLAN FROM PAPER TO GARDEN

Once the graph-paper design for a flower bed or border has been completed *(pages 42-43)*, it needs to be duplicated in the actual garden plot—and tested to make certain that it will in fact work out. The first step is to mark the bed- or border-to-be with lines corresponding to the divisions drawn on the plan, as shown in the drawing at top, opposite. The second step is to assemble the plants that have been bought or collected and set them out in their allotted spaces, as shown for a perennial border *(opposite, bottom)*. During the second step, the eye may catch problems not evident on the paper plan.

Ask yourself, are there too few of some species in evidence? Perennials, for example, look best when planted in groups of three, five, six and even more. Four plants grouped together tend to form a square and look boxy. Fewer than three and the group will not be large enough to notice.

Another problem may be overcrowding. On an average, each perennial needs a square foot of garden space to get its share of light, air and nutrients, and there should be a few inches of extra room between plant groups because some groups will grow larger than their neighbors. This is also the time to decide about the bed or border's overall plant density. Putting in a maximum number of plants will make a border look lush the first season—but will necessitate thinning in two or three years, when the grown plants begin to crowd each other. Less dense planting may give a thin look at first, but healthy perennials will fill the gaps in a couple of seasons.

The best time to plant in most regions is April or May, before the weather becomes punishingly warm. Early spring planting gives perennials time to put down roots before blooming season. Planting of perennials can also be done in the autumn, however, as long as it is done early enough for the plants to establish themselves before the onset of winter.

*Yellow yarrow and purple loosestrife, planted in clusters large enough to make the most of their colorful blooms, emerge from a bank of lavender cupid's-dart in a casual-seeming but carefully planned perennial border.*

## SET SEEDS FOR SONGBIRDS

Don't deadhead—that is, pluck off the faded blossoms of—aster, bee balm, campion, columbine and zinnia; let them go to seed instead. Finches, grosbeaks, sparrows, buntings, juncos, doves, thrashers, towhees, cardinals and other songbirds find the seeds of these flowers especially attractive, and will come to feed on them from late summer through the winter. When they do, you will hear them trilling their songs from morning until dusk.

1 Before starting to transfer your design from graph paper *(pages 42-43)* to garden plot, write the names of the plants you intend to use with indelible ink on small white plant stakes. Over the already prepared ground, use extra stakes and lengths of string to lay a simple grid that corresponds to heavy lines on the plan. Then, with the strings as guidelines, sketch in the various planting areas with sprinkled handfuls of bone meal or sand as shown above. Insert the marked stakes in the appropriate areas, indicating where the plant groups belong.

2 Place your plants (still in their pots) where the white stakes indicate; then stand back and study the design before doing any planting. Any overcrowded areas should quickly become evident, as should places where there are too few plants of any given sort. You should also check to be sure that the various species are located where you will want them to remain. Later transplanting should be avoided if possible. No plant is improved by being moved; some suffer if they are disturbed.

# LIGHTING THE GARDEN AFTER NIGHTFALL

*A circle of half-hidden flood lamps gives strong emphasis to the upward thrust of these California redwoods. Against the deeply shadowed background, the glowing bark and foliage suggest warmth and sanctuary.*

Lighting a garden for nighttime activity and viewing offers a rare opportunity to combine the practical and the dramatic. Unobtrusive ankle-high lamps that guide visitors down a flight of garden steps after sunset may open the way to a spotlit stand of trees whose branches cast fantastic shadows on the wall behind them.

There was a time when the obvious benefits of outdoor lighting—enhanced access, security and beauty—were beyond the means of most gardeners. Equipment was costly and hazardous to install, and even the smallest job called for an electrician or a landscape architect. The advent of low-voltage lighting systems has changed all that.

Low-voltage wiring carries only 12 volts, the same as your car's electrical system, instead of the 120 volts that household fixtures use. You can buy reasonably priced do-it-yourself kits from hardware stores or garden-supply centers. No permits or special skills are needed. A typical kit comes with a transformer box (for stepping down household current to 12 volts), a built-in timer, 100 feet of plastic-covered wire, a half-dozen weatherproof lighting fixtures and spikes to hold the fixtures in place.

Hang the transformer box on an outside wall near a three-pronged household outlet. Position the box at least 18 inches above the ground (you can mount it higher for more convenient access). If the wall is brick, hammer a masonry nail (with grooved sides to prevent slipping) into the mortar between bricks; leave ½ inch of nail projecting from the wall to support the transformer box.

Wire all lamps in daylight. Do not plug the transformer into the household outlet until the entire system is wired. Even a low-voltage electrical fixture can give you a small shock.

Lighting a garden is like painting with light and shadow. In general, less is better than more. Overlighting can make healthy plants appear sickly or artificial. Try for a natural look that brings out the drama inherent in the setting. This works best when the source of light is hidden from view. Mask fixtures behind trees, shrubs, branches and borders.

## UPLIGHTING

In this arrangement, a light concealed under shrubbery shines up from the ground, on plants or on a special point of interest like the sculpture at right. Uplighting can be dramatic, revealing contours unnoticed in ordinary light. It has its practical advantages, too, because it does not shine into people's eyes or into a neighbor's garden.

## SILHOUETTING

Light is placed at the base of a wall or a fence behind a tree or shrubs or other plants that you want to show off. The effect can be striking, especially if the plant or plants are unusual or interesting in shape. Open-branched plants show up best; pruning can help get the shape you want.

## MOONLIGHTING

As the name implies, the light comes from above, shining from a lamp hooked in a tree (as here) or a couple of them mounted high on a wall. Simulating light from the moon, this sort of arrangement makes the garden seem a natural and restful place at night.

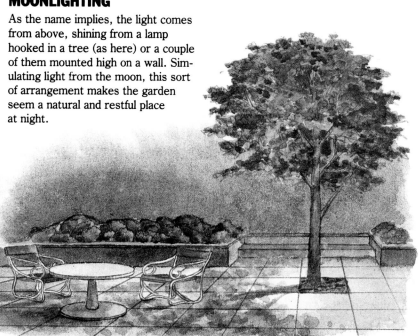

## SHADOWING

In this variant on uplighting, a lamp is hidden in a small shrub so that it illuminates a large shrub or tree nearby and throws a shadow on a wall or a fence. The closer you place the lamp to the object, the larger and more dramatic the shadow. Shadowing works best with plants that have space between their branches, such as the loose-limbed pine shown here. □

# 2

# TECHNIQUES FOR SUCCESSFUL GARDENING

*Small but already vigorous flowering dahlias are ready to move into the garden, thanks to several tried and true gardening techniques. Started from seed, then nurtured in individual pots, they are now hearty enough to thrive in a specially prepared garden bed.*

Successful gardening—whether that means growing luscious ripe tomatoes, keeping a green lawn thickly carpeted or tending to a vigorous and multicolored flower bed—depends on a handful of time-honored techniques. This chapter describes in detail some valuable methods that apply to the plants covered in the following chapters of this book.

Today, you have more gardening choices than ever before. A section on creating a "green" garden presents organic alternatives to chemical intervention with pesticides and herbicides. Next are some well-proven landscaping and soil improvement techniques for upgrading your garden environment. To help you establish a thriving garden in an area that may seem inhospitable to plants, there are suggestions for improving poor drainage and soil, and grading sloping or humped and hollow terrain. Hand in hand with soil improvement are directions for making compost as a supply of soil conditioner.

To keep established plants thriving, it helps to follow a program of regular maintenance. The key requirements of healthy plants—water and nutrient-rich soil—are the same no matter where they grow. The following pages include sections on how to water and fertilize plants efficiently and how to install a drip irrigation system and a soaker hose, allowing you to water a whole area at once while conserving this precious resource.

Plants need various sorts of protection, too—from staking to protect them from high winds and pelting rains, to averting the ravages of pests, to suffocating weeds and minimizing weed growth. These techniques are included along with others for nurturing plants—grooming to keep them healthier, bushier and eager to bloom, and using mulch to conserve moisture.

# CHAPTER CONTENTS

Propagating your own plants can be one of the most rewarding and intriguing parts of gardening. There is nothing difficult or arcane about propagating plants, and the rewards are legion. For one, the expense involved ranges from minimal to nonexistent. Many plants can be grown from seed, and virtually all the plants in your garden produce seeds from time to time. This chapter shows techniques for gathering and extracting seeds, and hastening their germination by reviving dormant ones. Most seeds can be started indoors and then successfully transplanted to the garden.

In addition, the chapter describes a number of methods that are collectively called vegetative propagation. These include dividing, layering, planting stem and leaf cuttings and scion grafting. Using these methods, you take a part of the parent plant and clone it into a separate plant. Alternatively, if you prefer to engage your own creativity in the reproductive process, refer to the section on hybridizing.

The propagation method you choose will depend upon both the type of plant you want to reproduce and the result you want. For example, the best way to produce the most offspring from a single parent is by sowing seeds. The new plants may not possess all the characteristics of the parent, but some may even be more colorful and vigorous. With vegetative techniques, you can duplicate a favored plant exactly, perpetuating the flowers and foliage of much-loved plants. Vegetative propagation usually gives you a mature plant faster than one you might grow from a seed of the same plant. Each propagation technique in this chapter works well with several types of plants. For additional techniques, refer to the chapters that are devoted to a specific type of plant.

# GROWING A "GREEN" GARDEN

*Banks of poppies with their rich green foliage and yellow blooms provide a colorful, contrasting background for a crisp row of white-blossomed perennial flowers. Like most plants, these thrive in a plot that is well mulched, watered and weeded. Mulching is an effective, chemical-free method of stifling the growth of weeds in a flower bed.*

As much as sunlight and rain are among gardeners' strongest natural allies, weeds and pests can be their greatest natural foes. Few things can spoil the effect of a rolling lawn like an invasion of dandelions or crabgrass; nothing can more systematically damage a colorful flower bed than an infestation of pests.

For years, the conventional defense against weeds and pests was limited to a chemical barrage—fighting weeds with herbicides and battling insects with pesticides. But in recent years, food growers, consumers' groups and home gardeners have begun to recognize that using chemicals can be dangerous. Formulated to kill living things, these substances can, in fact, do more harm than good—to the environment, to plants and, ultimately, to gardeners themselves.

Along with eradicating weeds and pests, chemicals can indiscriminately wipe out wildlife and vegetation the user did not intend to harm *(box, left)*—including beneficial insects that, eventually, would have fed on the pests *(opposite, top)*. In addition, pesticides and herbicides can be carried by the wind to cause damage in neighboring gardens. And some chemical residues can filter through the soil to groundwater, fouling drinking supplies. After use, the disposal of pesticide and herbicide containers and spray equipment can also lead to environmental contamination. Perhaps most disturbing, pests can become chemical-resistant over time, making their elimination even more difficult.

Many gardeners object to chemical control of pests and weeds on philosophical grounds: It runs counter, they say, to the idea that gardening should be harmonious with nature. This approach—called "organic" gardening—depends on the principle that you can grow a thriving and beautiful garden without using chemicals. Organic gardeners argue that weeds and pests are not the cause of problems, but rather symptoms of a poorly designed or maintained garden. A healthy, well-planned garden will generally be free of weeds and pests. Refer to the box at the bottom of the opposite page for tips on making your garden pest-, weed- and chemical-free.

## BEWARE OF PESTICIDES

Not only do pesticides kill the unwelcome insects that prey on your plants, including beetles and caterpillars. They also kill beneficial insects, such as bees and other insects, that do the vital work of pollinating flowers, as well as the spiders, mantises, ladybugs and birds that serve as pest controls in their own right. Beneficial insects also naturally aerate the soil by digging and burrowing; their droppings and dead bodies add up, acting as natural soil fertilizer. In most gardens, beneficial insects far outnumber pests. In a garden that is intended to attract wildlife, it is especially important to avoid using pesticides; insects are a main staple of many birds and fish.

## LIVE INSECT CONTROLS

Some destructive plant pests can be controlled with beneficial insects and lizards. Certain insects and lizards do not damage plants, but prey on the insects that do. These helpful creatures, which are available from specialized mail-order and greenhouse-supply firms, can be introduced into a garden. Since some insects feed on only one or two types of troublesome pests, select the right type of predator for the insects you need to control: Ladybugs and ladybug beetles feed on aphids; lacewings feed on aphids as well as mealybugs, spider mites, scales, thrips and whiteflies. Parasitic nematodes feed on fungus gnats and predatory mites feed on spider mites.

Lizards feed on a variety of insects, and they can be brought into a garden to help keep insect populations under control. The most commonly available lizard is the chameleon *(right)*, which can be purchased at pet stores. For most gardens, three or four chameleons should suffice.

Insecticides should not be used in combination with lizards and beneficial insects.

## STRATEGIES FOR A CHEMICAL-FREE GARDEN

The gardener dedicated to nurturing a lawn or garden without chemicals has many available options. Listed below are tips for growing chemical-free lawns, flower beds and vegetable plots. Many of the tips are preventive; it is easier to keep a healthy garden free of weeds and pests than to get rid of them after they have settled in. In some instances, you will be referred to another part of the book for more detailed information.

• Keep your soil healthy, upgrading it before it deteriorates *(pages 56-57)*. Pests tend to attack plants languishing in poor soil, and some weeds do better in poor soil than many desirable plants.

• Grow plants that are native to your area. Trying to coax a warm-weather plant to thrive in a northerly region or relocating a northern plant to the South often results in a weak plant that is vulnerable to pests. At the end of each subsequent chapter is a dictionary of plants; use the dictionaries in conjunction with the Zone Map *(inside front cover)* to select plants that will thrive in your climatic zone.

• Spread mulch around plants both to control weeds and to conserve moisture *(pages 70-71)*.

• Remove weeds by hand *(pages 70-71)* and, for small pest infestations, hand-pick them off plants, if possible. Refer to the Troubleshooting Guides in subsequent chapters for additional information on hand-picking pests.

• Set up yellow sticky traps—available at a garden-supply center—to control pests. Several insects, including winged aphids, fungus gnats, thrips and whiteflies, are attracted to the color yellow. The hue draws the insects to the traps, where they become trapped.

• Make your own compost *(pages 58-59)* and use it to fertilize soil.

• Use organic fertilizers—for example, well-rotted animal manure, compost and bone meal—rather than synthetic chemical products.

• Use natural pesticides rather than chemical ones. Some examples of natural pesticides are soft soap and pyrethrum, which is a plant extract. *Bacillus thuringiensis* (Bt), diatomaceous earth and horticultural oil are considered to be among the safest commercially available pesticides. Refer to the Troubleshooting Guides in subsequent chapters for specific directions.

• Experiment with companion planting. This entails planting together different species of flowers or vegetables that, in combination, keep pests away. Avoid planting too many of the same type of plant in the same part of the garden.

• Use water—a pond or basin, for example—to entice birds, frogs and toads into your garden *(page 52)*. These animals are natural predators of many pests, including slugs, snails and other ground-dwelling insects.

# LANDSCAPING: IMPROVING DRAINAGE

*A broad array of trees, shrubs, perennials and ornamental grasses flourish in a shaded garden, reflecting in their vigor and beauty the soil's good drainage. Even moisture-loving plants need proper drainage; sodden soil can cause their roots to rot.*

**G**ood drainage is essential to a healthy garden. When soil becomes waterlogged, plants cannot absorb the oxygen they need; roots suffocate and eventually rot *(box, below left)*. Even worse, excess water that collects around the foundations of your house may weaken the structure itself. But fortunately, drainage problems are easy to spot. Wherever puddles remain on the ground for several hours after a rain or a watering, you should take steps to improve drainage.

Preparing the soil *(pages 56-57)* may clear up the trouble. If your terrain slopes or has bumps or hollows, grading it *(pages 54-55)* may remedy the problem. If not, you will have to install a drainage system. For unusually severe or extensive problems, consult a professional contractor. But in most cases, you can do the job yourself with a simple drainage system consisting of a length of flexible, perforated plastic pipe in a gravel-filled trench. Excess water seeps down into the pipe and is carried away to an area where the drainage is more rapid.

You can buy drainage pipe, in 3- or 4-inch diameters, in most hardware stores. Lengths vary; you may have to cut a piece to size or connect several pieces together. To determine how much pipe you will need, measure the distance from the center of the trouble spot to the nearest area the water can be directed to.

Once the pipe is laid, grade the nearby soil so that water is directed away from your house, flower beds, vegetable plots, trees and shrubs, and into the trench. No major landscaping is required; all you have to do is shift enough soil to ensure that the ground slopes in the desired direction.

Puddling often occurs under a rain spout that carries water from the roof of a house. To eliminate such a problem, connect the drainage pipe to the spout with a plastic elbow or joint sold expressly for this purpose.

In time, any drainage system will become clogged by a buildup of silt and other debris. When this happens, replace the pipe.

---

### A WORD ABOUT WATER

• **Pooling water in a small garden**
The simple addition of a water element in a shady area can bring in and reflect light in a small garden. An easy way to do so without the fuss of pumps and pipes is to perch a shallow ceramic basin on a low wall, sink it into the ground, or place it near the side of the house or in the corner of a fence, where it will suggest the flowing harmony of a Japanese tea garden. The water will reflect flora and attract fauna such as birds, which are often drawn to a garden by the sight of water glistening in the sun; they come not only to drink but to bathe and preen themselves. Even butterflies sometimes need a drink and will flutter around the water's surface.

• **The dangers of poor drainage**
Too much water, caused by poor drainage, can kill your plants. Poor drainage can promote root rot, a soilborne fungus disease. If the leaves of your plants turn yellow and are stunted or wilted, or entire plants are wilting and dying, root rot may be the problem. Confirm the diagnosis by tugging on a small plant; if it can easily be pulled from the soil and reveals soft, wet, discolored, dark brown or black roots, it is afflicted with root rot. Before improving soil drainage, remove and discard affected plants and the surrounding soil and drench the soil with a fungicide.

**1** To lay a drainage pipe, dig a trench that is 12 to 18 inches wide; begin digging at the trouble spot to a depth of at least 1 foot. To ensure that water drains in the right direction, increase the depth gradually as the trench slopes away from the trouble spot. Unless the trench leads out directly to a paved street or some suitable catchment area, dig a small pit or dry well—2½ feet wide and deep—at the lower end of the trench. This will prevent water from draining onto a neighbor's property. Keep the soil you remove for later use as backfill *(step 2)*. To prevent silt and rocks from clogging the pipe, screen the opening at the upper end with a small piece of landscape fabric—available at a garden-supply center. The fabric will permit water to pass through but keep out larger particles. Lay the pipe in the trench so that the lower end extends 1 or 2 inches over the dry well *(left)*.

**2** Cover the pipe with a 4- to 6-inch layer of gravel and fill up the dry well with gravel to the same level. Then cut a piece of landscape fabric as long and wide as the trench and lay it on top of the gravel. This will prevent soil particles from clogging the perforations on top of the pipe. Fill the trench and dry well up to ground level; add organic matter, such as compost, to the backfill to encourage water to percolate down to the pipe. Using a shovel, regrade the area. Fill in any low spots—where puddles form—with soil removed from bumps and ridges that could block runoff. The ground should slope down slightly from the trouble spot. After this rough grading, use an iron rake to smooth the surface and remove rocks, clumps of grass and other debris *(right)*. To prevent soil erosion, plant flowers, shrubs or grass in the regraded area as soon as possible. If drainage is still poor, consider growing varieties that are resistant to excess water, or building a raised bed, as described in Chapter 1.

# LANDSCAPING: GRADING

*A lawn sweeps steeply, but at a regular pitch, past a house, carrying away rainwater and providing an interesting combination of planes and angles as background for the plantings.*

## SALVAGING A SLOPE

An area with a severe slope can be rescued for planting with ground covers or shrubs that have strong root systems. Roots help hold the soil in place and prevent erosion. Plants needing little care are also ideal on a slope; they require fewer trips on the hilly terrain for pruning and other maintenance chores. Good choices among ground covers *(Chapter 3)* are crown vetch, daylilies, hosta or English ivy. Among shrubs *(Chapter 8)*, choose juniper and cotoneaster.

G rading—the process of smoothing off land—is the basic earth-moving technique used to develop landscape. It provides adequate drainage and the smooth foundation necessary for lawns, walks and patios. It eliminates slopes so steep that they cause erosion of topsoil and make walking hazardous and planting impractical. But grading does not imply the creation of a surface that is perfectly horizontal or one that is unvaryingly flat; some slope is desirable so that rainwater will run off, and some contouring gives character to the landscape.

Good grading takes advantage of the leaning of the ground. The job may be as simple as evening out the odd high spot that looks unsightly and the random depression that tends to puddle (or to cause falls). Or it may be as elaborate as constructing stepped terraces (which simultaneously aid drainage and discourage soil-erosion by allowing land to drop considerably but in graduated stages). Refer to Chapter 1 for directions on terracing.

Changing a slope on a large scale is work for a professional landscape contractor. You can solve the soil-erosion problems associated with a steep slope by planting shrubs on it *(box, left)*. Minor irregularities can be easily fixed, using a flat-edged spade, a steel rake and a tarp to transfer soil from a spot that has too much to another that hasn't enough, as shown opposite.

1 Using a spade, cut the turf away from the area to be graded. Roll it up and place it on a tarp for later use. Dig out the topsoil and save it. Scrape the subsoil from the high spots and shovel it into the dips *(inset)*. Dig down about 6 inches. Remove stones and break up the subsoil to improve aeration and drainage *(right)*.

2 Tamp down the soil by treading on it. Add more soil and tamp again if necessary to achieve a solid base that is even with the adjoining subsoil. Shovel on the topsoil you saved, working in soil amendments, such as humus and fertilizer, to improve soil quality and drainage, and rake the surface smooth *(left)*. Finally, replace the turf and step on it to press it firmly into the topsoil.

# IMPROVING THE SOIL: CHEMICAL BALANCE AND TEXTURE

Plants grow best in nutrient-rich, chemically balanced and soft-textured soil that will retain enough water for the plants but will drain away any excess moisture. The logical first step is to analyze your soil's nutrient content and its acid-alkaline balance, the so-called pH level, measured on a scale of 0 to 14. The number 7 represents neutrality; the lower the number below that, the more acidic the soil is, and the higher the number, the more alkaline it is.

Although all plants prefer nutrient-rich soil, not all of them thrive in soil with the same pH level. Most plants prefer slightly acidic soil, whereas a few, like azaleas, grow best in more acidic conditions. Bulbs, on the other hand, thrive in alkaline soil, but will do well in slightly acidic soil. Fortunately, nutrient-poor soil can be enriched and soil pH can be adjusted, as shown opposite.

To determine the nutrient content and pH of your soil, gather a sample and test it—either with a do-it-yourself kit available at garden-supply centers or through mail-order suppliers, or by having the test done by an agricultural extension service or a fertilizer company. Gather the soil sample when the ground is moist but not wet. Dig down 4 to 6 inches with a trowel, remove a scoop of soil and put it in a clean bucket. Repeat in several places around the planting bed. Mix the scoopfuls together, remove a cupful and test it or seal it in a plastic bag and have it tested. The results will tell you whether you need to add fertilizer and lime or sulfur (to adjust soil pH), and what amounts of each are needed.

To test the texture of your soil, squeeze a fistful of it in your hand. If it fails to hold a shape and sifts through your fingers, the soil has too much sand. If it compacts into a tight ball, it has too much clay. In either case the remedy is the same—adding generous amounts of humus.

To save time, you can repair all soil deficiencies—in pH, texture and nutrient content—by double digging (*box, right and opposite*). For procedures on improving soil for a lawn, refer to pages 102-104; for improving vegetable plot soil, refer to pages 466-467.

*Fragrant annual herbs, with their lush green leaves and pleasing aroma, nestle beside some bright-blooming orange cosmos. These plants—and most others that give variety and color to a garden—will grow better if the soil has the proper texture and pH level and has been enriched with both organic matter and fertilizer.*

## DOUBLE DIGGING

Double digging is a process for improving soil that entails making a series of trenches and refilling one with soil from another. Remove a layer of topsoil from the first trench (*far right*), amend it and set it aside. Then break up and amend the subsoil in that trench. Transfer topsoil from the second trench (*center*) to the first trench and amend it. Continue digging, transferring and amending in this fashion until the topsoil set aside from the first trench is used to fill the last trench (*long arrow*). The operation may have any number of trenches, but in each step the subsoil stays in its own trench and the topsoil moves to another.

The best time to improve the soil of a planting bed is in late fall or early winter before the ground freezes. This will allow the amendments to decompose and give their nutrients to the soil over the winter, making the improved soil ready for spring planting. Whatever the season, do not dig a garden after a heavy rain; wet earth is hard to work with. Repeat the process every five years or so to give your plants a fresh lease on life.

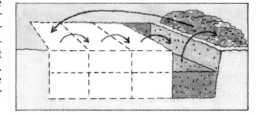

**1** To double dig a new bed, first use a flat-bladed spade to remove and discard any sod. Then dig a 2-foot-wide trench as long as you want the new bed to be *(left)*. Remove the top layer of soil to the depth of the blade, place it in a wheelbarrow or on a tarpaulin, discarding weeds, roots and large stones. Into the topsoil mix in the necessary amendments: lime for excess acidity; sulfur or humus (rotted leaves or manure, peat moss, blood meal, bone meal or compost) for excess alkalinity; fertilizer for nutrient-poor soil; and humus for soil that is too sandy or clayey.

**2** Using a garden fork, turn over the subsoil in the bottom of the trench to the depth of the fork tines; break up all clods thoroughly *(below)*. Work the same amendments into this layer of soil as you did for the topsoil layer you removed.

**3** Remove a spade's depth of topsoil from the second trench and transfer it to the first trench. Again, amend the soil with the necessary additives. Then turn over and break up the subsoil in the second trench and in successive trenches *(above)*, as described in step 2.

**4** Repeat the process—opening a new trench, moving soil to the previously opened trench and amending—until you have conditioned the entire bed. Fill the last trench with the soil removed from the first trench. When the entire bed has been turned over, break up any remaining clods and rake the surface smooth *(right)*.

57

# IMPROVING THE SOIL: MAKING COMPOST

*A pink-and-yellow perennial thrives in the dark, organically rich soil of its bed. Like virtually all plants, this one benefits from the extra nutrients that compost adds to the garden.*

## A VARIETY OF COMPOST BINS

Compost can be manufactured easily and neatly in many different types of containers. Ready-to-buy models are available at garden-supply centers, but you can make your own compost bin. For a small garden, an oil drum is large enough and has one advantage: The compost inside heats up fast and matures quickly. The drum should be open at the bottom and perforated on its sides to let air in. Larger bins can be made of cinder blocks or bricks, with spaces between the blocks (or bricks) for air circulation. Such bins may be mortared together, but at least one side should be left loose—that is, unmortared—so you can remove the blocks or bricks and easily get at the compost inside. No bin of any sort should have a floor; compost matures best if the pile rests on the ground. Each segment of a bin should measure at least 3 feet by 3 feet by 3 feet.

Most plants thrive in soil that is rich in humus—decaying organic matter—because humus holds moisture and provides nutrients to plants. The best way to give your plants the humus they need is to make your own in a compost pile assembled from fallen leaves and other organic matter. After the leaves are raked into piles, they can be shredded with a rotary lawn mower (shredding hastens their decomposition). Along with leaves, you can compost any organic matter that is handy—grass clippings, weeds, hay, straw, small twigs, vegetable refuse—so long as it has not been contaminated with herbicides or pesticides. Also eligible are kitchen scraps—spoiled lettuce, coffee grounds, eggshells, chopped-up corncobs. Meat scraps, dairy products, grease, bones and citrus fruits are not recommended, however; they turn rancid and attract rodents.

For a successful compost pile, you will have to add layers of garden soil (to supply the microorganisms that do the work of decomposition) and commercial fertilizer or blood meal (to supply the nitrogen that these microorganisms require). Water and aeration are also necessary to speed the rate of decomposition. While the pile decomposes, keep it moist but not waterlogged and stir it periodically with a shovel.

For neatness and efficiency, most compost piles are built inside simple enclosures. Four fencing stakes (which come with built-in hooks on one side) and a roll of chicken wire are sufficient to make a bin, as shown opposite. Other bin styles are possible, as described in the box at left.

After three or four months the material in the compost pile will no longer resemble the shredded leaves and other organic matter that you started with. It will be dark in color and crumbly to the touch—nutrient-rich humus ready to nourish your plants.

When you begin to use the compost, to ensure a continuous supply of humus, remove the fully composted material from the bottom of the pile by lifting up a section of chicken wire. Replace what you have taken by layering more organic matter, soil and fertilizer on top.

1 Choose an out-of-the-way site for your compost pile and break up the soil that will be under it, using a garden fork. This will promote good drainage from the bottom of the pile. To make a bin for a compost pile, buy four 4- to 5-foot-high fencing stakes and a roll of chicken wire, then mark out a 3-foot-square area and drive a stake into the ground at each marked corner *(right)*; use a sledgehammer, if necessary. Make sure the hooks on the stakes face outward so that you can attach the chicken wire to them.

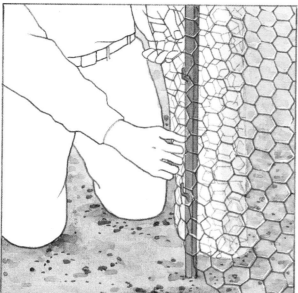

2 Wrap the wire around the first stake and loop the ends of the strands over the outward-facing hooks *(left)*; stretch the wire taut and repeat on each stake in turn. Cut away the rest of the roll, using wire cutters. If any wire extends above the stakes, bend the excess down. Secure the corners with lengths of wire cut from the chicken wire and twisted around each stake in three places.

3 Cover the bottom of the bin with 6 inches of organic matter—shredded leaves, twigs and branches, vegetable and kitchen scraps; top this with ¼ inch of high-nitrogen fertilizer or blood meal, bone meal or fish meal, then 2 inches of garden soil. Moisten thoroughly; moisture helps activate the bacteria in the pile, and also helps create heat—which speeds the process of decomposition, kills weeds and generally purifies the entire pile. Continue layering leaves, fertilizer and soil—moistening as you go—until the bin is full. If the weather is dry, water every two weeks and turn over the layers each week, using a garden fork to distribute the moisture and keep the material aerated. To conserve both moisture and warmth, you can cover the pile with an old blanket or rug, or with a sheet of black plastic. Cover the pile in heavy rain to keep it from becoming waterlogged, which will slow down decomposition. When the matter has turned dark and crumbly—usually in three to four months—it has turned into compost and is ready to use.

# MAINTAINING PLANTS: WATERING AND FERTILIZING

Garden plants have hearty appetites. To keep them healthy and looking their best, they need water and fertilizer regularly. Fertilizer labels carry three numbers that give the percentages of the nutrients—nitrogen, phosphorus and potassium (in that order)—that the mix contains. Only a soil test *(pages 56-57)* will tell you exactly what formulation is best for your garden. But plants generally have predictable requirements. The fertilizer most commonly used for roses, for example, is labeled 15-15-15, which means that 45 percent of the mix (by weight) consists of equal parts of the three main nutrients. The other 55 percent is filler, with traces of elements such as sulfur, calcium, magnesium, manganese, iron and zinc. A 5-10-10 fertilizer is ideal for annuals; a 5-10-5 for perennials; a 10-10-10 for bulbs. For the nutrition requirements of lawns, refer to pages 124-129; for trees and shrubs, pages 394-395; for vegetables, pages 468-469; and for houseplants, pages 536-538.

You can feed plants with granular fertilizer *(opposite)*, spikes or liquid fertilizer. The granular and spike forms may release their nutrients at once or little by little; the liquids nourish the soil right away. Whichever you use, be sure to read the label carefully to find out how much to apply. Inadequate nutrition stunts growth; too much can weaken plants and make them susceptible to disease.

Apply fertilizer at the start of the growing season (at planting time for annuals) and again in early summer for perennials and midsummer for annuals and roses. Give roses an additional application at the end of each bloom cycle. During their bloom cycle and for special occasions, a supplemental dose of liquid fertilizer for roses will brighten color and increase bloom size, with results within 10 days.

Water a plant immediately after feeding it so that the fertilizer reaches the roots. Also water most plants so they receive about 1 inch of water—including rainfall—per week; a rain gauge, available at garden-supply centers, can tell you how much rainfall your plants get. Trees are an exception: Water a newly transplanted sapling once a week for two or three years, an older tree only during droughts.

*Bursting with color and vigor, roses beautifully demonstrate the value of a thoughtful, timely program of nutrition.*

1 Before applying a fertilizer, remove weeds *(pages 70-71)*, leaves, old mulch and other debris from under and around the plant. Following the instructions on the label, spread the fertilizer near the base of the plant *(right)*; to protect your hands, wear gloves or use a trowel. Be careful not to let any fertilizer touch leaves, stems or flowers—unless you are using a foliage fertilizer that is specifically intended to be sprayed on foliage.

2 To water a plant with a hose, use a nozzle attachment that breaks up the flow into a gentle spray *(left)*. For more information on watering accessories, see the box below. Water until the ground is thoroughly wet; depending on weather and the type of soil, this may take five to 10 minutes. Then—foliage fertilizers excepted—give the leaves and stems a final rinse to make sure no fertilizer has landed on them; they can be damaged by the salts in fertilizer.

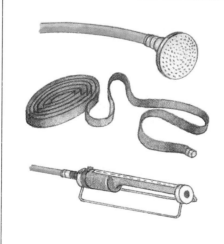

### WATERING ACCESSORIES

Whatever your watering chore, there is a tool available to help you do it right. To provide a gentle shower that will not wash away soil from the base of a plant, use a fine-spray nozzle *(top)* that attaches to your garden hose. To deliver moisture to the roots of plants with minimal evaporation loss, buy a soaker hose *(center)* made of permeable canvas or perforated rubber that oozes water from its entire length. Stretch out the soaker hose on the surface or bury it underground for a season of irrigation. If you use a sprinkler *(bottom)* to water plants, remember to leave it on long enough to give the soil a good, deep soaking.

# MAINTAINING PLANTS: DRIP IRRIGATION AND SOAKER HOSES

Almost no other care is more important to plants than watering. Nutrients from the soil must be dissolved in water before they can enter a plant. Plants take in water through their roots, so make sure the soil is moistened to a depth of 4 to 5 inches. To tell if your plants are getting enough water, dig to the base of the roots with a trowel and scoop up some soil. If it feels moist, you have watered sufficiently. Do not overwater. Saturated soil keeps air from reaching the roots; without air the roots will rot and die. Also, wet soil attracts slugs, snails and fungus.

If you water with an ordinary garden hose, do your watering in the morning, if possible, to allow the foliage to dry out by nightfall; at night, wet leaves tend to mildew.

Two far better ways to water are by drip irrigation or by using a soaker hose—methods that let water seep to many plant roots simultaneously. These methods don't wet plant leaves, and no water is lost to evaporation. Both are excellent methods of conserving water.

Soaker hoses *(page 64)* and the apparatus you need for drip irrigation *(below and opposite)* are available at garden-supply centers and by mail order. A drip irrigation system usually consists of an irrigation hose—one with several openings from which small, flexible mini-hoses, or ooze tubes, branch off to deliver water directly to the roots of individual plants. Both types of systems can be connected to an ordinary garden hose. And most come with instructions telling you how long to let them run for watering a given area, and with the parts needed to put the hose together. To determine how much irrigation or soaker hose you will need, draw a plan of your garden; measure the length of each row and of all turns between rows.

*Lying on either side of a row of tomato plants, a drip irrigation hose with ooze tubes lets water seep slowly into the soil where plants need it most—at their roots. Such a system is efficient because hardly any water is lost to evaporation.*

## DRIP IRRIGATION

1 Assemble a drip irrigation system following the manufacturer's instructions. For the model shown, first slip one of the clamps provided loosely around one end of the irrigation hose; then insert a plug *(right)*. Tighten the clamp around the plug, using a screwdriver to seal the end of the hose.

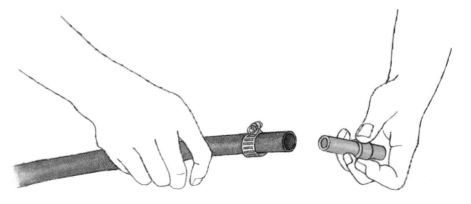

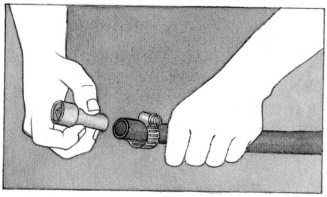

**2** Slip a second clamp loosely around the other end of the hose. Insert a female hose coupling *(above)*, then tighten the clamp over the coupling. Connect the coupling to your garden hose.

**3** Run the irrigation hose between rows of plants—in a vegetable plot, along the furrows lying between rows of vegetables, making a smooth curve at each end *(below)*. Smooth out any kinks in the hose and avoid right angles. Continue laying the irrigation hose until it lies alongside all plants to be watered.

**4** Punch a hole in the hose (using an awl or the tip of a nail, if necessary) at each plant location and insert an ooze tube into each hole *(left)*.

**5** Place the water-emitting end of the ooze tube on the ground directly under each plant *(below)*. To conserve moisture, cover the hose and tubes with mulch. Turn on the water at intervals recommended by the manufacturer. Check the water-emitting ends of the tubes periodically, clearing any clogged openings and securing any loosened tubes. Be careful to avoid damaging the hose or tubes when weeding or mowing.

## WATERING A LONE PLANT

To water a single plant, punch holes in a plastic jug and bury it near the plant. The top of the jug should protrude about 1 inch above the ground. Fill it with water. Water will seep to the roots. Refill the jug *(above)* when the soil feels dry.

## A SOAKER HOSE

1 Connect a soaker hose to a faucet near the planting bed. Lay the hose on the ground *(below)*. If your garden is planted in straight lines, run the hose between rows to supply plants on both sides. If the hose is new and resists lying flat, weight it down with bricks or stones while you work. To water a tree with a soaker hose, loop the hose around the tree's drip line— the point that lies just beneath the outermost edges of the branches.

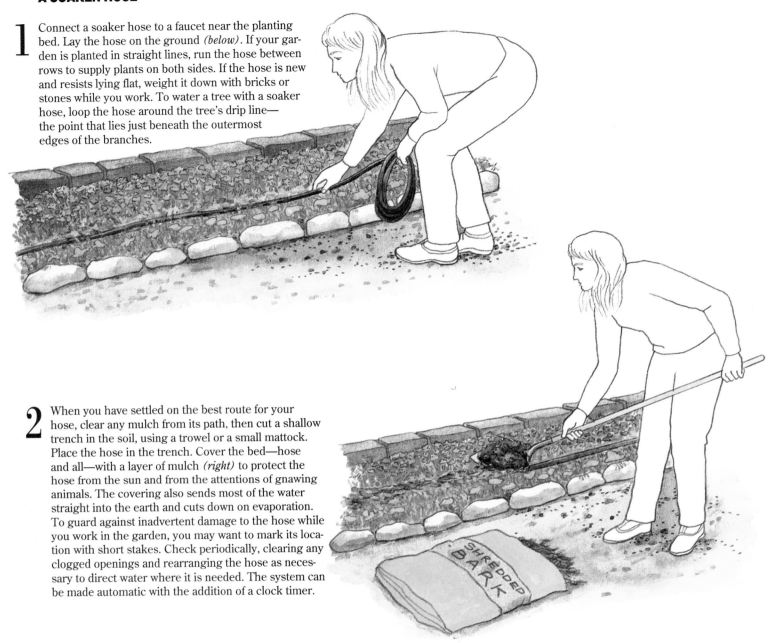

2 When you have settled on the best route for your hose, clear any mulch from its path, then cut a shallow trench in the soil, using a trowel or a small mattock. Place the hose in the trench. Cover the bed—hose and all—with a layer of mulch *(right)* to protect the hose from the sun and from the attentions of gnawing animals. The covering also sends most of the water straight into the earth and cuts down on evaporation. To guard against inadvertent damage to the hose while you work in the garden, you may want to mark its location with short stakes. Check periodically, clearing any clogged openings and rearranging the hose as necessary to direct water where it is needed. The system can be made automatic with the addition of a clock timer.

### WATER IN PEST CONTROL

Water isn't just essential to a plant's diet. It can also help you keep certain pests off your plants— without the use of pesticides. Aphids and leafhoppers are two pests that can do a great deal of damage to plants. Aphids are ⅛-inch semitransparent bugs that may be green, yellow, black, red or brown. They gather in clusters on buds, leaves and stems, and suck plant sap. Aphids can cause plant leaves to curl, wither and yellow, and buds and flowers to emerge deformed. Leafhoppers are ⅕-inch winged bugs that are light green or gray and wedge-shaped. They cause leaves to turn yellow or become speckled with white dots. They can also cause plant growth to be stunted. Although both pests can be combated with insecticidal soap or an insecticide, a strong, heavy stream of water from a garden hose can knock the insects off plants, and may even kill them.

# MAINTAINING PLANTS: STAKING

*Towering above a bed of cosmos, salvia and other plants, sunflowers nod in a breeze. Their tall stems need staking about halfway up.*

Some garden plants grow so tall, top-heavy or thin-stemmed that a stiff breeze may topple them. Especially vulnerable are those with large flower heads, such as dahlias, sunflowers and zinnias. Also endangered are slender plants such as cosmos, and tall, spiky plants such as delphinium and foxgloves. The best way to prevent broken stems and bedraggled blooms is to provide the plants with stakes—before the plants produce full-blown flowers and need support. One method, called peripheral staking, is to stake them in groups *(opposite)*. This works best with species that tend to sprawl sideways or grow upward—zinnias and marigolds, for example—and with slender plants like cosmos that are normally planted in clumps. Single staking—using one stake per plant *(page 67)*—is essential for spiky plants that grow very tall or have heavy blooms, or both. The time to single stake a spiky perennial is in spring, as soon as the plant shows signs of budding. Refer to pages 494-495 for directions on staking and caging tomato plants; for staking roses, refer to pages 336-337.

The stakes can be inconspicuous. Ideal are lengths of green-stained bamboo, which are thin but strong and blend into the surrounding foliage. They should be about ½ inch in diameter and long enough to support the height of the mature plants and leave an extra 8 inches to push into the ground.

## PERIPHERAL STAKING

1 To stake a small bed of slender-stemmed plants, drive a stake into the ground at each corner of the bed. A larger bed may require additional stakes, say three or more on each side. The stakes should be close enough to help the plants stay upright, without crowding them. Then loop a length of soft twine around the stakes about 1 foot above the ground and tie the ends *(right)*. This will help support the lower foliage as the plants grow taller. If you live in a windy area, you can give the plants extra support by running additional lengths of twine in a crisscross pattern through the flower bed, attaching the ends to diagonally opposite stakes.

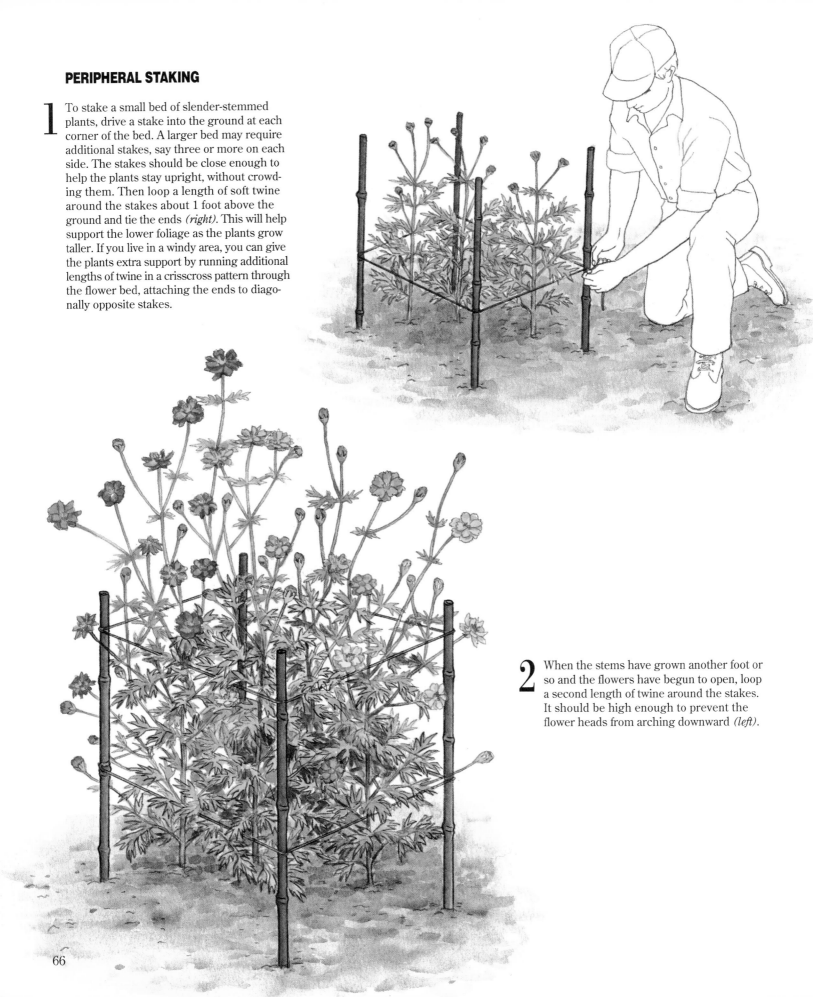

2 When the stems have grown another foot or so and the flowers have begun to open, loop a second length of twine around the stakes. It should be high enough to prevent the flower heads from arching downward *(left)*.

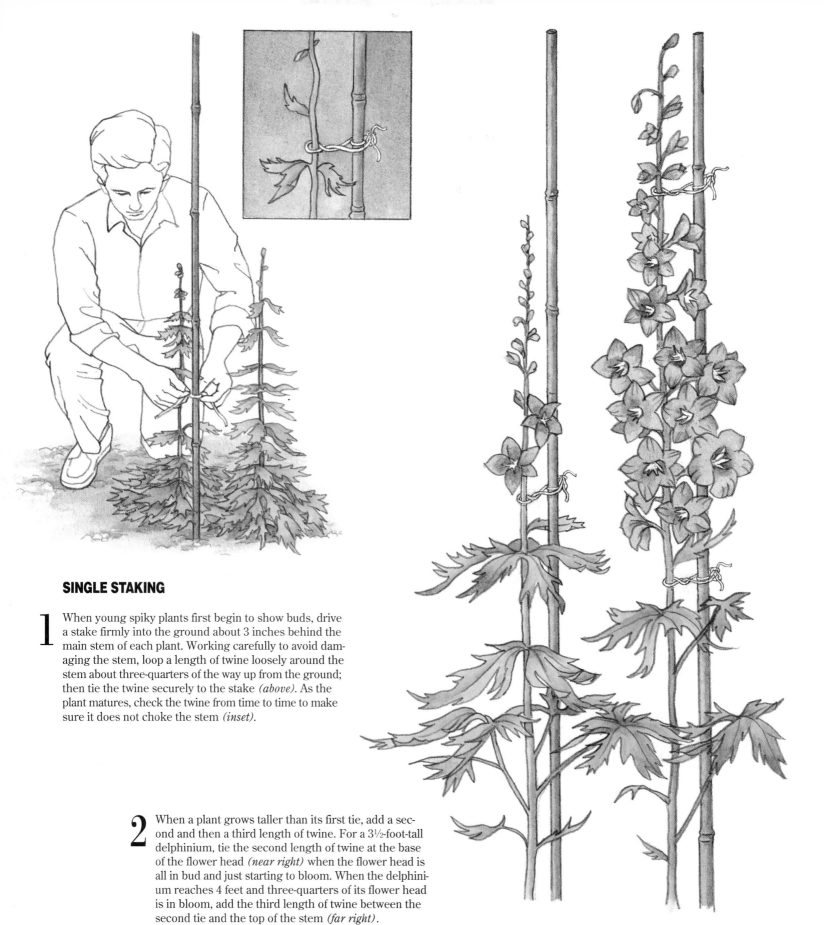

## SINGLE STAKING

1 When young spiky plants first begin to show buds, drive a stake firmly into the ground about 3 inches behind the main stem of each plant. Working carefully to avoid damaging the stem, loop a length of twine loosely around the stem about three-quarters of the way up from the ground; then tie the twine securely to the stake *(above)*. As the plant matures, check the twine from time to time to make sure it does not choke the stem *(inset)*.

2 When a plant grows taller than its first tie, add a second and then a third length of twine. For a 3½-foot-tall delphinium, tie the second length of twine at the base of the flower head *(near right)* when the flower head is all in bud and just starting to bloom. When the delphinium reaches 4 feet and three-quarters of its flower head is in bloom, add the third length of twine between the second tie and the top of the stem *(far right)*.

# MAINTAINING PLANTS: GROOMING

Every moment you spend in grooming your plants during the growing season will be generously repaid with a healthier, more beautiful garden. Pinching *(below, right)* promotes fuller, bushier foliage. And two methods of pruning—deadheading and disbudding *(opposite)*—encourage flowering plants to bloom longer and to produce larger or more abundant flowers.

Pinching involves nipping stem tips in the bud. Begun in springtime before flowers emerge, pinching encourages branching and results in larger growth for the plant.

Deadheading is the technique of removing faded flowers. Annuals, bulbs and repeat-blooming roses, such as hybrid teas, floribundas and grandifloras *(pages 322-323)*, all benefit from this technique; old garden roses *(pages 318-321)*, which have only a single burst of bloom, should not be dead-headed. If you want your plants to produce seeds, you should deadhead with every flush of bloom up until about three to five weeks before the first frost is expected. These last flowers can be allowed to produce seeds or, in the case of roses, rose hips for the fall. Rose hips are not only attractive; they are also essential to the health of the plant. As the rose hips develop, the plant slows its growth and prepares for winter.

Disbudding is the act of removing certain buds to redirect the energy of the plant. To produce one large single bloom, pinch back all side buds and leave just the terminal bud. To produce a large flower cluster, do just the opposite: remove the terminal bud and leave all the side buds.

Refer to pages 539-541 for directions on grooming houseplants; refer to pages 396-403 for directions on pruning, the art of grooming trees and shrubs.

*A floribunda rose blossoms profusely in hues of salmon blended with rose. As long as the faded flowers are regularly removed, these roses, like many flowering plants, bloom continually from midseason until the first autumn frost.*

## PINCHING FOR FULLNESS

To pinch back a stem, grasp the growing tip—the point of the stem above the top pair of mature leaves—between your thumb and forefinger *(right)* and remove it. This growing tip contains a plant hormone that inhibits the growth of buds farther down on the stem. By removing the tip, you allow the dormant buds to begin to grow. Seedlings can first be pinched when they have three or four sets of leaves. Transplants bought from a nursery can be pinched back as you plant them in the ground. Pinch the new growth on your plants after about three weeks to encourage them to become even bushier.

## DEADHEADING

Deadheading involves removing faded flowers. On a rose, as shown, a portion of the stem above the first strong dormant bud is also removed. This bud is located in the leaf axil of the upper-most set of leaves with five leaflets; leaves having fewer leaflets do not produce strong shoots. Once the dead flower is gone, the dormant bud will grow into a flowering shoot. When a flower blossom is spent, use pruning shears to cut the stem at a 45° angle, ¼ inch above the first set of leaves having five leaflets *(right)*; to avoid spreading disease, sterilize the shears in a water and bleach solution before using them. The dormant bud in the leaf axil *(inset)* will be stimulated to grow into a new shoot that will produce a flower within six weeks. For smaller plants, such as annuals, you can pluck off flowers with your fingers. On newly planted roses, remove just the flowers and leave the leafy stems during the first season of growth. Every available leaf is needed to manufacture sugar that will help build up the strength of the young plants. On bulbs, remove only the flower head, leaving the flower stalk which, as long as it remains green, manufactures food the bulb needs for future growth.

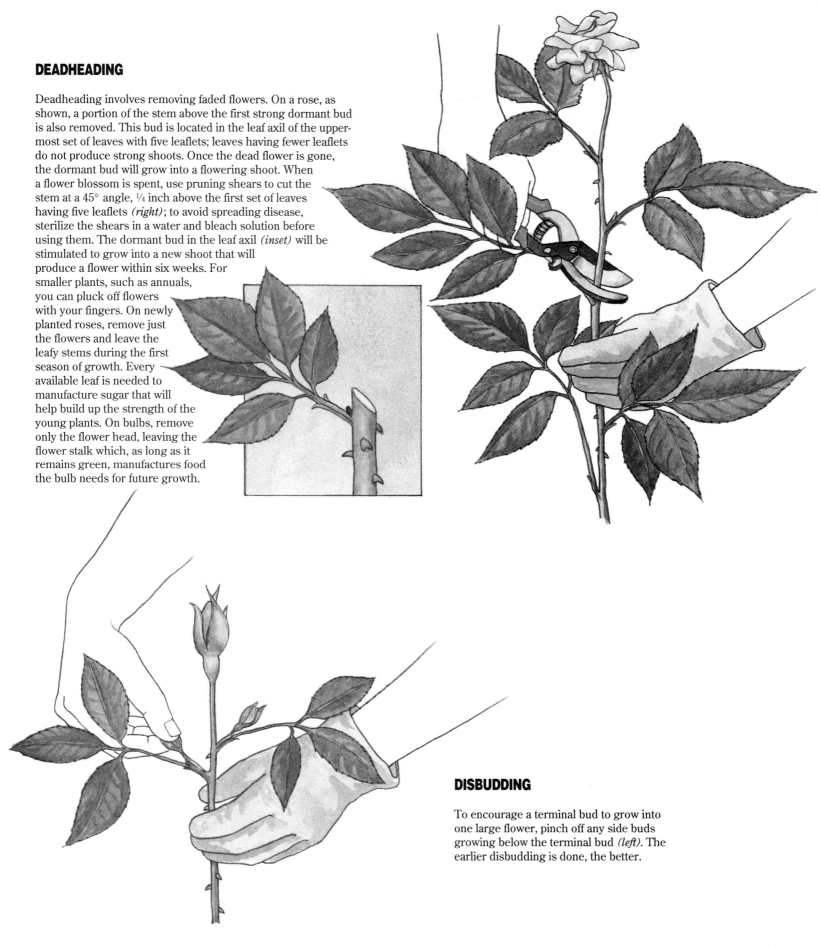

## DISBUDDING

To encourage a terminal bud to grow into one large flower, pinch off any side buds growing below the terminal bud *(left)*. The earlier disbudding is done, the better.

# MAINTAINING PLANTS: WEEDING AND MULCHING

Weeds are not only unattractive, they can hinder the growth of your favorite plants by competing aggressively for nutrients, light and moisture. To keep your garden healthy and good-looking, start weeding in early spring before undesirable plants can become established. To make sure a weed does not grow back, remove the entire plant, roots and all. This is best done by hand *(opposite)*; a hand weeding tool, available through mail-order catalogs and from garden-supply centers, extends your reach for the most tenacious roots.

A good way to keep weeds from gaining a foothold is to lay down fresh mulch every year. Few plants can survive without sun; a 1- to 4-inch layer of some suitable organic material—like shredded bark or leaves, pine bark chips or needles, decomposed grass clippings, salt marsh hay or peanut shells—discourages incipient weeds by denying them sunlight. At the same time mulch conserves soil moisture, reducing the need for water, and moderates soil temperature while adding visual appeal.

The best time to apply mulch to a garden bed is right after your early spring weeding, so that the mulch can work its unobtrusive magic throughout the growing season before the weeds grow large, produce seeds and propagate more weeds. Avoid mulching with fresh manure; it may be filled with weed seeds. Buy mulch at a garden-supply center, or use compost *(pages 58-59)*.

In the battle against weeds, there is no substitute for constant vigilance. Weeds can spring up any time during the year. If you want a weed-free garden, you will have to inspect your plantings on a regular basis—preferably daily but at least once a week—and immediately uproot any weeds you find, because weeds, especially perennials like dandelions, are very difficult to eradicate once they make themselves at home in a garden.

For directions on using black plastic mulch for a bed of ground covers, refer to pages 120-123; for a vegetable garden, refer to pages 486-489. For information on ridding a lawn of weeds, refer to pages 132-137. For directions on mulching roses, refer to pages 334-335.

*In a neat, space-saving mixture of vegetables and flowers, some pale pink roses bloom against a wooden fence behind rows of lettuce (foreground) and staked tomato plants. All the plantings grow well in a small bed that is kept weed-free and moist by a layer of shredded bark mulch.*

## WEEDING CONSIDERATIONS

If you can live with a flower garden that isn't perfectly manicured, you may not need to eradicate every last weed in sight. Certain weeds are advantageous; the larvae of butterflies and moths will eat thistle and nettle in preference to your flowers. Letting other weed types flourish, however, can be disastrous, since leaf miners and beetles breed in weeds. Leaf miners, the larvae of beetles, tunnel into leaves and eat leaf tissue, leaving foliage marked with yellow, light green, white or brown serpentine trails. Other beetles, including the Asiatic, Colorado potato and Japanese beetles, can strip plants of all their foliage. The best way to avoid leaf miners and beetles is to keep your garden weed-free.

1 To free a garden of weeds, attack them one by one. Insert a weeding tool at the base of a weed *(right)*. If the weed has an established tap-root, you may have to work the tool around the weed to loosen it. Lift the weed from the ground, knock off any soil from the roots and discard the entire plant. Repeat with all weeds you find.

2 Once a bed is free of weeds, level the soil using a rake or a hand cultivator—a short-handled, multipronged tool. Fill in any holes left by uprooted weeds. Then use the cultivator to scratch last year's old mulch into the soil *(left)*; the partly decomposed organic matter will add nutrients to the soil, reducing the need for fertilizer.

3 Add a fresh layer of organic mulch to the weeded, leveled bed; make the mulch 1 to 2 inches deep for small plants; 3 to 4 inches deep and 1 to 2 feet wide for larger plants and trees. Mulch should always go around plants, not on them, since plants whose crowns are covered with mulch may rot. If a plant has floppy foliage, gather the foliage together with one hand and lift it out of the way while you spread the mulch around the base with your other hand *(right)*. To spread mulch around a tree or shrub, leave a 6-inch-wide strip of bare ground directly around the trunk or stems; field mice and other small rodents hide under the mulch, and will gnaw at the bark if they find the trunk or stems too conveniently close. As the mulch decomposes or disperses with the wind, replenish it from time to time.

# MAINTAINING PLANTS:
# GETTING RID OF GARDEN PESTS

Spring and summer are prime seasons for insect infestations in the garden. Some insects attack foliage, others flowers, others bark. If the organic methods presented on pages 50-51 do not produce results, the right insecticide can help you fight back against the pests that threaten your plants and trees. But take care when choosing and using these powerful weapons; you want to make sure it's only the pests that get hurt.

There are many kinds of insecticides on the market, and not all are safe for home use. Read the label instructions of any insecticide carefully before buying it. Avoid synthetic insecticides. These are based on chemicals—chlorinated hydrocarbons, organophosphates and carbamates—that can harm people, animals and beneficial insects, and contaminate groundwater supplies.

Look for insecticides that are derived from natural sources and that are nontoxic except to the targeted pests. Some of these contain hormones that disrupt a pest's reproductive cycle; others rely on microorganisms that cause insect diseases or substances made by plants that have evolved natural defenses against pests—like the pyrethrins extracted from chrysanthemums.

The safest of all insecticides for home use is horticultural oil, available at garden-supply centers. A layer of it suffocates a variety of pests, especially scale insects that attack tree bark and twigs. Apply it in early spring on a windless day with a 1- to 1½-gallon compression sprayer *(opposite)*.

Roses should be sprayed twice during the dormant season, in late autumn and early spring, with a lime-sulfur solution that reduces fungus spores and kills insect eggs. During the growing season, spray every seven to 10 days with a fungicide, as a general protection against disease. At the first sign of insect or mite damage, apply a systemic pesticide.

Avoid applying a pesticide in temperatures above 80° F. Some are not effective in warm temperatures; others burn plant tissue. Even with nontoxic products, be sure to follow label instructions for recommended uses, application times and methods, and precautions.

*The lush blossoms and thick bark on this flowering cherry tree indicate a healthy tree (the horizontal striations on the bark are characteristic of the species). Scale insects sometimes invade tree bark in winter and can destroy the whole tree, but spraying with horticultural oil will smother them and any eggs they lay.*

**1** Before spraying a pesticide or fungicide, don a face mask and safety goggles to prevent particles from getting into your lungs and eyes. For added protection, wear long pants, a long-sleeved shirt and rubber gloves. Keep children and pets away from the area; do not allow them back into the area until the product label indicates it is safe. Prepare a compression sprayer following the manufacturer's instructions. For the model shown, unscrew the top and measure the pesticide or fungicide according to the instructions on the bottle and pour it into the sprayer *(left)*. Dilute as directed by filling the sprayer with water from a garden hose. To avoid inhaling concentrated chemical fumes, do not prepare the chemicals indoors.

**2** Replace the top of the compression sprayer and screw it on tightly. Holding onto the container with one hand, pressurize the container by pumping the handle several times with the other hand until you cannot pump any more *(right)*.

**3** To spray a tree, apply an even coat of the mixture over the bark *(left)*. To spray a rose, begin by coating the top surfaces of the leaves. Work quickly; one good pass over each area should be enough. Then coat the undersides of the leaves, where insects tend to congregate. Again, cover the surfaces evenly. After spraying with any pesticide or fungicide, unscrew the container top and dispose of any leftover mixture as recommended on the product label. Rinse the container thoroughly and hang it upside down to drain. Store it when it is dry.

# PROPAGATING PLANTS: GATHERING SEEDS

Most home gardens are sown from commercial seed because the seeds cast by many of the plants in your garden are likely to be hybrids, and hybrids will not breed true. What comes up, in fact, often bears little resemblance to the plants that produced the seed. The seeds of some normally unavailable varieties can be obtained from organizations specializing in seed exchanges *(box, opposite)*.

But if you are willing to experiment, planting seeds that you have gathered yourself can be a satisfying and inexpensive way to enlarge and enjoy your garden. Collecting should be done from your own garden, however, or that of a willing neighbor; collecting from public lands is against the law in many places, and collecting from plants in their natural habitat—woods and meadows, for example—can drastically limit the propagation potential of the species in its natural setting.

Plants vary greatly in their seed-bearing mechanisms. Some produce a few large seeds, with each encased in its own protective shell; the seedpods of other plants harbor a multitude of tiny seeds. Obviously, collection procedures vary from plant to plant. To collect seeds from a tree, for example, simply pick the cones, pods or berries it produces. Directions for collecting seeds from two types of flowering plants are illustrated here—annuals *(right)* and bulbs *(opposite)*.

By following a few general rules, you can improve your chances of raising new plants from seeds you have gathered. Only ripe seeds will germinate. Wait until your flowers mature and turn brown before you try to collect seeds from them. Always collect on a dry day so that the flower heads contain as little moisture as possible; moisture encourages the growth of mold, which can spoil stored seeds. Label each container of seeds with the name and location of the plant that the seeds are from. To extract and store the seeds properly, refer to pages 76-77.

*Zinnias are among the easiest flowers from which to collect seeds. When these rose pink blossoms turn brown, their seeds can be stripped by hand—and stored until the advent of a new planting season.*

## COLLECTING SEEDS: ANNUALS

Cut off old flower heads from an annual, such as the zinnia shown, using shears or scissors *(right)*. Group the flower heads by variety, place them in paper bags, fold over the tops of the bags and bring them indoors to dry.

# SAVING SEEDS FROM EXTINCTION

The universe of seeds available to the home gardener is ever-expanding—not merely with the new hybrids offered each year by the commercial seed companies—but also with the seeds of obscure, old-time plants that haven't been widely available for generations. The "rescue" from extinction of these seeds is due largely to the efforts of several nonprofit, nationwide organizations dedicated to preserving traditional varieties from disappearance. Organization members, who are primarily home gardeners drawn from all parts of the continent, exchange the seeds—and share the excitement of growing rare plants, usually flowers and vegetables. Listings of such organizations are readily available in most popular gardening magazines.

Since the discovery of North America by Europeans, settlers from every part of the world have been bringing non-native seeds to this continent, creating with indigenous varieties a horticultural melting pot. But due to a shrinking rural population and the preference of seed companies to sell new hybrids, many traditional native and foreign strains have become "endangered" or extinct.

One typical seed exchange organization, based in the Midwest, stocks the seeds of thousands of "heirloom" varieties—seeds passed down from generation to generation—as well as the seeds of traditional native Indian vegetable crops, Mennonite and Amish garden varieties, outstanding foreign seeds, and other vegetable seeds no longer offered in commercial seed catalogs. Each year, members distribute, plant and gather these seeds to ensure their survival.

The organization recruits gardeners who agree to "adopt" seeds from among the 4,000 varieties that are listed in the organization's annual inventory, plant and grow them for five years, and then return the same number of seeds back to the organization. As a result of the information and seed exchange between members, varieties believed to have been lost forever are periodically rediscovered and removed from the endangered list.

There is more to saving seeds from extinction than the novelty of growing rare plants. Some enthusiasts swear that vegetables grown from old-fashioned seeds taste better than the new hybrids. Perhaps more important, the practice promotes genetic diversity, which can be crucial to large-scale agriculture. In the early 1970s, for example, 15 percent of the U.S. corn crop was destroyed by a blight to which the hybrid variety being planted was particularly susceptible. But breeding the hybrid to a rare, recently rediscovered variety resulted in a new, blight-resistant hybrid.

Another benefit of saving seeds from extinction is the sense of history it inspires. Garden plants with a centuries-old heritage are living proof of the rich horticultural history of the continent.

## COLLECTING SEEDS: BULBS

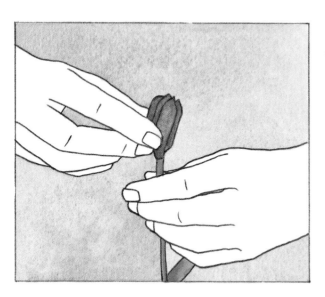

1 Check a bulb, like the lily shown, in late summer, after the petals have opened and fallen off. When the seedpod begins to turn brown (but before it splits open and the seeds disperse with the wind), snap it off where it joins the stem *(left)*.

2 To collect the individual seeds, cut open the seedpod lengthwise along a seam and shake out the seeds on a paper towel to dry *(right)*.

75

# PROPAGATING PLANTS: EXTRACTING AND STORING SEEDS

S eeds are living organisms. To remain viable, they need to be treated as nature treats them. Dry, non-fleshy seeds—from flowers, for example—should be stored dry *(below)*; fleshy-fruit seeds—such as from berries—should be stored moist *(opposite)*. Both kinds need to be extracted from their flower heads or fruit, cleaned as a precaution against rot and stored immediately after being collected. As soon as the weather permits, they will be ready to sow.

To make sure that the seeds of flower heads are fully dry before cleaning and storing them, remove the flower heads from the bags in which you collected them *(page 74)* and spread them out on a sheet of paper in a cool, well-ventilated area for two or three days. Label and date each type.

Each flower head or berry may contain one or more seeds. Large seeds are readily extracted; just pull them free with your fingers, plucking off any remaining petals from flower heads so that you can see the seeds more easily. Small seeds from flower heads are sometimes spontaneously released while they dry, but to make sure you get them all, you may need to shake the flower heads, or crush the pods with your fingers or the berry pulp with a wood block and then pick out the seeds one by one.

Unless the seeds can be planted right away *(box, opposite)*, they should be stored. But for best results, plant the seeds within one year.

*Attached to feathery puffs, the seeds of these just-opened asclepias pods are ready to be scattered by autumn breezes. These seeds can be stored for later sowing if they are removed from their pods and shorn of their feathery attachments.*

## DRY SEEDS

To prepare the seeds of a flower head for storage, first let the flower head dry for a few days. Then shake it over a sheet of paper and expel any loose seeds. Crush each seed capsule with your fingers to extract remaining seeds *(right)*, and place them on the paper. Carefully pour the seeds into a small paper envelope, recording the name of the plant, and the date and location of collection. To store the seeds, cover the bottom of a glass jar with a ½-inch layer of silica gel to absorb moisture and place the envelope in the jar; seal the jar and store it in the refrigerator until you are ready to plant next season.

## FLESHY-FRUIT SEEDS

1 To prepare the seeds of a berry or other fleshy fruit for storage, pick the pulp away from the seeds and set the seeds aside. For large quantities of fruit, first mash the pulp with a wooden block, then pick out the seeds *(below)*. Alternatively, use a food blender to separate the seeds from the pulp.

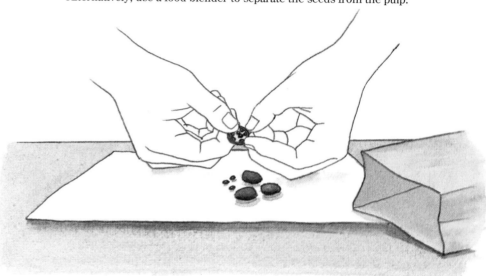

2 Clean the seeds in a bowl of water. The water will help separate the seeds from the pulp. Viable seeds, being heavy, will sink to the bottom of the bowl. The pulp and seeds lacking a solid healthy core will float to the top. Discard the pulp and the nonviable seeds and remove the viable seeds from the bowl. While they are still moist, wrap the viable seeds in a small sack cut from the feet of nylon hose. Dampen a handful of sphagnum moss and place the sack of seed on top; then fold the moss around the seed *(left)*. Put the moss-wrapped seed inside a small plastic bag, squeeze out as much air as possible, and record the name of the plant, and the date and location of collection. Store the bag in the refrigerator.

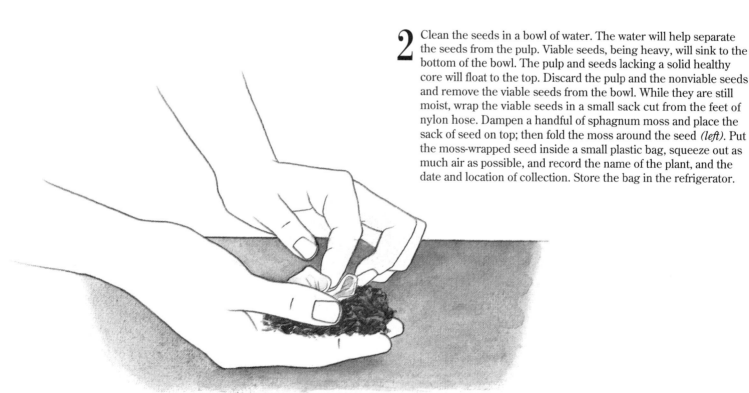

# PROPAGATING PLANTS: REVIVING DORMANT SEEDS

*A clump of flowering perennials puts forth white blossoms. Because the flowers are indigenous to the northern prairies, their seeds need a period of cold if they are to germinate.*

All seeds contain dormant embryos that are awaiting the right signals from the environment to start growing. Some tree seeds *(box, page 77)*, for example, should be planted immediately on being collected. Warmth and moisture will usually trigger germination. But some seeds require special treatment to break their dormancy.

Many seeds that ripen in the fall in temperate climates have developed mechanisms that prevent germination until after they have endured a period of cold; their seedlings would be killed by winter cold if they began growing too soon. Other plants—among them most trees—produce seeds with hard outer coats that must be worn down before germination can occur.

These survival mechanisms are among nature's wonders, but they can make growing plants from seed a frustrating experience for gardeners. Fortunately, dormancy can be overcome in each case by simulating the conditions that trigger germination naturally.

To wake up seeds that usually sleep through the winter, soak them in water and then store them in a refrigerator. This chilling process is known as stratification, and can take from three weeks to six months, depending on the species and on individual conditions. Flowering plant seeds need relatively brief periods of stratification: perennials, such as columbine and iris, three to four weeks and six to 12 weeks, respectively; roses, six weeks; an annual, like phlox, only two weeks. Trees, on the other hand, require lengthier periods: Fir, pine and sweet gum need one to three months, dogwood two to four months, and maple and prunus three to six months. As a rule of thumb, seeds are ready to move from stratification to planting when they have sprouted both roots and stems.

Seeds with hard outer coats remain dormant because moisture cannot penetrate to the embryo inside. In nature, the barrier is eventually breached by the action of microorganisms or by animals. You can achieve the same result with a process called scarification— nicking the seed coat with a file or a sharp knife.

## SOAKING VEGETABLE SEEDS

Most vegetable seeds germinate quickly, within 10 days, but a few, such as carrots, celery, okra and parsnips, have seeds that can take as long as three weeks to germinate. These seeds can be speeded along by soaking them in warm water—approximately 100° F—for 24 hours prior to sowing. The soaking also causes a slight increase in the percentage of seeds that will germinate. Tiny seeds that are difficult to handle, such as celery seeds, may be placed in a fine-mesh strainer or in a cheese-cloth bag for soaking. After soaking, the seeds should not be allowed to dry out, but should be sown immediately, while they are still damp. Bean seeds, which are extremely susceptible to rot and fungus, should never be soaked before sowing.

## SCARIFICATION

Whether it must be planted immediately or needs stratification, a seed with a hard outer coat will not sprout until the coat has broken down sufficiently to allow water to penetrate to the embryo. Scarify a seed if you cannot pierce its coat with your thumbnail. To scarify a seed, nick the seed coat carefully, using a sharp knife *(above)* or a file to expose the lighter-colored inner seed; alternatively, you can scarify a seed with a specially formulated chemical solution—available at a garden-supply center. After scarifying a seed, soak it in warm water overnight before planting or stratifying *(below)*.

## STRATIFICATION

Soak seeds in water for 12 to 24 hours (until they swell with moisture). Place them in a bag made from nylon hose, wrap the bag in damp sphagnum moss and slip it into a clear plastic bag *(right)*. Label the bag with the plant name, the date and the anticipated planting date. Check the bag periodically; if the seeds have started to sprout, remove them and sow them *(pages 80-81)*.

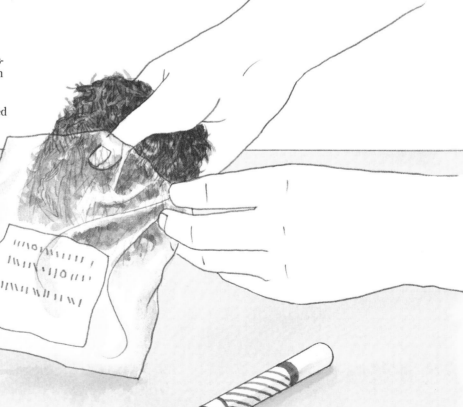

# PROPAGATING PLANTS: STARTING SEEDS INDOORS

Seeds can be sown directly in the garden, but insects, disease organisms in the soil, and cold spring weather may harm them and delay their growth. To protect seeds from the elements, start them indoors. Planting seeds indoors helps you get a jump on the season. In cold climates where spring comes late and summer is short, plants started indoors can be transplanted into the garden *(pages 82-83)* as soon as the soil warms, then have time to mature and flower or produce a crop before the first fall frost. Rushing into the season too eagerly, however, should be avoided. Seedlings that grow indoors too long before transplanting become weak and spindly.

Some plants have peculiar requirements that must be considered. Some annuals, for example, must be sown four to 12 weeks (depending on species) before the last frost date in your area *(inside back cover)*; refer to the Dictionary of Annuals *(page 200)* for precise timing. Not many gardeners grow bulbs from seed, largely because most bulbs take several years to progress from seed to flowering. But some bulbous plants—the tubers, the tuberous roots and the rhizomes *(pages 268-269)*, such as dahlias, begonias and achimenes—are easy to grow from seed and will produce flowers in their first summer.

Houseplant seeds, of course, can only be started indoors. The seeds of most common houseplants are available from seed catalogs, and the more exotic varieties can be ordered through specialized plant societies. Among the easiest houseplants to grow from seed are bromeliads, coleus and philodendrons.

Seeds can be planted in nursery flats, clay pots, cut-down milk cartons or, as illustrated at right and opposite, wooden boxes. Any container you use should have at least one drainage hole in the bottom, and be clean. You can sterilize a container with a bleach and water solution, and a final rinse with running water.

For directions on sowing annual seeds directly in the garden, refer to pages 188-189; for sowing grass seed, refer to pages 113-114; for sowing seeds in a vegetable plot, refer to pages 472-475.

*This brilliant multicolor border combines rows of three summer-blooming flowers. Tall cosmos plants form the backdrop for zinnias and marigolds. All three plants are annuals that can be started from seed sown indoors and then transplanted into the garden.*

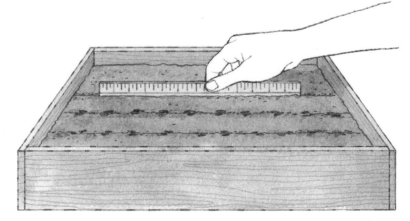

1 Buy a soilless potting mix that is specially formulated for starting seeds, moisten it, and fill a container to within ½ inch of the top with it. Use a straightedge to make indentations in the potting mix for rows *(above)*.

**2** Plant purchased seeds following the packet instructions. If you collected the seeds yourself, sprinkle them evenly into the rows, sowing about four seeds for every plant you expect to retain; not all seeds will germinate. In general, plant the seeds at a depth equal to twice their width. Unless the seeds require light to germinate, cover them with a thin layer of potting mix. Keep a record of the plant type.

Cover the container with a plastic bag to retain moisture, then set it in a warm place out of direct sunlight. Check it daily; if heavy water drops accumulate inside the bag, open it to allow air to enter *(right)*. The biggest problem with starting seeds is damping-off disease: The seeds will sprout, then flop over and die. The condition results from excessively moist potting mix, or insufficient air or excessive humidity in the bag, and is best avoided by providing seeds with the right conditions from the start. When the seeds sprout, generally after seven to 15 days, but as much as several months for some tree seeds, remove the bag, set the container in indirect sunlight and water daily.

**3** The seedlings should stand as far apart as they are tall. When they begin to crowd one another, thin them. Use scissors to snip off the least healthy looking plants *(above)*; discard them. Houseplants excepted, set the container outdoors a few hours each day to acclimate the seedlings; keep the potting mix moist. After one week, the seedlings can be transplanted.

## AN ALTERNATIVE METHOD FOR VEGETABLE SEEDS

With root crops, which do not transplant well, start seeds in peat pellets instead of a potting mix. First soak the pellets in water. Press two or three seeds into each pellet *(below)*; then put the pellets in a tray containing 1 inch of water. Don't let the tray dry out. When the seeds sprout, keep the strongest and snip the others. Then transplant the seedlings outdoors, pellets and all.

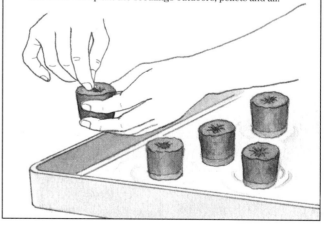

# PROPAGATING PLANTS: TRANSPLANTING SEEDLINGS

Given generous amounts of light and moisture, seeds started indoors produce regiments of brisk, green-topped little plants with astonishing swiftness. The trouble is, as the seedlings continue to grow, their ranks become overcrowded. At this point transplanting them into larger containers is necessary to give roots and leaves adequate space for further growth. Without this first indoor move, such plants may not be strong enough to survive the later shift into the garden.

The seedlings are large enough to transplant into individual containers when they have grown a second pair of leaves. The first step is to collect a supply of containers: peat pots, as shown at right and opposite, will do fine. So will clay pots, cell packs or even cutoff milk cartons and tin cans. Then purchase some commercial potting soil, which is sterile and loose enough for the delicate roots to grow in.

These supplies at hand, water the seedlings about to be transplanted. Moist soil will cling to the roots and protect them. For seedlings in flat trays, gently lift the plants with a small, flat tool such as a plastic knife, a wooden tongue depressor or a plastic strip of the sort garden-supply centers use as markers. For seedlings in pots, use one hand to scoop up a few at a time *(right)*. Replant the seedlings quickly so that their roots do not dry out. After a short period of additional growth, they will be ready to go outside, where they can mature in a cold frame *(opposite, bottom)*.

When the seedlings have grown—about 6 inches for a bulb, for example, about 12 inches for a rose, anywhere from 10 to 40 inches for a tree seedling (which, for a tree seedling, may take one to three years)—they can be transplanted into the garden. The planting bed should be prepared as shown on pages 56-57. In general, dig a hole for each seedling deep enough for it to sit at the same depth as it sat in its pot. Fill in around the roots with the soil you dug up, and tamp it down gently with your fingers. Refer to the following chapters for more detailed directions on planting individual plants into the garden.

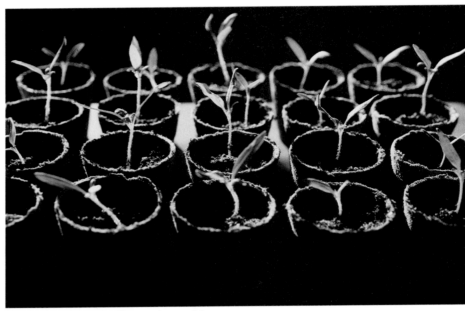

*Three-week-old tomato seedlings reach toward the light from peat pots. Started indoors, they have been transplanted to allow more growing room.*

1 To transplant a seedling, reach into the container in which the seeds were sown *(below)* and lift out a clump of seedlings on the palm of your hand. Be sure you don't pull up the stems, but get all the roots—and the soil around and underneath them as well.

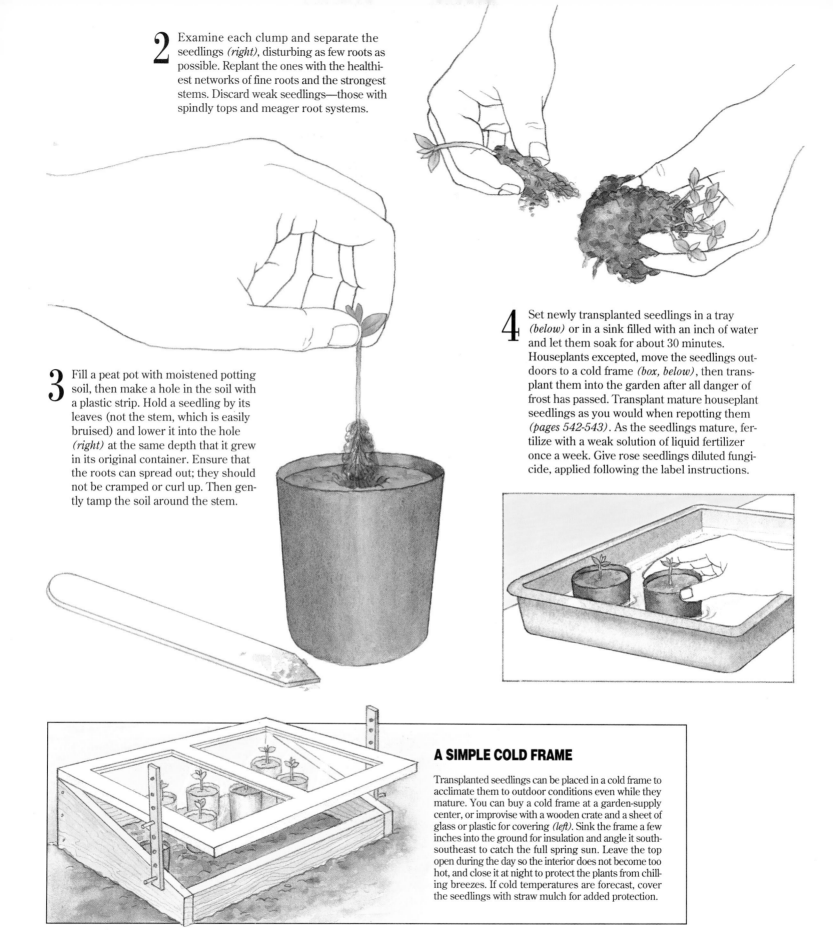

**2** Examine each clump and separate the seedlings *(right)*, disturbing as few roots as possible. Replant the ones with the healthiest networks of fine roots and the strongest stems. Discard weak seedlings—those with spindly tops and meager root systems.

**3** Fill a peat pot with moistened potting soil, then make a hole in the soil with a plastic strip. Hold a seedling by its leaves (not the stem, which is easily bruised) and lower it into the hole *(right)* at the same depth that it grew in its original container. Ensure that the roots can spread out; they should not be cramped or curl up. Then gently tamp the soil around the stem.

**4** Set newly transplanted seedlings in a tray *(below)* or in a sink filled with an inch of water and let them soak for about 30 minutes. Houseplants excepted, move the seedlings outdoors to a cold frame *(box, below)*, then transplant them into the garden after all danger of frost has passed. Transplant mature houseplant seedlings as you would when repotting them *(pages 542-543)*. As the seedlings mature, fertilize with a weak solution of liquid fertilizer once a week. Give rose seedlings diluted fungicide, applied following the label instructions.

## A SIMPLE COLD FRAME

Transplanted seedlings can be placed in a cold frame to acclimate them to outdoor conditions even while they mature. You can buy a cold frame at a garden-supply center, or improvise with a wooden crate and a sheet of glass or plastic for covering *(left)*. Sink the frame a few inches into the ground for insulation and angle it south-southeast to catch the full spring sun. Leave the top open during the day so the interior does not become too hot, and close it at night to protect the plants from chilling breezes. If cold temperatures are forecast, cover the seedlings with straw mulch for added protection.

# PROPAGATING PLANTS: DIVIDING

*This exuberant evergreen shrub shows the rejuvenating effect of repeated divisions—a brutal-seeming method of propagation that actually brings new life to many plants as they mature.*

A simple way to propagate many plants, including some ground covers, perennials and houseplants, and most bulbs, is to dig them up, break apart the clump of stems and replant the rooted (or bulbous) segments. As brutal as it sounds, this treatment does no harm and is actually beneficial to most plants. In the case of an older plant that has lost its shape as a result of unruly growth, propagation by division about once every three years serves a dual purpose: It not only creates new plants identical to the parent, it also restores the vigor of the original plant—provided the division is left with one or more stems and a mass of healthy roots (or a bulb).

Divide ground covers such as hosta and miscanthus. The perennials that are easiest to divide include aster, bellflower, gaillardia, phlox and yarrow. The shrubs that can be divided are generally those that are multi-stemmed and spreading, such as barberry, Aaron's-beard, leucothoe, paxistima and azalea. Houseplants that can be divided include African violet, asparagus fern, begonia, Boston fern, kafir lily and wandering Jew. Whatever the plant, choose one that is healthy and has well-developed stems growing from the crown.

The best time to divide plants is during their dormant period (early spring or late fall) when the plants are not actively growing. They divide most easily when they are two or three years old.

Before you uproot a plant, plan ahead so you are prepared to replant as soon as possible; roots exposed to the air for any length of time dry out and die.

While some shock to the root system is inevitable when a plant is removed from the soil, you can keep the disturbance to a minimum by working quickly and handling the plant gently at all times.

Repot divided houseplants immediately *(pages 542-543)*. For garden plants, transfer the divisions to individual containers—or to a protected area in your garden until they are ready to be moved to their permanent locations. For plants divided in spring, that means the fall immediately following. For those divided in fall, that means one year later.

## CUTTING AND PLANTING OFFSETS

Several houseplants—cacti, palms, bromeliads—reproduce by sending out small versions of themselves called offsets. The new little plants, which nestle at the base of the parent, make propagation easy; all you do is slice them from the parent plant, using a knife sterilized in a water and bleach solution, and place them in pots of their own. Do not do this, however, until the offsets are big enough to handle easily. If their roots are not fully formed, place them in a light propagating medium for a few weeks.

**1** To prepare a garden plant for dividing, water the soil around it thoroughly; then use a spading fork to dig all around the plant. When loosening the soil, work in a circle as broad as the plant's foliage so that the root system or bulbs will not be damaged. Work carefully, lifting it gently from the ground, using the spading fork *(right)*, or by hand. To prepare a house-plant for dividing, remove it from its pot *(page 542)*.

**2** In a protected location out of direct sunlight and strong wind, hold the plant at the crown area and gently shake off as much soil from the roots as possible. To divide a dug-up crown, cut it, using a sharp knife, or use your fingers to pull it apart into segments of roughly equal size *(left)*. Make the divisions at points that seem to separate easily, where crowns connect with healthy stems. Make sure each segment has plenty of roots (or a bulb) and top growth attached. Discard any dry, woody portion at the center of the old crown. Inspect each new division for insects, discolored roots (or bulbs) or foul odors.

**3** Discard plants that do not look and smell healthy. Use a sharp knife or pruning shears to trim off any old or dead roots. Dust the roots (or bulbs) with a fungicide. Cut off about a third of the top growth to compensate for root loss. Immediately replant the divisions, either in individual pots or in a protected area of your garden with enriched soil *(pages 56-57)*. When planting in the ground, leave about 1 foot between the divisions *(right)*. Refer to the following chapters for detailed planting instructions. Water the divisions daily, and feed them weekly through early summer with liquid fertilizer. Stop fertilizing in midsummer. Transplant the new plants to permanent locations the following fall.

# PROPAGATING PLANTS: LAYERING

The simplest and surest method of propagating plants with low-lying stems or branches, or roses with long and pliable canes, is layering, a technique that permits a plant to reproduce itself without grafting or cutting. Ideal candidates for layering are ground covers (Boston ivy, cotoneaster, English ivy, periwinkle), old garden roses and climbing roses, shrubs (azaleas, juniper, oleander and rhododendron), and houseplants (devil's ivy, grape ivy, philodendron and wandering Jew).

Layering is essentially a three-step process that begins early in the growing season, with the selection of a healthy plant. A single stem, branch or cane is stripped of foliage except for its tip. After the bark on the stripped portion is scarred and coated with hormone powder to stimulate root development, it is bent to the ground (or to the potting mix of another pot, for a houseplant) and buried in a shallow trench so that only the tip protrudes.

If the layering is done correctly, and if the buried stem, branch or cane is kept moist, roots will begin to develop by the end of the growing season (or in about three or four weeks, for a houseplant). By the beginning of the next season (or immediately, for a houseplant), it should be well rooted and ready for the second step of the soil-layering process—severance from the parent plant.

The severed stem, branch or cane, fortified by an application of liquid fertilizer, is then left in place for two or three weeks to adjust to its independence. It will then be safe to proceed with the next step, the removal and transplanting of the new plant to a new location. It is best to remove the plant with a generous root ball to a protected and fertilized interim site for the remainder of the season. The final transfer can then be carried out early in the following season.

*An old garden rose bears a profusion of pink blossoms in a raised garden bed. Old garden roses and climbing roses, having long, limber canes, as well as some ground covers, shrubs and houseplants with low-lying stems or branches, are easily propagated by soil layering—being buried under a thin layer of earth.*

1  To propagate a rose by layering, select a young, supple cane near the ground and strip it of leaves except for a few inches at the tip. Bend the cane to the ground *(right)* and use a trowel to dig a trench 3 to 4 inches deep and long enough to cover the part of the cane that touches the ground.

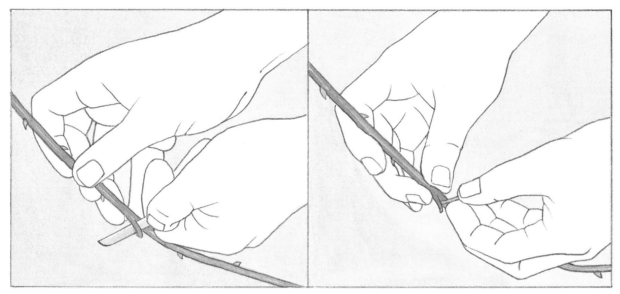

**2** At a point where the cane will be buried, and just below a bud, cut a notch *(above, left)* about twice as long as the cane is thick. Wedge the notch open with a bit of wood *(above, right)* and brush hormone powder, available at a garden-supply center, into the notch to promote root development.

**3** Bend the cane into the trench and secure the notched area against the soil with a wood prong *(left)*. Refill the trench with the original soil, mixed with compost, but leave the leafy tip protruding and pointing upward. Then mulch the buried portion. Check in the fall whether sturdy roots have formed. If a layered cane shows new growth and resists gentle tugging, it should thrive on its own.

**4** Early in the next growing season, sever the rooted cane, using shears; cut the cane on the parent just above the point where it disappears into the ground *(right)*. After two or three weeks, use a trowel to remove the new plant and the soil around the roots. Transplant it into the ground or to a container for further growth before removing it to a permanent site next season.

# PROPAGATING PLANTS: PLANTING STEM AND LEAF CUTTINGS

Any plant that has nonwoody stems—and many garden plants and most houseplants do—can be reproduced from stem cuttings. Several ground covers, perennials and shrubs that have woody or semiwoody stems, such as sedum, yarrow, lantana, yew, Russian cypress and English ivy, can also be propagated from stem cuttings. For propagating trees from stem cuttings, refer to pages 404-406. The few houseplants that have thick, fleshy leaves—African violets and begonias—can be reproduced by means of leaf cuttings *(box, below right)*. Either kind of cutting will send out new shoots that will signal the beginning of a new plant.

A stem cutting must include at least one node—the place where a leaf diverges from the stem; it is from the node that the new roots will develop. There are two kinds of stem cuttings. One is a tip cutting, which, as the name implies, is taken from the tip of the stem. To make one, cut just below a node that lies anywhere from 4 to 6 inches from the tip. Remove all flowers and flower buds, strip foliage from the lower third of the cutting, dip the cut end in rooting hormone powder, and insert it 1 to 2 inches deep in soilless potting medium, or vermiculite or perlite.

The other kind of stem cutting is a medial cutting—one taken from somewhere between the tip and the base of the stem. If the stem is long enough, you can take several of these after first removing the tip. Each medial cutting should include two nodes; make one cut just above a node and the other cut just below a second node. Remove flowers and foliage as with a tip cutting and insert the lower end 1 to 2 inches deep in rooting medium.

For garden plants, except bulbs, broad-leaved shrubs and conifers, stem cuttings should be taken in early spring. Take cuttings from bulbs and broad-leaved shrubs in late summer or early fall; from conifers in late fall or early winter.

*The soft but sturdy stems of this tropical houseplant provide ideal material for cloning—reliable reproduction of the parent plant through stem cuttings.*

## ROOTING A LEAF CUTTING

To propagate African violets and some begonias, select a healthy, mature leaf with a stalk that is 1 to 2 inches long. Dip the cut end in rooting hormone powder and insert the base of the stalk, at a 45° angle, into a standard rooting medium to a depth of 1 inch. Water thoroughly. Enclose the pot in a mini-greenhouse *(left)* and place it in bright indirect light. In a few weeks, a shoot will develop at the base of the parent leaf. When the plantlet is about 1 inch across and well formed, remove the mini-greenhouse and cut off the parent leaf at its base and discard it. Let the plantlet continue to grow in the same pot.

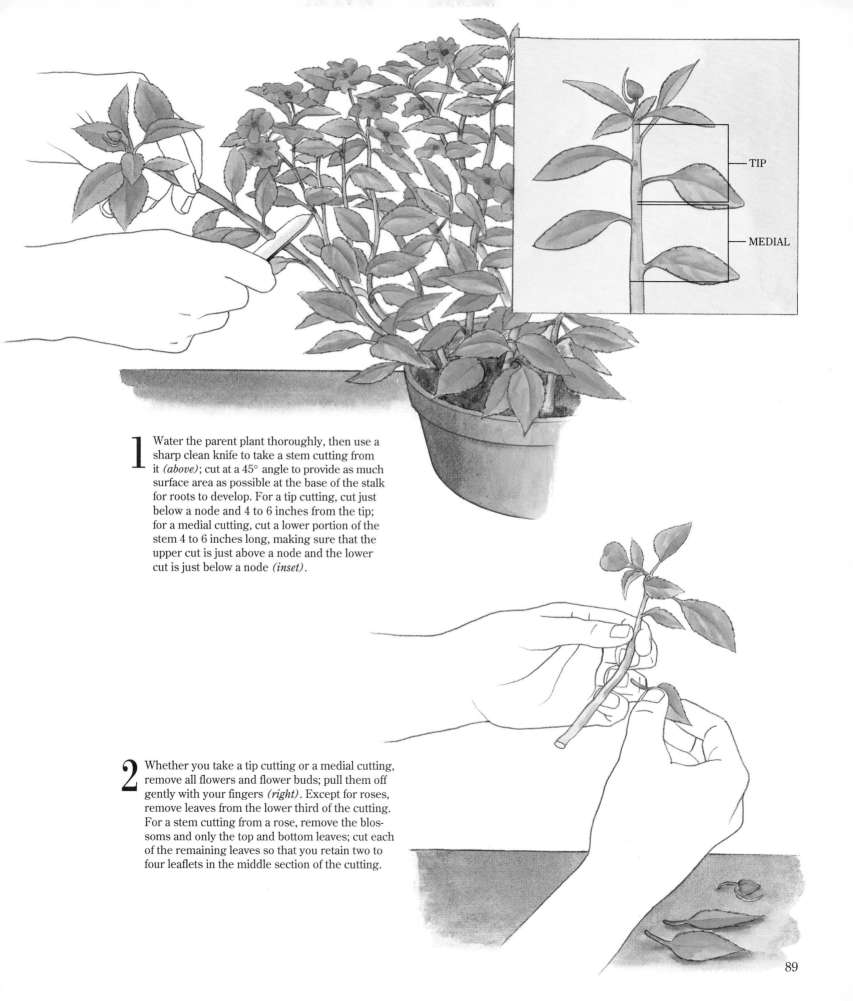

TIP

MEDIAL

1 Water the parent plant thoroughly, then use a sharp clean knife to take a stem cutting from it *(above)*; cut at a 45° angle to provide as much surface area as possible at the base of the stalk for roots to develop. For a tip cutting, cut just below a node and 4 to 6 inches from the tip; for a medial cutting, cut a lower portion of the stem 4 to 6 inches long, making sure that the upper cut is just above a node and the lower cut is just below a node *(inset)*.

2 Whether you take a tip cutting or a medial cutting, remove all flowers and flower buds; pull them off gently with your fingers *(right)*. Except for roses, remove leaves from the lower third of the cutting. For a stem cutting from a rose, remove the blossoms and only the top and bottom leaves; cut each of the remaining leaves so that you retain two to four leaflets in the middle section of the cutting.

**3** Buy a low-concentration rooting hormone powder at a garden-supply center and spread a small amount on a paper towel. To stimulate root development, lightly dust the bottom end of the cutting with the powder *(right)*.

**4** Fill a container to within ½ inch of the top with a soilless potting medium—available at a garden-supply center. Use a wooden dowel to poke a hole 1 to 2 inches deep in the medium. Insert the cutting into the hole and firm the medium around the stem. If you are taking multiple cuttings from a plant, you can root several in one container *(below)*. Water thoroughly. To maintain adequate humidity around the rooting area, enclose the cutting in a mini-greenhouse—a glass dome or a plastic bag supported by two or more dowels planted in the container. Place the container in bright indirect sunlight (direct sun could cause a damaging buildup of heat inside the mini-greenhouse). To check on the growth of the roots, gently tug on each cutting after 10 days to three weeks; with some garden plants, root development may take as long as four months. Once it has developed roots, the cutting will resist being pulled out. When the roots are 1 inch long, carefully lift the cutting from the medium and transplant it as you would a seedling *(pages 82-83)*.

# PROPAGATING PLANTS: SCION GRAFTING

The big, bold flowers of a saucer magnolia put on a spectacular spring performance. You can multiply the pleasure this showy but tender bloomer provides by grafting a shoot of it onto a healthy rootstock of a related but hardier species.

## GRAFTING CACTI

To graft two cacti together, select two plants of roughly equal size, one to serve as understock and the other as the scion. Using a sharp, sterilized knife, slice off the top portions of both the understock and the donor plant, then cut a V-shaped indentation into the top of the understock and a matching V-shaped wedge into the lower portion of the scion; fit the scion on top of the understock so that the wedge sits snugly in the indentation. Secure the graft with rubber bands stretched from the top of the scion to the bottom of the container. Leave the pot in a warm spot with indirect sunlight for two weeks or until the graft has taken; then move it to a sunny location and water as with any cactus.

Among the most common methods of grafting is scion grafting, in which a scion, or shoot, of one tree (called the donor tree) is joined atop the rootstock of another *(opposite and page 93)*. The key to the formation of a unified plant is the merging of the two trees' cambium *(box, page 407)*, the layer of cells beneath the bark responsible for growth. Whether the trunk of the new tree will bear a stronger resemblance to the rootstock or to the scion depends on how much rootstock you retain below the graft. At a minimum, at least 2 to 3 inches of the rootstock stem must remain to support the scion. This type of grafting can also be used to propagate a cactus *(box, left)*.

Grafting a tree should be done when both plants are dormant, so that they can become bonded together before either starts putting out new growth; grafting a cactus should be done during the growing season—spring and summer—when the transfer of life-giving sap through the cambium is most forceful. Grafting works best when both plants are of the same species; grafts between plants too different from one another rarely take. The scion and the rootstock should both be of the same diameter. The rootstock should be a year-old seedling still being grown in its pot.

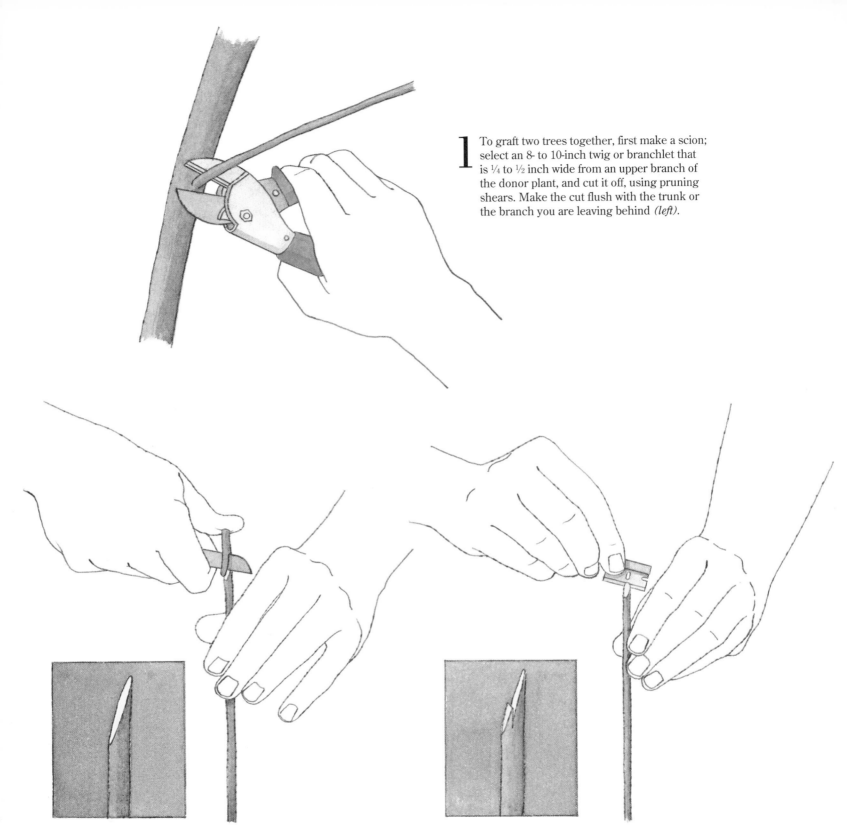

**1** To graft two trees together, first make a scion; select an 8- to 10-inch twig or branchlet that is ¼ to ½ inch wide from an upper branch of the donor plant, and cut it off, using pruning shears. Make the cut flush with the trunk or the branch you are leaving behind *(left)*.

**2** To prepare the scion for grafting, use a sharp knife to trim the scion's bottom surface on a slant *(above, left)* so that you form an oval-shaped surface and expose as much as possible of the cambium layer beneath the bark *(inset, left)*. Then, holding the stem steady with one hand and using a single-edged razor blade with the other, make a neat incision in the bottom surface of the scion *(above, right)*, pressing straight down to a depth of ¼ inch. Do not remove any wood. The result should be a tongue and groove *(inset, right)*.

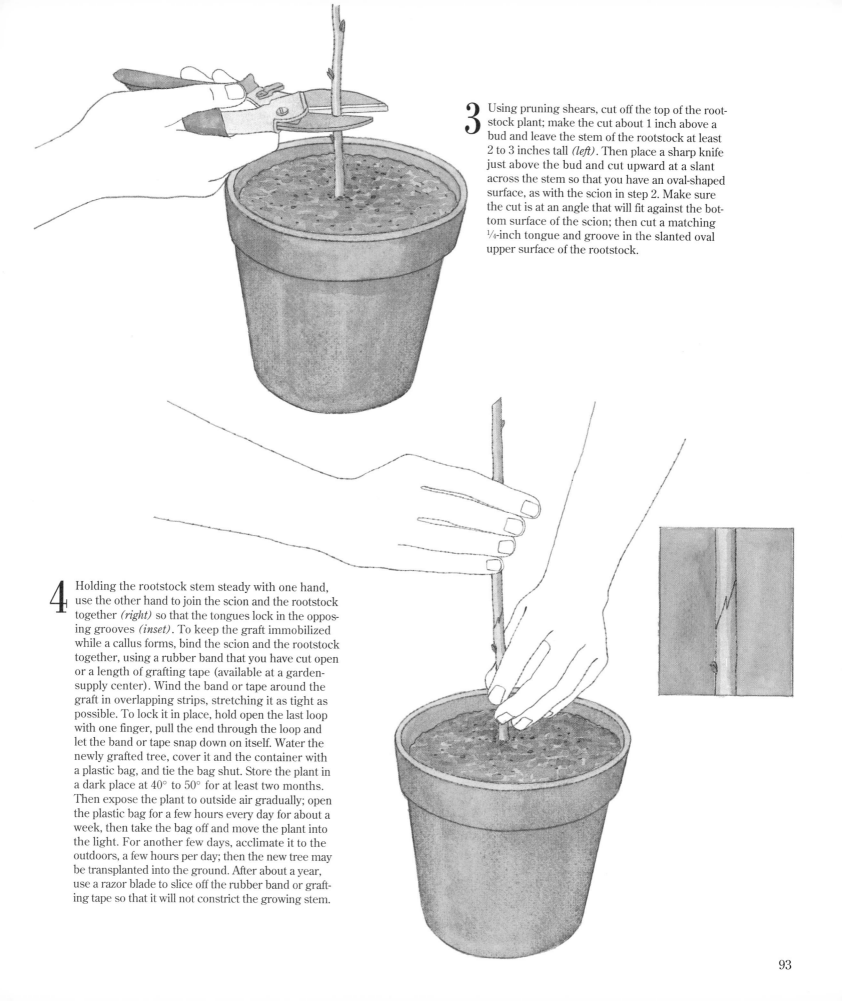

**3** Using pruning shears, cut off the top of the root-stock plant; make the cut about 1 inch above a bud and leave the stem of the rootstock at least 2 to 3 inches tall *(left)*. Then place a sharp knife just above the bud and cut upward at a slant across the stem so that you have an oval-shaped surface, as with the scion in step 2. Make sure the cut is at an angle that will fit against the bottom surface of the scion; then cut a matching ¼-inch tongue and groove in the slanted oval upper surface of the rootstock.

**4** Holding the rootstock stem steady with one hand, use the other hand to join the scion and the rootstock together *(right)* so that the tongues lock in the opposing grooves *(inset)*. To keep the graft immobilized while a callus forms, bind the scion and the rootstock together, using a rubber band that you have cut open or a length of grafting tape (available at a garden-supply center). Wind the band or tape around the graft in overlapping strips, stretching it as tight as possible. To lock it in place, hold open the last loop with one finger, pull the end through the loop and let the band or tape snap down on itself. Water the newly grafted tree, cover it and the container with a plastic bag, and tie the bag shut. Store the plant in a dark place at 40° to 50° for at least two months. Then expose the plant to outside air gradually; open the plastic bag for a few hours every day for about a week, then take the bag off and move the plant into the light. For another few days, acclimate it to the outdoors, a few hours per day; then the new tree may be transplanted into the ground. After about a year, use a razor blade to slice off the rubber band or grafting tape so that it will not constrict the growing stem.

# PROPAGATING PLANTS: HYBRIDIZING

Professional plant breeders are constantly introducing new hybrids that are distinguished by never-before-seen colors, greater vigor, more desirable growth habits and better resistance to disease. Improving specific traits through hybridizing is a time-consuming task best left to professionals. But using a simplified version of the method that commercial growers use, you can experiment with making your own hybrids—just for the fun of seeing what comes up.

The flowers of most plants contain both a male sex organ (the pollen-producing stamen) and a female sex organ (the egg-producing pistil). While many flowers are capable of self-pollination, their eggs can also be fertilized by pollen carried from other plants on the wind or on the bodies of insects like honeybees. Each offspring of such cross-pollination between different "parents" is a hybrid.

To create hybrids in your garden, you mimic this natural process—transferring pollen from the stamen of one plant to the pistil of another. For best results, choose parents that are members of the same species, and take care to guard against accidental pollination. You will be working outdoors, so you will need to work fast and cover your plants to protect them from being fertilized by wind-borne pollen. Hybridizing works well with flowering annuals, bulbs, roses and, as explained in the box at right, houseplants, such as African violets. Hybridizing should be done in the early spring so the female plant's seeds, should they germinate successfully, will have the entire growing season to ripen.

A reasonable goal for your first hybrid is the creation of a new petal color: for example, crossing a yellow-flowered portulaca with a red-flowered portulaca to make an orange-colored hybrid. The brand-new hybrid may be wholly unremarkable, or it may prove an outstanding combination of its parents. Not every pollination results in fertilization, however, so it pays to make several attempts at the same time. And be prepared for surprises; even experts have trouble predicting the outcome of a particular cross.

*Hybrid portulacas growing in a rock garden show some of the rich colors and double blooms that have been created by crossing carefully selected parents.*

## HYBRID HOUSEPLANTS

African violets are among the most popular flowering houseplants for a number of reasons. Their flowers come in many rich, bright colors; their leaves in interesting shapes—flat, ruffled, variegated. And the plants themselves vary in shape from large specimens to delicate miniatures to graceful trailing varieties. But African violets are gratifying to grow for another reason: It is both easy and exciting to make hybrids, creating new plants with unique blooms. The procedure is similar to that for garden plants *(opposite and pages 96-97)*, except it is unnecessary to cover the female flower *(step 4)* since accidental fertilization by wind- or insect-borne pollen indoors is highly unlikely. In addition, it takes six to nine months for the seedpod of a fertilized African violet ovary to mature, and 12 months more for the seeds to produce a new plant that will flower. But that is part of the excitement for African violet fanciers waiting to see what the results will be. If the new flowers are exceptionally handsome, you may wish to register your hybrid with the African Violet Society.

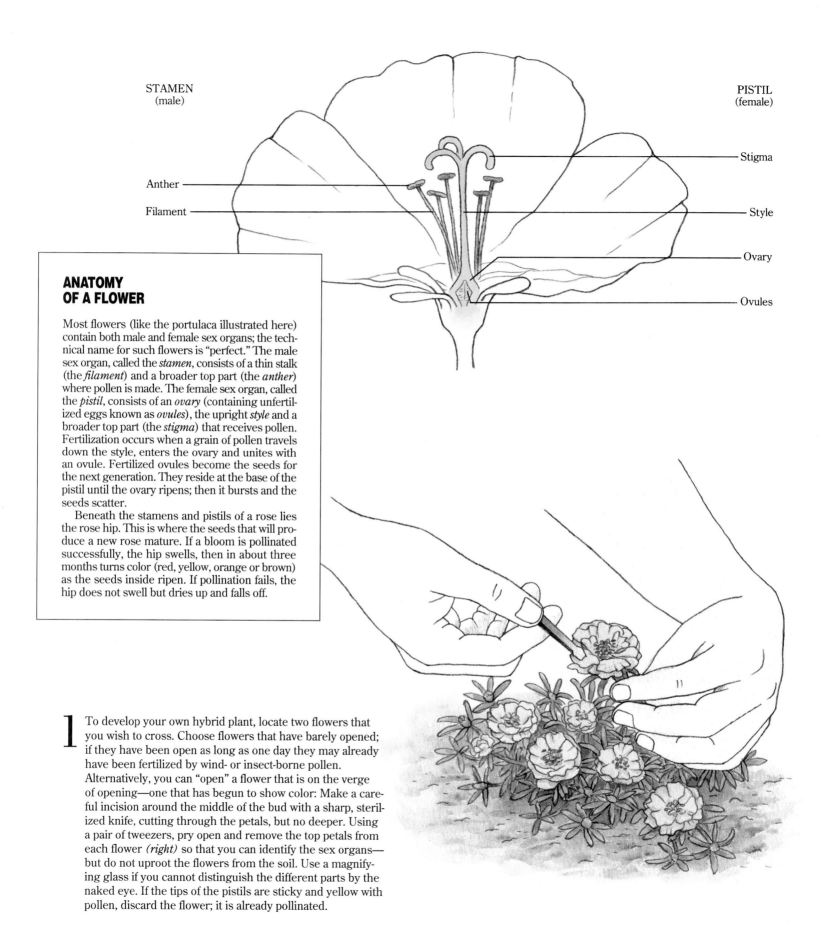

STAMEN
(male)

PISTIL
(female)

Anther

Filament

Stigma

Style

Ovary

Ovules

## ANATOMY
## OF A FLOWER

Most flowers (like the portulaca illustrated here) contain both male and female sex organs; the technical name for such flowers is "perfect." The male sex organ, called the *stamen*, consists of a thin stalk (the *filament*) and a broader top part (the *anther*) where pollen is made. The female sex organ, called the *pistil*, consists of an *ovary* (containing unfertilized eggs known as *ovules*), the upright *style* and a broader top part (the *stigma*) that receives pollen. Fertilization occurs when a grain of pollen travels down the style, enters the ovary and unites with an ovule. Fertilized ovules become the seeds for the next generation. They reside at the base of the pistil until the ovary ripens; then it bursts and the seeds scatter.

Beneath the stamens and pistils of a rose lies the rose hip. This is where the seeds that will produce a new rose mature. If a bloom is pollinated successfully, the hip swells, then in about three months turns color (red, yellow, orange or brown) as the seeds inside ripen. If pollination fails, the hip does not swell but dries up and falls off.

1 To develop your own hybrid plant, locate two flowers that you wish to cross. Choose flowers that have barely opened; if they have been open as long as one day they may already have been fertilized by wind- or insect-borne pollen. Alternatively, you can "open" a flower that is on the verge of opening—one that has begun to show color: Make a careful incision around the middle of the bud with a sharp, sterilized knife, cutting through the petals, but no deeper. Using a pair of tweezers, pry open and remove the top petals from each flower *(right)* so that you can identify the sex organs— but do not uproot the flowers from the soil. Use a magnifying glass if you cannot distinguish the different parts by the naked eye. If the tips of the pistils are sticky and yellow with pollen, discard the flower; it is already pollinated.

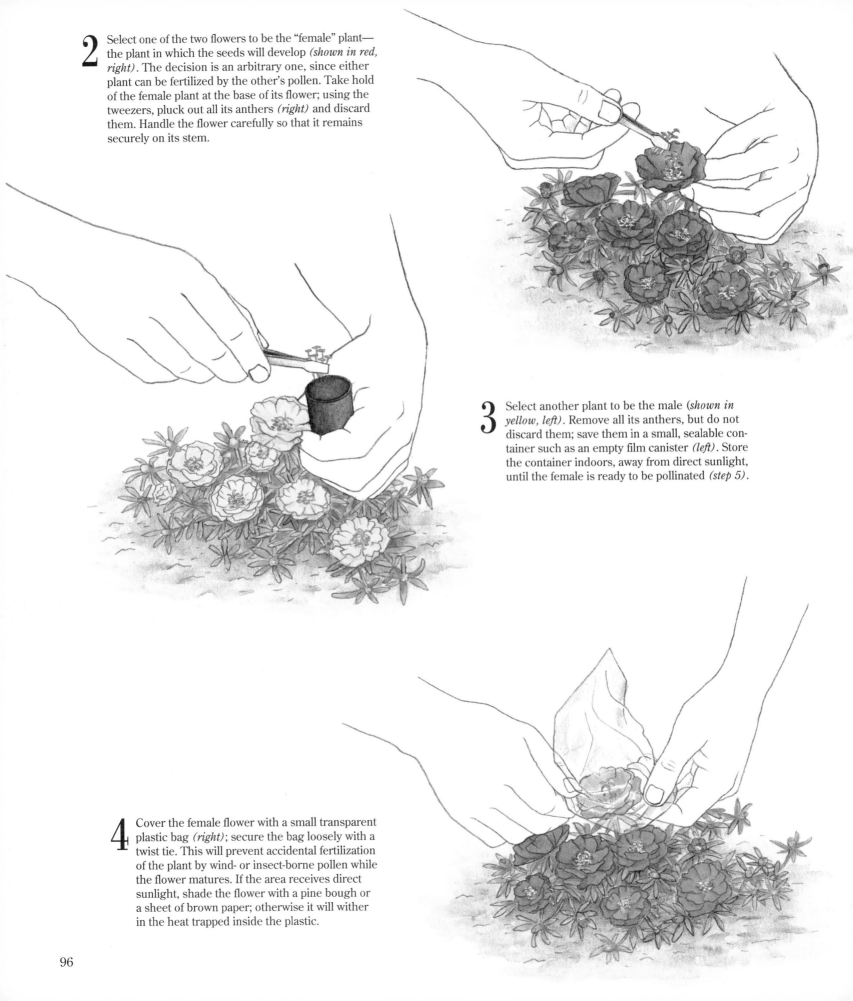

**2** Select one of the two flowers to be the "female" plant—the plant in which the seeds will develop *(shown in red, right)*. The decision is an arbitrary one, since either plant can be fertilized by the other's pollen. Take hold of the female plant at the base of its flower; using the tweezers, pluck out all its anthers *(right)* and discard them. Handle the flower carefully so that it remains securely on its stem.

**3** Select another plant to be the male *(shown in yellow, left)*. Remove all its anthers, but do not discard them; save them in a small, sealable container such as an empty film canister *(left)*. Store the container indoors, away from direct sunlight, until the female is ready to be pollinated *(step 5)*.

**4** Cover the female flower with a small transparent plastic bag *(right)*; secure the bag loosely with a twist tie. This will prevent accidental fertilization of the plant by wind- or insect-borne pollen while the flower matures. If the area receives direct sunlight, shade the flower with a pine bough or a sheet of brown paper; otherwise it will wither in the heat trapped inside the plastic.

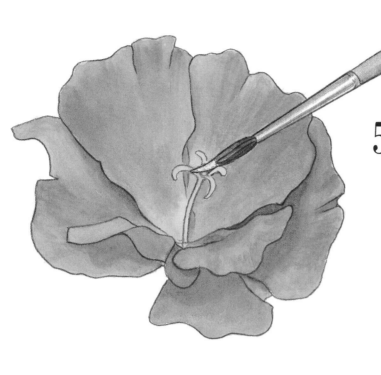

**5** Check the flower daily (for five or six days) to see if the pistil is ready to receive pollen. Look for a tiny drop of sticky substance—like a dewdrop—on the stigma. When this appears, dip a clean, fine-tipped paintbrush into the canister of anthers to bring out some pollen. With the brush-tip, "paint" the pollen onto the stigma *(left)*.

**6** Cover the newly pollinated flower with a clean plastic bag; discard the old bag, as it may contain pollen from other plants that could interfere with your cross. Secure the new bag loosely with a twist tie *(right)* and shade it from the sun again. Attach a tag to identify the cross for future reference in case you want to repeat or build on a particular success. Always list the female parent first: "Female Plant Name x Male Plant Name—Date."

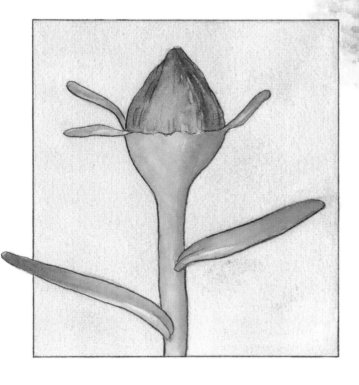

**7** Within a few days the petals of the pollinated flower will wither and fall off. Remove the plastic bag. Look for a swelling of the ovary *(left)*; this indicates the development of seeds within. To keep the swollen seedpod from bursting and scattering its seeds, wrap the pod in a piece of cheesecloth until you are ready to collect and store the seeds *(pages 74-75)*.

# 3

# LAWNS AND GROUND COVERS

*A lawn of heat-tolerant St. Augustine grass thrives in Florida, where the hot weather favors palm trees and other tropical plants. Like other warm-season grasses, St. Augustine can be started from chunks of sod, or plugs, which grow together to form a rugged lawn.*

Unlike most garden plants, grasses and ground covers are actively encouraged to spread well beyond their point of origin, blanketing a wide area in an expanse of green. Lawn grasses spread either by rhizomes, or underground stems, by aboveground stems called stolons or by an ever-widening crown that expands until it meets neighbor. Ryegrass and hard fescue are of this last type; zoysia and St. Augustine grass spread outward by means of stolons or rhizomes. Most of the popular ground covers, such as pachysandra, periwinkle, cotoneaster, ivy and juniper fall under one of three categories: vines, creeping plants whose long stems put down new roots wherever a leaf node touches the ground; perennials that grow by spreading on rhizomes; or prostrate shrubs that have wide-spreading branches.

Whether your lawn needs a simple patch or you are planting a new lawn, consider the climate and the tools available to you, as well as the expense that you are willing to incur; then choose a planting technique from the following pages. Before you begin work, the soil should be weeded, fertilized, tilled and, if necessary, treated with soil amendments *(pages 102-104).* Some young plants will require protection with moisture-conserving mulch *(pages 120-123).*

Anyone who has a lawn is familiar with chores such as mowing, watering, fertilizing and dealing with dandelions. When properly done this maintenance can not only increase the beauty of the garden setting, it can also boost the value of the house. This is true of a well-groomed ground cover as well. Although billed as easy-care, these lawn substitutes will benefit from a regular program of shearing and pruning to keep them vigorous.

In tackling these maintenance tasks, the operative word is "properly." Keep in

## CHAPTER CONTENTS

mind that, improperly done, maintenance tasks can do more harm than good. Grass cut too short during a siege of dry weather, for example, may suffer irreparable root damage. And grass cut when it is wet is apt to pick up waterborne disease spores spread by the whirling blades of the lawn mower. Similarly, too much fertilizer or too frequent watering can stimulate lush growth at the expense of stamina, and chemicals for controlling weeds can be useless if they are not geared to the particular weed. This chapter gives you the maintenance information you need to gain the best possible results.

Lawn grasses have been studied for so many years that almost nothing about them is a mystery. Their climate preferences, tolerance of sun and shade, the pests and diseases to which they are prone, and the weeds that can afflict them are all known in detail. Consequently, lawn care can be a predictable routine. Consult this chapter for the region map, the maintenance Checklist, the Troubleshooting Guide for lawns and the Gallery of Weeds. Use this information along with the step-by-step procedures, and you should be able to move through the cycle of sowing, mowing and spraying without any major crises.

Ground covers have their own problems. The zone map *(inside front cover)*, used in conjunction with the dictionary entries in this chapter, can help you to select plants that will thrive in your area. Similarly, the maintenance Checklist and Troubleshooting Guide can help you to prune, propagate, mulch and spray various kinds of ground covers. No matter how diligent the maintenance, ground cover plants do occasionally fail. Some methods of obtaining new plants are explained on page 142; others can be found in Chapter 2.

# FILLING IN THE BARE SPOTS

*A reseeded patch of lawn lies ready for a light covering of straw mulch. Given proper watering, the bare spot will start showing new green shoots within one to three weeks; about a month later, the patch will have become indistinguishable from the surrounding lawn.*

Bare spots can mar even the best-kept lawns. The most common cause is excessive foot traffic, which compacts soil and prevents grass roots from getting the air, water and nutrients they need. Grass may also die in places where you have accidentally spilled too much herbicide, too much fertilizer or some of the gasoline intended for your power mower.

Bare spots are easily repaired by reseeding. The best time to reseed a lawn is late August to mid-September; the soil will still be warm, but cooler than during midsummer and drier than in spring. In addition, the grass seeds you sow will encounter less competition from weeds at this time. Remember that simply spreading seed and raking it into the soil will waste a good deal of seed. For the best chance of its germinating, seed should be spread on bare spots only after the soil underneath has been reconditioned.

If a bare spot was caused by compacted soil, first break up the soil to a depth of 6 inches; then lighten the soil texture and add important nutrients by working in a few inches of peat moss and some fertilizer. A fertilizer that contains phosphorus will stimulate root production; you can buy a special high-phosphorus "starter" fertilizer designed to be used with newly sown grass seed. After adding the fertilizer, rake the patch until it is level with the surrounding lawn. Then scatter seed by the handful over the patch.

If the bare spot was caused by spilled chemicals, dig up and discard the contaminated soil and replace it with fresh, amended soil. Rake the area level with the surrounding lawn and spread seed over it.

Seed for the repair should match the seed you used to start the lawn. Planting different grasses side by side will result in a permanently unkempt look. If you don't have some of the original seed on hand, buy the same (or a similar) mix at a garden supply center. If you are unsure about the type of seed, choose a high-quality "blender" type for lawns.

After planting, keep the patch watered and exclude foot traffic until the grass is well established. If necessary, fence off the patch with stakes and string.

## USES FOR GRASS CLIPPINGS

After you mow the lawn, don't discard the clippings: They make an excellent no-cost mulch for flower beds and vegetable gardens alike. Grass clippings contain large amounts of nitrogen and organic matter that will benefit the soil, as long as you keep the following gardener's tips in mind.

• If you applied an herbicide to the lawn, go through at least four mowings before collecting the clippings for mulch; otherwise the herbicide will be transferred to the other plants in the garden.

• Once you have collected the clippings, set them aside and allow them to dry before they are used in the garden. (Clippings emit a great amount of heat as they dry; this heat can damage plants.) After they have dried, spread the grass clippings on the soil.

**1** Using a trowel, a shovel or a garden fork, loosen the top 3 to 6 inches of soil in the bare spot *(right)*. Into the loosened soil, work 2 inches of peat moss and a sprinkling of balanced phosphorus-rich lawn fertilizer. Level the patch. (For bare spots caused by spilled chemicals, dig up and discard the top 3 to 6 inches of soil, and substitute uncontaminated, amended soil.)

**2** Spread seeds thinly and evenly on the surface of the prepared soil *(left)*; use about 15 to 20 seeds per square inch. (Do not skimp; not all the seeds you sow will germinate.) Then scratch them into the soil with the teeth of a rake, lightly tamp them down with the flat side of the rake and smooth out the soil.

**3** Scatter a very thin layer of clean straw over the newly seeded area *(right)*; this mulch will help retain moisture in the soil. Water the patch lightly. Keep it moist and protect it from use until the new grass is well established.

# TILLING THE SOIL AND ENRICHING IT

There is only one sure way to grow velvety grass or vigorous ground covers: by preparing the soil carefully, before planting. Most soils need some enriching; all can benefit from the sort of care shown opposite and on page 104. It is also a good idea to test the quality of the existing soil before tilling it, to find out exactly what sort of enriching and amending it needs.

First test the soil's acid-alkaline balance, called the pH level. A level of 7.0 is neutral; below that the soil tends toward acidity. Turfgrasses prefer slightly acid surroundings in the 6.5 to 6.9 range, ground covers a more acidic 6.0 to 6.5. Take some samples of earth from several parts of the area to be planted, at a depth of about 6 inches, where roots are strongest; put the samples in small, labeled plastic bags, then send them to a county extension office, state university or ask for advice at a garden center. The laboratory report will indicate whether the various soil areas need to be made more alkaline by mixing in crushed dolomite limestone or more acidic by the addition of sulfur.

You can also use natural products to adjust soil pH: wood ashes, oystershells, or bonemeal to raise pH; finely ground cottonseed meal or calcium sulfate to lower it. Note that grasses planted along sidewalks can get doses of salt every winter, making their soil too alkaline over time. Calcium sulfate not only lowers pH, but soaks up gas, oil and pet urine as well as salt.

The lab report should also include measurements of vital minerals: calcium, potassium, phosphorus, sulfur and magnesium. If there are deficiencies, purchase a fertilizer that contains the needed nutrients (garden supply centers will help select the right type and amount).

Then evaluate the soil's texture. Ideally the soil should be a crumbly loam—firm enough to hold moisture, but neither dense and clayey nor too loose and sandy. To improve the soil's structure, add organic matter: rotted leaves, compost, peat moss. If using compost *(page 58)*, ensure that it is well aged and free of weed seeds. Even good soil can benefit from enrichment with some organic matter. Spread it over the area being planted and work it into the soil with a rotary tiller, along with the fertilizer and any other needed amendments.

*Growing thick and lush and bright green, a recently planted stretch of turfgrass has the look of a long-established lawn. Careful preparation of the ground before planting makes possible this sort of satisfying and speedy growth.*

## HOW A ROTARY TILLER WORKS

Motor-driven rotary tillers make working the soil a lot easier than doing it by hand, and they do it more efficiently. These tools can be rented from tool and garden centers, or purchased if the amount of gardening you do warrants the expense. The smaller and less costly sort—front-tine tillers with the rotary blades up front—are useful for tilling soil that has been worked before. Larger and more expensive rear-tine tillers are essentially the same, but have the power to break up earth that has never been tilled before and is likely to be compacted.

**1** Remove any visible rocks or sticks before operating the rotary tiller. Then start preparing your soil by churning it up with a rotary tiller, with the blades set to dig down 6 inches. If the site already has grass on it, make a preliminary run with the blades set for a 2- to 3-inch-deep surface till. Rake up and discard the cut-up grass before doing the regular 6-inch-deep tilling. Make sure the ground is moist before using the tiller; dry soil is difficult to till properly.

**2** Rake the tilled soil carefully, breaking up any clods and removing rocks, weeds, remaining bits of uprooted grass and all miscellaneous debris. For growing turfgrass especially, the soil should be as smooth and fine textured as you can make it. If any recent construction or renovation work has been done near the lawn area, remove any chunks of concrete or wood debris: These materials can cause dips in the soil, or react chemically with it; wood can rot and eventually give rise to mushrooms.

**3** Spread a layer of peat moss, grass clippings, animal manure, compost, sawdust, shredded leaves or other organic matter over the tilled area. The layer should be 2 to 4 inches thick; less than that will not much improve the soil's richness or texture. If your soil test indicated a need for amendments, a pH adjustment or fertilizers, this is the time to add them.

**4** Using the rotary tiller again, churn all the amendments into the soil thoroughly. Then smooth the plot once more with a rake *(right)*. Fill in any depressions where excess water might gather, and level off any mounds.

**5** As a finishing touch before planting, firm the tilled and amended soil with a light lawn roller. (Rollers are available by the day from tool rental agencies.) Rolling gets rid of air pockets as well as providing the smooth surface that lawns especially need. Next, water the soil to level it; be sure to remove any weeds before planting.

# GRASSES, GROUND COVERS AND THEIR USES

*Massed lilies-of-the-valley, showing scores of tiny, fragrant white flowers, crowd between two rocks in a sunny, secluded part of a landscape. Perennials that clump thickly and retain their vivid green foliage all summer, as these low-growing lilies-of-the-valley do, make fine ground covers.*

## FIRE-RESISTANT GROUND COVERS

If you live in an area where fire is a perennial threat, as it is in some of the arid regions of the West, you can reduce the risk to your property by using ground covers, especially ones that have fire-retardant qualities.

All ground covers have a natural advantage over other plants. Because their height is limited and they grow close to the soil, less of their surface area is exposed to air; consequently, they do not dry out as quickly as upright plants. And succulent ground covers, such as ice plant and sedum *(above)*, have an added virtue. Their foliage is thick and fleshy, and capable of holding water, and has a waxy coating that seals in moisture.

Turfgrasses and ground cover plants do essentially the same job. They carpet the land around a house and set off the rest of the landscaping—the trees and shrubs and flower beds. There are two large differences, though, between them. Grass can be walked on and played on, and a smooth lawn of it has a neat and manicured look matched by nothing else. Ground covers are looser and, like flower beds, are distinctly unsuited to foot traffic.

But ground covers have their advantages. For one, they do not have to be mowed and, once established, need only a minimum of other maintenance. For another, a number of ground covers will flourish where grass refuses to grow—in areas densely shaded by house or trees, in spots that are dry and hot or cool and wet. They are also ideal for narrow and odd-shaped places that, planted with grass, would be virtually impossible to mow, and for erosion control in wet or windy areas.

Ground covers come in many shapes, sizes, textures and even colors. They range from small shrubs—low-growing but woody— to creeping vines to a host of spreading perennial plants. A number of ornamental grasses have become popular for ground cover use. Ornamental grasses, which may or may not be relatives of the turfgrasses and are usually tall, shoot up in dense clumps of wonderfully varied shape and color. All of these types of ground covers are pictured on pages 107-108.

The turfgrasses themselves are also varied. They can be divided, though, into the two main classes shown on page 106—the so-called bunching grasses, which grow well only in cooler northern regions, and the creepers, which are usually suited to hot climates.

Grasses and ground covers need not be thought of as mutually exclusive. Although most homes have lawns around them, there is every reason to include ground covers in the landscape—to clothe difficult spots, to add variety or beauty, and to lighten the yard-keeping chores.

# TWO KINDS OF TURFGRASSES

On turfgrass, each grass blade grows from the base upward instead of from the tip, as most plants do; that is why turfgrasses are the most durable of ground covers and why they thrive despite traffic and regular close mowing. The base of each blade is partially below the soil surface and protected from damage. This is true of both bunching grasses, so-called since they grow in clumps or bunches, and the quite different creepers.

BUNCHING GRASSES
The classic cool-season lawn grasses—handsome but delicate fescue, ryegrass and others—generally grow upright in bunches, or clumps, from deep roots. Once planted, they spread by putting out new shoots called tillers, which rise from the crown and thicken the plant. The more the tillers are encouraged to grow by proper fertilizing, mowing and watering, the denser a lawn will be.

CREEPING GRASSES
All the grasses that are known as warm-season grasses and that grow best in hot climates—the Bermudas, zoysia, St. Augustine and Kentucky bluegrass—spread by means of stems that grow sideways. The stems are called stolons if they creep along the surface of the soil *(below)*, rhizomes if they tunnel beneath it *(right)*. In either case, these grasses spread far faster than the bunching grasses with their upright growth habit, and tend to stop weeds from growing near them.

# GROUND COVERS

The plants that make up the three main groups of ground covers *(below)* are remarkably diverse in texture, shape and growing habits. But they all form relatively low-growing and close-knit blankets of green—qualities that good ground covers should have. Most spread quickly, conserve moisture in the ground (and thus need little watering) and, by growing densely, keep out weeds. Among them, species can be found that will flourish in almost any soil and in the coolest shade or the hottest sun.

SHRUBS
Several sorts of woody shrubs—creeping juniper *(above)*, dwarf yew, dwarf azalea and cotoneaster among others—make good ground covers since their branches grow horizontally, allowing the plants to remain low and close to the soil. A number of these small shrubs are evergreens; such plants provide foliage through the year, and some of them put forth delicate but decorative blooms at various times during the growing season. Many are very hardy, and tolerant of wind, low temperatures and snow.

VINES
English ivy *(below)* and other vines are the quintessential ground covers because their stems root as they grow, and spread very swiftly. This rooting habit also makes them excellent for anchoring soil and stopping erosion. Some of them flourish in shaded areas where grass will not survive.

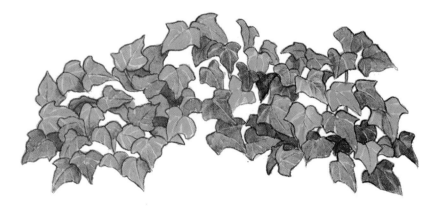

PERENNIALS
A considerable variety of perennials can be employed as ground covers, from modest-sized lily-of-the-valley *(left)* to taller daylilies, from twining strawberry plants to prickly pears. Like the turfgrasses, these plants are of two general types, those that grow in clumps and those that grow from rhizomes. The clumpy plants spread by forming new growth at their outer edges. The rhizomatous ones spread faster as the lateral-growing stems reach out and reroot. Some of them die back in the winter, but others are evergreens; most have decorative blooms. When used as ground covers, perennials need periodic dividing. Otherwise, dense growth decreases their vigor.

# ORNAMENTAL GRASSES

Grasses and grasslike sedges and rushes are increasingly used as ground covers, both for the decorative qualities of their long leaf blades and for their ability to grow fast over large areas. Often, they are used to achieve a romantic or naturalistic garden effect. Two or three species, of different shades and varying heights, can be banked one behind another for a wild billowing effect at the far borders of a landscape.

## GRASSES

The ornamental grasses that are properly called "ornamental grasses" are true grasses; their stems are round and jointed. Some of them, such as fountain grass *(left)*, grow 3 feet high and some are taller still. Planted in a mass, they make effective wind screens as well as handsome backgrounds for other plantings. Many grow feathery seed heads, which add to their decorative effect, and they generally stay erect through the winter, waving in the wind and lending interest to the landscape when virtually all growing things are dead or dormant. Ornamental grasses are easy to maintain; they should be cut back to the ground in early spring.

## SEDGES

Looking like grasses but belonging to a different botanical family—the stem structures of sedges are triangular and unjointed—various sedges make good ground covers in damp areas, where they thrive. You can mass them in a boggy part of the garden, or use them as accents near the margin of a pond or a small pool.

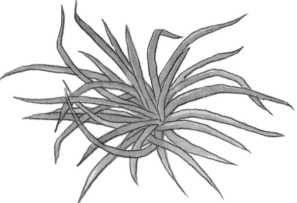

## RUSHES

Similar to sedges but having rounded unjointed stem structures, the rushes are also marsh plants and share the same preference for wet soil conditions. They are especially useful as ground covers where a property falls off toward a lake or the shore of a coastal inlet.

# STARTING A LAWN WITH PLUGS OR SPRIGS

Most of the so-called warm-season grasses—centipedegrass, St. Augustine and zoysia grass, for example—can withstand the blistering sun and high temperatures of southern and southwestern summers. Some strains are what experts call stoloniferous, which means they grow by spreading. They have lateral stems, or stolons, that creep and root and creep some more, sending up grassy shoots as they go. These grasses are best started by planting plugs—little chunks of sod—at regular intervals, as shown below and on the following pages, then letting the plugs grow together. The result will be patchy at first, but these grasses spread so fast that in less than a year a lawn will fill in.

An alternative to plugs is grass sprigs—small sections of stem. The short-term effect is even less orderly, but after a year the sprigs should grow together and fill in the lawn just as well. The first step is to decide when to do the planting. Spring and summer, when warm-season grasses do their most active growing, are best. Settle on a convenient week and begin preparing the soil *(pages 102-104)*. Order the sprigs accordingly, and plant them as soon as you receive them. The quickest way to plant sprigs is to spread them over the entire area, till them into the ground with a rotary tiller, then press them down with a roller. This, however, can be wasteful; some of the sprigs get buried. Pages 111-112 show another method, using furrows. Although more time-consuming, a higher percentage of the sprigs will take root and grow.

## STARTING A LAWN WITH PLUGS OF GRASS

1 To plant plugs of warm-season grass in prepared soil about 1 foot apart, you can measure with a ruler and mark the chosen spots with a trowel. It is easier, though, to use the grid-making device shown at right.

To make this rakelike tool, use an 8-foot length of 2-by-4 lumber; drive eight sixteen-penny nails through it on one of its 4-inch faces. The nails should be 12 inches apart; start 6 inches in from either end. Then add a 6-foot piece of 2-by-2 as a handle. Strengthen the joint by nailing a 3-foot-long support of 1-by-2 lumber on each side of the handle. Sand the handle to rid it of splinters.

Drag the tool across your plot in one direction, then crosswise at a 90° angle. The lines should intersect every 12 inches.

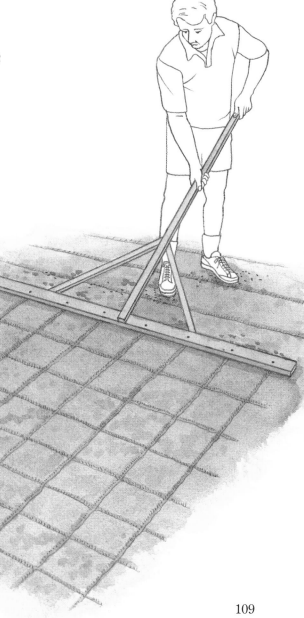

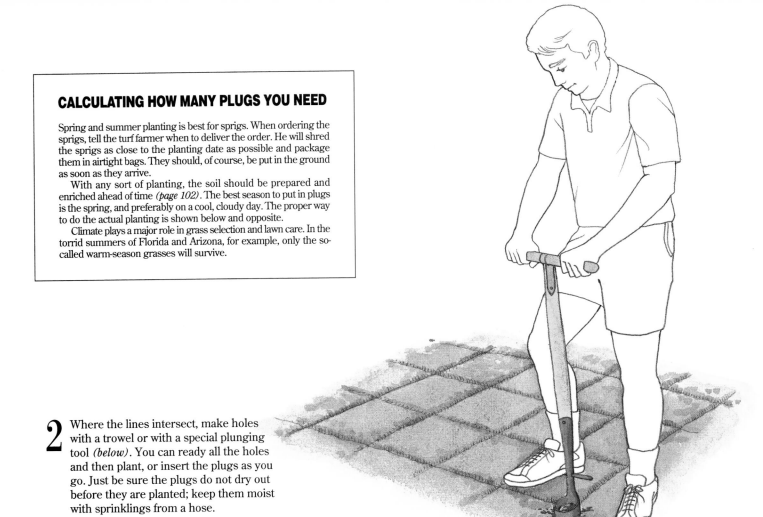

## CALCULATING HOW MANY PLUGS YOU NEED

Spring and summer planting is best for sprigs. When ordering the sprigs, tell the turf farmer when to deliver the order. He will shred the sprigs as close to the planting date as possible and package them in airtight bags. They should, of course, be put in the ground as soon as they arrive.

With any sort of planting, the soil should be prepared and enriched ahead of time *(page 102)*. The best season to put in plugs is the spring, and preferably on a cool, cloudy day. The proper way to do the actual planting is shown below and opposite.

Climate plays a major role in grass selection and lawn care. In the torrid summers of Florida and Arizona, for example, only the so-called warm-season grasses will survive.

**2** Where the lines intersect, make holes with a trowel or with a special plunging tool *(below)*. You can ready all the holes and then plant, or insert the plugs as you go. Just be sure the plugs do not dry out before they are planted; keep them moist with sprinklings from a hose.

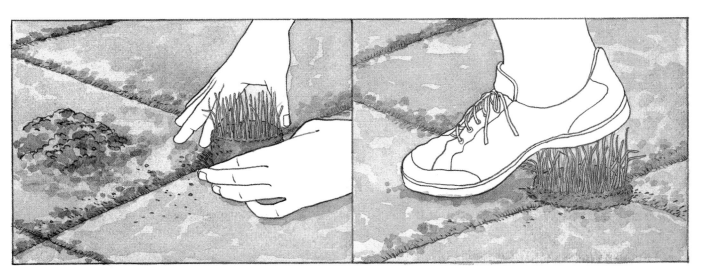

**3** Put a plug in its hole *(above, left)*, making sure that the grassy top sits ⅛ to ¼ inch above the soil line. If the plugs are too deep, the grass will not spread freely and make new roots in the surrounding earth. After the plug has been planted at the right depth, add some topsoil and organic matter around it, then tamp it down with your heel *(above, right)* to ensure good root-to-soil contact. Plant all your plugs in this fashion.

4 When all the plugs are in the ground, rake the areas between them. Whenever possible, stand outside the planting area while working. Smooth out any little hills and fill depressions so that the finished lawn will be smooth. Do not mound up earth around any of the plugs, however; they should remain above ground level.

As soon as the planting is finished, water the entire area thoroughly. An oscillating sprinkler is ideal because it spreads the water evenly without causing washouts. Continue watering liberally during the first couple of months, to be sure the plugs remain moist and become well established.

## STARTING A LAWN WITH GRASS SPRIGS

1 Before starting to plant freshly cut sprigs in furrows, prepare the lawn area and lightly water it; moist earth is easier to work with and better for the sprigs. Set up two stakes and connect them by string to mark a straight line for the first furrow. Then, with a mattock, dig the furrow 3 inches deep.

### ORDERING GRASS SPRIGS

Sprigs generally consist of sections of shredded stem 3 to 6 inches long. Most will include roots and blades of grass. Turf farms usually sell sprigs by the bushel; one bushel should be enough to plant 200 square feet. Alternatively, you can make your own sprigs from sod pieces. Keep in mind that a desirable sprig has roots and at least two to four nodes from which roots can develop.

If you buy the sprigs locally or by mail, ordering the right quantity is important; ordering at the right time is essential. Having no soil attached, they dry out quickly, so they should be planted soon after being shredded.

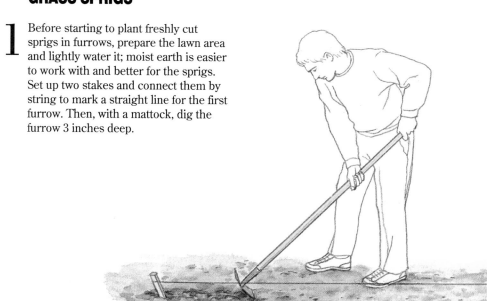

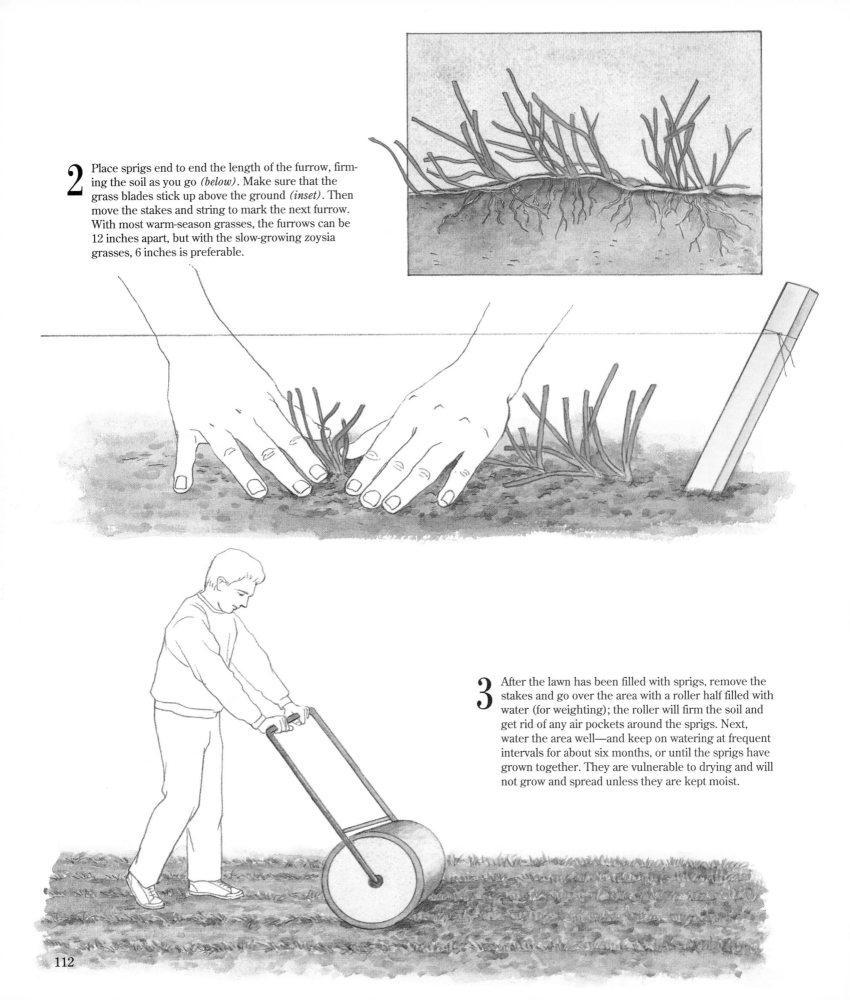

**2** Place sprigs end to end the length of the furrow, firming the soil as you go *(below)*. Make sure that the grass blades stick up above the ground *(inset)*. Then move the stakes and string to mark the next furrow. With most warm-season grasses, the furrows can be 12 inches apart, but with the slow-growing zoysia grasses, 6 inches is preferable.

**3** After the lawn has been filled with sprigs, remove the stakes and go over the area with a roller half filled with water (for weighting); the roller will firm the soil and get rid of any air pockets around the sprigs. Next, water the area well—and keep on watering at frequent intervals for about six months, or until the sprigs have grown together. They are vulnerable to drying and will not grow and spread unless they are kept moist.

# SOWING GRASS SEED — AN ECONOMICAL WAY TO BEGIN

Seeding is by far the most popular method of starting a new lawn. It is quick and easy; it costs much less than such methods as installing sod, plugs or sprigs; and commercially available seed offers the largest variety of both cool- and warm-season grass types.

To make sure you get the right kind of seed, think carefully about your needs before you buy. There are grasses that tolerate heavy wear (important if your lawn will double as a play area), as well as hot dry spells (for regions with low rainfall) and shade. The dictionary at the end of this chapter will help you find grasses with the specific characteristics you are looking for.

Be prepared to pay for quality. Avoid seed "bargains," which often have a low germination rate or contain a lot of "temporary" seeds that spring up fast and fade even faster. Quality grass seed contains only minimal amounts of filler material and weed seeds. The quality can to some extent be judged by the labels, so before buying, check the label carefully: Weed seed content should be less than 1 percent; inert matter, such as dirt, should be no higher than 2 to 4 percent; quality seed should contain no noxious weeds.

A good bet is any seed package labeled "Certified." This means that the state or, in Canada, the Federal government, has tested the contents and found that the seeds are accurately represented on the label. The label will also tell how many square feet the seeds in the package will cover.

Before seeding, prepare the soil as shown on pages 102-104. Never spread seed on wet soil, which can become compacted and hinder germination. Seeds can be sown by hand. But for neater, more even distribution, use a drop spreader, which deposits seeds through a long slot, or a broadcast spreader, which throws seeds in a half-circle *(page 114)*. Both kinds of spreaders can be rented at garden supply centers, as can lawn rollers, which make it easy to set the seeds firmly in place.

*Bright green shoots of new grass started from seed poke through a protective layer of straw mulch, which helps keep newly broadcast seeds from blowing away and conserves moisture while they germinate.*

## WHAT'S IN THE BAG

Grass seeds sometimes come packaged "straight" by the species or cultivar, such as Kentucky bluegrass—but most packages contain more than one kind of grass. The idea is to balance strengths and weaknesses. For example, some grasses are durable but slow-growing; others grow fast but are susceptible to disease or bad weather. A combination of traits should provide maximum satisfaction over the life of a lawn.

Packages labeled "mixture" contain seeds of more than one species (such as Kentucky bluegrass and fine fescue): "blends" bring together different cultivars of the same species. Both mixtures and blends combine grasses that have similar colors and textures.

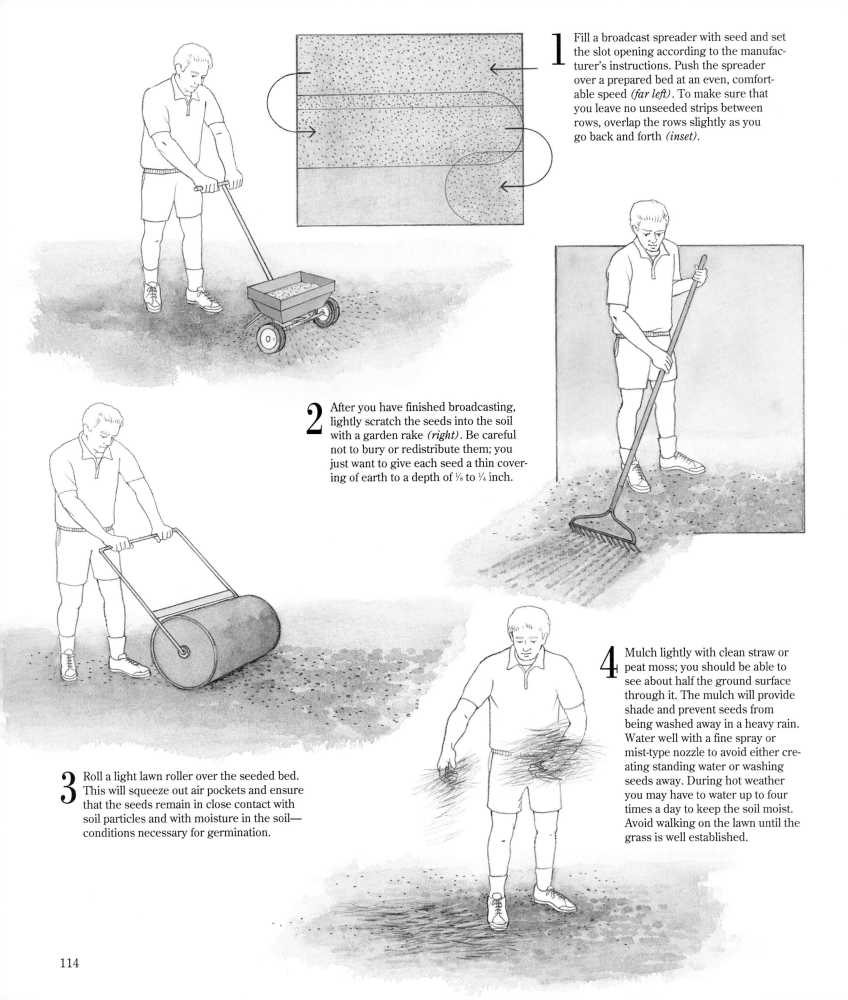

**1** Fill a broadcast spreader with seed and set the slot opening according to the manufacturer's instructions. Push the spreader over a prepared bed at an even, comfortable speed *(far left)*. To make sure that you leave no unseeded strips between rows, overlap the rows slightly as you go back and forth *(inset)*.

**2** After you have finished broadcasting, lightly scratch the seeds into the soil with a garden rake *(right)*. Be careful not to bury or redistribute them; you just want to give each seed a thin covering of earth to a depth of ⅛ to ¼ inch.

**3** Roll a light lawn roller over the seeded bed. This will squeeze out air pockets and ensure that the seeds remain in close contact with soil particles and with moisture in the soil—conditions necessary for germination.

**4** Mulch lightly with clean straw or peat moss; you should be able to see about half the ground surface through it. The mulch will provide shade and prevent seeds from being washed away in a heavy rain. Water well with a fine spray or mist-type nozzle to avoid either creating standing water or washing seeds away. During hot weather you may have to water up to four times a day to keep the soil moist. Avoid walking on the lawn until the grass is well established.

# INSTALLING SOD
# FOR AN INSTANT LAWN

**B**oth cool-season and warm-season grasses are available as sod. You can lay sod at any time, but it's best to avoid hot, dry spells. The ideal times for laying sod are late summer and early fall for cool-season grasses, and late spring and early summer for warm-season grasses. Careful site preparation is crucial; the soil must be turned, amended, leveled and watered ahead of time *(pages 102-104)*. When preparing the site, leave the soil surface 1 inch lower than adjacent driveways and walkways to accommodate the thickness of the sod. Spread high-phosphate fertilizer. Be ready to install the sod soon after it arrives; left rolled up, the strips will quickly dry out and die.

Sod strips are about 6 feet long, 2 feet wide, and between ¾ and 1 inch thick. Determine the square footage of your lawn; the sod dealer will tell you how many strips you need to cover the area. In sodding a very large lawn, mark off the site in manageable sections of 10 feet by 10 feet or so, and finish working on one section before moving on to the next.

Make sure the sod you order contains the type of grass you want. If you buy from a local dealer, examine the sod before you buy it. The grass itself should be dense, good in color, and free of disease, insects and weeds. The strips should be strong and intact. Lift one strip by an end; it should hold together like a piece of carpet. In some areas you can buy "certified" sod, the composition and quality of which are guaranteed.

*Rows of parallel lines are visible between the strips of turf on a newly sodded lawn. As the grass grows together, usually in two to four weeks, the lines will fade, creating an even surface color. Although sod costs up to five times more than a seeded lawn, it yields immediate results; it goes anywhere, including steep slopes; and the roots of properly laid sod quickly "knit" to the soil so erosion is halted.*

**1** A day or two before the sod is due to arrive, lightly rake the soil surface and water it well. Align the edge of a sod roll against a straight-edge such as a sidewalk—or set up stakes and strings for a guideline. Unroll the strip, checking the alignment and patting the sod down at every point to make sure it lies evenly on the damp soil surface. Lay a second strip of sod end to end with the first, taking care not to overlap the ends *(left)*. Don't pull or stretch the sod in any direction; stretched sod is more likely to shrink later on, leaving unsightly gaps in your lawn.

**2** Using fresh soil, fill in the joint between the two sod strips. First pull back the ends slightly, then work in the soil with a trowel and tamp it down *(left)*. Lay additional strips of sod end to end until you have finished the first row. Fill in and tamp down all joints. If you are working in hot temperatures, sprinkle newly laid sod pieces as soon as they are in place. Make sure that the sod still to be laid does not dry out while you are working.

**3** Lay a second row of sod alongside the first row. Stagger the strips—in a brickwork-like pattern—so that the joints in one row never line up with the joints in adjacent rows *(right)*. This will help make an even lawn.

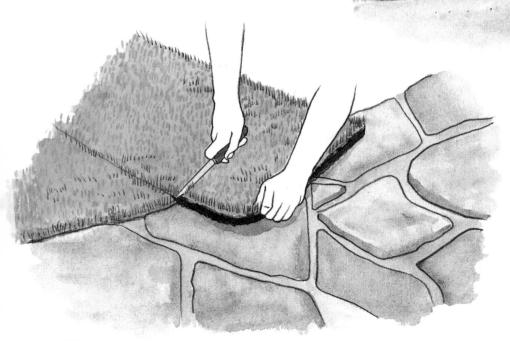

**4** When you come to odd-sized or unusually shaped areas like the ends of rows or curved corners—you will have to cut the strips of sod to fit *(left)*. Use a sharp-pointed tool, such as a spade, a knife or a mason's trowel. For a 3- to 4-inch gap, however, use soil to fill; small pieces of sod usually dry out and die.

**5** Roll the newly sodded lawn with a light roller to ensure good root-to-soil contact *(right);* then water thoroughly. If you roll as shown, and the sod pieces curl, try rolling perpendicular to the sod. For the next two weeks, water every other day (every day in a hot, dry spell) until the sod "knits" to the ground. Do not mow the new lawn until the grass is about 3 inches high. (**Gardener's Tip:** A roller should be used to firm the surface of an already-smooth lawn, not to iron out bumps.)

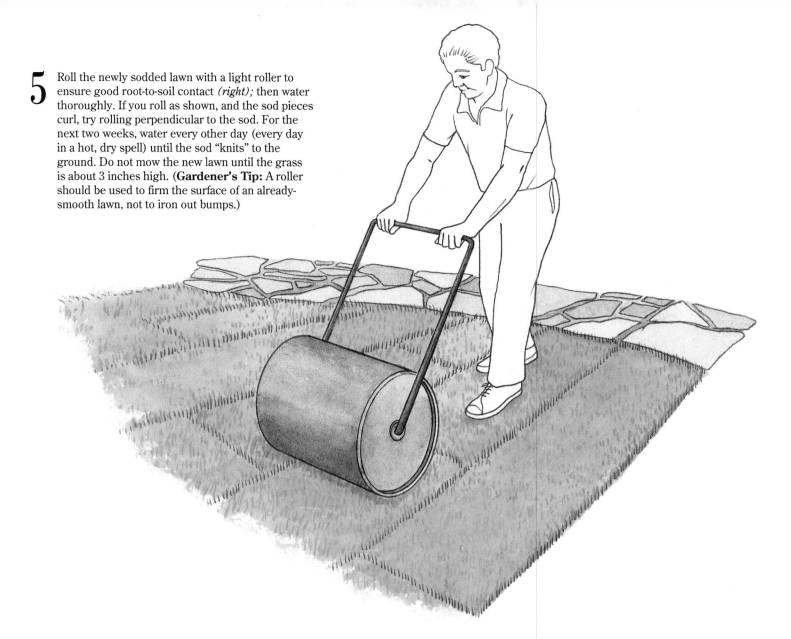

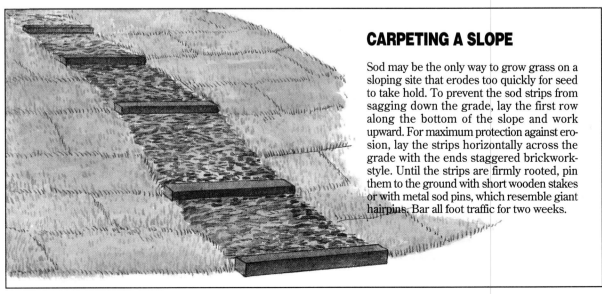

## CARPETING A SLOPE

Sod may be the only way to grow grass on a sloping site that erodes too quickly for seed to take hold. To prevent the sod strips from sagging down the grade, lay the first row along the bottom of the slope and work upward. For maximum protection against erosion, lay the strips horizontally across the grade with the ends staggered brickwork-style. Until the strips are firmly rooted, pin them to the ground with short wooden stakes or with metal sod pins, which resemble giant hairpins. Bar all foot traffic for two weeks.

# LOW-MAINTENANCE GROUND COVERS FROM BARE-ROOT PLANTS

The biggest and most important area you'll ever have to plant is likely to be the land directly around your house. Before settling for a traditional lawn, consider a sensible alternative: a sturdy, attractive, easy-to-maintain ground cover. A ground cover not only requires less care than a lawn, but its extensive root system does a better job of holding down soil on a slope. The principal drawback is that you can't walk on a bed of ground cover as you can on grass.

Mail-order catalogs offer ground cover plants in a wide selection of colors, shapes and growth habits. Ground covers most often come in containers, but some dealers ship them bare-root, that is, with little or no soil attached. These work just as well and cost less—a significant consideration, since it takes a substantial number of plants to serve as ground cover.

The optimal time for planting is spring to mid-summer. Before ordering plants, calculate the area you have to cover *(below, right)* and then figure how many plants you will need. The number will depend on the type of plant you select. As a rule, shrubs that spread should be placed no farther apart than a distance equal to their ultimate width. Perennials should be placed a distance about equal to their mature height. With vines you have a choice. If you are willing to wait a season or two for them to cover the ground completely, you can plant them 1 to 2 feet apart, and they will eventually grow together. If you are impatient and want the ground covered immediately, the vines can be planted as close together as you like—but be prepared to prune later.

To prevent erosion, especially on hills, arrange the plants in a staggered pattern so that those in one row will catch loosened soil and rain runoff from the rows above. To train plants to grow in a desired direction (toward the edge of a path, for example), secure them to the ground with pieces of bent wire or with sod pins.

*Clinging to a steep slope, a dense bed of periwinkle serves as an all-season bulwark against erosion. The small purple and white flowers are an early spring bonus.*

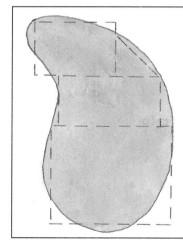

## DIVIDING A WHOLE INTO PARTS

To make calculating the area of an irregularly shaped garden space easy, divide it into simple geometric figures—squares, oblongs, triangles, half circles, as appropriate. Measure the area of each separately, and then add the areas together to get a total.

**1** Remove all weeds in the area, then prepare the soil for a ground cover bed as you would for a lawn *(pages 102-104)*. Then spread a 2-inch layer of organic mulch (such as pine needles that are disease-free) to resist erosion, reduce weed growth and conserve ground water *(right)*.

**2** Mark one edge of the bed with stakes and strings to help you lay out a straight row. Make an opening in the mulch for insertion of the first plant. With a trowel, dig a hole wide enough for the roots to spread out comfortably and deep enough so that the topmost roots will sit about ¼ inch below the surface *(left)*. Position the plant, firm the soil around it, replace the mulch and water well. Repeat for the other plants in the row. To maintain spacing, estimate visually or use a ruler.

**3** When you finish planting the first row, relocate the stakes and string to guide the planting of a second row. Arrange the second row parallel to the first, but with each plant offset from its first-row neighbors to create a staggered pattern. Then move the stakes and string again, and repeat the staggered pattern with succeeding rows *(right)* until the entire bed is covered.

# USING PLASTIC MULCH TO KEEP OUT WEEDS

The easiest way to keep ground covers weed-free is to deny weeds what all plants must have to live: a place in the sun. A thick layer of organic mulch (like peat moss, pine bark or straw) will hinder weed growth; for instructions on mulching, see page 70. But weed barriers made from plastic do an even better job than organic mulch since they leave fewer openings for weeds to exploit. The only breaks in the plastic are those you cut to let your own plants through. Be sure to use black-colored plastic; clear plastic will let the sun pass through.

The same property that makes plastic so effective a weed barrier—its impermeability—imposes some restrictions on its use. Ground covers that put down new roots as they sprawl, like ivy, or that multiply by spreading from their crowns, like hosta, will be frustrated by a plastic weed barrier. It should be used only with plants that grow from a central point—low-growing shrubs such as cotoneaster and dwarf varieties of yew and azalea.

It used to be that sealing off the ground with an impermeable plastic sheet also made it difficult to water and fertilize the soil around your plants. However, new materials have all but eliminated this problem. Some of the new plastics are perforated with thousands of tiny holes, and others are woven. Both kinds let air, water and fertilizer particles pass through in one direction but block weed seeds and seedlings from coming up in the other. You can also set up a soaker hose *(page 64)* before putting plastic mulch in place to ensure the soil gets enough water.

These new weed barriers are usually sold in sheets 3 feet wide and 50 to 100 feet long. Before installing any of them, prepare your ground cover bed for planting, as shown on pages 101-104. After planting the area with low-growing shrubs, cover the plastic weed barrier with some attractive camouflage such as shredded bark or pine bark chips. Warm sunny areas will require more frequent watering. Keep a watchful eye on the area covered with plastic. Look for signs of fungus and bacteria thriving in the warmer, moist soil, or any indication that a plant is not thriving under new conditions.

*Protected by an unseen sheet of plastic weed barrier, a juniper bed thrives. Holes have been cut in the plastic to let the juniper plants through, and a thin layer of organic mulch disguises the plastic.*

1 Spray a fungicide on the soil that you plan to cover; the plastic weed barrier will keep the soil under it warm and moist and will eliminate air circulation around the soil, predisposing plant stems and roots to rot. Set up any soaker hose you plan to use, then lay a large sheet of black-colored plastic weed barrier over a section of fully prepared bed *(below)*. Cut it to fit. Move to adjacent sections, and cut more plastic as needed to cover the entire bed. Adjacent pieces should overlap about 6 inches. Hold the plastic in place with stones or pegs, particularly in windy areas.

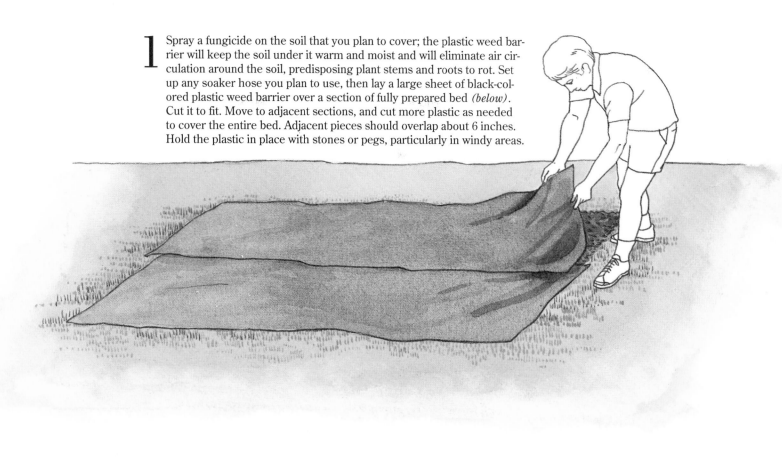

2 When choosing container-grown ground covers, avoid buying any with thick or tangled roots. Arrange the plants in their containers on top of the weed barrier in staggered rows *(below)*; check with your garden center for the recommended intervals between plants. If you are uncertain about distances, measure with stakes and string.

**3** Lift up each plant, and use a utility knife to cut an X through the weed barrier where the plant was standing. Make an X-shaped slit large enough for the plant's root ball to pass through *(right)*. Fold back the flaps of the slit and dig a hole in the exposed soil.

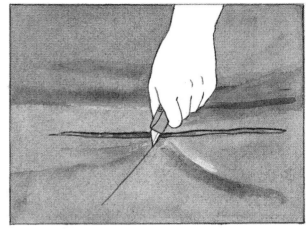

**4** Carefully remove a plant from its container. With one hand on the bottom of the container and the other hand covering the soil and supporting the plant, turn the container upside down. The plant should slide out smoothly *(right)*; if it doesn't, slap the side of the container several times and "tease" the roots out of the container. If the roots are thickly matted, gently untangle them with your fingers and cut their ends, using shears to encourage outward growth.

**5** Insert the plant in its hole, making sure it sits at the same depth in the ground as it did in its container. Firm some of the dug-up soil around the plant. Set aside excess soil for use elsewhere. Water well, then fold the flaps of the slit back in place around the plant *(left)*. Repeat until the entire bed is planted.

**6** To hide the sheets of plastic and make the bed look natural, sprinkle a decorative mulch over the weed barrier. You can use pine bark chips, shredded bark, pine straw—or whatever is cheap and readily available in your area.

PINE BARK

# WATERING:
# HOW MUCH, WHEN AND WHERE

The first and most essential part of caring for lawns and ground covers, of course, is making sure they have enough water to survive and thrive. The question is, how much is enough? To be fresh and vigorous, lawns need to get the right amount of moisture—not too much, not too little—and in the right way at the right times.

Fortunately, there is a handy rule to go by: the average lawn requires 1 inch of water each week during the growing season. Much of this inch, or all of it, may be supplied by rainfall. It is a good idea, in fact, to keep track of how much rain has come down during the season and in recent weeks—a rain gauge from a hardware store will help. If nature provides the needed weekly inch of rain, do not water the lawn any more. Excess moisture encourages weeds and makes grass more susceptible to fungi and other ailments.

But if rain has been infrequent, getting out hoses and sprinklers is very much in order. Too-dry grass exhibits several telltale signs: a wilted look, a dull gray-blue color and little resiliency when stepped on. Sprinklers should be turned on ideally once a week and allowed to run for the hour or so that it takes to supply an inch of water. One long soaking is far preferable to several short ones. It helps the water sink to a depth of 6 or 8 inches, which in turn encourages the grass roots to grow deep and strong. To check to be sure the water is getting down far enough, dig up a core of soil with a narrow trowel and examine it.

There are a few exceptions to the 1-inch rule. More water may be needed if the climate (or the summer season) is unusually hot or windy or both. And various parts of the landscape around a house may require extra moisture, as shown on page 125. Finally, there are ways to help save a lawn when drought and resulting water restrictions make normal watering impossible *(right)*.

*A pop-up sprinkler head from an underground watering system bathes the leaves of surrounding Bermudagrass with a fine vigorous spray. Underground systems, while not cheap to install, are efficient and convenient, and can be programmed to turn on and off automatically.*

## WHEN WATER IS SCARCE

Many parts of the country impose limits on lawn watering during dry seasons to save water for more vital uses. If you find that you cannot give your grass the moisture it needs, you can help it survive until wetter fall weather arrives by referring to the following suggestions:
• Schedule any permitted watering for early morning; the hot afternoon sun will accelerate evaporation of moisture.
• When watering, reposition the sprinkler carefully to avoid water runoff or excessive water in any one area.
• Aerate the lawn *(page 136)* to ensure that any water penetrates to the roots as rapidly as possible.
• Let the grass grow higher than normal by mowing less often and raising the height of the cut. This will reduce stress caused by frequent loss of plant tissue.
• Do not remove grass clippings after mowing the lawn; left on the grass, clippings act as a moisture-conserving mulch.
• Stop fertilizing. Fertilizers encourage grass to grow rapidly, increasing its need for water. Let growth slow down.
• Make a special effort to eliminate weeds, which compete with grass for moisture.
• In areas with frequent, prolonged dry spells, consider setting up a xeriscape garden *(page 36)* or planting a drought-resistant ground cover.

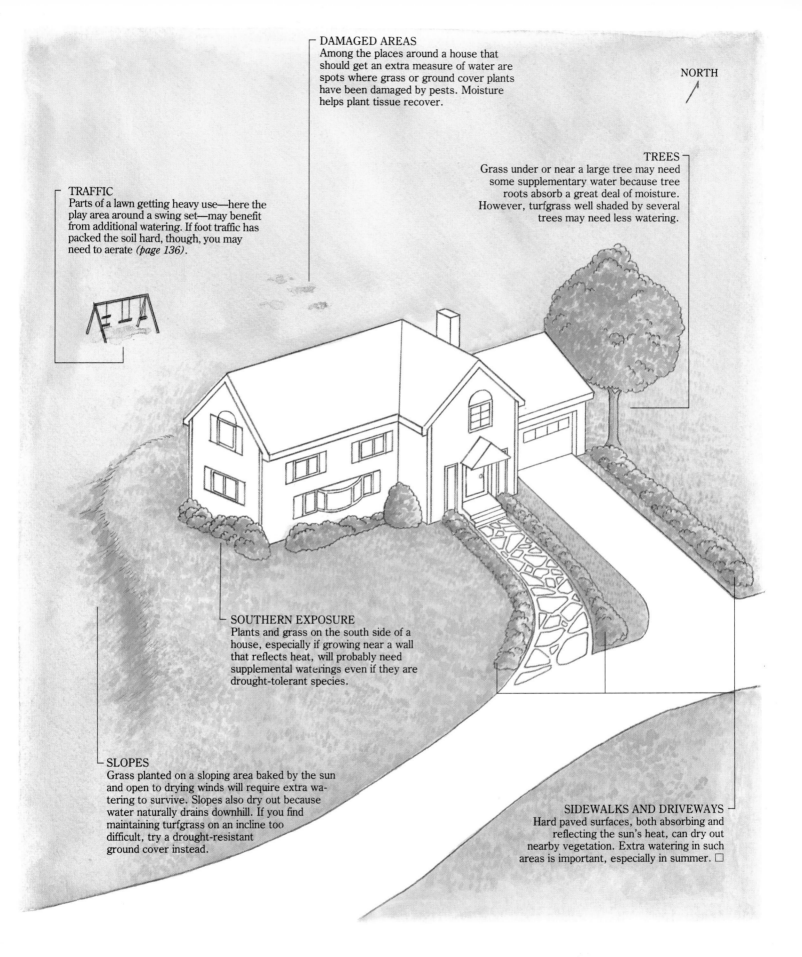

DAMAGED AREAS
Among the places around a house that should get an extra measure of water are spots where grass or ground cover plants have been damaged by pests. Moisture helps plant tissue recover.

NORTH

TREES
Grass under or near a large tree may need some supplementary water because tree roots absorb a great deal of moisture. However, turfgrass well shaded by several trees may need less watering.

TRAFFIC
Parts of a lawn getting heavy use—here the play area around a swing set—may benefit from additional watering. If foot traffic has packed the soil hard, though, you may need to aerate *(page 136)*.

SOUTHERN EXPOSURE
Plants and grass on the south side of a house, especially if growing near a wall that reflects heat, will probably need supplemental waterings even if they are drought-tolerant species.

SLOPES
Grass planted on a sloping area baked by the sun and open to drying winds will require extra watering to survive. Slopes also dry out because water naturally drains downhill. If you find maintaining turfgrass on an incline too difficult, try a drought-resistant ground cover instead.

SIDEWALKS AND DRIVEWAYS
Hard paved surfaces, both absorbing and reflecting the sun's heat, can dry out nearby vegetation. Extra watering in such areas is important, especially in summer. □

# A GUIDE
# TO FERTILIZING LAWNS

*A healthy, bright green lawn leads to a colorful border of flowers, shrubs and trees. Such a lawn results from a balanced diet of nutrients that produce strong roots and vigorous green grass blades.*

Because they are regularly subjected to overcrowding and mowing, turfgrasses require extra fertilizing care. An understanding of the basics of plant nutrition will help you avert problems and keep your lawn handsome and healthy.

There are 16 essential nutrients that all plants must have in order to live *(page 127)*. They get most of what they need from the soil, air and water. The purpose of fertilizers is to supplement the few essential nutrients that the environment does not supply in adequate amounts.

Plants absorb nutrients through their roots; how efficiently they use available nutrients is determined in part by soil composition. The best way to determine which nutrients are in short supply is a soil test, which you can make with a do-it-yourself kit, available at some garden centers, or have done at an agricultural extension service or other service recommended by your garden center.

The three nutrients that most often need to be added are nitrogen (for green leafy growth), phosphorus (for strong roots) and potassium (for general vigor). A "complete" fertilizer contains all three; the three numbers on the package (such as 21-7-14, or ratio of 3-1-2)) indicate the percentages of nitrogen, phosphorus and potassium (in that order) to be found in the product.

In general, the best time to apply fertilizer is just before a period of active growth—generally early spring. One application of general-purpose fertilizer per year will suffice for most ground cover beds. Established lawns should be fed more often, with a fertilizer that contains a higher percentage of nitrogen. For example, if the lawn begins to look run down and growth slows by June or July, a mid-summer feeding may be necessary. New lawns should be fed with a phosphorus-rich "starter" fertilizer to promote root growth. For all lawns and ground covers, avoid feeding during prolonged periods of dry weather.

Fertilizers come in liquid form and granular form. To apply a liquid fertilizer (and any product sold as water-soluble) use a watering can or, when recommended, the nozzle of a watering hose. Granular fertilizers are applied with spreaders. Whatever you use, be sure the grass is dry and the soil is moist when feeding; water in the soil is necessary to release the nutrients.

# THE ESSENTIALS OF PLANT NUTRITION

Plants get all the carbon, hydrogen and oxygen they need from the air and water. Of the remaining nutrients vital to growth and health, plants need relatively large amounts of nitrogen, phosphorus, potassium, sulfur, magnesium and calcium. These are the macronutrients. The nutrients required in much smaller amounts—iron, manganese, zinc, copper, molybdenum, boron and chlorine—are known as micronutrients, or trace elements. Most soils are rich enough in nutrients so that the only supplements you will have to consider are nitrogen, phosphorus and potassium (and, in certain locations, sulfur or iron). A soil test will tell you exactly what to do, but you can generally use a fertilizer for grass with nitrogen, phosphorus and potassium in a 3-1-2 ratio (for example, 21-7-14).

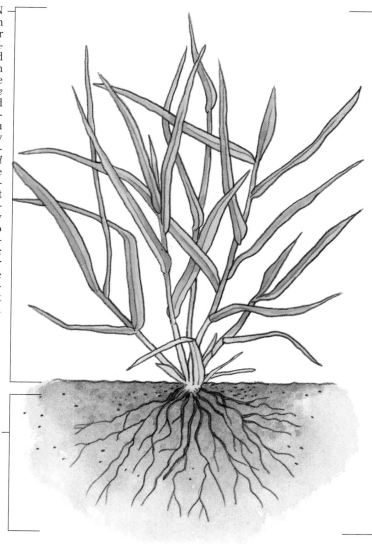

NITROGEN
Essential for leaf and shoot growth and to manufacture chlorophyll for green color. Nitrogen content of fertilizer should be high for spring and summer feeding, but low for autumn feeding. Fertilizer labels should give the source of the nitrogen. *Nitrate* nitrogen (nitrogen that does not need breaking down) is immediately available to plants and useful when you want quick greening, but it is easily washed away, so frequent supplements are necessary. *Ammoniacal* (ammonia-based) nitrogen must be converted to nitrate by microorganisms before it can be used; soil that is too cold or too wet slows microorganic activity. Decomposition by microorganisms is necessary to release *organic* nitrogen from sewage sludge and manure; but organic nitrogen remains in the soil longer than nitrates. Which type you choose depends on how fast you want results and how much time you want to spend fertilizing.

POTASSIUM
Needed for general vigor and for resistance to the stresses of drought, cold, heat and disease. Potassium content of fertilizer should be high for spring and autumn feeding. Potassium has been shown to be involved in such plant metabolic processes as protein synthesis and the maintenance of salt balance. Although potassium is washed from the soil by water, most soils contain sufficient quantities to make high supplements unnecessary. It is typically supplied in fertilizers in the form of potash.

PHOSPHORUS
Promotes root growth and flower bud formation. Extra-large quantities are needed for newly seeded lawns to help initiate root development. Since phosphorus does not wash easily out of soil as nitrogen does, frequent applications are not called for; fertilizers recommended for established lawns are typically low in phosphorus. The usual source of phosphorus in fertilizers is phosphoric acid.

# WHEN TO ADD FERTILIZER

Add fertilizer just before or during peak growth periods. The two graphs below compare the peak growth periods of warm-season and cool-season grasses. Warm-season grasses *(upper graph)* show a steady increase in growth to a peak in mid-summer, then a steady decline through late fall. Cool-season grasses *(lower graph)* have one peak in early spring and another, smaller peak in the fall. Within peak growth periods you can apply fertilizer in successive applications at your convenience, up to the total recommended for the year. But remember: never add more than 1 pound of nitrogen per 1,000 square feet in any one month; with too much nitrogen you risk burning the foliage and weakening growth. In addition, avoid applying a nitrogen-rich fertilizer near the end of the growing season; active autumn growth makes the grass more susceptible to winter damage.

**WARM-SEASON GRASSES**

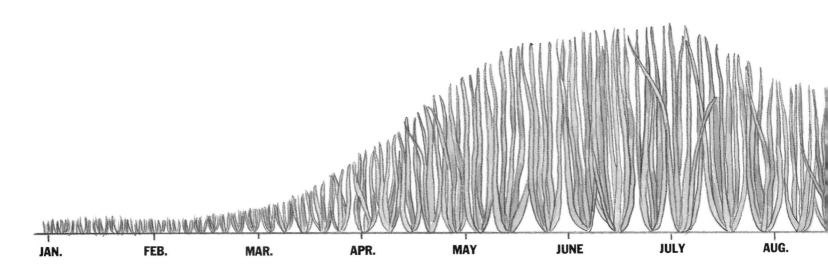

| JAN. | FEB. | MAR. | APR. | MAY | JUNE | JULY | AUG. |

**COOL-SEASON GRASSES**

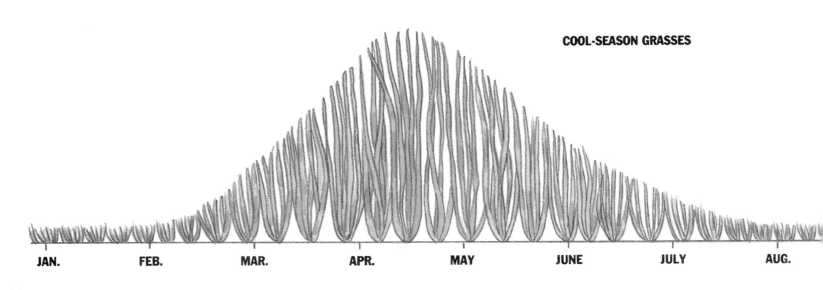

| JAN. | FEB. | MAR. | APR. | MAY | JUNE | JULY | AUG. |

128

| COMMON NAME | BOTANICAL NAME | TYPE | POUNDS OF NITROGEN PER 1,000 SQUARE FEET PER YEAR | |
|---|---|---|---|---|
| | | | MINIMUM | MAXIMUM |
| BERMUDAGRASS | CYNODON | WARM-SEASON | 3 LBS. | 6 LBS. |
| BLUEGRASS | POA | COOL-SEASON | 2 ½ LBS. | 6 LBS. |
| FESCUE | FESTUCA | COOL-SEASON AND TRANSITIONAL | | |
|   CREEPING RED FESCUE |   F. RUBRA RUBRA | COOL-SEASON AND TRANSITIONAL | 1 ¼ LBS. | 3 LBS. |
|   HARD FESCUE |   F. DURIUSCOLA | COOL-SEASON AND TRANSITIONAL | 1 ¼ LBS. | 3 LBS. |
|   TALL FESCUE |   F. ARUNDINACEA | COOL-SEASON AND TRANSITIONAL | 2 ½ LBS. | 6 LBS. |
| RYEGRASS | LOLIUM | COOL-SEASON | 2 LBS. | 6 LBS. |
| ST. AUGUSTINE GRASS | STENOTAPHRUM | WARM-SEASON | 3 LBS. | 6 LBS. |
| ZOYSIA | ZOYSIA | WARM-SEASON | 3 LBS. | 6 LBS. |

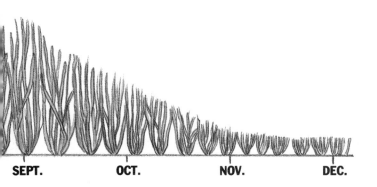

SEPT.    OCT.    NOV.    DEC.

## HOW MUCH TO USE

Almost all turfgrasses need higher doses of nitrogen than ornamental grasses or ground covers. In the Dictionary of Grasses and Ground Covers *(pages 160-177)*, you will find guidelines for fertilizing turfgrasses expressed in terms of nitrogen—specifically, pounds of nitrogen per 1,000 square feet of lawn per year. Depending on weather conditions and how much work you are willing to do, you can adjust the number of applications to achieve the total nitrogen dose recommended. The table above gives two choices: the lower figure is the minimum dose required for healthy growth, the higher figure is the maximum you can safely add for especially lush growth. (Keep in mind that extra growth means extra watering and mowing and, if you use chemical fertilizers, more acidic soil.) To determine how many square feet a bag of fertilizer will cover—at the rate of 1 pound of nitrogen per 1,000 square feet of lawn—multiply the weight of the bag by the nitrogen percentage stated on the label, then multiply by 1,000.

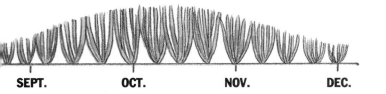

SEPT.    OCT.    NOV.    DEC.

# THREE BASICS OF LAWN CARE: MOWING, TRIMMING AND EDGING

Practically all gardeners think that they know how to mow a lawn. However, mowing is one of the least understood aspects of lawn care. How the grass is mowed and how often can vitally affect a lawn's health as well as its looks.

The first concern is how low to cut—and this depends on the type of grass. Some can safely be shaved down to half an inch in height, but others should be kept a good deal higher or they will sicken and burn out. Each sort of grass, in fact, has its own preferred height of cut (see the Dictionary of Grasses and Ground Covers, *pages 160-177*). As a general rule, most lawns should be mowed no lower than 1 ½ to 2 inches. Trying for a super-smooth carpet effect will damage the grass and its roots by removing too much energy-producing top growth.

There is also a general rule for how often to mow: when the grass has grown about one-third higher than its proper cutting level. This may mean more frequent mowings during the growing season than a once-a-week trim. But letting a lawn become shaggy is a mistake. When it is finally mowed, too much of the top growth gets cut at one time, which can put the grass in shock and cause some yellowing. Also, frequent mowings produce small snippets of cut leaves that can be left to sift down through the grass and return nitrogen to the soil. Longer cuttings must be collected in a catching bag or raked up; otherwise they will smother the lawn.

It is also wise to vary the cutting pattern *(page 131, step 1)* and to do some trimming and edging after mowing for a finished look. Three last provisos: clear the lawn of any stones, twigs, branches and other debris *before* mowing, be sure the mower blades are sharp *(inset, right)*—and for that reason be especially careful of fingers and toes. Wear heavy-duty shoes and never tinker in any way with a power mower while it is running. When making the finishing touches with a power trimmer and an edger *(page 131, steps 2 and 3)*, be sure to wear safety goggles as a precaution against flying stones.

*A curving corner of a lawn, neatly mowed and crisply trimmed, shows off a colorful flower bed of red tuberous begonias and clumpy, purple sweet alyssum.*

### KEEPING A LAWN MOWER IN CONDITION

Proper lawn care begins with proper care of your lawn mower. For a lush lawn, a well-sharpened mower is a must. If mower blades are not absolutely sharp, you risk injuring your lawn every time you mow it. Dull blades tear at grass instead of cutting it and leave ragged tips that can turn brown, making the lawn unattractive and susceptible to pests and diseases. After every four or five cuttings, examine the blades; if the edges are rounded or nicked, they need sharpening. If you have a reel-mower, take it to a professional blade sharpener. If you have a rotary mower, you can do the job yourself with a coarse file or an electric grinder. The grinder will give more even results. When grinding the blade of a rotary mower, be sure to maintain the original angle of its two cutting edges and the balance between them. Use a bevel square to establish the angle, then check after each pass through the grinder and correct any deviation on the next pass. To keep the blade in balance, the same amount of metal must be removed from each edge. Observe all safety precautions; wear safety goggles to protect your eyes against sparks and flying bits of metal shavings.

**1** To mow a good-sized lawn, follow a spiral pattern *(inset, above)*, one time going clockwise, the next time counter-clockwise. Mowing spirally eliminates tiring backtracking and stopping, and reversing directions from one mowing to the next keeps the grass from always being pressed down the same. It is easiest to move from the outside inward *(left)*. If your lawn has rocks or debris you cannot remove by hand, wear safety goggles when mowing.

**2** To trim grass next to walls, fences and trees that a lawn mower cannot reach, use grass shears or, to save time, a power trimmer. Some trimmers have small gasoline motors, but most run on electric current and require an outdoor extension cord *(right)*. If using an electric model, avoid getting the extension cord tangled and be careful not to trip over the cord; use a power cord shortener, available at a building supply center, to keep excess cord safely out of the way. Trimmers generally cut by means of a whirling nylon filament in the head. When trimming, hold the cutting head close to the ground.

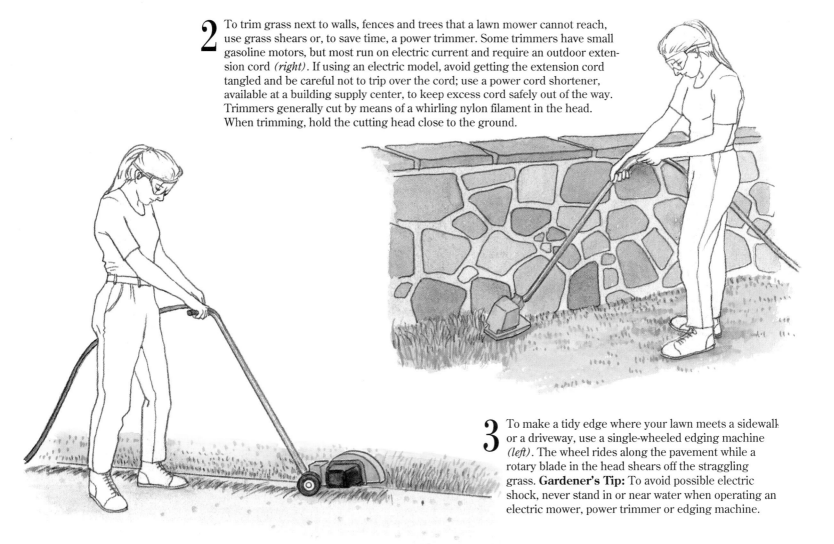

**3** To make a tidy edge where your lawn meets a sidewalk or a driveway, use a single-wheeled edging machine *(left)*. The wheel rides along the pavement while a rotary blade in the head shears off the straggling grass. **Gardener's Tip:** To avoid possible electric shock, never stand in or near water when operating an electric mower, power trimmer or edging machine.

# RIDDING A LAWN OF UNWELCOME WEEDS

All lawns are eventually attacked by weeds. The weeds differ in growth habits, but the basic techniques for combating them are the same. A few isolated weeds are best removed with a trowel or a fork-tongued weeding tool. But if a lawn is large and the weed invasion spreading, the only practical answer is a chemical herbicide. Choosing the right one calls for some knowledge of weed types.

Weeds are mainly of two sorts, annuals and perennials. The annuals grow from seed each year, produce seeds themselves and then die. The remedy is a preemergent herbicide—one that kills the seeds before the weeds can grow. For summer weeds, the preemergent should be applied about the time that forsythia blooms in the spring; for winter weeds, it should be spread in the fall.

Perennial weeds produce seeds, of course, but they also propagate themselves by spreading on their roots. They need a postemergent herbicide—one that kills weeds after they have emerged and begun to grow large. Most effective on most perennials are the so-called systemic herbicides, which poison a weed's entire system. For variations among weeds and specific information on fighting them, see pages 156-159.

Both preemergent and postemergent herbicides come in selective varieties, which are designed to kill only certain weeds, and in nonselective types that annihilate just about any plant they touch. For all ordinary purposes, the selective kinds are the best to use. Many herbicides, for example, are effective against either broad- or narrow-leaved weeds. Check the product label to ensure that you use the appropriate herbicide for the weed you wish to kill. To help you identify a weed, see pages 156-159 or consult a garden center or your state agricultural extension service.

To spray a herbicide as shown on page 133, always wear protective clothing: a long-sleeved shirt, trousers, rubber gloves and safety goggles. In addition, never spray a herbicide when it is windy; the spray can drift, killing any plant it touches—ornamental plants on a neighbor's lawn, for example.

*A smooth and virtually weed-free expanse of healthy lawn provides a handsome setting for a ranch-style house. The most practical way to control a large invasion of weeds is with chemical herbicides.*

## SPRAYERS FOR HERBICIDES

For a lawn of moderate size, a backpack tank *(below, left)* or a compression tank *(below, middle)* is large enough. With a backpack, which holds about 3 gallons of water-diluted herbicide, you need to pump with one hand while aiming the spray tube with the other. Compression tanks are pumped beforehand to build up pressure; they range in size from quart containers to 5-gallon ones. For large lawns, battery-powered, 12-gallon sprayers—available mounted on wheels *(below, right)*—make the task easier. There are also rotary spreaders *(not shown)* for dry granular herbicides.

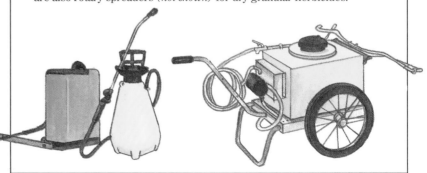

**1** A few days before applying a herbicide, mow your lawn *(right)*, wearing safety goggles for a lawn that has rocks or debris you cannot remove by hand, and give it a good watering. You should not mow it for several days after putting down the chemical because in mowing you will be cutting away treated foliage and thus reducing the effectiveness of the herbicide. Watering ahead of time will encourage the weeds to grow and make them more susceptible to the poison.

**2** Following the direction on the herbicide container, mix the chemical with water in your spray tank—here a backpack type. It is safer to put the water in first; this reduces the chance of splashing the herbicide about. Once the tank is full, begin spraying, keeping the nozzle close to the ground and hitting the weeds directly *(left)*. **Caution:** Never spray herbicide when it is windy.

**3** Keep children and pets away from an area treated with herbicide for several hours—until the herbicide is thoroughly dry; post warning signs or put up a temporary barrier to block access to the area. Do not water your lawn for a few days; watering will dilute the chemical and reduce its effect. In a week or so, when the weeds have died, rake them up *(right)* and throw them away to make room for new grass to grow.

133

# A BIOLOGICAL REMEDY FOR BEETLE GRUBS

The most devastating pests that can afflict a lawn are Japanese beetles or, more precisely, their larvae, or grubs. Hatching from eggs laid under the grass, the grubs feed voraciously on the roots until, in severe cases, the rootless grass can be rolled up like a rug. The most common signs of infestation are brown, dead patches in the lawn. To look for grubs, cut and fold back small sections of turf and examine the soil underneath. To be sure any uncovered grubs are those of Japanese beetles, bring or send a couple of them to a garden supply center or the nearest agricultural extension office.

The most effective way to battle the grubs is with a substance called milky spore, the dustlike dormant form of a bacterium called *Bacillus popilliae*, which was found back in the 1930s to be the natural bacterial enemy of Japanese beetles. Today it is the active ingredient in several insecticide powders sold in garden supply centers. As far as researchers know, the bacterium has no harmful effects on humans or warm-blooded animals.

The milky spore powder should be placed carefully under the grass of an infested lawn *(below and page 135)*. It need be applied only once in a decade because the bacteria multiply as they attack the grubs, becoming more numerous and effective in time. In fact, milky spore products only start working really well three years after application, but then continue working for 15 years or more.

Milky spore can be put down whenever the ground is not frozen, but the best time is either late spring, when new grubs are hatching, or early fall, before the grubs burrow into the soil for the winter. Choose a day that is not windy to apply milky spore to ensure that it goes where you intend. Note that treatment is most effective when it is performed on a community-wide basis.

*Showing no signs of the brown patches caused by Japanese beetle grubs, a handsome sun-dappled lawn thrives in the partial shade of well-spaced trees. Beetle grubs, archenemies of turfgrass, are best kept in check with milky spore, a bacteria-based powder that kills the invaders.*

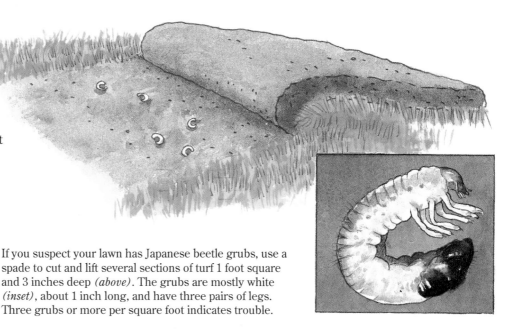

1 If you suspect your lawn has Japanese beetle grubs, use a spade to cut and lift several sections of turf 1 foot square and 3 inches deep *(above)*. The grubs are mostly white *(inset)*, about 1 inch long, and have three pairs of legs. Three grubs or more per square foot indicates trouble.

134

**2** Set up stakes and a string as a guide to applying the milky spore; the powder should not be scattered, but rather placed in rows of little pockets about 4 feet apart. Expect to use about 4 ounces of powder for every 1,000 square feet of lawn. To apply the powder, use a trowel to cut and lift a small, 1½-inch-deep patch of turf near one of the stakes and pour in a teaspoon of it *(below, left)*. Replace the grass. Repeat every 4 feet along the first row, then move the stakes 4 feet over and do the second row, and so on. The inset *(below, right)* shows the correct pattern of rows and holes.

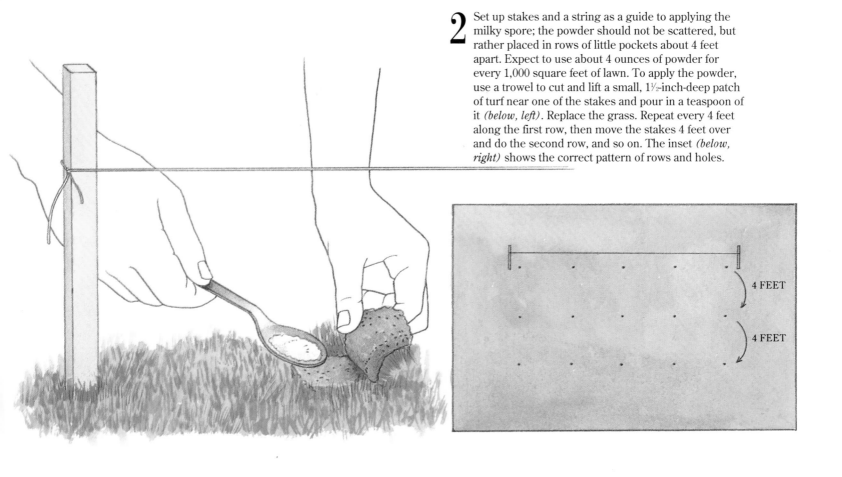

4 FEET

4 FEET

**3** After you have done enough rows to cover the infested turf, use a sprinkler *(right)* to thoroughly water the lawn for at least 20 minutes. This will help wash the spores into the soil and down to root level. Water again the next day, and the next; in fact, it is a good idea to keep the lawn moist for a week or two to help the milky spore compound spread and begin affecting the grubs.

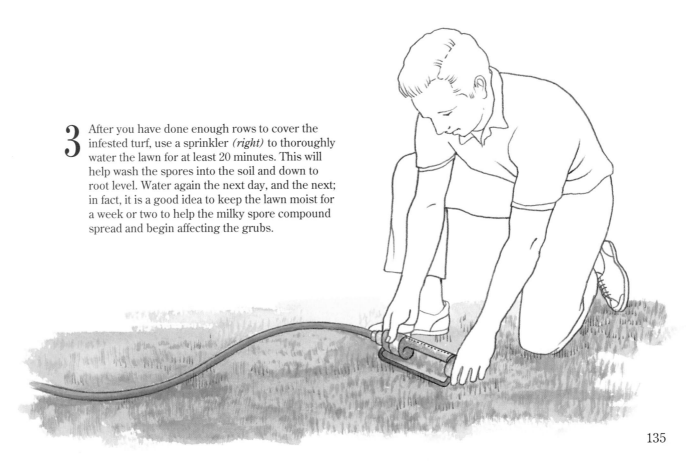

# A GRASS ROOTS CAMPAIGN TO LIVEN UP A FADED LAWN

*The close-knit, thriving grass of an extensive lawn looks half-gold, half-green in the slanting rays of an early-morning sun. To be this full and vigorous, lawn grasses need occasional aerating along with other care, to avoid compaction and to get oxygen and nutrients to the roots.*

Even the most carefully planted and tended stretches of lawn can, for no apparent reason, lose their velvety sheen and begin to look lackluster. The hidden cause of the malady is almost invariably compaction; the soil beneath the grass has become dense and hard, with the result that the air, water and fertilizer that grass needs cannot reach the roots. The sections of a lawn that are used most suffer worst and soonest.

The only reliable remedy is aeration—pulling out cores, or plugs of soil, so that moisture, nutrients and, above all, oxygen can get directly to root level. For a small lawn or a limited problem area, there are manual aerating tools similar in appearance to garden forks, but the prongs are hollow, and pull up plugs of soil. For a larger spread of grass, the sort of powered aerating machine shown on page 137 is a must for doing the job better, faster and with much less effort. Such machines can be rented from most garden supply centers.

In either case, the aerator should pull up plugs of soil that measure about ½ inch in diameter and 3 inches long, leaving good-sized holes that reach well into the root zone of the grass. The plugs can be broken up and used as topsoil or placed in a compost pile or bin. Similarly, the holes can be left to fill in naturally, or a top dressing can be sifted into them *(page 137, step 3)*.

The best time to aerate is when the lawn is actively growing—but not when the weather is very hot. And the ground should be moist. In most parts of the continent, these requirements point to spring and early fall. How often to do it depends on how fast the soil compacts and that depends in turn on the amount of traffic the lawn gets and on how dense and clayey the soil is. Conscientious golf course superintendents religiously aerate their greens and fairways twice a year, which is why golf course grass always looks so green and flawless despite the relentless pressure of feet, golf carts and golf clubs.

**Gardener's Tip:** Some homeowners do all of their mowing and gardening tasks wearing spiked athletic shoes. This seems to help aerate their lawns.

## WINTER COLOR FOR WARM-SEASON GRASSES

Warm-season grasses, which thrive in the heat of summer, become dormant and turn brown during the winter. Gardeners who grow these grasses in the Southern states don't have to settle for a brown lawn during the winter. They can overseed their lawns—that is, broadcast seed over the grass already growing in the soil. A lawn overseeded in the fall with a cool-season grass will sprout up as the warm-season grass goes dormant, and the cool-season grass will stay green throughout the winter. When high temperatures return the following spring, the cool-season grasses will die out as the warm-season grasses start to grow again.

To maintain such a green lawn year round, overseed in the fall as soon as the warm-season grasses begin to turn brown. Broadcast the seed as you would for a new lawn *(pages 113-114)*. Use a mix of various cool-season grasses and sow them at a rate twice that recommended for a new lawn, since about half the seeds will not germinate because of competition with the existing grass and foot traffic. After sowing, cover the lawn with a thin layer of topsoil and keep the lawn moist until the cool-season grasses are established.

**1** One day after giving the lawn a good watering, run the aerating machine back and forth across your entire lawn *(right)*. Examine the plugs that the aerator pulls up; if the soil is hard and dry, you may find they are crumbly and less than a full 3 inches long. If so, give the lawn another good watering, wait until the moisture has soaked in and try again.

**2** If the soil under your lawn is clayey, rake up the plugs *(right)* and throw them away. With lawns, the less clay the better. Plugs that seem to be good brown loam, however, can be broken up with the back of a garden rake; pulverized and sifted for stones, the cores make good topsoil or excellent compost additions. Alternatively, the plugs are handy for leveling uneven areas in the lawn.

**3** Scatter a top dressing of peat moss over the aerated lawn with a shovel *(left)*, then use the back of the rake to distribute it evenly and push it down into the aeration holes. Peat moss is light enough to let air into the root zone and helps retain moisture. This is also a good time to spread some fertilizer *(pages 126-129)*. Water the lawn thoroughly.

137

# DETHATCHING TO ADMIT AIR AND NUTRIENTS

Every lawn eventually accumulates a layer of old dead grass, unraked leaf bits and other detritus that is called thatch. It sits between the soil and the living grass, looking yellowish, matted and unattractive—and it can do a lawn real harm. If thick enough, thatch shuts off oxygen, moisture and fertilizer from the grass's roots and it provides a cozy home for pests and plant diseases. Getting rid of it is an important part of maintaining a healthy lawn.

The best way to tell whether a lawn needs dethatching is shown below, at right. A little thatch is no problem, and can even help by conserving moisture in the ground. But a mat that is ½ inch thick or more should be removed. Warm-season grasses—the zoysias and Bermudas commonly grown in the South—build up thatch more quickly than the blues and fescues used for lawns in northern areas. As a general rule, the denser warm-weather varieties should be dethatched every year, others perhaps once in three years.

Dethatching should be done when the grass is actively growing, so it will recover quickly afterward. Spring and fall are good times in the North, late spring and summer in the South.

There are tools for dethatching by hand: One, called a core cultivator, looks similar to a rake but the tines are sharp-pointed and somewhat curved. Another tool for small areas is called a cavex rake, or thatch rake. These hand tools are fine for a small plot. But for most lawns a motorized dethatcher is far preferable. Motorized dethatchers work much like gas-powered lawn mowers and can be rented from most garden supply centers. The illustrations on page 139 show how to use one. Another alternative is a newer dethatching device—a thatching/raking attachment that attaches to the front of a lawn mower to pull up thatch and keep the grass straight. These work best on self-propelled type mowers, and are reasonably priced.

*Looking like green broadloom, a manicured lawn stretches away from a handsome border of decorative shrubs and flowers. Dethatching plays an important part in keeping turfgrass bright by improving its oxygen intake and removing the underlying mat of old, dead and discolored plant material.*

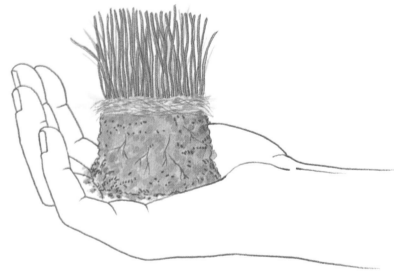

1 To see if your lawn needs dethatching, cut a small plug of turf about 2 inches deep with an old knife or a trowel. Examine its profile. You should see, from the bottom up, a layer of soil and roots, a stratum of thatch and then the green, growing grass *(above)*. If the thatch is more than ½ inch thick, dethatching is in order.

**2** Set the dethatching machine so that the adjustable rotating tines will dig down ½ inch. This should be deep enough to lift the top layer of thatch. Go over the entire lawn, making parallel passes *(right)*; move north-south first, for example, and then south-north.

**3** Rake up the thatch that has been dislodged *(left)* and throw it away. (You can put it in a compost pile if the grass has not been treated with chemicals.) If your lawn is generally healthy, a properly set dethatcher should not lift up a large amount of green grass. But some grass will come up with the thatch; this is normal and unavoidable.

**4** Set the tines on the dethatcher a fraction of an inch lower and go over the lawn again *(right)*, this time perpendicular to your first passes. If you initially moved north and south, go east and west this time. Again, rake up the thatch and discard it. After that, fertilize *(pages 126-129)*, and then give the lawn a good watering to help the grass recover.

139

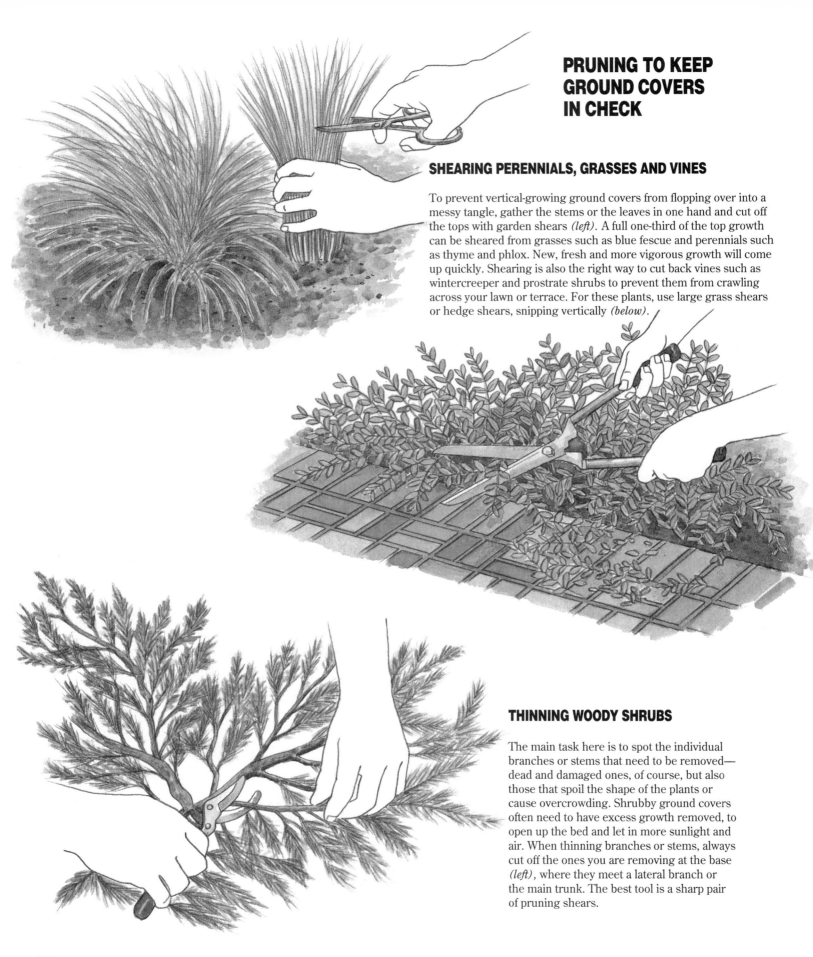

# PRUNING TO KEEP GROUND COVERS IN CHECK

### SHEARING PERENNIALS, GRASSES AND VINES

To prevent vertical-growing ground covers from flopping over into a messy tangle, gather the stems or the leaves in one hand and cut off the tops with garden shears *(left)*. A full one-third of the top growth can be sheared from grasses such as blue fescue and perennials such as thyme and phlox. New, fresh and more vigorous growth will come up quickly. Shearing is also the right way to cut back vines such as wintercreeper and prostrate shrubs to prevent them from crawling across your lawn or terrace. For these plants, use large grass shears or hedge shears, snipping vertically *(below)*.

### THINNING WOODY SHRUBS

The main task here is to spot the individual branches or stems that need to be removed—dead and damaged ones, of course, but also those that spoil the shape of the plants or cause overcrowding. Shrubby ground covers often need to have excess growth removed, to open up the bed and let in more sunlight and air. When thinning branches or stems, always cut off the ones you are removing at the base *(left)*, where they meet a lateral branch or the main trunk. The best tool is a sharp pair of pruning shears.

# SPRING RENOVATION FOR GROUND COVERS

*Following an early-spring mowing and raking, this bed of gazania has rebounded with new vigor—and a cheerful display of vibrantly colored blossoms.*

Winter can be hard on even winter-hardy ground covers. Although they survive the cold with their foliage largely intact, they often show ugly brown or straggly patches (the result of lack of moisture) when spring comes.

The first sign of warmer weather should be your signal to remove all dead or damaged stems and leaves. This not only improves the appearance of the bed but clears the way for the first vigorous growth of the new season. The pruning of ground covers makes them appear tidier, opens them up to better light penetration and air circulation, and stimulates lateral branching and growth. Prune spring-flowering plants immediately after they bloom, and summer- and fall-flowering plants in the spring.

Even ornamental grasses, whose weather-beaten foliage adds visual interest to a wintry landscape, will benefit from a thorough spring renovation.

You can clean up any ground cover bed with a pair of pruning shears—a time-consuming job. Fortunately, some evergreen ground covers grow low enough to the ground to be mowed. These include yarrow, Mondo grass and lily turf.

To avoid tearing up the plants, make sure the blades of your mower are absolutely sharp before you begin; if necessary, sharpen them. Set the mower to the highest setting (usually between 2½ and 3 inches) and run it once over the bed. Using a mower with a bag attachment to catch clippings will prevent the spread of disease organisms.

Whether you renovate a ground cover bed by hand pruning or with a mower, it is a good idea to fertilize immediately afterward. This will help nurture the emerging new growth. After fertilizing, lay down a fresh layer of mulch, such as pine straw, to slow evaporation from the soil surface and help control weeds.

## SPRING COLOR FOR GROUND COVERS

An area covered with herbaceous ground covers—those that die back in fall—looks barren in early spring, before the ground cover produces its warm-season growth. To enliven such an area, you can interplant groups of spring-flowering bulbs among the ground cover plants.

An herbaceous ground cover makes an ideal setting for a display of bulbs. The bulbs flower before the ground cover begins to grow, and they fade as the ground cover starts to fill in. After the bulbs bloom, their foliage turns brown, but the unattractive brown leaves are obscured by the sea of green.

For a natural-looking show of spring flowers against a ground cover, select early-blooming low-growing bulbs, such as squill and crocus. Plant them in the fall, between the ground cover plants.

# DIVISION: PROPAGATION AND REJUVENATION ALL IN ONE

Some perennial ground covers and ornamental grasses (like hosta and miscanthus) spread by establishing new clumps along their outer edges. With most of the plant's energy directed toward the perimeter, the center eventually becomes choked with old, woody growth. But that is easily remedied, because, fortunately, clumpy perennials lend themselves to periodic division—a process that not only restores their vigor but generates plenty of material for new beds.

Depending on the appearance of your plants, you'll probably want to divide every few years. If a plant has a woody center but healthy exterior clumps, it is ready for dividing. Division is also a good idea if your plants are overcrowded, a condition that stunts their growth, keeps them from growing to their full height and from flowering, and makes them more vulnerable to disease and pests. Each clump of plants has its own root system. If you keep these roots intact when you divide the plant, each newly separated clump will be capable of quickly establishing itself as an independent plant.

Before dividing a clumpy perennial *(page 84)*, water the ground well to make digging easier and to fortify the roots against the shock of transplanting. Then lift the plant with a spade and immediately pull apart the individual sections with your hands. If the clumps are bound together by intermeshed roots or crowns, cut them apart with a knife. Don't be afraid to exert some force if you encounter resistance; this will not cause damage to the plant.

Once you have removed all the vigorous outer clumps, examine what is left. Any center sections that look dry and lifeless should be discarded.

If you divide an entire bed of ground cover, you will end up with enough new plants to fill an additional bed. Since roots should not be exposed to the air a moment longer than necessary, prepare the new bed ahead of time and plant the new divisions as quickly as possible. Before planting the ground covers, improve the soil *(page 56)* of the existing bed or any new bed.

## A HOME-MADE BED FOR NURTURING CUTTINGS

The most convenient way to nurture a number of cuttings taken from ground cover plants is to put them in an easily made propagation bed such as the one shown above. The propagation bed keeps the cuttings both moist and warm—the conditions they need to develop roots and grow. The best time to make the bed and plant is spring or early summer, so the cuttings can be transplanted when they should be, in fall.

The bed shown measures 3 feet long and 2 feet wide, and can accommodate as many as 50 to 100 small cuttings. Once a few supplies have been collected, the bed should not take more than half an hour to construct, following the steps below:
• Spade out an area about 2 by 3 feet, about 1 foot deep, in a location that gets bright but not direct sunlight, and away from backyard traffic.
• Cover the bottom of the bed with at least 3 inches of coarse gravel for good drainage, then lay a sheet of window screening on top of the gravel. This will keep the rooting medium, which you will pour in next, from sifting down into the gravel layer.
• Fill the bed to the top with new, clean, weed-free builder's sand, a good rooting material because it is loose and drains well.
• Sink two precut weatherproofed 2-by-4s into the long sides of the bed; drill four small holes at 1-foot intervals in the tops of the boards to match up the two boards. Bank some soil against the outsides of the 2-by-4s to help hold them in place.
• Insert four 3-foot lengths of moderately stiff wire into corresponding holes in the 2-by-4s, making hoops that will support a plastic canopy.
• Cut a sheet of 4-foot by 6-foot clear plastic, so that it fits over the wires but has plenty of extra on both sides and at the ends.
• Using a staple gun, attach one side of the plastic to the outside of one of the 2-by-4s. Then staple the other side of the plastic to a third precut length of 2-by-4, as shown. This extra loose board can be lifted, allowing you to open the canopy at any time. Lift the plastic and plant your cuttings in the bed *(pages 88-89)*. When the cuttings are in place, water them well, then stretch the canopy back over the wire loops. Close the ends of the propagation bed by pulling the extra end sections of plastic to the ground and securing them with bricks or stones. Once the bed is closed, it will remain moist inside and seldom need more watering.

# REGION MAP FOR TURFGRASSES

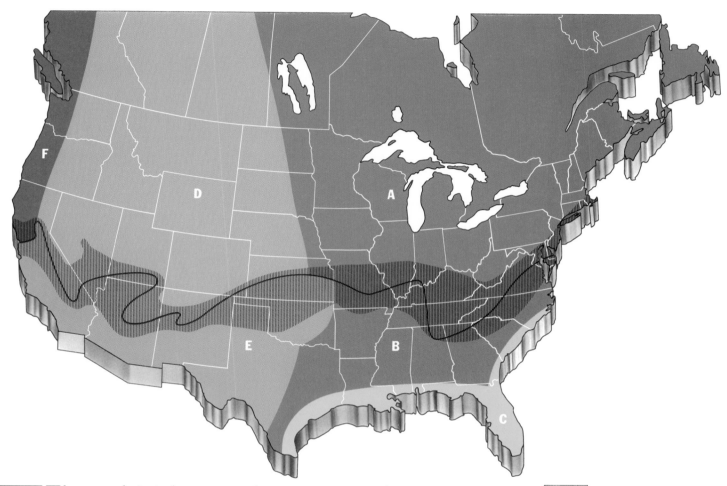

When you select a turfgrass, a ground cover or an ornamental grass for your yard, the most critical question to ask is whether the plant will survive in your climate. To find out if a ground cover or an ornamental grass will grow where you live, first determine the range of winter temperatures in your area. The zone map *(inside front cover)*, compiled by the U.S. Department of Agriculture, divides North America into 11 zones based on average minimum temperatures. Once you know which zone you live in, you can consult the Dictionary of Grasses and Ground Covers *(pages 160-177)* to find the winter climate a particular plant requires.

The ability of turfgrasses to survive the cold is easier to discern. All are categorized as either warm-season or cool-season grasses, and they grow in the type of climate the category name suggests. On the region map *(above)* the areas for cool- and warm-season grasses are separated by the black line that divides the country. The gray area indicates a transitional zone, where either type of grass may be used, depending on local conditions such as elevation and the amount of sun the lawn receives.

Winter temperature is but one factor that contributes to a healthy lawn; others such as humidity and rainfall also play major roles. The region map above divides North America into six regions based on year-round climates. Each turfgrass in the Dictionary has a letter that corresponds to one or more of these regions to indicate the areas in which that grass will flourish.

# A CHECKLIST FOR LAWNS

| | REGION A | REGION B | REGION C |
|---|---|---|---|
| **JAN./FEB.** | • Clean mower; repair if necessary<br>• Sharpen blades of mower and other tools | • Test soil pH; adjust if necessary<br>• Clean mower; repair if necessary<br>• Sharpen blades of mower and other tools<br>• Weed lawn or apply an herbicide<br>• Mow and edge as necessary<br>• Water if ground is dry<br>• Check for insects, diseases, moss, rodents<br>• Aerate compacted lawns<br>• Fill in bare spots | • Test soil pH; adjust if necessary<br>• Clean mower; repair if necessary<br>• Sharpen blades of mower and other tools<br>• Weed lawn or apply an herbicide<br>• Mow and edge as necessary<br>• Water if ground is dry<br>• Check for insects, diseases, moss, rodents<br>• Aerate compacted lawns<br>• Fill in bare spots |
| **MAR./APR.** | • Test soil pH; adjust if necessary<br>• Sow grass seed<br>• Lay sod<br>• Dethatch<br>• Aerate compacted lawn<br>• Weed lawn or apply an herbicide<br>• Mow and edge as necessary<br>• Water if ground is dry<br>• Check for insects, diseases, moss, rodents<br>• Apply fertilizer evenly | • Sow grass seed<br>• Lay sod<br>• Plant sprigs and plugs of warm-season grasses<br>• Dethatch<br>• Aerate compacted lawn<br>• Weed lawn or apply an herbicide<br>• Mow and edge as necessary<br>• Water regularly<br>• Check for insects, diseases, rodents<br>• Apply fertilizer evenly | • Sow grass seed<br>• Lay sod<br>• Plant sprigs and plugs of warm-season grasses<br>• Dethatch<br>• Aerate compacted lawn<br>• Weed lawn or apply an herbicide<br>• Mow and edge as necessary<br>• Water regularly<br>• Check for insects, diseases, rodents<br>• Apply fertilizer evenly |
| **MAY/JUNE** | • Sow grass seed<br>• Lay sod<br>• Dethatch<br>• Aerate compacted lawn<br>• Weed lawn or apply an herbicide<br>• Mow and edge regularly; adjust mower blades to summer cutting height<br>• Water regularly<br>• Check for insects, diseases, rodents<br>• Apply fertilizer evenly | • Lay sod<br>• Plant sprigs and plugs of warm-season grasses<br>• Dethatch<br>• Aerate compacted lawn<br>• Weed lawn or apply an herbicide<br>• Mow and edge as necessary; adjust mower blades to summer cutting height<br>• Water regularly<br>• Check for insects, diseases<br>• Apply fertilizer evenly | • Lay sod<br>• Plant sprigs and plugs of warm-season grasses<br>• Dethatch<br>• Aerate compacted lawn<br>• Weed lawn or apply an herbicide<br>• Mow and edge as necessary<br>• Water regularly<br>• Check for insects, diseases, rodents<br>• Apply fertilizer evenly |
| **JULY/AUG.** | • Lay sod<br>• Aerate<br>• Weed lawn or apply an herbicide<br>• Mow and edge regularly<br>• Water regularly<br>• Check for insects, diseases, rodents<br>• Till and enrich soil for new fall lawn | • Lay sod<br>• Dethatch<br>• Aerate<br>• Weed lawn or apply an herbicide<br>• Mow and edge regularly<br>• Water regularly<br>• Check for insects, diseases, rodents<br>• Till and enrich soil for new fall lawn | • Lay sod<br>• Dethatch<br>• Aerate<br>• Weed lawn or apply an herbicide<br>• Mow and edge regularly<br>• Water regularly<br>• Check for insects, diseases, rodents<br>• Till and enrich soil for new fall lawn |
| **SEPT./OCT.** | • Sow grass seed<br>• Lay sod<br>• Dethatch<br>• Aerate<br>• Weed lawn or apply an herbicide<br>• Mow and edge regularly; adjust mower blades to fall cutting height<br>• Water regularly<br>• Check for insects, diseases, rodents<br>• Rake leaves from the lawn | • Sow grass seed<br>• Overseed dormant warm-season grasses<br>• Lay sod<br>• Dethatch<br>• Aerate<br>• Weed lawn or apply an herbicide<br>• Mow and edge regularly; adjust mower blades to fall cutting height<br>• Water regularly<br>• Check for insects, diseases<br>• Rake leaves from the lawn | • Sow grass seed<br>• Overseed dormant warm-season grasses<br>• Lay sod<br>• Dethatch<br>• Aerate<br>• Weed lawn or apply an herbicide<br>• Mow and edge regularly<br>• Water regularly; adjust mower blades to fall cutting height<br>• Check for insects, diseases |
| **NOV./DEC.** | • Rake leaves from the lawn<br>• Clean mower for winter storage | • Overseed dormant warm-season grasses<br>• Weed lawn or apply an herbicide<br>• Mow and edge as necessary<br>• Water if ground is dry<br>• Check for insects, diseases<br>• Rake leaves from the lawn | • Overseed dormant warm-season grasses<br>• Weed lawn or apply an herbicide<br>• Mow and edge as necessary<br>• Water if ground is dry<br>• Check for insects, diseases<br>• Rake leaves from the lawn |

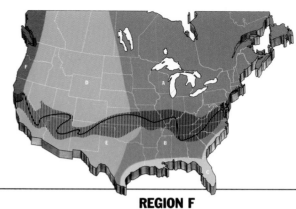

| REGION D | REGION E | REGION F | |
|---|---|---|---|
| • Clean mower; repair if necessary<br>• Sharpen blades of mower and other tools | • Test soil pH; adjust if necessary<br>• Clean mower; repair if necessary<br>• Sharpen blades of mower and other tools<br>• Weed lawn or apply an herbicide<br>• Mow and edge as necessary<br>• Water if ground is dry<br>• Check for insects, diseases, moss, rodents<br>• Aerate compacted lawns<br>• Fill in bare spots | • Clean mower; repair if necessary<br>• Sharpen blades of mower and other tools<br>• Aerate compacted lawns | JAN./FEB. |
| • Test soil pH; adjust if necessary<br>• Sow grass seed<br>• Lay sod<br>• Dethatch<br>• Aerate compacted lawn<br>• Weed lawn or apply an herbicide<br>• Mow and edge as necessary<br>• Water if ground is dry<br>• Check for insects, diseases, rodents<br>• Apply fertilizer evenly | • Sow grass seed<br>• Lay sod<br>• Plant sprigs and plugs of warm-season grasses<br>• Dethatch<br>• Aerate compacted lawn<br>• Weed lawn or apply an herbicide<br>• Mow and edge as necessary<br>• Water regularly<br>• Check for insects, diseases, rodents<br>• Apply fertilizer evenly | • Test soil pH; adjust if necessary<br>• Sow grass seed<br>• Lay sod<br>• Dethatch<br>• Aerate compacted lawn<br>• Weed lawn or apply an herbicide<br>• Mow and edge as necessary<br>• Water if ground is dry<br>• Check for insects, diseases, rodents<br>• Apply fertilizer evenly | MAR./APR. |
| • Sow grass seed<br>• Lay sod<br>• Dethatch<br>• Aerate<br>• Weed lawn or apply an herbicide<br>• Mow and edge regularly; adjust mower blades to summer cutting height<br>• Water regularly<br>• Check for insects, diseases, rodents<br>• Apply fertilizer evenly | • Lay sod<br>• Plant sprigs and plugs of warm-season grasses<br>• Dethatch<br>• Aerate<br>• Weed lawn or apply an herbicide<br>• Mow and edge as necessary; adjust mower blades to summer cutting height<br>• Water regularly<br>• Check for insects, diseases, rodents<br>• Apply fertilizer evenly | • Sow grass seed<br>• Lay sod<br>• Dethatch<br>• Aerate<br>• Weed lawn or apply an herbicide<br>• Mow and edge regularly; adjust mower blades to summer cutting height<br>• Water regularly<br>• Check for insects, diseases, rodents<br>• Apply fertilizer evenly | MAY/JUNE |
| • Lay sod<br>• Aerate<br>• Weed lawn or apply an herbicide<br>• Mow and edge regularly<br>• Water regularly<br>• Check for insects, diseases, rodents<br>• Till and enrich soil for new fall lawn | • Lay sod<br>• Dethatch<br>• Aerate<br>• Weed lawn or apply an herbicide<br>• Mow and edge regularly<br>• Water regularly<br>• Check for insects, diseases, rodents<br>• Till and enrich soil for new fall lawn | • Lay sod<br>• Aerate<br>• Weed lawn or apply an herbicide<br>• Mow and edge regularly<br>• Water regularly<br>• Check for insects, diseases, rodents<br>• Till and enrich soil for new fall lawn | JULY/AUG. |
| • Sow grass seed<br>• Dethatch<br>• Aerate<br>• Weed lawn or apply an herbicide<br>• Mow and edge regularly; adjust mower blades to fall cutting height<br>• Water regularly<br>• Check for insects, diseases<br>• Rake leaves from the lawn | • Sow grass seed<br>• Overseed dormant warm-season grasses<br>• Lay sod<br>• Dethatch<br>• Aerate<br>• Weed lawn or apply an herbicide<br>• Mow and edge regularly; adjust mower blades to fall cutting height<br>• Water regularly<br>• Check for insects, diseases | • Sow grass seed<br>• Lay sod<br>• Dethatch<br>• Aerate<br>• Weed lawn or apply an herbicide<br>• Mow and edge regularly; adjust mower blades to fall cutting height<br>• Water regularly<br>• Check for insects, diseases<br>• Rake leaves from the lawn | SEPT./OCT. |
| • Rake leaves from the lawn<br>• Clean mower for winter storage | • Overseed dormant warm-season grasses<br>• Weed lawn or apply an herbicide<br>• Mow and edge as necessary<br>• Water if ground is dry<br>• Check for insects, diseases<br>• Rake leaves from the lawn | • Mow and edge as necessary<br>• Water if ground is dry<br>• Rake leaves from the lawn<br>• Clean mower for winter storage | NOV./DEC. |

145

# A CHECKLIST FOR GROUND COVERS AND ORNAMENTAL GRASSES

| | ZONE 1 | ZONE 2 | ZONE 3 | ZONE 4 | ZONE 5 |
|---|---|---|---|---|---|
| **JANUARY/FEBRUARY** | • Spray broad-leaved ever-green ground covers with antidesiccant<br>• Replace mulch as needed<br>• Press into soil any plants that have heaved from ground | • Spray broad-leaved ever-green ground covers with antidesiccant<br>• Replace mulch as needed | • Spray broad-leaved ever-green ground covers with antidesiccant<br>• Replace mulch as needed<br>• Press into soil any plants that have heaved from ground<br>• Water plants if soil is dry and temperature is above freezing | • Spray broad-leaved ever-green ground covers with antidesiccant<br>• Replace mulch as needed<br>• Press into soil any plants that have heaved from ground<br>• Water plants if soil is dry and temperature is above freezing | • Replace mulch as needed<br>• Spray broad-leaved ever-green ground covers with antidesiccant<br>• Replace mulch as needed<br>• Press into soil any plants that have heaved from ground<br>• Water plants if soil is dry and temperature is above freezing |
| **MARCH/APRIL** | • Start seeds of ground covers and ornamental grasses indoors<br>• Prune or shear off damaged branches<br>• Press into soil any plants that have heaved from ground | • Start seeds of ground covers and ornamental grasses indoors<br>• Prune or shear off damaged branches<br>• Press into soil any plants that have heaved from ground | • Start seeds of ground covers and ornamental grasses indoors<br>• Prune or shear off damaged branches<br>• Press into soil any plants that have heaved from ground | • Start seeds of ground covers and ornamental grasses indoors<br>• Prune or shear off damaged branches<br>• Press into soil any plants that have heaved from ground | • Start seeds of ground covers and ornamental grasses indoors<br>• Plant ground covers and perennial ornamental grasses<br>• Prune or shear off damaged branches<br>• Press into soil any plants that have heaved from ground |
| **MAY/JUNE** | • Plant ground covers<br>• Plant annual and perennial ornamental grasses<br>• Take ground cover stem cuttings for propagation<br>• Layer ground cover stems for propagation<br>• Divide ground covers and perennial ornamental grasses<br>• Prune ground covers<br>• Cut back ornamental grasses to within 6 inches of ground<br>• Remove weeds or apply an herbicide<br>• Fertilize ground covers and ornamental grasses<br>• Replace mulch as needed<br>• Water as needed<br>• Check for insects, diseases | • Plant ground covers<br>• Plant annual and perennial ornamental grasses<br>• Take ground cover stem cuttings for propagation<br>• Layer ground cover stems for propagation<br>• Divide ground covers and perennial ornamental grasses<br>• Prune ground covers<br>• Cut back ornamental grasses to within 6 inches of ground<br>• Remove weeds or apply an herbicide<br>• Fertilize ground covers and ornamental grasses<br>• Replace mulch as needed<br>• Water as needed<br>• Check for insects, diseases | • Plant ground covers<br>• Plant annual and perennial ornamental grasses<br>• Take ground cover stem cuttings for propagation<br>• Layer ground cover stems for propagation<br>• Divide ground covers and perennial ornamental grasses<br>• Prune ground covers<br>• Cut back ornamental grasses to within 6 inches of ground<br>• Remove weeds or apply an herbicide<br>• Fertilize ground covers and ornamental grasses<br>• Replace mulch as needed<br>• Water as needed<br>• Check for insects, diseases | • Plant ground covers<br>• Plant annual and perennial ornamental grasses<br>• Take ground cover stem cuttings for propagation<br>• Layer ground cover stems for propagation<br>• Divide ground covers and perennial ornamental grasses<br>• Prune ground covers<br>• Cut back ornamental grasses to within 6 inches of ground<br>• Remove weeds or apply an herbicide<br>• Fertilize ground covers and ornamental grasses<br>• Replace mulch as needed<br>• Water as needed<br>• Check for insects, diseases | • Plant ground covers<br>• Plant annual and perennial ornamental grasses<br>• Take ground cover stem cuttings for propagation<br>• Layer ground cover stems for propagation<br>• Divide ground covers and perennial ornamental grasses<br>• Prune ground covers<br>• Cut back ornamental grasses to within 6 inches of ground<br>• Remove weeds or apply an herbicide<br>• Fertilize ground covers and ornamental grasses<br>• Replace mulch as needed<br>• Water as needed<br>• Check for insects, diseases |

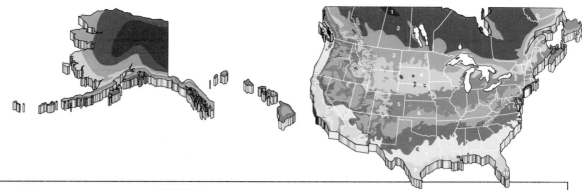

| | ZONE 6 | ZONE 7 | ZONE 8 | ZONE 9 | ZONE 10-11 | |
|---|---|---|---|---|---|---|
| | • Spray broad-leaved ever-green ground covers with antidesiccant<br>• Replace mulch as needed<br>• Start seeds of ground covers and ornamental grasses indoors<br>• Press into soil any plants that have heaved from ground<br>• Water plants if ground is dry and temperature is above freezing | • Spray broad-leaved ever-green ground covers with antidesiccant<br>• Replace mulch as needed<br>• Start seeds of ground covers and ornamental grasses indoors<br>• Press into soil any plants that have heaved from ground<br>• Water plants if ground is dry and temperature is above freezing | • Start seeds of ground covers and ornamental grasses indoors<br>• Water plants if ground is dry and temperature is above freezing | • Start seeds of ground covers and ornamental grasses indoors<br>• Plant ground covers<br>• Plant annual and perennial ornamental grasses<br>• Divide ground covers and perennial ornmental grasses<br>• Remove weeds or apply an herbicide<br>• Prune ground covers<br>• Water if ground is dry<br>• Check for insects, diseases | • Start seeds of ground covers and ornamental grasses indoors<br>• Plant ground covers<br>• Plant annual and perennial ornamental grasses<br>• Divide ground covers and perennial ornmental grasses<br>• Remove weeds or apply an herbicide<br>• Prune ground covers<br>• Water if ground is dry<br>• Check for insects, diseases | **JANUARY/FEBRUARY** |
| | • Start seeds of ground covers and ornamental grasses indoors<br>• Plant ground covers and perennial ornamental grasses<br>• Prune ornamental grasses<br>• Cut back perennial grasses to within 6 inches of ground<br>• Prune or shear off damaged branches<br>• Press into soil any plants that have heaved from ground | • Start seeds of ground covers and ornamental grasses indoors<br>• Plant ground covers and perennial ornamental grasses<br>• Fertilize ground covers and ornamental grasses<br>• Divide ground covers and perennial ornamental grasses<br>• Prune ground covers<br>• Remove weeds or apply an herbicide<br>• Cut back perennial grasses to within 6 inches of ground<br>• Prune or shear off damaged branches<br>• Press into soil any plants that have heaved from ground | • Plant ground covers<br>• Plant annual and perennial ornamental grasses<br>• Take ground cover stem cuttings for propagation<br>• Layer ground cover stems for propagation<br>• Divide ground covers and perennial ornamental grasses<br>• Prune ground covers<br>• Cut back ornamental grasses to within 6 inches of ground<br>• Remove weeds or apply an herbicide<br>• Fertilize ground covers and ornamental grasses<br>• Apply mulch for summer<br>• Water as needed<br>• Check for insects, diseases | • Plant ground covers<br>• Plant annual and perennial ornamental grasses<br>• Take ground cover stem cuttings for propagation<br>• Layer ground cover stems for propagation<br>• Divide ground covers and perennial ornamental grasses<br>• Prune ground covers<br>• Cut back ornamental grasses to within 6 inches of ground<br>• Remove weeds or apply an herbicide<br>• Fertilize ground covers and ornamental grasses<br>• Apply mulch for summer<br>• Water as needed<br>• Check for insects, diseases | • Plant ground covers<br>• Plant annual and perennial ornamental grasses<br>• Take ground cover stem cuttings for propagation<br>• Layer ground cover stems for propagation<br>• Divide ground covers and perennial ornamental grasses<br>• Prune ground covers<br>• Cut back ornamental grasses to within 6 inches of ground<br>• Remove weeds or apply an herbicide<br>• Fertilize ground covers and ornamental grasses<br>• Apply mulch for summer<br>• Water as needed<br>• Check for insects, diseases | **MARCH/APRIL** |
| | • Plant ground covers<br>• Plant annual and perennial ornamental grasses<br>• Take ground cover stem cuttings for propagation<br>• Layer ground cover stems for propagation<br>• Divide ground covers and perennial ornamental grasses<br>• Prune ground covers<br>• Cut back ornamental grasses to encourage new growth<br>• Remove weeds or apply an herbicide<br>• Fertilize ground covers and ornamental grasses<br>• Replace mulch as needed<br>• Water as needed<br>• Check for insects, diseases | • Plant ground covers<br>• Plant annual and perennial ornamental grasses<br>• Take ground cover stem cuttings for propagation<br>• Layer ground cover stems for propagation<br>• Divide ground covers and perennial ornamental grasses<br>• Prune ground covers<br>• Cut back ornamental grasses to encourage new growth<br>• Remove weeds or apply an herbicide<br>• Replace mulch as needed<br>• Water as needed<br>• Check for insects, diseases | • Plant ground covers<br>• Take ground cover stem cuttings for propagation<br>• Layer ground cover stems for propagation<br>• Prune ground covers<br>• Cut back ornamental grasses to encourage new growth<br>• Remove weeds or apply an herbicide<br>• Water as needed<br>• Check for insects, diseases | • Plant ground covers<br>• Take ground cover stem cuttings for propagation<br>• Layer ground cover stems for propagation<br>• Prune ground covers<br>• Cut back ornamental grasses to encourage new growth<br>• Remove weeds or apply an herbicide<br>• Water as needed<br>• Check for insects, diseases | • Plant ground covers<br>• Take ground cover stem cuttings for propagation<br>• Layer ground cover stems for propagation<br>• Prune ground covers<br>• Cut back ornamental grasses to encourage new growth<br>• Remove weeds or apply an herbicide<br>• Water as needed<br>• Check for insects, diseases | **MAY/JUNE** |

147

| | ZONE 1 | ZONE 2 | ZONE 3 | ZONE 4 | ZONE 5 |
|---|---|---|---|---|---|
| **JULY/AUGUST** | • Plant ground covers, perennial ornamental grasses<br>• Fertilize newly planted ground covers and ornamental grasses<br>• Prune ground covers<br>• Remove weeds or apply an herbicide<br>• Water as needed<br>• Check for insects, disease<br>• Collect seeds from selected ornamental grasses and ground covers<br>• Cut stalks of annual ornamental grasses for indoor display | • Plant ground covers, perennial ornamental grasses<br>• Fertilize newly planted ground covers and ornamental grasses<br>• Prune ground covers<br>• Remove weeds or apply an herbicide<br>• Water as needed<br>• Check for insects, disease<br>• Collect seeds from selected ornamental grasses and ground covers<br>• Cut stalks of annual ornamental grasses for indoor display | • Plant ground covers, perennial ornamental grasses<br>• Fertilize newly planted ground covers and ornamental grasses<br>• Prune ground covers<br>• Remove weeds or apply an herbicide<br>• Water as needed<br>• Check for insects, disease<br>• Collect seeds from selected ornamental grasses and ground covers<br>• Cut stalks of annual ornamental grasses for indoor display | • Plant ground covers, perennial ornamental grasses<br>• Fertilize newly planted ground covers and ornamental grasses<br>• Prune ground covers<br>• Remove weeds or apply an herbicide<br>• Water as needed<br>• Check for insects, disease<br>• Collect seeds from selected ornamental grasses and ground covers<br>• Cut stalks of annual ornamental grasses for indoor display | • Plant ground covers, perennial ornamental grasses<br>• Fertilize newly planted ground covers and ornamental grasses<br>• Prune ground covers<br>• Remove weeds or apply an herbicide<br>• Water as needed<br>• Check for insects, disease<br>• Collect seeds from selected ornamental grasses and ground covers<br>• Cut stalks of annual ornamental grasses for indoor display |
| **SEPTEMBER/OCTOBER** | • Water if the ground is dry<br>• Prepare soil for spring planting<br>• Apply mulch for winter<br>• Remove spent annual ornamental grasses<br>• Apply a slow-release fertilizer on newly planted ground covers and ornamental grasses | • Water if the ground is dry<br>• Prepare soil for spring planting<br>• Apply mulch for winter<br>• Remove spent annual ornamental grasses<br>• Apply a slow-release fertilizer on newly planted ground covers and ornamental grasses | • Water if the ground is dry<br>• Prepare soil for spring planting<br>• Apply mulch for winter<br>• Remove spent annual ornamental grasses<br>• Apply a slow-release fertilizer on newly planted ground covers and ornamental grasses | • Water if the ground is dry<br>• Prepare soil for spring planting<br>• Apply mulch for winter<br>• Remove spent annual ornamental grasses<br>• Apply a slow-release fertilizer on newly planted ground covers and ornamental grasses | • Water if the ground is dry<br>• Prepare soil for spring planting<br>• Apply mulch for winter<br>• Remove spent annual ornamental grasses<br>• Apply a slow-release fertilizer on newly planted ground covers and ornamental grasses |
| **NOVEMBER/DECEMBER** | • Spray broad-leaved evergreen ground covers with antidesiccant<br>• Replace mulch as needed | • Spray broad-leaved evergreen ground covers with antidesiccant<br>• Replace mulch as needed | • Spray broad-leaved evergreen ground covers with antidesiccant<br>• Replace mulch as needed | • Spray broad-leaved evergreen ground covers with antidesiccant<br>• Replace mulch as needed | • Spray broad-leaved evergreen ground covers with antidesiccant<br>• Water if the ground is dry<br>• Apply mulch for winter |

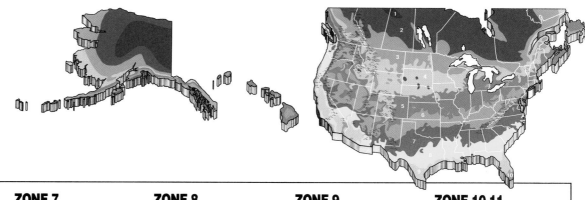

| | ZONE 6 | ZONE 7 | ZONE 8 | ZONE 9 | ZONE 10-11 | |
|---|---|---|---|---|---|---|
| | • Plant ground covers, perennial ornamental grasses<br>• Take ground cover stem cuttings for propagation<br>• Fertilize newly planted ground covers and ornamental grasses<br>• Prune ground covers<br>• Remove weeds or apply an herbicide<br>• Water as needed<br>• Check for insects, disease<br>• Collect seeds from selected ornamental grasses and ground covers<br>• Cut stalks of annual ornamental grasses for indoor display | • Plant ground covers, perennial ornamental grasses<br>• Take ground cover stem cuttings for propagation<br>• Fertilize newly planted ground covers and ornamental grasses<br>• Prune ground covers<br>• Remove weeds or apply an herbicide<br>• Water as needed<br>• Check for insects, disease<br>• Collect seeds from selected ornamental grasses and ground covers<br>• Cut stalks of annual ornamental grasses for indoor display | • Plant ground covers, perennial ornamental grasses<br>• Take ground cover stem cuttings for propagation<br>• Fertilize newly planted ground covers and ornamental grasses<br>• Prune ground covers<br>• Remove weeds or apply an herbicide<br>• Water as needed<br>• Check for insects, disease<br>• Collect seeds from selected ornamental grasses and ground covers<br>• Cut stalks of annual ornamental grasses for indoor display | • Plant ground covers, perennial ornamental grasses<br>• Take ground cover stem cuttings for propagation<br>• Fertilize newly planted ground covers and ornamental grasses<br>• Prune ground covers<br>• Remove weeds or apply an herbicide<br>• Water as needed<br>• Check for insects, disease<br>• Collect seeds from selected ornamental grasses and ground covers<br>• Cut stalks of annual ornamental grasses for indoor display | • Plant ground covers, perennial ornamental grasses<br>• Take ground cover stem cuttings for propagation<br>• Fertilize newly planted ground covers and ornamental grasses<br>• Prune ground covers<br>• Remove weeds or apply an herbicide<br>• Water as needed<br>• Check for insects, disease<br>• Collect seeds from selected ornamental grasses and ground covers<br>• Cut stalks of annual ornamental grasses for indoor display | **JULY/AUGUST** |
| | • Plant ground covers and perennial ornamental grasses<br>• Divide ground covers and perennial ornamental grasses<br>• Prune ground covers<br>• Remove weeds or apply an herbicide<br>• Water as needed<br>• Prepare soil for spring planting<br>• Apply mulch for winter<br>• Remove spent annual ornamental grasses<br>• Apply a slow-release fertilizer on newly planted ground covers and ornamental grasses | • Plant ground covers and perennial ornamental grasses<br>• Divide ground covers and perennial ornamental grasses<br>• Prune ground covers<br>• Remove weeds or apply an herbicide<br>• Water as needed<br>• Apply a slow-release fertilizer on newly planted ground covers and ornamental grasses | • Plant ground covers and perennial ornamental grasses<br>• Divide ground covers and perennial ornamental grasses<br>• Prune ground covers<br>• Remove weeds or apply an herbicide<br>• Water as needed<br>• Check for insects, diseases<br>• Apply a slow-release fertilizer on newly planted ground covers and ornamental grasses | • Plant ground covers and perennial ornamental grasses<br>• Take ground cover stem cuttings for propagation<br>• Divide ground covers and perennial ornamental grasses<br>• Prune ground covers<br>• Remove weeds or apply an herbicide<br>• Water as needed<br>• Apply a slow-release fertilizer on newly planted ground covers and ornamental grasses | • Plant ground covers and perennial ornamental grasses<br>• Take ground cover stem cuttings for propagation<br>• Divide ground covers and perennial ornamental grasses<br>• Prune ground covers<br>• Remove weeds or apply an herbicide<br>• Water as needed<br>• Apply a slow-release fertilizer on newly planted ground covers and ornamental grasses | **SEPTEMBER/OCTOBER** |
| | • Spray broad-leaved evergreen ground covers with antidesiccant<br>• Water if the ground is dry<br>• Apply mulch for winter<br>• Prepare soil for spring planting<br>• Check germination requirements of seeds ordered or purchased | • Spray broad-leaved evergreen ground covers with antidesiccant<br>• Water if the ground is dry<br>• Apply mulch for winter<br>• Prepare soil for spring planting<br>• Remove spent annual ornamental grasses | • Spray broad-leaved evergreen ground covers with antidesiccant<br>• Water if the ground is dry<br>• Apply mulch for winter<br>• Prepare soil for spring planting | • Plant ground covers and perennial ornamental grasses<br>• Divide ground covers and perennial ornamental grasses<br>• Prune ground covers<br>• Water as needed<br>• Apply a slow-release fertilizer on newly planted or prepared planting beds<br>• Remove spent annual ornamental grasses | • Plant ground covers and perennial ornamental grasses<br>• Divide ground covers and perennial ornamental grasses<br>• Prune ground covers<br>• Water as needed<br>• Apply a slow-release fertilizer on newly planted or prepared planting beds<br>• Remove spent annual ornamental grasses | **NOVEMBER/DECEMBER** |

# TROUBLESHOOTING GUIDE: LAWNS

| PROBLEM | CAUSE | SOLUTION |
|---|---|---|
| In late spring or early summer, the lawn becomes spotted with rounded patches of yellow or brown grass. Initially, the patches are only a few inches across, but during the summer they expand to cover several feet of turf. Affected grass can be pulled out of the soil easily. Damaged areas often appear first in lawn areas adjoining pavement. Small black insects may be visible on the pavement. Most damage is caused in late summer. | Billbugs, which are black weevils up to ¾ inch long. They emerge in spring, feed on the grass and lay their eggs in the grass stems. The larvae hatch and feed on the stems. As the larvae mature, they enter the soil and feed on the roots. Adults emerge again in the fall, feed briefly, and then hibernate in areas between the lawn and adjacent pavement. | Billbugs can be controlled with insecticide applied in spring, while the young larvae are still feeding on the stems and before they move down to the roots. Mow the lawn before using an insecticide, so the chemical can easily reach the soil. If the damage is limited to small areas, the grass may recover once the larvae are controlled. Large areas may need reseeding or resodding. |
| In early spring and late summer, irregular patches of brown grass appear throughout the lawn. The patches may be from several inches to several feet across. Within affected areas, the grass is easily pulled up and the turf can be rolled back. More birds or moles than usual may be a sign. | Grubs, which are white insects with curled bodies 1 to 1½ inches long. They are the larvae of beetles, including Japanese, European chafer, Asiatic garden, Oriental and June beetles. The grubs feed on grass roots, and are visible at the soil surface. | Japanese beetle grubs can be controlled organically with milky spore *(pages 134-135)*. Other grubs can be treated with insecticide applied in early spring or late summer, when the grubs are near the soil surface. To reach grubs in lower soil depths, apply the insecticide, then water heavily for deep penetration. |
| Beginning in spring and continuing through summer, small patches of the lawn turn brown and die. Within affected areas, the grass blades have jagged holes along the edges. Some blades may be severed at the soil surface. | Cutworms, gray, brown or black worms 1½ to 2 inches long. They are usually visible at the soil surface. The worms feed at night. The worms are the larvae of a night-flying moth that has striped wings. | Apply an insecticide in the evening or at night, when the worms and the moths are active. Repeat applications are necessary as long as cutworms are present. *Bacillus thuringiensis,* called Bt, a bacterium fatal to cutworms, caterpillars and other organisms kills the larvae. |
| The lawn thins out, turns light green or yellow, fails to grow, and wilts during heat or drought. The roots appear to be swollen, knotty and shallow. The lawn does not respond to fertilization, aeration or watering. | Nematodes, microscopic soil-dwelling worms that feed on grass roots. Their presence can be confirmed only by soil test. | No chemical controls are available to the homeowner. Consult your local extension service for soil testing information. When nematodes are present, soil treatment by a professional fumigator is necessary. |
| The lawn thins out and has a bleached, dried-out appearance. Grass blades turn yellow and are covered with tiny white spots. | Leafhoppers, ⅛- to ¼-inch wedge-shaped, yellow or light green insects that suck the juice from grass blades. They may be visible hopping from blade to blade or swarming in the grass. | Apply an insecticide as soon as symptoms appear. In the warm regions of the South and the West, leafhoppers may produce several generations per summer, and repeat applications are necessary if symptoms recur. |
| Large circular bare patches appear in the lawn. Jagged holes appear in grass blades. Caterpillars are visible on the grass. | Army worms, tan, green or black, 1½-inch insects with three stripes down their backs and a V on their heads. They are the larvae of a moth that lays its eggs on the grass. | Apply an insecticide in the evening, when the moths and the worms are active. Armyworms produce several generations per year; repeat applications if signs recur. *Bacillus thuringiensis* can be an effective organic control. |

| PROBLEM | CAUSE | SOLUTION |
|---|---|---|
| Circular or irregular yellow patches several feet across appear in the lawn during summer. The problem is especially severe in hot, dry areas of the lawn that receive extensive sunlight. | Chinch bugs, reddish brown or black insects 1/5 inch long that suck the juice from grass blades and stems. The insects are active in hot, dry summer weather. When conditions favor them, they can destroy a lawn in a few days. | Apply an insecticide as soon as symptoms appear, and again three weeks later to control successive generations. If symptoms recur or if hot, dry weather persists, continue treating the lawn with an insecticide throughout the summer. |
| Long, narrow ridges zigzag across the lawn. Mounds of soil may appear in the lawn beside holes that are the entrances to underground tunnels. | Animals such as moles, voles and gophers, which tunnel through the soil. Moles feed on insects such as grubs and ants; voles and gophers feed on roots and grass. | To get rid of moles, eliminate the grubs and ants they feed on. For other animals, several types of baits and traps are available. |
| Patches of grass up to 15 feet across take on an orange cast and then die. The problem appears first in shady areas of the lawn and then spreads to sunny areas. | Greenbugs, which are small, yellow or light green aphids that pierce grass blades and feed on them. The bugs then inject the blades with a toxic substance that turns them orange. Greenbugs prefer the cool, moist environment that shady areas provide. | Apply an insecticide once every seven days until symptoms disappear. Reduce the amount of fertilizer used in shady areas, because the insects feed heavily on lush new growth. |
| In spring, small patches of dead brown grass appear throughout the lawn. In summer, the patches enlarge to several feet across. Within affected areas, many grass blades have been cut off at the soil surface. Small whitish tunnels appear at the soil surface. At night, moths fly over the lawn in a zigzag pattern. The most severe damage occurs in July and August. | Sod webworms, the larvae of moths. The adult moths do not damage the lawn, but they drop their eggs onto the grass. When the larvae hatch, they construct the tunnels of soil and webbing. The worms usually feed at night, chewing off grass blades and pulling them into their tunnels. | Damaged grass may recover if the webworms are controlled as soon as symptoms appear. Apply an insecticide in the evening, when the worms and the moths are active. If symptoms persist, repeat applications may be necessary through the summer months. |
| Small hills of soil from 1 inch to 1 foot across appear throughout the lawn. The grass under and around the soil mounds dries out and dies. | Ants. The ants themselves do not damage an established lawn, but the anthills can smother the grass. The ants make underground tunnels among the grass roots that cause the soil to dry out and can kill the grass. Ants do eat grass seed. | Apply an insecticide to the anthills. Once the ants are controlled, reseed or resod any damaged or bare areas. Insecticides will, after one application, control ants for about 2 months. |
| The lawn is spotted with irregular patches of brown grass, first appearing in shady areas. Eventually, the patches may spread to cover the entire lawn. Within the patches, the grass blades have oval or round spots with tan centers and black or purple borders. | Leaf spot disease, also called helminthosporium disease and melting out. This fungus disease occurs primarily when the weather is humid, temperatures are moderate, and the lawn receives too much water or fertilizer. | When symptoms appear, apply a fungicide four times, seven to 10 days apart. Water in the morning; moisture evaporates from the grass blades more rapidly during the day than at night. Reduce shade, and improve aeration and water drainage. |
| Tufts of stunted, thick, yellow grass blades appear scattered throughout the lawn. | Yellow tuft, also called downy mildew, a fungus disease that is most active in cool, humid climates. The fungus spores spread in water. | Apply a fungicide as soon as symptoms appear. Mow only when the grass is dry; wet clippings on mowing tools can spread the disease. Avoid overwatering and overfertilization. |

| PROBLEM | CAUSE | SOLUTION |
|---|---|---|
| Grass blades are mottled with yellow. The mottling spreads over the blade until the entire blade turns yellow and withers. The discolored blades are coated with an orange powder. The lawn may begin to thin out. | Rust, a fungus disease most active in warm, humid weather. The fungus is most likely to attack lawns that have been underfertilized, underwatered or too closely mowed. The orange powder, which consists of fungus spores, spreads easily in wind. | Apply a fungicide every seven to 10 days until symptoms disappear. Make sure the lawn receives the recommended amounts of fertilizer and water. Mow the lawn at the recommended height. Collect and destroy grass clippings. Fertilize with nitrogen and water frequently. Mow every five to six days to dispose of rust clippings. |
| The lawn is spotted with brown patches of wilted grass blades. The patches are from 1 to 3 inches across. They may enlarge and coalesce rapidly, often within a few days. | Pythium blight, a fungus disease that is most active in warm, humid weather and when a lawn is overwatered or overfertilized. | Apply a fungicide every five to 10 days until the symptoms disappear. Do not water or fertilize more than the recommended amount. Mow only when the grass is dry; wet clippings on mowing tools can spread the disease. Seed the lawn late in the fall. |
| Grass is covered with a whitish gray powder. Eventually, the grass turns yellow, then brown, withers and dies. Lawns in the shade are most susceptible. | Powdery mildew, a fungus disease most active when nights are cool and damp, days are hot and humid, and air circulation is poor. | Apply a fungicide every seven to 10 days until symptoms disappear. Thin out the lower branches of large trees that shade the lawn. Water only in the morning; moisture evaporates from the grass blades more rapidly during the day than at night. |
| The lawn is spotted with penny-sized, copper-colored patches. The patches enlarge and coalesce to cover large areas. | Copper spot, a fungus disease most active in rainy weather when temperatures are between 50° and 75° F. The disease is most severe when a lawn is insufficiently fertilized or the soil is too acidic. | Apply a fungicide. Make sure that the lawn receives the recommended amount of fertilizer. Test the soil pH; if it is too acidic, apply lime. |
| A ring of lush, dark green grass appears in the lawn. The ring may be a few inches or several feet in diameter. Mushrooms may grow in the ring. | Fairy ring, caused by soil-dwelling fungi, generally in acid soils. The fungi do not attack grass; they feed on organic matter in the soil, depriving the grass roots of nutrients. The dark green growth is caused by the concentrated release of nutrients as fungi break down organic matter. | There are no effective chemical controls. Remove excess thatch, which is decomposing organic matter and attracts fungi. You can improve the appearance of the lawn by mowing more frequently and removing the mushrooms. Apply the recommended amounts of nitrogen, and aerate the area with spikes to improve water penetration. |
| Large, rounded patches of grass 2 feet across turn yellow and then brown. The border of each patch may turn purple. The blades in the center of the patch may be unaffected. | Rhizoctonia blight, also called brown patch, a fungus disease most active in hot, humid weather, when the lawn has been overfertilized or overwatered and has excessive thatch. | Apply a fungicide as soon as symptoms appear, and repeat the application at least three times, seven to 10 days apart. Continue as long as hot, humid weather persists. Remove excess thatch, which attracts the fungus. |
| The lawn is spotted with circular or irregular reddish brown patches from 2 inches to 2 feet across. Thin, red threads intertwine with the grass blades. | Red thread, a fungus disease that produces the red, threadlike growth. It is most active in humid weather and temperatures between 30° and 60° F. The disease spreads rapidly when a lawn does not receive adequate nitrogen or the soil pH is too acidic. | Apply a fungicide four times, seven to 10 days apart. Make sure the lawn receives the recommended amount of fertilizer. Test the soil pH; if it is too acidic, apply lime. Water only in the morning; moisture evaporates from the grass blades more rapidly during the day than at night. When fertilizing, increase nitrogen content. |

| PROBLEM | CAUSE | SOLUTION |
| --- | --- | --- |
| The lawn is spotted with silver-dollar-sized brown patches that may enlarge and coalesce to cover large areas. Within the affected areas, individual grass blades have yellow or tan spots with reddish brown borders. | Dollar spot, also called sclerotium rot, a fungus disease most active when the weather is humid and temperatures are mild, between 60° and 85° F. The disease is most likely to spread in lawns that are insufficiently watered or fertilized and have a heavy thatch. | Apply a fungicide twice, seven to 10 days apart. Make sure the lawn receives the recommended amount of fertilizer and water. Water only in the morning; moisture evaporates from the grass blades more rapidly during the day than at night. Water deeply; dethatch if necessary. |
| As winter snows melt, the lawn becomes spotted with patches of yellow or tan dry grass. The patches are 2 inches to 2 feet across. The grass blades within the patches are matted together, and a pink or grayish white, cottony growth may appear on them. | Snow mold, a fungus disease. There are two common types of snow mold: pink snow mold, also called fusarium patch; and gray snow mold, also called typhula blight. Both occur in winter and spring, when the ground remains wet from melting snow. | Apply a fungicide in early spring, when symptoms appear, and rake to break up the dry, matted blades. To prevent the disease, apply a fungicide in late fall or early winter. Do not fertilize in late fall; soft, lush growth is more susceptible to the disease. Avoid excessive use of lime. |
| Patches of yellow grass appear scattered throughout the lawn. Within the discolored areas, the grass blades are streaked with yellow and covered with stripes of black, sooty powder. Eventually, affected blades split lengthwise, wilt and die. | Stripe smut, a fungus disease most active in moderate temperatures, between 50° and 68° F. The disease usually occurs in spring and fall, especially in lawns that are overwatered or overfertilized. | Apply a fungicide when symptoms appear. If the disease occurs in spring, reduce the amount of water and fertilizer applied during the summer to help prevent its recurrence in fall. Hot and dry weather will usually stop the disease. Dethatch if necessary. |
| Patches of lawn acquire a yellow cast. Within the affected areas, individual grass blades are mottled with yellow. Eventually, the entire lawn turns yellow and begins to thin out. St. Augustine grass is the only susceptible turfgrass. | St. Augustine decline (SAD), a virus disease. The virus does not spread, but can be transmitted to healthy grass by greenbugs and other aphids and by diseased clippings carried on mowing tools. SAD occurs mostly in Texas and Louisiana. | There are no chemical controls for SAD. Greenbugs and other aphids should be controlled (pages 151, 155). Clean mowing tools thoroughly after each use. If damaged areas do not recover, they may be reseeded with disease-resistant varieties of St. Augustine. |
| Round patches of light green grass develop in scattered areas of the lawn. The patches may be up to 3 feet across, and the grass at the center of the patches may remain unaffected. Eventually, the light green grass turns brown and dies. | Fusarium blight syndrome, also called summer patch and necrotic ring spot, a fungus disease that occurs in hot, dry and windy weather. It is particularly severe when extended periods of heavy watering or rainfall are followed by drought. | When symptoms appear, apply a fungicide three times, 10 to 14 days apart. To prevent the disease from recurring the following year, apply a fungicide in late spring. Avoid excessive fertilization. Frequent light watering during dry periods helps halt the fungus. |
| The lawn becomes spotted with rings of dead brown grass. Eventually, the rings enlarge and merge. Within the rings, the grass blades become bronze-red before turning brown. Symptoms may appear in spring, but are most severe following periods of hot, dry weather in midsummer. Bentgrass is especially susceptible. | Take-all patch, also called ophiobolus patch, a fungus disease. The fungus is active in cool, humid weather, but the symptoms of the disease may not be apparent until the lawn is stressed by summer heat. The disease is especially severe in alkaline soils. This disease is generally found in the Pacific Northwest coastal regions. | There are no chemical cures. Applying an acid fertilizer to lower the soil pH may prevent the spread of the disease. If small areas are affected, they may be overseeded with less susceptible grasses, such as certain bluegrass and fescue species. Apply 2 pounds of sulfur per 1,000 square feet of lawn to lower the soil pH. |

# TROUBLESHOOTING GUIDE: GROUND COVERS

| PROBLEM | CAUSE | SOLUTION |
|---|---|---|
| Leaves are mottled with white, then lose their color and develop a dull bronze/silvery sheen. Tiny black specks are visible on the undersides of the leaves. Eventually, a fine white webbing appears on the plant. | Spider mites, nearly microscopic pests that suck the sap from plants. Mites are particularly active in hot, dry environments and they produce new generations every few days. Adult mites hibernate in debris or under bark. | Adult mites can be knocked off plants with a strong stream of water every three days; repeat treatment is necessary for control. In severe cases, spray with an insecticidal soap or a miticide three times, three days apart. To help prevent infestation, keep plants well watered and spray the undersides of the leaves with water every few days. Insect predators include lacewings and lady beetles. |
| Small, rounded or oblong holes appear in leaves and may appear in flowers. Eventually, plants may be stripped of foliage, or appear like veiny skeletons. | Beetles, including Asiatic, blister, chafer, flea and Japanese beetles. They are from ¼ to ¾ inch long and have hard shells. | Small colonies can be picked off plants by hand. The larvae of Japanese beetles can be controlled organically with milky spore *(pages 134-135)*. If the infestation is severe, apply an insecticide. Natural predators include tachinid flies and spring and fall tiphia wasps. |
| Leaf edges turn brown and then die. Leaves are spotted with irregular brown patches. Broad-leaved evergreens are especially susceptible. | Too much sun or too much wind, especially in winter. Wind and sun cause rapid water evaporation. When the ground is dry or frozen the roots cannot transfer sufficient water to the leaves. | Cut out affected leaves. Make sure ground covers are well watered in late fall. To lessen water evaporation, spray evergreens with an antidesiccant in fall. Construct low-level windbreaks in fall. |
| Jagged holes appear in leaves; stems may be chewed or broken off. The problem is especially severe in spring. Seedlings can be quickly wiped out or stunted. | Caterpillars, which are the larvae of butterflies and moths. Caterpillars emerge in spring and hide on the undersides of leaves. | Hand-pick and destroy large caterpillars. Spray affected plants with *Bacillus thuringiensis*. Apply in early spring to prevent infestation. |
| Upper leaf surfaces lose color and are mottled with white or yellow. The undersides of the leaves are covered with small black specks. Plants cease to grow. | Lace bugs, tiny flat bugs ¹⁄₁₆ to ⅛ inch long with clear, lacy wings and hoodlike coverings on their heads. The bugs suck the sap from the undersides of leaves. The black specks are deposited by the bugs as they feed. | Spray with an insecticide when symptoms appear and repeat the application two or three times, seven to 10 days apart. Direct spray to lower leaf areas where the bugs feed. Remove infected foliage. |
| Foliage is covered with a white powder. New growth is distorted in shape. Leaves may curl and turn yellow, die and fall off. The plant may be stunted. | Powdery mildew, a fungus disease that is most severe when nights are cool and humid, and days are warm, in shady areas with moderate temperatures. | Mildew can be eradicated with a lime-sulfur spray, provided the temperature is not above 80° F. Mildew can be prevented with a fungicide applied every 10 days when weather conditions are favorable for the disease. Try to plant resistant varieties, and follow clean cultivation practices: Rake leaves amid the ground cover in fall; avoid excess fertilization; prune out diseased foliage and discard as soon as possible. |

154

| PROBLEM | CAUSE | SOLUTION |
|---|---|---|
| Plants cease to grow and the plant tips die back. Leaves turn yellow and fall from the plant. Thin, white bumps appear on the undersides of the leaves and the stems. Dark brown, shell-shaped masses are scattered among the white bumps. Euonymus is especially susceptible, along with nearby pachysandra and English Ivy. | Euonymus scale, a tiny insect that sucks sap from plants. The male is white and the female develops a dark brown shell under which it lays eggs. | Prune out any dead or severely infested branches. Spray with an insecticide, repeating the application until all signs of scale disappear. To prevent infestation, spray plants with horticultural oil in spring, just before plant growth begins. Do not apply horticultural oil in early spring in temperatures 32°F or lower, or 90°F or higher. |
| Leaves suddenly wilt, turn brown or black, and appear to have been scorched by fire. Twigs may also turn black, and the bark at the base of the twigs becomes dark, dry and cracked. Cotoneaster is especially susceptible. | Fire blight *(Erwinia amylouvora)*, a bacterial disease that spreads rapidly in warm, wet conditions. The bacteria remain in the branches through winter, and can reinfect the plant in spring. | Prune out damaged branches and destroy them. Disinfect pruning tools with alcohol after each cut. To prevent the disease, spray plants with a bactericide every five to seven days from the time new growth appears until blooming is finished. Plant disease-resistant cotoneaster species. |
| Leaves turn pale green or yellow. The entire plant may wilt and can be pulled from the soil easily. The roots and the crown are discolored and have a sour odor. | Root rot or crown rot, fungus diseases that spread in waterlogged soil and hot, humid weather. The fungi thrive in water. | Remove and destroy infected plants and the surrounding soil. Apply a fungicide to the soil before replanting. Allow the soil to dry between waterings. Increase air circulation in the area, if possible. |
| Tan, brown or purple concentric circular spots appear on either or both upper and lower leaf surfaces. Eventually, the spots merge, and the entire leaf becomes discolored and falls from the plant. | Leaf spot disease, caused by several different fungi. The fungi spread easily in wind and water. | Remove damaged leaves and spray with a fungicide to control the disease. In fall, collect and destroy plant debris, where the fungi spend the winter. |
| Leaves curl, wither or are distorted in shape, and the plant is stunted, and may die. A clear, shiny substance appears on leaves and stems. | Aphids, green, yellow or brown insects ⅛ inch long. Aphids appear in clusters on buds, leaves and stems, where they suck sap from the plant. Aphids spread diseases. | Aphids can be knocked off plants with a strong stream of water on underside of leaves. Put out sticky yellow traps. If the infestation is severe, apply an insecticidal soap or an insecticide. Avoid excessive fertilization. |
| Large, jagged holes appear in leaves. Entire leaves and young seedlings may be eaten. Shiny silver trails appear on plants and on the ground, leaving behind a sticky trail of slime. | Snails and slugs, which are shell-less snails up to 3 inches long. They feed at night in cool, damp weather. | Hand pick at night, using a flashlight. Saucers of beer and inverted grapefruit halves set around plants will trap snails and slugs. Snail and slug bait is also available; it should be applied at dusk, and reapplied after plants have been watered and after a rainfall. Apply diatomaceous earth around ground covers and by stems. |
| Conifer needles turn brown, starting at the tips and progressing to the bases the needles. Eventually, needles may drop. Evergreen leaf edges and tips turn brown or black. Leaves may drop. Symptoms usually appear on older foliage. Plants along roads and walkways are especially susceptible. | Damage from salt applied to icy roads and walkways during winter snows. | Use sand or sawdust instead of salt to melt ice. To prevent damage, spray ground covers near roads with an antidesiccant in late fall. Plant salt-tolerant species, especially species recommended for coastal areas; these types of plants withstand heavy winter road saltings. |

# A GALLERY OF WEEDS

As every gardener knows, weeds proliferate with exasperating persistence, and if left unchecked will drive more timid plants out of a garden. Eliminate weeds as soon as they appear; they rob the lawn of water, sun and nutrients. In general, perennial weeds are broad-leaved and sprawling, and spread across the soil surface via stems or underground by means of roots. Annual weeds are either broad-leaved and sprawling or grassy and grow in clumps.

The question is, once you identify your weeds, how do you eliminate them? One way, as described here, is with an herbicide designed to interact with a weed's specific growth habit, cell structure and metabolism. As a rule, annual weeds can be checked with so-called preemergent herbicides, which are applied in advance to stop seeds from sprouting, and with postemergent contact herbicides, which kill whatever foliage they touch. Most perennials are best fought with postemergent systemic herbicides, which poison a plant's vascular system. For what to use, see the descriptions accompanying the pictures on these pages: For how to use it, see pages 132-133.

There is growing concern among gardeners, however, about the widespread use of herbicides—how they affect nearby water and wildlife. One alternative, of course, is old-fashioned hand weeding. Refer to pages 50-51 for tips on non-chemical weed-control.

**ANNUAL BLUEGRASS** *(Poa annua)* is a hardy grassy annual that grows in clumps of narrow, light green leaves and sprouts white, fluffy seed heads in spring and dies out in hot weather. To prevent seeds cast in summer from germinating in fall, use a preemergent herbicide in late summer.

**BLACK MEDIC** *(Medicago lupulina)* is a broad-leaved annual that forms dense mats of flat, branching stems, cloverlike foliage, small yellow spring flowers and black seeds. Use a postemergent systemic herbicide in early spring or in fall.

**CHICKWEED** is broad-leaved and may be either annual or perennial. Two prevalent varieties are common chickweed *(Stellaria media)*, an annual that has branching stems, small, pointed, light green leaves and small white flowers, and mouse-ear chickweed *(Cerastium vulgatum, left)*, a perennial that looks similar but has fuzzy, dark green leaves. Both can be controlled with a postemergent systemic herbicide applied when plants appear. Common chickweed can also be controlled with a preemergent herbicide applied in early spring or fall.

**CRABGRASS** is a grassy summer annual. Smooth crabgrass *(Digitaria ischaemum)* produces thick clumps of smooth, narrow, light green leaves; hairy or large crabgrass *(D. sanguinalis, left)* has shorter hairy leaves. Use a preemergent herbicide in spring or a postemergent contact herbicide as soon as plants appear.

**CURLY DOCK** *(Rumex crispus, right)* is a broad-leaved perennial that grows from a long taproot in a rosette of long, oval green leaves with curled edges. The leaves may be tinged with red seeds, are produced in a pyramidal seed head atop a slender stem. Use a postemergent systemic herbicide in spring or fall.

**DANDELION** *(Taraxacum officinale)* is a broad-leaved perennial with long, narrow, deeply notched green leaves that emerge in a rosette from a long taproot. It produces bright yellow flowers and fluffy white seed heads in spring. Use a postemergent systemic herbicide as soon as plants appear.

**GOOSEGRASS** *(Eleusine indica)*, also called silver crabgrass, is a grassy summer annual having low-growing clumps of flat, silver-green stems and narrow green leaves. It is found primarily in compacted soil and along walkways. To prevent it from taking hold, aerate compacted soil and use a preemergent herbicide in spring or a postemergent contact herbicide when the plants appear.

**HENBIT** *(Lamium amplexicaule)* is a broad-leaved annual that has small, scalloped leaves along stems that arch over and root where they touch the soil, and small purple spring flowers. Use a postemergent contact herbicide in spring or in fall when the plants appear.

**KNOTWEED** is a broad-leaved annual. Prostrate knotweed *(Polygonum aviculare)* has small, blue-green, lance-shaped leaves. The stems spread along the ground and form large, dense mats. Small white flowers blossom in late summer or early fall. Knotweed tends to grow in compacted soil. Aerate the soil and use a postemergent systemic herbicide when the plants appear.

**NUTSEDGE** is a grassy perennial that resembles turfgrass but has triangular instead of round stems. Yellow nutsedge *(Cyperus esculentus)* has shiny green leaves that grow upright from the base of the stem and small yellow flowers atop the stem. Purple nutsedge *(C. rotundus, above)* is similar, but its leaves are tinged with purple and its flowers are purple. Nutsedge spreads by seed and by underground tubers called nutlets. The nutlets do not respond to systemic herbicides; they require a postemergent contact herbicide.

**PLANTAIN** is a broad-leaved perennial. Buckhorn plantain *(Plantago lanceolata)* forms rosettes of narrow, dark green leaves up to 12 inches long and produces long, wiry stalks with bullet-shaped seed heads. Broadleaf plantain *(P. major, right)* forms rosettes of broad, oval leaves up to 6 inches long and produces short seed stalks. Both species have very long taproots. Use a postemergent systemic herbicide in fall or in early spring before the flowers appear.

**PROSTRATE SPURGE** *(Euphorbia supina, above)* is a broad-leaved annual that forms dense, multibranched mats of small dark green leaves along reddish stems. The sap is milky. Apply a preemergent herbicide twice in spring at six-week intervals or use a postemergent systemic herbicide before flowers appear.

**PURSLANE** *(Portulaca oleracea)* is a broad-leaved annual that thrives in summer heat. It forms mats of tiny succulent green leaves along thick reddish stems. Small yellow flowers bloom at the base of the leaves. Use a preemergent herbicide in early spring or a postemergent contact herbicide when the weeds appear.

**SPEEDWELL** *(Veronica serpyllifolia, below)* is a broad-leaved perennial that has small heart-shaped leaves and tiny white flowers in late spring. It thrives in shady, moist areas. Use a postemergent systemic herbicide when the plants are in bloom.

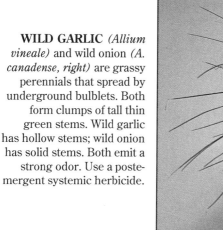

**RED SORREL** *(Rumex acetosella, above)*, also known as sheep sorrel, is a broad-leaved perennial that has arrow-shaped green leaves, reddish rhizomes and small reddish brown flowers atop slender stalks in spring. Use a postemergent systemic herbicide.

**WILD GARLIC** *(Allium vineale)* and wild onion *(A. canadense, right)* are grassy perennials that spread by underground bulblets. Both form clumps of tall thin green stems. Wild garlic has hollow stems; wild onion has solid stems. Both emit a strong odor. Use a postemergent systemic herbicide.

**YELLOW WOOD SORREL** *(Oxalis stricta, above)*, also called oxalis, is a broad-leaved perennial that has clover-like foliage, small yellow flowers and long narrow seedpods. Flowers bloom in spring and sometimes again in fall. Use a postemergent systemic herbicide.

AEGOPODIUM PODAGRARIA 'VARIEGATUM'

AJUGA REPTANS

ARABIS CAUCASICA

# DICTIONARY OF GRASSES AND GROUND COVERS

## Introduction

The dozens of entries in this dictionary embrace three diverse plant groups that are linked by their use in the garden—lawn turfgrasses, ground covers and ornamental grasses. The featured plants comprise the sturdiest and most beautiful and versatile species in their class. All plants are listed by their botanical names; common names are cross-referenced. The dictionary entries describe the climates in which each plant will grow. Ground covers and ornamental grasses are keyed to the Zone Map *(inside front cover)*; turfgrasses are keyed to the Region Map *(page 143)*.

**Achillea** see Dictionary of Perennials, page 264

**Aegopodium** (ee-go-PO-dee-um)
Goutweed

Fast-growing perennial ground cover that has divided leaves with toothed margins. Small white flowers bloom in flat-topped clusters in early summer. Zones 4-10.

**Selected species and varieties.** A. *podagraria* has light green foliage and grows 6 inches high. Flower heads 3 inches across bloom atop 12- to 14-inch stems. The cultivar 'Variegatum' has light green leaves edged in white and is not as aggressive a grower.

**Growing conditions.** Goutweed grows in any moist or dry, infertile garden soil. It tolerates sun but prefers partial shade. Remove flowers after they have bloomed. Goutweed may also be mowed. It spreads by underground runners and can be kept from becoming invasive by installing metal barriers in the ground 2 feet deep. Propagate by division.

**Landscape uses.** Goutweed is useful in a large area that needs to be covered, especially at the north side of a house, where it will receive some shade.

**Ajuga** (a-JOO-ga)
Bugleweed

Evergreen or semievergreen perennial ground cover with glossy, oval leaves that form mats of rosettes on the ground. Spikes of blue, violet, pink or white flowers bloom in spring. Some types spread by runners; others are clumping plants that spread more slowly by rhizomes. Zones 3-10.

**Selected species and varieties.** A. *genevensis* has 3-inch, coarse, toothed green leaves, hairy stems and spikes of blue flowers that grow 5 to 14 inches high in late spring. It spreads by rhizomes. A. *reptans,* carpet bugle, has dark green leaves 2 to 4 inches long and spikes of blue to purple flowers 3 to 6 inches high in midspring. The plants send out runners that form new plants at their ends.

**Growing conditions.** Plant bugleweed in full sun or in partial shade; in hot areas, it prefers partial shade. Bronze-leaved types will retain their coloring better if planted in full sun. Grow in any moist garden soil. Propagate by division.

**Landscape uses.** Use bugleweed as a ground cover under or in front of shrubs or in a rock garden. It is most effective planted under shrubs that flower at the same time.

**Arabis** (AR-a-bis)
Rock cress

Perennial ground cover that has hairy leaves and masses of small, single four-petaled flowers of white, pink or purple that bloom in midspring. Rock cress may be semievergreen or evergreen. Zones 4-8.

**Selected species and varieties.** A. *caucasica,* sometimes designated A. *albida,* wall rock cress, has mats of gray-green leaves that are borne in rosettes 4 to 6 inches high. Flowers are fragrant, white, ½ inch across and bloom in loose clusters 12 inches above the ground. The cultivar 'Flore Pleno' has double flowers; 'Rosabella' has pink flowers; 'Variegata' has green leaves that are edged in creamy white. Zone 6.

**Growing conditions.** Plant rock cress in full sun or light shade in sandy soil with excellent drainage. Soil for wall rock cress should be rich and may be dry or moist. As a rule rock cresses do not grow well where summers are hot or humid. Propagate by cuttings or division or from seeds.

**Landscape uses.** Plant rock cress as a ground cover on a slope or on top of a wall where it can gracefully spill down over the side.

## Arctostaphylos (ark-toh-STAF-i-los)

Wide-spreading, shrubby, evergreen ground cover that has glossy, smooth, oblong leaves. Flowers are small, bell-shaped, and pink or white. Red to brown branches grow in a crooked manner and root as they grow along the ground. Long-lasting red berries are ¼ inch wide. Zones 2-10.

**Selected species and varieties.** *A. uva-ursi,* bearberry, kinnikinick, grows 12 inches tall and has trailing branches that spread to 12 feet. Leaves are dark green, 1 inch long and turn bronze in winter. Pink flowers bloom in spring. Zones 2-7.

**Growing conditions.** Plant bearberry in full sun or partial shade in dry, sandy, acid soil with excellent drainage. Propagate by cuttings, by layering or from seeds.

**Landscape uses.** Bearberry is useful where a large area needs to be covered and is most attractive growing over and around rocks where the outline of its branches can be seen.

**Armeria** see Dictionary of Perennials, page 246

## Arundo (a-RUN-doh)

Perennial ornamental grass with an open, upright, arching habit, tall and woody stems, coarse and stiff leaves, and large silky plumes that last from summer into winter. Zones 7-10.

**Selected species and varieties.** *A. donax,* giant reed, grows 12 to 20 feet tall and has leaves 1 to 2 feet long and 2 ½ inches wide. Foliage is light green to blue-green. The variety 'Variegata,' striped giant reed, grows 3 to 8 feet tall and has foliage striped with white. Zones 8-10.

**Growing conditions.** Plant giant reed in full sun and moist, well-drained soil. Cut branches to the ground before new growth starts in spring. Propagate by division or from seeds.

**Landscape uses.** Giant reed does well by the side of a stream or a pool, and where soil erosion control is needed. Because of its large size, it is useful as a tall accent plant.

## Asarum (AS-a-rum)
Wild ginger

Fast-growing, spreading, evergreen or deciduous perennial ground cover that has shiny, leathery, heart-shaped aromatic leaves on long leaf-stalks. Flowers are small, ½ to 1 inch across, purplish to brown, bell-shaped, and usually hidden by the foliage in late spring and summer. Zones 3-9.

**Selected species and varieties.** *A. caudatum,* British Columbia wild ginger, has evergreen, 3- to 6-inch leaves and grows up to 6 to 7 inches tall. Zones 4-8. *A. europaeum,* European wild ginger, has evergreen, 2- to 3-inch leaves and grows 7 inches tall. Zones 6-8.

**Growing conditions.** Plant wild ginger in shade in slightly acid, moist, well-drained soil. Propagate by division, by root cuttings or from seeds.

**Landscape uses.** Wild ginger is a good choice to cover the ground under any trees.

**Avena grass** see *Helictotrichon*
**Azalea** see Dictionary of Trees and Shrubs, page 426
**Barrenwort** see *Epimedium*
**Bearberry** see *Arctostaphylos*
**Bellflower** see Dictionary of Perennials, page 246
**Bermudagrass** see *Cynodon*
**Bethlehem sage** see *Pulmonaria*
**Blood grass** see *Imperata*
**Blue oat grass** see *Helictotrichon*
**Boston ivy** see *Parthenocissus*
**Broom** see Dictionary of Trees and Shrubs, page 426
**Bugleweed** see *Ajuga*

## Calamagrostis (kal-a-ma-GROS-tis)
Feather reed grass

Vigorous perennial ornamental grass with erect clumps of rough leaves and lance-shaped seed heads on slender stems in summer. Zones 5-10.

ARCTOSTAPHYLOS UVA-URSI

ARUNDO DONAX 'VARIEGATA'

ASARUM EUROPAEUM

CALAMAGROSTIS ACUTIFLORA STRICTA

CALLUNA VULGARIS 'MULLION'

CAREX CONICA 'VARIEGATA'

CHASMANTHIUM LATIFOLIUM

**Selected species and varieties.** *C. acutiflora stricta* has dull green, 2-foot, slightly arching leaves. The seed head is 12 inches long, narrow, purplish in spring, wheat-colored in fall, and sits atop a 5-foot stem. *C. arundinacea brachytricha* has a wider, looser, pointed seed head that is white or pink, then changing to brown atop a 3-foot stem.

**Growing conditions.** Plant feather reed grass in full sun and moist, fertile soil. Sandy soil promotes spreading. Propagate by division.

**Landscape uses.** Plant feather reed grass as a screen or an accent plant, or alongside a pool or a stream.

**Calluna** (ka-LOO-na )
Heather

Evergreen shrubby ground cover that forms a spreading mound. Branches are covered with fine bright to dark green leaves and 10-inch spikes of tiny, single or double, nodding, bell-shaped flowers of white, pink or lavender. Zones 4-7.

**Selected species and varieties.** *C. vulgaris,* Scotch heather, grows 18 to 24 inches tall and spreads from 2 to 4 feet wide. Blooms appear in late summer and fall at the ends of ascending branches that are covered with scale-like leaves. 'Blazeway' is 18 inches tall with orange-yellow foliage. 'County Wicklow' grows 18 inches tall and has double, pale pink flowers. 'Kinlochruel' has double white flowers and bright green foliage. 'Mullion' is 18 inches high and has soft purplish pink to deep pink flowers.

**Growing conditions.** Grow Scotch heather in full sun or light shade in poor, moist, acid, well-drained soil. Roots are shallow and should be mulched. Protect from winter winds. Prune in early spring. Propagate by cuttings.

**Landscape uses.** Use Scotch heather as a ground cover on a sandy bank or in a seashore garden.

**Campanula** see Dictionary of Perennials, page 246
**Candytuft** see *Iberis*

**Carex** (KA-reks)
Sedge

Ornamental grass that has solid, triangular stems and tufted, arching leaves. Zones 3-8.

**Selected species and varieties.** *C. buchananii,* leatherleaf sedge, grows 12 to 24 inches tall. Leaves are narrow but heavy in texture. They are coppery brown in color and have curled tips. Zones 6-8. *C. conica* 'Variegata,' variegated miniature sedge, grows 6 inches tall and has dark green leaves with silver edges. Zones 5-10. *C. grayii,* Gray's sedge, grows 2 feet tall and has narrow, 18-inch, bright green leaves. The seedpod that develops in the fall is pyramidal to round with numerous pointed protrusions. *C. morrowii,* Japanese sedge, forms a 12-inch mound. 'Aureo-variegata' is green with a central yellow stripe. 'Variegata' is dark green with white margins. Zones 5-9. *C. pendula,* pendulous wood sedge, is 2 feet tall with bright green foliage and drooping gray-green seed heads that rustle in the breeze. Zones 5-9.

**Growing conditions.** Plant sedge in full sun or light shade in moist, fertile soil. Propagate by division.

**Landscape uses.** Grow sedge as an accent plant by the side of a pool, swamp or marsh. It will also do well in a container.

**Carpet bugle** see *Ajuga*
**Catmint** see Dictionary of Perennials, page 246
**Ceanothus** see Dictionary of Trees and Shrubs, page 426

**Chasmanthium**
(chas-MAN-thee-um)

Perennial ornamental grass that has an upright growth habit and thin stems. Flat, serrated leaf blades appear along the entire length of the stem. Zones 5-10.

**Selected species and varieties.** *C. latifolium,* northern sea oats, grows 3 to 5 feet tall. Flat leaves are 9 inches long and 1 inch wide. Seed heads are 8 to 12 inches long and appear on slender, drooping stalks. The foliage and the seed heads turn bronze after frost.

**Growing conditions.** Plant northern sea oats in full sun to partial shade in rich, fertile, moist soil. Propagate by division or from seeds.

**Landscape uses.** Plant northern sea oats as an accent plant or in a woodland garden.

## Chrysogonum (kri-SOG-o-num)

Perennial ground cover that has oval, toothed leaves and five-petaled yellow flowers. Zones 5-9.

**Selected species and varieties.** *C. virginianum* grows 4 to 12 inches tall. Hairy leaves are often tinged with purple. Yellow, 1 ½-inch flowers bloom in spring and summer.

**Growing conditions.** Plant chrysogonum in partial shade in rich, well-drained soil. It flowers best during cool summers. Propagate by division, by cuttings or from seeds.

**Landscape uses.** Chrysogonum may be planted as a ground cover under trees or shrubs.

**Cinquefoil** see Dictionary of Perennials, page 246

## Comptonia (komp-TOH-nee-a)

Deciduous shrubby ground cover that grows into a dense mass, spreading by underground runners. Zones 3-10.

**Selected species and varieties.** *C. peregrina*, sweet fern, grows 3 to 5 feet tall. Leaves are fragrant, 4 ½ inches long and ½ inch wide, hairy and notched along their entire length.

**Growing conditions.** Plant sweet fern in full sun to partial shade in sandy, well-drained soil. It will grow in rich soil but tolerates poor and dry soil as well. Propagate by layering, by division or from seeds.

**Landscape uses.** Plant sweet fern on a sandy or rocky bank, especially where soil erosion control is needed.

## Convallaria (kon-va-LAR-ee-a)
Lily-of-the-valley

Deciduous perennial ground cover that has upright, pointed leaves that grow from buds called pips that sprout on the rhizomes. Drooping bell-shaped, fragrant flowers bloom along one side of the flower stalk. Zones 4-8.

**Selected species and varieties.** *C. majalis* has leaves 6 to 8 inches high and 2 to 3 inches wide. Waxy, white or pink flowers are ¼ to ½ inch long and bloom in late spring.

**Growing conditions.** Plant lily-of-the-valley in partial to full shade and moist, rich, fertile, well-drained soil. Propagate from rhizomes, making sure that each division bears at least one pip.

**Landscape uses.** Grow lily-of-the-valley in the shade of a house or trees, or near water.

**Cord grass** see *Spartina*
**Cornus** see Dictionary of Trees and Shrubs, page 426

## Coronilla (kor-o-NIL-a)
Crown vetch

Fast-growing, deciduous, creeping perennial ground cover that has soft green feather leaves and pealike flowers. Zones 4-8.

**Selected species and varieties.** *C. varia* grows into a mat 18 to 24 inches high and 4 feet wide. Dense clusters of ½-inch pink flowers bloom in the summer. 'Penngift' has good drought tolerance and grows 12 to 18 inches high.

**Growing conditions.** Plant crown vetch in full sun or partial shade in dry, well-drained soil. Do not fertilize. It can be mowed in early spring to encourage new growth. Propagate by root divisions or from seeds. Seeds are often sown in combination with annual ryegrass, which will die out as the crown vetch becomes established.

**Landscape uses.** Plant crown vetch on a bank or a slope that cannot be easily mowed. It is a good plant to use where erosion control is needed.

CHRYSOGONUM VIRGINIANUM

COMPTONIA PEREGRINA

CONVALLARIA MAJALIS

CORONILLA VARIA

COTONEASTER HORIZONTALIS

CYNODON DACTYLON

CYPERUS ALTERNIFOLIUS

DICHONDRA MICRANTHA

## Cotoneaster (ko-toh-nee-AST-er)

Deciduous or evergreen shrubby ground cover that has stiff, spreading branches. Small white or pink flowers in bloom in spring, scattered among small, shiny, thick green leaves. Red or black berries ¼ inch across appear through autumn and winter. Zones 3-9.

**Selected species and varieties.** *C. adpressus,* creeping cotoneaster, is deciduous and grows 12 inches high. Its stems, which grow in a fish-bone pattern, root as it grows along the ground. Leaves are ½ inch long. Flowers are pink; berries are red. Zones 4-7. *C. horizontalis,* rockspray cotoneaster, is a deciduous shrub that grows 2 to 3 feet high and has fan-shaped branches. Foliage turns orange-red in fall and may be evergreen in Zones 8-10. Flowers are white or pink; berries are red. Zones 5-7. *C. salicifolius,* willow leaf cotoneaster, is an evergreen that has narrow, 1 ½ -to 3-inch leaves that turn purple in winter. White flowers bloom in 2-inch clusters; berries are red. The plant can reach 15 feet in height and width. Zones 6-8.

**Growing conditions.** Grow cotoneaster in full sun or partial shade in well-drained, neutral to slightly alkaline soil. Mature plants will tolerate drought and wind. Propagate by cuttings or by layering.

**Landscape uses.** Plant cotoneaster as a ground cover in a rocky area where the outline of its branches can be enjoyed, or where it can spill over the top of a wall.

**Cranesbill** see Dictionary of Perennials, page 246
**Crown vetch** see *Coronilla*

## Cynodon (SIN-o-don)
### Bermudagrass

Warm-season, medium- to high-maintenance turfgrass that is low-growing, vigorous and dense. It spreads by stolons and rhizomes and forms a tight sod. Regions B, C, E; it browns in the winter when temperatures drop below 50° F.

**Selected species and varieties.** *C. dactylon,* common Bermudagrass, is of fine to medium texture and ranges in color from light green to dark green.

**Growing conditions.** Bermudagrass will do well in full sun. Soil should be fine textured, fertile, well drained and have a pH that ranges between 5.5 and 7.5. The recommended mowing height is ½ to 1 inch. Fertilize Bermudagrass in early spring with 1 pound of nitrogen per 1,000 square feet and repeat in late spring and again in summer; or fertilize with ¾ pound of nitrogen per 1,000 square feet once a month for the eight-month season of active growth. Bermudagrass has good to excellent wear tolerance. It is susceptible to most turfgrass diseases and insects. The species can be propagated from seed, but named varieties must be grown from plugs or sprigs.

**Landscape uses.** Bermudagrass may be used in lawns that are subject to large volumes of foot traffic, as long as the high maintenance it requires is adequately provided.

## Cyperus (sy-PEER-us)

Semiaquatic ornamental grass that has long stems on top of which are sprays of foliage. Zone 10.

**Selected species and varieties.** *C. alternifolius,* umbrella plant, has slender stems 2 to 4 feet long. At the tops of the stems are 4- to 12-inch, lance-shaped leaves that hang down like the ribs of an umbrella.

**Growing conditions.** Cyperus will flourish in full sun or light shade in rich, very moist soil. It may also be grown in pots submerged in water. Propagate cyperus by division or by cuttings.

**Landscape uses.** Plant cyperus by the side of a pool or a stream, or in pots in an ornamental pool.

**Daylily** see Dictionary of Perennials, page 246
**Dead nettle** see *Lamium*
**Dianthus** see Dictionary of Annuals, page 200; Perennials, page 246

## Dichondra (dy-KON-dra)

Perennial ground cover used as a lawn substitute in warm-season turfgrass areas. It has round to kidney-shaped, light green leaves that are ½ to 1 inch across. It spreads by underground runners. Zones 9 and 10.

**Selected species and varieties.**
*D. micrantha* forms a low-growing, dense lawn. It has pale green flowers that are very small, sometimes inconspicuous, sometimes detracting noticeably from the appearance of the lawn.

**Growing conditions.** Grow dichondra in full sun to full shade in a fine-textured, rich, slightly acid, moist soil. Mow to a height of ½ to 1 inch whenever the cover looks uneven, which could be as infrequently as once per month. Fertilize with 1 pound of nitrogen per 1,000 square feet in early spring, late spring, summer and fall. Dichondra has limited wear tolerance and requires frequent watering. Leaf spot is the most serious disease problem. Propagate from seeds or with plugs.

**Landscape uses.** Choose dichondra as a substitute for turfgrass where foot traffic is limited. It grows well between stepping-stones.

**Dogwood** see Dictionary of Trees and Shrubs, page 426
**Dusty miller** see Dictionary of Annuals, page 200
**English ivy** see *Hedera*
**English yew** see Dictionary of Trees and Shrubs, page 426

**Epimedium** (ep-i-MEE-dee-um)
Barrenwort

Evergreen or deciduous woody perennial ground cover with clumps of finely toothed, heart-shaped leaves. Foliage is light green and often tinged with red in spring and fall. On evergreen species, the old leaves fall when new leaves are produced in spring. Flowers bloom in clusters in spring and very often are hidden under the foliage. Both leaves and flowers have wiry stems. Zones 4-10.

**Selected species and varieties.**
*E. grandiflorum*, long-spurred epimedium, grows 12 inches tall and is semievergreen. Flowers are 1 to 2 inches across, larger than other epimediums, and may be white, yellow, pink or violet. New foliage is red in spring, and leaves turn bronze in fall. 'Rose Queen' has large fuchsia-colored flowers with white-tipped spurs. Zones 3-8.

**Growing conditions.** Plant barrenwort in partial shade. It will tolerate full sun in a cool climate; where the climate is hot, the foliage will burn in the sun. Soil should be rich and slightly acid. Moist soil is best, but barren-

wort will tolerate dry conditions. Propagate by division.

**Landscape uses.** Plant barrenwort under trees and shrubs or as a ground cover in the front of a border.

**Erianthus** (er-ee-AN-thus)

Perennial, reedlike ornamental grass that has long, flat leaves and dense, silky, long seed heads in late summer. Zones 5-10.

**Selected species and varieties.**
*E. ravennae*, ravenna grass, is an upright grass with coarse, stiff, narrow leaves 3 feet long. Foliage is light green and turns brown after frost. Showy, 2-foot, silvery plumes appear on top of 7- to 14-foot stems and turn beige in fall.

**Growing conditions.** Plant plume grass in full sun in fertile, moist, well-drained soil. Propagate by division or from seeds.

**Landscape uses.** Grow plume grass as a tall accent plant or as a screen.

**Erica** (ER-i-ka)
Heath

Shrubby evergreen ground cover that has small, needlelike foliage that is held closely to the branches. Clusters of bell-shaped flowers of white, pink, rose, red or purple bloom in nodding spikes. Zones 3-9.

**Selected species and varieties.**
*E. carnea*, spring heath, grows 6 to 18 inches tall and spreads from 1 to 6 feet across. Flowers bloom from winter into spring and may last from three to five months. Foliage is dark green and shiny. Zones 6-9.

**Growing conditions.** Plant heath in full sun or, where summers are hot, partial shade. Soil should be sandy, rich and well drained, and may be acid or alkaline. Do not let soil remain dry in summer. The roots are shallow and should be mulched. Heath does best where humidity is high and where there are no drying winds. Shear the plant after it flowers. Propagate by cuttings, by division or by layering.

**Landscape uses.** Grow heath as a low border or as a ground cover, especially among rocks or on a bank.

EPIMEDIUM GRANDIFLORUM 'ROSE QUEEN'

ERIANTHUS RAVENNAE

ERICA CARNEA 'STARTLER'

EUONYMUS FORTUNEI 'SILVER QUEEN'

FESTUCA ARUNDINACEA 'REBEL'

FRAGARIA VESCA

**Eulalia grass** see *Miscanthus*

## Euonymus (yew-ON-i-mus)

Genus of deciduous and evergreen shrubs and vines, some of which make excellent ground covers. They are easy-care plants with smooth, waxy, leathery oval leaves. Flowers are green, yellow or white and are inconspicuous. Some species and varieties have berries. Zones 3-10.

**Selected species and varieties.** *E. fortunei,* wintercreeper, is an evergreen vine that roots as it grows along the ground. It grows to 12 to 24 inches tall and can spread to 20 feet. Foliage is ¾ to 2 inches across. Berries are round and pale pink. 'Colorata,' purple wintercreeper, is 12 to 18 inches tall. Its leaves turn purple in fall and winter. Cream-colored berries open to reveal orange seeds. 'Minima' grows 2 inches high and has ¼-inch leaves with white veins. It rarely sets berries. 'Silver Queen' grows 2 feet high and 6 feet wide and has green and off-white foliage. It does not produce berries. Zones 4-9.

**Growing conditions.** Plant euonymus in full sun to full shade. Varieties with white on the foliage do best in the shade and will turn pink in the sun. Euonymus can be grown in any well-drained garden soil but does best in acid soil. Propagate by cuttings, by layering or by division.

**Landscape uses.** Plant euonymus in large areas under trees and shrubs or on rocks. It is useful where soil erosion control is needed.

**Euphorbia** see Dictionary of Perennials, page 246
**Feather grass** see *Stipa*
**Feather reed grass** see *Calamagrostis*
**Fescue** see *Festuca*

## Festuca (fes-TOO-ka)
Fescue

Perennial cool-season and transitional zone turfgrass; also an ornamental grass. Regions A and F; northern parts of B and E; D with irrigation.

**Selected species and varieties.** *F. amethystina* large blue fescue, is an ornamental grass with upright tufts of fine blue foliage growing 18 inches high. Seed heads are small, fine textured and white. *F. arundinacea*, tall fescue, is a coarse, bunching, medium to dark green turfgrass with wide blades. 'Rebel' is medium green, fine textured and has good shoot density. *F. duriuscola*, hard fescue, is coarse textured, blue-green and grows in a tufted form. *F. rubra rubra,* creeping red fescue, is a fine-textured, medium to dark green grass that has a creeping habit. Creeping red and hard fescue are called "fine fescue" for their fine-textured leaves.

**Growing conditions.** Plant fescue in sun or partial shade. Creeping red fescue is the most shade-tolerant of the fescues, followed by hard fescue. Soil for tall fescue should be fertile, moist, rich and fine textured, with a pH of 5.5 to 6.5, although a pH as high as 8.5 will be tolerated. Tall fescue will tolerate wet soil. Soil for creeping red fescue and hard fescue should be dry and sandy and should have a pH of 5.5 to 6.5. Creeping red fescue will not tolerate wet soil. Mow tall fescue from 1½ to 2¼ inches high; hard fescue and creeping red fescue from 1 to 2½ inches high. Fertilize tall fescue with 2½ to 6 pounds of nitrogen per 1,000 square feet per year. Fertilize hard fescue and creeping red fescue with 1¼ to 3 pounds of nitrogen per 1,000 square feet per year. Tall fescue is one of the most drought- and wear-tolerant turfgrasses and is more heat-tolerant than most cool-season grasses. Most creeping red fescues are not heat-tolerant but are drought-tolerant, and have medium wear tolerance. Hard fescue is heat-, drought- and wear-tolerant.

**Landscape uses.** Tall fescue should be used in lawns that are subject to heavy traffic, and only the finer varieties blend well with other turfgrasses. Creeping red fescue is used in seed mixtures with other turfgrasses and is best suited to dry lawns that are located in the shade and have moderate foot traffic. Hard fescue lawns will tolerate more foot traffic than red fescue but not as much as tall fescue.

**Forget-me-not** see *Myosotis*
**Fountain grass** see *Pennisetum*

**Fragaria** (fra-GAR-ee-a)
Strawberry

Fast-growing perennial ground cover with three-part, dark green, oval leaves. White, six-petaled flowers are followed by edible, bumpy red fruit. Plants spread by runners at the ends of which new plantlets grow. Zones 5-10.

**Selected species and varieties.** *F. vesca* grows 8 to 12 inches tall. Flowers are ½ to ¾ inch across; fruits are ⅜ to ¾ inch in diameter. Both flowers and fruits are borne throughout the season. Zones 5 and 6.

**Growing conditions.** Plant strawberries in full sun in slightly acid, well-drained soil. Remove runners and plantlets to keep plants from becoming invasive. Propagate from seeds or from rooted plantlets.

**Landscape uses.** Grow strawberries in large, sunny areas. They are especially effective at the seashore and in informal gardens.

**Funkia** see *Hosta*

**Galium** (GAY-lee-um)

Perennial ground cover that spreads by creeping stems that are encircled with whorls of lance-shaped, 1-inch, shiny green leaves. Zones 5-10.

**Selected species and varieties.** *G. odoratum,* sweet woodruff, grows 6 to 12 inches tall and spreads to 24 inches across. White, star-shaped, four-part flowers bloom in clusters in spring.

**Growing conditions.** Plant sweet woodruff in partial to full shade in moist, well-drained, slightly acid soil. Prune back each spring to prevent the plant from becoming leggy. Propagate from seeds or by division.

**Landscape uses.** Grow sweet woodruff under trees or shrubs in a woodland garden. Its leaves and stems are aromatic when dried, and are used in flavoring May wine.

**Gaultheria** (gaul-THEER-ee-a)

Low-growing, evergreen shrubby ground cover that has small, drooping, bell-shaped white flowers in spring or early summer followed by attractive berries in fall. Zones 3-10.

**Selected species and varieties.** *G. procumbens,* wintergreen, grows 3 to 5 inches high and spreads 12 to 18 inches across. Foliage is oval, 2 inches long and glossy green, turning red or purple in cold winters. Berries are red and edible; they have a wintergreen aroma and flavor.

**Growing conditions.** Plant wintergreen in partially shaded location in rich, moist, acid, well-drained soil. Propagate from seeds or by cuttings, division or layering.

**Landscape uses.** Plant wintergreen as a ground cover under trees or shrubs or where it will cascade over a wall or rocks.

**Gazania** (ga-ZAY-nee-a)

Perennial ground cover grown as an annual in areas where it is not hardy. Oblong leaves grow from the base of the plant. Daisy-like flowers of yellow, gold, white, pink or orange bloom atop leafless stems that are 6 to 16 inches high. Blooms often have a black or white spot at the base of the petals and close at night and during cloudy weather. Zones 9 and 10.

**Selected species and varieties.** *G. rigens,* treasure flower, is a clumping plant with dark green leaves that have gray-green undersides. Flowers are 3 to 4 inches across. *G. rigens leucolaena* spreads by means of long, trailing stems. Foliage is silvery gray; flowers are 1 ½ to 2 ½ inches across.

**Growing conditions.** Grow gazania in full sun in dry, sandy, well-drained soil. Where grown as a perennial, it may be mowed every spring. Propagate by cuttings or division or from seeds.

**Landscape uses.** Clumping gazania is used as a filler between shrubs or as a ground cover along walkways. Trailing gazania is used in large areas and along slopes.

**Genista** see Dictionary of Trees and Shrubs, page 426
**Geranium** see Dictionary of Perennials, page 246
**Germander** see *Teucrium*
**Giant reed** see *Arundo*
**Ginger** see *Asarum*
**Goutweed** see *Aegopodium*

GALIUM ODORATUM

GAULTHERIA PROCUMBENS

GAZANIA RIGENS

HAKONECHLOA MACRA 'AUREOLA'

HEDERA HELIX

HELICTOTRICHON SEMPERVIRENS

HOSTA FORTUNEI 'AUREO-MARGINATA'

## Hakonechloa (hak-o-ne-KLO-a)

Perennial ornamental grass that spreads slowly by means of stolons and has soft, smooth leaves and delicate, open seed heads in late summer. Zones 5-10.

**Selected species and varieties.** *H. macra* grows 18 inches tall, with arching, dense, 9-inch, dark green leaves that grow with the appearance of being windswept. The cultivar 'Aureola' has bright yellow leaves with fine, warm green stripes.

**Growing conditions.** Grow hakonechloa in light shade; it tolerates full sun but will lose its color. Soil should be fertile and well drained. Propagate by division or from seeds.

**Landscape uses.** Plant hakonechloa in front of shrubs, as a specimen, as a ground cover or in a container.

**Heath** see *Erica*
**Heather** see *Calluna*

## Hedera (HED-e-ra)
Ivy

Woody evergreen vine that may be trained to grow either upright or as a ground cover. Ivies grown as ground covers generally have lobed leaves and seldom flower or set fruit. Stems root as they grow along the ground. Zones 5-10.

**Selected species and varieties.** *H. canariensis,* Algerian ivy, is a fast-growing vine that is 12 inches high when grown as a ground cover. Leaves are rounded to heart-shaped, shiny, rich green, have three to seven lobes and are 5 to 8 inches long. Zones 9-10. *H. helix,* English ivy, grows 6 inches high when grown as a ground cover. Leaves are dark green and dull on the upper surfaces, lighter on the undersides, 2 to 5 inches across and have three to five lobes. Zones 5-9.

**Growing conditions.** Grow ivy in sun or shade; variegated varieties are better grown in partial shade or their leaves will burn. Rich, moist, well-drained soil is preferred, although ivy will tolerate poor, dry soil. Prune ivy once or twice each year to control its growth, especially near low-growing shrubs. Ivy may also be mowed. Ivy may become a habitat for rodents and pests when thick. Propagate by cut-

tings. Cuttings rooted from stems with immature, lobed leaves will produce plants with lobed foliage only, unless allowed to climb.

**Landscape uses.** Plant ivy under and around trees and shrubs, on banks and level ground or where soil erosion control is needed. Algerian ivy should be used only in a large area since it grows so quickly.

## Helictotrichon (hel-ik-toh-TRY-kon)

Perennial ornamental grass that forms a clump of stiff, fine-textured and arching blades. Narrow seed heads form on one side of a tall, erect stem. Zones 5-10.

**Selected species and varieties.** *H. sempervirens,* sometimes designated *Avena sempervirens,* blue oat grass, avena grass, has narrow, blue leaves 12 to 24 inches tall and seed heads that form on 3- to 4-foot stems.

**Growing conditions.** Grow blue oat grass in full sun or light shade in well-drained, neutral soil. It is drought-resistant once established. Propagate by division or from seeds.

**Landscape uses.** Blue oat grass may be used either as a specimen or in a massed planting.

**Hemerocallis** see Dictionary of Perennials, page 246
**Hen-and-chickens** see *Sempervivum*
**Honeysuckle** see *Lonicera*

## Hosta (HOS-ta)
Plantain lily, funkia

Perennial ground cover that has mounds of foliage at the base of the plant. Leaves vary in size from several inches to more than a foot in length; vary in shape from long and narrow to round; and are known for their colors of green, blue, yellow and gold, which may be either solid or variegated. Many leaves are also deeply textured. Spikes of white, blue or lavender tubular flowers appear during the summer. Zones 4-9.

**Selected species and varieties.** *H. fortunei* grows 2 feet tall and has 5-inch, oval, ribbed leaves. Flowers are lavender, and appear in early summer in 3-foot spikes. *H. lancifolia,* narrow plantain lily, grows 12 inches high and has glossy, dark green, pointed, 6-inch leaves. Spikes of lavender flowers bloom on 2-foot stems in late summer. *H. plantaginea,* fragrant plantain lily, grows 18 inches tall and has bright green, rounded 10-inch leaves. Flowers are fragrant, 5 inches long, pale lavender to white and bloom on 2-foot stems in late summer.

**Growing conditions.** Plant most hostas in partial to full shade; wavy-leaf plantain lily will grow in full sun and shade. Soil should be moist, rich and well drained, but hostas will tolerate drought. Hostas are easy to grow but they are a favorite of slugs. Propagate by division. Hosta can be grown from seeds, but may not come true to variety.

**Landscape uses.** Plant hosta in a variety of locations: under trees, along a shady walkway, in a massed planting, as an edging or as a specimen.

**Houseleek** see *Sempervivum*
**Hypericum** see Dictionary of Trees and Shrubs, page 426

### Iberis (i-BER-is)
Candytuft

Annual or perennial ground cover that has clusters of small four-petaled flowers. Zones 4-10.

**Selected species and varieties.** *I. sempervirens* is an evergreen perennial that grows 9 to 12 inches tall and spreads into a mound 1½ to 3 feet across. Leaves are dark green, narrow, 1½ inches long and smothered by 1½-inch clusters of white flowers in midspring.

**Growing conditions.** Plant candytuft in full sun or partial shade in well-drained garden soil. It tolerates drought but grows better in moist soil. Shear the plant after it flowers to keep it compact. Do not plant it where it will be subjected to winter winds. Propagate by cuttings or layering or from seeds.

**Landscape uses.** Plant candytuft in a rock garden, atop a wall or as an edging.

### Imperata (im-per-AH-ta)

Perennial ornamental grass that has tufts of rigid, erect, flat leaf blades. Zones 5-10.

**Selected species and varieties.** *I. cylindrica rubra,* Japanese blood grass, is a tufted, upright plant with leaf blades that are green on the bottom and bright red on the top.

**Growing conditions.** Plant blood grass in full sun or light shade in moist, fertile and well-drained soil. Propagate by division.

**Landscape uses.** Plant blood grass as a specimen or accent, or in a border.

**Iris** see Dictionary of Perennials, page 246
**Ivy** see *Hedera*
**Japanese lawngrass** see *Zoysia*
**Japanese silver grass** see *Miscanthus*
**Japanese spurge** see *Pachysandra*
**Japanese yew** see Dictionary of Trees and Shrubs, page 426
**Juniper** see Dictionary of Trees and Shrubs, page 426
**Juniperus** see Dictionary of Trees and Shrubs, page 426
**Kentucky bluegrass** see *Poa*
**Kinnikinick** see *Arctostaphylos*
**Lamb's ears** see *Stachys*

### Lamium (LAY-mee-um)
Dead nettle

Perennial ground cover has square, hairy stems and coarsely toothed leaves. Flowers are lipped and resemble snapdragons. They bloom in late spring and early summer. Zones 4-9.

**Selected species and varieties.** *L. maculatum,* spotted dead nettle, grows 8 to 12 inches high and spreads to 2 feet across, rooting as it spreads. Leaves are heart-shaped to oval, 1½ to 2 inches long and dark green with white markings along the central vein. They may turn pink or purple in the fall. Flowers are purple and 1 inch long.

**Growing conditions.** Plant spotted dead nettle in partial to full shade. Any garden soil will do, but rich, moist soil is best. Spotted dead nettle is drought-tolerant once established. Propagate by division, by cuttings or from seeds.

**Landscape uses.** Plant spotted dead nettle under trees and shrubs in woodland gardens.

### Lantana (lan-TAN-a)

Perennial or shrubby ground cover that is often grown as an annual where it is not hardy. Small, tubular flowers bloom in dense, round clusters or spikes and change color as they age. Zones 9 and 10.

IBERIS SEMPERVIRENS

IMPERATA CYLINDRICA RUBRA

LAMIUM MACULATUM 'BEACON SILVER'

LANTANA MONTEVIDENSIS

LIRIOPE MUSCARI 'VARIEGATA'

LOLIUM PERENNE 'PALMER'

LONICERA JAPONICA 'HALLIANA'

**Selected species and varieties.**
*L. montevidensis,* trailing lantana, rapidly grows 12 to 18 inches tall and spreads from 3 to 6 feet wide. Leaves are rough textured, oval, 1 inch long and coarsely toothed. They are usually dark green but often turn purple in the winter. They have a sharp odor when crushed. Yellow, white, orange, pink, red or lilac flowers bloom on and off all year in round clusters at the ends of the branches.

**Growing conditions.** Plant lantana in full sun; it will mildew in shade. It will grow in any well-drained garden soil, but poor, dry soil is best. Fertilization will result in lush growth but few flowers. Prune back in early spring. Lantana will tolerate windy sites. Propagate by cuttings or from seeds.

**Landscape uses.** Plant lantana where it will cascade over walls and rocks or on dry banks, especially where soil erosion control is needed.

**Leiophyllum** see Dictionary of Trees and Shrubs, page 426
**Lily-of-the-valley** see *Convallaria*
**Lily turf** see *Liriope; Ophiopogon*

**Liriope** (li-RY-o-pee)
Lily turf

Perennial ground cover that forms tufts of grassy, dark green foliage. Some varieties are variegated. Flowers bloom in late summer or fall on 4- to 8-inch spikes. Zones 5-10.

**Selected species and varieties.**
*L. muscari,* blue lily turf, grows 12 to 18 inches tall and has ½-inch-wide-leaves that grow in non-spreading, upright, arching clumps. Flowers are lilac, purple or white. Zones 6-10. *L. spicata,* creeping lily turf, grows 8 to 10 inches tall and spreads to 18 inches across. Leaves are ¼ inch wide and often hide the flowers, which are lilac, blue or white.

**Growing conditions.** Lily turf grows in full sun to full shade and does best in rich, moist, well-drained soil; it tolerates dry, poor soil. It may be mowed. Propagate by division.

**Landscape uses.** Plant lily turf under trees and shrubs, as an edging, or on hot slopes or flat areas. It tolerates seashore conditions.

**Live forever** see *Sempervivum*

**Lolium** (LO-lee-um)
Ryegrass

Annual or perennial cool-season turfgrass that may be upright or bunching. Regions A and F where winters are not colder than -20°; D with irrigation; B, C and E to overseed warm-season grasses that turn brown in winter.

**Selected species and varieties.**
*L. perenne,* perennial ryegrass, is medium to dark green with light green undersides and medium texture. Improved varieties known as turf-type perennial ryegrasses have a darker green color, finer texture, increased weather tolerance and blend well with other grasses in mixtures. 'Palmer' is very dark green, of medium-fine texture and very wear-tolerant. Zones 5-7.

**Growing conditions.** Ryegrass should be grown in full sun to light shade. Soil should be fertile, moist and have a pH of 6.0 to 7.0. Mow ryegrass to a height of 1 ½ to 2 inches. It is difficult to mow because the leaf blades are tough, and the leaf tips often turn brown after mowing. Fertilize with 2 to 6 pounds of nitrogen per 1,000 square feet per year. Perennial ryegrass has greater wear tolerance than annual ryegrass. Ryegrass establishes very quickly from seed. Pythium blight is the most serious disease problem of ryegrass.

**Landscape uses.** Perennial ryegrasses are used in mixtures with other turfgrasses in lawns that receive average wear. Both annual and perennial ryegrasses are used to overseed dormant warm-season grasses during the winter.

**Lonicera** (lo-NIS-er-a)
Honeysuckle

Genus of fast-growing shrubs and vines, some of which are used as ground cover. Flowers are slender and tubular with prominent stamens, and are followed by non-showy black or red berries. Zones 5-10.

**Selected species and varieties.**
*L. japonica* is a fast-growing vine that reaches 2 to 3 feet in height and spreads to 10 feet across. Leaves are oval, 1 to 3 inches long, dark green and evergreen in warm climates. Fragrant flowers of white with a purple tint bloom in pairs all summer, fade to yellow as they age and are followed by black berries. 'Halliana,' Hall's honeysuckle, is the most rapid growing, spreading up to 30 feet across. Zones 7-10.

**Growing conditions.** Grow honeysuckle in sun or shade in any fertile, moist, well-drained soil. It likes heat and is drought-resistant when established. Honeysuckle can be hard to manage and needs to be pruned every year. Propagate by cuttings, layering or division, or from seeds.

**Landscape uses.** Plant honeysuckle on banks.

**Loosestrife** see Dictionary of Perennials, page 246
**Lungwort** see *Pulmonaria*

## Luzula (LOOZ-u-la)
Wood rush

Densely tufted, perennial ornamental grass that has a fine to medium texture. Leaves are soft and flat, and both leaves and stems are covered with soft, fine hairs. Single flowers bloom in spikes or clusters in spring. Zones 4-9.

**Selected species and varieties.** *L. nivea,* snowy wood rush, is an upright, arching plant that grows 18 to 24 inches tall. Flowers are white and bloom in round clusters. *L. sylvatica,* great wood rush, grows 12 inches tall and has narrow, pointed leaves. Flowers range from orange to brown in color and bloom in nodding clusters at the ends of the stems. *L. sylvatica marginata* has cream-colored margins on its foliage.

**Growing conditions.** Grow wood rush in partial to full shade in rich, moist, acid soil. Propagate by division from seeds.

**Landscape uses.** Plant wood rush as a ground cover, in a rock garden or in a woodland garden. It is especially useful for soil erosion control.

**Lysimachia** see Dictionary of Perennials, page 246
**Maiden grass** see *Miscanthus*
**Mascarenegrass** see *Zoysia*

## Mentha (MEN-tha)
Mint

Upright or low-growing perennial that has square stems, aromatic foliage, and lavender or white tubular flowers in spikes or clusters at the ends of the stems. Zones 3-10.

**Selected species and varieties.** *M. requienii,* Corsican mint, creeping mint, grows ½ to 1 inch tall and spreads 6 to 12 inches across. Foliage is bright green, flat, round, ⅛ inch in diameter and has a mossy appearance. Very tiny, light purple flowers bloom in early summer. Zones 5-10.

**Growing conditions.** Grow Corsican mint in sunny or partial shade locations, in moist soil. All mints can become very invasive. Propagate by division or from seeds.

**Landscape uses.** Plant Corsican mint as a mat under shrubs or between stepping-stones.

**Microbiota** see Dictionary of Trees and Shrubs, page 426
**Mint** see *Mentha*

## Miscanthus (mis-KAN-thus)

Perennial ornamental grass that forms clumps of upright, stiff leaves and has showy, feathery seed heads in fall. Zones 5-10.

**Selected species and varieties.** *M. floridulis,* giant miscanthus, is a coarse-textured plant growing 10 feet tall. Leaves are pale green and 3 feet long; seed heads are white. *M. saccariflorus,* eulalia grass, forms a narrow clump 6 to 10 feet high. Leaves are 3 feet long and 1 inch wide and turn rusty brown in fall. Plumes are silvery white. *M. sinensis,* Japanese silver grass, Chinese silver grass, grows to 8 feet or more. Leaves 2 to 3 feet long and 1 inch wide grow in narrow clumps and turn beige or orange-brown in fall. Seed heads are pink. 'Gracillimus,' maiden grass, is fine textured and grows 5 feet high in a graceful, arching habit. Leaves are narrow and curl at the ends. 'Variegatus,' striped eulalia grass, grows 5 feet tall and has narrow green foliage striped in white and yellow. 'Zebrinus,' zebra grass, grows 6 to 8 feet tall in a narrow form. Foliage has yellow horizontal stripes.

**Growing conditions.** Plant miscanthus in full sun or light shade in a moist, moderately fertile soil. Tall varieties may need staking if the soil is too fertile or if light is too low. Eulalia grass is invasive and may need to be restricted with underground barriers. Propagate by division or from seeds.

**Landscape uses.** Plant miscanthus as a barrier plant or specimen, or near the water.

LUZULA NIVEA

MENTHA REQUIENII

MISCANTHUS SINENSIS 'ZEBRINUS'

MOLINIA CAERULEA 'VARIEGATA'

MYOSOTIS SCORPIOIDES

OPHIOPOGON JAPONICUS

PACHYSANDRA TERMINALIS

## Molinia (mo-LIN-ee-a)

Perennial ornamental grass that forms tufted clumps of upright and arching leaves. Leaf blades are soft, narrow and flat. Flowers and seed heads appear in panicles on stiff stems. Zones 5-8.

**Selected species and varieties.** *M. caerulea*, moor grass, has erect leaves 6 to 12 inches long and green or purple spikes of flowers and seeds on 3-foot stems. 'Variegata,' variegated purple moor grass, has mounds of soft, fine-textured leaves striped in creamy yellow. Seed heads are purplish green on 1- to 2-foot stems.

**Growing conditions.** Moor grass will flourish in full sun or light shade locations, in rich, moist, acid soil. Propagate by division.

**Landscape uses.** Plant moor grass as an accent or as a specimen plant. Tall plants may be used in background plantings; low ones as edgings.

**Mondo grass** see *Ophiopogon*
**Moor grass** see *Molinia*
**Mother of thyme** see *Thymus*

## Myosotis (my-o-SO-tis)
Forget-me-not

Annual, biennial or perennial ground cover that has narrow oblong leaves and clusters of small, tubular, five-lobed flowers. Zones 4-10.

**Selected species and varieties.** *M. scorpioides* is a perennial that grows 18 inches tall and wide, spreading by creeping roots. Flowers are blue with a pink, yellow or white eye and bloom in delicate, airy clusters at the ends of the stems in spring and summer. *M. scorpioides semperflorens* grows 8 inches high.

**Growing conditions.** Grow forget-me-not in partial to full shade in rich, moist soil. It may be short-lived but it self-sows readily. Forget-me-not is prone to spider mite and mildew. Propagate by division or from seeds.

**Landscape uses.** Plant forget-me-not as a filler plant under bulbs or other perennials or near the water.

**Myrtle** see *Vinca*
**Nepeta** see Dictionary of Perennials, page 246
**Northern sea oats** *see Chasmanthium*
**Oat grass** *see Helictotrichon*

## Ophiopogon (o-fi-o-PO-gon)
Mondo Grass, lily turf

Evergreen perennial that has tufts of basal, grasslike leaves and loose, erect clusters of ¼-inch nodding flowers that are often hidden by the foliage. Zones 7-10.

**Selected species and varieties.** *O. japonicus* grows 6 to 12 inches high and has dark green, soft, curved foliage that is 8 to 16 inches long and ⅛ inch wide. It spreads quickly by underground stolons. Flowers are white or pale lavender and bloom in summer. *O. planiscapus* 'Arabicus,' black mondo grass, grows 8 to 10 inches wide. Leaves are arching; they are green when new but purplish black when mature. Flowers are white, pink or purple and bloom in summer.

**Growing conditions.** Mondo grass may be grown in full sun to full shade, but partial shade is preferred where summers are hot. Any garden soil is acceptable; mondo grass will tolerate both heat and drought. Propagate by division.

**Landscape uses.** Plant mondo grass under trees, on slopes or flat areas, or as an edging. It also tolerates seashore conditions.

## Pachysandra (pak-i-SAN-dra)
Spurge

Woody, perennial ground cover that may be deciduous or evergreen. It has oval leaves in whorls along the stems. The outer half of the leaf has a toothed margin. Flowers bloom in spikes and are not showy. Zones 4-8.

**Selected species and varieties.** *P. procumbens*, Allegheny spurge, trails at first and then forms erect clumps 8 to 10 inches high. It spreads to 15 inches across. Fuzzy greenish white to purple flowers appear in early spring. Leaves are 3 inches long and dull green mottled in gray. Deciduous Zones 4-7; evergreen Zones 8-9. *P. terminalis,* Japanese spurge, is an evergreen growing 9 to 12 inches high and spreading to 3 feet across by underground stems. Leaves are thick, dark green, glossy and 2 to 4 inches long. White flowers bloom in late spring. 'Silver Edge' has narrow silver margins on the leaves. Zones 5-8.

**Growing conditions.** Grow pachysandra in partial to full shade; leaves will turn yellow in the sun. Soil should be rich, cool, moist and neutral to acid. Pachysandra tolerates drought once established. Protect from winter sun and wind. Pachysandra is susceptible to euonymus scale. Propagate by cuttings or division.

**Landscape uses.** Plant pachysandra under trees and shrubs, as an edging, on slopes or on flat areas.

**Panic grass** see *Panicum*

**Panicum** (PAN-i-kum)
Panic grass

Annual or perennial, erect or creeping ornamental grass that is grown for its panicles of flowers and seed heads, which are light, open and feathery. Zones 5-10.

**Selected species and varieties.** *P. virgatum,* switch grass, is a perennial that grows vigorously 5 to 6 feet high. Leaves are green, narrow, 1 to 2 feet long and have rough margins. In autumn, they change to bright yellow or golden orange. Large beige or brown panicles grow on erect stems.

**Growing conditions.** Grow switch grass in full sun and light, well-drained soil. Dry soil is best, but switch grass tolerates moist soil and poor drainage. Propagate by seeds or division.

**Landscape uses.** Plant switch grass as a screen, as an accent plant or in a massed planting in a large area.

**Parthenocissus** (parth-e-no-SIS-us)

Woody deciduous vine that climbs to 60 feet or more but can be used as a ground cover. Foliage is either three-lobed or made up of three to five leaflets. Small, inconspicuous, greenish white flowers bloom among the leaves and are followed by blue to black berries. Zones 4-9.

**Selected species and varieties.** *P. tricuspidata,* Boston ivy, climbs to 60 feet on a support, but as a ground cover is 9 inches high, spreading to 8 feet across. Foliage is three-lobed, 8 to 10 inches across, shiny dark green in spring and summer, and bright scarlet in fall. 'Robusta' is a very vigorous grower with waxy leaves. Zones 4-8.

**Growing conditions.** Grow Boston ivy in full sun to light shade in rich, moist soil. Propagate by cuttings, layering or seeds.

**Landscape uses.** Plant Boston ivy in large areas, either sloped or flat. If it encounters trees, shrubs or walls, it will climb.

**Paxistima** (pak-SIS-ti-ma)

Neat, compact, fine-textured, shrubby ground cover that has small, shiny, dark green evergreen leaves. Inconspicuous flowers bloom in midspring to early summer. Zones 4-9.

**Selected species and varieties.** *P. canbyi,* Canby paxistima, grows 12 inches high and spreads 3 to 5 feet across. Wiry stems root as they grow. Leaves are narrow, ½ to 1 inch long and turn bronze in winter. Flowers are tiny and may be either greenish white or reddish. *P. myrsinites,* Oregon boxwood, grows 18 to 24 inches high and spreads to 6 feet across. Its flowers are 1 ½ inches long; otherwise it is similar to Canby paxistima. Zones 6-9.

**Growing conditions.** Grow paxistima in full sun to partial shade in moist, rich slightly acid, well-drained soil. It prefers high humidity. Propagate by division or cuttings.

**Landscape uses.** Plant paxistima under trees, in front of a shrub border or in a rock garden.

PANICUM VIRGATUM

PARTHENOCISSUS TRICUSPIDATA

PAXISTIMA CANBYI

PENNISETUM ALOPECUROIDES

POA PRATENSIS

PULMONARIA ANGUSTIFOLIA

## Pennisetum (pen-i-SEE-tum)

Annual or perennial ornamental grass with narrow, flat leaf blades that grow in a graceful, arching habit and nodding seed heads. The seed heads are spiked and slightly plumed. Zones 5-9.

**Selected species and varieties.** *P. alopecuroides,* fountain grass, is a perennial that grows 2 to 3 feet fall in a mounded form. Leaves are bright green and of fine to medium texture. Seed heads are cylindrical, silvery white and 6 to 8 inches long. 'Hameln' is more compact and 2 ½ feet high. *P. setaceum,* crimson fountain grass, grows 3 feet high and has graceful, arching, narrow leaves with a fine texture. Seed heads are 6 to 10 inches long and purple to red. 'Rubrum' has red foliage. It is perennial in Zones 8 and 9 but can be grown as an annual in other zones.

**Growing conditions.** Grow pennisetum in full sun or light shade in fertile, well-drained soil. Propagate by division or from seeds.

**Landscape uses.** Grow pennisetum as a hedge, as a specimen or in a flower border.

**Periwinkle** see *Vinca*
**Phlox** see Dictionary of Perennials, page 246
**Plantain lily** see *Hosta*

## Poa (PO-a)
### Bluegrass

Cool-season turfgrass that may be either bunching or stoloniferous in its habit. Regions A and F; D with irrigation.

**Selected species and varieties.** *P. pratensis,* Kentucky bluegrass, forms a high-quality turf of medium texture, with medium to dark green color and smooth, soft, shiny blades. It spreads vigorously by rhizomes. 'Adelphi' is very dark green, medium textured and has excellent disease resistance. 'Baron' is dark green, medium to coarse textured and needs frequent fertilizing. 'Bonnieblue' is dark green and medium textured, shade-tolerant and has excellent disease resistance. 'Challenger' is dark green and medium to fine textured, has excellent cold tolerance and disease resistance, and is one of the most drought-resistant Kentucky bluegrasses. 'Eclipse' is dark green, medium textured, very cold-tolerant and somewhat shade-tolerant and has

excellent disease resistance. 'Fylking' is dark green and medium to fine textured and needs little fertilizing. 'Merion' is dark green and medium to coarse in texture. It is very resistant to helminthosporium disease but very susceptible to other diseases. It requires heavy fertilization. 'Mystic' is medium to dark green and fine textured. 'Nassau' is dark green and medium to coarse textured and has excellent disease resistance. It turns green earlier in spring than most Kentucky bluegrasses.

**Growing conditions.** Grow Kentucky bluegrass in full sun or light shade. Soil should be moist, fertile, medium textured and have a pH of 6.0 to 7.0. Bluegrass prefers humid climates. Mow Kentucky bluegrass to a height of 1 to 2 inches. Fertilize with 2 ½ to 6 pounds of nitrogen per 1,000 square feet per year. Kentucky bluegrass has medium to good wear tolerance. Propagate Kentucky bluegrass from seed or sod. Bluegrass is prone to most turf diseases; helminthosporium is the most serious.

**Landscape uses.** Plant Kentucky bluegrass on lawns receiving average to heavy foot traffic and located in open, sunny areas.

**Potentilla** see Dictionary of Perennials, page 246
**Prairie cord grass** see *Spartina*

## Pulmonaria (pul-mo-NAR-ee-a)
### Lungwort

Perennial ground cover that spreads by creeping roots. Leaves are broad to lance-shaped and hairy; they have long stems and form at the base of the plant. Flowers are long and narrow, five-lobed and funnel-shaped. They bloom in nodding clusters at the tops of almost leafless stems in late spring or early summer. Zones 4-8.

**Selected species and varieties.** *P. angustifolia,* blue lungwort, grows 6 to 12 inches high and spreads from 12 to 18 inches across. Foliage is narrow and dark green. Flowers are blue, rose or white, and ¾ to 1 inch long. *P. saccharata,* Bethlehem sage, grows from 8 to 18 inches high and spreads to 24 inches across. Leaves are oval, pointed and dark green spotted with white. Flowers are white, blue or purplish red and ¾ to 1 inch across. 'Mrs. Moon' has pink buds that open into large blue flowers.

**Growing conditions.** Grow lungwort in partial to full shade in cool, moist, well-drained soil. Propagate by division or from seeds.

**Landscape uses.** Plant lungwort in woodland gardens, under trees or under shrubs.

**Ravenna grass** see *Erianthus*
**Red fescue** see *Festuca*
**Rhododendron** see Dictionary of Trees and Shrubs, page 426
**Rock cress** see *Arabis*
**Rosemary** see Dictionary of Trees and Shrubs, page 426
**Russian cypress** see Dictionary of Trees and Shrubs, page 426
**Ryegrass** see *Lolium*
**St. Augustine grass** see *Stenotaphrum*
**St.-John's-wort** see Dictionary of Trees and Shrubs, page 426
**Sand myrtle** see Dictionary of Trees and Shrubs, page 426
**Sarcococca** see Dictionary of Trees and Shrubs, page 426
**Scotch heather** see *Calluna*
**Sea oats** see *Chasmanthium*
**Sedge** see *Carex*
**Sedum** see Dictionary of Perennials, page 246

**Sempervivum** (sem-per-VEE-vum)
Live forever, houseleek

Genus of succulent perennials, some of which are used as ground covers. Leaves are thick and grown in small rosettes; new plants form around the base of the parent plant. Flowers are white, yellow, pink or red, and star-shaped. They bloom in clusters in summer, but often are not showy. Zones 4-10.

**Selected species and varieties.** *S. tectorum*, hen-and-chickens, grows 6 inches high and 3 to 6 inches across. Foliage is gray-green and the pointed leaf tips are often tinged with purple. Flowers are pink to purplish red, 1 inch across and bloom somewhat unreliably on 12- to 18-inch stems.

**Growing conditions.** Grow hen-and-chickens in full sun in any well-drained soil. It tolerates poor soil, heat and drought, but should be watered in summer. Propagate from seeds or by removing the offsets from the parent rosette and rooting them.

**Landscape uses.** Plant hen-and-chickens in small areas, in rock gardens and in rock walls.

**Silver spike grass** see *Spodiopogon*

**Spartina** (spar-TEE-na)
Cord grass

Upright, perennial ornamental grass that spreads by rhizomes. Leaf blades are long and coarse. Stems are thin and wiry and topped with one-sided, narrow seed heads in branched clusters. Zones 5-10.

**Selected species and varieties.** *S. pectinata* 'Aureo-marginata', prairie cord grass, grows 3 to 8 feet tall and has a coarse texture. Leaves are narrow, 2 feet long, arching and shiny green with rough, yellow margins. The leaves turn yellow before dropping from the plant after frost. Seed heads are 6 to 15 inches long on 5- to 8-foot stems and turn yellow in autumn.

**Growing conditions.** Grow prairie cord grass in full sun or light shade. It will grow in salt and fresh water marshes or in sandy garden soil. It is invasive when grown in water, less so when grown in soil. Propagate by division or from seeds.

**Landscape uses.** Plant prairie cord grass as a water plant, as a background plant or as a specimen. It has a heavy root system and is useful where soil erosion control is needed.

**Speedwell** see Dictionary of Perennials, page 246

**Spodiopogon** (spo-dee-o-PO-gon)

Deciduous, perennial ornamental grass that has arching, stiff foliage and erect stems that carry seed heads in late summer. Zones 5-10.

**Selected species and varieties.** *S. Sibericus*, silver spike grass, grows to a height of 3 feet. Leaves are 12 inches long and 1 inch wide. They are dark green, a red to purple in midsummer and then completely red or purple in fall. Silvery seed heads grow 12 inches long on 5-foot stems.

**Growing conditions.** Grow silver spike grass in full sun or light shade in moist to wet soil. Propagate by division or from seeds.

**Landscape uses.** Plant silver spike grass as a specimen near the water.

**Spring heath** see *Erica*
**Spurge** see *Pachysandra*

SEMPERVIVUM HYBRID

SPARTINA PECTINATA 'AUREO-MARGINATA'

SPODIOPOGON SIBERICUS

STACHYS BYZANTINA

STENOTAPHRUM SECUNDATUM

STIPA GIGANTEA

## Stachys (STAK-is)

Annual or perennial ground cover. Oval or lance-shaped leaves clothe square stems. Tubular flowers of purple, scarlet, yellow, white or pink bloom in whorled spikes at the ends of the stems. Zones 4-10.

**Selected species and varieties.** *S. byzantina*, sometimes designated *S. lanata* or *S. olympica*, lamb's ears, forms a mat of foliage 8 inches high and 36 inches across. Leaves are soft, white, woolly and 4 inches long. Pink or purple flowers that are ½ inch wide and 1 inch long bloom in summer on 18-inch stems. Evergreen Zones 7-10.

**Growing conditions.** Grow lamb's ears in full sun or light shade in light, sandy, well-drained soil. Good drainage during winter is critical. Propagate by division or from seeeds.

**Landscape uses.** Plant lamb's ears on slopes, under high-branched trees, as edgings or in rock gardens.

## Stenotaphrum (sten-o-TAF-rum)
St. Augustine grass

Warm-season turfgrass that is low-growing and very coarse textured. It is very aggressive and spreads by thick stolons. Region C; southern parts of B and E.

**Selected species and varieties.** *S. secundatum* is blue-green in color and spongy in character.

**Growing conditions.** Grow St. Augustine grass in full sun to full shade. it is the most shade-tolerant warm-season turfgrass. It has fair drought resistance and good wear tolerance. It prefers humid climate and tolerates seashore conditions. Soil should be rich, moist, fertile, sandy and well drained, with a pH of 6.5. Mow to a height of 1½ to 2½ inches. Fertilize with 3 to 6 pounds of nitrogen per 1,000 square feet per year. The grass discolors in the winter when temperatures drop below 55° F. Propagate by plugs or sod. Brown patch, St. Augustine decline (SAD) virus, leaf spot and dollar spot are the most serious diseases; chinch bug is the most serious insect problem.

**Landscape uses.** Plant St. Augustine grass in warm, humid climates on lawns receiving average foot traffic.

## Stipa (STY-pa)
Feather grass

Perennial ornamental grass that has narrow leaves and large, showy, feathery seed heads. Zones 5-10.

**Selected species and varieties.** *S. gigantea* has a tufted mound of arching foliage 3 feet high at the base of the plant. Leaves are 18 inches long. Seed heads are thin and drooping, 15 inches long and appear in late summer on 6-foot, wide-spreading stems.

**Growing conditions.** Grow feather grass in full sun to partial shade in light, well-drained, fertile soil. Propagate by division or from seeds.

**Landscape uses.** Plant feather grass as a specimen or a background plant.

**Stonecrop** see Dictionary of Perennials, page 246
**Strawberry** see *Fragaria*
**Sweet box** see Dictionary of Perennials, page 426
**Sweet fern** see *Comptonia*
**Sweet woodruff** see *Galium*
**Switch grass** see *Panicum*
**Tall fescue** see *Festuca*
**Taxus** see Dictionary of Trees and Shrubs, page 426

## Teucrium (TOO-kree-um)
Germander

Perennial or small evergreen shrub that is used as a ground cover. Stems and foliage are covered with white to silver hairs. Two-lipped, tubular flowers bloom in showy spikes at the ends of the stems. Zones 5-10.

**Selected species and varieties.** *T. chamaedrys* grows 10 to 12 inches high and spreads to 2 feet across from underground stems. Leaves are shiny, dark green, toothed and ¾ inch long. White, pink or purplish red flowers bloom in summer in loose spikes. 'Prostratum' grows 6 inches high and spreads to 2 feet wide.

**Growing conditions.** Grow germander in full sun or light shade in well-drained soil. Water deeply but infrequently. It tolerates poor soil, but dislikes drying winds. Propagate by division, by cuttings or from seeds.

**Landscape uses.** Germander tolerates shearing and so is used as a neat edging or a low, formal edge.

**Thyme** see *Thymus*

## Thymus (TY-mus)
Thyme

Low-growing woody perennial or small shrub that spreads to form a mat 18 inches across. Leaves are small and aromatic. Lilac or purple flowers bloom in small clusters in the summer. Zones 4-10.

**Selected species and varieties.** *T. praecox arcticus,* mother of thyme, grows 1 to 2 inches high. It has ¼-inch dark green, leathery evergreen leaves and ½-inch, globe-shaped or hemispherical flower heads. Blooms are white, pink, rose or purple and appear on 4-inch stems. *T. vulgaris,* common thyme, is a shrub 6 to 15 inches tall and has ½-inch, evergreen, gray-green leaves and white to lilac flowers in whorls. Zones 4-9.

**Growing conditions.** Thyme may be grown in full sun in dry, well-drained soil. It is heat-tolerant. Propagate by cuttings or division, or from seeds.

**Landscape uses.** Plant thyme in a rock garden, between stepping-stones, as a border, as a lawn substitute or on a dry slope. Common thyme is also used as a culinary herb.

**Treasure flower** see *Gazania*
**Veronica** see Dictionary of Perennials, page 246

## Vinca (VINK-a)

Genus of erect or trailing evergreen shrubs and vines, usable as ground covers. The trailing types root as they grow along the ground. Single, five-petaled, flat flowers of blue or white bloom in the leaf axils in early spring. Foliage is oval and shiny. Zones 5-10.

**Selected species and varieties.** *V. major,* big periwinkle, forms an open mound 6 to 18 inches high and 48 inches across. Leaves are oval to heart-shaped, dark green, 3 inches across and formed on wiry stems. Flowers are blue, white, pink or red, and 1 to 2 inches across. Zones 7-10. *V. minor,* periwinkle, myrtle, forms a dense cover 6 to 10 inches high and 24 inches across. Leaves are leathery, oblong, dark green.

**Growing conditions.** Grow vinca in full sun to partial shade; partial shade is preferred where summers are hot. Soil should be sandy, moist and well drained. Vinca can be mowed. Big periwinkle is more invasive than periwinkle. Propagate by cuttings, division or layering, or from seeds.

**Landscape uses.** Vinca may be planted on slopes or under trees and shrubs.

**Viola** see Dictionary of Annuals, page 200
**Violet** see Dictionary of Annuals, page 200
**Wild ginger** *see Asarum*
**Wild lilac** see Dictionary of Trees and Shrubs, page 426
**Wintercreeper** see *Euonymus*
**Wintergreen** see *Gaultheria*
**Woodruff** see *Galium*
**Wood rush** see *Luzula*
**Wood sedge** see *Carex*
**Yarrow** see Dictionary of Perennials, page 246
**Yew** *see* Dictionary of Trees and Shrubs, page 426
**Zebra grass** see *Miscanthus*

## Zoysia (ZOY-zee-a)

Warm-season and transitional zone turfgrass that spreads by thick stolons and rhizomes and develops slowly into a uniform, dense, low-growing, high-quality lawn that remains evergreen above 50° F. Stems and leaves are tough and stiff. Regions B, C and E; coastal areas of A and F.

**Selected species and varieties.** *Z. japonica.* Japanese lawngrass, is dark green and has prostrate leaf blades 3 inches wide. It is the coarsest-textured zoysia. 'Meyer' is medium dark green and medium textured. *Z. tenuifolia,* mascarenegrass, is very light green and has erect leaf blades 1 inch wide. It is the finest-textured zoysia. Zones 9 and 10.

**Growing conditions.** Grow zoysia in full sun or partial shade. Mascarenegrass is the most shade-tolerant zoysia. All are very tolerant of heat and drought. Soil should be fine textured, fertile, well drained and have a pH of 6.0 to 7.0. Mow to a height of ½ to 1 inch. Zoysia is difficult to mow because of its tough leaf blades. Fertilize with 1 pound of nitrogen per 1,000 square feet in spring, and again in summer and fall; or ¾ pound of nitrogen per 1,000 square feet monthly throughout the eight-month growing season. All zoysias are very wear-tolerant when growing, except during the winter, when they are dormant. Zoysia turns straw brown below 50° F but can be overseeded with cool-season turfgrasses. Propagate by plugs or by sod. Zoysia is relatively free of major insect and disease problems.

**Landscape uses.** Plant zoysia in lawns that are actively used in the humid warm and transitional regions.

TEUCRIUM CHAMAEDRYS 'PROSTRATUM'

THYMUS PRAECOX ARCTICUS

VINCA MINOR

ZOYSIA JAPONICA 'MEYER'

# 4

# ANNUALS

*A massed planting of golden yellow marigolds and pink petunias makes a dazzling mid-summer show. Both these annuals are free-flowering plants that, with a little maintenance in spring and summer, will make a fine display all season long.*

Annuals are among the most cheerful flowers in the garden, and because they are here this year and gone the next, they allow endless opportunities for experimenting. Beginning in spring with brightly colored early-blooming petunias and ending in late fall with the frost-denying foliage of ornamental cabbage, annuals bloom continuously, often under conditions that other, less sturdy plants cannot tolerate.

This chapter will show you how to take full advantage of annuals' flexibility and variety. Annuals are natural candidates for all sorts of decorative uses. They can be massed together in formal, geometrical beds *(page 180)*. Tucked among spring bulbs, spring-flowering shrubs and other plants *(page 182)*, they mask the inevitable decline of these seasonal blooms. Annual vines make handsome quick-growing covers for trellises and fences. Along with these many uses for annuals, the chapter includes helpful guidelines for putting together window boxes that provide the best conditions for growing annuals in confined spaces. Refer to Chapter 2 for directions on improving the soil of your flower bed as well as on handling the routine gardening tasks that will benefit even the sturdiest of annuals, including watering and fertilizing, staking and grooming, weeding and mulching and getting rid of garden pests. A little tender care will help your plants look their best—bushier, fuller, with larger and more abundant flowers.

Starting plants from seed may not be the quickest way to create a garden but it is the most magical. The following pages describe the common practice of sowing annual seeds in the garden. Refer to Chapter 2 for instructions on gathering

# CHAPTER CONTENTS

seeds and starting seeds indoors as well as for other methods of propagating annuals, including planting stem cuttings and creating your own hybrids.

Annuals are more likely to stay healthy and look their best if the gardener pays attention to such fundamental matters as timing and troubleshooting. Some annuals are hardy enough to withstand—even to need—cool soil, and thus should be planted early in spring or late in fall; others are tender and must not be put in the ground till after all danger of frost is past. For a general guide to timely planting in your area, see the frost-date map *(inside back cover)*; it indicates the average date of the last frost in nine regions across the United States and Canada. Then, for a checklist of chores to do and when to do them, see the chart on pages 192-195; for information about what to do at summer's end to give your annuals a head start for next year, see page 190.

Even in the best of gardens, trouble arises from time to time, and any plant may look sickly or distressed. Pages 196-199 provide a collection of common garden ailments. The text and illustrations are designed to help you identify such garden pests as beetles and scale, for instance—or how to distinguish the damage done by particular pests if, like leaf miners, they are too small to be seen with the naked eye. The text also gives information on how to correct the damage that such pests inflict.

The chapter concludes with a dictionary describing the genus and species of dozens of the beautiful flowers that grow as annuals. Use the dictionary in conjunction with the frost-date map to help you determine the ideal time for sowing and planting annuals in your area.

# PLANTING ANNUALS IN A FLOWER BED

Despite its intimidating connotations, the term "formal garden" refers merely to a flower bed laid out in a geometric design and filled as often as not with old-fashioned, everyday annuals like marigolds and petunias. Because many annuals are densely flowered, they perfectly suit a formal, symmetrical bed, and look their best framed in one. Such a precisely shaped garden cannot be bent to fit in a yard where slopes or rocks make the ground uneven. But in an open, level area, a formal bed with strong, straight lines can be striking. The bold design makes the most of a small lot, and the plot's regular shape makes it easy to plant, even for a beginning gardener. (If desired, you can smooth out a bumpy or an uneven area, as described on pages 54-55 in Chapter 2.)

The equipment needed to lay out a formal bed is simple to gather and use: stakes, some string and a length of ordinary board, as shown below and opposite. The board, marked to serve as a spacing guide, helps you plant the annuals in the precise rows the design calls for.

To make the formal pattern, plant the annuals in blocks of colors and limit the kinds of plants you use. Two or three varieties are enough; more shapes and colors can spoil the visual effect. Favorite candidates besides petunias and marigolds include dusty miller, wax begonias and snapdragon. Be sure to pick plants that have similar space requirements, so that the rows will be even (see the Dictionary of Annuals, pages 200-221). All is not lost, however, should two plants with different spacing needs—one of 12 inches, and the other 10, for example—prove irresistible. You can plant them both either 10 or 12 inches apart, whichever seems better suited to the overall spacing of the bed.

*Rows of silvery dusty miller enclose several inner bands of purple and white salvia, giving a formal garden an orderly but pleasing geometric design.*

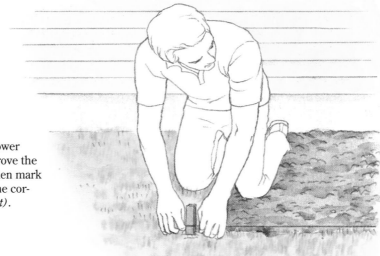

**1** After deciding on the size of your formal flower bed—it should be at least 3 feet by 6—improve the soil of the bed as shown on pages 56-57. Then mark out one straight side by sinking stakes at the corners and connecting them with string *(right)*.

**2** To plant the annuals in straight rows, buy a board as wide as the spacing required by the annuals you have chosen. For plants needing 10 inches between them, for example, get a 10-inch-wide board. To properly space plants in the same row, mark the board: starting 5 inches in from the end of the board, cut notches into one long end at 10-inch intervals *(inset, above)*. Place the board so that one short end lies against the string defining the plot's long side, and so that at least 5 inches of soil show between the board and the short edge of the bed. Kneel on the board and begin planting your annuals *(right)*.

**3** When you have planted one row, lift the board and move it back one full width *(left)*. The impression left by the board in the soil will help you realign it. Continue planting and moving the board until the bed is finished. Water the plants generously to help their roots recover quickly from the stress of transplanting.

181

# CHANGING COLORS FROM SEASON TO SEASON

Annuals can be used to fill out flower beds that are devoted mainly to other sorts of plants, like perennials or bulbs. Most perennials bloom for only a few weeks each year. Bulbs generally flower only in the early spring. A bed or a border containing just these types of plants can go through dull periods when nothing much blooms.

The remedy is to interplant with annuals, which provide color when all the other plants are strictly green. Many annuals are known for their bright season-long blooms. Some others, such as violets, enjoy cool weather and bloom in the spring. Marigolds and zinnias, on the other hand, are warm-weather plants and bloom on through the fall. A judicious mixture of early bloomers with later-flowering species will give a garden color throughout the growing season.

Annuals are usually added to the beds of more permanent plants in the spring. Planting is easy, as the drawings opposite demonstrate. Simply select fairly open spots between clumps of perennials or clusters of bulbs—and dig carefully to avoid injuring the roots of the established plants.

*Nestled in front of a row of perennial lilies and iris that retain only their green foliage after their blooming season has ended, annuals such as deep purple and rose pink petunias and light purple ageratum add mid-summer color.*

## ACCENT ON FOLIAGE

Most gardeners plant annuals for their colorful flowers, but the main features of some varieties are the rich textures and patterns of their foliage. Coleus leaves have splashes of color ranging from pale green to red. Dusty miller foliage has a silver tone and a soft, feltlike texture. Both of these low-growing annuals can be used for edging and borders *(right)*. To fill garden beds, foliage annuals such as bloodleaf and kochia grow to 5 feet in height. Bloodleaf has deeply veined, bright red leaves, while kochia has light green leaves until fall, when the foliage turns a bright pinkish red.

1 When adding flowering annuals to an established bed, plant them one at a time in the bare spots. First, clear away any mulch from each planting spot and loosen the soil, using a trowel. Then, add a teaspoonful of all-purpose fertilizer and a handful of compost *(page 58)* or other fine organic matter. Mix the amendments thoroughly into the soil *(right)*.

2 Dig a hole in the loosened, amended soil, using the trowel. Loosen the roots of a new annual and the soil around them, and place the plant in the hole. Be sure the plant sits at the same depth as it did in its container; adjust the depth of the hole by hand, if necessary *(left)*. Once the annual is planted, firm the soil around it and respread the mulch you cleared away. Water the plant generously to help its roots recover quickly from the stress of transplanting.

# PLANTING ANNUALS IN A WINDOW BOX

*Standing tall above a mix of purple heliotrope and nierembergia, deep pink geraniums highlight this overflowing window box. Lacy white artemisia, a perennial, provides a cool contrast.*

Window boxes of annuals in bloom can do more than beautify windowsills. They can also brighten porch railings or add decorative accents to outdoor staircases. In addition, they offer an opportunity to create beauty on a small scale and enable the gardener to control the planting environment by determining the location and exposure of the box. When choosing a window box, avoid oversized containers; they will be much heavier when filled with soil and difficult to mount. Make sure to affix securely any window box you mount, bolting it in place, if necessary.

Since plants in window boxes are more exposed to the drying effects of sun and wind than plants in the ground, they need more water. During the summer you may have to give them several good soakings every day. All that water will quickly wash away nutrients, so enrich the soil once a week with diluted fertilizer *(page 60)*. For sunny locations, use only boxes made of wood or clay; soil in metal or thin plastic containers can overheat in direct sunlight and "bake" roots to death.

When combining different annuals in one window box, include only plants with similar sun and shade requirements. Place taller, more upright varieties in the back of the box, and shorter plants in front of them. For a cascading effect, fill the front of the box with trailing plants like lobelia. Follow the instructions opposite to set up a window box and arrange plants in it.

1 If you make your own wooden window box or buy one without drainage holes, make a series of holes in the bottom. Set the box upside down on a secure surface, then use an electric drill fitted with a ¼-inch bit to bore a hole every 3 to 4 inches along the bottom of the box about 1 inch from each edge of it *(right)*. To keep soil from washing out of the drainage holes when you water your plants, line the inside surface of the bottom of the box with a piece of window screening cut to fit.

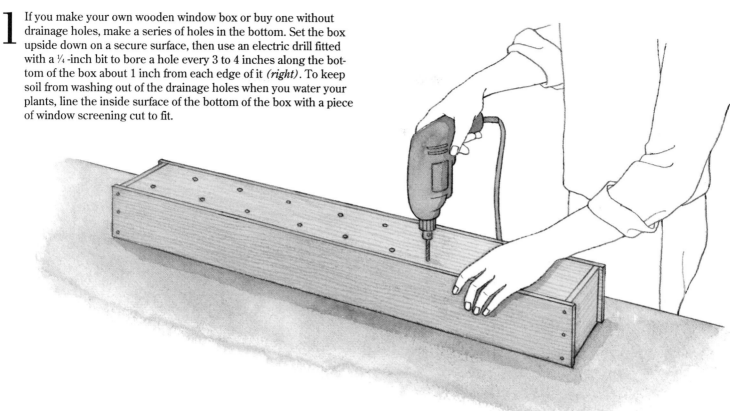

2 To prepare the box for your plants, spread a 1-inch layer of gravel on top of the liner to allow excess water to drain away safely instead of pooling around plant roots. On top of the gravel, place several inches of commercial potting soil so that the soil line is about 1 inch below the rim of the box. To fit the plants into the window box you may have to pare some soil from their root balls with your fingers; take care not to disturb the roots too much. Next arrange the plants in the window box and fill in around each plant with potting soil *(right)*; make sure that each plant is sitting at the same depth in the window box as it did in its container. Mount the window box at the location you selected, then water the plants thoroughly until water begins running out of the drainage holes.

# TRAINING VINES ON A TRELLIS

A number of bright-blooming annuals are essentially vines that can be trained up trellises, fences or similar frameworks with wonderful effect. A trellis interlaced with flowers and lush foliage can provide a vertical garden of head-high color at the edge of a terrace or in front of a porch, and can also serve as a sun-shade, a windbreak or a screen to afford extra privacy. Annual vines are ideal climbers, grow-ing swiftly in the spring, then conveniently dying back in the autumn to allow the pre-cious rays of the winter sun to pass.

Climbing annuals include several much-loved standbys: nasturtiums, sweet peas and morning glories. Each one has unique fea-tures and requirements. Nasturtiums are a horticultural rarity; they positively thrive on neglect. They need little if any fertilizer, and not much water either, to produce flowers in abundance. Once nasturtiums are sown as seeds in early spring *(page 188)*, they will grow and flower all summer long.

Sweet peas, with their sweet-scented and many-colored flowers, require a little more attention. Growing well in cool weather—and disliking heat—they should be planted early, right after the last hard frost. During the hot months, they should be protected by a 2- to 4-inch-thick carpet of mulch *(page 70)* laid around their stems, which will keep down the soil temperature.

The all-time favorites are morning glories, shown at right and opposite. Their blooms are large and festive, and the plants produce thick foliage with astonishing rapidity. They do not begin to grow, however, until the spring sun has warmed the earth to about 50° F. In tem-perate zones, therefore, they should (unlike sweet peas) be planted late, in mid-May at the earliest.

*Lavender-and-white morning glories climb and trail and drip luxuriantly as they cling to an open, trellis-like garden fence. A freestanding trellis is easy to tack together from similar slats of painted wood; fiberglass ones can be purchased at garden supply centers.*

1 Improve the soil *(page 56)* of the planting area, then firmly anchor your trellis in the ground. Use a trowel to dig a 4- or 5-inch-deep trench in front of the trellis and plant your seeds in the trench *(right)*. Cover the seeds with soil and water them. Once the seedlings have sprouted, thin them out as you would when sowing seeds in the garden *(page 189, step 4)*.

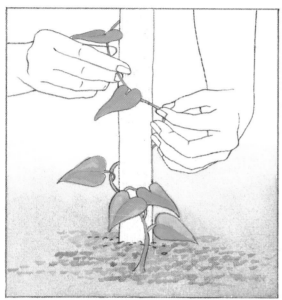

2 Once your vines have grown high enough to reach the trellis, you can begin helping the stems wrap themselves around the framework. Some plants naturally twist clockwise, some the reverse. Note the direction your vines naturally incline to and help them twine around the framework that way *(above)*. If they do not take hold, secure them to the framework with string.

3 When the vines have climbed about a third of the way up the trellis, start pinching back the stem tips *(page 68)* to encourage branching. As the plant grows taller and produces flowers, remove dead blooms *(right)* to maintain the appearance of the trellis and promote continued flowering.

# SOWING SEEDS
# IN THE GARDEN

There are many good reasons for sowing seeds directly in the garden. Some annuals grow so fast that nothing is gained by starting them indoors. Some—such as poppy and larkspur—do not flourish when moved. And some, like sweet peas and forget-me-nots, do better when started in cool soil.

There are equally good reasons for sowing seeds indoors *(page 80)*. Some annuals have tiny seeds that may be lost if sown outdoors. Others need a long time to grow before they flower. If you want such flowers as marigold, zinnia, geranium and verbena blooming in your garden in early summer, they must be sown indoors—four to 12 weeks before the last frost date in your area.

Before sowing seeds outdoors in spring, test the soil's condition. Take a handful of soil and squeeze it; if it sticks together, it is too wet. Wait a few days and test it again. When the soil is moist but crumbles in your hand, it is ready for planting.

There are two methods of sowing seeds outdoors. One is to broadcast seeds—toss them into the soil at random and water lightly. This method is useful for such fine seeds as portulaca and petunia.

A second method is to sow seeds in furrows, as shown below and opposite. This requires more work, but enables you to control the arrangement of the flowers. That may be important if you are planting a formal bed *(page 180)* and want precise geometric lines.

*A crowd of gloriosa daisies—some with solid yellow petals, others splashed with orange—nod in the midsummer sun. As hardy annuals, they do well when sown directly in the soil, early in the seaon.*

## MAKE A COZY NOOK
## FOR BUTTERFLIES

Butterflies are not particular about the color of the flowers on which they feed, but they do care about atmosphere. They like sun, and since their bodies are so light they welcome shelter from the wind. To accommodate them, sow annuals whose nectar they find most delectable, such as coreopsis, phlox, sage and zinnia, and surround the flowers with a windbreak of taller plants and shrubs.

1 Improve the soil of your flower bed *(page 56)*. Then mark its boundaries using stakes and string as when laying out a formal garden *(page 180, step 1)*. Use the edge of a mattock *(right)* or a hoe to loosen the surface soil and make a furrow about 1 inch deep—or, if you purchased the seeds, as deep as the seed packet instructions indicate. Follow the seed packet instructions or refer to the Dictionary of Annuals *(pages 200-221)* for spacing between furrows.

**2** Sprinkle the seeds evenly into the furrows *(right)*. To ensure that enough seedlings sprout, sow about four seeds for every plant you expect to retain. Cover the seeds with a thin layer of soil if directed to do so on the seed packet.

**3** Tamp the surface soil lightly with a rake to eliminate hollows and air pockets and to press the seeds gently into the ground below so they will make contact for rooting *(left)*. Use a hose with an adjustable spray nozzle to dampen the bed lightly. Water the bed daily so the ground does not dry out.

**4** After a week or 10 days, when the seedlings begin to crowd one another, thin them out. Retain the seedlings with the stoutest stems and the greenest leaves. To avoid disturbing a seedling while you pull out an adjacent plant, place a finger on each side of the base of its stem and apply light pressure to the soil to keep its root system intact *(right)*.

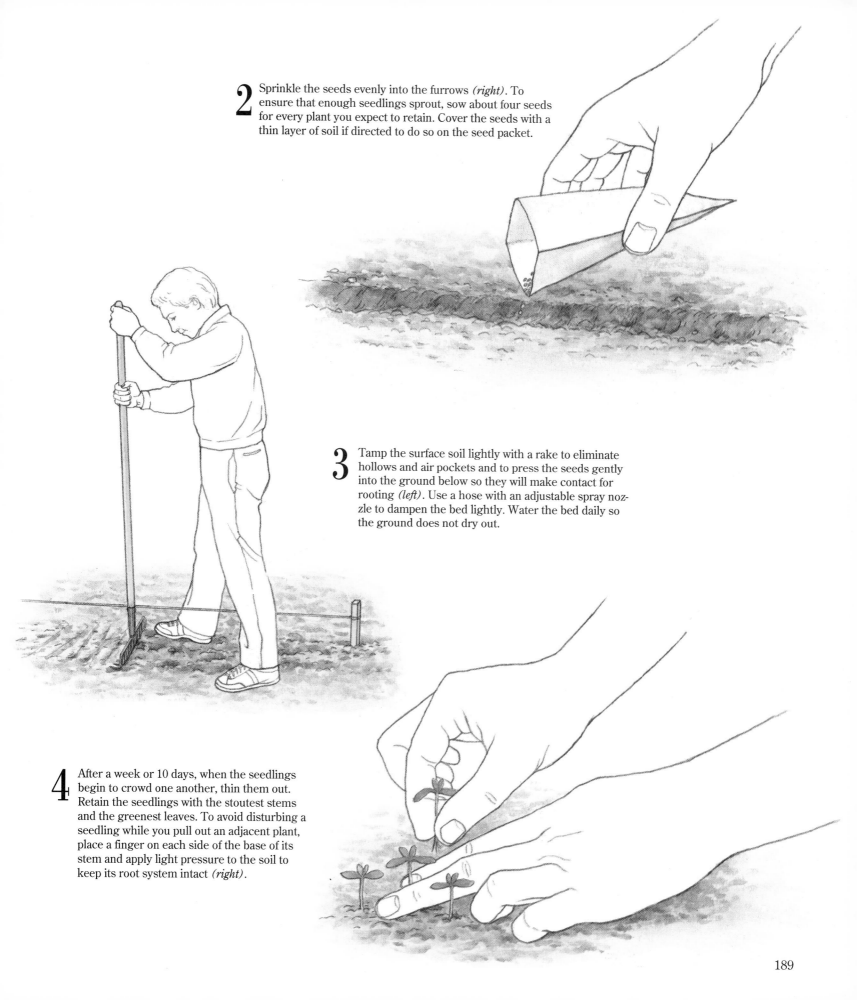

# PREPARING AN ANNUAL GARDEN FOR THE WINTER

The first frost of fall spells the end for most annuals. An exception is the geranium, an annual in North America that is a perennial in its native Africa—meaning that it cannot survive cold winters, but will bloom, season after season, in a warm climate. If dug up *(inset)* a few weeks before the onset of cold weather, a geranium can be potted and brought indoors, kept alive through the winter in a dormant state and returned to the ground in spring to bloom again.

Even for other annuals, fall is by no means the end of the gardener's year. By taking proper precautions before winter, you can ensure an early rebirth of your spring garden. Since frost-killed plants may harbor pests and disease-causing organisms, remove all dead foliage from your annual flower bed as soon as possible. If the entire bed is devoted to annuals, simply pull up the plants and discard them on your compost heap *(page 58)* or as trash.

If the bed also contains perennials or bulbs that will survive the winter, cut the annuals off at the ground with shears so that you can remove them without injuring the plants that remain. Leave the roots of the cut annuals in the ground to die.

A bed emptied of annuals can be brightened by filling in the bare spots with pansies or hardy annuals like ornamental cabbage. In many climates, these plants will bring color to your garden until the end of December. Buy them at a garden supply center or start your own from seed *(page 80)* in mid-summer and plant them outdoors in fall.

Use a winter mulch to protect these plants and any others that have evergreen foliage. The mulch helps maintain a stable ground temperature; without it, alternate freezing and thawing can cause roots to heave above the surface, where the cold dry air will quickly kill them.

*In a late-autumn bed where frost-killed annuals have been removed, foxgloves and newly transplanted pansies poke above a winter mulch of pine needles.*

## HOLDING GERANIUMS OVER WINTER

Dig up only a geranium that is disease- and insect-free. Moisten the soil at the base of the plant and use a spade to dig it up carefully *(right)*, leaving the major roots intact and keeping as much soil as possible around them. Pot the geranium *(page 542)*. Using clippers, remove any dead leaves and flowers and cut back about a third of the plant. Put the pot in a shady spot for a week, then bring it indoors and set it in a cool place out of direct sunlight. Mist the soil when it is dry. At winter's end, expose the plant gradually to direct sunlight and to the outdoors.

**1** Where pulling up an annual by the roots would disturb the roots of neighboring perennials or bulbs, remove a dead plant by cutting its stem off at the ground *(right)*. Gather the cut plants in bundles and throw them into your compost bin or discard them with the trash. The roots of the cut annuals will die in the ground.

**2** To protect the roots of a perennial or bulb during the winter months, mulch with straw, shredded leaves, pine needles or other readily available insulating material. Use no more than 2 to 3 inches of mulch; too thick a layer can harm plants by blocking the passage of air, sunlight and water. Work the mulch under the foliage, taking care not to bury it *(left)*. For more information on mulching, see page 70.

**3** If you live in a region where winter temperatures drop below 20° F, lay an extra cover of very thin mulch on top of the plants *(right)*. If your region has high winds, shelter the plants with small boughs cut from evergreens. For information on pruning boughs from an evergreen tree, see page 400; for information on shearing boughs from a hedge, see page 402. When spreading mulch or boughs on top of plants, particularly evergreens, make sure the protective cover is thin enough to permit air, sunlight and water to pass through.

191

# A CHECKLIST FOR ANNUALS

| | REGION 1 | REGION 2 | REGION 3 | REGION 4 | REGION 5 |
|---|---|---|---|---|---|
| **JANUARY/FEBRUARY** | • Study seed catalogs and order seeds<br>• Check germination requirements of seeds ordered (Check Dictionary of Annuals, pages 200-221)<br>• Plan and design flower beds and other uses for annuals, including window boxes and, for climbing annuals, trellises and fences<br>• Clean, sharpen and repair tools | • Study seed catalogs and order seeds<br>• Check germination requirements of seeds ordered (Check Dictionary of Annuals, pages 200-221)<br>• Plan and design flower beds and other uses for annuals, including window boxes and, for climbing annuals, trellises and fences<br>• Clean, sharpen and repair tools | • Study seed catalogs and order seeds<br>• Check germination requirements of seeds ordered (Check Dictionary of Annuals, pages 200-221)<br>• Plan and design flower beds and other uses for annuals, including window boxes and, for climbing annuals, trellises and fences<br>• Clean, sharpen and repair tools | • Study seed catalogs and order seeds<br>• Check germination requirements of seeds ordered (Check Dictionary of Annuals, pages 200-221)<br>• Plan and design flower beds and other uses for annuals, including window boxes and, for climbing annuals, trellises and fences<br>• Clean, sharpen and repair tools<br>• Start tender annual seeds indoors if they require 12 weeks or more to develop<br>• Start annual herb seeds indoors<br>• Accelerate warming of flower beds by spreading sheet of black plastic over them<br>• Start hardy annual seeds indoors for planting outdoors as soon as the soil can be worked | • Study seed catalogs and order seeds<br>• Check germination requirements of seeds ordered (Check Dictionary of Annuals, pages 200-221)<br>• Plan and design flower beds and other uses for annuals, including window boxes and, for climbing annuals, trellises and fences<br>• Clean, sharpen and repair tools<br>• Start tender annual seeds indoors if they require 10 weeks or more to develop<br>• Start annual herb seeds indoors<br>• Accelerate warming of flower beds by spreading sheet of black plastic over them<br>• Start hardy annual seeds indoors for planting outdoors as soon as the soil can be worked |
| **MARCH/APRIL** | • Start any seeds indoors<br>• Start dahlias indoors<br>• Start annual herb seeds indoors | • Start any seeds indoors<br>• Start dahlias indoors<br>• Start annual herb seeds indoors | • Start any seeds indoors<br>• Start dahlias indoors<br>• Start annual herb seeds indoors | • Start tender annual seeds indoors if they require 12 weeks or more to develop<br>• Start dahlias indoors<br>• Prepare and fertilize soil of flower beds as soon as ground can be worked<br>• Place hardy annuals in cold frame, then plant outdoors<br>• Sow hardy annual seeds outdoors<br>• Weed flower beds<br>• Thin seedlings<br>• Bring container plants indoors or mulch tender annuals if below average temperatures are forecast | • Start tender annual seeds indoors<br>• Start dahlias indoors<br>• Prepare and fertilize soil of flower beds as soon as ground can be worked<br>• Place hardy annuals in cold frame, then plant outdoors<br>• Sow annual seeds outdoors<br>• Weed flower beds<br>• Thin seedlings<br>• Bring container plants indoors or mulch tender annuals if below average temperatures are forecast |
| **MAY/JUNE** | • Prepare and fertilize soil of flower beds as soon as ground can be worked<br>• Place any annuals in cold frame, then plant outdoors<br>• Plant annuals in window boxes<br>• Weed and mulch flower beds<br>• Thin seedlings<br>• Water as necessary<br>• Combat pests and fungal diseases using organic means, applying insecticides and fungicides only if necessary | • Prepare and fertilize soil of flower beds as soon as ground can be worked<br>• Place any annuals in cold frame, then plant outdoors<br>• Plant annuals in window boxes<br>• Weed and mulch flower beds<br>• Thin seedlings<br>• Water as necessary<br>• Combat pests and fungal diseases using organic means, applying insecticides and fungicides only if necessary | • Prepare and fertilize soil of flower beds as soon as ground can be worked<br>• Place any annuals in cold frame, then plant outdoors<br>• Plant annuals in window boxes<br>• Weed and mulch flower beds<br>• Thin seedlings<br>• Water as necessary<br>• Combat pests and fungal diseases using organic means, applying insecticides and fungicides only if necessary | • Plant tender annuals outdoors<br>• Plant annuals in window boxes<br>• Sow tender annual seeds outdoors<br>• Weed flower beds<br>• Thin seedlings<br>• Water as necessary<br>• Place snail and slug bait and protect seedlings from birds<br>• Combat pests and fungal diseases using organic means, applying insecticides and fungicides only if necessary<br>• Train vines and climbing annuals<br>• Mulch flower beds | • Plant tender annuals outdoors<br>• Plant annuals in window boxes<br>• Sow tender annual seeds outdoors<br>• Weed flower beds<br>• Thin seedlings<br>• Water as necessary<br>• Place snail and slug bait and protect seedlings from birds<br>• Combat pests and fungal diseases using organic means, applying insecticides and fungicides only if necessary<br>• Train vines and climbing annuals<br>• Mulch flower beds |

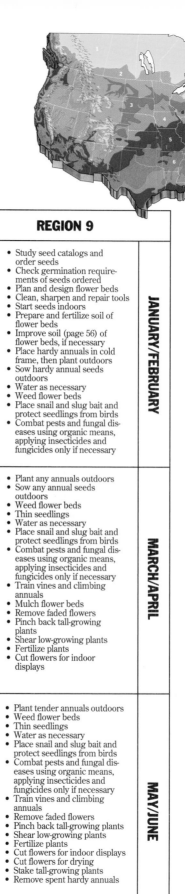

| REGION 6 | REGION 7 | REGION 8 | REGION 9 | |
|---|---|---|---|---|
| • Study seed catalogs and order seeds<br>• Check germination requirements of seeds ordered (Check Dictionary of Annuals, pages 200-221)<br>• Plan and design flower beds and other uses for annuals, including window boxes and, for climbing annuals, trellises and fences<br>• Clean, sharpen and repair tools<br>• Start any seeds indoors<br>• Accelerate warming of flower beds by spreading sheet of black plastic over them | • Study seed catalogs and order seeds<br>• Check germination requirements of seeds ordered (Check Dictionary of Annuals, pages 200-221)<br>• Plan and design flower beds and other uses for annuals, including window boxes and, for climbing annuals, trellises and fences<br>• Clean, sharpen and repair tools<br>• Start any seeds indoors<br>• Accelerate warming of flower beds by spreading sheet of black plastic over them<br>• Prepare and fertilize soil of flower beds as soon as ground can be worked<br>• Improve soil (page 56) of flower beds, if necessary | • Study seed catalogs and order seeds<br>• Check germination requirements of seeds ordered (Check Dictionary of Annuals, pages 200-221)<br>• Plan and design flower beds<br>• Clean, sharpen and repair tools<br>• Start seeds indoors<br>• Prepare and fertilize soil of flower beds<br>• Improve soil (page 56) of flower beds, if necessary<br>• Place hardy annual seedlings in cold frame, then plant outdoors<br>• Sow hardy annual seeds outdoors<br>• Water as necessary<br>• Weed flower beds<br>• Thin seedlings<br>• Place snail and slug bait and protect seedlings from birds | • Study seed catalogs and order seeds<br>• Check germination requirements of seeds ordered<br>• Plan and design flower beds<br>• Clean, sharpen and repair tools<br>• Start seeds indoors<br>• Prepare and fertilize soil of flower beds<br>• Improve soil (page 56) of flower beds, if necessary<br>• Place hardy annuals in cold frame, then plant outdoors<br>• Sow hardy annual seeds outdoors<br>• Water as necessary<br>• Weed flower beds<br>• Place snail and slug bait and protect seedlings from birds<br>• Combat pests and fungal diseases using organic means, applying insecticides and fungicides only if necessary | **JANUARY/FEBRUARY** |
| • Start dahlias indoors<br>• Prepare and fertilize soil of flower beds as soon as ground can be worked<br>• Place hardy and tender annuals in cold frame, then plant outdoors<br>• Sow any annual seeds outdoors<br>• Weed flower beds<br>• Thin seedlings<br>• Water as necessary<br>• Bring container plants indoors or mulch tender annuals if below average temperatures are forecast | • Start dahlias indoors<br>• Prepare and fertilize soil of flower beds as soon as ground can be worked<br>• Place hardy and tender annuals in cold frame, then plant outdoors<br>• Sow any annual seeds outdoors<br>• Weed flower beds<br>• Thin seedlings<br>• Water as necessary<br>• Place snail and slug bait and protect seedlings from birds<br>• Combat pests and fungal diseases using organic means, applying insecticides and fungicides only if necessary<br>• Train vines and climbing annuals | • Plant any annuals outdoors<br>• Sow any annual seeds outdoors<br>• Weed flower beds<br>• Thin seedlings<br>• Water as necessary<br>• Place snail and slug bait and protect seedlings from birds<br>• Combat pests and fungal diseases using organic means, applying insecticides and fungicides only if necessary<br>• Train vines and climbing annuals<br>• Mulch flower beds<br>• Remove faded flowers<br>• Pinch back tall-growing plants<br>• Shear low-growing plants<br>• Fertilize plants<br>• Cut flowers for indoor displays | • Plant any annuals outdoors<br>• Sow any annual seeds outdoors<br>• Weed flower beds<br>• Thin seedlings<br>• Water as necessary<br>• Place snail and slug bait and protect seedlings from birds<br>• Combat pests and fungal diseases using organic means, applying insecticides and fungicides only if necessary<br>• Train vines and climbing annuals<br>• Mulch flower beds<br>• Remove faded flowers<br>• Pinch back tall-growing plants<br>• Shear low-growing plants<br>• Fertilize plants<br>• Cut flowers for indoor displays | **MARCH/APRIL** |
| • Plant tender annuals outdoors<br>• Plant annuals in window boxes<br>• Sow tender annual seeds outdoors<br>• Weed flower beds<br>• Thin seedlings<br>• Water as necessary<br>• Place snail and slug bait and protect seedlings from birds<br>• Combat pests and fungal diseases using organic means, applying insecticides and fungicides only if necessary<br>• Train vines and climbing annuals<br>• Mulch flower beds<br>• Remove faded flowers<br>• Pinch back tall-growing plants<br>• Shear low-growing plants<br>• Fertilize plants | • Plant tender annuals outdoors<br>• Weed flower beds<br>• Thin seedlings<br>• Water as necessary<br>• Place snail and slug bait and protect seedlings from birds<br>• Combat pests and fungal diseases using organic means, applying insecticides and fungicides only if necessary<br>• Train vines and climbing annuals<br>• Mulch flower beds<br>• Remove faded flowers<br>• Pinch back tall-growing plants<br>• Shear low-growing plants<br>• Fertilize plants<br>• Cut flowers for indoor displays<br>• Cut flowers for drying | • Plant tender annuals outdoors<br>• Weed flower beds<br>• Thin seedlings<br>• Water as necessary<br>• Place snail and slug bait and protect seedlings from birds<br>• Combat pests and fungal diseases using organic means, applying insecticides and fungicides only if necessary<br>• Train vines and climbing annuals<br>• Remove faded flowers<br>• Pinch back tall-growing plants<br>• Shear low-growing plants<br>• Fertilize plants<br>• Cut flowers for indoor displays<br>• Cut flowers for drying<br>• Stake tall-growing plants<br>• Remove spent hardy annuals | • Plant tender annuals outdoors<br>• Weed flower beds<br>• Thin seedlings<br>• Water as necessary<br>• Place snail and slug bait and protect seedlings from birds<br>• Combat pests and fungal diseases using organic means, applying insecticides and fungicides only if necessary<br>• Train vines and climbing annuals<br>• Remove faded flowers<br>• Pinch back tall-growing plants<br>• Shear low-growing plants<br>• Fertilize plants<br>• Cut flowers for indoor displays<br>• Cut flowers for drying<br>• Stake tall-growing plants<br>• Remove spent hardy annuals | **MAY/JUNE** |

|  | REGION 1 | REGION 2 | REGION 3 | REGION 4 | REGION 5 |
|---|---|---|---|---|---|
| **JULY/AUGUST** | • Weed flower beds<br>• Water as necessary<br>• Combat pests and fungal diseases using organic means, applying insecticides and fungicides only if necessary<br>• Train vines and climbing annuals<br>• Remove faded flowers<br>• Pinch back tall-growing plants<br>• Shear low-growing plants<br>• Fertilize plants<br>• Cut flowers for indoor displays<br>• Cut flowers for drying<br>• Take cuttings to root indoors<br>• Stake tall-growing plants<br>• Deadhead flowers<br>• Collect seeds from selected flower heads | • Weed flower beds<br>• Water as necessary<br>• Combat pests and fungal diseases using organic means, applying insecticides and fungicides only if necessary<br>• Train vines and climbing annuals<br>• Remove faded flowers<br>• Pinch back tall-growing plants<br>• Shear low-growing plants<br>• Fertilize plants<br>• Cut flowers for indoor displays<br>• Cut flowers for drying<br>• Take cuttings to root indoors<br>• Stake tall-growing plants<br>• Deadhead flowers<br>• Collect seeds from selected flower heads | • Weed flower beds<br>• Water as necessary<br>• Combat pests and fungal diseases using organic means, applying insecticides and fungicides only if necessary<br>• Train vines and climbing annuals<br>• Remove faded flowers<br>• Pinch back tall-growing plants<br>• Shear low-growing plants<br>• Fertilize plants<br>• Cut flowers for indoor displays<br>• Cut flowers for drying<br>• Take cuttings to root indoors<br>• Stake tall-growing plants<br>• Deadhead flowers<br>• Collect seeds from selected flower heads<br>• Sow biennial seeds indoors or outdoors<br>• Plant biennals outdoors<br>• Thin biennial seedlings | • Weed flower beds<br>• Water as necessary<br>• Combat pests and fungal diseases using organic means, applying insecticides and fungicides only if necessary<br>• Train vines and climbing annuals<br>• Remove faded flowers<br>• Pinch back tall-growing plants<br>• Shear low-growing plants<br>• Fertilize plants<br>• Cut flowers for indoor displays<br>• Cut flowers for drying<br>• Take cuttings to root indoors<br>• Stake tall-growing plants<br>• Deadhead flowers<br>• Collect seeds from selected flower heads<br>• Sow biennial seeds indoors or outdoors<br>• Thin biennial seedlings | • Weed flower beds<br>• Water as necessary<br>• Combat pests and fungal diseases using organic means, applying insecticides and fungicides only if necessary<br>• Train vines and climbing annuals<br>• Remove faded flowers<br>• Pinch back tall-growing plants<br>• Shear low-growing plants<br>• Fertilize plants<br>• Cut flowers for indoor displays<br>• Cut flowers for drying<br>• Stake tall-growing plants<br>• Deadhead flowers<br>• Collect seeds from selected flower heads<br>• Sow hardy annual seeds indoors or outdoors<br>• Sow biennial seeds indoors or outdoors<br>• Thin biennial seedlings |
| **SEPTEMBER/OCTOBER** | • Remove annuals killed by frost<br>• Check and repair trellises and raised beds<br>• Dig up dahlias and store them<br>• Harvest tender herbs, or dig them up and store them<br>• Apply a phosphorus source to soil of flower beds<br>• Condition soil of flower beds using compost | • Water as necessary<br>• Cut flowers for indoor displays<br>• Cut flowers for drying<br>• Remove annuals killed by frost<br>• Check and repair trellises and raised beds<br>• Dig up dahlias and store them<br>• Harvest tender herbs, or dig them up and store them<br>• Apply a phosphorus source to soil of flower beds<br>• Condition soil of flower beds using compost<br>• Collect seeds from selected flower heads | • Weed flower beds<br>• Mulch biennials<br>• Water as necessary<br>• Cut flowers for indoor displays<br>• Cut flowers for drying<br>• Remove annuals killed by frost<br>• Check and repair trellises and raised beds<br>• Dig up dahlias and store them<br>• Harvest tender herbs, or dig them up and store them<br>• Apply a phosphorus source to soil of flower beds<br>• Condition soil of flower beds using compost<br>• Collect seeds from selected flower heads<br>• Fertilize plants with a slow-release fertilizer | • Weed flower beds<br>• Water as necessary<br>• Cut flowers for indoor displays<br>• Cut flowers for drying<br>• Remove faded flowers<br>• Remove annuals killed by frost<br>• Check and repair trellises and raised beds<br>• Dig up dahlias and store them<br>• Harvest tender herbs, or dig them up and store them<br>• Apply a phosphorus source to soil of flower beds<br>• Condition soil of flower beds using compost<br>• Collect seeds from selected flower heads<br>• Fertilize plants with a slow-release fertilizer<br>• Plant and mulch hardy biennials<br>• Plant ornamental kale and cabbage | • Weed flower beds<br>• Water as necessary<br>• Cut flowers for indoor displays<br>• Cut flowers for drying<br>• Remove faded flowers<br>• Take cuttings to root indoors<br>• Plant hardy annuals outdoors<br>• Plant biennials outdoors<br>• Harvest tender herbs, or dig them up and store them<br>• Apply a phosphorus source to soil of flower beds<br>• Condition soil of flower beds using compost<br>• Collect seeds from selected flower heads<br>• Fertilize plants with a slow-release fertilizer |
| **NOVEMBER/DECEMBER** | • Use dried flowers for holiday season decorations<br>• Consult gardening books for unfamiliar plant varieties or gardening techniques | • Use dried flowers for holiday season decorations<br>• Consult gardening books for unfamiliar plant varieties or gardening techniques | • Use dried flowers for holiday season decorations<br>• Consult gardening books for unfamiliar plant varieties or gardening techniques | • Use dried flowers for holiday season decorations<br>• Consult gardening books for unfamiliar plant varieties or gardening techniques | • Use dried flowers for holiday season decorations<br>• Consult gardening books for unfamiliar plant varieties or gardening techniques<br>• Remove annuals killed by frost<br>• Check and repair trellises and raised beds<br>• Dig up dahlias and store them<br>• Plant ornamental kale and cabbage<br>• Mulch hardy annuals, providing extra mulch covering if severe winter weather is forecast<br>• Mulch biennials |

194

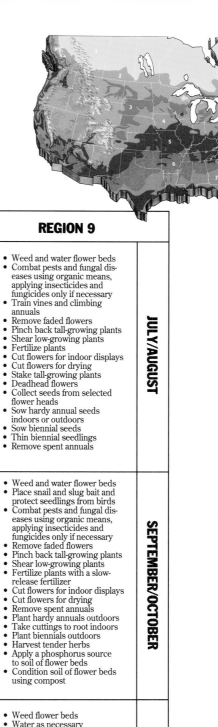

| | REGION 6 | REGION 7 | REGION 8 | REGION 9 | |
|---|---|---|---|---|---|
| | • Weed flower beds<br>• Water as necessary<br>• Combat pests and fungal diseases using organic means, applying insecticides and fungicides only if necessary<br>• Train vines and climbing annuals<br>• Remove faded flowers<br>• Pinch back tall-growing plants<br>• Shear low-growing plants<br>• Fertilize plants<br>• Cut flowers for indoor displays<br>• Cut flowers for drying<br>• Stake tall-growing plants<br>• Deadhead flowers<br>• Collect seeds from selected flower heads<br>• Sow hardy annual seeds indoors or outdoors<br>• Sow biennial seeds indoors or outdoors<br>• Thin biennial seedlings | • Weed flower beds<br>• Water as necessary<br>• Combat pests and fungal diseases using organic means, applying insecticides and fungicides only if necessary<br>• Train vines and climbing annuals<br>• Remove faded flowers<br>• Pinch back tall-growing plants<br>• Shear low-growing plants<br>• Fertilize plants<br>• Cut flowers for indoor displays<br>• Cut flowers for drying<br>• Stake tall-growing plants<br>• Deadhead flowers<br>• Collect seeds from selected flower heads<br>• Sow hardy annual seeds indoors or outdoors<br>• Sow biennial seeds<br>• Thin biennial seedlings<br>• Remove spent annuals | • Weed and water flower beds<br>• Combat pests and fungal diseases using organic means, applying insecticides and fungicides only if necessary<br>• Train vines and climbing annuals<br>• Remove faded flowers<br>• Pinch back tall-growing plants<br>• Shear low-growing plants<br>• Fertilize plants<br>• Cut flowers for indoor displays<br>• Cut flowers for drying<br>• Stake tall-growing plants<br>• Deadhead flowers<br>• Collect seeds from selected flower heads<br>• Sow hardy annual seeds indoors or outdoors<br>• Sow biennial seeds<br>• Thin biennial seedlings<br>• Remove spent annuals | • Weed and water flower beds<br>• Combat pests and fungal diseases using organic means, applying insecticides and fungicides only if necessary<br>• Train vines and climbing annuals<br>• Remove faded flowers<br>• Pinch back tall-growing plants<br>• Shear low-growing plants<br>• Fertilize plants<br>• Cut flowers for indoor displays<br>• Cut flowers for drying<br>• Stake tall-growing plants<br>• Deadhead flowers<br>• Collect seeds from selected flower heads<br>• Sow hardy annual seeds indoors or outdoors<br>• Sow biennial seeds<br>• Thin biennial seedlings<br>• Remove spent annuals | **JULY/AUGUST** |
| | • Weed flower beds<br>• Water as necessary<br>• Combat pests and fungal diseases using organic means, applying insecticides and fungicides only if necessary<br>• Cut flowers for indoor displays<br>• Cut flowers for drying<br>• Remove faded flowers<br>• Take cuttings to root indoors<br>• Plant hardy annuals outdoors<br>• Plant biennials outdoors<br>• Harvest tender herbs, or dig them up and store them<br>• Apply a phosphorus source to soil of flower beds<br>• Condition soil of flower beds using compost<br>• Collect seeds from selected flower heads<br>• Fertilize plants with a slow-release fertilizer | • Weed and water flower beds<br>• Place snail and slug bait and protect seedlings from birds<br>• Combat pests and fungal diseases using organic means, applying insecticides and fungicides only if necessary<br>• Remove faded flowers<br>• Pinch back tall-growing plants<br>• Shear low-growing plants<br>• Fertilize plants with a slow-release fertilizer<br>• Cut flowers for indoor displays<br>• Cut flowers for drying<br>• Remove spent annuals<br>• Plant hardy annuals outdoors<br>• Take cuttings to root indoors<br>• Plant biennials outdoors<br>• Harvest tender herbs<br>• Apply a phosphorus source to soil of flower beds<br>• Condition soil of flower beds using compost | • Weed and water flower beds<br>• Place snail and slug bait and protect seedlings from birds<br>• Combat pests and fungal diseases using organic means, applying insecticides and fungicides only if necessary<br>• Remove faded flowers<br>• Pinch back tall-growing plants<br>• Shear low-growing plants<br>• Fertilize plants with a slow-release fertilizer<br>• Cut flowers for indoor displays<br>• Cut flowers for drying<br>• Remove spent annuals<br>• Plant hardy annuals outdoors<br>• Take cuttings to root indoors<br>• Plant biennials outdoors<br>• Harvest tender herbs<br>• Apply a phosphorus source to soil of flower beds<br>• Condition soil of flower beds using compost | • Weed and water flower beds<br>• Place snail and slug bait and protect seedlings from birds<br>• Combat pests and fungal diseases using organic means, applying insecticides and fungicides only if necessary<br>• Remove faded flowers<br>• Pinch back tall-growing plants<br>• Shear low-growing plants<br>• Fertilize plants with a slow-release fertilizer<br>• Cut flowers for indoor displays<br>• Cut flowers for drying<br>• Remove spent annuals<br>• Plant hardy annuals outdoors<br>• Take cuttings to root indoors<br>• Plant biennials outdoors<br>• Harvest tender herbs<br>• Apply a phosphorus source to soil of flower beds<br>• Condition soil of flower beds using compost | **SEPTEMBER/OCTOBER** |
| | • Use dried flowers for holiday season decorations<br>• Consult gardening books for unfamiliar plant varieties or gardening techniques<br>• Remove annuals killed by frost<br>• Check and repair trellises and raised beds<br>• Dig up dahlias and store them<br>• Plant ornamental kale and cabbage<br>• Mulch hardy annuals, providing extra mulch covering if severe winter weather is forecast<br>• Mulch biennials | • Take cuttings to root indoors<br>• Use dried flowers for holiday season decorations<br>• Consult gardening books for unfamiliar plant varieties or gardening techniques<br>• Remove annuals killed by frost<br>• Check and repair trellises and raised beds<br>• Dig up dahlias and store them<br>• Plant ornamental kale and cabbage<br>• Mulch hardy annuals, providing extra mulch covering if severe winter weather is forecast<br>• Mulch biennials<br>• Study seed catalogs and order seeds<br>• Check germination requirements of seeds ordered | • Take cuttings to root indoors<br>• Use dried flowers for holiday season decorations<br>• Consult gardening books for unfamiliar plant varieties or gardening techniques<br>• Remove annuals killed by frost<br>• Check and repair trellises and raised beds<br>• Dig up dahlias and store them<br>• Plant ornamental kale and cabbage<br>• Mulch hardy annuals, providing extra mulch covering if severe winter weather is forecast<br>• Mulch biennials<br>• Study seed catalogs and order seeds<br>• Check germination requirements of seeds ordered<br>• Start any seeds indoors | • Weed flower beds<br>• Water as necessary<br>• Place snail and slug bait and protect seedlings from birds<br>• Combat pests and fungal diseases using organic means, applying insecticides and fungicides only if necessary<br>• Fertilize plants<br>• Remove spent annuals<br>• Check and repair trellises and raised beds<br>• Dig up dahlias and store them<br>• Take cuttings to root indoors<br>• Mulch hardy annuals<br>• Mulch biennials<br>• Study seed catalogs and order seeds<br>• Check germination requirements of seeds ordered<br>• Start any seeds indoors<br>• Prepare and fertilize soil of flower beds for spring | **NOVEMBER/DECEMBER** |

195

# TROUBLESHOOTING GUIDE: ANNUALS

| PROBLEM | CAUSE | SOLUTION |
|---|---|---|
| Dark brown blotches appear on the leaves of calendula, chrysanthemum, geranium, heliotrope, lobelia, pansy and zinnia. Foliage eventually yellows, dies and falls off the plant. | Leaf spot disease, which is caused by various fungi. The fungi, which thrive in cool, moist conditions, are spread by wind and water. | Remove and destroy all infected leaves. Thin plants to increase air circulation. Water plants in the morning; damp soil and cool night air foster the spread of the disease. Several fungicides will prevent leaf spot, but they will not cure infected plants. Another method of preventing leaf spot is to plant only seeds that are disease-free; soak them in hot water for 30 minutes before sowing. |
| Seedlings suddenly topple over and die. Any annual is susceptible, but annual phlox, salvia and sweet alyssum are especially prone. | Damping-off, a disease caused by fungi that live in the soil and attack roots and stems. A weblike growth on the soil surface confirms the diagnosis. Using unsterile or poorly draining soil, or overwatering soil can contribute to the disease. | Before sowing seeds indoors, drench the flats with an approved fungicide. Use a sterile, soilless planting medium. Do not overwater seedlings. Ensure that the germination area has adequate air circulation. Plant only in garden soil that has good drainage. |
| Orange or brown powdery spots develop primarily on the undersides of leaves. Leaves may wilt; plant growth may be stunted. Susceptible annuals include carnation, chrysanthemum, cornflower, lobelia, morning glory, primula, snapdragon and viola. | Rust, a disease caused by a fungus that thrives when days are hot and humid and nights are cool. | Remove and destroy infected plants. Water only in the morning to prevent spreading the disease. Sulfur and a number of approved fungicides will help control the disease. When staking plants, use new stakes each year. Rust-resistant varieties of snapdragon are available. |
| Color fades from African daisy, forget-me-not, geranium, pansy, sweet pea and other annuals. Plants may be stunted and may wilt. Roots are damp, soft and discolored. | Root rot, caused by one of several fungi that thrive in heavy wet soil. | Remove and discard infected plants, and flush the soil with an approved fungicide. Plant in a raised bed or only in well-drained soil; improve soil and drainage, if necessary. |
| Leaves, stems and flower buds are coated with a fine, white powder. Plants and flowers may be distorted in shape. Annual phlox, dahlia, fuchsia, spider flower, sweet pea, verbena and zinnia are particularly susceptible. | Powdery mildew, a disease caused by a fungus. The fungus is spread by wind and water, and it thrives in both hot, dry weather and periods of high humidity. | Remove and destroy infected plant parts. Sulfur-based fungicides can both prevent the disease and eliminate it on infected plants. Plants should not be crowded; good air circulation reduces the spread of the disease. Avoid overwatering plants. To avoid spreading the disease from infected to healthy plants, do not water plants from above. Mildew-resistant varieties of zinnia are available. |

| PROBLEM | CAUSE | SOLUTION |
|---|---|---|
| Tips, leaves and the centers of carnation, dahlia, forget-me-not, fuchsia, geranium, heliotrope, lobelia, petunia, snapdragon and strawflower turn black or brown, often accompanied by a fuzzy, gray growth. The problem occurs most often in cool, damp conditions. | Botrytis blight, also called gray mold, a disease caused by the fungus *Botrytis cinerea*. | Cut away any infected plant parts and destroy them. A number of approved fungicides can control the disease. Provide good air circulation and avoid overhead watering; use drip irrigation or a soaker hose. Water in the morning to allow daytime heat to dry foliage quickly. |
| Foliage turns yellow, plants may be stunted and new growth is distorted. Flower buds may not open or may be deformed. Chrysanthemum, cosmos, kochia and marigold can be affected. | Aster yellows, a disease caused by mycoplasmas, organisms similar to bacteria. The mycoplasmas are spread by leafhoppers. | Remove and destroy infected plants. To control aster yellows, leafhoppers must be controlled with an organic spray or an approved insecticide. Keep the garden weeded to deter leafhoppers. |
| Yellow or brown streaks and spots or mottling develop on the foliage of calendula, chrysanthemum, coleus, cosmos, dahlia, forget-me-not, geranium, marigold or petunia. Plant may be stunted. | A virus infection. There are several different virus infections, including the common mosaic virus. Infections can be unsightly, but they usually cause little damage to plants and may subside by themselves. | Remove damaged plant parts, using a clean tool. To avoid spreading infection from diseased to healthy plants, avoid handling plants when they are wet. There are no chemical products for viruses, but they can be spread by aphids, which should be controlled by applying an approved chemical insecticide or insecticidal soap. Keep the garden weeded to deter viruses. |
| Wilting occurs in Cape marigold, chrysanthemum, coleus, cosmos, dahlia, impatiens, lobelia, marigold, nasturtium and pansy; plants stop growing and eventually die. A cross section of a stem will show dark brown spots or streaks. | Wilt, a disease caused by soil-dwelling fungi or bacteria that penetrate plants through the roots or the base of the stem and clog plant tissue, restricting the plant's ability to take up water. | Remove infected plants and destroy them, using a clean tool. In replanting, choose wilt-resistant varieties. There are no chemical preventatives or controls for wilt. If the soil is heavily infested and the problem recurs, the soil may need professional fumigation. |
| Irregular dark brown, red or black spots appear on the leaves and stems of foxglove, pansy, primula, snapdragon and viola. | Anthracnose, a disease caused by a fungus that thrives in warm, wet weather. | Remove and discard any infected plant parts; to avoid spreading infection from diseased to healthy plants, avoid handling plants when they are wet. Spray remaining plants with a recommended fungicide or lime sulfur when the temperature is below 85° F. |
| Upper surfaces of leaves have yellowish flecks or streaks of a bleached, whitish color. Leaf edges may curl. | Air pollution and smog. | There are no controls for pollution. Provide good air circulation. In high heat and humidity, provide shade for plants; these conditions, combined with intense sunlight, cause leaf pores to open, making them more susceptible to pollutants. If you live in a smoggy area, plant varieties that are resistant to smog and pollution. |

197

| PROBLEM | CAUSE | SOLUTION |
|---|---|---|
| Leaves curl, wither and may turn yellow. Flowers may be distorted in shape. A shiny substance appears along stems and leaves. If roots are attacked, plant growth is stunted and leaves wilt and discolor. Many annuals are susceptible. | Aphids, also called plant lice, ⅛-inch-long, semitransparent insects found in colonies along buds and stems. They may attack roots. Aphids secrete a sticky, shiny substance that attracts ants. | Aphids can be knocked off plants with a strong stream of water. Control them by dusting diatomaceous earth on plants or hanging yellow sticky traps. If infestation is severe, apply an approved chemical insecticide or insecticidal soap. Control root-attacking aphids using a recommended insecticide; ladybugs and green lacewings are natural predators. Try planting nasturtium and petunia to help deter aphids. |
| Foliage turns yellow on African daisy, browallia, lobelia, marigold, salvia and strawflower. Plants may be stunted or deformed. | Leafhoppers, gray or green, wedge-shaped, winged insects up to ⅕ inch long. | Leafhoppers spread disease and should be controlled with an organic spray or an approved insecticide. Heavy sprays of water will knock them off plants but may not kill them. Keeping the garden area clean may help to keep them away. Try planting geranium and petunia to help deter leafhoppers. |
| Oblong or irregular-shaped holes appear in leaves and flowers. Eventually, plants may be stripped of all foliage. Many annuals, including balsam, nicotiana, phlox and zinnia are susceptible. | Any of several beetles, including Colorado potato, cucumber and Japanese, which are ¼- to ½-inch insects with hard shells. They can spend the winter in the soil and move upward as conditions warm up. | Beetles can be hand-picked and destroyed. The easiest way to control beetles is to destroy their larvae with milky spore, a bacterium fatal to beetles but harmless to plants and other animals. Plants may be sprayed with an approved insecticide. Turn the soil in the fall to expose grubs to predatory birds. Try planting geranium, marigold, nasturtium or petunia to help deter beetles. |
| Leaf surfaces have colorless areas with light green or brown tunnels. Castor bean, chrysanthemum, dahlia, morning glory, nasturtium and verbena can be affected. | Leaf miners, flies that lay their eggs on the leaves; when the eggs hatch, the larvae tunnel into the leaves. | Cut off and destroy infested leaves. Keep the garden well weeded; flies lay eggs in weedy areas. Leaf miner eggs, or the insects themselves, can be crushed between the fingers. If the problem persists, use an approved insecticide. |
| Plants suddenly lose their color and wilt. Roots are damaged or deformed and have knots and swellings. African daisy, chrysanthemum, cornflower, statice and sweet pea can be affected. | Nematodes, microscopic worms that live in the soil and attack plant roots. Since they cannot be seen, only a soil test can confirm their presence. | Remove and destroy affected plants. Large plantings of marigold will kill nematodes. Make liberal use of compost and organic matter in flower beds. Do not plant susceptible annuals in an area that has been infested within the past three years. If the problem persists, professional soil treatment may be needed. |
| Leaves of many annuals turn yellow or reddish and their surface becomes dull. Foliage may curl and wither. Tiny black specks are visible on the undersides of foliage. Eventually, webs will appear on plants. | Spider mites, tiny pests that suck the juice from leaves. | Keep plants well watered; mites thrive in hot, dry conditions. To avoid spreading infection, avoid handling healthy plants after handling diseased ones. A heavy spray of water can knock mites off plants. They can be controlled with an approved miticide or an insecticidal soap. Ladybugs are natural predators. |

| PROBLEM | CAUSE | SOLUTION |
| --- | --- | --- |
| Leaves of chrysanthemum, gaillardia, mignonette and pansy develop small patches of white, yellow or brown around the edges, curl up, then wither and die. Flower buds are discolored and may not open; if they do open, the petals will have brown edges. | Thrips, slender winged insects just visible to the eye, resembling tiny gnats. Thrips scrape holes in leaves and suck the juice from them. | Remove infected flower buds and plant tips; remove severely infested plants altogether. Spray remaining plants with an approved chemical insecticide or an insecticidal soap. Keep plants well watered; thrips can be knocked off plants with a strong stream of water. Green lacewings are natural predators. |
| Entire plants, especially calendula and coleus, become discolored. When a plant is shaken, a cloud of white specks appears. | Whitefly, a white, $1/16$-inch insect that collects in colonies on the undersides of leaves. Whiteflies suck the juice from leaves, secreting a substance on foliage that attracts certain fungus diseases. | Whitefly may be controlled with insecticidal soap, an organic spray or approved chemical insecticide. Whitefly is attracted to the color yellow; hang yellow flypaper or sticky traps. Check for signs of whitefly before buying plants. Green lacewings and ladybugs are natural predators. Try planting marigold or nasturtium to help deter whitefly. |
| Large holes are eaten in the foliage of coleus, forget-me-not, geranium, hibiscus, marigold, nicotiana, pansy and petunia. Entire young seedlings may be eaten. Shiny silver streaks appear on plants and garden paths. | Slugs (shell-less snails) and snails, gray, black, brown or yellow pests up to 3 inches long. They feed at night, especially in cool and damp conditions. They can spend the winter in the soil. | Bait can be purchased and applied at dusk; it will need to be reapplied after rain or watering. Shallow saucers of beer or inverted grapefruit halves will trap slugs and snails. They can also be picked up by hand, especially at night. Control them by dusting diatomaceous earth around plants. |
| The upper leaf surfaces of balsam, calendula, dahlia, gaillardia, marigold, snapdragon and zinnia become spotted. Foliage may lose color, wilt and fall from the plant. Flower buds may be deformed. | Plant bugs, also called true bugs, orange, green or black insects $1/4$ inch long that suck plant juices. | Spray with soapy water or use an organic spray or an approved chemical insecticide. |
| Light green oval spots and white patches resembling cotton appear on leaves and stems of hibiscus and impatiens. Plants become discolored and may wilt. | Scale, a $1/8$- to $1/4$-inch insect with an oval shell. The white patches are egg sacs. | Scale can be controlled with insecticidal soap or an approved chemical insecticide. |
| Leaves are eaten and entire plants may be stripped, primarily in late spring. Castor bean, heliotrope, mignonette, ornamental kale and verbena are the most susceptible annuals. | Any number of caterpillars. | *Bacillus thuringiensis*, called Bt, a bacterium that kills caterpillars but does not harm plants or other animals. If caterpillars return to your garden every spring, Bt can be sprayed in anticipation of the problem. |
| A white, foamy substance appears between leaves and stems. | Spittlebugs. When their eggs hatch, the young green insects produce the foam for protection while they feed on leaves and stems. | Wash bugs off plants with a heavy spray of water. If infestation is severe, spray with an approved insecticide. |

AGERATUM HOUSTONIANUM

# DICTIONARY OF ANNUALS

### Introduction

The dictionary entries that follow describe some of the hardiest and most beautiful annuals available to gardeners as well as some biennials and perennials that behave like annuals in North America—germinating, blooming, producing seeds and dying in one year only. All plants are listed by their botanical names; common names are cross-referenced. Each entry contains a broad description of the genus, a more detailed description of one or more selected species and varieties, and useful information about growing conditions—whether the plant does best in sun or shade, and what kind of soil it requires.

**African daisy** see *Arctotis; Lonas*

### Ageratum (ah-jer-AY-tum)
Ageratum, floss flower

A group of 30 species, most with oval-shaped leaves and scalloped edges, and tiny, compact flowers. One species is among the most popular of all edging plants.

**Selected species and varieties.** *A. houstonianum:* bears fluffy, powder-puff-like flower heads, primarily purplish-blue but sometimes pink or white; plants are mounded, short and compact with heart-shaped leaves.

**Growing conditions.** For best results, grow ageratums by setting plants into the garden, using either purchased bedding plants or seedlings you have grown indoors. Start seeds six to eight weeks before the outdoor planting date and do not cover them; they need light during their five- to 10-day germination. Space plants 6 to 8 inches apart in a warm location, in full sun or light shade. Where summers are long and hot, ageratums grow best in light shade. They dislike excessive heat and humidity; in the South and in hot areas of the West they make better plants for spring and fall than for summer. Ageratums are not fussy about soil, but will perform best if soil is rich, moist and well drained. Water when the ground starts to become dry. Fertilize with 5-10-5 at planting time and again monthly. Ageratums are low-maintenance plants; their flowers fall cleanly as they fade. If plants become leggy, shear them back.

ANTIRRHINUM MAJUS

ARCTOTIS HYBRID

### Antirrhinum (an-ti-RY-num)
Snapdragon

A perennial often grown as an annual, valued for its showy flowers in shades of red, bronze, pink, white, rose, yellow, scarlet, primrose, apricot, orange, crimson, magenta, or lilac. Snapdragons do best in borders, beds and rock gardens, and make exquisite and long-lasting cut flowers.

**Selected species and varieties.** *A. majus:* blooms have a light, spicy fragrance and appear on showy, erect spikes over dark, straplike foliage. When snapdragon was so named, its pouch-shaped, two-lipped flowers resembled the jaws of a dragon ready to snap. Today, however, the traditional snapdragons have been joined by cultivars with open-faced trumpet-like ruffle-edged blooms as well as some with fully double flowers.

**Growing conditions.** In midspring, when the soil has begun warming up, snapdragon seeds may be sown where plants are to bloom. However, for best results, sow indoors six to eight weeks before the outside planting date. Do not cover seeds, as they need light for germination, which takes 10 to 14 days. Snapdragon seedlings and bedding plants tolerate light frosts, so they can be set into the garden about four weeks before the last expected frost. Plant them in full sun or light shade, spacing them 6 to 15 inches apart, depending on their ultimate height. Avoid overcrowding, which invites disease. Soil should be light, rich in organic matter and well drained. Fertilize with 5-10-5 before planting and repeat monthly; water when ground starts to dry out. Pinch young plants to induce branching and more abundant flowers. To encourage reblooming, cut off faded flower spikes.

### Arctotis (ark-TOE-tis)
African daisy

A daisy-family member native to South Africa; has toothed or deeply cut basal leaves and bears flower heads on long, leafless stalks. Used in beds and borders.

**Selected species and varieties.** *A.* hybrids: yellow, white, pink, bronze, red, purple, brown and orange flowers on plants 10 to 12 inches tall.

**Growing conditions.** Seeds can be sown outdoors in early spring as soon as the soil can be worked, but for best results, sow them indoors six to eight weeks before the last frost and set seedlings outside just after last frost. Germination takes 21 to 35 days. Space plants 12 inches apart in full sun. African daisies do best in poor, dry, sandy soil, so avoid overwatering and fertilize little, if at all. They also prefer cool nights. In hot areas, therefore, grow them in spring or fall; in coastal areas and at high elevations, grow them in summer. To prolong flowering and improve appearance, keep faded blooms removed.

### Asarina (ass-ah-REE-nah)

A genus of vine that can quickly grow to 10 feet. Generally has soft, hairy triangular leaves and trumpet-shaped flowers resembling those of snapdragons. May be grown on trellises, in hanging baskets or other containers, or as annual ground covers.

**Selected species and varieties.** *A. barclaiana:* bears pink 1 ¼-inch flowers that fade to purple as they age. *A. erubescens,* creeping gloxinia: produces 3-inch rose to pink flowers. *A. procumbens:* pale pink 1 ½-inch flowers. *A. scandens:* 2-inch lavender blooms.

**Growing conditions.** Seeds may be started indoors 10 or 12 weeks before planting outdoors; germination takes 10 to 15 days. Stem cuttings may be taken at the end of the summer and overwintered in a cold frame or a greenhouse. Plant seedlings or rooted cuttings in the garden several weeks before the last frost. Grow in full sun and a rich, well-drained soil. Fertilize with 5-10-5 at planting time and again during the growing season; keep well watered.

### Bachelor's button see *Centaurea*
### Balsam see *Impatiens*
### Basket flower see *Centaurea*

### Begonia (be-GON-ee-ah)

More than 1,000 species of plants have single or double flowers of white, pink, rose or red. Many are spectacular in beds, in edgings, in containers and can be grown indoors as well.

**Selected species and varieties.** *B.* x *semperflorens-cultorum,* wax begonia: flowers appear continuously over waxy green, bronze, brown or variegated foliage. Plants grow 6 to 12 inches high and 4 to 8 inches wide, and many varieties are heat- and sun-tolerant. Avalanche series cultivars are specifically bred for hanging baskets and for use as ground covers; they are sun- and heat-tolerant. Cocktail series cultivars, 6 to 8 inches tall, have bronze leaves, large blooms and good heat tolerance. Double Ruffles series cultivars produce fluffy ball-like red, pink or white flowers on 12-inch plants with green foliage. These cultivars are heat-resistant. Party series cultivars have large, 2-inch flowers with good weather tolerance. Pizzazz series cultivars have medium-sized red, white or pink flowers and green leaves on 10-inch plants. These heat-resistant cultivars can be grown in sun or shade. Prelude series cultivars, green-leaved and early-blooming, are uniform 6-inch plants with small flowers of white, pink, rose and scarlet. These cultivars are very rain-tolerant.

**Growing conditions.** Wax begonias can be propagated from seeds started indoors 12 to 16 weeks before they are planted outside after the last frost. Bedding plants are also readily available in spring. Space plants 6 to 8 inches apart. Begonias prefer partial shade, but can be set in full sun if temperature does not exceed 90° F. In hot areas, select bronze-leaved wax begonias over the green-leaved forms for their greater heat resistance. Soil should be very rich and well drained; wax begonias will tolerate a somewhat dry soil. Fertilize with 5-10-5 before planting and again monthly.

### Bellflower see Dictionary of Perennials, page 246
### Black-eyed Susan vine see *Thunbergia*
### Blanket flower see *Gaillardia*
### Bloodleaf see *Iresine*
### Blueweed see *Echium*

### Brassica (BRASS-ih-kah)

A genus that includes the vegetables cabbage, kale, broccoli, mustard greens and cauliflower.

**Selected species and varieties.** *B. oleracea* (Acephala Group), ornamental cabbage, ornamental kale: open rosettes of green leaves with centers of white, pink or purple. Plants measure 12 to 15 inches across and 10 to 12 inches high. They are most unusual and decorative bedding plants, used primarily for their foliage in the fall and winter.

**Growing conditions.** Ornamental cabbage and kale are most often used in the garden in fall and winter, because they need cool temperatures to grow. Sow seeds indoors in late

ASARINA ERUBESCENS

BEGONIA × SEMPERFLORENS-CULTORUM

BRASSICA OLERACEA (ACEPHALA GROUP)

BROWALLIA SPECIOSA 'BLUE BELLS'

CALENDULA OFFICINALIS

CENTAUREA CYANUS

summer, six to eight weeks before the first expected fall frost. The seeds of ornamental cabbage must be chilled for three days in the refrigerator before sowing and then left uncovered, as they need light to germinate. Ornamental kale needs neither light nor chilling. Seeds germinate in 10 to 14 days. Set the seedlings into the ground about one month before the first expected fall frost, spacing them 12 to 15 inches apart in full sun, in a soil rich in organic matter. Fertilize with 5-10-5 before planting and once a month after that, and keep the soil moist. The foliage begins to turn color when temperatures reach 50° F, and color is intensified by frost. In areas where temperatures do not drop below 20° F, plants will last all winter. Some say that ornamental kale is edible, but it tastes very bitter.

## Browallia (bro-WAL-ee-ah)
Browallia, bush violet

Browallias are grown for their abundant 2-inch flowers—starlike, bell-shaped blossoms that are velvety in texture and come in purple, blue or white. Stems grow from 8 to 18 inches long. Browallia is a good choice as a bedding plant in a shaded area, but it is spectacular as a container plant on a patio or a deck; it fills out its container and cascades over the sides.

**Selected species and varieties.** *B. speciosa* 'Major,' sapphire flower: the most common garden browallia. From this cultivar the Bells series cultivars were produced, with stems that trail 10 to 12 inches from the center of the plant. The mix of all available cultivars is called 'Jingle Bells'; individual members of the series include 'Blue Bells' (amethyst).

**Growing conditions.** Sow seeds indoors six to eight weeks before frost danger has passed. Seeds should not be covered as they need light for their 14- to 21-day germination period. Transplant seedlings or purchased bedding plants into the garden when night temperatures will not drop below 65° F. Space plants 6 to 10 inches apart in part shade in a rich, well-drained soil. Fertilize with 5-10-5 before planting. Mulch to keep soil moist and cool.

**Bugloss** see *Echium*
**Burning bush** see *Kochia*
**Bush violet** see *Browallia*

## Calendula (kah-LEN-du-lah)

A genus from the Mediterranean having large flower heads with rays of yellow, orange or cream.

**Selected species and varieties.** *C. officinalis*, pot marigold: grown for its bright orange or yellow blooms, which make a conspicuous display in pots and in massed plantings; sometimes used as an ingredient of teas and a colorful garnish on food. The crisp, 3- to 4-inch flower heads, on fuzzy stems, are either single or double and daisy-like or chrysanthemum-like. Bon Bon series has large, 2 ½- to 3-inch flowers on compact, 10-inch early-blooming plants. Available in orange or yellow or a mix of these colors with apricot.

**Growing conditions.** Sow seeds indoors four to six weeks before the last expected frost. Seeds may also be sown outdoors where plants are to grow, in midspring—about four weeks before the last frost. Germination takes 10 to 14 days. Move hardened seedlings or purchased bedding plants to the garden two weeks before the last frost. Space them 12 to 15 inches apart. As calendula does best where temperatures remain below 80° F, it is used as a spring or fall plant in hot climates, and as a summer plant where summers are cool. It prefers full sun but will grow in light shade. Soil should be rich in organic matter, fertilized with 5-10-5 before planting and kept well watered. Cut off flowers as they fade. Note: if you use calendula in tea or as a garnish for food, avoid spraying your garden with any pesticide not recommended for vegetables.

**Calliopsis** see *Coreopsis*
**Canary bird flower** see *Tropaeolum*
**Candytuft** see Dictionary of Grasses and Ground Covers page 160
**Campanula** see Dictionary of Perennials, page 246
**Cape marigold** see *Dimorphotheca*
**Cardinal climber** see *Ipomoea*
**Carnation** see *Dianthus*
**Castor bean** see *Ricinus*
**Cathedral bells** see *Cobaea*

## Centaurea (sen-TAW-ree-ah)

These popular garden plants produce double, frilly, ruffled or tufted blooms, primarily blue but also in shades of pink, rose, lavender, yellow and white. Blooms are borne atop wiry stems with long, thin foliage. Centaureas work well in a border, and they provide both long-lasting cut flowers and excellent dried flowers.

**Selected species and varieties.** *C. cyanus,* cornflower, bachelor's button: grows up to 36 inches tall with 1 ½-inch blooms that are usually blue, sometimes purple or pink.

**Growing conditions.** Cornflower is very hardy and will withstand frost, so seeds or well-hardened plants may be put into the garden in midspring as soon as the soil can be worked. For earlier bloom, start seeds indoors four weeks before the outdoor planting date. Germination will take seven to 14 days, and seeds must be completely covered because they require darkness to germinate. Where winters are mild, seeds can be sown in autumn for early-spring bloom. Cornflowers are not long-blooming plants; for a continuous supply of color, sow seeds every two weeks through spring and summer. To prolong blooming, remove spent flowers.

## Cheiranthus (kae-RAN-thus)
Wallflower

Fragrant flowers borne in clusters on bushy 12- to 30-inch plants. Leaves are narrow and bright green.

**Selected species and varieties.** *C. cheiri,* English wallflower: yellow, orange or mahogany-colored 1-inch blooms borne in erect, showy clusters. Wallflower is a perennial, but does not tolerate heat and can survive only in areas—such as the Pacific Northwest—with cool, moist summers; elsewhere it is treated as an annual. Used in beds, borders and rock gardens.

**Growing conditions.** Sow seeds indoors in midwinter, six to eight weeks before transplanting outdoors. Germinate wallflowers at a cool (60° F) temperature; seedlings will appear five to seven days after sowing. Hardened seedlings or purchased bedding plants may be set in the garden in early spring as soon as soil can be worked. Where winter temperatures do not drop below 20° F, seeds may also be sown in late summer for bloom the following spring; move plants into place two months before the first fall frost. Space plants 12 to 15 inches apart in full sun or light shade in an average, well-drained soil, and use a protective mulch against possible frost damage. Fertilize with 5-10-5 before planting. Keep the soil well watered and mulched.

## Chrysanthemum
(krih-SAN-the-mum)

Chrysanthemums are among the most popular garden plants. Although the fall-blooming perennial is probably best-known, it has many annual relatives that can brighten the summer border. These colorful plants have single or double daisy-like blooms in all colors except blue and purple. The flowers range from large and showy to diminutive and button-like; foliage is generally divided and strong-smelling. One species is grown not for its flower heads but instead for its silver-gray foliage.

**Selected species and varieties.** *C. frutescens,* white marguerite, Paris daisy: a bushy, 3-foot plant with lacy gray-green leaves and 2-inch white or pale yellow flowers with dark yellow centers. A tender perennial that can be grown as an annual.

**Growing conditions.** Annual chrysanthemums do best where summers are mild and moist, through they will tolerate moderate heat and drought. Sow seeds or most species outdoors after all danger of frost has passed, or indoors eight to 10 weeks before the last frost date. Germination takes eight to 18 days, depending on species. Annual chrysanthemums are also generally available in spring as bedding plants, which can be set in the garden after all danger of frost is past. Set plants 4 to 18 inches apart, depending on the ultimate size of the species, in full sun and a well-drained, average soil. Fertilize at planting time and again every month during the growing season. To ensure continuous bloom, pick flowers as they fade.

## Cigar flower see *Cuphea*

## Cleome (klee-OH-me)

More than 300 species of tropical plants, only one of which is useful to the gardener.

**Selected species and varieties.** *C. hasslerana,* spider flower: strong-scented white, rose, pink or lavender florets; the protruding clusters of 2- to 3-inch stamens look somewhat spidery. Seedpods are conspicuously long and slim. Spider flower is perfect for the back of a border, where its waving 3- to 6-foot stems are most attractive.

**Growing conditions.** Sow seeds where plants are to grow after all danger of frost has passed, or sow them

CHEIRANTHUS CHEIRI

CHRYSANTHEMUM FRUTESCENS

CLEOME HASSLERANA

COBAEA SCANDENS

COLEUS × HYBRIDUS

CONSOLIDA AMBIGUA

indoors four to six weeks before last frost. Germination will take 10 to 14 days. Space plants 2 to 3 feet apart in a warm spot with full sun and average soil. They will withstand high summer heat and are very drought-resistant. Feed very lightly, if at all, and do not overwater. In the South, spider flower will reseed itself from year to year.

## Cobaea (koe-BEE-ah)

A tropical climbing vine that has showy flowers.

**Selected species and varieties.** *C. scandens,* cup-and-saucer vine, Mexican ivy, monastery bells: has 2-inch cup-shaped flowers that open a pale green and darken to purple as they mature. Foliage is dark green. 'Alba': a cultivar with white flowers. Cup-and-saucer vine, a very fast-growing plant, can reach 20 feet in a year and is very suitable for use on screens and trellises. In frost-free areas it is a perennial, but it can be grown in the North as an annual.

**Growing conditions.** Start seeds indoors in pots six to eight weeks before the last frost date. Set the large, flat seeds on edge, barely covering the top edges with soil. Germination takes 15 to 20 days. After all danger of frost is past, transplant to a location with full sun or light shade, a rich, moist, well-drained soil and a support on which the vine will climb. Cup-and-saucer vine tolerates wind; in areas with hot summers, however, it prefers after-noon shade.

## Coleus (KO-lee-us)

A popular, shade-loving plant grown for its striking foliage. Use coleus in shady beds, borders or containers.

**Selected species and varieties.** *C.* x *hybridus;* foliage is edged, blotched or patterned in splashy combinations or green, chartreuse, white, gold, bronze, scarlet, ivory, orange, rose, copper, yellow and purple. Leaf edges may be lacy, smooth, fringed wavy or toothed. Dragon series cultivars bear large heart-shaped serrated leaves on 12-inch plants that have a ridged texture and an exotic look. Saber series cultivars have lobed, sword-shaped leaves that cascade and look well in hanging baskets.

**Growing conditions.** Either purchase bedding plants or start seeds indoors six to eight weeks before the last frost date. When sowing, do not cover seeds; they need light for germination, which takes 10 to 15 days. Coleus can also be propagated by stem cuttings. Take cuttings in fall before the first frost or in spring from plants over-wintered indoors. Move plants to the garden after all danger of frost has passed. Coleus prefers partial to deep shade and should be spaced 10 to 12 inches apart. Plants will survive in full sun if they are adequately watered, but foliage color will fade. Soil should be rich in organic matter, and kept moist. Fertilize with 5-10-5 before planting and repeat during the season. Flowers may be left on the plants as they form, but removing them will help maintain bright foliage color.

## Coneflower see *Rudbeckia*

## Consolida (kon-SO-lih-dah)
Larkspur

Stately 1- to 5-foot flower spikes covered with beautiful 1- to 3-inch flowers. Flowers are white, blue, purple, pink or yellow and appear throughout spring and early summer. Use them for the back of a border or against a fence. They make fine cut flowers and dried flowers.

**Selected species and varieties.** *C. ambigua*, rocket larkspur (sometimes incorrecly sold as *Delphinium ajacis*): has erect braches, most growing to 2 feet, but some reaching 5 feet. *C. orientalis* (sometimes incorrectly sold as *D. orientale* or *D. consolida*) is similar, but the branches are more horizontal. 'Giant Imperial' is a mixture of plants that produce double, closely spaced feathery flowers on low-branching plants 4 to 5 feet tall.

**Growing conditions.** Larkspur does best in cool climates, and is a good choice for spring in warm areas. Seeds may be sown outdoors where plants are to grow in early spring; in mild areas, sow outdoors in fall. Indoors, start six to eight weeks before the last frost date, but sow in peat pots, since plants do not transplant well. The seeds need darkness during their eight- to 15-day germination period, so cover them with a thin layer of soil. Since the seeds are short-lived, plant only fresh seeds and do not store seeds for later use. Space plants 12 to 36 inches apart in full sun and rich, loose, slightly alkaline soil. Fertilize at planting time and again monthly during the growing season. Larkspurs will reseed themselves from year to year. Water and mulch to keep soil moist and cool. To extend bloom, remove flowers as they fade. If plants grow tall, they may need to be staked.

## Coreopsis (core-ee-OP-sis)

A genus of approximately 100 species, a dozen of which are grown for their showy blooms.

**Selected species and varieties.** *C. tinctoria,* calliopsis, golden coreopsis: flower heads to 1¼ inches across, with centers of red or purple and rays of yellow, brown or red-purple. Blooms may be bright red, yellow, pink or purple. The blooms, solid-colored or banded, are borne atop slender, wiry stems 8 to 36 inches tall. With their long flowering season, calliopsis are perfect for borders; they are also excellent cut flowers.

**Growing conditions.** Sow seeds outdoors in early spring where plants are to grow; then thin seedlings to 6 to 8 inches apart. Or purchase bedding plants; or start seeds indoors six to eight weeks before the last frost date. Seeds germinate in five to 10 days and need light to germinate, so do not cover them. When transplanting, take care not to disturb their roots. Calliopsis likes full sun, a light sandy soil with excellent drainage, little or no fertilizer and sparse watering. To keep plants neat and encourage them to produce more flowers, clip flowers as they fade.

## Cornflower see *Centaurea*

## Cosmos (KOS-mos)

Cosmos will fill the garden from early summer until frost with clusters of single or double daisy-like flower heads in white, gold, yellow, orange, pink or crimson. Ray florets are wide and serrated, on slender stems 4 to 6 feet in height. Taller types are excellent for the back of a border; use shorter ones in the middle of a border and in massed plantings. All make excellent cut flowers.

**Selected species and varieties.** *C. bipinnatus,* garden cosmos, common cosmos: tall, with lacy foliage and brightly colored 1- to 2-inch flowers. 'Sensation Mixed': grows 36 to 48 inches tall and bares single flowers that are 3 to 6 inches across in a mix of lavender, pink, red and white. *C. sulphureus,* yellow cosmos, orange cosmos: has

denser, broader foliage and generally shorter plants than *C. bipinnatus.* 'Bright Lights' has semidouble flowers of flame red, bright yellow, gold or orange on 30- to 36-inch plants. 'Diablo' has scarlet-orange 2- to 3-inch flowers on 24- to 36-inch plants. 'Sunny Red' has bright orange-red single 2-inch blooms that fade to scarlet as they age. It is the first truly dwarf cosmos, growing only 12 to 14 inches tall, and is very heat-resistant. 'Sunny Red' has yielded a series of dwarf cultivars including: 'Sunny Gold,' 'Sunny Orange' and 'Sunny Yellow.'

**Growing conditions.** Cosmos seeds may be sown outdoors where plants are to grow after all danger of frost has passed. Use purchased bedding plants, or start seeds indoors five to seven weeks before the last frost date. Germination takes five to 10 days. Space plants 9 to 24 inches apart depending on their ultimate size, in full sun and a warm spot. Soil should be dry and infertile; rich soil will produce foliage but no flowers. Do not overwater or overfertilize. To keep plants trim, cut off faded flowers. Tall types may need some wind protection.

**Creeping gloxinia** see *Asarina*
**Crown daisy** see *Chrysanthemum*
**Cup-and-saucer vine** see *Cobaea*
**Cupflower** see *Nierembergia*

## Cuphea (KU-fee-ah)

A compact tender perennial that is usually grown as an annual. The brightly colored, tubular 1-inch flowers resemble small cigars or firecrackers and are borne in the leaf axils. Plants grow 12 to 18 inches high, are well-suited for bedding or hanging baskets.

**Selected species and varieties.** *C. ignea,* cigar flower, firecracker plant: bears fiery red tubular flowers, each with a ring of violet or black near the tip and an ash white mouth. *C.* x *purpurea:* has flowers of bright rose or red, tinged with either violet or purple. 'Firefly' has clusters of crimson blooms.

**Growing conditions.** Seeds of both species may be sown outdoors after all frost danger has passed, but for best results, start seeds indoors six to eight weeks before the last frost date. Germination takes eight to 10 days. Plant 9 to 12 inches apart in sun or light shade in a light, well-drained soil. Keep well watered. Fertilize with 5-10-5 before planting; no further feeding is needed. These plants do best in hot climates with high humidity.

COREOPSIS TINCTORIA

COSMOS BIPINNATUS 'SENSATION MIXED'

CUPHEA IGNEA

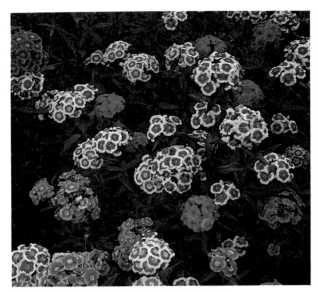

DIANTHUS BARBATUS

DIGITALIS PURPUREA

DIMORPHOTHECA SINUATA HYBRID

**Cypress vine** see *Ipomoea*
**Dahlia** see Dictionary of Bulbs, page 292
**Daisy** see *Arctotis; Chrysanthemum; Rudbeckia*

## Dianthus (die-AN-thus)

The dianthus genus is a large one, with members knows as pinks, sweet William and carnation. The name "pinks" comes not from the flowers' color, but from their serrated petals, which look as if they might have been cut with pinking shears. Most dianthus have a delicious fragrance reminiscent of cloves; plant them where their aroma can be enjoyed, in rock gardens, rock walls, beds or borders.

**Selected species and varieties.** *D. barbatus,* sweet William: a biennial or perennial often grown as an annual; grows to 12 inches. Pinked blooms are red, white, pink or rose-purple, many with a contrasting "eye"; they appear in dense round clusters over green leaves. 'Roundabout' has mixed colors on dwarf, spreading plants. 'Wee Willie' is only 3 inches high and colorful all season. *D. chinensis,* China rainbow pink, grows from 6 to 18 inches tall, has single or double flat-topped, frilled flowers of red, white, pink, rose or lilac. Blooms are 1 inch across, some in solid colors, others two-toned. Foliage is grasslike and gray-green. 'China Doll' produces clusters of double flowers in a wide color range, on 12- to 15-inch plants. Magic Charms series cultivars bear large, abundant blooms on dwarf plants; available in five separate colors; crimson, scarlet, coral, pink and white. Princess series cultivars are among the most reliable for compactness, neatness and all-summer flowering; colors include ruby, salmon, crimson, scarlet, white. 'Snowfire': a dwarf cultivar bearing snow white blooms with cherry red centers; is rain- and heat-tolerant. 'Telstar' is a cheerful mix of crimson, pink, rose, scarlet, white and bicolors; withstands light frost and heat.

**Growing conditions.** Sow seeds indoors six to eight weeks before the last frost date; germination takes five to 10 days. Set seedlings or purchased bedding plants into the garden after danger of frost has passed. Space plants 6 to 9 inches apart in full sun and a light, rich, well-drained soil. Dianthus prefers alkaline conditions, so check soil and raise pH with lime if necessary. Incorporate 5-10-5 into the soil before planting, and feed monthly thereafter. Cut back plants after they bloom to encourage further flowering.

Dianthus perform best in areas with a cool to moderate climate and high humidity. Some of those sold as annuals, particularly the newer hybrids, may be perennials in areas where winter temperatures do not go below 0° F.

## Digitalis (didge-ih-TAL-iss)
Foxglove

A dramatic plant that grows up to 6 feet tall and bears spikes of nodding 1- to 3-inch bell-shaped flowers, in colors including white, yellow, pink, purple or red. The blooms resemble the end of a glove finger, and many have spots of contrasting colors inside. The leaves may be round or tapered. Use foxglove as a bold accent plant or in the back of a flower border. Although a biennial or perennial plant, it can be grown as an annual.

**Selected species and varieties.** *D. purpurea* 'Gloxiniiflora': robust and large-flowered, has flower spikes longer than those of other cultivars.

**Growing conditions.** To grow foxgloves as annuals, start them indoors 10 to 12 weeks before the last frost, and move them to the garden two weeks before the last frost date. To grow them as biennials, set plants or seeds in the garden in late summer, two months before the first expected frost. Germination takes 15 to 20 days. Plant foxgloves in part shade, 15 to 24 inches apart, in rich, loose, well-drained soil. Avoid excessive heat. Water the plants well, without making soil soggy and never let it dry out. Fertilize at planting time with 5-10-5, and again as blooming begins. Apply mulch in fall after the ground freezes. To propagate as biennials, divide the plants in early spring.

## Dimorphotheca
(die-more-foe-THEE-kah)
Cape marigold, star-of-the-veldt

Cape marigolds are cheerful-looking 4- to 16-inch plants with 1 ½- to 3-inch daisy-like flowers of white, yellow, orange, salmon or pink. The undersides of the petals are blue or lavender; centers are a contrasting dark color or yellow. During the day, they make a bright addition to any bed, border or ground cover. The flowers close at night.

**Selected species and varieties.** *D. sinuata* grows 12 inches tall. Its 1½-inch flowers are orange-yellow with violet at the base and yellow centers.

**Growing conditions.** After all danger of frost has passed, sow seeds outdoors where plants are to grow. For earlier bloom, purchase bedding plants or start seeds indoors four to five weeks before the outside planting date. Germination takes 10 to 15 days. To ensure success, use only fresh seeds. Set plants 4 to 8 inches apart in full sun and a light, sandy, well-drained soil. Cape marigolds prefer dry soil, so water them lightly. Fertilize plants every other month. Cape marigolds are easy to grow, preferring cool weather, but tolerating heat and drought.

**Dusty miller** see *Centaurea Chrysanthemum; Senecio*

## Echium (EK-ee-um)
Viper's bugloss

Two biennial species of viper's bugloss are grown as annuals for their erect spikes of small five-lobed flowers of blue, purple, red, pink or white. The 1- to 3-foot plants have broad, hairy, tongue-shaped leaves and hairy stems. These are best used in borders and rock gardens.

**Selected species and varieties.** *E. lycopsis:* grows to 2 feet, bears red flowers that change to bluish purple as they age. *E. vulgare,* blueweed, blue devil: grows to 3 feet, has blue flowers. 'Blue Bedder' reaches only 12 inches in height, is covered with ½-inch, cup-shaped blooms.

**Growing conditions.** Sow seeds outdoors in early spring as soon as the soil can be worked, or start them indoors four to six weeks earlier. Germination takes seven to 14 days and requires a temperature of about 60° F. In the garden, space the plants 12 to 15 inches apart in full sun and in dry, well-drained, poor soil. Avoid overwatering buglosses and fertilize little, if at all; in rich soil, the buglosses produce few flowers.

**Euphorbia** see Dictionary of Perennials, page 246
**Everlasting** see *Helichrysum; Helipterum*
**Firecracker plant** see *Cuphea*
**Floss flower** see *Ageratum*
**Flowering tobacco** see *Nicotiana*
**Forget-me-not** see *Myosotis*
**Foxglove** see *Digitalis*

## Fuchsia (FEW-sha or FEWKS-ee-ah)
Fuchsia, lady's eardrop

Fuchsias bear delicate drooping flowers shaped like hoop skirts, generally two-toned with long, showy stamens. They are splendid in hanging baskets.

**Selected species and varieties.** *F.* x *hybrida:* blooms, usually single but sometimes double, come in shades of pink, red, white, lavender, blue, orange, yellow and fuchsia.

**Growing conditions.** Fuchsia plants are generally sold in baskets ready to use, but it is possible to grow them from seeds or cuttings. Sow seeds indoors six months before desired blooming time. Do not cover seeds, as they need light during the 21- to 28-day germination period. Stem cuttings may be taken at any time and rooted. Grow fuchsia in full or partial shade in rich soil with excellent drainage. Keep soil well watered and mist the plants frequently; they need high humidity and cool temperatures to perform adequately. Either work a slow-release fertilizer into the soil at planting time, or fertilize every two weeks thereafter. The plants benefit from regular pinching, which keeps them compact. In fall, you can lift the plants from the garden, let them dry out and then store them, dormant, in a cool, dry spot for the winter. For more reliable results, however, start fresh each year with new seeds, cuttings or plants.

## Gaillardia (gah-LAR-dee-ah)
Gaillardia, blanket flower

Showy 2 ½-inch flower heads on plants from 10 to 24 inches tall. Blooms have ray florets of red, bronze, butterscotch and maroon, often tipped with yellow. Use them in beds and borders and as cut flowers indoors. They are also heat- and drought-tolerant and therefore especially useful in seaside gardens.

**Selected species and varieties.** *G. pulchella:* plants are neat and covered with flowers until frost. Some of the flowers are double; those of newer cultivars are almost ball-shaped. 'Lollipops': a 10- to 12-inch mounded cultivar covered with ball-shaped flowers in solids and bicolors.

**Growing conditions.** Sow seeds outdoors where plants are to grow, after all danger of frost has passed. For earlier bloom, start with bedding plants or sow seeds indoors four to six weeks before outdoor planting date. Germination takes 15 to 20 days. Gaillardias grow as wide as they are tall,

ECHIUM VULGARE

FUCHSIA × HYBRIDA

GAILLARDIA PULCHELLA

HELIANTHUS ANNUUS

HELICHRYSUM BRACTEATUM

HELIOTROPIUM ARBORESCENS 'MARINE'

so plant them 10 to 24 inches apart, depending on the ultimate height of the species you grow. Soil should be light, sandy and well drained. These annuals are an excellent choice where hot sun beats on the garden, because they prefer full sun, heat and dry soil. Fertilize little, if at all, and to keep plants in best condition, remove flowers as they fade.

**Gazania** see Dictionary of Grasses and Ground Covers, page 160
**Geranium** see *Pelargonium*
**Gloriosa daisy** see *Rudbeckia*

## Helianthus (heel-ee-AN-thus)
Sunflower

Large, coarse, hairy, somewhat sticky leaves on stalks topped with very large flower heads. Traditional sunflowers are yellow, but newer cultivars have yellow-orange, white or bronze ray florets and dark red, purple, yellow or brown centers; some bear double flowers. Traditional sunflowers reach 4 to 12 feet, but modern dwarf forms grow to only 15 inches. Very attractive to birds. Easy to grow, good for cutting, fun for young gardeners because it grows so fast they will see results soon.

**Selected species and varieties.** *H. annuus,* common sunflower: grows 12 feet high; flowers, in white, yellows, oranges, browns and bicolored, may be 1 foot or more across. 'Italian White' has 4-inch cream-colored ray florets with a ring of yellow around a black center on a 4-foot plant. 'Sunburst Mixed': deep crimson, lemon, bronze or gold 4-inch blooms on a 4-foot plant. 'Teddy Bear': an 8- to 12-inch cultivar, bears golden yellow flower heads with hundreds of ray florets on a sturdy 2-foot plant.

**Growing conditions.** Sow seeds outdoors in the spring where the plants are to grow, after all danger of frost has passed. Seeds can be started indoors and will germinate in 10 to 14 days, but sunflowers grow so fast that indoor sowing is not necessary. Space plants 2 to 4 feet apart in full sun and a light, dry, well-drained soil. Fertilize sparingly, keeping the soil fertility low. Do not overwater. Sunflowers thrive in hot temperatures. Taller cultivars require staking.

## Helichrysum (hel-ee-CRY-sum)
Helichrysum, everlasting

More than 300 species of plants having stiff, papery bracts that hold their color long after drying.

**Selected species and varieties.** *H. bracteatum,* strawflower: grows 12 to 30 inches tall, with narrow leaves and wiry stems. Showy flower heads, composed of colorful bracts, not petals, around centers of tiny disc florets. The bracts may be bright red, salmon, yellow, pink or white; the centers come in these colors plus purple. May be used in beds or for cut flowers, but is usually grown for drying.

**Growing conditions.** Although seeds can be sown outdoors where plants are to grow, after all danger of frost has passed, better results will be achieved by using bedding plants or by starting seeds indoors four to six weeks before planting outside. Do not cover the seeds, which need light during the seven- to 10-day germination. Space plants 9 to 15 inches apart, in full sun, in a porous, well-drained soil. Fertilize every two weeks during the growing season. Strawflower thrives where summers are hot and dry. To dry flowers, cut them up before the center petals open, strip off the foliage and hang the flowers to dry upside down in a shaded area.

**Heliotrope** see *Heliotropium*

## Heliotropium (he-lee-oh-TRO-pee-um)
Heliotrope

A mainly tropical or subtropical genus with more than 200 species, one of which is widely cultivated for its fragrant flowers.

**Selected species and varieties.** *H. arborescens:* can grow as tall as 6 feet, but generally only reaches 24 inches. Bears tiny white, dark blue or purple flowers in flat 6-inch clusters. Foliage is dark green and textured. 'Marine': bushy, compact cultivar bearing large flower heads of deep purple up to 15 inches across, over dark green foliage. Pretty as bedding plants, heliotropes are often used in pots and hanging baskets, placed where their alluring fragrance can be enjoyed. Also used to attract bees to vegetable gardens and orchards.

**Growing conditions.** Start with purchased plants or sow seed started indoors 10 to 12 weeks before the last frost date. Germination takes 21 to 25 days. Heliotropes are very sensitive to frost, so wait until two weeks after the last average frost date to set plants outside. Space the plants 12 inches apart in full sun and a rich, well-drained soil. Fertilize with 5-10-5 before planting heliotropes and feed again every other month. Keep well watered. When grown in containers, heliotropes do best in light shade.

## Helipterum (he-LIP-ter-um)
Everlasting, strawflower

As the common names of the genus suggest, helipterums are grown for their durable paper-like flowers. The blooms of these daisy-family members are dense heads of tiny yellow disc florets surrounded by showy, petal-like bracts of yellow, white or pink. Blooms are borne on long stalks above felty white leaves. Helipterums dry very well; they also make good bedding plants and good cut flowers.

**Selected species and varieties.** *H. manglesii,* Swan River everlasting: 18 inches tall, with long, slender stems and 1½-inch flowers of pink, silver-white or violet with golden centers. 'Maculatum' is taller and more vigorous and has pink flowers.

**Growing conditions.** Everlasting seed may be sown outdoors where plants are to grow, after frost danger has passed. However, for best results, use purchased bedding plants or start seeds indoors six to eight weeks before outdoor planting time. Germination takes 14 to 21 days. Transplant after all danger of frost has passed, working very gently, as everlastings dislike transplanting. Space plants 8 to 12 inches apart, in full sun and an average, dry, sandy soil with excellent drainage. Do not overwater. Fertilize 5-10-5 at planting time and again every other month. To dry, cut stems before the flowers are fully opened, tie in bunches and hang with blossoms upside down in a dry, shady, well-ventilated area. In areas with long growing seasons, make several plantings at two-week intervals to lengthen the harvest period.

## Hibiscus (hi-BIS-kus)
Hibiscus, mallow

Shrubby plants of varying heights that are filled during summer with large usually single, five-petaled flowers, whose prominent stamens protrude in a tubular formation. Many hibiscus are perennials and some are woody shrubs; others are annuals or grown as annuals. Many are useful as hedges or accents; they bring an exotic, tropical look to the garden.

**Selected species and varieties.** *H. moscheutos,* rose mallow: a perennial that can be grown as an annual. Varies in height from 18 inches to 6 feet, has downy stems and hairy leaves, and 4-inch flowers of pink, red or white; flowers in summer if started early indoors. 'Dixie Belle' grows to 24 inches tall, with 8- to 9-inch flowers of rose, red, pink and shell pink with a red eye; it is an early bloomer. 'Disco Belle' series cultivars are available in white, rosy red and a mixture, with all flowers having dark red eyes. Plants grow to 20 inches; their flowers are 10 inches across. 'Southern Belle' grows 4 to 6 feet, with 1-inch flowers of red, rose, pink, pink-and-white, and white with a red eye.

**Growing conditions.** Annual hibiscus seeds may be sown outdoors where they are to grow, after all danger of frost has passed, or sown indoors six to eight weeks before the outside planting date. The seeds are hard-coated; score each one with a knife or scissors before planting, or soak them all in water. They will sink when they are ready for planting. Germination takes 15 to 30 days. Set seedlings or purchased bedding plants into the garden after frost danger is past. To grow perennial hibiscus as an annual, buy bedding plants, or start seeds indoors three months before the outside planting date for mid- to late-summer bloom. Space dwarf hibiscus a distance apart equal to their ultimate height, as they are very bushy plants. Taller hibiscus should be planted a distance apart equal to about two-thirds of their ultimate height; for example, hibiscus that will grow to 6 feet should be planted 4 feet apart. Hibiscus like full sun or light shade and a rich, well-drained, moist soil. Plants tolerate heat in summer as long as they are kept well watered. Native to swampy areas, they do well in wet spots. Fertilize with 5-10-5 before planting; no further feeding will be necessary. Where winter temperatures drop below 20° F, protect perennial hibiscus with a 6-inch mulch of straw if you wish to keep it over the winter.

## Impatiens (im-PAY-shens)
Balsam, jewelweed

Showy plants, primarily from the African and Asian tropics, bearing bright, spurred flowers in their leaf axils. Flowers come in shades of pink, red, purple, lavender, yellow and white,

HELIPTERUM MANGLESII

HIBISCUS MOSCHEUTOS

IMPATIENS BALSAMINA

IMPATIENS × 'NEW GUINEA'

IMPATIENS WALLERANA

IPOMOEA TRICOLOR 'HEAVENLY BLUE'

and may be single or double. Except for one group grown for its brightly variegated foliage, impatiens have simple green leaves. Especially valuable for their tolerance of shade. Use them in beds, borders or planters.

**Selected species and varieties.** *I. balsamina,* garden balsam: a favorite in Victorian gardens; bears waxy blooms close to the stem. Flowers can be single but most are double; some new cultivars have double blooms resembling camellias. Flowers come in white, pink, red, purple, lavender, salmon or yellow, sometimes solid colors, sometimes spotted. Plants grow 10 to 36 inches tall and have toothed, pointed, 6-inch leaves. 'Tom Thumb' is a drought-tolerant compact cultivar 10 to 12 inches tall, with ruffled flowers at the top of the plant.

*I.* x *'New Guinea'*: a special strain discovered in the 1970s by botanists visiting New Guinea and brought back to the United States; many cultivars have been developed from it. Grown not so much for its flowers as for its showy, often red-veined leaves of maroon or of variegated green, yellow and cream. Plants grow 12 to 24 inches high and bloom moderately, with flowers resembling those of garden impatiens in lavender, orange, pink, red, salmon and purple. The Sunshine series cultivars have large flowers and compact plants, most with variegated foliage. 'Sweet Sue,' the first New Guinea impatiens that can be grown from seed, bears flaming orange flowers 2 to 3 inches across; its foliage is lance-shaped and deep green and has a touch of bronze.

*I. wallerana,* garden impatiens, busy Lizzie, patience plant: one of the most popular annuals, beloved for its rainbow of colors, variety of sizes, nonstop bloom from spring to frost, easy care, shade tolerance, uniform habit and dependability. Varieties of garden impatiens range from short ground covers to tall, mounded plants reaching 18 inches. Most flowers are flat, 1 to 2 inches across, five-petaled and single, although there are double-flowered cultivars. Flower colors divide into seven shades: pink, white, salmon, orange, scarlet, red and violet. There are also bicolors, with white, starlike centers. 'Accent': at 6 to 8 inches, a flat-growing, ground-hugging plant with early-blooming flowers 2 inches across. 'Blitz': the largest flowering impatiens, with 2 ½-inch blooms on a 12- to 18-inch plant. Very tolerant of heat and sun, excellent for containers. 'Duet' blooms are available in bicolors of red, orange, scarlet or deep rose with white. Flowers are 1 ¼ inches across on 10- to 12-inch plants.

**Growing conditions.** All impatiens are planted outside in spring after all danger of frost has passed. Either grow your own seedlings indoors, or use purchased bedding plants. Do not sow garden impatiens seeds outdoors; start them indoors 10 to 14 weeks before outdoor planting and expect germination to take 14 days. Balsam seeds may be sown outdoors where plants are to grow, after all danger of frost has passed, or started indoors six to eight weeks before the outdoor planting date; germination takes eight to 14 days. All New Guinea impatiens (except 'Sweet Sue') are propagated by stem cuttings in a mixture of peat moss and perlite. Start seeds of 'Sweet Sue' New Guinea impatiens indoors 12 to 16 weeks before the last frost. Temperatures must be very warm during the 14- to 28-day germination period. Normally, only about half of the seeds will germinate, so sow more heavily than usual.

Space plants 6 to 15 inches apart, depending on their ultimate height. Plant balsam in full sun or part shade in a rich, well-drained soil. Fertilize with 5-10-5 before planting and again monthly. Balsam loves heat and should be watered heavily. Plant New Guinea impatiens in partial to full sun and very rich, well-drained soil. Keep well watered; dryness causes plant stress and may produce leaf burn and defoliation. Mulch plants at planting time; they need cool soil for best growth. Fertilize at planting time with 5-10-5 and again every other month during the season. Overfertilizing will discourage flowering.

Garden impatiens will perform well in a wide range of temperatures including high heat, especially when the humidity is high. Soil should be rich in organic matter to retain moisture, and fertilized lightly with 5-10-5 before planting. Feed garden impatiens only sparingly; if overfed, they stop blooming. Water all impatiens when the ground starts to become dry. In extreme heat or sun, impatiens foliage will wilt during the day, but this does not necessarily mean the plants need watering. If the foliage perks up when the sun goes down, do not water. If the foliage stays limp or starts to turn yellow, more water is necessary. A mulch will help retain water and keep the ground cool. Although impatiens is known as a shade plant, thriving in anything from four hours of direct light to all-day dappled light, it can be grown in part or full sun if it is heavily watered. Faded flowers fall cleanly, so impatiens plants do not require deadheading.

## Ipomoea (ip-oh-MEE-ah)
Morning glory

A large group of fast-growing annual and perennial vines, some growing as much as 30 feet per year, with showy tubular flowers. They are excellent for covering fences, trellises or other areas where privacy is needed, and good in hanging baskets.

**Selected species and varieties.** *I. alba,* moonflower, moon vine: a tender perennial grown as an annual; climbs to 15 feet and has bright green, shiny leaves. Fragrant, trumpet-shaped white flowers open in the evening. *I. coccinea,* red morning glory or star ipomoea: has 1½-inch scarlet flowers with yellow throats; vines grow to 10 feet. *I. nil, I. purpurea* and *I. tricolor:* three species of common morning glory. All grow to 10 feet, with heart-shaped leaves and tubular single or double flowers. Colors include blue, purple, pink, red and white; flowers open in the morning and fade by afternoon, to be replaced by others the next day. Blooms are solid-colored, striped, bicolored or tricolored. *I. tricolor* 'Heavenly Blue' has intense blue flowers with lighter blue centers.

**Growing conditions.** To sow indoors, plant seeds four to six weeks before the last frost date; for best results, start them in individual pots. Germination takes only five to seven days; to hasten germination, nick the hard seed coats with a file before sowing, or soak the seeds in water for 24 hours. Transplant gently, so as not to disturb roots. To plant seeds directly outdoors, wait until all danger of frost has passed, and set seeds 12 to 18 inches apart in full sun and a sandy, light, well-drained soil. Too-rich soil will produce all vine and no flowers. Water very moderately, and provide a trellis or other support for all but the bush types. Some tying may be necessary, as not all morning glories are natural climbers.

## Iresine (eye-res-EYE-nee)
Iresine, bloodleaf

Primarily grown for its ornamental foliage, but sometimes bears clusters of tiny flowers.

**Selected species and varieties.** *I. herbstii,* chicken gizzard: a tender perennial used as an annual bedding plant. Has blood-red foliage, some with purple tinge and prominent veining; seldom flowers. 'Aureo-reticulata' has green or greenish red leaves with yellow veins. Used in borders, as an edging plant and especially in designs.

**Growing conditions.** Bloodleaf is grown from cuttings, since foliage color does not come true from seeds. Bedding plants can be purchased. To grow your own plants, take stem cuttings in late winter and root them in a mixture of perlite and peat moss. Transfer the rooted cuttings outside after all danger of frost has passed. Set the plants 12 to 15 inches apart in a warm location with full sun and an average garden soil. Water them well; iresine thrives in soil that is too wet for many other plants. Fertilize with 5-10-5 at planting time; no further feeding is needed.

**Johnny-jump-up** see *Viola*

## Kochia (KOE-kee-ah)

A genus of 80 species, all having narrow leaves and insignificant flowers. Used as a hedge or garden novelty. However, the blooms are thought to cause hay fever.

**Selected species and varieties.** *K. scoparia trichophylla,* summer cypress, burning bush: a globe-shaped, 3-foot plant with dense, narrow, feathery leaves and greenish flowers that are all but invisible. Although Kochia looks like a conifer from a distance, in early autumn, it turns a bright cherry red and becomes a real attraction.

**Growing conditions.** Start from bedding plants or seeds. Sow seeds outdoors after all danger of frost has passed, where plants are to bloom. To start seeds indoors, sow them in individual peat pots four to six weeks before the outdoor planting date. Do not cover seeds; they need light during the 10- to 15-day germination period. Space kochia plants 18 to 24 inches apart in full sun and a dry soil with excellent drainage. Hot weather is preferred; in fact, the plant is slow to develop when weather is cool. Shear to keep plants symmetrical. Fertilize with 5-10-5 before planting and monthly thereafter. Seeds drop easily and sprout quickly, which can be a nuisance. Keep well weeded.

**Lantana** see Dictionary of Grasses and Ground Covers, page 160
**Larkspur** see *Consolida*

## Lathyrus (LATH-ih-rus)

A group of more than 100 species belonging to the pea family. Most are vinelike and bear tendrils.

IRESINE HERBSTII 'AUREO-RETICULATA'

KOCHIA SCOPARIA TRICHOPHYLLA

LATHYRUS ODORATUS

211

LIMONIUM SINUATUM

LOBELIA ERINUS

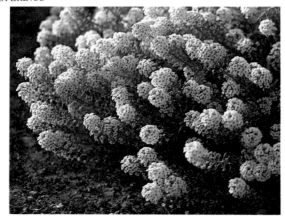

LOBULARIA MARITIMA

**Selected species and varieties**. *L. odoratus,* sweet pea: may be either tendril-bearing vines that climb to 6 feet, or bushy dwarf plants reaching 2 ½ feet. The pealike, 2-inch flowers of this old-fashioned garden favorite are deliciously fragrant and come in purple, rose, red, white, pink and blue; solid or bicolored.

**Growing conditions**. Sow seeds outdoors in early spring as soon as the soil can be worked; in mild areas, sow seeds in fall for early color the following spring. Even for spring sowing, prepare the seedbed the previous fall. Soil should be deeply prepared, rich in organic matter and slightly alkaline. Before sowing seeds, soak them in water for 24 hours, or file the hard seed coat, to shorten germination time to 10 to 14 days. Cover seeds completely; they need darkness to germinate. Seeds can also be started indoors four to six weeks before outdoor planting; sow in individual peat pots, because sweet peas dislike being transplanted. Harden seedlings off by gradually exposing them to cool spring air before transplanting outdoors. Plant dwarf sweet peas 15 inches apart; vining types should be planted 6 to 8 inches apart. Sweet peas do best where it's cool, and will not tolerate drying winds. Provide a trellis or other support for the climbers, and give both types full sun. Feed with 5-10-5 when planting and feed again monthly during the growing season. Water heavily, and mulch to keep soil cool and damp. Keep faded flowers picked in order to prolong flowering.

**Limonium** (lih-MOWN-ee-um)
Statice, sea lavender

A genus of 150 species that grow on sea coasts of all seven continents.

**Selected species and varieties**. *L. sinuatum:* an everlasting grown for its delicate panicles of tiny, papery, funnel-shaped flowers in shades of purple, blue, yellow, red or white. Plants grow to 30 inches tall on winged stems. A biennial grown as an annual, the plant makes an attractive temporary hedge and excellent dried flowers.

**Growing conditions**. Sow seeds outdoors where plants are to bloom, after all danger of frost has passed. Or sow seeds indoors, using peat pots to minimize the shock of transplantation, eight to 10 weeks before the last frost date. Germination takes 15 to 20 days. Move seedlings or purchased bedding plants to the garden after danger of frost has passed. Space the plants 18

to 24 inches apart in full sun and a sandy, light, well-drained soil. Statice tolerates drought, high temperatures and salt spray. Fertilize at planting time with 5-10-5, and water moderately. To dry, cut when flowers are fully open; hang in bunches in a cool and dry area.

**Lobelia** (loe-BEE-lee-ah)

An alternate-leaved plant that has spires of brightly colored flowers.

**Selected species and varieties**. *L. erinus:* ½-inch flowers are blue or violet with yellow or white throats. Plants grow only 3 to 8 inches tall and spread to 10 inches across. Use for edgings, borders, ground covers, rock gardens and containers. 'Blue Moon,' an early-blooming, heat-tolerant cultivar, bears bright blue flowers with green foliage. Cascade series cultivars are ideal trailing plants for containers; flowers come in shades of blue, red, ruby, white, purple and lilac. 'Crystal Palace' is the most popular lobelia, with eye-catching dark blue flowers and bronze leaves. 'White Lady' has sparkling snow white flowers.

**Growing conditions**. Ten to 12 weeks before the last frost, sow seeds indoors in vermiculite, and do not cover them. Provide a warm (75° F) environment during germination, which takes 15 to 20 days, and water only from the bottom, as the species is vulnerable to damping off. You may prefer to use purchased bedding plants. Transfer plants to the garden after the last frost date; space them 8 to 10 inches apart in full sun or part shade in a rich, well-drained soil. Lobelias do best where summers are cool; in warm areas, keep them out of full sun. Fertilize with 5-10-5 before planting, and keep moist during the growing season. If plants get leggy, cut them back to encourage compact growth and heavier bloom. Flowers fall cleanly as they fade.

**Lobularia** (lob-you-LAIR-ee-ah)

A genus of plants native to the Mediterranean; most have white flowers. Used for borders, edgings or containers, especially where their fragrance can be appreciated.

**Selected species and varieties**. *L. maritima,* sweet alyssum, domed clusters of tiny, sweetly scented flowers of white, rose, lavender or purple, covering 3- to 4-inch plants that spread to 12 inches. Foliage is linear, almost needle-like. A perennial that is usually grown as a hardy annual, sweet alyssum reseeds itself readily. 'Carpet of Snow' is a very uniform cultivar with pure white flowers. 'Rosie O'Day' is more heat-resistant than others, bears an abundance of nonfading, rose pink blooms. 'Royal Carpet' is slightly taller than others; bears flowers in clusters that are deep violet at the edges and lighter toward the center. 'Snow Cloth' is similar to 'Carpet of Snow' but earlier to flower, more compact, bears more flowers. 'Wonderland' is an early-blooming mixture of compact plants with cherry-rose, purple and white flowers.

**Growing conditions.** Sow seeds outdoors several weeks before the last expected frost. Or start seeds indoors four to six weeks before the last frost date. Do not cover seeds, as they need light for germination, which takes eight to 15 days. You may prefer to purchase bedding plants. Sweet alyssum seedlings are particularly prone to damping off, so do not overmoisten the soil. Move plants into the garden after the last spring frost; only small plants transplant well. Space plants 10 to 12 inches apart, in full sun or partial shade and an average, well-drained soil. Fertilize with 5-10-5 before planting. Sweet alyssum tolerates drought but prefers to be kept moist. It prefers cool weather. While sweet alyssum will grow in hot areas, it will not flower abundantly. Flowers fall cleanly as they fade. If plants become leggy, cut them back to encourage compact growth and further bloom.

### Lonas (LOE-nas)

A Mediterranean plant having flat-topped flower heads. It adds brightness to a rock garden or border, and tolerates wind and salt spray; lonas is thus a good choice for a seaside garden. It also makes excellent cut or dried flowers.

**Selected species and varieties.** *L. annua,* yellow ageratum, African daisy: fluffy, button-like ¼-inch flower heads of golden yellow, in dense 2-inch clusters. Flowers appear over finely cut leaves on upright, spreading plants growing 10 to 18 inches tall.

**Growing conditions.** Seeds can be sown outdoors where the plants are to grow, after all danger of frost has passed; but for best results start seeds indoors six to eight weeks before the last frost date. Germination takes five to seven days, and seeds should be covered completely as they need darkness to germinate. Space seedlings or purchased bedding plants 6 to 8 inch-

es apart, in full sun and average, well-drained soil. Incorporate 5-10-5 fertilizer into the soil before planting; no further feeding will be needed. Yellow ageratums will not withstand excessive heat. Plant as early as possible, so plants can become established before hot weather. Keep yellow ageratums well watered and mulched.

**Mallow** see *Hibiscus*
**Marguerite** see *Chrysanthemum;*
**Marigold** see *Calendula;*
*Dimorphoteca, Tagetes*
**Mignonette** see *Reseda*
**Moon vine** see *Ipomoea*
**Morning glory** see *Ipomoea*
**Moss rose** see *Portulaca*

### Myosotis (my-oh-SOW-tiss)
Forget-me-not

Prostrate plants with hairy foliage and stems, and clusters of small flowers. Use forget-me-nots at the front of a border, as edging, or as ground cover to contrast with spring bulbs and early-blooming perennials.

**Selected species and varieties.** *M. sylvatica,* garden forget-me-not: profuse quantities of ¼-inch flowers, usually blue with a yellow eye, but may be rose, pink or white. Plants grow 6 inches high and 10 inches wide.

**Growing conditions.** For early-spring bloom, scatter seeds outdoors in early fall; they will germinate and bloom the following year. For fall bloom, sow seeds outdoors in early spring. Plants can be started indoors in winter for transplanting outside in early spring, but this is not an easy method, as the seeds must be kept at 55° F during the eight- to 14-day germination period. Cover them completely, as they also need darkness to germinate. Space plants 6 to 8 inches apart in a rich, very moist, well-drained soil. Grow in a cool spot with light shade. Fertilize every other month during the growing season, and keep plants well watered. Forget-me-not plants will die back in the heat of summer. They self-seed very easily, so if you want flowers to return, allow them to go to seed after they bloom.

### Nasturtium see *Tropaeolum*

### Nicotiana (nih-koe-she-AN-ah)

An upright-growing plant with somewhat fuzzy, sticky foliage and fragrant, trumpet-shaped flowers.

LONAS ANNUA

MYOSOTIS SYLVATICA

NICOTIANA ALATA 'NICKI ROSE'

NIEREMBERGIA HIPPOMANICA VIOLACEA

PAPAVER NUDICAULE

PELARGONIUM × DOMESTICUM

PELARGONIUM × HORTORUM

**Selected species and varieties**. *N. alata,* flowering tobacco: a relative of the commercially grown tobacco plant, with loose bunches of flowers of yellow, purple, green, red, pink or white. 'Domino' is a compact cultivar that grows 10 to 14 inches tall and has early-blooming flowers of purple, pink with a white eye, red, lime green, crimson and white. Nicki series grows 16 to 18 inches tall, with pink, red, rose, white, yellow or lime green blooms.

**Growing conditions**. Flowering tobacco seeds can be sown outdoors where they are to grow, after all danger of frost has passed. For earlier bloom, buy bedding plants or sow seeds indoors six to eight weeks before the last frost date. Germination takes 10 to 20 days. Leave seeds uncovered; they need light to germinate. Flowering tobacco flourishes in full sun or part shade. Choose a rich, well-drained soil, fertilize with 5-10-5 before planting and space plants 10 to 12 inches apart. Plants will tolerate hot summer weather as long as the humidity is high and they are well watered. Keep them neat by cutting off dead flower stalks; new blooms will quickly replace old ones until frost. Flowering tobacco reseeds freely, so if you let the plants go to seed after blooming, they will return.

**Nierembergia** (nee-ram-BER-gee-ah)
Cupflower

A summer-blooming plant with multiple branches and cup-shaped flowers of white, lilac or blue. Used in beds, borders, edgings and rock gardens. An annual in the North, it is a perennial in the South.

**Selected species and varieties**. *N. hippomanica violacea:* 1-inch yellow-centered violet blooms on mounded plants with hairy, fernlike leaves; height ranges from 6 to 15 inches. 'Purple Robe': a 6-inch cultivar that forms a dense mat; its purple-blue flowers have good heat resistance.

**Growing conditions**. Use purchased bedding plants, or start seeds indoors 10 to 12 weeks before the last spring frost. Germination takes 15 to 20 days. Seedlings can be moved outdoors after the last frost date, or, if they are hardened off by gradual exposure to cool spring air, two to three weeks before the last frost date. Space plants 6 to 9 inches apart in full sun to light shade in a light, moist, well-drained soil. Fertilize with 5-10-5 before planting, and feed again monthly during the growing season.

**Oenothera** see Dictionary of Perennials, page 246
**Ornamental cabbage** see *Brassica*
**Ornamental kale** see *Brassica*
**Pansy** see *Viola*

**Papaver** (pa-PA-ver)
Poppy

Annual poppies look just like their perennial cousins. They bear single or double 1- to 3-inch flowers in red, purple, white, pink, salmon or orange, with a texture like crepe paper. Poppy stems are tall and emerge from deeply cut basal leaves.

**Selected species and varieties**. *P. nudicaule,* Iceland poppy: a perennial that can be grown as an annual; bears 1- to 3-inch white, pink, yellow-orange or red flowers and reaches 1 foot in height. *P. rhoeas,* corn poppy, Flanders poppy, Shirley poppy: grows to 3 feet, and bears 2-inch flowers of red, purple or white.

**Growing conditions**. Sow poppy seeds outdoors where the plants are to grow, either in late fall or as soon as the ground can be worked in spring. Seeds may also be started indoors, but they need cool temperatures (55° to 60° F) and the seedlings do not transplant well. Cover poppy seeds completely, as they need darkness for germination, which takes 10 to 15 days. Sow Shirley poppy seeds successively every two weeks during spring and early summer for continuous bloom. They will do best before hot weather. Iceland poppy must be started early if it is to bloom the first year. Set plants 9 to 12 inches apart, in full sun and a rich soil with excellent drainage. Do not overwater. Fertilize with 5-10-5 before planting; no additional fertilizing is recommended.

**Pelargonium** (pel-ar-GOE-nee-um)
Geranium

Showy clusters of white, pink, salmon or scarlet flowers, above roundish, hairy, toothed and slightly ruffled foliage. Plants may be trailing or upright and somewhat woody. Good in garden beds, borders and containers of all kinds.

**Selected species and varieties**. *P.* x *domesticum,* Martha Washington, Lady Washington, regal geranium: has deeply lobed and serrated leaves, large flowers with dark blotches on the upper petals; can be grown only in cool areas of the northern United States. *P.* x *hortorum,* zonal geranium, bedding geranium: single or double flowers in 5-inch round clusters atop leafless stems. Leaves are heart-shaped with scalloped edges; some have brown or black markings called "zoning," some are solid green, others are variegated with white, yellow, bronze, purple, pink or orange. Flower colors include white, pink, rose, salmon, coral, lavender and red. Grown as annuals, plants reach 24 inches high. Sunbelt is a series specially bred for southern climates. It is medium to tall and comes in coral, dark red, hot pink, salmon and scarlet. Ringo is a series having mostly zoned leaves and a compact, uniform plant. Sprinter is a series of compact plants that bloom profusely; among its cultivars are 'Merlin' (crimson with an orange eye) and 'Bright Eyes' (red with a white eye). *P. peltatum,* ivy geranium, hanging geranium: trailing stems that reach 3 feet in length. Flowers range in color from white to deep pink and are borne in five- or seven-flowered clusters. The 2- to 3-inch leaves are ivy-shaped and may have a reddish zone. Ivy geraniums are used in pots and hanging baskets and as ground cover.

**Growing conditions**. All geraniums can be propagated from cuttings, and this method ensures that flower color and leaf form remain the same. If you choose to propagate from seeds, sow them indoors 12 to 16 weeks before the last expected frost. Cover the fine seeds sparsely, and keep the flat in a warm spot (70° to 80° F) during the five- to 15-day germination period. Set seedlings in the garden after all danger of frost has passed. Space plants 8 to 12 inches apart in a very rich, slightly acid, well-drained soil. Zonal geraniums need full sun; ivy and Martha Washington geraniums benefit from dappled shade. Geraniums perform best when well fertilized, so incorporate 5-10-5 into the soil before planting and feed again monthly. Keep well watered, applying water to the ground only, and not to the foliage and flowers. In northern climates, geraniums may be dug up at the end of the growing season, stored indoors in a cool, dark place and replaced outdoors the following spring.

Geraniums that are grown in containers respond best to a rich, soilless mixture and prefer to be potbound. To keep the plants neat and encourage further blooming, cut off the faded flowers.

**Periwinkle** see Dictionary of Grasses and Ground Covers, page 160

**Petunia** (pe-TOON-ee-ah)

A genus of approximately 30 species, nearly all from Argentina, having bright-colored flowers and small, fuzzy leaves. Petunia may be grown as a spreading or a cascading plant, and used in beds, borders, containers or hanging baskets.

**Selected species and varieties**. *P.* x *hybrida:* blooms in every color of the rainbow; blossoms are solid or splashed, starred, zoned, speckled, striped, veined or edged in white. Petunias come in two basic classes: grandiflora and multiflora. Grandifloras have flowers up to 5 inches across; multifloras produce greater numbers of smaller (2- to 3-inch) blossoms and are more disease-resistant. Blooms in both classes may be single and trumpet-shaped, perhaps with fringed or ruffled petals; or double, having extra petals in the center and somewhat resembling carnations. Ultra series has many 3-inch flowers in various reds, white and blue, sometimes bicolored, on compact, very weather-tolerant 8-inch plants. 'Purple Pirouette' is a grandiflora double with deep purple petals ruffled and edged in white; plants are 12 inches high and 18 inches across; blooms are 3 ½ to 4 inches. 'Madness' is a very popular, compact multiflora, with flowers rather large for the class. Resisto series, also multiflora, were developed to withstand cool, wet summers; flattened by a heavy rain, the 12-inch plants will spring right back.

**Growing conditions**. Start these very fine seeds indoors 10 to 12 weeks before the last frost date. Do not cover them, as they need light for the 10-day germination; they also need warmth (70° to 85° F) to germinate. If you purchase bedding plants, choose ones not yet in bloom—they will grow better and bloom more vigorously. Set plants in the garden in spring after all frost danger has passed. Space petunias 8 to 12 inches apart in a sunny or lightly shaded spot. Average, well-drained garden soil with 5-10-5 incorporated before planting will suffice. Petunias do very well in sandy and dry soil. Where soil is heavy, poor or alkaline, choose singles over doubles. Petunias will benefit from pinching at planting time to encourage bushy growth. If plants become leggy, cut them back and they will soon rebloom. Grandiflora petunias are susceptible to botrytis, a disease that kills blossoms, especially in rainy, humid areas. The multiflora types are resistant.

PELARGONIUM PELTATUM

PETUNIA × HYBRIDA 'ULTRA CRIMSON STAR'

PETUNIA × HYBRIDA
PURPLE PIROUETTE'

PETUNIA × HYBRIDA 'RESISTO BLUE'

PHASEOLUS COCCINEUS

PHLOX DRUMMONDII

PORTULACA GRANDIFLORA

PORTULACA OLERACEA HYBRID

## Phaseolus (fay-zee-OH-lus)
Bean, phaseolus

A vine related to the snap bean and other beans grown in the vegetable garden for food.

**Selected species and varieties**. *P. coccineus,* scarlet runner bean: 1-inch, showy scarlet flowers on 8- to 12-foot vines. Edible foot-long beans follow the flowers, but scarlet runner bean is used in flower gardens for its quick growth and handsome flowers and foliage. Plant it against a wall or a trellis to provide a quick screen. Very attractive to hummingbirds.

**Growing conditions**. Sow seeds outdoors where plants are to grow, after all danger of frost has passed. Germination takes six to 10 days. Space plants 2 inches apart in full sun and a rich, moist, well-drained soil. Fertilize at planting time and repeat monthly. Keep well watered. To keep plants flowering, pick off spent blooms before beans can form.

## Phlox (FLOCKS)

A genus of about 60 species, having lance-shaped leaves and terminal clusters of flowers.

**Selected species and varieties**. *P. drummondii,* annual phlox, Drummond phlox, Texan pride: compact, mounded 6- to 18-inch plant with long, thin leaves and round or star-shaped 1-inch flowers in white, pink, blue, red, salmon, lavender and sometimes yellow. Good for edging, bedding borders, rock gardens and containers. 'Twinkle, Dwarf Star': a ball-shaped, 8-inch plant covered with star-shaped blooms composed of pointed, fringed petals. Solids and bicolors in red, pink, salmon, rose, lavender, blue and white.

**Growing conditions**. Sow seeds outdoors where plants are to grow, in spring as soon as the ground can be worked. Indoors, start 10 weeks before the outside planting date and sow seeds in individual peat pots, because the seedlings do not transplant well. Cover seeds well, for they need darkness to germinate. Cool temperatures (55° to 65° F) are also critical for the 10- to 15-day germination period. To prevent killing by damping-off, take care not to overwater seedlings. Harden off seedlings or bedding plants by exposing them gradually to cool spring air, then transplant them to the garden two to three weeks before the last frost date. When transplanting, select some of the weaker seedlings; these tend to produce more interesting colors. Plant in full sun, 6 inches apart, in a rich, light, well-drained sandy soil. Fertilize with 5-10-5 before planting, and feed monthly throughout the blooming season. Keep soil moist but not wet, watering in the morning to reduce risk of disease. Keep faded flowers removed; shearing the plants back encourages compact growth and more flowers. Though phlox is fairly heat-tolerant, flowering may decline in midsummer.

**Pinks** see *Dianthus*
**Poppy** see *Papaver*

## Portulaca (por-tu-LAK-ah)
Portulaca, moss rose

Low-growing, ground-hugging plants 4 to 6 inches tall, with fleshy stems and leaves and generally showy flowers. Most flowers close up at night, in the shade and on cloudy days. Best used as edgings, borders, ground covers or in containers.

**Selected species and varieties**. *P. grandiflora:* 1- to 2-inch ruffled flowers in pink, red, gold, yellow, cream, orange, white or salmon. Single flowers are wide-open and cup-shaped; semidouble and double flowers resemble tiny full-blown roses. Leaves are needle-like. 'Calypso,' 'Double,' 'Sunnyboy' and 'Sunnyside' are mixes, producing mostly double flowers in a variety of colors. 'Sundance' is a cultivar with 2-inch flowers in mixed colors; its flowers stay open longer than most other varieties. *P. oleracea:* has 18-inch-long trailing stems and bright yellow ³⁄₈-inch flowers; hybrids are available in mixed colors.

**Growing conditions**. Sow moss rose seeds outdoors where plants are to grow, after all danger of frost has passed. Sow seeds indoors eight to 10 weeks before the last frost date. Germination takes 10 to 15 days. Transplant seedlings or bedding plants after danger of frost has passed. Space plants 12 to 15 inches apart, in full sun and a dry, sandy, well-drained soil. Fertilize with 5-10-5 before planting and do not feed again. Moss rose withstands heat and drought and should be watered very lightly. Moss rose is a low-maintenance plant; its flowers fall cleanly as they fade, and plants self-seed from year to year.

**Pot marigold** see *Calendula*
**Purple ragwort** see *Senecio*

## Reseda (re-SEE-dah)
Mignonette

A genus of more than 50 species that are native to the Mediterranean region, having small flowers that generally grow in long spikes.

**Selected species and varieties.** *R. odorata,* common mignonette: a 12- to 18-inch plant bearing thick 6- to 10-inch spikes of small, highly fragrant flowers that are yellowish white, sometimes touched with red. Use mignonette in borders and beds, or as a pot plant on a deck or a patio where its fragrance can be appreciated; or plant it under windows to fill the house with its sweet scent.

**Growing conditions.** Sow seeds outdoors in the spring as soon as the ground can be worked. Seeds can be started indoors four to six weeks before the outdoor planting date, but mignonette is hard to transplant and not much is gained by starting it early. Do not cover the seeds because they need light for germination, which takes five to 10 days. In mild climates, seeds can be sown outdoors in fall for germination early the following spring. Space plants 10 to 12 inches apart. Select a location with soil that is rich and well drained. Mignonette likes sun but will thrive in light shade as well. Water well to keep soil moist, and mulch to keep it cool. Mignonette will flourish in warm climates; where summers are hot, it should be treated as a spring and fall plant.

## Ricinus (rye-SIGN-nus)

A single species of fast-growing plant native to Africa; produces a bean that yields castor oil and a poison. Used as an accent plant, background or screen; adds a tropical look to the garden.

**Selected species and varieties.** *R. communis,* castor bean: a shrubby 5- to 8-foot plant grown for its deeply lobed leaves. Young leaves have a red or bronze tinge; as they mature, they darken to green and eventually reach 3 feet in width. The plant produces reddish brown or white flowers, but these are insignificant.

**Growing conditions.** Sow seeds outdoors after all danger of frost has passed, or start seeds indoors six to eight weeks before the last frost date. Germination takes 15 to 20 days. Space plants 4 to 5 feet apart in full sun and a rich, well-drained, sandy or clay soil. Plants do best where climate is hot and humid; they like to be heavily watered. Fertilize with 5-10-5 before planting and again monthly during the summer. In mild climates, castor bean will grow as a perennial.

## Rudbeckia (rude-BEK-ee-ah)
Coneflower

A genus of about 25 species native to North America; flower heads are usually yellow. Coneflowers work well in a border, but are especially effective in a wildflower garden. Excellent for cut flowers.

**Selected species and varieties.** *R. hirta,* 'Gloriosa daisy': developed from the black-eyed Susan that blooms along rural roadsides in the summer. The daisy-like flower heads are 3 to 6 inches across; their yellow or black cone-shaped centers, consisting of tiny disc florets, are surrounded by a single or double row of petal-like ray florets of gold, yellow, bronze, orange, brown or mahogany, often with zones or bands of contrasting colors. Plants reach 8 to 36 inches in height. Although gloriosa daisies can be perennial in many parts of the country, they are easily grown from seed to bloom the first year and thus make good annuals. 'Goldilocks' bears 3- to 4-inch semidouble flower heads on 8- to 10-inch plants. 'Marmalade' is wind-resistant. It grows to 2 feet and has 3-inch flowers of bright gold with contrasting dark centers.

**Growing conditions.** Sow seeds indoors six to eight weeks before the last frost date or outdoors as soon as the soil can be worked; germination takes five to 10 days. Or purchase bedding plants. Seedlings should be moved to the garden after danger of frost has passed; space the seedlings 12 to 24 inches apart, in full sun or light shade. Any well-drained garden soil will do. Although gloriosa daisies do best in a rich soil kept evenly moist, they will tolerate drought and heat. Fertilize with 5-10-5 at planting time. No further feeding is needed. Gloriosa daisies freely reseed, so plants may reappear from year to year if spent blooms are not removed.

RESEDA ODORATA

RICINUS COMMUNIS

RUDBECKIA HIRTA

SALVIA FARINACEA

SALVIA SPLENDENS

SENECIO CINERARIA 'CIRRUS'

**Sage** see *Salvia*

## Salvia (SAL-vee-ah)
Salvia, sage

Salvia is a large genus of plants used in both flower gardens and herb gardens. The flowers are two-lipped and generally red, but may be purplish blue, white, reddish purple, deep purple or rose. Blooms are borne in showy terminal spikes; leaves are borne in pairs. Most salvias are perennials grown as annuals. Use them in massed plantings, beds, borders, containers and as cut flowers.

**Selected species and varieties.** *S. farinacea,* mealy-cup sage: has narrow spikes profusely covered with violet-blue or white flowers. Leaves are gray-green; plants grow to 24 inches. *S. splendens,* scarlet sage: grown primarily for its spikes of red flowers borne over dark green leaves; plants reach 6 to 24 inches in height. 'Bonfire' is tall, to 24 inches, and bears scarlet blooms. 'Carabiniere' comes in orange, scarlet, purple and white, as well as reds. 'Hotline' series cultivars are very early and very compact. The flowers, available in red, salmon, white and violet, are the most heat-resistant of all salvias. 'Red Hot Sally' is very early to flower, and reaches only 10 inches in height.

**Growing conditions.** Start seeds indoors eight to 10 weeks before the date of the last spring frost. Do not cover seeds of *S. splendens* as they need light to germinate. Germination takes 10 to 15 days. *S. farinacea* needs to be started indoors 12 weeks before transplanting outdoors. Salvia transplants best before it comes into bloom, so don't start seeds too early. Space plants 8 to 12 inches apart; dwarf cultivars can be planted closer together. Salvias like full sun or part shade and a rich, well-drained soil. Although plants will tolerate dry soil, they do better if kept evenly watered. Salvia is very sensitive to fertilizer burn, so feed lightly but often throughout the summer. Salvia will reseed, but self-sown plants rarely reach blooming size during the summer except in the South.

**Scabiosa** see Dictionary of Perennials, page 246
**Scarlet runner bean** see *Phaseolus*
**Sea lavender** see *Limonium*

## Senecio (se-NEE-shee-o)

A large genus of 2,000 to 3,000 species. Many have showy flower heads borne in clusters; some have decorative foliage.

**Selected species and varieties.** *S. cineraria,* dusty miller: produces flowers of yellow or cream in small terminal clusters, but is grown primarily for its foliage, woolly and white with rounded lobes. Grows 2 ½ feet high and is used in beds and borders. 'Cirrus' has broad, oak-shaped, very white leaves and is heat-, rain- and frost-tolerant. *S.* x *hybridus,* florists' cineraria: hairy, heart-shaped leaves and dense clusters of 2-inch single or double flower heads in white, pink, red, purple, violet or blue, many with contrasting rings. The 1- to 3-foot plant is often used as a houseplant, but can be successfully grown outdoors in the cool, mild climate of the Northwest. *S. elegans*, purple ragwort: bears loose clusters of 1-inch flower heads having purple ray florets around yellow centers. Plants are 2 feet tall, with deeply cut foliage.

**Growing conditions.** For dusty miller, sow seeds indoors eight to 10 weeks before the last frost date. For purple ragwort, sow indoors six to eight weeks before the last frost date. Germination for both takes 10 days to two weeks. Florist's cineraria may be sown indoors and will germinate in 10 to 15 days, but the plant will not bloom for five to six months; sow seeds in late summer or early fall for blooming the following spring. Or start with purchased bedding plants. Either way, set plants in the ground when they are just coming into bud; plants already in flower will not adjust to the outdoors. All senecio plants should be set in the ground after the last frost, spaced 12 inches apart, and fertilized with 5-10-5 at planting time. Dusty miller likes full sun or light shade, a sandy, light and well-drained soil, and light watering when soil has dried out. If plants start to get leggy, they can be sheared back. Purple ragwort needs full sun and a rich, moist, well-drained soil—but only occasional watering. Florist's cineraria needs partial shade to full shade, a soil that is rich, moist and well-drained, and mulching and frequent watering. It should be fertilized monthly during the blooming season, and flowers should be picked off as they fade.

**Snapdragon** see *Antirrhinum*
**Spider flower** see *Cleome*
**Spurge** see Dictionary of Perennials, page 246
**Star-of-the-veldt** see *Dimorphotheca*
**Statice** see *Limonium*
**Strawflower** see *Helichrysum; Helipterum*
**Sunflower** see *Helianthus;*
**Sweet alyssum** see *Lobularia*
**Sweet pea** see *Lathyrus*
**Sweet William** see *Dianthus*

## Tagetes (ta-JEE-tees)
Marigold

A member of the daisy family, native to Mexico; the common name is a translation of the Spanish conquistadors' term for it, "Mary's gold." Showy flower heads of yellow, gold, orange or maroon, strongly scented foliage and deeply cut leaves. Used in beds, borders, massed plantings, edgings and containers; for cut flowers; and sometimes in vegetable gardens, because they are thought to repel certain beetles and nematodes.

**Selected species and varieties.** *T. erecta:* African marigold, American marigold, Aztec marigold: generally the tallest of marigolds, most varieties growing from 12 to 36 inches tall, but there are some dwarf varieties that reach only 6 inches. Flowers are very full, double or carnation-like, and up to 5 inches across. Crush series, the smallest of the dwarf African marigolds, with 4-inch, flattened flowers on 6- to 8-inch plants, includes 'Pumpkin' (orange), 'Papaya' (gold) and 'Pineapple' (yellow). Jubilee series includes 'Orange,' 'Golden' and 'Diamond' (primrose yellow) varieties. Round, 4- to 5-inch, carnation-like flowers are weather-resistant and cover the tops of the plants, which grow to 24 inches tall. Lady series cultivars come in pale and golden yellows, and orange. The curved petals form a 3-inch ball on a 20-inch rounded plant. Monarch series cultivars have yellow, gold and orange, intricately spaced petals on a slightly flattened, 4-inch double flower. Plants reach 20 inches and are exceptionally weather-tolerant. *T. patula,* French marigolds: 6- to 16-inch plants with a profusion of small flower heads in various shapes. Some are crested, having a tufted center surrounded by a collar of ray florets; others have broad, flat petals; still others are carnation-like. Aurora is the largest-flowered French marigold of the flat-petaled type, bearing 2-inch

double blossoms. Early-blooming, 10 to 12 inches tall, it comes in two varieties, 'Gold' and 'Fire' (a glowing red-and-orange bicolor). Bonanza series has 2-inch crested, heat-resistant blooms on 8- to 10-inch plants. Varieties include 'Gold,' 'Yellow,' 'Orange,' 'Spry' (yellow crest with mahogany rays), 'Harmony' (orange crest with maroon rays) and 'Flame' (maroon petals bordered with gold). Janie series includes 'Gold,' 'Janie Bright Yellow,' 'Flame' (red-and-orange bicolor) and 'Harmony' (mahogany with gold-orange centers); blooms are double, crested, and 1½ inches across on an 8-inch heat-resistant plant. 'Red Marietta' bears single, gold-edged red flowers, which stay red all summer when many others soften in color. Flowers are 2½ inches across on 16-inch plants. *T. patula* x *erecta:* unlike other marigolds, blooms all summer, even in the hottest part of the country. The plant is sterile and does not set seed. Nuggets series comes in yellow, orange and red, sometimes bicolored, bearing 2-inch double flowers on 10-inch plants. *T. tenuifolia,* signet marigold, dwarf marigold: has fine, lacy, lemon-scented foliage on 12-inch plants with tiny, single flowers in gold, lemon yellow or orange.

**Growing conditions.** Sow seeds indoors four to six weeks before the last frost date. Germination takes five to seven days. Seeds of most marigolds can also be sown outdoors where they are to grow, after danger of frost has passed. Two exceptions are African marigold, which takes longer than other marigolds to bloom, and sterile types, which have such a low germination rate that you can control them better by starting indoors. Transplant seedlings or purchased bedding plants to the garden after danger of frost has passed. Space plants a distance apart about half their ultimate height; for example, African marigolds expected to grow to 24 inches should be spaced 12 inches apart. Marigolds thrive in full sun and relatively high temperatures, but some will stop flowering when temperatures exceed 90° F. They generally bloom until fall frost and will do well in any average not-too-rich garden soil. Fertilize with 5-10-5 prior to planting, and repeat monthly through the blooming season. Water when the soil is dry. To promote continuous bloom, pick off faded flowers regularly; this, of course, does not apply to sterile types, which do not set seed.

SENECIO × HYBRIDUS

TAGETES ERECTA 'PRIMROSE LADY'

TAGETES PATULA × ERECTA (NUGGETS SERIES)

THUNBERGIA ALATA (SUSIE SERIES)

TROPAEOLUM MAJUS

VERBENA × HYBRIDA 'TRINIDAD'

## Thunbergia (thun-BER-gee-ah)

A genus of about 100 species, many of them vines, having showy flowers.

**Selected species and varieties.** *T. alata,* black-eyed Susan vine: a tender perennial that can be grown as an annual. Trumpet-shaped, 1 ½-inch flowers in white, yellow or orange, with dark purple or black throats in most cultivars. The vine grows fast and will reach 5 or 6 feet; bears dense, dark green, arrowhead-shaped leaves.

**Growing conditions.** Sow seeds indoors, six to eight weeks before the last frost date; germination takes 15 to 20 days. In mild climates, seed can be sown outdoors where plants are to grow, when danger of frost has passed. Bedding plants are also readily available. Plant in full sun or very light shade in a light, rich, moist, well-drained soil. Set plants about 6 inches apart, and provide a support, such as a pole, lamp post or trellis, if you wish the plants to climb. Do not prune plants during the growing season, but pick off flowers as they fade in order to keep the plants trim and productive. Water when the ground starts to become dry.

## Tropaeolum (tro-pee-OH-lum)
Nasturtium

A genus of plants that come in three basic forms: bushy, growing to 12 inches; semitrailing, to 24 inches; and vining, to 8 feet. All grow rapidly and bear single, semidouble or double funnel-shaped flowers in tones of red, yellow and orange, each with a spur extending from the back. The flowers generally droop; some are fragrant. Foliage is round or lobed; stems are fleshy and curl around trellises and other objects. Depending on plant habit, nasturtiums may be used as bedding plants, in containers and hanging baskets, on a trellis or to overhang a wall. They are often included in children's gardens. Sometimes they are planted in vegetable gardens, as they are thought to repel squash bugs and some beetles.

**Selected species and varieties.** *T. majus,* the common garden nasturtium, has showy yellow, orange, scarlet or mahogany blooms 2 to 2 ½ inches across.

**Growing conditions.** Sow seeds outdoors where they are to grow, after all danger of frost has passed. Seeds may be started indoors, but seedlings do not transplant well. Space plants 8 to 12 inches apart in full sun or light shade, in soil that is light and well drained. Do not fertilize; rich soil produces lush foliage but no flowers. Water when soil is dry, but do not overwater. Nasturtium does best where temperatures are cool; in warm climates, the bush types outperform the vining types. Where vines are grown, they need to be tied to their supports.

## Verbena (ver-BEE-nah)

Verbenas bear stunning brightly colored flowers in red, white, violet, purple, blue, cream, rose or pink. The individual flowers are small and tubular, but they appear in clusters 2 ½ to 4 inches across on spreading or upright plants. Use for edgings, beds, ground covers, rock gardens, in hanging baskets; they also make fine cut flowers.

**Selected species and varieties.** *V.* x *hybrida,* common garden verbena: the most popular species in the genus. Upright or slightly creeping plants grow to 24 inches tall. Flowers come in all verbena colors, many with a contrasting white eye; leaves are deeply quilted or textured. 'Trinidad': an upright grower, 10 inches tall, with shocking pink flowers.

**Growing conditions.** Verbena seeds are small and take a long time to germinate, so do not sow them outdoors. Buy bedding plants in spring, or sow seeds indoors 10 to 12 weeks before the last expected frost. Refrigerate seeds for seven days before sowing, and sow extra heavily, because verbena seeds' germination percentage is usually low, especially with the older cultivars. Cover the seed flat with black plastic until germination occurs, after 20 to 25 days. Verbena is particularly prone to damping-off, so make sure the medium is not overly wet. Plants are also easy to root from stem cuttings. Move plants outside after all danger of frost is past; select a spot with full sun and a rich, light, well-drained soil. Space spreading types 12 to 15 inches apart, and upright types 8 to 10 inches apart. Fertilize with 5-10-5 at planting time and feed monthly. Verbena is one of the best annuals to use where weather is hot and dry and soil is poor.

**Viola** (vie-OH-lah)
Violet, viola

Dainty, flat, single flowers with five round petals; foliage is usually round to heart-shaped. Depending on species and cultivar, flowers are ½ to 4 inches across, and plants grow 6 to 15 inches tall. Most violets are biennials grown as annuals. All prefer cool weather; in hot climates they are generally grown as spring and fall plants, to be replaced in summer by more heat-resistant annuals. Viola is used in massed plantings, edgings, rock gardens and containers, and for spot color.

**Selected species and varieties.** *V. odorata,* sweet violet, English violet: the violet that is sold by florists; a perennial sometimes grown as an annual. Plants grow 12 inches high; flowers are ¾ inch across, fragrant, usually violet in color. *V. tricolor,* Johnny-jump-up: a perennial grown as a hardy annual; its ¾ -inch flowers are purple, white and yellow. *V.* x *wittrockiana,* pansy, heartsease: flower colors include red, white, blue, pink, bronze, yellow, purple, lavender or orange.

**Growing conditions.** Sow seeds indoors 14 weeks before the last frost date. Germination takes 10 to 20 days. Seeds benefit from several days' refrigeration in a moist medium before sowing. Purchased bedding plants and seedlings that have been hardened off—that is, gradually acclimated to outdoor conditions—can be set in the garden as soon as the ground can be worked in spring. In the South and warm parts of the West, where winter temperatures do not drop below 20° F, pansies planted and mulched in fall will survive the winter and bloom again the following spring. Pansy plants can also be overwintered in cold frames and transplanted in early spring. Space plants of all species 6 to 8 inches apart in a moist, rich soil. Except for sweet violet, all prefer full sun but will grow in part shade. Sweet violet needs part shade in most areas and full shade in very hot climates. Fertilize with 5-10-5 before planting and again every month during the blooming period. Water the plants well; mulch to keep the soil moist and cool. Where nights are hot, they seldom thrive. To extend pansies' bloom time, pick the flowers before they go to seed. If plants become leggy, pinch them back to keep them compact.

**Violet** see *Viola*
**Wallflower** see *Cheiranthus*

**Zinnia** (ZIN-ee-ah)

Flowers of these popular garden annuals range from tiny button-like heads to large double-petaled flower heads with quill-like ray florets. The flower heads come in pink, rose, red, cherry, lavender, purple, orange, salmon, gold, yellow, white, cream and light green—virtually every color except true blue. Plants range in size from 6-inch dwarfs to varieties almost 4 feet high. Use zinnias in edgings, borders or beds; they also make excellent cut flowers and good container plants. Plants start to bloom when still very short and continue blooming as they grow, until frost.

**Selected species and varieties.** *Z. elegans,* common zinnia: heights up to 3 feet with stiff single or double flower heads from 1 to 7 inches across. Blooms in all colors. Some are solid-colored, others muticolored or zoned. Some are round, domed or ball-shaped; others are shaped like dahlia or chrysanthemum flowers. *Z. haageana,* Mexican zinnia: grows from 12 to 18 inches high and bears 1 ½ to 2-inch, single or double flower heads in tones of red, mahogany, yellow and orange; some blooms are solid-colored; others are two-toned.

**Growing conditions.** Sow zinnia seeds outdoors after all danger of frost has passed, where plants are to grow. Or sow seeds indoors four weeks before the last frost. Germination takes five to seven days. Move seedlings or purchased bedding plants to the garden after the danger of frost has passed. Space plants from 6 to 24 inches apart—whatever their height will be at maturity. Do not crowd plants; they are susceptible to mildew. For maximum growth and flowering, incorporate 5-10-5 into the soil at planting time and feed again twice monthly. Zinnias like full sun and a rich, fertile and well-drained soil. Encourage bushiness by pinching the plants when they are young. Cutting flowers for indoor use and removing blooms as they fade also encourages new growth and keeps the plants bushy. Zinnias thrive in hot, dry climates, but they need regular watering. Water them in the morning; to prevent disease, avoid wetting the foliage.

VIOLA TRICOLOR

ZINNIA ELEGANS

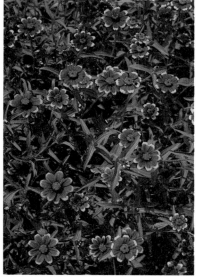

ZINNIA HAAGEANA

# 5

# PERENNIALS

*A broad band of 'Mary Todd' daylilies brightens the base of a white picket fence. Each bloom lasts only a day—hence the name—but fresh new flowers appear day after day for three weeks or more. The daylily is one of the quickest plants to take hold in a garden.*

Perennials are arguably the most rewarding sorts of plants a gardener can cultivate. They are long-lived, reappearing uncoaxed year after year. They are wonderfully varied in their foliage, and the flowers offer a broad palette of colors. And perennials are marvelously versatile. Many will thrive in the hottest, sunniest spot in your garden; others do well brightening a cool, shady corner. A number are downright theatrical, with broad, saucer-sized blooms.

You might start with a single showy bloomer—to highlight a doorway, adorn a mailbox or provide a splash of brightness under a tree. For other limited spaces, you can use small groups of perennials in pots or planters. For somewhat larger areas and for damp ones that need help with drainage, you can create compact rock gardens with perennials.

Perennials as a rule are not temperamental plants, and few demand extensive care. In fact, many varieties, once planted in nourishing soil, display an almost disconcerting abundance of rude health, growing upward and outward with increasing exuberance each season. But perennials do require a gardener's attention periodically. A number of the old tried-and-true favorites—delphiniums and peonies, for example—become so tall that they need supports to keep their long stems from bending under the weight of their extravagant blooms. The best (and least conspicuous) ways to stake these and other lofty plants are shown in Chapter 2.

This chapter gives you directions for other tasks, most of them required because perennials retain their vigor year after year. There are ways, for example, to reclaim a neglected perennial bed. As for new plants, they need to be put in the ground with special care from the start, since they will stay there for many seasons. For the same reason, perennial beds

# CHAPTER CONTENTS

require some tidying up and renewing of the soil, especially in spring, in order to keep them fresh and comfortable for their long-term tenants. The last task of the year is winterizing. Done as outlined here, it should keep your perennials alive through the cold, dormant months and help get them ready to burst upward with renewed energy when spring returns.

Propagating your own perennials can be one of the most rewarding parts of gardening. To watch the growth of plants that you have nurtured from seed is exciting in itself. Even more creative is the process of multiplying the perennials already growing in your garden by dividing their roots, or by cultivating cuttings. Either way, follow the propagation instructions in Chapter 2, and you will soon possess a wealth of fresh and healthy perennials with which to start a new garden.

Perennials are well known for their ruggedness and adaptability. Some varieties easily survive the long, hard winters of Maine and Minnesota, yet tolerate the torrid summers of North Carolina and Mississippi. But not many perennials thrive in every climate. To find out about temperatures in your part of the country, consult the Zone Map (*inside front cover*), which divides North America into 11 climatic zones. To find out which zones plants flourish in, consult the Dictionary of Perennials (*pages 246-263*).

Wherever you live and whatever perennials you grow, your garden will go through seasonal changes—which bring with them regular seasonal tasks such as cutting back and mulching. To help you schedule the maintenance of your garden, the checklist on pages 238-241 lays out the gardening year month by month and zone by zone. Refer to pages 242-245 for a list of common bugs and diseases that can assail your plants, and effective remedies for the problems they create.

# CONTAINER-GROWN PLANTS — CHOOSING WISELY, PLANTING WELL

The quickest way to get perennials started in a garden is to buy them, container grown, from a nursery. But check carefully to make sure that the plants are healthy. The leaves should have fresh, uniform color; obvious blemishes indicate trouble with pests or disease. Buds, if present, should be tight; any flowers that have bloomed should be bright and crisp-looking. Look for straight stems; droopy stems may indicate overcrowding or lack of light. Tall plants are not necessarily desirable; they may have sent up spindly stems to reach the sunlight in a crowded greenhouse. It is better to select plants with several shorter, more vigorous shoots.

Buy in the early spring. Nurseries have the largest selection then—and spring is the right time to put most potted perennials into the ground. The sun and earth are not too hot, and early planting allows the new arrivals several weeks to adjust after the transition from pot to flower bed before they bloom. If perennials are to be transplanted in the summer, choose a day that is cool, even drizzly. The plants should be watered liberally and then shaded for some days afterward.

Spring is best for another reason too: A perennial may have been in its container about a year before being sold and its roots may already be crowded. The plant may be rootbound—the ends of the roots twining around one another, beginning to form a tight knot. No harm will have been done as long as numerous small, pale, healthy-looking feeder roots are still visible. And there is an easy cure for the problems presented by bound roots; separating them *(right)* will ensure that the perennial is planted properly and will help its chances for a long, healthy life.

*Ranks of clearly labeled perennials, their foliage crisp and their flowers bright-hued and healthy-looking, stand in a clean and neatly organized nursery—ready for transplanting to a garden.*

To separate bound roots, cut the root ball vertically partway up with the blade of a trowel. Gently pull the two halves apart and loosen the plant's roots. Dig a hole at least half again as wide as the root ball and somewhat deeper. If very dry, soak the hole with water before planting. Mix the soil you have removed with some organic matter—humus or compost—and also add a few spoonfuls of a phosphate fertilizer. Put some of this soil mixture in the hole—enough so that the top of the root ball will be level with the ground. Add soil until the hole is filled and water well.

# PUTTING BARE-ROOT PERENNIALS INTO THE GROUND

**M**any gardeners order perennials from mail-order nurseries—and for good reason. Selections are much wider than at local suppliers, and prices are often lower. In addition, mail-order nurseries offer the latest and most interesting varieties that are hard to find anywhere else.

Mail-order plants are usually shipped in a dormant state with bare roots or with a small soil plug attached to the roots. Dormant plants may look dead; do not be put off if they look spindly, even sticklike.

Most nurseries plan shipments so that the plants arrive at the beginning of the best planting season for your area. Plant them as soon as possible; bare-root plants dry out quickly and should never be left exposed to either the sun or the wind.

If weather or other reasons prevent you from planting immediately, unpack the boxes immediately. Water well and keep them moist; store in a cool, shady area until you can plant them. Provided they haven't produced new green growth, bare-root perennials will survive in these wrappings in a cool, dark place (35° to 45° F) for up to two weeks. Then, if further delay is unavoidable, transplant them to a pot and keep them in a well-sheltered place or in a cold frame *(page 83)*.

Read the instructions that come with the plant to see if organic matter should be added before the soil is put back in the hole. The instructions will also tell you how deep to plant. The placement of the crown—the area where the roots and stems meet—is crucial. Hosta, for example, does best when the crown is 1 or 2 inches below the soil surface, but depth varies with other species. The plant has spent millennia evolving, and if planted at an unfamiliar level will spend so much energy trying to adapt that it will not survive.

## MAKING GARDENING EASY

If you want to keep gardening chores to a minimum, select plants that require little maintenance. Among the perennials rarely bothered by pests and diseases are butterfly weed, coreopsis, bleeding heart, coneflower, daylily, candytuft, veronica, globeflower, sedum, coralbells, poppy and yarrow.

The time that you must devote to gardening chores will be reduced even further if you plant perennials that do not need staking, frequent deadheading, dividing or thinning. In this category are butterfly weed, coneflower, bleeding heart, daylily, coralbells, gay-feather, Virginia bluebells, geum, hosta and veronica.

Using a trowel, dig a hole 10 to 12 inches deep and wide enough to accommodate the fully extended roots. Add organic matter to the removed soil if needed. When you are ready to begin planting, unwrap the plant. Save the identifying marker. Check for dryness, damage or disease; cut off any unhealthy roots with a pruner or scissors. Then trim excessively long roots so they will fit in the hole without bending or curling. With soil you have previously removed, build a cone in the bottom of the hole. Set the plant over the cone; adjust the height of the cone so that the crown of the plant—the junction of roots and stems—sits at the recommended depth. Separate the roots and spread them down over the cone in an evenly spaced arrangement *(below)*. Refill the hole, working soil between the roots with your fingers to eliminate air pockets. Firm the soil with your hands, water well and insert an identifying marker.

# THE PERENNIAL BORDER—
# MAINSTAY OF THE GARDEN

*Outlining a broad strip of sunlit lawn, two perennial borders form a fluid design by mixing and matching heights and textures as well as colors—among them mounds of purple verbena, carpets of pinks and spires of white salvia.*

The most eye-catching area of any garden may well be the perennial border—the flowering plants that run in a broad swath along a fence, a wall, a pathway, the edge of the lawn, the property line; in fact, the line demarcating any boundary. Use the method shown in Chapter 1 to plan and lay out a perennial border. You can use a combination of flowers that will bloom at the height of summer and make a spectacular display of colors: yellows, purples and blues, for example, and a few splashes of white and orange for accent. With only graph paper and tracing paper, colored pencils, a ruler and the Dictionary of Perennials *(pages 246-263)* for tools, you can follow the same technique to fashion a border of any combination of colors and textures. If you want bold colors, for instance, you can plant coreopsis for yellow, bellflower for blue, bee balm for red, phlox for an assertive pink, candytuft for standout white. If pastels are more to your liking you can use foxglove for yellow, astilbe for peach and lamb's-ears for silvery foliage.

Choose an area that has good drainage, light and space. An unshaded southern or southeastern exposure is ideal because most perennials like lots of sun. A site measuring 4 feet by 12 feet is appropriate; that is enough space to allow you to mass plants for effective displays of color, but not so large as to be unmanageable.

# BRIGHT ACCENTS
# IN SHADY LOCATIONS

*Pale pink astilbes with feathery, delicate blossoms and handsome foliage, provide a textural accent in a shady area at the edge of a lawn. When the blooms are gone, the brown seed heads of the spikes can be picked for dried arrangements.*

Perennials are surprisingly adaptable. Although most of them thrive in full sun, some flourish in shade *(box, below)*. With their combination of colorful flowers and lush foliage, they make wonderful accents in a garden that has light to medium shade.

Light shade lasts for two or three hours between 10 a.m. and 6 p.m. in the summer; medium shade lasts for four or five hours. The shade need not be constant. If you have tall deciduous trees that cast lacy patterns of shadow on and off throughout the course of the day, for example, or a slatted fence or a hedge that filters the afternoon sun, you have light to medium shade.

Walls provide shade, too—but some walls are better at doing so than others. A wall that faces east is preferable to one that faces west; in facing east it allows the plants sun in the morning and shades them in the afternoon, when the sun is hottest. A wall that faces west will cancel out the benefits of the shade it gives in the morning; not only does it leave the plants exposed to afternoon sun but redoubles the heat by absorbing the rays of the sun and reflecting them back upon the plants.

Shade-loving plants not only require respite from the heat of the sun, they also have certain other requirements. They need rich soil with plenty of humus. Most of them need fertilizing in spring, when their buds are forming, and once or twice again in summer, as the plants continue growing. And all of them need plenty of moisture. Water them well and often, and mulch them to help the soil remain moist.

To plant perennials, use a trowel to dig a hole for each plant, making the hole slightly larger than the pot. Amend the soil by combining 3 parts soil with 1 part humus, compost or other enrichment, and partially refill the hole. Knock on the bottom of the pot to loosen the plant, and lift off the plant. If the roots are tightly bound, cut them apart *(page 224)*. Set the plant in its hole, placing it at the same depth as it was in its pot. Using your hands, press the soil down firmly around the base of the plant *(right)*. When you have finished, water all plants thoroughly.

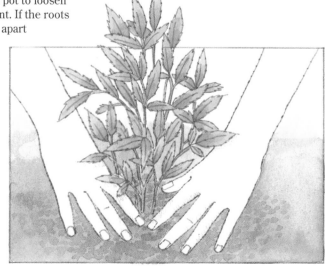

## SOME PERENNIALS FOR SHADE

| | |
|---|---|
| Astilbe | Goatsbeard |
| Hosta | Bethlehem sage |
| Lenten rose | Bleeding heart |
| Coralbells | Columbine |

*\* See Dictionary of Perennials (pages 246-263)*

# AN ISLAND BED FOR SHOWING OFF PERENNIALS

Few spots in a garden make a more spectacular showplace for bright-blooming perennials than an island bed—that is, a garden standing alone on a broad swath of lawn—which can be viewed and appreciated from different vantage points.

An island bed can be oval or rectangular, or it can flow in curves that follow the contours of the land. It can be small or large. But within the bed, the plants must be carefully chosen and placed for height. As a rule of thumb, the tallest plants should grow about half as tall as the plot is wide—4 feet tall, for example, in an island bed that is 8 feet across. In general, tall plants should go in the center of the bed, shorter ones at the outer edges—but not so rigidly as to produce a conical effect. The rippling contours of tall and short plants interspersed will provide interest.

Among the most dramatic of plants for an island bed are peonies, which produce magnificent flowers in a broad range of colors and grow tall enough to show to advantage. The best time to plant them is in the fall, after the roots have been divided *(Chapter 2)*. Like most perennials, they require well-prepared soil and plenty of light. But peonies make some special demands *(opposite)*. Each plant has one or more "eyes," sometimes called growth buds, the pinkish protrusions that grow on the crown. For the plant to bloom, the eyes need below-freezing temperatures for a minimum of six weeks. They should be planted from just below the surface (in the south) to 2 inches below the surface (in the north); the soil insulates the roots, and in a warm climate, too thick a layer of soil will prevent the necessary chilling.

*The fuchsia-colored blooms and rounded shape of a peony plant make it stand out in an island bed.*

## A GUIDE TO PLANT HEIGHTS

Fifteen perennials that would make a handsome island garden are shown and named below, with taller and shorter species interspersed so they provide hills and valleys in the flower bed.

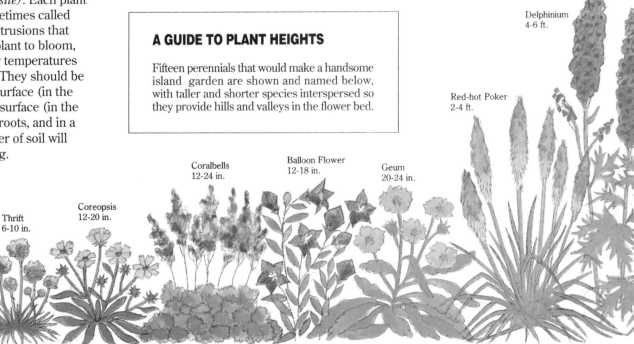

Delphinium
4-6 ft.

Red-hot Poker
2-4 ft.

Coralbells
12-24 in.

Balloon Flower
12-18 in.

Geum
20-24 in.

Coreopsis
12-20 in.

Thrift
6-10 in.

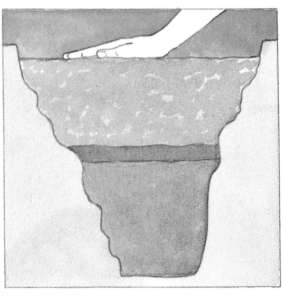

**1** To plant a peony, first dig a hole 18 to 20 inches deep and 20 inches wide. Fill the hole to within 8 inches of the top with a mixture of composted cow manure and garden soil. Add a 1-inch layer of plain soil (to separate the peony roots from direct contact with the manure, which would burn them) and then a 6-inch layer of soil mixed with about four trowelfuls of bone meal. Firm with your hand *(left)*. Allow 3 feet between holes; peonies grow large and need room.

**2** Place the peony root on the top soil layer so that the eyes, or buds *(inset)*, are below the surface of the ground—immediately below the surface if you live in the south, where winters are mild; up to 2 inches if you live in the north. Add or remove soil to get the depth correct. Spread the roots evenly over the soil *(below)*. Fill the hole with more soil, tamp it down and water it.

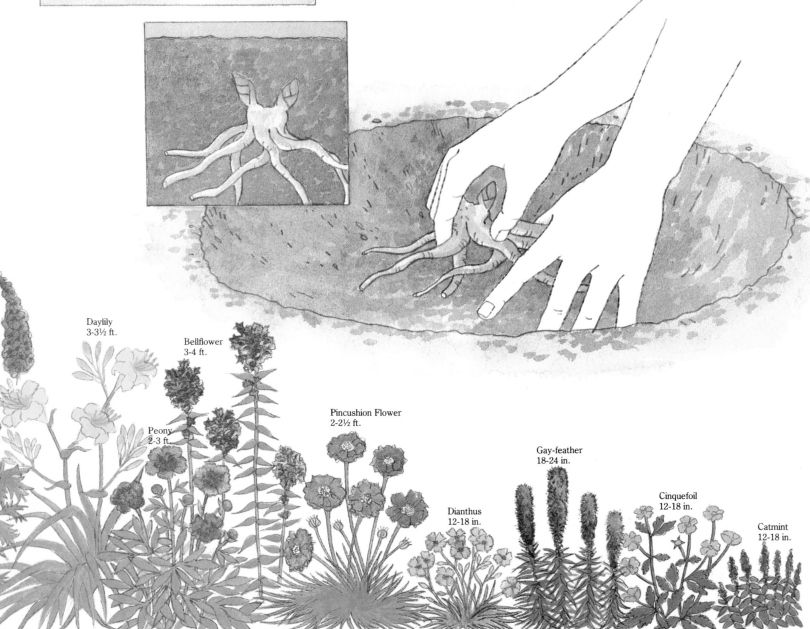

Daylily
3-3½ ft.

Bellflower
3-4 ft.

Peony
2-3 ft.

Pincushion Flower
2-2½ ft.

Dianthus
12-18 in.

Gay-feather
18-24 in.

Cinquefoil
12-18 in.

Catmint
12-18 in.

# THE SCREE GARDEN—
# A BED OF STONES FOR EASY DRAINAGE

An easy way to reclaim a poorly drained plot is a scree garden, so called because its layers of stone chips resemble a real scree, a collection of loose broken rocks that are deposited by erosion at the foot of mountain slopes.

A scree garden is a small, man-made rock garden specially constructed to drain efficiently. It can have much of the variety and beauty of a full-fledged rock garden, and offer the same welcome contrast to regular beds and borders. A list of scree-loving plants appears in the box below.

A scree garden will look its best if it simulates nature, sloping like a real scree and seeming to emerge from a rock outcrop. If your yard has some large rocks in place, situate the scree garden around them. Locating the garden where it will get some shade is also a good idea; a stony scree can get hot. It is also important to choose species that are compatible with the predominant stone being used in the underlayers and on the surface. Lime-loving plants grow best around limestone; perennials favoring acid soils do better with acid sandstone. For a neutral environment, neither acid nor alkaline, try granite. If you live in the Northwest, where the climate is moist, you might need to add more stone chips and sand; in the Southwest, where it is arid, more peat moss may be required.

*Appearing to flow naturally from a stone outcropping, a scree garden blooms with shrubs and perennials that need well-drained soil, which the scree garden provides.*

To make a scree garden, dig out your area to a depth of 2 feet. Shovel in a drainage layer of large chips and coarse gravel 6 inches deep *(left)*. Add a 1-inch layer of straw. Fill the excavation to within 1 inch of the top with mixed stone and soil. The mixture should include loam, compost or leaf mold, peat moss, stone chips and sand as well as some slow-release fertilizer in proportions that depend on climate. After letting the main stone-loam layer settle for a week to 10 days, spread on a 1-inch covering layer of stone chips *(diagram)*. Use a trowel to make holes in the top stone layer for the plants you have chosen. Plant them, and water well for several days.

## SAMPLING OF PLANTS FOR A SCREE GARDEN

| | |
|---|---|
| Sea Pink | Basket-of-gold |
| Sedum | Candytuft |
| Crested Iris | Yarrow |

*\*See Dictionary of Perennials (pages 246-263)*

# RESTORING AN ABANDONED FLOWER BED

*A well-tended bed of black-eyed Susans and bright pink phlox makes a handsome display in front of a Victorian veranda. These flowers are so hardy that they can be brought back from near extinction by dividing and transplanting.*

A neglected perennial bed is a sad sight to behold. Crowded by weeds and grass, plants become embroiled in exhausting competition for breathing room and nutrients. Some plants actually force themselves half out of the ground to escape overcrowding; then, with the roots exposed, they are likely to die. Others are so weakened by the struggle to survive that they scarcely bloom. Undoing the ravages of neglect takes hard work. First, look for clues to the original design of the bed. Was it organized around certain colors, textures, fragrances? Identify and label plants that are in bloom; without flowers, it's hard to tell a purple from a yellow iris. Make sketches or record seasonal changes with a camera. Decide what to keep and what to discard. Some plants, such as bee balm and aster, grow new shoots on their outer edges and develop bare centers as they mature. They can be restored to health by a process called root division *(Chapter 2)*. Use a spade to redefine the bed's edges. Remove all weeds. Check for invasive plants such as daylily and phlox, which may have overrun their neighbors; divide these and transplant them.

Test the soil; add lime or sulfur if needed. Work organic matter around plants, or dig up plants and set them aside while you amend the soil.

## MAXIMIZING ON MUMS

Chrysanthemums are favorite perennials for the fall garden, but from early spring until late August, they take up space and do not provide blossoms. To solve this problem without purchasing new mums every fall, and still have flower beds that are filled with color all summer long, take stem cuttings from the chrysanthemums in spring, when new mum growth begins. As soon as the cuttings have taken root, remove the mother plants from the ground and discard them. In their place, fill the beds with annuals for color that lasts throughout the summer. In early fall, when the annuals begin to fade and the new chrysanthemums begin to bloom, remove the annuals from the beds. Plant the mums, leave them in the ground for the winter and start the process over again the following spring.

# BRINGING RHIZOMES BACK TO LIFE

A rhizome is a stem that behaves like a root. It grows laterally along or just under the soil surface, and it consists of fleshy tissue that stores nutrients the plant lives on. It has many fine, hairlike feeder roots that extend downward and draw nutrients from the soil.

Rhizomes need dividing because they are voracious feeders and vigorous spreaders that eventually exhaust and outgrow the soil they were planted in. Since they are located at or near the soil surface, they are easy to get at.

The most common perennials with rhizomes propagated by division are varieties of bearded iris (*opposite*). They need to be divided about once every four years. When they are ready for rejuvenation by division, they will give visible signals; the number and quality of blooms will decline, and the rhizomes themselves will begin to push out of the soil.

The time for division is after the flowers fade. Because the rhizomes are so close to the surface, the entire plant is easily lifted with a spading fork. After gently shaking the plant and rinsing off any clinging soil, you can distinguish the vigorous new rhizomes from the older, exhausted portions, which will be shriveled, hollow or darker in color. Cut out old or diseased growth with a sharp knife and discard, and then cut the remaining rhizome into as many sections as you want. Make sure each division has healthy leaves and a complement of roots attached to it.

Plant new divisions in soil improved with compost. The roots should be covered with 2 to 4 inches of soil; the rhizomes themselves sit half in, half out, of the ground. Sprinkle fertilizer around the new plants.

*Hybrid bearded irises greet the spring with colorful, aromatic blossoms. Through periodic divisions, bearded iris and other plants with rhizomes can flourish in the same garden for 50 years or more.*

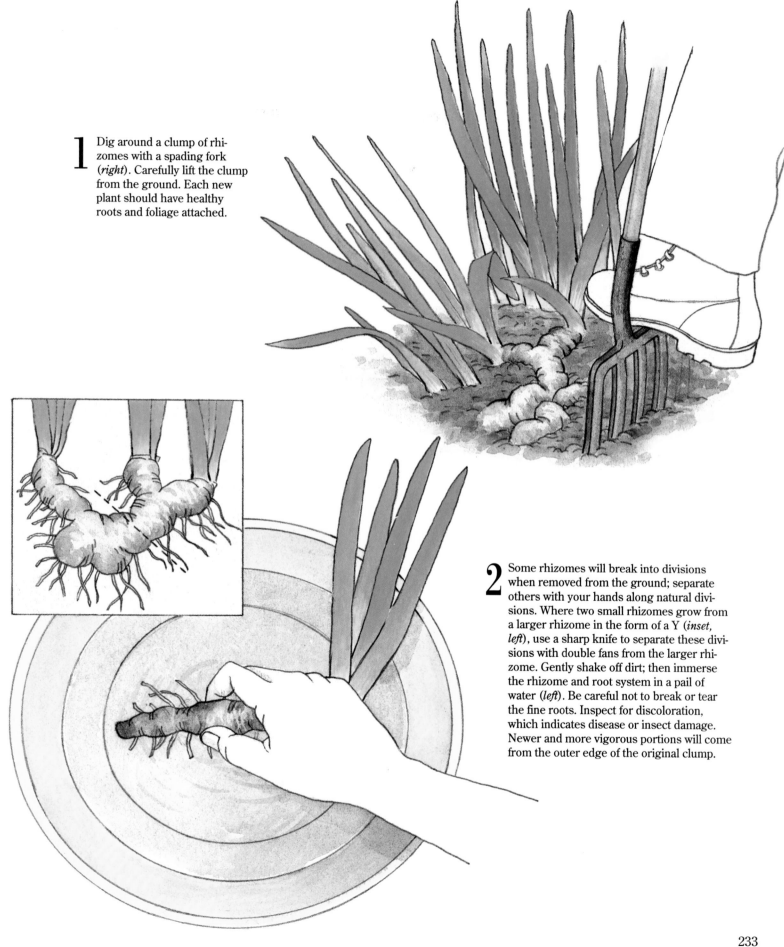

1 Dig around a clump of rhizomes with a spading fork (*right*). Carefully lift the clump from the ground. Each new plant should have healthy roots and foliage attached.

2 Some rhizomes will break into divisions when removed from the ground; separate others with your hands along natural divisions. Where two small rhizomes grow from a larger rhizome in the form of a Y (*inset, left*), use a sharp knife to separate these divisions with double fans from the larger rhizome. Gently shake off dirt; then immerse the rhizome and root system in a pail of water (*left*). Be careful not to break or tear the fine roots. Inspect for discoloration, which indicates disease or insect damage. Newer and more vigorous portions will come from the outer edge of the original clump.

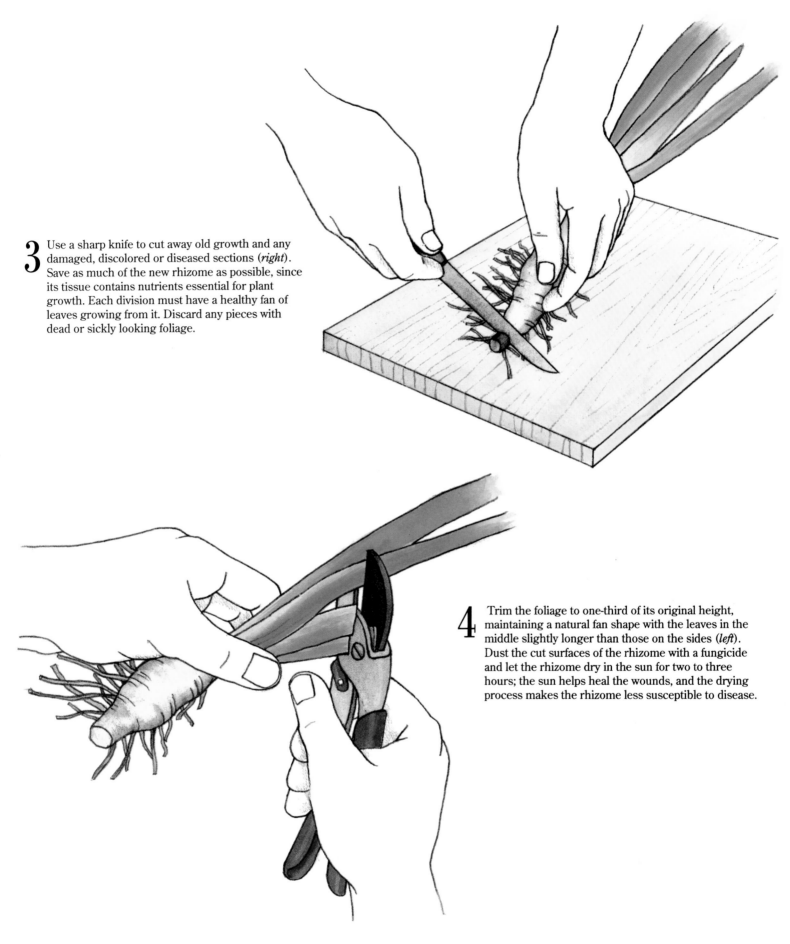

**3** Use a sharp knife to cut away old growth and any damaged, discolored or diseased sections (*right*). Save as much of the new rhizome as possible, since its tissue contains nutrients essential for plant growth. Each division must have a healthy fan of leaves growing from it. Discard any pieces with dead or sickly looking foliage.

**4** Trim the foliage to one-third of its original height, maintaining a natural fan shape with the leaves in the middle slightly longer than those on the sides (*left*). Dust the cut surfaces of the rhizome with a fungicide and let the rhizome dry in the sun for two to three hours; the sun helps heal the wounds, and the drying process makes the rhizome less susceptible to disease.

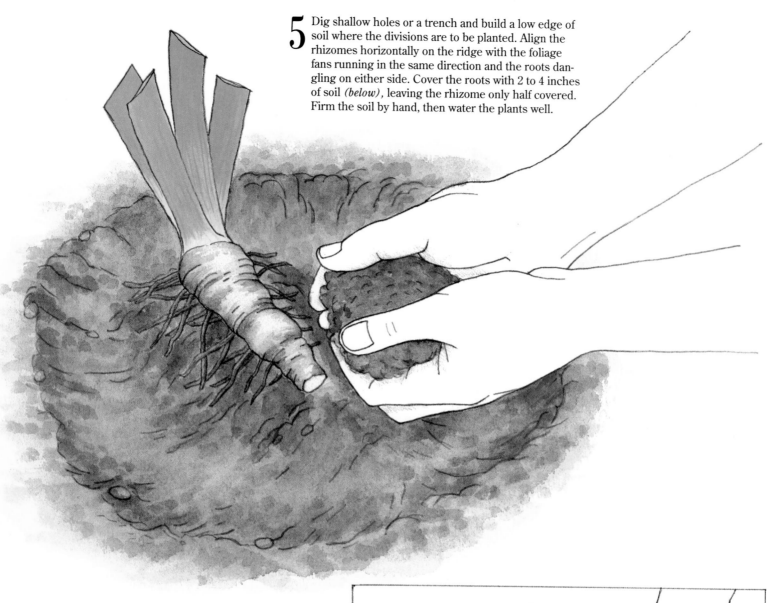

**5** Dig shallow holes or a trench and build a low edge of soil where the divisions are to be planted. Align the rhizomes horizontally on the ridge with the foliage fans running in the same direction and the roots dangling on either side. Cover the roots with 2 to 4 inches of soil *(below)*, leaving the rhizome only half covered. Firm the soil by hand, then water the plants well.

**6** Sprinkle bone meal or low-nitrogen fertilizer in a ring around each division *(right)*, taking care not to get any fertilizer on the rhizome itself. Apply fertilizer again in early spring, before the plants bloom, and in late summer or fall, after they have flowered.

# BEDDING DOWN PERENNIALS FOR THE WINTER

A perennial garden needs an annual cleanup in the fall to make it look neater through the winter and to promote healthy growth the next season. After the first killing frost, the stems of perennials that die back to the underground crown (chrysanthemums, peonies, coreopsis) should be cut back so that only 3 or 4 inches of stalk remain (*opposite*). The dead stems and other detritus should then be raked up, cleared away and disposed of with trash to rid your garden of any lingering insects or diseases.

After cold weather has frozen the ground hard, mulches should be spread for winter protection. Mulches put down too soon make cozy homes for rodents, which will feast on the plants and their roots. Once the ground is hard, rodents will seek shelter elsewhere.

In most regions where winters are cold, mulching is needed not to keep plants warm but, paradoxically, to make sure that they stay solidly frozen in the ground. The perennials that are normally grown in the cooler zones can survive frigid weather. What they cannot tolerate is sharp variations: freezes followed by thaws followed by more freezes. Such changes cause the ground to heave, to move the plants and break their roots. Winter mulches prevent heaving by shading the soil from the sun so that it stays frozen, while also allowing air and moisture to penetrate. Snow does the same job perfectly, and in regions where a winter-long cover of 4 or 5 inches of snow is predictable, no mulching is required.

Some of the best mulches provide nutrients as well as protection: shredded leaves from deciduous trees, shredded tree bark, partially decomposed organic matter. In the spring, such mulches can be worked into the soil after being carefully removed from the crowns of the emerging plants. For more information on mulching, see page 70.

*An autumn mulch of pine needles blankets the ground around cut-back stems of goldenrod, insulating the plant's roots for the coming winter.*

## ACCENTS AT NIGHT

One of the most delightful times of day in a garden is the evening, when the air is still and cool. To make the most of it, select perennials with white or pastel flowers, because pale colors show up better against the night sky than dark ones. Garden lighting will help to accent them and show off their beauty. Some flowers become more fragrant at night.

The gas plant is a perennial that can lend a little fun to the night garden. Its foliage and flowers exude a volatile gas that can be ignited. For a momentary flare that is bright (but not hot enough to be dangerous), hold a lighted match alongside the plant. Choose a still night; wind disperses the gas and you won't get any flare at all.

**1** Cut back your perennials following the first hard frost so that only 3 or 4 inches of stalk remain *(left)*; diseases and insects will be removed with the dead and dying foliage, and the stubble will serve to mark the locations of your plants until they burst forth with new growth in the spring.

**2** After waiting for the ground to freeze hard—it may be as long as two months after the initial killing frost—shovel a 2- to 3-inch layer of shredded tree leaves *(right)* or other good mulch over your garden. Keep in mind that maple leaves are alkaline and oak leaves are acid. Delphiniums are a special case; they like an inch of coal ashes or sand to fend off their enemies, snails.

# A CHECKLIST FOR PERENNIALS

| | ZONE 1 | ZONE 2 | ZONE 3 | ZONE 4 | ZONE 5 |
|---|---|---|---|---|---|
| **JANUARY/FEBRUARY** | • Study seed and plant catalogs for new ideas for spring<br>• Sharpen and repair garden tools<br>• Press heaved plants back into soil<br>• Check winter mulch; add extra, including Christmas tree boughs, if necessary | • Study seed and plant catalogs for new ideas for spring<br>• Sharpen and repair garden tools<br>• Press heaved plants back into soil<br>• Check winter mulch, add extra, including Christmas tree boughs, if necessary | • Study seed and plant catalogs for new ideas for spring<br>• Sharpen and repair garden tools<br>• Press heaved plants back into soil<br>• Check winter mulch; add extra, including Christmas tree boughs, if necessary | • Study seed and plant catalogs for new ideas for spring<br>• Sharpen and repair garden tools<br>• Press heaved plants back into soil<br>• Check winter mulch; add extra, including Christmas tree boughs, if necessary | • Study seed and plant catalogs for new ideas for spring<br>• Sharpen and repair garden tools<br>• Press heaved plants back into soil<br>• Check winter mulch; add extra, including Christmas tree boughs, if necessary |
| **MARCH/APRIL** | • Sow perennial seeds indoors | • Sow perennial seeds indoors | • Sow perennial seeds indoors | • Sow perennial seeds indoors<br>• Plant bare-root perennials<br>• Complete bed preparation for planting | • Remove fallen leaves, twigs and branches from garden<br>• Repair fences, edging<br>• Remove winter mulch<br>• Sow perennial seeds outdoors<br>• Plant bare-root perennials<br>• Complete bed preparation for planting |
| **MAY/JUNE** | • Remove fallen leaves, twigs and branches from garden<br>• Repair fences, edging<br>• Remove winter mulch<br>• Sow perennial seeds outdoors<br>• Set seedlings outdoors<br>• Plant bare-root perennials<br>• Plant container perennials<br>• Divide and transplant perennials<br>• Root chrysanthemums; then plant<br>• Thin out overgrown plantings<br>• Fertilize as growth starts<br>• Cut back ornamental grasses<br>• Stake plants<br>• Apply summer mulch<br>• Weed flower beds<br>• Water if ground is dry<br>• Check for insects, disease<br>• Apply summer mulch<br>• Plant chrysanthemums<br>• Disbud peonies | • Remove fallen leaves, twigs and branches from garden<br>• Repair fences, edging<br>• Remove winter mulch<br>• Sow perennial seeds outdoors<br>• Set seedlings outdoors<br>• Plant bare-root perennials<br>• Plant container perennials<br>• Divide and transplant perennials<br>• Root chrysanthemums; then plant<br>• Thin out overgrown plantings<br>• Fertilize as growth starts<br>• Cut back ornamental grasses<br>• Stake plants<br>• Apply summer mulch<br>• Weed flower beds<br>• Water if ground is dry<br>• Check for insects, disease<br>• Apply summer mulch<br>• Plant chrysanthemums<br>• Disbud peonies | • Remove fallen leaves, twigs and branches from garden<br>• Repair fences, edging<br>• Remove winter mulch<br>• Complete bed preparation<br>• Sow perennial seeds outdoors<br>• Set seedlings outdoors<br>• Plant bare-root perennials<br>• Plant container perennials<br>• Divide and transplant perennials<br>• Root chrysanthemums; then plant<br>• Thin out overgrown plantings<br>• Fertilize as growth starts<br>• Cut back ornamental grasses<br>• Stake plants<br>• Apply summer mulch<br>• Weed flower beds<br>• Water if ground is dry<br>• Check for insects, disease<br>• Apply summer mulch<br>• Plant chrysanthemums<br>• Disbud peonies | • Remove fallen leaves, twigs and branches from garden<br>• Repair fences, edging<br>• Remove winter mulch<br>• Complete bed preparation<br>• Sow perennial seeds outdoors<br>• Set seedlings outdoors<br>• Plant bare-root perennials<br>• Plant container perennials<br>• Divide and transplant perennials<br>• Root chrysanthemums; then plant<br>• Thin out overgrown plantings<br>• Fertilize as growth starts<br>• Cut back ornamental grasses<br>• Stake plants<br>• Apply summer mulch<br>• Weed flower beds<br>• Water if ground is dry<br>• Check for insects, disease<br>• Apply summer mulch<br>• Plant chrysanthemums<br>• Disbud peonies | • Complete bed preparation<br>• Sow perennial seeds outdoors<br>• Set seedlings outdoors<br>• Plant container perennials<br>• Divide and transplant perennials<br>• Root chrysanthemums; then plant<br>• Thin out overgrown plantings<br>• Fertilize as growth starts<br>• Cut back ornamental grasses<br>• Stake plants<br>• Apply summer mulch<br>• Weed flower beds<br>• Water if ground is dry<br>• Check for insects, disease<br>• Apply summer mulch<br>• Plant chrysanthemums<br>• Disbud peonies |

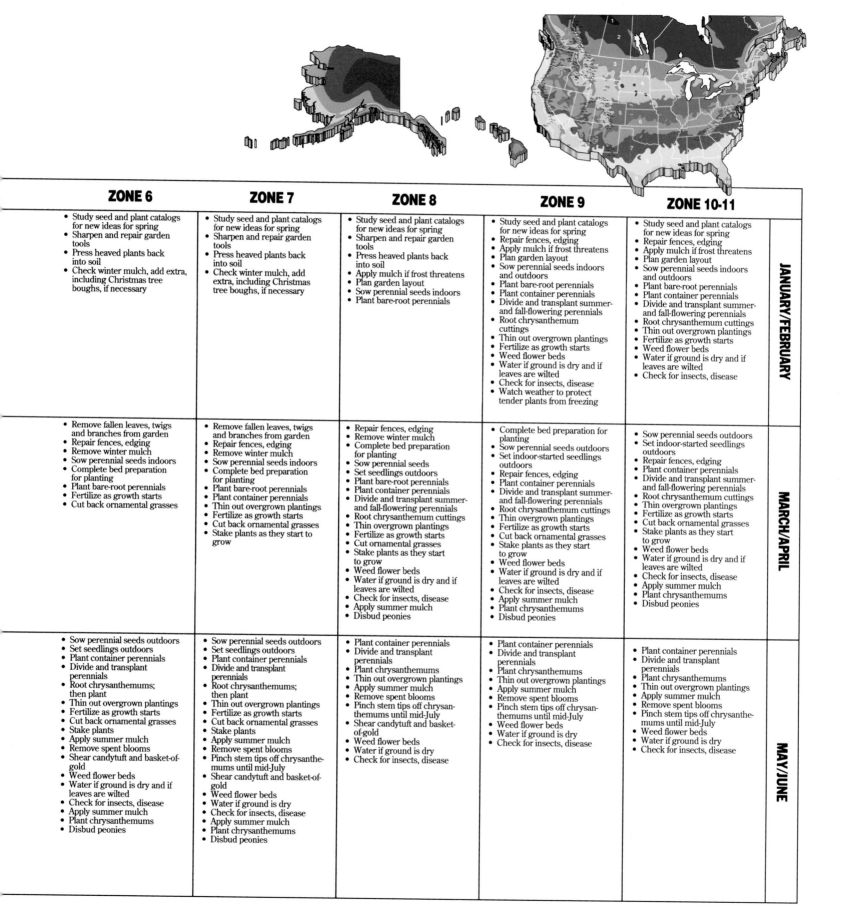

| | ZONE 6 | ZONE 7 | ZONE 8 | ZONE 9 | ZONE 10-11 | |
|---|---|---|---|---|---|---|
| | • Study seed and plant catalogs for new ideas for spring<br>• Sharpen and repair garden tools<br>• Press heaved plants back into soil<br>• Check winter mulch, add extra, including Christmas tree boughs, if necessary | • Study seed and plant catalogs for new ideas for spring<br>• Sharpen and repair garden tools<br>• Press heaved plants back into soil<br>• Check winter mulch, add extra, including Christmas tree boughs, if necessary | • Study seed and plant catalogs for new ideas for spring<br>• Sharpen and repair garden tools<br>• Press heaved plants back into soil<br>• Apply mulch if frost threatens<br>• Plan garden layout<br>• Sow perennial seeds indoors<br>• Plant bare-root perennials | • Study seed and plant catalogs for new ideas for spring<br>• Repair fences, edging<br>• Apply mulch if frost threatens<br>• Plan garden layout<br>• Sow perennial seeds indoors and outdoors<br>• Plant bare-root perennials<br>• Plant container perennials<br>• Divide and transplant summer- and fall-flowering perennials<br>• Root chrysanthemum cuttings<br>• Thin out overgrown plantings<br>• Fertilize as growth starts<br>• Weed flower beds<br>• Water if ground is dry and if leaves are wilted<br>• Check for insects, disease<br>• Watch weather to protect tender plants from freezing | • Study seed and plant catalogs for new ideas for spring<br>• Repair fences, edging<br>• Apply mulch if frost threatens<br>• Plan garden layout<br>• Sow perennial seeds indoors and outdoors<br>• Plant bare-root perennials<br>• Plant container perennials<br>• Divide and transplant summer- and fall-flowering perennials<br>• Root chrysanthemum cuttings<br>• Thin out overgrown plantings<br>• Fertilize as growth starts<br>• Weed flower beds<br>• Water if ground is dry and if leaves are wilted<br>• Check for insects, disease | **JANUARY/FEBRUARY** |
| | • Remove fallen leaves, twigs and branches from garden<br>• Repair fences, edging<br>• Remove winter mulch<br>• Sow perennial seeds indoors<br>• Complete bed preparation for planting<br>• Plant bare-root perennials<br>• Fertilize as growth starts<br>• Cut back ornamental grasses | • Remove fallen leaves, twigs and branches from garden<br>• Repair fences, edging<br>• Remove winter mulch<br>• Sow perennial seeds indoors<br>• Complete bed preparation for planting<br>• Plant bare-root perennials<br>• Plant container perennials<br>• Thin out overgrown plantings<br>• Fertilize as growth starts<br>• Cut back ornamental grasses<br>• Stake plants as they start to grow | • Repair fences, edging<br>• Remove winter mulch<br>• Complete bed preparation for planting<br>• Sow perennial seeds<br>• Set seedlings outdoors<br>• Plant bare-root perennials<br>• Plant container perennials<br>• Divide and transplant summer- and fall-flowering perennials<br>• Root chrysanthemum cuttings<br>• Thin overgrown plantings<br>• Fertilize as growth starts<br>• Cut ornamental grasses<br>• Stake plants as they start to grow<br>• Weed flower beds<br>• Water if ground is dry and if leaves are wilted<br>• Check for insects, disease<br>• Apply summer mulch<br>• Disbud peonies | • Complete bed preparation for planting<br>• Sow perennial seeds outdoors<br>• Set indoor-started seedlings outdoors<br>• Repair fences, edging<br>• Plant container perennials<br>• Divide and transplant summer- and fall-flowering perennials<br>• Root chrysanthemum cuttings<br>• Thin overgrown plantings<br>• Fertilize as growth starts<br>• Cut back ornamental grasses<br>• Stake plants as they start to grow<br>• Weed flower beds<br>• Water if ground is dry and if leaves are wilted<br>• Check for insects, disease<br>• Apply summer mulch<br>• Plant chrysanthemums<br>• Disbud peonies | • Sow perennial seeds outdoors<br>• Set indoor-started seedlings outdoors<br>• Repair fences, edging<br>• Plant container perennials<br>• Divide and transplant summer- and fall-flowering perennials<br>• Root chrysanthemum cuttings<br>• Thin out overgrown plantings<br>• Fertilize as growth starts<br>• Cut back ornamental grasses<br>• Stake plants as they start to grow<br>• Weed flower beds<br>• Water if ground is dry and if leaves are wilted<br>• Check for insects, disease<br>• Apply summer mulch<br>• Plant chrysanthemums<br>• Disbud peonies | **MARCH/APRIL** |
| | • Sow perennial seeds outdoors<br>• Set seedlings outdoors<br>• Plant container perennials<br>• Divide and transplant perennials<br>• Root chrysanthemums; then plant<br>• Thin out overgrown plantings<br>• Fertilize as growth starts<br>• Cut back ornamental grasses<br>• Stake plants<br>• Apply summer mulch<br>• Remove spent blooms<br>• Shear candytuft and basket-of-gold<br>• Weed flower beds<br>• Water if ground is dry and if leaves are wilted<br>• Check for insects, disease<br>• Apply summer mulch<br>• Plant chrysanthemums<br>• Disbud peonies | • Sow perennial seeds outdoors<br>• Set seedlings outdoors<br>• Plant container perennials<br>• Divide and transplant perennials<br>• Root chrysanthemums; then plant<br>• Thin out overgrown plantings<br>• Fertilize as growth starts<br>• Cut back ornamental grasses<br>• Stake plants<br>• Apply summer mulch<br>• Remove spent blooms<br>• Pinch stem tips off chrysanthemums until mid-July<br>• Shear candytuft and basket-of-gold<br>• Weed flower beds<br>• Water if ground is dry<br>• Check for insects, disease<br>• Apply summer mulch<br>• Plant chrysanthemums<br>• Disbud peonies | • Plant container perennials<br>• Divide and transplant perennials<br>• Plant chrysanthemums<br>• Thin out overgrown plantings<br>• Apply summer mulch<br>• Remove spent blooms<br>• Pinch stem tips off chrysanthemums until mid-July<br>• Shear candytuft and basket-of-gold<br>• Weed flower beds<br>• Water if ground is dry<br>• Check for insects, disease | • Plant container perennials<br>• Divide and transplant perennials<br>• Plant chrysanthemums<br>• Thin out overgrown plantings<br>• Apply summer mulch<br>• Remove spent blooms<br>• Pinch stem tips off chrysanthemums until mid-July<br>• Weed flower beds<br>• Water if ground is dry<br>• Check for insects, disease | • Plant container perennials<br>• Divide and transplant perennials<br>• Plant chrysanthemums<br>• Thin out overgrown plantings<br>• Apply summer mulch<br>• Remove spent blooms<br>• Pinch stem tips off chrysanthemums until mid-July<br>• Weed flower beds<br>• Water if ground is dry<br>• Check for insects, disease | **MAY/JUNE** |

| | ZONE 1 | ZONE 2 | ZONE 3 | ZONE 4 | ZONE 5 |
|---|---|---|---|---|---|
| **JULY/AUGUST** | • Sow perennial and biennial seeds outdoors<br>• Remove spent blooms<br>• Shear ground covers and rock-garden plants<br>• Cut off phlox blooms before seeds drop<br>• Pinch stem tips off chrysanthemums until early July<br>• Dig up iris; check for borers and root rot<br>• Divide and replant iris<br>• Cut flowers and ornamental grasses for drying<br>• Weed; check summer mulch<br>• Water if ground is dry<br>• Check for insects and diseases; treat immediately<br>• Plant chrysanthemums in bud and bloom<br>• Plant poppies and peonies<br>• Harvest cut flowers for indoor displays | • Sow perennial and biennial seeds outdoors<br>• Remove spent blooms<br>• Shear ground covers and rock-garden plants<br>• Cut off phlox blooms before seeds drop<br>• Pinch stem tips off chrysanthemums until mid-July<br>• Dig up iris; check for borers and root rot<br>• Divide and replant iris<br>• Cut flowers and ornamental grasses for drying<br>• Weed; check summer mulch<br>• Water if ground is dry<br>• Check for insects disease<br>• Plant chrysanthemums in bud and bloom<br>• Plant poppies and peonies<br>• Harvest cut flowers for indoor displays | • Sow perennial and biennial seeds outdoors<br>• Remove spent blooms<br>• Shear ground covers and rock-garden plants<br>• Cut off phlox blooms before seeds drop<br>• Pinch stem tips off chrysanthemums until mid-July<br>• Dig up iris; check for borers and root rot<br>• Divide and replant iris<br>• Cut flowers and ornamental grasses for drying<br>• Weed; check summer mulch<br>• Water if ground is dry<br>• Check for insects, disease<br>• Plant chrysanthemums in bud and bloom<br>• Plant poppies and peonies<br>• Harvest cut flowers for indoor displays | • Sow perennial and biennial seeds outdoors<br>• Remove spent blooms<br>• Shear ground covers and rock-garden plants<br>• Cut off phlox blooms before seeds drop<br>• Pinch stem tips off chrysanthemums until mid-July<br>• Dig up iris; check for borers and root rot<br>• Divide and replant iris<br>• Cut flowers and ornamental grasses for drying<br>• Weed; check summer mulch<br>• Water if ground is dry<br>• Check for insects, disease<br>• Plant chrysanthemums in bud and bloom<br>• Plant poppies and peonies<br>• Harvest cut flowers for indoor displays | • Sow perennial and biennial seeds outdoors<br>• Remove spent blooms<br>• Shear ground covers and rock-garden plants<br>• Cut off phlox blooms before seeds drop<br>• Pinch stem tips off chrysanthemums until mid-July<br>• Dig up iris; check for borers and root rot<br>• Divide and replant iris<br>• Cut flowers and ornamental grasses for drying<br>• Weed; check summer mulch<br>• Water if ground is dry<br>• Check for insects, disease<br>• Plant chrysanthemums in bud and bloom<br>• Plant poppies and peonies<br>• Harvest cut flowers for indoor displays |
| **SEPTEMBER/OCTOBER** | • Water if ground is dry and if leaves are wilted<br>• Cut back tops of withered plants<br>• Apply slow-acting fertilizer to perennial beds<br>• Move semihardy young plants to a cold frame<br>• Clean up leaves and other litter<br>• Turn off water; drain hose<br>• Apply winter mulch after a hard freeze<br>• Install wind/soil erosion controls<br>• Compost spent plant materials | • Water if ground is dry and if leaves are wilted<br>• Cut back tops of withered plants<br>• Apply slow-acting fertilizer to perennial beds<br>• Move semihardy young plants to a cold frame<br>• Clean up leaves and other litter<br>• Turn off water; drain hose<br>• Apply winter mulch after a hard freeze<br>• Install wind/soil erosion controls<br>• Compost spent plant materials | • Water if ground is dry and if leaves are wilted<br>• Cut back tops of withered plants<br>• Apply slow-acting fertilizer to perennial beds<br>• Move semihardy young plants to a cold frame<br>• Clean up leaves and other litter<br>• Turn off water; drain hose<br>• Apply winter mulch after a hard freeze<br>• Install wind/soil erosion controls<br>• Compost spent plant materials | • Water if ground is dry and if leaves are wilted<br>• Cut back tops of withered plants<br>• Apply slow-acting fertilizer to perennial beds<br>• Move semihardy young plants to a cold frame<br>• Clean up leaves and other litter<br>• Turn off water; drain hose<br>• Apply winter mulch after a hard freeze<br>• Divide and transplant summer-flowering perennials<br>• Install wind/soil erosion controls<br>• Compost spent plant materials | • Sow perennial and biennial seeds outdoors<br>• Remove spent blooms<br>• Prepare soil for fall planting<br>• Divide and transplant spring-flowering perennials<br>• Water if ground is dry and if leaves are wilted<br>• Move semihardy young plants to a cold frame<br>• Install wind/soil erosion controls<br>• Compost spent plant materials |
| **NOVEMBER/DECEMBER** | • Order seed catalogs for next year | • Order seed catalogs for next year | • Order seed catalogs for next year | • Rake leaves from perennial beds<br>• Order seed catalogs for next year | • Rake leaves from perennial beds<br>• Order seed catalogs for next year<br>• Water if ground is dry<br>• Turn off water; drain hose<br>• Apply winter mulch after a hard freeze |

240

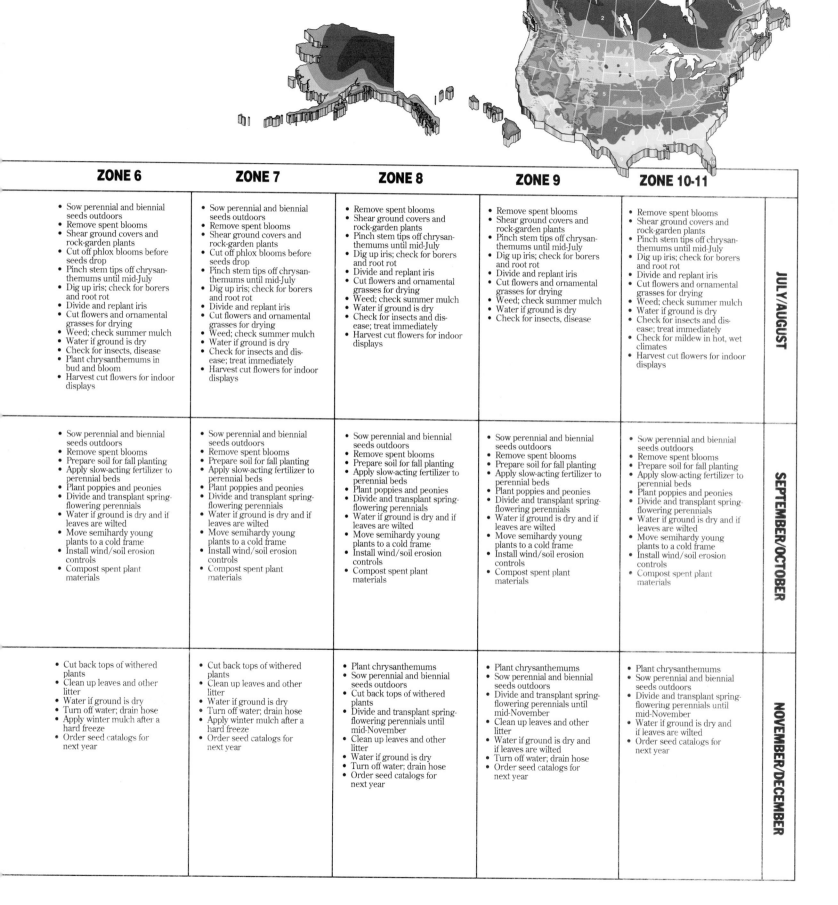

| | ZONE 6 | ZONE 7 | ZONE 8 | ZONE 9 | ZONE 10-11 | |
|---|---|---|---|---|---|---|
| | • Sow perennial and biennial seeds outdoors<br>• Remove spent blooms<br>• Shear ground covers and rock-garden plants<br>• Cut off phlox blooms before seeds drop<br>• Pinch stem tips off chrysanthemums until mid-July<br>• Dig up iris; check for borers and root rot<br>• Divide and replant iris<br>• Cut flowers and ornamental grasses for drying<br>• Weed; check summer mulch<br>• Water if ground is dry<br>• Check for insects, disease<br>• Plant chrysanthemums in bud and bloom<br>• Harvest cut flowers for indoor displays | • Sow perennial and biennial seeds outdoors<br>• Remove spent blooms<br>• Shear ground covers and rock-garden plants<br>• Cut off phlox blooms before seeds drop<br>• Pinch stem tips off chrysanthemums until mid-July<br>• Dig up iris; check for borers and root rot<br>• Divide and replant iris<br>• Cut flowers and ornamental grasses for drying<br>• Weed; check summer mulch<br>• Water if ground is dry<br>• Check for insects and disease; treat immediately<br>• Harvest cut flowers for indoor displays | • Remove spent blooms<br>• Shear ground covers and rock-garden plants<br>• Pinch stem tips off chrysanthemums until mid-July<br>• Dig up iris; check for borers and root rot<br>• Divide and replant iris<br>• Cut flowers and ornamental grasses for drying<br>• Weed; check summer mulch<br>• Water if ground is dry<br>• Check for insects and disease; treat immediately<br>• Harvest cut flowers for indoor displays | • Remove spent blooms<br>• Shear ground covers and rock-garden plants<br>• Pinch stem tips off chrysanthemums until mid-July<br>• Dig up iris; check for borers and root rot<br>• Divide and replant iris<br>• Cut flowers and ornamental grasses for drying<br>• Weed; check summer mulch<br>• Water if ground is dry<br>• Check for insects, disease | • Remove spent blooms<br>• Shear ground covers and rock-garden plants<br>• Pinch stem tips off chrysanthemums until mid-July<br>• Dig up iris; check for borers and root rot<br>• Divide and replant iris<br>• Cut flowers and ornamental grasses for drying<br>• Weed; check summer mulch<br>• Water if ground is dry<br>• Check for insects and disease; treat immediately<br>• Check for mildew in hot, wet climates<br>• Harvest cut flowers for indoor displays | **JULY/AUGUST** |
| | • Sow perennial and biennial seeds outdoors<br>• Remove spent blooms<br>• Prepare soil for fall planting<br>• Apply slow-acting fertilizer to perennial beds<br>• Plant poppies and peonies<br>• Divide and transplant spring-flowering perennials<br>• Water if ground is dry and if leaves are wilted<br>• Move semihardy young plants to a cold frame<br>• Install wind/soil erosion controls<br>• Compost spent plant materials | • Sow perennial and biennial seeds outdoors<br>• Remove spent blooms<br>• Prepare soil for fall planting<br>• Apply slow-acting fertilizer to perennial beds<br>• Plant poppies and peonies<br>• Divide and transplant spring-flowering perennials<br>• Water if ground is dry and if leaves are wilted<br>• Move semihardy young plants to a cold frame<br>• Install wind/soil erosion controls<br>• Compost spent plant materials | • Sow perennial and biennial seeds outdoors<br>• Remove spent blooms<br>• Prepare soil for fall planting<br>• Apply slow-acting fertilizer to perennial beds<br>• Plant poppies and peonies<br>• Divide and transplant spring-flowering perennials<br>• Water if ground is dry and if leaves are wilted<br>• Move semihardy young plants to a cold frame<br>• Install wind/soil erosion controls<br>• Compost spent plant materials | • Sow perennial and biennial seeds outdoors<br>• Remove spent blooms<br>• Prepare soil for fall planting<br>• Apply slow-acting fertilizer to perennial beds<br>• Plant poppies and peonies<br>• Divide and transplant spring-flowering perennials<br>• Water if ground is dry and if leaves are wilted<br>• Move semihardy young plants to a cold frame<br>• Install wind/soil erosion controls<br>• Compost spent plant materials | • Sow perennial and biennial seeds outdoors<br>• Remove spent blooms<br>• Prepare soil for fall planting<br>• Apply slow-acting fertilizer to perennial beds<br>• Plant poppies and peonies<br>• Divide and transplant spring-flowering perennials<br>• Water if ground is dry and if leaves are wilted<br>• Move semihardy young plants to a cold frame<br>• Install wind/soil erosion controls<br>• Compost spent plant materials | **SEPTEMBER/OCTOBER** |
| | • Cut back tops of withered plants<br>• Clean up leaves and other litter<br>• Water if ground is dry<br>• Turn off water; drain hose<br>• Apply winter mulch after a hard freeze<br>• Order seed catalogs for next year | • Cut back tops of withered plants<br>• Clean up leaves and other litter<br>• Water if ground is dry<br>• Turn off water; drain hose<br>• Apply winter mulch after a hard freeze<br>• Order seed catalogs for next year | • Plant chrysanthemums<br>• Sow perennial and biennial seeds outdoors<br>• Cut back tops of withered plants<br>• Divide and transplant spring-flowering perennials until mid-November<br>• Clean up leaves and other litter<br>• Water if ground is dry<br>• Turn off water; drain hose<br>• Order seed catalogs for next year | • Plant chrysanthemums<br>• Sow perennial and biennial seeds outdoors<br>• Divide and transplant spring-flowering perennials until mid-November<br>• Clean up leaves and other litter<br>• Water if ground is dry and if leaves are wilted<br>• Turn off water; drain hose<br>• Order seed catalogs for next year | • Plant chrysanthemums<br>• Sow perennial and biennial seeds outdoors<br>• Divide and transplant spring-flowering perennials until mid-November<br>• Water if ground is dry and if leaves are wilted<br>• Order seed catalogs for next year | **NOVEMBER/DECEMBER** |

# TROUBLESHOOTING GUIDE: PERENNIALS

| PROBLEM | CAUSE | SOLUTION |
|---|---|---|
| Leaves curl, are distorted in shape and may have a black, sooty appearance; plant is stunted. Many perennials may be affected, including columbine, delphinium, iris, poppy and chrysanthemum. | Aphids (plant lice), ⅛-inch cream, green, red, black or brown semitransparent insects found on buds, leaves and stems. | Wash plants with a spray of water and a diluted soap solution or with an insecticide. Ladybug beetles, which eat aphids, may also be introduced into the garden. |
| Peony flowers fail to open or have browned petals. Other perennials, such as chrysanthemum, foxglove, daylily and delphinium, have darkened buds and leaves with a silvery appearance. The plants may be stunted. | Thrips, which are tiny, thin insects barely visible to the naked eye. | Destroy damaged buds and foliage. Spray plants with an insecticide. |
| Small, round holes are eaten into leaves and flowers. | Japanese, Asiatic, snout, blister or other beetles—dark red, brown or bronze-colored, hard-shelled insects ¼ to ½ inch long. | Small colonies can be handpicked. Japanese beetles can be caught in baited traps. The larval stage can be controlled with *Bacillus popilliae,* a bacterium, called milky spore, that causes milky disease, which is lethal to beetles but harmless to plants. |
| Chrysanthemum buds are distorted and do not open; stems and leaves are severely twisted. | Midges, maggots that bore into leaves and stems; not visible to the naked eye. | Pick off and destroy affected buds and foliage. |
| Iris plants wilt, discolor and eventually die. Leaves become loose at the base and the rhizomes become soft and rotten. | Iris borer, a 1 ½ -inch-long, fat, wormlike larva. | In fall, pick off and destroy damaged leaves. In spring, young borers are visible in the leaves and may be removed by hand. Heavily infested rhizomes should be dug out and discarded. |
| Leaves become speckled with white dots, which later turn yellowish brown. Leaves and stems curl or become distorted. | Leafhoppers, small, yellow-green, cricket-like insects. | Damaged foliage should be removed and destroyed. Spray plants with an insecticide. |
| White or light green tunnels are bored into leaves of columbine, chrysanthemum or delphinium. Older tunnels turn black. Leaves may lose color, dry up and eventually die. | Leaf miners, microscopic, pale green fly maggots. | Control is difficult. Pick off and destroy infested leaves as they appear. In the fall, cut the plant to the ground and discard it. Since organic waste attracts maggots, keep the garden well weeded. |

| PROBLEM | CAUSE | SOLUTION |
|---|---|---|
| Foliage of columbine, or chrysanthemum turns yellow and plants are stunted. Shaking of the plants causes a white cloud to appear. | Whiteflies, insects 1/16 inch long that generally collect on the undersides of young leaves. | Keep the garden weeded. Spray affected plants with a diluted soap solution or an insecticide. Whiteflies are attracted to yellow, so flypaper can be hung in the garden to help control the population. |
| Leaves become speckled, then discolored and curled; flowers and buds discolor or dry up and webbing is seen. This is particularly evident in hot, dry weather. Susceptible plants are columbine, daylily, delphinium, iris, phlox, foxglove, candytuft and chrysanthemum. | Mites, which are pinhead-sized, insect-like creatures. | Keep the plants well watered, and spray the undersides of the leaves with water or a diluted soap solution regularly. An insecticide may also be used. |
| Holes appear in leaves; buds, flowers and stems may also be eaten. | Any variety of caterpillar. | Small populations can be destroyed by hand. *Bacillus thuringiensis,* called Bt, causes milky disease, which kills many types of caterpillars but does not harm plants. If caterpillars return to your garden every spring, Bt can be sprayed in anticipation of the problem. |
| Light-colored spots appear on the upper surfaces of leaves. Foliage may wilt or discolor and fall from the plant. Flower buds may be deformed. | Plant bugs, also called true bugs, green or shiny black insects, 1/4 inch long, with antennae and wings. | Spray with an insecticide. |
| A sudsy, white substance resembling foam appears in the area between leaf and stem. | Spittlebugs. Eggs hatch in spring and young insects produce the foamy substance for protection while they feed on sap from tender leaves and stems. | Wash plants off with water and a diluted soap solution or use an insecticide. |
| Chrysanthemum or phlox plants wilt, stop growing and may die. Sometimes brown or yellow blotches appear on leaves. | Nematodes, very tiny worms that live in the soil and feed on roots. | Since nematodes cannot be seen, only a soil test will confirm their presence. Be suspicious if roots appear swollen or stunted. There are no effective chemical controls; remove and dispose of infected plants and the soil that surrounds them. |
| Holes are eaten in leaves, starting with leaves at the bottom of plants. Entire young seedlings may disappear. Telltale silver streaks appear on leaves and garden paths. | Slugs or snails, which hide during the day and feed at night. | Slug and snails can be trapped in saucers of beer. Slugs will also collect under grapefruit halves or melon rinds turned upside down. Both slugs and snails are killed by salt, but salt may damage plants. Bait is available at garden supply centers. |

| PROBLEM | CAUSE | SOLUTION |
|---|---|---|
| Leaves develop spots or lesions that can lead to yellowing and the death of the plant. Aster, chrysanthemum, delphinium, foxglove, iris and phlox are particularly susceptible. | Leaf spot disease, caused by a number of fungi or bacteria and spread by insects, contaminated tools or even splashing water. The organisms thrive in moisture. | Remove infected leaves as they appear and do not allow infected material to remain in the garden through winter. Water overhead only in the morning; damp foliage in cool night air fosters the spread of the disease. Do not overcrowd plants. A fungicide can protect healthy foliage but will not destroy fungus on infected leaves. |
| Young seedlings suddenly topple over, especially when started indoors. | Damping-off, a disease caused by a fungus that forms in the soil and attacks seeds and the roots of young seedlings at ground level. | Use a fresh, sterile planting medium. Do not overwater seed flats. Provide good air circulation. Drench the seed flat with a systemic fungicide before sowing. |
| Upper leaf surfaces have pale spots; undersides of leaves are covered with an orange or reddish brown powder. Plants may be stunted in severe cases. Bee balm, black-eyed Susan, chrysanthemum, columbine and liatris are susceptible. | Rust, a disease cause by fungus. | Water early in the day so plants can dry before nightfall; cool air and damp foliage foster the spread of the disease. In the fall, collect and discard all infected leaves and stems. Spray with sulfur or a garden fungicide. Some varieties of chrysanthemum are rust-resistant. |
| Leaves turn yellow or are stunted and wilted. Entire plant may wilt and die. Roots are discolored, dark brown or black. Many perennials, especially aster, chrysanthemum and delphinium, may be affected. | Root rot, caused by pythium, rhizoctonia or sclerotinia fungus in the soil. | Remove and discard affected plants and the surrounding soil. These fungi grow in moist soils; improved soil drainage is one means of control. Drench the soil with a garden fungicide. |
| White, powdery growth appears on upper leaves, causing leaf distortion. Signs may also be seen on stems and buds—especially in late summer and fall, when nights are cool. Susceptible plants include aster, bee balm, delphinium and phlox. | Powdery mildew, a disease caused by fungus. | Plant susceptible plants in full sun with good air circulation. Water overhead only in the early morning. Cut off infected plants to the ground in fall and discard. Fungicides may be used; also effective are lime-sulfur sprays and antidesiccants. |
| Foliage of gaillardia, coreopsis and delphinium suddenly yellows; flowers are stunted and have a greenish color; new growth is distorted in shape. | Aster yellows, a disease caused by microscopic organisms similar to bacteria. | Aster yellows is often spread by leafhoppers; spray plants with an insecticide. Remove and destroy infected plants; do not use the same type of plant in the same spot. Keep the garden weeded; aster yellows and leafhopper eggs thrive in untended, weedy areas. |

| PROBLEM | CAUSE | SOLUTION |
|---|---|---|
| Entire plant becomes yellow, wilts, fails to grow and eventually dies; a cut across a stem reveals dark streaks or other discoloration on the inside. Chrysanthemum, peony, bleeding heart, aster, coreopsis, poppy, phlox and delphinium may be affected. | Vascular wilt, caused by fungi or bacteria in the soil. | Remove and destroy infected plants; substitute wilt-resistant varieties. There are no effective chemical controls. |
| Tips and leaves of peonies blacken. Buds may not open; if they do, flowers are likely to be streaked with brown. | Botrytis blight, a disease caused by various fungi. | Cut stalks to the ground in fall and destroy. As growth starts in spring, spraying with a systemic fungicide can help prevent recurrence. |
| Leaves of peony, columbine, delphinium, iris, aster or gaillardia become mottled with light green or yellow discoloration. Plant growth is often stunted. | Mosaic virus. | Virus infections cannot be controlled, but since they are often spread by aphids, treat affected areas for aphids; wash plants with a spray of water and a diluted soap solution or with an insecticide. Keep the garden well weeded. Remove infected plants. |
| Iris plants fall over; rhizomes are soft to the touch. | Soft rot, a disease caused by bacteria. | Cut out the infected parts of the rhizomes with a sharp knife or scrape them out with a spoon. Mix a 10 percent solution of chlorine bleach in water and pour it over the rhizomes and the surrounding soil. |
| Leaves and stems of iris or columbine turn yellow, wilt and rot, then die. White fibers are visible at the base of the plant. Roots show signs of decay. | Crown rot, a disease caused by a fungus that enters stems at soil level. | Remove and discard all infected plants and the surrounding soil. Thin out overcrowded plants and improve soil drainage. Clean and disinfect all garden tools, which can spread the disease. |
| Foliage of peony develops irregular, purplish brown spots. Purplish lesions form along the stem; plant growth is often stunted. | Anthracnose, a disease caused by fungus. | The best control is preventive spraying with a fungicide in early spring. Remove and discard any infected plant parts. |
| Leaves of aster, geum, veronica, and potentilla turn yellow. The undersides of the foliage develop gray or tan fuzzy growths that resemble tufts of cotton. | Downy mildew, a disease caused by fungus. | Do not water plants overhead after morning. Remove and destroy infected plant parts or the entire plant if the infection is severe. Spray with fungicide. |

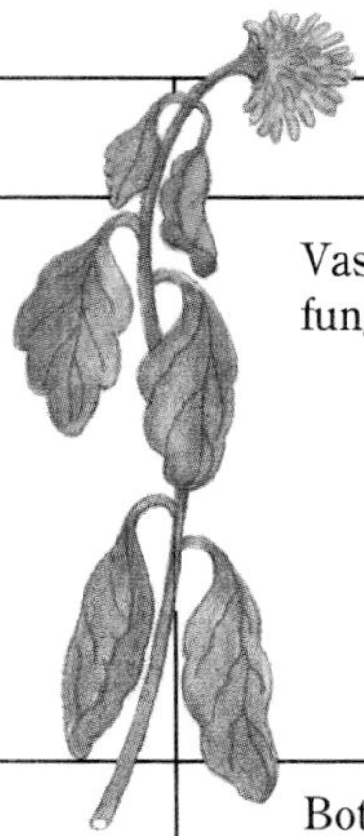

ACHILLEA MILLEFOLIUM 'FIRE KING'

ANEMONE × HYBRIDA

AQUILEGIA CHRYSANTHA

# DICTIONARY OF PERENNIALS

## Introduction

The entries in this dictionary present a variety of the most colorful and long-lasting perennial plants. All plants are listed by their botanical names; common names are cross-referenced. Within each entry is a description of what the plant looks like, what climatic zone it flourishes in, when it blooms, and what it requires in the way of soil conditions, sunlight, moisture and special care; to determine the zone in which you live, refer to the Zone Map *(inside front cover)*.

## Achillea (ak-il-EE-a)
Yarrow

Sun-loving plant with ferny foliage and flat clusters of white or yellow flowers. Noted for its ability to grow in poor soil and dry conditions. Zones 3-9.

**Selected species and varieties.** *A. filipendulina*, fernleaf yarrow: grayish green foliage and showy clusters of small yellow flowers that blossom throughout the summer on plants 4 feet tall. Varieties include 'Coronation Gold,' with 3-inch deep-yellow flower clusters that bloom on stiff, upright 3-foot stems from late spring through midsummer; and 'Gold Plate,' the tallest of the achilleas, with 6-inch yellow flower heads on 4 ½-foot stems from late spring to midsummer. *A. millefolium*, common yarrow: small, flat, clusters of grayish white flowers, and foliage that smells spicy when crushed. Height 2 feet. The variety 'Fire King' has clusters of bright pink flowers with white centers growing on 2-foot stems rising from a low mat of light green leaves. Blooms middle to late summer.

**Growing conditions.** Plant yarrow in full sun in a well-drained soil. Although it tolerates poor soil, yarrow will flourish in soil enriched with organic matter. Stake tall species. Divide clumps every three or four years or whenever they become crowded. If the dead flowers are cut off, the plant will bloom again later in the season.

**Landscape uses.** Low forms of yarrow make good rock garden plants. Grow the taller kinds in a perennial border or in a cutting garden. The large, flat flower heads are long-lasting as cut flowers and are easily dried for winter bouquets.

**Adam's-needle** see *Yucca*
**Aegopodium** see Dictionary of Grasses and Ground Covers, page 160
**Agapanthus** see Dictionary of Bulbs, page 292
**Alumroot** see *Heuchera*

## Anemone (a-NEM-o-ne)
Windflower

Graceful single or double flowers in white, cream, and shades of red, purple and blue. Sizes range from 3-inch alpines to 2-foot hybrids. Branched stems with leaves composed of several divided or ferny leaflets. Zones 4-8.

**Selected species and varieties.** *A.* x *hybrida*, Japanese anemone: single pink or white flowers 2 to 3 inches wide from late summer into fall on 3-foot stems. Zones 5-8. *A. pulsatilla*, pasque flower: blue or purple bell-shaped flowers on foot-tall plants in the spring. Zones 5-8. *A. vitifolia* 'Robustissima,' grape-leaved anemone: branching clusters of pink flowers on 2- to 3- foot stalks. Blooms from late summer into fall. Zones 4-8.

**Growing conditions.** Grow anemones in partial shade in moist, but not soggy, woodland soil or in garden soil supplemented with organic matter such as compost or well-rotted leaves. Pasque flower requires full sun and well-drained soil in cool locations. Grape-leaved anemone also thrives in ordinary garden soil and tolerates both full sun and drought. Japanese anemones should have some protection from the wind. Space the smaller anemones 1 foot apart and the taller ones 2 feet apart. New plants can be started from seed or by dividing established plants carefully in the spring. Japanese and grape-leaved anemones will all grow quickly under good conditions and may require division every three years or so. The other anemones grow more slowly and division is rarely needed except for propagation purposes.

**Landscape uses.** It is possible to have anemones flowering in three seasons. Plant the spring-blooming pasque flower in a rock garden or in a partially shaded border. Plant Japanese anemones for late-summer and autumn bloom. Use grape-leaved anemone for late-season flowers in sun or light shade.

**Aquilegia** (ak-wil-EE-jee-a)
Columbine

Graceful plants with attractive ferny foliage and yellow, blue, lavender, red, white or bicolored flowers. Long narrow spurs extend backward from the flower. Zones 3-9.

**Selected species and varieties.** *A. chrysantha*, golden columbine: large yellow flowers up to 3 inches across with exceptionally long spurs bloom from late spring to midsummer. The variety 'Silver Queen' is 2½ to 3 feet tall with showy white spring flowers. *A. flabellata*, fan columbine: a low-growing species with blue to purple flowers 2 inches wide on 1- to 1½-foot stems. The variety 'Nana Alba' is barely 1 foot tall with white spring flowers.

**Growing conditions.** Plant in full sun or light shade in well-drained soil. After several years the plants will begin to deteriorate. Discard and replace them. To start plants from seed, sow outdoors early in the spring in fine soil and transplant into the garden the following autumn or spring. Set plants 1½ feet apart.

**Landscape uses.** Fan columbine is an appealing plant for a rock garden or the front of a flower border. Use the taller forms in the middle of a border, where they will bloom for several weeks. The flowers are excellent for cutting. Columbines have abundant nectar and attract hummingbirds.

**Arabis** see Dictionary of Grasses and Ground Covers, page 160
**Arisaema** see Dictionary of Bulbs, page 292

**Armeria** (ar-MEER-ee-a)
Thrift, sea pink

White, pink or rose globe-shaped clusters of flowers borne on leafless stems above low tufts of grassy evergreen leaves in spring or summer. Zones 3-8.

**Selected species and varieties.** *A. plantaginea*, plantain thrift: 1- to 1¾-inch clusters of rosy pink or white flowers on 2-foot stems above 4- to 6-inch clumps of grassy leaves from late spring through midsummer.

**Growing conditions.** Plant thrift in full sun in a well-drained sandy soil. Plants will flower less if soil is too rich. Clumps eventually die out in the center. To rejuvenate old plants and prop-

agate new ones, divide thrift every three to four years in spring or fall, and space new plants 9 to 12 inches apart.

**Landscape uses.** Plantain thrift is a good plant for the front of a border.

**Aruncus** (a-RUNK-us)
Goatsbeard

Robust shrubby plant with ferny foliage and large plumes of small white flowers for about two weeks in late spring or early summer. Zones 4-9.

**Selected species and varieties.** *A. dioicus*, goatsbeard: foliage clump grows up to 4 feet tall and 3 feet across. Flower stalks are 4 to 6 feet tall. The broad, handsome leaves remain in good condition for many months. *A. dioicus* 'Kneiffii' is a smaller and slower-growing plant and has more finely cut leaves. Its flower stalks are 2 to 3 feet tall.

**Growing conditions.** Grow goatsbeard in partial shade in rich, moist soil. Plant it in a permanent site, since the tough root system makes transplanting and dividing difficult. Space plants 4 feet apart.

**Landscape uses.** Plant singly as a specimen, at the back of a large perennial border or in a lightly shaded woodland garden. Goatsbeard makes an impressive display when several plants are grouped together.

**Asarum** see Dictionary of Grasses and Ground Covers, page 160

**Asclepias** (as-KLEE-pee-as)

Showy flat flower clusters on stems with milky sap in summer and early fall. Ornamental seedpods packed with many seeds attached to silky hairs, carried by the wind. Zones 3-9.

**Selected species and varieties.** *A. tuberosa,* butterfly weed: showy 2-inch clusters of bright orange ⅓-inch flowers from early to late summer. Broad 4½-inch-long leaves on stems 2 to 3 feet high. Favored by the monarch butterfly. Leaves and stems poisonous to animals. Zones 3-9.

ARMERIA PLANTAGINEA

ARUNCUS DIOICUS

ASCLEPIAS TUBEROSA

ASTER × FRIKARTII

ASTILBE × ARENDSII 'FANAL'

AURINIA SAXATILIS

**Growing conditions.** Plant butterfly weed in full sun. Butterfly weed grows best in dry soil. It is resistant to drought and needs to be watered only during an extended dry spell. It can also be grown in ordinary garden soil. Space plants 1 ½ to 2 feet apart. Propagate by seed or from root cuttings.

**Landscape uses.** Plant butterfly weed in a border or a wildflower garden, where its brilliant color is most effective in groups of three or more plants. Its flowers are excellent for drying. The seedpods are attractive when used in dried arrangements.

### Aster (AS-ter)

A large group of dependable plants whose daisy-like yellow-centered flowers come in white and a variety of blues, purples and pinks. Blooming time ranges from early summer to late fall. Zones 3-9.

**Selected species and varieties.** *A.* x *frikartii*: fragrant lavender-blue flowers 2 to 2 ½ inches wide on stems 2 to 3 feet high. Exceptionally long blooming period from early summer through fall. Zones 4-8. *A. novae-angliae*, New England aster: purple flowers 1 ½ inches wide and lance-shaped leaves on branching stems 5 feet tall or more. Blooms summer through fall. Zones 3-8. Varieties of *A. novae-angliae* include 'Harrington's Pink,' with pink flowers on 4-foot stems in fall. *A. novi-belgii*, Michaelmas daisy: bluish violet flowers 1 inch across on 3- to 5-foot stems from late summer until frost. Zones 2-8.

**Growing conditions.** Asters are sturdy plants that are easy to grow. Plant them in full sun in well-drained fertile soil. If soil is chronically wet in winter, they are prone to rot. Space low-growing asters 1 to 1 ½ feet apart and the taller ones 2 to 3 feet apart. Remove fading flowers before they set seed, since the seedlings will not be identical to the original plant. Divide asters every three or four years, or when they become crowded. To propagate, remove sections from the outside of the clump and replant in spring or fall.

**Landscape uses.** Asters are important perennials for summer and autumn bloom. Plant species asters in a wildflower garden. Grow the cultivated varieties in a flower border, and use the dwarf forms as edging plants. Whether they are wild or cultivated, asters are lovely in arrangements, by themselves and combined with other cut flowers.

### Astilbe (as-TIL-be)

Graceful, glossy ferny foliage in loose mounds below fluffy summer flower spikes in white and shades of pink, red and lavender on erect stems. Zones 4-8.

**Selected species and varieties.** *A.* x *arendsii*, garden spirea: a varied group of 1 ½ to 3 ½ foot-tall hybrids. 'Fanal' is a 2-foot variety with early-summer to midsummer deep red flowers above finely divided foliage tinged with red. *A. chinensis* 'Pumila': a dwarf astilbe 8 to 12 inches tall with numerous spikes of pink flowers that bloom from midsummer to late summer. Zones 5-8.

**Growing conditions.** Plant astilbes in light shade in moist soil that is rich in organic matter. Although they do best in shade, astilbes can be grown successfully in full sun if they are given plenty of water and mulch in summer. *A. chinensis* 'Pumila' tolerates drought better than the others. The plants multiply rapidly and should be divided in spring or fall every two or three years. Space new plants 1 ½ to 2 feet apart.

**Landscape uses.** Plant astilbes in groups in a perennial border or mass them as ground cover in a shady location. Plant the tall forms singly, as specimen plants. If the weather is not too hot, the shiny foliage will remain attractive all summer.

### Aurinia (o-RIN-ee-a)
Basket-of-gold

Low-growing plant topped with frothy clusters of yellow or apricot flowers above rosettes of silver-gray foliage in early spring. Zones 3-8.

**Selected species and varieties.** *A. saxatilis*, basket-of-gold: forms mat 6 to 12 inches high with open clusters of dainty four-petaled yellow flowers.

**Growing conditions.** Plant basket-of-gold in full sun in a well-drained sandy or gravelly soil that is not too fertile, spacing plants 9 to 12 inches apart. It does not grow well where summers are hot and humid. Cut plants back by a third after they flower. Basket-of-gold is difficult to divide but is easily propagated from seed sown in spring or fall.

**Landscape uses.** Mass basket-of-gold in a rock garden, use as an edging plant for a border, or allow it to cascade over a low retaining wall or the edge of a raised bed.

**Avena grass** see Dictionary of Grasses and Ground Covers, page 160
**Azure sage** see *Perovskia*
**Baby's-breath** see *Euphorbia*; see *Gypsophila*
**Balloon flower** see *Platycodon*

**Baptisia** (bap-TIZ-ee-a)
Wild indigo

Blue or white spring flowers shaped like small butterflies in loose spikes on mounded 3- to 4-foot plants with bluish green to gray-green foliage. Zones 3-8.

**Selected species and varieties.** *B. australis*, blue wild indigo, blue false indigo: large clumps of stems with clover-like leaves and spires of 1-inch blue flowers. Zones 3-8.

**Growing conditions.** Grow wild indigos in full sun in well-drained to dry sandy soil. In partial shade they will grow but not flower profusely. They may need to be staked. Propagate by seed, cuttings or division in spring. Set new clumps 2 to 3 feet apart.

**Landscape uses.** Wild indigos are valuable for both their beautiful form and their flowers in drier sections of a wildflower garden or a perennial border. The flowers and foliage are excellent in arrangements.

**Basket-of-gold** see *Aurinia*
**Bee balm** see *Monarda*
**Begonia** see Dictionary of Annuals, page 200; Bulbs, page 292

**Belamcanda** (bel-am-CAN-da)
Blackberry lily

Sprays of lily-like summer flowers on branched stems above 1½-foot grass-like leaves. Seedpods open to reveal columns of shiny seeds that resemble blackberries. Zones 5-10.

**Selected species and varieties.** *B. chinensis*: red-spotted orange flowers up to 2 inches wide on 3-foot stems.

**Growing conditions.** Plant blackberry lilies in full sun or light shade in a moist but well-drained soil enriched with organic matter. Provide mulch where winters are severe. Propagate from seed, by division of the tubers in spring, or by digging up and replanting the seedlings that crop up. Space them 1 foot apart.

**Landscape uses.** Use blackberry lilies in a perennial border or an island bed, where they will bloom for at least two weeks. The plant's unusual seed-pods are attractive in the garden and in arrangements, either fresh or dried.

**Bellflower** see *Campanula*
**Bethlehem sage** see Dictionary of Grasses and Ground Covers, page 160
**Blackberry lily** see *Belamcanda*
**Black-eyed Susan** see *Rudbeckia*
**Blanket flower** see Dictionary of Annuals, page 200
**Blazing star** see *Liatris*
**Bleeding heart** see *Dicentra*
**Blue oat grass** see Dictionary of Grasses and Ground Covers, page 160

**Boltonia** (bowl-TO-nee-a)

White daisy-like flowers with bright yellow centers from late summer into fall. Zones 3-8.

**Selected species and varieties.** *B. asteroides* 'Snowbank,' white boltonia: many ¾-inch white flowers grow on sturdy 3- to 5-foot branched stems lined with narrow bluish green leaves.

**Growing conditions.** Plant white boltonia in full sun in either dry or moist garden soil. Plants do not require staking. Propagate by division. Space new plants 3 feet apart.

**Landscape uses.** Use white boltonia in a naturalistic meadow garden or at the back of a border. Pick flowers for fall bouquets.

**Burnet** see *Sanguisorba*
**Butterfly weed** see *Asclepias*
**Calamagrostis** see Dictionary of Grasses and Ground Covers, page 160

**Campanula** (kam-PAN-ew-la)
Bellflower

Spikes or clusters of showy blue, violet, purple or white bell- or star-shaped flowers in spring, summer or fall, depending on the species. Broad oval, toothed leaves in tufts at the bases of stems, becoming thinner and smaller toward the tips. Zones 3-9.

BAPTISIA AUSTRALIS

BELAMCANDA CHINENSIS

BOLTONIA ASTERIODES 'SNOWBANK'

CAMPANULA GLOMERATA

249

CERATOSTIGMA PLUMBAGINOIDES

CLEMATIS RECTA 'PURPUREA'

DELPHINIUM

DIANTHUS

**Selected species and varieties.** *C. carpatica*, Carpathian bellflower: many delicate blue 2-inch bell-shaped flowers on compact plants less than 1 foot tall from late spring to early summer, followed by a few flowers throughout the summer. Zones 3-9. *C. glomerata*, clustered bellflower, Danesblood bellflower: clusters of up to 12 deep purple inch-wide flowers blossom on 2-foot stems from spring through early summer, followed by another show of blossoms late in the season. Zones 3-8.

**Growing conditions.** Most bellflowers thrive in sun or light shade in a moist but well-drained soil enriched with organic matter such as peat moss or compost. Dig up and divide bellflowers every three or four years to maintain plant vigor. Space small species and cultivars 9 to 12 inches apart and larger ones up to 2 feet apart. Clip faded flowers to encourage further bloom. In winter protect bellflowers with a light mulch.

**Landscape uses.** Plant dwarf and trailing bellflowers in a rock garden or in the crevices of a wall, next to steps or in a wildflower garden. Use taller species of bellflower in a perennial border. The flower sprays are excellent for cutting.

**Candytuft** see Dictionary of Grasses and Ground Covers, page 160
**Catmint** see *Nepeta*

**Ceratostigma** (ser-at-OS-tig-ma)
Plumbago

Spreading 1-foot plants with clusters of brilliant blue flowers from late summer through midfall. Zones 5-9.

**Selected species and varieties.** *C. plumbaginoides*, blue plumbago, leadwort: cobalt blue flowers ¾ inch across. Handsome bright green leaves lining wiry, slightly zigzag stems turn reddish in fall.

**Growing conditions.** Plant blue plumbago in full sun or light shade in a moist, well-drained light soil. Its creeping roots spread rapidly and may be invasive. Propagate by division in spring. Space new plants 1½ feet apart. Protect with a winter mulch in Zone 5.

**Landscape uses.** Use blue plumbago to edge a sunny flower border, or plant clumps in a lightly shaded shrub border, or grow it as a ground cover where its spreading habit can be used to advantage.

**Chrysanthemum** see Dictionary of Annuals, page 200
**Chrysogonum** see Dictionary of Grasses and Ground Covers, page 160
**Cinquefoil** see *Potentilla*

**Clematis** (KLEM-a-tis)

Fragrant, showy blue or white flowers shaped like bells or stars in summer. Zones 3-9.

**Selected species and varieties.** *C. recta*, ground clematis: starry white flowers up to 1 inch wide in fluffy clusters near the top of rangy 3- to 5-foot plants from early summer to midsummer. The variety 'Purpurea' has white flowers and purple-tinted leaves. Zones 4-9.

**Growing conditions.** Plant clematis in full sun in moist, well-drained soil enriched with organic matter. Apply 2 to 3 inches of mulch to keep the soil around the roots evenly moist and to grow ground clematis as an erect plant, provide stakes to support.

**Landscape uses.** Use clematis in a border; allow ground clematis to tumble over the edges of raised beds or retaining walls. Use both the flowers and seed heads in arrangements.

**Columbine** see *Aquilegia*
**Coneflower** see *Echinacea*; see *Rudbeckia*
**Coralbells** see *Heuchera*
**Coreopsis** see Dictionary of Annuals, page 200
**Cranesbill** see *Geranium*
**Daisy** see *Aster*
**Daylily** see *Hemerocallis*
**Dead nettle** see Dictionary of Grasses and Ground Covers, page 160

**Delphinium** (del-FIN-ee-um)
Larkspur

Tall, heavy spikes of spurred early-to late-summer blossoms, usually in shades from blue to purple but also in white and pink, often with a contrasting center called a bee. Handsome deeply cut foliage. Zones 3-10.

**Selected species and varieties.** *D. elatum*, candle larkspur, bee larkspur: bluish purple blossoms up to 2 inches across in dense spikes on stalks to 6 feet tall. The parent of many hybrids including the Belladonna delphiniums, with branched 3- to 5-foot stalks bearing multiple spikes of 2-inch white or blue flowers. Zones 3-10.

**Growing conditions.** Grow delphiniums in full sun in moist but well-drained slightly acid to alkaline soil enriched with organic matter. Protect from wind and stake tall stems. Cut stems back after summer blooming for a second crop of flowers in fall. Propagate from seed or by division. Set new plants 2 feet apart for good air circulation. Delphiniums prefer cool summers and do well in Zones 8-10 only on the West Coast.

**Landscape uses.** Plant relatively short delphiniums in the middle of a perennial border and the taller ones at the back. Tall hybrids are also grown in beds of their own

### Dianthus (dy-AN-thus)
Pink

Fragrant red, pink or white spring and early-summer flowers above handsome clumps of blue or gray-tinted grassy leaves that are evergreen in mild climates. Zones 3-9.

**Selected species and varieties.** *D.* x *allwoodii*, Allwood pink: red, pink or white, usually 2-inch blossoms, sometimes with one color splotched on another. Plants grow up to 1 ½ feet tall. Zones 3-8. *D. barbatus*, sweet William: white, red, pink or multicolored blossoms in dense heads on 2-foot plants with broad leaves. Zones 3-9.

**Growing conditions.** Pinks do best in full sun in a well-drained, slightly alkaline sandy soil but will tolerate slightly acid soil. Space plants 12 to 18 inches apart. Shear mat-forming types in fall. In cold areas, protect with evergreen boughs in winter. Do not use a dense mulch, such as leaves, that fosters rot by reducing air circulation and trapping moisture. Propagate from seed or by division every three years in spring. Sweet William grows well in Zone 9 on the West Coast only.

**Landscape uses.** Grow pinks in the front of a perennial border or in a rock garden, plant as a ground cover in a small sunny area, or use to edge a walk or a terrace.

### Dicentra (dy-SEN-tra)
Bleeding heart

Heart-shaped red, pink or white blossoms and attractive clumps of ferny foliage. Zones 3-9.

**Selected species and varieties.** *D. spectabilis*, common bleeding heart: pink to purple flowers along arching 3-foot stems in spring. Zones 3-9. The cultivar 'Alba' bears pure white blooms.

**Growing conditions.** Plant bleeding hearts in light shade in a well-drained soil enriched with organic matter. Space plants 1 ½ to 2 feet apart. Common bleeding heart dies down in summer. Propagate by division in early spring or from seed.

**Landscape uses.** Use bleeding heart in a shady border or allow it to naturalize in a woodland garden.

### Dictamnus (dik-TAM-nus)
Gas plant, dittany

Loose spires of airy white or pinkish purple blossoms on shrubby 2- to 3-foot plants in late spring to early summer. Zones 3-8.

**Selected species and varieties.** *D. albus*, gas plant: white blossoms up to 2 inches across. A lighted match held under the blossoms will sometimes ignite the gas they give off and produce a slight flash of light, thus the common name. Glossy, aromatic dark green compound leaves are attractive all season long. Gas plant is a long-lived perennial. The variety 'Purpureus' has pinkish purple blossoms.

**Growing conditions.** Grow gas plant in full sun in a well-drained soil enriched with organic matter. Space plants 8 feet apart, setting them in their permanent locations. Gas plant should not be disturbed, since it is difficult to transplant or divide it successfully. It grows slowly and takes several years to become established. Propagate from seed, which will produce blooming plants in three or four years.

**Landscape uses.** Set gas plant in the middle of a perennial border, where its shrubby form and dark leaves form a good backdrop for shorter plants. White gas plants are attractive in a monochromatic border.

### Digitalis see Dictionary of Annuals, page 200
### Dittany see *Dictamnus*

### Echinacea (ek-in-AY-see-a)
Purple coneflower

Summer-blooming large daisy-like flowers with gracefully drooping pink to purple or white petals and prominent conical centers. Zones 3-10.

DICENTRA SPECTABILIS

DICTAMNUS ALBUS 'PURPUREUS'

ECHINACEA PURPUREA

ECHINOPS RITRO

ERYNGIUM GIGANTEUM

EUPHORBIA EPITHYMOIDES

**Selected species and varieties.** *E. purpurea*: flowers up to 6 inches across in white and shades of pink and purple on stems up to 4 feet tall. Zones 3-10. 'Bright Star' is a variety with rose-colored petals surrounding a deep purple center. 'The King' has deep reddish purple petals and a brown center. 'White Lustre' has creamy white petals surrounding a bronze center.

**Growing conditions.** Grow purple coneflowers in full sun or light shade. Set new plants 2 feet apart in well-drained sandy soil. Purple coneflower is easy to grow and flourishes even in dry, windy sites. It may need staking if soil is fertile. Propagate from root cuttings or by division in spring or fall. Plants also seed themselves freely.

**Landscape uses.** Use purple coneflowers at the back of a border or along the sunny edges of woodland areas for many weeks of color. They make excellent cut flowers, and stripped of petals, their prickly centers add textural variety to dried arrangements.

**Echinops** (EK-in-ops)
Globe thistle

Bristly blue globes bloom in summer on plants with spiny, deeply scalloped leaves that are glossy above and covered with downy white hairs on their undersides. Zones 3-9.

**Selected species and varieties.** *E. ritro*: spherical bright blue flower heads 1 ½ to 2 inches in diameter on stems to 2 feet tall.

**Growing conditions.** Plant globe thistle in full sun in well-drained soil. Because of its deep roots, it will tolerate drought; soggy soil will kill it. In very fertile soil it may require staking. Clumps can be left undisturbed or new plants can be propagated by division every three or four years in spring. Set new plants 18 to 24 inches apart.

**Landscape uses.** Stiff and sculptural in appearance, globe thistle makes a bold statement in the middle of a border or at the back of one. Use it as the focal point of an island bed. If the flowers are cut before they are fully open, they can be hung upside down to dry for winter bouquets.

**Eryngium** (e-RINJ-ee-um)
Sea holly

Collars of spiny leaflike bracts surrounding conical centers of many tightly packed tiny blue or green flowers in summer. Silvery gray-green leaves and stiff stems up to 3 feet tall give the plants a bristly, architectural quality. Zones 5-9.

**Selected species and varieties.** *E. giganteum*: large blue or pale green centers 2 to 4 inches long surrounded by spiny gray-green bracts on stems to 2 feet or more. Zones 5-8.

**Growing conditions.** Sea hollies do best in full sun in a well-drained sandy soil that is not too rich in organic matter. *E. giganteum* dies out after flowering but self-sows freely to replace itself. Sea hollies are difficult to divide because of their long taproots. Propagate from seed sown in spring or fall or from root cuttings.

**Landscape uses.** The stiff, sculptural leaves and flowers of sea hollies make them superb specimen plants. Use them as accents in a border, in a sunny rock garden or border composed of silver-, white- or gray-leaved plants.

**Eulalia grass** see Dictionary of Grasses and Ground Covers, page 160

**Euphorbia** (yew-FOR-bee-a)
Spurge

Clusters of tiny flowers surrounded by colorful petal-like bracts in white, yellow, chartreuse or red-orange in spring or summer. Zones 4-10.

**Selected species and varieties.** *E. epithymoides*, cushion spurge: 1- to 1 ½-foot hemispherical mound of neat foliage. Dense clusters of flowers are surrounded by bright chartreuse bracts in spring. Foliage reddens in autumn. Zones 4-10.

**Growing conditions.** Grow spurges in full sun in well-drained to dry soil. Where summers are hot, provide some light shade. Cushion spurge does not do well in hot, humid conditions. Spurges are seldom propagated by division because they are difficult to transplant. They sow themselves freely, however, and small seedlings can be moved with a large soil ball. The milky sap of euphorbia stains and sometimes irritates skin. Wear gloves when picking spurges for arrangements and seal the cut end of each stem by searing it with a flame.

**Landscape uses.** Feature cushion spurge at the front of a border for its symmetrical mounded form, bright spring bracts and reddish fall foliage.

**Feather reed grass** see Dictionary of Grasses and Ground Covers, page 160

**Five-finger** see *Potentilla*

**Fountain grass** see Dictionary of Grasses and Ground Covers, page 160

**Foxglove** see Dictionary of Annuals, page 200

**Gaillardia** see Dictionary of Annuals, page 200

**Garden heliotrope** see *Valeriana*

**Gas plant** see *Dictamnus*

**Gay-feather** see *Liatris*

## Geranium (jer-AY-nee-um)
Cranesbill

Flat blossoms from 1 to 2 inches across in shades of pink, magenta, violet and blue on thin stems above clumps of attractively toothed and lobed leaves. The frost-sensitive bedding plants commonly called geraniums are members of the genus *Pelargonium*. Zones 3-10.

**Selected species and varieties.** *G.* x 'Johnson's Blue': prolific crop of bright blue 1½- to 2-inch flowers veined in a deeper blue above a 1-foot mound of foliage in spring or early summer. Zones 4-8. *G. sanguineum*, bloody cranesbill: deep magenta 1-inch spring or early-summer flowers above a 12-inch mound of finely cut lobed leaves that redden in fall. Zones 4-10.

**Growing conditions.** Plant hardy geraniums in full sun or light shade in a moist but well-drained soil. Where summers are hot and dry, grow them in light shade. Bloody cranesbill tolerates more heat and drought than other species. Allow 1½ to 2 feet for geraniums. Propagate by dividing plants every three or four years in spring. Hardy geraniums do not grow well in Zones 9 and 10 in the Southern states.

**Landscape uses.** Use low-growing geraniums such as bloody cranesbill in rock gardens. Plant other geraniums in a lightly shaded woodland garden or at the front of a border, where their foliage makes them an asset after flowering ceases.

## Geum (JEE-um)
Avens

One- to 1½-inch-wide flowers in red, yellow or white with softly ruffled petals surrounding conspicuous center from spring into summer. Clumps of attractively toothed and lobed downy foliage. Zones 5-10.

**Selected species and varieties.** Hybrid geums include *G.* x 'Borisii,' with yellow-orange to deep orange flowers on 12-inch stems above neat low clumps of foliage. Zones 5-9.

**Growing conditions.** Plant geums in full sun or light shade in a moist but well-drained soil enriched with organic matter. Propagate by division every two or three years in fall. Set new plants 1 to 1½ feet apart.

**Landscape uses.** Use the low-growing geums such as *G.* x 'Borisii' in a rock garden.

**Globeflower** see *Trollius*

**Globe thistle** see *Echinops*

**Goatsbeard** see *Aruncus*

**Goldenray** see *Ligularia*

**Goldenrod** see *Solidago*

**Goutweed** see Dictionary of Grasses and Ground Covers, page 160

## Gypsophila (jip-SOFF-ill-a)
Baby's-breath

Thousands of minute, dainty summer flowers scattered on a lacy mass of wiry branched stems with tiny pointed leaves. Zones 4-9.

**Selected species and varieties.** *G. paniculata*: a mound of tangled stems 3 to 4 feet tall and wide with ¼-inch white flowers that become pinkish with age. Zones 4-9. The variety 'Bristol Fairy' has flowers with double rows of petals. 'Pink Fairy' grows to 1½ feet with double-petaled light pink flowers. *G. repens*, creeping baby's-breath: trailing branched stems 6 to 8 inches tall with white, pale purple or pink flowers. The variety 'Alba' has white flowers; 'Rosea' has pink blossoms. Zones 6-8.

**Growing conditions.** Plant baby's-breath in full sun in a moist, well-drained alkaline soil, allowing 3 to 4 feet of space for *G. paniculata* and 18 inches for *G. repens*. The deep root system makes baby's-breath difficult to transplant or divide. Propagate from seed sown in spring. If plants are sheared before the flowers go to seed, they will flower again where growing seasons are long. Stake taller plants to avoid a straggly appearance. Baby's-breath does well in Zone 9 only on the West Coast.

**Landscape uses.** Baby's-breath makes an excellent filler plant in a border, a rock garden or bouquets.

GERANIUM × 'JOHNSON'S BLUE'

GEUM × 'BORISII'

GYPSOPHILA REPENS 'ROSEA'

HELENIUM AUTUMNALE

HELLEBORUS ORIENTALIS

HEMEROCALLIS

## Helenium (hel-EE-nee-um)
Sneezeweed

Prominent pompoms of dark yellow, orange or red-brown encircled by drooping, narrow fan-shaped petals in lighter shades. Profuse flower clusters in summer and early fall at the tips of branched stems. Narrow leaves in clumps at the base of the plant, becoming sparser near the top of the stem. Zones 3-9.

**Selected species and varieties.** *H. autumnale*, common sneezeweed: flowers up to 2 inches across on rangy 5- to 6-foot stems in late summer and early fall.

**Growing conditions.** Sneezeweed flourishes in full sun in a moist but not wet soil enriched with organic matter. Pinch taller sneezeweeds in spring to restrict their height and increase the number of flowers, and stake them for support. Propagate and renew plants by division every three to four years in spring. Space new plants 1½ to 2 feet apart.

**Landscape uses.** Use common sneezeweed at the back of an informal border, where it blends nicely with creamy white- or yellow-flowered perennials such as goldenrod. Sneezeweeds make good cut flowers.

**Helianthus** see Dictionary of Annuals, page 200
**Helictotrichon** see Dictionary of Grasses and Ground Covers, page 160
**Heliotrope** see *Valeriana*
**Hellebore** see *Helleborus*

## Helleborus (hell-e-BOR-us)
Hellebore

Winter to early-spring flowers on thick stems rising from rosettes of usually evergreen leaves composed of leaflets arranged like the fingers on a hand. Cup- or bell-shaped flowers 1 to 3 inches across in white, pale green, pink or purple. Zones 3-10.

**Selected species and varieties.** *H. orientalis*, Lenten rose: nodding cup-shaped flowers of cream, green, pink, rose or purple up to 2 inches across on 18-inch stems. Saw-toothed glossy leaves. Zones 4-9.

**Growing conditions.** Hellebores need partial shade and a constantly moist but well-drained soil enriched with organic matter. Water well and provide mulch where summers are dry.

At the northern end of the range, hellebores may need protection from the weight of winter snows. They do not do well in Zones 9 and 10 in the Southern states. Set plants out in spring, leaving 2 feet between Lenten roses. Propagate from seed or by division after flowering, although brittle roots make division of mature clumps difficult and older plants may not bloom for a year after being disturbed. Lenten rose self-sows readily. All parts of the plant are poisonous and the juices from bruised stems may cause skin irritation.

**Landscape uses.** Grow hellebores in a shaded perennial or shrub border or plant them in the shade of a wall. Allow Lenten rose to spread in a naturalistic woodland garden. Flowers are long-lasting, and the foliage is attractive most or all of the year.

## Hemerocallis (hem-er-o-KAL-is)
Daylily

Bold trumpet-shaped flower from 1 to 10 inches across, sometimes with double row of petals or ruffled edges, in spring, summer or fall. The hundreds of hybrids offer a broad choice of hues, from off-white or cream through yellow, melon, pink and red to mauve and orchid, often with two or three colors in the same blossom. Clusters of up to 30 flowers grow on stiff 1- to 7-foot stalks rising from a thick clump of narrow, arching leaves. The long flower buds in each cluster open successively, and each flower lasts only a day, hence the name. Zones 3-10.

**Selected species and varieties.** *H.* hybrids: 'Stella de Oro' is another dwarf, with light yellow 2½-inch flowers with pale green throats and ruffled petals blooming on 12- to 18-inch stalks from late spring into fall. Species and hybrids vary in hardiness but there are daylilies suitable for each zone from 3 to 10.

**Growing conditions.** Daylilies thrive in full sun in any well-drained soil. They compete well with tree roots and will grow in light shade but may flower less. Propagate by dividing clumps every three to six years in fall or early spring. Space dwarf hybrids 1 to 1½ feet apart and the taller hybrids 2 to 3 feet apart. If small plantlets appear along the flower stalks, they can be removed and rooted as cuttings.

**Landscape uses.** Use daylilies as border plants; place them in the front, middle or back of the border according to their height. By selecting hybrids with different flowering times, it is possible to have daylilies in bloom continuously from spring to fall. Allow them to spread in an informal naturalistic garden. Planted in large groups, daylilies make an excellent ground cover under trees, in large sunny areas or on steep banks where their dense foliage will shade out weeds and their roots will slow erosion. Plant special hybrids as specimen plants.

## Heuchera (hew-KAIR-a)

Spikes of tiny white, pink or red bell-shaped flowers from spring to mid-summer on wiry stems rising from low-growing clumps of evergreen leaves with scalloped edges. Zones 3-10.

**Selected species and varieties.** *H. sanguinea*, coralbells: flowers in white or shades of pink and red on stems up to 2 feet tall.

**Growing conditions.** Plant coralbells in full sun or light shade in a moist, well-drained soil enriched with organic matter. Coralbells tend to die out where summers are hot and dry. Space coralbells 1 foot apart. Crowns become woody after several years. Renew plants and propagate them by division every three years in spring or fall, setting divisions about a foot apart. Heucheras do not grow well in Zone 10 in the Southern states.

**Landscape uses.** Use coralbells as edgings for sunny or shady borders where their attractive foliage will show to advantage even when plants are not in bloom. They are excellent plants for a lightly shaded area in a woodland garden and make good cut flowers.

**Hosta** see Dictionary of Grasses and Ground Covers, page 160
**Iberis** see Dictionary of Grasses and Ground Covers, page 160

## Iris (EYE-ris)

Clumps of stiff, narrow, swordlike leaves and upright stalks of striking spring or summer blooms. Flowers are composed of erect petals called standards and drooping petals called falls. Petals may be ruffled, crested like a cockscomb down the centers of the falls or bearded, with colorful hairs at the base of the falls. The flowers are available in shades of almost every color except red, often with two or more colors in the same blossom. Zones 3-10.

**Selected species and varieties.** *I.* hybrids, bearded iris: a huge group of plants named for the small hairy patches, or beards, at the base of the falls. There is a color for every garden. Zones 3 to 10. Bearded irises are divided into dwarf, intermediate and tall classes based on plant size. The variety 'Hall of Fame' is salmon pink. *I. cristata*, crested iris: 6 to 8 inches tall with 2 ½-inch lilac summer flowers marked with white or orange and white crests on the falls. Zones 4-8. *I. ensata*, also called *I. kaempferi*, Japanese iris: clusters of beardless 4- to 10-inch mid-summer flowers shaped like small orchids on 2- to 4-foot plants. There are hundreds of hybrids in white, blue, pink, violet and purple, often with yellow markings. Zones 5-9. *I. pseudacorus*, yellow flag: delicate 2-inch yellow beardless flowers marked with brown on stalks up to 5 feet tall in summer. Zones 5-10.

**Growing conditions.** Irises do best in full sun although they will tolerate light shade. Plant bearded, crested and dwarf bearded irises in a moist, well-drained soil with their rhizomes level with the soil surface. Japanese irises and yellow flag prefer constantly moist soils. Pacific Coast hybrids tolerate drought and heat. Japanese irises do best when soil is slightly acid. Space the low-growing crested irises and dwarf bearded irises 1 foot apart and the taller irises 1 ½ feet apart. Winter mulch is unnecessary. Propagate irises by dividing their rhizomes after the flowers fade. Bearded, Japanese, and yellow flag irises grow well in Zone 10 only on the West Coast.

**Landscape uses.** Use dwarf bearded or crested at the front of a border or in a rock garden. Plant Japanese irises or yellow flag irises in moist soils at the edge of a stream, pool or moist woodland garden. Grow bearded irises in a border or plant them along a wall or in front of evergreen shrubs.

**Jack-in-the-pulpit** see Dictionary of Bulbs, page 292

## Kniphofia (ny-FO-fee-a)
Red-hot poker, torch lily

Tall, leafless flower stalks tipped with long, densely packed clusters of drooping summer or fall flowers in vivid colors. Clumps of arching gray-green grassy leaves 1 inch wide and up to 3 feet long. Zones 6-10.

HEUCHERA SANGUINEA

IRIS 'HALL OF FAME'

KNIPHOFIA UVARIA

LIATRIS 'KOBOLD'

LIGULARIA PRZEWALSKII 'THE ROCKET'

LYSIMACHIA PUNCTATA

**Selected species and varieties.** *K. uvaria*: deep scarlet flowers up to 2 inches long that fade to yellow. Blossoms are crowded in dense 12-inch spikes on 3-foot stalks.

**Growing conditions.** Plant red-hot poker in full sun in moist, well-drained sandy soil, choosing locations that are sheltered from wind. Tie up the leaves and mulch the crowns to protect plants during winter in areas at the northern end of its range. Propagate red-hot poker by division every three to four years in the spring, setting new plants 1 ½ to 2 feet apart. Red-hot poker grows well in Zone 10 only on the West Coast.

**Landscape uses.** Use red-hot poker as a striking specimen at the middle or back of a border, where its foliage will also serve as a filler throughout the season.

**Lamb's-ears** see Dictionary of Grasses and Ground Covers, page 160
**Lamium** see Dictionary of Grasses and Ground Covers, page 160
**Larkspur** see *Delphinium*
**Lavandula** see Dictionary of Trees and Shrubs, page 426
**Lavender** see Dictionary of Trees and Shrubs, page 426
**Lavender cotton** see *Santolina*
**Leadwort** see *Ceratostigma*
**Lenten rose** see *Helleborus*

## Liatris (ly-AY-tris)
Blazing star, gay-feather

Long wands of late-summer or fall flowers crowded at the top of upright stems above narrow swordlike foliage. Translucent green balloon-shaped buds open to purple or white flowers. The flowers have threadlike projections that give them a fuzzy appearance. The blooms open from top to bottom. Zones 3-10.

**Selected species and varieties.** *L. spicata*, spiked gay-feather: stems 3 to 6 feet tall tipped with foot-long spikes of ½-inch purple or white flowers. Zones 3-10. 'Kobold' is a compact form growing only 18 inches tall with deep purple flowers.

**Growing conditions.** Plant gay-feathers in full sun or light shade in a moist, well-drained sandy soil, spacing plants 1 foot apart. Propagate from seed or by division in spring. Gay-feathers grow well in Zones 9 and 10 only on the West Coast.

**Landscape uses.** *L. spicata* 'Kobold' is suitable for the front of a border.

## Ligularia (lig-yew-LAY-ree-a)

Large, rounded heart- or kidney-shaped leaves, sometimes toothed or splotched with color, forming graceful clumps of foliage 2 to 4 feet tall. Bright yellow or orange flowers in summer. Zones 4-10.

**Selected species and varieties.** *L. przewalskii* 'The Rocket': prominently toothed, dark green, triangular to round leaves in 4-foot mounds. 6-foot flower stalks with 12- to 18-inch spires of yellow ½-inch summer flowers. Zones 4-8.

**Growing conditions.** Plant ligularias in full sun in a constantly moist but not wet soil amply enriched with organic matter. Ligularias grow in light shade but the flower stalks will lean toward the sun.

**Landscape uses.** Use ligularia singly as a specimen plant or as a bold feature in a perennial border. Use the leaves of the leopard plant in floral arrangements.

**Lilyturf** see Dictionary of Grasses and Ground Covers, page 160
**Liriope** see Dictionary of Grasses and Ground Covers, page 160
**Lobelia** see Dictionary of Annuals, page 200
**Loosestrife** see *Lysimachia*
**Lungwort** see Dictionary of Grasses and Ground Covers, page 160

## Lysimachia (Ly-si-MAK-ee-a)
Loosestrife

Vigorous, easy-to-grow plant with spikes of small white flowers or cup-shaped yellow flowers on erect stems in spring or summer. The genus *Lythrum* has the same common name. Zones 4-8.

**Selected species and varieties.** *L. punctata*, yellow loosestrife: deep yellow flowers marked inside with a brown circle on stems to 3 feet tall. Large, deeply veined, pointed oval leaves crowd the stems. Zones 5-7.

**Growing conditions.** Loosestrifes thrive in moist soil in full sun or light shade. Space plants 2 feet apart. They can spread quickly and overcrowd neighboring plants. Propagate by dividing the thick mat of roots in early spring.

**Landscape uses.** Loosestrifes may be planted in a border if their spread is kept in check with frequent division. They require less attention in a naturalistic garden where they can spread freely into wide clumps.

**Marguerite** see Dictionary of Annuals, page 200
**Marjoram** see *Origanum*

**Mertensia** (mer-TEN-see-a)
Bluebells

Pink buds open to trumpet-shaped blue flowers in spring. Zones 4-8.

**Selected species and varieties.** *M. virginica*, Virginia bluebells: loose nodding clusters of 1-inch flowers on plants from 1 to 2 feet high. Flowers may be various shades of blue and are occasionally pink or white. A plant often has buds and open flowers at the same time. Long, blue-green leaves.

**Growing conditions.** Virginia bluebells grow best in partial shade where the soil is acid, moist, well drained and rich in organic matter. They can tolerate full sun. Space them 1 foot apart. The plants go dormant in summer and need drier soil then. They can be propagated by seed or by division after they go dormant. They may self-sow.

**Landscape uses.** Virginia bluebells can be used in a woodland garden or a shady perennial bed and are attractive in drifts under trees at the edge of a lawn. Because they are dormant in summer, they should be interplanted with plants that fill up the spaces they leave, such as hostas.

**Michaelmas daisy** see *Aster*
**Miscanthus** see Dictionary of Grasses and Ground Covers, page 160

**Monarda** (mo-NARD-a)

Small, tubular red, pink, lavender or yellow flowers blooming from summer to early fall in dense 2- to 3-inch clusters surrounded by aromatic leaves on square stems. Monarda belongs to the mint family. Zones 4-9.

**Selected species and varieties.** *M. didyma*, bee balm: red flowers on 3-foot plants. The variety 'Cambridge Scarlet' has flowers in a clearer, more brilliant red; 'Croftway Pink' bears rose pink flowers.

**Growing conditions.** Monardas do best in moist, rich soil in full sun or light shade. They grow rapidly in these conditions and may in fact become invasive. In drier soil they are shorter and less invasive. Space plants 1 ½ to 2 feet apart. Divide plants in spring.

**Landscape uses.** Monardas are well suited to naturalizing in a meadow or woodland garden. *M. didyma* and its varieties are also attractive in small groups in a border. Do not plant monardas where they may crowd out smaller or less vigorous plants. Monardas of all sorts attract bees and hummingbirds.

**Mullein** see *Verbascum*
**Myosotis** see Dictionary of Grasses and Ground Covers, page 160; Annuals, page 200

**Nepeta** (ne-PEE-ta)
Catmint

Tiny blue flowers in spikes on a low-growing plant with gray-green triangular or heart-shaped aromatic foliage loved by cats. Blooms spring to mid-summer. Zones 4-8.

**Selected species and varieties.** *N. mussinii,* catmint: soft blue or lavender-blue flowers on 1-foot stems . The plant spreads to 1 ½ feet in width.

**Growing conditions.** Grow catmint in full sun in sandy, well-drained soil. Poor soil keeps it compact and attractive; in rich soil it is likely to sprawl. Space plants 1 to 1 ½ feet apart. Stems may be cut back by half after flowering to encourage a second blooming. Increase by division or by seed.

**Landscape uses.** Catmint is a fine ground cover. It may also be used in the front of a border, in a rock garden or in an herb garden. Its subtle blues and lavenders combine well with soft pinks, yellows and other blues.

**New Zealand flax** see *Phormium*
**October daphne** see *Sedum*

**Oenothera** (ee-no-THEE-ra)

Showy four-petaled summer flowers in yellow, white or pink. Zones 3-9.

**Selected species and varieties.** *O. fruticosa*, common sundrops: 1- to 2-inch yellow flowers in clusters at the tops of 1- to 2-foot stems. Zones 4-8. *O. tetragona*, common sundrops: lemon

MERTENSIA VIRGINICA

MONARDA DIDYMA 'CROFTWAY PINK'

NEPETA MUSSINII

OENOTHERA FRUTICOSA

ORIGANUM VULGARE 'AUREUM'

PAEONIA 'KANSAS'

PEROVSKIA ATRIPLICIFOLIA

yellow flowers on a plant about 3 feet high; may be perennial or biennial. Zones 4-8. *O. tetragona* and *O. fruticosa* are often confused with each other.

**Growing conditions.** Grow sundrops in full sun and well-drained soil. They do well even in poor and dry soils and can become invasive. Allow 1 to 1 ½ feet between sundrops. Propagate by seed or by division in spring.

**Landscape uses.** Use sundrops as border plants; their bright yellow flowers contrast well with other colors.

## Origanum (o-RIG-an-um)
Marjoram

Low, neat mat of aromatic, oval 1 ½-inch leaves and wiry, branching flower stalks bearing small spikes of rose to purple flowers in late summer. Zones 4-10.

**Selected species and varieties.** *O. vulgare* 'Aureum,' variegated pot marjoram: a cultivar valued mainly for its foliage, which is golden yellow until midsummer and then turns green. Flower stalks are 1 ½ to 2 feet tall.

**Growing conditions.** Pot marjoram needs full sun and moist, well-drained soil. Space plants 1 ½ feet apart. Propagate in spring by division or from seed.

**Landscape uses.** Use variegated pot marjoram as a colorful, aromatic edging for a border. Pick the leaves for use as a culinary herb.

## Paeonia (pee-O-nee-a)
Peony

Showy spring and early-summer blossoms on bushy plants that grow up to 4 feet in height and may thrive for decades. Blossoms range from white and creamy yellow through pinks and dark purple-red and may have single, double or semidouble rows of petals. Shoots emerge red and ferny in spring, then develop into lush, deeply divided foliage. Zones 3-10.

**Selected species and varieties.** *P. tenuifolia*, fernleaf peony: the smallest and most delicate of the peonies, growing about 1 foot high, that has finely divided foliage and single red-purple flowers in early summer. Zones 6-8. The variety 'Kansas' possesses bright red blossoms on very strong stems in midseason.

**Growing conditions.** Peonies need well-drained soil enriched with organic matter. They thrive in sun and grow in light shade but become leggy and weak in heavy shade. Plant container-grown peonies whenever the ground is not frozen, any time from late August until the ground freezes. Space plants 3 feet apart. Set crowns an inch below the soil surface; planting too deep results in failure to bloom. Divide in fall; cut roots apart with a knife and leave at least three eyes to each piece.

**Landscape uses.** Use peonies in a border or in front of shrubs, as specimens, as hedges, or along a wall or a fence. Their foliage is an asset after the flowers have faded. Use fernleaf peony in a rock garden. Peonies are excellent cut flowers.

**Panicum** see Dictionary of Grasses and Ground Covers, page 160
**Pansy** see Dictionary of Annuals, page 200
**Pasque flower** see *Anemone*
**Pennisetum** see Dictionary of Grasses and Ground Covers, page 160
**Peony** see *Paeonia*

## Perovskia (per-OV-skee-a)

Three- to 5-foot-high shrubby plant with aromatic silvery leaves and small blue blossoms that appear in late summer. Zones 4-8.

**Selected species and varieties.** *P. atriplicifolia*, azure sage, Russian sage has flowers densely packed at the ends of stems, clustered more loosely below. Silvery foliage and small blossoms give sage a lacy effect. The leaves and stems smell like sage when crushed. The plant spreads to about 3 feet across.

**Growing conditions.** Azure sage grows best in well-drained soil in full sun. Space plants 2 to 3 feet apart. Propagate by seed. Cutting the plant to the ground in early spring promotes good bloom.

**Landscape uses.** Plant azure sage in a border or island bed, where it combines well with ornamental grasses. Azure sage can also be used as any airy hedge or screen.

## Phlox (FLOX)

Clusters of five-petaled flat-faced flowers in orange, red, pink, lavender, purple, blue or white on stems that trail or grow erect to 4 feet. Some phlox bloom in spring, others in summer or early fall. Zones 3-10.

**Selected species and varieties.** *P. bifida*, prairie phlox: grows to 10 inches with spring flowers that have white to light blue deeply cut petals. Zones 5-8. *P. paniculata*, border phlox: the common phlox of the summer garden. Grows to 4 feet high with white, pink, red, orange, lavender or purple flowers in heavy clusters. Zones 4-9. The variety 'Mt. Fujiyama' has large heads of white flowers; 'Orange Perfection' has orange flowers, and 'Starfire' has early blooms of intense red. *P. subulata*, moss pink: low-growing mat of stiff needle-like evergreen leaves smothered in spring with blooms of white, pink, blue, lavender or red flowers, depending on the variety. Zones 4-10.

**Growing conditions.** Phlox species have varied cultural needs. Moss pink and prairie phlox do best in full sun and sandy soil. The other species require moist, well-drained soil rich in organic matter. Border phlox does best in full sun and needs plenty of water in the summer. Remove about half of the young shoots from border phlox in spring for best blossoming. Border phlox needs good air circulation to prevent powdery mildew, so space plants at least 2 feet apart. Divide them every three to four years to keep them robust. Space the other tall-growing phlox 1 ½ to 2 feet apart and the lower-growing phlox 1 to 1 ½ feet apart. Propagate by division.

**Landscape uses.** Border phlox is a mainstay of any perennial border for summer color. Prairie phlox and moss pink can be used as rock garden plants, as ground covers or at the front of a border.

## Phormium (FORM-ee-um)

Bold fan-shaped plant with leathery swordlike leaves and red flowers on tall stalks up to 15 feet in height. Zones 8-10.

**Selected species and varieties.** *P. tenax* 'Variegatum,' New Zealand flax: stiff gray-green leaves up to 9 feet long striped with yellow. Plum red flowers appear in clusters on stalks that rise several feet above the foliage.

**Growing conditions.** New Zealand flax grows best in moist soil in full sun or light shade. It tolerates windy sites and does well in seaside gardens. In Zone 8 plant it in a warm, sheltered spot. Space plants 3 to 5 feet apart. Propagate New Zealand flax by seed or by division.

**Landscape uses.** Use New Zealand flax alone as a specimen plant, combine it with shrubs or plant it in a perennial border for a spiky accent.

**Pincushion flower** see *Scabiosa*
**Pink** see *Dianthus*
**Plantain lily** see Dictionary of Grasses and Ground Covers, page 160

## Platycodon (plat-i-KO-don)
Balloon flower

Fat, balloon-like buds open into cup-shaped blue, pink or white flowers that bloom all summer. Zones 3-9.

**Selected species and varieties.** *P. grandiflorus mariesii*, Maries' balloon flower: 1 ½- foot plant with either blue or white flowers.

**Growing conditions.** Plant balloon flowers in a light, moist, well-drained acid soil enriched with organic matter such as peat moss, compost and leaf mold. They grow best in full sun, although light shade helps the flowers to retain their color. Space plants 1 ½ feet apart. Propagate by division in spring or by seed. Plants started from seed will bloom their second year. New growth is late to appear in spring.

**Landscape uses.** Balloon flower is a good plant for dependable color all summer long in a perennial border. The smaller Maries' balloon flower is suitable for a rock garden.

**Plumbago** see *Ceratostigma*
**Poppy** see Dictionary of Annuals, page 200

PHLOX BIFIDA

PHORMIUM TENAX 'VARIEGATUM'

PLATYCODON GRANDIFLORUS MARIESII

POTENTILLA RECTA 'WARRENII'

RUDBECKIA FULGIDA

SANGUISORBA CANADENSIS

**Potentilla** (po-ten-TILL-a)
Cinquefoil, five-finger

Spring or summer blossoms resembling small roses in white, yellow, pink or shades of red. Leaves are composed of three or five leaflets arranged like the fingers on a hand. Zones 4-9.

**Selected species and varieties.** *P. recta*, sulfur cinquefoil: pale yellow inch-wide summer flowers on 2 ½-foot plants with hairy gray leaves. Zones 4-7. The variety 'Warrenii' has bright yellow flowers on bushy 2-foot plants. *P. tridentata*, wineleaf cinquefoil: clusters of tiny ¼-inch white flowers from spring through summer above neat foot-high mats of leaves with three shiny dark green leaflets that turn brilliant wine red in fall and are sometimes evergreen. Zones 4-8.

**Growing conditions.** Plant cinquefoils in sun or light shade in well-drained sandy soil. Sulfur cinquefoil does best in hot, dry spots and can be invasive. The leaves of wineleaf cinquefoil show their best fall color in an acid soil. Allow 1 foot between sulfur and wineleaf cinquefoils.

**Landscape uses.** Use cinquefoils in a border or in a rock garden. Allow sulfur cinquefoil to spread in a naturalistic garden. Plant wineleaf cinquefoil in a rock garden, use it as a ground cover or underplant it with plants, such as small spring bulbs.

**Pulmonaria** see Dictionary of Grasses and Ground Covers, page 160
**Red-hot poker** see *Kniphofia*
**Rock cress** see Dictionary of Grasses and Ground Covers, page 160

**Rudbeckia** (rood-BEK-ee-a)
Coneflower

Masses of large daisy-like yellow flowers with a raised dark cone at the center from midsummer into fall on vigorous, easy-to-grow plants. Zones 4-9.

**Selected species and varieties.** *R. fulgida*, orange coneflower, black-eyed Susan: flowers 1 to 1 ½, inches across with orange-yellow petals surrounding a brownish black central cone that is decorative after the petals fall. Height 2 to 3 feet.

**Growing conditions.** Plant coneflowers in full sun or light shade in almost any moist, well-drained fertile soil. Space plants 1 ½ to 2 feet apart.

They tend to spread quickly and may need to be divided every two years. Propagate by division in early spring or from seed.

**Landscape uses.** Use coneflowers in the front or middle of a border or plant them in large drifts in a naturalistic meadow garden. Their dark cones provide interest in the garden in late fall and winter.

**Russian sage** see *Perovskia*
**Sage** see *Perovskia*
**Salvia** see Dictionary of Annuals, page 200

**Sanguisorba** (san-gwi-SOR-ba)
Burnet

Creamy white or rose pink summer or fall flowers in dense spikes like bottle brushes, and lacy foliage composed of several paired leaflets. Zones 4-9.

**Selected species and varieties.** *S. canadensis*, American burnet, great burnet: creamy flowers in dense, stiff spikes up to 8 inches long above bright green leaves in late summer or fall. Plants grow to 3 feet in a garden, up to 6 feet in boggy ground. Zones 4-8.

**Growing conditions.** Burnets do best in full sun or light shade in moist, well-drained soil enriched with peat moss. Space plants 2 feet apart. Propagate by division in early spring or fall, or grow from seed.

**Landscape uses.** Use burnets near the back of the border, where American burnet is especially valuable for its late-season bloom. American burnet grows well in wet soil and can be used beside streams or in a bog garden.

**Santolina** (san-to-LEE-na)
Lavender cotton

Low shrubby mounds of aromatic, finely cut evergreen leaves and yellow flowers in early summer. Zones 6-10.

**Selected species and varieties.** *S. chamaecyparissus*, lavender cotton: mounds of silvery foliage up to 2 feet tall and 2 feet wide; ¾-inch flowers on slender 6-inch stalks. Zones 6-9. *S. virens*, green lavender cotton: spreading plants 18 inches tall with narrow toothed green leaves 2 inches long and creamy yellow ½-inch flowers on 10-inch stalks. Zones 7-10.

**Growing conditions.** Plant lavender cotton in full sun in any well-drained garden soil. It tolerates seaside conditions. Space plants 1 ½ to 2 feet apart. Cut them back heavily in spring or after flowering to keep them bushy and compact. Provide winter mulch at the northern end of the range. Propagate from seed or by rooting cuttings in spring.

**Landscape uses.** Use lavender cotton as an edging plant for paths and beds or as a foliage plant in a border or rock garden. Lavender cotton responds well to pruning and can be sheared into formal shapes.

## Scabiosa (skab-i-O-sa)
Pincushion flower

Blue, lavender or white summer flowers up to 3 inches across with centers like tiny pincushions surrounded by ruffly petals. Flower stalks 2 ½ feet long rising from tufts of narrow light green leaves. Zones 4-10.

**Selected species and varieties.** *S. caucasica*, pincushion flower: flat blue or white frilled blossoms. The variety 'Miss Willmott' has creamy white blossoms.

**Growing conditions.** Plant pincushion flower in full sun in a light, moist, well-drained neutral to alkaline soil. In hot areas it does better in light shade; it grows well in Zones 9 and 10 only on the West Coast. Space plants 1 ½ to 2 feet apart. Remove faded blossoms to encourage flower production. Propagate pincushion flower from seed or by division in spring.

**Landscape uses.** Since individual plants produce only a few flowers each, group pincushion flowers for more impact in a bed or border. The blossoms make good cut flowers.

**Scottish bluebells** see *Campanula*
**Sea holly** see *Eryngium*
**Sea pink** see *Armeria*

## Sedum (SEE-dum)
Stonecrop

Drought-tolerant plant with clusters of tiny star-shaped flowers in yellow, white or pink and plump, fleshy overlapping leaves. Zones 3-10.

**Selected species and varieties.** *S.* x 'Autumn Joy': 2-foot plant with toothed gray-green leaves and flat clusters of pink fall flowers that turn rusty red and remain colorful throughout winter. *S. maximum* 'Great Stonecrop': greenish white late-summer flowers on 1- to 2-foot plants with fat oval gray-green leaves. Zones 4-10. *S. maximum* 'Atropurpureum' bears flat reddish flower heads and has maroon-purple leaves. *S.* x 'Ruby Glow': bright pink fall flowers and gray-blue leaves on compact 8-inch plants. Zones 4-10. *S. sieboldii*, Siebold stonecrop, October daphne: small dense heads of bright pink flowers from late summer through fall on low, arching 9-inch stems with blue-gray, nearly triangular leaves. Zones 3-10. *S. spectabile*, showy stonecrop: large dense heads of bright pink fall flowers on 1 ½ foot stems with 8-inch gray-green leaves. Zones 8-10.

**Growing conditions.** Sedums flourish in full sun or light shade in any well-drained garden soil. They will grow in poor, dry soils. Space Siebold stonecrops 1 foot apart and the other species and cultivars 1 ½ to 2 feet apart. Sedums are easily increased by division or by rooting leaf or stem cuttings.

**Landscape uses.** Use sedums in a rock garden or border, where they are valuable for both flowers and foliage. The maroon leaves of *S. maximum* 'Atropurpureum' make an interesting accent among green-leaved perennials, and the dried flower heads and stems of 'Autumn Joy' sedum are handsome additions to a winter garden. Butterflies flock to sedum flowers.

**Sneezeweed** see *Helenium*
**Soapweed** see *Yucca*

## Solidago (sol-i-DAY-go)
Goldenrod

Plumy clusters of tiny flowers in shades of yellow from middle or late summer into fall. Zones 3-10.

**Selected species and varieties.** *S. canadensis*, Canada goldenrod: branching plumes of shaggy yellow flowers on 5-foot stems with narrow, pointed 6-inch leaves. The variety 'Peter Pan' has canary yellow blossoms on compact plants only 2 ½ feet tall. Zones 3-10.

**Growing conditions.** Plant goldenrods in full sun in any well-drained soil that is not too rich. They also tolerate light shade and considerable dryness. Space plants 1 to 2 feet apart. Propagate by division or from seed. Goldenrods self-sow prolifically and may be invasive, especially in very fertile soil.

SANTOLINA CHAMAECYPARISSUS

SCABIOSA CAUCASICA 'MISS WILLMOTT'

SEDUM × 'AUTUMN JOY'

SOLIDAGO CANADENSIS 'PETER PAN'

TANACETUM VULGARE

TRILLIUM GRANDIFLORUM

TROLLIUS × CULTORUM

VALERIANA OFFICINALIS

**Landscape uses.** Use goldenrods in a naturalistic meadow garden or group them in a border with other late-season perennials such as asters or sneezeweed.

**Speedwell** see *Veronica*
**Spurge** see *Euphorbia*
**Stachys** see Dictionary of Grasses and Ground Covers, page 160
**Stonecrop** see *Sedum*
**Sundrops** see *Oenothera*
**Sunflower** see Dictionary of Annuals, page 200
**Sweet William** see *Dianthus*
**Switch grass** see Dictionary of Grasses and Ground Covers, page 160

## Tanacetum (tan-a-SEE-tum)
Tansy

Clusters of ¼-inch button-like yellow flowers from late summer to early fall above strongly scented ferny foliage. Zones 4-10.

**Selected species and varieties.** *T. vulgare*, tansy: 2- to 3-foot plant with finely divided leaves. The variety *crispum*, fernleaf tansy, has more finely cut leaves. Flowers are longlasting. Leaves can be safely used as a flavoring only in very small quantities; larger amounts are poisonous.

**Growing conditions.** Tansy thrives in full sun or partial shade in well-drained average soil. In moist, fertile soil it can become invasive. Space plants 1 ½ to 2 feet apart. Propagate by division or from seed. Tansy does not do well in Zone 10 in Florida.

**Landscape uses.** Use fernleaf tansy in a perennial border for both its foliage and its flowers or plant it in an ornamental herb garden.

**Tansy** see *Tanacetum*
**Thrift** see *Armeria*
**Torch lily** see *Kniphofia*

## Trillium (TRILL-ee-um)

White spring flowers with three petals on 6- to 18-inch stems above a whorl of three broad, oval pointed leaves. Zones 3-8.

**Selected species and varieties.** *T. grandiflorum*, snow trillium: pure white flowers 3 to 6 inches across turn slowly to pink as they age. The deep green leaves are up to 6 inches long and have conspicuous veins and wavy edges.

**Growing conditions.** Plant trillium in light to deep shade in a moist, well-drained, slightly acid soil enriched with organic matter, spacing plants 1 foot apart. Propagate trillium by division or from seed.

**Landscape uses.** Plant snow trillium in groups for luminous patches of white in a naturalistic woodland garden or a shady border.

## Trollius (TROL-ee-us)
Globeflower

Waxy orange or yellow flowers with curving, overlapping petals in spring and occasionally in summer or fall. Low clumps of deeply cut dark green leaves. Zones 5-10.

**Selected species and varieties.** *T. ledebourii*, Ledebour globeflower: stems up to 3 feet tall with orange 2 ½-inch flowers with long petal-like orange stamens filling their centers. The variety 'Golden Queen' has deep orange flowers on 2-foot-long stems. *T.* x *cultorum*: globe-shaped yellow or orange flowers on 3-foot stems.

**Growing conditions.** Plant globeflowers in partial shade in a constantly moist, even wet soil enriched with organic matter such as peat moss or compost. They can take full sun if the soil is not allowed to dry out. Globeflowers grow naturally in swampy places and will not tolerate dryness. Space plants 1 ½ feet apart. Propagate by division in fall or from seed. Remove fading flowers to prolong the blooming season. Globeflowers grow well in Zones 9 and 10 on the West Coast only.

**Landscape uses.** Use globeflowers at the edges of ponds, streams or boggy meadows or in moist, shady wildflower gardens. The foliage of both species remains attractive all season long. Both species' flowers and foliage are suitable for use in arrangements.

## Valeriana (val-ee-ri-AY-na)

Rounded clusters of fragrant white, pink or lavender flowers in summer on stems 3 to 4 feet tall with attractive ferny leaves. Zones 4-10.

**Selected species and varieties.**
*V. officinalis*, common valerian, garden heliotrope: tiny 3/16-inch flowers in airy heads above foliage composed of paired pointed leaflets.

**Growing conditions.** Common valerian thrives in full sun or light shade in almost any soil. Space plants 1½ to 2 feet apart. Propagate from seed or by division in spring or fall.

**Landscape uses.** Use common valerian in the middle or back of a border for both its flowers and its fragrance. Common valerian's flowers are good for cutting.

## Verbascum (ver-BAS-cum)
Mullein

Branched spikes with densely packed yellow or white blossoms on stems 3 feet tall in summer. Zones 5-9.

**Selected species and varieties.**
*V. chaixii*, Chaix mullein: inch-wide yellow flowers with woolly purple centers. Woolly silvery green leaves up to 6 inches long grow in a mound at the base of plants and become smaller and sparser toward the top of the stem. The cultivar 'Album' has white flowers with purple centers.

**Growing conditions.** Choose a site in full sun in well-drained sandy soil and space plants 1½ to 2 feet apart. Propagate from seed or root cuttings, or by division.

**Landscape uses.** Use Chaix mullein as a stately vertical feature in a sunny border. The attractive woolly leaves are semi-evergreen.

**Verbena** see Dictionary of Annuals, page 200

## Veronica (ver-ON-i-ka)

Small blue, pink or white flowers clustered in 6-inch spikes at the tips of erect stems in summer. Zones 4-10.

**Selected species and varieties.**
*V. spicata*, spike speedwell: pink or blue ¼-inch flowers on 1½-foot plants. Zones 4-8.

**Growing conditions.** Veronicas grow well in full sun or light shade in a moist, well-drained soil. Allow 1 to 1½ feet of space for spike speedwell. Remove fading spikes to prolong flowering. Propagate by division in fall.

**Landscape uses.** Plant veronicas in a border for a long period of color. Their strong spiky forms make an interesting contrast with airy, fine-textured plants such as Russian sage.

**Violet** see Dictionary of Annuals, page 200
**Virginia bluebells** see *Mertensia*
**Wild ginger** see Dictionary of Grasses and Ground Covers, page 160
**Wild indigo** see *Baptisia*
**Windflower** see *Anemone*
**Yarrow** see *Achillea*

## Yucca (YUK-ka)

Spikes of fragrant, waxy white bell-shaped flowers in summer over a stiff rosette of sword-shaped evergreen foliage between 2 and 3 feet tall. Yuccas are actually shrubs, but they are used as perennials. Zones 3-10.

**Selected species and varieties.**
*Y. filamentosa*, Adam's-needle: white or cream blossoms 2 inches in diameter in branched 1- to 3-foot spikes on stalks that range up to 10 feet in height. One-inch-wide gray-green leaves with curly white threads along the edges. Zones 5-10. *Y. glauca*, soapweed: greenish white 2-inch flowers in slender spikes above grayish green ½-inch-wide leaves edged in white or pale gray with curly threads. Zones 3-10.

**Growing conditions.** Yuccas do best in full sun and a fast-draining, sandy soil, but they can also be planted in light shade or in a heavier soil. Space new plants 2 to 3 feet apart. Propagate by digging up and replanting the suckers that spring up around the base.

**Landscape uses.** The bold form of its leaves makes yucca a dramatic focus year-round and its tall flower spikes stand out in summer. Plant yucca as a specimen, at the corner or end of a bed or border, or next to an architectural feature such as a gate or flight of steps. Yuccas are mainstays of desert gardens.

**Zebra grass** see Dictionary of Grasses and Ground Covers, page 160

VERBASCUM CHAIXII 'ALBUM'

VERONICA SPICATA

YUCCA FILAMENTOSA

# 6

# BULBS

*With crisp foliage and bright shiny blooms, a border of orange and yellow Greigii tulips thrives in a bed of good, enriched soil. Tulips are "true bulbs," one of five plant types that are commonly called bulbs.*

The term "bulb" generally refers to any plant that stores food underground in specially modified leaves, stems or roots. Besides true bulbs, included in the category are corms, tubers, rhizomes and tuberous roots. As shown on pages 266-269, all of these plants stockpile everything needed for a new growth cycle, and most of them can outlast adverse climatic conditions—and then burst into bloom as soon as the weather improves. They are among the easiest and most reliable plants that a gardener can grow.

Few garden plants mark the passage of the seasons more clearly than flowering bulbs. Crocuses pushing through the snow herald the coming of spring, and tulips and daffodils announce that spring has truly arrived. Lilies are a sure sign of mid-summer. Finally, with autumn's arrival, the spectacular blossoms of dahlias grow ever more brilliant.

Happily for gardeners, it is easy to incorporate this cyclical display into a garden plan, for flowering bulbs are among the most rewarding of plants. Because they carry within their underground structures all the nutrients needed to bring them into flower, they are, in effect, self-perpetuating. This chapter provides detailed descriptions of various popular options for growing bulbs, including planting them in a flower bed or on a lawn. Refer to Chapter 2 for directions on performing the regular maintenance tasks that will help your bulbs look their best—watering and fertilizing, grooming and staking, weeding and mulching, and combating pests.

For avid gardeners who suffer through the long winter months deprived of flowers, bulbs can be a godsend. Through a technique called forcing, they can be encouraged to speed up their normal cycle of growth and bloom indoors long before nature intended.

## CHAPTER CONTENTS

Not all bulbs respond equally well to forcing, and for those that do, the forcing procedure has different requirements. Some bulbs, after being potted, need a mandatory chilling period of anywhere from six to 15 weeks at temperatures barely above freezing. Others need eight to 12 weeks at 50° to 60° F. Refer to the Dictionary of Bulbs at the end of this chapter for details concerning plants that can be forced.

Bulbs, especially exotic hybrids, can be expensive. One way to bypass the expense is to propagate new plants from existing plants or from purchased seed. Bulbs acquired in this way are not only less costly, but they can duplicate exactly a much-loved flower.

Several methods of propagating bulbs, such as planting cormels *(page 278)*, scaling, slicing, scoring and scooping are explained on the following pages. For other methods of propagating bulbs, such as starting seeds indoors, dividing, planting stem cuttings and creating hybrids, refer to Chapter 2. Any propagation technique is best done when a bulb is at its prime, full of the nutrients it has been collecting all summer long. Gardeners should not expect immediate results; most young bulbs do not reach flower-bearing age for two or three years.

Keep your bulbs vibrant and healthy by following the monthly checklist of maintenance chores for bulbs on page 286. For the pests and diseases that afflict bulbs, there are standard remedies, and these are described in the Troubleshooting Guide. When choosing bulbs that will flourish in your garden, refer to the Zone Map *(inside front cover);* locate your zone, then consult the Dictionary for plants suited to where you live.

# A GALLERY OF BULBS AND HOW THEY GROW

What true bulbs, corms, tubers, rhizomes and tuberous roots have in common is that they grow from underground storage structures that are made up of modified plant parts. These structures are shown in detail opposite and on pages 268-269. True bulbs store food in modified leaf tissue; corms, tubers and rhizomes store it in modified stem tissue; tuberous roots store it in roots. All five storage structures serve the same purpose; by building up a reserve of nutrients during the growing season, they enable the plant to survive a long dormant period—and then put out fresh foliage and flowers as soon as weather conditions permit.

Once they have done so, photosynthesis, the process whereby plants manufacture food, takes place only in green tissue. As long as it remains alive and green, the foliage of a bulb will continue to make food. This food is needed for the underground storage structure to produce next year's flower. That is why the foliage of a bulb should not be removed from the plant when the flower fades; it should be allowed to die back naturally.

Most bulbs available from garden supply centers and mail-order sources are designated winter-hardy. Examples include tulips, lilies and daffodils. These natives of temperate climes normally go dormant when the weather turns cold and are ready to blossom in the spring. Other bulbs, among them amaryllis, begonias, dahlias and gladioli, are known as tender bulbs; they come from the tropics, where dry weather triggers dormancy and wet weather prompts renewed growth. Whichever kind they are, bulbs are usually purchased in their dormant phase. When buying bulbs, select the largest samples you can find; big bulbs are full of reserve food energy, which can be counted on to produce luxuriant foliage and bright flowers when the spring growing season arrives. Small bulbs may not bloom in the first year. For more rules on choosing bulbs, see the box opposite.

*Around the shapely trunk of a crape myrtle, blue spring starflowers, pink and purple anemones, and yellow daffodils herald spring. All these flowers are classed as bulbs, though they arise from different structures: anemones from tubers, daffodils and spring starflowers from tunicate bulbs.*

# TRUE BULBS

A true bulb has a basal plate that consists of compressed stem tissue. Roots descend from the bottom, and modified leaves (scales) grow upward from it. The scales store food. One kind of true bulb, which includes daffodils and tulips, is called tunicate *(left)*; such bulbs have an outer tunic of dry, papery scales covering fleshy inner scales and a tiny flower bud. The flower bud and inner scales will elongate and emerge to form the flower and foliage. The other kind of bulbs are scaly bulbs *(below)*, like the lily. They consist of overlapping fleshy scales that surround an apical bud that will develop into flowers and foliage. They have no common covering. Both kinds of true bulbs produce offspring bulbs from lateral buds located near the basal plate.

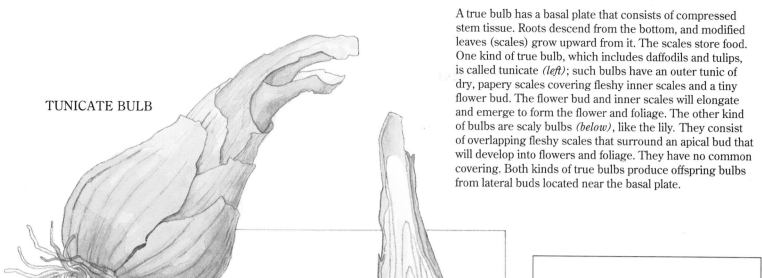

TUNICATE BULB

TUNIC
SCALE
FLOWER BUD
BASAL PLATE
LATERAL BUDS
ROOTS

## RULES FOR CHOOSING BULBS

Select bulbs that are heavy and feel solid. Lightness means a bulb has dried out inside. Similarly, softness indicates disease—and nicks may mean damage. Avoid bulbs packaged in bags or boxes labeled "mixed bulbs" or "bargain assortment." The bulbs inside could be low-grade leftovers hardly worth the trouble to plant. Instead of going to a nursery, you can choose bulbs from mail-order catalogs. Bulbs bought by mail tend to be more costly than the assortment in nursery bins, but those shipped by reputable firms are usually of high quality.

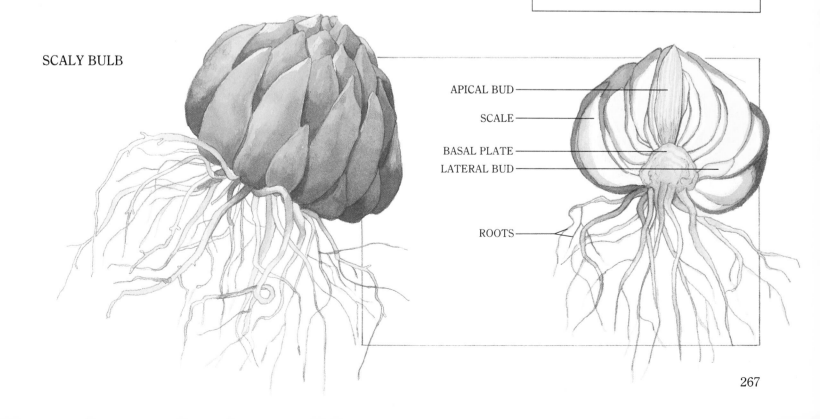

SCALY BULB

APICAL BUD
SCALE
BASAL PLATE
LATERAL BUD

ROOTS

## CORMS

A corm (*left and directly below*) is a swollen stem base. On the bottom it has roots; at or near the top it has an apical bud, or growth bud, that will develop both foliage and flowers. Peacock orchids are examples of corms. Like a tunicate bulb, a corm has a papery covering (a tunic) that protects food that is stored in the stem tissue inside. At the base of the corm, lateral buds (which are not visible to the naked eye) will produce tiny corms called cormels.

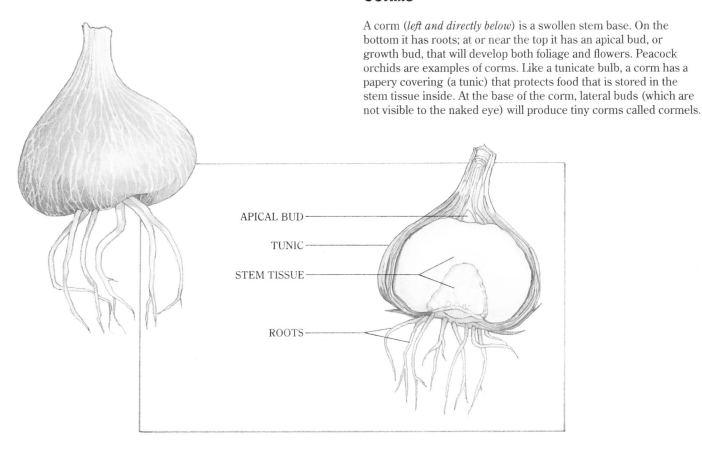

APICAL BUD

TUNIC

STEM TISSUE

ROOTS

## TUBERS

A tuber *(below)* consists of thickened stem tissue with a cluster of growth buds protruding from its top. Foliage and flowers grow from these buds. Roots extend from the bottom of the tuber. Most tubers, like the tuberous begonia, simply grow larger from year to year and produce more and more growth buds.

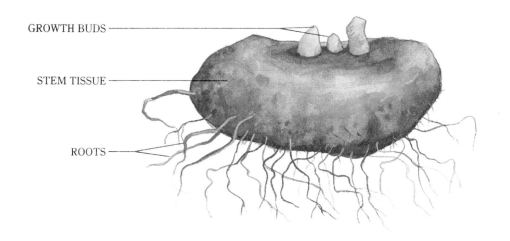

GROWTH BUDS

STEM TISSUE

ROOTS

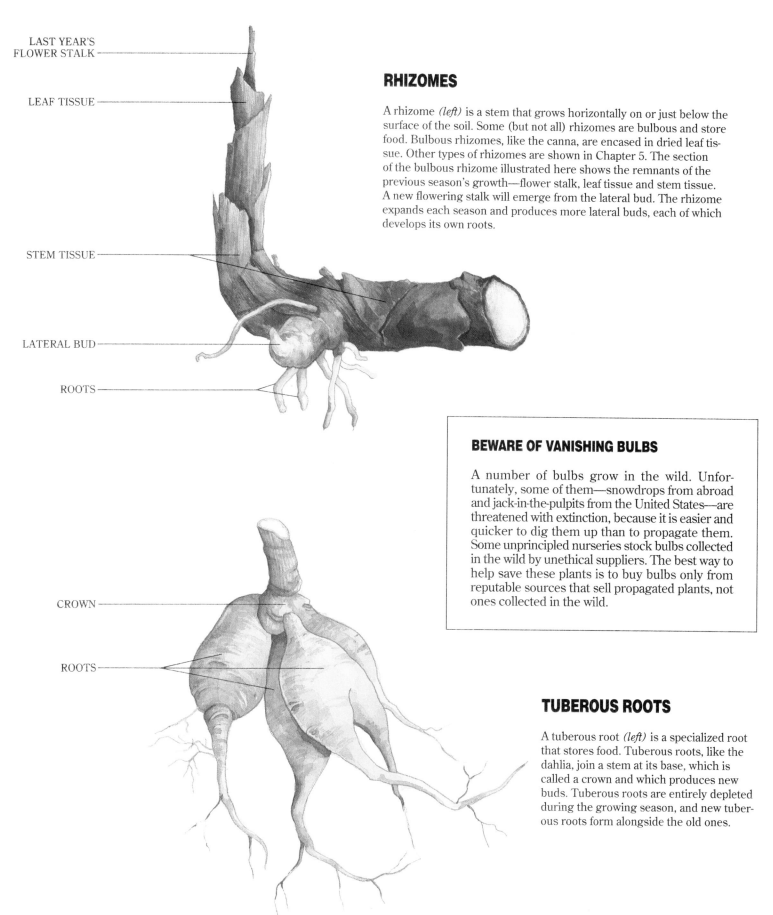

LAST YEAR'S
FLOWER STALK

LEAF TISSUE

STEM TISSUE

LATERAL BUD

ROOTS

## RHIZOMES

A rhizome *(left)* is a stem that grows horizontally on or just below the surface of the soil. Some (but not all) rhizomes are bulbous and store food. Bulbous rhizomes, like the canna, are encased in dried leaf tissue. Other types of rhizomes are shown in Chapter 5. The section of the bulbous rhizome illustrated here shows the remnants of the previous season's growth—flower stalk, leaf tissue and stem tissue. A new flowering stalk will emerge from the lateral bud. The rhizome expands each season and produces more lateral buds, each of which develops its own roots.

### BEWARE OF VANISHING BULBS

A number of bulbs grow in the wild. Unfortunately, some of them—snowdrops from abroad and jack-in-the-pulpits from the United States—are threatened with extinction, because it is easier and quicker to dig them up than to propagate them. Some unprincipled nurseries stock bulbs collected in the wild by unethical suppliers. The best way to help save these plants is to buy bulbs only from reputable sources that sell propagated plants, not ones collected in the wild.

CROWN

ROOTS

## TUBEROUS ROOTS

A tuberous root *(left)* is a specialized root that stores food. Tuberous roots, like the dahlia, join a stem at its base, which is called a crown and which produces new buds. Tuberous roots are entirely depleted during the growing season, and new tuberous roots form alongside the old ones.

# PLANTING BULBS
# IN A FLOWER BED

Some bulbs flourish best in sunny beds of good-textured loamy soil that drains well, is rich in nutrients and is also chemically balanced. This sounds like a tall order, but with a little thought and planning—followed, inevitably, by a bit of good old-fashioned digging—it is not that hard to create these optimum conditions.

First, choose the bed's location. A few bulbs can tolerate shade, but most like it sunny and warm. So select an area that has full sun and is protected from harsh winds by shrubs, a fence, a wall or some other windbreak.

Then analyze the soil's texture, nutrient content and pH level—that is, its acid-alkaline balance; refer to pages 56-57 for the analysis procedure. One reason bulbs grow so well in the Netherlands is that the soil is full of crushed seashells, which make it alkaline. If analysis shows that your soil needs amendment—lime for acidic soil (a pH of 5.9 or below), fertilizer for nutrient-poor soil, organic matter for clayey or sandy soil—follow steps 1 and 2 opposite to improve it, then plant your bulbs *(step 3)*.

## COMBINING BULBS
## WITH OTHER PLANTINGS

Bulbs look especially handsome when put in a bed that is already planted with perennials. The bulbs' bright, waxy blooms show up dramatically against a background of mixed flowers and foliage. They will also lengthen a bed's yearly color display, since a number of bulbs pop up before winter is over, and others are the last to bloom in the fall. The trick to mixing bulbs in a bed with other plants is to put suitable bulbs in the right places—to achieve a season-long display and to be sure the bulbs thrive. Before you start, note the exposure of the site. Most bulbs need at least four hours of direct sun each day, and they will get it if the bed faces south or west. Consider the bulbs' season of bloom, planting them to fill gaps where other plants will not be in full bloom at those times. For choices, see the Dictionary of Bulbs *(page 292)*. Consider the bulbs' color, planting bulbs whose blooms will harmonize with neighboring clumps of flowers. Finally, consider plant height. Tall plants like lilies should go at the back of a border, looking over the heads of shorter plants, and low growers such as grape hyacinth in front.

*In a sunny flower bed alongside a white dowel fence, rows of white tulips and cream-colored daffodils nod their heads above a rank of massed grape hyacinths. The bulbs are somewhat shielded from spring breezes by the fence.*

1 Determine where you want your bed of flowering bulbs; select a location that you will be able to view from a favorite vantage point. Also determine how large it should be; use a hose or rope to outline a free-flowing shape for the bed. Then turn the earth to a depth of 9 to 12 inches. As you dig, turn over each spadeful of earth and chop up the clods *(left)*. Remove all weeds, old roots and rocks as you go.

2 After turning the bed, pour a layer of organic matter on top *(right)*; use compost, peat moss or shredded leaves. A 1-inch layer is enough for good soil, but use at least 3 inches to improve the composition of earth that is too sandy or clayey. Work the organic matter into the bed with your spade. Sprinkle some 10-10-10 fertilizer or some slow-release bulb fertilizer on the amended soil—about ¾ pound for every 25 square feet. Work it into the soil along with any lime the soil analysis deemed necessary.

3 When the earth is ready, dig 6- to 8-inch-deep individual holes in it for your bulbs *(left)*; plant five large bulbs, or 10 to 15 small bulbs, per square foot—growing tip up *(box, below)*. Larger bulbs such as daffodils should be spaced 5 to 9 inches apart, depending on how close you want the blooms, but tiny bulbs (crocus or grape hyacinth) can be far closer—2 or 3 inches apart and only 2 to 4 inches deep. Cover the bulbs with soil and water the bed well.

## WHICH WAY IS UP

Many bulbs have obvious top and bottom sides. Daffodils, for example, have flat undersides with remnants of roots attached, and pointed tips from which growth will come. But some plants are harder to be sure about, such as dahlias, which grow from tuberous roots, and anemones, which spring from odd-shaped tubers. With such bulbs, look for the remains of roots, then for growing points, to determine which way is up. If you are still unsure, plant the bulb sideways; the growing stems will seek light and head upward while the roots will descend in search of moisture and food.

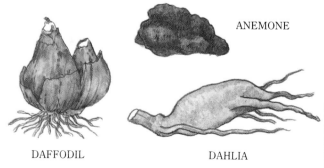

ANEMONE

DAFFODIL

DAHLIA

271

# PLANTING BULBS ON A LAWN

Nothing more cheerfully signals the coming of spring than the bright blooms of crocuses and daffodils, and nowhere do they look better than poking their heads up through an expanse of lawn that is just turning green. The flowers, growing from bulbs planted under the grass, can shoot up in early spring, even in an icy, late-season snowfall. But these uniquely hardy blooms and their bulbs somehow survive the winter's last blasts to proclaim that the sun is high again and a season of rebirth has arrived.

This dramatic annual show is not hard to produce. Choose an open stretch of lawn that gets plenty of sunlight. Then select the bulbs and get them into the ground in the fall. Besides crocuses and daffodils, spring starflowers, early narcissus, scilla, snowdrop and glory-of-the-snow are excellent choices for planting on a lawn. (For more exact planting times, see the Dictionary at the end of this chapter.) The planting itself *(opposite)* should look casual and informal, as if nature, rather than human hands, had done the job. To accelerate the process of digging multiple holes for planting bulbs, you can use a bulb planter *(below)*.

Once planted, the bulbs will repeat their performance season after season. Crocuses, daffodils, scilla and other early-season bulbs can remain in the ground for years. They do not need to be dug up and divided like many other plants; in fact they multiply freely on their own underground. They also need a bare minimum of care: a sprinkling of fertilizer each autumn as new roots develop and another application in the spring.

The lawn where the bulbs are planted should not be mowed, of course, while the plants are blooming and their foliage is young and fresh; the leaves manufacture food that is vital to the bulbs' survival and flowering. So wait to trim the grass until the foliage has turned yellow and begun to die back—about eight to 12 weeks after the flowers have peaked. Gardeners anxious to mow should choose the earliest-blooming bulbs, which should have flowered and faded before the grass gets out of hand.

*Clouds of white and yellow daffodils shoot up in an orchard beneath gnarled fruit trees. The daffodils flourish, their bulbs reproducing and spreading underground, because they bloom early in the spring, before the trees leaf out and cast too much shade.*

## USING A BULB PLANTER

The common spade and trowel are adequate for planting a few handfuls of bulbs, but when you are planting a great many, a special tool called a bulb planter can save you time and effort. A bulb planter is a cylindrical tool that is particularly useful if you are planting bulbs on a lawn or in a bed that already contains other plants. It is available in a hand-held model, as shown, and in larger, spade-sized models that feature a side bar for pushing the planter into the ground by foot and handlebars for pulling the planter out of the ground. Both types of planters create bulb-sized planting holes by removing plugs of soil from the ground.

1 To give the spring blooms in your lawn a natural look, grab a handful of bulbs of the same sort and gently toss them on the grass *(left)*. Some should fall in rough clusters, some singly. Take care not to mix different cultivars in the same cluster; they may bloom at different times and make the cluster look ragged. But it is a good idea to plant different cultivars in separate areas, so that some clusters will bloom early, some late.

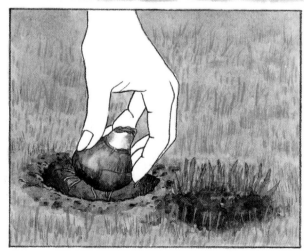

2 Use a trowel *(right)* or a bulb planter to cut a round plug of grass everywhere that a bulb or a cluster of bulbs has fallen. The opening should be slightly larger in diameter than the bulb or the cluster. Set the plug aside, then dig a hole that is two or three times as deep as the bulb is wide—about 6 to 8 inches deep for most daffodils but shallower for miniatures and for crocuses and scilla.

3 As you dig the holes, set the soil aside on a sheet of newspaper. For each hole's worth of soil, thoroughly mix in a tablespoon of a balanced fertilizer such as 10-10-10 *(below)* or a slow-release bulb fertilizer. Drop some of the amended soil in the bottom of each hole—an inch or so of the mix per hole should be enough.

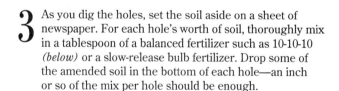

4 Place the bulbs, growing tip up, in the holes *(above)* and cover them with the remaining soil. Firm the soil with your hands and water it lightly. Replace the grass plug, tamp it down and water again. Repeat the scattering and planting in as many places as you wish until you have the spring display you want.

# FORCING BULBS

You can force bulbs to flower out of season indoors by exposing them to a speeded-up version of their normal growth cycle. Among the hardy spring-blossoming bulbs that respond well to forcing are tulips, daffodils, crocuses and hyacinths.

The bulbs of these flowers need to experience a dormant season of cold (but not freezing) temperatures before they are ready to bloom. The easiest way to satisfy this requirement is to store them in a refrigerator.

Most suppliers ship bulbs to arrive for fall planting, usually in late September or early October. To ensure a good selection and to allow ample forcing time for winter blossoming, order early. Choose cultivars that are especially recommended for forcing.

As soon as the bulbs arrive, plant them in a container of moist potting mix so that just the bulbs' growing tips are visible. Mix in a tablespoon of 10-10-10 fertilizer or a slow-release bulb fertilizer. Don't combine different cultivars in the same containers; they may bloom at different times.

Before refrigerating the container of bulbs, check the temperature. The ideal temperature and duration of chilling varies for different species of bulbs; check the Dictionary of Bulbs *(pages 292-313)* for storage requirements of bulbs that respond well to forcing.

One good way to store a large number of potted bulbs is to chill them in a covered outdoor trench *(opposite)*. Since bulbs are best stored at a uniformly cold temperature, the challenge is to chill them in a trench dug below the frost line where winter temperatures are constant.

Not all bulbs are ready to flower at the same time. By taking advantage of nature's own schedule, you can provide a steady supply of colorful accents for your home all winter long. Before you bury potted bulbs, divide them into groups according to their natural blooming times. Label each pot with the name of the bulb and the date for removal from the trench. Then load the pots into the trench by groups so that you can easily dig out the earliest bloomers first. Depending on the species, the bulbs must remain chilled for 8 to 16 weeks.

*A weathered wooden box bursts with sprays of dark pink hyacinths. Such a box can be planted with hardy bulbs, buried in an outdoor trench to keep the bulbs chilled, then dug up and brought indoors when top growth emerges from the soil.*

## FORCING AMARYLLIS BULBS

Amaryllis bulbs are easily forced and can provide many years of spectacularly colored flowers. The bulbs are sold from late fall to early spring. Always choose the largest bulbs available; they will produce the largest flowers. Good-sized bulbs may be as large as medium grapefruits. Plant each bulb soon after you buy it in a good-draining pot that is 2 to 4 inches wider than the diameter of the bulb; use a potting mix of 3 parts peat, 1 part vermiculite and 1 part perlite with a tablespoon of 10-10-10 fertilizer or a slow-release bulb fertilizer, leaving about half the bulb exposed above the soil line. The bulb should bloom in four to six weeks. Cut off the flowers as soon as they fade and remove the flower stalk, but continue watering the plant through spring and summer. Stop watering in late fall to induce dormancy. The foliage will turn yellow and wilt. When the leaves are totally dry and dead, cut them. Then store the potted bulb in a dark, cool place at about 50° to 60° F for about 8 weeks. When new growth emerges, replace the top layer of old soil with fresh soil and add fertilizer. Move the pot to a bright location to begin a new growth cycle.

**1** Plant the bulbs in any kind of container that has drainage holes. Strawberry jars—cylindrical pots with holes around the sides for plants to grow through—make attractive containers for unusual displays of several bulbs at once. To use a strawberry jar to force bulbs, fill the jar up to the lowermost holes with sand or a potting mix made of 3 parts peat, 1 part vermiculite and 1 part perlite. Place one bulb—crocus corms are shown—in each hole with the growing tip angled up and slightly outward *(right)*. Add more sand or potting mix and bulbs until all the holes are filled. Place several bulbs across the top of the container and cover them with 1 inch of sand or potting mix. Water well.

**2** With a garden spade, dig a trench *(left)* on a site that has good drainage; to ensure adequate drainage, position the trench on a slight slope. To ensure that the trench is dug below the frost line, make it 6 to 12 inches deep, depending on the area in which you live. Make sure the trench is big enough and deep enough to allow you to bury a number of pots in the ground.

**3** Place the containers in the trench and fill in around them with loose soil *(right)*. Tamp the soil down lightly with your foot. Cover with mulch. If the weather is very dry, water occasionally; moisture in the soil stimulates root growth. But don't overwater; constant dampness can cause bulbs to rot. For the crocus corms shown, move away some of the mulch in eight to 12 weeks; if shoots are beginning to emerge in the containers, the corms are ready to lift. Dig up the containers and place them indoors in a bright, warm location. Flowers should appear in three to six weeks.

# PROPAGATING BULBS: BULBLETS

One of the easiest and most economical ways to increase your stock of some bulbs—lilies, fritillaries and onions among them—is to take advantage of their propensity for generating offspring bulbs. These small bulbs, each of which can be separated from the parent and raised as an independent plant, are of two sorts: bulblets and bulbils. Bulblets appear spontaneously on the sides of the parent bulb or along the underground portion of the stem. Bulbils form in the leaf axils or flower heads. The typical places where you might find bulblets and bulbils on a lily are shown in the box opposite.

You can encourage the formation of bulblets and bulbils by removing flower buds and flowers from a lily plant. Deprived of its flowers and hence of its seeds, the plant is unable to reproduce sexually through pollination, and is therefore more likely to turn its energies to asexual reproduction.

If left on the parent, few bulblets or bulbils will survive to develop into mature plants. They should be "harvested" in the late summer or early fall, and planted immediately—to prevent their drying out.

All lily bulbs need a period of chilling before they are ready to grow again. You can give offspring bulbs the necessary chilling by planting them in a raised nursery bed in your garden in a sheltered corner that receives plenty of light. Refer to Chapter 1 for directions on setting up a raised bed in your garden. The soil of the bed should be rich in organic matter and well turned *(page 271, steps 1 and 2)*. Cover the bulblets to a depth of 2 to 3 inches; as they increase in size, their roots will pull them deeper below the soil surface.

Mulch after planting and water well to keep the soil moist. The plants will take three to five years to mature and reach flowering size.

*A clump of majestic fritillaries stands tall in a sunny bed. Fritillaries are among a few bulbs that form small bulblets underground; harvested, planted and carefully nurtured for a few years, the bulblets will give rise to another generation of beautiful flowering plants.*

1 To harvest lily bulblets, dig up a mature lily; carefully work a spading fork around the plant until it begins to heave from the soil *(right)*. Gently remove the soil; look for bulblets on the side of the parent bulb or on the stem between the top of the bulb and the soil surface.

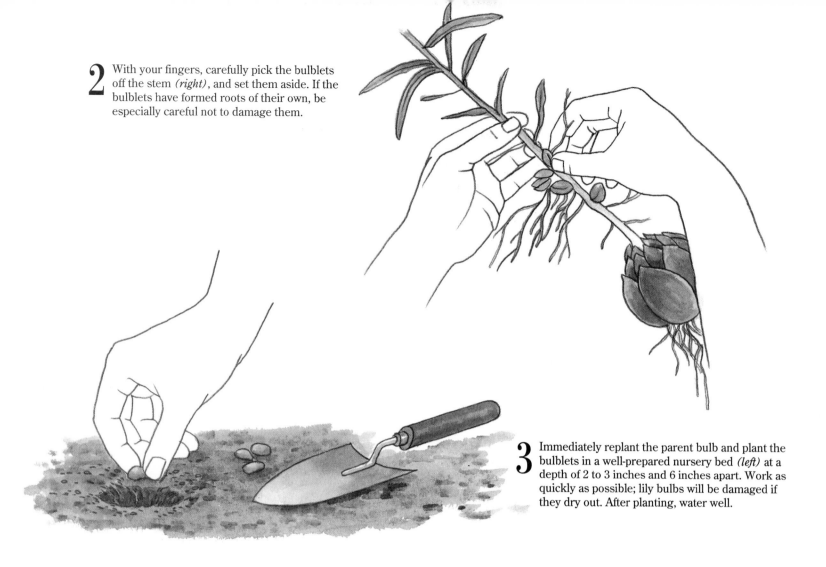

**2** With your fingers, carefully pick the bulblets off the stem *(right)*, and set them aside. If the bulblets have formed roots of their own, be especially careful not to damage them.

**3** Immediately replant the parent bulb and plant the bulblets in a well-prepared nursery bed *(left)* at a depth of 2 to 3 inches and 6 inches apart. Work as quickly as possible; lily bulbs will be damaged if they dry out. After planting, water well.

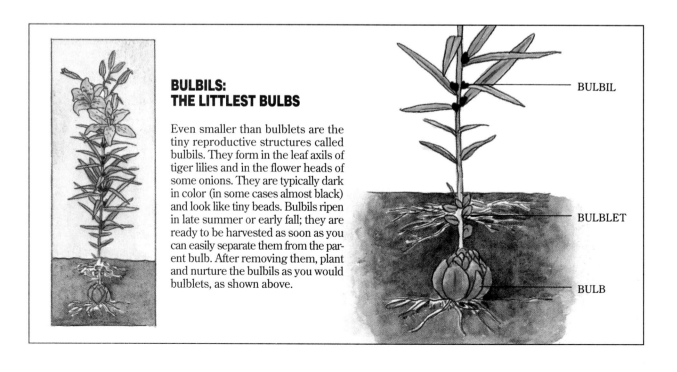

## BULBILS: THE LITTLEST BULBS

Even smaller than bulblets are the tiny reproductive structures called bulbils. They form in the leaf axils of tiger lilies and in the flower heads of some onions. They are typically dark in color (in some cases almost black) and look like tiny beads. Bulbils ripen in late summer or early fall; they are ready to be harvested as soon as you can easily separate them from the parent bulb. After removing them, plant and nurture the bulbils as you would bulblets, as shown above.

BULBIL

BULBLET

BULB

# PROPAGATING BULBS: CORMS AND THEIR PROGENY

Gladioli, freesias and some other flowering plants that grow from the fleshy underground stems known as corms are peculiarly easy to propagate. The corms themselves wither each year, and in the process make new corms to replace the old ones. While engaged in this odd self-reproduction, they also give birth to small offspring called cormels. In nature, most cormels die for lack of space to grow. But if human hands collect and nurture them, they will produce in turn an extra new generation of plants. It usually takes up to two years for these plants to flower; after that they will be just as colorful and vigorous as those started from full-fledged, nursery-bought corms.

Digging up mature corms and picking off their cormels, shown below and opposite, should be done in the fall, after the growing season is over. Hardy cormels need to be planted right away, like the bulblets described on pages 276-277; tender cormels should be stored over the winter and put in the ground the following spring. The best place to do the storing is in an unheated garage or basement or other cool place where the temperature hovers around 50° F.

When spring comes, the cormels should be planted first in a raised nursery bed in your garden in a sheltered corner that receives plenty of light. Plant the cormels in a raised bed as you would bulblets *(page 276)*. Mulch after planting and water well to keep the soil moist. After about two years of this pampered existence, when they start to produce flower buds, they will be strong enough for transplanting into a garden bed of well-prepared soil.

*The startlingly bright and complex blooms of a cormous plant seem to explode amid the plants' bright green, spiky foliage. Cormous plants can be propagated easily by separating small cormels from the plants' corms and nurturing these offspring.*

1 To start collecting cormels, carefully dig up a cormous plant—here a gladiolus—with a spading fork when the foliage has yellowed in the autumn *(right)*.

**2** Gently work the soil from the new corm with your fingers; the old one will be a withered structure attached to the bottom, and will probably come off with the soil. Locate the tiny cormels clinging to the new corm's base. Carefully pick off the cormels *(right)* and set them aside.

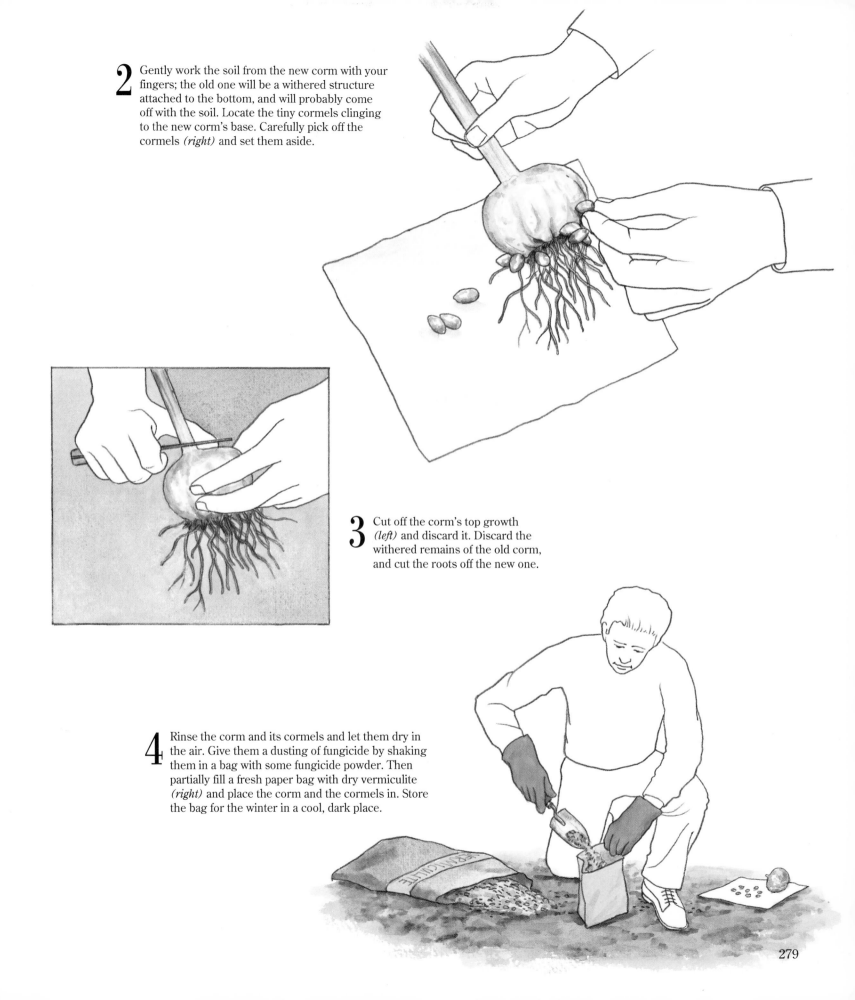

**3** Cut off the corm's top growth *(left)* and discard it. Discard the withered remains of the old corm, and cut the roots off the new one.

**4** Rinse the corm and its cormels and let them dry in the air. Give them a dusting of fungicide by shaking them in a bag with some fungicide powder. Then partially fill a fresh paper bag with dry vermiculite *(right)* and place the corm and the cormels in. Store the bag for the winter in a cool, dark place.

# PROPAGATING BULBS: SCALING LILIES

lthough it sounds like a drastic procedure, "scaling" simply means reproducing a plant by taking apart the bulb and making the parts produce new little bulbs. It works with those plants, notably lilies and the ones called fritillaries, that have bulbs resembling artichokes—compact clusters of plump, pointed, overlapping leaves or scales. It is an easy way to get choice bulbs to produce numerous offspring, and at no cost whatsoever.

Scaling can be done to bulbs newly purchased from a nursery. Just remove a few outer leaves from the parent bulbs, breaking them off near the bottom of the bulb and including a bit of the basal plate—the area where roots grow. The parent bulbs can still be planted, and will reproduce normal, full-sized stalks and flowers. Or scaling can be done to established bulbs by digging them from the ground, then plucking off four to six healthy leaves *(below and opposite)*. Again, the parent bulbs, once replanted in the garden, will continue to flourish.

The rest of the scaling process is equally uncomplicated. If you place the scales in a flat full of a sterile propagating medium such as vermiculite or sand, they will give birth to new bulbs that, when large enough, can be moved to a protected nursery bed in your garden in a sheltered corner that receives plenty of light. Or they can be transplanted to a sunny spot outdoors and insulated with a thick cover of mulch. For more information on mulching, refer to page 70.

The ideal time to begin the process is after the plants have flowered, usually mid-summer. The parent bulbs should be full of growing energy then, and their offspring can be planted in their final outdoor beds early enough to become established before winter comes. Scaling's one drawback is that the new bulblets will not be mature enough to produce flowers for three years or so.

*Living up to their name, regal lilies dominate a garden plot with their tall stems—up to 5 feet—and their theatrical white blossoms, streaked with purplish red and having yellow centers. These choice bulbs are easy to multiply by the scaling method, a single bulb yielding many small offspring.*

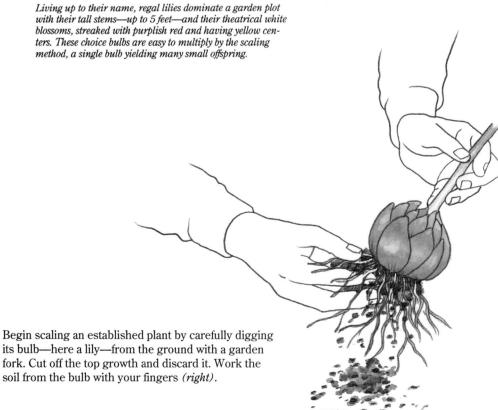

1 Begin scaling an established plant by carefully digging its bulb—here a lily—from the ground with a garden fork. Cut off the top growth and discard it. Work the soil from the bulb with your fingers *(right)*.

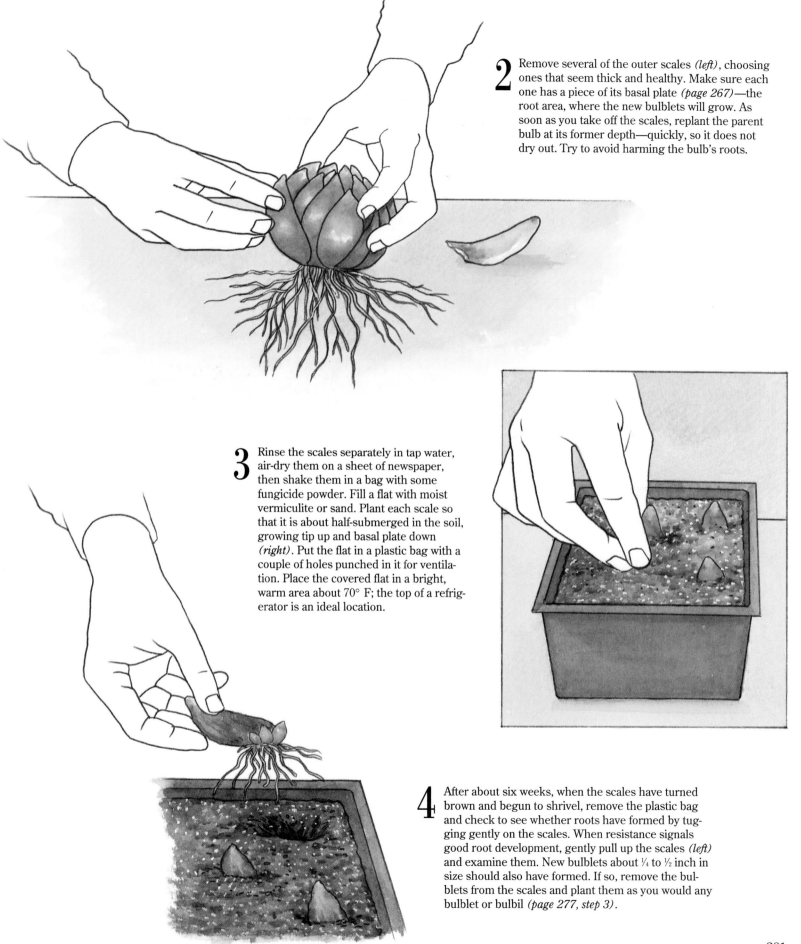

**2** Remove several of the outer scales *(left)*, choosing ones that seem thick and healthy. Make sure each one has a piece of its basal plate *(page 267)*—the root area, where the new bulblets will grow. As soon as you take off the scales, replant the parent bulb at its former depth—quickly, so it does not dry out. Try to avoid harming the bulb's roots.

**3** Rinse the scales separately in tap water, air-dry them on a sheet of newspaper, then shake them in a bag with some fungicide powder. Fill a flat with moist vermiculite or sand. Plant each scale so that it is about half-submerged in the soil, growing tip up and basal plate down *(right)*. Put the flat in a plastic bag with a couple of holes punched in it for ventilation. Place the covered flat in a bright, warm area about 70° F; the top of a refrigerator is an ideal location.

**4** After about six weeks, when the scales have turned brown and begun to shrivel, remove the plastic bag and check to see whether roots have formed by tugging gently on the scales. When resistance signals good root development, gently pull up the scales *(left)* and examine them. New bulblets about ¼ to ½ inch in size should also have formed. If so, remove the bulblets from the scales and plant them as you would any bulblet or bulbil *(page 277, step 3)*.

281

# PROPAGATING BULBS: SLICING TUNICATE BULBS

Daffodils, tulips, squill and several similar plants can be made to reproduce by a simple process of slicing up their bulbs and planting the pieces, as shown opposite. These are the plants whose bulbs are called "tunicate" *(page 267)*; they are smooth, neat structures that rather resemble onions. Like onions, they consist of fleshy scales laminated in concentric rings and having a papery outer coating (the tunic). Trying to propagate them as you would lilies by peeling the layers, however, does not work; the scales have no way to root and grow. But slicing the bulbs from top to bottom does work. Planted in vermiculite or sand, the vertical sections will produce tiny new bulblets—providing each section includes part of what is called the basal plate, the gnarled area on the bottom of the bulb where roots form.

The right season to propagate these tunicate bulbs is late summer or early fall—August or September. The bulbs are then dormant but their tissues contain a summer's worth of stored food energy, which helps produce the new bulbs. The only potential difficulty is digging the bulbs up efficiently. Most tunicate bulbs are spring bloomers. By fall their foliage has died back and disappeared, leaving little indication where the bulbs are located beneath the soil. So it is important—and this is true for other bulbs as well—to put some markers—golf tees, for example—in the bed over each bulb when planting, to pinpoint the exact spots for future digging. Alternatively, you can dig up these bulbs when their foliage begins to turn yellow. The foliage will guide you to the location of the bulbs and help you avoid cutting them.

When the bulbs have been dug up, they should be sliced with a sharp knife, its blade sterilized in a solution of 1 part bleach to 9 parts water. The entire process, including planting the sliced sections, need take only a minute or two per bulb, a small investment of time to multiply a stock of tulips or daffodils four times over or even more.

*Dramatic-looking with their bright blooms and long, leafless stems, belladonna lilies grow profusely by a plain slat fence. These plants, like tulips, grow from tunicate bulbs, which are easily cut up for propagation, but they flourish only in the warmth of climatic zones 9, 10 and 11.*

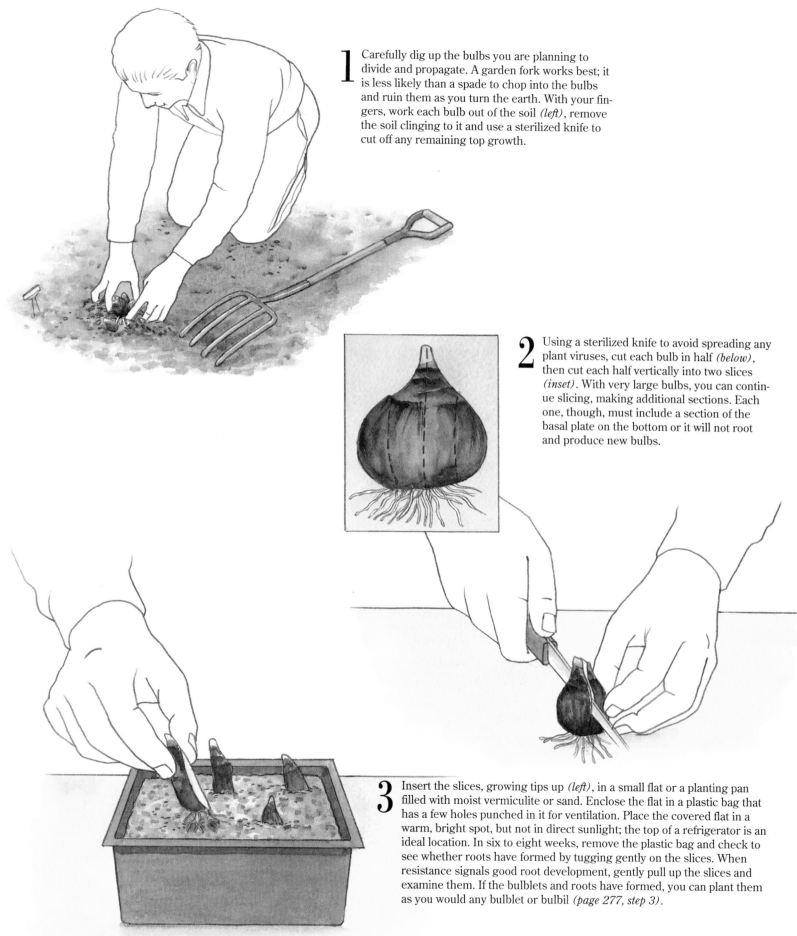

**1** Carefully dig up the bulbs you are planning to divide and propagate. A garden fork works best; it is less likely than a spade to chop into the bulbs and ruin them as you turn the earth. With your fingers, work each bulb out of the soil *(left)*, remove the soil clinging to it and use a sterilized knife to cut off any remaining top growth.

**2** Using a sterilized knife to avoid spreading any plant viruses, cut each bulb in half *(below)*, then cut each half vertically into two slices *(inset)*. With very large bulbs, you can continue slicing, making additional sections. Each one, though, must include a section of the basal plate on the bottom or it will not root and produce new bulbs.

**3** Insert the slices, growing tips up *(left)*, in a small flat or a planting pan filled with moist vermiculite or sand. Enclose the flat in a plastic bag that has a few holes punched in it for ventilation. Place the covered flat in a warm, bright spot, but not in direct sunlight; the top of a refrigerator is an ideal location. In six to eight weeks, remove the plastic bag and check to see whether roots have formed by tugging gently on the slices. When resistance signals good root development, gently pull up the slices and examine them. If the bulblets and roots have formed, you can plant them as you would any bulblet or bulbil *(page 277, step 3)*.

# PROPAGATING BULBS: SCORING AND SCOOPING

Two of the choicest of the tunicate *(page 267)*, or onionlike, bulbs—colorful, fragrant hyacinths and squill—are best propagated by techniques descriptively known as scoring and scooping. Either method can be used; both involve cutting the bottom portions of large, healthy bulbs with a small, sharp knife *(opposite, step 1)*. The purpose is to destroy the basal plate's main shoot, or growing point. Oddly, with this gone, the bulbs will engender numerous new bulblets along the exposed interior scales. Note that scooping produces more bulblets than scoring. A single good-sized hyacinth bulb, carefully scooped and then incubated, can produce as many as 60 offspring—which makes this a wonderfully economical way to acquire enough bulbs for a big, glorious, spring-blooming hyacinth bed. The only drawback is that the bulblets need to mature for three years or so before they can produce flowers.

Nursery-bought bulbs can be scored or scooped; in fact, it is a good idea when buying bulbs to set aside two or three for propagation purposes. Or mature bulbs can be dug from the garden in summer when their foliage has died back. After the cutting has been done, the bulbs should be dusted with fungicide and placed in dry vermiculite or other fine planting medium for a few weeks until protective calluses form over the cuts; the medium must be dry, or the callus will not form. Then the bulbs should be incubated further in a planting tray for six to eight weeks in a dark area at about 85° F, and the air should be humid.

After about three months, the bulblets should have formed inside the parent bulbs and be ready for planting in a nursery bed set aside for the purpose.

*Large, snowy hyacinth blossoms, cupped by their own spiky foliage, stand out handsomely against a background of deep green ivy. A dozen or more hyacinths like these can be propagated by either scoring or scooping a single mother bulb, which will produce clusters of new bulblets.*

## GROWING BULBS HYDROPONICALLY

A good way to give children the fun of seeing roots develop—and a painless lesson in botany—is to grow bulbs hydroponically: that is, in nothing but water. Hyacinths, paperwhite narcissus and some tulips can be grown and displayed in transparent containers of clean water. Each container should have a neck narrow enough to hold the bulb firmly just above the water's surface. Some containers, called hyacinth glasses *(right)*, are especially made for hydroponic forcing. Bud vases and some flower vases work nicely, as do wine carafes and even some salad dressing and vinegar containers. If you use a recycled container, just make sure that it is absolutely clean. Fill the container with water to the level where the bottom of the bulb will rest, and then set the bulb into place. Add water as it evaporates, gently lifting the bulb from the neck, if necessary.

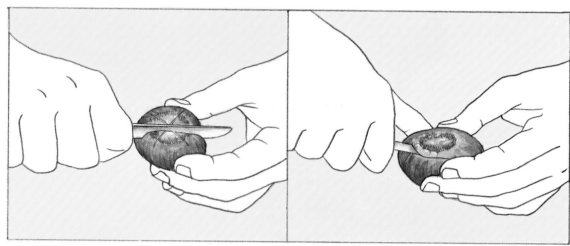

**1** You can propagate a hyacinth or squill by either scoring or scooping it with a small, sharp knife. To score a hyacinth, make three ½-inch-deep intersecting cuts across the basal plate *(above, left)*. To scoop a hyacinth, slice out the entire plate *(above, right)*.

**2** Place the scored or scooped bulb on a rack and keep it at room temperature for a day while it dries and the bulb splits open. Wearing rubber gloves, dust the bulb with a fungicide; place it, bottom down, in a tray of dry vermiculite *(left)* or sand and keep it at 65° to 70° F for about two weeks. Then raise the temperature to 85° F and provide some humidity by lightly misting the tray.

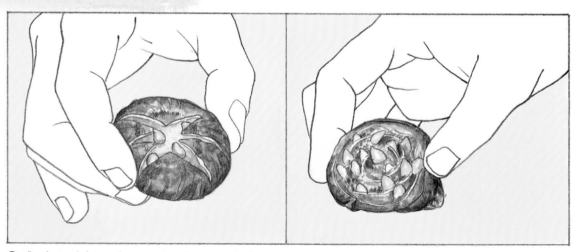

**3** In six to eight weeks, examine the parent bulb to see whether bulblets have formed along the scored edges *(above, left)* or inside the scooped interior *(above, right)*. When the bulblets are ¼ to ½ inch in size, pick them off and plant them as you would any bulblet or bulbil *(page 277, step 3)*.

# A CHECKLIST FOR BULBS

| | ZONE 1 | ZONE 2 | ZONE 3 | ZONE 4 | ZONE 5 |
|---|---|---|---|---|---|
| **JANUARY/FEBRUARY** | • Check mulch; add if necessary<br>• Lightly mulch emerging tips of early daffodils and tulips<br>• Order summer-flowering bulbs<br>• Pot tender bulbs for indoor spring bloom<br>• Discontinue chilling hardy bulbs and place them in a well-lit area to force foliage and flowers<br>• Start tuberous begonia seeds indoors<br>• Pot lilies for early spring forcing | • Check mulch; add if necessary<br>• Lightly mulch emerging tips of early daffodils and tulips<br>• Order summer-flowering bulbs<br>• Pot tender bulbs for indoor spring bloom<br>• Discontinue chilling hardy bulbs and place them in a well-lit area to force foliage and flowers<br>• Start tuberous begonia seeds indoors<br>• Pot lilies for early spring forcing | • Check mulch; add if necessary<br>• Lightly mulch emerging tips of early daffodils and tulips<br>• Order summer-flowering bulbs<br>• Pot tender bulbs for indoor spring bloom<br>• Discontinue chilling hardy bulbs and place them in a well-lit area to force foliage and flowers<br>• Start tuberous begonia seeds indoors<br>• Pot lilies for early spring forcing | • Check mulch; add if necessary<br>• Lightly mulch emerging tips of early daffodils and tulips<br>• Order summer-flowering bulbs<br>• Pot tender bulbs for indoor spring bloom<br>• Discontinue chilling hardy bulbs and place them in a well-lit area to force foliage and flowers<br>• Start tuberous begonia seeds indoors<br>• Pot lilies for early spring forcing | • Check mulch; add if necessary<br>• Lightly mulch emerging tips of early daffodils and tulips<br>• Order summer-flowering bulbs<br>• Pot tender bulbs for indoor spring bloom<br>• Discontinue chilling hardy bulbs and place them in a well-lit area to force foliage and flowers<br>• Start tuberous begonia seeds indoors<br>• Pot lilies for early spring forcing |
| **MARCH/APRIL** | • Remove mulch from new growth and flowers<br>• Fertilize spring-flowering bulbs with fast-release fertilizer<br>• Start tuberous begonias from tubers indoors<br>• Start cannas from rhizomes indoors<br>• Start dahlias from seeds or from tuberous roots indoors<br>• Start tuberoses from tubers indoors<br>• Prepare beds for planting | • Remove mulch from new growth and flowers<br>• Fertilize spring-flowering bulbs with fast-release fertilizer<br>• Start tuberous begonias from tubers indoors<br>• Start cannas from rhizomes indoors<br>• Start dahlias from seeds or from tuberous roots indoors<br>• Start tuberoses from tubers indoors<br>• Prepare beds for planting | • Start tuberous begonias from tubers indoors<br>• Start cannas from rhizomes indoors<br>• Start dahlias from seeds or from tuberous roots indoors<br>• Start tuberoses from tubers indoors<br>• Plant summer-flowering bulbs after frost<br>• Remove faded flowers<br>• Remove yellowed foliage<br>• Apply mulch for summer<br>• Water as necessary | • Start tuberous begonias from tubers indoors<br>• Start cannas from rhizomes indoors<br>• Start dahlias from seeds or from tuberous roots indoors<br>• Start tuberoses from tubers indoors<br>• Continue to plant hardy summer-flowering bulbs<br>• Remove faded flowers<br>• Remove yellowed foliage<br>• Apply mulch for summer<br>• Water as necessary | • Continue to plant hardy summer-flowering bulbs<br>• Remove faded flowers<br>• Remove yellowed foliage<br>• Apply mulch for summer<br>• Water as necessary |
| **MAY/JUNE** | • Prepare beds for planting<br>• Plant summer-flowering bulbs after frost<br>• Remove faded flowers<br>• Remove yellowed foliage<br>• Apply mulch for summer<br>• Water as necessary<br>• Fertilize summer-flowering bulbs | • Prepare beds for planting<br>• Plant summer-flowering bulbs after frost<br>• Remove faded flowers<br>• Remove yellowed foliage<br>• Apply mulch for summer<br>• Water as necessary | • Prepare beds for planting<br>• Plant summer-flowering bulbs after frost<br>• Remove faded flowers<br>• Remove yellowed foliage<br>• Dig and store bulbs that cannot tolerate wet soil in summer in a cool, dry location<br>• Apply mulch for summer<br>• Water as necessary | • Prepare beds for planting<br>• Plant summer-flowering bulbs after frost<br>• Remove faded flowers<br>• Remove yellowed foliage<br>• Dig and store bulbs that cannot tolerate wet soil in summer in a cool, dry location<br>• Apply mulch for summer<br>• Water as necessary | • Prepare beds for planting<br>• Plant summer-flowering bulbs after frost<br>• Remove faded flowers<br>• Remove yellowed foliage<br>• Dig and store bulbs that cannot tolerate wet soil in summer in a cool, dry location<br>• Apply mulch for summer<br>• Water as necessary |

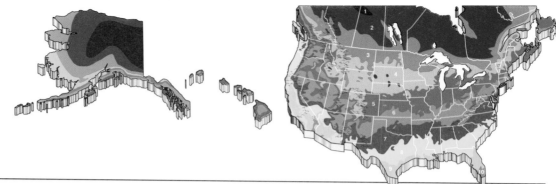

| **ZONE 6** | **ZONE 7** | **ZONE 8** | **ZONE 9** | **ZONE 10-11** | |
|---|---|---|---|---|---|
| • Check mulch; add if necessary<br>• Lightly mulch emerging tips of early daffodils and tulips<br>• Order summer-flowering bulbs<br>• Pot tender bulbs for indoor spring bloom<br>• Discontinue chilling hardy bulbs and place them in a well-lit area to force foliage and flowers<br>• Start tuberous begonia seeds indoors<br>• Pot lilies for early spring forcing | • Check mulch; add if necessary<br>• Lightly mulch emerging tips of early daffodils and tulips<br>• Order summer-flowering bulbs<br>• Pot tender bulbs for indoor spring bloom<br>• Discontinue chilling hardy bulbs and place them in a well-lit area to force foliage and flowers<br>• Start tuberous begonia seeds indoors<br>• Pot lilies for early spring forcing | • Remove mulch from new growth and flowers<br>• Fertilize spring-flowering bulbs with fast-release fertilizer<br>• Order summer-flowering bulbs<br>• Pot tender bulbs for indoor spring bloom<br>• Discontinue chilling hardy bulbs and place them in a well-lit area to force foliage and flowers<br>• Start tuberous begonia seeds indoors<br>• Prepare beds for planting<br>• Pot lilies for early spring forcing | • Order summer-flowering bulbs<br>• Pot tender bulbs for indoor spring bloom<br>• Discontinue chilling hardy bulbs and place them in a well-lit area to force foliage and flowers<br>• Start tuberous begonia seeds indoors<br>• Prepare beds for planting<br>• Plant refrigerated bulbs outdoors<br>• Plant summer-flowering bulbs after frost<br>• Fertilize spring-flowering bulbs with fast-release fertilizer<br>• Water as necessary<br>• Pot lilies for early spring forcing | • Order summer-flowering bulbs<br>• Pot tender bulbs for indoor spring bloom<br>• Discontinue chilling hardy bulbs and place them in a well-lit area to force foliage and flowers<br>• Prepare beds for planting<br>• Plant refrigerated bulbs outdoors<br>• Plant summer-flowering bulbs<br>• Fertilize spring-flowering bulbs with fast-release fertilizer<br>• Water as necessary<br>• Pot lilies for early spring forcing | **JANUARY/FEBRUARY** |
| • Remove mulch from new growth and flowers<br>• Fertilize spring-flowering bulbs with fast-release fertilizer<br>• Start tuberous begonias from tubers indoors<br>• Start cannas from rhizomes indoors<br>• Start dahlias from seeds or from tuberous roots indoors<br>• Start tuberoses from tubers indoors<br>• Remove faded flowers and yellowed foliage from spring-flowering bulbs<br>• Place potted lilies outdoors | • Remove mulch from new growth and flowers<br>• Fertilize spring-flowering bulbs with fast-release fertilizer<br>• Start tuberous begonias from tubers indoors<br>• Start cannas from rhizomes indoors<br>• Start dahlias from seeds or from tuberous roots indoors<br>• Start tuberoses from tubers indoors<br>• Remove faded flowers and yellowed foliage from spring-flowering bulbs<br>• Place potted lilies outdoors | • Remove mulch from new growth and flowers<br>• Fertilize spring-flowering bulbs with fast-release fertilizer<br>• Start tuberous begonias from tubers indoors<br>• Start cannas from rhizomes indoors<br>• Start dahlias from seeds or from tuberous roots indoors<br>• Start tuberoses from tubers indoors<br>• Remove faded flowers and yellowed foliage from spring-flowering bulbs<br>• Place potted lilies outdoors | • Remove mulch from new growth and flowers<br>• Fertilize spring-flowering bulbs with fast-release fertilizer<br>• Start tuberous begonias from tubers indoors<br>• Start cannas from rhizomes indoors<br>• Start dahlias from seeds or from tuberous roots indoors<br>• Start tuberoses from tubers indoors<br>• Remove faded flowers and yellowed foliage from spring-flowering bulbs<br>• Place potted lilies outdoors | • Remove mulch from new growth and flowers<br>• Fertilize spring-flowering bulbs with fast-release fertilizer<br>• Start tuberous begonias from tubers indoors<br>• Start cannas from rhizomes indoors<br>• Start dahlias from seeds or from tuberous roots indoors<br>• Start tuberoses from tubers indoors<br>• Remove faded flowers and yellowed foliage from spring-flowering bulbs<br>• Place potted lilies outdoors | **MARCH/APRIL** |
| • Plant summer-flowering bulbs after frost<br>• Remove faded flowers<br>• Remove yellowed foliage<br>• Dig and store bulbs that cannot tolerate wet soil in summer in a cool, dry location<br>• Apply mulch for summer<br>• Water as necessary | • Plant summer-flowering bulbs after frost<br>• Remove faded flowers<br>• Remove yellowed foliage<br>• Transplant and divide spring-flowering bulbs<br>• Dig and store bulbs that cannot tolerate wet soil in summer in a cool, dry location<br>• Apply mulch for summer<br>• Water as necessary | • Continue to plant summer-flowering bulbs<br>• Remove faded flowers<br>• Remove yellowed foliage<br>• Transplant and divide spring-flowering bulbs<br>• Dig and store bulbs that cannot tolerate wet soil in summer in a cool, dry location<br>• Apply mulch for summer<br>• Water as necessary | • Continue to plant summer-flowering bulbs<br>• Remove faded flowers<br>• Remove yellowed foliage<br>• Transplant and divide spring-flowering bulbs<br>• Dig and store bulbs that cannot tolerate wet soil in summer in a cool, dry location<br>• Apply mulch for summer<br>• Water as necessary | • Continue to plant summer-flowering bulbs<br>• Remove faded flowers<br>• Remove yellowed foliage<br>• Transplant and divide spring-flowering bulbs<br>• Dig and store bulbs that cannot tolerate wet soil in summer in a cool, dry location<br>• Apply mulch for summer<br>• Water as necessary | **MAY/JUNE** |

| | ZONE 1 | ZONE 2 | ZONE 3 | ZONE 4 | ZONE 5 |
|---|---|---|---|---|---|
| **JULY/AUGUST** | • Order spring-flowering bulbs<br>• Prune side branches of dahlias to produce large flowers<br>• Stake tall plants<br>• Plant fall-flowering bulbs<br>• Water as necessary<br>• Fertilize summer-flowering bulbs | • Order spring-flowering bulbs<br>• Prune side branches of dahlias to produce large flowers<br>• Stake tall plants<br>• Plant fall-flowering bulbs<br>• Water as necessary<br>• Fertilize summer-flowering bulbs | • Order spring-flowering bulbs<br>• Prune side branches of dahlias to produce large flowers<br>• Stake tall plants<br>• Plant fall-flowering bulbs<br>• Water as necessary<br>• Fertilize summer-flowering bulbs | • Order spring-flowering bulbs<br>• Prune side branches of dahlias to produce large flowers<br>• Stake tall plants<br>• Plant fall-flowering bulbs<br>• Water as necessary<br>• Fertilize summer-flowering bulbs | • Order spring-flowering bulbs<br>• Prune side branches of dahlias to produce large flowers<br>• Stake tall plants<br>• Plant fall-flowering bulbs<br>• Water as necessary<br>• Fertilize summer-flowering bulbs |
| **SEPTEMBER/OCTOBER** | • Prepare beds for planting<br>• Plant spring-flowering bulbs<br>• Protect newly planted bulbs from squirrels, birds and other pests<br>• Dig and store tender bulbs in a cool, dry location<br>• Discard diseased, dug-up bulbs<br>• Take stem cuttings from achimenes, tuberous begonias and dahlias for propagation<br>• Fertilize hardy summer-flowering and other established bulbs<br>• Apply mulch for winter<br>• Water if necessary<br>• Pot hardy bulbs for forcing and begin chilling them | • Prepare beds for planting<br>• Plant spring-flowering bulbs<br>• Protect newly planted bulbs from squirrels, birds and other pests<br>• Dig and store tender bulbs in a cool, dry location<br>• Discard diseased, dug-up bulbs<br>• Take stem cuttings from achimenes, tuberous begonias and dahlias for propagation<br>• Fertilize hardy summer-flowering and other established bulbs<br>• Apply mulch for winter<br>• Water if necessary<br>• Pot hardy bulbs for forcing and begin chilling them | • Prepare beds for planting<br>• Plant spring-flowering bulbs<br>• Protect newly planted bulbs from squirrels, birds and other pests<br>• Dig and store tender bulbs in a cool, dry location<br>• Discard diseased, dug-up bulbs<br>• Take stem cuttings from achimenes, tuberous begonias and dahlias for propagation<br>• Fertilize hardy summer-flowering and other established bulbs<br>• Apply mulch for winter<br>• Water if necessary<br>• Pot hardy bulbs for forcing and begin chilling them | • Prepare beds for planting<br>• Plant spring-flowering bulbs<br>• Protect newly planted bulbs from squirrels, birds and other pests<br>• Dig and store tender bulbs in a cool, dry location<br>• Discard diseased, dug-up bulbs<br>• Take stem cuttings from achimenes, tuberous begonias and dahlias for propagation<br>• Fertilize hardy summer-flowering and other established bulbs<br>• Apply mulch for winter<br>• Water if necessary<br>• Pot hardy bulbs for forcing and begin chilling them | • Prepare beds for planting<br>• Plant spring-flowering bulbs<br>• Protect newly planted bulbs from squirrels, birds and other pests<br>• Dig and store tender bulbs in a cool, dry location<br>• Discard diseased, dug-up bulbs<br>• Take stem cuttings from achimenes, tuberous begonias and dahlias for propagation<br>• Fertilize hardy summer-flowering and other established bulbs<br>• Apply mulch for winter<br>• Water if necessary<br>• Pot hardy bulbs for forcing and begin chilling them |
| **NOVEMBER/DECEMBER** | • Check mulch; add if necessary<br>• Pot tender bulbs for indoor winter bloom<br>• Pot paperwhite narcissus at two-week intervals for indoor bloom throughout fall<br>• Discard diseased, dug-up bulbs | • Check mulch; add if necessary<br>• Pot tender bulbs for indoor winter bloom<br>• Discard diseased, dug-up bulbs | • Check mulch; add if necessary<br>• Pot tender bulbs for indoor winter bloom<br>• Pot paperwhite narcissus at two-week intervals for indoor bloom throughout fall<br>• Discard diseased, dug-up bulbs | • Check mulch; add if necessary<br>• Pot tender bulbs for indoor winter bloom<br>• Pot paperwhite narcissus at two-week intervals for indoor bloom<br>• Discard diseased, dug-up bulbs | • Check mulch; add if necessary<br>• Pot tender bulbs for indoor winter bloom<br>• Pot paperwhite narcissus at two-week intervals for indoor bloom<br>• Discard diseased, dug-up bulbs |

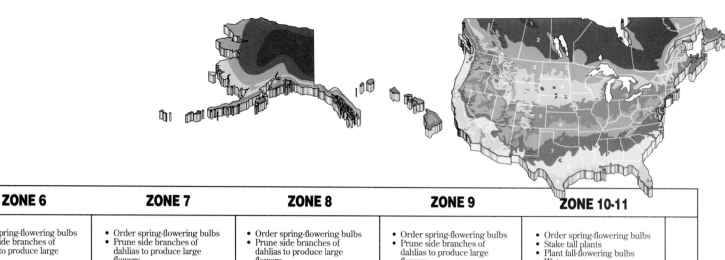

| | ZONE 6 | ZONE 7 | ZONE 8 | ZONE 9 | ZONE 10-11 | |
|---|---|---|---|---|---|---|
| | • Order spring-flowering bulbs<br>• Prune side branches of dahlias to produce large flowers<br>• Stake tall plants<br>• Plant fall-flowering bulbs<br>• Water as necessary<br>• Fertilize summer-flowering bulbs | • Order spring-flowering bulbs<br>• Prune side branches of dahlias to produce large flowers<br>• Stake tall plants<br>• Plant fall-flowering bulbs<br>• Water as necessary<br>• Fertilize summer-flowering bulbs | • Order spring-flowering bulbs<br>• Prune side branches of dahlias to produce large flowers<br>• Stake tall plants<br>• Plant fall-flowering bulbs<br>• Water as necessary<br>• Fertilize summer-flowering bulbs | • Order spring-flowering bulbs<br>• Prune side branches of dahlias to produce large flowers<br>• Stake tall plants<br>• Plant fall-flowering bulbs<br>• Water as necessary<br>• Fertilize summer-flowering bulbs | • Order spring-flowering bulbs<br>• Stake tall plants<br>• Plant fall-flowering bulbs<br>• Water as necessary<br>• Fertilize summer-flowering bulbs | **JULY/AUGUST** |
| | • Prepare beds for planting<br>• Plant spring-flowering bulbs<br>• Protect newly planted bulbs from squirrels, birds and other pests<br>• Dig and store tender bulbs in a cool, dry location<br>• Discard diseased, dug-up bulbs<br>• Take stem cuttings from achimenes, tuberous begonias and dahlias for propagation<br>• Fertilize hardy summer-flowering and other established bulbs<br>• Water if necessary<br>• Pot hardy bulbs for forcing and begin chilling them<br>• Pot tender bulbs at two-week intervals | • Prepare beds for planting<br>• Plant spring-flowering bulbs<br>• Protect newly planted bulbs from squirrels, birds and other pests<br>• Dig and store tender bulbs in a cool, dry location<br>• Discard diseased, dug-up bulbs<br>• Take stem cuttings from achimenes, tuberous begonias and dahlias for propagation<br>• Fertilize hardy summer-flowering and other established bulbs<br>• Water if necessary<br>• Pot hardy bulbs for forcing and begin chilling them<br>• Pot tender bulbs at two-week intervals | • Prepare beds for planting<br>• Plant spring-flowering bulbs<br>• Protect newly planted bulbs from squirrels, birds and other pests<br>• Dig and store tender bulbs in a cool, dry location<br>• Discard diseased, dug-up bulbs<br>• Take stem cuttings from achimenes, tuberous begonias and dahlias for propagation<br>• Fertilize hardy summer-flowering and other established bulbs<br>• Water if necessary<br>• Pot hardy bulbs for forcing and begin chilling them<br>• Pot tender bulbs at two-week intervals | • Prepare beds for planting<br>• Protect newly planted bulbs from squirrels, birds and other pests<br>• Dig and store tender bulbs in a cool, dry location<br>• Take stem cuttings from achimenes, tuberous begonias and dahlias for propagation<br>• Fertilize hardy summer-flowering and other established bulbs<br>• Water if necessary<br>• Pot hardy bulbs for forcing and begin chilling them<br>• Pot tender bulbs at two-week intervals<br>• Plant paperwhite narcissus and other tender bulbs for early bloom | • Prepare beds for planting<br>• Protect newly planted bulbs from squirrels, birds and other pests<br>• Dig and store tender bulbs in a cool, dry location<br>• Take stem cuttings from achimenes, tuberous begonias and dahlias for propagation<br>• Fertilize hardy summer-flowering and other established bulbs<br>• Water if necessary<br>• Pot hardy bulbs for forcing and begin chilling them<br>• Pot tender bulbs at two-week intervals<br>• Plant paperwhite narcissus and other tender bulbs for early bloom | **SEPTEMBER/OCTOBER** |
| | • Continue to plant spring-flowering bulbs<br>• Protect newly planted bulbs from squirrels, birds and other pests<br>• Continue to dig and store tender bulbs in a cool, dry location<br>• Pot paperwhite narcissus at two-week intervals for indoor bloom throughout fall<br>• Discard diseased, dug-up bulbs<br>• Apply mulch for winter<br>• Pot tender bulbs for indoor winter bloom | • Continue to plant spring-flowering bulbs<br>• Protect newly planted bulbs from squirrels, birds and other pests<br>• Continue to dig and store tender bulbs in a cool, dry location<br>• Discard diseased, dug-up bulbs<br>• Apply mulch for winter<br>• Pot tender bulbs for indoor winter bloom | • Continue to plant spring-flowering bulbs<br>• Protect newly planted bulbs from squirrels, birds and other pests<br>• Continue to dig and store tender bulbs in a cool, dry location<br>• Discard diseased, dug-up bulbs<br>• Apply mulch for winter<br>• Pot tender bulbs for indoor winter bloom | • Plant spring-flowering bulbs<br>• Plant paperwhite narcissus and other tender bulbs for early bloom<br>• Protect newly planted bulbs from squirrels, birds and other pests<br>• Continue to dig and store tender bulbs in a cool, dry location<br>• Discard diseased, dug-up bulbs<br>• Pot tender bulbs for indoor winter bloom<br>• Water if necessary<br>• Refrigerate hardy bulbs that require a chilling period | • Plant spring-flowering bulbs<br>• Plant paperwhite narcissus and other tender bulbs for early bloom<br>• Protect newly planted bulbs from squirrels, birds and other pests<br>• Continue to dig and store tender bulbs in a cool, dry location<br>• Discard diseased, dug-up bulbs<br>• Pot tender bulbs for indoor winter bloom<br>• Water if necessary<br>• Refrigerate hardy bulbs that require a chilling period | **NOVEMBER/DECEMBER** |

# TROUBLESHOOTING GUIDE: BULBS

| PROBLEM | CAUSE | SOLUTION |
| --- | --- | --- |
| Bulbs fail to grow or they have been dug out of the ground and eaten. If bulbs have grown, the flowers and stems have been chewed off or eaten. | Field mice, rabbits, gophers, voles, chipmunks, deer and squirrels. Field mice, rabbits, gophers and voles make underground tunnels to reach bulbs; chipmunks, deer and squirrels dig them out of the ground and may eat the foliage and flowers. | Before planting bulbs, dig a bed or a trench and line the bottom and the sides with chicken wire. Add a handful of sharp-edged gravel to the hole after planting the bulbs, or plant bulbs the animals do not eat, such as onion and daffodils. Alternatively, plant bulbs in raised beds or containers. |
| Leaves develop silvery white or brown streaks and flecks, and leaf tips turn brown. Eventually, leaves wither and die. Flower buds turn brown and may not open; if they do open, they are streaked and distorted. A sticky brown substance appears on stored bulbs. White and pastel-colored flowers are especially susceptible. | Thrips, nearly microscopic insects that suck sap from the flowers and leaves. | Remove and discard infested buds, flowers and foliage. Apply a systemic insecticide two or three times, seven to 10 days apart. Dust bulbs with diazinon before storing them. |
| Large, jagged holes appear in established leaves. New leaves may disappear entirely. Shiny silver trails appear on plants and on the ground. | Snails and slugs, which are brown shell-less snails up to 3 inches long. They feed at night. | Shallow saucers of beer and inverted grapefruit halves set around plants will trap snails and slugs. Snail and slug bait is also available; it should be applied at dusk, and may need to be reapplied after plants have been watered and after a rainfall. |
| Leaves curl, yellow or are distorted in shape, and the plant is stunted. Flowers may be streaked and malformed. A clear, sticky substance appears on the foliage. | Aphids, which are green, yellow, black or brown insects ⅛ inch long. Aphids appear in clusters on buds and leaves and at the base of the plant, where they feed on sap. They also carry and spread diseases, and their secretions attract ants. | Aphids can be knocked off plants with a strong stream of water. If the infestation is severe, spray with an insecticidal soap or an insecticide approved by government agencies for use on bulbs. |
| Leaves and stems lose their color. The entire plant collapses and dies. | Wireworms, which are brown worms with segmented bodies ¾ inch long. They are the larvae of click beetles. They bore into bulbs and up the stems of plants. | Apply an insecticide to the plants and the surrounding soil. To prevent infestation, apply an insecticide to the soil and to the bulbs before planting them. |
| Small, rounded or oblong holes appear in leaves and may also appear in flowers. Eventually, the leaf surface between veins disappears. | Beetles, including Asiatic garden, blister, cucumber, Japanese and rose chafer beetles. They are from ¼ to ¾ inch long and have hard shells. They chew into and damage leaves, stems and flowers. | Beetles can be picked off plants by hand. If the adult population is large, apply an insecticide. To control beetles in the larval stage, use a grub-proofing insecticide. The larvae of Japanese beetles can be controlled with milky spore, a bacterium fatal to beetles but harmless to plants and other animals. |

| PROBLEM | CAUSE | SOLUTION |
|---|---|---|
| Leaves become speckled, then turn dry and lose their color. The plant is stunted. Eventually, a fine white webbing appears on the plant. | Spider mites, nearly microscopic red, black, yellow or green pests that suck the sap from foliage. | Spray the undersides of the leaves with a strong stream of water every three days. If symptoms persist, apply a miticide three times, three days apart. Destroy and discard heavily infested plants. |
| Plants wilt and foliage loses its color. Bulbs are soft and spongy. Flowers are deformed, or fail to develop or bloom. | Bulb mites, tiny white pests that feed on drying bulbs. Colonies of mites may be contained within the bulb, or they may be visible on an exterior portion of the bulb. | There are no chemical cures for bulb mites. Discard infested bulbs. To prevent infestation, apply an insecticide to bulbs you have stored before planting them. |
| Leaves curl, split and are covered with yellow or brown blotches. In severe cases, plants cease to grow. Small knotty growths appear on the roots. Bulb tissue appears brown. | Nematodes, microscopic worms that feed on both foliage and bulbs. | Dig up and discard infested plants. Consult your local extension service or a garden supply center for soil testing information. Do not plant bulbs in an area that is infested with nematodes. Soil treatment by a professional fumigator may be necessary. |
| Leaves, stems and flower buds are covered with a white powder. Foliage and buds are distorted in shape. The plant may be stunted. | Powdery mildew, a fungus disease that is most severe when nights are cool and days are warm. Mildew spreads rapidly among crowded bulbs. | Mildew can be both eradicated and prevented with a fungicide applied once every 10 days when nights are cool and days are warm. Allow adequate space between bulbs when planting them. |
| Yellow, red, brown, gray or black spots appear on the leaves. Eventually, the spots merge and the leaf turns yellow and dies. Bulbs weaken and die after a few years. | Leaf spot, a fungus disease that is most severe in warm, humid weather. | Prune and discard infected leaves. To prevent leaf spot from spreading, apply a fungicide every seven to 10 days. Do not plant in the same area for several years. |
| Leaves turn red or yellow, wilt and die. Growth is stunted. Flowers may not develop. Bulbs are either soft and mushy, or hard and dried out. They may be covered with sunken lesions. White, pink, gray or black mold may form on the bulb or on the stem near the soil line. Roots are dark and slimy. | Root rot and bulb rot, fungus and bacterial diseases that may occur either while the bulb is in the ground or during storage. | Discard all infected bulbs and the surrounding soil. Be careful not to damage bulbs when digging or handling them; damaged bulbs are susceptible to disease. To prevent root or bulb rot, dust bulbs with a powdered fungicide or soak them in a fungicide solution before storage and before replanting. Plant in well-drained soil. |
| Fuzzy gray or brown mold appears on buds, flowers and foliage. Leaves develop brown or gray spots and eventually turn yellow and die. Flowers may not open. Bulbs have dark, sunken areas and are covered with a brown growth. Tulips are especially susceptible. | Botrytis blight, also called gray mold, a fungus disease most prevalent in cool, wet weather. | Remove and discard infected leaves and flowers. Apply a fungicide every seven to 10 days during cool, wet weather. Before planting them, dust bulbs with a powdered fungicide or soak them in a fungicide solution. Provide air circulation around plants; avoid overcrowding plants. Remove foliage and flowers after they die back. |
| Leaves become mottled with yellow and eventually turn completely yellow. Leaves curl or are misshapen. Flowers are smaller than normal and may be streaked or spotted with yellow, blue or green. The plant ceases to grow. Lilies are especially susceptible. | Virus diseases, including mosaic, yellows and ring spot viruses. | There are no chemical controls for viruses. Remove and discard infected bulbs. Disinfect tools with rubbing alcohol after working on infected plants. To help prevent virus, control aphids, which spread virus diseases, using a water stream, or an approved insecticide. Plant virus-resistant species of lilies. |

# DICTIONARY OF BULBS

## Introduction

This dictionary features a wide range of plants in five different groups: true bulbs, corms, tubers, tuberous roots and rhizomes. The most beautiful, resistant and self-sufficient plants in each class are highlighted. All plants are listed by their botanical names; common names are cross-referenced. The dictionary entries describe the climate zone in which each plant will grow; refer to the Zone Map *(inside front cover)* to locate your zone.

## Achimenes (a-KIM-e-neez)
Monkey-faced pansy, orchid pansy

A genus of species distributed throughout the American tropics. They are in the gesneriad family and are related to African violets and gloxinias. Plants have fibrous roots with scaly rhizomes and are 1 to 2 feet tall. The blooms are trumpet-shaped with flaring lobes and flat, pansy- or impatiens-like faces. Grow achimenes outdoors in beds or baskets as annuals, indoors as potted plants. Zones 10 and 11.

**Selected species and varieties**. *A. longiflora* has large, red-purple, white-throated flowers that are 1½ inches long and 1½ inches wide. Leaves are hairy and up to 3 inches long and 1½ inches wide. 'Blauer Planet' is more compact than the species. It has 1½- to 2-inch blue-purple flowers with white throats.

**Growing conditions.** Grow achimenes in bright light but out of direct sun and in rich, well-drained soil to which organic matter and coarse sand or vermiculite have been added. Keep soil evenly moist after plants begin to grow. Plant the rhizomes in pots or baskets in early spring for summer bloom, three or four rhizomes per 6-inch pot. Place the rhizomes horizontally, ½ to 1 inch below the surface. Rhizomes can also be started in flats filled with moist peat moss and moved to pots or beds when growth is 3 inches high. Achimenes can also be grown from stem cuttings. Plants perform best when temperatures remain above 60° F at night and below 80° F during the day. In fall, gradually withhold water and dry the plants out. Store the rhizomes in a cool, dry place over winter. In spring, resume watering and repot if necessary. To force for summer bloom, store potted in dry soil at 50° to 60° F for 8 to 12 weeks in winter.

## Acidanthera (a-si-DAN-ther-a)
Peacock orchid

Tender, summer-blooming plants native to tropical and South Africa. Flowers are graceful and delicate-looking, somewhat resembling butterflies or orchids. They are borne in loose spikes and open in succession. Foliage is sword-shaped. Plants arise from corms. Effective when grown in clumps of 10 or more. Plant where the fragrance of the flowers can be appreciated. Zones 9-11.

**Selected species and varieties.** *A. bicolor* (sometimes listed as *A. murieliae*) bears spikes with three or more white flowers with chocolate-brown centers. Plants are 2 to 3 feet tall. Peacock orchid blooms are 3 inches across and very fragrant, and make excellent cut flowers.

**Growing conditions.** Plant peacock orchids in full sun in a location protected from high winds. Space corms about 6 inches apart at a depth of 3 to 4 inches. Enrich the soil with compost and fertilize with 5-10-5 when plants emerge and again one month later. North of Zone 9, start peacock orchids indoors and move them to the garden after danger of frost has passed (See the Frost Date Map on the inside back cover). They can be difficult to transplant, so start the plants in peat pots that can go directly into the ground or grow them in tubs. North of Zone 9, peacock orchids should be dug after the first hard frost. Shake off excess soil and allow them to dry for several days in a cool, dry place out of direct sun. Cut back the tops of the plants, discard the remains of the previous season's corms and separate the cormels. Store the corms and cormels in dry peat moss or vermiculite at a temperature of 55° to 60° F. Peacock orchids require a long growing season to bloom. Propagate plants from the small cormels that are borne around old corms. Small corms take up to two seasons to bloom.

## Agapanthus (ag-a-PAN-thus)

Amaryllis-family members from South Africa with thick rhizomes and fleshy roots. Strap-shaped or linear leaves are borne at the base of the stems and may be deciduous or evergreen. Flowers are tubular and borne in umbels on leafless stalks. They come in blue, purplish blue or white. Zones 8-11.

ACHIMENES LONGIFLORA 'BLAUER PLANET'

ACIDANTHERA BICOLOR

AGAPANTHUS ORIENTALIS

**Selected species and varieties.**
*A. orientalis* (also listed as *A. praecox*) is an evergreen species reaching 3 feet in height. Flowers are blue, funnel-shaped and borne in 40- to 100-bloom umbels. 'Peter Pan' is a free-blooming dwarf type, with foliage 8 to 12 inches in height and blue blooms reaching 18 inches.

**Growing conditions.** Agapanthuses are grown outdoors year round in Zones 9, 10 and 11. North of these zones, they are grown in greenhouses in tubs or large pots and moved outdoors during the summer. Plants will grow in full sun or light shade. Pot-grown plants require regular applications of fertilizer during the growing season. Keep soil evenly moist during the growing season; dry off gradually in fall for winter rest. Divide plants only when overcrowding causes reduced flowering. To force for summer bloom, store potted in dry soil at 50° to 60°F for 8 to 12 weeks in winter.

## Allium (AL-ee-um)
Onion

A large genus best known for its edible members: chives, onions, garlic and leeks. Leaves are usually grasslike or cylindrical and hollow. Like the vegetables to which they are related, ornamental onions arise from rhizomes or bulbs and are onion-scented when bruised. Small flowers are borne in few- to many-flowered umbels on leafless stems. Blooms appear in spring and summer and are yellow, white, pink, red, violet and blue. Excellent for beds and borders; smaller species are fine for the rock garden. All make excellent cut flowers, and also can be used for dried arrangements. Zones 2-11.

**Selected species and varieties.**
*A. aflatunense* bears 4-inch globes of rose-purple flowers on 2½- to 5-foot stalks. Flowers appear in spring. Zones 5-11. *A. christophii*, stars-of-Persia, is a 3-foot plant bearing lacy-looking, 8- to 12-inch umbels of star-shaped flowers that are lilac and have a metallic sheen. Blooms appear in late spring. Zones 4-11. *A. giganteum*, giant onion, produces 4- to 5-inch, ball-shaped umbels of flowers carried on leafless 4-foot stems. Lilac flowers appear in early midsummer. Zones 5-8.
*A. moly*, lily leek, golden garlic, bears 3-inch clusters of yellow, star-shaped flowers in June. Zones 3-8. *A. neapolitanum*, daffodil garlic, Naples onion, is a spring-blooming, 1½-foot plant with fragrant, white starlike flowers borne in 2- to 3-inch umbels. 'Grandiflorum' is a large-flowered cultivar. Zones 7-9. *A. rosenbachianum*, rosenbach onion, white stamens contrast with dark violet flowers on 24-inch stems; blooms in early summer. Zone 5. *A. schoenoprasum*, chive, is a 12-inch plant with tubular, aromatic leaves. It is widely used as an herb. Flowers appear in spring, are rose-pink and are borne in dense, 1-inch, many-flowered umbels. Zones 4-9. *A. sphaerocephalum*, ballhead onion, produces dense, ball-shaped, 2-inch umbels of reddish purple flowers in midsummer. Plants reach 2 to 3 feet. Zones 5-9. *A. tuberosum*, Chinese chive, Chinese garlic, is an edible, 1½-foot plant producing small, fragrant, white flowers in summer. Zone 4.

**Growing conditions.** Plant onions in full sun at a depth of two to three times the diameter of the bulbs. Space plants 6 to 18 inches apart, depending on the height of the species. Bulbs can be planted in spring or fall. Onions will grow in any good garden soil. Bulbs multiply easily. Clumps may be left undisturbed in the garden for years, requiring division only when crowding reduces flower production. Many onions can be propagated by bulbils produced in the flower clusters or the small bulbs that appear around the larger bulbs underground.

## Amaryllis (am-a-RIL-is)

A one-species South African genus that once contained many species now classified as *Hippeastrum*. Flowers are funnel-shaped and appear in clusters on solid stems. (*Hippeastrum* bears its flowers on hollow stems.) The bulbs produce strap-shaped leaves after the flowers have begun to fade. Amaryllis can be grown in beds and borders in frost-free areas and in greenhouses where not hardy. Zones 9-11.

**Selected species and varieties.**
*A. belladonna*, belladonna lily, naked lady, bears fragrant rose, pink or white blooms that are 3½ inches across. Flowers appear atop naked 18-inch stalks; foliage appears after the flowers.

**Growing conditions.** Grow belladonna lilies outdoors in a sunny site with deeply prepared, rich, well-drained soil. Plant the bulbs in spring or early summer, before the leaves develop, at a depth of 4 to 6 inches. Do not disturb the bulbs unless absolutely necessary. Pot-grown plants should be set with the neck of the bulb at the soil surface. Keep the soil moist but not wet. To force for late summer or fall bloom, store potted in dry soil at 50° to 60° F for 8 to 12 weeks in winter.

ALLIUM AFLATUNENSE

ALLIUM MOLY

AMARYLLIS BELLADONNA

ANEMONE BLANDA 'BLUE STAR'

ANEMONE CORONARIA 'DE CAEN'

ARISAEMA SIKOKIANUM

BEGONIA GRANDIS

## Anemone

(a-NEM-o-nee or a-ne-MO-nee)
Windflower, lily-of-the-field

A large genus, belonging to the buttercup family, that contains many popular perennials, some of which grow from tubers. Fernlike leaves are divided or composed of two or more leaflets. Flowers may be daisylike or poppylike and double or single, but have petal-like sepals, not true petals. Clustered stamens at the center of the flowers are also often showy. Blossoms are usually borne singly on stems that rise above the foliage. They close at night and during cloudy weather. Anemones are fine for beds and borders as well as rock gardens. Zones 3-11.

**Selected species and varieties.** *A. blanda,* Greek anemone, does not have any hair on its foliage. Flowers are daisylike and deep blue. Plants are 2 to 8 inches tall. Once endangered, millions of *A. blanda* are now raised and sold by nurseries in the Netherlands. 'Blue Star' bears violet-blue flowers on 3-inch stems; 'Pink Star' has pink blooms on 6- to 10-inch stems; 'White Splendor' has white flowers on 6-inch stems. Zones 6-9. *A. coronaria,* poppy anemone, bears 1½- to 2½-inch flowers on 6- to 18-inch stalks. Flowers are red, lavender, blue or white, and may be single or double. 'St. Brigid' and 'De Caen' are cultivars that have especially showy flowers. Zones 6-11.

**Growing conditions.** The tubers of these anemones look like bark chips and it is often difficult to tell which end is up. Soak them overnight in warm water and put them in the ground on their sides. Anemones prefer humus-rich soil and a site shaded from midday sun. Where they are hardy they are planted in the fall and mulched over winter. To grow them where they are not hardy, plant them outdoors in early spring; dig them in fall and store the roots in dry sand or peat moss indoors over winter.

## Angel's tears see *Narcissus*

## Arisaema (ar-i-SEE-ma)
Jack-in-the-pulpit, Indian turnip

A genus of nearly 200 tuberous herbs grown for their lush, spear-shaped leaves, which are three-lobed. The flowers, which are tiny and insignificant, are borne on a fleshy spike called a spadix, commonly referred to as the Jack. The spadix is surrounded by a showy spathe, or pulpit, that is cuplike at the bottom but expands into a flap or lid that shelters the spadix. The spathe is green or white and may be marked with purple. Ripened fruit is often red and showy. Arisaemas are fine plants for a shady wildflower garden. Buy from reputable nurseries that sell only propagated flowers. Zones 4-9.

**Selected species and varieties.** *A. dracontium,* green dragon, dragonroot, bears a single leaf that is divided into seven to 19 segments. Plants reach 3 feet in height. The flowering stalk is shorter than the leafstalk. The spathe is slender and surrounds the spadix, which has a tail-like tip that reaches 2 to 4 inches in length. Zones 4-9. *A. sikokianum* has a spathe that is maroon-striped on the outside; the spadix and the inside of the spathe are ivory-white. The foliage is marked with cream. Zones 5-9. *A. thunbergii* has foliage variegated with red or purple. The spathe is striped with purplish brown and the spadix has an 8- to 12-inch, threadlike tip. Zones 8 and 9. *A. triphyllum,* Jack-in-the-pulpit, Indian turnip, bears two leaves, each with three leaflets. Plants reach 2 feet in height. The spathe is greenish on the outside. It bears brilliant red berries in spikes in early fall. Zones 4-9.

**Growing conditions.** Plant arisaemas in dappled to full shade in a location with rich, well-drained soil that has plenty of organic matter, such as humus. They require a regular supply of moisture during the growing season. Plant the tubers in fall and place them deep enough to accommodate the roots, which arise from the top of the tuber. Propagate by division or by seed sown outdoors in fall.

**Atamasco lily** see *Zephyranthes*
**Autumn crocus** see *Colchicum*
**Aztec lily** see *Sprekelia*
**Ballhead onion** see *Allium*
**Basket flower** see *Hymenocallis*

## Begonia (be-GO-nee-a)

A genus of succulent tropical and subtropical plants that are grown for their ornamental foliage or showy blossoms. Flowers may be pink, red, yellow or white, and have a succulent or fleshy texture. Male and female flowers are borne on the same plant.

**Selected species and varieties.** *B. grandis* (also listed as *B. evansiana*), hardy begonia, Evans begonia, bears pink flowers on 2-foot plants. Leaves are dark green on top and maroon underneath. Hardy in Zones 7-9, but with mulching and a protected location hardy as far north as Zone 5. *B. x tuberhybrida,* tuberous begonia, is a group of hybrids developed by crossing several different species from the Andes in South America. Flowers are brilliant red, pink, orange, yellow or white and may be marked with contrasting colors. The cultivars are classified into divisions according to flower form and plant habit. Groups include rosebud, or rose-flowered, which have large, double flowers with raised roselike centers. Camellia-flowered tuberous begonias bear double, camellia-like blooms up to 6 inches across.

**Growing conditions.** Grow *B. grandis* outdoors in a shady location with moist, rich soil high in organic matter. Mulch plants in winter. *B. grandis* can be propagated from seeds, cuttings or bulbils. Tuberous begonias perform well in areas with cool, moist summers; for best results, day temperatures should remain below 80° F and night temperatures should be below 60° F. Start tubers indoors in February or March in a shallow container with adequate drainage filled with 2 inches of peat or sphagnum moss. Place the tubers concave side up and lightly cover with peat or sphagnum moss. Place the container in a warm (60°-70° F), bright place. Sprinkle the surface of the medium lightly with water when it dries out. When growth begins, water more often. Carefully move the tubers to pots, planters or beds when the shoots are about 4 inches tall. Plant tubers 1 inch below the surface. Soil mixture should be rich and perfectly drained: ⅔ peat moss and ⅓ sand is ideal. Pots should be at least 6 inches wide and 6 inches deep; planters 8 inches wide by 6 inches deep to provide adequate room for roots. Do not set plants outside until danger of frost has passed. Place plants in light shade or a location with early-morning or late-afternoon sun only. Water in the morning, and to prevent mildew, avoid sprinkling foliage and flowers. Soil should be moist but allowed to dry slightly between waterings. Plants that are kept too wet or too dry will drop their flower buds. Stake plants to keep them from breaking; place the stake 3 inches from the tuber and tie the stems with yarn or rags; string will cut the fleshy stems. Fertilize every other week with a balanced fertilizer. Remove fallen petals and leaves, to avoid rot. Allow frost to kill the foliage in fall, then dig the tubers and set them indoors in a cool, dry place. To force *B. x tuberhybrida* for fall bloom, store boxed in dry peat moss at 50° to 60° F for 8 to 12 weeks in winter.

**Belladonna lily** see *Amaryllis*
**Bell-flowered squill** see *Endymion*
**Brodiaea** see *Ipheion*

## Caladium (ka-LAY-dee-um)

A genus of tropical plants in the arum family grown for their showy leaves. Flowers are borne on a spadix surrounded by a sometimes showy spathe. Caladiums make fine additions to shady beds and borders. Where they are not hardy, they are often dug and stored indoors in winter or grown as annuals. Zones 10 and 11.

**Selected species and varieties.** *C.* x *hortulanum,* fancy-leaved caladium, is grown for its large, arrow- or heart-shaped leaves that are variegated or shaded with pink, deep rose, maroon, green and white. Plants range from 8 to 36 inches in height; leaves range from 6 to 24 inches in length. The flowers are often removed to prevent the plants from setting seed. Many cultivars are available, including 'Postman Joyner,' which has deep red leaves with green margins.

**Growing conditions.** Plant caladiums outdoors in a shady location with rich soil at a depth of about 1 inch. North of Zones 10 and 11, grow them in containers or as annuals for the shade. Start plants indoors in late winter in the pots or tubs in which they are to grow or in peat pots. Plant tubers at a depth of 2 to 3 inches. Caladiums prefer day temperatures above 70° F, so do not move plants to the garden until late spring. Keep caladiums evenly moist throughout the growing season. At the end of the season allow the plant to dry out. Dig the tubers and store them indoors in a cool, dry place over winter. To force for summer bloom, store boxed in dry peat moss at 50° to 60° F for 8 to 12 weeks in winter.

**Caladium** see also *Colocasia*

## Canna (KAN-a)
Indian shot, canna

A heat-loving, tropical genus of large, showy plants that have been widely hybridized. The plants are 4 to 8 feet tall, arise from thick rhizomes and have broad, 18- to 25-inch-long leaves. Flowers reach 4 inches in diameter and are borne in terminal clusters. They consist of small greenish petals and showy, petal-like sterile stamens. Cannas are fine for beds or borders and are often grown as annuals where they are not hardy. Zones 7-11.

BEGONIA × TUBERHYBRIDA

CALADIUM × HORTULANUM 'POSTMAN JOYNER'

CANNA × GENERALIS 'CHALLENGER'

CHIONODOXA LUCILIAE

CLAYTONIA VIRGINICA

CLIVIA MINIATA

**Selected species and varieties.** *C. flaccida,* golden canna, is native to marshes in the eastern United States. Plants are 5 feet in height and bear showy spikes of yellow flowers. *C.* x *generalis,* common garden canna, is a group of large-flowered hybrids with flowers that come in red, yellow, cream, orange and pink, and may also be marked with contrasting colors. Height ranges from 2 feet for dwarf cultivars to 8 feet for full-sized cultivars. 'Challenger' has salmon-colored flowers and green foliage. 'City of Portland' is a rose-pink-flowered selection. The Pfitzer series cultivars, which come in apricot, red, yellow and pink, are dwarf plants generally under 2½ feet tall. Zones 9-11. *C. indica,* Indian shot, is a 4-foot plant with bright red flowers that have orange lips spotted with red. Zones 9-11. *C.* x *orchiodes,* orchid-flowered canna, produces very large yellow or red flowers that are marked with contrasting colors. Zones 9-11. *C. warscewiczii* bears purplish or brownish purple foliage on 5-foot plants. Flowers are red. Zones 9-11.

**Growing conditions.** Plant cannas in a sunny location in a bed that has rich, well-drained soil with plenty of organic matter. To improve drainage, mound the bed so that the center is 4 to 6 inches above the edge. Cannas will not tolerate poor, dry or rocky soil. Provide plenty of water during the growing season. Cannas are heat–loving plants and most cannot tolerate frost. In Zones 9, 10 and 11, grow them outdoors year round. North of Zone 9, start rootstocks indoors four weeks before plants are to be moved outside, which should be done after all danger of frost has passed. Or, plant outdoors after soil temperature has warmed to 60° or 70° F; place them several inches below the surface. In fall, once the tops have been killed by the first frost, dig the plants, cut the tops off, shake the soil off the roots and dry the plants in the sun for several hours. Store the roots in dry sand or vermiculite in a cool, dry place over winter. In spring, cut the stored rootstocks into sections, each with one or two buds, and replant. To force *C.* x *generalis* for summer bloom, store potted in dry soil at 50° or 60° F for 8 to 12 weeks in winter.

**Checkered lily** see *Fritillaria*
**Chinese chive** see *Allium*
**Chinese garlic** see *Allium*

**Chionodoxa** (ky-on-o-DOK-sa)
Glory-of-the-snow

A genus of early-flowering, bulbous plants with blue, white or pink flowers borne in terminal spikes. Leaves are long and narrow. Glory-of-the-snow is planted in rock gardens, under deeply rooted trees such as oaks and in wildflower gardens. Zones 4-9.

**Selected species and varieties.** *C. luciliae* is a 3- to 6-inch species with narrow foliage that bears spikes of four to six 1-inch flowers. Blooms are usually blue with a white center, but 'Alba' is a white-flowered cultivar. 'Gigantea' is a large-flowered selection. 'Pink Giant' bears pink, 1-inch flowers with white centers. Zones 4-9. *C. sardensis* is a 6-inch plant with slightly smaller blue flowers. Collection in the wild has endangered the species; purchase from reputable dealers that sell only propagated bulbs. This species is widely produced in the Netherlands. Zones 4-9.

**Growing conditions.** Plant glory-of-the-snow in autumn in a location with rich, well-drained soil at a depth of 3 inches. It will grow in full sun or light shade and perform best if left undisturbed. Divide only if plants become overcrowded and flowering declines.

**Chive** see *Allium*

**Claytonia** (klay-TOH-nee-a)
Spring beauty

A small genus of fleshy-foliaged, spring-blooming plants related to the annual portulaca. The plants bear small clusters of pink or white flowers, and most arise from corms. Most spring beauties are native American wildflowers and are fine subjects for wildflower and rock gardens. Zones 5-9.

**Selected species and varieties.** *C. virginica,* Virginia spring beauty, has loose spikes of two to 15 flowers that are pink or white marked with pink and borne atop 6- to 12-inch plants. The foliage is grasslike and narrow. Zones 5-9.

**Growing conditions.** Plant spring beauties in a location with rich, moist soil that is high in organic matter. Spring beauties prefer a site with light shade. Plants can be propagated by seed or by division.

## Clivia (KLY-vee-a)
Kafir lily

A genus of evergreen perennials from South Africa with fleshy roots and fan-like clumps of dark green, leathery, strap-shaped leaves. Flowers, which are reddish yellow, orange or red, are funnel-shaped and carried in umbels on leafless stalks. Kafir lilies are grown as houseplants or as greenhouse plants in the North, in borders and in containers in the South. Zones 10 and 11.

**Selected species and varieties.** *C. miniata,* scarlet kafir lily, is a 2-foot plant bearing umbels of up to 20 trumpet-shaped flowers that are orange-red on the outside and yellowish inside. *C.* x *cyrtanthiflora* produces clusters of nodding, narrow, tube-shaped flowers that are red and yellow.

**Growing conditions.** Outdoors in Zones 10 and 11, grow kafir lilies in shady borders that have rich, well-drained soil and receive bright light but not direct sun. They bloom in winter or early spring. Clumps should remain undivided and undisturbed. North of Zones 10 and 11, plants can be grown indoors in winter and be brought out to a shady spot in summer. Fertilize in spring and propagate by division or from seed.

## Colchicum (KOLE-chi-kum)
Meadow saffron, autumn crocus

Despite the common name autumn crocus, colchicum is not a true crocus but a member of the lily family. It produces foliage in spring and showy white, rosy purple or yellow flowers in fall after the foliage has died down. They make fine additions to a rock or wildflower garden and also can be planted under trees. Zones 4-11.

**Selected species and varieties.** *C. autumnale,* common autumn crocus, meadow saffron, bears one to four white to light purple flowers up to 4 inches long. *C. speciosum* produces long, narrow (12- to 16-inch by 3- to 4-inch) foliage in spring and showy, cup-shaped flowers in fall. Blooms are up to 4 inches across and 6 to 12 inches long and are rose to purple with white throats. Many hybrids are available, and these are often showier than the species. 'The Giant' produces pinkish mauve flowers with white bases.

**Growing conditions.** Plant colchicums in late summer, as soon as possible after receiving the corms, or they will begin blooming before they are planted. Select a planting location with rich, well-drained soil and plant the corms at a depth of 2 to 3 inches. Allow the foliage to die back naturally; cutting the foliage back prematurely will prevent future bloom. Colchicum corms are poisonous.

## Colocasia (ko-lo-KAY-see-a)
Elephant's ear

A small genus of large tropical plants in the arum family. One species is grown as an ornamental for its enormous foliage. The flowers are borne on a fleshy spadix surrounded by a leafy spathe. Zones 9-11.

**Selected species and varieties.** *C. esculenta* (also listed as *Caladium esculenta*), taro, dasheen, is cultivated in the tropics for its fleshy tubers, which to be edible must be thoroughly cooked. (In Hawaii the cooked dish is known as poi.) The leaves can also be cooked and eaten like spinach. The plants are 3 to 7 feet in height. Leaves are arrow-shaped, up to 2 feet in length and borne on 4- to 6-foot stems. The foliage may be green or marked with red-purple or bluish black.

**Growing conditions.** Grow elephant's ear in partial shade in a location with deep, moist, fertile soil. Select a site protected from high winds, which can damage the foliage. Plant the fleshy tubers at a depth of 6 inches and space them 3 to 6 feet apart. North of Zones 9-11, elephant's ear can be planted in late spring, when the soil is warm, and dug up when the tops are killed by the first frost. Dry the roots and store them in dry peat or sand in a cool, frost-free place over winter.

## Corn flag see *Gladiolus*

## Crinum (KRY-num)
Crinum, crinum lily, spider lily

Crinums are tropical, lilylike plants grown for their showy white, pink or red flowers, which appear in spring or summer. Contrary to their common names, they are actually members of the amaryllis family. They have long, strap-shaped leaves that may be deciduous or evergreen. Flowers are trumpet-shaped and borne in umbels atop leafless stalks. Plants arise from bulbs. Crinums are planted alone as specimen plants and allowed to form large clumps, or grouped in borders or along pools or ponds. They can be grown in large tubs as well. Zones 7-11.

COLCHICUM SPECIOSUM 'THE GIANT'

COLOCASIA ESCULENTA

CRINUM ASIATICUM

297

CRINUM × POWELLII 'ALBUM'

CROCUS TOMASINIANUS

CROCUS VERNUS 'STRIPED BEAUTY'

**Selected species and varieties.** *C. americanum,* southern swamp crinum, swamp lily, bears white flowers that are 3 inches across and 3 to 4 inches long. Leafless flower stalks, which appear before the foliage, carry up to six flowers and reach 1½ to 2 feet in height. Southern swamp crinum is native to wet places in the southern United States. Zones 9-11. *C. asiaticum,* poison bulb, produces a clump of 3- to 4-inch-wide leaves and umbels of 20 to 50 fragrant white flowers with greenish tubes. Zones 9-11. *C. x powellii* bears clumps of leaves that are 3 to 4 feet long and 3 to 4 inches wide and produce umbels of about eight flowers. 'Album' is a white-flowered cultivar. Zones 8-11.

**Growing conditions.** Crinums prefer rich, moist soil and light shade. Plant the bulbs 2 to 3 feet apart with the tips just beneath the surface of the soil. Leave in place, since digging and dividing can interrupt flowering. North of Zone 8, plant in a protected location and mulch heavily in winter. Or overwinter the bulbs indoors.

### Crocus (KRO-kus)

Crocuses are traditional harbingers of spring that bear grasslike leaves and cup-shaped, white, yellow, pink, lilac or deep purple flowers held close to the ground. The stigmas in the centers of the blooms are often showy. In some species, the leaves appear after the flowers; in others, with the flowers. All arise from corms and are generally 3 to 6 inches in height. There are autumn-flowering species in this genus, which is classified in the iris family. These true crocuses should not be confused with the so-called autumn crocuses, or *Colchicum* species, which are members of the lily family. Crocuses can be planted at the front of beds and borders, in woodland gardens around the bases of deep-rooted trees such as oaks or in rock gardens. Zones 3-11.

**Selected species and varieties.** *C. ancyrensis* bears golden yellow, ¾-inch flowers in late winter. 'Golden Bunch' is a free-flowering cultivar with orange-yellow flowers. Zones 5-11. *C. biflorus,* Scotch crocus, bears 4-inch-long flowers that may be white or lilac and can be striped or veined with purplish blue. Flowers appear in early spring. Zones 5-11. *C. chrysanthus* bears 4-inch-long blooms that range from pale yellow to orange-yellow. The flowers are fragrant and appear in early spring. 'Advance' has pale yellow flowers striped with purple. 'Blue Pearl'

bears pale blue flowers. 'Cream Beauty' has pale yellow blooms. Zones 4-9. *C. etruscus* bears 4-inch-long lilac flowers with yellow throats in early spring. Zones 3-9. *C. flavus* produces golden yellow flowers that range from 2½ to 7 inches in early spring. Zones 4-9. *C. goulimyi* is an autumn-blooming species that does well in Southern California. Blooms are star-shaped, deep pinkish purple and fragrant. Zones 8-11.

*C. laevigatus* bears very fragrant white flowers with orange-yellow throats in autumn or winter. 'Fontenayi' bears buff-colored blooms that are rose-lilac on the outside. *C. medius* is an autumn-blooming species with lilac to purple blooms that are 4 to 10 inches in length. Zones 6-11. *C. niveus* is a robust autumn-flowering species bearing white flowers with golden orange throats. Zones 5-8.

*C. ochroleucus* produces pale cream flowers that are orange on the inside in fall. Zones 5-9. *C. sativus,* saffron crocus, bears large, fragrant purple or white blooms in fall. The orange-red stigmas and styles, when dried, are the source of the herb saffron. Zones 6-11. *C. sieberi,* Sieber crocus, has 1½-inch-long lilac flowers in late winter or early spring. Zones 7-11. *C. speciosus* is a very showy fall-blooming species with violet-blue flowers and bright orange stigmas. Zones 5-11. *C. tomasinianus* has lilac to purple flowers with white throats. Flowers 2½ to 5½ inches long appear in early spring. 'Whitewell Purple' has reddish purple flowers. 'Ruby Giant' is a squirrel-resistant cultivar. *C. vernus,* common crocus, Dutch crocus, has been the most commonly grown species in the United States for many years. It bears flowers that are lilac or white and are often striped with purple and blooms in early spring. Cultivars include 'Purpurea,' which has purple flowers; 'Remembrance,' which has blue flowers; 'Snowstorm,' which has white flowers; 'Striped Beauty,' which has lilac flowers with white stripes; and 'Yellow Mammouth,' which bears large golden yellow blooms. Zones 4-11.

**Growing conditions.** Grow crocuses in a location that has full sun at least during the season the foliage is apparent (spring or fall). Crocuses require good drainage and perform best in well-drained sandy or gritty soil. They will not grow well in wet clay soil. For best results, prepare the soil to a depth of about 6 inches. Plant corms with the bases 3 to 4 inches below the surface. Crocuses do not need dividing and can be left undisturbed for many years. Feed annually in spring with a balanced bulb fertilizer. The foliage must be allowed to mature and yellow naturally if the plants are to produce corms and blooms for the following year; do not mow it or cut it back. Crocuses planted in a lawn or any other location where they must compete with plants other than shallow-rooted annuals will need to be replaced every few years. Mow the lawn to a height of 3 inches for the first few mowings to allow the foliage to mature. Gophers, voles and squirrels all eat the corms. Crocuses require varying periods of cold temperatures to bloom, and gardeners in Zones 9, 10 and 11 should experiment with small quantities of bulbs to determine which bloom most reliably in their area. To force for winter or spring bloom, store potted in moist soil at 35° to 48°F for 15 to 16 weeks in fall.

**Crown imperial** see *Fritillaria*
**Cuban lily** see *Scilla*
**Daffodil** see *Narcissus*
**Daffodil garlic** see *Allium*

### Dahlia (DAL-ya)

Although commonly grown as annuals, dahlias actually are tender, tuberous-rooted perennials that can be saved and grown year after year. Plants range in size from 1 to 6 feet in height, and flowers range from 2 to 10 inches across. Dahlias are members of the daisy family and bear flower heads made up of showy ray florets, or "petals," surrounding tightly packed, buttonlike centers. Blooms come in many flower forms. Colors range from white to rose, red, orange, yellow and purple, and blooms may be bicolored. Zones 9-11.

**Selected species and varieties.** All of the dahlias grown today are of hybrid origin, most descending from crosses between *D. pinnata* and *D. coccinea*. So many different flower forms have been developed that dahlias have been classified into groups according to the type of bloom by the American Dahlia Society. Single dahlias bear daisylike blooms that have an open center and a single row of ray florets. They may be one color or two-toned. Anemone-flowered dahlias have open centers with one or more rows of ray florets and tubular disc florets that give a pincushion effect. 'Brookside Snowball' is a ball dahlia with 4- to 4½-inch white flowers. 'Fable' is an anemone-flowered cultivar. Cactus-flowered dahlias are fully double blooms with ray florets that either curve in toward the center of the flower or out toward its base. 'Keewatin

Pioneer' is a cactus-flowered cultivar with red and yellow 4- to 6-inch flowers. There are two types of so-called decorative dahlias; formal and informal. Both have fully double blooms, but formal decoratives have broad ray florets that are regularly arranged, pointed or rounded on the tips, and curved in toward the center of the flower and out at the base. Informal decoratives have ray florets that are long and twisted and irregularly arranged. Mignon dahlias bear single flowers and are under 18 inches in height.

**Growing conditions.** Grow dahlias in full sun or light shade in a location with light, rich, well-drained soil. Dahlias should be planted outdoors after all danger of frost has passed. Space plants 8 to 24 inches apart, depending on their ultimate height, and feed with 5-10-5 fertilizer at planting and repeat monthly during the growing season. Mulch and water heavily; never let the soil dry out completely. Most dahlias require staking. For best results, place stakes in the ground before planting the dahlias, and as the plants grow tie the stems to the stake with rags or yarn. To store dahlias over winter north of Zone 9, dig the tuberous roots after the tops of the plants have been blackened by frost, shake off the excess soil and dry them in the sun for several hours. Remove the tops of the plants and store the roots in a cool, dry place over winter. Check them periodically to make sure they do not dry out. Plants that begin to grow are receiving too much heat or light. Most dahlia cultivars are propagated by cuttings or division. To divide dahlias, cut the stored roots into sections in spring before planting. Make sure that each root section has a bud. Dahlias can also be started from seed, but the colors and forms will not breed true.

**Dasheen** see *Colocasia*
**Dragonroot** see *Arisaema*
**Elephant's ear** see *Colocasia*

### Endymion (en-DIM-ee-on)
Wood hyacinth

A genus of bulbous, spring-blooming plants with spikes of nodding, bell-shaped flowers that are blue, pink or white. Foliage is narrow and grasslike. Wood hyacinths, which are also listed as *Hyacinthoides* and *Scilla,* are used in woodland gardens and in borders and make excellent cut flowers. Zones 5-9.

DAHLIA 'BROOKSIDE SNOWBALL'

DAHLIA 'KEEWATIN PIONEER'

ENDYMION HISPANICUS

ERANTHIS HYEMALIS

EUCOMIS AUTUMNALIS

FREESIA × HYBRIDA

**Selected species and varieties.** *E. hispanicus* (also listed as *Hyacinthoides hispanicus, Scilla campanulata* and *S. hispanicus)*, Spanish bluebell, bell-flowered squill, bears strap-shaped leaves that are 1 foot long and 1½ inches wide. Squill plants reach about 20 inches and produce 10- to 30-flowered spikes of bell-shaped, ¾-inch flowers that come in blue, rose-purple, white and pink. 'Alba Maxima' has white flowers. 'Blue Queen' and 'Excelsior' produce profuse quantities of blue flowers; 'Rosabella' has pink flowers.

**Growing conditions.** Grow wood hyacinths in medium to heavy shade, such as under deciduous trees, in humus-rich soil that is moist. Plant the bulbs in fall 3 inches deep and 6 inches apart. Do not dig or divide the plants unless absolutely necessary. They will multiply by offsets and self-seeding.

## Eranthis (e-RAN-this)
### Winter aconite

Winter aconites are early-spring-blooming members of the buttercup family that arise from tuberous roots. The foliage is deeply divided and borne at the base of the plant, with the exception of one dissected leaf that is carried just below the flower. Flowers are borne one per stem and consist of showy sepals (usually yellow, occasionally white) surrounding small, nectar-producing petals. Winter aconites make fine additions to woodland and rock gardens and also can be used for naturalizing. Zones 4-9.

**Selected species and varieties.** *E. hyemalis* is an upright, 3- to 8-inch species with brilliant yellow flowers. Collection in the wild has endangered the species; purchase from reputable dealers that sell only propagated tuberous roots.

**Growing conditions.** Winter aconites require rich, well-drained soil that remains moist during the summer months. The tuberous roots should be in the ground when growth begins in early fall, so plant in late summer or early fall. Soak the tubers overnight in water before planting, and select a location with full sun or light shade. Plant at a depth of 3 inches and space plants 3 to 4 inches apart. Mulch to preserve soil moisture. Plants will die down in middle to late spring and can be overplanted with shallow-rooted annuals or perennials. Mark the plantings to avoid inadvertently digging them up, and do not divide them.

## Eucomis (YEW-ko-mis) or
## (yew-KO-mis)
### Pineapple lily

Pineapple lilies are summer-blooming lily-family members native to South Africa. They arise from bulbs and bear a rosette of leaves topped by a spike of greenish white, starlike flowers. The flower spikes are topped by a cluster of 10 to 30 leaflike bracts. Use pineapple lilies in flower borders in Zones 7-11, or in pots or tubs in the North. They make fine cut flowers. Zones 7-11.

**Selected species and varieties.** *E. autumnalis* is a 1- to 2-foot species with strap-shaped leaves having wavy margins and spikes of ¾-inch flowers.

**Growing conditions.** Grow pineapple lilies in a location with full sun or light shade. They should be planted in fall at a depth of 3 to 4 inches and will grow in most well-drained soils. Soil should be evenly moist when the leaves are above ground, but can be allowed to dry out after plants die down. Plants do not need dividing and can be left undisturbed for years. Multiply best by self-seeding.

**Fairy lily** see *Zephyranthes*

## Freesia (FREE-zha)

Freesias are extremely fragrant plants native to South Africa. They arise from tapered corms and bear narrow, sword-shaped leaves and spikes of funnel-shaped flowers that may be white, yellow, pink or purple. Freesias are generally grown as greenhouse plants or as annuals, except in the Deep South and Southern California. They make excellent cut flowers. Zones 9-11.

**Selected species and varieties.** *F.* x *hybrida* is a group of 1½- to 2-foot hybrids with single or double, 2-inch flowers that come in white or yellow but may be veined or shaded with pink, purple or orange. Many cultivars are available. 'Ballerina' has large, pure white flowers. *F. refracta* is an 8- to 18-inch species with very fragrant, greenish white flowers that are 1 inch long.

**Growing conditions.** In frost-free areas, plant freesias in the fall 2 to 3 inches deep. They require full sun and rich, well-drained soil, and do best where temperatures are cool (45° to 55°F) at night. In the North, they can be grown in pots in sunny windows. To force for winter or spring bloom, store potted in dry soil at 50° to 60°F for 8 to 12 weeks in summer.

## Fritillaria (fri-ti-LAIR-ee-a)
Fritillary

Fritillarias are spring-flowering, bulbous plants in the lily family. The flowers are nodding, funnel- to bell-shaped, and may be borne singly or in loose spikes or clusters. Blooms may be solid-colored or checkered. Most fritillarias are best used in rock gardens because they are intolerant of wet soil, especially in winter. A few species, such as *F. imperialis,* can be planted in borders. Zones 3-9.

**Selected species and varieties.** *F. imperialis,* crown imperial, is a showy, 2- to 4-foot plant that is very popular despite its skunklike odor. The leaves are borne on the bottom two-thirds of the stem. The flowers are 2 inches long, bell-shaped, borne in a downward-pointing cluster at the top of the stem, and are orangish red, yellow or purplish. A number of cultivars are available. 'Lutea Maxima' bears large yellow flowers; 'Orange Brilliant,' orange; and 'Rubra Maxima,' large red flowers. Collection in the wild has endangered the species; purchase from reputable dealers that sell only propagated bulbs. Zones 5-9. *F. lanceolata,* checker lily, mission bells, bears one to four 1½-inch flowers that are purple mottled with greenish yellow. Plants reach 2 feet in height. Zones 6-9. *F. meleagris,* guinea-hen flower, checkered lily, bears solitary, bell-shaped blooms that are 1½ inches long and have a checkered white and purplish or maroon pattern. Plants are 1 to 1½ feet tall. 'Alba' is a white flowered form. Zones 3-9. *F. pallidiflora* bears bluish green foliage and 1½-inch, bell-shaped flowers that are yellowish white on the outside and dotted with purple inside. Zones 5-9. *F. persica* is a 3-foot plant that bears 10 to 30 bell-shaped, ¾-inch flowers that are violet-blue in color. 'Adiyama' bears 1-inch flowers that are plum-colored. Zones 5-9, but plants require protection from late frosts in the North. Collection in the wild has endangered the species; purchase from reputable dealers that sell only propagated bulbs. *F. pudica,* yellow fritillary, yellow bell, is a 9-inch species with grasslike leaves. It bears one to three yellow or orange bell-shaped flowers that are ¾ inch long. Zones 4-9.

**Growing conditions.** Fritillarias will grow in full sun or light shade and prefer a location with rich, well-drained soil. Plant bulbs at a depth of 4 to 6 inches as soon as they are available in the fall. They dry out quickly, so plant them as soon as possible. Most fritillarias from the western United States will not tolerate wet eastern winters. The best species for the East are *F. imperialis* and *F. pudica,* although in the East the latter requires full sun and extremely well-drained soil that has little humus. Do not cultivate around the plants and leave them undisturbed for as long as possible. Divide only if plants become so crowded that flowering ceases. To force for late winter or early spring bloom, store potted in dry soil at 50° to 60°F for 8 to 12 weeks in summer.

## Fritillary see *Fritillaria*

## Galanthus (ga-LAN-thus)
Snowdrop

Snowdrops are members of the amaryllis family that bloom in late winter or very early spring. They are small, bulbous plants that have two or three grasslike leaves and nodding, waxy white flowers borne one per stem. Each bloom consists of six petal-like segments; there are three large outer segments that are white and three inner ones that are marked with green and appear tubular. Snowdrops are grown in rock gardens and naturalized under deciduous trees and shrubs. Collection in the wild has endangered some species in the genus; purchase from reputable dealers that sell only propagated bulbs. Zones 3-11.

**Selected species and varieties.** *G. byzantinus* has 5½-inch leaves and nodding, ½- to 1-inch flowers. Zones 5-9. *G. elwesii,* giant snowdrop, bears leaves that are 1 inch wide and 4 inches long. Its blooms are 1¼ to 2 inches long. Zones 5-9. *G. nivalis,* common snowdrop, bears 4-inch leaves that are ¼ inch wide. It has 1-inch-long flowers. 'Flore Pleno' bears double flowers; 'Magnet' is a large-flowered form; 'Sam Arnott' is large-flowered but also has fragrant flowers. Zones 4-9. *G. reginae-olgae* is a fall-blooming species from Greece. Zones 5-11.

**Growing conditions.** Grow snowdrops in a location that has full sun or light shade, at least during the spring, when the foliage is apparent, and moist, rich, well-drained soil. Plant bulbs in late summer or early fall at a depth of 3 inches. Space plants 3 inches apart. They do not need dividing and if left undisturbed will form large colonies. The foliage must be allowed to mature and yellow naturally if the plants are to produce blooms the following year; do not mow or cut the foliage back.

FRITILLARIA MELEAGRIS

FRITILLARIA PERSICA

GALANTHUS NIVALIS

GLADIOLUS BYZANTINUS

GLADIOLUS × COLVILLEI

HYACINTHUS ORIENTALIS 'VANGUARD'

**Giant onion** see *Allium*

## Gladiolus (gla-dee-O-lus)
Corn flag, sword lily

A genus of showy, summer-blooming members of the iris family, most of which are native to South Africa. They arise from corms and have long, narrow, sword-shaped leaves. Flowers are borne in few- to many-flowered spikes covered with leaflike bracts. Individual blooms are flaring or trumpet-shaped. Gladioli are grown in beds and borders. In areas where they are not hardy, they can be dug and overwintered indoors. Zones 5-11.

**Selected species and varieties.** *G. byzantinus* is a 3-foot plant with many-flowered spikes of pinkish purple flowers that may be striped with white. White- and scarlet-flowered forms are also available. *G.* x *colvillei,* Colville gladiolus, is a fairly hardy species with red flowers that have a yellow central blotch. 'The Bride' is a pure-white-flowered cultivar.

**Growing conditions.** Grow gladiolus in full sun, in deeply prepared soil that is rich and well drained. Dig a trench for planting that is 2 inches deeper than the recommended planting depth. Apply a balanced fertilizer such as 5-10-10 and cover it with 2 inches of soil. Plant small corms (under 1 inch) at a depth of 3 to 4 inches; larger corms 6 to 8 inches. When planting, cover the corms with several inches of soil and fill in the trench as the plants grow. Space corms 3 to 6 inches apart. Side-dress plants with fertilizer when they emerge and again when flowers start to show color. Stake gladioli to protect them from high winds. To prolong the blooming season, corms can be started at 10- to 14-day intervals from early spring to midsummer up until 90 days before the first killing frost. Dig the corms six weeks after blooming, when the foliage begins to brown; or, in areas where the plants are hardy, the corms can be left in the ground over winter. Where the corms are not hardy, dig the last crop of corms before the first hard frost. Shake off excess soil and cut back the tops of the plants. Allow the corms to dry out of direct sun, discard the remains of the previous season's corms and dust the corms with fungicide before storing in a cool (40° F), dry place for the winter. In the warmest part of Zones 9, 10 and 11, corms benefit from three months of cold storage in the refrigerator. Propagate plants from the small cormels borne around old corms. The cormels take up to two seasons to bloom.

**Glory-of-the-snow** see *Chionodoxa*
**Golden garlic** see *Allium*
**Grape hyacinth** see *Muscari*
**Green dragon** see *Arisaema*
**Guinea-hen flower** see *Fritillaria*
**Hyacinth** see *Hyacinthus*
**Hyacinth-of-Peru** see *Scilla*

## Hyacinthus (hy-a-SIN-thus)
Hyacinth

A one-species genus in the lily family with colorful, heavily scented spikes of flowers that appear in spring. Leaves are strap-shaped, and the bulbs often have purplish coverings. Hyacinths are grown in beds and borders and can also be forced indoors. Zones 6-9.

**Selected species and varieties.** *H. orientalis,* common hyacinth, Dutch hyacinth, garden hyacinth, bears dense spikes of very fragrant flowers. The individual flowers are bell-shaped and blue, pink or white. Blooms are carried in stiff, football-shaped spikes. Many cultivars are available: 'L'Innocence' is white; 'Pink Pearl' is pink; 'Vanguard' is lilac-colored.

**Growing conditions.** Grow hyacinths in full sun in a location with rich, well-drained soil. Plant bulbs in fall at a depth of 6 to 8 inches. Mulch heavily, especially in the North, to protect the shoots that emerge in early spring. Fertilize monthly during the growing season. Large, newly planted bulbs will produce extra-large flower clusters the first season after planting, smaller clusters thereafter. To force for spring bloom, store potted in moist soil at 35° to 48°F for 13 to 15 weeks in fall.

## Hymenocallis (hy-men-o-KAL-is)
Spider lily, basket flower, Peruvian daffodil

Spider lilies belong to a small genus of plants in the amaryllis family. They have thick, strap-shaped leaves that may be evergreen or deciduous. The white or yellow flowers, borne in umbels atop stout stalks, are fragrant and somewhat resemble daffodils. They have a central, funnel-shaped cup that is surrounded by six petallike lobes or segments, which are attached at the base of the bloom. The lobes are narrow and curve out around the trumpetlike base. They also have long, spidery stamens. Spider lilies are grown in beds and borders. Zones 5-11.

**Selected species and varieties.**
*H. caribaea* is an evergreen species with narrow, foot-long leaves and eight- to 10-flowered clusters of fragrant white flowers that have 2½-inch-long, funnel-shaped bases and narrow, 4-inch lobes. *H. narcissiflora,* basket flower, Peruvian daffodil, is a 2-foot-tall plant with two- to five-flowered clusters of fringed, 2-inch trumpets surrounded by curving lobes. Zones 7-11. *H.* x *'Sulfur Queen'* is a hybrid cultivar resembling *H. narcissiflora,* which is one of its parents, with yellow flowers. Zones 7-11.

**Growing conditions.** Plant spider lilies in rich, fertile soil that is well drained but remains moist throughout the growing season. Deciduous species should remain dry during dormancy. Spider lilies will tolerate full sun or light shade. In areas where they are hardy, these plants can be left in the ground throughout the year. Where they are not hardy, plant them indoors in large pots and move the pots outdoors after all danger of frost has passed. Or plant them outdoors in spring and dig the bulbs in fall before the first frost. Leave the roots attached to the bulbs and dry them upside down so that any water runs away from the plants. Bulbs can be packed in nearly dry peat or stored in open trays at a temperature of 55° to 60° F. Tub-grown plants are set with the tip of the bulb 1 inch below the surface; bulbs planted in the ground should be set at a depth of 3 to 4 inches. To force for late spring or summer bloom, store potted in slightly moist soil at 50° to 60° F for 8 to 12 weeks in fall or winter.

**Indian shot** see *Canna*
**Indian turnip** see *Arisaema*

**Ipheion** (i-FEE-on)

A small genus of bulbous plants in the amaryllis family that are native to South America. Plants have narrow, grasslike leaves that have an onion-like odor when bruised. Flowers are solitary, funnel-shaped and borne on leafless stalks. Zones 6-11.

**Selected species and varieties.**
*I. uniflorum* (formerly *Brodiaea uniflora, Leucocoryne uniflora* and *Milla uniflora*), spring starflower, has ⅜-inch-wide leaves and 6- to 8-inch stalks topped by star-shaped, 1½-inch flowers that are whitish blue or blue. 'Wisley Blue' is fragrant and has light blue flowers with white centers. Zones 6-9.

**Growing conditions.** Spring starflower requires full sun and rich, extremely well-drained, somewhat sandy soil. Plant the bulbs in late summer or early fall, 3 inches deep and 3 inches apart. Leave the plants undisturbed for as long as possible. Divide only if flowering ceases. Plants flower in spring, and the foliage disappears after flowering only to reappear in fall and persist through winter. In the northern zones, spring starflowers benefit from a light winter covering of cut evergreen branches. A good bulb to plant on a lawn, it is widely available.

**Iris** see Dictionnary of Perennials, page 246
**Jack-in-the-pulpit** see *Arisaema*
**Jacobean lily** see *Sprekelia*
**Jonquil** see *Narcissus*
**Kafir lily** see *Clivia*
**Leucocoryne** see *Ipheion*

**Leucojum** (lew-KO-jum)
Snowflake

A very small genus of European natives in the amaryllis family that have small bulbs and narrow leaves. Flowers are nodding and bell-shaped, and borne alone or in umbels atop hollow stalks. Snowflakes are used in rock gardens, in borders and for naturalizing. Collection in the wild has endangered most species in the genus; purchase from reputable dealers that sell only propagated bulbs. Zones 4-11.

**Selected species and varieties.**
*L. aestivum,* giant snowflake, summer snowflake, is a spring-blooming species that produces two- to eight-flowered spikes of white, cup-shaped flowers tipped with green. Blooms are borne on 9- to 12-inch stalks. 'Gravetye' is a large-flowered cultivar. *L. vernum,* spring snowflake, has white ¾-inch flowers with green tips. Blooms are borne atop 6- to 12-inch stalks during early spring.

**Growing conditions.** Grow snowflakes in rich, well-drained soil in a location protected from hot sun. For best results, dig a generous quantity of organic matter such as compost or leaf mold into the soil at planting time. Keep plants evenly moist while they are actively growing. Plant bulbs in late summer or fall 2 inches deep; space 3 inches apart. Leave plants undisturbed for as long as possible; divide only for propagation.

HYMENOCALLIS CARIBAEA

IPHEION UNIFLORUM 'WISLEY BLUE'

LEUCOJUM VERNUM

LILIUM CANADENSE

LILIUM CANDIDUM

LILIUM PHILADELPHICUM

## Lilium (LIL-ee-um)
Lily

The genus of the true lilies, from which so many plants in other genera have taken their common names. True lilies are very showy plants with trumpet- or bell-shaped flowers borne pointing up or down, and singly or in many-flowered clusters. Each has six petal-like segments called tepals that are usually the same color, and may be white, yellow, orange, red, maroon or purple. Tepals generally curve backward at the tips; species with reflexed petals have tepals that curve in a semicircle. Blooms have six stamens and are often spotted on the inside. The bulbs are scaly and the flowers are borne on erect, leafy stems.

There are between 80 and 90 species of lilies and many more cultivars. In addition to true species lilies, which are listed below by botanical name, many hybrids have been developed. Hybrids, which are generally easier to grow than the species, have been divided into groups according to the origin of the parent species. Within these groups the plants are further divided according to the form of the flowers. Lilies make fine additions to borders, can be planted in clumps as specimen plants and also are used for naturalizing. Zones 4-11.

**Selected species and varieties.**
*L. amabile,* Korean lily, is a 3-foot species with one- to six-flowered spikes of orange-red, 2-inch blooms with dark spots. Flowers have an unpleasant scent and appear in late spring. 'Luteum' has pure yellow flowers. *L. auratum,* gold-band lily, has lance-shaped leaves and flaring, fragrant, 6- to 12-inch flowers that are white with red spots and a gold stripe down the center of each tepal. Blooms appear in summer atop 3- to 9-foot plants in spikes of up to 35 flowers. Zones 5-11. *L. canadense,* Canada lily, meadow lily, is a summer-blooming, 5-foot-tall plant native to bogs and wet meadows in eastern North America. Blooms are bell-shaped and nodding with very reflexed tepals, 3 inches across, and yellow, orange or red in color. *L. canadense editorum* is native to drier sites than the species and bears red flowers. *L. candidum,* Madonna lily, Annunciation lily, is a 6-foot-tall plant bearing five to 20 fragrant, pure white blooms with yellow anthers in spring or early summer. Unlike most lilies, it dies down after blooming and develops new growth in the fall. Madonna lilies are susceptible to botrytis blight. Zones 5-11.

*L. columbianum,* Columbia lily, Oregon lily, is a summer-blooming, West Coast native reaching 5 feet and bearing few- to many-flowered spikes of nodding, 2-inch flowers. Blooms have very reflexed tepals and are yellow to red with maroon spots. Zones 7-11. *L. concolor,* star lily, morning-star lily, is a scarlet-flowered species that reaches 3 to 4 feet in height. The cup-shaped blooms point upward and are 3½ inches wide and 2 inches long. Zones 5-11. *L. formosianum,* Formosa lily, is a late-summer- to early-autumn-blooming species with white, funnel-shaped blooms that are fragrant and marked with purple on the outside. It is very susceptible to virus diseases. Zones 6-11. *L. hansonii,* Hanson lily, Japanese Turk's-cap, is a 5-foot species with loose spikes of fragrant, nodding, 2½-inch-wide flowers. The blooms appear in late spring and are orange-yellow spotted with purplish brown. *L. henryi* bears spikes of 10 to 20 bright orange, nodding flowers in August. It tolerates virus diseases and is resistant to wilt. 'Citrinum' is a bright-yellow-flowered cultivar. Zones 5-11.

*L.* x *hollandicum,* candlestick lily, is a hybrid between *L. bulbiferum* and *L. maculatum* that bears 4-inch-wide, upward-pointing blooms on 1½-foot plants. Flowers are cup-shaped and yellow to red in color. Zones 5-11. *L. japonicum,* Japanese lily, is a 3-foot species with fragrant, funnel-shaped flowers that are 6 inches long and 6 inches wide. Blooms appear in summer, one to five per stalk, and are pale pink in color. Japanese lily is susceptible to virus diseases. Zones 6-11. *L. lancifolium* (also listed as *L. tigrinum*), tiger lily, produces 6-foot stems of one to 25 flowers in July. Blooms are nodding, 5 inches wide, and orange or red spotted with purple. Small, black bulbils are often borne in the leaf axils. 'Splendens' has larger, deep red flowers with prominent dark spots; it blooms in August. Tiger lilies are often infected with lily mosaic virus. It does not harm them but spreads easily to other bulbs, so tiger lilies should be planted in isolation from other lilies.

*L.* x *maculatum* (also listed as *L.* x *elegans*) is a hybrid with erect, cup-shaped flowers borne atop 2-foot plants, blooms are borne in summer, are 4 inches wide and are yellow to deep red in color. Zones 5-11. *L. martagon,* Turk's-cap lily, Martagon lily, has drooping, ill-smelling flowers borne three to 50 per spike in late spring. Blooms are usually purple spotted with black, but may be white to pink. 'Album' has pure white flowers. Collection in the wild has endangered the species; purchase from reputable dealers that sell only propagated bulbs.

*L. michiganense,* Michigan lily, is a 5-foot plant with nodding, 3-inch-wide flowers that have reflexed petals. Blooms are borne one to eight per plant and are orange-red spotted with maroon. Zones 5-11. *L. monadelphym,* Caucasian lily, bears many-flowered spikes of bell-shaped, fragrant flowers in late spring atop 5-foot plants. Blooms are 5 inches across and golden yellow, sometimes spotted with purple. *L. parryi,* lemon lily, has 4-inch, funnel-shaped blooms that are lemon yellow and may be spotted with maroon. Flowers are fragrant and borne atop 4- to 6-foot plants. Zones 7-11.

*L. philadelphicum,* wood lily, orange-cup-lily, produces upward-pointing, cup-shaped blooms that are 4 inches long and orange-red with dark spots. Flowers are borne in late spring to summer atop 2- to 3-foot plants. Zones 5-11. *L. pyrenaicum,* yellow Turk's-cap lily, is a 4-foot species with unpleasantly scented 1½- to 2-inch flowers with reflexed petals. Blooms are sulfur yellow and appear in late spring. 'Rubrum' is an orange-red flowered cultivar. Zones 5-11. *L. regale,* regal lily, royal lily, produces umbels of fragrant, 6-inch-long flowers purplish outside and white with a yellow throat inside. Blooms are borne in summer atop 6-foot plants. *L. speciosum,* Japanese lily, showy lily, is a late-summer or early-fall-blooming species with fragrant flowers that have tepals so spreading the flowers appear flat. Blooms are white marked with red or pink. *L. speciosum* is susceptible to virus. Many cultivars are available. 'Rubrum' has deep pink and red flowers. 'White Glory' has white blooms. Zones 5-11. *L. superbum,* Turk's-cap lily, bears nodding, 3-inch-wide, yellow to orange-red blooms atop 5- to 8-foot-tall plants. Flowers are spotted with maroon and appear in summer.

*L.* x *testacum,* nankeen lily, bears up to 12 fragrant, nodding, 3-inch flowers that are apricot to yellow atop 6-foot plants. It is susceptible to botrytis blight and basal rot. *L. washingtonianum,* Washington lily, is a 3- to 6-foot species with white to greenish white flowers. Blooms are fragrant, funnel-shaped, up to 8 inches across and borne in summer. Zones 7-11.

American Hybrid Lilies are cultivars developed from native American species. The Bellingham cultivars, which are typical of this group, are 4- to 6-foot plants that produce nodding, 4- to 6-inch flowers with reflexed petals in pink, red, orange or yellow and spotted with reddish brown. Blooms are borne up to 20 per plant in summer.

Asiatic Hybrid Lilies are compact, 2- to 5-foot plants that bear many-flowered spikes of 4- to 6-inch flowers that may point up, out or down. Blooms may be red, pink, orange, yellow, lavender or white and appear in summer. 'Connecticut King' grows 3 to 4 feet tall and has upright lemon yellow flowers with gold throats. 'Connecticut Yankee' has nodding orange flowers with deeply reflexed petals. 'Enchantment' bears dark-spotted orange blooms that point upward. 'Melon Time' grows 3 feet tall and has upward-facing salmon to orange flowers. 'Rose Fire' has coppery rose blooms that are deep red at center with gold flashes.

Aurelian Hybrid Lilies, which are sometimes called Trumpet or Olympic hybrids, have fragrant flowers up to 8 inches long that may be trumpet-shaped, bowl-shaped or even flat and are borne in summer. Blooms may be greenish or pure white, yellow, orange or pink, and are carried atop 3- to 8-foot plants. 'Black Dragon' is an Aurelian Hybrid with nodding, trumpet-shaped blooms that are purplish on the outside and white with a yellow throat on the inside. 'Golden Splendor' has rich golden yellow blooms. 'Pink Perfection' has nodding, deep rose-pink trumpets. Zones 4-7.

Oriental Hybrid Lilies were developed from crosses between *L. auratum, L. speciosum* and *L. japonicum,* among others. The flowers are fragrant, 3 to 10 inches wide and are the last of the lilies to flower, in late summer. They come in pure white or white with pink, yellow or red stripes. Plants are 2½ to 7 feet tall. 'Imperial Crimson' has flat-faced blooms that are white blushed with rose-pink edged in white. 'Imperial Gold' is white dotted with maroon and has a yellow stripe down the center of each tepal. 'Stargazer' has fragrant crimson flowers with white borders and dark spots. Unlike the blooms of most Oriental Hybrids, the flowers of 'Stargazer' face upward Zones 5-11.

**Growing conditions.** Grow lilies in rich, well-tilled porous soil that is very well drained. They will grow in full sun or light shade, although flowers sometimes fade if they are exposed to hot sun. Plants prefer soil that remains moist and cool at all times. If possible, select a site where the bases of the plants will remain shaded; choose companion plants such as small rhododendrons or azaleas, tall ferns or other perennials that will not provide too much competition. Mulch also helps keep the soil moist and cool. Lilies also require staking and a location protected from strong wind.

Plant lilies in beds that are dug to a depth of at least 1 foot. Add generous quantities of organic matter such as compost, peat moss or humus. Lily bulbs, which are very fragile and must be handled with care, may have roots

LILIUM 'CONNECTICUT KING'

LILIUM 'ROSE FIRE'

LILIUM 'PINK PERFECTION'

LILIUM 'IMPERIAL CRIMSON'

LYCORIS RADIATA

MUSCARI ARMENIACUM

along the stem that arises on top of the bulb. Plant in fall or early spring, leaving all roots intact. Dust the bulbs with fungicide before planting to prevent rot. Set bulbs in the ground with the base of the bulb three times as deep as the bulb is high. (For example, a 3-inch-tall bulb should be planted with the base 9 inches below the soil surface.) Hybrids and cultivars of *L. candidum* are an exception to this rule; plant them in late summer or early fall only, with no more than 1 inch of soil over the tops of the bulbs.

Fertilize all lilies with a slow-release fertilizer or well-rotted manure when growth emerges in spring. Tall plants may require staking; be sure to keep stakes well away from the base of the plant to avoid damaging the bulbs. Lilies should not be dug or divided unless absolutely necessary. Many lilies are susceptible to virus diseases, which are transmitted by aphids from lily to lily and from other infected plants. There is no cure for infected plants, so it is important to control aphid populations and destroy any infected plants. Streaked, spotted or stunted foliage; dwarfed plants; or distorted, misshapen flowers are all indications of virus disease. Dig and discard all portions of any infected plants. Do not add infected plant material to the compost heap. To force for late winter or spring bloom, store potted in moist peat moss at 40° to 45°F for 6 weeks in fall.

**Lily** see *Lilium*
**Lily leek** see Allium
**Lily-of-the-field** see *Anemone*

## Lycoris (ly-KOR-is)

A genus of bulbous species in the amaryllis family that are native to China and Japan. Plants bear umbels of spider-shaped flowers that are fragrant and have a short tube at the base. Blooms are white, yellow or pink, and generally appear when the plants are leafless. The leaves are strap-shaped and narrow and either die down before the flowers appear or arise after the flowers have faded. Lycoris can be planted in beds and borders, and can also be grown in tubs or large pots in areas where it is not hardy. Zones 5-11.

**Selected species and varieties.** *L. radiata*, spider lily, short-tube lycoris, bears dark pink to bright red flowers that are 1½ inches long. The petal-like lobes of each flower are nar-

row and curve backward, and together with the long stamens they give the blooms a spidery appearance. Zones 7-11. *L. squamigera,* magic lily, hardy amaryllis, is a 2-foot plant with trumpet-shaped flowers that are 3 inches long and appear in summer and are rose-lilac or pink.

**Growing conditions.** Plant lycoris in a location with sun and rich, well-drained soil. Plant the bulbs at a depth of 5 inches, and leave plants undisturbed as long as possible. Digging and dividing can prevent flowering for several years.

**Magic lily** see *Lycoris*
**Meadow lily** see *Lilium*
**Meadow saffron** see *Colchicum*
**Milla** see *Ipheion*
**Mission bells** see *Fritillaria*
**Monkey-faced pansy** see *Achimenes*
**Morningstar lily** see *Lilium*

## Muscari (mus-KAR-ee)
Grape hyacinth

A genus of spring-blooming, lily-family members with small bulbs and narrow leaves. Flowers are blue or white, may be musky or sweet-scented, and are urn-shaped or nearly spherical. The blooms are borne in dense spikes that in some species resemble clusters of grapes. Grape hyacinths can be used as edgings, in beds and borders, and are also fine for naturalizing. Zones 3-11.

**Selected species and varieties.** *M. armeniacum* is a 9-inch-tall species with narrow, foot-long leaves that appear in fall. The flowers, which appear in early spring, are 5/16 inch long, deep violet-blue with white tips and borne in dense spikes of 30 to 40 blooms. *M. azureum* blooms in early spring, with 6-inch-long leaves and bright blue, 3/16-inch flowers. Blooms are fragrant and are borne in dense, 8-inch-tall spikes of 20 to 40 flowers. 'Album' is a white-flowered cultivar. Zones 4 to 11.

**Growing conditions.** Grow grape hyacinths in full sun or light shade in a location with deep, rich, well-drained soil that is somewhat sandy. Plant bulbs in fall 3 inches deep and 3 to 4 inches apart. Plants thrive if left undisturbed, and will multiply rapidly. To force *M. armeniacum* for late winter or early spring bloom, store potted in moist soil at 40° to 48°F for 15 to 16 weeks in fall.

**Naked lady** see *Amaryllis*
**Naples onion** see *Allium*


**Narcissus** (nar-SIS-sus)
Daffodil

Daffodils are among the best known of spring-flowering bulbs, and although there are only about 70 species in the genus, there are hundreds of hybrids with varying flower forms. Members of the amaryllis family, daffodils arise from bulbs and generally have flat, narrow leaves. The flowers are usually nodding and may be white, yellow or bicolored. They are borne alone or several per stem. The bloom consists of a corona, or crown, which is cup- or trumpet-shaped, stands in the center, and may be long and tubular or short and ringlike. The corona is surrounded by six petallike segments that are referred to collectively as the perianth. Most daffodils bloom in spring, but two species bloom in fall. They are used in beds or borders, in rock gardens and for naturalizing. Zones 4-9.

**Selected species and varieties.** There are so many species and hybrid daffodils that horticulturists classify them in divisions according to flower form and size or to the species from which they were developed. The divisions are further subdivided according to the color of the floral parts.

Division I. Trumpet Daffodils bear one bloom per stem, and flowers have trumpets, or coronas, that are at least as long as the perianth segments. Blooms appear in early to middle spring. 'Cantatrice' grows 16 inches tall and has white flowers.

'Foresight' has white perianth segments and golden yellow trumpets. 'Lunar Sea' grows 18 inches tall and blooms in midseason with a yellow perianth and white corona (the reverse of most daffodils). 'Unsurpassable' bears golden yellow flowers with 5-inch-wide perianths atop 18-inch plants. Miniature cultivars are included in this class as well: 'Little Beauty' grows 6 inches tall and has white perianth segments and pale yellow trumpets. 'Little Gem' is 5 inches tall with yellow blooms. 'W.P. Milner' is a miniature that grows 5 inches tall and blooms in early to middle spring with all-white blossoms. Zones 4-8.

Division II. Large Cup Daffodils have one flower per stem, and bloom in early to midspring. The corona is more than one-third the length of the perianth segments, but less than their total length. Plants generally are 16 to 18 inches tall, and the flowers are 3½ to 4½ inches wide. 'Carlton' has bright yellow blooms. 'Ceylon' grows 14 inch-

es tall and blooms in early to middle spring; it has yellow perianth segments and an orange corona. 'Daydream' grows 16 inches tall and blooms in middle to late spring.

Division III. Small Cup Daffodils have coronas that are less than one-third the length of the perianth segments. They bear one flower per stem and bloom in early spring. Plants generally are 14 to 16 inches tall and flowers are 2 to 3 inches wide. 'Birma' grows 16 inches tall and blooms early; it has yellow perianth segments and a red corona. It naturalizes easily. 'Verger' grows 18 inches tall, blooms in midseason with white perianth segments and a red corona, and naturalizes easily. Zones 4-8.

Division IV. Double Daffodils do not look like typical daffodils; there is usually no defined corona but instead a cluster of petaloids at the center, and there may be more than one bloom per stem. Plants range from 14 to 18 inches tall, and blooms are from 1 to 3 inches across. 'Acropolis' grows 18 inches tall, usually blooms late in the season, and is white with red and white petaloids. 'Cheerfulness' bears clusters of double white flowers that are fragrant. 'Tahiti' grows 16 inches tall and usually blooms late in the season; it is yellow with red petaloids. 'White Marvel' has pure white, double blooms on 14-inch plants. 'Pencrebar' is a miniature that grows to 10 inches and has 2-inch, all-yellow flowers. Zones 4-8.

Division V. Triandrus Hybrid Daffodils are hybrids and cultivars developed from *N. triandrus*. Flowers generally are smaller than those in the first four divisions, and are fragrant and nodding, and borne one or more per stem. Blooms of Triandrus Hybrids appear in middle to late spring, at the end of the daffodil season. 'Liberty Bells' bears two- to four-flowered clusters of dark lemon yellow blooms atop 12-inch stems. Blooms are nodding and have long trumpets. 'Petrel' grows 12 inches tall, usually blooms late, and has an abundance of flowers that are all-white and fragrant. 'Thalia' is a late-flowering cultivar that has fragrant, pure white flowers borne in two- to four-flowered clusters atop 16-inch stems. There are also miniature Triandrus Hybrids; 'Hawera' is an 8-inch plant with yellow, 1-inch-long flowers. Zones 4-8.

Division VI. Cyclamineus Hybrid Daffodils are hybrids and cultivars of *N. cyclamineus*. Plants bloom in early spring and are 6 to 10 inches tall. Flowers are ½ to 2 inches wide and have reflexed perianth segments. 'Dove Wings' has creamy white perianth segments and canary yellow coronas. 'February Gold' has pure yellow

NARCISSUS 'CARLTON'

NARCISSUS 'THALIA'

NARCISSUS 'JACK SNIPE'

NARCISSUS 'GRAND SOLEIL D'OR'

NARCISSUS POETICUS 'ACTAEA'

NARCISSUS BULBOCODIUM

blooms. 'February Silver' has cream-colored trumpets and white perianth segments. 'Jack Snipe' has white flowers with lemon yellow trumpets. 'Jet Fire' grows 12 inches tall, blooms from early to middle spring and is yellow with a red corona. Among miniatures, 'Jumblie' grows 6 inches tall, blooms from early to middle spring and is yellow with a red corona; 'Quince' grows 5 inches tall, blooms in midseason and is all yellow.

Division VII. Jonquilla Hybrid Daffodils are hybrids and cultivars of *N. jonquilla.* They generally have fragrant ½- to 1-inch flowers with small cups and thin, reedlike leaves. 'Pueblo' grows 14 inches tall and usually blooms late with all-white blossoms. 'Quail' bears fragrant, golden yellow flowers with two or three blooms per stalk. 'Stratosphere' grows 24 inches tall, usually blooms late and has all-yellow flowers. 'Suzy' bears two- to four-flowered clusters of fragrant blooms with orange-red cups and broad yellow perianth segments. 'Trevithian' bears two- to four-flowered stalks of fragrant, lemon yellow blooms with broad, overlapping perianth segments. Flowers are borne atop 18-inch stems and appear in midspring. Zones 4-8.

Division VIII. Tazetta Hybrid Daffodils are hybrids and cultivars of *N. tazetta,* and are sometimes called Poetaz or Polyanthus daffodils. Flowers are ½ to 1¼ inches across, have small cups, are usually fragrant and are borne in four- to eight-flowered clusters. The plants range from 12 to 18 inches in height. 'Grand Soleil d'Or' is a nonhardy cultivar used in the North for forcing indoors on pebbles. It can be grown outdoors in gardens in Zones 8-11. It bears clusters of fragrant, golden yellow flowers.

Division IX. Poeticus Hybrid Daffodils are hybrids and cultivars of *N. poeticus.* They have pure white perianth segments and small, cuplike centers, or "eyes," that may be yellow with red margins or all red or may have greenish throats. All are fragrant and bloom in middle to late spring. 'Actaea' bears pure white, 3-inch-white flowers with yellow centers edged in red atop 18-inch plants.

Division X. Species and Wild Forms includes all daffodil species and wild hybrids and forms. *N. asturiensis* is a 5-inch species with solitary, 1-inch-long, pale yellow flowers borne in early spring. The trumpets are longer than the perianth segments. Zones 5-9. *N. bulbocodium,* hoop-petticoat daffodil, bears small, bright yellow flowers in early spring with very narrow perianth segments and 1-inch-long trumpets.

Plants range from 4 to 18 inches tall, have tubular-shaped leaves and naturalize easily. *N. bulbocodium conspicuous* is a large-flowered form. Zones 6-9. *N. cyclamineus* has narrow, 12-inch leaves and solitary, nodding, yellow flowers that are 1 to 2 inches long. Zones 6-9. *N. jonquilla,* common jonquil, grows to 18 inches and bears two- to six-flowered clusters of fragrant, 1-inch long flowers. Blooms are yellow and have coronas that are half as long as the perianth segments.

*N.* x *odorus,* campernelle jonquil, grows to 12 inches and has fragrant, two- to four-flowered clusters of yellow, 2-inch blooms with ¾-inch cups. Zones 6-9. *N. poeticus,* poet's narcissus, pheasant's-eye narcissus, is an 18-inch species bearing fragrant, pure white flowers with small, shallow cups edged in red. Blooms are 2 to 3 inches across and appear in late spring. Zones 4-7. *N. pseudonarcissus,* daffodil, trumpet narcissus, produces solitary, yellow, 2-inch flowers with trumpets as long as the perianth segments atop 12- to 18-inch plants. *N. rupicola* is a 6-inch species with very short cupped, fragrant, yellow, ¾- to 1¼-inch-wide flowers borne one per stem. Zones 6-11. *N. scaberulus* is a 4-inch-tall species with deep orange-yellow flowers. Zones 7-11. *N. tazetta,* polyanthus narcissus, is an 18-inch species bearing clusters of fragrant, 1-inch flowers that are white with light yellow coronas. *N. tazetta papyraceus,* paperwhite narcissus, has all-white fragrant flowers that bloom in clusters. It is easily forced.

*N. triandrus,* angel's-tears, has nearly round, 12-inch leaves and white, 1- to 1½-inch-long flowers with reflexed petals and cuplike coronas without waxy edges. The corona is half as long as the perianth segments. 'Albus' grows 4 inches tall and has all-white flowers that bloom in early to middle spring. *N. triandrus concolor* has pale yellow blooms. Collection in the wild has endangered many species in the genus; purchase from reputable dealers that sell only propagated blulbs. Zones 5-9.

Division XI. Split Corona Daffodils have coronas that are split at least one-third of their length. 'Cassata' grows 16 inches tall and blooms in early to middle spring; the blossoms are white with a yellow and white corona. 'Dolly Mollinger' grows 16 inches tall and blooms in midseason; the flowers are white with an orange and white corona. 'Orangerie' has a bright orange corona that lies against the white perianth segments. 'Valdrome' has bright yellow coronas that nearly conceal the yellow perianth segments. Zones 4-8.

**Growing conditions.** Grow daffodils in a site with full sun or light shade during the spring season, when the foliage is apparent. Soil should be rich in organic matter and well drained; bulbs will rot in wet soil. For best results, prepare the soil to a depth of 1 foot before planting and add generous quantities of compost. If drainage is a problem or if the planting is in wet clay soil, also add sand before planting. Plant bulbs in middle to late fall, but before the soil freezes so plants can develop roots before winter. In Zones 7-11, plant after the soil has cooled to under 60° F. Set bulbs at a depth of 3½ times the height of the bulb. Daffodils can be left undisturbed for years. They need dividing only when the plants become so crowded that flowering ceases. Mulch annually with well-rotted manure or compost. Daffodil foliage must be allowed to yellow naturally after the flowers fade if the plants are to produce blooms for the following season; do not mow or cut it back. Fertilize in fall with a slow-release fertilizer that is low in nitrogen and high in potash (a 5-10-20, for example). Plant annuals or perennials in front of the bulbs to mask their maturing foliage. Tazetta species of narcissus and hybrids cannot be stored. To force any other species for late winter or early spring bloom, store potted in moist soil at 40° to 48° F for 13 to 15 weeks in fall.

**Onion** see *Allium*
**Orchid amaryllis** see *Sprekelia*
**Orchid pansy** see *Achimenes*
**Peacock orchid** see *Acidanthera*
**Peruvian daffodil** see *Hymenocallis*
**Peruvian jacinth** see *Scilla*
**Pineapple lily** see *Eucomis*

## Polianthes (pol-ee-AN-theez)

A genus of about a dozen species, native to Mexico, in the agave family. Plants have bulblike bases and often thick rhizomes and roots. Polianthes foliage is grasslike; the flowers are tubular and borne in spikes. Polianthes species are grown in beds and borders, especially where their fragrance can be enjoyed. Zones 9-11; grown as annuals in the North.

**Selected species and varieties.** *P. tuberosa,* tuberose, is a 3-foot-tall plant with 12- to 18-inch leaves that are borne at the base of the plant. Flowers are extremely fragrant, waxy white and

borne in loose spikes. Blooms appear in summer to fall. 'Single Mexican' has fragrant, single flowers and grows 3 to 4 feet high.

**Growing conditions.** Tuberoses can be grown outdoors in beds and borders in Zones 9-11. Elsewhere they are generally planted outdoors when danger of frost has passed, then dug and stored indoors over winter. Plant the bulblike tubers in a site with full sun or light shade and rich, well-drained soil to which abundant amounts of compost have been added. Full-sized tubers should be planted 3 inches deep and 6 inches apart; smaller offsets should be planted 2 inches deep and 4 inches apart. Offsets will not bloom the first year. Healthy tubers will always show a green growing point. Mulch and water heavily through the growing season. Withhold water near the end of the season, when the foliage will begin to yellow, and dig and store the tubers indoors in a cool, dry place. Tubers can also be started indoors in February or March in 4-inch pots filled with porous, quickly draining potting medium. Lightly cover the tubers with peat or sphagnum moss. Place the container in a warm (60° to 70° F), bright place. Water sparingly until growth begins, then water more often. Do not set plants outside until danger of frost has passed.

**Rain lily** see *Zephyranthes*

## Scilla (SIL-a)
Squill

A genus of bulbous lily-family members grown for their early-spring blooms. Narrow, grasslike leaves are borne at the base of the plant. Foliage usually appears with the flowers, which are small and bell-shaped. Blooms are borne in few- to many-flowered racemes and are blue, white or purple. Squills are grown in rock and woodland gardens, under deciduous shrubs and trees, and can be easily naturalized. Zones 4-11.

**Selected species and varieties.** *S. bifolia,* twinleaf squill, bears two or sometimes three narrow, 8-inch-long leaves. Flowers, which are borne in clusters of three to eight, are starlike, ½-inch-wide, and blue in color. 'Alba' bears white flowers. 'Rosea' is a pink-

NARCISSUS CYCLAMINEUS

POLIANTHES TUBEROSA 'SINGLE MEXICAN'

SCILLA PERUVIANA

SCILLA SIBERICA

SPREKELIA FORMOSISSIMA

TRITELEIA LAXA 'QUEEN FABIOLA'

flowered cultivar. *S. peruviana,* Cuban lily, Peruvian jacinth, hyacinth-of-Peru, is an 18-inch plant with 1-foot-long, 1-inch-wide leaves. Flowers are ½-inch long, purple or reddish, although white forms also exist. Blooms are borne in spikes of 50 or more. Zones 9-11.

*S. siberica,* Siberian squill, is a 4- to 6-inch plant with deep blue, ½-inch-wide flowers that are nodding and bell-shaped. Blooms are borne three to five per cluster. 'Alba' is a white-flowered cultivar. 'Spring Beauty' is a large-flowered form with deep blue blooms. Collection in the wild has endangered the species; purchase from reputable dealers that sell only propagated bulbs. *S. tubergeniana* resembles *S. siberica* but is only 5 inches tall. Flowers are cup-shaped, 1½ inches wide, and white or pale blue. Zones 5-11. Collection in the wild has endangered the species; purchase from reputable dealers that sell only propagated bulbs.

**Growing conditions.** Grow squill in full sun or partial shade in a location with rich, well-drained, somewhat sandy soil. Siberian squill is able to grow under evergreens, where few other plants are able to survive. Plant bulbs in early fall at a depth of three times the height of the bulb. Plants will multiply rapidly, and benefit from an occasional fall mulching with well-rotted manure or compost.

**Scilla** see also *Endymion*
**Snowdrop** see *Galanthus*
**Snowflake** see *Leucojum*
**Spanish bluebell** see *Endymion*
**Spider lily** see *Crinum; Hymenocallis; Lycoris*

**Sprekelia** (spre-KEE-lee-a)

A one-species genus native to Mexico and classified in the amaryllis family. Plants arise from bulbs and have long narrow leaves and solitary, two-lipped flowers. Sprekelia can be grown outdoors in beds or borders in the South and Southwest; grown indoors in the North. Zones 9-11.

**Selected species and varieties.** *S. formosissima,* Aztec lily, Jacobean lily, orchid amaryllis, is a 1-foot-tall species with narrow leaves that appear with the flowers. *Sprekelia* blooms are bright red, 4 inches long and borne one per leafless, 12-inch-tall stalk. Flowers, which appear in summer, have three upright petal-like segments and three lower segments that form an orchidlike lip.

**Growing conditions.** Sprekelia species can be grown outdoors in the warmest parts of Zones 9-11, where they prefer a sunny site with rich, sandy, well-drained soil. When they are grown outdoors, flowers appear in late spring. In the North, plant bulbs indoors in pots in late fall or winter for late-winter bloom. Leave a 2-inch space between the bulb and the edge of the pot, and plant the bulbs with the upper half above the soil surface. Use a rich, sandy potting soil to which bone meal has been added. Keep plants barely moist and in a warm, dark place until growth begins. Move plants to a bright spot out of direct sun for flowering. Remove stalks after flowering, feed twice a month with a weak fertilizer and keep watering until fall, when the leaves will begin to yellow. Store plants dry and repot them in late fall or early winter. To force for spring bloom, store potted in dry soil at 50° to 60°F for 8 to 12 weeks in winter.

**Spring beauty** see *Claytonia*
**Spring starflower** see *Ipheion*
**Squill** see *Scilla*
**Star lily** see *Lilium*
**Stars-of-Persia** see *Allium*
**Swamp lily** see *Crinum*
**Sword lily** see *Gladiolus*
**Taro** see *Colocasia*

**Triteleia** (try-TEL-ee-a)

A genus of North American amaryllis-family members that arise from corms and have narrow leaves and umbels of small, six-petaled flowers. In the West, they make fine additions to native plant gardens, naturalized areas and perennial borders. In the East, they can be grown in rock gardens. Zones 6-11.

**Selected species and varieties.** *T. hyacinthina,* wild hyacinth, has narrow, grasslike leaves and 2½-foot flower stalks topped with umbels of ½-inch flowers that are white, blue or lilac. *T. laxa,* grass nut, triplet lily, Ithuriel's spear, is a 2½-foot-tall plant with umbels of 1¼- to 1¾-inch flowers that are trumpet-shaped and violet-purple, blue or sometimes white. The cultivar 'Queen Fabiola' has deep blue or violet flowers with darker midribs. It grows 12 inches tall and has grasslike leaves.

**Growing conditions.** Plant triteleias outdoors in fall in a location with full sun and well-drained sandy or gritty soil. Plant the corms at a depth of 3 to 5 inches and space them 2 to 3 inches apart. These plants are easy to grow in the West, but are intolerant of wet eastern summers. In the East, keep the plants evenly moist while the flowers are in bloom and the foliage is green, in spring and early summer. After the foliage dies down, dig the corms and store them in a dry place over the summer. Replant in fall. In the West, plants can be left undisturbed for many years.

**Tiger lily** see *Lilium*
**Tuberose** see *Polianthes*
**Tulip** see *Tulipa*

**Tulipa** (TOO-lip-a)
Tulip

A genus of hardy, spring-blooming bulbs in the lily family. Leaves are usually borne at the base of the plant but occasionally on the stem, and are generally thick and leathery. Most tulips have bluish green foliage; a few species and hybrids have mottled foliage. Flowers are showy, erect and cup-shaped. Each has six tepals (three petal-like sepals and three true petals) that are identical. Blooms come in most colors except true blue.

There are between 50 and 150 species of tulips as well as thousands of hybrids, which have been developed by breeders over the centuries. Hybrid tulips are much more commonly grown than the species. All of the species and hybrid tulips have been separated into 15 divisions according to bloom time, flower form and parent species. The divisions have been further organized into four groups: Species and their hybrids; Early; Midseason; and Late, or May-Flowering. By selecting a variety of tulips from several divisions and each of the four groups, gardeners can plan for a long spring tulip display. Tall hybrid tulips are grown in beds and borders. Species Tulips and their cultivars are grown as edging plants at the front of borders and in rock gardens. Most make fine cut flowers. Zones 4-11.

**Selected species and varieties.** Species Tulips, *T. acuminata,* Turkish tulip, is a 1- to 1 ½-foot-tall species with 4-inch-long flowers that are yellow or light pink. The tepals are very narrow and pointed, and blooms appear in late spring. Zones 4-8. *T. batalinii* is a 5- to 6-inch species with grasslike leaves and yellow, 2-inch-long flowers that appear in early spring. Zones 4-8. *T. clusiana,* lady tulip, candy-stick tulip, is 15 inches tall and has small, fragrant, 2-inch-long flowers that appear in late spring. Blooms reddish purple at the base, white or yellowish at the tip, and striped with pinkish red on the outside. Zones 4-8. *T. humilis* bears 2½-inch-long flowers with pointed tepals atop 4-inch plants. Blooms are reddish green outside, pale purple with a yellow blotch at the base inside. Zones 4-8. *T. kolpakowkiana* is a 6-inch species that bears one or two early-spring flowers that are 2 inches long and yellow and slightly reddish outside. Zones 4-8.

*T. orphanidea* is an 8- to 12-inch species with narrow leaves and solitary flowers that appear in early spring. Blooms are orange to brown or yellow and marked with green outside. Tepals are pointed at the tips and the flowers are 2 inches long. Zones 5-8. *T. praestans* bears one to four 2-inch-long flowers atop 12-inch plants. Blooms are red without a central blotch and appear in early spring. 'Fuselier' bears stems of three or four scarlet-orange flowers. Zones 5-8.

*T. pulchella* bears cup-shaped flowers that open flat atop 4- to 6-inch plants in early spring. Blooms are 1½ inches long and red to purple in color, paler inside. Zones 5-8. *T. saxatilis* produces bulbs at the end of creeping stolons and blooms in midspring. Flowers are borne one to three per 12-inch stem and are cup-shaped, fragrant, 2 inches long and pale pinkish-purple with a large yellow blotch at the base. Zones 4-8.

*T. sylvestris* is an 8- to 12-inch-tall species with strap-shaped leaves and weak stems that blooms in late spring. Flowers are 2 inches long, somewhat starlike, fragrant and bright yellow in color. *T. tarda* has narrow, strap-shaped leaves and few-flowered clusters of yellow, starlike flowers edged in white. Blooms are 2 inches long and appear in early spring atop 5-inch plants. The species is long-lived. Zones 4-8. *T. turkestanica* is an 8-inch species

TULIPA HUMILIS

TULIPA PRAESTANS 'FUSELIER'

TULIPA FOSTERANA 'PURISSIMA'

TULIPA GREIGII 'YELLOW DAWN'

TULIPA 'DUTCH FAIR'

TULIPA 'ELIZABETH ARDEN'

that bears one to six 1¼-inch-long flowers that are white with an orange-yellow base. Blooms are star- or lily-like and appear in early spring. Zones 4-8. *T. wilsoniana* bears bright red flowers with a black blotch at the base of the bloom. Blooms are 2 inches long and appear atop 8-inch plants. Zones 4-8.

There are three divisions of tulips that have been developed from specific species and closely resemble the parent species. These are Fosterana Tulips, Greigii Tulips and Kaufmanniana Tulips.

Fosterana Tulips are hybrids and varieties of *T. fosterana,* a species with scarlet blooms marked with a black blotch edged in yellow at the base inside the flowers. Fosterana Tulips are early-flowering, 16- to 18-inch plants with three or four broad leaves and very large blooms that are dark at the base inside. 'Purissima' is a white-flowered variant of 'Red Emperor' and is streaked with yellow at the base inside. Zones 4-8.

Greigii Tulips, hybrids and varieties of *T. greigii*, have large flowers that appear in midspring and attractive foliage mottled with maroon. They exhibit characteristics of *T. greigii*, a 6- to 9-inch species with broad, waxy-margined leaves that are mottled with purple brown. The species has 3-inch-long, scarlet-orange flowers with a black blotch edged in yellow at the base inside the flower. 'Yellow Dawn' has rose-red petals edged with yellow. Zones 4-8.

Kaufmanniana Tulips are hybrids and varieties of *T. kaufmanniana* and are commonly called water lily tulips because of the flowers' resemblance to water lilies. *T. kaufmanniana* is an 8-inch species with 3-inch-long flowers that open flat and are somewhat starlike. Kaufmanniana Tulips are generally the earliest tulips to bloom and range from 5 to 10 inches tall. Blooms may be white, pink, red or yellow, and have a yellow blotch at the base. Plants have three to five broad leaves that are pointed at the tip and may be solid green or mottled with maroon. Zones 4-8.

Early Tulips, comprising both Single Early Tulips and Double Early Tulips, bloom in early spring and are good for forcing in pots. They are the first of the hybrid tulips to bloom and are somewhat shorter than other hybrids, ranging from 9 to 16, or sometimes 20, inches tall.

Single Early Tulips have large, long-lasting flowers that are single (six-petaled), cup-shaped, 2 to 4 inches long and often fragrant. Blooms come in a wide variety of colors, including red, yellow, orange and white. Zones 4-8.

Double Early Tulips have many-petaled flowers that somewhat resemble peonies and come in a wide range of colors. Blooms are 3 to 4 inches wide. Zones 4-8.

Midseason Tulips comprise the Triumph Tulips and Darwin Hybrid Tulips. These bloom in middle to late spring.

Triumph Tulips are generally crosses between Single Early Tulips and later-flowering hybrids. They have large, strong, 1- to 2-foot stems and 2- to 4-inch-long flowers. Triumph Tulips come in a variety of colors and may be striped or edged with contrasting colors. Zones 4-8.

Darwin Hybrid Tulips are the result of crosses between Darwin hybrids and *T. fosterana*. They bear single, 3-to 4-inch-long blooms atop sturdy, 2-foot stems. Flowers come in a wide variety of colors and often have a dark central blotch. 'Dutch Fair' flowers are golden yellow streaked with scarlet, except at the base, which is bluish black. 'Elizabeth Arden' produces rose-pink blooms. Zones 4-8.

Late, or May-Flowering, Tulips include Single Late Tulips, Lily-Flowered Tulips, Rembrandt Tulips, Parrot Tulips, and Double Late Tulips (also called Peony-Flowered Tulips).

Single Late Tulips are 2- to 2½-foot plants with sturdy stems and single, 3- to 4-inch-long flowers that have a satiny texture and come in a wide variety of colors, including many pastels not available in other hybrid groups. In profile, the blooms look square-based and rectangular.

Lily-Flowered Tulips bloom just before the Single Late Tulips and are crosses between Cottage Tulips and *T. retroflexa*. They bear single 2- to 4-inch-long blooms with pointed tepals that curve outward. 'West Point' has golden yellow blooms. Zones 4-8.

Rembrandt Tulips are 1½- to 2½-foot plants with white, yellow or red blooms striped or marked with black, brown, purple, red or pink. Zones 4-8.

Parrot Tulips have fringed, ruffled tepals that give the flowers an orchid-like form. Blooms appear in late spring, are 6 to 7 inches wide and come in a variety of colors. The stems are often weak, so Parrot Tulips should be planted where they are protected from wind. Zones 4-8.

Double Late Tulips are from 1 to 2 feet tall and have long-lasting, many-petaled blooms that are 6 inches wide and come in a variety of colors. 'Clara Carder' has rose-purple flowers that are white at the base. Zones 4-8.

**Growing conditions.** Tulips perform best when grown in sun, and require a minimum of five to six hours of full sun per day. Grow them in very well-drained, deeply prepared soil that is somewhat sandy and rich in organic matter. Plant the bulbs in late fall, and be sure to store them in a cool place before planting. Bulbs exposed to temperatures above 70° F for even a short time will produce flowers that are one-half to one-third normal size. It is also a good idea to purchase from dealers who have proper cool-storage facilities. Set bulbs at a depth of 4 to 8 inches, depending on the size of the bulb. (Smaller bulbs are planted closer to the surface than larger ones.) Tulips planted at a depth of 1 foot will bloom for several years but will produce fewer offsets than bulbs planted closer to the surface. Feed plants in spring with a balanced fertilizer. Allow the foliage to ripen naturally, allowing it to produce food for the following years' bloom. Bulbs can be dug and divided if they have become crowded after the foliage has faded.

Many gardeners treat tulips as annuals, because they tend to bloom less reliably after the first year. In that case, they are dug after the flowers have faded and are discarded. Tulips are eaten by mice and chipmunks. They can also be infected with virus diseases, which will cause the flowers to be striped with white or green. Infected bulbs should be dug and discarded. In Zones 9-11 tulips can be grown as annuals, provided the bulbs are stored for six to eight weeks at 40° to 45° F before planting in late fall or early winter. To force Single and Double Early tulip hybrids for late winter or early spring bloom, store potted in moist soil at 40° to 48° F for 13 to 15 weeks in fall.

**Turk's-cap lily** see *Lilium*
**Windflower** see *Anemone*
**Winter aconite** see *Eranthis*
**Wood hyacinth** see Endymion
**Wood lily** see *Lilium*
**Yellow bell** see *Fritillaria*
**Zantedeschia** see Dictionary of Houseplants, page 552

**Zephyranthes** (zef-i-RAN-theez)
Zephyr lily, rain lily, fairy lily

A genus of bulbous species in the amaryllis family with grasslike leaves and solitary, funnel-shaped flowers that have flaring segments. Blooms may be white, yellow, pink or red. Zephyr lilies are planted at the front of borders and in rock gardens, and are used for naturalizing. Zones 7-11; in the North, bulbs can be dug in fall and replanted in spring.

**Selected species and varieties.** *Z. atamasco,* atamasco lily, fairy lily, has narrow, 12-inch leaves and white flowers that may be tinged with purple. Blooms are borne atop 12-inch stems and have flaring, lilylike perianth segments. Plants bloom in early spring. *Z. candida* bears grasslike, 1-foot-long leaves and white, 1-inch-long flowers that appear from summer to fall. Zones 9-11. *Z. citrina* has bright yellow, 2-inch-long flowers that somewhat resemble crocuses. Blooms appear from late summer to fall. Zones 9-11. *Z. grandiflora* bears 1-foot-long leaves and rose or pink flowers that are 4 inches across and 3 inches long. Blooms appear in late spring to summer. Zones 9-11. *Z. longifolia* is a 6-inch-tall species that has 1-inch-long flowers that are bright yellow inside and copper-colored outside. Zones 9-11. *Z. rosea* resembles *Z. grandiflora* but has broader leaves and rose-pink, 1-inch-long flowers. Blooms appear in fall. Zones 9-11.

**Growing conditions.** Grow zephyr lilies in full sun and rich, well-drained soil that remains moist while the foliage is above the ground. Plant the bulbs in spring (in fall in the Deep South and the Southwest) at a depth of three to four times the height of the bulbs. Space plants 2 to 3 inches apart. *Z. atamasco* requires a site that is very well drained in winter and should be planted in a warm, sheltered location near the northern limit of its hardiness. In the North, bulbs can be dug after flowering and stored in moist sand during the winter.

**Zephyr lily** see *Zephyranthes*

TULIPA 'WEST POINT'

TULIPA 'CLARA CARDER'

ZEPHYRANTHES GRANDIFLORA

# 7

# ROSES

*The smooth, shapely petals of a pink and yellow 'Granada' rose gleam above a strong, straight stem. Evenly shaded coloring, symmetrical form and spiraling flower centers are characteristic of prizewinning roses.*

Symbol of love and beauty for thousands of years, the rose probably has more admirers than any other flower. Most roses are descended from a handful of classic types, some of them dating back to pre-Biblical times. And for all their varied forms, most require essentially the same kind of treatment. They need sun and a soil rich in nutrients that encourage healthy roots and blossoms.

The plants should go into the ground early enough for the roots to become established before top growth starts—a planting time that varies with climate and geography. But planting time also depends on the form in which the rose is delivered. Dormant plants, delivered "bare-root," without soil, should go into the ground earlier than those that are potted in a growing medium when purchased. Details on such matters are discussed in this chapter, along with the special handling required for growing roses in containers, and for using roses as a screen or a hedge.

Although there is no mystery to growing roses, keep in mind that instructions will constantly refer to operations performed on rose *canes*—the horticulturist's term for rose stems. Keep in mind too that many modern roses are actually two plants in one, a cultivated top grafted onto a sturdier root. The graft—called a bud, or graft, union—is visible as a thickening, knotlike growth at the top of the rootstock, and should never be tampered with. Depending on locale, this graft should be planted either slightly above or below the level of the soil *(page 324)*.

Roses typically reward their owners with such an amazing display of bloom that no amount of work involved in their care seems wasted. The care begins in early spring, while the plant is still dor-

# CHAPTER CONTENTS

mant, and lasts until about a month before the first hard frost. This involves a regular program of feeding and watering, and a rigorous program of spraying, for roses are prone to attack by mildew and fungus, and by pests such as aphids, mites and the infamous Japanese beetle. For some roses, such as tree roses and climbers, the routine chores include staking and tying. And, as winter approaches, almost all roses need some kind of protection. Finally, there are the season-long jobs of deadheading and disbudding *(Chapter 2)* and the related job of pruning.

Sooner or later, most gardeners who take roses seriously are tempted to try their hands at creating a new rose or duplicating an old favorite. They embark on a botanical adventure that is very likely to be fascinating every step of the way. Propagating roses involves familiar tools and materials, and the simple procedures described in this chapter. Refer to Chapter 2 for additional techniques for propagating roses, including starting plants from seeds, layering, planting stem cuttings and creating your own hybrids.

For roses to succeed they need a helping hand, a willing heart and what may seem at times like constant attention. In fact, with a little intelligent planning, many of the traditional problems of rose culture can be bypassed or simplified. Winter cold, for example, will be easier to deal with if the rose variety is suited to the zone in which it is to be planted; the zone map *(inside front cover)* will clarify this correlation. Using the same map in conjunction with the checklist of chores on pages 352-355, gardeners can fit their seasonal activities to local climate conditions. Intelligent planning can also minimize the problems of pests and diseases; using the Troubleshooting Guide may help you beat trouble before it starts.

# ROSES—
# AN ANCIENT AND EXTENDED FAMILY

*Shimmering with brilliant color, the petals of an 'Apothecary's Rose' look much as they did in medieval times, when this ancient plant was much prized by alchemists for its sweet and lasting perfume and for its medicinal properties; potions made from it were used to soothe upset stomachs and heal skin lesions. The 'Apothecary' is a member of the old strain of roses called gallica.*

Part of the fascination of planting and nurturing roses is selecting which ones to put in the garden. The choices are rich and varied almost beyond counting. Mankind was cultivating roses at the dawn of history 5,000 years ago and has been busy at it ever since. The ancient Chinese bred roses, as did the Greeks and Romans; Europeans of the Renaissance made rose culture a quasi-religious passion. In more recent times, growers from many nations have steadily added more varieties by crossbreeding some of the earth's original wild roses, or crossing them with antique Oriental and European hybrids, or mating recent hybrids with older ones or with one another. The result has been untold thousands of varieties, many of them relatively new, others dating back to the Middle Ages and before.

The roses illustrated at right and on the following six pages show, first, the basic types of blooms and, second, the most interesting and significant classes—both historically and botanically—that are available today. From among them a rose enthusiast should be able to choose an intriguing mixture of the best, most beautiful and most fascinating of the world's roses.

# THE FOUR TYPES OF BLOSSOMS

The blooms of all roses assume one or another of the four shapes or forms illustrated below. The main differences are in the number of petals—which varies from as few as five to more than 200—and in the petals' arrangement. It is from the arrangement—the number of petal layers—that the blossom types get their descriptive if not very elegant names: single, semidouble, double and very double.

## SINGLE BLOSSOM
The simplest of rose blossoms, the single has five to 12 petals arranged on the same plane and not enclosing one another. All wild roses have single flowers.

## THE SEMIDOUBLE
As its name implies, this sort of bloom is a halfway stop between a single and a double. It has two strata of 13 to 24 petals, but they are neither as numerous nor as closely furled as the petals in the true double.

## DOUBLE FLOWER
A double flower has two complete and concentric rings of outer petals—and almost invariably a prominent central portion of more petals that encloses the pistils and stamens. The number of petals may vary from 25 or so to about 50 in the most lavish ones.

## VERY DOUBLE BLOOM
Far the most extravagant-looking form of rose blossom, the very double grows anywhere from 50 to 200 small petals, which cluster in a number of tight rings or layers. It may be what rosarians call "button-eyed," having a single center formed by very tiny unopened petals *(above)*, or it may be "quartered," with petals arranged somewhat like a pinwheel, in three, four or five separate clusters.

# THE WILD ROSES

The earth's wild varieties, called species roses, are the ancestors of all the cultivated roses, and they continue to flourish around the world. In fact, 200 species of them still exist. Some grow as shrubs, some as climbers. All are hardy and they self-pollinate, producing seedlings that (unlike those of hybrids) duplicate the parent plant. The wild roses native to Europe and North America bloom only once a season, but those of the Orient bloom repeatedly.

**SPECIES ROSE**
Wild roses are always single, have only five petals and all show yellow stamens at the center. They can be showy, with bright shades of yellow, pink or red.

# OLD GARDEN ROSES: THE HISTORIC CLASSES

The most ancient of the classes is one simply called China, which was bred by Chinese gardeners perhaps 5,000 years ago. The oldest of the European classes is gallica, which dates back at least to the first century A.D. It was only after traders brought Chinese roses back to Europe and crossbred them that Western roses became repeat bloomers. The finest and most important of the older cultivated roses are shown below, at right and opposite. Some have been favorite garden roses for many centuries.

**GALLICA**
Hardy plants that bloom once a season, members of the gallica family have single or double blossoms in pink, red, or red and white stripes. The Red Rose of Lancaster, symbol of one faction in the 15th Century Wars of the Roses, was a gallica.

**DAMASK**
An ancient class of roses brought from the Middle East to Europe by Crusaders, damasks are hardy and have double or semidouble blooms that may be white, pink or red.

318

## MUSK
Named for their often strong musky fragrance, these roses have been cultivated in Europe and the Mediterranean basin for many centuries. Musks are hardy plants with arching canes and flowers that may be either single or double and either white or pink in color. Like most other old Western roses, most musks bloom only once in each growing season, usually in the spring. A few bloom in summer, then again in autumn.

## CHINA
The most important variety brought to Europe from the Orient by British traders in the late 18th Century, the China rose became popular both for crossbreeding and for its own small but decorative semidouble pink or red flowers.

## TEA
Another ancient Chinese plant, the tea rose came to the West in the 19th Century. It has been repeatedly crossbred with other varieties, producing today's large and varied class of hybrid tea roses. Not particularly hardy, the typical tea has large, showy blooms in lovely shades of cream, yellow and pink. Its fragrance suggests tea leaves, thus the name.

## ALBA

Cultivated at least since the Middle Ages, alba is a natural hybrid of gallica and a Mediterranean species rose called *Rosa canina*. The alba produces a handsome show of blossoms that may be pale pink or white (alba means "white" in Latin) once a year. The White Rose that symbolized the House of York, enemy of the Lancastrians in England's Wars of the Roses, is thought to have been a cultivar known as 'Alba Semi-Plena.'

## CENTIFOLIA

As the name implies, centifolias produce luxuriant very double blooms with 100 petals or more. They may be red, pink or white. These old roses, which date back to the 16th Century, are also known as cabbage roses because their petals overlap rather like the leaves on a head of cabbage, and as Provence roses for the part of France where they were once widely grown.

## MOSS

Originally a mutation of centifolia, this 17th Century rose is also hardy and produces similarly large, globular blossoms of pale pink or red. The difference is that the moss has patches of velvety green mosslike sheen on its sepals and stems.

## PORTLAND
The first European rose to bloom more than once a season, it was originally bred in Italy by crossing damask and China strains, then brought to England, where it was named for an 18th Century rose fancier, the Duchess of Portland. The plant is not very hardy, but it produces lovely double blooms that may be pink, red or purple.

## BOURBON
Another descendant of the damask and China classes, this rose was first grown by French colonists on the Isle of Bourbon in the Indian Ocean, then brought to France in the early 1800s. Bourbons like Portlands, are repeat bloomers, producing single or double blossoms of white, pink, red or purple.

## NOISETTE
First bred in 1828 by a South Carolina planter who crossed musk and China roses, the plant was soon taken to France by a man named Noisette, hence the roses' name. The flowers are quite varied, some cultivars producing single blooms, others producing very doubles, and the colors range from white through various pinks to purple.

## HYBRID PERPETUAL
Among the most complex of older hybrids—their ancestry includes Chinas, Bourbons, Portlands and Noisettes—the perpetuals became the favorite garden roses of Victorian times for their ability to bloom more frequently than any roses bred in the West before. More than 1,000 varieties were bred then and perhaps 100 are still grown today. They are hardy plants, producing very double flowers of white, pink and maroon.

# THE MODERN CULTIVARS

Over the last century and a quarter, botanists and rose breeders have developed the half-dozen new families or classes of roses shown here—the moderns that dominate today's plant catalogs and gardens. They are a varied group, ranging from splashy hybrid teas and large shrubs to small, adaptable miniatures. Most have been crossbred for hardiness as well as for beautiful blooms, and for increased resistance to disease. The modern cultivars come in a profusion of colors and forms, and most of them put on luxuriant, season-long shows of flowers.

POLYANTHA
Descended from China roses and an Asian species rose called *Rosa multiflora,* polyanthas are very hardy and produce large clusters of small flowers that may be single or double, and white, pink, yellow and even orange in color.

HYBRID TEA
Among the best of modern roses, with their full, handsome blossoms, hybrid teas were also the first, dating back to 1867, when a French botanist crossed hybrid perpetuals with older tea roses. Hundreds of varieties of hybrid teas have appeared since. They are distinguished by their long stems and their flowers ranging in shape from singles to high-centered doubles and very doubles, and in color from white, pink and red to an unusual brilliant yellow.

FLORIBUNDA
These roses, descended from polyanthas and hybrid teas, were first developed in Denmark in 1911. True to their name, which means flowering in abundance, they grow clusters of blooms—some of them rich very doubles—throughout the season. The blooms may be high-centered or cupped; the stems are long; the colors are white, yellow, orange, pink, red and lavender.

## SHRUB

Answering a need for tall, tough, bushlike roses, the shrub varieties were first bred shortly after World War I from a wide mixture of antecedents. Some shrubs reach 10 feet tall, most at least 6, and all are very hardy, which makes them useful for many landscaping purposes. The blossoms are single to double and may be white, pink, red, yellow, orange or purple.

## MINIATURES

The opposite of large shrub roses, miniatures reach only 10 to 18 inches in height and their blooms are to scale: clusters of small single to very double flowers varying from white to orange to purple. The first ones were bred early in this century by a Colonel Roulet from a dwarf Chinese rose that was later given the Latin name *Rosa rouletti* in his honor. They only became widely available, however, in the 1960s.

## GRANDIFLORA

The newest class of roses, introduced in Great Britain in 1954, grandifloras are descended from hybrid teas and floribundas. The best varieties grow up to 10 feet tall and produce large double flowers in white, pink, red, yellow or orange. The first cultivar was 'Queen Elizabeth,' named for the recently crowned Elizabeth II.

# CHOOSING BARE-ROOT ROSES AND PLANTING THEM RIGHT

alf the job of growing handsome roses is selecting trouble-free plants in the first place. This means checking them over carefully, starting with the roots. Most roses stocked by nurseries and mail-order houses, although grown in soil beds, are sold with bare roots—that is, with the roots removed from the earth and wrapped in peat moss and plastic. Undo the wrapping and look to see if there is any breakage. Minor damage that can be trimmed is acceptable; battered roots are not. The plant roots should also be firm, supple and moist; dry, brittle ones are clearly unhealthy.

Next, examine the top part. The canes, or stalks, should also be strong and firm, and the buds must be dormant, looking plump but tightly closed. Roses showing signs of imminent blooms will not acclimate well and grow. Equally important are the so-called bud, or graft, unions *(below, right)*, which should be firm and solid. A soft, corky growth indicates a bacterial disease called crown gall, which is fatal to roses. If plants bought by mail order have badly damaged roots or indications of disease and rot, they should be returned for a refund. A problem plant seen in a nursery should not be bought.

A rose that passes inspection should have its roots soaked in water as soon as you remove it from the peat moss packing. Roses need a good drink before being planted, and at least 2 gallons of water per week for the rest of the growing season. (They need no watering in winter, when they are dormant.) The spot chosen for planting should be sunny; roses need an average of six hours of sun a day in order to prosper. And the ground itself needs to be well worked and rich. If the area has not been double-dug recently *(pages 56-57)*, the soil will require some attention. How to do this—and all the other steps in planting a rosebush—are shown opposite and on the following two pages.

A 'Trumpeter' rose—one of the floribunda hybrids—bursts with theatrically brilliant scarlet blooms. Planted bare-root in the early spring, floribundas quickly establish themselves in a garden and flower luxuriantly in about eight weeks.

## BUD UNIONS

Many commercially available roses are cultivars, which means one sort of plant was grafted into the rootstock of another. Bud unions, also called bud grafts, are the sites of the grafting—where there are knots or swellings about 4 to 6 inches above the roots. When planting roses according to the instructions on the following pages, the position of the bud union is important.

BUD ONION

324

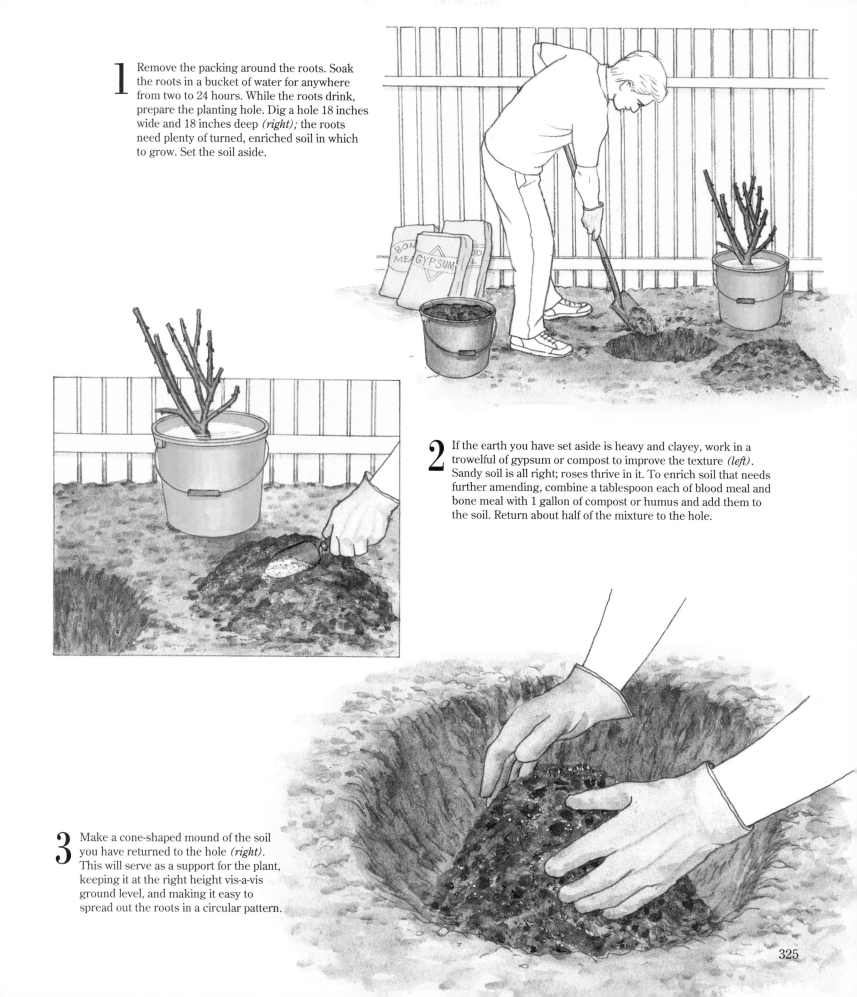

**1** Remove the packing around the roots. Soak the roots in a bucket of water for anywhere from two to 24 hours. While the roots drink, prepare the planting hole. Dig a hole 18 inches wide and 18 inches deep *(right)*; the roots need plenty of turned, enriched soil in which to grow. Set the soil aside.

**2** If the earth you have set aside is heavy and clayey, work in a trowelful of gypsum or compost to improve the texture *(left)*. Sandy soil is all right; roses thrive in it. To enrich soil that needs further amending, combine a tablespoon each of blood meal and bone meal with 1 gallon of compost or humus and add them to the soil. Return about half of the mixture to the hole.

**3** Make a cone-shaped mound of the soil you have returned to the hole *(right)*. This will serve as a support for the plant, keeping it at the right height vis-a-vis ground level, and making it easy to spread out the roots in a circular pattern.

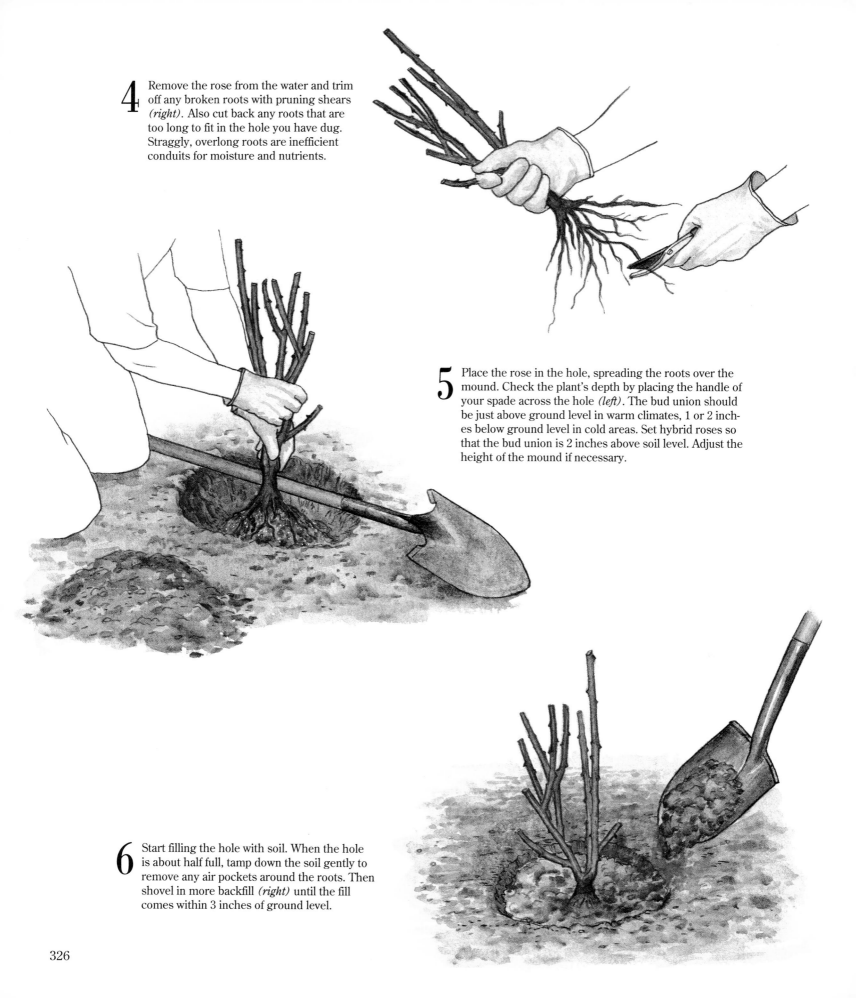

4 Remove the rose from the water and trim off any broken roots with pruning shears *(right)*. Also cut back any roots that are too long to fit in the hole you have dug. Straggly, overlong roots are inefficient conduits for moisture and nutrients.

5 Place the rose in the hole, spreading the roots over the mound. Check the plant's depth by placing the handle of your spade across the hole *(left)*. The bud union should be just above ground level in warm climates, 1 or 2 inches below ground level in cold areas. Set hybrid roses so that the bud union is 2 inches above soil level. Adjust the height of the mound if necessary.

6 Start filling the hole with soil. When the hole is about half full, tamp down the soil gently to remove any air pockets around the roots. Then shovel in more backfill *(right)* until the fill comes within 3 inches of ground level.

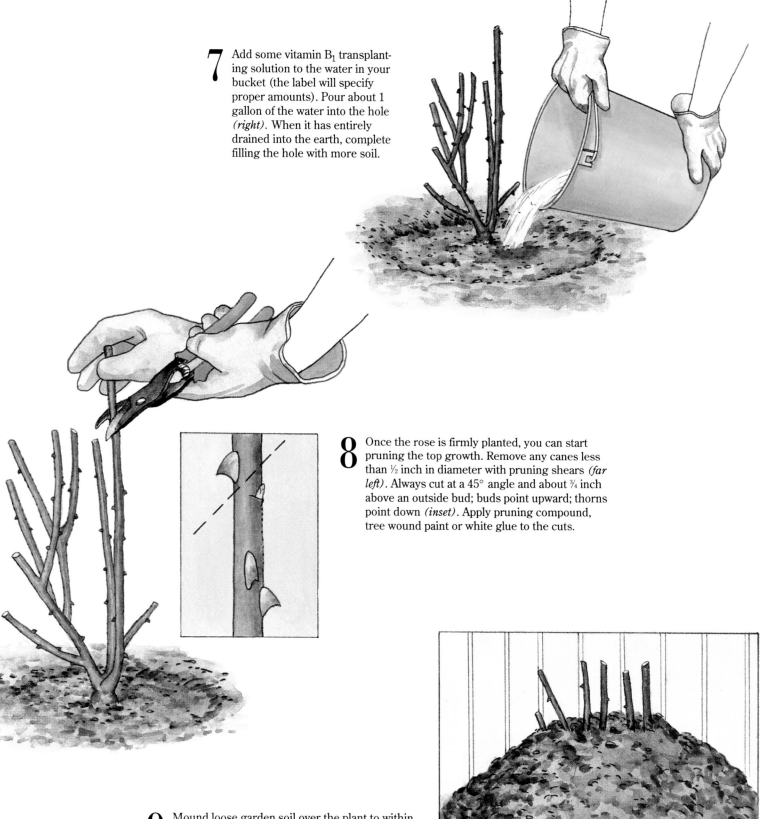

**7** Add some vitamin B$_1$ transplanting solution to the water in your bucket (the label will specify proper amounts). Pour about 1 gallon of the water into the hole *(right)*. When it has entirely drained into the earth, complete filling the hole with more soil.

**8** Once the rose is firmly planted, you can start pruning the top growth. Remove any canes less than ½ inch in diameter with pruning shears *(far left)*. Always cut at a 45° angle and about ¾ inch above an outside bud; buds point upward; thorns point down *(inset)*. Apply pruning compound, tree wound paint or white glue to the cuts.

**9** Mound loose garden soil over the plant to within 3 inches of the tips of the canes *(right)*. Water the mound thoroughly. When new growth appears, remove the mound and cover the area around the plant with a 3-inch layer of mulch, to deflect excess heat and conserve moisture.

# FILLING OUT A GARDEN WITH CONTAINER-GROWN ROSES

Container-grown roses are more expensive to buy than bare-root roses *(pages 324-327)*, but they offer an advantage. Unlike bare-root stock, which must be purchased and planted early, container-grown roses may be planted any time during the growing season. That makes them useful either as midseason additions or as replacements.

Removal from the container is usually a simple matter of sliding out the root ball if the container is plastic *(opposite)* or peeling away the cover if it is paper. If the container is metal, it may be advisable to have the sides slit at the time of purchase to facilitate removal. If the container is made of biodegradable paper or fabric, it need not be removed; it will disintegrate in the soil.

Container-grown roses should be carefully inspected. First make sure the top growth is not diseased and that the canes show no signs of damage. If any leaves or buds have sprouted, inspect them: They should be well formed and healthy. To make sure the plant is not potbound, inspect the holes at the bottom of the container; there should be no roots protruding from them. Then ask the nursery salesperson to pull the plant from its container so you can make sure that the roots are not circling the root ball.

The key to the successful planting of a container-grown rose is its proper placement in the prepared hole. Since the nursery has already established the correct position of the bud union in relation to the soil surface in the container, it is important to maintain that relationship. The bud union should be slightly above ground level in warm climates, 1 or 2 inches below ground level in cold areas. Set hybrid roses so that the bud union is 2 inches above soil level.

*A profusely blooming pale yellow 'Rise 'n' Shine' miniature rose borders a stone walk. Because of their diminutive size, miniature roses are easily grown and maintained in containers, and are often sold that way.*

**1** To plant a potted rose, use a trowel to dig a hole slightly wider and deeper than the pot *(right)*. If the site was not prepared earlier, dig 6 inches deeper and fill the space with organic matter.

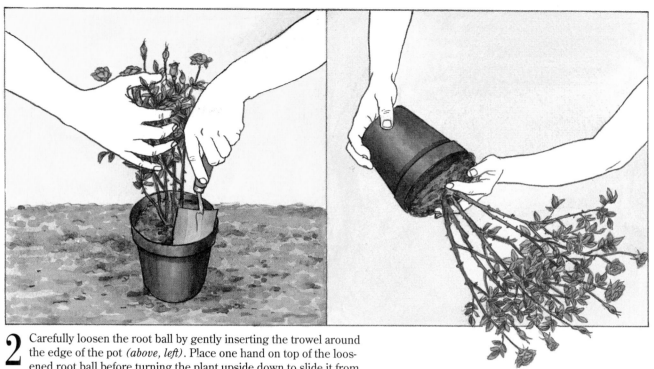

**2** Carefully loosen the root ball by gently inserting the trowel around the edge of the pot *(above, left)*. Place one hand on top of the loosened root ball before turning the plant upside down to slide it from the pot in a single compact cylinder *(above, right)*.

**3** Set the plant in the hole so that the root ball is level with the surface, removing or adding soil if necessary. Fill in around the root ball and tamp down with your hands *(below)*. Water thoroughly and add a layer of mulch around the base to retain moisture.

# A HEDGE OF SHRUB ROSES FOR A BORDER

An informally shaped hedge of 'Simplicity' floribunda roses in bloom creates a bold pink and green border at the edge of a lawn—and provides privacy from the neighbors.

A hedge is a group of plants put to work in the garden. It can protect the garden boundaries, provide a backdrop for other plants or screen an unwanted view. It can also direct people to the path where the gardener wants them to go. With their spreading shapes, shrub roses lend themselves well to use in informal hedges. Instead of being sheared as some formal evergreen hedges are, a rose hedge is allowed to grow naturally. After the hedge has been planted, a light pruning of straggling branches at the beginning of the growing season is all that is needed. Shrub roses will form a dense wall that will be spectacular when in bloom. Only occasional summer grooming may be necessary if the hedge is of a repeat-blooming variety; refer to Chapter 2 for information on deadheading and disbudding.

Shrub roses are apt to come in bare-root form. For the best effect, use roses of one kind so that the shape and flower color are uniform the length of the hedge. In selecting a shrub rose, think not only about color, but also about the shrub's ultimate height at maturity and its growing habit—whether it will give you one big show of flowers or bloom repeatedly, whether it blooms singly or in clusters, whether it produces hips (or seedpods) that remain on the canes into the winter. For the characteristics of different roses, consult the Dictionary of Roses *(pages 360-379)*.

First mark off the area with stakes and string. Measure the length in feet and divide by 2 to calculate the number of plants you need; each rose plant needs 2 feet of room to spread. While the bare-root plants soak in water (for at least two hours before planting), mark the locations where the planting holes should be dug—at 2-foot intervals along the string. Plant as you would any bare-root roses *(pages 324-327)*.

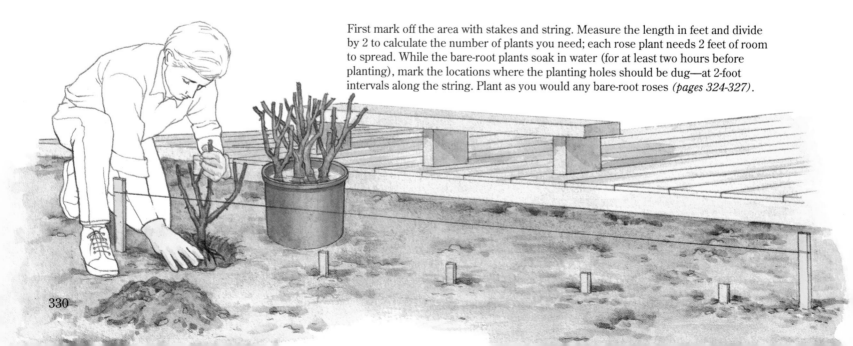

# TRANSPLANTING TO GIVE A ROSE NEW LIFE

A rosebush that is otherwise healthy may fail to thrive because it stands in the shade of taller plants, or because its roots cannot compete for nutrients with the roots of nearby plants. By transplanting to a more hospitable environment, you can give a languishing rosebush a new lease on life. When a few precautions are taken, the procedure is so simple and safe that you may want to employ it for purely esthetic purposes—to brighten up a bare wall or fence, highlight a newly planted bed or revamp the design of your entire garden.

The key to success in transplanting roses is proper care of the root system, which should be kept moist at all times. The best time to transplant is in late winter or early spring, while the plant is dormant. With few if any leaves to keep supplied with water, the roots can devote most of their energy to the job of establishing themselves in the new site.

If you transplant early enough, the root system should be ready to support new foliage when warm weather triggers the next growth. Begin preparations as soon as the ground is workable. Water the plant thoroughly several days in advance; during the move the moistened soil will cling to the roots and help shield them from the drying effects of sun and wind. To further minimize the risks of exposure, wrap the root ball in a plastic sheet or a piece of burlap.

Follow the planting procedure for bareroot roses outlined on pages 324-327. Be sure to dig the new hole and prepare the soil before you lift the plant from the ground.

*Transplanted from cramped quarters to a spacious location in spring, a young 'Keepsake,' a hybrid tea rose is established and blooming well before autumn leaves fall. Transplanting in late winter or early spring when they are dormant gives the plants time to adjust to a new site before they have to use their energy producing summer foliage and flowers.*

# ROSES IN POTS
# TO ENHANCE SMALL SPACES

Small and middle-sized roses can be planted in pots or other containers as well as in the ground. This allows town-house dwellers with limited backyard space to have any number of potted roses on a deck or patio. Householders with bigger gardens can move clusters of pot-grown roses around for variety, or use them to provide color in areas where other plants have finished blooming. Gardeners in northerly regions can bring their potted miniature roses indoors for the winter—where they will thrive as houseplants until spring—and store larger plants in a garage or a cellar.

Containers 12 inches wide and deep are about right for miniatures and other small varieties; larger roses require 16-inch pots. Clay and plastic pots both work well. So do tubs made of decay-resistant woods such as cedar and redwood. Metal containers get too hot in summer. All must have drainage holes in the bottom to keep the roots from getting waterlogged. Potted roses must stand on some sort of pedestal, so excess water will not collect underneath.

Planting roses in containers differs little from putting them in the ground *(pages 324-329)*. The depth of planting varies slightly, however, and using a special potting mixture is vital *(box opposite)*.

Transfer your potting mixture into the planting container until it is about three-fourths full. Then form a mound with the mix to accommodate the rose plant's roots. The top of the mound should be 2 inches or so below the container's rim. Trim off any dead or damaged roots, and spread the healthy roots over the mound. Spread more mix over the roots until the mix reaches the bud union *(page 324)*. Prune back the canes to about 6 inches, as directed on page 327, step 8. Water the plant immediately, then give it a weekly soaking. Roses should never dry out completely. Apply liquid or dry fertilizer every month or so.

*In a large terra-cotta pot on a brick terrace, the pink blossoms of a floribunda rise above a cascading, purple lobelia. Growing in containers, the plants can be moved about from time to time to change the look of the garden.*

## HYBRIDS FOR THE HOBBYIST

To the delight of rose enthusiasts everywhere, new rose hybrids from various classes enter the marketplace every year. Most of these flowers undergo a rigorous, 2-year testing process that evaluates characteristics such as disease-resistance, bud and flower form, color and fragrance. Only the most highly rated flowers carry the All-American Rose Selection (AARS) tag of approval. Some former AARS winners include: 'Europeana,' 'Mister Lincoln,' 'Peace,' 'Pink Parfait,' 'Queen Elizabeth' and 'Tiffany' (see Dictionary of Roses, pages 360-379).

The avid amateur can enter a successful hybrid in competition. For example, 'Sheer Elegance' *(right)*, a 1991 AARS winner, entered by a commercial nursery, was hybridized by a nonprofessional. Competitions are held at the local, regional and national levels. Consult your local American Rose Society member for specific regulations and entrance requirements.

# A ROUNDED DIET FOR HEALTHY ROSES

Roses have hearty appetites. To keep on producing beautiful blooms, sturdy stems and healthy foliage, they require three indispensable nutrients: nitrogen, phosphorus and potassium. Fertilizer labels carry three numbers that give the percentages of nitrogen, phosphorus and potassium (in that order) that the mix contains. Only a soil test will tell you exactly what formulation is best for your garden. But the fertilizer most commonly used for roses in northerly climates is labeled 15-15-15, which means that 45 percent of the mix (by weight) consists of equal parts of the three main nutrients. The other 55 percent is filler, with traces of elements such as sulfur, calcium, magnesium, manganese, iron and zinc. In the South, 10-10-10 fertilizer is commonly used.

You can feed roses with granular fertilizer, spikes or liquid fertilizer. The granular and spike forms release their nutrients at once or little by little; the liquids act right away. Whichever you use, read the label carefully: Inadequate nutrition stunts growth; too much can weaken plants, making them susceptible to disease.

Roses should be fed on a regular schedule. Apply granular fertilizer at the start of the growing season, at the end of each bloom cycle (roughly six weeks) and nine to 12 weeks before the first frost in your area. One caution: If you have just planted roses in spring, give them about four weeks to establish themselves before starting to fertilize; young roots are fragile and can be burned if they are fertilized before they have time to establish themselves. Time-release fertilizer delivers nutrients to the soil slowly but steadily over a four-month period. Apply it twice, once at the beginning and once again at the end of the growing season, six to eight weeks before the first frost.

During the bloom cycle and for special occasions, a supplemental dose of liquid fertilizer will brighten color and increase bloom size; with results visible within 10 days.

A day before you plan to apply a granular fertilizer, thoroughly water the soil under each rose plant. When you are ready to fertilize, measure the precise amount of fertilizer called for on the label and sprinkle it evenly on the drip line—the circle directly below the outermost foliage, from which rainwater drips into the soil. Next, with a trowel or a garden fork, break up the soil surface and work the grains of fertilizer into the top 2 inches of soil all around the plant. Sprinkle water on the area around the plant to dissolve the nutrients and make them available to the plant's roots.

## POTTING MIXTURE FOR ROSES

To make the potting mixture that roses thrive on, combine 1 gallon of organic matter (peat moss, shredded bark and leaf mold) with ½ gallon of perlite, ½ gallon of vermiculite, 1 trowelful of superphosphate and ½ trowelful each of dolomite lime and trace minerals (manganese, zinc, sulfur, calcium, magnesium and iron) with 1 gallon of soil.

# HYBRIDS AND CLIMBERS— PREPARING FOR THE WINTER

Species roses, shrub roses and many old garden roses are hardy and live unharmed through the coldest Maine and Minnesota winters. But a majority of the modern hybrids such as teas, floribundas, grandifloras and large flowering climbers are highly sensitive to frigid weather. If hit with a deep North Country freeze, they can turn black and die virtually overnight. They need protection anywhere that winter temperatures get down around zero or below. To find out about temperature ranges and which roses require winterizing, consult the Zone Map *(inside front cover)* and the Dictionary of Roses *(pages 360-379)*.

For the less hardy roses, winter preparations should begin right after autumn's initial hard frost. First comes some cutting back *(below)*. Then, in extremely cold areas, bush roses and especially tall tree varieties may need to be buried for the duration in a trench with a thick covering of earth *(pages 336-339)*. In regions with less punishing temperatures, rose plants can be adequately shielded simply by piling earth around the base. For more protection in northern climates, a thick covering of leaves can be added. Both of these steps are shown on the opposite page. So is a method of using burlap to wrap climbing roses, which grow too tall for the earth-and-leaf method.

When spring comes, do not be hasty uncovering roses. An early thaw can bring out buds, which will be badly nipped if a last cold snap follows. Only when all danger of frost is past is it safe to uncover the roses. They should be pruned for spring and summer, as explained on pages 342-343.

*Responding to the chill of autumn, a 'Bonica' shrub rose has produced hips, shed its leaves and dropped all but one blossom. Following the first hard frost, shrub roses can be cut back and protected for the onset of winter.*

1 After the first frost, trim your rosebushes back until the canes are 1 or 2 feet in length in the north, 3 feet in the south. Do not worry about the location of buds (as you do in spring pruning); this fall cutting back, in reducing the size of the bush, lessens its vulnerability to drying winds and freezing.

**2** Insulate the bottom portions of the canes, the bud union and the roots by mounding up 12 inches of loose, disease-free earth from another part of the garden. Firm the mound with your hands, but do not pack it down; crumbly soil aids drainage.

**3** For still more insulation, form a cylinder out of a sheet of wire mesh and enclose your bush and its mound of earth in it. Fasten the mesh by bending the protruding horizontal wires around each other *(above)*. To make sure the cylinder stays put, pack another couple of inches of earth around the bottom of the wire.

**4** Pack the wire cylinder with mulch until it is almost full *(above)*. Old leaves, pine needles and bark chips all provide good insulation. In the spring, lift off the wire and the mulch and brush away the mounded earth. Then rinse off the canes with a light spray of water.

### A WINTER BLANKET FOR A CLIMBER

Climbing roses are too tall to bury underneath mounded earth or encase in wire cylinders. Still, their long canes need shielding from desiccating cold and wind. The best protection is burlap. First, pull the canes into a bundle at the base, leaving the tops pinned *(left)*. Wrap some twine around the lower 2 or 3 feet of the canes. Then wrap a burlap sheet around the tied canes, stretching it at least halfway up the plant. Tie the burlap in place with some more twine. In spring, remove the burlap, untie the canes and reposition the canes as necessary.

# YEAR-ROUND CARE FOR TREE ROSES: SPRING STAKING, WINTER BURIAL

*This pink-blossomed 'Duet,' here grown as a tree rose and securely staked against the threat of high winds, commands a colorful mosaic of begonia beds and evergreen shrubs.*

A tree rose is a standard made by grafting together parts from three different plants. The first provides the rootstock, the second a trunk and the third a flowering top. Perched on its slender "trunk," the top may reach a height of 3 feet, allowing you to bring the excitement of roses into a garden otherwise too small for ordinary rose plants. You can buy tree roses at garden-supply centers or by mail order. The flowering tops are usually cut from hybrid teas, floribundas or miniatures because they are compact and can be supported by long, thin trunks. Even so, the tops tend to be heavy, and tree roses are always at risk of bending or breaking in strong wind. They should therefore be supported with 1-by-1 stakes just after planting. Remove the stakes only when you are getting the plants ready for winter.

Although as a rule roses tolerate the cold better than most ornamental plants, tree roses are sensitive to the drying effects of winter wind, sun and temperature fluctuations around the freezing point. And they cannot survive without protection where temperatures drop below 10° F.

The surest protection against wintry conditions is burial. After the first frost, cut back the canes to a length no greater than 2 feet, as shown on page 334. Dig a narrow ditch as long as the plant is tall. After loosening the soil around the roots, gently bend the trunk down until the entire plant is lying in the ditch. Backfill, then cover the plant with a mound of soil several inches high. If you expect subzero temperatures during the winter, cover the mound with several more inches of organic mulch or a plastic sheet. If you use plastic, weight it down with stones or pieces of wood.

In spring, when the ground has completely thawed and all danger of frost is past, remove the mulch and the soil, and gently raise the plant to an upright position. Firm the soil around the root ball. Stake as before; water and mulch. Prune as shown on page 343.

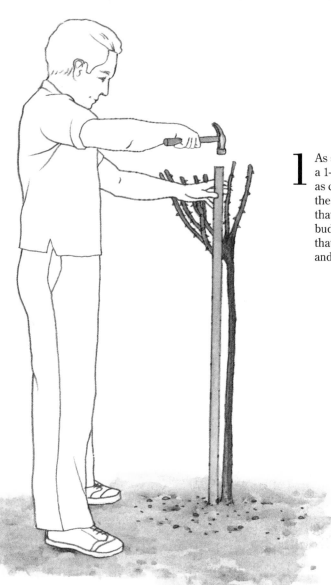

1 As soon as you plant a tree rose, support it with a 1-by-1 wooden or metal stake. Place the stake as close to the upright trunk as possible. Drive the stake about 1 foot into the ground *(left)*, so that the top of the stake is just below the upper bud union (also called bud graft, the swelling that marks the union between the trunkstock and flowering top).

2 Secure the stake to the trunk by wrapping plant tape (the kind that stretches to let a plant grow) around the lower, middle and upper sections *(right)*. Leave the tape and stake in place at all times—unless you need to protect the plant for winter *(pages 338-339)*.

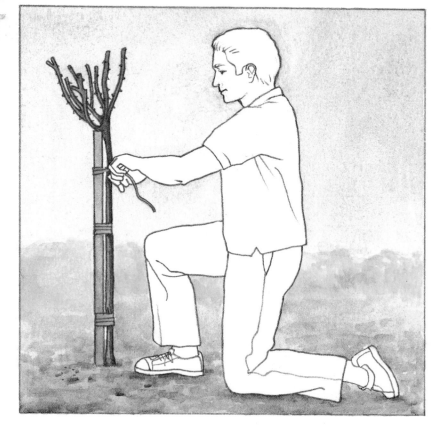

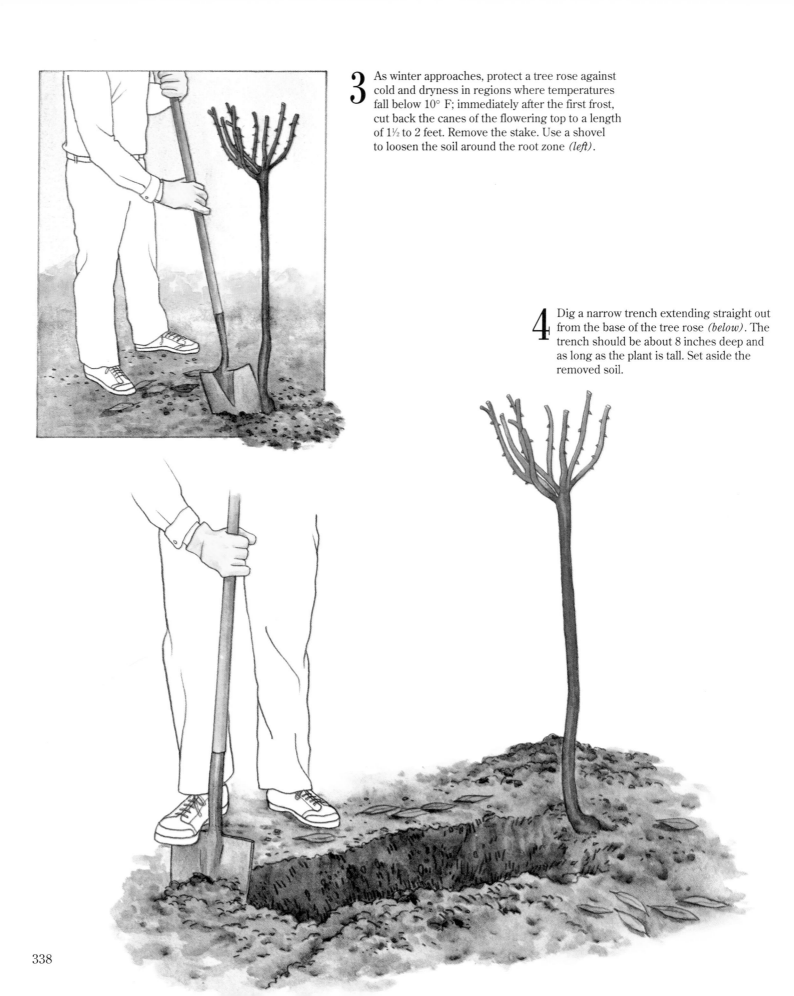

**3** As winter approaches, protect a tree rose against cold and dryness in regions where temperatures fall below 10° F; immediately after the first frost, cut back the canes of the flowering top to a length of 1½ to 2 feet. Remove the stake. Use a shovel to loosen the soil around the root zone *(left)*.

**4** Dig a narrow trench extending straight out from the base of the tree rose *(below)*. The trench should be about 8 inches deep and as long as the plant is tall. Set aside the removed soil.

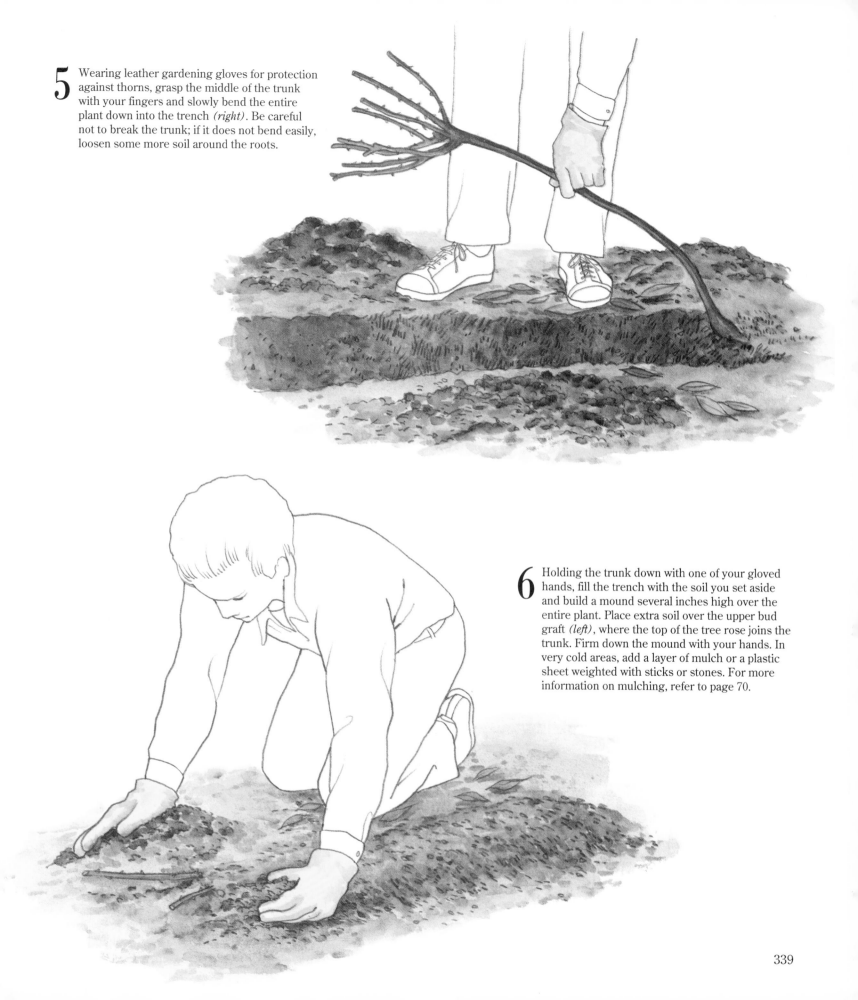

**5** Wearing leather gardening gloves for protection against thorns, grasp the middle of the trunk with your fingers and slowly bend the entire plant down into the trench *(right)*. Be careful not to break the trunk; if it does not bend easily, loosen some more soil around the roots.

**6** Holding the trunk down with one of your gloved hands, fill the trench with the soil you set aside and build a mound several inches high over the entire plant. Place extra soil over the upper bud graft *(left)*, where the top of the tree rose joins the trunk. Firm down the mound with your hands. In very cold areas, add a layer of mulch or a plastic sheet weighted with sticks or stones. For more information on mulching, refer to page 70.

# TIMELY PRUNING FOR HARDY ROSES

Although all roses can benefit from regular pruning, the extent and timing vary with different types of plants. Roses that flower on year-old growth, including shrub roses, species roses, and such old garden roses as gallicas, damasks, centifolias, Noisettes, Bourbons and Portlands, are usually hardier than their hybrid relatives and require less care. Pruning in the early spring, as the buds begin to swell, will make even the sturdiest specimen healthier and more attractive. As soon as you have finished pruning, resume the watering you suspended while the plant was dormant; new growth will wilt if it has insufficient water.

The first pruning target should be canes that are dead, diseased or damaged. Discolored and rough-textured, they are easily spotted among green, smooth-textured healthy canes and should be completely removed or cut back to the good wood.

The next target should be unproductive canes, especially those that crowd each other or are too weak and spindly to produce flowers. Removing them opens the plant's interior to air and sunlight while permitting plant energy to be concentrated on productive growth.

Finally, judicious pruning can also improve the shape and the flowering potential of plants. A uniform trimming of all cane tips and a more severe pruning of lateral canes promotes outward growth and a greater quantity of rose blossoms.

When pruning roses, always wear leather gardening gloves for protection against thorns, and use sharp, clean tools.

Pruning shears can handle most cuts; loppers may be needed for large canes, and a thin pruning saw is best for use in tight and hard-to-reach spaces. Refer to page 398 for detailed descriptions of a selection of pruning tools. Cuts that are ½ inch or more in diameter should be given a protective coating of pruning compound or white glue. Refer to the large drawing opposite to determine where to prune a typical rose; the step-by-step procedure *(right and opposite)* provides a close-up view of how to make each pruning cut.

*A handsome 'Golden Wings' shrub rose—upright, compact, with healthy new growth and a profusion of blooms—shows the effects of regular annual pruning in early spring.*

1 To remove an entire cane *(designated A in the large drawing opposite)*, cut it from the base at a 45° angle *(right)* so that rainwater will run off. Use pruning shears for small canes, loppers for canes more than ½ inch in diameter.

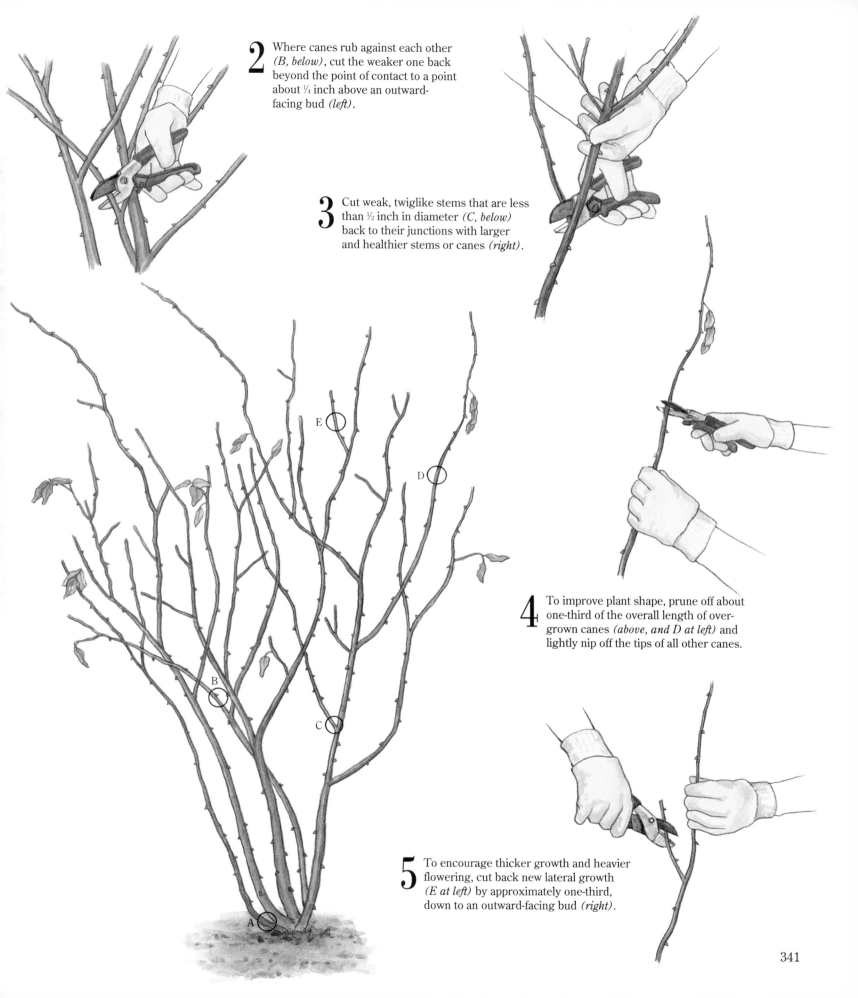

**2** Where canes rub against each other *(B, below)*, cut the weaker one back beyond the point of contact to a point about ¼ inch above an outward-facing bud *(left)*.

**3** Cut weak, twiglike stems that are less than ½ inch in diameter *(C, below)* back to their junctions with larger and healthier stems or canes *(right)*.

**4** To improve plant shape, prune off about one-third of the overall length of over-grown canes *(above, and D at left)* and lightly nip off the tips of all other canes.

**5** To encourage thicker growth and heavier flowering, cut back new lateral growth *(E at left)* by approximately one-third, down to an outward-facing bud *(right)*.

341

# PRUNING TO BRING OUT THE BEST IN MODERN ROSES

Since modern roses such as hybrid teas, polyanthas, floribundas, grandifloras and miniatures flower only on new wood, vigorous pruning is necessary to get the most out of each blooming season. The ideal time to prune such roses is in early spring, just before the growing season. First, discard all dead, diseased or damaged canes, and remove any that are less than ½ inch in diameter; thinner canes will neither support new growth nor produce any quality blooms. Then thin out the remaining canes to open up the plant and force it to concentrate its energy on a few young, strong canes. While thinning, keep in mind that you are also determining the shape of the plant for the summer.

Next, cut back the remaining canes to about two-thirds of their original length. To encourage new growth in the proper direction, place each cut ¼ inch above an outward-facing bud. Always cut at a 45° angle so that rainwater will run off instead of collecting on the wound. For larger, exhibition-quality blooms, you can shorten canes to one-third of their length— but be aware that such severe pruning may also shorten the plant's life span; in reducing the plant's foliage, you rob it of sugar it needs for strength and vigor.

Look closely at the pith, or center, of each cane. Any discoloration is a sign that the cane has been damaged by frost. Cut back a little more until the pith shows a solid cream color. Once the growing season begins, you will have to keep a sharp eye out for suckers— robust shoots that emerge from the rootstock below the bud graft. Left unchecked, they will sap a plant's energy. The best way to remove suckers is to rip them off at the base.

As shown opposite, always wear leather gardening gloves for protection against thorns, and use sharp, clean tools.

*The first result of early spring pruning, a 'Tiffany' hybrid tea rose blooms on new wood at the tip of a carefully cropped cane.*

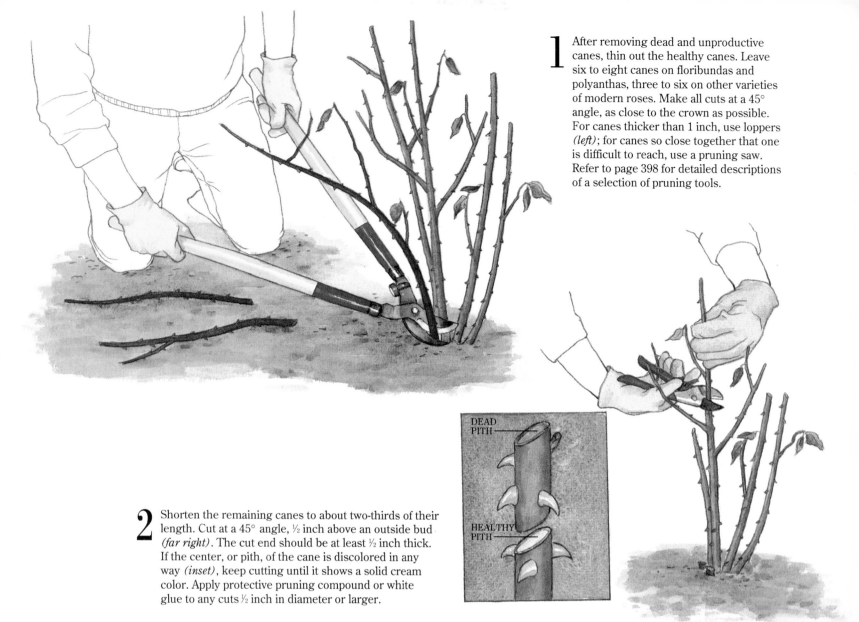

**1** After removing dead and unproductive canes, thin out the healthy canes. Leave six to eight canes on floribundas and polyanthas, three to six on other varieties of modern roses. Make all cuts at a 45° angle, as close to the crown as possible. For canes thicker than 1 inch, use loppers *(left)*; for canes so close together that one is difficult to reach, use a pruning saw. Refer to page 398 for detailed descriptions of a selection of pruning tools.

DEAD PITH

HEALTHY PITH

**2** Shorten the remaining canes to about two-thirds of their length. Cut at a 45° angle, ½ inch above an outside bud *(far right)*. The cut end should be at least ½ inch thick. If the center, or pith, of the cane is discolored in any way *(inset)*, keep cutting until it shows a solid cream color. Apply protective pruning compound or white glue to any cuts ½ inch in diameter or larger.

## THE WAR ON SUCKERS

Energy-draining suckers—stems that grow from a rootstock and do not share the desirable characteristics of the top growth—should be removed when they are a few inches long. Otherwise, they will eventually dominate the plant.

Attempts to control suckers with shears or loppers are bound to end in frustration; they will only grow back. Instead, use a trowel to expose the base of the sucker where it is attached to the bud graft; then, wearing leather gardening gloves, take hold of the sucker with both hands and rip it off the rootstock *(left)*.

# CLIMBING ROSES FOR A WALL OF BRIGHT COLOR

Hardly anything that can be grown in a garden looks more dramatic than a rose plant laden with blooms growing up a trellis, a wall or a weathered wooden fence. Climbing roses provide bright, graceful spreads of color that can camouflage an unsightly view.

Persuading roses to climb in an eye-pleasing fashion, however, sometimes presents a problem. The term "climber" is misleading; with some exceptions, roses do not climb of their own accord. Unlike vines, they produce no tendrils that cling, and rose canes cannot twine about a trellis. In short, roses need help to climb well—some pruning and training as well as tying *(opposite)*. The main requirement is that the plant have long, supple canes.

After the climber is well established in the ground—but before training begins—some pruning is called for. It should be done at the start of the growing season. Remove all unproductive canes *(pages 340-341)* and cut some of the laterals—the stems that branch off the main canes (or basal canes) back to the second bud; pruning encourages the remaining two buds to develop. When training time comes, there is an interesting fact to remember. The vertically growing canes of most climbing roses produce flowers only at their tips. But canes that are bent to grow horizontally produce blooms all along their length. It is not fully understood why this occurs, but the reason has to do with a botanical phenomenon known as apical dominance, which means that terminal buds—those formed at the branch tips, which naturally grow upright—dominate plant growth and inhibit lateral buds from developing. When the canes of a rose bush are spread out, the lateral buds face upward and are therefore able to bloom. Thus, when training a rose up a trellis or a fence, if you bend a number of canes toward the horizontal, you will get a richer, brighter panoply of flowers.

*Its growth encouraged by having its canes trained horizontally along a wooden fence, a choice climbing cultivar called 'Joseph's Coat' produces extravagant clusters of blossoms. The rose was named for the Biblical garment of many colors because its flowers combine several tones of yellow, pink and red.*

## BLOSSOMS THROUGHOUT THE GROWING SEASON

When roses are dormant, as most of them are from fall through winter and spring, the rose garden can be a barren scene. But a rose garden interspersed with other types of plants can be colorful from early spring to late fall. In early spring, when rose plants are merely bare canes, bulbs such as crocus, daffodil, hyacinth and squill will blossom until the roses begin to develop leaves. Plant them between rosebushes and along the border of the rose bed. Refer to Chapter 6 for directions on planting bulbs.

For early summer, when the bulbs die back, plant annuals *(Chapter 4)* such as petunia, salvia and sweet alyssum, or perennials *(Chapter 5)* such as basket of gold and candytuft; they will add different colors, shapes and textures to your garden before your roses bloom. For fall color, plant late-blooming bulbs such as agapanthus, autumn crocus and autumn daffodil.

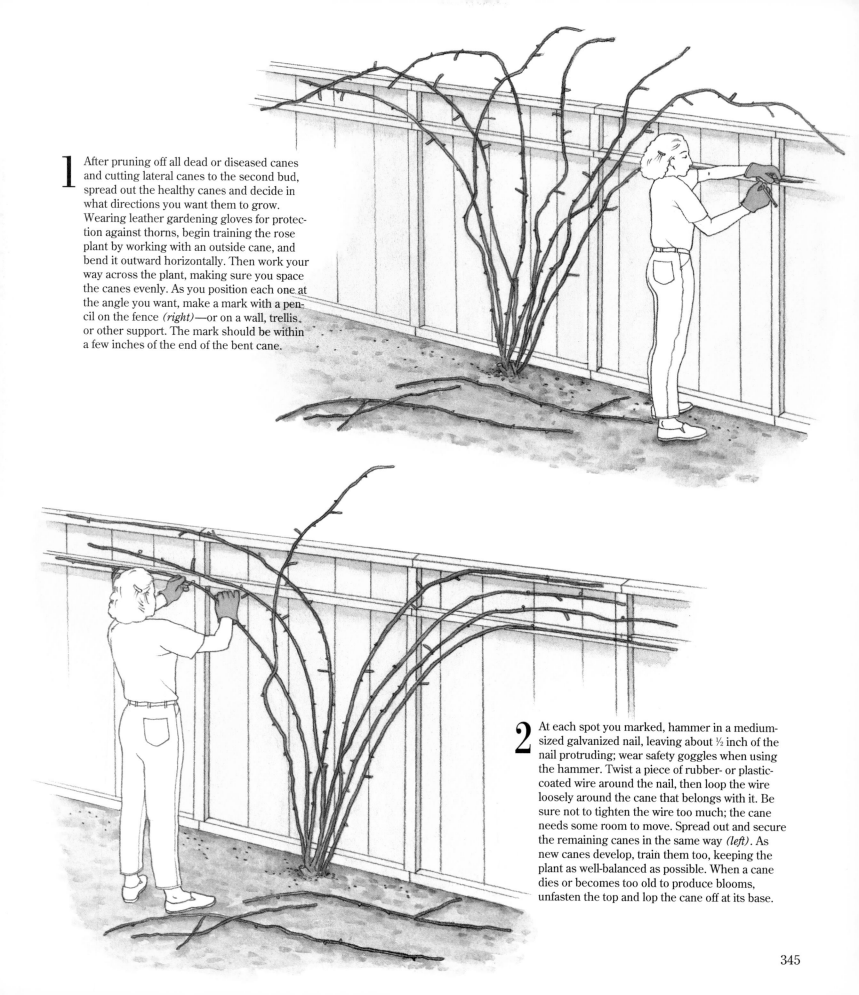

**1** After pruning off all dead or diseased canes and cutting lateral canes to the second bud, spread out the healthy canes and decide in what directions you want them to grow. Wearing leather gardening gloves for protection against thorns, begin training the rose plant by working with an outside cane, and bend it outward horizontally. Then work your way across the plant, making sure you space the canes evenly. As you position each one at the angle you want, make a mark with a pencil on the fence *(right)*—or on a wall, trellis, or other support. The mark should be within a few inches of the end of the bent cane.

**2** At each spot you marked, hammer in a medium-sized galvanized nail, leaving about ½ inch of the nail protruding; wear safety goggles when using the hammer. Twist a piece of rubber- or plastic-coated wire around the nail, then loop the wire loosely around the cane that belongs with it. Be sure not to tighten the wire too much; the cane needs some room to move. Spread out and secure the remaining canes in the same way *(left)*. As new canes develop, train them too, keeping the plant as well-balanced as possible. When a cane dies or becomes too old to produce blooms, unfasten the top and lop the cane off at its base.

# BUD GRAFTING
# TO DUPLICATE A FAVORITE HYBRID

Grafting roses sounds like a job best left to professional growers or botanists. But grafting is in fact surprisingly easy to do and, further, is the only workable way to propagate choice hybrid cultivars. Trying to grow hybrid roses from seed is an uncertain proposition because the seeds will not necessarily reproduce the desired qualities of the parent.

Grafting involves little more than taking a bud from the cultivar and attaching it to a rose of another, hardier species. The key to the process is finding this parent plant, or understock, as rose fanciers call it. The plant should be one that produces good strong roots. Favored as an understock, or rootstock, today is *Rosa multiflora*, whose roots are remarkably disease-resistant and will tolerate many types of soil. If you already have a multiflora or other usable understock growing in the garden, you can use it for grafting. Or one can be bought from a nursery—or even started from cuttings *(pages 348-349)*.

The actual grafting is a relatively simple matter of doing a bit of cutting and fitting with a knife and some elastic tape. All the necessary steps are shown on these and the following three pages. This sort of grafting—called T budding from the shape of the cuts that are made in the understock—should always be done in early summer, when the cambium, a layer just under a rose's bark, is full of growth cells. Joining the cambium belonging to the bud to that of the understock is what makes a graft take hold and produce a fresh, new copy of the cultivar.

The only potential problem with T budding is a legal one. Hybrid roses are protected by 17-year patents that prevent anyone from propagating and selling them without permission from the person who first bred them. There is no reason, however, why a cultivar cannot be cloned for private use and enjoyment.

*The grandiflora 'Gold Medal' displays the best of two worlds—lush gold blossoms and the sturdy rootstock of a hardier variety. Hybrids are best propagated by bud grafting because their seeds do not breed true.*

1 To begin the grafting process, snip a healthy shoot from the rose you are planning to reproduce. The shoot should be young and fresh-looking but mature enough to have flowered. Wearing leather gardening gloves to protect your hands from thorns, cut off the shoot at a point about 12 inches below the top leaves *(right)*.

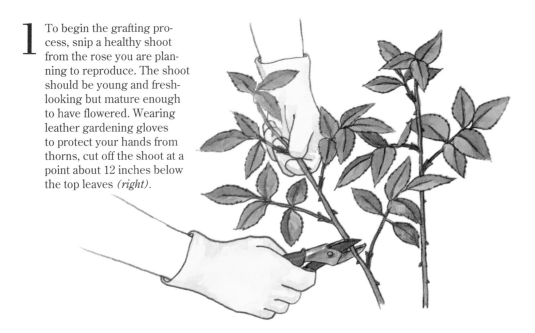

**2** Remove the shoot's leaves and thorns. Use pruning shears for the leafstalks *(left)*. Be sure you leave behind a ½-inch stub each time; the buds you want to preserve and use for grafting are nestled in the stubs (or leaf axils). Remove the thorns by snapping them off with your thumb.

**3** Using a small, sharp knife, slice a bud and its surrounding bark—a "bud shield"—from the middle portion of the shoot. Begin by making a horizontal cut about ⅛ inch deep through the bark roughly ½ inch below the bud *(above, left)*. Make an identical cut ½ inch above the bud. Slip the knife blade downward from the top cut *(above, right)* until the knife reaches the bottom cut. You should end with a neat slice of bark with the bud intact.

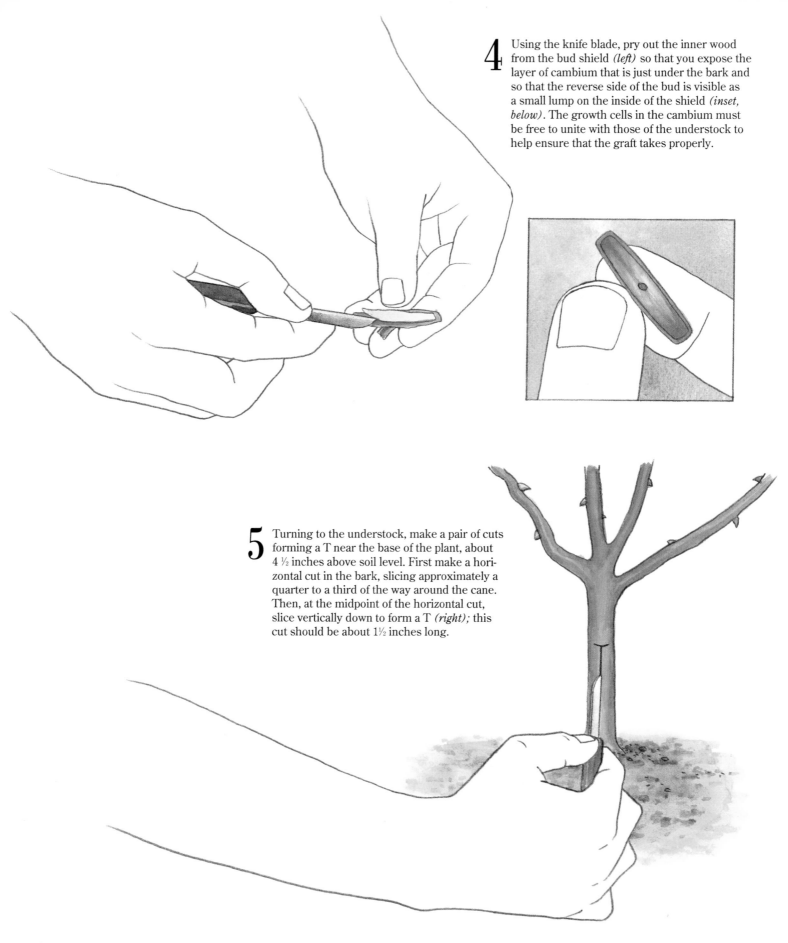

**4** Using the knife blade, pry out the inner wood from the bud shield *(left)* so that you expose the layer of cambium that is just under the bark and so that the reverse side of the bud is visible as a small lump on the inside of the shield *(inset, below)*. The growth cells in the cambium must be free to unite with those of the understock to help ensure that the graft takes properly.

**5** Turning to the understock, make a pair of cuts forming a T near the base of the plant, about 4 ½ inches above soil level. First make a horizontal cut in the bark, slicing approximately a quarter to a third of the way around the cane. Then, at the midpoint of the horizontal cut, slice vertically down to form a T *(right);* this cut should be about 1½ inches long.

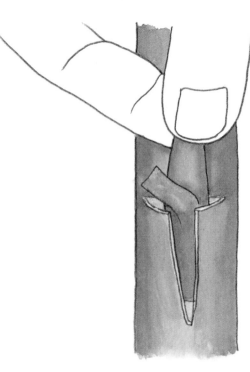

**6** With your fingers, bend the corners of the T cut away from the cane to form a slot or pocket. Insert the bud shield into the slot *(left)*. The flaps of the slot should enclose most of the bark portion of the shield. If any of the bud shield protrudes above the top of the slot, slice off the excess for a snug fit.

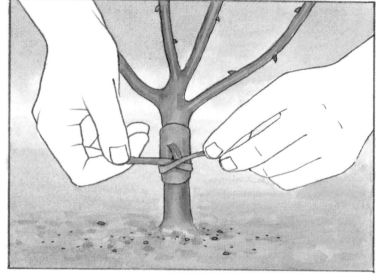

**7** Secure the graft with a rubber band that has been cut open or with budding tape *(right)*, a rubber strip that has a hole in the center. Place the tape on the shield so that the hole fits over the stub sheltering the bud, or wrap the band around the shield, in either case leaving the bud exposed, and tie the ends securely

**8** After about three weeks, when the bud has begun to sprout, remove whatever wrapping material you employed—if it has not already disintegrated on its own. Cut the wrapping using a knife on the side of the cane opposite the bud and peel it off. Then cut the top of the rootstock just above the graft *(left)*.

# TAKING ADVANTAGE OF SUCKERS: AN EASY WAY TO PROPAGATE

During the growing season roses often put forth suckers—those thin shoots that grow straight up from roots. On rose plants that have been grafted, suckers are merely nuisances to be removed as soon as possible, since neither their foliage nor their flowers will resemble the desirable top growth. But roses that grow on their own roots—as do species roses and plants that were started from seed or stem cuttings—produce suckers that share all the characteristics you see in the top growth. These suckers can be easily detached and raised as independent plants.

The ideal time to propagate from such suckers is at the start of the growing season so that the new plants will have ample opportunity to establish themselves before the onset of winter. Choose ones that are growing at some distance from the point at which the rest of the canes emerge. Such outside suckers are younger than interior suckers and tend to be more vigorous. They are also easier to work with, and can be separated from the parent with far less trauma to the main plant and to the prospective new plant.

For best results, try to dig up each sucker with its root system largely intact. Start by loosening the soil around a sucker with a shovel. Then dig down through the loosened soil, severing the sucker's roots from those of the parent. In lifting the sucker, keep as much soil as possible around the roots to prevent them from drying out. Plant the sucker immediately in a container where the roots can recover from the shock of division. Keep the soil moist and feed once a week with diluted liquid fertilizer.

An 'Apothecary's Rose' displays a broad mound of color in a sunny garden location. As an old garden rose that grows on its own roots, it throws up suckers that can be used to start new plants that will have the traits of the parent plant.

Look for a vigorous sucker, several inches long, growing approximately 1 foot from the main part of the plant. With the blade of a shovel, loosen a few inches of soil all around the sucker *(right)*. Then dig down several inches into the sucker's root area and use the shovel blade to sever its roots from the parent. Ease the shovel under the sucker and lift it out of the ground. After three weeks in a container, the sucker can be transplanted to a prepared bed.

# CUTTING BLOOMS
# AND KEEPING THEM BRIGHT

**1** Wearing leather gardening gloves for protection against thorns, use clean, sharp pruning shears to cut the stem below a just-opening bloom; cut at a 45° angle about ¼ inch above an outside leaf *(left)*. Keep the length of the cut stem in proportion to the flower. There is no point in taking extra stem, because the foliage produces nutrients and distributes them throughout the plant. The loss of too much foliage will weaken the rose plant. With repeat-blooming roses, snip above a pair of five-leaflet leaves. The buds in these leaf axils will grow the strongest flowering stems.

Cutting roses for indoor bouquets takes delicate care. It has to be done in the right way and at the right time and with a touch of artistic flair as well. First, there is the matter of timing. With many varieties, roses can be cut any time during the growing season. In fact, taking a bloom here and there can, like judicious pruning, rejuvenate the plant. With repeat-blooming varieties, it can also encourage new flowering shoots to develop. However snipping late in the season is a bad idea. The blossoms of repeat bloomers start to produce seeds a month or so before the first hard frost. Seed production slows the plants' metabolism, preparing them for winter dormancy. Cutting late blooms upsets their seasonal rhythm.

Roses are best cut late in the afternoon, probably because at that hour the blooms contain a full ration of the natural sugars the plant has created during the day. The flower itself should be just opening, and its sepals—the leaflike coverings of the rosebuds—should have unfurled.

**2** To help preserve the flower, quickly plunge its stem into water heated to about 110° F. Then, while the stem is still in the water, make a fresh cut in its base, taking off about ¼ inch *(right)*. Leave the stem submerged for 30 minutes to stop the flow of air to the blossom. Then, take the cutting out of the water and remove any leaves from the lower two-thirds of the stem with your fingers. Place the rose in a vase filled with water and a preservative of two teaspoons of sugar plus a few drops of bleach. Place the vase in a cool, dark room for a few hours before displaying it. Renew the water and preservative daily.

# A CHECKLIST FOR ROSES

| | ZONE 1 | ZONE 2 | ZONE 3 | ZONE 4 | ZONE 5 |
|---|---|---|---|---|---|
| **JANUARY/FEBRUARY** | • Read catalogs; order roses for spring planting<br>• Clean, oil, sharpen tools | • Read catalogs; order roses for spring planting<br>• Clean, oil, sharpen tools | • Read catalogs; order roses for spring planting<br>• Clean, oil, sharpen tools | • Read catalogs; order roses for spring planting<br>• Clean, oil, sharpen tools | • Read catalogs; order roses for spring planting<br>• Clean, oil, sharpen tools |
| **MARCH/APRIL** | • Test soil pH; adjust if necessary<br>• Plant bare-root roses<br>• Plant container-grown roses<br>• Transplant any roses that need to be moved<br>• Remove winter protection<br>• Begin pruning in mid-April<br>• Apply granular fertilizer after pruning<br>• Water as necessary<br>• Install or repair supports for climbing roses<br>• Mulch newly planted roses | • Test soil pH; adjust if necessary<br>• Plant bare-root roses<br>• Plant container-grown roses<br>• Transplant any roses that need to be moved<br>• Remove winter protection<br>• Begin pruning in mid-April<br>• Apply granular fertilizer after pruning<br>• Water as necessary<br>• Install or repair supports for climbing roses<br>• Mulch newly planted roses | • Test soil pH; adjust if necessary<br>• Plant bare-root roses<br>• Plant container-grown roses<br>• Transplant any roses that need to be moved<br>• Remove winter protection<br>• Begin pruning in mid-April<br>• Apply granular fertilizer after pruning<br>• Water as necessary<br>• Install or repair supports for climbing roses<br>• Mulch newly planted roses | • Test soil pH; adjust if necessary<br>• Plant bare-root roses<br>• Plant container-grown roses<br>• Transplant any roses that need to be moved<br>• Remove winter protection<br>• Begin pruning in mid-April<br>• Apply granular fertilizer after pruning<br>• Water as necessary<br>• Install or repair supports for climbing roses<br>• Mulch newly planted roses | • Test soil pH; adjust if necessary<br>• Plant bare-root roses<br>• Plant container-grown roses<br>• Transplant any roses that need to be moved<br>• Remove winter protection<br>• Begin pruning in mid-April<br>• Apply granular fertilizer after pruning<br>• Water as necessary<br>• Install or repair supports for climbing roses<br>• Mulch newly planted roses |
| **MAY/JUNE** | • Remove suckers<br>• Plant container-grown roses<br>• Remove side buds to encourage large single blossoms, or remove terminal buds to encourage clusters of blossoms<br>• Deadhead faded flowers<br>• Apply granular fertilizer<br>• Apply supplemental liquid fertilizer<br>• Begin spraying regularly with a fungicide and watch for black spot, mildew and rust<br>• Weed soil<br>• Apply mulch for summer<br>• Water as necessary<br>• Spray against insect pests | • Remove suckers<br>• Plant container-grown roses<br>• Remove side buds to encourage large single blossoms, or remove terminal buds to encourage clusters of blossoms<br>• Deadhead faded flowers<br>• Apply granular fertilizer<br>• Apply supplemental liquid fertilizer<br>• Begin spraying regularly with a fungicide and watch for black spot, mildew and rust<br>• Weed soil<br>• Apply mulch for summer<br>• Water as necessary<br>• Spray against insect pests<br>• Remove and burn diseased leaves | • Remove suckers<br>• Plant container-grown roses<br>• Remove side buds to encourage large single blossoms, or remove terminal buds to encourage clusters of blossoms<br>• Deadhead faded flowers<br>• Apply granular fertilizer<br>• Apply supplemental liquid fertilizer<br>• Begin spraying regularly with a fungicide and watch for black spot, mildew and rust<br>• Weed soil<br>• Apply mulch for summer<br>• Water as necessary<br>• Spray against insect pests<br>• Remove and burn diseased leaves | • Remove suckers<br>• Plant container-grown roses<br>• Remove side buds to encourage large single blossoms, or remove terminal buds to encourage clusters of blossoms<br>• Deadhead faded flowers<br>• Apply granular fertilizer<br>• Apply supplemental liquid fertilizer<br>• Begin spraying regularly with a fungicide and watch for black spot, mildew and rust<br>• Weed soil<br>• Apply mulch for summer<br>• Water as necessary<br>• Spray against insect pests<br>• Remove and burn diseased leaves | • Remove suckers<br>• Plant container-grown roses<br>• Remove side buds to encourage large single blossoms, or remove terminal buds to encourage clusters of blossoms<br>• Deadhead faded flowers<br>• Apply granular fertilizer<br>• Apply supplemental liquid fertilizer<br>• Begin spraying regularly with a fungicide and watch for black spot, mildew and rust<br>• Weed soil<br>• Apply mulch for summer<br>• Water as necessary<br>• Spray against insect pests<br>• Remove and burn diseased leaves |

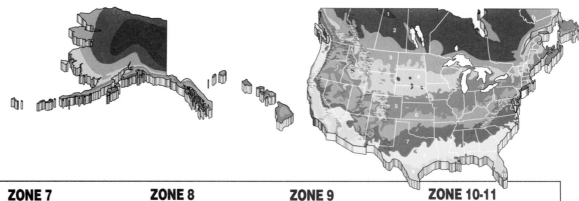

| | ZONE 6 | ZONE 7 | ZONE 8 | ZONE 9 | ZONE 10-11 | |
|---|---|---|---|---|---|---|
| | • Read catalogs; order roses for spring planting<br>• Clean, oil, sharpen tools | • Read catalogs; order roses for spring planting<br>• Clean, oil, sharpen tools | • Plant bare-root roses<br>• Plant container-grown roses<br>• Transplant any roses that need to be moved<br>• Begin pruning in mid-February<br>• Apply granular fertilizer after pruning<br>• Resume watering<br>• Mulch newly planted roses<br>• Test soil pH; adjust to about 6.0-6.5<br>• Clean and sterilize pruning shears<br>• Install trellis or fence support for climbing roses | • Plant bare-root roses<br>• Plant container-grown roses<br>• Transplant any roses that need to be moved<br>• Begin pruning in mid-February<br>• Apply granular fertilizer after pruning<br>• Resume watering<br>• Mulch newly planted roses<br>• Test soil pH; adjust to about 6.0-6.5<br>• Clean and sterilize pruning shears<br>• Install trellis or fence support for climbing roses | • Plant bare-root roses<br>• Plant container-grown roses<br>• Transplant any roses that need to be moved<br>• Begin pruning in late January<br>• Apply granular fertilizer after pruning<br>• Resume watering<br>• Mulch newly planted roses<br>• Test soil pH; adjust to about 6.0-6.5<br>• Clean and sterilize pruning shears<br>• Install trellis or fence support for climbing roses | JANUARY/FEBRUARY |
| | • Test soil pH; adjust if necessary<br>• Plant bare-root roses<br>• Plant container-grown roses<br>• Transplant any roses that need to be moved<br>• Remove winter protection<br>• Begin pruning in mid-April<br>• Apply granular fertilizer after pruning<br>• Water as necessary<br>• Install or repair supports for climbing roses<br>• Mulch newly planted roses | • Test soil pH; adjust if necessary<br>• Plant bare-root roses<br>• Plant container-grown roses<br>• Transplant any roses that need to be moved<br>• Remove winter protection<br>• Begin pruning in mid-April<br>• Apply granular fertilizer after pruning<br>• Water as necessary<br>• Install or repair supports for climbing roses<br>• Mulch newly planted roses<br>• Spray for aphids | • Plant container-grown roses<br>• Remove side buds to encourage large single blossoms, or remove terminal buds to encourage clusters of blossoms<br>• Deadhead faded flowers<br>• Apply granular fertilizer<br>• Apply supplemental liquid fertilizer<br>• Begin spraying regularly with a fungicide<br>• Weed soil<br>• Apply mulch for summer<br>• Water as necessary<br>• Install or repair supports for climbing roses<br>• Spray for aphids<br>• Remove suckers | • Plant container-grown roses<br>• Remove side buds to encourage large single blossoms, or remove terminal buds to encourage clusters of blossoms<br>• Deadhead faded flowers<br>• Apply granular fertilizer<br>• Apply supplemental liquid fertilizer<br>• Begin spraying regularly with a fungicide<br>• Weed soil<br>• Apply mulch for summer<br>• Water as necessary<br>• Install or repair supports for climbing roses<br>• Spray for aphids<br>• Remove suckers | • Plant container-grown roses<br>• Remove side buds to encourage large single blossoms, or remove terminal buds to encourage clusters of blossoms<br>• Deadhead faded flowers<br>• Apply granular fertilizer<br>• Apply supplemental liquid fertilizer<br>• Begin spraying regularly with a fungicide<br>• Weed soil<br>• Apply mulch for summer<br>• Water as necessary<br>• Install or repair supports for climbing roses<br>• Spray for aphids<br>• Remove suckers | MARCH/APRIL |
| | • Remove suckers<br>• Plant container-grown roses<br>• Remove side buds to encourage large single blossoms, or remove terminal buds to encourage clusters of blossoms<br>• Deadhead faded flowers<br>• Apply granular fertilizer<br>• Apply supplemental liquid fertilizer<br>• Begin spraying regularly with a fungicide and watch for black spot, mildew and rust<br>• Weed soil<br>• Apply mulch for summer<br>• Water as necessary<br>• Spray against insect pests<br>• Remove and burn diseased leaves | • Remove suckers<br>• Plant container-grown roses<br>• Remove side buds to encourage large single blossoms, or remove terminal buds to encourage clusters of blossoms<br>• Deadhead faded flowers<br>• Apply granular fertilizer<br>• Apply supplemental liquid fertilizer<br>• Begin spraying regularly with a fungicide and watch for black spot, mildew and rust<br>• Weed soil<br>• Apply mulch for summer<br>• Water as necessary<br>• Spray against insects<br>• Remove and burn diseased leaves | • Remove suckers<br>• Plant container-grown roses<br>• Remove side buds to encourage large single blossoms, or remove terminal buds to encourage clusters of blossoms<br>• Deadhead faded flowers<br>• Apply granular fertilizer<br>• Apply supplemental liquid fertilizer<br>• Continue spraying regularly with a fungicide and watch for black spot, mildew and rust<br>• Weed soil<br>• Apply mulch for summer<br>• Water as necessary<br>• Spray against insect pests<br>• Remove and burn diseased leaves | • Remove suckers<br>• Plant container-grown roses<br>• Remove side buds to encourage large single blossoms, or remove terminal buds to encourage clusters of blossoms<br>• Deadhead faded flowers<br>• Apply granular fertilizer<br>• Apply supplemental liquid fertilizer<br>• Continue spraying regularly with a fungicide and watch for black spot, mildew and rust<br>• Weed soil<br>• Apply mulch for summer<br>• Water as necessary<br>• Spray against insect pests<br>• Remove and burn diseased leaves | • Remove suckers<br>• Plant container-grown roses<br>• Remove side buds to encourage large single blossoms, or remove terminal buds to encourage clusters of blossoms<br>• Deadhead faded flowers<br>• Apply granular fertilizer<br>• Apply supplemental liquid fertilizer<br>• Continue spraying regularly with a fungicide and watch for black spot, mildew and rust<br>• Weed soil<br>• Apply mulch for summer<br>• Water as necessary<br>• Spray against insect pests<br>• Remove and burn diseased leaves | MAY/JUNE |

|  | ZONE 1 | ZONE 2 | ZONE 3 | ZONE 4 | ZONE 5 |
|---|---|---|---|---|---|
| **JULY/AUGUST** | • Remove and burn diseased leaves<br>• Plant container-grown roses<br>• Remove side buds to encourage large single blossoms, or remove terminal buds to encourage clusters of blossoms<br>• Deadhead faded flowers<br>• Apply granular fertilizer until mid-August<br>• Apply supplemental liquid fertilizer until mid-August<br>• Continue spraying regularly with a fungicide<br>• Weed soil<br>• Water as necessary<br>• Watch for and spray against insect pests<br>• Propagate by budding<br>• Continue mulching | • Remove and burn diseased leaves<br>• Plant container-grown roses<br>• Remove side buds to encourage large single blossoms, or remove terminal buds to encourage clusters of blossoms<br>• Deadhead faded flowers<br>• Apply granular fertilizer until mid-August<br>• Apply supplemental liquid fertilizer until mid-August<br>• Continue spraying regularly with a fungicide<br>• Weed soil<br>• Water as necessary<br>• Watch for and spray against insect pests<br>• Propagate by budding<br>• Continue mulching | • Remove and burn diseased leaves<br>• Plant container-grown roses<br>• Remove side buds to encourage large single blossoms, or remove terminal buds to encourage clusters of blossoms<br>• Deadhead faded flowers<br>• Apply granular fertilizer until mid-August<br>• Apply supplemental liquid fertilizer until mid-August<br>• Continue spraying regularly with a fungicide<br>• Weed soil<br>• Water as necessary<br>• Watch for and spray against insect pests<br>• Propagate by budding<br>• Continue mulching | • Remove and burn diseased leaves<br>• Plant container-grown roses<br>• Remove side buds to encourage large single blossoms, or remove terminal buds to encourage clusters of blossoms<br>• Deadhead faded flowers<br>• Apply granular fertilizer until mid-August<br>• Apply supplemental liquid fertilizer until mid-August<br>• Continue spraying regularly with a fungicide<br>• Weed soil<br>• Water as necessary<br>• Watch for and spray against insect pests<br>• Propagate by budding<br>• Continue mulching | • Remove and burn diseased leaves<br>• Plant container-grown roses<br>• Remove side buds to encourage large single blossoms, or remove terminal buds to encourage clusters of blossoms<br>• Deadhead faded flowers<br>• Apply granular fertilizer until mid-August<br>• Apply supplemental liquid fertilizer until mid-August<br>• Continue spraying regularly with a fungicide<br>• Weed soil<br>• Water as necessary<br>• Watch for and spray against insect pests<br>• Propagate by budding<br>• Continue mulching |
| **SEPTEMBER/OCTOBER** | • Discontinue deadheading in early September<br>• Discontinue watering in early October<br>• Prepare soil for spring planting<br>• Apply winter protection in October<br>• Install wind breaks if needed<br>• Take hardwood cuttings for propagation in October<br>• Sweep up leaves to control diseases | • Discontinue deadheading in early September<br>• Discontinue watering in early October<br>• Prepare soil for spring planting<br>• Apply winter protection in October<br>• Install wind breaks if needed<br>• Take hardwood cuttings for propagation in October<br>• Sweep up leaves to control diseases | • Discontinue deadheading in early September<br>• Discontinue watering in early October<br>• Prepare soil for spring planting<br>• Apply winter protection in October<br>• Install wind breaks if needed<br>• Take hardwood cuttings for propagation in October<br>• Sweep up leaves to control diseases | • Discontinue deadheading in early September<br>• Discontinue watering in early October<br>• Prepare soil for spring planting<br>• Apply winter protection in October<br>• Install wind breaks if needed<br>• Take hardwood cuttings for propagation in October<br>• Sweep up leaves to control diseases | • Discontinue deadheading in early September<br>• Transplant any roses that need to be moved<br>• Discontinue watering in early October<br>• Weed soil<br>• Prepare soil for spring planting<br>• Install wind breaks if needed<br>• Take hardwood cuttings for propagation in October<br>• Sweep up leaves to control diseases |
| **NOVEMBER/DECEMBER** | • Lightly prune roses<br>• Continue taking hardwood cuttings<br>• Pot roses for forcing | • Lightly prune roses<br>• Continue taking hardwood cuttings<br>• Pot roses for forcing | • Lightly prune roses<br>• Continue taking hardwood cuttings<br>• Pot roses for forcing | • Lightly prune roses<br>• Continue taking hardwood cuttings<br>• Pot roses for forcing | • Lightly prune roses<br>• Apply winter protection in November<br>• Continue taking hardwood cuttings<br>• Pot roses for forcing |

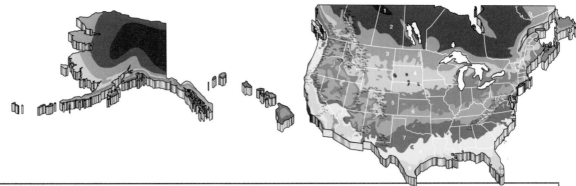

| | ZONE 6 | ZONE 7 | ZONE 8 | ZONE 9 | ZONE 10-11 | |
|---|---|---|---|---|---|---|
| | • Remove and burn diseased leaves<br>• Plant container-grown roses<br>• Remove side buds to encourage large single blossoms, or remove terminal buds to encourage clusters of blossoms<br>• Deadhead faded flowers<br>• Apply granular fertilizer until mid-August<br>• Apply supplemental liquid fertilizer until mid-August<br>• Continue spraying regularly with a fungicide<br>• Weed soil<br>• Water as necessary<br>• Watch for and spray against insect pests<br>• Propagate by budding<br>• Continue mulching | • Remove and burn diseased leaves<br>• Plant container-grown roses<br>• Remove side buds to encourage large single blossoms, or remove terminal buds to encourage clusters of blossoms<br>• Deadhead faded flowers<br>• Apply granular fertilizer until mid-August<br>• Apply supplemental liquid fertilizer until mid-August<br>• Continue spraying regularly with a fungicide<br>• Weed soil<br>• Water as necessary<br>• Watch for and spray against insect pests<br>• Propagate by budding<br>• Continue mulching | • Remove and burn diseased leaves<br>• Plant container-grown roses<br>• Remove side buds to encourage large single blossoms, or remove terminal buds to encourage clusters of blossoms<br>• Deadhead faded flowers<br>• Apply granular fertilizer<br>• Apply supplemental liquid fertilizer<br>• Continue spraying regularly with a fungicide<br>• Weed soil<br>• Water as necessary<br>• Watch for and spray against insect pests<br>• Propagate by budding<br>• Continue mulching | • Remove and burn diseased leaves<br>• Plant container-grown roses<br>• Remove side buds to encourage large single blossoms, or remove terminal buds to encourage clusters of blossoms<br>• Deadhead faded flowers<br>• Apply granular fertilizer<br>• Apply supplemental liquid fertilizer<br>• Continue spraying regularly with a fungicide<br>• Weed soil<br>• Water as necessary<br>• Watch for and spray against insect pests<br>• Propagate by budding<br>• Continue mulching | • Remove and burn diseased leaves<br>• Plant container-grown roses<br>• Remove side buds to encourage large single blossoms, or remove terminal buds to encourage clusters of blossoms<br>• Deadhead faded flowers<br>• Apply granular fertilizer<br>• Apply supplemental liquid fertilizer<br>• Continue spraying regularly with a fungicide<br>• Weed soil<br>• Water as necessary<br>• Watch for and spray against insect pests<br>• Propagate by budding<br>• Continue mulching | **JULY/AUGUST** |
| | • Discontinue deadheading in early September<br>• Discontinue watering in early October<br>• Weed soil<br>• Read catalogs; order roses for late-fall planting<br>• Install wind breaks if needed<br>• Take hardwood cuttings for propagation in October<br>• Sweep up leaves to control diseases | • Plant container-grown roses<br>• Continue spraying regularly with a fungicide<br>• Discontinue deadheading in early October<br>• Discontinue watering in mid-October<br>• Weed soil<br>• Read catalogs; order roses for late-fall planting<br>• Install wind breaks if needed<br>• Take hardwood cuttings for propagation in October<br>• Sweep up leaves to control diseases | • Plant container-grown roses<br>• Apply granular fertilizer until early September<br>• Continue spraying regularly with a fungicide<br>• Discontinue deadheading in early October<br>• Discontinue watering in mid-October<br>• Weed soil<br>• Read catalogs; order roses for late-fall planting<br>• Take hardwood cuttings for propagation in October<br>• Sweep up leaves to control diseases | • Plant container-grown roses<br>• Apply granular fertilizer until early September<br>• Continue spraying regularly with a fungicide<br>• Discontinue deadheading in early October<br>• Discontinue watering in mid-October<br>• Weed soil<br>• Read catalogs; order roses for late-fall planting<br>• Take hardwood cuttings for propagation in October<br>• Sweep up leaves to control diseases | • Plant container-grown roses<br>• Apply granular fertilizer until early September<br>• Continue spraying regularly with a fungicide<br>• Discontinue deadheading in early October<br>• Discontinue watering in mid-October<br>• Weed soil<br>• Read catalogs; order roses for late-fall planting<br>• Take hardwood cuttings for propagation in October<br>• Sweep up leaves to control diseases | **SEPTEMBER/OCTOBER** |
| | • Lightly prune roses<br>• Plant bare-root roses<br>• Transplant any roses that need to be moved<br>• Prepare soil for spring planting<br>• Apply winter protection in November<br>• Continue taking hardwood cuttings<br>• Pot roses for forcing | • Lightly prune roses<br>• Plant bare-root roses<br>• Transplant any roses that need to be moved<br>• Prepare soil for spring planting<br>• Apply winter protection in November<br>• Continue taking hardwood cuttings<br>• Pot roses for forcing | • Lightly prune roses<br>• Plant bare-root roses<br>• Plant container-grown roses<br>• Transplant any roses that need to be moved<br>• Prepare soil for spring planting<br>• Read catalogs; order roses for spring planting<br>• Clean, oil, sharpen tools<br>• Continue taking hardwood cuttings<br>• Pot roses for forcing | • Lightly prune roses<br>• Plant bare-root roses<br>• Plant container-grown roses<br>• Transplant any roses that need to be moved<br>• Prepare soil for spring planting<br>• Read catalogs; order roses for spring planting<br>• Clean, oil, sharpen tools<br>• Continue taking hardwood cuttings | • Lightly prune roses<br>• Plant bare-root roses<br>• Plant container-grown roses<br>• Transplant any roses that need to be moved<br>• Prepare soil for spring planting<br>• Read catalogs; order roses for spring planting<br>• Clean, oil, sharpen tools<br>• Continue taking hardwood cuttings | **NOVEMBER/DECEMBER** |

# TROUBLESHOOTING GUIDE: ROSES

| PROBLEM | CAUSE | SOLUTION |
|---|---|---|
| Circular black spots ¼ inch in diameter appear on upper leaf surfaces. Each black spot is surrounded by a yellow halo. As the spots enlarge and coalesce, the entire leaf turns yellow and falls from the plant. Easily spread by rain or overhead watering. Some leaves of resistant varieties will remain green and on the cane. | Black spot, a fungus disease. The disease is most common in humid and rainy conditions; the fungus spores germinate in water. Once a plant is infected, the fungus will remain on old leaves left on the ground or in the canes through the winter and reappear on the next season's growth. | There is no chemical cure for infected plants. In the early spring, after an infection, prune the canes back lower than normal to eliminate fungus spores that remained on the canes over winter, and apply a lime-sulfur spray before the leaves open. To prevent black spot from infecting new plants, spray with a synthetic chemical fungicide once every 10 days, starting in midspring. If symptoms appear, remove and destroy all infected leaves, including those on the ground. Water plants in the morning so that they will dry before evening. Do not water plants from above; wet leaves are hospitable to germinating spores. |
| Leaves, especially new leaves, become twisted or curled and are covered with a white powder. Young shoots are misshapen and foliage may be stunted. Flower buds and canes may also be affected. | Powdery mildew, a fungus disease carried by wind, most severe when nights are cool and humid, and days are warm and dry. The disease remains on bud scales, inside stems and on old fallen leaves in winter. | Remove and destroy all infected leaves, including those on the ground. To prevent mildew or to arrest its spread, apply a fungicide once every 10 days, starting in midspring. |
| Small red, brown or purple spots develop on the upper leaf surfaces. The center of each spot eventually dries out, turns white and may fall out of the leaf. Leaves eventually turn yellow and fall from the plant. Sometimes, bumpy brown spots will appear on stems. | Spot anthracnose, a fungus disease. The fungus spreads in water, especially in spring rains. Fungus remains in infected rose canes through the winter. | When symptoms appear, begin spraying with a fungicide once every seven days until all signs of the disease are eliminated. Prune away diseased canes in the spring. Do not water plants from above, since the fungus spreads in splashing water. |
| Rosebuds fail to open and are covered with a grayish brown, fuzzy mold. Open flowers are flecked with yellow or brown and lower petals are wilted and brown. The stems below infected flowers become discolored. Infected flowers easily fall apart when handled. | Botrytis blight, also called gray mold, a fungus disease that spreads in moist air and cool temperatures. Disease remains in infected plant parts through the winter. | There are no chemical cures for blight once it occurs. If symptoms appear, cut off and destroy all infected plant parts. Spray with a fungicide to keep the disease from spreading. To prevent blight, regularly deadhead flowers and destroy the infected plant parts. Do not overmulch plants in the fall, as this keeps the canes moist and encourages fungus growth. |

| PROBLEM | CAUSE | SOLUTION |
|---|---|---|
| Red or brown sunken spots with dark margins develop on canes. Cracks may appear within the spots. The spots enlarge and eventually encircle the cane. Leaves and stems above the damaged area turn yellow, wilt and die, or growth is poor around area of lesion. | Canker, a fungus disease. The fungus spreads in water and enters the plant through cuts or wounds in the canes. The problem is most severe in early to middle spring, when plants come out of dormancy. | There is no chemical preventive or cure for canker. When symptoms appear, prune infected canes below the canker and burn the diseased plant parts. Use sharp pruning shears and make the cut just above a node at a 45° angle. Cover cut area with a pruning paint or spray to prevent infection. Disinfect tools with alcohol or household bleach after each cut. |
| Orange, powdery spores appear on the undersides of the leaves. Eventually, yellow or brown spots appear on upper leaf surfaces. Infected leaves mottle, and may wilt or curl. | Rust, a fungus disease that spreads in moist air, wind and moderate temperatures. The problem is most severe in the Pacific Northwest, where the climate is cool and humid. | Remove and destroy all infected leaves, including those on the ground. Avoid overhead watering because the fungus spreads in water. To prevent the disease, spray with a fungicide every seven to 10 days in cool, wet weather. Consider rust-resistant rose varieties when planting new roses. |
| Round growths about 2 inches in diameter appear at the base, or crown, of the plant. The growths are light green when young and turn brown and woody as they age. Plant growth is stunted, foliage is abnormally small and few buds are produced. Flowers are misshapen and plant dies. | Crown gall, a disease that is caused by bacteria living in the soil. The bacteria enter a plant through the roots or through wounds at the root area. The bacteria cause abnormal cell growth, which produces the galls. | There are no chemical controls for crown gall. Small galls may be pruned out with a sharp knife or pruning shears. After pruning, burn the diseased plant parts. Disinfect tools with alcohol or household bleach after each cut. After pruning, cover cut area with pruning paint or spray to prevent infection. In severe cases, remove the plant and the soil surrounding the roots to prevent the bacteria from spreading. Before buying plants, inspect their crowns for any swellings or rough-surfaced growths in the crown area. Do not propagate diseased plants. |
| Leaves are mottled or streaked with yellow (A) or they develop a pattern of yellow netting (B). Plant growth slows. | Mosaic, a virus disease that is often transmitted by aphids and other insects, or by propagation of infected plants. Although the virus does not affect flowers, it detracts from the overall appearance of the plant. | There are no chemical controls or cures. In mild cases, symptoms often disappear by themselves. In severe cases, infected plants should be removed to prevent the virus from spreading. Do not propagate diseased plants. Before buying new plants, inspect them for signs of infection. |

| PROBLEM | CAUSE | SOLUTION |
|---|---|---|
| Holes appear in flowers and then in leaves and stems. Light-colored flowers are especially susceptible. Affected plant parts are chewed or entirely eaten, or have small holes. | Japanese beetles, shiny copper-and-green, hard-shelled insects up to ½ inch long. Beetles move from flower to flower, consuming the petals before they eat the leaves. They seem to be attracted to light-colored blossoms. Beetle larvae may eat plant roots. | Pick beetles off plants by hand and destroy the beetles. Spray the plants with an insecticide. In late summer and in spring, treat the ground around affected roses with a grub-controlling insecticide or with milky spore. In the fall, rake up fallen leaves; adult beetles spend the winter in plant debris. |
| Small, rounded holes appear in leaves. Eventually, the entire leaf surface between the veins disappears, creating a skeleton-like appearance. | Rose slugs, the larvae of sawfly wasps. The slug is light green with a dark brown head and is up to ½ inch long. Some species have shiny bodies; others are covered with hair. Rose slugs generally feed at night on the undersides of leaves; they do not eat buds and flowers. | At the first sign of slug infestation, spray the plant with an insecticide and make sure the insecticide covers the undersides of leaves. Rose slugs can quickly damage plants; inspect roses frequently. Practice clean cultivation. |
| Roses fail to blossom or existing buds suddenly turn black and die. The foliage and the stem surrounding affected buds may also become deformed, blacken and die. | Rose midge, a fly larva that is yellow-white and ¹⁄₁₂ inch long. The larvae feed in clusters at the bases of rosebuds. Flies lay eggs in growing tips of rose canes. | Prune off and destroy all infested plant parts. Spray plants with an insecticide and apply a systemic insecticide to the ground around the plants where the larvae pupate. |
| Buds do not open, or flowers are deformed. Petals have brownish yellow streaks and small dark spots or bumps. White and pastel roses are particularly susceptible. | Thrips, tiny winged orange to brownish-yellow insects with elongated bodies. Thrips feed at the bases of rosebuds and on the petals of open flowers. They seem to be attracted to light-colored blossoms. | Early prevention is very important. To discourage thrips from attacking, spray plants with a systemic insecticide just before the buds open. If signs of thrip damage appear, remove and destroy infected flowers and buds. Spray infected plants with an insecticide. If the infestation is severe, repeat applications may be necessary. |
| Leaves curl, rosebuds and foliage wither or become distorted in shape. A clear, sticky substance that attracts ants appears on foliage. | Aphids, semitransparent insects ⅛ inch long that cluster on new growth and flower buds. They suck the juice from the plant and secrete the sticky substance. Aphids can carry and spread diseases. | Aphids may be knocked off plants with a stream of water especially directed to the underside of the leaves. In severe infestations, spray with an insecticide or an insecticidal soap. Introduce ladybugs to the area; they are natural aphid predators, although harmless to roses. |
| Plant growth slows. Leaves and flowers are smaller than normal. Leaves may turn yellow, wilt and drop. The roots are discolored and have small, knotty growths at the tips. Tiny white eggs can be seen inside the knotty growths. | Nematodes, microscopic worms that dwell in the soil and feed on plant roots. A soil analysis is needed to confirm the presence of nematodes. | Remove infested plants and the surrounding soil. Do not plant roses in the same area for three years. If the problem persists, consult a local extension service or garden-supply center for advice. |

| PROBLEM | CAUSE | SOLUTION |
|---|---|---|
| Small circles or ovals appear in leaf margins. | Leafcutter bees, which are shiny black, blue or purple bees. The bees do not eat the foliage; they use leaf material to build their nests. | Prune out canes that have damaged foliage. Since leafcutter bees are pollinators of several crops, the use of chemicals to destroy the bees is not recommended. |
| Round or oval masses appear on stems and canes. Stems appear encrusted with whitish-gray shelled insects. Foliage wilts, turns yellow and drops from the plant. Growth is stunted and flowers are not produced. | Rose scales, ⅛-inch, white, gray or brown insects with crusty shells. Scales usually appear in clusters and suck out sap from the plant. | Prune out and destroy heavily infested canes. Spray plants with an insecticide. To prevent scale infestation, spray plants with dormant horticultural oil in early spring. |
| Upper surfaces of leaves are covered with small yellow specks. Leaves may curl and turn pale. Damage is similar to that of the spider mite. | Leafhoppers, which are triangular, white or light yellow insects ⅛ to ⅝ inch long. They feed on the undersides of leaves and suck the sap from the leaves. Leafhoppers can carry and spread diseases. | Spray with an insecticide or insecticidal soap. In the fall, rake up leaves and remove weeds that can harbor leafhopper eggs through the winter. |
| Holes appear in un-opened rosebuds. Leaves and stems may also have holes or may be chewed off. Problem often occurs in late spring. | Caterpillars, the larvae of moths and butterflies. Most are yellow or green and up to 1 inch long. Some, such as budworms, attack only the flowers; others eat the leaves and canes. | Spray with *Bacillus thuringiensis,* called Bt, a bacterium fatal to caterpillars but harmless to plants and other animals. If caterpillars return to your garden every spring, Bt can be sprayed in anticipation of the problem. Prune out infected plant parts and destroy them. |
| Leaves become dry and have a dull bronze sheen. Tiny specks may be visible on the undersides of the leaves. Eventually, thin webbing appears on the foliage. | Spider mites, nearly microscopic pests that may be red, black, yellow or green. To confirm their presence, shake a leaf over a piece of white paper; the mites will be visible moving against the white background. These mites suck out leaf juices from the underside of the leaf. Mites proliferate in hot, dry weather. | Knock adults off plants with a strong stream of water. Spray with a miticide three times, three days apart. Use different miticides; mites may build up resistance to a single miticide. Mites produce new generations in a few days, so repeat treatments will be necessary. In the early spring, rake and clean up old leaves, weeds and debris. |
| Growing tips, foliage and canes wilt. Swollen areas up to 1 inch long appear on canes. There may be punctures in the cane or holes in the pruned area of the stem. | Borers, moth larvae that are white or yellow worms up to 1 inch long. Borers enter the canes through wounds and through pruned stem tips, and lay their eggs in the canes. When hatched, larvae will eat through the canes. | Cut off the affected area. Make the cut below the swelling on the cane to be sure you remove the borer. To prevent borers from entering canes, apply shellac or white glue to the exposed tips after pruning. |

'ALBA SEMI-PLENA'

'ALTISSIMO'

'AMERICA'

# DICTIONARY OF ROSES

### Introduction

The dictionary entries that follow present a wide variety of the most beautiful and widely cultivated roses. They are listed alphabetically by individual rose names. Each entry describes the class to which the rose belongs and the type of blossom it produces. Other qualities such as fragrance and characteristics of leaf or flower are included where appropriate. Some roses are sensitive to low temperatures; these roses are labeled tender and need protection where temperatures fall below 10° F. Each entry also suggests where best to plant roses and also provides information on whether a rose is most suitable for cut flowers or exhibition.

### 'Alba Semi-Plena'

Introduced 16th Century or earlier

#### Class
Old Garden Rose: Alba

#### Flowers
Semidouble, 2½ inches, soft white. Short buds quickly open to cupped flowers displaying prominent gold stamens. Flowers borne in clusters, usually of six to eight flowers. Pure, sweet fragrance. This was the White Rose of the House of York during the Wars of the Roses.

#### Bloom
Midseason; does not repeat.

#### Plant
Sturdy and arching, 6 to 8 feet, with gray-green, matte foliage. A large crop of long, orange-red rose hips ripen in late summer or fall. The plant will support itself in a vase-shaped form, rather bare at the base; or it may be trained against a wall, fence or trellis. Alba roses will grow and bloom well in more shade than most roses. They are immune to the common rose fungus diseases. The plant is extremely hardy.

#### Landscape and other uses.
In borders, on walls, fences, trellises, and as a specimen shrub. 'Alba Semi-Plena' has only one season of bloom, but the disease-free gray-green foliage makes it a good garden shrub all season, and the orange-red rose hips add a late show.

### 'Altissimo'

Introduced 1966

#### Class
Large-flowered climber

#### Flowers
Single, having seven petals, 4 to 5 inches. Blossoms are velvety blood-red, cupped to flat. Stamens are yellow and show up brightly against the red; they darken slightly with age. Flowers are borne in small clusters and sometimes singly. Flowers have little scent.

#### Bloom
Midseason; repeats all season.

#### Plant
Tall, 6 to 8 feet, with large, matte, dark green leaves; young shoots are purplish red. Hips are large. Semihardy. Training the canes to grow horizontally will increase blossoming.

#### Landscape and other uses
On pillars, walls, and fences, and as a free-standing shrub.

### 'America'

Introduced 1976

#### Class
Large-flowered climber

#### Flowers
Double, 4 to 5 inches, rich, unfading coral pink. Very full, high-centered form, opening from spiraled, pointed-ovoid buds. Flowers are generally borne in clusters, sometimes singly, and last well. Flowers have strong fragrance.

#### Bloom
Midseason; repeats fairly well.

#### Plant
Upright and bushy, 9 to 12 feet, with dark, semiglossy foliage. Unlike most other large-flowered climbers, 'America' produces flowers on new shoots as well as on older ones. Semihardy.

**Landscape and other uses**
On pillars, fences and walls, and as long-lasting cut flowers.

## 'Angel Face'
Introduced 1968

**Class**
Floribunda

**Flowers**
Double, 3 to 4 inches, deep mauve with ruffled petal edges toned ruby. Flowers are flat to cupped, showing yellow stamens and long-lasting. Blossoms are borne in small clusters and singly. Strong old-rose fragrance with slight spiciness.

**Bloom**
Midseason; repeats well during entire season.

**Plant**
Bushy and compact, 2 to 3 feet, with leathery, glossy, dark green leaves. In some areas 'Angel Face' suffers from black spot and mildew, which weaken the plants and reduce their winter hardiness. Otherwise plant is semihardy.

**Landscape and other uses**
In beds, borders and low hedges, and as cut flowers and exhibition flowers.

## 'Apothecary's Rose'
Sometimes designated *Rosa gallica officianalis*
Known in ancient times

**Class**
Old Garden Rose: Gallica

**Flowers**
Semidouble, 3 to 3½ inches, flat-cupped. The color is pink to modern eyes, but historically this is the Red Rose of the House of Lancaster in the Wars of the Roses. Before the importation of the first China roses, about 1700, this was as red as European roses came. Yellow stamens show brightly against the petals. Flowers are borne singly or in clusters of three or four; the flower stems are strong and erect. Quite fragrant. Gallica roses are spicier and less sweet than other old roses, and their fragrance intensifies as the flower dries. This characteristic, and medieval belief in the medicinal powers of scented roses, made the 'Apothecary's Rose' the basis of the perfume industry in Provins, France. It was cultivated there for conserves as early as the 14th Century.

**Bloom**
Profuse at midseason and reasonably long-lasting in flower; does not repeat.

**Plant**
Upright and bushy, 3 to 4 feet. Canes are almost thornless, with a few small prickles and a general coating of harmless, tiny bristles. Leaves are matte, even rough, and medium green. The plant spreads freely by suckers if grown on its own roots. When bud-grafted onto an understock, the plant does not spread, but grows taller, to 4 or 4½ feet. Extremely hardy.

**Landscape and other uses**
In hedges, in beds with other plants and as specimens. Round red hips provide late summer interest. Dried petals are good for potpourri.

## 'Baby Darling'
Introduced 1964

**Class**
Miniature

**Flowers**
Double, 1 to 1½ inches, blended of orange and salmon. Small, pointed bud. Flowers are borne singly and several together on short stems. They are long-lasting provided they are shaded from afternoon sun. Flowers are moderately fragrant.

**Bloom**
Midseason; blooming repeats intermittently.

**Plant**
Bushy and spreading, plant is 12 inches, with small, light green foliage. Tender.

**Landscape and other uses**
In borders, edgings, beds and containers.

'ANGEL FACE'

'APOTHECARY'S ROSE'

'BABY DARLING'

'BONICA'

'CECILE BRUNNER'

'CENTURY TWO'

'CHICAGO PEACE'

## 'Bonica'
Introduced 1981

**Class**
Shrub

**Flowers**
Double, 2½ to 3½ inches, light pink. Buds are spiraled, deeper in color towards the center, and open to cupped flowers with ruffled petals. Blossoms are borne in large, loose clusters. Flowers have little scent.

**Bloom**
Midseason; repeats well during entire season.

**Plant**
Spreading, 3 to 5 feet, with small, glossy, dark green leaves. Orange fruit develops in fall and persists through winter. Hardy and considerably disease-resistant; plant requires less spraying than most roses.

**Landscape and other uses**
In beds, borders and hedges.

## 'Cecile Brunner'
Introduced 1881

**Class**
Polyantha; Climbing Polyantha

**Flowers**
Double, 1 to 1½ inches, pale pink flowers with yellow at the base. Little spiraled buds that open to high-centered or rather loose flowers. Flowers are borne in loose clusters. Often known as the 'Sweetheart Rose.' The flower fragrance is tealike, light but definite.

**Bloom**
Late. The bush form repeats very steadily all season; the climbing form repeats intermittently after a heavy initial bloom.

**Plant**
Shrub form is 3 to 4 feet; climbing form reaches 15 to 25 feet tall. The bush form has sparse, semiglossy dark green foliage. The climber has foliage so dense that it may sometimes hide some of the flowers. Both forms have rather smooth wood and few thorns. Tender.

**Landscape and other uses**
In beds, borders and arbors, on large trellises and walls, and climbing up tree trunks. Flowers make excellent cut roses and boutonnieres.

## 'Century Two'
Introduced 1971

**Class**
Hybrid Tea

**Flowers**
Double, 4½ to 5 inches, medium pink with violet overtones. Long pointed buds open to cupped flowers that are borne singly or in small clusters, with long-lasting quality. Moderate fragrance.

**Bloom**
Midseason; repeats all season.

**Plant**
Upright and bushy, 4 feet, with leathery, green foliage. Plant is semi-hardy.

**Landscape and other uses**
In beds and borders, and as cut flowers and exhibition flowers.

## 'Chicago Peace'
Introduced 1962

**Class**
Hybrid Tea

**Flowers**
Very double, 5 to 5½ inches, with strong deep pink blended with yellow. Ovoid buds open to flowers that are deep, full and cupped. Flowers are usually borne singly. Slight fragrance.

**Bloom**
Midseason; repeats well during entire season.

**Plant**
Upright, 4½ to 5 feet, with stout canes and large, dark green, leathery leaves. Semihardy.

**Landscape and other uses**
In beds and borders, and also as cut flowers.

### 'Chrysler Imperial'
Introduced 1952

**Class**
Hybrid Tea

**Flowers**
Double, 4½ to 5 inches, rich crimson with darker shadings (later fading to magenta) and a velvety texture. Buds are spiraled and are borne singly. Heavy, old-rose fragrance.

**Bloom**
Midseason; repeats well during entire season.

**Plant**
Upright, 4 to 5 feet, with semiglossy, dark green leaves. Somewhat subject to mildew. Semihardy.

**Landscape and other uses**
In beds and borders, and also as cut flowers.

### 'Cinderella'
Introduced 1953

**Class**
Miniature

**Flowers**
Very double, ¾ to 1 inch, white with touches of light pink. The petals are tightly and evenly arranged. Flowers are borne singly and in clusters. Spicy and tealike fragrance.

**Bloom**
Abundant in midseason; repeats well all season.

**Plant**
Upright, vigorous and compact, 10 inches, almost thornless, with semiglossy green leaves. Semihardy and easy to grow.

**Landscape and other uses**
In borders, edgings, beds and containers. Plant also grows very well indoors.

### 'Color Magic'
Introduced 1978

**Class**
Hybrid Tea

**Flowers**
Double, 5 inches, ivory to deep rose color. Long, spiraled buds open to flat-cupped blossoms that show amber stamens. Flowers are borne mostly singly. Slight fragrance.

**Bloom**
Midseason; repeats all season.

**Plant**
Upright and well-branched, 3½ to 4 feet, with large, glossy dark green foliage. Semihardy.

**Landscape and other uses**
In beds and borders, and as cut flowers and exhibition flowers.

### 'Cornelia'
Introduced 1925

**Class**
Shrub: Hybrid Musk

**Flowers**
Double, 1 to 1½ inches coppery coral or apricot to strawberry pink. Tight buds open quickly to rosette blossoms showing yellow stamens. Colors are softer in the heat of summer, more vivid in cool autumn weather. Flowers are borne in small to very large (18-inch) clusters. Strong fragrance of spiced honey and fruit.

**Bloom**
Late midseason; repeats well all season, sometimes giving its best display in autumn.

**Plant**
Arching, 6 to 8 feet, with brown canes and bronzy foliage. Grows and blooms well in partial shade. Semihardy.

**Landscape and other uses**
As a specimen, in borders and in combination with other plants. May be trained to grow on walls, trellises and fences.

'CHRYSLER IMPERIAL'

'CINDERELLA'

'COLOR MAGIC'

'CORNELIA'

'CUPCAKE'

'DON JUAN'

'DOUBLE DELIGHT'

'DUET'

### 'Cupcake'
Introduced 1981

**Class**
Miniature

**Flowers**
Very double, 1½ inches, clear, medium pink that holds well. Buds open to high-centered, long-lasting flowers. Flowers are borne singly and in clusters of two to five. No fragrance.

**Bloom**
Heavy in midseason; repeats well all season.

**Plant**
Bushy, 12 to 14 inches, with semiglossy, green foliage. Plant is semihardy.

**Landscape and other uses**
In borders, edgings and containers, and as cut flowers and exhibition flowers.

### 'Don Juan'
Introduced 1958

**Class**
Large-flowered climber

**Flowers**
Double, 4 to 5 inches, dark, velvety red, sometimes brushed with nearly black markings. Oval buds open slowly to long-lasting, high-centered or cupped blossoms. Flowers are borne singly and in small clusters. Flowers have strong fragrance.

**Bloom**
Midseason; repeats all season.

**Plant**
Upright, 8 to 10 feet, with glossy, dark green foliage. Semihardy.

**Landscape and other uses**
On pillars, trellises, fences and walls, and as cut flowers.

### 'Double Delight'
Introduced 1977

**Class**
Hybrid Tea

**Flowers**
Double, 5½ inches, cherry red surrounding a creamy white center. Buds open to high-centered blossoms. Flowers are borne singly. Strong, spicy fragrance.

**Bloom**
Midseason; repeats all season.

**Plant**
Bushy, 4 feet, with matte green foliage. Semihardy.

**Landscape and other uses**
In beds and borders, and as cut flowers and exhibition flowers.

### 'Duet'
Introduced 1960

**Class**
Hybrid Tea

**Flowers**
Double, 4 inches, in two shades of pink, the tops of the petals being light and the undersides dark. Buds are urn-shaped and open to loose blossoms displaying the two colors. Nonfading. Flowers are borne mostly in clusters. Slight fragrance.

**Bloom**
Midseason; repeats very well all season.

**Plant**
Upright, vigorous and bushy, plant is 4 to 5½ feet, with glossy, green leaves.

**Landscape and other uses**
In beds, borders and hedges, and as cut flowers.

### 'Escapade'
Introduced 1967

**Class**
Floribunda

**Flowers**
Semidouble, 3 inches, rosy violet blending to white at the center, with long, dark amber stamens showing prominently against the white. Flowers are saucer-shaped and have about 12 petals. They are borne in clusters.

**Bloom**
Midseason; repeats consistently all season.

**Plant**
Upright and bushy, 2½ to 3 feet, with glossy, light green leaves. Semihardy.

**Landscape and other uses**
In beds, borders and low hedges, and as cut flowers.

**'Esmeralda'** see 'Keepsake'

### 'Europeana'
Introduced 1963

**Class**
Floribunda

**Flowers**
Double, ruffled, 3 inches, deep crimson. Blossoms are neat, full, cupped and long-lasting. Flowers are borne in large clusters. Little fragrance.

**Bloom**
Midseason; bloom repeats strongly all season.

**Plant**
Bushy and spreading, 2 to 3 feet. Foliage is dark red when young and matures to a glossy, dark green with reddish tints. Large flower clusters are sometimes top-heavy; planting in groups lets the stems support each other. Semihardy.

**Landscape and other uses**
In beds, borders and low hedges, and as cut flowers.

### 'Evening Star'
Introduced 1974

**Class**
Floribunda

**Flowers**
Double, 4 to 4½ inches, pure white with light yellow bases. Buds are pointed and open to spiraled, high-centered blossoms. Flowers are borne singly and in clusters. Slight fragrance.

**Bloom**
Midseason; repeats all season.

**Plant**
Upright and bushy, 3 to 3½ feet, with dark, bluish green leaves. Tender.

**Landscape and other uses**
In beds, borders and low hedges, and as cut flowers and exhibition flowers.

### 'First Edition'
Introduced 1976

**Class**
Floribunda

**Flowers**
Double, 2 to 2½ inches. Buds are coral-orange and pointed, and open to coral-rose cupped flowers that usually show yellow anthers. The color is richest in cool weather. Flowers are borne mostly in large, flat-topped clusters. Slight fragrance.

**Bloom**
Midseason; repeats all season.

**Plant**
Upright, 3½ feet, with glossy, light green foliage. Semihardy.

**Landscape and other uses**
In beds, borders and low hedges, and as cut flowers and exhibition flowers.

'ESCAPADE'

'EUROPEANA'

'EVENING STAR'

'FIRST EDITION'

'FIRST PRIZE'

'FOLKLORE'

'GENE BOERNER'

'FRAGRANT CLOUD'

### 'First Prize'
Introduced 1970

**Class**
Hybrid Tea

**Flowers**
Double, 5 to 6 inches, pink with ivory centers. Long, pointed buds open to high-centered flowers. Blossoms are borne singly or in small clusters. Flowers have moderate fragrance.

**Bloom**
Midseason; repeats all season.

**Plant**
Upright and spreading, 5 feet, with leathery, dark green foliage. Susceptible to fungus diseases. Plant is tender.

**Landscape and other uses**
In beds and borders, and as cut flowers and exhibition flowers.

### 'Folklore'
Introduced 1977

**Class**
Hybrid Tea

**Flowers**
Double, 4½ inches, blending tones of orange. Long, pointed buds open gradually to high-centered, long-lasting blossoms. Flowers are borne singly or in clusters. Strong fragrance.

**Bloom**
Midseason; repeats all season, slowly but in strong flushes.

**Plant**
Upright and bushy, 4 to 5 feet, with glossy, medium green leaves. New canes may have a spurt of growth in late summer. Plant is semihardy.

**Landscape and other uses**
In beds and borders, and as cut flowers and exhibition flowers.

### 'Fragrant Cloud'
Introduced 1963

**Class**
Hybrid Tea

**Flowers**
Double, 5 inches, varying shades of orange-red. Color fades in hot sun. Flowers are high-centered and borne in clusters of up to 10 blooms. The scent is among the strongest of all roses, blending the fragrances of tea and old rose.

**Bloom**
Midseason; repeats well during entire season.

**Plant**
Upright and vigorous, 4 to 5 feet tall, with large, glossy, dark green leaves. Easy to grow. Semihardy.

**Landscape and other uses**
In beds and borders, and also as cut flowers.

### 'Gene Boerner'
Introduced 1968

**Class**
Floribunda

**Flowers**
Double, 2½ to 3½ inches, pink. Pointed buds open to high-centered blossoms; petal edges turn back to form points. Flowers are borne singly or in clusters. Flowers have slight fragrance.

**Bloom**
Midseason; repeats all season.

**Plant**
Upright, 3½ to 5 feet, with glossy, green foliage. Plant is semihardy.

**Landscape and other uses**
In beds, borders and hedges, and as cut flowers and exhibition flowers.

## 'Gold Medal'
Introduced 1982

**Class**
Grandiflora

**Flowers**
Double, 3½ to 4 inches, deep yellow, sometimes flushed with orange-red. Long, pointed buds open to high-centered, long-lasting blossom. Flowers are borne singly or in clusters. Slight tea fragrance.

**Bloom**
Midseason; repeats all season.

**Plant**
Upright and bushy, 4 to 5½ feet, with glossy, dark green foliage. Plant is semihardy.

**Landscape and other uses**
In beds and borders, and as cut flowers and exhibition flowers.


## 'Golden Wings'
Introduced 1956

**Class**
Shrub

**Flowers**
Single, generally having five petals but sometimes up to 10, 4 to 5 inches, clear pale yellow becoming ivory. Long, pointed buds open to saucer-shaped blossoms that have dark amber stamens in the centers. Flowers are borne singly and in clusters, with a light fragrance of clover and spice.

**Bloom**
Early; repeats continuously all season.

**Plant**
Upright, branching and vigorous, 5 feet, with matte, light green leaves and moderately thorny canes. Hips are orange and showy. Plant is hardy. Shortening canes by about a third at spring pruning encourages compactness.

**Landscape and other uses**
Borders, hedges and in combination with other plants, and as cut flowers.

## 'Granada'
Introduced 1963

**Class**
Hybrid Tea

**Flowers**
Double, 4 to 5 inches, yellow flushed with pink and red. Spiraled buds open to high-centered blossoms that flatten as they mature. Flowers are borne singly and in clusters. Strong spicy fragrance.

**Bloom**
Midseason; repeats very well all season.

**Plant**
Upright, 4½ to 5½ feet, with glossy, dark green foliage. The leaf edges are distinctively serrated. Susceptible to mildew. Plant is tender.

**Landscape and other uses**
In beds and borders, and as cut flowers and exhibition flowers.


## 'Handel'
Introduced 1965

**Class**
Large-flowered climber

**Flowers**
Double, 3½ inches, creamy white edged with bright rose pink that deepens on exposure to hot sunshine. Spiraled buds open to blossoms that may be high-centered or cupped. Flowers are borne in clusters. Slight fragrance.

**Bloom**
Midseason; repeats all season.

**Plant**
Upright, 12 to 15 feet, with glossy, dark green foliage. Plant is semihardy.

**Landscape and other uses**
On trellises, walls and fences.

'GOLD MEDAL'

'GOLDEN WINGS'

'GRANADA'

'HANDEL'

'HANSA'

'HERITAGE'

'ICEBERG'

'IVORY FASHION'

## 'Hansa'
Introduced 1905

**Class**
Shrub: Hybrid Rugosa

**Flowers**
Double, 3 to 3½ inches, bright red-violet. Long, slender bud quickly opens to a loose, crumpled flower. Flowers are borne in clusters on short stems. Flowers have strong fragrance of clove and old rose.

**Bloom**
Early; repeats well all season.

**Plant**
Upright and bushy, 4 to 5 feet, with dark green, crinkled foliage. Canes are gray and extremely thorny. Hips are large, round and orange-red. Like other Rugosa roses, 'Hansa' grows well even in sandy soil and salt spray, and is good for a seashore garden. Its foliage is immune to the common rose fungus diseases and resists most insect damage. But it seems allergic to some fungicides. Spare Rugosas when spraying other roses. Extremely hardy.

**Landscape and other uses**
In hedges, in combination with other plants, and as specimens. The crinkled, disease-free foliage is an asset in the garden. Use 'Hansa' where the penetrating fragrance can be enjoyed—near a doorway, a window, a porch or a patio.

## 'Heritage'
Introduced 1985

**Class**
Shrub

**Flowers**
Double, 3 inches, blush pink, a little deeper toward the centers. The outer petals open to a deep cup surrounding a profusion of inner petals. Flowers are borne singly and in clusters. Strong and unusual fragrance that is a blend of old rose, myrrh and lemon.

**Bloom**
Midseason; repeats all season.

**Plant**
Upright, 4 feet, with semiglossy, dark green foliage. May be pruned like a hybrid tea to produce a smaller plant with larger flowers. Semihardy.

**Landscape and other uses**
In beds, borders and in combination with other plants, and as cut flowers.

## 'Hidcote Yellow'
see 'Lawrence Johnston'

## 'Iceberg'
Sometimes designated 'Schneewittchen'
Introduced 1958

**Class**
Floribunda

**Flowers**
Double, 2½ to 3½ inches, pure white. Spiraled buds open to loosely cupped blossoms. Flowers are borne in small and large clusters. Flowers have mild, sweet fragrance.

**Bloom**
Abundant in early part of midseason; repeats well all season.

**Plant**
Upright and bushy, 3 to 4½ feet, with glossy, light green foliage and few thorns. Forms a rounded bush if given room to spread. Plant is hardy.

**Landscape and other uses**
In beds, borders and hedges, and as cut flowers and exhibition flowers. Makes an excellent tree rose.

## 'Ivory Fashion'
Introduced 1958

**Class**
Floribunda

**Flowers**
Semidouble, 3½ to 4½ inches, ivory white flowers. Oval buds open to wide, slightly cupped flowers showing dark amber and yellow stamens. Flowers are borne in clusters. Flowers have moderate fragrance.

**Bloom**
Midseason; repeats all season.

**Plant**
Upright and branching, 3 feet, with semiglossy, green foliage. Plant is semihardy.

**Landscape and other uses**
In beds, borders and low hedges, and as cut flowers and exhibition flowers.

### 'Jean Kenneally'
Introduced 1984

**Class**
Miniature

**Flowers**
Double, 1½ inches, apricot blended with yellow and pink. Blossoms are spiraled, high-centered and long-lasting; petals fold back to form points. Flowers are borne singly and in clusters. Slight fragrance.

**Bloom**
Midseason; repeats very well all season.

**Plant**
Upright, bushy and vigorous, 22 to 30 inches (tall for a miniature). Semihardy.

**Landscape and other uses**
In borders, beds and containers, and as cut flowers and exhibition flowers.

### 'Joseph's Coat'
Introduced 1964

**Class**
Large-flowered climber

Flowers. Double, 3 inches, with changing tones of yellow, pink and red. Urn-shaped buds open to cupped blossoms. Flowers are borne in clusters. Flowers have slight fragrance.

**Bloom**
Midseason; repeats all season.

**Plant**
Upright, 8 to 10 feet, with glossy, dark green foliage. Unlike most climbers, 'Joseph's Coat' blooms on new wood. Plant is tender.

**Landscape and other uses**
On pillars, trellises, walls and fences. Can be grown as a free-standing shrub of about 6 feet.

### 'Keepsake'
Sometimes designated 'Esmeralda'
Introduced 1981

**Class**
Hybrid Tea

**Flowers**
Double, 5 inches, blended light and dark pink. Oval buds open to high-centered blossoms. Flowers are borne singly or in clusters of two or three. Moderate fragrance.

**Bloom**
Midseason; repeats all season.

**Plant**
Upright and bushy, 5 to 6 feet, with glossy, green foliage and large, heavy thorns. Semihardy.

**Landscape and other uses**
In beds and borders, and as cut flowers and exhibition flowers.

### 'Lady X'
Introduced 1966

**Class**
Hybrid Tea

**Flowers**
Double, 4½ to 5 inches, pale mauve. Long, pointed buds open to high-centered blossoms. Flowers are generally borne singly on long stems. They are easily damaged by rain, and petal edges may burn in very hot weather. Slight fragrance.

**Bloom**
Midseason; repeats all season.

**Plant**
Upright and branching, 5 to 7 feet, with sparse, semiglossy foliage. Semihardy.

**Landscape and other uses**
In beds and borders, and also as cut flowers.

'JEAN KENNEALLY'

'JOSEPH'S COAT'

'KEEPSAKE'

'LADY X'

'LAWRENCE JOHNSTON'

'MADAME HARDY'

'MARY MARSHALL'

### 'Lawrence Johnston'
Sometimes designated
'Hidcote Yellow'
Introduced after 1923

**Class**
Large-flowered climber

**Flowers**
Semidouble, 3 to 3½ inches, bright yellow. Blossoms are cupped and show prominent yellow stamens. Flowers are borne in clusters. Rich fragrance.

**Bloom**
Early to midseason; repeats sparsely and intermittently.

**Plant**
Upright, 20 feet, with glossy, light green leaves and thorny canes. Susceptible to black spot in warm climates. Hardy.

**Landscape and other uses**
On trellises, fences and walls. Can be grown as a free-standing shrub 6 to 10 feet tall.

### 'Madame Hardy'
Introduced 1832

**Class**
Old Garden Rose: Damask

**Flowers**
Very double, 3 to 3½ inches. Bud is flesh pink and opens to an ivory white blossom. The many petals are intricately folded in sections, with a green button eye at the center. Leafy sepals ornament the unopened buds. Flowers are borne in clusters. Soft, delicate fragrance.

**Bloom**
Abundant in midseason; does not repeat.

**Plant**
Upright, bushy and vigorous, 5 feet, with green leaves and thorny canes. Canes may droop under the weight of the flowers. To keep them upright, bind the canes together, stake them or situate several plants together for mutual support. Disease-resistant. Extremely hardy.

**Landscape and other uses**
In borders, in combination with other plants, and as cut flowers.

### 'Mary Marshall'
Introduced 1970

**Class**
Miniature

**Flowers**
Double, 1½ inches, blended tones of orange, yellow and coral. Long, pointed buds open to cupped, long-lasting blossoms. Flowers are borne singly and in clusters. Flowers have moderate fragrance.

**Bloom**
Midseason; bloom repeats well all season.

**Plant**
Upright and bushy, 10 to 14 inches, with semiglossy, green foliage. Semihardy.

**Landscape and other uses**
In borders, edgings, beds and containers, and also as cut flowers and exhibition flowers. Although may be grown indoors, is slow to repeat.

### 'Mary Rose'
Introduced 1983

**Class**
Shrub

**Flowers**
Double, 3 to 4 inches, soft, rose pink that pales with age. Short buds open quickly to loosely cupped flowers having short petals. Flowers are borne in clusters. Sweet fragrance.

**Bloom**
Abundant in early midseason; repeats well all season.

**Plant**
Upright and arching, 4½ feet, with matte, light to medium green foliage. Pruned severely in the manner of a hybrid tea, 'Mary Rose' will make a smaller bush with larger flowers; pruned very lightly it makes a larger, looser shrub. Disease-resistant. Plant is hardy.

**Landscape and other uses**
In beds, borders and in combination with other plants, and as a specimen.

### 'Minnie Pearl'
Introduced 1982

**Class**
Miniature

**Flowers**
Double, 1½ inches, light pink blended with apricot; petal bases are light yellow. Color deepens slightly in hot sun. Long, pointed buds open to high-centered blossoms. Flowers are borne singly. Slight fragrance.

**Bloom**
Midseason; repeats well during entire season.

**Plant**
Upright and branching, 18 to 24 inches, with semiglossy, green foliage. Semihardy.

**Landscape and other uses**
In borders, edgings, beds and containers, and as cut flowers and exhibition flowers.

### 'Mister Lincoln'
Introduced 1964

**Class**
Hybrid Tea

**Flowers**
Double, 5 to 6 inches, dark, unfading red with velvety petal texture. Pointed buds open to high-centered, long-lasting blooms that become cupped or globular. Flowers are borne singly on long, stiff stems. Strong, rich fragrance.

**Bloom**
Midseason; repeats all season, but sparsely.

**Plant**
Upright, branching and vigorous, 4½ to 5½ feet, with matte or semiglossy, dark green leaves. The foliage is less disease-prone than other dark red Hybrid Teas and the plant is easy to grow. Semihardy.

**Landscape and other uses**
In beds and borders, and as cut flowers and exhibition flowers.

### 'Mrs. John Laing'
Introduced 1887

**Class**
Old Garden Rose:
Hybrid Perpetual

**Flowers**
Double, 4 inches, soft, silvery pink. Short, pointed buds open to full, cupped blossoms, having the inner petals a little shorter than the outer. Flowers borne singly and in small clusters. Strong fragrance.

**Bloom**
Midseason; repeats well all season.

**Plant**
Upright, 3 to 4 feet, with matte, light green leaves and few thorns. Hardy.

**Landscape and other uses**
In beds, borders and in combination with other plants, and as cut flowers.

'MARY ROSE'

'MINNIE PEARL'

'MISTER LINCOLN'

'MRS. JOHN LAING'

'OLYMPIAD'

'ORANGEADE'

'ORANGE SUNBLAZE'

'PARTY GIRL'

### 'Olympiad'
Introduced 1984

**Class**
Hybrid Tea

**Flowers**
Double, 4 to 5 inches, bright, unfading red with velvety petal texture. Unlike most red roses, 'Olympiad' does not turn bluish with age. Pointed buds open to high-centered, long-lasting blossoms. Flowers are borne singly or in small clusters. Very slight fragrance.

**Bloom**
Abundant in midseason; repeats well all season.

**Plant**
Upright and bushy, 3 to 5 feet, with semiglossy, green foliage and thorny canes. Semihardy.

**Landscape and other uses**
In beds and borders, and as cut flowers and exhibition flowers.

### 'Orangeade'
Introduced 1959

**Class**
Floribunda

**Flowers**
Semidouble, 2½ to 3½ inches, clear orange. Small buds open quickly to blossoms showing bright yellow stamens. Flowers are borne in clusters. Flowers have slight fragrance.

**Bloom**
Midseason; repeats all season.

**Plant**
Bushy and vigorous, 2½ to 3 feet, with round, dark green leaves. Susceptible to mildew. Semihardy.

**Landscape and other uses**
In beds and borders, and also as cut flowers.

### 'Orange Sunblaze'
Introduced 1982

**Class**
Miniature

**Flowers**
Double, 1½ inches, bright, unfading orange-red. Short buds open to flat rosettes. Flowers have no fragrance.

**Bloom**
Midseason; repeats well during entire season.

**Plant**
Upright and bushy, 12 to 16 inches, with large, matte, light green foliage. Semihardy.

**Landscape and other uses**
In beds, borders, edgings and containers.

### 'Party Girl'
Introduced 1979

**Class**
Miniature

**Flowers**
Double, 1½ inches, soft yellow with tones of apricot-pink. Long, pointed buds open to high-centered blossoms. Flowers are usually borne singly, sometimes in large clusters. Spicy fragrance.

**Bloom**
Midseason; repeats all season.

**Plant**
Upright and bushy, 12 to 15 inches, with semiglossy, dark green foliage. Semihardy.

**Landscape and other uses**
In beds, borders, edgings and containers, and as cut flowers and exhibition flowers. Grows well indoors.

### 'Pascali'
Introduced 1963

**Class**
Hybrid Tea

**Flowers**
Double, 3 to 4 inches, creamy white, sometimes spotted with pink in wet weather. Pointed buds open to high-centered blossoms. Flowers are borne singly or in clusters. Little fragrance.

**Bloom**
Midseason; repeats well during entire season.

**Plant**
Upright, 3½ to 4 feet, with semiglossy, dark green leaves.

**Landscape and other uses**
In beds and borders, and as cut flowers and exhibition flowers.

### 'Peace'
Introduced 1945

**Class**
Hybrid Tea

**Flowers**
Double, 5 to 6 inches, light yellow edged with pink, except in cool weather, when the pink may be missing. Plump, spiraled buds open to high-centered blossoms. Flowers are borne singly or in clusters. Slight fragrance.

**Bloom**
Midseason; repeats well during entire season.

**Plant**
Upright and bushy, 4 to 5½ feet, with large, glossy, dark green foliage and thick, moderately thorny canes. Semihardy.

**Landscape and other uses**
In beds, borders and in combination with other plants, as cut flowers and for exhibitions.

### 'Perfume Delight'
Introduced 1973

**Class**
Hybrid Tea

**Flowers**
Double, 4 to 5 inches, rose pink. Long, pointed buds open to cupped blossoms. Flowers are borne singly or in clusters. Strong, spicy fragrance.

**Bloom**
Midseason; repeats all season.

**Plant**
Upright and bushy, 3 to 4½ feet, with large, green leaves and strong, thick, thorny canes. Semihardy.

**Landscape and other uses**
In beds and borders, and also as cut flowers.

### 'Pink Parfait'
Introduced 1960

**Class**
Grandiflora

**Flowers**
Double, 3½ to 4 inches, in blended tones of pinks and cream, lighter toward the centers. Spiraled buds open to high-centered blossoms that become cupped. Flowers are borne singly and in clusters. Slightly musky fragrance.

**Bloom**
Midseason; repeats well during entire season.

**Plant**
Upright and bushy, 3½ to 4½ feet, with semiglossy, green foliage. Semihardy.

**Landscape and other uses**
In beds and borders, and also as cut flowers.

'PASCALI'

'PEACE'

'PINK PARFAIT'

'PERFUME DELIGHT'

'POPCORN'

'PRISTINE'

'QUEEN ELIZABETH'

**'Popcorn'**
Introduced 1973

**Class**
Miniature

**Flowers**
Semidouble, ¾ inch, white. Buds open to cupped blossoms that show prominent yellow stamens. Flowers are borne in clusters. Honey fragrance.

**Bloom**
Abundant in midseason; repeats well all season.

**Plant**
Upright and vigorous, 12 to 14 inches, with small, glossy, green foliage. Semihardy.

**Landscape and other uses**
In beds, borders, edgings and containers.

**'Pristine'**
Introduced 1978

**Class**
Hybrid Tea

**Flowers**
Double, 4½ to 6 inches, pink shading from pale at the centers to deep at the petal edges. Long, spiraled buds open to high-centered blossoms that are short-lived. Flowers are generally borne singly. Slight fragrance.

**Bloom**
Midseason; repeats sparsely.

**Plant**
Upright and spreading, 4 to 5 feet tall, with glossy, dark reddish green foliage. Tender.

**Landscape and other uses**
In beds and borders, and as cut flowers and exhibition flowers.

**'Queen Elizabeth'**
Introduced 1954

**Class**
Grandiflora

**Flowers**
Double, 3½ to 4 inches, blended shades of soft pink. Pointed buds open to cupped blossoms. Flowers are borne singly or in clusters. Slight tea fragrance.

**Bloom**
Abundant in midseason; repeats well all season.

**Plant**
Upright and vigorous, 5 to 7 feet, with glossy, dark green foliage. Somewhat disease-resistant, and easy to grow. Semihardy.

**Landscape and other uses**
In beds, borders and in combination with other plants, as cut flowers and for exhibitions.

**'Rainbow's End'**
Introduced 1984

**Class**
Miniature

**Flowers**
Double, 1½ inches, yellow blending to deep pink or red where full sunlight strikes the petal edges; flowers remain pure yellow if grown in shade or indoors. Pointed buds open slowly to high-centered blossoms. Flowers are borne singly and in clusters. No fragrance.

**Bloom**
Midseason; repeats all season.

**Plant**
Upright and bushy, 14 to 18 inches, with glossy, dark green foliage. Semihardy.

**Landscape and other uses**
In beds, borders, edgings and containers, and as cut flowers and exhibition flowers. Grows well indoors.

**'Rise 'n' Shine'**
Introduced 1977

**Class**
Miniature

**Flowers**
Double, 1½ to 2 inches, yellow. Long, pointed buds open to high-centered blossoms. Flowers are borne singly and in clusters. Slight fragrance.

**Bloom**
Midseason; repeats well all season.

**Plant**
Upright and bushy, 14 to 16 inches, with matte, green leaves. Disease-resistant. Semihardy.

**Landscape and other uses**
In beds, borders, edgings and containers, and as cut flowers and exhibition flowers.

**Rosa damascena versicolor**
see 'York and Lancaster'

**Rosa gallica officianalis**
see 'Apothecary's Rose'

**'Rosa Mundi'**
Sometimes designated *Rosa gallica versicolor*
Introduced before 1581

**Class**
Old Garden Rose: Gallica

**Flowers**
Semidouble, 3 to 3½ inches, deep pink streaks on pale pink or soft white. Buds open to wide, flat cups that effectively show off the streaking. Flowers are borne singly or in clusters of three or four on erect stems. Legend has it that 'Rosa Mundi' was named for Rosamunde, the mistress of Henry II of France. It is a sport of the 'Apothecary's Rose,' to which a branch will occasionally revert. Strong fragrance.

**Bloom**
Abundant in midseason; does not repeat.

**Plant**
Upright and bushy, 3 to 4 feet, with matte, green leaves and almost thornless canes. Round, red hips appear in late summer. Watch for and remove canes that sport back to the 'Apothecary's Rose.' Plant is extremely hardy.

**Landscape and other uses**
In beds, hedges and in combination with other plants.

**Rosa rugosa alba**
Introduced 1870

**Class**
Species

**Flowers**
Single, having five petals, 2½ to 4 inches. Long, pointed buds are tinted blush and open quickly to pure white blossoms with creamy stamens. Flowers are generally borne in clusters. Strong clovelike fragrance.

**Bloom**
Early; repeats well all season.

**Plant**
Spreading and vigorous, 4 to 6 feet tall, with bright green, crinkled foliage. Canes are gray and extremely prickly. Large, orange-red hips form in late summer without preventing new flower's growth; often fruit and flowers are borne side by side. *Rosa rugosa alba* grows wild in New England. It flourishes in sandy soil and salt spray and is a good rose for a seashore garden. The foliage is immune to the common rose fungus diseases and resists most insect damage. But it seems allergic to some fungicides; spare your Rugosas when spraying other roses. Plant is very hardy.

**Landscape and other uses**
In borders, hedges and in combination with other plants, and as a specimen. The crinkled, disease-free foliage is an asset in the garden.

'RAINBOW'S END'

'RISE 'N' SHINE'

'ROSA MUNDI'

ROSA RUGOSA ALBA

375

'ROYAL HIGHNESS'

'ROYAL SUNSET'

'SEA PEARL'

'SIMPLICITY'

## 'Royal Highness'
Introduced 1962

**Class**
Hybrid Tea

**Flowers**
Double, 5 to 5½ inches, light pink. Spiraled buds open slowly to high-centered blossoms. Flowers are borne singly on long stems. Strong tea fragrance.

**Bloom**
Midseason; repeats all season.

**Plant**
Upright and bushy, 4 to 5 feet, with glossy, dark green foliage. Very susceptible to rust. Tender.

**Landscape and other uses**
In beds and borders, and as cut flowers and exhibition flowers.

## 'Royal Sunset'
Introduced 1960

**Class**
Large-flowered climber

**Flowers**
Double, 4½ to 5 inches, apricot that fades in hot weather. Oval, spiraled buds open to cupped blossoms. Flowers are borne singly and in small clusters. Fruity fragrance.

**Bloom**
Midseason; repeats all season.

**Plant**
Upright, 6 to 10 feet, with glossy, deep green foliage. Tender.

**Landscape and other uses**
On pillars, trellises, fences and walls, and as cut flowers.

## 'Schneewittchen'
see 'Iceberg'

## 'Sea Pearl'
Introduced 1964

**Class**
Floribunda

**Flowers**
Double, 4½ inches, shades of pink blended with yellow and peach. Buds open slowly to high-centered blossoms. Flowers are borne singly and in small clusters. Slight fragrance.

**Bloom**
Early midseason; repeats during entire season.

**Plant**
Upright and bushy plant, 3½ to 4 feet, with semiglossy, dark green foliage.

**Landscape and other uses**
In beds and borders, and as cut flowers and exhibition flowers.

## 'Simplicity'
Introduced 1979

**Class**
Floribunda

**Flowers**
Semidouble, 3 to 4 inches, medium pink. Pointed buds open to blossoms that may be flat or cupped and show dark yellow stamens that turn light brown with age. Flowers are borne in small clusters. Little fragrance.

**Bloom**
Abundant in midseason; repeats well all season.

**Plant**
Upright and bushy, 2½ to 3½ feet, with semiglossy, light to medium green foliage. Hardy.

**Landscape and other uses**
In beds, borders and hedges, and as cut flowers.

## 'Snow Bride'
Introduced 1982

**Class**
Miniature

**Flowers**
Double, 1½ inches, white. Long, pointed buds open to high-centered flowers that show yellow stamens. Flowers are borne singly and are long-lasting. Little fragrance.

**Bloom**
Midseason; repeats all season.

**Plant**
Compact, 18 inches, with semiglossy, green foliage.

**Landscape and other uses**
In beds, borders, edgings and containers, and as cut flowers and exhibition flowers.

## 'Sombreuil'
Introduced 1850

**Class**
Old Garden Rose: Climbing Tea

**Flowers**
Very double, 3½ to 4 inches, ivory white with distinctive beige tones toward the center. Short buds open to flat, saucer-shaped blossoms that are quartered in form. Flowers are borne in clusters on nodding stems. Strong tea fragrance.

**Bloom**
Midseason; repeats well.

**Plant**
Upright and vigorous, 8 to 12 feet, with semiglossy, green leaves and moderately thorny canes. Semihardy.

**Landscape and other uses**
On walls, fences, trellises and arbors, and as cut flowers.

## 'Sonia'
Sometimes designated 'Sonia Meilland,' sometimes 'Sweet Promise'
Introduced 1974

**Class**
Grandiflora

**Flowers**
Double, 4 to 4½ inches, pink suffused with coral. Long, slender buds open to high-centered blossoms. Flowers (which may not appear for a year after planting) are borne singly or in small clusters. Mildly fruity fragrance.

**Bloom**
Midseason; repeats all season.

**Plant**
Upright, 4 feet, with glossy, deep green foliage. Semihardy.

**Landscape and other uses**
In beds and borders, and also as cut flowers.

## 'Starglo'
Introduced 1973

**Class**
Miniature

**Flowers**
Double, 1¾ inches, white. Long, pointed buds open slowly to high-centered, star-shaped blossoms. Flowers are borne singly and in clusters. Slight fragrance.

**Bloom**
Midseason; repeats all season.

**Plant**
Compact, 12 to 16 inches, with semiglossy, green foliage. Semihardy.

**Landscape and other uses**
In beds, borders, edgings and containers and as cut flowers and exhibition flowers.

'SNOW BRIDE'

'SOMBREUIL'

'SONIA'

'STARGLO'

'SUNFIRE'

'SUNSPRITE'

'THE FAIRY'

'TIFFANY'

## 'Sunfire'
Introduced 1974

**Class**
Floribunda

**Flowers**
Double, 3½ inches, bright orange-red that holds its color. Oval buds open to high-centered blossoms. Flowers are borne singly or in clusters. Flowers have slight fragrance.

**Bloom**
Midseason; repeats all season.

**Plant**
Upright and bushy, 4 feet, with leathery, green foliage. Disease-resistant. Semihardy.

**Landscape and other uses**
In beds, borders and hedges, and as cut flowers.


## 'Sunsprite'
Introduced 1977

**Class**
Floribunda

**Flowers**
Double, 3 inches, deep yellow that holds its color. Oval buds open to high-centered blossoms. Flowers are borne in clusters. Moderate to strong fragrance.

**Bloom**
Early midseason; repeats well all season.

**Plant**
Compact, 3 feet, with glossy, light green leaves. Semihardy.

**Landscape and other uses**
In beds and borders, and as cut flowers and exhibition flowers.


**'Super Star'** see 'Tropicana'

**'Sweet Promise'** see 'Sonia'


## 'The Fairy'
Introduced 1932

**Class**
Polyantha

**Flowers**
Double, 1 to 1½ inches, light pink that turn nearly white in hot sun. Small buds open to slightly cupped blossoms that are long-lasting. No fragrance.

**Bloom**
Late; repeats well all season.

**Plant**
Spreading and vigorous, 1½ to 2½ feet tall and somewhat wider, with tiny, glossy, dark green leaves and thorny canes; usually rounded and bushy in form, but sometimes trailing and ground-hugging. Disease-resistant, but somewhat susceptible to spider mites in hot weather. Plant is hardy.

**Landscape and other uses**
In beds, borders and hedges, and as cut flowers and tree roses. In its trailing form 'The Fairy' is among the few roses that can be used as ground cover.


## 'Tiffany'
Introduced 1954

**Class**
Hybrid Tea

**Flowers**
Double, 4 to 5 inches, soft rose pink with a glow of yellow at the petal bases. Long, pointed buds open to high-centered blossoms. Flowers are borne singly or in clusters. Flowers have strong old-rose fragrance.

**Bloom**
Midseason; repeats well during entire season.

**Plant**
Upright and bushy, 4½ feet, with glossy, dark green foliage. More disease-resistant than most hybrid teas. Performs best where summers are hot. Plant is semihardy.

**Landscape and other uses**
In beds and borders, and also as cut flowers.

### 'Touch of Class'
Introduced 1986

**Class**
Hybrid Tea

**Flowers**
Double, 4½ to 5½ inches, pink blended with cream and coral. Spiraled buds open to high-centered blossoms. Flowers are generally borne singly on long stems. Slight fragrance.

**Bloom**
Midseason; repeats all season.

**Plant**
Upright, 4 feet, with small, semiglossy, dark green leaves. Semihardy.

**Landscape and other uses**
In beds and borders, and also as cut flowers.

### 'Trumpeter'
Introduced 1977

**Class**
Floribunda

**Flowers**
Double, 3½ inches, vivid orange-scarlet that holds its color well even in hot sun. Oval buds open to high-centered blooms. Flowers are borne singly and in clusters. Flowers have light fragrance.

**Bloom**
Abundant in midseason; repeats well all season.

**Plant**
Upright and bushy, 3 to 4½ feet, with glossy, dark green foliage. Semihardy.

**Landscape and other uses**
In beds, borders and hedges, and as cut flowers.

### 'Uncle Joe'
Sometimes designated 'Toro'
Introduced 1971

**Class**
Hybrid Tea

**Flowers**
Very double, 6 inches, medium to dark red. Buds open slowly to high-centered blossoms. Flow-ers are borne singly on long stems. Cool, damp weather sometimes stunts flower production. Strong fragrance.

**Bloom**
Midseason; repeats all season.

**Plant**
Upright, 5 feet, with glossy, dark green foliage. Semihardy.

**Landscape and other uses**
In beds and borders, and also as cut flowers.

### 'York and Lancaster'
Sometimes designated *Rosa damascena versicolor*
Introduced before 1551

**Class**
Old Garden Rose: Damask

**Flowers**
Double, 2 to 3 inches, all white, all pink, or white and pink combined. Moderate fragrance. The flower is named for the adversaries in the Wars of the Roses in 15th Century England; the white rose was the symbol of the royal house of York and the red rose the symbol of the royal house of Lancaster. Buds open to loosely cupped blossoms. Flowers are borne in clusters.

**Bloom**
Midseason; does not repeat.

**Plant**
Upright and bushy, 3 to 5 feet, with slightly gray-green leaves and thorny canes. Difficult to grow; needs cool conditions and good soil. Extremely hardy.

**Landscape and other uses**
In borders and in combination with other plants.

'TOUCH OF CLASS'

'TRUMPETER'

'UNCLE JOE'

'YORK AND LANCASTER'

379

# 8

# TREES AND SHRUBS

*A small Japanese maple casts shade on a grassy lawn in summer, with a variety of shrubs lining the foundation of a home. Trees and shrubs can serve several purposes, offering shade, beauty and a measure of privacy to any yard or garden.*

Whether you choose them for the seasonal color provided by their flowers, fruits and leaves, or for the unchanging beauty of evergreens, the trees and shrubs you have will dominate your garden. Trees form the living architecture of the landscape, shaping its space in three dimensions—and doing so over long spans of time. Shrubs can afford the privacy of an impenetrable hedge or simply present a pleasing pattern of greenery or a spectacular show of flowers and foliage. It therefore pays to choose trees and shrubs with forethought, plant them with care and maintain them faithfully.

As described on the following pages, planting is the first step in getting trees and shrubs off to a good start. Planting must be done in timely fashion, in a well-chosen and well-prepared site, and with good stock. In buying new trees or shrubs, it is best to deal with a reputable nursery or mail-order house and to buy the best plants you can find. Think not only about appearance, but also about the nature of each plant itself. Although trees and shrubs have a well-deserved reputation for hardiness, many are adversely affected by extreme weather conditions. Trees do best in areas to which they are indigenous; taking a tree out of its accustomed environment will decrease its chances of survival. The Zone Map *(inside front cover)* will help you select trees and shrubs that are adapted to your climate. Find your zone; then consult the Dictionary of Trees and Shrubs *(pages 426-459)* to see which plants will thrive in your garden.

Compared with other plants, trees and shrubs may seem relatively self-sufficient. But if they are to thrive, they need a little attention. This chapter describes how to

# CHAPTER CONTENTS

water and fertilize trees and shrubs as well as how to prune and propagate them. Refer to Chapter 2 for other nurturing tasks for your trees and shrubs, including weeding and mulching and averting the ravages of pests.

Pruning is the art of gently guiding a tree or shrub into its best possible shape, not by drastically altering its natural growth habit, but by skillfully modifying and making the most of it. Too often, though, pruning turns into a confrontation between gardener and plant, and the plant comes out the worse for wear. Learning just a few simple techniques will give you the skill to tackle any pruning job. Refer to this chapter for directions on pruning trees, removing limbs from a mature tree, pruning a needle-leaved evergreen tree and shearing a hedge to keep it dense, compact and shapely.

Propagation may seem a mysterious science best left to professional growers. But if you enjoy experimenting and are patient, you may find that propagating your own plants holds many rewards. Two methods of propagating trees and shrubs are shown in this chapter—planting stem cuttings and cleft grafting. Refer to Chapter 2 for other methods of propagating trees and shrubs, including starting seeds indoors, dividing and layering shrubs, and grafting trees from scions.

You can take the guesswork out of caring for your trees and shrubs by following the month-by-month maintenance checklists on pages 410-417. Then on pages 418-425 is a veritable rogues' gallery of pests and diseases that may threaten your trees and shrubs. The entries are keyed to common danger signs and, in each case, detailed information is provided to help you identify the problem and take swift corrective action.

# PLANTING A TREE

A young sycamore maple rises past the roof of a low-lying suburban house, its rounded shape contrasting with the flat planes of house and lawn, its leafy branches providing shade. The sycamore maple is a fast-growing tree that reaches approximately 70 feet at maturity.

A tree can dramatically alter the character of your yard or garden, imposing structure on the landscape and creating a focal point of interest. But choosing the right tree can be a simple matter if you avoid a few common pitfalls.

First, select a suitable shape. If you want to frame a path, tall evergreens would make a good choice. If you want to shade a sunny patio, choose a rounded deciduous tree.

Next, consider scale: Select a tree that will still fit its context when fully grown. Plant it where it has room to grow safely; branches overhanging a chimney can be a fire hazard, and spreading roots may interfere with buried pipes that pass through the yard. A tree too big for its site or in the wrong place may eventually have to be cut down. Your nursery can tell you how much space to allow for each species of tree. Although the recommended spacing may seem exaggerated, remember that a young sapling will develop into an imposing tree in just a few years.

Trees come from the nursery in three different ways: bare-rooted, in containers and—the most expensive option—with the root ball wrapped in burlap. If you buy a container-grown tree, the principal risk is a tree that has become too old and large for its container. The result will be overcrowded roots, with the major ones showing pretzel-like contortions. Ask the nursery assistant to remove at least part of the root ball from its container and check for excessive compaction and crowding.

If you buy a balled-and-burlapped tree, ask whether the wrapping is natural burlap. If it is not, ask for planting instructions. Examine the burlap before buying. More than one layer of wrapping may mean the tree was dug up so long ago that the original burlap began to fall apart. Such a tree has remained in the nursery too long. Similarly, roots growing through the burlap indicate the tree has been out of the ground for weeks. Avoid it and look for something fresher. A method for planting an oriental flowering dogwood sapling wrapped in natural burlap is shown opposite and on the following page.

1 Dig a hole for the sapling that is twice as wide as and 6 inches deeper than its root ball. Pile the excavated soil beside the hole for later use as backfill. Improve the soil in the hole *(pages 56-57)* if the soil or drainage is poor. In the center of the hole, build a firmly packed mound of backfill 6 inches high for the root ball to rest on; the mound will allow the roots to spread out and will help to drain away excess water. Combine the remaining backfill with dehydrated cow manure, peat or some other organic soil amendment, mixing 3 parts backfill to 1 part amendment. Pick up the sapling and set the root ball on the mound. **Gardener's Tip:** Handle the sapling by its root ball, not by its trunk; if it is held by the trunk, the weight of the soil in the root ball might break off some of the roots. To confirm that the sapling is at the correct depth, lay a stake across the hole *(right)*; if the stake is aligned with the old soil mark on the sapling's trunk, the sapling will be at the correct depth when the hole is filled in. Otherwise, adjust the depth of the hole.

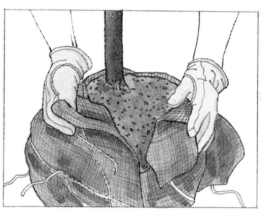

2 Cut the twine holding the burlap in place but do not remove the burlap—it will rot away eventually. Fill the hole almost to the top with amended backfill and tamp it down well. Fold the cloth back into the soil *(above)* so that it will not wick moisture away from the roots. Continue filling the hole to the level of the old soil mark on the trunk and tamp the soil once again. Soak the root ball with water.

3 If the planted sapling is more than 6 feet tall or will be subject to high winds, buy two 6-foot-long, 1-by-2 stakes to support it. Use a sharp knife to cut a notch in each stake about 3 inches from the top *(right)*.

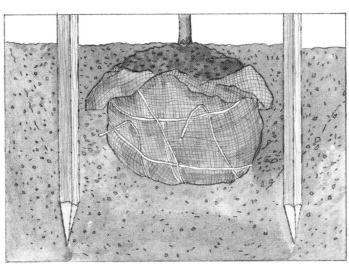

**4** Drive the stakes straight into the ground on either side of the root ball; they must go deep enough to reach into the firm soil below the filled hole *(above)*. Form a basin at the inner edge of the stakes to concentrate water on the roots, where it is needed most. Spread mulch 2 to 3 inches deep around the sapling, leaving a small space between the mulch and the trunk. For more information on mulching, refer to page 70.

## PROTECTING TREES FROM WINTER

Sturdy though they may seem, trees are susceptible to winter damage. The thin bark of trees such as birch and silver maple is prone to frost cracks, especially when the trees are young. The foliage of broad-leaved evergreen trees loses water through evaporation, and if a tree is unable to replace the water, the leaves can turn brown and drop off. And the limbs of needle-leaved evergreens can be broken by the weight of snow and ice.

But you can take precautions against all these hazards. In late fall, cover the trunks of birches and silver maples with strips of burlap tied with string or with adhesive tree wrap (available at garden supply centers); wind it diagonally around each trunk. Water your broadleaved evergreens well and spray them with an antidesiccant, as you would a shrub *(page 390)*. If ice or snow remains on a pine or spruce after a storm, knock it off with a broom as soon as possible.

**5** To secure the sapling to the stakes, cut two pieces of garden hose, each 1 foot long, and slip each one over a 3- or 4-foot length of wire; the hose will protect the tree trunk. Bend one hose-covered section of the wire around the trunk; loop the protruding wire ends into a figure eight and secure them in the notch of one stake *(inset)*. Repeat with the other piece of hose, wire and stake. Leave the wires loose enough for the tree to flex with the wind *(right)*. The stakes may be removed after a year. For tips on protecting your trees from winter damage, refer to the box above.

# TRANSPLANTING A TREE

The tried-and-true way to transplant a tree with a substantial root system is to borrow a trick from tree farmers: wrap the roots in a good-sized sheet of burlap. Provided you choose a tree with a trunk no bigger than 1 inch in diameter (bigger than that will be too heavy), no serious problems are involved. The main requirements—illustrated below and on pages 386-387—are to free the root ball from the earth without harming it, and to get the burlap under and around it.

This sort of transplanting has several advantages. First, the burlap wrapping helps keep the bulky root ball and its earth in one solid piece. The burlap also helps protect any bruised or exposed root tips from wind and sun while the tree is being moved, lessening water loss (and thus stress) to the tree. Further, a well-wrapped root ball can be maneuvered easily into its new location.

The best times of the year to do the digging and moving are late fall and early spring, that is, when the tree is dormant. An evergreen, although it will not shed all its foliage in autumn and winter, transpires less moisture during the cool months. This protects the tree in winter when ground water may not be available to replace transpired water. In very cold regions spring is probably preferable, because it spares the fresh transplant winter's punishing weather.

The best time to transplant is when the ground is moist but not waterlogged. Moist soil will cling to the roots. Sodden ground is too heavy to work.

*Laden with spring blooms, the boughs of a small cherry tree arch gracefully toward the lawn. Such trees, when young, are easily moved with the aid of a burlap sheet.*

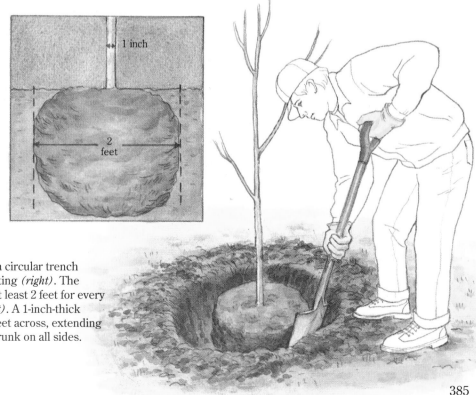

1 Using a curved-blade shovel, dig a circular trench around the tree you are transplanting *(right)*. The diameter of the circle should be at least 2 feet for every inch of the trunk's diameter *(inset)*. A 1-inch-thick trunk requires a trench that is 2 feet across, extending at least 12 inches away from the trunk on all sides.

**2** Dig the trench to a depth equal to its width—here 24 inches. Then to avoid having to lift the weight of too much moist soil unnecessarily, use a spade to shave the sides of the ball of earth around the roots *(left)* until you reach the roots. Work carefully and do not chop at the root ball; you can easily injure the delicate outer root tips. To free the root ball from the earth, place the spade under the ball on one side of the tree, then push the blade with your foot under the ball. Repeat the process on the other side of the tree, gradually lifting the root system from the ground. You may sever the bottom end of the taproot, but it will grow again.

## HOW TO HELP TREES UNDER SIEGE

Nothing is quite so damaging to trees as an attack by pests or disease—particularly when entire communities are afflicted by the same culprit. Three current "tree epidemics" are among the most worrisome, causing widespread concern across the United States:
• **Eastern U.S.** In the early spring, trees are infested by gypsy moth caterpillars, which can nibble through tree leaves, stopping only when a tree is defoliated. In fact, a single tree can be destroyed within a few years. Although you should consult a certified pest control professional for a heavily-infested tree, you can handle less severe problems yourself, as advised on page 418. If you live in the East, take preventative action: Help keep gypsy moths away by keeping your yard and garden clean of debris, and plant varieties of trees that are gypsy-moth-resistant, such as ash, dogwood, honey locust or yellow poplar.
• **Southern and Western U.S.** Bark beetles in these areas target pines that are damaged by wind, drought or flooding, and can destroy them in months. The main sign of bark beetle appears on the tree trunk as small lumps of pitch, the size of popcorn. By the time a pine's needles discolor, it is almost too late to save the tree. To discourage the beetles from attacking, avoid damaging tree bark when gardening.

• **Florida, Texas and California.** Lethal Yellowing (LY) and butt rot are diseases that afflict palm trees like the Washington fan palm. An LY-infected tree drops all of its nuts, and its flower pods die in their shells. Later, the leaves turn yellow and die; if more than half a dozen leaves are affected, the tree must be cut down. But, with early detection, an infected tree can be saved. Consult a local tree nursery or a professional arborist for advice on a diagnosis and treatment. Butt rot is a tough, leathery, yellow to deep red or brown fungus that masses at or near the base of palm trees, causing gradual decay. Although there is no cure for butt rot, you can take precautions to prevent it. Minimize damage to a palm tree's roots and base when gardening. Do not plant palms in areas exposed to butt rot without first having the soil fumigated. Finally, ensure adequate drainage and avoid planting in shady locations.

The best defense against tree pests and diseases is faithful maintenance of your trees; be on the lookout for problems or any change in a tree's appearance. For more information about pests and diseases in your area, contact your local county extension service or a local branch of the American Forestry Association.

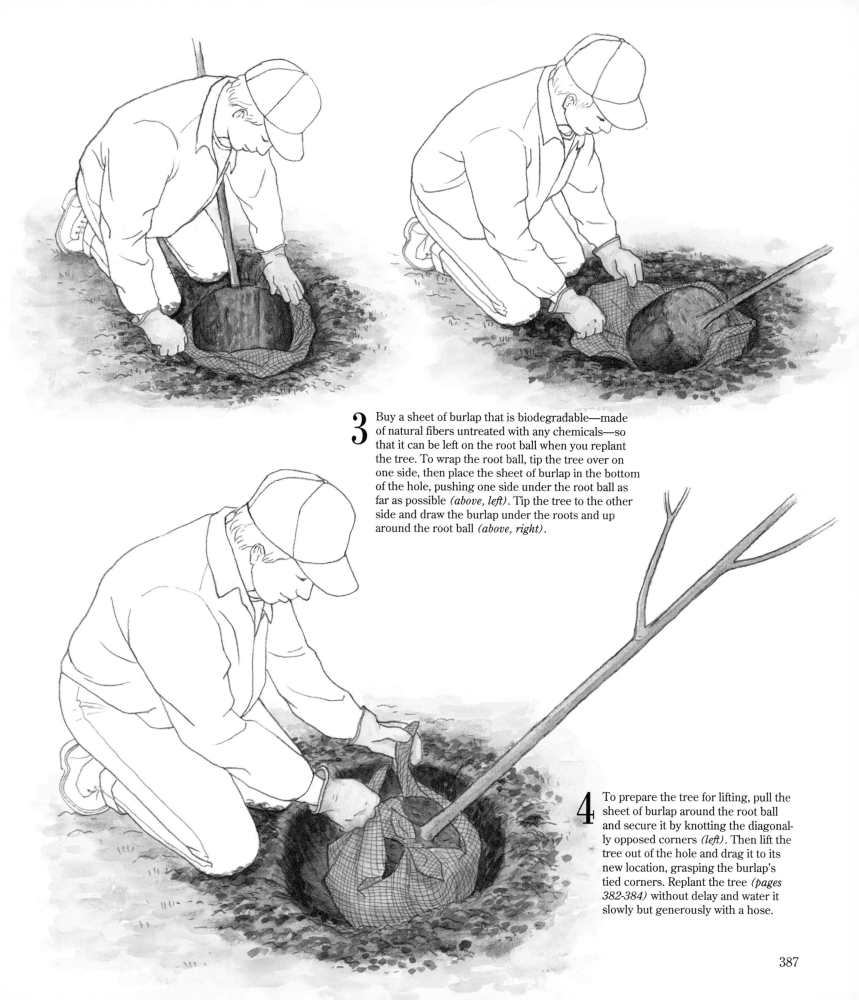

**3** Buy a sheet of burlap that is biodegradable—made of natural fibers untreated with any chemicals—so that it can be left on the root ball when you replant the tree. To wrap the root ball, tip the tree over on one side, then place the sheet of burlap in the bottom of the hole, pushing one side under the root ball as far as possible *(above, left)*. Tip the tree to the other side and draw the burlap under the roots and up around the root ball *(above, right)*.

**4** To prepare the tree for lifting, pull the sheet of burlap around the root ball and secure it by knotting the diagonally opposed corners *(left)*. Then lift the tree out of the hole and drag it to its new location, grasping the burlap's tied corners. Replant the tree *(pages 382-384)* without delay and water it slowly but generously with a hose.

387

# PLANTING SHRUBS

*The white and pink flowers of low-lying azaleas accent the entrance to this field-stone and shingle house. Azaleas bloom best when shielded from excessive sun and wind, so they make ideal additions to yards dominated by large shade trees.*

S hrubs that will enhance your yard season after season, year after year, are available in three categories: deciduous shrubs, which lose their leaves in the fall; broad-leaved evergreens, such as rhododendron; and needle-leaved evergreens, such as juniper. Shrubs also come from the nursery in three different ways: with their roots covered in burlap, or planted in baskets or plastic containers. When buying shrubs, choose smaller, younger plants, which are usually less expensive and easier to plant than older ones. Look for healthy plants with crisp and green top growth and foliage that shows no signs of pests, disease or breakage, and roots that are white and springy.

Check the burlap of a burlap-covered shrub. It should look new and intact, indicating that the shrub has been wrapped recently. Avoid plants that have roots sticking through the burlap or a second layer of burlap hiding an earlier layer; in both cases the shrubs have been out of the ground too long. If the roots are wrapped in chemically treated or synthetic burlap, request specific planting instructions. Beware of a root ball that seems soft and crumbly. Good root balls have a solid feel. Shop for burlap-covered shrubs in early fall or in spring when better nurseries traditionally put them on sale.

Plant shrubs in cool weather to avoid subjecting them to high temperatures and intense sunlight. Early spring and fall are ideal planting times, since the roots can get established before the shrub blossoms or the ground freezes. The shorter the branches, the better the shrub can expend its energy establishing roots. When you buy a new shrub, ask if it has already been pruned. If not, prune off one-third to one-half the branches' length before planting the shrub.

Shrubs less than 3½ feet high can be set in the ground by hand. A bigger shrub should be rolled onto its side and eased into place with the aid of its burlap wrapping *(opposite)*; do not handle a shrub by its branches or they may break. For guidelines on planting container-grown shrubs, refer to the box at left.

## PLANTING CONTAINER-GROWN SHRUBS

Container-grown shrubs demand some special treatment because they have spent their lives in narrow confines and have been pampered with more than the usual quantities of nutrients. The transition from pot to earth is stressful. First, they need to be planted in extra-large holes—at least twice the size of their root balls, but preferably three times as large. The additional space is filled with generous amounts of good loose soil. The extra room gives the long-confined roots plenty of space to search out nutrients and grow.

Second, the roots themselves need to be "destressed," that is, pried open and pruned here and there. A shrub that shows lots of healthy foliage is likely to have a healthy root ball, but even so, the roots may be growing in tight circles that follow the contours of the pot, and will need to be loosened and spread out before being put in the ground. Container-grown shrubs can be put in the ground any time the soil can be worked, but the best time to plant them is the early fall.

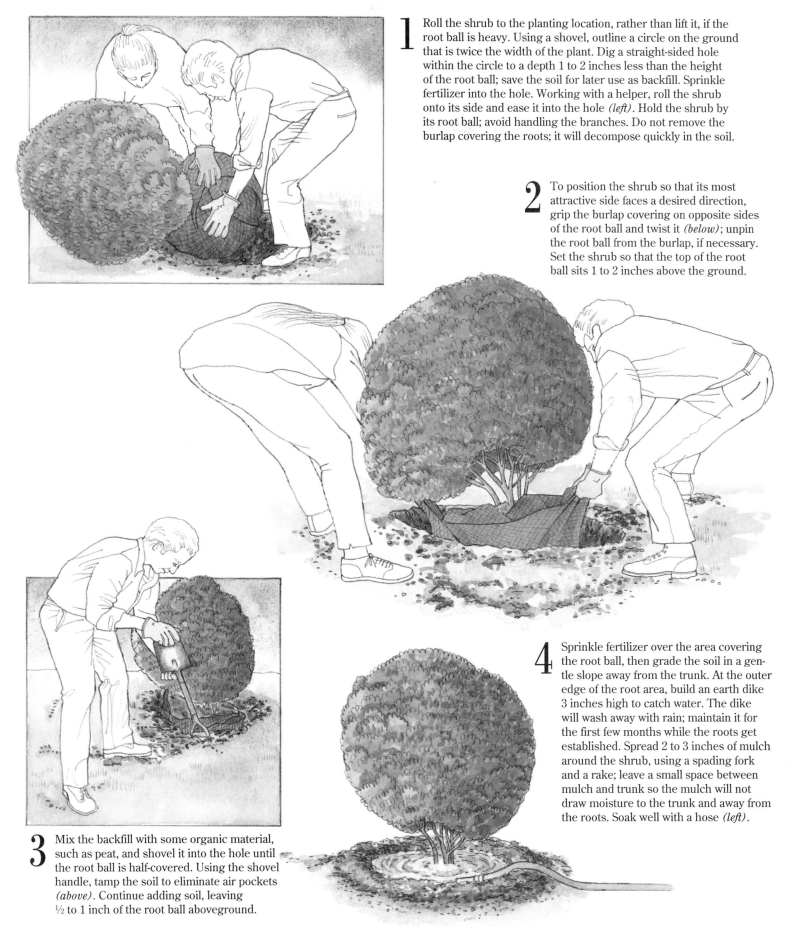

**1** Roll the shrub to the planting location, rather than lift it, if the root ball is heavy. Using a shovel, outline a circle on the ground that is twice the width of the plant. Dig a straight-sided hole within the circle to a depth 1 to 2 inches less than the height of the root ball; save the soil for later use as backfill. Sprinkle fertilizer into the hole. Working with a helper, roll the shrub onto its side and ease it into the hole *(left)*. Hold the shrub by its root ball; avoid handling the branches. Do not remove the burlap covering the roots; it will decompose quickly in the soil.

**2** To position the shrub so that its most attractive side faces a desired direction, grip the burlap covering on opposite sides of the root ball and twist it *(below)*; unpin the root ball from the burlap, if necessary. Set the shrub so that the top of the root ball sits 1 to 2 inches above the ground.

**4** Sprinkle fertilizer over the area covering the root ball, then grade the soil in a gentle slope away from the trunk. At the outer edge of the root area, build an earth dike 3 inches high to catch water. The dike will wash away with rain; maintain it for the first few months while the roots get established. Spread 2 to 3 inches of mulch around the shrub, using a spading fork and a rake; leave a small space between mulch and trunk so the mulch will not draw moisture to the trunk and away from the roots. Soak well with a hose *(left)*.

**3** Mix the backfill with some organic material, such as peat, and shovel it into the hole until the root ball is half-covered. Using the shovel handle, tamp the soil to eliminate air pockets *(above)*. Continue adding soil, leaving ½ to 1 inch of the root ball aboveground.

# TRANSPLANTING SHRUBS

*Graceful juniper branches look feathery but are prickly to the touch; the needles are fine and grow close together but are sharply pointed at the ends. This coniferous evergreen prefers hot, dry, sunny conditions and is an ideal shrub to transplant.*

## PROTECTING SHRUBS FROM WINTER DAMAGE

Broad-leaved evergreen shrubs—azaleas, mountain laurel, rhododendrons and others—can shrivel and die in cold climates for want of water. Winter winds draw moisture from the leaves, and so does winter sunshine. And dormant roots cannot replace the lost moisture. To defend shrubs against winter damage, be sure they get extra waterings as the date of the first hard frost approaches. This will send them into winter with a good supply of moisture. Then spread a thick layer of mulch around them to help keep the water from evaporating and to provide insulation for the roots. For more information on mulching, refer to page 70. In northerly areas, there are two further useful maneuvers. One is to spray the leaves with an antidesiccant—a milky-looking waxy liquid that coats the leaves and retards water loss. Another is to build temporary screens using wood stakes and burlap sheets on the windward sides of exposed evergreens.

There are many reasons for transplanting a shrub. Its present site may be overcrowded; you may have an empty spot elsewhere you would like to fill; or you may simply want to change the look of your garden. Transplanting is easy to do—but it causes a shock even to healthy plants. To minimize the shock, prune the plant before moving it, because the less top growth it has to support, the better its roots can take hold. Cut off a third to a half of the branch growth. Then wrap the pruned plant in burlap as shown on the following pages to protect its branches during transplanting.

When you dig into the soil, be careful not to cut into the fine "feeder" roots, the ones at the outer limits of the root system. They carry nutrients to the plant, and a shrub cannot afford to lose many of them. To safeguard them, keep a large ball of soil around the root system and wrap the root ball in two more pieces of burlap. The only expendable part of the root system of many shrubs is the taproot, which extends straight down into the ground and anchors the plant. It must be severed before the shrub can be removed from the ground. Slice through it with a sharp blow of a spade.

The best time to move a shrub is in the early spring, before the year's new growth has begun. Cool, moist weather is ideal. Carry small shrubs by hand, gripping them just above the root ball, where the branches are strongest. Transplanting a large shrub is a two-person job. You can use a wheelbarrow or a cart, but you may find it easier to slide the shrub onto a dropcloth and drag it along like a sled.

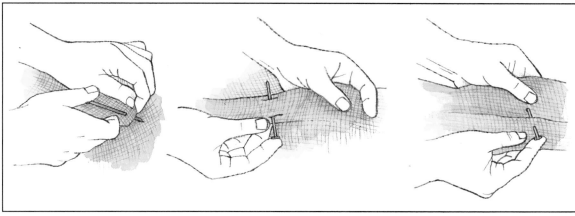

## PINNING IT UP

For safe transplanting, wrap a shrub in natural-fiber burlap, using 4-inch-long common nails to secure the burlap. Pinch together two pieces of overlapping burlap and insert the point of a nail through both pieces *(far left)*. Reverse the direction of the nail and push the point back through both pieces *(middle)*. Press the point of the nail into the burlap again to keep it from protruding *(near left)*.

**1** Wrap the shrub in a rectangular piece of burlap long enough to reach from the bottom branches of the plant to the top and wide enough to go around the circumference; first, trim any low branches that might get in your way. Wrap one short edge of the burlap piece around the base of the shrub *(right)* and fasten the corners together with nails, following the technique shown in the box above.

**2** Pull the other short edge of the burlap piece over the top of the shrub so that it hangs in a flap. Grasp the corners of the flap and pin them together *(left)*. Pull firmly on the long edges of the piece until they overlap in front of the shrub. Starting from the base of the shrub and working toward the top, pin the overlapping edges together. To begin digging up the shrub, use a spade to mark a circle in the ground about one-third wider than the shrub's diameter. Dig a trench around the outside of the circle; keep the blade of the spade facing away from the plant to avoid damaging the feeder roots. When the trench is dug, turn the spade so that the blade faces the plant at a slight angle to the roots and dig deep under them in order to loosen the soil around and under the plant's root system.

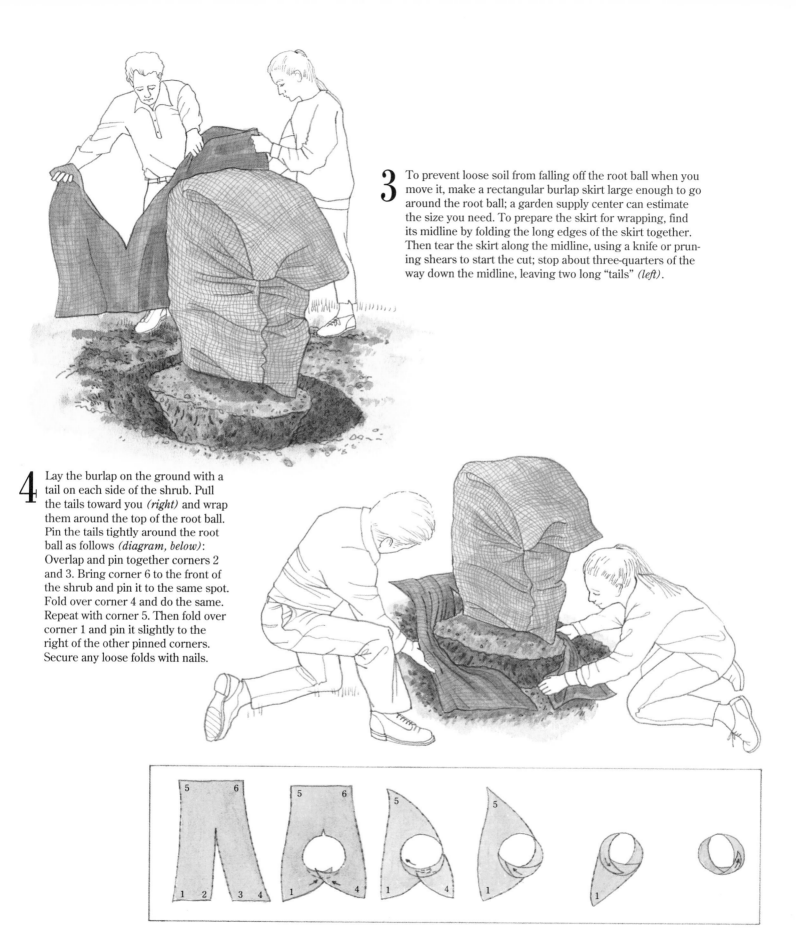

**3** To prevent loose soil from falling off the root ball when you move it, make a rectangular burlap skirt large enough to go around the root ball; a garden supply center can estimate the size you need. To prepare the skirt for wrapping, find its midline by folding the long edges of the skirt together. Then tear the skirt along the midline, using a knife or pruning shears to start the cut; stop about three-quarters of the way down the midline, leaving two long "tails" *(left)*.

**4** Lay the burlap on the ground with a tail on each side of the shrub. Pull the tails toward you *(right)* and wrap them around the top of the root ball. Pin the tails tightly around the root ball as follows *(diagram, below)*: Overlap and pin together corners 2 and 3. Bring corner 6 to the front of the shrub and pin it to the same spot. Fold over corner 4 and do the same. Repeat with corner 5. Then fold over corner 1 and pin it slightly to the right of the other pinned corners. Secure any loose folds with nails.

**5** Determine whether the shrub has a taproot: Rock the shrub over on its side, exposing the bottom of the root ball. If there is a taproot, chop it off, as close as possible to the root ball, using the front edge of the spade. Cover the exposed bottom of the root ball with another piece of burlap. To secure this piece to the root ball, take hold of diagonally opposing corners of it *(right)* and pin them together across the top of the root ball. Before pinning the last two free corners together, pull them up firmly and shake the root ball to make sure that it is as tightly packed as possible. Then pin together any remaining loose flaps and openings.

**6** To lift the shrub, tip it to one side. Shovel some of the soil you removed back into the hole *(above)*. Tip the shrub onto this backfill and shovel soil from the other side into the hole *(right)*. Tip the shrub again and add more soil from the first side. Continue alternately tipping the shrub and backfilling until the hole is full and the plant has been raised to ground level. Plant the shrub *(page 388)* at the desired location.

# WATERING AND FERTILIZING TREES AND SHRUBS

Supplementing the diet of young trees does wonders for their development. When fertilized three times a year, they shoot up fast—some species may grow as much as 5 to 6 feet in one season. Fertilizer also benefits mature trees; a dose applied every two or three years will maintain all-round vigor. Shrubs, to be at their healthiest and most attractive, need to be fertilized as well.

All trees and shrubs take in nutrients through their roots, most of which extend laterally from the trunk and branches to beyond the drip line—the point that lies just beneath the outermost edges of the branches.

The three most important nutrients are nitrogen (for healthy leaves), phosphorus (for healthy roots and blossoms) and potassium (for overall strength and resistance to cold and disease). Fertilizers labeled "complete" contain all three nutrients in any of several ratios. For example, the label "5-10-10" on a bag means it contains 5 percent nitrogen, 10 percent phosphorus and 10 percent potassium. The remaining 75 percent is mostly inert filler—to aid in application—plus trace amounts of other nutrients.

Fertilizer comes in three forms—liquid, which can be sprayed; solid, which may be slow-release pellets or spikes, which are placed underground; and granulated, which is broadcast by hand. Of the three forms, granulated is the simplest to use. No special equipment is required to apply it. You merely sprinkle the granules evenly on the ground above the plant's roots.

Young trees should be fertilized once in the spring just before new growth starts, once just after the tree has blossomed and once in the fall just after the leaves start to drop. Fertilize shrubs in the spring before growth starts, or in the fall after the plant has stopped producing new shoots. In all seasons, wait until the ground cover is dry before broadcasting; fertilizer will burn wet grass and the leaves of any living plant on contact. Always follow the label instructions when applying fertilizer.

*The large, abundant and healthy leaves of a variegated Norway maple indicate a tree that has been fertilized with a sufficient diet of nitrogen.*

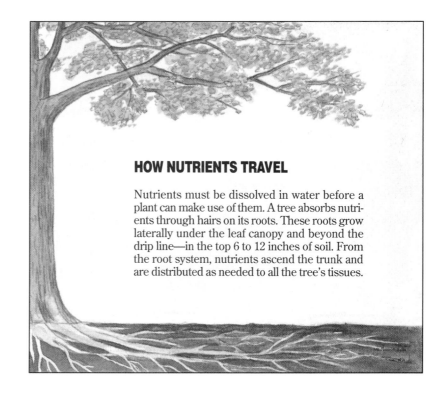

## HOW NUTRIENTS TRAVEL

Nutrients must be dissolved in water before a plant can make use of them. A tree absorbs nutrients through hairs on its roots. These roots grow laterally under the leaf canopy and beyond the drip line—in the top 6 to 12 inches of soil. From the root system, nutrients ascend the trunk and are distributed as needed to all the tree's tissues.

# ONE WAY TO FERTILIZE

Sprinkle fertilizer in a ring about 6 inches from a tree trunk—keeping the fertilizer a safe distance from the trunk to avoid damaging the bark. A foot or two beyond the drip line, sprinkle a second ring of fertilizer. Fill the area between the two rings with fertilizer, distributing it evenly, a handful at a time. Fertilize a shrub near the base of the plant. Water immediately so that the fertilizer soaks into the soil.

## AERATING ROOTS

To give a tree's roots a breath of fresh air, you can aerate the soil at the base of the trunk in spring. Aeration consists of making small holes in the soil so that more oxygen can get to the roots, most of which extend from the trunk to the drip line in the top 6 to 12 inches of soil. It is especially helpful for trees that are in the path of heavy foot traffic, which compresses the soil, or for trees in soil with high clay content. Aeration can be done with an ordinary pitchfork. There are also tools designed especially for the purpose—available at garden supply centers. The best tools lift plugs of soil out of the ground. Also available are automated aerating machines, which are useful if you have an orchard of large, established trees.

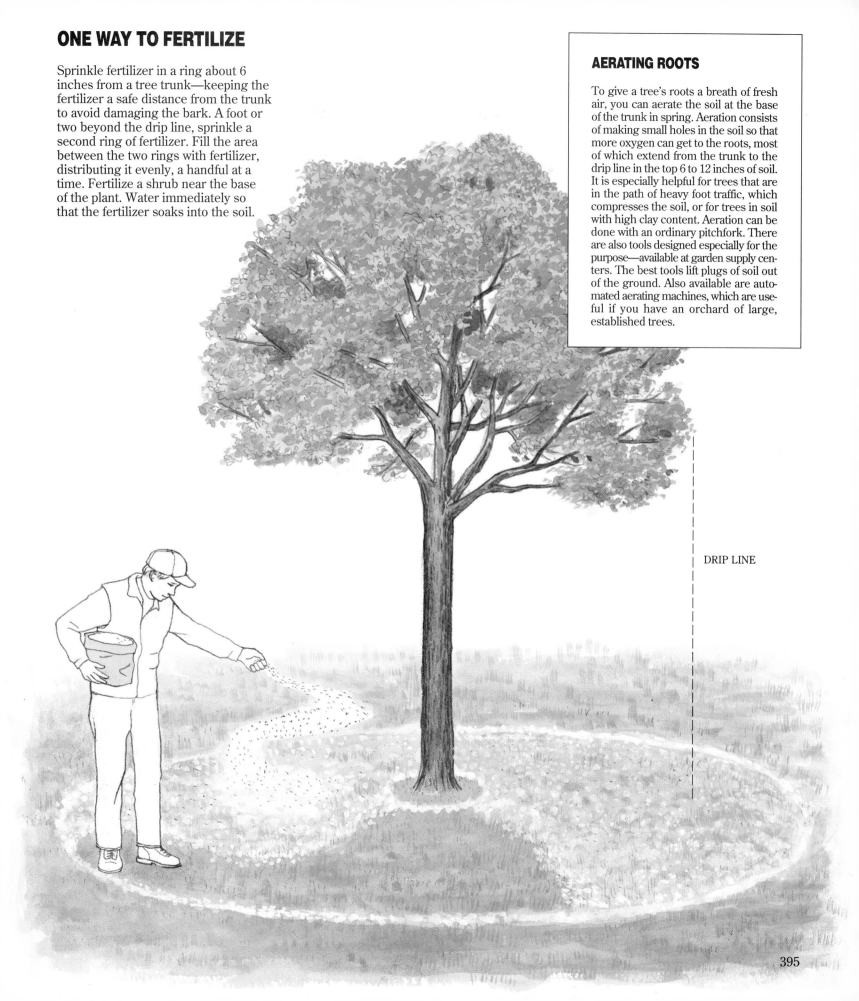

DRIP LINE

# PRUNING A TREE

All trees, no matter what sort of garden they are grown in, require some pruning from time to time, if only to remove dead and diseased limbs, so that they stay healthy and retain graceful, pleasing shapes. This applies especially to deciduous trees. Needle-leaved evergreens usually need only a modicum of care *(page 400)*; they grow rather neatly and their shapes are symmetrical.

The ideally shaped leafy tree generally has one main leader (the trunk) and a number of major lateral branches extending from it. But the typical tree is seldom so orderly, sending out overlong limbs and producing other sorts of superfluous growth. Keeping a leafy tree healthy involves pruning this extra clutter—to let sunlight reach the tree's interior, as well as to remove dead wood and any branches that have discolored bark or other signs of disease. The sorts of situations requiring pruning are pictured in the box opposite.

When pruning a tree for looks, any extraneous growth should be snipped off to simplify the tree's structure, bring it into balance and perhaps keep it small enough for its allotted space. The first year after a major pruning a tree may look a bit bare, but the next season it should have a fresh, clean form as well as renewed vigor.

How to do the snipping itself is shown at top, opposite. Pruning tools are pictured on pages 398-399. For your own safety, wear sturdy gloves, long pants and a long-sleeved shirt when pruning a tree. Light pruning—lopping off a dead branch—can be done at any time of year, but a major job should be postponed until the tree is dormant, usually in the winter. Some exceptions are birches, beeches and maples, which tend to bleed sap when cut. They should be pruned in late spring or early summer; they bleed less when in full leaf. For a flowering tree, prune just after the flowers have faded, to avoid removing the next year's flower buds. To avoid stripping bark when cutting a large branch, remove the heaviest branches in sections with a sequence of carefully spaced cuts *(pages 398-399)* and support the branch with one hand while cutting or sawing with the other hand.

*A young Japanese maple grows straight and strong, and with a pleasingly irregular but balanced shape. Careful pruning has opened up the tree so that the pattern of its trunks and limbs can be seen clearly through the brilliant foliage.*

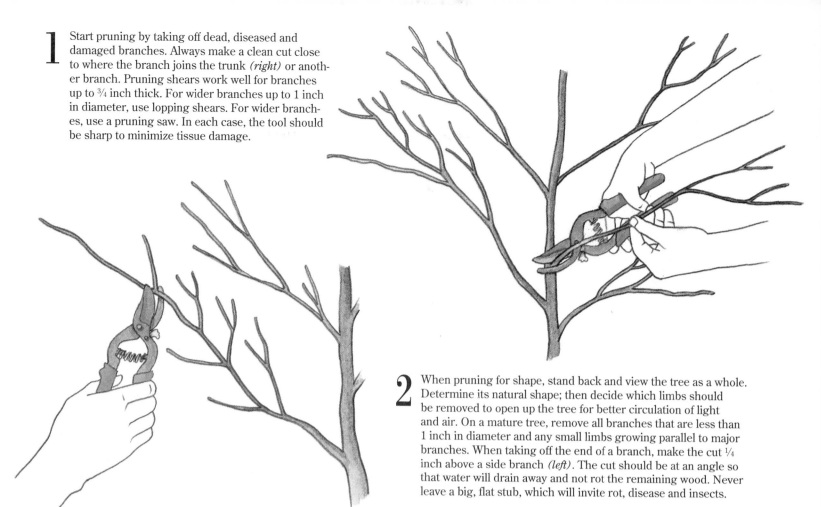

**1** Start pruning by taking off dead, diseased and damaged branches. Always make a clean cut close to where the branch joins the trunk *(right)* or another branch. Pruning shears work well for branches up to ¾ inch thick. For wider branches up to 1 inch in diameter, use lopping shears. For wider branches, use a pruning saw. In each case, the tool should be sharp to minimize tissue damage.

**2** When pruning for shape, stand back and view the tree as a whole. Determine its natural shape; then decide which limbs should be removed to open up the tree for better circulation of light and air. On a mature tree, remove all branches that are less than 1 inch in diameter and any small limbs growing parallel to major branches. When taking off the end of a branch, make the cut ¼ inch above a side branch *(left)*. The cut should be at an angle so that water will drain away and not rot the remaining wood. Never leave a big, flat stub, which will invite rot, disease and insects.

## WHAT TO CUT

Problem areas to look at when pruning a deciduous tree are shown here. It is easiest and best to do a major pruning job when a tree is young. Once it is well shaped, the tree should need little more attention except for the removal of dead branches.

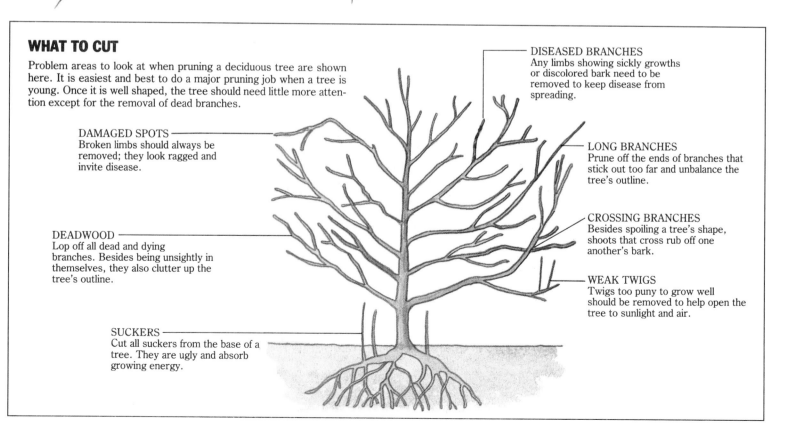

DAMAGED SPOTS
Broken limbs should always be removed; they look ragged and invite disease.

DEADWOOD
Lop off all dead and dying branches. Besides being unsightly in themselves, they also clutter up the tree's outline.

SUCKERS
Cut all suckers from the base of a tree. They are ugly and absorb growing energy.

DISEASED BRANCHES
Any limbs showing sickly growths or discolored bark need to be removed to keep disease from spreading.

LONG BRANCHES
Prune off the ends of branches that stick out too far and unbalance the tree's outline.

CROSSING BRANCHES
Besides spoiling a tree's shape, shoots that cross rub off one another's bark.

WEAK TWIGS
Twigs too puny to grow well should be removed to help open the tree to sunlight and air.

# REMOVING LIMBS FROM A MATURE TREE

There are a number of reasons for pruning a large limb from a mature tree. The limb may be diseased or damaged; it may be interfering with a view, growing into a roof or a chimney (which makes it a fire hazard) or casting unwanted shadows. Or the limb may be a hazard to the tree itself. A branch that forms a narrow V-shaped crotch with the trunk instead of a wide-angled L is vulnerable to injury from accumulated ice and snow, and may have to be removed before it breaks off.

For most trees, the best time to do such surgery is when they are dormant, usually winter or early spring. Before cutting off a large branch, examine it carefully. Look for its branch collar—a swelling where the branch attaches to the trunk. Make your cut close to the branch collar—about 1 inch away—but never into it; the collar contains substances that will help the tree seal and heal the wound. Leave the wound open to the sun and air; tree "dressings" only hinder the natural healing process. To keep the wound as small as possible, avoid tearing off surrounding bark. If the branch is a heavy one, remove it as shown opposite. For limbs up to 10 inches in diameter, use a curved pruning saw *(box, below)*; for ones larger than that, use a bow saw *(box, opposite)*.

*A Babylon weeping willow shows strong limbs and rounded crown—characteristics preserved by periodic pruning of crossing, damaged and weak branches.*

---

**TOOLS FOR PRUNING**

**PRUNING SHEARS**
For removing slender suckers or branches. The best shears have stainless-steel blades. Most are 7 to 9 inches including the handle, and fit in a pocket. Be sure the shears are closed and locked before pocketing them.

**CURVED SAW**
For removing thick suckers or branches. The best saws have flexible blades of tempered steel, with six teeth per inch. The teeth usually have beveled cutting edges and are angled so that they do all the work on the pull, not the push.

**FOLDING SAW**
Works like a standard, curved-blade pruning saw and is made of the same materials: tempered steel for the blade, ash or hickory for the handle. When the blade is folded and secured, the saw can be safely carried in a pocket.

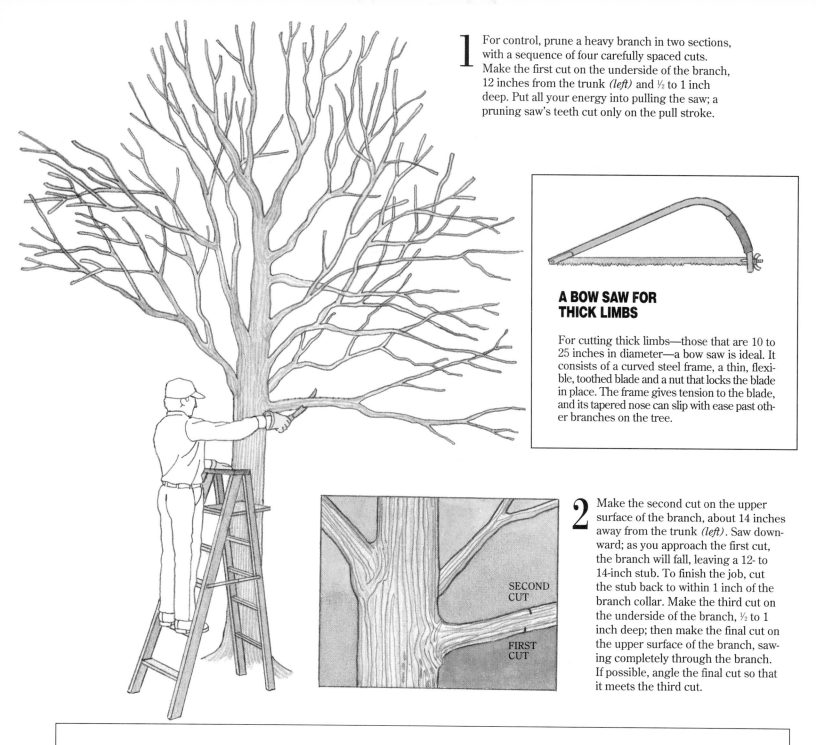

**1** For control, prune a heavy branch in two sections, with a sequence of four carefully spaced cuts. Make the first cut on the underside of the branch, 12 inches from the trunk *(left)* and ½ to 1 inch deep. Put all your energy into pulling the saw; a pruning saw's teeth cut only on the pull stroke.

### A BOW SAW FOR THICK LIMBS

For cutting thick limbs—those that are 10 to 25 inches in diameter—a bow saw is ideal. It consists of a curved steel frame, a thin, flexible, toothed blade and a nut that locks the blade in place. The frame gives tension to the blade, and its tapered nose can slip with ease past other branches on the tree.

SECOND CUT

FIRST CUT

**2** Make the second cut on the upper surface of the branch, about 14 inches away from the trunk *(left)*. Saw downward; as you approach the first cut, the branch will fall, leaving a 12- to 14-inch stub. To finish the job, cut the stub back to within 1 inch of the branch collar. Make the third cut on the underside of the branch, ½ to 1 inch deep; then make the final cut on the upper surface of the branch, sawing completely through the branch. If possible, angle the final cut so that it meets the third cut.

### ADOPTING AN HISTORIC TREE

That lawn or garden tree you've been caring for may also be worth preserving on historic grounds. Although historic trees—unlike historic houses and other structures—are not protected by legislation, they are accorded historic value. A tree is deemed valuable on historic grounds if it is located at the site of an historic event or on a property that is registered for preservation, or if it embodies certain distinguishing characteristics of its species or has an unusual shape.

Until protecting legislation is enacted, tree activists in some communities across the country are taking steps to establish local programs designed to protect historic trees on private property. While this movement is especially important in areas steeped in history, such as Maryland, Virginia, Massachusetts and the District of Columbia, trees with historic value can be found in other areas as well.

Sometimes, a home renovation or other unavoidable cause can require a perfectly healthy tree to be cut down. But any tree, particularly an historic one, on private property can be "adopted"—dug up and transplanted to another locality. So, before letting the ax fall on a healthy tree, contact your municipal public works or planning department. Someone may be interested in adopting your tree, with all transplanting costs borne by its new "parent."

# PRUNING A NEEDLE-LEAVED EVERGREEN

Some judicious pruning, especially in the early years, will help promote the health of almost any tree or shrub and encourage it into a compact yet natural-looking silhouette. The techniques of pruning, however, differ with different kinds of plants. Deciduous trees, broad-leaved evergreens and soft-needled conifer shrubs put out buds all along their branches. Cutting just beyond a bud will promote new growth in a predictable direction; it will encourage the remaining buds to bloom and the branch to put out more buds.

In general, needle-leaved evergreens need less training than their broad-leaved cousins to keep them in shape. Those that are fine-needled and send shoots out in all directions along their branches—such as hemlocks, yews and arborvitae—need only be sheared at the tips from time to time. But certain others—pines, spruces and firs—put out new growth only at the ends of their limbs. Every spring each branch tip produces a new growth called a candle—a cylindrical shoot that develops into a branch during the summer.

Pruning pines, spruces, firs and similar needle-leaved evergreens involves selective and careful cutting of the candles. When done correctly, it can help control a tree's size and shape. Pruning the candles of a shrub will promote the growth of more candles and hence a denser, bushier plant in the long run. If you cut off part of a candle, the remainder develops and becomes a branch; and that branch will produce a new candle the following spring. But if you cut off a branch to the inside of a candle it cannot produce a new one.

Pruning is most effective when started early in the life of a tree. Damaged and unshapely branches can be pruned any time of the year *(right)*. Pruning for shape *(opposite)* should be done in spring.

Pruning mature branches on a stiff-needled conifer shrub should be done sparingly and selectively because mature wood has few buds to produce new growth. Try to follow the natural form of the shrub as closely as possible, and cut inside the desired silhouette, rather than at its edge, so that the stub is concealed.

*Upright candles on this Austrian pine are made for pinching off. Similar pruning in previous springs has resulted in the close, dense growth seen here.*

## WHERE TO PRUNE

A branch pruned from a needle-leaved evergreen will never grow beyond the cut. Candidates for pruning include weather-damaged branches, branches that stray from a desired silhouette *(right)* and branches that obstruct a pathway. Cut 1 inch above a fork formed by two lateral branches *(above)*. For branches thicker than 1 inch in diameter, use a pruning saw.

**1** To train a young pine to assume a compact shape as it matures, prune its candles every spring *(right)*. Wait until the candles reach a length of about 4 inches; then break them in half *(above)*.

**2** Once a needle-leaved evergreen has grown to within inches of the size you want it to be, you can prevent further growth by breaking off each of its candles close to its base *(left)*. Repeat every spring as soon as new candles appear. The tree will maintain its height, shape and vigorous appearance.

# SHEARING A HEDGE FOR A FORMAL EFFECT

Many hedges planted as windbreaks, privacy screens and backdrops for flower beds look best if they are sheared rather than allowed to grow shaggy and untamed. With clean, sharp lines, they give a landscape definition and an eye-pleasing symmetry, and if they are tapered so that they are narrower at the top than they are at the bottom, the lower branches get the light and air they need to develop. The clipping need only be done twice a year or so, and the job, shown opposite, is surprisingly easy to do well.

The task is made far easier if you have top-quality cutting tools. Hedge shears with long blades give the most control and are best for hedges of moderate size. They should have drop-forged, heat-treated steel blades and ash or hickory handles, and be kept sharp *(box, below)*. Power shears do not cut as neatly but are more practical for extensive hedges that would simply take too long to trim by hand. Small pruning shears are needed to cut stems too thick or tough for other clippers.

Not all shrubs are good candidates for shearing. Trimming large-leaved shrubs involves cutting many leaves in half, which results in a lot of unsightly brown edges. A hedge made of such shrubs is better left unsheared. In general, small-leaved plants make the best formal hedges. Traditional favorites include juniper, boxwood and privet.

Trimming should be done in the spring, when new growth has appeared, and followed up with a second pruning later in the season. At neither time should new shoots be completely cut back. A hedge of shrubs must be allowed to grow slightly each year if it is to remain vigorous.

*The geometric lines of two Japanese boxwoods frame a neatly shaped small brush cherry. Both kinds of shrubs, with their small leaves, are ideal for shearing.*

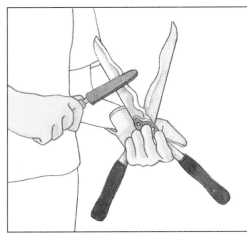

## SHARP BLADES FOR CLEAN CUTS

Keen-edged shears make hedge trimming not only easier, but also far neater; dull blades can tear stems and produce uneven cuts. To sharpen them, use a medium-grit stone lubricated with oil to start, then follow with a fine-grit stone. For wavy-edged blades, which are superior since they have more cutting edge than straight ones, employ a stone that has a rounded surface.

1 Decide how wide you want the bottom of your hedge to be, and how much you want it to taper inward toward the top. Begin clipping at the bottom. To aid in making a tapered edge as you move upward, hold the shears with the blades tilted slightly inward *(right)*. Trust your eye, and step back periodically to see how the shrubs are shaping up.

2 Shear a flat plane across the top surface of the hedge *(left)*. After you have finished shearing, remove clippings that have not fallen to the ground by running a leaf rake over the surface of the hedge. Finally, clean your clipping tools, making sure to remove encrusted sap or resin.

# PROPAGATING TREES: STEM CUTTINGS

*Their tips bathed in sunlight, three fig trees stand like sentinels along a fence. Figs are among the leafy trees that root most readily from cuttings.*

The surest method of propagating trees is by means of softwood cuttings from the soft new shoots at the ends of branches that healthy trees produce in the spring. Softwood shoots can be snipped from oriental flowering dogwood, magnolia, weeping willow and many other deciduous trees, and from a variety of evergreens including hollies and yews, then allowed to root in a planting mixture, as shown on the following pages. Cuttings should be made about two months after the shoots have begun to grow. If shoots first appear in mid-April, softwood cuttings from them can be taken in mid-July on into the fall.

After cuttings have been growing in pots for two months, they will need to be transplanted into larger containers to relieve crowding. Transplant the cuttings as you would seedlings *(pages 82-83)*. They should then be allowed to grow in their new containers until the end of their third season before being planted in the ground *(pages 382-384)*. Plant them when dormant, preferably in the spring. Cuttings will survive best if the tree from which they are taken has recently absorbed water, and if they are made during the cool morning hours, not in the drying heat of mid-afternoon.

1 Select a few bright-leaved softwood stems and snip each one off about 6 inches from the tip *(right)*. Make the cut 1 inch below a node, where a leaf emerges from the stem, and cut at an angle *(above)* so that you provide maximum stem surface for new roots to grow from. New roots will form at and above the node.

2 Remove the leaves from the bottom two-thirds of each stem you have cut. Then roughen the bottom ½ inch of each cutting by scraping away the bark using shears *(left)* or a knife. This will enable the cuttings to absorb moisture and nutrients and hasten the growing of roots. To further stimulate root development, pour some rooting hormone powder—available at a garden supply center—into a plastic bag, and dip the ends of the cuttings in the bag; apply a thin, even coating of powder to each cutting.

**3** Plant the cuttings in a pot filled to within ¾ inch of the top with a planting mixture of peat moss and vermiculite. Space the cuttings 4 to 6 inches apart, and press them down so that the bottom leaves of each cutting are flush with the top of the potting mixture. To keep the environment around the cuttings moist, push a pair of wood dowels into the planting mixture and place the pot in a plastic bag, tying off the end of it. The dowels will keep the plastic away from the cuttings. Keep the cuttings in the plastic covering until new top growth is visible—probably in about one to two months. Water only if the planting mixture dries out. Then begin acclimating the new plants to the outdoor environment; for about a week, open the bag in the evenings *(left)* and close it again during the warm daylight hours. After that, remove the plastic.

## ROOTING DECIDUOUS HARDWOOD STEMS

An alternative method of propagating trees is to cut and plant hardwood stems in the late fall and winter, when the shoots have weathered a full growing season and are no longer soft. Curiously, hardwood cuttings from evergreens are planted in the same way as softwood shoots. But hardwood stems taken from deciduous trees must be 8 to 10 inches long and they require a storage period of about six weeks before planting. First, dip the stems in a rooting hormone powder and a fungicide. Then place them in a plastic bag and put the bag in the refrigerator.

After the storage period, put the cuttings in pots of planting mixture with only the top bud visible *(right)*; this will secure the cuttings and in addition will prevent the buds from developing before the roots. Wrap the pots in plastic and keep them at 70° F. New top growth will appear in two to three months. When the temperature turns warm outdoors, move the pots and acclimate the plants as you would for stem cuttings *(above)*.

# PROPAGATING SHRUBS: CLEFT GRAFTING

Grafting is a method of propagation in which pieces of two healthy plants are united to produce one vigorous offspring. It is usually done for the purpose of combining the best characteristics of two different varieties—say hardiness or disease resistance (generally provided by the rootstock of one plant) with color, texture or flowers (provided by a shoot—called a scion—from another plant). While grafting is challenging, and not all attempts are successful, the reward can be a superior plant.

There are many different methods of grafting. Scion grafting *(pages 91-93)* works well with trees and some houseplants. Cleft grafting *(pages 408-409)* is done by removing the top growth of the rootstock, making an incision in the upper surface of the remaining stem and inserting a stem cutting (the scion) in the incision.

Cleft grafting is often done with broad-leaved flowering evergreens because the process generally produces mature plants that will flower earlier than plants propagated by other means. Cleft grafting can be done indoors or out, and with container-grown plants or plants growing in the ground. The rootstock may be wider in diameter than the scion; if so, two scions can be started on one rootstock and the weaker of the two can be discarded later. But the rootstock and the scion must be of the same genus. And to ensure a union between scion and rootstock, you must make sure to match up the cambium of one with the cambium of the other *(box, right)*. It is also important to work quickly; the scion must not be allowed to dry out.

After the two plants have been attached and until the bond is secure, provide a warm, humid environment by covering the attached scion and rootstock with a clear plastic bag or a large glass jar. Once new growth appears on the scion, gradually begin to accustom the grafted plant to outdoor air by poking holes in the plastic. Do not remove the bag for two or three months.

*A 50-year-old broad-leaved evergreen shrub makes an arresting specimen. These types of shrubs are often propagated by grafting young shoots of a colorful variety, like this one, onto the rootstock of another, hardier variety.*

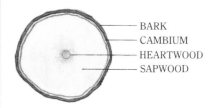

## INSIDE A WOODY STEM

The main divisions of the stem of a woody plant are seen here in cross section. Just inside the protective bark is the thin layer of cambium, where all new growth takes place. Inside that is sapwood, which transmits water and nutrients from the roots to the stem tips. At the center is heartwood.

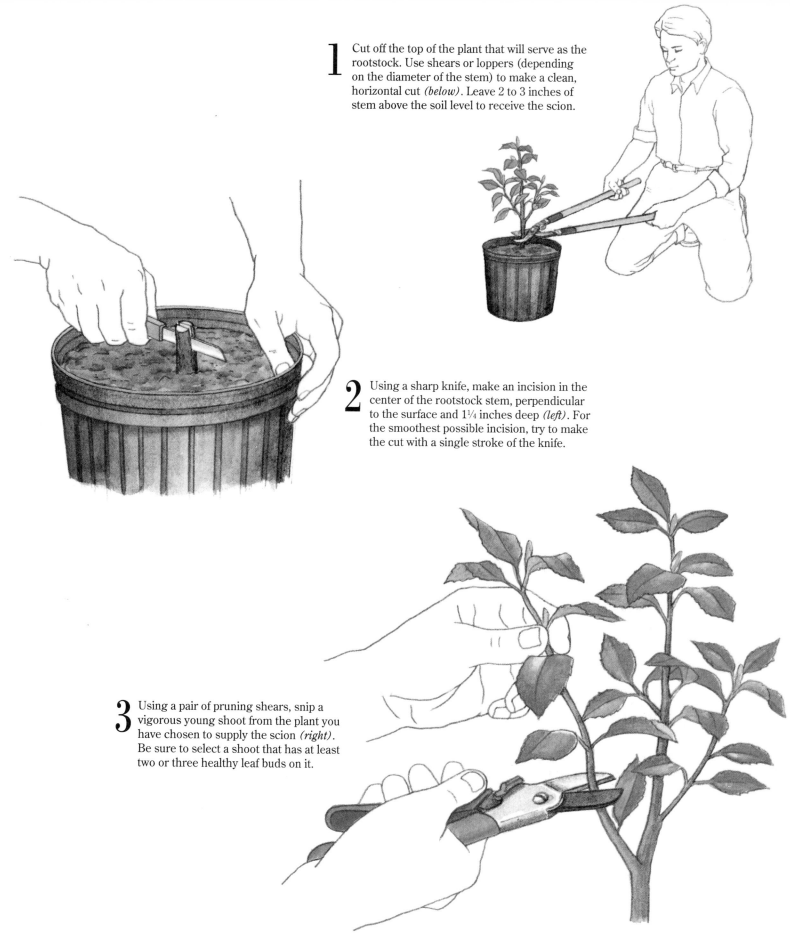

**1** Cut off the top of the plant that will serve as the rootstock. Use shears or loppers (depending on the diameter of the stem) to make a clean, horizontal cut *(below)*. Leave 2 to 3 inches of stem above the soil level to receive the scion.

**2** Using a sharp knife, make an incision in the center of the rootstock stem, perpendicular to the surface and 1¼ inches deep *(left)*. For the smoothest possible incision, try to make the cut with a single stroke of the knife.

**3** Using a pair of pruning shears, snip a vigorous young shoot from the plant you have chosen to supply the scion *(right)*. Be sure to select a shoot that has at least two or three healthy leaf buds on it.

**4** Use a knife to form a tapered wedge shape on the end of the scion *(inset, left)*: Make a slanting cut on each side of the scion 1½ inches from the bottom end of it *(above)*. Pare off bark and some wood with each cut, exposing a portion of the cambium layer.

**5** Insert the wedge-shaped end of the scion into the incision in the rootstock *(inset, right)*, holding the incision open with a screwdriver, if necessary *(far right)*. Make sure the cambium layers of the scion and rootstock meet. For extra protection, seal the opening in the rootstock with warm paraffin. Using shears, snip off the outer half of all the scion's leaves; this will reduce their need for nourishment while the plants are working to form a permanent union. If there is room, insert two scions into the incision—on opposite sides of it—to double the chances of a successful graft. Label the graft with the names of both rootstock and scion. If you are storing a graft indoors, cover it with a plastic bag; if outdoors, cover it with a large glass jar and shield it from the sun with a paper bag. When new growth begins, poke holes in the plastic —or prop up the jar—to accustom the plant to a less sheltered environment. Keep the plastic or jar on for two or three months. After the union is firmly established, remove the weaker of the two scions.

# A CHECKLIST FOR TREES

|  | ZONE 1 | ZONE 2 | ZONE 3 | ZONE 4 | ZONE 5 |
|---|---|---|---|---|---|
| **JANUARY/FEBRUARY** | • Prune dormant trees<br>• Spray evergreens with antidesiccant<br>• Remove snow and ice from evergreens after every snowfall<br>• Replace mulch as needed<br>• Check supports for recently planted trees | • Prune dormant trees<br>• Spray evergreens with antidesiccant<br>• Remove snow and ice from evergreens after every snowfall<br>• Replace mulch as needed<br>• Check supports for recently planted trees | • Prune dormant trees<br>• Spray evergreens with antidesiccant<br>• Remove snow and ice from evergreens after every snowfall<br>• Replace mulch as needed<br>• Check supports for recently planted trees | • Prune dormant trees<br>• Spray evergreens with antidesiccant<br>• Remove snow and ice from evergreens after every snowfall<br>• Replace mulch as needed<br>• Check supports for recently planted trees | • Prune dormant trees<br>• Spray evergreens with antidesiccant<br>• Remove snow and ice from evergreens after every snowfall<br>• Replace mulch as needed<br>• Check supports for recently planted trees |
| **MARCH/APRIL** | • Clean, oil, sharpen tools<br>• Take hardwood cuttings for propagation | • Clean, oil, sharpen tools<br>• Take hardwood cuttings for propagation | • Clean, oil, sharpen tools<br>• Take hardwood cuttings for propagation | • Plant bare-root trees<br>• Plant container and balled-and-burlapped trees<br>• Apply horticultural oil<br>• Clean, oil, sharpen tools<br>• Install supports for newly planted trees<br>• Water and mulch newly planted trees<br>• Take hardwood cuttings for propagation<br>• Transplant evergreens | • Prune out winter damage<br>• Plant bare-root trees<br>• Plant container and balled-and-burlapped trees<br>• Remove winter mulch and burlap wrappings<br>• Apply horticultural oil<br>• Clean, oil, sharpen tools<br>• Install supports for newly planted trees<br>• Water and mulch newly planted trees<br>• Take hardwood cuttings for propagation<br>• Transplant evergreens |
| **MAY/JUNE** | • Remove trees that are weak, rotted or tangled in utility wires<br>• Prune trees<br>• Prune out winter damage<br>• Shear fine-needled evergreens<br>• Fertilize trees with slow-release fertilizer as growth starts<br>• Plant bare-root trees<br>• Plant container and balled-and-burlapped trees<br>• Install supports for newly planted trees<br>• Water and mulch newly planted trees<br>• Transplant trees<br>• Remove winter mulch and burlap wrappings<br>• Apply horticultural oil<br>• Weed soil around trees; apply preemergent herbicide<br>• Apply summer mulch<br>• Check for insects, diseases | • Remove trees that are weak, rotted or tangled in utility wires<br>• Prune trees<br>• Prune out winter damage<br>• Shear fine-needled evergreens<br>• Fertilize trees with slow-release fertilizer as growth starts<br>• Plant bare-root trees<br>• Plant container and balled-and-burlapped trees<br>• Install supports for newly planted trees<br>• Water and mulch newly planted trees<br>• Transplant trees<br>• Remove winter mulch and burlap wrappings<br>• Apply horticultural oil<br>• Weed soil around trees; apply preemergent herbicide<br>• Apply summer mulch<br>• Check for insects, diseases | • Remove trees that are weak, rotted or tangled in utility wires<br>• Prune trees<br>• Prune out winter damage<br>• Shear fine-needled evergreens<br>• Fertilize trees with slow-release fertilizer as growth starts<br>• Plant bare-root trees<br>• Plant container and balled-and-burlapped trees<br>• Install supports for newly planted trees<br>• Water and mulch newly planted trees<br>• Transplant trees<br>• Remove winter mulch and burlap wrappings<br>• Apply horticultural oil<br>• Weed soil around trees; apply preemergent herbicide<br>• Apply summer mulch<br>• Check for insects, diseases | • Remove trees that are weak, rotted or tangled in utility wires<br>• Prune trees<br>• Prune out winter damage<br>• Shear fine-needled evergreens<br>• Fertilize trees with slow-release fertilizer as growth starts<br>• Plant bare-root trees<br>• Plant container and balled-and-burlapped trees<br>• Install supports for newly planted trees<br>• Water and mulch newly planted trees<br>• Transplant trees<br>• Remove winter mulch and burlap wrappings<br>• Weed soil around trees; apply preemergent herbicide<br>• Apply summer mulch<br>• Check for insects, diseases | • Remove trees that are weak, rotted or tangled in utility wires<br>• Prune trees<br>• Shear fine-needled evergreens<br>• Fertilize trees with slow-release fertilizer as growth starts<br>• Plant container and balled-and-burlapped trees<br>• Install supports for newly planted trees<br>• Water and mulch newly planted trees<br>• Transplant trees<br>• Remove winter mulch and burlap wrappings<br>• Weed soil around trees; apply preemergent herbicide<br>• Apply summer mulch<br>• Check for insects, diseases |

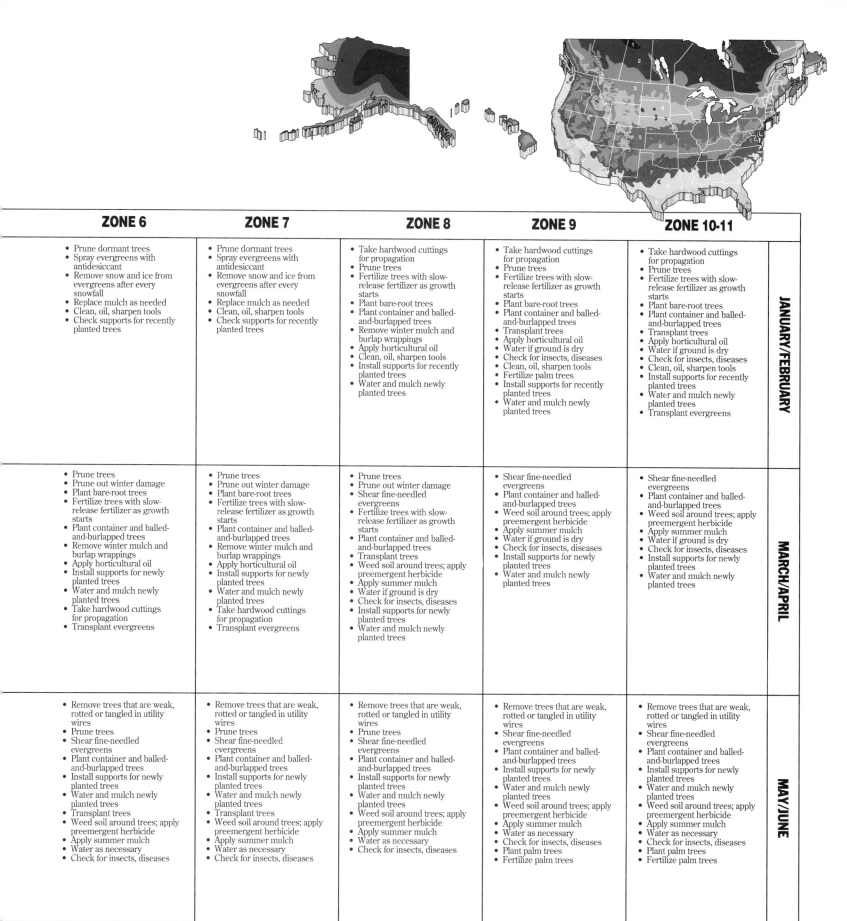

| | ZONE 6 | ZONE 7 | ZONE 8 | ZONE 9 | ZONE 10-11 | |
|---|---|---|---|---|---|---|
| | • Prune dormant trees<br>• Spray evergreens with antidesiccant<br>• Remove snow and ice from evergreens after every snowfall<br>• Replace mulch as needed<br>• Clean, oil, sharpen tools<br>• Check supports for recently planted trees | • Prune dormant trees<br>• Spray evergreens with antidesiccant<br>• Remove snow and ice from evergreens after every snowfall<br>• Replace mulch as needed<br>• Clean, oil, sharpen tools<br>• Check supports for recently planted trees | • Take hardwood cuttings for propagation<br>• Prune trees<br>• Fertilize trees with slow-release fertilizer as growth starts<br>• Plant bare-root trees<br>• Plant container and balled-and-burlapped trees<br>• Remove winter mulch and burlap wrappings<br>• Apply horticultural oil<br>• Clean, oil, sharpen tools<br>• Install supports for recently planted trees<br>• Water and mulch newly planted trees | • Take hardwood cuttings for propagation<br>• Prune trees<br>• Fertilize trees with slow-release fertilizer as growth starts<br>• Plant bare-root trees<br>• Plant container and balled-and-burlapped trees<br>• Transplant trees<br>• Apply horticultural oil<br>• Water if ground is dry<br>• Check for insects, diseases<br>• Clean, oil, sharpen tools<br>• Fertilize palm trees<br>• Install supports for recently planted trees<br>• Water and mulch newly planted trees | • Take hardwood cuttings for propagation<br>• Prune trees<br>• Fertilize trees with slow-release fertilizer as growth starts<br>• Plant bare-root trees<br>• Plant container and balled-and-burlapped trees<br>• Transplant trees<br>• Apply horticultural oil<br>• Water if ground is dry<br>• Check for insects, diseases<br>• Clean, oil, sharpen tools<br>• Install supports for recently planted trees<br>• Water and mulch newly planted trees<br>• Transplant evergreens | **JANUARY/FEBRUARY** |
| | • Prune trees<br>• Prune out winter damage<br>• Plant bare-root trees<br>• Fertilize trees with slow-release fertilizer as growth starts<br>• Plant container and balled-and-burlapped trees<br>• Remove winter mulch and burlap wrappings<br>• Apply horticultural oil<br>• Install supports for newly planted trees<br>• Water and mulch newly planted trees<br>• Take hardwood cuttings for propagation<br>• Transplant evergreens | • Prune trees<br>• Prune out winter damage<br>• Plant bare-root trees<br>• Fertilize trees with slow-release fertilizer as growth starts<br>• Plant container and balled-and-burlapped trees<br>• Remove winter mulch and burlap wrappings<br>• Apply horticultural oil<br>• Install supports for newly planted trees<br>• Water and mulch newly planted trees<br>• Take hardwood cuttings for propagation<br>• Transplant evergreens | • Prune trees<br>• Prune out winter damage<br>• Shear fine-needled evergreens<br>• Fertilize trees with slow-release fertilizer as growth starts<br>• Plant container and balled-and-burlapped trees<br>• Transplant trees<br>• Weed soil around trees; apply preemergent herbicide<br>• Apply summer mulch<br>• Water if ground is dry<br>• Check for insects, diseases<br>• Install supports for newly planted trees<br>• Water and mulch newly planted trees | • Shear fine-needled evergreens<br>• Plant container and balled-and-burlapped trees<br>• Weed soil around trees; apply preemergent herbicide<br>• Apply summer mulch<br>• Water if ground is dry<br>• Check for insects, diseases<br>• Install supports for newly planted trees<br>• Water and mulch newly planted trees | • Shear fine-needled evergreens<br>• Plant container and balled-and-burlapped trees<br>• Weed soil around trees; apply preemergent herbicide<br>• Apply summer mulch<br>• Water if ground is dry<br>• Check for insects, diseases<br>• Install supports for newly planted trees<br>• Water and mulch newly planted trees | **MARCH/APRIL** |
| | • Remove trees that are weak, rotted or tangled in utility wires<br>• Prune trees<br>• Shear fine-needled evergreens<br>• Plant container and balled-and-burlapped trees<br>• Install supports for newly planted trees<br>• Water and mulch newly planted trees<br>• Transplant trees<br>• Weed soil around trees; apply preemergent herbicide<br>• Apply summer mulch<br>• Water as necessary<br>• Check for insects, diseases | • Remove trees that are weak, rotted or tangled in utility wires<br>• Prune trees<br>• Shear fine-needled evergreens<br>• Plant container and balled-and-burlapped trees<br>• Install supports for newly planted trees<br>• Water and mulch newly planted trees<br>• Transplant trees<br>• Weed soil around trees; apply preemergent herbicide<br>• Apply summer mulch<br>• Water as necessary<br>• Check for insects, diseases | • Remove trees that are weak, rotted or tangled in utility wires<br>• Prune trees<br>• Shear fine-needled evergreens<br>• Plant container and balled-and-burlapped trees<br>• Install supports for newly planted trees<br>• Water and mulch newly planted trees<br>• Weed soil around trees; apply preemergent herbicide<br>• Apply summer mulch<br>• Water as necessary<br>• Check for insects, diseases | • Remove trees that are weak, rotted or tangled in utility wires<br>• Shear fine-needled evergreens<br>• Plant container and balled-and-burlapped trees<br>• Install supports for newly planted trees<br>• Water and mulch newly planted trees<br>• Weed soil around trees; apply preemergent herbicide<br>• Apply summer mulch<br>• Water as necessary<br>• Check for insects, diseases<br>• Plant palm trees<br>• Fertilize palm trees | • Remove trees that are weak, rotted or tangled in utility wires<br>• Shear fine-needled evergreens<br>• Plant container and balled-and-burlapped trees<br>• Install supports for newly planted trees<br>• Water and mulch newly planted trees<br>• Weed soil around trees; apply preemergent herbicide<br>• Apply summer mulch<br>• Water as necessary<br>• Check for insects, diseases<br>• Plant palm trees<br>• Fertilize palm trees | **MAY/JUNE** |

411

|  | ZONE 1 | ZONE 2 | ZONE 3 | ZONE 4 | ZONE 5 |
|---|---|---|---|---|---|
| **JULY/AUGUST** | • Shear fine-needled evergreens<br>• Plant container and balled-and-burlapped trees<br>• Transplant evergreens<br>• Weed soil around trees; apply preemergent herbicide<br>• Aerate compacted soil around roots<br>• Take cuttings for propagation<br>• Apply summer mulch<br>• Water as necessary<br>• Check for insects, diseases<br>• Remove trees that are weak, rotted or tangled in utility wires | • Shear fine-needled evergreens<br>• Plant container and balled-and-burlapped trees<br>• Transplant evergreens<br>• Weed soil around trees; apply preemergent herbicide<br>• Aerate compacted soil around roots<br>• Take cuttings for propagation<br>• Apply summer mulch<br>• Water as necessary<br>• Check for insects, diseases<br>• Remove trees that are weak, rotted or tangled in utility wires | • Shear fine-needled evergreens<br>• Plant container and balled-and-burlapped trees<br>• Transplant evergreens<br>• Weed soil around trees; apply preemergent herbicide<br>• Aerate compacted soil around roots<br>• Take cuttings for propagation<br>• Apply summer mulch<br>• Water as necessary<br>• Check for insects, diseases<br>• Remove trees that are weak, rotted or tangled in utility wires | • Shear fine-needled evergreens<br>• Plant container and balled-and-burlapped trees<br>• Transplant evergreens<br>• Weed soil around trees; apply preemergent herbicide<br>• Aerate compacted soil around roots<br>• Take cuttings for propagation<br>• Apply summer mulch<br>• Water as necessary<br>• Check for insects, diseases<br>• Remove trees that are weak, rotted or tangled in utility wires | • Shear fine-needled evergreens<br>• Plant container and balled-and-burlapped trees<br>• Transplant evergreens<br>• Weed soil around trees; apply preemergent herbicide<br>• Aerate compacted soil around roots<br>• Water as necessary<br>• Check for insects, diseases<br>• Remove trees that are weak, rotted or tangled in utility wires |
| **SEPTEMBER/OCTOBER** | • Plant container and balled-and-burlapped deciduous trees<br>• Transplant deciduous trees<br>• Water if ground is dry<br>• Rake leaves and use in compost<br>• Apply winter mulch and wrap tree trunks in burlap<br>• Turn off water, drain hose<br>• Remove trees that are weak, rotted or tangled in utility wires<br>• Take hardwood cuttings for propagation | • Plant container and balled-and-burlapped deciduous trees<br>• Transplant deciduous trees<br>• Water if ground is dry<br>• Rake leaves and use in compost<br>• Apply winter mulch and wrap tree trunks in burlap<br>• Turn off water, drain hose<br>• Remove trees that are weak, rotted or tangled in utility wires<br>• Take hardwood cuttings for propagation | • Plant container and balled-and-burlapped deciduous trees<br>• Transplant deciduous trees<br>• Water if ground is dry<br>• Rake leaves and use in compost<br>• Apply winter mulch and wrap tree trunks in burlap<br>• Turn off water, drain hose<br>• Remove trees that are weak, rotted or tangled in utility wires<br>• Take hardwood cuttings for propagation | • Plant container and balled-and-burlapped deciduous trees<br>• Transplant deciduous trees<br>• Water if ground is dry<br>• Rake leaves and use in compost<br>• Apply winter mulch and wrap tree trunks in burlap<br>• Turn off water, drain hose<br>• Remove trees that are weak, rotted or tangled in utility wires<br>• Take hardwood cuttings for propagation | • Plant container and balled-and-burlapped deciduous trees<br>• Transplant deciduous trees<br>• Water if ground is dry<br>• Take hardwood cuttings for propagation<br>• Water if ground is dry<br>• Rake leaves and use in compost<br>• Remove trees that are weak, rotted or tangled in utility wires |
| **NOVEMBER/DECEMBER** | • Prune dormant trees<br>• Fertilize dormant trees<br>• Spray evergreens with antidesiccant<br>• Put wire mesh around tree trunks for protection against animals<br>• Remove snow and ice from evergreens after every snowfall<br>• Protect young trees<br>• Check supports for newly planted trees | • Prune dormant trees<br>• Fertilize dormant trees<br>• Spray evergreens with antidesiccant<br>• Put wire mesh around tree trunks for protection against animals<br>• Remove snow and ice from evergreens after every snowfall<br>• Protect young trees<br>• Check supports for newly planted trees | • Prune dormant trees<br>• Fertilize dormant trees<br>• Spray evergreens with antidesiccant<br>• Put wire mesh around tree trunks for protection against animals<br>• Remove snow and ice from evergreens after every snowfall<br>• Protect young trees<br>• Check supports for newly planted trees | • Prune dormant trees<br>• Fertilize dormant trees<br>• Spray evergreens with antidesiccant<br>• Put wire mesh around tree trunks for protection against animals<br>• Remove snow and ice from evergreens after every snowfall<br>• Protect young trees<br>• Check supports for newly planted trees | • Prune dormant trees<br>• Fertilize dormant trees<br>• Spray evergreens with antidesiccant<br>• Apply winter mulch and wrap tree trunks in burlap<br>• Put wire mesh around tree trunks for protection against animals<br>• Remove snow and ice from evergreens after every snowfall<br>• Water if ground is dry<br>• Turn off water, drain hose<br>• Rake leaves and use in compost<br>• Protect young trees<br>• Check supports for newly planted trees |

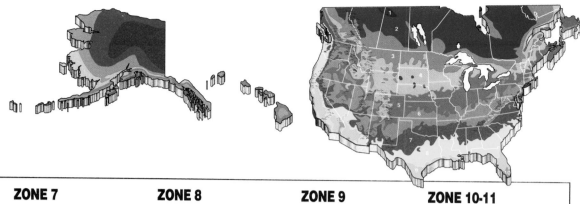

| | ZONE 6 | ZONE 7 | ZONE 8 | ZONE 9 | ZONE 10-11 | |
|---|---|---|---|---|---|---|
| | • Shear fine-needled evergreens<br>• Plant container and balled-and-burlapped trees<br>• Transplant evergreens<br>• Weed soil around trees; apply preemergent herbicide<br>• Aerate compacted soil around roots<br>• Water as necessary<br>• Check for insects, diseases<br>• Remove trees that are weak, rotted or tangled in utility wires | • Shear fine-needled evergreens<br>• Plant container and balled-and-burlapped trees<br>• Transplant evergreens<br>• Weed soil around trees; apply preemergent herbicide<br>• Aerate compacted soil around roots<br>• Water as necessary<br>• Check for insects, diseases<br>• Remove trees that are weak, rotted or tangled in utility wires | • Shear fine-needled evergreens<br>• Plant container and balled-and-burlapped trees<br>• Transplant evergreens<br>• Weed soil around trees; apply preemergent herbicide<br>• Aerate compacted soil around roots<br>• Water as necessary<br>• Check for insects, diseases<br>• Remove trees that are weak, rotted or tangled in utility wires | • Shear fine-needled evergreens<br>• Plant container and balled-and-burlapped trees<br>• Transplant evergreens<br>• Weed soil around trees; apply preemergent herbicide<br>• Aerate compacted soil around roots<br>• Water as necessary<br>• Check for insects, diseases<br>• Plant palm trees<br>• Remove trees that are weak, rotted or tangled in utility wires | • Shear fine-needled evergreens<br>• Plant container and balled-and-burlapped trees<br>• Transplant evergreens<br>• Weed soil around trees; apply preemergent herbicide<br>• Aerate compacted soil around roots<br>• Water as necessary<br>• Check for insects, diseases<br>• Plant palm trees<br>• Remove trees that are weak, rotted or tangled in utility wires | JULY/AUGUST |
| | • Plant container and balled-and-burlapped deciduous trees<br>• Transplant deciduous trees<br>• Water if ground is dry<br>• Take hardwood cuttings for propagation<br>• Rake leaves and use in compost<br>• Remove trees that are weak, rotted or tangled in utility wires | • Plant container and balled-and-burlapped deciduous trees<br>• Transplant deciduous trees<br>• Water if ground is dry<br>• Take hardwood cuttings for propagation<br>• Rake leaves and use in compost<br>• Remove trees that are weak, rotted or tangled in utility wires | • Plant container and balled-and-burlapped deciduous trees<br>• Transplant deciduous trees<br>• Water if ground is dry<br>• Take hardwood cuttings for propagation<br>• Rake leaves and use in compost<br>• Remove trees that are weak, rotted or tangled in utility wires | • Plant container and balled-and-burlapped deciduous trees<br>• Transplant deciduous trees<br>• Water if ground is dry<br>• Take hardwood cuttings for propagation<br>• Rake leaves and use in compost<br>• Plant palm trees<br>• Fertilize palm trees<br>• Remove trees that are weak, rotted or tangled in utility wires | • Plant container and balled-and-burlapped deciduous trees<br>• Transplant deciduous trees<br>• Water if ground is dry<br>• Take hardwood cuttings for propagation<br>• Rake leaves and use in compost<br>• Plant palm trees<br>• Fertilize palm trees<br>• Remove trees that are weak, rotted or tangled in utility wires | SEPTEMBER/OCTOBER |
| | • Prune dormant trees<br>• Fertilize dormant trees<br>• Plant bare-root trees<br>• Transplant deciduous trees<br>• Spray evergreens with antidesiccant<br>• Apply winter mulch and wrap tree trunks in burlap<br>• Put wire mesh around tree trunks for protection against animals<br>• Water if ground is dry<br>• Turn off water, drain hose<br>• Rake leaves and use in compost<br>• Water and mulch newly planted trees<br>• Protect young trees<br>• Remove trees that are weak, rotted or tangled in utility wires<br>• Check supports for newly planted trees | • Prune dormant trees<br>• Fertilize dormant trees<br>• Plant container, bare-root and balled-and-burlapped trees<br>• Spray evergreens with antidesiccant<br>• Apply winter mulch and wrap tree trunks in burlap<br>• Put wire mesh around tree trunks for protection against animals<br>• Take hardwood cuttings for propagation<br>• Water if ground is dry<br>• Turn off water, drain hose<br>• Rake and compost leaves<br>• Water and mulch newly planted trees<br>• Protect young trees<br>• Remove trees that are weak, rotted or tangled in utility wires<br>• Check supports for newly planted trees | • Prune dormant trees<br>• Fertilize dormant trees<br>• Plant container, bare-root and balled-and-burlapped trees<br>• Spray evergreens with antidesiccant<br>• Apply winter mulch and wrap tree trunks in burlap<br>• Put wire mesh around tree trunks for protection against animals<br>• Take hardwood cuttings for propagation<br>• Water if ground is dry<br>• Turn off water, drain hose<br>• Rake and compost leaves<br>• Water and mulch newly planted trees<br>• Protect young trees<br>• Remove trees that are weak, rotted or tangled in utility wires<br>• Check supports for newly planted trees | • Prune trees<br>• Fertilize dormant trees<br>• Plant container and balled-and-burlapped trees<br>• Transplant deciduous trees<br>• Take hardwood cuttings for propagation<br>• Water if ground is dry<br>• Rake leaves and use in compost<br>• Water and mulch newly planted trees<br>• Remove trees that are weak, rotted or tangled in utility wires<br>• Check supports for newly planted trees | • Prune trees<br>• Fertilize dormant trees<br>• Plant container and balled-and-burlapped trees<br>• Plant bare-root trees<br>• Transplant deciduous trees<br>• Take hardwood cuttings for propagation<br>• Water if ground is dry<br>• Rake leaves and use in compost<br>• Water and mulch newly planted trees<br>• Remove trees that are weak, rotted or tangled in utility wires<br>• Check supports for newly planted trees | NOVEMBER/DECEMBER |

413

# A CHECKLIST FOR SHRUBS

| | ZONE 1 | ZONE 2 | ZONE 3 | ZONE 4 | ZONE 5 |
|---|---|---|---|---|---|
| **JANUARY/FEBRUARY** | • Remove snow and ice from weak-limbed or tall-growing shrubs after every snowfall<br>• Replace mulch as needed<br>• Reapply antidesiccant to broad-leaved evergreens<br>• Check windbreaks and protection<br>• Select shrubs with winter color for spring planting | • Remove snow and ice from weak-limbed or tall-growing shrubs after every snowfall<br>• Replace mulch as needed<br>• Reapply antidesiccant to broad-leaved evergreens<br>• Check windbreaks and protection<br>• Select shrubs with winter color for spring planting | • Remove snow and ice from weak-limbed or tall-growing shrubs after every snowfall<br>• Replace mulch as needed<br>• Reapply antidesiccant to broad-leaved evergreens<br>• Check windbreaks and protection<br>• Select shrubs with winter color for spring planting | • Remove snow and ice from weak-limbed or tall-growing shrubs after every snowfall<br>• Replace mulch as needed<br>• Reapply antidesiccant to broad-leaved evergreens<br>• Check windbreaks and protection<br>• Select shrubs with winter color for spring planting | • Remove snow and ice from weak-limbed or tall-growing shrubs after every snowfall<br>• Replace mulch as needed<br>• Reapply antidesiccant to broad-leaved evergreens<br>• Check windbreaks and protection<br>• Select shrubs with winter color for spring planting |
| **MARCH/APRIL** | • Replace mulch as needed<br>• Prune shrubs<br>• Start grafts for propagation<br>• Remove undesirable shrubs<br>• Clean, oil, sharpen tools<br>• Protect delicate shrubs from late frost | • Replace mulch as needed<br>• Prune shrubs<br>• Start grafts for propagation<br>• Remove undesirable shrubs<br>• Clean, oil, sharpen tools<br>• Protect delicate shrubs from late frost | • Replace mulch as needed<br>• Prune shrubs<br>• Start grafts for propagation<br>• Divide multistemmed shrubs<br>• Remove undesirable shrubs<br>• Clean, oil, sharpen tools<br>• Protect delicate shrubs from late frost | • Propagate shrubs by layering<br>• Replace mulch as needed<br>• Prune shrubs<br>• Plant shrubs<br>• Start grafts for propagation<br>• Divide multistemmed shrubs<br>• Apply horticultural oil spray<br>• Remove undesirable shrubs<br>• Clean, oil, sharpen tools<br>• Protect delicate shrubs from late frost<br>• Water and mulch newly planted shrubs<br>• Plant new climbing shrubs<br>• Check supports for established climbing shrubs | • Propagate shrubs by layering<br>• Replace mulch as needed<br>• Prune shrubs<br>• Prune out winter damage<br>• Plant shrubs<br>• Start grafts for propagation<br>• Divide multistemmed shrubs<br>• Remove burlap screens<br>• Apply horticultural oil spray<br>• Remove undesirable shrubs<br>• Clean, oil, sharpen tools<br>• Protect delicate shrubs from late frost<br>• Water and mulch newly planted shrubs<br>• Plant new climbing shrubs<br>• Check supports for established climbing shrubs |
| **MAY/JUNE** | • Prune spring-flowering shrubs<br>• Prune out winter damage<br>• Shear formal hedges<br>• Fertilize shrubs as growth starts<br>• Test soil pH around established shrubs and adjust, if necessary<br>• Plant shrubs<br>• Remove burlap screens<br>• Transplant shrubs<br>• Weed soil around shrubs<br>• Apply horticultural oil spray<br>• Apply mulch for summer<br>• Check for insects, diseases<br>• Water and mulch newly planted shrubs<br>• Propagate shrubs by layering<br>• Check supports for climbing shrubs<br>• Plant new climbing shrubs<br>• Remove faded flowers from shrubs | • Prune spring-flowering shrubs<br>• Prune out winter damage<br>• Shear formal hedges<br>• Fertilize shrubs as growth starts<br>• Test soil pH around established shrubs and adjust, if necessary<br>• Plant shrubs<br>• Remove burlap screens<br>• Transplant shrubs<br>• Weed soil around shrubs<br>• Apply horticultural oil spray<br>• Apply mulch for summer<br>• Check for insects, diseases<br>• Water and mulch newly planted shrubs<br>• Propagate shrubs by layering<br>• Check supports for climbing shrubs<br>• Plant new climbing shrubs<br>• Remove faded flowers from shrubs | • Prune spring-flowering shrubs<br>• Prune out winter damage<br>• Shear formal hedges<br>• Fertilize shrubs as growth starts<br>• Test soil pH around established shrubs and adjust, if necessary<br>• Plant shrubs<br>• Remove burlap screens<br>• Transplant shrubs<br>• Weed soil around shrubs<br>• Apply horticultural oil spray<br>• Apply mulch for summer<br>• Check for insects, diseases<br>• Water and mulch newly planted shrubs<br>• Propagate shrubs by layering<br>• Check supports for climbing shrubs<br>• Plant new climbing shrubs<br>• Remove faded flowers from shrubs | • Prune spring-flowering shrubs<br>• Prune out winter damage<br>• Shear formal hedges<br>• Fertilize shrubs as growth starts<br>• Test soil pH around established shrubs and adjust, if necessary<br>• Plant shrubs<br>• Remove burlap screens<br>• Transplant shrubs<br>• Weed soil around shrubs<br>• Apply mulch for summer<br>• Check for insects, diseases<br>• Remove faded flowers from shrubs | • Prune spring-flowering shrubs<br>• Shear formal hedges<br>• Fertilize shrubs as growth starts<br>• Test soil pH around established shrubs and adjust, if necessary<br>• Plant shrubs<br>• Remove burlap screens<br>• Transplant shrubs<br>• Weed soil around shrubs<br>• Apply mulch for summer<br>• Check for insects, diseases<br>• Remove faded flowers from shrubs |

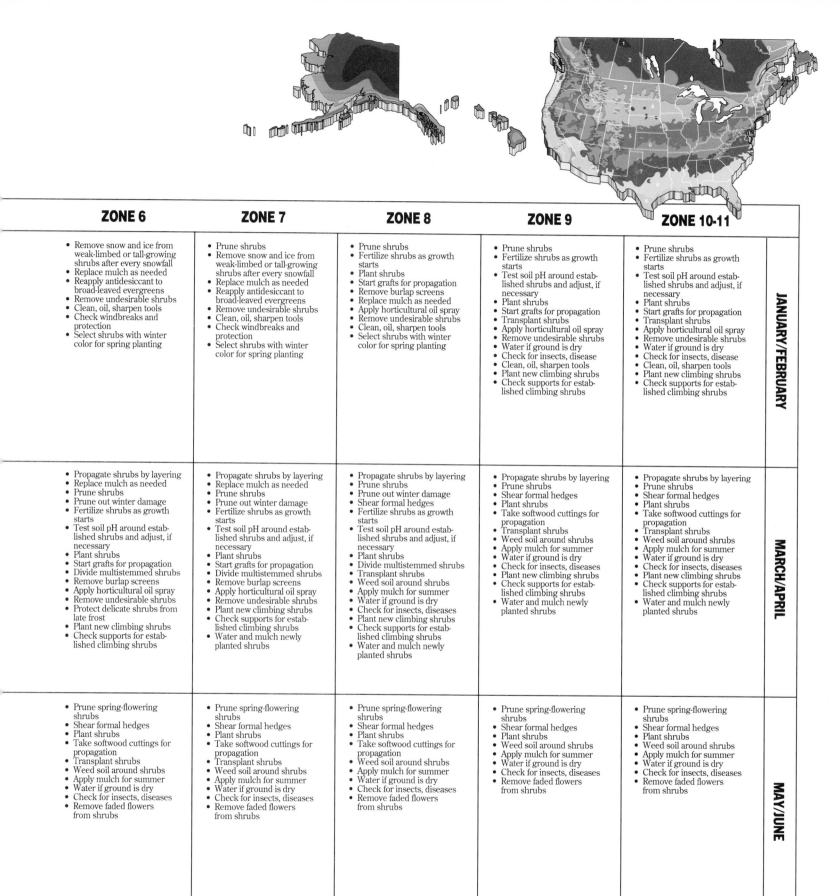

| | ZONE 6 | ZONE 7 | ZONE 8 | ZONE 9 | ZONE 10-11 | |
|---|---|---|---|---|---|---|
| | • Remove snow and ice from weak-limbed or tall-growing shrubs after every snowfall<br>• Replace mulch as needed<br>• Reapply antidesiccant to broad-leaved evergreens<br>• Remove undesirable shrubs<br>• Clean, oil, sharpen tools<br>• Check windbreaks and protection<br>• Select shrubs with winter color for spring planting | • Prune shrubs<br>• Remove snow and ice from weak-limbed or tall-growing shrubs after every snowfall<br>• Replace mulch as needed<br>• Reapply antidesiccant to broad-leaved evergreens<br>• Remove undesirable shrubs<br>• Clean, oil, sharpen tools<br>• Check windbreaks and protection<br>• Select shrubs with winter color for spring planting | • Prune shrubs<br>• Fertilize shrubs as growth starts<br>• Plant shrubs<br>• Start grafts for propagation<br>• Remove burlap screens<br>• Replace mulch as needed<br>• Apply horticultural oil spray<br>• Remove undesirable shrubs<br>• Clean, oil, sharpen tools<br>• Select shrubs with winter color for spring planting | • Prune shrubs<br>• Fertilize shrubs as growth starts<br>• Test soil pH around established shrubs and adjust, if necessary<br>• Plant shrubs<br>• Start grafts for propagation<br>• Transplant shrubs<br>• Apply horticultural oil spray<br>• Remove undesirable shrubs<br>• Water if ground is dry<br>• Check for insects, disease<br>• Clean, oil, sharpen tools<br>• Plant new climbing shrubs<br>• Check supports for established climbing shrubs | • Prune shrubs<br>• Fertilize shrubs as growth starts<br>• Test soil pH around established shrubs and adjust, if necessary<br>• Plant shrubs<br>• Start grafts for propagation<br>• Transplant shrubs<br>• Apply horticultural oil spray<br>• Remove undesirable shrubs<br>• Water if ground is dry<br>• Check for insects, disease<br>• Clean, oil, sharpen tools<br>• Plant new climbing shrubs<br>• Check supports for established climbing shrubs | **JANUARY/FEBRUARY** |
| | • Propagate shrubs by layering<br>• Replace mulch as needed<br>• Prune shrubs<br>• Prune out winter damage<br>• Fertilize shrubs as growth starts<br>• Test soil pH around established shrubs and adjust, if necessary<br>• Plant shrubs<br>• Start grafts for propagation<br>• Divide multistemmed shrubs<br>• Remove burlap screens<br>• Apply horticultural oil spray<br>• Remove undesirable shrubs<br>• Protect delicate shrubs from late frost<br>• Plant new climbing shrubs<br>• Check supports for established climbing shrubs | • Propagate shrubs by layering<br>• Replace mulch as needed<br>• Prune shrubs<br>• Prune out winter damage<br>• Fertilize shrubs as growth starts<br>• Test soil pH around established shrubs and adjust, if necessary<br>• Plant shrubs<br>• Start grafts for propagation<br>• Divide multistemmed shrubs<br>• Remove burlap screens<br>• Apply horticultural oil spray<br>• Remove undesirable shrubs<br>• Plant new climbing shrubs<br>• Check supports for established climbing shrubs<br>• Water and mulch newly planted shrubs | • Propagate shrubs by layering<br>• Prune shrubs<br>• Prune out winter damage<br>• Shear formal hedges<br>• Fertilize shrubs as growth starts<br>• Test soil pH around established shrubs and adjust, if necessary<br>• Plant shrubs<br>• Divide multistemmed shrubs<br>• Transplant shrubs<br>• Weed soil around shrubs<br>• Apply mulch for summer<br>• Water if ground is dry<br>• Check for insects, diseases<br>• Plant new climbing shrubs<br>• Check supports for established climbing shrubs<br>• Water and mulch newly planted shrubs | • Propagate shrubs by layering<br>• Prune shrubs<br>• Shear formal hedges<br>• Plant shrubs<br>• Take softwood cuttings for propagation<br>• Transplant shrubs<br>• Weed soil around shrubs<br>• Apply mulch for summer<br>• Water if ground is dry<br>• Check for insects, diseases<br>• Plant new climbing shrubs<br>• Check supports for established climbing shrubs<br>• Water and mulch newly planted shrubs | • Propagate shrubs by layering<br>• Prune shrubs<br>• Shear formal hedges<br>• Plant shrubs<br>• Take softwood cuttings for propagation<br>• Transplant shrubs<br>• Weed soil around shrubs<br>• Apply mulch for summer<br>• Water if ground is dry<br>• Check for insects, diseases<br>• Plant new climbing shrubs<br>• Check supports for established climbing shrubs<br>• Water and mulch newly planted shrubs | **MARCH/APRIL** |
| | • Prune spring-flowering shrubs<br>• Shear formal hedges<br>• Plant shrubs<br>• Take softwood cuttings for propagation<br>• Transplant shrubs<br>• Weed soil around shrubs<br>• Apply mulch for summer<br>• Water if ground is dry<br>• Check for insects, diseases<br>• Remove faded flowers from shrubs | • Prune spring-flowering shrubs<br>• Shear formal hedges<br>• Plant shrubs<br>• Take softwood cuttings for propagation<br>• Transplant shrubs<br>• Weed soil around shrubs<br>• Apply mulch for summer<br>• Water if ground is dry<br>• Check for insects, diseases<br>• Remove faded flowers from shrubs | • Prune spring-flowering shrubs<br>• Shear formal hedges<br>• Plant shrubs<br>• Take softwood cuttings for propagation<br>• Weed soil around shrubs<br>• Apply mulch for summer<br>• Water if ground is dry<br>• Check for insects, diseases<br>• Remove faded flowers from shrubs | • Prune spring-flowering shrubs<br>• Shear formal hedges<br>• Plant shrubs<br>• Weed soil around shrubs<br>• Apply mulch for summer<br>• Water if ground is dry<br>• Check for insects, diseases<br>• Remove faded flowers from shrubs | • Prune spring-flowering shrubs<br>• Shear formal hedges<br>• Plant shrubs<br>• Weed soil around shrubs<br>• Apply mulch for summer<br>• Water if ground is dry<br>• Check for insects, diseases<br>• Remove faded flowers from shrubs | **MAY/JUNE** |

| | ZONE 1 | ZONE 2 | ZONE 3 | ZONE 4 | ZONE 5 |
|---|---|---|---|---|---|
| **JULY/AUGUST** | • Prune shrubs after flowering<br>• Shear formal hedges<br>• Plant shrubs<br>• Take softwood cuttings for propagation<br>• Transplant shrubs<br>• Weed soil around shrubs<br>• Replace mulch as needed<br>• Water as necessary<br>• Check for insects, diseases | • Prune shrubs after flowering<br>• Shear formal hedges<br>• Plant shrubs<br>• Take softwood cuttings for propagation<br>• Transplant shrubs<br>• Weed soil around shrubs<br>• Replace mulch as needed<br>• Water as necessary<br>• Check for insects, diseases | • Prune shrubs after flowering<br>• Shear formal hedges<br>• Plant shrubs<br>• Take softwood cuttings for propagation<br>• Transplant shrubs<br>• Weed soil around shrubs<br>• Replace mulch as needed<br>• Water as necessary<br>• Check for insects, diseases | • Prune shrubs after flowering<br>• Shear formal hedges<br>• Plant shrubs<br>• Take softwood cuttings for propagation<br>• Transplant shrubs<br>• Weed soil around shrubs<br>• Replace mulch as needed<br>• Water as necessary<br>• Check for insects, diseases | • Prune shrubs after flowering<br>• Shear formal hedges<br>• Plant shrubs<br>• Take softwood cuttings for propagation<br>• Weed soil around shrubs<br>• Replace mulch as needed<br>• Water as necessary<br>• Check for insects, diseases |
| **SEPTEMBER/OCTOBER** | • Propagate conifers from stem cuttings<br>• Divide multistemmed shrubs<br>• Adjust soil pH and add amendments for spring planting<br>• Spray broad-leaved evergreens with antidesiccant<br>• Apply mulch for winter and install burlap screens<br>• Water if ground is dry<br>• Turn off water, drain hose<br>• Protect shrubs from wind if necessary | • Propagate conifers from stem cuttings<br>• Divide multistemmed shrubs<br>• Adjust soil pH and add amendments for spring planting<br>• Spray broad-leaved evergreens with antidesiccant<br>• Apply mulch for winter and install burlap screens<br>• Water if ground is dry<br>• Turn off water, drain hose<br>• Protect shrubs from wind if necessary | • Propagate conifers from stem cuttings<br>• Divide multistemmed shrubs<br>• Adjust soil pH and add amendments for spring planting<br>• Spray broad-leaved evergreens with antidesiccant<br>• Apply mulch for winter and install burlap screens<br>• Water if ground is dry<br>• Turn off water, drain hose<br>• Protect shrubs from wind if necessary | • Propagate conifers from stem cuttings<br>• Divide multistemmed shrubs<br>• Adjust soil pH and add amendments for spring planting<br>• Spray broad-leaved evergreens with antidesiccant<br>• Apply mulch for winter and install burlap screens<br>• Water if ground is dry<br>• Turn off water, drain hose<br>• Weed soil around shrubs<br>• Protect shrubs from wind if necessary | • Plant shrubs<br>• Propagate conifers from stem cuttings<br>• Divide multistemmed shrubs<br>• Transplant shrubs<br>• Adjust soil pH and add amendments for spring planting<br>• Water if ground is dry<br>• Weed soil around shrubs |
| **NOVEMBER/DECEMBER** | • Put wire mesh around shrubs for protection against animals<br>• Remove snow and ice from weak-limbed or tall-growing shrubs after every snowfall<br>• Apply deer repellant if necessary<br>• Pot flowering shrubs for winter bloom indoors<br>• Take hardwood cuttings for propagation<br>• Check mulch<br>• Check wind protection | • Put wire mesh around shrubs for protection against animals<br>• Remove snow and ice from weak-limbed or tall-growing shrubs after every snowfall<br>• Apply deer repellant if necessary<br>• Pot flowering shrubs for winter bloom indoors<br>• Take hardwood cuttings for propagation<br>• Check mulch<br>• Check wind protection | • Put wire mesh around shrubs for protection against animals<br>• Remove snow and ice from weak-limbed or tall-growing shrubs after every snowfall<br>• Apply deer repellant if necessary<br>• Pot flowering shrubs for winter bloom indoors<br>• Take hardwood cuttings for propagation<br>• Check mulch<br>• Check wind protection | • Put wire mesh around shrubs for protection against animals<br>• Remove snow and ice from weak-limbed or tall-growing shrubs after every snowfall<br>• Apply deer repellant if necessary<br>• Pot flowering shrubs for winter bloom indoors<br>• Take hardwood cuttings for propagation<br>• Check mulch<br>• Check wind protection | • Spray broad-leaved evergreens with antidesiccant<br>• Apply winter mulch and install burlap screens<br>• Put wire mesh around shrubs for protection against animals<br>• Remove snow and ice from weak-limbed or tall-growing shrubs after every snowfall<br>• Water if ground is dry<br>• Turn off water, drain hose<br>• Protect shrubs from wind if necessary<br>• Apply deer repellant if necessary<br>• Pot flowering shrubs for winter bloom indoors<br>• Take hardwood cuttings for propagation |

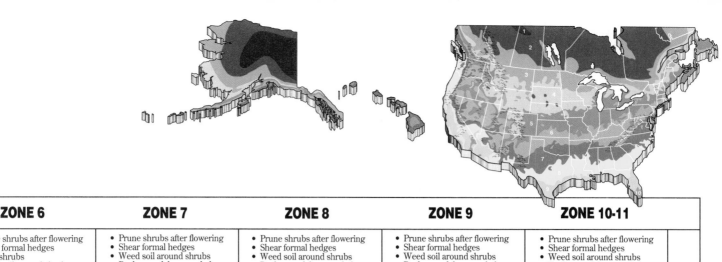

| | ZONE 6 | ZONE 7 | ZONE 8 | ZONE 9 | ZONE 10-11 | |
|---|---|---|---|---|---|---|
| | • Prune shrubs after flowering<br>• Shear formal hedges<br>• Plant shrubs<br>• Weed soil around shrubs<br>• Replace mulch as needed<br>• Water as necessary<br>• Check for insects, diseases | • Prune shrubs after flowering<br>• Shear formal hedges<br>• Weed soil around shrubs<br>• Replace mulch as needed<br>• Water as necessary<br>• Check for insects, diseases | • Prune shrubs after flowering<br>• Shear formal hedges<br>• Weed soil around shrubs<br>• Replace mulch as needed<br>• Water as necessary<br>• Check for insects, diseases | • Prune shrubs after flowering<br>• Shear formal hedges<br>• Weed soil around shrubs<br>• Replace mulch as needed<br>• Water as necessary<br>• Check for insects, diseases | • Prune shrubs after flowering<br>• Shear formal hedges<br>• Weed soil around shrubs<br>• Replace mulch as needed<br>• Water as necessary<br>• Check for insects, diseases | **JULY/AUGUST** |
| | • Plant shrubs<br>• Propagate conifers from stem cuttings<br>• Divide multistemmed shrubs<br>• Transplant shrubs<br>• Adjust soil pH and add amendments for spring planting<br>• Water if ground is dry<br>• Weed soil around shrubs | • Prune shrubs<br>• Plant shrubs<br>• Propagate conifers from stem cuttings<br>• Divide multistemmed shrubs<br>• Water if ground is dry<br>• Weed soil around shrubs | • Prune shrubs<br>• Plant shrubs<br>• Propagate conifers from stem cuttings<br>• Divide multistemmed shrubs<br>• Water if ground is dry<br>• Weed soil around shrubs | • Prune shrubs<br>• Plant shrubs<br>• Propagate conifers from stem cuttings<br>• Divide multistemmed shrubs<br>• Water if ground is dry<br>• Weed soil around shrubs | • Prune shrubs<br>• Plant shrubs<br>• Propagate conifers from stem cuttings<br>• Divide multistemmed shrubs<br>• Water if ground is dry<br>• Weed soil around shrubs | **SEPTEMBER/OCTOBER** |
| | • Spray broad-leaved evergreens with antidesiccant<br>• Apply winter mulch and install burlap screens<br>• Put wire mesh around shrubs for protection against animals<br>• Water if ground is dry<br>• Turn off water, drain hose<br>• Protect shrubs from wind if necessary<br>• Apply deer repellant if necessary<br>• Pot flowering shrubs for winter bloom indoors<br>• Take hardwood cuttings for propagation | • Prune shrubs<br>• Fertilize shrubs<br>• Spray broad-leaved evergreens with antidesiccant<br>• Apply winter mulch and install burlap screens<br>• Put wire mesh around shrubs for protection against animals<br>• Remove undesirable shrubs<br>• Water if ground is dry<br>• Turn off water, drain hose<br>• Protect shrubs from wind if necessary<br>• Apply deer repellant if necessary<br>• Pot flowering shrubs for winter bloom indoors<br>• Take hardwood cuttings for propagation | • Prune shrubs<br>• Fertilize shrubs<br>• Propagate conifers from stem cuttings<br>• Adjust soil pH and add amendments for spring planting<br>• Spray broad-leaved evergreens with antidesiccant<br>• Apply winter mulch and install burlap screens<br>• Put wire mesh around shrubs for protection against animals<br>• Remove undesirable shrubs<br>• Water if ground is dry<br>• Turn off water, drain hose<br>• Protect shrubs from wind if necessary<br>• Apply deer repellant if necessary<br>• Pot flowering shrubs for winter bloom indoors<br>• Take hardwood cuttings for propagation | • Prune shrubs<br>• Fertilize shrubs<br>• Plant shrubs<br>• Propagate conifers from stem cuttings<br>• Transplant shrubs<br>• Remove undesirable shrubs<br>• Water if ground is dry<br>• Pot flowering shrubs for winter bloom indoors<br>• Take hardwood cuttings for propagation | • Prune shrubs<br>• Fertilize shrubs<br>• Plant shrubs<br>• Propagate conifers from stem cuttings<br>• Transplant shrubs<br>• Remove undesirable shrubs<br>• Water if ground is dry<br>• Pot flowering shrubs for winter bloom indoors<br>• Take hardwood cuttings for propagation | **NOVEMBER/DECEMBER** |

# TROUBLESHOOTING GUIDE: TREES

| PROBLEM | CAUSE | SOLUTION |
|---|---|---|
| Trees lose their foliage in late spring. Translucent egg clusters several inches in diameter may be seen on the tree trunks. Many trees, including alder, birch, elm, hawthorn, linden, maple, oak, pine, poplar, sassafras and willow may be affected. | Gypsy moth caterpillars, which are 2 inches long and have hairy brown bodies with red and blue spots. | Scrape egg clusters off trunks and destroy them. Spray caterpillars with an insecticide or *Bacillus thuringiensis*, called Bt, a bacterium fatal to caterpillars but harmless to plants and other animals. Loosely tie a piece of burlap around each affected trunk; the caterpillars will be trapped under the burlap and can then be collected and destroyed. Parasitic wasps are natural predators. |
| Leaves curl, buds and flowers are deformed, and tree growth is stunted. Leaves may be coated with a black, sooty powder. Branches may die. Beech, birch, crabapple, elm, flowering fruit, linden, maple, oak, pine and willow trees are susceptible. | Aphids, ⅛-inch, semitransparent insects that may be green, yellow, black, brown or red. Aphids carry bacterial, fungal and viral diseases. They pierce foliage and suck sap from foliage, stems and roots. They often form large colonies on trees. | In early spring, before the leaf buds open, spray the foliage with horticultural oil, which smothers insects and their eggs. Treat infestations as they appear with an insecticide. Repeat applications at one-week intervals, if necessary. |
| Silky, weblike nests that resemble tents appear in the crotches of birch, elm, flowering fruit, hawthorn, maple, oak, poplar and willow trees. Caterpillars may be visible on the foliage during the day. | Tent caterpillars, hairy, 2-inch-long insects with blue spots and red stripes. | Spray with an insecticide or *Bacillus thuringiensis*, or introduce parasitic wasps, which are natural predators. |
| Trees weaken and cease to grow; twigs, branches or entire trees may die. White, cottony patches and small, brown round or oval shells appear on branches, twigs, and sometimes leaves and fruit. Any tree may be affected. | Any of a number of scale insects, from ¹⁄₁₀ to ⅜ inch long, with gray, white, yellow, green, black, brown, red or purple shells. The cottony patches, often misdiagnosed as fungus, are egg sacs. | In midspring, spray with horticultural oil, which will smother the eggs and young insects. The precise timing of spraying may depend on the type of scale; check with a garden supply center. Treat infestations as they appear with an insecticide. Repeat applications at one-week intervals, if necessary. |
| Upper surfaces of leaves lose color and are covered with white or yellow speckles; undersides of leaves are covered with small, dark specks. Susceptible trees are ash, birch, elm, hawthorn, honey locust, linden, oak, sycamore and willow. | Lace bugs, tiny flat bugs ¹⁄₁₆ to ⅛ inch long with transparent, lacy wings and hoodlike coverings on their heads. They pierce foliage and suck sap. | Spray with an insecticide in midspring and again in midsummer to control successive generations of lace bugs, which mature in six to eight weeks. |
| Cocoonlike, 1- to 2-inch bags that look like brown, dry foliage hang from branches. The most susceptible trees are conifers such as hemlock and pine, but linden, locust and maple can also be affected. | Bagworm, a 1-inch caterpillar with a brown or black body and a white or yellow head. It uses pieces of leaves and twigs to construct a bag around itself. | In winter or spring, the bags may be hand-picked and destroyed before the caterpillars emerge. In late spring or early summer, when caterpillars emerge, apply an insecticide or *Bacillus thuringiensis*. |

| PROBLEM | CAUSE | SOLUTION |
|---------|-------|----------|
| Trees become defoliated. Eggs appear on the undersides and the bases of the leaves. Both evergreen and deciduous trees are susceptible. | Sawfly larvae, caterpillar-like insects 1 to 1½ inches long. Most are green, with stripes or spots, and resemble the needlelike foliage of conifers. | Spray with an insecticide when the insects appear in early spring and summer. Repeat applications may be needed to control successive generations. |
| Bark on lower sections of trunks is missing or ragged. | Deer, rabbits or other animals. | Tree trunks can be wrapped in burlap or encased in cylinders of wire mesh or tar paper. Protection should reach 20 inches higher than the average snowfall line. Spread blood meal near the tree; reapply after rain. |
| Light green or brown serpentine markings appear on leaves; leaves eventually turn brown and die. Some species of birch are susceptible; so are aspen, crabapple, elm, flowering fruit, hawthorn, holly, locust, oak, pine, spruce and tupelo trees. | Leaf miners, which are the larvae of flies, moths or beetles that tunnel into leaf surfaces. | Spray with a systemic pesticide in spring. Apply pesticide to the ground out to the drip line under infested trees. If the infestation is severe, consult a professional arborist. |
| Irregular holes appear in leaves of elm and other shade trees. Eventually, entire trees may be defoliated. Trees become vulnerable to pests and diseases. | Beetles, including the Japanese beetle, a ½-inch, metallic green insect; the larva of the elm leaf beetle, a ½-inch yellow grub striped or spotted with black; and the elm bark beetle, which is ⅛ inch long and reddish brown. | Adult forms of beetles can be controlled with insecticide. Larvae should be controlled with insecticides applied to trees and to the lawn around trees. For Japanese beetles, spray in June and July; for elm leaf beetles, spray in May and June. Spraying for a second generation five to six weeks later may also be necessary. |
| Trees are suddenly defoliated. Insects can be seen hanging from branches on thin, silklike threads. Beech, elm and other shade trees may be affected. | Cankerworm, also called inchworm, a ½-inch moth larva that is usually green, but may be brown or black. Larvae can be identified by the way they arch their backs as they move. Cankerworms chew on foliage. | Spray with an insecticide or *Bacillus thuringiensis*, called Bt. In an area having a history of infestation by the pest, spray in early spring before the insect appears. Wrap trunks with a sticky material to trap female adults before they lay eggs. |
| Leaves lose their color and upper leaf surfaces take on a dull silver or bronze sheen. Tiny black specks, small translucent blisters and pest eggs and eggshells may be seen on the undersides of leaves. Eventually, leaves wither and drop and fine webs may appear on branches. Linden, locust, maple, oak and pine are susceptible. | One of a number of mites, microscopic spiderlike pests. They rupture plant cells when feeding on leaf tissue. | Spray with horticultural oil in spring before leaf buds open. If symptoms appear in summer, apply a miticide. Repeat applications three days apart are usually necessary for control. |
| Leaves are small or sparse. Tree growth slows or stops. Small round holes may appear in the bark. Dogwood is particularly susceptible, but ash, birch, elm, hemlock, honey locust, linden, locust, maple, oak, pine and poplar are also susceptible. | Borers, ½- to 2½-inch-long caterpillars that work their way into the bark and destroy the tree from inside the trunk. They are difficult to kill when they penetrate tree bark. Borers prosper in unhealthy, nonvigorous trees or in trees in poor growing conditions. | Stressed trees are particularly vulnerable to borer attack, so keep trees well watered, fertilized and disease-free. Wrap paper or plastic around the tree trunks to discourage borers. Once they have entered the trunk, they can be cut out with a knife if they are near the surface. Prune infested branches. An insecticide may be applied to the bark where holes appear; check with a garden supply center for correct timing. |

419

| PROBLEM | CAUSE | SOLUTION |
|---|---|---|
| Leaves at the ends of branches suddenly wilt, turn black and appear to have been scorched by fire. Twigs may also turn black. Dark brown cankers several inches long develop on trunks and main branches. Crabapple, flowering fruit and hawthorn trees are susceptible. | Fire blight, a bacterial disease. The bacteria overwinters in infected tree parts. | There are no chemical controls, but avoid nitrogen-rich fertilizer. Prune out damaged branches when the tree is dormant, cutting well below infected areas, and disinfect pruning tools with alcohol after each cut. Prune out root suckers. Spray with an antibiotic every five to seven days when the trees are in bloom to prevent the disease. |
| Leaves are distorted in shape, turn yellow, dry up and drop. Leaves and twigs are covered with a whitish gray powder. Symptoms are most severe when days are warm and nights are cool. Many deciduous trees can be affected. | Powdery mildew, a fungal disease. | Prune out infected tree parts and rake up leaves promptly. To prevent or control the disease, spray with a fungicide once a week during periods of warm days and cool nights. Increase air circulation and sunlight to trees. |
| Leaves on one branch, several branches or an entire tree first turn yellow, then brown, wilt and may drop. A cross section of a branch reveals a dark ring or rings. Maples are the most susceptible, but many types of trees can be affected. | Verticillium wilt, a fungal disease. The fungus lives in the soil and can enter plants through wounds. Its presence can be confirmed only by a laboratory test of a damaged branch. | There are no chemical controls. Remove damaged tree parts. If infection is severe, the tree cannot be saved and must be removed to prevent the spread of the disease. Plant wilt-resistant varieties, such as beech, birch, crabapple, ginkgo, holly, hawthorn, plane tree and willow. |
| Small brown spots form on new leaves and spread until entire leaves are brown and look scorched. Leaves drop and are succeeded by a set of healthy leaves. If this occurs in successive years, the trees will become stressed and may die. Ash, birch, elm, linden, maple, oak, plane tree, sycamore and tulip tree may be affected. | Anthracnose, a fungal disease that is particularly severe in wet weather because the fungus is spread by splashing water. Cool, wet weather promotes infection of twigs and branches; warm, wet weather promotes infection of foliage. | A fungicide can be used both to prevent and to control the disease. Spray in spring when leaf buds start to open and repeat two or three times, 10 to 14 days apart. Prune out infected twigs and branches and promptly rake up and destroy fallen leaves and twigs. |
| Rough, round swellings up to several inches across appear on tree trunks, branches and roots. Trees may cease to grow, leaves may yellow and branches may die back. Young trees may die. Susceptible trees are flowering fruit, oak, poplar, sycamore and willow. | Crown gall, a bacterial disease that inhabits the soil. The bacteria enters plants mainly through wounds, stimulating abnormal cell growth. | There are no chemical controls. Prune out damaged branches on affected trees. Do not plant susceptible trees in an area with a history of the disease. To keep from spreading the disease, avoid wounding trees when gardening. |
| Areas between the veins or along the margins of leaves turn white, brown or yellow. Leaves may also be speckled or streaked or have a silvery sheen. | Air pollution, but consult a garden supply center to rule out pests or disease as a cause. | There are no controls for pollution. Pollution-tolerant trees are available, such as elm, ginkgo, linden, Norway maple, pin oak, sycamore and tulip tree. |
| Red, brown or black patches appear on stems, branches and trunks. Infected areas expand and eventually may kill the tree. Trees weaken, becoming susceptible to trunk breakage. | Canker, a fungal or bacterial disease. | Stressed trees are particularly susceptible to canker, so keep trees well watered, fertilized and free of insects. Prune out infected parts as soon as they appear and disinfect tools with alcohol after each cut. If infection is severe, the tree must be removed to prevent the spread of the disease. Avoid wounding trees. |

| PROBLEM | CAUSE | SOLUTION |
| --- | --- | --- |
| Yellow spots appear on upper surfaces of leaves, and the undersides are covered with reddish orange blisterlike pustules. Crabapple, hawthorn, pine, poplar and red cedar trees are susceptible. When a pine is infected, small cankers appear on the trunk and branches *(right)*. Leaves may drop. | Rust, a fungal disease. | Rust develops only when certain plants are grown near each other, and these combinations should be avoided. Do not plant pine trees near gooseberry or currant. Do not plant crabapple or hawthorn near red cedar or juniper. Do not plant poplar trees near hemlock. If symptoms appear, spray with a fungicide three times, 10 days apart. |
| Leaves at the tops of trees and toward the ends of long branches begin to droop and lose their color and shine. Young trees are especially susceptible. | Insufficient water or overly compacted soil around the root zone. | Check the soil in the upper 12 inches around the base of an affected tree. If the soil is so dry that it crumbles in your hand, the tree needs water. Soak thoroughly and apply mulch to help retain moisture. Aerate the root zone, if necessary, to ensure that water can reach roots. |
| Small, round dark spots, sometimes surrounded by yellow rings, appear on leaves. As the spots expand in size, the entire leaves become dark and usually drop. Catalpa, dogwood, elm, flowering fruit, hawthorn and oak trees are susceptible. | Leaf spot, caused by a number of fungi or bacteria. The disease is particularly severe in wet weather because the fungi and bacteria are spread by splashing water. | Rake and destroy all fallen leaves. A fungicide can be used both to prevent and to control leaf spot. Spray once every 10 days, starting when leaf buds begin to open, again when they unfurl, once again when they are half-grown and finally when they are full-grown. |
| Malodorous sap flows from wounds in bark. The sap, which damages tree cambium and bark, may be either brown or white and foamy. Birch, elm, maple, oak, poplar, sycamore and willow are susceptible. | Slime flux, a bacterial infection. The bacteria enter the tree through wounds caused by injury, such as lawn-mower cuts or from insects, and then they infect the sap. | There are no chemical controls for slime flux. Paint wounds with tree-wound paint. Drill a hole slanted upward into the tree just below the wound and insert a plastic tube into the hole; this will allow infected sap to drain away from the tree and promote healing of the wound. Cut away loose, dead bark to allow the area to dry out. |
| Leaves wilt and drop. Branches stop growing and may die. A white, fan-shaped fungal growth appears just under the bark near the base of the tree or just under the soil line. Eventually, long, round black strands of tissue form under the bark and on or near the roots. Many trees are susceptible, especially maple and oak trees. | Shoestring root rot, a fungal disease. | Stressed trees are particularly susceptible to shoestring root rot, so keep trees well watered, fertilized and free of insects and diseases. Remove the damaged parts of partially infected trees. If the entire root system is infected, the tree must be removed and the soil around it replaced. Avoid replanting susceptible varieties. |
| Leaf edges appear scorched. Fall coloration of leaves occurs prematurely in summer, and leaves drop. Trees along roadways and footpaths are the most susceptible. | Salt injury. This occurs when roots take in salt applied to the ground to melt ice and snow. The salt bonds with water in the soil, making the water unavailable to roots. | Use sand or sawdust instead of salt. Plant salt-tolerant trees, such as black cherry, black locust, paper birch, red oak, white ash, white oak or yellow birch, along roadways. |

421

# TROUBLESHOOTING GUIDE: SHRUBS

| PROBLEM | CAUSE | SOLUTION |
|---|---|---|
| A brownish gray moldy growth appears on flowers and foliage. Flowers collapse, foliage loses its color and new growth dies back. Most shrubs are susceptible. | Botrytis blight, also known as gray mold, a fungus disease. The problem is especially severe during cool, humid weather. | Spray with a fungicide once a week until symptoms disappear. Prune out and discard damaged flowers and foliage. Provide good air circulation and avoid overhead watering; use drip irrigation or a soaker hose. |
| New leaves are yellow, but leaf veins remain green. Older foliage may turn yellow around the leaf margins. Shrubs planted near the foundation of the house may be severely affected. Acid-loving broad-leaved evergreens such as azalea, gardenia, mountain laurel and rhododendron are susceptible. | Iron deficiency, which occurs when soil is too alkaline. The elements in alkaline soil bond with iron to form an insoluble salt and thus prevent the iron from being absorbed by plants. | Add shredded pine bark to the soil; the bark's acid content keeps the iron from bonding and enables it to be available to plants. Test the soil pH and adjust the level to between 4.5 and 5.5. Spray the foliage and the soil around the shrub with a solution of chelated iron, or work coffee grounds, which are highly acidic, into the soil. |
| Leaves are covered with round spots or uneven blotches. On azalea, leucothoe, mountain laurel, rhododendron and wild lilac, the spots may be yellow, red, brown or gray. On photinia, the spots are purple, and as they enlarge, they turn brown with purple margins. On all shrubs, the markings will grow together until the entire leaf is covered, turns yellow and dies. | Leaf spot, a fungus disease. The fungus is spread by water and wind, particularly during hot, humid weather. | There are no chemical cures for infected leaves; they should be pruned off and destroyed. To prevent the disease, spray shrubs with a fungicide when new growth develops in spring, and continue spraying once every two weeks as long as the weather is hot and humid. Avoid overcrowding plants; try to increase their exposure to sunlight. Add mulch and set up windbreaks. Control insects; uninfested plant tissue is less vulnerable to attack. |
| Foliage and branches of conifers turn brown. Needles may drop. Entire sections of the shrub may die back. | Twig and needle blight, a fungus disease that is common in damp, humid conditions. The fungus spreads in water. | Prune out infected areas and sterilize pruning tools after each cut. In spring, spray shrubs with a fungicide and repeat the application until the symptoms disappear. |
| Conifer needles turn orange or are mottled with orange. Broad-leaved evergreen foliage develops small water-filled blisters that burst, leaving brown areas on the leaf surface. Leaves may be flecked with yellow, and the leaf margins and areas between veins turn brown. Symptoms usually appear first on new growth. Over time shrubs may lose leaves and their growth may be stunted. | Air pollution, exhaust fumes and, in northerly areas, acid rain. | There are no cures for damage from pollution or acid rain. Plant pollution-tolerant shrubs such as arborvitae, cotoneaster, juniper or privet. |

| PROBLEM | CAUSE | SOLUTION |
|---|---|---|
| Upper surfaces of leaves are covered with small yellow spots. Undersides of leaves are covered with an orange powder. Affected leaves may drop from the shrub. Azalea and rhododendron are susceptible. | Rust, a fungus disease that spreads rapidly among damp leaves. | There are no chemical cures or preventives for the rust that attacks azalea and rhododendron. Remove infected leaves to prevent spread of the disease. |
| Leaves wilt, turn yellow, then brown and die without dropping from the plant. Roots are dark and decayed. Many evergreen shrubs are susceptible. | Root rot, caused by a fungus that thrives in wet soil. | There are no chemical controls. Infected shrubs and the surrounding soil should be removed. Before planting shrubs, make sure that your soil has good drainage. Avoid wounding bark when gardening; maintain shrubs faithfully. |
| Azalea and rhododendron flower petals develop small, rounded brown spots, beginning on the undersides of flower petals; flowering shrub petals (right) develop brown streaks and blotches. The brown markings spread rapidly until the entire flower turns brown and collapses. | The fungus diseases azalea petal blight and camellia petal blight. Symptoms can be distinguished from normal fading because flowers turn brown almost overnight. | There are no chemical cures. Remove diseased flowers and rake up any debris on the ground under the shrub. To prevent the disease, spray with a fungicide as soon as the flower buds start to show color, and repeat applications every five days until flowering ends. |
| Conifer needles turn brown, starting at the tips and progressing to the bases. Broad-leaved evergreen leaf tips and margins turn brown or black. The symptoms usually appear first on older needles and leaves, and eventually may also appear on new growth. | Damage caused by salt applied to icy roads and walkways during winter. | To melt ice, use sand or sawdust instead of salt. Spray shrubs near roadsides with an antidesiccant. Plant salt-tolerant shrubs such as euonymus, oleander, pyracantha and viburnum. |
| Cotoneaster and pyracantha foliage suddenly wilts, turns brown or black, and appears to have been scorched. Bark at the base of affected areas may turn dark, dry out and crack. | Fire blight, a bacterial disease that spreads in warm, wet conditions. Insects, particularly bees, spread the disease. | There are no chemical cures. Prune out damaged branches well below the diseased area and disinfect pruning tools after each cut. To prevent the disease, spray shrubs with a recommended antibiotic every five to seven days in spring while new growth develops; check with a garden supply center. Plant fire blight-resistant varieties. |
| Leaves of broad-leaved evergreens have a dull, silvery appearance. The leaves may wilt and fall from the shrub. Foliage may be covered with black specks. Bud tips may turn brown and drop. | Thrips, tiny insects that feed on the sap of leaf tissue. | During the summer, spray shrubs every two weeks with an insecticide until all signs of infestation are gone. |
| Opening buds and needles on branch tips have been chewed. Eventually, the damaged needles are webbed together with silk. The branch tips die back and the entire shrub may die. | Spruce budworms, 1-inch caterpillars that have dark reddish brown bodies with yellow stripes along the sides. | Spray with an insecticide in midspring when new growth and buds start to open. |

423

| PROBLEM | CAUSE | SOLUTION |
|---|---|---|
| New foliage of azalea, boxwood, gardenia or rhododendron may have a distorted shape. Eventually, leaves may become speckled with yellow or gray (A). Needles of arborvitae or juniper lose their sheen and are streaked with yellow (B). Eventually, the needles turn brown and may drop from the plant. Thin, silken webs appear on the branches of all susceptible shrubs. | Mites, microscopic spiderlike pests that may be red, green, black, yellow, pink or white. Mites thrive in a hot, dry environment. | Keep shrubs well watered to discourage the pests. Spray with an approved miticide in spring and summer when symptoms appear. Repeat applications may be necessary. After an infestation, spray shrubs with horticultural oil early the following spring to smother eggs. |
| Leaves have yellow spots and leaf margins may curl. Affected areas may be covered with a clear, sticky substance. When an infested shrub is shaken, a cloud of tiny flying insects appears. Azalea, gardenia, privet and rhododendron are susceptible. | Whiteflies, $\frac{1}{12}$-inch white insects that feed on the undersides of leaves. | When symptoms appear, spray with an insecticide and be sure to cover the undersides of leaves; synthetic pyrethrins are very effective against whitefly. Repeat the application at one-week intervals until all signs of infestation are gone. |
| Shrubs do not develop new growth in spring. Needles turn yellow, then brown and holes appear in the margins (A). Branches wilt, and the shrub may die. Azalea and rhododendron leaves turn yellow, wilt and curl up; leaf edges appear scalloped. Holes appear in the leaf margins (B). | Black vine weevils, also called taxus weevils. In early spring, the grubs feed on roots. In early summer, the weevils, which have $\frac{3}{8}$-inch black or brown bodies covered with yellow hair, feed on foliage at night. | Remove weeds and fallen leaves around shrubs in the fall; weevils lay their eggs in weedy areas during the winter. When symptoms appear, spray the foliage and the ground around the shrub with an insecticide, starting in early summer. Repeat applications three times, three weeks apart. |
| Shrubs cease to grow and the tips of branches may die. Foliage wilts and loses its color. Branches, twigs or leaves are covered with small round or oval masses. Most evergreen shrubs are susceptible. | Scale insects, which have hard or soft shells ranging in size from $\frac{1}{10}$ to $\frac{3}{8}$ inch. The shells may be white, yellow, green, red, brown or black. | Prune out severely infested branches. Spray shrubs with horticultural oil in early spring to smother the eggs. If insects appear in summer, spray with an insecticide. |
| Azalea, rhododendron or mountain laurel leaves turn yellow, then brown. Main branches have small holes from which sawdust emerges. Patches of bark may peel off. Entire branches may wilt or break off. | Rhododendron borers, $\frac{1}{2}$-inch yellow-white caterpillars that bore into and under the bark after shrubs bloom. | There are no controls for borers once they get under the bark. Cut off infested branches. In spring, spray or paint the bark at two-week intervals with an insecticide developed especially for borers; this will kill the larvae when they hatch. |
| Upper surfaces of leaves are speckled with white or yellow. Undersides of the leaves are covered with dark specks. Shrubs may fail to grow. The most susceptible shrubs are azalea, cotoneaster, pieris and rhododendron. | Lace bugs, small flat bugs that are $\frac{1}{16}$ to $\frac{1}{8}$ inch long and have clear, lacy wings and hoodlike coverings on their heads. | Spray the undersides of leaves with an insecticide in late spring. Repeat the application two or three times, 10 days apart, until all signs of infestation are gone. |

424

| PROBLEM | CAUSE | SOLUTION |
|---|---|---|
| Leaf tips of conifers such as arborvitae and juniper turn yellow, then brown (A). Boxwood leaves are spotted with yellow. The spots enlarge to blisterlike patches and turn brown. The spots first appear on the undersides of leaves, and then as they enlarge, they penetrate the upper leaf surfaces (B). Shrub leaves are marked with yellowish or brown serpentine trails (C). | Leaf miners, the larvae of beetles, flies or moths. The larvae are $\frac{1}{8}$ to $\frac{1}{4}$ inch long and may be yellow or green. They hatch from eggs laid inside the leaves and feed on leaf tissue. | Prune out severely infested branch tips and leaves. Spray conifers with an insecticide in early summer. Spray boxwoods in late May. |
| Foliage turns yellow and wilts. Entire branches may die back. Roots are covered with small, irregular swellings. The most susceptible shrubs are boxwood and gardenia. | Nematodes, microscopic worms that feed on shrub roots. The only way to confirm their presence is by a soil test. | Remove damaged shrubs and the surrounding soil. In severe cases, professional soil treatment may be necessary. Consult a local county extension office or a garden supply center about soil fumigation. |
| Leaves turn yellow. Cottonlike white masses appear on branches and stems. Affected areas may be covered with a clear, sticky substance that attracts ants. Azalea and gardenia are the most susceptible shrubs. | Mealybugs, $\frac{1}{8}$- to $\frac{1}{4}$-inch oval insects covered with white, waxy hairs. | Spray with horticultural oil in mid-spring. If insects appear in early summer, spray with an insecticide. Repeat applications may be necessary. |
| New growth on needle-leaved evergreen shrubs is deformed and bends downward instead of growing straight. Branch ends turn yellow, then brown and may die back. A mass of resin forms at the base of needles. | European pine shoot moths, which lay their eggs on branch tips. The eggs hatch $\frac{3}{4}$-inch-long brown caterpillars that bore into the base of the needles. | Prune off the deformed growth as soon as it appears. Hand-pick eggs off infested buds. Spray shrubs with an insecticide in early spring and again in early summer. |
| Green, bulblike galls from $\frac{1}{2}$ inch to 2 inches long appear at the base of needles on the tips of conifer branches in spring. The galls turn brown as they age and eventually split open. Colonies of small insects are visible along the branches. In severe cases, entire branches may die and break off. Conifers may be affected. | Spruce gall aphids, $\frac{1}{8}$-inch insects that have dark bodies often covered with a white, waxy substance. When the aphids feed on the foliage, they deposit a toxin that causes the galls. In spring, adult females deposit eggs from which galls develop. | In midspring, apply horticultural oil to the ends of twigs and branches to smother egg masses. In late spring, spray the same areas with an insecticide. If galls appear, spray with an insecticide in early fall as soon as the galls break open. The galls should not be pruned off, since removal of branch tips may destroy the shape of the shrub. |
| Cocoonlike, 1- to 2-inch bags that look like brown, dry foliage hang from branches. The most susceptible shrubs are arborvitae and juniper. | Bagworm, a caterpillar that grows to 1 inch long and has a brown or black body with a white or yellow head. It uses leaves and twigs to construct its shelter. | In winter or spring, the bags can be hand-picked off shrubs before caterpillars appear. In late spring, if caterpillars appear, spray with an insecticide or with *Bacillus thuringiensis*. |

425

ABIES CONCOLOR

ACACIA BAILEYANA

ACER GRISEUM

# DICTIONARY OF TREES AND SHRUBS

The dictionary entries that follow present a wide variety of beautiful and practical trees and shrubs. Trees are listed on pages 426-448; shrubs on pages 449-459.

## Introduction to trees

The trees are listed by their botanical names; common names are cross-referenced. Each entry describes the characteristics shared by members of the genus and points out the special traits of individual species, such as unusual foliage coloration. Each entry also suggests appropriate ways to use trees in the landscape, such as for streetside planting, specimens or shade.

### Abies (AY-beez)
Fir

Pyramidal evergreen that rises to heights of 30 to 150 feet. Branches are open and upright; needles are aromatic, flat, blunt-pointed and marked on the underside of most species by two whitish lines. Cones mature in a single season and grow upright, mostly near the top of the tree, on spreading branches. Zones 2-8.

**Selected species and varieties.** *A. concolor,* white fir: grows 30 to 50 feet in height and 15 to 30 feet in spread. Upward-curving needles are bluish or grayish green and 2 inches long. Zones 4-8.

**Growing conditions.** Firs prefer full sun, but they will grow in partial shade. They require moist, well-drained, sandy, acid soil and should be sheltered from wind.

**Landscape uses.** Firs make good specimen trees, screens, accents and background plants on properties large enough to accommodate their massive size.

### Acacia (a-KAY-sha)
Acacia, wattle

Broad-leaved evergreens that range from 5-foot shrubs to 90-foot trees. The trees have rounded crowns of feathery foliage, and clusters of fragrant yellow flowers that blossom in spring and are followed by dry pods. Zones 8-11.

**Selected species and varieties.** *A. baileyana,* Bailey's acacia, Cootamundra wattle: slender tree that grows 25 to 30 feet tall. Has billows of small, bright, golden cotton-ball-like flowers that cluster over ferny, grayish blue foliage from January to March. Zones 10 and 11.

**Growing conditions.** Acacia is fast growing, 4 feet or more per year. It requires full sun and moist soil, and a warm, dry climate. Bailey's acacia is drought-tolerant once established. Cool summer nights and relatively dry winters produce quality blooms. Prune trees after they have flowered.

**Landscape uses.** Acacia is a good street tree or accent plant in frost-free climates. In cold climates it should be container-grown to protect its tender roots from freezing.

### Acer (AY-ser)
Maple

Deciduous trees 15 to 75 feet tall. All have dense, round crowns and colorful fall leaves that are palmately lobed and long-stalked. In most species, non-showy flowers appear in early spring before leaves emerge. Fruits are paired winged seeds called samaras, or keys; they mature either in spring or in fall. Zones 2-9.

**Selected species and varieties.** *A. buergeranum,* trident maple: bushy, small tree that grows 15 to 30 feet. It has flaking orange-brown bark and 3-inch, pointed, shiny trilobed leaves, which are glossy dark green in summer and yellow, orange and red in fall. Greenish yellow flowers appear in May. Zones 6-8. *A. campestre,* hedge maple: reaches 35 feet or more. Leaves have three to five rounded lobes, stems are corky, and greenish flower heads appear in early spring. Zones 5-8. *A. ginnala,* Amur maple: grows 15 to 20 feet tall. Fragrant flowers are pale yellow. Leaves are simple, toothed and trilobed, with the largest lobe in the center; they are glossy green in spring and summer, and turn red or orange in fall. Winged seeds are red in fall. Zones 2-6. *A. griseum,* paperbark maple: so called because its cinnamon to red-brown bark peels in papery strips. Grows 20 to 30 feet or more in height with an open branching habit. Leaves are composed of three coarsely toothed leaflets; they often turn scarlet in fall. Zones 5-7.

*A. negundo,* box elder, ash-leaved maple: grows 30 to 50 feet in height and spread. Has a rounded crown and irregular branches. Leaves are ovate to oblong, 2 to 4 inches long, and turn yellow-green to brown in autumn. Gray-brown bark is slightly furrowed. Zones 5-8. *A. palmatum,* Japanese maple: grows 15 to 20 feet tall. Leaves are saw-toothed and turn brilliant yellow, bronze or purplish in fall. Zones 6-8.

*A. platanoides,* Norway maple: grows to 50 feet with large, five-lobed, leathery leaves that are broader than they are long and sometimes turn yellow in fall. Greenish yellow flower clusters appear in spring. Winged paired fruit are shaped like coat hangers. Bark is dark and uniformly fissured. Zones 3-7. 'Columnare' has leaves that are smaller than those of the species; it is columnar in shape, with branches that spread at a 30° to 60° angle from a central trunk. 'Crimson King' has deep red leaves.

*A. pseudoplatanus,* sycamore maple: grows 40 to 60 feet tall and has light gray bark that peels to expose orange-brown inner bark. Zones 5-7. *A. rubrum,* red maple: grows 40 to 50 feet and is one of the first trees to flower in spring. Leaves are usually trilobed, toothed, whitish underneath and turn red in fall. Bark is light gray on young trees; becomes dark gray with vertical, platelike ridges as the tree ages. The tree has red flowers in spring and red winged pods in fall. Zones 3-9. 'October Glory' has shiny leaves that turn brilliant orange to red in autumn but fade before they drop from the tree. 'Red Sunset' has bright green leaves that turn orange or scarlet in early fall.

*A. saccharinum,* silver maple: a large, spreading tree that grows 50 to 70 feet tall and 35 to 45 feet across. It has long, pendulous branches; deeply cut, pointed five-lobed leaves; and twigs that emit an unpleasant odor when bruised. Bark exfoliates to show orange undertones. Suckers emerge at the base of the trunk. Silver maple has little, if any, fall color. It is short-lived, but hardy and aggressive and a good tree for poor soils where hardly anything else will grow. Zones 3-9. *A. saccharum,* sugar maple: a relatively short-trunked tree with a large crown that gives it a total of 60 to 75 feet in height and a 40- to 50-foot spread. Leaves are three- to five-lobed, as broad as they are long, and turn yellow, burnt orange and tones of red in autumn. Chartreuse flowers emerge in April, and fruit is produced in fall. Zones 3-8. 'Bonfire' is a heat-tolerant, vigorous maple with leaves that turn carmine red in fall. 'Fairview' has lighter colored bark than other maples and leaves that turn yellow in fall. *A. tataricum,* tatarian maple: grows 20 to 30 feet tall and just as wide.

Leaves are 2 to 4 inches wide, toothed, dark green in summer and turn yellow to red in fall. Zones 4-7.

**Growing conditions.** All maples can grow in full sun or partial shade except for Japanese maple, which grows only in partial shade. Most need moist, well-drained soil. Trident maple tolerates a variety of soil conditions—wetness, salt and compaction. Hedge maple adapts to alkaline soil. Amur maple tolerates drought and cold. Paperbark will grow in clay, and it should be pruned in summer for its attractive branching habit to show. Red maple and silver maple may split in winter storms. Sugar maple cannot tolerate road salt. Tatarian tolerates drought.

**Landscape uses.** Trident maple makes a good medium-size patio plant, street tree or specimen. Hedge maple is best used as a screen or hedge. Amur maple is a good specimen tree; it is also small enough to be container-grown and makes a good bonsai subject. The bright-colored peeling bark and the open branching of paperbark maple make it an attractive specimen tree all year round. Japanese maple, because it is diminutive in size, makes a good accent in patio gardens and courtyards. Norway maple tolerates urban pollution better than most maples and is therefore useful as a street tree. Grass is difficult to grow underneath Norway, red and sugar maples because of their shallow surface roots. Silver maple grows so fast it provides quick shade, but it should not be used as a street tree because its limbs break easily in winter storms, and its roots push up sidewalks and buckle drain tiles. Sugar maple is a good shade tree.

**Aesculus** (ES-kew-lus)
Horse chestnut, buckeye

Deciduous flowering tree that grows 20 to 50 feet tall. It has compound leaves shaped like the spokes of a wheel, and glossy brown husked nuts. Zones 4-8.

**Selected species and varieties.** *A.* x *carnea* 'Briotii': a cultivar that grows 25 to 40 feet, has large, ruby red flower heads and pointed palmate leaves that are dark, glossy green. It is pyramidal as a young tree but becomes roundheaded when mature. Zones 5-8. *A. octandra,* sometimes designated *A. flava,* yellow buckeye, sweet buckeye: grows up to 70 feet tall in an oval, upright form with spreading branches. Fruit is 2 to 2½ inches long and pear-shaped. Bark is mottled gray

ACER RUBRUM

ACER SACCHARUM

AESCULUS × CARNEA 'BRIOTII'

ALBIZIA JULIBRISSIN 'ROSEA'

ALNUS CORDATA

AMELANCHIER LAEVIS

ARBUTUS UNEDO

and brown. Zones 5-8. *A. pavia,* pavia, red buckeye: small tree that reaches 20 feet. It produces loose clusters of red flowers in June. Zones 6-8.

**Growing conditions.** Horse chestnut needs full sun and deep, moist, fertile soil.

**Landscape uses.** Horse chestnuts are good shade trees for wide, open spaces. They are not for small city lots or sidewalks because their flowers and fruit produce litter.

## Albizia (al-BIZ-ee-a)

Deciduous flowering tree that grows from 20 to 120 feet tall or more. It is flat-topped, wide-spreading and low-branched. It blooms in midsummer, has feathery, fernlike foliage that folds inward when touched and produces long, beanlike seedpods in autumn. Zones 6-11.

**Selected species and varieties.** *A. julibrissin,* silk tree, mimosa: grows to 40 feet with 9- to 12-inch-long leaves and pink flowers. Zones 7-9. The cultivars 'Charlotte' and 'Tryon' have rosy pink, powder-puff-like flowers and are resistant to mimosa wilt disease. 'Rosea' has deeper pink blossoms and is hardier than 'Charlotte' or 'Tryon.' Zones 6-9.

**Growing conditions.** Silk tree does best in full sun and well-drained soil. It tolerates dry, hot summers and polluted areas.

**Landscape uses.** Albizia makes a good shade tree, ornamental or accent plant.

## Alder see *Alnus*

## Alnus (AL-nus)
Alder

Deciduous tree that grows 40 to 70 feet tall. It has flowers that emerge in spring and are followed by toothed leaves and cone-like fruits. Zones 2-7.

**Selected species and varieties.** *A. cordata,* Italian alder: grows 30 to 50 feet tall in a pyramidal to rounded form. Leaves are ovate and 2 to 4 inches long. Zones 5-7. *A. glutinosa,* common alder, black alder: grows up to 60 feet tall and sometimes develops an oval or oblong crown. Flowers are red or purple. Bark is glossy and dark brown. Zones 3-7. 'Imperialis' has deeply cut leaves. 'Pyramidalis' grows to 50 feet;

it is narrow, upright, dense and low-branched. *A. incana,* white alder: grows 40 to 60 feet tall. It has dull, dark green foliage.

**Growing conditions.** Alder grows in full sun or partial shade. It does best in wet or moist soil but tolerates dry soil.

**Landscape uses.** In mass plantings, alders make good screens.

## Amelanchier (am-e-LANK-ee-er)
Serviceberry, Juneberry, shadbush

Small deciduous flowering tree that grows 20 to 30 feet tall in a rounded shape. Has snowy white 1-inch flowers that are among the first to bloom in spring and are followed in summer by sweet red or purple berry-like fruit. Leaves turn yellow, orange or red in fall. Smooth gray bark is streaked with reddish longitudinal fissures. Zones 3-8.

**Selected species and varieties.** *A. arborea,* downy serviceberry: pointed, finely toothed leaves are grayish green in spring and turn a deeper green in summer. *A.* x *grandiflora,* apple serviceberry: a naturally occurring hybrid between downy serviceberry and Allegheny serviceberry with larger flowers than either. Zones 4-8. *A. laevis,* Allegheny serviceberry: leaves are purplish when they emerge and later turn dark green. Fruit is purple to black. Zones 4-8.

**Growing conditions.** Serviceberry tolerates either full sun or partial shade. It prefers moist soil but can adapt to a wide variety of soils. It seldom needs fertilizing and needs pruning only to control suckers.

**Landscape uses.** Serviceberry lends itself to naturalizing at the edge of a wood. As a specimen tree it has four-season interest with its colorful flowers, fruit, leaves and bark.

## Arborvitae see *Thuja*

## Arbutus (ar-BEW-tus)
Manzanita

Ornamental broad-leaved evergreen that grows 20 to 100 feet tall. Flowers are white or pale pink, fruits are berry-like and rounded, and foliage is glossy. Zones 7 and 8.

**Selected species and varieties.** *A. menziesii,* madrone: grows up to 75 feet tall. Has small, white, 9-inch-long flower clusters in May and red-orange berries in fall. Older bark peels back to reveal lighter cinnamon bark underneath. Zone 7. *A. unedo,* strawberry tree: slow growing to 20 to 30 feet. Has serrated leaves, drooping flower clusters of white or pink from October to December, and edible but tasteless fruit that looks something like strawberries. 'Compacta' has deep green foliage tinted with amber and abundant white flowers in fall. 'Elfin King' is a dwarf and has a reddish cast to its new growth. Zone 8.

**Growing conditions.** Arbutus needs sun and protection from wind. It prefers dry, sandy and acid soil.

**Landscape uses.** *Arbutus is a good specimen or accent plant, but its shedding can cause litter.*

**Ash** see *Fraxinus*
**Aspen** see *Populus*
**Basswood** see *Tilia*
**Beech** see *Fagus*

## Betula (BET-yew-la)
Birch

Deciduous tree that grows 40 to 100 feet tall. Has slender branches, flowers borne in catkins and double-toothed leaves that turn yellow in autumn. Bark varies in color from white, silver, yellow-orange, reddish brown to near black. Zones 4-9.

**Selected species and varieties.** *B. albo-sinensis septentrionalis,* Chinese paper birch: grows 40 to 60 feet tall and has curling, red-orange bark. Zones 5-7. *B. alleghaniensis,* yellow birch: grows 60 to 70 feet tall. Leaves are dull, dark green on upper surfaces and pale yellow-green on the undersides in summer, and change to yellow in fall. Bark on young trees is yellow or bronze and shreds; on older trees it is reddish brown and peels off. Zones 3-5. *B. maximowicziana,* monarch birch: grows 45 to 50 feet tall. Leaves are heart-shaped and bark is orange-gray. Zones 5 and 6. *B. nigra,* river birch: reaches 100 feet in height. Bark is shaggy and tannish with pink and orange undertones. 'Heritage' has salmon white, peeling bark. Zones 4-9. *B. papyrifera,* paper birch, canoe birch, white birch: reaches 50 feet or more and has striking white bark. Zones 2-5. *B. pendula,* European white birch: grows 40 to 50 feet tall. The crown is pyramidal in youth and becomes oval as the tree matures. Leaves are up to ¾ inch long. Zones 2-6. 'Dalecarlica,' silver birch: has particularly pendulous branches and leaves that are deeply lobed to within ⅛ inch of the midrib. 'Purpurea,' purple-leaf European birch: grows to 50 feet. Young leaves emerge deep purple in spring and fade in summer. Zones 3-5. *B. platyphylla japonica* 'Whitespire,' whitespire birch: grows 40 to 50 feet in a pyramidal shape. Zones 4-7.

**Growing conditions.** Most birches grow in full sun. They prefer moist, cool soil but can tolerate poor soil in the North. Canoe birch should be planted on a slope that faces north. Monarch birch tolerates urban pollution. River birch should not be planted in alkaline soil.

**Landscape uses.** Birch is a good shade tree. It can be naturalized in a woodsy border.

**Birch** see *Betula*
**Box elder** see *Acer*
**Buckeye** see *Aesculus*
**Buttonwood** see *Platanus*
**California incense cedar** see *Calocedrus*

## Calocedrus (kal-o-SEE-drus)

Stately, columnar, needle-leaved evergreen that grows 30 to 100 feet tall. It has tiny, scalelike green foliage and flattened stems. Zones 6-9.

**Selected species and varieties.** *C. decurrens,* California incense cedar: aromatic tree that grows 50 feet or more. Lower branches grow close to the ground. Needles retain their shiny green color year round. Bark is reddish brown and peels. Cones appear in autumn and persist until spring.

**Growing conditions.** California incense cedar must have full sun, humid atmosphere and moist soil. It cannot tolerate smog or wind.

**Landscape uses.** The columnar form of calocedrus makes the tree suitable for formal plantings in large areas. It may be used singly as a specimen, or in massed planting as a screen.

## Carpinus (kar-PY-nus)
Hornbeam

Deciduous tree that grows slowly to heights ranging from 20 to 60 feet. It has toothed, prominently ribbed leaves, spring-flowering catkins and nutlets in leafy bracts that ripen in autumn. Trunks are short and covered with fluted gray bark. Zones 3-9.

BETULA PAPYRIFERA

CALOCEDRUS DECURRENS

CARPINUS BETULUS

CATALPA BIGNONIOIDES

CEDRUS ATLANTICA 'GLAUCA'

CELTIS LAEVIGATA

CERCIS CANADENSIS 'ALBA'

**Selected species and varieties.** *C. betulus,* European hornbeam: grows to 40 to 60 feet in height and 30 to 40 feet in width. The tree is rounded in shape and has dark green leaves that sometimes turn yellow. Zones 5-7. 'Columnaris' is slow growing, narrow, steeple-shaped and has dense foliage. 'Fastigiata' becomes oval to vase-shaped with age and has dense, ascending branches. *C. caroliniana,* American hornbeam, blue beech, ironwood, musclewood, water beech: a small tree that grows to 35 feet with an irregular branching habit and dark bluish gray bark. In autumn, leaves become red-orange and bracts containing nutlets turn brown. Zones 4-7.

**Growing conditions.** Hornbeam grows in sun or shade and in any moist, well-drained soil.

**Landscape uses.** Hornbeam makes a good street tree, shade tree or specimen. Several together in a massed planting make a good windbreak. European hornbeam takes heavy shearing as a hedge. American hornbeam is useful as a patio tree, and because of its size, can grow as an understory plant—a small tree under the cover of taller trees.

## Catalpa (ka-TAL-pa)

Deciduous shade tree that grows 30 to 90 feet tall. It has opposite, sometimes whorled, leaves that are heart-shaped and are downy on the underside, conspicuous summer flowers and long, beanlike seed capsules known as Indian cigars that hang on throughout the winter. Zones 4-9.

**Selected species and varieties.** *C. bignonioides,* southern catalpa: ornamental tree of broad, spreading growth, with stout, brittle branches, 30 to 40 feet tall. Leaves are 4 to 8 inches long, unfurl in late June and turn black before falling. Flowers are white, spotted with yellow and purple, and emerge in midsummer. Foot-long seedpods decorate the tree in fall. Bark has loose, thin scales. Zones 5-9. *C. speciosa,* northern catalpa: grows 50 to 80 feet. It has an upright, irregular silhouette and conspicuous twigs, especially in winter. Stems are knobby. Masses of early-summer blooms are followed by hard, long seedpods. Gray-brown bark has coarse, elongated ridges and furrows.

**Growing conditions.** Catalpa likes sun and thrives in hot, dry summers. It is a tough tree and adapts to a wide variety of soil types.

**Landscape uses.** Catalpa makes a good shade tree on a lawn that is large enough to accommodate it.

## Cedar see *Cedrus*

## Cedrus (SEE-drus)
Cedar

Needle-leaved evergreen that grows 40 to 60 feet or more. It has graceful, wide-spreading branches and fragrant wood. Zones 5-9.

**Selected species and varieties.** *C. atlantica* 'Glauca,' atlas cedar: grows to 60 feet. It is conical in youth, becoming flat-topped as it matures. Its needles are smooth and silvery blue. Zones 6-9. *C. deodara,* deodar cedar: reaches 50 feet in height. Has graceful horizontal branches that droop at their tips. Its needles are soft and green. Zones 7-9. *C. libani,* cedar-of-Lebanon: has a shorter crown than atlas cedar. It is the hardiest of the true cedars. Zones 5-8.

**Growing conditions.** Deodar cedar and cedar-of-Lebanon need sun and like dry soil; atlas cedar is adaptable and can take sun or partial shade. Any good garden soil will support them all.

**Landscape uses.** Singly, cedars make outstanding specimen trees. Their branches are spread so wide that three together can make an effective screen. Atlas cedar is used as an accent plant when silvery blue is wanted.

## Celtis (SEL-tis)
Hackberry

Deciduous tree that grows 70 to 80 feet in height with a rounded crown. Leaves are ovate and generally toothed. Fruit is fleshy, berry-like and orange-red to blue-black. Zones 4-9.

**Selected species and varieties.** *C. laevigata,* sugar hackberry: has a crown that spreads up to 80 feet in width. Zones 6-9. *C. occidentalis,* common hackberry: has a tall, oval crown, bark that is gray and vertically ridged, and leaves that turn yellow in fall. Zones 4-8.

**Growing conditions.** Hackberries need full sun. They prefer moist soil, but they will grow in dry, heavy, sandy and rocky soil and tolerate wind and pollution.

**Landscape uses.** Hackberries make good shade trees; they grow rapidly and thus can provide shade in a few years' time. They also make good street trees because of their resistance to pollution and because their deep roots do not crack sidewalks.

## Cercis (SER-sis)
Redbud

Graceful, 20- to 40-foot deciduous tree having branches that arch horizontally. After a shower of small flowers in spring, lush, heart-shaped foliage appears. Zones 5-9.

**Selected species and varieties.** *C. canadensis,* eastern redbud: grows 20 to 30 feet with a 30-foot spread. Has magenta pink flowers on zigzagging branchlets. Fruits are in small, papery seedpods. Falling leaves exude a pleasant, spicy scent. Zones 5-8. 'Alba' has white flowers. 'Forest Pansy' has leaves that emerge reddish purple and turn dark green in summer. Flowers are darker than the standard magenta pink. 'Wither's Pink Charm' has soft pink blossoms, paler than those of the species, and is hardier than 'Alba.' *C. reniformis,* Texas redbud: has rounded, leathery foliage and is less cold-hardy than eastern redbud. Zones 8 and 9.

**Growing conditions.** Redbud grows in full sun and partial shade and in any well-drained soil.

**Landscape uses.** Redbud makes a good lawn accent or specimen tree. It is also effective naturalized in a woodland border.

## Chamaecyparis (kam-a-SIP-a-ris)
False cypress

Pyramidal evergreen conifer that grows 40 to 100 feet. It has flat sprays of scalelike leaves marked with white on the undersides. Reddish brown bark shreds. Zones 5-9.

**Selected species and varieties.** *C. nootkatensis,* Nootka false cypress: dense evergreen that grows to 100 feet or more. It lacks the white underside markings typical of most species; leaf sprays are rough to the touch and emit a pungent odor when bruised. Cones are pointed. 'Pendula' is fast growing, with graceful, drooping branchlets and soft, blue-green foliage, without the white markings typical of most false cypresses. It can live for hundreds of years under the right climatic conditions. *C. pisifera,* sawara false cypress: grows up to 70 feet. Leaves can be feathery or mosslike; colors range from bright green to dark green to bluish green. Zones 5-8. 'Golden Thread' grows to 10 feet tall and has weeping, golden threadlike foliage.

**Growing conditions.** False cypress needs sun, but cool temperatures, high humidity and protection from wind. Soil should be moist and well drained.

**Landscape uses.** Tall species of false cypress provide vertical accents as specimen trees. Medium-tall species make good screens. Short species are useful as foundation plants.

**Cherry** see *Prunus*
**Chinese flame tree** see *Koelreuteria*
**Chinese scholar tree** see *Sophora*

## Cladrastis (klad-RAS-tis)
Yellowwood

Deciduous flowering ornamental tree that grows 20 to 50 feet or more. It has a graceful, rounded crown and fragrant blossoms that cascade from slender, zigzagging branches in late May and early June. Zones 4-8.

**Selected species and varieties.** *C. lutea:* leaves are composed of seven to nine leaflets; they emerge yellowish green, turn bright green in summer and yellow in autumn. Flowers are white; thin, flat, drooping seedpods follow in autumn. The bark is smooth and gray. Zones 4-8.

**Growing conditions.** Yellowwood needs full sun and is drought-resistant once established. It thrives in most well-drained soils. It needs a few years after planting before it flowers; then the flowering is best every other year or two. Prune yellowwood only in summer to avoid sap bleeding.

**Landscape uses.** Yellowwood's combination of springtime flowers and crooked branches make it an attractive specimen tree all year round, and in summer it provides good shade. But it lures bumblebees; beware of planting it where children play.

**Cork tree** see *Phellodendron*

## Cornus (KOR-nus)
Dogwood

Deciduous ornamental trees that grow from 15 to 40 feet and are generally wider than they are tall. They have year-round interest: flowers in spring, fruit in summer, wine-colored foliage in autumn and a picturesque silhouette in winter. Zones 3-8.

CHAMAECYPARIS NOOTKATENSIS

CLADRASTIS LUTEA

CORNUS FLORIDA 'WELCHII'

CORYLUS COLURNA

COTINUS OBOVATUS

CRATAEGUS PHAENOPYRUM

**Selected species and varieties.** *C. alternifolia,* pagoda dogwood: open-branched tree that grows 15 to 25 feet. Leaves tend to be concentrated near the ends of the branches. Abundant, flat-topped flower clusters appear in May with bluish black fruit following in July or August. Zones 3-7. *C. florida,* flowering dogwood: reaches 15 to 40 feet. Minuscule yellow true flowers are surrounded by white, sometimes pink, showy bracts that open in spring. Clustered red fruits follow, and leaves turn scarlet in fall. Bark is blocky and coarse. Zones 6-9. 'Welchii' has variegated creamy white, pink and green leaves. *C. kousa,* Kousa dogwood, oriental flowering dogwood: has pointed, white flower-like bracts that appear in June, later than flowering dogwood, and turn pink with age. Red, raspberry-like, dangling fruit follows from August to October. *C. kousa chinensis:* includes Chinese cultivars, such as 'Milky Way,' which flowers heavily, and 'Summer Stars,' which has bracts that hang on for about six weeks. Zones 5-8.

**Growing conditions.** Dogwoods need partial shade and cool, acid, well-drained soil.

**Landscape uses.** Dogwoods make spectacular specimens and accents—in spring for their showy flowers, in summer for their fruits, and some species in winter for their colorful bark. They are small enough to use on patios; and because they do best in partial shade, they thrive as understory plants—small trees under the cover of taller ones.

**Corylus** (KOR-il-us)
Filbert, hazelnut

Group of deciduous nut trees that are related to the birch family and grow from 25 to 120 feet tall. Zones 4-8.

**Selected species and varieties.** *C. colurna,* Turkish filbert: a pyramidal tree that reaches 50 feet or more, grown for its tasty nuts, which are enveloped in leafy, ragged-edged husks. Leaves are handsome and green in summer. Bark is corky and rough. Zones 4-7.

**Growing conditions.** Filbert grows in full sun or partial shade. It prefers well-drained, loamy soil, tolerates drought and thrives in hot summers and cold winters.

**Landscape uses.** Filbert makes a good shade tree and accent tree. It can be naturalized in a woodsy border or used as a street tree.

**Cotinus** (ko-TY-nus)
Smoke tree

Deciduous tree that grows 15 to 30 feet tall and may be vase-shaped or rounded in form. It often seems to be enveloped in a smoky haze, which is created by masses of curious, hairy flower stalks that persist long after the inconspicuous greenish yellow flowers have faded in June. Zones 5-8.

**Selected species and varieties.** *C. obovatus,* American smoke tree: a small tree, generally 20 to 30 feet tall, that has a rounded crown and orange stems. Bark is gray and scaly. Leaves are a striking blue-green in spring and summer and turn intense shades of yellow and red in autumn. Male plants produce showy flower stalks.

**Growing conditions.** Smoke tree prefers sun but can tolerate partial shade. It thrives in average, well-drained soil. Soil that is too rich or the application of too much fertilizer will encourage foliage production at the expense of flowering.

**Landscape uses.** Smoke tree may be used as an accent plant in a shrub border.

**Crabapple** see *Malus*
**Crape myrtle** see *Lagerstroemia*

**Crataegus** (kra-TEE-gus)
Hawthorn

Broad-crowned deciduous tree that grows up to 30 feet tall. It has prickly thorns, flowers late in spring or in early summer, and produces small, fleshy fruit that persists into winter. Leaves are lobed and toothed. Bark may be smooth or scaly. Zones 4-9.

**Selected species and varieties.** *C. phaenopyrum,* Washington hawthorn: a vase-shaped tree having a spread nearly as wide as it is tall. It bears white blossoms in June and thorns that are up to 3 inches long. Fruits are glossy reddish orange. Leaves are glossy green, turning orange to red in autumn. Zones 4-8. *C. viridis* 'Winter King,' winter king hawthorn: similar to Washington hawthorn but with larger fruit and fewer and shorter thorns. Fruit is persistent, but not glossy. Zones 5-7.

**Growing conditions.** Hawthorns prefer full sun and well-drained loamy soil but adapt well to adverse conditions.

**Landscape uses.** Hawthorns make good screens, hedges or accent plants.

## Cryptomeria (krip-toh-MEER-ee-a)

Tall, pyramidal, needle-leaved evergreen native that grows rapidly to 50 or 60 feet in height and 20 to 30 feet in width. Foliage is fine-textured, soft and lush. Bark is reddish brown and shreds in vertical strips. Cones are globe-shaped and approximately 1 inch in diameter. Zones 6-9.

**Selected species and varieties.** *C. japonica,* Japanese cedar: foliage is soft and long when young, maturing to shorter, stiffer needles. Needles are awl-shaped and arranged spirally on ropelike drooping branchlets. They are green in spring and summer, turning reddish brown in fall, bronze in winter, or brown if exposed to drying wind. 'Lobbii' is hardier and more compact than the species and holds its green leaf color throughout the winter. 'Yoshino' is columnar and grows to 30 feet tall. It has bronze-green needles in winter.

**Growing conditions.** Japanese cedar grows in sun or partial shade, and in moist, acid soil. It requires protection from wind in open areas and does not tolerate salt spray in coastal areas.

**Landscape uses.** Japanese cedar makes a good specimen tree and in massed plantings makes a good screen.

## Cucumber tree see *Magnolia*

## x Cupressocyparis
(kew-pres-o-SIP-a-ris)
Leyland cypress

Narrow pyramidal evergreen that reaches 50 to 70 feet in height. It is a hybrid that combines the rapid growth and resistance to sea winds of one parent, Monterey cypress, with the ability to resist winter damage of its other parent, Nootka false cypress. Zones 7-11.

**Selected species and varieties.** x *C. leylandii* 'Naylor's Blue': has blue-green leaves. 'Castlewellan' is a conifer with yellow foliage.

**Growing conditions.** Leyland cypress needs full sun and adapts to many soils. It can tolerate salt spray but needs protection from drying and from winter winds.

**Landscape uses.** Leyland cypress can be used singly as a specimen and in massed plantings as a screen.

## Cupressus (kew-PRES-us)
Cypress

Large, long-lived, fragrant evergreen that grows 40 to 90 feet tall. Leaves are scalelike; cones are small and round. Zones 6-9.

**Selected species and varieties.** *C. arizonica,* Arizona cypress: has rough, red bark, small blue-green leaves that are fetid when bruised. It is one of the hardier cypresses. Zones 6-8. *C. glabra,* smooth-barked Arizona cypress: similar to Arizona cypress, but the bark shreds annually, exposing smooth, inner red bark. Zones 7-9. *C. macrocarpa,* Monterey cypress: long-lived native Californian that grows along the seaside and reaches 40 feet or more. Trees are pyramidal in youth; as they age, massive limbs widen into an umbrella-like form and eventually sprawl, bend and gnarl in picturesque fashion. Zones 8 and 9. *C. sempervirens,* Italian cypress: a regal Mediterranean that is a slender, formal column 40 to 70 feet or more. It has dark green foliage and thin bark. Zones 8 and 9.

**Growing conditions.** Arizona cypress, smooth-barked Arizona cypress and Italian cypress need full sun and well-drained soil. All are suitable for mild, dry climates. Monterey cypress needs moist, well-drained soil and does best in the coastal areas of the West; it is difficult to grow on the East Coast.

**Landscape uses.** Singly, cypresses can be used as specimen trees, and in massed plantings they make good screens and windbreaks.

## Cypress see *Cupressus; Taxodium*

CRYPTOMERIA JAPONICA 'YOSHINO'

× CUPRESSOCYPARIS LEYLANDII

CUPRESSUS MACROCARPA

433

DAVIDIA INVOLUCRATA

DELONIX REGIA

EUCALYPTUS FICIFOLIA

FAGUS GRANDIFOLIA

**Davidia** (da-VID-ee-a)

Deciduous 20- to 60-foot-tall ornamental tree with a wide-spreading crown and white, pointed bracts that blossom inconsistently. Zones 6-8.

**Selected species and varieties.** *D. involucrata,* dove tree, handkerchief tree: grows 50 to 60 feet. When the tree is mature—about 10 years of age—it has unusual, hooded, floral bracts surrounding a center head of tiny brushlike yellow flowers. The bracts are white and flutter in the breeze, hence the common name, handkerchief tree. They are of unequal length, the lower being about 6 to 8 inches, the upper one 3 to 4 inches. Leaves are heart-shaped at the base and persist until frost turns them brown and kills them.

**Growing conditions.** Dove tree prefers partial shade and a moist, well-drained soil.

**Landscape uses.** Dove tree makes a spectacular specimen with its fluttering white bracts.

**Dawn redwood** see *Metasequoia*

**Delonix** (del-O-niks)
Poinciana

Deciduous subtropical tree that grows 20 to 40 feet tall with an even wider spread. It produces flamboyant red or yellow flowers in summer and fall. Zones 10 and 11.

**Selected species and varieties.** *D. regia,* royal poinciana, flame tree, flamboyant, peacock flower: a fast-growing, flat-topped tree with scarlet and yellow flowers that are 3 inches across and have petals shaped like claws. Royal poinciana is one of the showiest flowering trees in the world. The flowers are followed by 2-foot-long pods, which persist long after the leaves drop from the tree. Leaves are fine-textured, ferny and 1 to 2 feet long.

**Growing conditions.** Royal poinciana demands full sun and frost-free temperatures but is undemanding as to soil. It does not tolerate shade from trees nearby, and it does best along the seashore.

**Landscape uses.** Royal poinciana makes a striking specimen and can be used as a street tree.

**Dogwood** see *Cornus*
**Douglas fir** see *Pseudotsuga*
**Dove tree** see *Davidia*
**Elm** see *Ulmus*

**Eucalyptus** (yew-ka-LIP-tus)
Gum tree

Large genus of fast-growing, shallow-rooted evergreens that range in height from 20 to 100 feet. The leaves are blue-green and fragrant and go through distinct changes in shape; they are round or ovate when young and become elongated as they mature. Flowers bloom in small, feathery heads. Zones 9-11.

**Selected species and varieties.** *E. cinerea,* silver dollar tree: grows 20 to 50 feet tall. Leaves are coin-shaped and silvery when young. Bark is reddish brown and peels in ribbons on smaller branches. White flowers bloom in spring. Zones 10 and 11. *E. ficifolia,* flaming gum, red-flowering gum: tree that grows to 30 feet with a dense, broad crown and rough, persistent bark. Noted for its showy red flowers, which bloom in midsummer.

**Growing conditions.** Eucalyptus needs full sun and dry soil. With young trees, cut back on water and fertilizer in fall, or roots may freeze and die.

**Landscape uses.** Gum trees make good small accent plants. Flaming gum tree serves as a street tree.

**Fagus** (FAY-gus)
Beech

Lofty deciduous shade tree that grows 50 to 100 feet tall and wide. It has a dense, rounded head, oval leaves that are toothed and pointed, and smooth, light gray bark. Spring flowers are followed by small triangular nuts enclosed in prickly cases. Zones 3-9.

**Selected species and varieties.** *F. grandifolia,* American beech: grows to a height of 50 to 70 feet or more with a short trunk, conspicuous surface roots and a wide-spreading crown. Leaves are 2 to 6 inches long and sharply toothed, and turn golden copper in autumn. Zones 3-8.
*F. sylvatica,* European beech: grows 70 to 80 feet tall. Has smaller leaves, 2 to 4 inches long, which turn a russet color in autumn. Branches are low and leafy, and often sweep the ground. Zones 5-8. The cultivar 'Dawyckii' is column-shaped; it grows 80 feet or more in height and only 10 feet in width. 'Pendula,' weeping beech: has

branches that sweep down at angles of 60° to 45°. 'Riversii,' Rivers purple beech: has leaves that are deep purple in color.

**Growing conditions.** Beech does best in full sun and in moist, well-drained acid soil.

**Landscape uses.** Its great height and massive spread make beech a spectacular specimen. It provides shade so dense that few plants will grow beneath it.

## False cypress
see *Chamaecyparis*

## Ficus (FY-kus)
Fig

Broad-leaved evergreen and deciduous trees that grow 10 to 75 feet tall. They have short, stout branches that grow downward to the ground and take root, thus developing into additional stems. The foliage discharges a milky sap when bruised. Zones 8-11.

**Selected species and varieties.** *F. benjamina,* weeping fig: evergreen that reaches 30 to 50 feet in height in approximately 30 years. Leaves are leathery, pointed and 5 inches long. Bark is smooth and gray. Zones 10-11.

**Growing conditions.** Weeping fig prefers filtered sun and loamy garden soil.

**Landscape uses.** Weeping fig can be used as a specimen tree or lawn accent in mild climates. In temperate or cold climates it can be container-grown for the patio and brought indoors for the winter.

**Fig** see *Ficus*
**Filbert** see *Corylus*
**Fir** see *Abies*
**Flamboyant** see *Delonix*
**Flame tree** see *Delonix*

## Franklinia (frank-LIN-ee-a)

Deciduous tree that grows 10 to 30 feet tall with multiple trunks and upright-spreading branches. Bark is fissured. Foliage is shiny and dark green, and it changes to shades of orange and red in fall. Woody, capsuled fruit produces flat, wingless seed. Zones 6-8.

**Selected species and varieties.** *F. alatamaha,* Franklin tree: bears fragrant, white, five-petaled blossoms that are frilly and cupped, and nearly 3 inches across. They bloom from late summer to fall.

**Growing conditions.** Franklin tree flowers best in full sun. It needs moist, well-drained, acid soil.

**Landscape uses.** Because it blossoms late when few ornamentals are flowering and has attractive bark, Franklin tree is well suited for use as an accent or a specimen tree.

## Fraxinus (FRAK-sin-us)
Ash

Tall, usually deciduous, rapid-growing, round-crowned shade tree that grows to 80 feet. Clusters of small flowers appear in early spring and are followed by clusters of 1-inch, paddle-shaped winged seeds that cling until fall. Leaves are generally compound with up to 11 leaflets. Zones 2-9.

**Selected species and varieties.** *F. americana,* white ash: grows 50 to 80 feet. Leaves turn orange to purple in fall. Bark is diamond-patterned and gray on mature trees. Zones 3-9. 'Autumn Purple' grows to 60 feet. It is a cultivar bred to be nonfruiting and litterless. It has glossy deep green leaves that turn reddish purple to mahogany in fall. 'Rosehill' is a seedless ash that grows to 50 feet. Its leaves turn bronze-red in fall. Zones 5-9. *F. excelsior,* European ash: grows 70 to 80 feet tall with a 60- to 90-foot spread. Lower branches curve upward. Leaves are dark green in summer and drop when they are still green or after fading to yellow. Zones 4-6. 'Aurea' grows slowly and is noted for its yellow twigs, yellow older bark and yellow fall color. 'Hessei' has a straight trunk and flat-topped crown. Leaves, unlike most ash leaves, are simple, ovate, pointed and deeply toothed. Zone 4. *F. ornus,* flowering ash: grows to 40 to 50 feet and has small, but profuse, fragrant white flowers in long, dense clusters, which distinguish it from other ash trees. Zones 5-7. *F. pennsylvanica,* green ash: is distinguished from white ash by its narrow crown and tan diamond-patterned bark. Zones 3-9. *F. uhdei,* shamel ash, evergreen ash: grows fast to 30 to 50 feet. It is densely branched and has glossy leaves. Zone 9.

**Growing conditions.** Most ashes adapt to any soil if they get full sun.

**Landscape uses.** Ashes make good specimen trees and provide dense shade.

FAGUS SYLVATICA 'PENDULA'

FICUS BENJAMINA

FRANKLINIA ALATAMAHA

FRAXINUS EXCELSIOR 'AUREA'

GINKGO BILOBA

GLEDITSIA TRIACANTHOS INERMIS 'SHADEMASTER'

GYMNOCLADUS DIOICUS

**Frijolito** see *Sophora*

### Ginkgo (GINK-o)
Ginkgo, maidenhair tree

Deciduous tree that grows to 80 feet in an irregular form. It has exotic fan-shaped leaves that are often deeply notched at the center of the outer margin. Zones 4-8.

**Selected species and varieties.** *G. biloba,* maidenhair tree: grows between 30 to 80 feet tall. Leaves appear on short branchlets and turn bright yellow in autumn. Bark is gray-brown and ridged. Male and female flowers are produced on separate trees; female trees are undesirable because the seeds have an unpleasant odor. 'Autumn Gold' is a nonfruiting cultivar that is medium-size. Zones 5-8. 'Fastigiata,' sentry ginkgo, is narrowly pyramidal in form.

**Growing conditions.** Ginkgo will grow in full sun or partial shade and needs well-drained, moist, slightly acid soil.

**Landscape uses.** Ginkgo makes a good specimen tree and provides dappled shade.

### Gleditsia (gle-DIT-see-a)
Honey locust

Fast-growing deciduous tree that grows 30 to 70 feet tall with a broad, open crown and a short trunk. Branches are spreading, sometimes drooping; branchlets are slender and armed with long, pointed, forked spines. Pods are long and narrow and contain a sweet, gummy sap. Zones 3-9.

**Selected species and varieties.** *G. triacanthos inermis,* thornless honey locust: has smooth stems and delicate, lacy, compound foliage that provides filtered shade. Bark is brown and furrowed. Fragrant greenish flower clusters appear in May. Foliage turns yellow in fall. The fruit is a strap-like pod that forms in late summer and twists spirally before it falls. 'Moraine' is a sterile cultivar that produces no pods. 'Shademaster' is a podless cultivar with a strong central trunk and ascending branches. 'Skyline' has an upright shape and leaves that turn gold in fall. 'Sunburst' grows 30 to 35 feet tall and has an upright spreading shape. Foliage emerges yellow in early summer and then turns green, but it retains a tinge of yellow at the twig tips. Zones 4-9.

**Growing conditions.** Honey locust needs full sun and prefers alkaline soil. It tolerates flooding and is resistant to wind damage, highway salting and urban pollution.

**Landscape uses.** Honey locust makes a good specimen tree. It provides dappled shade; grass and ground cover will grow beneath it.

**Golden chain tree** see *Laburnum*
**Golden rain tree** see *Koelreuteria*
**Gum** see *Eucalyptus*

### Gymnocladus (jim-no-KLA-dus)

Deciduous tree that grows 50 to 75 feet, occasionally to 100 feet, with a spread of 40 feet. It has stout branches and feather-like foliage. Fragrant flower clusters appear in spring. Zones 4-8.

**Selected species and varieties.** *G. dioicus,* Kentucky coffee tree: generally grows to 60 to 75 feet, but can reach 90 feet. Leaves are 36 inches long, 24 inches wide and doubly compound, with many leaflets per leaf. Bark is scaly, ridged and dark gray to black. Flowers are greenish white. On female trees, thick, reddish brown pods appear in fall and persist into winter.

**Growing conditions.** Kentucky coffee tree grows in full sun or partial shade. It prefers fertile soil but tolerates dry soil. It also tolerates urban pollution.

**Landscape uses.** Kentucky coffee tree makes a good specimen tree on land large enough to accommodate it. Male trees, because they produce no pods, may be used as street trees.

**Hackberry** see *Celtis*

### Halesia (ha-LEE-zha)
Silverbell, snowdrop tree

Deciduous ornamental, 20 to 80 feet tall, with drooping flower clusters that form on the previous year's wood, and four-winged fruit that emerges green and ripens to brown. Zones 4-8.

**Selected species and varieties.** *H. carolina,* Carolina silverbell: grows 20 to 30 feet in a wide-spreading, rounded or irregular form. Long, white, bell-shaped flower clusters appear in late April and early May. Leaves are bright green, simple and finely toothed, and turn yellow in fall. Bark is gray to brown and vertically furrowed. *H. diptera,* two-winged silverbell: 20- to 30-foot tree with low-branching, multiple-stem form. Fruit has two wings instead of four. Zones 6-8. *H. monticola,* mountain silverbell: grows up to 80 feet and is similar to Carolina silverbell but has larger flowers and fruits. Zone 5.

**Growing conditions.** Silverbell grows in full sun or partial shade and moist, well-drained, acid soil. It needs protection from wind.

**Landscape uses.** Silverbell makes a good accent on a patio. It may also be used in a woodland border and as an understory plant—that is, interspersed among taller trees.

**Handkerchief tree** see *Davidia*
**Hawthorn** see *Crataegus*
**Hazelnut** see *Corylus*
**Hemlock** see *Tsuga*
**Holly** see *Ilex*
**Honey locust** see *Gleditsia*
**Hornbeam** see *Carpinus*
**Horse chestnut** see *Aesculus*

**Ilex** (I-leks)
Holly

Genus of deciduous and evergreen trees, 10 to 50 feet tall, that grow all over the world. They are pyramidal in shape and have leathery leaves. Male and female trees bear red or yellow berry-like fruit in fall; trees of both sexes must be planted together to produce. Zones 3-9.

**Selected species and varieties.** *I. aquifolium,* English holly: grows to 20 feet and has leaves that are wavy-edged and spiny when the tree is young; as the tree ages the leaves on its upper branches lose their spines and become smooth. Zones 6-8. *I. x attenuata* 'Fosteri' #2 and #3, Foster holly: both are compact, have glossy green, small leaves with spiny edges, and abundant fruit. Zones 6-9. *I. latifolia,* lusterleaf holly: grows up to 40 feet tall. Leaves are glossy and spineless. Fruit is red and occurs in dense clusters. Zones 7 and 8. *I. x* 'Nellie R. Stevens': fast-growing cultivar bred to produce fruit without the assistance of a male. It grows 25 feet tall and its leaves have only two to three teeth on each side. Zones 6-9. *I. opaca,* American holly: slow-growing tree that reaches 40 to 50 feet. Form is pyramidal in youth and becomes irregular with age. Branches are short and

crooked. Leaves are ovate and spiny-toothed. Fruit is red in fall. Zones 7-9. *I. pedunculosa,* longstalk holly: grows to 20 feet or more, with shiny, pointed, dark green, spineless leaves and red berries. Zones 5-7. *I. vomitoria* 'Pendula,' weeping yaupon: grows to 20 feet in a weeping form and bears abundant scarlet fruit that persists into spring. Zones 8 and 9.

**Growing conditions.** Hollies grow in full sun or partial shade. They need moist, well-drained soil and protection from winter sun and winds.

**Landscape uses.** Hollies can be used as specimens or accents, and in hedges and borders.

**Japanese cedar** see *Cryptomeria*
**Japanese pagoda tree** see *Sophora*
**Japanese umbrella tree**
see *Sciadopitys*
**Juneberry** see *Amelanchier*
**Kentucky coffee tree**
see *Gymnocladus*

**Koelreuteria** (kol-ru-TEER-ee-a)
Golden rain tree

Rapidly growing deciduous tree that reaches 45 to 60 feet. It has feather-like leaves and 12- to 15-inch clusters of small, yellow flowers that fall to the ground. Zones 5-9.

**Selected species and varieties.** *K. bipinnata:* upright, roundheaded tree that grows to 60 feet. Seedpods emerge pink and dry to tan. Zones 7-9. *K. elegans,* Chinese flame tree: grows to 60 feet with a flat-topped, spreading crown. Seedpods are bright orange-red and resemble Chinese lanterns. Zone 9. *K. paniculata,* panicled golden rain tree: roundheaded tree that grows to 30 feet tall and spreads as wide. Seedpods are balloon-like in shape and greenish in color. They turn yellow, then brown, in fall. Zones 5-7.

**Growing conditions.** Golden rain tree grows in full sun to partial shade and in well-drained soil. It adapts to a wide range of conditions and tolerates urban pollution.

**Landscape uses.** Golden rain trees make good specimens, and are also suited for use as shade and street trees.

HALESIA MONTICOLA

ILEX × 'NELLIE R. STEVENS'

KOELREUTERIA PANICULATA

437

LABURNUM × WATERERI 'VOSSII'

LAGERSTROEMIA INDICA

LIQUIDAMBAR STYRACIFLUA

## Laburnum (la-BER-num)

Small deciduous tree that grows 10 to 30 feet tall and is noted for its 20-inch pendulous clusters of 1-inch yellow flowers. Bark is smooth, dark olive green to brown with black patches. Leaves are composed of three small oval leaflets. Pods are brown and leathery and persist until winter. Zones 4-7.

**Selected species and varieties.** *L. x watereri,* golden chain tree: grows 10 to 15 feet with yellow blossoms that dangle like chains from its branches. The tree may be rounded or vase-shaped and is open in form. Foliage is bright blue-green in summer. Zones 5-7. 'Vossii' was bred to have a dense form. Zones 6 and 7.

**Growing conditions.** Golden chain tree grows in full sun or partial shade and in well-drained soil. It needs shelter from drying winds and from hot afternoon sun, especially in winter.

**Landscape uses.** Golden chain tree is best used as an accent tree in a massed planting. Plant it with discretion; its seeds and leaves are toxic.

## Lagerstroemia
(la-ger-STREEM-ee-a)
Crape myrtle

Small to large deciduous trees ranging in height from 10 to 60 feet. They have multiple stems and broad, spreading crowns, and they bloom profusely in white and a broad range of pinks, reds and purples. Flower petals are crinkled like crepe paper. Zones 7-11.

**Selected species and varieties.** *L. indica:* grows to about 20 feet and has smooth, exfoliating bark that exposes gray-brown underbark. Flowers bloom recurrently from July through September. Leaves are elliptic to oblong, yellowish green to bronze when emerging, then dark green in summer, and yellow, orange or red in autumn. Zones 7-9. 'Muskogee' grows up to 21 feet high and 15 feet wide. Bark is medium brown, leaves are green in summer and turn red in autumn, flowers are pale lavender. 'Natchez' grows up to 21 feet high and 21 feet wide. Bark is dark cinnamon brown and mottled, flowers are white, and leaves turn orange and red in fall. 'Tuscarora' grows up to 15 feet high and 15 feet wide with leaves that emerge red-tinged, turn dark green in summer and then orange-red in fall. Flowers are dark coral pink.

**Growing conditions.** Crape myrtle needs full sun; it does not flower well in shade. It will grow in any well-drained soil but prefers slightly acid loam. Once established, it tolerates drought. Encourage repeated blooming by removing spent flowers.

**Landscape uses.** Crape myrtle makes a fine specimen or border plant. It provides dappled shade; grass and other ground covers can grow underneath its canopy.

**Leyland cypress** see *Cupressocyparis*
**Lilac** see *Syringa*
**Limetree** see *Tilia*
**Linden** see *Tilia*

## Liquidambar (lik-wid-AM-bar)
Sweet gum

Deciduous tree that grows 25 to 80 feet tall with star-shaped leaves having five to seven lobes and toothed edges. Fruits are woody, spiny capsules containing a gummy sap that hang from long stems. Bark is ridged and resembles cork. Zones 5-9.

**Selected species and varieties.** *L. styraciflua:* grows 70 to 80 feet tall. The tree is symmetrical and pyramidal in shape when young but develops a rounded crown with age. Leaves hang on the tree until late in autumn and turn rich shades of yellow, purple and red. Zones 6-9.

**Growing conditions.** Sweet gum grows in full sun to partial shade and needs moist, well-drained acid soil. It tolerates saltwater spray if sheltered from strong winds.

**Landscape uses.** Sweet gum makes a good specimen and shade tree.

## Liriodendron (leer-ee-o-DEN-dron)
Tulip tree

Massive deciduous tree that grows 25 to 30 feet tall in eight years and may eventually reach more than 100 feet with a spread half as wide. It branches high on the trunk and is noted for its upright, tulip-like flowers in spring. Zones 5-9.

**Selected species and varieties.** *L. tulipifera,* tulip tree, yellow poplar, tulip magnolia, tulip poplar, whitewood: grows 60 to 90 feet tall. The crown is conical in youth and becomes oval with age. Leaves are 5 inches across, lobed and blunt along the top edge. They turn yellow in autumn. When the tree reaches 10 years of age, it produces tulip-like blossoms that are yellowish green with a deep orange blotch at the base of the petals. Fruits are slim, winged and conelike, and persist into winter. Bark is ridged and furrowed. The cultivar 'Aureo-marginatum' has leaves that are variegated with yellow or greenish yellow margins.

**Growing conditions.** Tulip tree grows in full sun. It requires moist, well-drained, slightly acid soil that is deep enough to accommodate the tree's massive root system.

**Landscape uses.** Tulip tree is a good specimen tree in an area large enough to contain its enormous root system and broad branching habit.

**Live oak** see *Quercus*
**Locust** see *Robinia*
**Madrone** see *Arbutus*

### Magnolia (mag-NO-lee-a)

Genus of deciduous or evergreen trees, 20 to 80 feet tall, having large showy blossoms and large, leathery, dark green leaves. Zones 4-9.

**Selected species and varieties.** *M. acuminata,* cucumber tree: deciduous tree that grows to 50 to 80 feet tall or more, and nearly as wide. It has massive, wide-spreading branches, is pyramidal in youth and becomes broadly rounded in age. Leaves are 4 to 10 inches in length. Flowers are 3 inches long, loosely cup-shaped and yellowish green. Fruit is knobby, cucumber-like and slits open in early fall to reveal red, pea-size seeds that dangle on slender threads. Zones 4-8. *M. grandiflora,* southern magnolia, bull bay: broad-leaved evergreen that grows 60 to 80 feet in height and 30 to 50 feet in spread with a low-branching habit. The tree may take 15 to 20 years to blossom; flowers, when they emerge, are white, nearly 1 foot in diameter and fragrant. Leaves are 4 to 10 inches long, ovate and pointed. Zones 6-9. *M.* x *loebneri,* Loebner magnolia: deciduous, compact tree, 20 to 30 feet tall, that casts dense shade. Flowers have 12 white to blush pink petals, and the bark is silver-gray. 'Merrill' has 15 white petals per blossom. *M.* x *soulangiana,* saucer magnolia: deciduous tree that grows 20 to 30 feet tall. Flowers are 5 to 10 inches in diameter, white inside and tinged with pink or purple outside. Bark is smooth and gray.

**Growing conditions.** Magnolias grow in full sun or partial shade. They need deep, moist, slightly acid, well-drained soil and protection from wind. To maintain shape, prune trees after they have flowered.

**Landscape uses.** Magnolias make spectacular specimen trees where there is room to accommodate their deep roots and broad-spreading branches.

**Maidenhair tree** see *Ginkgo*

### Malus (MAY-lus)
Flowering crabapple

Deciduous flowering tree that grows 15 to 25 feet tall. It produces abundant clusters of white to pink or purplish single flowers, and yellow, orange, or red to purple fruits that are 2 inches or smaller. Some species bloom only in alternate years. Zones 2-6.

**Selected species and varieties.** *M. floribunda,* Japanese flowering crabapple: grows to 15 to 25 feet tall and just as wide. It has a rounded, arching outline, is densely branched and has fine-textured foliage. Fragrant pink to red buds bloom in midspring, fade to white as the blossoms open, and are followed by red or yellow fruit. 'Snowdrift' grows 15 to 20 feet tall in a dense, rounded form. Red buds open to white flowers. Fruit appears annually and is orange-red. *M. sieboldii zumi* 'Calocarpa,' redbud crab: grows to 25 feet tall. It has a rounded crown, spreading, drooping branchlets and a dense canopy of dark green foliage. Bright red flower buds open to fragrant white blossoms and are followed by glossy red fruits that are persistent.

**Growing conditions.** Crabapples need full sun for best flowering and fruit. They should have well-drained, moist, acid soil, and they need pruning in spring. Of all flowering fruit trees, crabapples are the easiest to grow and the most cold-hardy.

**Landscape uses.** Singly, crabapples make good specimen trees, and in massed plantings they make good borders.

**Manzanita** see *Arbutus*
**Maple** see *Acer*
**Mescal bean** see *Sophora*

LIRIODENDRON TULIPIFERA

MAGNOLIA × SOULANGIANA

MALUS FLORIBUNDA

METASEQUOIA GLYPTOSTROBOIDES

NYSSA SYLVATICA

OXYDENDRUM ARBOREUM

PARROTIA PERSICA

## Metasequoia (met-a-se-KWOY-a)
Dawn redwood

Deciduous tree that grows 70 to 80 feet or more. It has long, feathery needles. Zones 5-8.

**Selected species and varieties.** *M. glyptostroboides*: grows in a pyramidal outline. Foliage is green in summer and turns orange-brown to red-brown in autumn. Cones are globular in shape, about ¾ inch across, and hang from long stalks. Bark is reddish brown and peels in long, narrow strips.

**Growing conditions.** Dawn redwood needs full sun and grows best in deep, moist, slightly acid soil.

**Landscape uses.** Dawn redwood makes a good specimen tree on properties that are large enough to accommodate its great size.

**Mimosa** see *Albizia*
**Musclewood** see *Carpinus*

## Nyssa (NIS-a)
Tupelo

Deciduous tree that grows 25 to 75 feet tall with a spread half as wide. It has a tall domed crown and its leaves turn scarlet in fall. Zones 5-9.

**Selected species and varieties.** *N. sylvatica*, pepperidge, sour gum, black gum, black tupelo: grows 30 to 50 feet tall or more. It has horizontal branching that gives it a spreading form in youth but becomes somewhat weeping and irregular with age. Leaves are bright, shiny, dark green in summer and change to bright yellow, orange, scarlet or purple in fall. Female flowers are small, greenish white and borne in clusters. Fruit is fleshy, blue-black and bittertasting. Older trees have dark, furrowed bark.

**Growing conditions.** Tupelo grows in full sun to partial shade. It must have deep, acid soil and a moist location that is sheltered from winds.

**Landscape uses.** Tupelo makes a good specimen, shade tree or street tree. It can also be naturalized in a woodsy border.

**Oak** see *Quercus*

## Oxydendrum (ok-see-DEN-drum)
Sourwood, sorrel tree

Deciduous slow-growing tree that generally reaches 25 to 30 feet; over a long period of time it may attain 50 to 75 feet. It has multiple stems and a pyramidal crown. It is ornamental in four seasons. It has glossy, leathery leaves in spring; white, bell-shaped flowers in summer; scarlet foliage and yellow to brown persistent fruit in fall; and dark, deeply furrowed bark that shows up in winter. Zones 6-9.

**Selected species and varieties.** *O. arboreum*, sourwood: has gracefully drooping branches bearing leaves that are ovate and 3 to 8 inches long, and flower clusters that are 10 inches long or more.

**Growing conditions.** Sourwood grows in full sun or partial shade and in moist, well-drained, very acid soil. It needs shelter from winds and does not tolerate urban pollution.

**Landscape uses.** With its large flower clusters, sourwood makes a spectacular specimen tree. It can also be used as a shade tree, and it grows well as an understory plant among taller trees.

## Parrotia (pa-ROT-ee-a)

Deciduous tree that grows 20 to 40 feet tall. It is low-branched and conical in shape, and may be single or multiple-stemmed. Zones 5-9.

**Selected species and varieties.** *P. persica*, Persian parrotia, Persian witch hazel: leaves are ovate, glossy green in summer and bright yellow, orange and scarlet in fall. Bark is mottled gray, green, white and brown, and it peels year round when the tree is mature.

**Growing conditions.** Persian witch hazel needs morning sun, shade from other plants in the heat of the afternoon in summer, and protection from winter sun and windburn. It prefers well-drained, loamy, slightly acid soil.

**Landscape uses.** Persian witch hazel may be used as a specimen, shade, accent or street tree.

**Peacock flower** see *Delonix*
**Pear** see *Pyrus*
**Pepperidge** see *Nyssa*
**Persian witch hazel** see *Parrotia*

## Phellodendron (fel-o-DEN-dron)
Cork tree

Deciduous tree that grows rapidly 30 to 60 feet tall. It has a short trunk and tortuous branches that give it a sculptured look. Zones 3-7.

**Selected species and varieties.** *P. amurense,* Amur cork tree: broad, spreading tree that grows 30 to 45 feet tall. Corky, furrowed bark is gray-brown. Leaves are glossy dark green in summer and yellow briefly in fall. Fleshy black fruit is ½ inch in diameter. Both leaves and fruit give off a scent like turpentine when crushed.

**Growing conditions.** Cork tree needs full sun and will adapt to almost any kind of soil. It is generally trouble-free and maintenance-free.

**Landscape uses.** Cork tree makes a good specimen or shade tree on areas large enough to accommodate it.

## Picea (py-SEE-a)
Spruce

Evergreen conifer that grows 20 to 100 feet tall in a pyramidal shape with sharp-pointed, spirally arranged needles that are ½ to 1 inch long. Zones 1-7.

**Selected species and varieties.** *P. abies,* Norway spruce: grows rapidly, reaching 40 to 80 feet in height and 20 to 30 feet in spread. Needles are lustrous green, branchlets are pendulous and cones are up to 6 inches long. Zones 3-7. 'Cupressina,' Cupress Norway spruce: grows to 50 feet in a narrow, upright form with ascending branches. *P. glauca,* white spruce: similar in appearance to Norway spruce, but its cones are only 1 to 2 inches long and its needles are blue-green with a whitish tinge. Zones 1-5. *P. omorika,* Serbian spruce: grows 60 to 70 feet or more in a graceful, narrow pyramid. Needles are glossy dark green on the upper surface and lined in white on the underside. Cones have fine-toothed scales; they are purplish blue-black when young and mature to reddish brown. Zones 4-8. *P. orientalis,* Oriental spruce: grows 50 to 60 feet. Needles are glossy dark green and only ¼ to ½ inch long. Cones are 2 to 4 inches long; they are reddish purple when young and turn brown when mature. Zones 5-7. *P. pungens,* Colorado spruce: grows 30 to 75 feet tall with stiff, horizontal branches. Leaves vary in color; they may be green, bluish or silvery white. Cones are 2 to 4 inches long. Zones 2-7.

**Growing conditions.** Most spruces need full sun and sandy, acid, moist but well-drained soil. White spruce is the hardiest species; it survives winters of -70° F and summers of 110° F. Serbian spruce needs to be protected from cold wind. Oriental spruce is an exception in that it prefers clay soil; it cannot tolerate extremely wet or extremely dry soil, strong winds or polluted air. Colorado spruce prefers cool soil.

**Landscape uses.** Singly, spruces make majestic specimen trees, and in massed plantings they make good screens and windbreaks.

## Pine see *Pinus*

## Pinus (PY-nus)
Pine

Diverse genus of evergreen conifers that grow from 10 to more than 100 feet tall. They are generally conical when young and develop rounded tops with age; but of all needle-leaved evergreens, pines have the widest range of characteristics, habit and distribution. Zones 2-9.

**Selected species and varieties.** *P. bungeana,* lacebark pine: grows 30 to 50 feet tall, generally in a bushy shape, with multiple trunks and mottled, exfoliating bark. Needles are 4 inches long on gray-green twigs. Cones are 2 to 3 inches long. Zones 5-8. *P. cembra,* Swiss stone pine: grows very slowly to 25 to 40 feet or more with 2- to 3-inch lustrous, dark green needles having white lines. Cones are 2 to 3 inches long. Young stems are covered with orange hair that turns gray-black as they age. Zones 3-7. *P. contorta,* shore pine: grows 25 to 30 feet tall and has yellowish green needles that are 1½ inches long and twisted. Cones are 1½ inches long. Zones 5-8. 'Latifolia,' lodgepole pine: grows tall, 70 to 80 feet, and has longer, broad, light green needles.

*P. densiflora,* Japanese red pine: grows slowly to 50 to 60 feet. It has an irregular crown and a twisted, often leaning, trunk with orange-red bark. Needles are 3 to 5 inches long. Cones are 2 inches long. Zones 3-7. 'Oculus-draconis,' dragon's eye pine, has variegated foliage, each needle having two yellow bands. Zones 6 and 7. *P. flexilis,* limber pine: grows slowly to 30 to 50 feet tall. Zones 4-7. Needles are 2½ to 3½ inches long, cones are up to 6 inches long, and branchlets are so supple that they can be twisted for decorations.

PHELLODENDRON AMURENSE

PICEA ABIES

PINUS BUNGEANA

441

PINUS STROBUS

PISTACIA CHINENSIS

PLATANUS OCCIDENTALIS

*P. koraiensis,* Korean pine, is hardy enough to grow in Zone 3. *P. nigra,* Austrian pine: grows 50 to 60 feet in height and 20 to 40 feet in spread and has multiple stems. Needles are 4 to 6 inches long with fine-toothed margins. Cones are 2 to 3 inches long and 1 to 1¼ inches wide, and tawny yellow when young. Zones 4-7. *P. palustris,* longleaf pine, Florida pine, Georgia pine: grows 80 to 90 feet tall. Needles are 8 to 18 inches long. Cones are 10 inches long and remain on the tree up to 20 years. Zones 7-10. *P. parviflora,* Japanese white pine: grows to 50 feet or more. Needles are 1½ inches long and are bluish green; cones are 3 inches long. Zones 4-7. 'Glauca' has fine-textured, twisted, whitened, blue-green foliage.

*P. strobus,* eastern white pine: grows 50 to 80 feet tall or more. Leaves are 3 to 5 inches long and blue-green. Cones are cylindrical, 6 to 8 inches long and 1⅗ inches wide. Zones 3-8. *P. thunbergiana,* Japanese black pine: grows 20 to 40 feet tall and has multiple stems. Needles are dark green, 2½ to 7 inches long, twisted and densely crowded. Zones 6-9.

**Growing conditions.** Pines need full sun and moist, well-drained soil. Lodgepole pine tolerates wet soil; limber pine tolerates dry soil. Japanese white pine and Japanese black pine tolerate salt. Eastern white pine needs a humid atmosphere. Austrian pine withstands urban pollution.

**Landscape uses.** All pines can be used singly as specimen trees and in massed plantings for screens. Austrian pine makes a good street tree because of its tolerance for pollution. Japanese black pine is an excellent tree for the seashore.

**Pistache** see *Pistacia*

**Pistacia** (pi-STAY-sha)
Pistache

Deciduous and evergreen trees that grow 30 to 60 feet tall, have rounded crowns, feather-like leaves, inconspicuous flowers and fruit that is berry-like. Zones 7-11.

**Selected species and varieties.** *P. chinensis,* Chinese pistache: grows rapidly to 30 to 45 feet in height. Leaves are dark green in summer and turn bright red to orange in autumn. Fruit is ¼ inch in diameter; it is red at first and matures to robin's egg blue. Zones 7-9.

**Growing conditions.** Chinese pistache needs full sun and does best in moist, well-drained soil, but it can tolerate drought.

**Landscape uses.** Chinese pistache is suited for use as a specimen, accent, shade or street tree.

**Plane tree** see *Platanus*

**Platanus** (PLAT-a-nus)
Sycamore, buttonwood, plane tree

Deciduous shade tree that grows 75 to 100 feet in height and spreads as wide. It has a massive trunk and crooked branches. Zones 4-11.

**Selected species and varieties.** *P.* x *acerifolia,* London plane tree: similar to sycamore but does not spread quite so wide and bears its fruit in twos and threes. Zones 6-9. *P. occidentalis,* American plane tree, American buttonwood, eastern sycamore, button-ball: leaves are large, 4 to 9 inches wide, with three to five triangular lobes, and coarsely toothed. Fruits occur in tight, spiny, round balls that hang singly from long stalks and often persist through winter. Bark is grayish brown and flakes off to reveal a cream-colored inner bark, giving a mottled appearance. Zones 4-9.

**Growing conditions.** Plane trees prefer full sun and moist, well-drained soil, but are extremely adaptable and will grow almost anywhere.

**Landscape uses.** Plane trees make good specimen and shade trees on areas large enough to accommodate them.

**Plum** see *Prunus*
**Poinciana** see *Delonix*
**Poplar** see *Populus*

**Populus** (POP-u-lus)
Poplar

Fast-growing deciduous tree that grows 40 to 100 feet tall. It has dangling catkins that emerge before the leaves. Fruit is usually a small capsule. Bark is gray and furrowed. Zones 1-9.

**Selected species and varieties.** *P. alba,* white poplar: grows 40 to 80 feet tall with an irregular, broadly rounded crown. Leaves are dark green, 2 to 5 inches long, three- to five-lobed, and white to silvery and felty on the undersides. They usually fall early in autumn before showing color. Zones

3-8. 'Pyramidalis,' bolleana poplar: a tall, narrow, columnar tree that grows 45 to 50 feet tall. It becomes pyramidal in old age. Leaves are shiny white on the undersides. *P. tremuloides,* quaking aspen: grows 40 to 50 feet tall with a 20- to 30-foot spread. It is narrow and pyramidal when young and develops a rounded crown with age. Leaves are 1½ to 3 inches long and wide, dark green in summer and yellow in the fall. Bark is smooth and pale green on young trees, and fissured and dark on mature ones. Zones 1-5.

**Growing conditions.** Poplar and aspen grow best in full sun and deep, moist, well-drained soil, but they adapt to a wide variety of growing conditions. They tolerate drought, urban pollution and salt spray. Pruning should be done in summer to avoid bleeding.

**Landscape uses.** Poplars make good screens, windbreaks and property dividers. Because they have invasive roots, they serve well for erosion control.

### Prunus (PROO-nus)

Large genus of deciduous flowering fruit trees that includes plum, cherry, peach, apricot and almond. They grow from 15 to 60 feet tall. Zones 2-9.

**Selected species and varieties.** *P.* x *blireiana,* blireiana plum: grows 25 feet tall. It has a rounded densely branched crown, small purple leaves that fade to green and double 1¼-inch pink flowers. Zones 6-9. *P. cerasifera,* cherry plum: rounded tree that grows to 25 feet with spreading branches. Flowers are white; fruit is 1 inch in diameter and may be yellow or reddish. 'Atropurpurea' has narrow-leaved, reddish purple foliage that tends to fade, and light pink flowers. Zones 5-9. 'Thundercloud' is similar to 'Atropurpurea,' but it holds its purple leaf color throughout the season. Zones 6-9. *P. maackii,* Amur chokecherry: 35- to 45-foot roundheaded, densely branched ornamental with coppery brown bark that peels in thin, curly strips. Small, white flowers bloom profusely in May and are followed by small, black fruit. Foliage emerges early in spring and falls early in autumn. Zones 2-6. *P. sargentii,* Sargent cherry: upright, rounded tree that grows to 40 to 50 feet tall with saw-toothed, 3- to 5-inch leaves; they are dark green in summer and turn red to bronze in fall. Bark is glossy and red to chestnut brown. Pink flowers are followed by purplish black fruit that opens in June and July. Zones 4-7. *P. serotina,* black cherry: grows 50 to 60 feet with an oval

crown and pendulous branches. Leaves are dark green in summer and turn yellow to red in fall. Flowers are white. Fruits emerge red; in August they ripen to black and are edible. Zone 4-9. *P. serrula,* paperbark cherry: grows up to 30 feet tall and has shiny mahogany-colored bark that peels. Zones 6-8. *P. serrulata,* Japanese flowering cherry: vase-shaped tree that grows to 50 to 75 feet tall. Flowers are ½ to 2½ inches in diameter and range from single to double, white to pinks. Leaves turn bronze in fall. Zones 6-8. 'Kwanzan' grows to 40 feet and produces an abundance of 2½-inch deep-pink flowers. 'Shirotae,' also designated 'Mt. Fuji,' has a spreading habit with 2-inch fragrant, white flowers. *P. subhirtella,* Higan cherry: grows 20 to 30 feet tall and half as wide in a weeping form. Flowers are ½ inch in diameter. Fruits are ⅓ inch in diameter and shiny black. Zones 4-8. 'Autumnalis' has a forked trunk, and slender stems with pink flowers that sometimes bloom in fall as well as in the spring. 'Pendula,' weeping Higan cherry: has graceful, drooping branches. Zones 6-8. *P.* x *yedoensis,* Yoshino cherry: grows up to 40 feet in a spreading, rounded form and produces fragrant 1-inch flowers that open pink and change to white. Zones 5-8.

**Growing conditions.** Most cherries will flourish in full sun or partial shade, except purple leaf cultivars, which need full sun to bring out their color. Cherry plums adapt to any good, well-drained soil. Chokecherries require sandy, well-drained soil.

**Landscape uses.** Cherry plums make good specimen, accent and patio trees. The tall species provide shade.

### Pseudotsuga (soo-doh-TSOO-ga)

Evergreen conifer that grows up to 100 feet tall in a conical to pyramidal shape. It is related to the pine family. Zones 3-7.

**Selected species and varieties.** *P. menziesii,* Douglas fir: grows 40 to 60 feet tall. It is pyramidal in shape and has wide-spreading branches; the upper branches ascend and the lower branches descend. Needles are 1 to 1½ inches long and blunt; they are dark green on the upper sides and banded in white on the undersides. Cones are oval-shaped and 2 to 4 inches long; they are purplish when young and turn yellow-brown when they mature. Zones 4-6. *P. menziesii glauca,* Rocky Mountain Douglas fir: slower growing, more compact variety with bluish green needles. Zones 4-7.

POPULUS TREMULOIDES

PRUNUS SUBHIRTELLA 'PENDULA'

PSEUDOTSUGA MENZIESII

443

PYRUS CALLERYANA 'BRADFORD'

QUERCUS VIRGINIANA

ROBINIA PSEUDOACACIA

**Growing conditions.** Douglas fir needs full sun, a humid climate and moist, well-drained acid to neutral soil. It should have protection from winds because its roots are shallow and it can easily be uprooted.

**Landscape uses.** Singly, Douglas fir makes a spectacular specimen tree; several together make a good windbreak.

### Pyrus (PY-rus)
Pear

Deciduous and semievergreen trees, 20 to 60 feet tall, grown for their ornamental white flowers. Zones 4-11.

**Selected species and varieties.** *P. calleryana,* Callery pear: has an open, oval to conical crown that is 15 to 30 feet in spread. Leaves have scalloped edges; they are glossy dark green in summer and turn crimson red in autumn. 'Aristocrat' has attractive leathery leaves that turn yellow to red in autumn. 'Bradford' grows 30 to 50 feet. It has a compact pyramidal crown and a cloudlike cover of flowers in early spring. Its leaves turn scarlet or purple in autumn. Zones 5-8. 'Capital' has an upright habit and leaves that turn coppery brown in autumn. 'Red Spire' is pyramidal in form and has leaves that turn yellow in fall. *P. kawakamii,* evergreen pear: grows in an irregular shape to 30 feet tall. Flowers appear on the tree from late winter through spring. Zones 8-11. *P. salicifolia,* willowleaf pear: grows 15 to 25 feet tall and has silvery, willow-like leaves. Zones 4-7. 'Pendula' has drooping branches.

**Growing conditions.** Pear trees prefer full sun but are easy to grow and adapt to nearly all soils. They can withstand air pollution, drought and wind.

**Landscape uses.** Pear trees make good street and shade trees. Small species can be container-grown for use on patios.

### Quercus (KWER-kus)
Oak

Deciduous and broad-leaved evergreen trees, 35 to 100 feet tall, that are distributed across the North American continent in both cold and tropical regions. Zones 2-11.

**Selected species and varieties.** *Q. acutissima,* sawtooth oak: grows 35 to 45 feet tall. It is pyramidal when young and ages to a broadly rounded, spreading form. Leaves are 3½ to 7½ inches long, 1 to 2¼ inches wide; they emerge yellow in spring, turn dark green in summer and change to yellow or golden brown in fall. Acorns are 1 inch long. Zones 6-9. *Q. agrifolia,* California live oak: evergreen that grows to 50 feet. It has a rounded crown, broadly spreading branches, shiny, spine-tipped green leaves and dark gray to black bark. Acorns are pointed. Zones 9-11. *Q. alba,* white oak: grows to 75 feet in an erect form. It has wide-spreading branches and round-lobed leaves that turn wine to crimson in fall. Acorns are ½ to ¾ inches long with rounded ends. Bark is light gray and shallowly fissured. Zones 3-9. *Q. bicolor,* swamp white oak: deciduous tree that grows 50 to 60 feet tall and has a broad, round crown. Six-inch-long leaves are coarsely toothed, shiny green on the upper surfaces and felty white on the undersides. Bark is grayish brown, vertically fissured and flaky. Zones 4-8. *Q. coccinea,* scarlet oak: grows to 75 feet. Deeply lobed leaves turn scarlet in fall. Zones 5-9. *Q. imbricaria,* shingle oak: grows 50 to 60 feet in height and width. Leaves are 2½ to 6 inches long, shiny and unlobed, and turn russet in fall. Zones 5-8. *Q. macrocarpa,* bur oak, mossy cup oak: deciduous tree that grows 70 to 90 feet tall. Leaves are 4 to 10 inches long, rounded on the tips and yellow in fall. Acorns are up to 1½ inches long. Bark is dark gray, thick and deeply furrowed. Zones 2-8. *Q. myrsinifolia,* Chinese evergreen oak: compact, roundheaded tree that grows to 30 feet. Leaves are narrowly ovate, 2 to 4½ inches long, ¾ to 1¼ inches wide and pointed at the tip. Zones 7-9. *Q. palustris,* pin oak: grows 60 to 75 feet tall in a pyramidal shape. The lower branches are pendulous, and the upper ones are upright; mature trees lose their lower branches. Leaves are 3 to 6 inches long and have five to seven lobes with deep U-shaped indentations between the lobes. They turn soft tan in fall. Acorns are ½ inch in diameter and globe-shaped. Zones 4-8. *Q. phellos,* willow oak: grows up to 60 feet tall and wide. It is pyramidal in youth and develops a rounded form as it ages. Leaves are 2 to 5½ inches long and only ½ inch wide; they turn yellowish brown to russet red in fall. Acorns are ½ inch long and rounded. Zones 6-9. *Q. robur,* English oak, truffle oak: deciduous tree that grows 75 to 100 feet tall and wide. It has a rounded crown and a short trunk. Leaves are 2 to 5 inches long and ¾ to 2½ inches wide and have rounded lobes. Zones 5-9. 'Fastigiata' grows 50 to 60 feet tall in a narrow, columnar form. *Q. rubra,* red oak: grows 60 to 80 feet in height, 40 to 50 feet in spread, and has a round crown. Leaves are 4½ to 8½ inches long, 4 to 6 inches wide and sometimes have as many as 11 lobes. They emerge pink to red in spring, turn dark green in summer and change to bright red in fall. Zones 3-9. *Q. virginiana,* southern live oak: evergreen tree that grows 40 to 80 feet in height, 60 to 100 feet in spread. Branches are contorted. Leaves are elliptic, 1¼ to 3 inches long and ⅜ to 1 inch wide. They are dark green and leathery on the upper surfaces, gray-green and woolly on the undersides. Zones 8-11.

**Growing conditions.** Nearly all oaks need full sun and moist, acid, well-drained, rich, deep soil. Swamp white oak and pin oak prefer wet soil. Only shingle oak tolerates dry soil.

**Landscape uses.** Oaks make majestic specimens and cast deep shade. They may be used as street trees. Fastigiate English oak can provide a vertical accent.

### Redbud see *Cercis*

### Robinia (ro-BIN-ee-a)
Locust

Deciduous shade tree that grows 25 to 80 feet tall. It has feather-like leaves, stems that may be armed with spines, clusters of pea-shaped flowers, and dry pods. Zones 3-8.

**Selected species and varieties.** *R. pseudoacacia,* black locust: grows 50 to 75 feet tall with upright branches and a slender, oblong crown. Fragrant, white flowers appear from May to early June. Leaves consist of six to 19 rounded leaflets. Pods are 2 to 4 inches long, smooth and brownish black. Zones 4-8.

**Growing conditions.** Black locust needs full sun but thrives in poor soil.

**Landscape uses.** Black locust is a good tree for difficult terrain; it has tenacious roots that will take hold on a steep slope and prevent soil erosion.

### Salix (SAY-liks)
Willow

Deciduous tree that grows 15 to 75 feet tall with arched branches that sweep the ground. Leaves are long and narrow. Small flowers are borne in dense catkins. Zones 2-9.

**Selected species and varieties.** *S. alba* 'Trista,' golden weeping willow: grows 50 to 75 feet tall and wide. It has pendulous golden twigs and narrow leaves. Zones 2-8. *S. babylonica,* Babylon weeping willow: grows 30 to 40 feet on a short, stout trunk and has a rounded crown. Leaves emerge pale green in spring and turn dull green in summer and yellow in autumn. Light green catkins appear among the leaves in spring. Zones 7-9. *S. matsudana* 'Tortuosa,' corkscrew willow: grows 30 to 50 feet tall. Unlike most willows, it has branches that ascend rather than droop. Twigs occur in twisted spirals. Zones 5-9.

**Growing conditions.** Willows grow in full sun or partial shade and need wet soil.

**Landscape uses.** Willows make good specimens and accent trees. They are especially suited to planting alongside rivers and lakes.

### Sassafras (SAS-a-fras)

Deciduous tree that grows up to 60 feet tall. It is noted for its aromatic bark, roots, branches, leaves, flowers and fruit. Zones 5-9.

**Selected species and varieties.** *S. albidum*: grows 30 to 60 feet in an irregular shape with horizontal, contorted branching. Leaves are sometimes mitten-shaped, sometimes three-lobed, sometimes unlobed; all shapes may appear on the same tree at the same time. They turn shades of orange and red in fall. Bark is reddish brown and furrowed. Flowers are yellowish green and bloom in spring. Fruits are fleshy and blue, and appear on red stalks.

**Growing conditions.** Sassafras grows in full sun or partial shade. It prefers moist, loamy, acid, well-drained soil and needs protection from wind.

**Landscape uses.** Sassafras makes a good specimen or shade tree. Several together can be used in a woodsy border.

### Sciadopitys (sy-a-DOP-i-tis)

Pyramidal evergreen conifer that grows 20 to 40 feet tall with branches that rise upward at the tips. Zones 5-8.

**Selected species and varieties.** *S. verticillata,* Japanese umbrella tree: has branches that are horizontal when young and become pendulous with

SALIX BABYLONICA

SASSAFRAS ALBIDUM

SCIADOPITYS VERTICILLATA

SOPHORA JAPONICA 'REGENT'

STEWARTIA PSEUDOCAMELLIA

STYRAX OBASSIA

SYRINGA RETICULATA

age. Leaves may be spirally arranged, scalelike and crowded near the branchlet tips, or linear, flat and whorled in clusters of 20 to 30. Cones are 2 to 4 inches long and take up to two years to mature.

**Growing conditions.** Japanese umbrella tree grows in full sun or shade and in moist, well-drained acid soil. It needs protection from wind.

**Landscape uses.** Japanese umbrella tree makes a good specimen or accent. Several together can be planted in a border.

**Serviceberry** see *Amelanchier*
**Shadbush** see *Amelanchier*
**Silk tree** see *Albizia*
**Silver bell** see *Halesia*
**Silver dollar tree** see *Eucalyptus*
**Smoke tree** see *Cotinus*
**Snowbell** see *Styrax*
**Snowdrop tree** see *Halesia*

## Sophora (so-FOR-a)

Deciduous and evergreen trees that grow 20 to 75 feet tall with rounded crowns, showy flowers and beanlike seeds. Zones 5-8.

**Selected species and varieties.** *S. japonica* 'Regent,' Japanese pagoda tree, Chinese scholar tree: deciduous tree that grows 20 to 60 feet tall. Flowers are slightly fragrant, ½ inch long and creamy white, and appear in 15-inch-long sprays in summer. Seedpods are 2 to 4 inches long and greenish yellow; they ripen in October and persist through winter. Leaves are 6 to 10 inches long and have seven to 17 leaflets. *S. secundiflora*, mescal bean, frijolito: broad-leaved evergreen tree that grows up to 35 feet tall. Flowers are 1 inch long and violet-blue. Pods are up to 8 inches long and emit red seeds.

**Growing conditions.** Sophoras need full sun and fertile, well-drained soil. Once established they can tolerate heat, drought and air pollution.

**Landscape uses.** Sophoras can be used for specimens, accents, shade trees and street trees.

**Sorrel tree** see *Oxydendrum*
**Sour gum** see *Nyssa*
**Sourwood** see *Oxydendrum*
**Southern magnolia** see *Magnolia*
**Spruce** see *Picea*

## Stewartia (stew-ART-ee-a)

Deciduous tree that grows slowly to 20 to 40 feet tall in a pyramidal shape. It has waxy white flowers that bloom in summer and flaking bark that gives it a mottled appearance. Zones 5-8.

**Selected species and varieties.** *S. koreana,* Korean stewartia: grows 20 to 25 feet tall with branches that zigzag. Flowers are 3 inches in diameter. Leaves are oval, 2 to 4 inches long, ¾ to 3 inches wide and toothed; they turn orange-red in fall. Bark is mottled grayish brown and orange-brown. Zones 6 and 7. *S. pseudocamellia*, Japanese stewartia: grows to 30 to 40 feet tall. Leaves are 1½ to 3½ inches long and turn yellow, red or purplish red in fall.

**Growing conditions.** Stewartias need partial shade from hot afternoon sun, and grow best in moist, loamy, acid soil. Once planted, they should not be moved.

**Landscape uses.** Stewartias make good specimen and accent trees.

## Styrax (STY-raks)
Snowbell

Deciduous tree that grows 20 to 30 feet tall and bears showy white flowers. Zones 5-9.

**Selected species and varieties.** *S. japonicus,* Japanese snowbell: has horizontal branches and pendulous clusters of fragrant, bell-shaped flowers. Leaves are 1 to 3½ inches long and often turn yellow in autumn. The bark is dark gray and smooth. Zones 6-8. *S. obassia,* fragrant snowbell: similar to Japanese snowbell, but has 8-inch-long leaves and upright branches. Zones 5-8.

**Growing conditions.** Snowbell grows in sun or shade and does best in moist, well-drained, acid soil.

**Landscape uses.** Snowbell may be used as a specimen, on a patio or in a border.

**Sweet gum** see *Liquidambar*
**Sycamore** see *Platanus*

## Syringa (si-RING-ga)
Lilac

Deciduous tree that grows 20 to 30 feet tall and wide. It has showy flowers that may be white, lilac pink, red or purple. Zones 2-7.

446

**Selected species and varieties.**
*S. reticulata,* Japanese tree lilac: has spreading branches and reddish brown bark. Flowers are white and fragrant, and appear in 6- to 12-inch-long clusters in summer after other lilacs have faded. Leaves are heart-shaped, 2 to 7 inches long. Zones 3-7. 'Ivory Silk' grows 20 feet in a compact oval shape.

**Growing conditions.** Japanese tree lilac needs full sun and loose, slightly acid, well-drained soil. It should be pruned after it has flowered.

**Landscape uses.** Japanese tree lilac makes a good specimen, accent or street tree.

## Taxodium (tak-SO-dee-um)
Cypress

Genus of deciduous and evergreen conifers that grow 50 to 80 feet tall in a conical or columnar shape. Trunks are fluted and flared at the base. Zones 5-9.

**Selected species and varieties.**
*T. ascendens,* pond cypress, pond bald cypress: deciduous tree that grows 70 to 80 feet tall. Leaves are awl-shaped and up to ½ inch long. Cones are purple when young; they are up to 1¼ inches in diameter and may be round or ovoid. Zones 6-9. *T. distichum,* bald cypress: deciduous tree that grows 50 to 70 feet tall with graceful, horizontal branches. Foliage is fine-textured and needle-like, up to ¾ inch long; it is delicate green in spring and summer, and bronze in fall. Bark is reddish brown and fissured.

**Growing conditions.** Cypresses grow in full sun or partial shade. They are among the few trees that can live with permanently wet roots; they often grow in swampy areas. They will adapt to soil, but the soil must be acid, sandy and moist.

**Landscape uses.** Pond cypress makes a good vertical accent. Bald cypress may be used as a specimen tree or in a woodsy border.

## Taxus (TAK-sus)
Yew

Evergreen trees that grow 10 to 60 feet tall. They have needle-like leaves and fleshy, bright-colored fruit. Zones 4-7.

**Selected species and varieties.**
*T. baccata,* English yew: grows 35 to 60 feet tall and 15 to 25 feet wide. Leaves are ¼ inch long, dark green and shiny on the upper sides, and paler on the undersides. Fruit is red. Zones 6 and 7. *T. cuspidata,* Japanese yew: grows 10 to 40 feet tall and wide. Branches may be spreading or upright. Inch-long leaves are dull green on the upper surfaces and have yellow bands on the undersides. Zones 4-7.

**Growing conditions.** Yews grow in full sun or partial shade and need moist, fertile, well-drained soil.

**Landscape uses.** Yews make good specimens, foundation plants, hedges and screens.

## Thuja (THOO-ya)
Arborvitae

Genus of evergreen conifers that grow up to 70 feet tall. They have flattened branchlets with soft needle-like leaves and small cones. Zones 2-9.

**Selected species and varieties.**
*T. occidentalis,* American arborvitae, eastern white cedar: narrow 40- to 60-foot columnar tree having dense, compact, aromatic foliage that is yellow-green to bright green. Bark is reddish brown, fibrous and shreddy. Zones 3-7. 'Lutea' grows 30 to 35 feet tall in a pyramidal shape and has bright yellow foliage. Zones 4-7. 'Nigra' has a pyramidal shape and dark green foliage. Zone 4. 'Spiralis' grows 30 to 45 feet tall in a narrow pyramidal form. Leaves are dark green and branches are spiral-shaped. 'Techny' is also a pyramidal form and has dark green foliage. Zones 3-7. *T. orientalis,* sometimes designated *Pladycladus orientalis,* Oriental arborvitae: grows 18 to 25 feet in height and 10 to 12 feet in width. It may be conical or pyramidal; it is compact in youth and becomes open with age. Leaves are bright green to yellow when the tree is young and darken as the tree matures. Zones 5-9. 'Semperaurescens' has shoots that emerge golden yellow in spring and turn bronze in winter. *T. plicata,* western arborvitae, western white cedar: grows 50 to 70 feet high and 15 to 25 feet wide. It is pyramidal and has glossy green foliage. Zones 5-7.

**Growing conditions.** All arborvitaes need full sun. Most will adapt to any average, well-drained soil, but eastern and western arborvitaes need deep, moist, well-drained soil and high humidity. They are vulnerable to snow and ice damage and need protection from winter sun scorch.

**Landscape uses.** Arborvitaes are suitable for use as accents, hedges, screens and foundation plants.

TAXODIUM ASCENDENS

TAXUS BACCATA

THUJA OCCIDENTALIS

TILIA CORDATA

TSUGA CANADENSIS

ULMUS AMERICANA

WASHINGTONIA FILIFERA

## Tilia (TIL-ee-a)
Linden, basswood, limetree

Deciduous shade tree that grows 50 to 80 feet tall with a straight trunk and narrow crown. Flowers are fragrant, leaves are heart-shaped and branchlets zigzag. Zones 2-8.

**Selected species and varieties.** *T. americana,* American linden, basswood: fast-growing tree, 60 to 80 feet tall, with a rounded crown. Toothed leaves are 4 to 8 inches long and nearly as wide. Yellow flowers occur in early summer. *T. cordata,* littleleaf linden: grows slowly to 60 to 70 feet. Three-inch-long leaves have hairy undersides. Zones 3-8. 'Greenspire' has a pear-shaped crown. Zones 4-8. *T. tomentosa,* silver linden: 50 to 70 feet tall. White hairs on the leaf undersides, stems and buds give the tree a silvery appearance. Zones 4-7.

**Growing conditions.** Linden needs full sun and moist, well-drained soil. It cannot tolerate urban pollution.

**Landscape uses.** Linden makes a good specimen and shade tree.

## Tsuga (TSOO-ga)
Hemlock

Needle-leaved evergreen conifer that grows 30 to 70 feet tall. It has slender leading shoots and irregular horizontal to drooping branches that nod in the breeze. Zones 3-7.

**Selected species and varieties.** *T. canadensis,* Canada hemlock: broadly pyramidal tree with a forked trunk that grows 40 to 70 feet tall. Needles are ¼ to ⅔ inch long, rich green on the upper surfaces and banded in white on the undersides. Cones are ½ to 1 inch long. *T. caroliniana,* Carolina hemlock: grows 40 to 60 feet with dark green needles that radiate around the stems. Cones are 1 to 1½ inches long. Zones 5-7.

**Growing conditions.** Hemlock prefers partial shade; moist, well-drained soil, and a cool and humid climate. It needs shelter from winds and cannot tolerate air pollution.

**Landscape uses.** Hemlock makes a graceful specimen tree; several together make good hedges, screens, windbreaks and background plantings.

**Tulip tree** see *Liriodendron*
**Tupelo** see *Nyssa*

## Ulmus (UL-mus)
Elm

Mainly deciduous tree that grows 40 to 90 feet tall. Generally vase-shaped, it has gray, furrowed bark and saw-toothed leaves. Zones 2-9.

**Selected species and varieties.** *U. americana,* American elm: grows 60 to 80 feet tall with a spreading crown. Leaves are 3 to 6 inches long, shiny dark green in summer and yellow in fall. *U. parvifolia,* Chinese elm, lacebark elm: reaches 50 feet. It has a forked trunk, arching branches and mottled, flaking bark. Leaves are ¾ to 2½ inches long, leathery and may turn yellow or reddish purple in fall. Zones 5-9.

**Growing conditions.** Elm needs full sun and moist, deep, well-drained soil.

**Landscape uses.** Elm makes a good specimen tree and provides deep shade.

**Washington fan palm**
see *Washingtonia*

## Washingtonia (wash-ing-TOH-nee-a)
Washington fan palm

Tropical evergreen that grows 30 to 80 feet tall with a long trunk and rounded crown. Zones 9 -11.

**Selected species and varieties.** *W. filifera,* desert fan palm, petticoat palm: grows 50 to 70 feet tall. The trunk is usually obscured by a skirt of withered leaves. The crown has light green leaves that form a fan up to 6 feet wide. Fibrous threads hang in the leaf margins. In summer, fragrant flowers bloom in clusters along 9-foot branches. Fruit is berry-like, ¼ inch in diameter, black, and ripens in fall.

**Growing conditions.** Washington fan palm needs full sun and moist soil.

**Landscape uses.** Washington fan palm makes a good specimen tree.

**Wattle** see *Acacia*
**Weeping willow** see *Salix*
**White cedar** see *Thuja*
**Whitewood** see *Liriodendron*
**Willow** see *Salix*
**Yaupon** see *Ilex*
**Yellow poplar** see *Liriodendron*
**Yellowwood** see *Cladrastis*
**Yew** see *Taxus*

## Introduction to Shrubs

The shrubs included in this dictionary are prized for their foliage, which comes in many shades of green and other colors. The featured plants are versatile, serving as formal or informal hedges, screens, foundation plantings and mixed shrub borders. Some shrubs make an ideal focal point in a garden; others offer attractive seasonal displays of flowers or fruit. The shrubs are listed by their botanical names; common names are cross-referenced.

**Aaron's-beard** see *Hypericum*

### Abelia (a-BEE-lee-a)

Graceful, rounded shrub that bears 1-inch clusters of fragrant, bell-shaped white to pink flowers from early summer through autumn. Foliage is glossy. Evergreen Zones 8-11; deciduous or semievergreen Zones 6 and 7.

**Selected species and varieties.** *A.* x *grandiflora,* glossy abelia, is 2 to 6 feet tall and wide, with arching stems. Leaves are oval-shaped, 1 inch long, bronze when young, dark green in summer and reddish bronze in winter.

**Growing conditions.** Plant abelia in full sun or partial shade in moist, acid, well-drained fertile soil. Leaves are more evergreen if protected from wind. Prune the plant in early spring. To rejuvenate an overgrown shrub, prune out stems at ground level.

**Landscape uses.** Plant abelia in a foundation planting, shrub border, mass planting or hedge.

**Arborvitae** see *Platycladus*
**Azalea** see *Rhododendron*
**Banana shrub** see *Michelia*
**Barberry** see *Berberis*
**Bay laurel** see *Laurus*

### Berberis (BER-ber-is)
Barberry

Deciduous or evergreen, rounded, thorny shrub that has clusters of glossy leaves at the end of short spurs. Flowers are yellow and bloom in spring. Zones 3-8.

**Selected species and varieties.** *B. julianae,* wintergreen barberry, grows 6 to 8 feet tall and has spiny, narrow, 4-inch-long leaves that are dark green in summer. Zones 6-8.

**Growing conditions.** Grow barberry in sun or partial shade in average, moist, well-drained garden soil. Prune lightly to shape the plant. Mature shrubs do not transplant well.

**Landscape uses.** Because of its thorns, barberry makes an excellent barrier plant. It can also be planted as a hedge or in a foundation planting or a shrub border. Low-growing varieties may be used as ground cover and in rock gardens.

**Bottlebrush** see *Callistemon*
**Boxwood** see *Buxus*
**Broom** see *Genista*
**Brush cherry** see *Syzygium*
**Butcher's-broom** see *Ruscus*

### Buxus (BUK-sus)
Boxwood

Dense, compact shrub with small, round, leathery leaves and inconspicuous flowers that bloom in spring. The stems arch slightly, giving the shrub a soft appearance. Zones 4-9.

**Selected species and varieties.** *B. microphylla,* littleleaf box, has leaves 1 inch long and grows 3 feet high. Zones 6-9. The variety *japonica,* Japanese boxwood, grows to 6 feet tall and has light green, 1-inch leaves. Zones 5-9. *B. sempervirens,* common or English boxwood, can grow to 20 feet. Leaves are larger than those of littleleaf box, up to 1¼ inches long. Flowers are sweetly scented. 'Arborescens,' American box, is conical in form. Zones 5-8.

**Growing conditions.** Grow boxwood in sun or partial shade in well-drained, rich, moist soil. The roots are shallow and should be heavily mulched. Plants withstand pruning and shearing. Protect from winds.

**Landscape uses.** Boxwood is a formal plant that is best used in a hedge, an edging or a foundation planting. Taller varieties make good screens.

**Calico bush** see *Kalmia*

### Callistemon (kal-i-STEE-mon)
Bottlebrush

Shrub that may be upright or weeping; both forms have hundreds of silky, 1-inch stamens that protrude from tiny flowers on long, tubular spikes. Blooms appear primarily in summer but may form on and off throughout

ABELIA × GRANDIFLORA

BERBERIS JULIANAE

BUXUS SEMPERVIRENS 'ARBORESCENS'

CALLISTEMON CITRINUS

CEANOTHUS FOLIOSUS 'ITALIAN SKIES'

ELAEAGNUS PUNGENS 'FRUITLANDII'

FEIJOA SELLOWIANA

GARDENIA JASMINOIDES

the year. Leaves are leathery, long and narrow, bronze when young and later dark green. Zones 9-11.

**Selected species and varieties.** *C. citrinus*, crimson bottlebrush, grows upright and has 4-inch spikes of red flowers and 2-inch leaves. The plant generally grows 10 to 15 feet tall, but sometimes reaches 25 feet.

**Growing conditions.** Plant bottle-brush in full sun in well-drained acid or alkaline soil. It does best when well watered, but will tolerate drought. It also tolerates wind and salt spray. For maximum flowering, prune the plant heavily every three years.

**Landscape uses.** The striking flowers of bottlebrush make it a good specimen plant. Because of its height, it is a useful screen or hedge. It is a good plant for a seashore garden.

**Calluna** see Dictionary of Grasses and Ground Covers, page 160
**Cape honeysuckle** see *Tecomaria*

## Ceanothus (see-a-NO-thus)
Wild lilac

Upright shrub or ground cover grown for its showy, dense, cone-shaped clusters of flowers, which may be blue, white or lavender. Zones 7-11.

**Selected species and varieties.** *C. foliosus* grows 1 foot or more in height and is densely branched. Leaves are oblong, ¾ inch in length and pale on the undersides. Clusters of blue flowers bloom in spring. 'Italian Skies' has lavender-blue flowers and light green leaves.

**Growing conditions.** Plant wild lilac in full sun in sandy, light soil. Water deeply but infrequently. Prune the plant before it flowers.

**Landscape uses.** Use wild lilac in a mass planting or as a ground cover. It also makes a good seashore plant.

**Cotoneaster** see Dictionary of Grasses and Ground Covers, page 160
**Devilwood** see *Osmanthus*
**Echium** see Dictionary of Annuals, page 200

## Elaeagnus (el-ee-AG-nus)

Broad genus of deciduous and ever-green trees and large, spreading shrubs grown primarily for their showy foliage, which is silvery on the undersides. Inconspicuous tubular flowers may bloom in spring or fall. Zones 2-11.

**Selected species and varieties.** *E. pungens,* thorny elaeagnus, is 15 feet tall. Its leaves are 2 to 4 inches long, olive green on the upper surfaces and have wavy margins. The flowers are fragrant, and the plant is often thorny. 'Fruitlandii' is more compact, with larger, more silvery leaves and bears edible red fruit in spring. Zones 7-11.

**Growing conditions.** Grow elaeagnus in sun or partial shade. It prefers sandy soil, but will grow in any garden soil, including poor and dry soil. Do not overwater. Do not fertilize. Elaeagnus tolerates wind. Prune or shear to shape and control growth.

**Landscape uses.** Elaeagnus may be used singly as an accent plant, or massed in hedges, screens and borders. It tolerates seashore conditions well. Thorned varieties make effective barriers.

**Erica** see Dictionary of Grasses and Ground Covers, page 160
**Euonymus** see Dictionary of Grasses and Ground Covers, page 160

## Feijoa (fay-JO-a)

Broad, fast-growing multistemmed shrub with oblong leaves and small, single flowers with long, showy stamens that bloom in spring and summer. Egg-shaped, edible, yellow or green fruit with white flesh follows in fall. Zones 9-11.

**Selected species and varieties.** *F. sellowiana*, pineapple guava, grows 10 to 20 feet tall and has glossy green 2- to 3-inch leaves with white undersides. Flowers are white with a purple cast on the inside.

**Growing conditions.** Grow pineapple guava in full sun or light shade in sandy, rich, well-drained soil. Fertilize in early spring and again in early summer. Prune the plant before it flowers.

**Landscape uses.** The tall, bushy habit of pineapple guava makes it a good background for other plants and useful in hedges and screens.

**Fire thorn** see *Pyracantha*
**Fragrant tea olive** see *Osmanthus*

## Gardenia (gar-DEEN-ya)

Compact shrub with glossy, leathery leaves and very fragrant, white, waxy flowers. Zones 8-11.

**Selected species and varieties.** *G. jasminoides* grows 2 to 5 feet tall and has 2½- to 3-inch flowers in spring and summer. Leaves grow to 2 to 4 inches long.

**Growing conditions.** Grow gardenia in full sun in cool areas and in partial shade where summers are hot. Soil should be moist, acid, rich and well drained. The roots are shallow; mulch well and be careful when weeding near them. Fertilize heavily during the growing season. Protect from winds. Gardenia blooms best where days are hot and humid and nights are below 65° F.

**Landscape uses.** Gardenia makes a handsome accent or specimen plant. It also adds beauty to foundation plantings and to hedges. In areas colder than Zone 8, it can be grown in a container and moved indoors for the winter.

**Gaultheria** see Dictionary of Grasses and Ground Covers, page 160

## Genista (je-NIS-ta)
Broom

Small, spreading shrub with many slender, almost leafless, green stems. Foliage, where present, is very small. Yellow flowers bloom at the ends of the branches in spring. Zones 2-11.

**Selected species and varieties.** *G. pilosa,* silky-leaved woodwaxen, grows 12 to 18 inches tall and spreads to 7 feet wide. Gray-green branches root along the ground and are covered with tiny, silvery leaves. The plant may be deciduous in cold climates. It gives the appearance of being evergreen because its dense branches retain their gray-green color all winter. Zones 6-11.

**Growing conditions.** Grow silky-leaved woodwaxen in full sun in dry, infertile, well-drained acid or alkaline soil. Prune the plant after it has flowered to encourage a second bloom. Silky-leaved woodwaxen does not transplant well.

**Landscape uses.** Its spreading habit makes silky-leaved woodwaxen good as a ground cover and in mass plantings on slopes and banks.

**Germander** see Dictionary of Grasses and Ground Covers, page 160
**Heath** see Dictionary of Grasses and Ground Covers, page 160
**Heather** see Dictionary of Grasses and Ground Covers, page 160
**Honeysuckle** see Dictionary of Grasses and Ground Covers, page 160

## Hypericum (hy-PER-i-kum)
St.-John's-wort

Low-growing, spreading shrub with oval to oblong leaves. In summer it bears cup-shaped yellow flowers that have five petals and many showy stamens that give the center of the flower a crested look. Zones 8-11; semi-evergreen Zone 7.

**Selected species and varieties.** *H. calycinum,* Aaron's-beard, grows 12 to 18 inches tall and spreads by underground stems. Leaves are 4-inch oblongs, green with pale undersides, and turn purple in winter. Flowers are 2 inches across. *H.* x 'Hidcote' has 3-inch fragrant flowers, the largest flowers of all St.-John's-worts. The plant grows 2 to 6 feet tall and spreads to 4 to 6 feet wide. Foliage is 2½ inches long, dark green above and pale green underneath.

**Growing conditions.** Grow St.-John's-wort in sun or partial shade in a light, well-drained soil. Most species prefer acid soil, but Aaron's-beard will grow in alkaline soil as well. Prune before growth starts. Heavy pruning can keep the plants more compact.

**Landscape uses.** Use St.-John's-wort as a ground cover on a flat expanse or on a slope. It also makes a colorful informal hedge.

**Juniper** see *Juniperus*

## Juniperus (joo-NIP-er-us)
Juniper

Vast group of coniferous trees and both upright and prostrate shrubs. Juvenile foliage is sharp and needle-like; mature foliage is softer and scale-like. Some plants have only one or the other; other plants have both. Foliage ranges from light to dark green, to blue-green, to blue or silver and often turns purplish in winter. Female plants produce small, round, blue berries that are used to flavor gin. Zones 2-11.

GENISTA PILOSA

HYPERICUM × 'HIDCOTE'

JUNIPERUS CONFERTA

451

KALMIA LATIFOLIA

LAURUS NOBILIS

LAVANDULA ANGUSTIFOLIA

LEIOPHYLLUM BUXIFOLIA

**Selected species and varieties.** *J. chinensis,* Chinese juniper, is an upright, broad pyramidal tree with smaller-growing cultivars. Foliage may be scalelike or needlelike. Zones 4-9.

*J. conferta,* shore juniper, has soft, blue-green needlelike foliage and grows 1 foot high and 6 to 8 feet across. Zones 6-9.

*J. horizontalis,* creeping juniper, has blue-green, mostly scalelike foliage that turns purple in winter. 'Wiltonii,' blue rug juniper, is a creeping plant 6 inches high and 8 feet wide and has steel gray foliage. Zones 3-9.

*J. sabina,* savin juniper, has stiff branches that arch in a vase shape. The plant grows 4 to 5 feet tall and 10 feet wide and has dark green, scalelike foliage. 'Skandia' has dark green foliage and grows 12 inches high and 4 feet wide. 'Tamariscifolia,' tam juniper, is mounded and feathery in appearance, 18 inches high and 10 feet across, and has blue-green leaves. Zones 3-9.

*J. scopulorum,* Rocky Mountain juniper, is a narrow, erect tree that grows to 30 feet and has scalelike, light green to rich blue leaves. Several of its cultivars are useful shrubs. Zones 3-9. *J. squamata,* singleseed juniper, is a 3-foot shrub with blue-green, needlelike foliage. Its branch tips arch and slightly nod. 'Blue Star' is more rounded, 2 feet high and 4 feet wide, and has blue-green leaves. Zones 4-8. *J. virginiana,* eastern red cedar, is a large tree with deep green, scale-like or needlelike foliage. It has several dwarf cultivars. Zones 3-9.

**Growing conditions.** Plant junipers in full sun in acid to neutral, dry, well-drained soil. Do not overwater. Prune in spring as growth starts.

**Landscape uses.** Junipers are so diverse in habit that there is one to fit any landscape need. Low-growing forms make excellent ground covers on flat surfaces and on slopes. They also do well spilling over rocks and walls. Spreading types make excellent hedges and screens. Any of them can find a place in a foundation planting, and those with unique shape or coloration can be used as specimens and accents. They also do well in seashore gardens.

**Kalmia** (KAL-mee-a)
Laurel, calico bush

Dense, rounded shrub that has shiny, leathery, dark green leaves. Flowers are cup-shaped and appear in clusters at the ends of the branches in late spring; they may be white, pink or pur-

ple, and the petals are often spotted in purple or maroon. The stamens curl back and are attached to the petals until they are released by bees or other insects. Zones 3-8.

**Selected species and varieties.** *K. angustifolia,* sheep laurel, grows 2 to 3 feet tall. It has 1- to 2-inch narrow, oblong leaves and 2- to 3-inch clusters of lavender to rose flowers. *K. latifolia,* mountain laurel, is 7 to 12 feet tall. It has 2- to 4-inch oval leaves and 4- to 6-inch clusters of white or rose flowers. Zones 5-8.

**Growing conditions.** Grow laurel in full sun or partial shade in moist, rich, acid, well-drained soil. It has shallow roots and will benefit from a mulch to keep them cool and moist. Prune the plant after it flowers.

**Landscape uses.** Use laurels in a foundation planting, in a massed planting or as specimens. They also fit well in a woodland garden beneath tall trees.

**Lantana** see Dictionary of Grasses and Ground Covers, page 160
**Laurel** see *Kalmia; Laurus*

**Laurus** (LAW-rus)
Laurel, sweet bay

Broad-based, multistemmed shrub that grows in a conical shape. Leaves are dark green, dull, leathery and aromatic. Inconspicuous white flowers bloom in spring and are followed by ½-inch black berries. Zones 8-11.

**Selected species and varieties.** *L. nobilis,* bay laurel, grows 8 to 12 feet tall. Its 2- to 4-inch leaves are the bay leaves used in cooking.

**Growing conditions.** Grow bay laurel in full sun or partial shade in any rich, moist, well-drained soil. Water heavily in spring but keep the soil dry the rest of the year. Prune or shear the plant in summer.

**Landscape uses.** Several bay laurels together make good hedges and good background plantings. They take well to pruning. Singly, laurel also grows well in containers.

**Lavandula** (la-VAN-dew-la)
Lavender

Small, mounded shrub or perennial with long, narrow, hairy, aromatic, gray-green leaves. Fragrant lavender, purple or blue flowers appear in dense spikes during the summer and off and on all year in frost-free areas. Lavender is hardy in Zones 5-11, but will be an herbaceous perennial in Zones 5-8.

**Selected species and varieties.** *L. angustifolia,* English lavender, grows 2 to 3 feet tall and has 2½-inch leaves. Lavender or purple flowers bloom in 3- to 3½-inch spikes. *L. dentata,* French lavender, is a 1- to 3-foot shrub. It has 1½-inch gray, toothed leaves and 1½- to 2½-inch spikes of lavender flowers. Zones 9-11.

**Growing conditions.** Plant lavender in full sun in loose, well-drained soil. Water and fertilize sparingly. Prune the plant after it flowers to keep it compact. To dry the flowers, cut them as they open and hang them in a cool, dry area.

**Landscape uses.** Lavender is used as an edging, a low hedge or in the front of a shrub border. It is also used in flower gardens and herb gardens.

**Lavender** see *Lavandula*

**Leiophyllum** (ly-o-FIL-um)
Sand myrtle

Neat, compact shrub with upright branches and shiny, leathery, oval ½-inch leaves. Waxy, ¼-inch pink or white flowers bloom in 1-inch clusters in late spring. Zones 6-8.

**Selected species and varieties.** *L. buxifolia* grows 18 to 36 inches high in rounded form. Foliage turns bronze in the winter.

**Growing conditions.** Grow sand myrtle in partial shade in acid, moist, rich, well-drained soil. Prune the plant after it flowers.

**Landscape uses.** Because of its small size and neat appearance, sand myrtle does well in rock gardens and as a low edging. It tolerates seashore conditions.

**Leucothoe** (loo-KOTH-o-ee)

Multistemmed mounded shrub that has graceful, arching branches. Foliage is narrow and pointed, bronze in spring, green in summer and red in winter. White, tiny, bell-shaped flowers bloom in slender, drooping clusters at the ends of the branches in midspring. Zones 5-9.

**Selected species and varieties.** *L. fontanesiana,* drooping leucothoe, is 3 to 6 feet tall. It has 2- to 5-inch leaves and 3- to 4-inch flower clusters. Young branches are red. 'Girard's Rainbow' has variegated foliage of pink, yellow, green and copper.

**Growing conditions.** Plant leucothoe in partial to full shade in moist, acid, rich, well-drained soil. Shelter it from drying winds. Prune the plant after it flowers. To rejuvenate an old plant, cut out older stems at the base.

**Landscape uses.** Leucothoe is attractive in a foundation planting, shrub border, a woodland garden or massed on banks and slopes. It is a good foil for taller plants that have lost their lower branches.

**Ligustrum** (li-GUS-trum)
Privet

Deciduous or evergreen shrub that has a dense, erect habit. The evergreen species have smooth, shiny, leathery, dark green, round to oval foliage and spiked clusters of small, scented, white flowers in late spring or early summer. Zones 7-11.

**Selected species and varieties.** *L. japonicum,* Japanese privet, is 6 to 10 feet high and has 4- to 6-inch flower clusters. 'Rotundifolium' is 4 to 5 feet high and has round leaves. 'Texanum Silver Star' is 6 feet tall and has leaves edged in creamy white. 'Variegatum' has leaves edged with white and grows to 10 feet.

**Growing conditions.** Plant privet in full sun or partial shade in any soil except one that is constantly wet. It is very tolerant of air pollution and drought. Pruning in early spring will reduce or eliminate flowering. If flowers are desired, wait until after the plant has flowered to prune.

**Landscape uses.** Privet is used mainly in hedging because it withstands heavy shearing, but it also makes a good background plant.

**Michelia** (my-KEE-lee-a)

Dense tree or shrub that has narrow leaves and fragrant, saucer-shaped flowers that bloom among the leaves. Zones 9-11.

**Selected species and varieties.** *M. doltsopa* grows to 15 to 20 feet and can be either a wide or a narrow shrub. Leaves are dark green, 6 to 7 inches

LEUCOTHOE FONTANESIANA

LIGUSTRUM JAPONICUM

MICHELIA FIGO

453

MICROBIOTA DECUSSATA

MYRTUS COMMUNIS

NERIUM OLEANDER

long, thin and leathery. Fragrant 5- to 7-inch whitish flowers bloom in winter and spring. *M. figo,* banana shrub, grows 6 to 20 feet tall with shiny, 3-inch leaves. Dark yellow flowers with maroon edges bloom in spring; they are 1½ inches across and have a strong banana fragrance.

**Growing conditions.** Plant michelia in full sun or partial shade in moist, acid, fertile, well-drained soil. It is very heat-tolerant. Prune the plant after it flowers.

**Landscape uses.** Plant michelia as a specimen where its fragrance can be enjoyed.

## Microbiota (my-kro-by-O-ta)

Widely spreading conifer with bright green, feathery, scalelike foliage that turns copper in fall. Zones 2-11.

**Selected species and varieties.** *M. decussata,* Russian cypress, Siberian cypress, grows 18 to 24 inches tall and spreads to 4 to 6 feet across.

**Growing conditions.** Plant Russian cypress in sun or shade in a dry, well-drained soil. Prune or shear at any time.

**Landscape uses.** Use Russian cypress as a ground cover, a low hedge or in a massed planting.

**Mountain laurel** see *Kalmia*
**Myrtle** see *Myrtus*

## Myrtus (MER-tus)
Myrtle

Dense, rounded shrub that has shiny, thick, dark green, aromatic leaves. Flowers are saucer-shaped with five petals and several prominent stamens that give the center of the bloom a delicate, fluffy look. Zones 9-11.

**Selected species and varieties.** *M. communis* grows 5 to 12 feet tall with 1- to 2-inch oval, pointed leaves. Fragrant flowers of white or pink are ¾ inch across and bloom in clusters during the summer, followed by showy, ½-inch blue-black berries.

**Growing conditions.** Grow myrtle in sun or partial shade in any well-drained acid or alkaline soil. It tolerates heat and drought. Prune or shear the plant in early spring before growth starts.

**Landscape uses.** The neat, dense habit of myrtle makes it useful as a hedge, edging, screen or massed planting. It tolerates salt spray and wind and is a good seashore plant.

## Nerium (NEER-ee-um)
Oleander

Broad, dense, rounded shrub with thick, leather, glossy, pointed, narrow leaves that appear in whorls of three. Tubular flowers with five petals bloom in showy clusters at the ends of the branches. Zones 8-11.

**Selected species and varieties.** *N. oleander* grows 8 to 20 feet tall with 4- to 10-inch leaves that are dark green above and light green below. Yellow, red, white, pink or purple flowers 2 to 3 inches across bloom in clusters of four or five blooms during spring and summer. Some flowers are fragrant. All parts of the oleander plant are poisonous if ingested, and the leaves may cause a skin rash.

**Growing conditions.** Grow oleander in full sun or light shade in any soil. Regular watering in spring encourages flowering, but water should be decreased in fall so the foliage matures before winter. Oleander tolerates heat, drought, wind, air pollution and poor soil. Prune the plant in early spring.

**Landscape uses.** Oleander's density and wind tolerance combine to make it a good choice for a screen, windbreak, hedge or seashore garden. It also does well in shrub borders and in containers.

**Oleander** see *Nerium*
**Oriental arborvitae** see *Platycladus*

## Osmanthus (os-MAN-thus)

Upright, rounded shrub with foliage that varies in size and shape and may be smooth-margined or toothed. Fragrant white, yellow or orange flowers are ¼ to ½ inch across, tubular to bell-shaped and bloom in clusters. The flowers are not showy, but they emit a strong, sweet fragrance. Zones 7-11.

**Selected species and varieties.** *O. americanus,* devilwood, grows to 20 feet, and has 4- to 6-inch narrow, shiny leaves. White flowers bloom in spring and are followed by dark blue berries. *O. delavayi* is 6 feet tall and has graceful, arching branches and 1-inch toothed leaves. White flowers are 1 inch across and the largest of any osmanthus, and bloom in spring. Zones 8-11. *O.* x *fortunei,* fortune's osmanthus, grows 10 to 20 feet tall and has 3- to 4-inch oval, thick, toothed leaves. White flowers bloom in fall. 'San Jose' is similar but has yellow to orange blooms. *O. fragrans,* fragrant tea olive, grows to 10 feet tall and has 2- to 4-inch slightly toothed leaves. Flowers are white, the most fragrant of any osmanthus, and bloom most abundantly in spring and summer and off and on throughout the year where winters are mild. *O. fragrans aurantiacus* is similar, but has foliage that is narrower, less shiny and toothless, and cream to orange fragrant flowers. Zones 8-11. *O. heterophyllus,* holly osmanthus, grows 10 to 15 feet tall, and has 1½- to 2½-inch oval, spiny leaves. White flowers bloom in summer and fall. 'Myrtifolius' is 5 feet tall and has 1- to 2-inch narrow, spineless leaves. 'Rotundifolius' is 5 feet high with round, spineless foliage. 'Variegatus' is 10 feet tall with spined leaves that have white margins.

**Growing conditions.** Grow osmanthus in full sun or partial shade in rich moist acid and well-drained soil. Osmanthus can be pruned or sheared at any time.

**Landscape uses.** Plant osmanthus in a hedge, a screen or a background planting. It can also be grown in containers. Locate it where its fragrance can be enjoyed.

**Paxistima** see Dictionary of Grasses and Ground Covers, page 160

### Photinia (fo-TIN-ee-a)
Red tip

Genus of large deciduous and evergreen shrubs. The evergreen species are prized for their shiny, leathery, toothed foliage, which is bright red when young. Single, white flowers have five petals and bloom in the spring. Berries are ¼ inch across and are often inconspicuous. Zones 5-11.

**Selected species and varieties.** *P.* x *fraseri,* Fraser photinia, is 15 feet tall and has 3- to 5-inch oblong leaves and 3- to 5-inch flower clusters. Zones 7-11. *P. glabra,* Japanese photinia, is 12 feet tall. It has 2- to 4-inch clusters of fragrant flowers. Zones 8-11. *P. serrulata,* Chinese photinia, is 10 to 30 feet high. It has 4- to 8-inch oblong, toothed leaves and 4- to 6-inch flower clusters. Berries are red and showy. Zones 8-11.

**Growing conditions.** Grow photinia in full sun to light shade in rich, fertile, well-drained soil. Chinese photinia will tolerate alkaline soil; other photinias need acid soil. Water heavily in spring and summer, then taper off in fall to allow the foliage to mature before winter so it will not be damaged. Repeated pruning throughout the year will encourage new, red growth and keep the plants low-growing.

**Landscape uses.** Because it is so showy, photinia makes a good specimen. It is also useful as a hedge, a screen or a background plant.

### Pieris (py-ER-is)
Andromeda

Upright, rounded shrub with dark green foliage that is red or bronze when young. Urn-shaped, ¼-inch, white or pink flowers bloom in clusters in spring. Red flower buds are evident and decorative all winter. Zones 4-9.

**Selected species and varieties.** *P. floribunda,* mountain andromeda, is 3 to 6 feet tall and has oval, 1½- to 3½-inch dull foliage. Flower clusters are slightly fragrant, white, 2 to 4 inches high and upright. Zones 4-8. *P. forrestii,* Chinese andromeda, is 5 to 10 feet tall and has 4½-inch narrow, shiny leaves and exceptionally red new growth. Flower clusters are slightly fragrant, white, 4 to 6 inches long and pendulous. Zones 8 and 9. *P. japonica,* Japanese andromeda, is 3 to 10 feet tall and has lance-shaped to oval, shiny 1½- to 3½-inch foliage. Flowers are slightly fragrant and bloom in drooping clusters. 'Bonsai' is compact and 2 feet tall. 'Mountain Fire' has bright red new foliage and white flowers. 'Pygmaea' looks nothing like other andromedas; it grows only 12 inches tall, has ½- to 1-inch leaves and rarely blooms. 'Valley Rose' is 3 feet tall and has pink flowers. 'Valley Valentine' is 4 feet tall and has deep rose flowers. 'Variegata' is 3 feet tall; its foliage is pink when young, then changes to green with white markings. Zones 5-9. *P. japonica* x *floribunda* 'Brouwer's Beauty' is a cross between mountain andromeda and Japanese andromeda. It grows 3 to 6 feet tall. Zones 4-9. *P. taiwanensis,* Formosa andromeda, is 6 feet tall and has oval, dull, 5-inch leaves and 4- to 6-inch clusters of upright flowers. 'Snow Drift' is 3 feet tall and has pure white flowers. Zones 7-9.

**Growing conditions.** Most andromedas will grow in full sun or partial shade. Chinese andromeda will tolerate full shade. Soil should be rich,

OSMANTHUS HETEROPHYLLUS

PHOTINIA SERRULATA

PIERIS JAPONICA

PLATYCLADUS ORIENTALIS

PODOCARPUS MACROPHYLLUS MAKI

PYRACANTHA COCCINEA

sandy, moist, acid and well drained. Roots are shallow and should be mulched to keep them moist and cool. Shelter from winter wind and sun. Prune in spring immediately after the plant flowers.

**Landscape uses.** Use andromeda in a foundation planting or border, or as an accent.

**Pineapple guava** see *Feijoa*

## Platycladus (plat-i-CLAD-us)
Oriental arborvitae

Pyramidal or globe-shaped conifer with scalelike green, blue-green or yellow foliage held vertically. Zones 6-11.

**Selected species and varieties.** *P. orientalis* is a densely branched, erect shrub with sprays of foliage that curve inward. Leaves are slightly fragrant when rubbed.

**Growing conditions.** Plant Oriental arborvitae in full sun or light shade in moist, rich, fertile, neutral, well-drained soil. Remove snow and ice from the branches promptly to avoid breakage or disfiguring. Oriental arborvitae is heat- and drought-resistant but not very winter-hardy. Prune or shear the plant in spring.

**Landscape uses.** Use upright forms of Oriental arborvitae as hedges, screens, foundation plants and at entryways. Globe-shaped varieties fit well into rock gardens.

## Podocarpus (pod-o-KAR-pus)

Coniferous tree or shrub that may be columnar or broad. It has narrow to slightly oval, soft needles 1 to 3 inches long. Zones 7-11.

**Selected species and varieties.** *P. macrophyllus maki*, Chinese podocarpus, grows 6 to 8 feet tall and has 3-inch, dark green, narrow leaves.

**Growing conditions.** Plant podocarpus in full sun in cool areas, or in partial shade where summers are hot. Soil should be rich, fertile, moist and well drained. Prune or shear the plant at any time.

**Landscape uses.** Use podocarpus as a hedge or a windbreak. Podocarpus is tolerant of seashore conditions, and is one of the best shrubs available for containers because it does not mind a restricted root area.

**Privet** see *Ligustrum*

## Pyracantha (py-ra-KAN-tha)
Fire thorn

Thorny, upright or spreading shrub that has dark green leaves. Small white flowers bloom in 1- to 1½-inch clusters in spring and are followed by showy clusters of red, orange or yellow berries in fall and winter. Zones 6-11.

**Selected species and varieties.** *P. coccinea,* scarlet fire thorn, grows from 6 to 12 feet tall with an irregular branching habit. Leaves are oblong and 1 to 1½ inches long. Fruits are bright red. Zones 5-11. The hybrid 'Mohave' is 8 to 10 feet tall and has berries that turn orange-red very early in the fall. Zones 7-11.

**Growing conditions.** Plant fire thorn in full sun in fertile, well-drained soil. Protect the plant from winter wind. It will tolerate drought and air pollution once it is established. Prune back leggy branches at any time to keep the plant bushy.

**Landscape uses.** Fire thorn makes a good barrier plant since it is so thorny. It may also be grown as a hedge, in a massed planting or against a north or east wall, as it does not like reflected heat.

**Red cedar** see *Juniperus*
**Redwood** see *Sequoia*

## Rhododendron (ro-do-DEN-dron)
Azalea, rhododendron

Extremely large genus of deciduous and evergreen shrubs known commonly as rhododendrons and azaleas. Plants vary in size, foliage and form, but all have showy flowers that bloom from early spring to midsummer in all colors of the rainbow.

All azaleas are rhododendrons, but not all rhododendrons are azaleas. One way to distinguish between them is that azaleas generally have leaves that are small, narrow, pointed and hairy along the midrib; rhododendron leaves occur in whorls and are generally large, broad, long and leathery. Azalea flowers are borne along the sides and at the tips of the branches; some are single, having one ring of petals, some are double, having numerous overlapping petals, and some have one single flower set inside another single flower, a configuration called hose-in-hose. Rhododendron flowers are generally single; they are borne in dome-shaped clusters known as trusses and appear only at the ends of the branches. Azalea flowers are generally funnel-shaped and have five to 10 stamens; rhododendron flowers are usually bell-shaped and have 10 or more stamens. Azaleas are usually smaller than rhododendrons and grow in a spreading form; rhododendrons generally grow upright.

For the purposes of description, azaleas and rhododendrons may be divided into four categories: azalea species, which are found in nature; azalea hybrid groups, which have been bred by crossing two or more species; rhododendron species, which occur in nature; and rhododendron hybrids, which have been bred by crossing two or more species. Zones 2-11.

**Azalea species.** *R. kaempferi,* torch azalea, blooms in mid- to late-spring, grows 6 to 8 feet high and has 2½-inch hairy, oblong to oval leaves that often turn bronze during winter. Flowers are 2 inches across and may be white, pink, orange, red or salmon. Zones 6-8.

**Azalea hybrid groups.** Back Acre Hybrids have single to double flowers. 'Margaret Douglas' grows 4 to 6 feet tall and has 3-inch flowers of salmon with white throats; they bloom in middle to late spring. Flowers are 2 to 3 inches across; some have frilled petals. 'Chimes' has dark red flowers in midspring. Zones 8 and 9.

**Rhododendron species.** *R. augustinii* is 6 feet tall and has 3-inch leaves. Flowers of blue or purple are 2 to 2½ inches across. Zones 7-9.

*R. catawbiense,* Catawba rhododendron, is 6 to 8 feet high and wide. Leaves are oval, 3 to 6 inches long and pointed, and have white undersides. White to purplish pink flowers that have olive green throats appear in late spring and early summer and are 2 inches across. Zones 5-8.

*R. fortunei* is 12 feet tall and has 4- to 8-inch, oblong leaves that have gray undersides. Flowers are fragrant, pale purple to pink, 3½ inches across in 8-inch trusses and bloom in late spring. Zones 6-9.

*R. yakusimanum* is a 3-foot, spreading plant that has narrow, 3-inch leaves. Pink or white, 2½-inch flowers bloom in late spring. Zones 6-8.

**Rhododendron hybrids.** 'Anna Rose Whitney' is 5 feet tall and has rich, deep pink flowers in late spring. Zones 7-9. 'English Roseum' is 5 to 6 feet high and has bright lilac to purple flowers with yellow-green throats in early summer. Zones 6-8.

'Gomer Waterer' is 6 feet tall and has white flowers blushed with pink or lilac in early summer. Zones 5-8. 'Janet Blair' is 4 to 6 feet tall and has clear pink flowers in middle to late spring. Zones 5-8. 'Loder's White' grows to 5 feet and has flowers that open pink and fade to white in mid-spring. Zones 7 and 8.

'Mrs. Furnival' is 4 feet tall and has light pink flowers with red to brown blotches in late spring. Zones 6-8. 'Nova Zembla' is 5 feet tall and has red flowers with dark centers in midspring. Zones 4-8.

'P.J.M.' is 3 to 5 feet tall and has purplish pink flowers in early spring. The plant may bloom in fall in warmer areas. Foliage turns bronze in winter. Zones 5-8. 'Ramapo' is 1½ to 3 feet high and has violet-blue flowers in early spring. Zones 6-8. 'Roseum Elegans' is 6 to 8 feet tall and has rose pink to purplish pink flowers in late spring. Zones 4-8. 'Scintillation' is 8 feet tall and has light pink flowers with gold throats in late spring. Zones 7 and 8.

**Growing conditions.** Plant azaleas and rhododendrons in partial shade. Azaleas will tolerate full sun if the ground is constantly moist, and rhododendrons will tolerate full shade. Soil for both should be rich, high in organic matter, acid and well drained. Roots are shallow and should be mulched to keep them cool. Do not cultivate around the roots or they will be damaged.

Feed lightly and infrequently. If leaves become yellow, check to make sure that the soil is acidic and correct the pH if it is not. Application of chelated iron to the soil will also correct yellowing leaves.

Prune azaleas and rhododendrons immediately after they flower to control size and shape the plants. On rhododendrons, cut to the next lower whorl of leaves; on azaleas cut just above a leaf. Faded flowers of azaleas will fall cleanly from the plant. Faded trusses of rhododendrons should be manually removed; be careful not to damage the new growing tips.

Protect from drying winds and winter sun. Apply an antidesiccant to large rhododendron leaves at the beginning of winter in the colder limits of their hardiness.

**Landscape uses.** Rhododendrons and azaleas make good foundation plantings. They are also effective lining driveways and walkways, as hedges, in massed plantings and in woodland gardens. The small varieties do well in rock gardens. They will also grow well in containers, a fact that is useful in areas where soil conditions are not conducive to their growth.

RHODODENDRON CATAWBIENSE

RHODODENDRON × 'LODER'S WHITE'

RHODODENDRON × 'MRS. FURNIVAL'

RHODODENDRON × 'SCINTILLATION'

ROSMARINUS OFFICINALIS

RUSCUS ACULEATUS

SARCOCOCCA HOOKERANA HUMILIS

SEQUOIA SEMPERVIRENS
'ADPRESSA'

**Rosemary** see *Rosmarinus*

## Rosmarinus (ros-ma-RY-nus)
Rosemary

Upright or trailing shrub that has aromatic stems and foliage. Leaves are needlelike, ½ to 1 inch long, glossy green on the upper surfaces and gray on the undersides. Fragrant, pale blue, tubular, ½-inch flowers appear in upright spikes during winter and spring. Zones 7-11.

**Selected species and varieties.** *R. officinalis* grows upright, 2 to 6 feet tall. Foliage has white hairs on the undersides. Zones 8-11.

**Growing conditions.** Plant rosemary in full sun in dry, well-drained soil. It tolerates heat, drought and poor soil. Water sparingly and do not fertilize. Pinch out growing tips to control plant size.

**Landscape uses.** Rosemary is useful as a border plant or a hedge. It may also be grown in a flower garden or an herb garden. The trailing cultivars may be used as ground covers or to spill over walls, and all varieties tolerate seashore conditions.

## Ruscus (RUS-kus)
Butcher's-broom

Low-growing shrub that spreads into a thick clump by underground stems. The actual leaves are tiny and scalelike. Small, greenish flowers bloom on the middle of the flattened stems in spring, and are followed by ½-inch red or yellow berries on the female plants. Zones 7-11.

**Selected species and varieties.** *R. aculeatus* grows 1½ to 3 feet tall. The leaflike branches are oval, thick, leathery, ¾ to 1 inch long and dull green, and have spiny tips. Zones 8-11.

**Growing conditions.** Butcher's-broom may be grown in full sun in cool climates and in partial shade where summers are hot. Soil should be moist and well drained. Both male and female plants are usually necessary to produce berries. Cut out branches at ground level to control plant size.

**Landscape uses.** The upright spreading habit of butcher's-broom makes it useful as a ground cover and as a low hedge; its unusual blooming habit makes it a good accent plant.

**Russian cypress** see *Microbiota*
**St.-John's-wort** see *Hypericum*
**Sand myrtle** see *Leiophyllum*
**Santolina** see Dictionary of Perennials, page 246

## Sarcococca (sar-ko-KOK-a)
Sweet box

Small genus of shrubs that may be erect or spreading. Leaves are thin, leathery and glossy dark green. Small, white, fragrant flowers bloom among the leaves in late winter and spring. Berries are ¼ inch across and may be black or red. Zones 6-9.

**Selected species and varieties.** *S. hookerana digyna* is slender and has narrow leaves. Zones 7-9. The variety *humilis,* dwarf Himalayan sweet box, grows 2 feet high and spreads to 8 feet wide. Zones 6-9.

**Growing conditions.** Grow sweet box in partial to full shade in rich, fertile, moist, well-drained soil. Prune out old stems to the ground in early spring.

**Landscape uses.** Sweet box is best used as a hedge or a border. Dwarf Himalayan box is a good ground cover.

## Sequoia (se-KWOY-a)
Redwood

Broad genus of conifers from large trees to small shrubs. Needles are arranged on both sides of the branches. They are pointed, ¼ to 1 inch long, and blue-green or dark green with two white lines on the undersides. Bark is reddish brown. Cones are round and 1 inch in diameter. Zones 7-9.

**Selected species and varieties.** *S. sempervirens* 'Adpressa,' dwarf redwood, is a 6-foot, broad pyramidal shrub; growing tips are creamy white in spring and summer.

**Growing conditions.** Grow dwarf redwoods in full sun or partial shade in very moist, rich, well-drained soil. They do best where humidity is high. Prune in spring to keep compact.

**Landscape uses.** Use dwarf redwoods as accent plants or in foundation plantings. The low-growing cultivars may be used as ground covers and in rock gardens.

**Sheep laurel** see *Kalmia*
**Siberian cypress** see *Microbiota*
**Silky-leaved woodwaxen** see *Genista*

## Skimmia (SKIM-ee-a)

Dense, mounded shrub that has oblong, 3- to 5-inch leaves and small white flowers that bloom in spring. Round, ½-inch red berries form in clusters in fall and winter. Zones 7-9.

**Selected species and varieties.** *S. japonica,* Japanese skimmia, is a densely branched shrub 2 to 4 feet high and 6 feet wide. Foliage forms at the ends of the branches; it is yellow-green, leathery and has wavy margins.

**Growing conditions.** Plant skimmia in partial to full shade in moist, rich, acid, well-drained soil. It tolerates air pollution. Little if any pruning is necessary. Both male and female plants are needed to produce berries on the Japanese skimmia; plant one male for every six to eight females.

**Landscape uses.** Skimmias are effective in foundation plantings, shrub borders, mass plantings, edging and hedges, and can be used in seashore gardens.

**Sweet bay** see *Laurus*
**Sweet box** see *Sarcococca*

## Syzygium (sy-ZIJ-ee-um)

Genus of 400 to 500 trees and shrubs that have deep green foliage that is often tinged with copper, especially when young. Flowers have tufts of stamens that look brushy. Berries are soft and edible. Zones 10-11.

**Selected species and varieties.** *S. paniculatum*, brush cherry, is a 40-foot tree that can be pruned into a 20-foot shrub. Leaves are oblong and 2 to 3 inches long. Flowers are white, ½ to 1 inch wide and appear in clusters in spring. Berries are purple and ½ to ¾ inches across.

**Growing conditions.** Grow brush cherry in full sun or partial shade in any well-drained soil. Prune both the branches and the roots frequently to keep the plant in shrub form.

**Landscape uses.** Use brush cherry in a background planting or in a hedge. It can be pruned into formal shapes.

## Tecomaria (tek-o-MAIR-ee-a)

Vining shrub that has finely divided leaves and yellow, red or orange flowers that bloom in loose clusters at the ends of the branches. Blooms are trumpet-shaped and five-lobed. Zones 9-11.

**Selected species and varieties.** *T. capensis,* cape honeysuckle, is a sprawling 15-foot semivine that can be pruned to a 6-foot shrub. Flowers are 2 inches long, bright orange, and appear in fall and winter. Leaves are glossy, 6 inches long and have five to nine 2-inch leaflets. Two-inch seedpods follow the flowers.

**Growing conditions.** Plant cape honeysuckle in full sun in sandy, well-drained soil. It is tolerant of heat and wind, and of drought once it is established.

**Landscape uses.** If unpruned, cape honeysuckle can be grown on a trellis, against a wall or as a ground cover on a bank. Pruned, it is used as a hedge or screen. It is tolerant of seashore conditions.

**Teucrium** see Dictionary of Grasses and Ground Covers, page 160

## Viburnum (vy-BER-num)

Deciduous or evergreen, upright, rounded shrub with lush foliage, showy clusters of bell-shaped, white or pink flowers that bloom in spring, and bright clusters of berries in autumn and winter. Zones 4-11.

**Selected species and varieties.** *V.* x *burkwoodii*, Burkwood viburnum, grows 6 to 8 feet high and wide. Leaves are pointed, dark green, 4 inches long, glossy on the top surfaces and hairy on the undersides. Flower clusters are white, fragrant and 3 inches long. Fruits are red at first and change to black. Evergreen in Zones 8-11; semievergreen in Zones 5-7.

**Growing conditions.** Plant viburnum in partial to full shade in moist, rich, slightly acid, well-drained soil. Mulch to keep the roots cool. Protect from drying winds. Decrease watering in autumn to let foliage mature before winter cold sets in. Prune to shape the plant and stimulate branching in early spring before growth starts.

**Landscape uses.** Plant the fragrant viburnums near a window where their sweet scent can be enjoyed. They serve well as foundation plantings, screens, hedges or accent plants.

**Wild lilac** see *Ceanothus*
**Wintergreen** see Dictionary of Grasses and Ground Covers, page 160

SKIMMIA JAPONICA

SYZYGIUM PANICULATUM

TECOMARIA CAPENSIS

VIBURNUM × BURKWOODII

# 9

# VEGETABLES

*Butterhead lettuce flourishes in a partially shaded garden patch. Lettuce and other leafy vegetables need some protection from hot summer sun and can grow successfully in the shade of taller plants.*

From the first crisp carrots of early summer to the last sweet squash of fall, a vegetable garden is a constantly changing delight. There is the pleasure of anticipation, of watching as beets and carrots shoulder their way into view. Then there is the enjoyment of consuming the harvest, fresh-picked and full of flavor.

But good vegetable gardens never arrive at this perfection unassisted. They produce bumper crops because someone has paid attention to the important preliminaries: to siting and soil preparation. To be succulent, vegetables need sun, preferably throughout the day, and they need a friable, well-drained soil rich in the nutrients that promote healthy growth.

Like all living things, vegetables benefit from tender loving care when young. Given a good send-off, they are much more likely to mature into healthy, heavy-bearing plants. Nature of course plays a critical role, providing the warm sun and gentle rain that encourage seeds to sprout and young seedlings to develop strong roots. But human intervention can abet the process in a surprising number of ways. Seeds can be encouraged to germinate, for instance, by being planted when soil conditions are at their optimum—warm enough, moist enough and sufficiently friable to give the emerging sprouts the best of all possible environments. For an extra boost, the seeds can even be started indoors *(pages 80-81)* in a minigreenhouse and a sterile growing medium that eliminates many of the bacterial dangers that plague young plants.

In other ways, too, vegetables profit from early attention to their needs. Upright supports can increase yield, as can staggering a particular vegetable's planting dates, or pairing, in a single row, two compatible vegetables with different maturing dates. In the 70 to 90 days it

## CHAPTER CONTENTS

takes head lettuce to mature, for example, green peppers will be germinating; and when the lettuce has been harvested the slower-growing peppers will be just approaching maturity and able to spread out in the space vacated by the lettuce. Crop rotation, too, can improve vegetable quality by varying the demands made on the soil by different plants. Information for giving plants a good start can be found in this chapter.

Lending vegetables a helping hand at the right time can actually reduce the amount of work you have to do in your garden in the long run. It's much easier to smother weeds before they appear than it is to pull them up later; it's more efficient to strengthen a tender young shoot than to prop up a top-heavy stalk; it's easier, more efficient and a lot more satisfying to arrange for the right amounts of sun and water and the right kind of protection against insects and disease than it is to try to salvage sun-scalded, desiccated or pest-ridden seedlings.

Along with good soil, good seeds and good care, a successful vegetable garden depends on good timing. Because some seeds must stay cool to germinate and some seedlings shrink from the slightest hint of frost, your decisions about when to plant which crops will be critical in determining the size of your harvest. Plan ahead, using the frost-date map *(inside back cover)* to determine the average date of the last frost in your region. For more specific guidance, turn to the table of Planting Dates for Vegetables *(pages 498-501)* and the Dictionary of Vegetables starting on page 506.

In the battle against garden pests, victory goes to those who know their enemy. The knowledge you need can be found on pages 502-505. Entries are arranged to help you identify a problem, pinpoint the cause and take effective action.

# STARTING A VEGETABLE PLOT

**W**herever you live, you can grow vegetables. Whether your climate is warm or cold, your terrain hilly or flat, your property large or small, you can have the satisfactions of raising and eating your own fresh vegetables.

To begin, select the site with care. The vegetable garden as a whole must be located where it will have sunlight—at least for seven hours of the day. Within the garden, the placement of specific vegetables is important, too; a few vegetables, such as lettuce, need the cooling relief of part-time shade *(page 480)*.

Vegetables need protection from other elements as well. If possible, the garden should be placed on the sheltered side of a hedge or a row of trees that can serve as a windbreak, because strong winds can uproot tender seedlings and blow down crops that are top-heavy when ripe. Wind can also dry out soil, and vegetables need plenty of moisture. But vegetables also need well-drained soil, so avoid placing the garden where too much water collects. In some suburban and rural areas, wildlife can ravage a garden: Fences may be needed to keep out deer, rabbits and raccoons, or netting to keep out birds.

Next, consider the space requirements. Asparagus needs 18 inches between plants and 36 inches between rows; beans need only 6 inches between plants and 24 inches between rows, and yield more vegetables per plant besides. Seed packet instructions generally use a 15-foot row as a measure for determining yield. From that you can judge how much space to devote to vegetables and which ones you have room to grow.

When you have selected the site and size for your garden, you are ready to prepare the ground for planting. The best time to do so is when the soil is soft—after the last spring frost in your area *(map, inside back cover)*. Pick up a handful of soil, make a ball and drop it. If it falls apart, the soil is workable; if it sticks together, it is too hard or too wet. Once you have determined that the soil can be worked, follow some basic steps *(right and opposite)* for laying out the bed, tilling the soil and marking the placement of your rows.

*Neat rows of beans, leaf vegetables and root crops soak up sunlight in a garden bordered with eye-pleasing iris and peonies. Wide paths between rows allow for easy fertilizing, weeding and—the reason for it all—harvesting.*

1 Mark the perimeter of your vegetable garden with stakes and string. Facing into the garden, dig down with a spade just inside the marked perimeter to the depth of the blade; then turn the sod over into the garden area *(below)*. Repeat all along the perimeter. Remove the stakes and string for easy access.

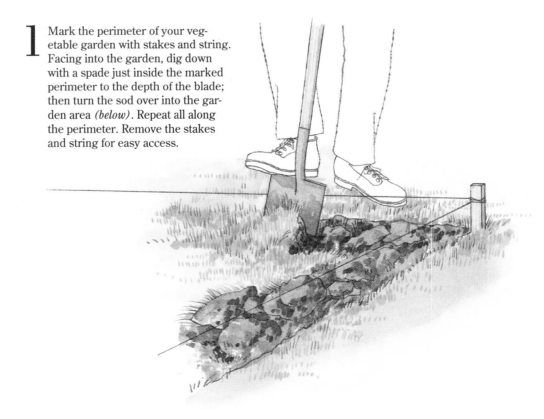

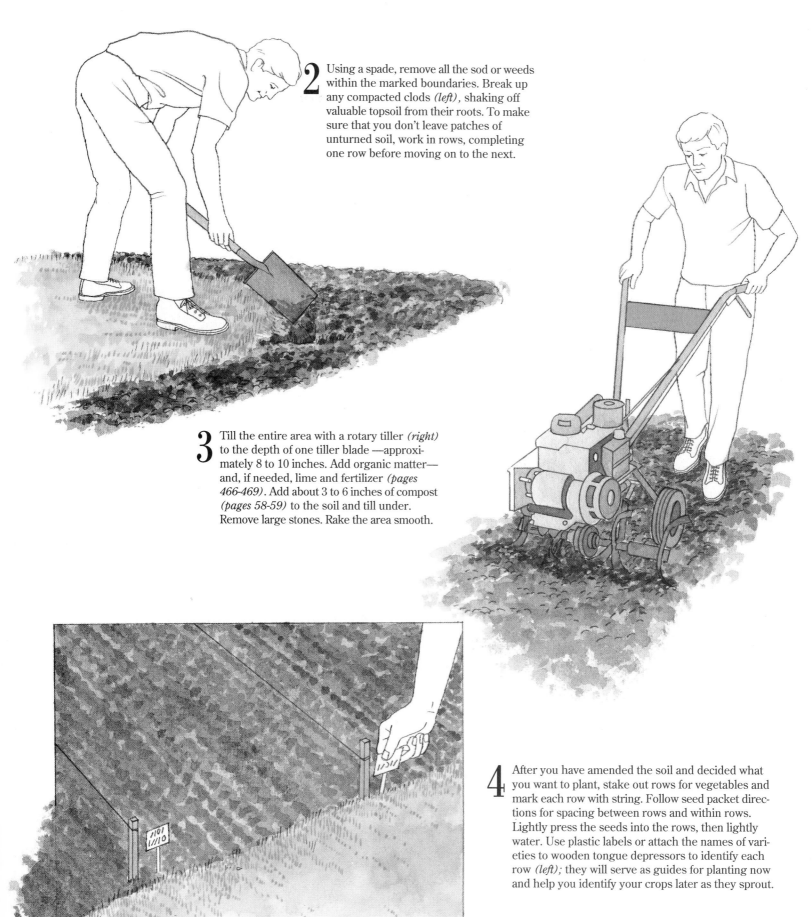

**2** Using a spade, remove all the sod or weeds within the marked boundaries. Break up any compacted clods *(left)*, shaking off valuable topsoil from their roots. To make sure that you don't leave patches of unturned soil, work in rows, completing one row before moving on to the next.

**3** Till the entire area with a rotary tiller *(right)* to the depth of one tiller blade —approximately 8 to 10 inches. Add organic matter— and, if needed, lime and fertilizer *(pages 466-469)*. Add about 3 to 6 inches of compost *(pages 58-59)* to the soil and till under. Remove large stones. Rake the area smooth.

**4** After you have amended the soil and decided what you want to plant, stake out rows for vegetables and mark each row with string. Follow seed packet directions for spacing between rows and within rows. Lightly press the seeds into the rows, then lightly water. Use plastic labels or attach the names of varieties to wooden tongue depressors to identify each row *(left);* they will serve as guides for planting now and help you identify your crops later as they sprout.

# SITING A GARDEN
# TO MAKE THE MOST OF THE SUN

Plants need sunlight, even more than compost and fertilizer, to grow. Most need at least seven hours of it each sunny day, or they may be stunted. So a vegetable garden should ideally be placed in full sun, and planted in such a fashion that the sunlight does the most good.

This is not always easy to achieve, especially in restricted backyard plots. Houses, walls and trees cast shadows that can be tricky to calculate. For example, in northern latitudes shadows stretch longer in all seasons than they do in, say, the Middle Atlantic states or the Deep South because of the sun's lower angle. For the same reason, shadows grow longer in all regions during the early spring and the autumn than they do during the bright days of June and July.

When siting a vegetable plot, therefore, take into account the sun's angle at various seasons and figure out in advance where plant-stunting shadows will fall. A wall that looks innocent in the brightness of May may throw part of a plot into deep shadow by late summer. Especially avoid a site where an obstruction will block the sun during the hot mid-day hours when sunlight does vegetables the most good. The best strategy, then, is to locate a garden as far from obstructions as possible, and to try to angle the plot so that it faces south—toward the sun—with any walls or trees on its northern border.

This is good advice in fact for siting any garden, even one in an ideal open area with no trees or walls anywhere about. A plot angled north-south, as in the example opposite, gives all the vegetables an equal share in the straight-on rays of the mid-day sun, and the canted light of morning and afternoon as well, as the sun's position moves from east to west.

Some shading by one plant of another is all right. If your garden is shaded part of the time, remember that leafy vegetables like lettuce and spinach, and the root vegetables, can get by with less than a full day's sun. But day-long sunshine is a necessity for plants that throw extra energy into producing fruit, such as tomatoes, squash and peppers.

*Tall-growing cornstalks shade a row of lettuce plants from the sharply slanted beams of an afternoon sun. In midsummer, lettuce needs partial shade during a portion of each day.*

464

# HOW THE SHADOWS FALL

The drawing at right shows the pattern of light and shade in an imaginary, but ideal, garden located at 40° north latitude—that is, along the line that runs more or less through New York, Indianapolis, Topeka and Denver to Sacramento. The garden is oriented north *(top)* to south, with the rows running east-west to catch the full benefit of the sun. The time is 10 a.m., as the west-leaning shadows indicate. The vegetables are planted so that they do not shade one another. The tallest, corn, is at the north end of the plot; the shortest, lettuce, is at the southern end.

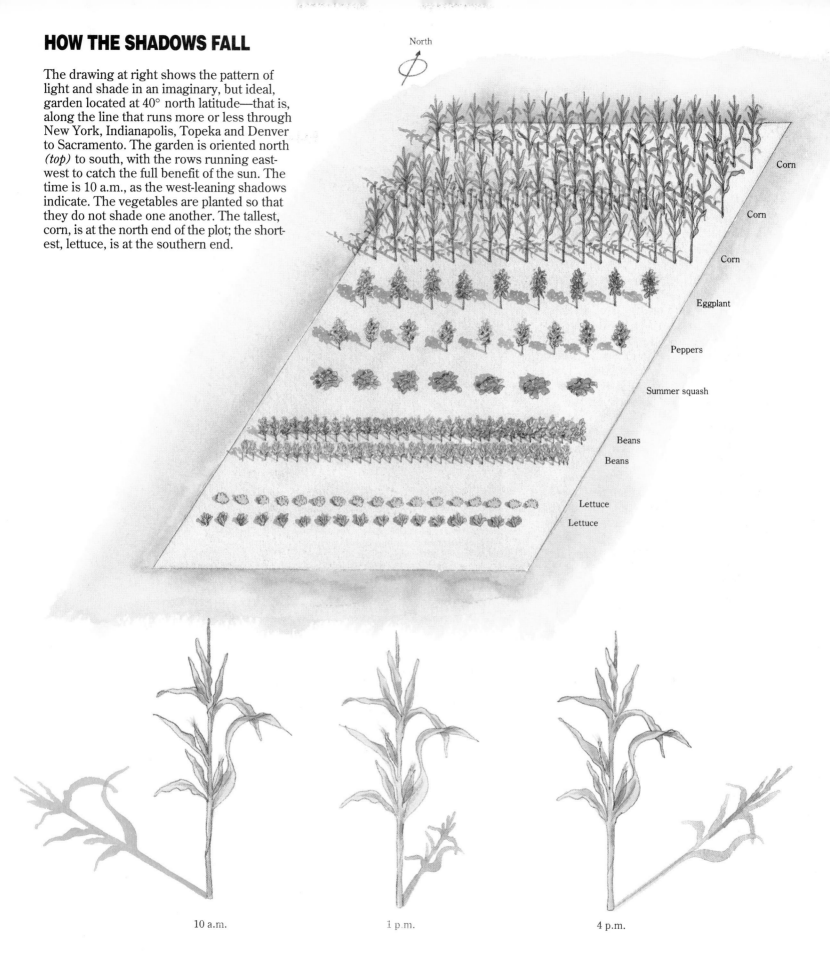

North

Corn

Corn

Corn

Eggplant

Peppers

Summer squash

Beans

Beans

Lettuce

Lettuce

10 a.m.

1 p.m.

4 p.m.

# YOUR SOIL AND ITS pH—
# AN ACID TEST

Among the most important factors in vegetable gardening is the pH level of the soil. The term "pH" represents a measurement of the soil's acidity or alkalinity on a scale of 0 to 14. The number 7 represents neutrality; the lower the number below that, the more acid the soil; the higher the number, the more alkaline it is. Most vegetables prefer a more acid soil with a pH around 6.5. If too alkaline, the soil does not promote the chemical activity that attracts the nutrients required for vegetable growth. If soil is too acidic, the soil attracts nutrients but does not release them. Excess acidity can be corrected by adding lime to the soil, and alkalinity can be controlled by adding sulfur.

In general, areas with clayey soil and high rainfall tend to be acidic; areas with sandy soil and low rainfall have a high salt content, which makes them alkaline. To determine the pH of your soil, gather a soil sample and test it with a do-it-yourself kit purchased at a garden supply center or through mail-order suppliers. Alternatively, your local agricultural extension service will test your soil for a nominal fee; fertilizer companies often perform a soil test free of charge.

Gather the soil sample when the ground is moist but not wet. Dig down 4 to 5 inches, and with a trowel, remove a scoop of soil and put it in a clean plastic bucket. Repeat in several places around the garden. Mix the scoopfuls together, remove a cupful, seal it in a plastic bag and mail it to the extension service. The test results will tell you the pH ratio, whether you should add lime or sulfur, and what amounts of either are needed. You can spread them by hand or, for best results, use a drop spreader *(opposite)*.

*Rows of lettuce and Chinese cabbage grow fat and leafy in a neatly tended garden. The soil's pH can be maintained at a level congenial to vegetables by periodic applications of lime (to correct acidity) or sulfur (if the soil is too alkaline).*

## GARDENING WITH CHILDREN

If you teach children to garden, they will experience a joy that will be with them the rest of their lives. To encourage children to garden, it is important to have them grow vegetables that will mature quickly so that they can see the results of their efforts right away.

Large vegetable seeds are the easiest for children to handle; corn, beans, beets, carrots and seed potatoes are all good choices. Children also enjoy raising colorful tomato plants. There are varieties of both full-sized beefsteak and cherry tomatoes that mature quickly: see pages 525-526. Interplanting natural insect repellants like easy-to-grow marigolds and nasturtiums with vegetables helps introduce children to garden planning.

**1** After turning over the soil and calculating how much lime or sulfur you need to add (based on pH test results, soil type and the size of your garden), set the calibration device *(inset)* on the drop spreader. Some spreaders come with recommended settings; if yours does not, set it at the medium opening *(right)*. Open and close the hopper to make sure the mechanism works. Fill the hopper with lime or sulfur.

**2** Working at an even pace, walk the spreader around the perimeter of the garden, then up and down in rows *(below)*. Don't let rows of lime (or sulfur, if that is what you are adding) overlap, or you will overcorrect the problem. Keep the hopper closed on turns between rows. If any lime (or sulfur) is left over, it means your calibration was off. Reset the calibration to a small opening and walk the entire site again so you will have given the garden its full measure of lime or sulfur. Then till it into the soil.

# NUTRIENTS FOR HEALTHY SOIL

Like growing children, growing vegetables need a balanced diet. Most soils lack sufficient nutrients to keep vegetables healthy. To find out what's missing and what supplements to add, gather a soil sample *(page 466)* and have it tested by your agricultural extension service. Or purchase a home-testing kit and do it yourself. Since soil conditions change over time, retest every three to four years.

The three most important nutrients for vegetables are nitrogen (for healthy leaves), phosphorus (for healthy roots) and potassium (for strong stalks and resistance to disease). The test results will tell you exactly how much of these nutrients to add to the soil before planting the vegetables.

Commercial fertilizers that are sold as "complete" contain all three major nutrients in a predetermined ratio; for example, the numbers 5-10-5 on a label refer to the percentages of nitrogen, phosphorus and potassium in the product. Follow the manufacturer's instructions for application. Too much of any nutrient can be as harmful to plants as too little. Organic fertilizers such as animal manure, fish meal and alfalfa meal are also good sources of nutrients. If possible, use aged, dry manure; unless it is plowed into the soil in the fall and allowed to decompose over the winter, fresh manure can injure roots; it also begets weeds that will compete with the crops.

There are several alternative methods of applying fertilizer. One is to spread fertilizer evenly over the site with a drop spreader and then turn the soil under to a depth of 3 to 4 inches; for the best results, this should be done in the fall. Another is to fertilize row by row just before spring planting *(opposite)*.

A third method is called side-dressing *(opposite)*—placing fertilizer alongside rows— and a variation of that is band-dressing, placing fertilizer in a ring around an individual plant *(box, opposite)*. One or the other of these two methods should be done when plants blossom, and again at three- to four-week intervals until harvest time.

*Celery grows crisp and green in soil that has been well-fertilized with nitrogen, phosphorus and potassium.*

## CROPS TO IMPROVE THE SOIL

After the garden is harvested in autumn, planting a cover crop, also called green manure, will prevent erosion, add nutrients to the soil, improve drainage and choke out weeds. Green manure is a crop not grown for its edible or ornamental value.

If you have a large vegetable garden and will not be growing crops on the entire space during summer, plant a cover crop instead of allowing the land to stand fallow. Move the cover crop from one area to another each year for a regular program of soil improvement.

Annual ryegrass is a popular cover crop that grows during the fall and can be tilled under just before spring planting so the soil is at its best for the new growing season. Legumes such as soybeans are good summer cover crops because they add nitrogen to the soil.

**1** To concentrate fertilizer under a seed row before planting, dig a trench along the marked row with a mattock *(left)* or a hoe. The trench should be 2 inches deeper than the recommended depth of the seeds you will plant. This will vary from crop to crop; follow the instructions on the seed packet.

**2** Spread 1 to 1½ pounds of complete fertilizer (containing nitrogen, phosphorus and potassium in a ratio such as 5-10-5) into every 100 feet of trench. Use a rake *(below)* to cover the fertilizer with 2 inches of soil. Tamp down. Sow the seeds on top of the soil and cover them with more soil according to instructions on the packet. To release the fertilizer nutrients, water the soil.

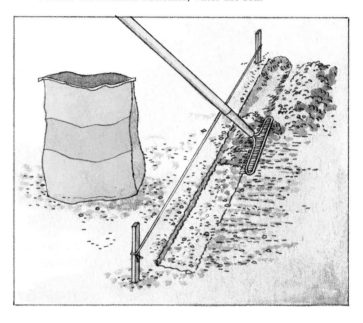

**3** Once your plants have blossomed, fertilize them again, applying a side-dressing row by row. Use a mattock or a hoe to dig a 2-inch-deep trench alongside each row at the drip line (the outermost edge of the foliage). By hand, spread 1 to 1½ pounds of complete fertilizer per 100 feet of trench *(left)*. Cover with 2 inches of soil. Tamp down.

## FERTILIZING PLANT BY PLANT

To band-dress individual plants, dig a trench 2 inches deep around each plant at the drip line. Sprinkle 2 tablespoons of complete fertilizer inside the trench; then refill it with soil. Or, apply half a handful of slow-release fertilizer around the plant stem; then add water to release the fertilizer's nutrients.

469

# CROP ROTATION—A DEFENSE AGAINST PESTS AND DISEASES

The phrase "crop rotation" brings to mind huge fields of wheat and corn stretching across the Kansas plains. But rotating crops, long known to be essential for good yields on large-scale farms, pays off even in relatively small vegetable gardens. It is a good idea before planting seedlings outdoors *(pages 476-477)* to map out a rotation scheme that will be useful in the coming years.

First of all, rotating crops yearly from one part of a garden to another helps control insect pests and the plant diseases they carry. It works because most pests are attracted to only one family of plants. For example, hornworms, whiteflies and Colorado potato beetles zero in solely on members of the potato family (which includes eggplant, peppers and tomatoes). These pests and those that attack other vegetables live in the soil through the winter and attack again the next spring. But if the crops they feed on are moved next season, the pests will be left behind and die for want of food and the vacated plot will be safe for plants of another family.

Crop rotation also avoids depleting the soil of nutrients. Some plants, such as corn, soak up nutrients at a ferocious rate.

*Healthy, pest-free lettuce, beet greens and carrots share space in a thriving garden. Carrots and beets attract the same pests and should be rotated into a new bed each year. Lettuce and other leaf crops should be moved because they consume large amounts of nutrients, especially nitrogen.*

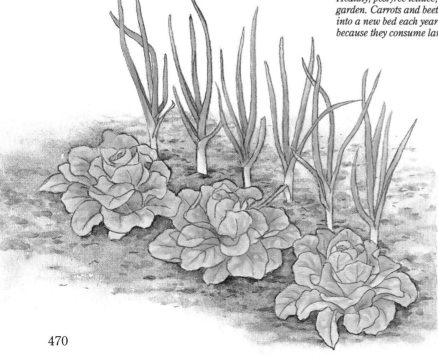

## NATURAL INSECT REPELLANT

Certain plants will help to keep unwanted insects out of your vegetable garden. Garlic *(left, behind lettuce)* repels aphids. Radishes can be planted near beans, cucumbers, eggplants, squash and tomatoes to discourage beetles and mites. Rosemary wards off moths and Mexican bean beetles.

Nasturtiums keep aphids, beetles and squash bugs away. Plant beans near potatoes to repel Mexican bean beetles. Marigolds can be fatal to nematodes and will deter Colorado potato beetles. Locate tomato plants near asparagus to discourage asparagus beetles. Petunias control leafhoppers, Mexican bean beetles and some aphids.

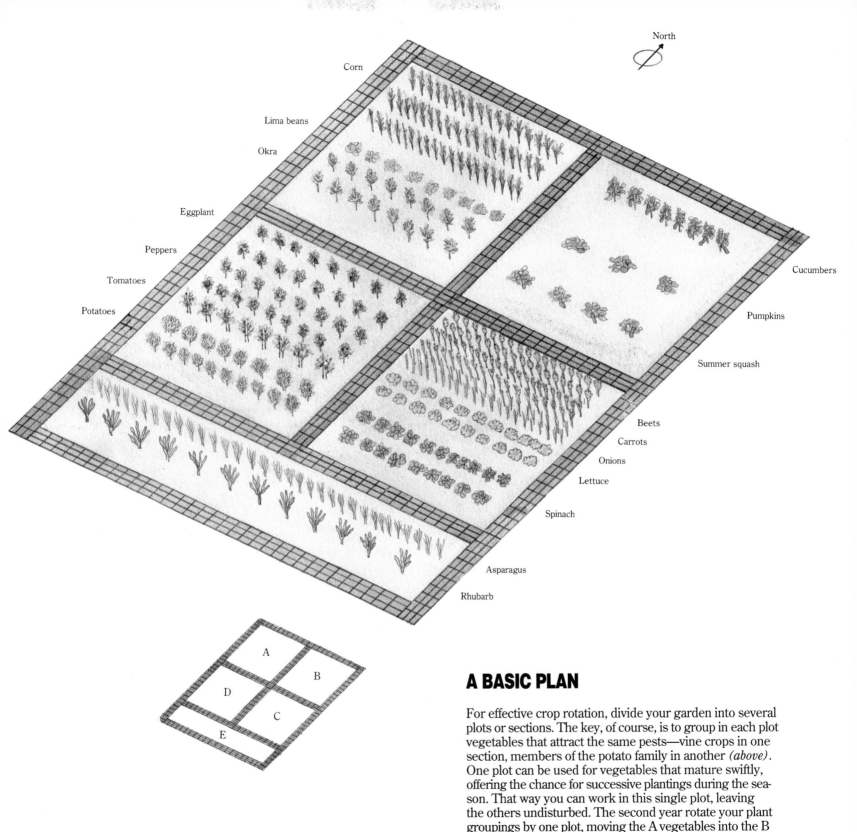

North

Corn

Lima beans

Okra

Eggplant

Peppers

Tomatoes

Potatoes

Cucumbers

Pumpkins

Summer squash

Beets

Carrots

Onions

Lettuce

Spinach

Asparagus

Rhubarb

A

B

D

C

E

## A BASIC PLAN

For effective crop rotation, divide your garden into several plots or sections. The key, of course, is to group in each plot vegetables that attract the same pests—vine crops in one section, members of the potato family in another *(above)*. One plot can be used for vegetables that mature swiftly, offering the chance for successive plantings during the season. That way you can work in this single plot, leaving the others undisturbed. The second year rotate your plant groupings by one plot, moving the A vegetables into the B section, the B into the C and so on *(left)*. Continue the same progression each successive season. The exceptions to this rotation are the perennials, asparagus and rhubarb, which should remain quiet in their own isolated bed (E).

# PREPARING THE GARDEN FOR SOWING

*Evenly spaced and standing in an orderly row, bush bean seedlings sprout about two weeks after having been sown directly in garden soil.*

Before you put seeds in the ground, make sure that the soil has been properly tilled and amended *(pages 466-469)*. The texture should be fine and crumbly, moist but not soggy. Remove clods and stones; rake until the surface is smooth and level.

Test the temperature of the soil with a soil thermometer before sowing. Soil that is too cold will inhibit germination and stunt growth. If the soil temperature is below 65° F, lay a light mulch of leaves or straw over the soil and test again a few days later.

Lay out and mark seedbeds in straight rows, using stakes and string or a ready-made row marker, a device consisting of stakes with coiled string attached; you unwind the string as you walk along the row. For guidance on how deep to plant seeds, follow instructions on the seed packets. Seeds that are planted even a few inches deeper than recommended will not germinate. Consult the Dictionary of Vegetables on page 506 for details on many vegetables.

After covering the seeds with soil, water the bed immediately, but use a light spray to avoid either dislodging the seeds or disturbing the soil surface. Continue spraying to keep the ground moist during and after germination. To retain moisture and block intense sunlight, cover the seedbed with a thin layer of grass clippings or compost.

When seeds start to sprout, thin the seedlings to the spacing indicated on the seed packet; when overcrowded, they will never mature into healthy plants. Remove the least vigorous seedlings. Instead of pulling them up by the roots—which can damage nearby plants—cut them off at the base of the stem with a knife or a pair of scissors.

There are two ways to sow seeds outdoors: by hand, or with an all-in-one-operation wheel seeder like the one shown on page 475.

To get a jump on the season, you can start seeds early indoors *(pages 80-81)*, and then transplant the seedlings into your garden.

## TESTING SOIL TEMPERATURE

To germinate, most summer vegetable seeds need to be planted in warm soil. A soil temperature of 75° F is just right for the majority of vegetables. As soil temperatures dip toward 65° F, however, fewer seeds germinate, and the early growth and mature development of many crops is inhibited.

On any given day, air temperature and soil temperature may vary by as much as 10 degrees or more. To get a reliable reading of the soil temperature, insert a soil thermometer into the ground to a depth of 2 to 3 inches *(right)*. Delay planting if the soil is too cold. A light mulch of leaves or straw will keep the soil from drying out in the wind and from becoming waterlogged from spring rains.

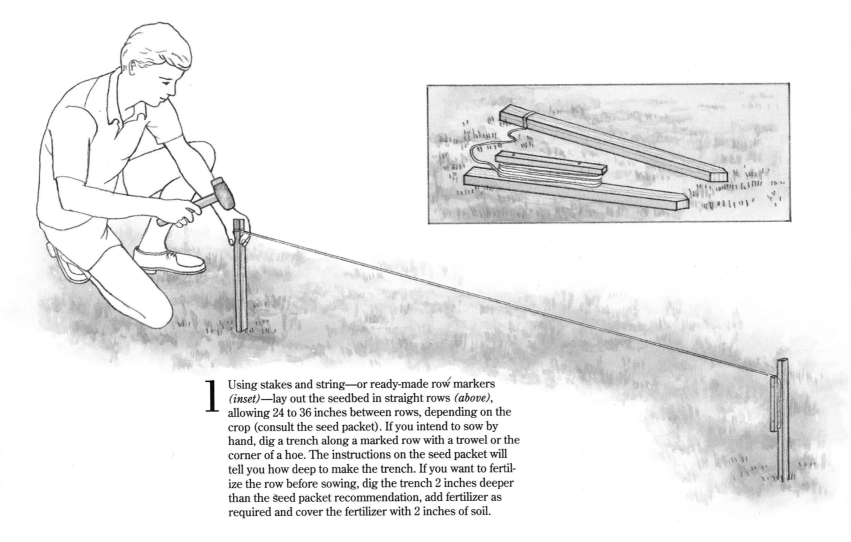

**1** Using stakes and string—or ready-made row markers *(inset)*—lay out the seedbed in straight rows *(above)*, allowing 24 to 36 inches between rows, depending on the crop (consult the seed packet). If you intend to sow by hand, dig a trench along a marked row with a trowel or the corner of a hoe. The instructions on the seed packet will tell you how deep to make the trench. If you want to fertilize the row before sowing, dig the trench 2 inches deeper than the seed packet recommendation, add fertilizer as required and cover the fertilizer with 2 inches of soil.

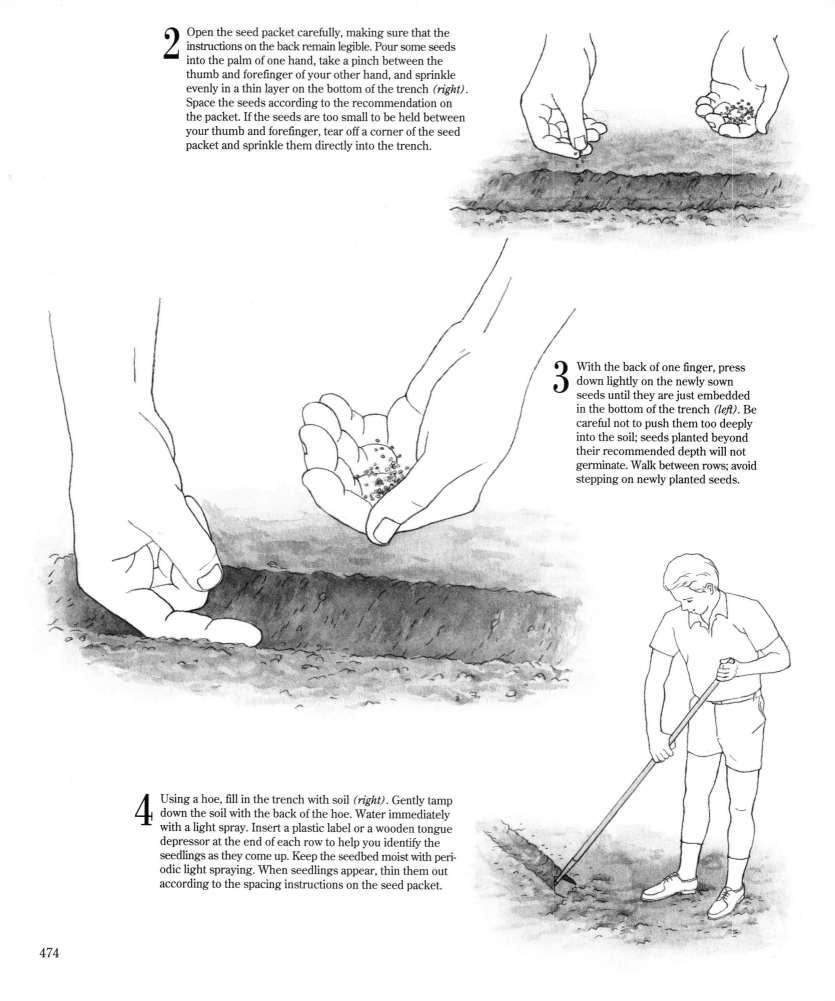

**2** Open the seed packet carefully, making sure that the instructions on the back remain legible. Pour some seeds into the palm of one hand, take a pinch between the thumb and forefinger of your other hand, and sprinkle evenly in a thin layer on the bottom of the trench *(right)*. Space the seeds according to the recommendation on the packet. If the seeds are too small to be held between your thumb and forefinger, tear off a corner of the seed packet and sprinkle them directly into the trench.

**3** With the back of one finger, press down lightly on the newly sown seeds until they are just embedded in the bottom of the trench *(left)*. Be careful not to push them too deeply into the soil; seeds planted beyond their recommended depth will not germinate. Walk between rows; avoid stepping on newly planted seeds.

**4** Using a hoe, fill in the trench with soil *(right)*. Gently tamp down the soil with the back of the hoe. Water immediately with a light spray. Insert a plastic label or a wooden tongue depressor at the end of each row to help you identify the seedlings as they come up. Keep the seedbed moist with periodic light spraying. When seedlings appear, thin them out according to the spacing instructions on the seed packet.

# ONE-STEP SOWING

A wheel seeder is a simple but ingenious device that allows you to combine all the steps involved in sowing seeds into a single operation. As you push the wheel seeder up and down each marked row *(right)*, it digs a trench to a preset depth, automatically drops and spaces the seeds, fills in the trench and tamps down the soil. You can buy many different models of wheel seeders at garden-supply centers: but most share the features illustrated below.

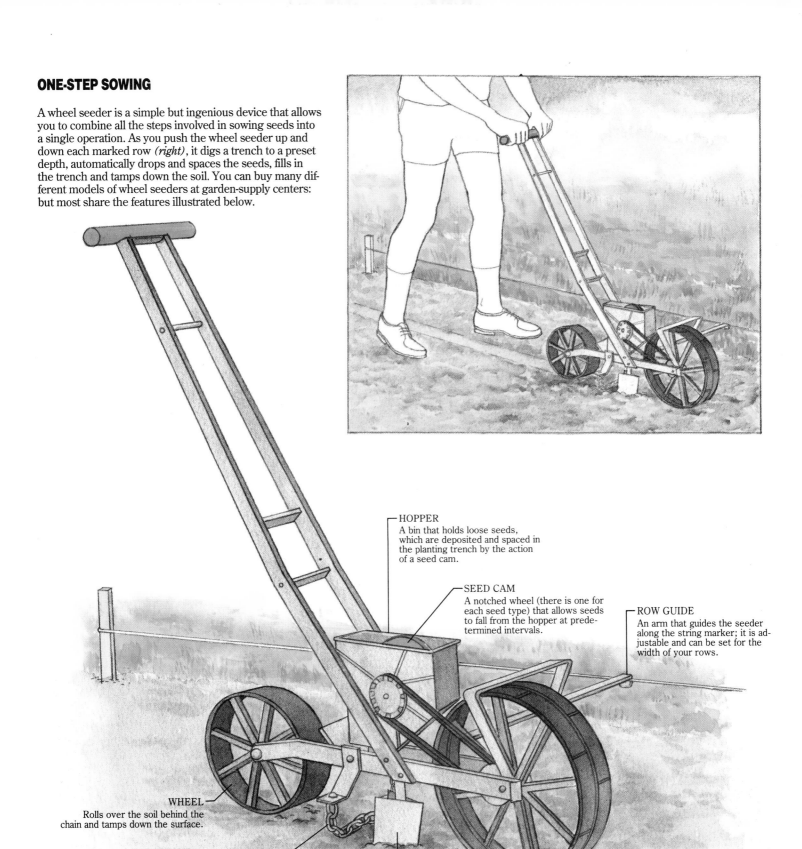

HOPPER
A bin that holds loose seeds, which are deposited and spaced in the planting trench by the action of a seed cam.

SEED CAM
A notched wheel (there is one for each seed type) that allows seeds to fall from the hopper at predetermined intervals.

ROW GUIDE
An arm that guides the seeder along the string marker; it is adjustable and can be set for the width of your rows.

WHEEL
Rolls over the soil behind the chain and tamps down the surface.

CHAIN
Drags on the ground behind the plow and covers the seeded trench with soil.

PLOW
A small blade that can be set to dig a trench at a depth appropriate to the seeds you are planting.

# RELIEVING STRESS ON YOUNG PLANTS

**F**or vegetable seedlings begun indoors, the move into the strong sun, brisk breezes and a garden full of busy pests can be hazardous and stressful. But there are several ways to ease the passage and get the seedlings off to a good start. One is a process called hardening off—gradually acclimating young plants to their new, rougher environment. About 10 days before the recommended time for transplanting arrives, move the seedlings outdoors for an hour, then for two hours the second day, then for three and so on until they have been in the sun for a full 10 hours. If you buy seedlings from a greenhouse, acclimate them the same way. If you buy them at a nursery, ask whether they have been hardened off. If they have not, harden them off before you plant them. This sort of gradual, gentle treatment is especially important for tender plants such as tomatoes, eggplant and peppers.

When they are ready for transplanting, choose a cool, cloudy day or a time in the late afternoon, when the sun is waning. Seedlings begun in peat pots can be planted pot and all; those begun in plastic cell packs should be watered and then removed before being set in the ground *(below and opposite)*. After the transplants' leaves begin to droop slightly, water them. A good soaking diminishes stress and the root balls will slip out of the containers more easily.

*A strong, leafy young tomato plant wears a collar of newspaper to fend off cutworms. The paper will eventually crumble away, will not harm the plant and will prevent cutworms from climbing the stem.*

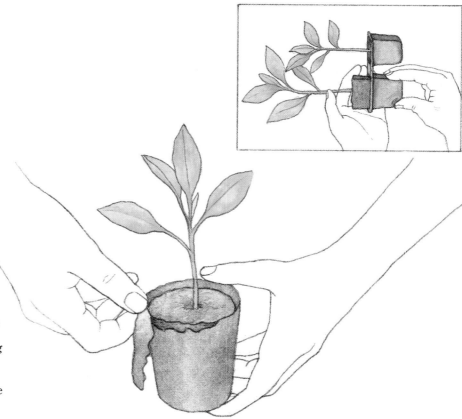

1 Before planting a seedling grown in a small peat pot, tear off about ½ inch of the pot's rim, as shown at right; an exposed rim will siphon moisture from the roots. To remove a seedling from a plastic cell pack *(inset)*, squeeze the bottom of the pack gently and ease the plant out. If the seedling roots are curled around the pot sides, gently tease the roots apart.

476

**2** To protect your plants from the menace of cutworms, rip newspaper into 3-inch squares. Wrap each square around a plant's main stem *(right)*. About half of a collar should protrude above ground when the seedling is planted.

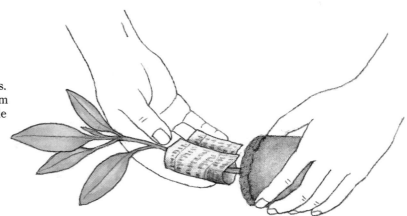

**3** To plant a seedling, dig a hole with a trowel a couple of inches deeper than the depth of the peat pot—or the root ball, if the seedling has been removed from its container. Into the bottom of the hole sprinkle ½ teaspoon of fertilizer. Cover the fertilizer with 2 inches of soil that has been well mixed with compost or a small amount of general-purpose fertilizer. Plant the seedling and firm the soil around it *(left)*. Water immediately and then water some more for at least five days.

## TOMATOES ON THE SIDE

Tomato seedlings often become too tall and spindly. The best way to plant one of these precocious, leggy plants is on its side, the long stem in the ground and only 6 inches of foliage in the air. First, dig a small trench about 4 inches deep and as long as the stem. Sprinkle in some fertilizer and cover the fertilizer with a 2-inch layer of enriched soil. Remove any leaves from the stem and then lay it horizontally in the trench. Cover the roots and stem with more soil. The top 6 inches of the plant's foliage will soon turn upward toward the sun.

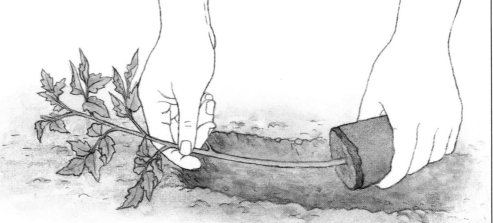

# INTERPLANTING CROPS FOR BONUS YIELDS

**W**ild grasses and other plants in an uncultivated field manage to prosper even though they often grow almost on top of one another. They survive the crowding in part because some of the plants shoot up early, mature swiftly and then die back, allowing their slower-growing neighbors an unimpeded chance at the sun.

This principle can be applied in a vegetable garden. A number of vegetables are spring growers and mature early. Others are best planted in midseason. You can overlap them, planting some midseason vegetables well before the early growers have finished producing. By the time the new plants need a full measure of space, light and air, the older ones will have gone to seed.

This technique, called interplanting, makes maximum use of a garden's space and can dramatically increase its yield. And it can be done with a variety of crops. Green peppers grow with lettuce in the photograph at right; the drawings show how to interplant peppers with broccoli. For other successful pairings, see the box on the opposite page.

A parallel method of extending a garden's harvest is to stagger the times certain crops mature. Planting a few summer squash on, say, June 15 and then another batch on July 1 will produce two separate crops a couple of weeks apart. Similarly, the harvest can be lengthened by planting several different versions of the same vegetable at the same time. Tomatoes, for example, are available in early-, mid- or late-season varieties. And some hybrid corns ripen in only 54 days; others take as long as 80 days. Growing both ensures a long season of sweet, homegrown corn.

*The shiny green leaves of young sweet pepper plants emerge between rows of butterhead lettuce (bottom) and red leaf lettuce (top). Both lettuces will have been harvested long before the peppers mature.*

**1** To interplant green pepper seedlings with mature broccoli plants, first use a trowel to clear away any weeds that have grown up, then make room for the peppers by trimming the lower broccoli leaves with a knife or garden shears as shown.

**2** Dig holes for the seedlings in a staggered pattern between broccoli plants *(inset, below)*. To the soil you have removed, add organic matter. Sprinkle fertilizer in the holes, then pour in some amended soil. Put a seedling in each hole, add more soil and tamp lightly. Water well.

**3** After a few weeks, if your timing has been right, the pepper seedlings should have begun to mature—and the broccoli plants will have ceased yielding. At that stage, remove the older plants by cutting them off at ground level *(left)*. Do not bother to dig up the roots; let them stay in the ground to rot, and thus enrich the garden soil.

### GOOD COMBINATIONS

Cucumbers and Peppers
Spinach and Onions
Broccoli and Peppers
Carrots and Beets or Radishes
Corn and Squash or Cucumbers
Lettuce and Onions, Radishes or Beets

# ASPARAGUS: A PERENNIAL SPRING TREAT

*Crisp asparagus spears shoot up shortly after the ground has thawed. Spears are ready for harvest when they are 6 to 8 inches high. They should be cut off at ground level with a knife—but carefully, so that the blade does not slice into roots or spears forming underground.*

## SHADING LETTUCE FROM MIDSUMMER SUN

Lettuce and other leafy vegetables like the sun—in moderation. To keep your lettuce growing and harvestable throughout the summer, shelter the plants from direct sunlight beneath a temporary shade structure. A typical shade structure consists of white screening material—cheesecloth is ideal—stretched across a semirigid framework. The screening material must be thin enough to let light through while blocking much of the sun's heat. The framework must be sturdy enough to withstand winds.

Grown since ancient times, asparagus is treasured not only because it is the first green vegetable to pop up each spring and a delectable one, but also because its tender spears grow of their own accord year after year. Unlike most other vegetables, asparagus is a perennial and a hardy one at that. Well cared for beds produce for 15 years and more.

Such a marvel naturally has its quirks. Asparagus thrives only where winters have enough bite to cause freezing, since the roots must become dormant to renew themselves. That rules out the Deep South (Florida and Louisiana, for example) and other warm regions. Yet asparagus plants need plenty of hot summer sun. A bed should be located in full sunlight, and in a spot where there is shelter from chill spring winds.

Asparagus also requires a good deal of space. Growing enough to satisfy a family of four takes two rows about 20 feet long and spaced at least 4 feet apart. The soil should be light, loose and well drained. Planting should be done in the spring. In buying stock to plant, select the largest one-year-old crowns your nursery has for sale. They should look crisp and have moist, healthy roots. How to cultivate a bed and plant the rows is shown opposite and on the following pages. Asparagus does not compete well with weeds, so keep the bed area weed-free.

A last quirk of asparagus is that the roots must mature in the ground for two years before spears are harvested. None should be cut the year of planting and few, if any, the next spring. The third year, spears can be cut for four weeks. After that, asparagus can be harvested for six to eight weeks each spring.

The uncut spears of the first years, and some every year afterward, should be allowed to continue growing. They will form handsome ferny bushes about 5 feet tall. Besides being decorative, the foliage creates sugars that, stored in the roots through the winter, increase the next spring's crop. When the bushes turn brown in the fall, they should be cut back—and added to the compost pile to make mulch for another season.

1 To begin planting asparagus, first spade the bed to a depth of 18 inches and work in generous amounts of well-seasoned manure or weed-free compost. In the spaded area, dig trenches about 8 inches deep and 12 inches wide, with ample space (4 to 6 feet) between them. Set the soil from the trenches aside. If it is heavy, amend it: Make it more crumbly with extra compost, sand, leaf mold or fine topsoil. Make a series of 3-inch-high mounds in each trench at 18-inch intervals *(left)*.

2 Gently hold the crown you have bought and snip off any broken or rotted roots with a garden clipper *(right)*. Then trim the roots again, removing a maximum of 2 or 3 inches, to make them roughly equal in length. Note: Nurseries often sell crowns that are two and three years old. Avoid them. Although large, they do not produce a crop any sooner than one-year-old crowns, can carry disease and are harder to plant successfully.

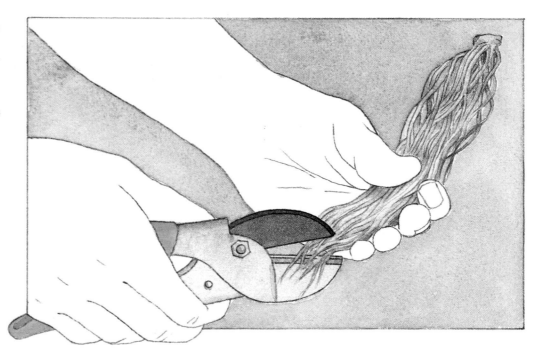

**3** Place the crowns over the soil mounds you have made in the trenches. Spread the roots apart carefully *(left)*. It is important that the soil in the trenches be free of weeds; asparagus suffers from the competition weeds offer for water and nutrients. Large ones entangled in asparagus roots are particularly harmful.

**4** Cover each crown with 3 inches of the soil that was dug from the trench *(right)*. Gently sprinkle the mounds with water. Moderate but frequent watering works best. You do not want to flood the trenches, and asparagus roots do not thrive if they are too wet.

**5** When purplish shoots appear, cover them with more soil *(below)*. Repeat the process each time shoots come up until the trenches are filled. Then add a bit more; the finished trenches should be slightly mounded and the roots should be no more than 8 or 9 inches underground *(inset)*. A few weeks after you have finished planting, apply some general-purpose fertilizer and cover the bed with a layer of mulch to conserve water and retard weeds. A second application of fertilizer in the fall is also a good idea. Continue fertilizing each year, pulling back the mulch while you work the fertilizer into the soil.

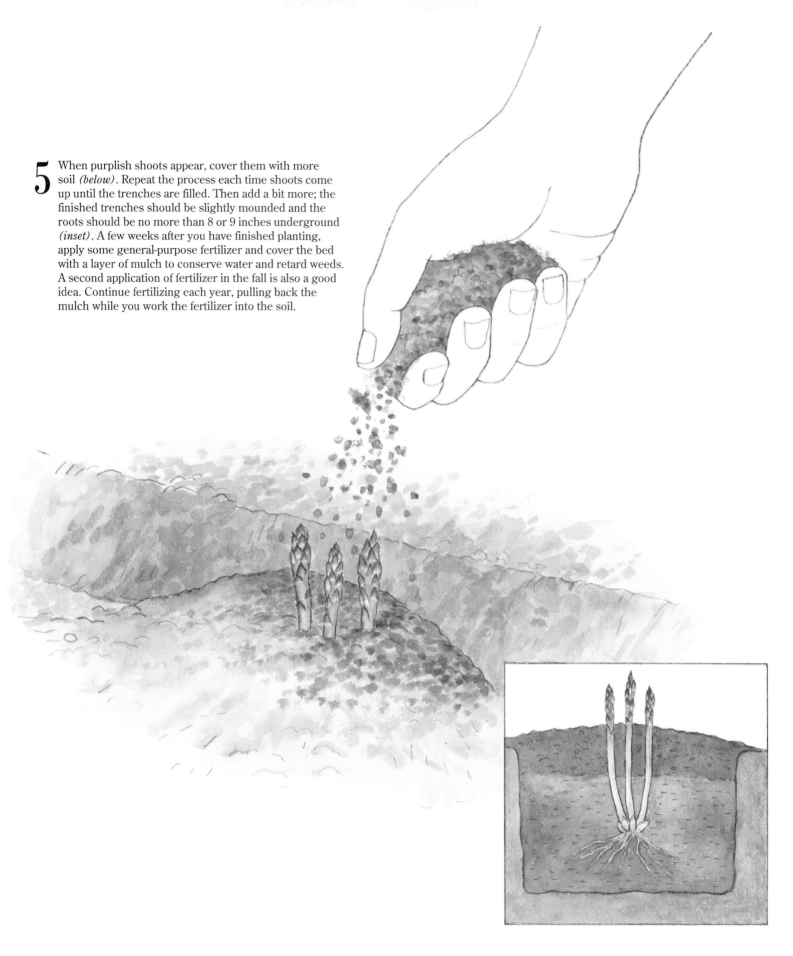

# PREPARING A BED FOR ROOT CROPS

*Cornstalks, carrot tops, lettuce and other vegetable greens stand together in a raised bed—along with a row of marigolds, which help repel bugs.*

Vegetables that are grown for their edible roots—carrots, beets, parsnips—are among the tastiest and most healthful of all vegetable. They also offer some practical advantages to the home gardener. They have the effect of lengthening the summer growing season. Most can be planted earlier in the spring than other vegetables because, lodged snugly underground, they do not suffer from the season's last frosty cold snaps. Similarly, they continue growing, waiting to be harvested, even after the first hard frosts of autumn have shriveled most other crops. And after having been harvested, they keep remarkably well. They stay fresh for months if they are stored in a cold cellar or in some other cool place, so they provide homegrown vegetables for the table throughout the winter.

Because the roots are the most important part of these vegetables, good soil conditions are critical. A raised bed is ideal: It has good drainage and the roots will develop undisturbed by hard, compacted earth. But root crops can also be started from seed in any well-prepared area of the garden.

For an easy start, the seeds should planted in a light, loose growing medium such as a mixture of vermiculite and dry peat moss *(opposite)*, which allows the roots to grow evenly and without resistance. In establishing their nourishing roots, these plants consume soil nutrients at a rapid clip, so before planting them it is a good idea to sprinkle fertilizer on the bed and work it into the soil with a spade. The type of fertilizer used depends on the particular vegetable being planted. After the planting is done, the bed should be mulched, to retard weeds and conserve moisture, and treated to frequent waterings.

## A RAISED VEGETABLE BED

If space is limited, the soil is unfit for use or has poor drainage, you can grow vegetables in a raised vegetable bed *(above)*. The bed can be any length, but no more than 6 feet wide, so that all parts of it will be within easy reach. To construct such a bed:

• Outline the area with stakes and string.
• Buy lengths of 6-by-6 landscape timbers of rot-resistant redwood or cedar and wire mesh to keep out tunneling animals.
• Lay the timber in two courses beside the outlined area, then bolt the timber together.
• Staple a piece of mesh (slightly larger than the area enclosed by the timber) to the wood.
• Fill the bed with soil. Your vegetable bed is now ready for planting.

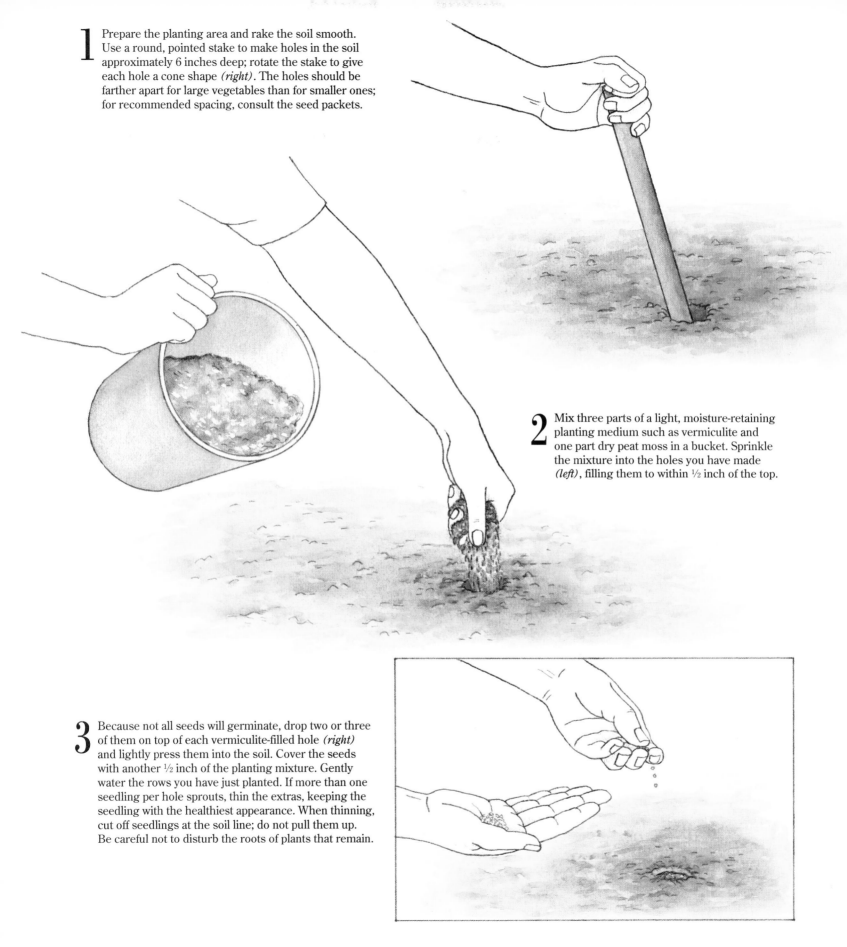

1 Prepare the planting area and rake the soil smooth. Use a round, pointed stake to make holes in the soil approximately 6 inches deep; rotate the stake to give each hole a cone shape *(right)*. The holes should be farther apart for large vegetables than for smaller ones; for recommended spacing, consult the seed packets.

2 Mix three parts of a light, moisture-retaining planting medium such as vermiculite and one part dry peat moss in a bucket. Sprinkle the mixture into the holes you have made *(left)*, filling them to within ½ inch of the top.

3 Because not all seeds will germinate, drop two or three of them on top of each vermiculite-filled hole *(right)* and lightly press them into the soil. Cover the seeds with another ½ inch of the planting mixture. Gently water the rows you have just planted. If more than one seedling per hole sprouts, thin the extras, keeping the seedling with the healthiest appearance. When thinning, cut off seedlings at the soil line; do not pull them up. Be careful not to disturb the roots of plants that remain.

# PLASTIC MULCH
# FOR WEED CONTROL

*Sweet potato plants spread their leaves above a protective sheet of black plastic. By conserving water, holding heat and eliminating weeds, plastic mulch gives vegetables a head start on the growing season.*

W hat's good for one plant in a garden tends to be good for other plants. That's why it can be difficult to encourage the growth of vegetables while trying to discourage the growth of weeds. Fortunately, there is one way to do both at the same time: Lay down a mulch.

A mulch is any layer of material, organic or inorganic, that you place on the ground around plants. Mulches not only keep weed seeds from germinating by blocking sunlight, they conserve moisture by inhibiting evaporation and act as insulation against extremes in soil temperature. Mulches also act as excellent soil erosion prevention, and can serve to warm up the soil in spring to speed up the growth of seeds and transplants.

Organic mulches, such as well-rotted compost, hay, shredded leaves, ground corncobs and bark chips, also improve soil texture and fertility. But they have drawbacks as well; hay harbors weed seeds, bark can be infested with ants and termites, and some of the organic mulches actually leach nitrogen from the soil as they decompose.

Inorganic mulches range from old newspapers to large rolls of aluminum foil and black plastic available at garden-supply centers. A major drawback of paper and foil is that they look unnatural in a garden; foil is also costly and hard to handle.

Many home gardeners mulch with plastic because it is inexpensive, easy to install and unsurpassed for weed control. Laid down at planting time, sheets of plastic also keep foliage clean, which can prevent disease. And by helping to warm the soil, a plastic mulch can hasten the ripening of warm-season crops like peppers and tomatoes by as much as 14 days.

Black plastic sheets are relatively unobtrusive; to hide them entirely, cover them with a thin layer of organic material. Plastic mulch is sold in rolls 1½ to 3 feet wide, just right for a broad row of vegetables.

## MAKING THE MOST OF SMALL SPACES

When garden space is limited, the right combination of compact plants and a variety of containers can be used to produce vegetables. Anything from clay pots to wooden barrels, plastic buckets and discarded tires will hold your crops. Patios, balconies and porches can be transformed into vegetable gardens.

Hot peppers *(right)* and eggplant are compact plants that are suitable for container growing. Full-sized tomatoes and cucumbers are available on compact plants. Root crops such as beets and carrots take up little space, and some vegetables—garlic, leeks and onions—don't mind being crowded.

Summer annuals may be mixed with vegetables in containers to add a colorful finishing touch to your garden.

1 After tilling and preparing the soil for planting, use a rake to build a low mound of soil the length of the row *(left)*. Rake the soil up from the two long sides, leaving a shallow depression on either side. Smooth the soil on top of the mound. Remove clods and large stones. If you plan to use drip irrigation *(pages 62-64)*, install it at this time. Drip irrigation coupled with black plastic mulch is the most efficient way to maintain soil moisture, especially in drought-prone areas such as California and the southwestern U.S.

2 Unroll a length of black plastic mulch to match the length of the row *(right)*. Secure the plastic at one end with a few small stones and drape it over the earthen mound. Use a pair of scissors to cut the roll to fit.

**3** With your fingers, work the edge of the plastic sheet into the ground on both sides of the row and at the ends to a depth of 2 inches *(right)*. To anchor the plastic against wind and rain, push loose soil over the edge of the sheet and tamp it down.

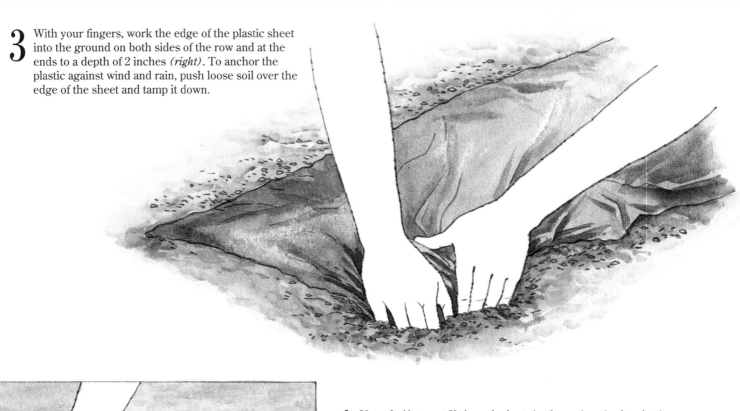

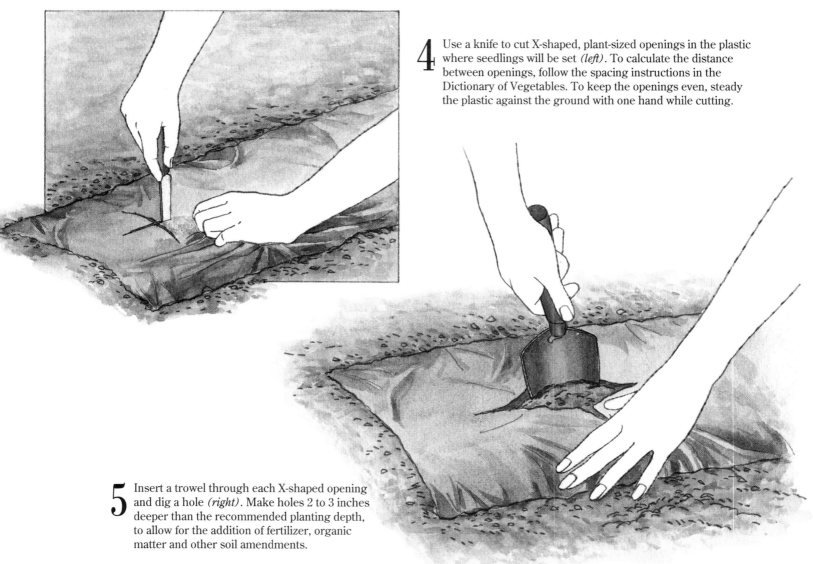

**4** Use a knife to cut X-shaped, plant-sized openings in the plastic where seedlings will be set *(left)*. To calculate the distance between openings, follow the spacing instructions in the Dictionary of Vegetables. To keep the openings even, steady the plastic against the ground with one hand while cutting.

**5** Insert a trowel through each X-shaped opening and dig a hole *(right)*. Make holes 2 to 3 inches deeper than the recommended planting depth, to allow for the addition of fertilizer, organic matter and other soil amendments.

**6** Fill each hole with water to give the soil a good soaking *(below)*. Let the water drain out the bottom of each hole. Since the plastic mulch will inhibit evaporation from the soil surface, much of the water will remain available to the roots of the plant as it grows. Continue digging holes and filling them with water until you have completed the row.

**7** When the water in the first hole has drained away, add about 2 tablespoons of complete fertilizer. This is fertilizer that contains the three major plant nutrients—nitrogen, phosphorus and potassium—in percentages listed on the label (for example, 5-10-5). To guard the roots from direct contact with the fertilizer, cover them with at least 2 inches of soil mixed with organic matter. Insert the seedling. Fill in the hole with enriched soil and gently firm with your fingers *(left)*. During the season, use granular fertilizers, spread directly on the soil around the root zone. Inspect the black plastic mulch after heavy rains, winds or storms to see if it is still secure, especially when the seedlings are young.

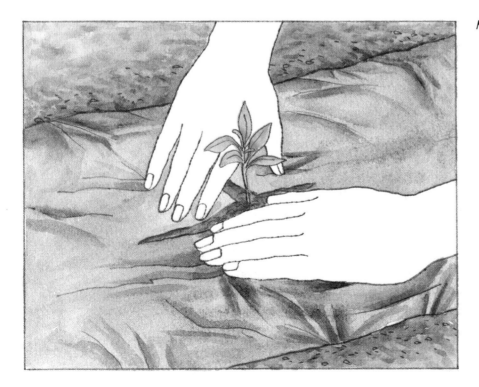

# GROWING POTATOES UNDER STRAW

mericans consume a staggering 128 pounds of potatoes per person per year. And there are good reasons why this is so. The potato is tasty on its own, but its flavor is subtle and able to blend with the flavors of almost any other foods it is served with. It is also rich in vitamins and iron.

The home gardener can easily grow potatoes. They are best grown from so-called seed potatoes—potatoes that have been cut into pieces *(below),* and then planted so that their eyes, or buds, will sprout new leaves, stems, roots and tubers.

If you plant seed potatoes, it is better to buy specially prepared seed potatoes from a garden-supply center or through mail order than to use grocery store potatoes. Special seed potatoes are certified healthy and free of disease; grocery store potatoes may be carrying disease without showing it, and they may have been treated to prevent sprouting.

Don't plant potatoes too early: They can withstand a light frost, but not a heavy freeze. Test your soil *(page 466-467)* before planting. Potatoes do best in acid soil; lower the pH if the soil is too alkaline.

Seed potatoes can be started in either of two ways. One is to plant them in hilled rows, the same way that corn is planted *(page 496)*. The other is to lay them on top of the soil—either on the ground or in a raised bed—with a covering of straw *(opposite)*. In the latter method, the potatoes will grow only about half as big as ones sown in the soil and hilled, but you will get more of them—especially if you live in an area where soil drainage is slow or one where the soil is rocky, such as New England. Just make sure you use straw (which is dried wheat, and seed-free), not hay (which is dried grass, and full of seeds).

*A blanket of straw conceals a crop of new potatoes— their ripening signaled by the lush green leaves that have surfaced above the insulating straw.*

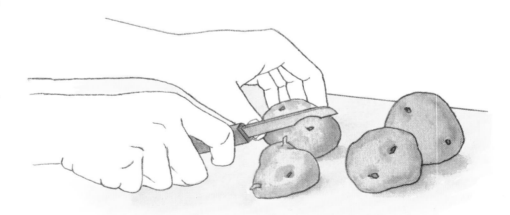

1 Cut seed potatoes into chunks about 1½ inches thick, making sure that each chunk has at least one eye *(above)*. Discard any chunks that appear moldy or diseased. Small potatoes may be left whole, but slice a bit off one side to serve as a bottom so the seed potato will stay put when laid on the soil. Dusting the chunks with sulfur will deter rotting in the ground. Leave the pieces in a warm place for a day or two so the cut surfaces can heal and dry.

**2** Prepare the soil by working in organic matter and fertilizer. Rake the bed smooth. Place the potato pieces on
the soil, 12 to 15 inches apart, with the cut side down
and the eyes pointing upward and outward *(right)*.
Press each piece firmly into the soil about ½ inch deep.

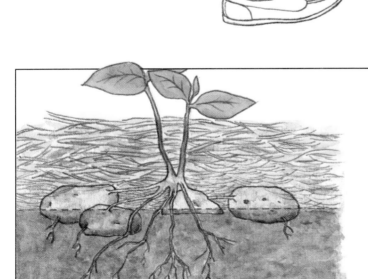

**3** Cover the bed with about 18 inches
of clean straw *(left)*. If the bed is in
a windy location, cover the straw
with about ½ inch of soil to hold it
in place. Water regularly to keep
the soil from drying out; if it does
the potatoes are likely to be knobby.

### A DEVELOPING
### POTATO PLANT

About 13 weeks after planting under
straw, a seed potato has sent up
some upright stems with leafy green
foliage. Along the soil line it has
formed specialized stems with
swellings called tubers. These are
a fresh crop of potatoes. From both
the stems and the tubers, many hairlike feeder roots descend into the
soil to absorb nutrients.

# HARVESTING POTATOES FROM UNDERGROUND

When the foliage of potato plants turns brown, thrust a potato rake into the hill beneath the plants and gently pull up the potatoes *(left)*. Choose a time when you have had a few days of dry weather so the plants and the soil will not be waterlogged. If the ground has hardened, carefully loosen the soil around the plants, then dig underneath to lift out potatoes. Shake off loose soil but do not wash the potatoes. Leaving potatoes in the ground over the winter invites disease that can harm next year's crop; feel around in the hill with your hand to make sure you have got them all. Spread unearthed potatoes on the ground for one or two days to dry out and harden their skins. Store only unblemished potatoes, and eat the rest as soon as possible.

There are many reasons to grow potatoes. They take up little space in your garden, they can be harvested through much of the summer, they store well and they taste better than the ones you buy. Despite appearances, the potato is not a root but a tuber, an underground stem swollen with nutrients. The plant concentrates all its goodness in the tuber; the green parts of the potato plant—seeds, leaves, fruit and aboveground stems—are poisonous.

The small, thin-skinned potatoes called new potatoes are actually immature potatoes. Before harvesting them, wait until the flowers are fully opened; new potatoes should be about the size of a hen's egg. You can gather them seven or eight weeks after planting; picking some will not harm the crop. The plants will be leafy and green; to be sure the potatoes are ready for eating, reach into the soil below the foliage, feel around for some boiling-size potatoes and detach them from their roots. Don't try to store these early pickings; eat them at once for their tender texture and delicate flavor.

When the plants turn brown and start to die, the potatoes are no longer new. They can be harvested as full-grown potatoes any time from then until the first frost. But be sure to dig them before the first frost; they cannot withstand the cold. Remove them one by one from the soil or raise several at once with a rounded potato rake *(left)* or with a garden fork.

With proper care, potatoes can be stored all winter. Do not wash them. Store only potatoes that have no cuts or bruises, which beget infection. Before storing the potatoes, cure them for two weeks in a dark, humid room at 50° to 60° F. Then move them to a dark, dry, cool, well-ventilated place, like a basement. To prevent sprouting, keep stored potatoes away from light and make sure the temperature remains below 50° F.

Potatoes will suffocate in airtight containers; store them in wooden barrels, crates or bushel baskets, or in metal or plastic garbage cans with holes punched in the sides and bottom. You can even pile potatoes loosely in a corner, as long as it is dark, dry and cool.

# PICKING SQUASH AND STORING IT

All members of the squash family are planted the same way; you can sow seeds indoors *(pages 80-81)* or outdoors *(pages 472-475)*. Many grow on vines and show other marks of kinship. But when it comes to harvesting, the family breaks into a pair of distinct branches. Summer squashes, as the name implies, should be picked during the warm months, when they are dewy fresh and their skins are tender. In fact, zucchini and the tubular yellow varieties taste best when only about 6 inches long, and disc-shaped scallop squash should be picked early, too. After picking, any of these can be stored in a refrigerator, but only for about a week.

The winter squashes are an entirely different matter. Acorn squash, Hubbards, butternuts, turban and spaghetti squash, and pumpkins—which are really just large squash—can all be stored without any refrigeration for months and make excellent eating throughout the winter. If harvested when young, they will be watery inside and lack sweetness. Instead, they should be allowed to mature on the vine as long as possible —almost until the first hard frost. Partly because they take so long to mature, they need special treatment *(right)* at harvest time. After picking, leave the squash outside for a day if the weather is sunny and there is no threat of frost. This will begin the curing process that hardens the skin.

All winter squashes need to be cured for a few weeks in a dark, warm, well-ventilated room to dry and harden their skins. In the basement, near the furnace will do, with perhaps a house fan turned on to help circulate the air.

After curing, squashes should be stored in a single layer—again for ventilation—on open shelves in a dry place that stays about 50° or 55° F all winter. Preserved in this way, acorns and Hubbards and turbans remain deliciously fresh into the dark months, and pumpkins can provide pies long after Thanksgiving and even Christmas are past. Never wash a winter squash or a pumpkin except just before cooking; water removes a natural preservative coating from the skin and the vegetables will spoil quickly.

1 When winter squash and pumpkins approach full development in late summer, place them on small boards or shingles. Off the ground, they will stay dry and free of rot. Roll them a quarter turn once a week for even color and well-rounded shape. To test whether a squash or a pumpkin is ready for picking, try to pierce the skin with your thumbnail *(above)*. If the skin breaks, the pumpkin is unripe (but don't worry; the wound will heal). If it is impervious to your nail, the vegetable is ready to pick.

2 To harvest squash or pumpkins, cut them off the vine, leaving 3 to 5 inches of stem attached *(below)*. Do not carry any of these vegetables by its stem; the weight will weaken the connection and the vegetable will spoil. If you do break off a stem, eat that squash first, since it will not keep well.

# STAKES AND CAGES TO SUPPORT TOMATOES

The tomato is the most popular home garden crop in America—partly because it tastes good, partly because it is one of the easiest crops to grow. It is also among the most diverse of crops; it comes in several hundred varieties. Yet all of those varieties can be divided into two general types: what horticulturalists call "determinate" and "indeterminate."

Determinate tomatoes are so called because they are bushlike in form and generally yield a single crop of fruit. Indeterminate tomatoes—the more common of the two—have vinelike growth habits; they sprawl in any direction where they meet no interference, and with sufficient sun, water and nutrients they will keep growing and producing fruit until the first frost of autumn.

Which kind of tomato you plant will influence how you grow them in your garden. Indeterminate tomatoes can be left to sprawl, but if they are they will be susceptible to rot, disease and insect pests. You can minimize these dangers if you stake the plants *(box, right)*. Staking has the further advantage of saving space; stakes can be set as close as 18 inches apart, whereas a sprawling plant may cover as much as 8 feet of ground. If you stake, however, you must prune the plants regularly every week to ensure vigorous growth. And as the plant rises in height, the new growth must be repeatedly tied to help keep the plant vertical.

Determinate tomatoes can be allowed without risk to stand on their own. They cannot, however, be staked; they are all too compact and many are too short.

For all indeterminate tomatoes, and for determinate tomatoes that grow from 2 to 3 feet tall, there is a third alternative—caging *(opposite)*. Caging requires a minimum of pruning. It also does away with the need for repeated tying; the cages serve to contain the plants as they grow.

You can buy tomato cages at a garden-supply center or make your own from pieces of wire mesh *(inset, opposite)*.

1 When a tomato seedling has had time to establish itself outdoors—about three weeks after transplanting—prepare it for caging. Use a clean, sharp knife to cut off the less vigorous shoots near the base of the plant *(below)*; leave one or two strong main stems. By concentrating the plant's energy in fewer stems, you will increase the yield of tomatoes later on.

## A TIMELY STAKE

To stake a tomato plant, insert a 6-foot wooden stake into the ground about 4 inches from the plant when it is a three-week-old seedling. Drive the stake 10 inches deep. Tie the plant to the stake with a length of soft cord or plastic-covered twist tie. First loop the cord tightly around the stake so that it will not slip down. Then loop it loosely around the stem, just below a branch or bud, leaving ½ inch of slack; this will keep the cord from choking the stem as it grows thicker. Check periodically; add a new tie whenever the plant grows another foot.

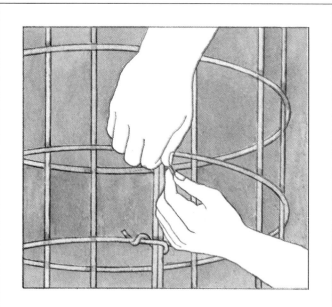

## AN ENCIRCLING CAGE

To make your own cage, buy a 5-foot square of concrete-reinforcing wire mesh with 6-inch squares. Bring two edges of the mesh together to make a cylinder and secure them by twisting the horizontal wires that protrude from one edge around the wires on the other edge *(above)*. The diameter of the cylinder will be between 18 and 24 inches. With a wire cutter, cut off the last horizontal wire on the bottom end of the cylinder, leaving vertical wire "spikes" that can be pushed into the ground to anchor the cage.

**2** Make an encircling cage *(box, left)*, and push it into the ground around the tomato plant. Gently gather all stems inside the cage *(above)* so that their growth will be guided upward along the interior surface of the mesh cylinder.

**3** As the plant grows, check periodically for suckers—small side shoots that sprout in the crotch between a main stem and a branch. When the suckers are 3 to 4 inches long, pinch them off at the base with your fingers or cut them off with a clean, sharp knife *(left)*. This minimal pruning will encourage earlier fruit production and more bountiful harvests.

# MOUNDING SOIL
# FOR STRONG CORNSTALKS

*Five weeks after planting, corn growing in neat rows is about 18 inches tall. The sweetest varieties take up to 12 weeks to mature.*

Corn has been a staple of the American diet ever since the Indians taught the Pilgrims to grow it, and it has been cultivated in much the same way since then. For example, settlers learned to "hill" corn—to make mounds around the bases of the stalks to support them—and this is still done today *(opposite)*. Farmers have long known that a first crop can be planted early—even before the last spring frost—because the young plants can stand some cold. But corn also needs lots of warmth and should get full, day-long sun—preferably in a site sheltered from the wind. Corn also soaks up nutrients, and a nitrogen-rich fertilizer should be worked into the soil. Then the seeds should be planted in furrows 2 inches deep and 36 inches apart. Plant five seeds per foot; not all will germinate, and extra plants can be snipped off when they are about 6 inches high *(opposite, top)*.

Seeds of one particular variety should not be planted in a single long row, but rather in a compact block of several shorter rows. The plants pollinate each other to produce ears and they need to be close together. By the same token, different varieties should be kept far apart; cross-pollination between them can spoil the ears' taste and texture.

A last trick: a single planting of corn produces ears for only about one week, so if you want to have corn all summer, plant several crops two weeks apart until 12 weeks before the first frost in your area.

## TIPS FOR INCREASING THE YIELD

• Make sure that plants have adequate moisture during tasseling (flowering).
• To help pollinate the corn crop, tap the corn tassels when fully developed in late June or July.
• Have your soil tested *(pages 466-467)*, and amend if necessary. The optimum pH for corn is 5.8 to 6.5.

496

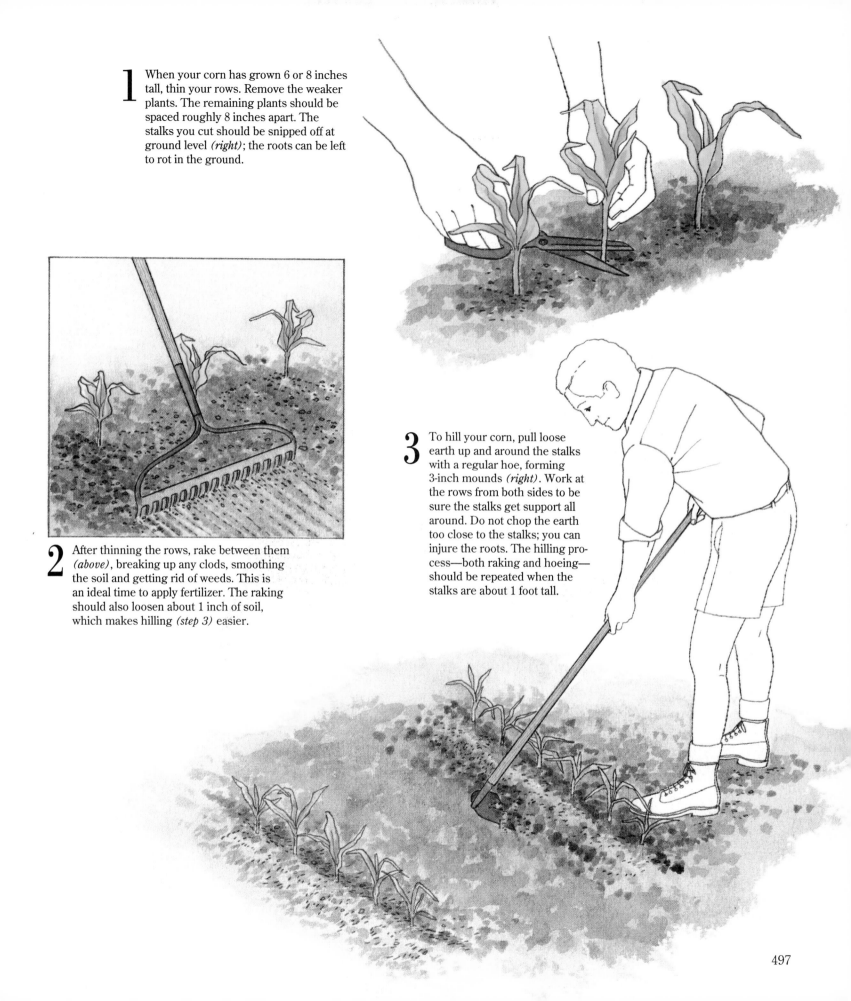

1 When your corn has grown 6 or 8 inches tall, thin your rows. Remove the weaker plants. The remaining plants should be spaced roughly 8 inches apart. The stalks you cut should be snipped off at ground level *(right)*; the roots can be left to rot in the ground.

2 After thinning the rows, rake between them *(above)*, breaking up any clods, smoothing the soil and getting rid of weeds. This is an ideal time to apply fertilizer. The raking should also loosen about 1 inch of soil, which makes hilling *(step 3)* easier.

3 To hill your corn, pull loose earth up and around the stalks with a regular hoe, forming 3-inch mounds *(right)*. Work at the rows from both sides to be sure the stalks get support all around. Do not chop the earth too close to the stalks; you can injure the roots. The hilling process—both raking and hoeing—should be repeated when the stalks are about 1 foot tall.

# PLANTING DATES
# FOR VEGETABLES

| | | REGION 1 | REGION 2 | REGION 3 | REGION 4 |
|---|---|---|---|---|---|
| ARTICHOKES | Seeds and roots | Not recommended | Not recommended | Not recommended | May 10–May 30 |
| ASPARAGUS | Roots | May 15–June 10 | May 1–June 1 | Apr. 20–May 15 | Mar. 30–Apr. 30 |
| BEETS | Seeds | May 15–June 15 | May 1–June 15 | Apr. 25–June 15 | Apr. 15–July 15 |
| CARROTS | Seeds | May 20–June 15 | May 10–June 15 | May 1–July 1 | Apr. 20–July 10 |
| CELERIAC AND CELERY | Seedlings | June 1–June 15 | May 20–June 15 | May 10–July 1 | Apr. 20–July 5 |
| CHICORY | Seeds | May 30–June 15 | May 15–June 15 | May 15–June 15 | June 1–July 1 |
| CORN | Seeds | Not recommended | May 20–June 10 | May 15–June 15 | May 5–June 15 |
| CUCUMBERS | Seeds | Not recommended | Not recommended | June 1–June 15 | May 20–July 1 |
| DRY BEANS | Seeds | Not recommended | May 25–June 15 | May 15–June 30 | May 10–July 10 |
| EGGPLANTS | Seedlings | Not recommended | Not recommended | June 1–June 15 | May 20–June 15 |
| GARBANZO BEANS | Seeds | Not recommended | May 25–June 15 | May 15–June 30 | May 10–July 10 |
| GARLIC | Cloves | May 15–June 1 | May 1–May 30 | Apr. 15–May 15 | Apr. 1–May 1 |
| HORSERADISH | Roots | May 15–June 1 | May 1–May 30 | Apr. 20–May 20 | Apr. 15–May 15 |
| HORTICULTURAL BEANS | Seeds | Not recommended | June 10–July 1 | May 30–July 1 | May 25–July 15 |
| JERUSALEM ARTICHOKES | Tubers | Not recommended | Not recommended | May 20–June 20 | May 10–June 30 |
| LEEKS | Seeds | May 1–June 1 | May 1–June 1 | May 1–May 20 | Apr. 15–May 15 |
| LETTUCE (HEAD) | Seedlings | May 20–June 30 | May 10–June 30 | May 1–July 15 | Apr. 15–May 15<br>June 15–Aug. 1 |
| LETTUCE (LEAF) | Seeds and seedlings | May 20–July 15 | May 10–July 15 | May 1–Aug. 1 | Apr. 15–Aug. 1 |
| LIMA BEANS | Seeds | Not recommended | Not recommended | Not recommended | May 25–June 15 |
| OKRA | Seeds | Not recommended | Not recommended | June 1–June 20 | May 20–July 1 |
| ONIONS | Seedlings | May 1–June 10 | May 1–May 30 | Apr. 20–May 15 | Apr. 10–May 1 |

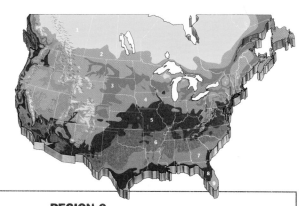

| REGION 5 | REGION 6 | REGION 7 | REGION 8 | REGION 9 | |
|---|---|---|---|---|---|
| Apr. 30–May 30 | Apr. 10–May 30 | Mar. 20–Apr. 30 | Feb. 28–Apr. 30 | Jan. 30–Apr. 30<br>Jan. 1 in frost-free areas | ARTICHOKES |
| Mar. 15–Apr. 15 | Feb. 15–Apr. 10 | Dec. 1–Mar. 10 | Dec. 1–Feb. 28<br>Certain varieties only;<br>see Dictionary | Dec. 1–Feb. 1<br>Certain varieties only;<br>see Dictionary | ASPARAGUS |
| Mar. 20–Aug. 15 | Mar. 1–Sept. 1 | Feb. 15–Oct. 1 | Jan. 10–Dec. 1 | Jan. 10–Dec. 1 | BEETS |
| Apr. 1–Aug. 1 | Mar. 1–Apr. 20<br>July 15–Aug. 15 | Feb. 10–Mar. 20<br>Aug. 15–Sept. 1 | Jan. 10–Mar. 1<br>Sept. 1–Dec. 1 | Jan. 10–Mar. 1<br>Sept. 15–Dec. 1 | CARROTS |
| Apr. 10–June 15 | Mar. 15–May 30 | Feb. 20–Apr. 1 | Jan. 10–Mar. 1 | Sept. 1–Feb. 1 | CELERIAC AND CELERY |
| June 15–July 15 | June 1–July 1 | June 1–July 1 | Sept. 1–Oct. 1 | Sept. 15–Oct. 15 | CHICORY |
| Apr. 25–June 1 | Mar. 25–June 1 | Mar. 15–May 1 | Feb. 10–Apr. 15 | Feb. 1–Mar. 15 | CORN |
| May 1–July 15 | Apr. 10–Aug. 1 | Mar. 20–May 1<br>June 1–Aug. 15 | Feb. 15–Apr. 15<br>June 1–Sept. 15 | Feb. 15–Mar. 15<br>Aug. 15–Oct. 1 | CUCUMBERS |
| Apr. 25–Aug. 1 | Apr. 1–Aug. 15 | Mar. 15–Sept. 1 | Feb. 1–Sept. 20 | Feb. 1–Nov. 1 | DRY BEANS |
| May 10–July 1 | Apr. 15–July 1 | Mar. 25–July 15 | Mar. 1–Sept. 1 | Feb. 1–Sept. 30 | EGGPLANTS |
| Apr. 25–Aug. 1 | Apr. 1–Aug. 15 | Mar. 15–Sept. 1 | Feb. 1–Sept. 20 | Feb. 1–Nov. 1 | GARBANZO BEANS |
| Mar. 10–Apr. 15 | Feb. 10–Mar. 20 | Feb. 1–Mar. 1<br>Aug. 1–Oct. 1 | Aug. 15–Nov. 15 | Sept. 15–Nov. 15 | GARLIC |
| Mar. 20–Apr. 30 | Mar. 1–Apr. 10 | Aug. 30–Oct. 30 | Sept. 15–Nov. 25 | Oct. 1–Dec. 15 | HORSERADISH |
| May 10–July 15 | Apr. 15–July 25 | Mar. 25–July 25 | Mar. 1–July 25 | Feb. 15–July 25 | HORTICULTURAL BEANS |
| Apr. 30–July 10 | Apr. 10–July 10 | Mar. 20–July 10 | Feb. 28–July 10 | Jan. 1–July 10 | JERUSALEM ARTICHOKES |
| Mar. 15–May 1 | Feb. 15–Apr. 1 | Jan. 25–Mar. 15 | Jan. 1–Mar. 1 | Jan. 1–Feb. 15 | LEEKS |
| Mar. 20–May 1<br>July 15–Aug. 30 | Mar. 1–Apr. 1<br>Aug. 1–Sept. 15 | Feb. 1–Mar. 10<br>Aug. 15–Oct. 15 | Jan. 1–Feb. 15<br>Sept. 1–Dec. 1 | Sept. 15–Feb. 1 | LETTUCE (HEAD) |
| Mar. 20–June 1<br>July 15–Sept. 1 | Feb. 15–Mar. 15<br>Aug. 15–Oct. 1 | Jan. 15–Apr. 1<br>Aug. 25–Oct. 1 | Jan. 1–Mar. 15<br>Sept. 1–Dec. 1 | Sept. 15–Feb. 1 | LETTUCE (LEAF) |
| May 1–June 30 | Apr. 1–Aug. 1 | Mar. 20–Aug. 15 | Feb. 10–Sept. 15 | Feb. 1–Oct. 1 | LIMA BEANS |
| May 1–Aug. 1 | Apr. 10–Aug. 10 | Mar. 20–Aug. 20 | Mar. 1–Sept. 20 | Feb. 15–Oct. 1 | OKRA |
| Mar. 15–May 1 | Feb. 15–Apr. 1 | Jan. 15–Mar. 10 | Oct. 1–Feb. 1 | Oct. 1–Jan. 15 | ONIONS |

|  |  | REGION 1 | REGION 2 | REGION 3 | REGION 4 |
|---|---|---|---|---|---|
| ONIONS | Seeds | May 1–June 10 | May 1–May 30 | Apr. 20–May 15 | Apr. 1–May 1 |
| ONIONS | Sets | May 1–June 10 | May 1–May 30 | Apr. 20–May 15 | Apr. 10–May 1 |
| PARSNIPS | Seeds | May 20–June 10 | May 10–June 15 | May 1–June 15 | Apr. 15–July 1 |
| PEPPERS | Seedlings | Not recommended | June 10–June 20 | May 25–June 20 | May 20–July 1 |
| POTATOES | Tubers | May 5–June 1 | Apr. 30–June 1 | Apr. 15–June 10 | Apr. 1–June 10 |
| PUMPKINS | Seeds | Not recommended | Not recommended | May 20–June 10 | June 1–June 15 |
| RHUBARB | Roots | May 15–June 1 | May 1–May 20 | Apr. 15–May 10 | Apr. 1–May 1 |
| SALSIFY | Seeds | May 25–June 1 | May 10–June 10 | May 1–June 20 | Apr. 15–June 20 |
| SHALLOTS | Cloves | May 20–June 10 | May 1–June 10 | Apr. 20–May 20 | Apr. 10–May 1 |
| SNAP BEANS | Seeds | Not recommended | May 25–June 15 | May 15–June 30 | May 10–July 10 |
| SORREL | Seeds | May 20–June 15 | May 1–June 15 | May 1–July 1 | Apr. 15–July 15 |
| SOUTHERN PEAS | Seeds | Not recommended | Not recommended | Not recommended | Not recommended |
| SOYBEANS | Seeds | Not recommended | Not recommended | Not recommended | May 25–June 10 |
| SUMMER SPINACH | Seeds | Not recommended | June 10–June 20 | May 20–July 1 | May 10–July 1 |
| SUMMER SQUASH | Seeds and seedlings | June 10–June 20 | June 10–June 20 | May 20–July 1 | May 10–July 1 |
| SWEET POTATOES | Slips | Not recommended | Not recommended | Not recommended | Not recommended |
| SWISS CHARD | Seeds | May 30–June 15 | May 10–June 30 | May 1–July 1 | Apr. 20–July 5 |
| TAMPALA | Seeds | June 10–June 30 | June 10–July 10 | May 20–July 20 | May 10–July 30 |
| TOMATOES | Seedlings | June 15–June 30 | June 10–June 30 | May 25–June 30 | May 15–June 30 |
| WATERCRESS | Seeds | Not recommended | May 20–Aug. 15 | May 10–Aug. 15 | May 1–Aug. 30 |
| WINTER SQUASH | Seeds and seedlings | Not recommended | Not recommended | May 20–June 10 | June 1–June 15 |

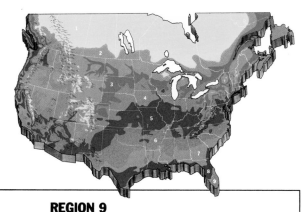

| REGION 5 | REGION 6 | REGION 7 | REGION 8 | REGION 9 | |
|---|---|---|---|---|---|
| Mar. 15–Apr. 15 | Feb. 20–Apr. 1 | Feb. 1–Mar. 10 | Jan. 1–Feb. 15 | Jan. 1–Jan. 15 | ONIONS |
| Mar. 10–Apr. 10 | Feb. 15–Apr. 1 | Not recommended | Not recommended | Not recommended | ONIONS |
| Mar. 20–July 10 | Mar. 1–Apr. 10 | Jan. 15–Mar. 15 | Jan. 1–Feb. 15 | Sept. 1–Dec. 1 | PARSNIPS |
| May 10–July 10 | Apr. 15–July 20 | Apr. 1–Aug. 1 | Feb. 15–May 1 | Feb. 1–Apr. 1 | PEPPERS |
| Mar. 15–June 1 | Feb. 20–Apr. 15 | Feb. 1–Mar. 15<br>July 25–Aug. 20 | Jan. 1–Mar. 1<br>Aug. 1–Sept. 15 | Jan. 1–Feb. 15<br>Aug. 1–Sept. 15 | POTATOES |
| May 15–July 1 | May 30–July 10 | June 15–July 20 | July 1–Aug. 15 | Aug. 1–Sept. 1 | PUMPKINS |
| Mar. 10–Apr. 15 | Mar. 1–Apr. 1 | Not recommended | Not recommended | Not recommended | RHUBARB |
| Mar. 20–July 1 | Mar. 1–July 10 | Feb. 1–June 15 | Jan. 10–Mar. 1 | Jan. 1–Feb. 1 | SALSIFY |
| Mar. 15–May 1 | Feb. 15–Apr. 10 | Jan. 15–Mar. 20<br>Aug. 15–Oct. 1 | Jan. 1–Mar. 1<br>Sept. 1–Oct. 15 | Jan. 1–Feb. 1<br>Sept. 15–Nov. 1 | SHALLOTS |
| Apr. 25–Aug. 1 | Apr. 1–Aug. 15 | Mar. 15–May 15<br>July 1–Sept. 1 | Feb. 1–May 1<br>July 15–Sept. 20 | Feb. 1–Apr. 1<br>Sept. 1–Nov. 1 | SNAP BEANS |
| Mar. 15–May 15 | Feb. 20–Apr. 15 | Feb. 10–Mar. 20 | Jan. 15–Mar. 10 | Jan. 1–Mar. 1 | SORREL |
| May 10–July 1 | Apr. 15–Aug. 1 | Mar. 25–Sept. 1 | Mar. 1–Sept. 10 | Feb. 15–Sept. 20 | SOUTHERN PEAS |
| May 10–June 25 | Apr. 20–July 15 | Apr. 10–July 25 | Mar. 1–July 30 | Mar. 1–July 30 | SOYBEANS |
| May 1–Aug. 1 | Apr. 10–Aug. 1 | Mar. 20–Aug. 15 | Feb. 15–Aug. 15 | Feb. 1–Apr. 15 | SUMMER SPINACH |
| May 1–July 20 | Apr. 10–Aug. 1 | Mar. 15–Aug. 10 | Feb. 15–Sept. 1 | Feb. 1–Oct. 1 | SUMMER SQUASH |
| May 10–June 10 | Apr. 20–June 15 | Apr. 1–June 1 | Mar. 1–June 1 | Feb. 15–May 15 | SWEET POTATOES |
| Apr. 1–Aug. 1 | Mar. 1–Sept. 10 | Feb. 15–Sept. 1 | Jan. 10–Oct. 1 | Jan. 1–Nov. 1 | SWISS CHARD |
| Apr. 30–Aug. 1 | Apr. 10–Aug. 15 | Mar. 20–Sept. 1 | Feb. 28–Sept. 1 | Jan. 1–Oct. 1 | TAMPALA |
| May 5–July 1 | Apr. 10–June 1 | Mar. 20–May 20 | Feb. 28–May 1 | Feb. 1–Apr. 1 | TOMATOES |
| Apr. 10–Sept. 15 | Mar. 20–Sept. 30 | Mar. 1–Oct. 15 | Jan. 30–Nov. 1 | All year | WATERCRESS |
| June 1–July 1 | June 10–July 10 | June 20–July 20 | July 1–Aug. 15 | Aug. 1–Sept. 1 | WINTER SQUASH |

# TROUBLESHOOTING GUIDE: VEGETABLES

| PROBLEM | CAUSE | SOLUTION |
|---|---|---|
| Brown spots ringed with yellow appear on leaves of tomatoes or potatoes. Tomatoes may rot at the stem end and have dark, leathery, sunken spots that can spread over the rest of the fruit. Potatoes will develop brown, corky, dry spots. Yields are sometimes reduced. | Early blight, caused by the fungus *Alternaia*. Called early blight because it occurs in the spring. *(See late blight, below.)* | Rotate crops and destroy infected plants at the end of the season. Treat with a fungicide safe for vegetables. When planting seed potatoes, use only those certified disease-free by the state or provincial agricultural department. Choose resistant varieties; use a generous amount of compost in preparing soil beds. |
| Dark, irregular spots appear on leaves and stems of tomatoes and potatoes, and there may be a white mold on the lower leaf surface. Fruits and tubers can also be affected with darkened, rotting spots. | Late blight, caused by the fungus *Phytophthora*. Called late blight because it occurs in fall. | Treat with a fungicide recommended for vegetables. Rotate crops and destroy all infected plants in fall. When planting seed potatoes, use only those certified disease-free. Plant resistant varieties. Destroy culled fruit. |
| Dark red, black-brown pockmarks on bean pods; sunken spots with rings on ripe tomatoes. Also affects cucumbers and other vegetables. | Anthracnose, a fungus disease. | Keep the garden free of weeds and debris. Rotate crops every three years. Spray with sulfur, starting in early spring, or with a fungicide recommended for vegetables. |
| If affected before germination, seeds become brown and mushy, and rot in the soil, or young seedlings suddenly wilt, fall over and die. | Damping-off, a fungus disease. Any vegetable can be affected. Fungi present in the soil primarily attack growing seedlings that are least resistant to cold, wet soil conditions. | Use a sterile, soilless medium to start seeds indoors, and do not overwater flats. Make sure the garden soil has good drainage. Use treated seeds or treat the medium with a recommended fungicide. Do not plant outdoors if soil is too damp or too cold. |
| White dust develops on the lower surfaces of leaves and spreads over the entire leaf and stem, causing distortion on beans, cucumbers, squash, pumpkins, eggplants, tomatoes and peppers. | Powdery mildew, a fungus disease. Spores are carried by the wind to new hosts, where moderate temperatures and shade favor powdery mildew. | Space plants so air can circulate between them. Thin seedlings to avoid crowding. Avoid watering late in the day; damp soil fosters spread of disease. Spray with sulfur when temperature is below 85° F, or treat with a fungicide safe for vegetables. |
| Vegetable foliage, especially that of rhubarb, develops tiny yellow spots that later turn brown or purplish-gray, enlarge and have red margins. Leaves turn yellow and die. | Leaf spot, a fungus disease. | Rotate crops. Treat with a recommended fungicide, beginning in spring when growth starts. Avoid watering late in the day. Remove all diseased and damaged foliage and debris from the garden in fall. |
| Foliage of beans, cucumbers, squash, pumpkins or peppers becomes mottled, yellowed, white or curled. Fruits may be discolored or streaked. Foliage looks spotted, streaked or ringed. There may be discoloration along leaf veins. | Mosaic, a virus disease spread by plant sap during propagation, pruning, or when plants are rubbed together. | Remove diseased vegetable plants immediately. Plant varieties resistant to mosaic virus. As the virus is spread by aphids, leafhoppers and whiteflies, control these insects and remove all weeds where they may live and breed. Use certified, high-quality plants and seeds. Rotate crops. |

| PROBLEM | CAUSE | SOLUTION |
|---------|-------|----------|
| Tiny white or silvery white-green growths, or galls, form on corn ears, stalks and tassels, usually at the top of the plant. At maturity, the galls turn black and burst open, releasing large numbers of black powdery spores. | Smut, a fungus disease, that can be spread by overhead watering. May be more prevalent in soils that have had high nitrogen additions. | There are no chemical controls for smut. Remove and burn or otherwise destroy diseased plant parts. Remove the galls before they burst open. Rotate crops and plant resistant varieties. Avoid excessive additions of nitrogen to the soil. |
| At first, edges of lettuce leaves get small yellowish spots, which then darken and appear to be burned. | Tip burn, a condition caused by high heat, lack of calcium and uneven soil moisture. | Grow lettuce in moist soil in a partially shaded location during the heat of summer. Maintain an even supply of water to lettuce. Plant resistant varieties. |
| Sunken pockmarks with black mold form on cucumbers, squash and pumpkins; plants and fruits may be distorted. Rough, corky scabs appear on potatoes. | Scab, a bacterial or fungus disease. | Rotate crops. Plant disease-free, scab-resistant seeds and seed potatoes that are certified scab-resistant. There is no chemical cure for bacterial scab, which affects potatoes, but a soil pH under 5.5 will prevent the disease. Cucumbers, squash and pumpkins may be treated with a recommended fungicide. |
| Sunken, dry areas develop on onions just before harvest or while they are in storage. A crusty layer of hard black tissue forms around the neck, and gray, moldy growth forms between the inside layers. | Neck rot, a fungus disease. | There are no chemical controls for neck rot. Do not harvest bulbs until the tops brown and fall over, and dry the bulbs completely before storing them. Keep the area well weeded. Incorporate compost and organic matter into the soil. |
| Both sides of leaves on asparagus and bean plants develop small, rust-colored spots or pustules; then they turn yellow and drop. | Rust, a fungus disease. | Water early in the day to prevent disease spread on wet leaves. Dust or spray with sulfur when the temperature is below 85° F or use a fungicide safe for vegetables. Destroy infected plants in fall. Use new stakes each year for climbing bean plants. |
| Brown cracks and lesions appear on the inner and outer surfaces of celery stalks. Leaves are small. | Brown check, which is caused by a boron deficiency. | Add 2 ounces of borax to every 30 pounds of fertilizer before applying it to celery, or make a dilute borax solution and apply it to the base of the plant. |
| Vine crops such as cucumbers, squash and pumpkins, as well as potatoes, spinach and rhubarb suddenly wilt and die. Leaves usually turn yellow at tops, then brown, curl and wilt. Seedlings of vine crops, tomatoes and eggplants are stunted, and eventually wilt and die. | Wilt caused by bacteria or by *Fusarium* or *Verticillium* fungus. A cross section of the affected plant's stem will show brown streaks. | Bacterial wilt is spread by cucumber beetles, which must be controlled. To control fusarium and verticillium wilt in tomatoes, plant only resistant varieties. Fusarium wilt does not affect eggplants; there are no verticillium-resistant varieties of eggplants. Remove any diseased plants immediately and clean up the garden completely in the fall. Rotate crops. Acid soil will deter these fungi. |
| Blossom ends of tomatoes have sunken, tough, black patches. Blossom end of the fruit looks shrunken. | Blossom-end rot, caused by a calcium deficiency caused by uneven moisture levels in the soil. Watch for blossom-end rot when drought follows an excess of spring rain. | Make sure that the garden receives an inch of water per week. Mulch during dry periods. Have your soil pH checked to make sure it is between 5.5 and 7.0. Cut back on nitrogen fertilizers. |

| PROBLEM | CAUSE | SOLUTION |
| --- | --- | --- |
| Small holes appear in the leaves, flowers and fruit of many vegetables. Eventually, plants may be stripped of all foliage. | Beetles, including asparagus, flea, cucumber, Colorado potato, Mexican bean and Japanese beetles, 1/4- to 1/2-inch insects with hard shells. | Hand-pick larger beetles from the plant. Control larvae with milky spore, a bacterium fatal to beetles but harmless to plants and other animals. Keep the garden weeded; beetles lay eggs in weedy areas. Spray with a pesticide recommended for vegetables. Aromatic marigolds repel many beetles. |
| Leaves of plants are withered, curled, mottled or distorted; ants appear on stems and leaves. Plants grow poorly or die. Any vegetable can be affected. | Aphids, 1/8-inch insects, of various colors, that suck plant juices and secrete a sticky substance that can spread disease and attract ants. | Introduce natural predators: ladybugs, green lacewings and syrphid flies. Wash aphids off leaves with a heavy stream of water or spray them with a pesticide recommended for vegetables. Install yellow sticky traps. |
| Vine crops wilt, dry out and turn black. Leaf tips and stem joints of beans, beets, Swiss chard, celery or potato plants and their roots are deformed and turn black. | Plant bugs—1/4-inch tarnished plant bugs or 5/8-inch squash bugs. Green to brown with dark brown and yellow markings, they suck sap and damage plant tissue. | Hand-pick the bugs and remove damaged leaves. Apply an insecticide that is recommended for vegetables. Remove all infested plants in fall. Cover plants with row covers, commonly available at garden-supply centers. |
| Plants, especially young transplants, are eaten or cut off at the base at soil level. | Cutworms, gray, brown or black caterpillars up to 2 inches long. Rarely seen during daylight hours. Some have stripes or spots. Damaging larvae winter in the soil. | Place a protective collar made out of a milk container around seedlings. Wood ashes around the base of the plant are a deterrent. Use *Bacillus thuringiensis*. Hand-pick cutworms at night. Remove infested plants in fall, and till deeply to expose and kill larvae. |
| Corn kernels are eaten within the husk. Insides of tomatoes, beans, peppers and squash are eaten away; foliage of vegetables is chewed. | Corn earworm (also known as tomato fruitworm), a 1- to 2-inch caterpillar with dark, lengthwise stripes. | Hand-pick worms by pulling back corn husks after pollination. Spray with a pesticide recommended for vegetables. Remove and destroy all infested plants in fall. *Bacillus thuringiensis* kills larvae. Tachinid flies and trichogramma wasps are natural predators. |
| Large holes are eaten in leaves; ripe fruits are destroyed; seedlings may be eaten. Tomatoes are especially susceptible. Silver streaks appear on leaves and garden paths. | Snails or slugs (shell-less snails), night-feeding pests up to 3 inches long. Prefer cool, moist locations. | Trap slugs in saucers of beer or grapefruit halves turned upside down. Salt kills snails and slugs, but may damage crops. Bait is available; choose one safe for vegetables. Spread diatomaceous earth around plants. Hand-pick snails and slugs, especially at night. Mulch with cedar or oak bark. |
| Plants wilt on warm days or become stunted, light in color or low in yield. Roots are swollen and knotted. Any summer vegetable except corn and beans may be affected. Most damage is done in hot weather. | Nematodes, microscopic worms too small to be visible to the eye; only a soil test will confirm their presence. They feed on roots. Some form nutrient-blocking galls on roots. | Contact your local extension service for diagnosis. Rotate crops or relocate the garden every three years. Use compost to encourage predatory fungi. Interplant with marigolds. Professional soil fumigation may be needed. Plant resistant varieties. |
| Holes appear in leaves, stalks or stems of beans, beets, celery, peppers and potatoes, and at the bottom of corn ears, breaking the stems. | European corn borer, a 1-inch spotted caterpillar that moves through the stem; stems must be cut to see the borer. | Borers can be removed by hand. Spray plants with a pesticide recommended for vegetables. Remove all infested plants from the garden in fall. Grow resistant corn varieties. Natural predators are braconid wasps, ladybugs and tachinid flies. |

| PROBLEM | CAUSE | SOLUTION |
|---|---|---|
| Plants do not develop; full-grown plants may wilt and die, or develop fungal or bacterial diseases. Root crops, especially onions, have tunnels and rot. | Maggots—legless, wormlike, white or yellow pests ⅓ inch long that enter the plant through the roots. | Wood ashes around plant bases deter maggots. Or use an insecticide recommended for vegetables in the soil. Do not fertilize with manure, which attracts maggot-breeding flies. Spread diatomaceous earth around plants. |
| Colorless areas appear on the leaf surfaces of peppers, tomatoes, cucumbers, eggplants, squash, spinach and beet greens. | Leaf miners, which are tiny pale-green or whitish maggots. | Cut off and destroy infested leaves. Keep the area well weeded. Treat with a pesticide recommended for vegetables. Remove and destroy infested plants in fall. Crush the eggs or miners between fingers. Cultivate soil in fall, exposing maggots to the birds. Rotate crops. |
| Plants, especially tomatoes, weaken and become discolored. When plants are shaken, a large cloud of white insects appears. | Whitefly, a tiny, ¹⁄₁₆-inch insect that sucks on plant leaves, especially young growth, secreting a substance on plants that attracts fungus. | Knock off with a heavy water spray. Treat plants with an insecticidal soap. Hang yellow sticky traps nearby; flypaper may attract and kill whiteflies. Do not buy plants that show signs of whitefly. |
| Foliage of beans, carrots, lettuce, potatoes, squash and tomatoes starts to yellow, beginning at the edges; leaves begin to curl up. Plants may be stunted or deformed. | Leafhoppers, light green or gray winged insects up to ⅕ inch long, suck out plant juices, restricting nutrient flow and spreading disease. | Heavy sprays of water can knock the insects off plants. Or use an insecticide recommended for vegetables. Plant geraniums and petunias nearby to repel leafhoppers. Cover young plants with cheesecloth or a row cover, available at garden-supply centers. |
| Vines of squash, pumpkins and cucumbers suddenly wilt; little piles of a yellowish substance appear on stems where insect entered plant. | Squash vine borer, a 1-inch white caterpillar with a brown head. Stems must be cut to see the borer. | Hand-pick borers. Cut out damaged stems and pile soil over the tips to foster new growth. Destroy vines after harvest. Grow resistant varieties. Plant in midsummer to avoid the early summer peak infestation time. |
| Leaves of beans, cucumbers, eggplants or tomatoes have yellow blotches and are mottled with black specks on the undersides. Later, webs form on plants. Infested leaves turn silvery or yellow. | Spider mites, almost microscopic pests. The black specks are the mites. Eggs are laid at the base of the plant, and on buds and leaves. | As mites thrive in hot, dry weather, keep plants well watered and mist the undersides of the foliage. Spray with an insecticidal soap or a miticide recommended for vegetables. Mites prefer hot conditions; spray cold water on leaves. |
| Small, round holes with brown edges appear in artichoke buds, stems and foliage. Caterpillars chew plants, especially in spring. | Artichoke plume moth. The moth lays eggs on the plant and the larva bores into the artichoke. Green or yellowish larvae with black markings. | Destroy infested plants. Apply an insecticide safe for vegetables; do so repeatedly until all signs of the moth and larva disappear. |
| Foliage and fruit of tomatoes, potatoes, eggplants and peppers are devoured. Sometimes fruit is eaten. | Tomato hornworm, a 3- to 4-inch green worm with white bands and horns. | Hand-pick. Treat plants with *Bacillus thuringiensis*. Introduce natural predators such as braconid wasps or trichogramma wasps. Plant in midsummer to avoid the early summer peak infestation time. |
| Leaves develop white, yellow or brown blotches, distortion or curling, then wither, turn brown and die. Any vegetable, but primarily onions, may be affected. | Thrips, slender insects just barely visible to the eye, make holes in foliage and fruit, then suck out plant juices. They can transmit other diseases, such as wilt, to crops. | Keep plants well watered. Treat with an insecticide recommended for vegetables when damage first occurs. If the problem persists, remove infested plants. Aluminum foil mulch is a deterrent. Introduce natural predators, such as green lacewings. |

# DICTIONARY OF VEGETABLES

## Introduction

The following dictionary entries present a variety of popular garden vegetables. They are arranged alphabetically by their common names; their botanical names follow. Many have hybrid varieties specially bred for higher yields, better flavor and greater disease-resistance. Information is included on common diseases and how to harvest vegetables. Most vegetables are annuals, meaning they must be planted anew each year; their life cycles are completed in one season. Others, such as asparagus and rhubarb, are perennial and appear year after year. Biennials—beets, for example—develop roots and foliage one year and produce flowers and fruit the next.

**Acorn Squash** see Winter Squash

## Artichokes
Cynara scolymus

Artichokes are large, succulent flower buds with thick, heavy scales. The buds are the edible parts of the plant and are harvested before they open. Some gardeners leave a bud or two on the plant for their ornamental value; the buds open into broad, bright purple, thistle-like flowers. The plant grows to 4 feet wide and 4 feet tall with silvery green, fernlike foliage. Artichokes are perennial plants in mild-winter areas where temperatures do not drop below 20° F and damage or kill them. In cold-winter areas that have a long growing season, artichokes must be planted year after year.

**Selected varieties.** *'Green Globe,'* 100 days from seed to ripe fruit. The standard artichoke variety. Plant produces large, round buds with solid centers and green bracts (petal-like leaves that surround the heart), which sometimes have a purple base.

**Growing conditions.** Artichokes may be started from seeds or from root divisions. Seeds can be started outdoors in spring after all danger of frost has passed; germination requires 12 to 15 days. Sow the seeds ½ inch deep and 1 to 2 feet apart. When the seedlings are several inches tall, thin them to about 4 feet apart. In cold areas that have a short growing season, the seeds should be started indoors six to eight weeks before the last frost date, then transplanted into the garden.

Seedlings started indoors and root divisions can be planted in the garden after all danger of frost has passed. Plant them 6 inches deep and about 4 feet apart.

Artichokes do best in regions with long, cool summers, such as the California coast. They require rich, well-drained soil. They will not grow where their roots are waterlogged. When growing artichokes as perennials in areas with cool winter temperatures, apply mulch to protect the plants.

Fertilize perennial artichokes in fall after the last harvest or in spring when growth starts. Feed artichokes grown as annuals when they are first planted and then again when they are 24 inches high.

Artichokes grown as perennials need to be divided every three to four years or they will cease to produce. This can be done by cutting the roots of old artichoke plants into several sections and planting the new divisions.

Artichokes are susceptible to damage from aphids, slugs, snails and the artichoke plume moth.

**Harvesting.** Artichokes should be harvested when the flower buds are still closed and about 4 inches across. With a sharp knife, cut the stem 1 to 2 inches below the base of the bud. To encourage further growth, cut the stalks of perennial artichokes to the ground after harvest.

## Asparagus
Asparagus officinalis

Asparagus is a perennial vegetable that takes three years to start producing edible spears and then continues producing for 12 or more years. From the first spring, spear tips will push through the soil, but the gardener must be patient. If the plant is to develop a strong root system, the first spears must be left unharvested. From them will develop lateral branches and sprawling fernlike foliage up to 3 feet tall. In the third year, when new spears emerge and grow to about 7 inches high, they can be harvested.

**Selected varieties.** *'Mary Washington,'* three years from seed to harvest. The variety most widely available to the home gardener. Thick, heavy, straight green stalks tinged with purple. Resistant to asparagus rust. *'UC 157,'* three years. Produces from three to five spears in a cluster rather than the open, random pattern of other varieties. The spears are deep green,

'GREEN GLOBE' ARTICHOKE

'MARY WASHINGTON' ASPARAGUS

smooth and cylindrical. Resistant to fusarium root rot. *'Waltham Washington,'* three years. This is an improved hybrid descendant of *'Mary Washington'* with increased resistance to asparagus rust.

**Growing conditions.** Most varieties of asparagus must be grown where winter temperatures fall below 20° F. Without freezing soil the plants will not produce.

Asparagus can be grown from seeds or from purchased roots. Neither type can be harvested before the third year, but plants started from roots will produce more spears in that year than plants started from seeds. Seeds should be started indoors in winter or outdoors after the soil has warmed to the 70s. Germination takes from two to three weeks. Seeds started indoors should be set into the soil 3 to 5 inches apart. The second year, plants should be thinned or transplanted to 15 inches apart.

Purchased roots are designated as either one- or two-year plants. The designation refers to the age of the roots; either type must grow in the garden for two years before harvesting is possible. Healthy roots have a spread of about 15 inches; they should be firm and turgid. Plant the roots in late spring, 15 inches apart.

Soil for asparagus should be rich in organic matter and well drained. Add fertilizer to the soil before planting. In subsequent years, fertilize in spring, as growth starts, and in fall, after harvesting. Water regularly, especially when the foliage is developing.

Because asparagus foliage is dense, weeding is difficult. Since asparagus does not compete well with weeds, mulch should be used to keep beds weed-free.

Pests and diseases that can affect asparagus are the asparagus beetle, thrips, rust and fusarium root rot.

**Harvesting.** Snap spears off with your fingers or cut them with a knife at or just below the soil line. Spears should be cut when they are 6 to 8 inches long, but do not harvest until the plants' third year in the garden. During the first two years, allow the spears to develop into foliage. During the third year, harvest only those spears that are at least 7 inches long and ½ inch thick. Harvest for a period of four weeks. After that, allow new spears to grow into foliage, which will strengthen the plant. In the fourth and later years, harvest for a period of six weeks, leaving later spears to produce foliage.

## Beans

Beans are a main staple of kitchens all over the world. They come in a broad range of shapes, sizes and colors and have a variety of uses. Although each type of bean has characteristics of its own, members of the bean family share certain traits.

Beans are legumes—plants having roots bearing nodules that contain nitrogen-fixing bacteria. Unless you are sowing in spring, make sure you buy bean seeds that have been treated with a bacterial culture called an inoculant, which stimulates chemical action that enables the beans to make use of the nitrogen in the soil; otherwise they will not yield well.

In soil that is cool and damp bean seeds are subject to fungus and rot. If they are started in spring, therefore, they should be treated with a fungicide instead of an inoculant; the fungicide cancels the effect of the inoculant. Whichever you choose, purchase treated seeds from a garden-supply center or a seed catalog; saving seeds from your old plants is not recommended.

All beans are susceptible to damage from certain diseases and insects. To help control these problems, rotate the crops every year, and at the end of the growing season, remove and destroy all dried plant growth.

For specific varieties, see Dry Beans; Garbanzo Beans; Horticultural Beans; Lima Beans; Snap Beans; Southern Peas; Soybeans.

## Beets
Beta vulgaris, Crassa Group

Beets are sweet-tasting, globular or tapering roots in shades of deep red or purple; a few varieties have gold roots and some have white roots. The flesh of some varieties is marked with concentric circles called zones. The tops are reddish green and leafy and grow to about 18 inches; they can be cooked and eaten as greens. Beets can be left in the soil for two years, but roots produced the second year are usually less tender and less tasty than those of the first year.

**Selected varieties.** *'Golden,'* 55 days. Fast-growing. Its golden roots do not bleed during cooking. Retains its tender texture even when allowed to grow large. Sow seeds heavily; germination is not high. *'Lutz Green Leaf,'* 80 days. Also called *'Winter Keeper'* because it stores well. Tapered, with purplish red skin; flesh is dark red and zoned. Retains its sweetness even if allowed to grow to a larger size. *'Ruby Queen,'* 52

'GOLDEN' BEET

'RUBY QUEEN' BEET

'JUWAROT' CARROT

'SHORT 'N SWEET' CARROT

'UTAH 52-70R IMPROVED' CELERY

days. Early variety. Globe-shaped, solid red, with short, dark green leaves that redden over time.

**Growing conditions.** Beets are started from seeds. In early spring, as soon as the soil can be worked, the seeds should be sown in their permanent location. Like other root crops, they cannot be transplanted; a move would cause root deformity.

Sow seeds ½ inch deep and 1 inch apart. As a beet seed is actually a fruit containing two or three seeds, thinning will need to be done soon after germination, which takes 10 to 14 days, or overcrowding will occur. Seedlings should be thinned to 3 to 4 inches apart. The thinnings may be used in soups and stews.

Beets are tolerant of heat and resistant to light frosts, so they have a long growing season. For a continuous supply of beets, sow seeds every three weeks from early spring until two months before the first fall frost date.

The best flavor is obtained when beets mature quickly, which requires a rich, loose, well-drained soil. Beets do best in neutral soil; apply lime to acid soil. Add 5-10-5 fertilizer to the soil before sowing. Water regularly to prevent toughness, especially during hot spells.

Beets are relatively insect- and disease-free; the one pest that may damage the plants is the leaf miner.

**Harvesting.** Pull beets from the ground when they are 2 to 3 inches across; gently move the soil away from the root to check the size. Light frost will not damage beets, but they should be harvested before the ground freezes hard. Leave 1 inch of stem on the beet to prevent bleeding during cooking.

**Black-eyed Peas** see Southern Peas

### Carrot
Daucus carota sativis

Carrots are yellow-orange roots that grow beneath bright green, finely cut foliage that can reach 20 inches in height. The roots are generally long, slender and tapered, although some varieties have round, short or wedge-shaped roots. Carrot plants can be left in the garden for two years, but they are usually less tender and less tasty in the second year. Selection of a carrot variety should be based on soil characteristics. The shorter types should be chosen in areas where the soil is heavy; the smaller roots are less likely to be deformed by heavy soil.

**Selected varieties.** *'Juwarot,'* 70 days. Dark orange, tapered carrot up to 8 inches in length. *'Short 'n Sweet,'* 68 days. Bright orange to the center, 4 inches long and 2 inches thick. Excellent for container growing.

**Growing conditions.** Carrots are grown from seeds, which can be sown directly in the garden in spring, as soon as the soil can be worked. Carrot plants cannot be transplanted; a move can cause deformities in the roots.

Sow seeds ½ inch deep. Germination takes two to three weeks. When plants begin to develop, thin them to 3 inches apart. The thinnings can be used in cooking. To have a continuous supply of carrots, sow seeds in succession every three weeks until two months before the first fall frost is expected.

Carrots do best in temperatures between 40° and 80° F. They should not be grown during the summer in areas of extreme heat.

If the soil is not light and loose, carrots will not form properly. Incorporate large amounts of organic matter and add 5-10-10 fertilizer to the soil before sowing. Keep the soil evenly moist to prevent the carrots from splitting.

Carrot plants can be damaged by damping-off, aster yellows, root maggots and leafhoppers.

**Harvesting.** Carrots should be harvested when they are 2 inches or less in diameter; gently move the soil away from the root to check its size. Smaller carrots generally have better flavor. Although carrots will not be harmed by light frost, they should be harvested before the ground freezes hard.

### Celery
Apium graveolens dulce

Celery is a leafy, bushy plant that grows to 30 inches tall and produces edible, elongated, light green or yellow leaf stalks usually from 6 to 9 inches long. The stalks are crisp, crunchy and high in fiber, and can be eaten raw or cooked. Celery is a biennial, but it is grown as an annual.

**Selected varieties.** *'Utah 52-70R Improved,'* 105 days. Grows 26 inches high and has crisp, thick, dark green stalks 12 inches long. Resistant to brown check, Western celery mosaic and black heart.

**Growing conditions.** Celery needs a growing season of approximately four months of 70° F weather; it is therefore a good summer crop for the northern United States. It does not thrive in areas with hot, dry summers.

Celery is grown from purchased seedlings or from seeds, which may be started indoors 10 to 12 weeks before being transplanted into the garden. Germination takes 21 to 25 days. When seedlings are 3 to 4 inches tall, plant them outdoors 9 to 12 inches apart.

Celery needs soil that is moist, rich in organic matter and has a pH of 6.0 to 7.0. Celery is also a heavy feeder; it requires twice the amount of fertilizer that most vegetables do. Fertilize with 5-10-5 prior to planting and once a month thereafter.

Celery plants can be affected by late blight, black heart, mosaic, brown check, aphids, nematodes and plant bugs.

**Harvesting.** Celery can be harvested by lifting the entire plant from the ground or by cutting the stalks off at the soil line; or outer stalks can be pulled off without damage to the plant, which will remain intact and continue to grow. Do not let celery continue growing past its maturity date or it will become pithy and hollow.

**Chick-peas** see Garbanzo Beans

## Chicory
Cichorium intybus

Chicory is a cousin of endive and escarole. Its basal foliage is oblong and grows to 18 inches in a head of large, loosely wrapped, dark green leaves. The leaves are used as salad greens. Chicory can be grown as a perennial in areas where winter temperatures drop to -20° F. It is generally grown as an annual because if it is left in the ground for more than a season, its roots become invasive.

**Selected varieties.** *'Sugarhat,'* 86 days. Grown for tender, sweet yet tangy leaves that are long and oval, resembling romaine lettuce.

**Growing conditions.** Chicory is grown from seeds planted directly in the soil about the time of the last spring frost. In the hot South and West, it can be sown in late summer for a winter crop. Seeds should be planted ½ inch deep and 4 inches apart. After germination, which takes seven to 10 days, plants should be thinned to 12 inches apart.

Soil for chicory should have a neutral pH. When plants are grown for foliage, average soil is adequate. When plants are grown for roots, soil must be rich in organic matter and constantly moist. Fertilize prior to plant-

ing and again after two months. A fertilizer low in nitrogen, such as 5-10-10, should be used when growing plants for roots; 5-10-5 should be used for foliage crops. Chicory is free of insects and diseases.

**Harvesting.** Chicory foliage can be harvested as often as needed up until just before the first frost, when the leaves begin to acquire a bitter taste. If the roots are left in the ground all winter they will produce new leaves for harvest in spring. After the leaves have been harvested, the plant will produce a tall stem with light blue flowers.

## Corn
Zea mays rugosa

Corn is a grassy plant that grows up to 9 feet tall and usually produces one or two ears with yellow, white or bicolored kernels. The kernels are square, and varieties with larger kernels have fewer rows of kernels per cob.

Corn is sweetest and most flavorful when it is cooked within minutes of picking, which is why home gardeners give so much space to this space-taking vegetable.

Beginning in the early 1970s, seed breeders developed varieties of "supersweet" corn. These varieties—also called "shrunken" for the appearance of their seeds—remain sweet for a longer period of time (10 to 14 days) after harvest because their sugar content is slow to convert to starch. The home gardener who cooks corn as soon as it is harvested does not need to grow one of the supersweet corns. These varieties are meant for corn that will be stored before cooking.

**Yellow varieties.** *'Early Sunglow,'* 63 days. Four-foot plant that produces 6- to 7-inch ears with 12 rows of very sweet kernels. A good variety for areas with cool spring weather, since seeds can survive in cold soil. Hybrid. *'Iochief,'* 89 days. This hybrid is more drought-tolerant and wind-resistant than most corns. Ears are 9 to 10 inches long with 14 to 18 kernels of corn on a 6½-foot plant.

**White varieties.** *'How Sweet It Is,'* 80 days from seed to ripe fruit. This supersweet hybrid keeps well. Plants grow to 7 feet. Cobs are 8 inches long, with 16 to 18 rows of kernels.

**Bicolored varieties.** *'Butterfruit Bicolor,'* 76 days. A supersweet hybrid. Small kernels in 16 to 18 rows on 8-inch ears. Plant grows to 7 feet. Good for freezing and canning.

'SUGARHAT' CHICORY

'EARLY SUNGLOW' YELLOW CORN

'HOW SWEET IT IS' WHITE CORN

509

'BUTTERFRUIT BICOLOR' CORN

'WHITE WONDER' SLICING CUCUMBER

'SALADIN' PICKLING CUCUMBER

**Growing conditions.** Corn is grown from seed. It does not transplant well, and should be sown directly in the soil after all danger of frost has passed and the soil has warmed to 50° F. Seeds should be planted 2 inches deep and 4 to 6 inches apart in rows 2 to 3 feet apart. Once plants are a few inches high, thin them to 12 to 14 inches. Do not grow corn plants too close together; crowding reduces yield.

To guarantee a supply of corn throughout the summer, either plant several varieties of early-, midseason- and late-maturing corn, or plant seeds in succession every two weeks until early summer.

Corn must be planted in a block of the same type and of at least three rows rather than in a straight line; this ensures pollination and development. Yellow hybrid corn must be planted downwind from white corn, or cross-pollination will occur and the white corn will not develop. The supersweet hybrids should be grown in a separate area at least 700 feet away from other varieties to prevent cross-pollination, which will result in tough, tasteless kernels.

Some corn seed is treated with a fungicide to prevent rotting before germination. This is necessary where the soil is damp and cold in spring.

Corn does best in areas with long, hot summers. Soil should be rich and neutral. Fertilize with 5-10-5 prior to planting, then when the plants are 8 inches tall and again when they are 18 inches tall. If supersweet hybrids are to germinate, the soil must be warm and twice as moist as would be needed for a regular variety of corn.

Corn is a shallow-rooted plant, so be careful when weeding not to disturb the roots. Mulch can be applied to the soil, or you can follow the Indian custom of interplanting corn with pumpkins or squash; these vegetables prevent weeds from developing.

Problems that can develop with corn are corn borer, corn earworm, corn maggot, smut and wilt. Wilt is generally a problem only with nonhybrid varieties.

**Harvesting.** The cobs are ready to harvest when the silks—the hairlike growths that emerge at the tips of the husks—start to turn brown and damp. To test for readiness, open a husk slightly and prick a kernel with your fingernail. If it bursts with its milk, it is ready to pick.

To harvest, hold the ear near the bottom and break it off the plant with a downward, twisting motion. If there are two ears per plant, the top ear will be ready a day or two before the lower one.

**Cowpeas** see Southern Peas
**Cress** see Watercress

## Cucumbers
Cucumis sativus

Most cucumbers are cylindrical, dark green fruits; most of them grow on sprawling, vining plants that reach 6 to 8 feet long and have rough, medium green, three-pointed leaves and 1-inch yellow flowers. There are also several varieties that grow on compact, bushy plants; these are ideal for gardens with limited space.

Varieties of cucumbers have been developed specifically for slicing and for pickling. Slicing cucumbers are cylindrical and can grow to 10 inches long. Pickling cucumbers are shorter and more blocky.

Cucumbers are also classed according to their reproductive traits. Most plants have both male and female flowers. Some have only female flowers; those that do yield more cucumbers and mature earlier than plants that have both male and female flowers. When you buy seeds for female-flowering plants, the packet will contain a pollinator. There are also self-fertilizing varieties, which form fruit without pollination and are truly seedless. These varieties must be isolated to prevent cross-pollination by other varieties. The varieties listed below have both male and female flowers, except where noted.

**Slicing varieties.** 'White Wonder,' 60 days. A novelty; the cucumber has snow white skin. Grows 8 to 10 inches long; meat is firm and crisp. Nonhybrid.

**Pickling varieties.** 'Saladin,' 55 days. Bright green, 5-inch fruit has only female flowers. Tolerant of powdery mildew and bacterial wilt; resistant to cucumber mosaic virus. Hybrid.

**Bush varieties.** 'Bush Crop,' 60 days from seed to ripe fruit. Slicing. A compact, bushy plant with short vines and cucumbers 7 inches long. Hybrid.

**Growing conditions.** Cucumbers are started from seeds planted directly in the soil in spring, after all danger of frost has passed. Seeds should be sown 1 inch deep and 4 to 6 inches apart. Germination takes about seven days. When seedlings are 2 inches tall, thin them to 12 inches apart.

When varieties having all female flowers are used, be sure to mark the male pollinator so that it is not accidentally thinned out. Male plants have green seeds; female plants have beige seeds. Use one male plant for every five or six females. The male flowers will blossom first. The fruit will not form until after the female flowers have bloomed.

Where the growing season is five months or more, try a second sowing in midseason for a second crop.

Cucumber vines can be left to grow along the ground or they can be trained on a trellis, pole, fence or other support.

Cucumbers do best in warm, mild climates. The soil must be rich in organic matter, light, moist and well drained. Fertilize the soil before planting and then monthly with 5-10-5.

Cucumbers are susceptible to damage from a number of diseases and insects. These include cucumber mosaic virus, downy mildew, powdery mildew, scab, bacterial wilt, angular leaf spot, anthracnose, striped cucumber beetles, aphids and mites.

**Harvesting.** Pickling cucumbers are usually harvested when small, 1½ to 3 inches long, but they can be allowed to grow longer for large dill pickles. Slicing cucumbers are harvested when they are about 7 inches long. Cut the cucumber from the vine with a knife rather than breaking it off. Cucumbers should be harvested regularly to keep the plant productive.

## Dry Beans
Phaseolus vulgaris

Dry beans are certain varieties of the snap bean family *(see Snap Beans)* that are left on the vine until dried by the sun. When the pods of these varieties mature, they split and the dry beans fall out. The plants grow to about 20 inches tall. Beans are from ¼ to ¾ inch long and are white, yellow, pink, brown, black or speckled, with somewhat variable flavor and many uses in cooking.

**Selected varieties.** *'Great Northern,'* 90 days. Also called navy beans. Pods 3 to 4 inches long filled with large white beans that retain a firm consistency when cooked.

**Growing conditions.** Dry beans mature and produce over a short period of time; to have a continuous supply of beans, make successive plantings every two to three weeks.

After all danger of frost has passed, sow seeds directly in the soil—1 inch deep in heavy soils, 1½ inches deep in sandy soils. Germination takes six days. Seedlings should be thinned to about 5 inches apart, except for the flat-podded varieties, which take slightly more space.

Dry beans do best in areas where summers are warm. The beans will grow in any average, well-drained garden soil with a pH higher than 6.0. Fertilize prior to planting with 5-10-10; no further feeding is needed.

**Harvesting.** Dry beans can be harvested by pulling pods off the plant just as they begin to split open, or by holding the plant at the base and shaking the beans off into a cheesecloth or a bag. Or the entire plant may be lifted from the soil.

## Eggplant
Solanum melongena

Eggplant is so named because its fruit was originally small, whitish and egg-shaped. Although some varieties retain this shape, the modern eggplant may be round or elongated and generally has shiny dark purple fruit. The plant is bushy, grows 2 to 3 feet tall, has fuzzy leaves and produces attractive pink flowers that develop into the fruit. Each plant usually produces four or five fruits. There are also varieties called Oriental eggplants, which produce a more slender fruit with a dull skin. The calyx (the end of the stem that looks like a cap on the eggplant) on Oriental eggplant is purple; the calyx of the others is green.

**Selected varieties.** *'Beauty Hybrid,'* 69 days. Glossy black skin covers firm flesh and rounded fruit. Resistant to fusarium and tobacco mosaic virus.

**Growing conditions.** Eggplant must have a long, warm growing season and is ideal for the Deep South and hot West. It is grown from seeds generally started indoors, eight weeks before the last frost and when night temperatures will not drop below 55° F. Sow seeds ¼ inch deep. Seeds germinate in 10 to 15 days. The seedlings should be planted in the garden 18 to 24 inches apart once the weather has settled and the soil has warmed. Eggplant may also be grown in containers.

Soil for eggplants should be slightly acid, well drained and rich in organic matter. Fertilize lightly with 5-10-5 at planting time and again when the plants bloom.

Eggplant is susceptible to damage from verticillium wilt, cutworm, flea beetle and Colorado potato beetle. To keep disease to a minimum, do not plant eggplant where tomatoes, peppers or strawberries have been grown in the last three years; all are susceptible to verticillium wilt.

'BUSH CROP' CUCUMBER

'GREAT NORTHERN' DRY BEAN

'BEAUTY HYBRID' EGGPLANT

511

GARBANZO BEAN

GARLIC

'MALINER KREN' HORSERADISH

**Harvesting.** Although an eggplant can grow up to 10 inches in diameter, it is best harvested when 4 to 5 inches across and when the skin is still glossy; when the skin becomes dull the fruit is apt to be bitter.

Cut the fruit from the plant with shears, leaving a small piece of stem on the eggplant. Harvesting early will encourage further fruit production within the season.

## Garbanzo Beans
Cicer arietinum

Garbanzo beans, also called chickpeas, grow on plants that are 12 to 24 inches tall, bushy and somewhat weedy in appearance. Tan-colored beans with a nutty flavor form in short, 1-inch swollen pods. As only one or two wrinkled beans form in each puffy pod and plants are bushy, garbanzo beans require a lot of space for a relatively low yield. The beans are a rich source of starch and protein, and they benefit the soil by replenishing its nitrogen supply.

**Selected varieties.** There are no named varieties of garbanzo beans; the seeds are sold under the common name. They mature in 100 days from seed to ripe bean.

**Growing conditions.** Garbanzo beans do best in the hot, dry conditions of the South and West. Start the plants from seeds sown directly in dry, sandy soil 1 to 1½ inches apart. Germination takes six days. As plants develop, thin them to 6 inches apart.

Garbanzo beans produce and mature over a short period of time; successive plantings ensure a continuous supply.

Plants are susceptible to mosaic, rust, anthracnose, blight, powdery mildew, aphids, leafhoppers, mites and bean beetles.

**Harvesting.** Harvest individual pods as they begin to split, or pull the entire plant out of the soil and allow the beans to dry and fall off onto a catch cloth.

## Garlic
Allium sativum

Garlic, a pungent member of the onion family, has a bulb made up of seven to 10 cloves encased in a papery white skin. Large leaves grow up to 15 inches tall. If allowed to flower, garlic produces clusters of tiny white blooms. Flowering does not affect the quality of the edible cloves. Garlic is a perennial, but in areas of extreme cold it may not survive the winter.

**Selected varieties.** Although a few varieties of garlic have been developed, they are not widely available to home gardeners. Garlic is usually sold under its common name. The plant matures in 90 days from clove to bulb.

**Growing conditions.** Garlic is grown from individual cloves, available from garden-supply centers or you can use cloves from the supermarket. Break cloves off carefully from the main bulb and plant them directly in the soil 3 to 4 inches apart, with the pointed side up and deep enough so their tips are just covered.

Garlic is planted in early to middle spring as soon as the ground can be worked for harvest in the fall. In the hot South and West, garlic can be planted in fall for a spring harvest. Cloves will begin to show signs of growth within seven days; the tip of a green stem will emerge from the soil.

Soil for garlic should be well drained, light, sandy and enriched with organic matter. The best growth is obtained when the soil is loose; the pH level can be anywhere in the 5.5 to 8.0 range. Fertilize at planting time and again when the tops are 6 inches tall, using a fertilizer low in nitrogen. Too much nitrogen will cause lush top growth at the expense of the bulbs.

Garlic plants actually repel insects; the plants are also free of disease.

**Harvesting.** When the foliage starts to turn yellow at the end of the season, bend the tops over at the base without breaking them. This will hasten ripening and drying. Leave the bulbs in the soil for two to three days; then lift them carefully and allow them to dry in the sun. After harvesting, save several bulbs for cloves to plant for next year's crop.

**Green Beans** see Snap Beans

## Horseradish
Armoracia rusticana

The root of the horseradish plant is the source of the hot and zesty grated sauce of the same name. The plant grows to 30 inches tall, has large, coarse leaves and white, seedless flowers. The roots are long, thick and white. Horseradish is a perennial hardy to 10° F, but it is generally grown as an annual, because roots become tough and stringy the second year.

**Selected varieties.** 'Maliner Kren,' 150 days from root cuttings to mature fruit. The standard variety of horseradish, also known as Bohemian horseradish. Straight white roots up to 18 inches in length.

**Growing conditions.** Horseradish is grown from root cuttings, which may be planted in spring or fall. If you take cuttings from a larger root, cut 6-inch sections as thick as a pencil. Purchased roots have tapered ends; plant them at an angle, with the slanted end pointing down and the upper end 2 to 3 inches below the soil surface. Space the roots about 1 foot apart. Horseradish does not do well in extreme summer heat or sandy soil.

Soil should be loose, rich and well drained for straight root formation. Add fertilizer to the soil at planting time.

The flea beetle can cause damage to horseradish plants.

**Harvesting.** Dig up horseradish roots in autumn and winter as needed; they are best used when fresh. Be sure to remove all roots that will not be used before growth starts the next spring, since remaining roots can become invasive weeds.

### Horticultural Beans
Phaseolus vulgaris

Horticultural beans, also called field beans or shell beans, are very similar to snap beans, but they are grown for the seeds inside their pods, like peas. Although it is possible to harvest young beans and eat the pods, the pods are tough.

Some varieties have colorful pods splashed with crimson or maroon, and some have bicolored beans. The beans range in size from $\frac{1}{4}$ to $\frac{1}{2}$ inch long, and their texture is mealy and nutty.

**Selected varieties.** *'French Horticultural,'* 68 days. The plant produces short runners but does not need staking. Pods have splashes of red and cream; beans are buff and red.

**Growing conditions.** Beans are grown from seeds planted directly in the garden after all danger of frost has passed and the soil is warm. Seeds should be sown 1 inch deep in heavy soils and $1\frac{1}{2}$ inches deep in sandy soils. Germination takes about six days. Seedlings should be thinned to about 5 inches apart.

Beans can be grown in any average, well-drained soil with a pH over 6.0. Before planting, fertilize with 5-10-10; no further feeding is necessary.

Beans are susceptible to damage from anthracnose, blight, powdery mildew, aphids, bean beetles, leafhoppers and mites.

**Harvesting.** When the beans are mature, either pull the pods off the plant or lift the entire plant from the ground. The beans should be full and plump. Test by harvesting a few as their maturity date approaches; it may be necessary to let some beans become overripe so that the majority are ripe enough for easy shelling. The overripe beans can be used in the same ways as dry beans.

### Jerusalem Artichoke
Helianthus tuberosus

The Jerusalem artichoke is a relative of the sunflower. It is an edible, crunchy round tuber about one-fourth the size of a large potato. The plant forms stalks that reach 6 to 8 feet in height and has 3-inch, sunflower-like blooms. Jerusalem artichokes are perennials hardy to -10° F but are grown as annuals because they become invasive if they are left in the garden.

**Selected varieties.** There are no named varieties of Jerusalem artichoke; it is sold under its common name. The artichokes mature in 110 days from root cuttings to tubers.

**Growing conditions.** Jerusalem artichokes sprout from the eyes—buds embedded in small indentations—in their own tubers. Small tubers can be planted whole; large tubers should be cut into pieces that have at least one growing eye. In spring, cuttings should be planted 4 to 6 inches deep and 12 inches apart. If flower buds form on the plant, they should be removed before they blossom to encourage root growth.

Soil should be dry and sandy. Fertilize very sparingly and water only when the ground is dry.

Jerusalem artichoke is resistant to insects and diseases.

**Harvesting.** In the late fall, remove the tubers from the ground by digging a large, circular hole around each stalk, then lifting them from the soil by hand. Remove all of the tubers to prevent the plant from becoming an invasive weed.

### Leeks
Allium ampeloprasum,
Porrum Group

Leeks are members of the onion family with a mild, delicate, sweet flavor. Unlike onions, leeks do not form bulbs, but grow into thick, cylindrical, edible stalks that can reach 18 inches tall. The foliage, which is dark green, flat and straplike, can also be used in cooking.

'FRENCH HORTICULTURAL' BEAN

JERUSALEM ARTICHOKE

'BROAD LONDON' LEEK

'BUTTERCRUNCH' BUTTERHEAD LETTUCE

'ICEBERG' CRISPHEAD LETTUCE

'RED SAILS' LEAF LETTUCE

**Selected varieties.** *'Broad London,'* 150 days from seed to mature root. Also called *'Large American Flag.'* Blue-green leaves top thick, 9-inch-long stems. Tolerates cold; the best variety if plants will remain in the garden through winter.

**Growing conditions.** Leeks are grown from seeds. Because they take a long time to mature, leek seeds are usually started indoors six to 10 weeks before transplanting into the garden. Germination takes about 10 days. The seedlings can be transplanted when they are about the thickness of a pencil; they should be spaced 3 to 6 inches apart.

Soil for leeks must be fertile, rich and constantly moist to ensure stem development. The soil pH must be in the 6.0 to 8.0 range. Fertilize at planting time with 5-10-5, and again when the tops are 6 to 9 inches tall.

It is possible to leave leeks in the ground over winter and harvest them the following spring. When this is done, apply mulch or some other winter protection if the temperature drops below 10° F.

Leeks are susceptible to damage from aphids and maggots; they are relatively disease-free.

**Harvesting.** Leeks can be harvested in the fall any time after they have reached ¾ inch in diameter; but if they are allowed to grow to 1½ inches in diameter, they will have a sweeter flavor. In areas with mild climates, leeks can be left in the ground all winter and harvested as needed, or harvested the following spring.

## Lettuce
Lactuca sativa

What would a salad be without lettuce? Although several other greens are used as salad bases, lettuce is still the number one choice for salads.

There are four types of lettuce: butterhead, crisphead, leaf and romaine (also called cos). Butterhead lettuce has crisp, fleshy, delicate leaves of light to dark green that form a small, loose head; the interior of the head is creamy in color. Crisphead, also called iceberg lettuce, has a tight, firm head of brittle leaves. Since the plants cannot be crowded and are slow to mature, this is the most difficult type of lettuce to grow. Leaf lettuce is a nonheading lettuce with rumpled, frilled or oaklike leaves of light to dark green or bronzered. It matures quickly and is the easiest lettuce to grow. Romaine lettuce has an upright, cylindrical head with firmly wrapped leaves that are light to medium green with a cream-colored interior. Romaine leaves have a slightly sweeter flavor than leaf or butterhead varieties.

Although lettuce is grown in summer, it does not do well in hot weather or warm soil. High temperatures can make lettuce bolt, meaning the plant produces flowers, which causes the leaves to wilt and become very bitter. Some types and varieties are less prone to bolting than others. Generally, leaf and romaine types are the most heat-resistant.

**Butterhead varieties.** *'Buttercrunch,'* 65 days. Thick, juicy, dark green, crumpled leaves form a compact head. This variety stays sweet even in hot weather and is very slow to bolt. Developed to tolerate summer heat, it is the most bolt-resistant butterhead.

**Crisphead varieties.** *'Iceberg,'* 85 days. Crisp, tender heads of silver-white are surrounded by light green, crinkled leaves with edges often tinged in brown. Tolerates some heat. Resistant to tip burn.

**Leaf varieties.** *'Red Sails,'* 42 days. Ruffled and fringed red-bronze leaves form a compact, open head with a full center.

**Romaine varieties.** *'Parris Island,'* 70 days from seed to mature leaves. Dark green, slightly crinkled leaves form a tight, erect, 10-inch head. Slow to bolt. Resistant to tip burn and tolerant of lettuce mosaic.

**Growing conditions.** Lettuce can be grown from seed or from purchased seedlings. Leaf lettuce is almost always grown from seed because it matures quickly. Butterhead and romaine varieties can be grown from either seed or seedlings. Crisphead lettuce requires a longer growing season and is almost always grown from purchased seedlings.

When lettuce is planted in spring, it should be done as soon as the ground can be worked; lettuce does better in cool temperatures. For a continuous harvest, lettuce can be planted successively every two weeks until hot weather arrives. After the high heat of summer is past, lettuce can be planted again if there is enough time for it to mature between planting and the first fall frost date. In mild-climate areas, lettuce can be planted throughout the winter.

Lettuce can be started from seeds sown indoors or directly in the garden; in either case, the seeds should not be covered with soil because they need light to germinate. To start crisphead varieties indoors, sow seeds 10 weeks before the last frost date; butterhead and romaine varieties need only six weeks before transplanting. Or, after the last frost, sow seeds directly in the soil, 3 inches apart. Germination takes seven to 10 days. Thin leaf lettuce to 6 inches apart, butterhead and romaine to 10 inches apart, crisphead to 12 inches apart. The thinnings can be used in salads and cooking.

Soil for lettuce must be neutral in pH, fertile and well drained. Soil must be kept uniformly and constantly moist, or the head-lettuce varieties will develop pinkish brown interiors. Fertilize before planting and again every three weeks to promote fast growth, which enhances the flavor. Frequent weeding is necessary; lettuce does not compete well with weeds. Mulch will reduce weed growth and keep the soil cool and moist.

Lettuce plants can be damaged by slugs and snails, aphids, mosaic, downy mildew and tip burn.

**Harvesting.** Leaves of leaf varieties can be picked from the outside of the plant any time they are large enough. With butterhead and romaine, outer leaves may be picked or the entire plant can be lifted from the soil when it matures. Crisphead lettuce is harvested when the center is firm; squeeze the head to test for firmness.

## Lima Beans
Phaseolus limensis

Two types of lima beans are grown in home gardens: large-seeded and baby limas, also called butter beans. Both types are flat, light-colored beans from ½ to 1 inch long and have a mealy or nutlike flavor. Both are shelled before eating. Lima beans are available in both bush and pole varieties, but all baby limas grow on bush-type plants. The pole varieties mature later but bear over a longer period of time than the bush varieties.

Most of the northern part of the United States is not suited for growing the large-seeded limas; these beans need a long growing season of high temperatures. The baby limas mature faster and can be planted in areas where the growing season is short. Baby limas are also a good crop for the hot regions of the South and West because they are more heat-resistant than large-seeded varieties.

**Bush varieties.** 'Fordhook 242,' 75 days. A large-seeded lima. High-yielding plant produces many pods with three or four plump, thick beans. Resistant to heat and rot.

**Pole varieties.** 'King of the Garden,' 88 days. Pods are 5 inches long and an inch wide; they contain three or four large, flat beans.

**Growing conditions.** Lima beans are grown from seeds sown directly in the soil because they do not transplant well. Sow the seeds in the spring, when the soil is 70° F or warmer. If the soil is cool, use a fungicide to prevent seeds from rotting.

Plant seeds 1 inch deep in clay soils and 1½ inches deep in sandy soils. Germination takes seven days. Thin both bush and pole varieties to about 8 inches apart.

Bush limas can be planted in succession every two weeks until approximately two months before the first fall frost. Pole lima beans will require staking; stake them as soon as the plants begin to develop so that they do not become tangled and damaged.

Soil should be light and well drained and have a pH higher than 6.0. Fertilize with 5-10-10 before planting but do not feed again during the season.

Lima beans are susceptible to damage from aphids, leafhoppers, mites, anthracnose, blight and mildew. Pole varieties are especially susceptible to damage from the bean beetle.

**Harvesting.** Beans can be picked as soon as pods are full-sized, between 3 and 5 inches long. Harvest pole lima beans carefully to prevent the vines from breaking; hold the vine in one hand while harvesting with the other. Pods should be picked as they mature to keep the plant productive. Late in the season, some limas can be left on the plant and harvested as dry beans.

**Navy Beans** see Dry Beans
**New Zealand Spinach**
see Summer Spinach

'PARRIS ISLAND' ROMAINE LETTUCE

'FORDHOOK 242' BUSH LIMA BEAN

'KING OF THE GARDEN' POLE LIMA BEAN

'ANNIE OAKLEY' OKRA

'STOCKTON RED' BULBING ONION

'YELLOW SWEET SPANISH' BULBING ONION

## Okra
Hibiscus esculentus

Okra is a fast-growing plant that ranges from 3 to 8 feet in height and produces attractive, yellow, hollyhock-like blooms that have maroon centers. The flowers grow into slender, pointed, edible green seedpods up to 8 inches long. Their skin is either smooth or ribbed. The leaves are large, lush and lobed.

**Selected varieties.** *'Annie Oakley,'* 52 days from seed to ripe fruit. Compact plant produces long, slender pods; pods remain tender even if they are left on the plant longer than their maturity date. A good choice for areas where the climate is cool. Hybrid.

**Growing conditions.** Okra is started from seed. In warm areas with a long growing season, the seeds can be sown directly in the soil; they should be planted ½ to ¾ inch deep. In areas with a short growing season, the seeds can be started indoors four to six weeks before the last frost date. Germination takes 10 to 14 days. Thin the seedlings to 12 inches apart for the shorter varieties and 18 inches apart for the taller ones.

Okra will grow in any average clay soil with a neutral pH. Fertilize with 5-10-5 when the plants are 8 inches tall, and again when pods start to form.

Okra plants can be damaged by cold winds and in windy areas may require some protection, such as a location behind a fence. The plants are also susceptible to damage from fusarium wilt, corn earworms and nematodes.

**Harvesting.** Although okra pods can grow to 8 inches in length, they should generally be picked when they are 2 to 3 inches long, or they will become tough and tasteless. Harvesting should be done every two or three days to keep the plant producing. After the first harvest, remove the bottom leaves from the plant; this will help keep it productive. In regions of the South and West where summers are hot, plants can become extremely tall, which makes harvesting difficult. Tall plants can be cut down to 12 to 18 inches; they will resprout and continue to produce.

## Onions
Allium cepa, Cepa Group

Whether it be green, red, purple, yellow or white, the onion is one of the mainstays of the kitchen. It can be eaten raw or cooked.

Onions are categorized in two groups: bulbing onions and bunching onions. Bulbing onions are grown for the 1- to 5-inch edible bulbs that form at the base of 20-inch foliage shoots. These bulbs, available in a variety of colors, are enclosed in papery skins. Bunching onions have either small bulbs or no bulbs at all; they are grown for their edible, tubular, multiple green stems that grow to 12 inches tall. They are called bunching onions because the stems grow in a bunch from the base. They continue to divide and sprout new stems throughout the growing season. Both bulbing and bunching onions harvested at an immature stage are called scallions.

Bulbing varieties are classified as either long-day or short-day onions. This is a critical distinction based on their growth habits; long-day onions will form bulbs only during the long days of summer in the northern parts of the United States, and short-day onions will form bulbs only during the short days of winter or the shorter days that occur in summer in the South.

**Bulbing varieties.** *'Stockton Red,'* 100 days. Medium-sized, round onion with thick, dark purple skin. *'Yellow Sweet Spanish,'* 120 days. Long-day. Very large, globe-shaped onion with golden yellow skin and white flesh. Does not store well.

**Bunching varieties.** *'Japanese Bunching,'* 110 days. Long, slender green stems. Plant forms little or no bulb.

**Growing conditions.** Onions can be grown from seeds, transplants or sets. Sets are dry bulbs whose growth has been temporarily halted. These are usually long-day onions and are grown only in the northern regions of the United States. Onions started from seeds are usually sown indoors 10 to 12 weeks before the last frost date. In areas with a long growing season, they can be sown directly in the soil, ¼ to ½ inch deep. Germination takes 10 to 14 days. Transplants and sets should be planted about 1 inch deep.

The final spacing for plants, regardless of how they were started, depends on the type of onion. Bulbing onions should be spaced a distance slightly larger than their ultimate diameter. Bunching onions and those grown for scallions should be spaced 2 to 3 inches apart.

The soil must be well drained, high in organic matter, fertile and loose. Onions do not grow well in clay soils. The soil pH should be as close to neutral as possible. Fertilize heavily at the time of planting and feed twice more during the growing season.

Bulbing onions may poke their way out of the soil as they grow; the sunlight on the top of the onion will help increase the bulb size.

Onions can be damaged by neck rot, maggots and thrips.

**Harvesting.** Bunching onions and onions grown for scallions may be harvested as soon as they are large enough. Remove only half of the bunch at one time; this allows new shoots to form within four to six weeks. Bunching onions do not store well, so they should be harvested as needed. The longer they remain in the ground, the more pungent they will be.

Bulbing onions are ready for harvesting when their tops begin to turn brown. To hasten ripening, bend the tops over gently without breaking them. Several days later, dig around the onions carefully and lift the bulbs from the soil. Leave them in the sun for a week, until their necks are dry.

## Parsnips
Pastinaca sativa

Parsnips are long, carrot-like, yellowish white roots with leafy tops of lacy green foliage. The root can grow to 12 inches long and to 3 inches thick at the shoulder. Compound-leaved foliage grows to 18 inches tall. Parsnips are biennials and can remain in the ground through winter, but plants not harvested until spring lose some flavor and tenderness.

**Selected varieties.** *'Harris Model,'* 110 days. A medium-length root; this is the smoothest and whitest variety.

**Growing conditions.** Parsnips are grown from seeds sown directly in the soil in early spring, as soon as the soil can be worked. Sow the seeds ¼ to ½ inch deep, and sow them generously; only a small percentage will germinate. The seeds may take as long as 18 days to sprout. When the seedlings are 1 inch tall, thin them to about 5 inches apart.

Parsnip seeds are short-lived. They should be stored in the refrigerator until sowing, and they cannot be saved from one year to the next.

Parsnips need warm but not excessively hot temperatures, so they are not a good summer crop in hot regions of the South and West.

Soil for parsnips should be light, loose, slightly acid and evenly moist to prevent root distortion. Fertilize with 5-10-5 prior to planting and again every month during the growing season. Keep the area weeded; parsnips do not compete well with weeds.

Parsnips are susceptible to damage from aphids, beetles, leafhoppers and leaf miners.

**Harvesting.** Parsnips are harvested in fall after the first frost; freezing temperatures help make the root sweet. Loosen the soil around the plant and then pull the root out of the soil. Parsnips can be harvested all at once and stored or harvested as needed. If they remain in the soil in winter, a straw mulch will help keep the ground warm.

## Peppers
Capsicum annuum

Peppers are among the most versatile vegetables; they can be used for slicing and eating raw, and for frying, pickling, stuffing or spicing. They are available in a wide variety of shapes, colors, sizes and tastes. Peppers form from white flowers on a bushy plant that grows 20 to 30 inches tall and wide.

Pepper varieties are classified as either sweet or hot. Most bell-shaped peppers are sweet peppers. Most long, thin, tapered peppers are hot peppers. The color of the pepper has nothing to do with its spiciness; all peppers, even the familiar green bell pepper, will eventually turn red or gold if left on the plant.

Pimentos are the sweetest peppers; when dried, they are ground to make paprika. Hot peppers are the source of cayenne pepper and Tabasco sauce.

**Sweet varieties.** *'Better Belle,'* 65 days. A blocky, four-lobed medium green bell pepper with thick walls; 4½ by 3½ inches. Resistant to tobacco mosaic virus. Hybrid.

**Hot varieties.** *'Anaheim TMR23,'* 77 days from transplanting to ripe fruit. A long, tapered, flat pepper 8 by 2½ inches. One of the mildest hot peppers. Nonhybrid.

**Growing conditions.** Peppers can be grown either from seeds or from purchased seedlings. Since peppers require a long, warm growing season, seeds are generally started indoors, eight to 10 weeks before transplanting. Seeds should be sown ⅛ inch deep. Germination takes 10 days. Transplanting can be done when temperatures are consistently in the 60s. The plants should be set 18 to 24 inches apart, so that they will just touch each other when mature.

Soil should be rich, moist, well drained and slightly acid. Do not overfertilize peppers; this will cause lush foliage growth and no fruit. Feed lightly at planting time and again in six weeks.

'JAPANESE BUNCHING' ONION

'HARRIS MODEL' PARSNIP

'BETTER BELLE' SWEET PEPPER

'ANAHEIM TMR23' HOT PEPPER

'KATAHDIN' BAKING POTATO

'NORLAND' BOILING POTATO

Pepper plants can be damaged by sunscald, tobacco mosaic virus, aphids, borers and cutworms.

**Harvesting.** The pepper is a unique plant because it will produce only a certain number of fruits at one time. Once that number is reached, the plant stops producing blossoms. When some of the fruits are harvested, the plant will resume production.

Sweet varieties are usually harvested when they are immature, green, full-sized and firm, but if they are allowed to mature and turn red on the vine, the peppers will be sweeter and higher in vitamins A and C. Hot varieties are picked after they have reached maturity. The fruit of both varieties can be cut or picked from the stem; in either case be sure to leave a piece of stem on the pepper.

## Potatoes
Solanum tuberosum

The potato is an edible underground tuber that forms between the base of an underground stem and the roots. Tubers can be either round or oblong, with brown or red skin and with white or cream-colored flesh. Varieties are classified by the way they are to be cooked—boiled or baked. The flesh of the two types is different in texture; boiling varieties are moist and baking varieties are dry and mealy. The plant grows 30 inches high and 4 feet wide. Its flowers are pale pink to white with protruding yellow centers; leaves are large and compound. Potatoes are annuals.

**Baking varieties.** *'Katahdin,'* 115 days from seed potato to mature potato. Large, round to oblong potato with cream-colored skin.

**Boiling varieties.** *'Norland,'* 90 days from seed potato to mature potato. Red-skinned potato with shallow eyes and smooth white flesh. Resistant to scab.

**Growing conditions.** Although there are a few varieties of potato that are grown from true seed, the plant is most frequently grown from a seed potato— a portion of a mature potato that has at least one eye, or bud, in an indentation on the potato skin.

When you purchase seed potatoes, be sure they are certified disease-free by the state or provincial agricultural department. Growing plants from store-bought potatoes is not recommended because the risk of disease is high, and store-bought potatoes are usually treated with a sprout inhibitor.

Seed potatoes come in various sizes. The optimum seed potato is about 1½ by 2 inches in size, weighs 2 to 3 ounces and has one to three eyes. Larger seed potatoes need to be cut into blocks of roughly these dimensions; if you do so, be sure that each piece has at least one eye. The pieces should be placed in a light, airy location for one or two days to dry.

Plant seed potatoes in early spring about five weeks before the last frost. Set them 4 to 5 inches deep with the eyes facing up. Space them 12 to 15 inches apart.

Potatoes do best in mild, warm-summer climates. Since cool nights aid the final stages of the ripening process, potatoes are grown as fall and spring crops in hot regions of the South and West.

Soil must be sandy, rich in organic matter, well drained, loose and acid, with a pH between 4.5 and 5.5. At planting time, mix 5-10-5 into the soil before setting the potatoes in place. No further fertilizing is needed.

If you plant potatoes in the soil, as opposed to laying them under straw *(page 490)*, the soil must be tilled, or mounded up, around the potatoes to keep them from poking through the soil and being exposed to light. Light turns potatoes green, bitter and slightly poisonous. Any potatoes having a greenish cast should be discarded.

Potatoes can be damaged by the Colorado potato beetle, flea beetle, aphid, leafhopper, scab and blight.

**Harvesting.** Immature potatoes, also called new potatoes, are harvested in midsummer about the time the plants are in bloom. Harvest them by digging gently around the plant and removing some tubers, leaving the rest to grow to full size.

Mature potatoes are harvested in the fall, when the plant tops die back. Use a potato rake or a garden fork to loosen the soil first and minimize damage to the tubers; then gently lift out the potatoes.

Cure potatoes by storing them in a warm, dark place for 14 days; then move them to a cool—about 50° F— dry location.

## Pumpkin
Cucurbita

This Halloween favorite is a member of the squash family. It grows on large, sprawling vines that can spread to 10 feet, and on bush-type plants that reach 3 feet in width. The plant stems are prickly. The leaves are large, triangular and slightly lobed. The yellow flowers develop into large round fruits with orange skin.

Pumpkins belong to one of two species. *C. pepo,* the smaller, ranges from 6 to 20 pounds and is used for baking and carving. *C. maxima,* the larger, ranges from 20 to 100 pounds and is grown primarily for exhibition.

**Selected varieties.** *'Big Max,'* 120 days from seed to ripe fruit. A globe-shaped pumpkin that can grow to 100 pounds. The skin is rough and reddish pink; underneath is a layer of orange-yellow flesh that is 4 inches thick and stringy. Nonhybrid.

**Growing conditions.** Although pumpkin seedlings generally do not transplant well, they can be started indoors if the seeds are planted in individual peat pots that can go with them into garden soil and thus reduce transplant shock. Pumpkin seeds should be started four or five weeks before the last frost date and planted outdoors after all danger of frost has passed.

Sow seeds ½ to 1 inch deep, either in groups in mounded hills or in rows. Space the hills 6 to 8 feet apart for vining plants and 3 to 4 feet apart for bush plants. Plant four to six seeds per hill. After germination, which takes seven to 10 days, thin the hills to two plants per hill. If seeds are sown in rows, space the seeds 6 inches apart. After germination, thin vining plants to 4 feet apart and bush plants to 3 feet apart.

Soil for pumpkins must be rich in organic matter, well drained and have a neutral pH. Fertilize with 5-10-5 at planting time and again every four weeks until harvest. Pumpkins are among the few summer vegetables that will tolerate light shade.

Approximately one month before harvest, pinch back any new tips and remove the smaller fruits from the plant so the largest pumpkins can develop to full size.

To raise large, exhibition pumpkins, select one of the large-fruited varieties and allow only one pumpkin to develop on the plant.

Pumpkins can be damaged by vine borers and cucumber beetles.

**Harvesting.** As pumpkins mature, they should be raised off the ground on boards to prevent the bottoms from rotting *(page 493).* Pumpkins are harvested in the fall, when the rind becomes hard and the foliage starts to die. They will tolerate light frost but must be harvested before a hard frost. Leave a piece of the stem on the pumpkin to prevent rotting.

## Rhubarb
Rheum rhabarbarum

Rhubarb is usually grown for its edible stalks, which are used to make tart-flavored pies, preserves and sauces. It is also an attractive ornamental in perennial borders. Its green, pink or red leaf stalks grow from 18 to 26 inches high and to 2 inches thick. The leaves are heart-shaped, textured, curled and deep green tinged with red. Though attractive, the leaves are poisonous and should be stripped from the stalks when they are harvested.

**Selected varieties.** *'Valentine'* has deep red stalks that retain their color when cooked. The sweetest variety.

**Growing conditions.** Rhubarb can be grown only in areas with cold winters and mild summers. It must have at least two months of freezing temperatures in order to produce and does not tolerate temperatures above 90° F.

Rhubarb is generally grown from root divisions. It can be started from seed, but this is risky, since a plant grown from seed may not grow true to the variety, is not as strong as a plant started from a root division and takes longer to mature.

Root divisions may be either purchased at a garden-supply center or taken from old plants in your own or a friend's garden. The plants should be divided every four years or when stalks start to grow thin. Early spring is the best time for dividing. Cut the roots of old plants into clumps, each of which has at least one bud, or eye—a whitish, red-tinted protrusion pointing upward from the root. Plant the clumps 36 inches apart, with the eye set 3 inches deep in the soil.

Soil should be neutral, moist, well drained and rich in organic matter. Incorporate 5-10-5 into the soil before planting. After the first year, feed plants in spring, when growth starts, and again in fall, after harvest. Add mulch for protection during winter in areas where temperatures drop below 10° F.

Rhubarb plants can be damaged by slugs, snails, earwigs, beetles or leaf spot.

**Harvesting.** Stalks should not be harvested for at least one year after plants are grown from root cuttings. Outer stalks can be harvested in spring and early summer when they are 18 to 24 inches long. Pull or break them off at the base instead of cutting them, because cutting may damage the roots located at the soil surface. Any stalks less than 1 inch thick should be left on the plant.

'BIG MAX' PUMPKIN

'VALENTINE' RHUBARB

'SANDWICH ISLAND MAMMOTH' SALSIFY

SHALLOT

'ROMANO' BUSH BEAN

Rhubarb can be harvested over a six- to eight-week period. Do not at any time remove more than half of the plant's stalks; some foliage is necessary to strengthen the plant and encourage future growth.

## Salsify
Tragopogon porrifolius

Salsify is grown for its 8-inch, tapered, smooth, thick taproot, which in its appearance resembles a parsnip, with dull, creamy white flesh. Because it tastes something like an oyster, salsify is also called oyster plant or vegetable oyster. The foliage looks like clumps of thick grass.

**Selected varieties.** *'Sandwich Island Mammoth,'* 120 days from seed to mature root. The most widely available variety of salsify.

**Growing conditions.** Salsify is started from seeds sown directly in the soil about two weeks before the last spring frost. The seeds should be sown ¼ inch deep and 2 inches apart. Germination takes seven days. When the plant tops are 3 inches high, the plants should be thinned to about 5 inches apart.

Soil must be light, sandy, deep and rich in organic matter—but manure should not be used because it causes the roots to split. The roots also crack in dry soil; soil should be kept moist. Fertilize with 5-10-5 at planting time and again in two months.

Salsify is generally insect- and disease-free; but if aphids or tarnished plant bugs are in the garden, they may attack salsify plants.

**Harvesting.** Dig up the roots in fall, just before the ground freezes. Soaking the soil first will make the roots easier to remove. Some roots can also be left in the ground all winter and then harvested in spring.

## Scallions see Onions

## Shallots
Allium cepa, Aggregatum Group

Shallot is the onion substitute called for in many French gourmet recipes; it has a more delicate, subtle flavor than the standard onion.

The plant is grown primarily for its bulb, which is shaped like garlic but is smaller and chestnut brown rather than white. Each bulb may have three

to four cloves. The foliage is also edible; it resembles immature green onions with long, tube-shaped leaves.

**Selected varieties.** Shallot has no specific varieties; it is sold under its common name. It develops in 90 days from clove to mature bulb.

**Growing conditions.** The shallot grows from a bulb, which can be purchased from a garden-supply center or from a gourmet market. The bulb should be broken into separate cloves. Each clove is inserted into the soil so that the tip is just below the soil surface. Cloves should be spaced about 3 inches apart.

The cloves can be planted in early spring, as soon as the soil can be worked. In the hot South and West, they can be planted in the fall for harvest the following spring.

Soil should be loose and rich with a neutral pH. Add a low-nitrogen fertilizer such as 5-10-10 to the soil at planting time. Feed again halfway through the growing season.

Shallots are generally insect- and disease-free but may be attacked by aphids and maggots.

**Harvesting.** Young shallots can be harvested and used like green onions. To harvest full-sized bulbs, wait until fall, when the foliage starts to turn brown. To encourage the bulb to ripen, bend the foliage down without breaking it off. After five days, dig up the bulbs and store them in a cool, airy, dry spot.

After harvesting, save several bulbs for cloves to start next year's crop.

## Snap Beans
Phaseolus vulgaris

Snap beans are pods of seeds harvested before the seeds mature. Most varieties of snap beans are green and are also called green beans, French beans or string beans. Very few of them are true string beans. This is a name once given to the bean because the seam of the pod used to have a string that needed to be removed before cooking, a nuisance eliminated by modern breeding. Some varieties of snap beans are yellow; these are also called wax beans. A few varieties of snap beans are purple.

Snap beans are oval, round, or broad and flat pods ranging from 5 to 12 inches long. They grow on one of two types of plants: bush plants and vines. The vine types are also called pole beans because they must be supported. Bush varieties are full, stocky plants that grow to 20 inches tall. The plants produce beans for only about three weeks; for a continuous supply, they must be planted successively every two to three weeks. Pole varieties grow 6 to 8 feet tall. Once they mature, they produce beans over a period of about eight weeks.

Whether you select bush beans or pole beans will depend on how you intend to use the crop. Bush beans mature over a concentrated period of time, which is an advantage if you can or freeze them. Pole beans grow more slowly and produce more pods over a longer period of time, which is preferable if you want to eat them fresh.

**Bush varieties.** 'Blue Lake,' 57 days from seed to ripe bean. Smooth, medium green, round, 6-inch pods with white seeds on a 16-inch plant. The entire crop matures at once. Resistant to common bean mosaic. 'Brittle Wax,' 52 days. A high-yielding wax bean plant. The pod is lemon yellow, rounded, slightly curved and 7 inches long.

'Romano,' 53 days. Also known as 'Roma II.' This is the bush form of the 'Romano' pole bean. The bush variety matures earlier and is more disease-resistant. Flat green pods are 4 inches long and filled with buff seeds. Flavor is stronger and sharper than other varieties. Resistant to common bean mosaic and mildew.

**Pole varieties.** 'Scarlet Runner' Bean, (Phaseolus coccineus), 65 days. A vegetable that is frequently grown for its ornamental value. The vine grows to 15 feet. Its scarlet blossoms are attractive. The pods grow to 12 inches long. Can be grown as a perennial where winter temperatures do not drop below 20° F.

**Growing conditions.** Snap beans are grown from seeds sown directly in the soil in spring, when the ground is warm and all danger of frost has passed. Seeds should be sown 1 inch deep in heavy soil and 1½ inches deep in sandy soil. Germination will take six days. White-seeded beans may not germinate as well as others and thus should be sown more heavily than other varieties.

The spacing for bush beans should be 3 to 4 inches between plants, except for the flat-podded varieties, which require slightly more space. The spacing for pole beans depends on the type of support used. In general, several seeds should be sown at the base of each support and then thinned to keep only the strongest seedling per support.

Beans do best in areas with warm summers, but they will not produce in extreme heat. In the South and West, beans are generally grown as spring and fall crops. Bush beans are more heat- and drought-resistant than pole beans.

Beans will grow in any average, well-drained garden soil with a pH over 6.0. Fertilize prior to planting with 5-10-10; no further feeding will be needed.

Bean plants can be damaged by mosaic, rust, anthracnose, blight, powdery mildew, aphids, bean beetles, leafhoppers and mites.

**Harvesting.** Snap beans can be harvested when they are large enough to eat; the seeds should be starting to fill out. Hold the plant stem in one hand while pulling the pods off with the other; do not let the stem break.

### Sorrel
Rumex acetosa

Sorrel, also called sour grass, is grown for its tart, tangy, citrus-flavored leaves, which are used in soups and salads. Its arrow-shaped foliage, 8 to 16 inches long and high in vitamin C, grows on upright plants in large, dense clumps. When in bloom, the plants can reach 4 feet in height, but without flowers they are 18 inches high. Although sorrel is a perennial hardy to -20° F in winter, it is generally grown as an annual because it becomes invasive.

**Selected varieties.** Although a few varieties of sorrel have been developed, sorrel is most often sold under its common name. The plants mature in 100 days from seed to ripe leaves.

**Growing conditions.** Sorrel is usually grown from seeds planted directly in the soil in spring. Seeds should be sown ⅛ inch deep and 4 inches apart. After germination, which takes 10 days, the plants should be thinned to 10 inches apart. If sorrel is left in the ground and grown as a perennial, new plants can be started from root divisions of old plants. Because sorrel is a rapid spreader, it can be divided every two to three years.

Although sorrel will grow in areas of high heat, its flavor is best when it matures in cool temperatures. It is one of the relatively few vegetables that will tolerate partial shade.

Soil should be well drained and have a neutral pH; acid soil encourages the weedy characteristics of the plant. To help control its invasiveness, cut off the flower heads as soon as they appear so seeds will not spread.

Sorrel plants are susceptible to slug and snail damage.

'SCARLET RUNNER' BEAN

SORREL

'CALIFORNIA BLACKEYE' SOUTHERN PEA

'PINKEYE PURPLE HULL' SOUTHERN PEA

'PRIZE' SOYBEAN

NEW ZEALAND SPINACH

**Harvesting.** Individual leaves can be cut from the sorrel plant as needed, or the entire plant can be cut off at ground level and the leaves removed. If sorrel is grown as a perennial, it can be cut to the ground after the spring harvest and allowed to regrow for harvest in the fall.

## Southern Peas
Vigna unguiculata

Southern peas, also called black-eyed peas or cowpeas, are legumes, like beans; they are called peas because the seeds are round. The plant grows to 24 inches tall. Most varieties are erect and bushy, but a few are sprawling with short runners. The pods are either slender or plump and smooth or lumpy, depending on the variety. They splay out like fingers above shiny, dark green leaves on long, smooth stems. The beans are white, cream or purple and from ½ to ⅜ inch long. They can be harvested and shelled when mature or left on the plant to be used as dry beans.

**Selected varieties.** *'California Blackeye,'* 75 days from seed to ripe bean. Large, smooth, 8-inch pods are filled with white beans that have black eyes, or spots. Resistant to wilt and nematodes. *'Pinkeye Purple Hull,'* 78 days. Slender, rounded, deep purple pods to 8 inches long. White seeds have small purple eyes.

**Growing conditions.** Southern peas are grown from seeds planted directly in the soil after all danger of frost has passed and soil is 70° F. Seeds should be sown from ½ to 1 inch deep, depending on the soil; heavier soils call for a shallower planting depth. Germination takes 10 days. The percentage of germination is not high, so seeds should be sown generously. Seedlings should be thinned to 6 inches apart.

Southern peas do well in heat and drought, and are a good crop to grow where it is too hot for snap beans. Soil should be average to rich and well drained. Fertilize prior to planting with 5-10-10 and do not fertilize again.

Southern peas can be damaged by anthracnose, blight, powdery mildew, aphids, bean beetles, leafhoppers, mites and nematodes.

**Harvesting.** Individual pods can be picked for shelling as they mature. The beans will expand and form lumps within the pod. The pods will change color. Some of the pods may be left on the plant and harvested later for dry beans.

## Soybeans
Glycine max

Soybean plants are 3 feet tall, bushy and erect with round, furry leaves. They produce short, hairy pods that cling close to the stem. Each pod contains two or three round, pea-sized, black or yellow beans. Soybeans are rich in fat and have three times the protein of other beans.

**Selected varieties.** *'Prize,'* 85 days from seed to ripe shell bean. Plant produces from two to four yellow beans per pod.

**Growing conditions.** Sow soybeans directly in the soil in spring, after all danger of frost has passed and the soil is warm. In sandy soil, sow the seeds 2 inches deep; in heavy soil, sow them 1 inch deep. Seeds will germinate within 12 days. Thin the seedlings to 4 inches apart.

Soybeans do well in areas with a long, hot growing season. Soybeans thrive in almost any soil, but they are not drought-resistant and should be watered regularly. Fertilize the soil with 5-10-10 before planting and do not feed the plants again. Although soybeans are erect, bushy plants, they will need some sort of a support if they are planted in a windy area.

Soybeans can be damaged by anthracnose, blight, mosaic, powdery mildew, aphids, bean beetles, mites and leafhoppers.

**Harvesting.** Soybeans can be picked for shelling when they are full-sized, plump and still green. Beans may also be left on the plant so that they can be harvested when they are dry.

**Spinach** see Summer Spinach
**Squash** see Summer Squash;
Winter Squash
**String Beans** see Snap Beans

## Summer Spinach
Tetragonia tetragonioides

True spinach cannot be grown in summer heat, but New Zealand spinach, also called summer spinach, is a warm-weather spinach substitute. It has triangular, dark green, shiny leaves that are thick and succulent and have a flavor similar to spinach. The plant is bushy; in cool climates, it produces runners that form a dense mat 2 to 3 feet wide, and in warm climates the runners grow to several feet long and can be trained on a trellis. Slender clusters of tiny yellow flowers appear above the foliage.

**Selected varieties.** There are no named varieties of New Zealand spinach; it is sold under its common name. The spinach matures in 60 days from seed to ripe leaves.

**Growing conditions.** New Zealand spinach is usually started from seeds sown directly in the soil in spring, after all danger of frost has passed. The seeds are planted 1 inch deep and 12 inches apart. Germination takes eight days. As a seed is actually a small fruit containing two or three seeds, thinning must be done soon after germination. When the plants are 4 inches tall, they should be thinned again to stand 18 inches apart.

Seeds can also be started indoors; but since they do not transplant well, they should be sown in individual peat pots that can go with them into the garden to reduce transplant shock. They can be started 6 weeks before the last frost date and then, when all danger of frost has passed, planted in the garden 18 inches apart.

Soil should be an average, sandy garden loam. Fertilize with 5-10-5 before planting and once again in midsummer. The plant is heat- and drought-resistant and can be grown as a perennial in mild climates.

New Zealand spinach is resistant to most insects and diseases.

**Harvesting.** Pick off new and tender leaves from the tips of the branches about once a week to keep the plant producing new foliage.

### Summer Squash
Cucurbita pepo

Squash is among the most commonly homegrown vegetables and it does well in almost all of the United States. It is a space-consuming, bushy plant that spreads to 3 feet and has large, dark green leaves. Fruit may be round or oblong with white, yellow, green or orange edible flesh and skin.

There are four types of summer squash varieties: crookneck, scallop, straightneck and zucchini. Crookneck varieties have tapering bodies and curved necks. Scallop varieties are round and bowl-shaped with scalloped edges. Straightneck varieties are long and tapering without distinctive necks. Zucchini varieties are straight, cylindrical fruits with yellow, gray, green or black skin.

The types listed below are standard varieties except where noted.

**Crookneck varieties.** *'Early Golden Summer,'* 53 days from seed to ripe fruit. Small, curved-neck fruit with warted, bright yellow skin and soft, light yellow flesh.

**Scallop varieties.** *'Sunburst Hybrid,'* 53 days. Bright, golden yellow fruit is lightly scalloped and has a green sunburst pattern at both ends. Buttery taste. Firm but tender flesh.

**Straightneck varieties.** *'Butterstick Hybrid,'* 50 days. Evenly tapered golden fruit with creamy white flesh of firm texture and a sweet, nutty flavor.

**Zucchini varieties.** *'Black Jack,'* 48 days. Fruit grows to 7 inches long and has dark green skin with pale green flecks. *'Burpee Hybrid,'* 50 days. Medium green fruit with shiny skin on a bush-type plant. *'Zucchini Elite,'* 48 days. Fruit grows to 8 inches long, and has glossy, dark green skin with pale green flecks. Hybrid.

**Growing conditions.** Squash can be started from seeds or from purchased seedlings, but neither should be transplanted outdoors until all danger of frost has passed and the soil is warm. Seeds that are sown directly in the soil should be sown ½ inch deep. Seeds can also be started indoors in spring, approximately three weeks before the last frost date, and then moved into the garden. Germination takes 10 days. The seedlings should be thinned to a spacing of 3 feet apart.

Summer squash thrives in hot weather and is heat-resistant. Soil for squash should be rich, well drained and fertile. Mix 5-10-5 into the soil before planting and fertilize again every three weeks.

Squash plants are susceptible to damage from the squash borer, squash bug, aphid, cucumber beetle, mildew, wilt and damping-off.

**Harvesting.** The fruit of summer squash is harvested when it is still immature, meaning the skin is still soft and can be pierced with a fingernail. Although squash can be left to grow as large as desired, the flavor of cylindrical types is best when the fruit is about 5 inches long and 1½ to 2 inches in diameter; the flavor of scallop types is best when they are 3 to 4 inches across. Squash grows quickly, and the plant should be checked daily to see if the fruit needs harvesting. Frequent harvesting ensures that the plant will keep producing.

'EARLY GOLDEN SUMMER' CROOKNECK SQUASH

'SUNBURST HYBRID' SCALLOP SQUASH

'ZUCCHINI ELITE' SQUASH

'CENTENNIAL' SWEET POTATO

'FORDHOOK GIANT' SWISS CHARD

TAMPALA

## Sweet Potatoes
Ipomoea batatus

The sweet potato is an oblong edible root with flesh that ranges from pale yellow to orange. The plant is a low-growing vine with dark green, pointed leaves on short runners. It produces petunia-like blossoms in early summer. Sweet potatoes are sometimes called yams, but this is a misnomer. The yam is a tropical vegetable of the genus *Dioscorea*.

**Selected varieties.** *'Centennial,'* 95 days. Copper-colored skin and orange flesh. Matures faster than other varieties and is the best choice for areas with a short growing season.

**Growing conditions.** Sweet potatoes are grown from slips—seed potatoes (pieces of potatoes) that have already sprouted and developed roots. Slips should be certified disease-free by the provincial or state agriculture department. The slips can be planted outdoors in spring after all danger of frost has passed and the soil is warm. They should be spaced 15 to 18 inches apart. The bottom of the cutting should be placed 5 to 6 inches deep in the soil; some of the lower leaves on the stem can be buried.

Sweet potatoes are heat-tolerant and drought-resistant. They need a long growing season in which night temperatures will not drop below 60° F.

Soil should be well drained, dry, sandy and slightly acid. Fertilize with 5-10-5 prior to planting and do not fertilize again during the season. Too much fertilizer will cause the plant to produce lush foliage instead of full-sized potatoes.

Sweet potatoes are susceptible to damage from aphids, cucumber beetles, flea beetles, leafhoppers and nematodes.

**Harvesting.** Sweet potatoes are harvested at the time of the first fall frost. All potatoes should be removed from the ground then because frost can damage them.

Dig carefully around the potatoes so their skin is not damaged. Lift them out of the soil and allow them to dry out on the ground for several hours. Keep the potatoes in a warm, humid, dark place for two weeks; then move them to a cool area—approximately 50° F—for storage.

## Swiss Chard
Beta vulgaris, Cicla Group

Swiss chard is a relative of the beet. Unlike the beet, it is not grown for its root; it is grown for its edible stems and leaves. The leaves, which have thick midribs and wide veins, can be eaten either raw or cooked. The plant grows from 24 to 28 inches high.

**Selected varieties.** *'Fordhook Giant,'* 60 days from seed to mature leaves. Dark green, crumpled leaves are thick and fleshy. Stems are 2½ inches wide and white; leaf veins are also white. Drought-resistant. Does not do well in sandy soil. *'Large White Rib,'* 60 days. Broad, flat stems are silvery white; medium green leaves are smooth, thick and tender with white veins. This variety does well in sandy soils. *'Lucullus,'* 50 days. Light yellow-green leaves are heavily curled and crumpled; slender stalks are creamy white.

**Growing conditions.** Swiss chard is grown from seeds sown directly in the soil in early spring, about three weeks before the last spring frost is expected. Seeds should be sown 2 to 3 inches apart and ½ inch deep. Germination takes 10 days. A chard seed, like a beet seed, is actually a small fruit that contains several seeds. To prevent overcrowding, thinning must be done immediately after germination. Then, when the seedlings are 6 to 8 inches high, thin them again to stand 6 inches apart. The thinnings can be eaten.

Swiss chard will tolerate poor soil conditions, but for the best growth and flavor, soil should be loose, rich and well drained, and have a pH that is close to neutral. Fertilize prior to planting with 5-10-5, and again every six weeks during the growing season. Swiss chard is one of the most heat-resistant greens.

Although Swiss chard is generally free of insects and diseases, it may be attacked by leaf miners and plant bugs.

**Harvesting.** Cut off the outer leaves when they are 6 to 8 inches long, and leave the inner leaves to develop for later harvesting. Or cut the entire plant off about 1 inch above the ground; the plant will then produce new leaves, which will be ready for cutting in a few weeks.

## Tampala

Amaranthus tricolor

Tampala is a leafy green vegetable similar to spinach, but unlike spinach, the plant can withstand summer heat. Leaves are heart-shaped, 4 inches long, and green with orange, red or purple tips. The leaves can be used in cooking or in salads. The full-grown plant is bushy and can reach 6 feet tall, but tampala is usually harvested at an immature stage.

**Selected varieties.** There are no named varieties of tampala; it is sold under its common name. The plant matures in 70 days from seed to ripe leaves.

**Growing conditions.** Tampala is grown from seed planted directly in the soil in spring, after all danger of frost has passed. The seed should be sown ¼ inch deep and 2 inches apart. Germination takes seven to 10 days. When seedlings are 4 inches tall, they should be thinned to about 6 inches apart. The thinnings can be used in salads and soups. To have a continuous supply of tampala all summer, seeds can be sown every two weeks until one month prior to the first frost date.

Tampala thrives in high heat and is drought-tolerant. Soil should be average and well drained. Before planting, mix 5-10-5 into the soil. No further fertilizing will be needed during the growing season.

**Harvesting.** When the plant is 6 to 8 inches high, remove the entire plant by cutting it off at ground level. If tampala is allowed to grow into a large, shrubby plant, only the top 5 inches of the branch tips should be cut for harvest.

## Tomatoes

Lycopersicon lycopersicum

The most widely homegrown vegetable is the tomato. The tomato is available in sizes ranging from the ¾-inch cherry tomato to the beefsteak tomato that can grow to 5 inches across. There are more varieties of tomato than of any other vegetable. The fruit can be round, oval, globular, oblate or pear-shaped. Although most tomatoes are red, some varieties are yellow and others are orange.

Tomato plants generally belong to either of two groups: determinate or indeterminate. This grouping is based on the plant's growth habits. The determinate tomato is a bushy plant whose terminal growth develops flowers and fruit. When the plant reaches full size, it stops growing, and all the fruit ripens at the same time. This type of tomato is used for canning, juice and other processing. The indeterminate tomato is a vine that continues to grow, flower and produce fruit until it is killed by frost. This type of fruit is best for slicing and salads. Modern seed breeders have developed a variation on those two, a type called intermediate short internode (abbreviated in seed catalogs as ISI). It combines the traits of the other two; it flowers indefinitely, like the indeterminate tomato, but it grows as a compact bush plant and as such can be caged but not staked *(page 494)*.

Many varieties are resistant to certain diseases and insects. The resistance is part of the variety's name and is indicated by the letters V, F, N or T. These initials stand for the variety's resistance to verticillium wilt, fusarium wilt, nematodes or tobacco mosaic. There are two types of fusarium wilt. Those varieties marked F are resistant to one type of the disease and those marked FF are resistant to both types.

**Standard varieties.** *'Ace 55 VF,'* 80 days from seed to ripe fruit. Determinate. Large fruit on a compact plant. *'Beefsteak,'* 90 days. Indeterminate. Large, round fruit can grow to 1 pound. *'Heinz 1350 VF,'* 75 days. Determinate. Excellent for canning. Tomatoes do not crack. *'Long-Keeper,'* 78 days. Determinate. Light golden to orange-red skin. Not as tasty or juicy as others, but stores well. *'Marglobe Improved VF,'* 75 days. Determinate. Medium-sized fruit. *'New Yorker V,'* 60 days. Determinate. Small to medium-sized fruit. Early variety, especially good for areas with a short growing season. *'Roma VF,'* 76 days. Determinate. Deep red, plum-shaped fruit; good for juice and tomato paste. *'Rutgers VF,'* 75 days. Determinate. Medium-sized fruit. *'Tropic VF,'* 80 days. Indeterminate. Large fruit. Good for areas with a hot climate.

**Hybrid varieties.** *'La Roma VFF,'* 62 days. Determinate. Used for making tomato paste; more productive than the older, nonhybrid *'Roma.'*

'LONG-KEEPER' STANDARD TOMATO

'LA ROMA VFF' HYBRID TOMATO

'SWEET 100' CHERRY TOMATO

'YELLOW PLUM' TOMATO

'TINY TIM' CONTAINER TOMATO

WATERCRESS

'TABLE ACE' ACORN SQUASH

**Cherry varieties.** *'Sweet 100,'* 68 days. Indeterminate. Extremely sweet cherry tomato produced in long, heavy clusters of 100 fruits. One of the earliest to mature. Very high in vitamin C content. Hybrid.

**Yellow-fruited varieties.** *'Yellow Plum,'* Indeterminate. Plum-shaped. Best yellow variety for cooking and preserving. Nonhybrid.

**Container varieties.** *'Tiny Tim,'* 55 days. Determinate. Plant grows to only 15 inches tall and produces ¾-inch cherry tomatoes. Nonhybrid.

**Growing conditions.** Tomatoes are grown from seeds or purchased plants. Seeds should be started indoors because the germination rate is much higher than it would be if they were planted directly in the soil. Seeds can be started from six to eight weeks before the last frost date. Germination takes six to 10 days. Seedlings can be transplanted into the garden or into individual containers after all danger of frost has passed and nights are above 60° F. The plants should be set into the soil deeper than they grew in the pot or flat so roots will form along the stem and produce a stronger plant.

The spacing of plants depends on the type of tomato and the manner of support. Planting distance should be 24 inches for determinate or ISI tomatoes, which should not be staked. Indeterminate tomatoes that are staked should be spaced 18 inches apart, and indeterminate tomatoes that are caged *(page 494)* should be spaced 30 to 36 inches apart. Indeterminate tomatoes that are not staked or caged should be spaced 40 to 48 inches apart. Although indeterminate tomatoes can be allowed to grow on the ground and will produce twice as much fruit as indeterminate tomatoes that are supported, the supported plants produce larger tomatoes that ripen faster.

Soil for tomatoes should be evenly moist, well drained, with a pH of 5.5 to 7.0 and high in organic matter. Fertilize before planting and then once a month until harvest. Mulch should be applied after planting to keep the soil evenly moist and prevent blossom-end rot. The plants should not be watered just prior to harvesting; watering at this time would cause the fruit to crack and acquire a bland, watery taste.

Fruit production will decrease if the soil becomes cool, during periods of heavy rain and when there are hot, dry winds. Plant leaves may curl up, especially in hot weather. This is a normal occurrence and does not affect the plant's production.

Tomatoes can be damaged by aphids, whiteflies, Colorado potato beetles, leafhoppers, cutworms, tomato hornworms, spider mites, slugs, nematodes, blight and blossom-end rot.

**Harvesting.** Tomatoes can be picked from the plant as they ripen. Just prior to the first fall frost, pick all of the remaining full-sized tomatoes and ripen them indoors. To ripen, the fruit needs two weeks at a temperature of 70° F and another four weeks at 55° F. The tomatoes can be ripened on a windowsill out of direct sunlight and then stored in the refrigerator.

## Watercress
Nasturtium officinale

Watercress is an aquatic plant that needs a moist environment. Each plant grows to 4 inches tall and spreads into a mat about 12 inches across. The plant has small, thin, round green leaves; it blooms in spring, producing tiny, pale flowers that resemble nasturtiums. Watercress is grown for its pungent, peppery-tasting foliage, which can be used in salads or as a garnish. It is a perennial in areas with winter temperatures as low as -10° F; in areas with colder temperatures, it must be replanted each spring.

**Selected varieties.** There are no named varieties of watercress; it is sold under its common name. Plants mature in 60 days from seed to ripe leaves.

**Growing conditions.** Watercress can be grown from seed or from started plants, which can be purchased at a nursery or a grocery store. Seeds are started indoors in early spring and should be kept out of direct sunlight in a cool area where the temperature does not exceed 55° F. The planting medium must be light and constantly moist; the seeds should not be covered. Germination takes seven to 10 days.

Seeds or started plants may also be planted outdoors in early spring. They can be sown in a sandy garden bed or in water, in a garden pond or a stream.

The plants should be set 8 to 12 inches apart. Seedlings started in a stream or other source of running water can be held in place with small stones or pebbles at the base of their stems until the roots take hold.

Watercress can tolerate full sun if it is grown in water. If it is in soil, it needs partial shade, or heat and dryness will cause the leaves to acquire a bitter taste. Soil should be fertile, sandy and well drained, with a pH of 7.0. The roots require a constant supply of moisture, so plants should be watered every day. Watercress can become invasive, and may need to be pruned or thinned each spring.

Watercress is insect- and disease-free.

**Harvesting.** Stems may be cut after the plant has bloomed. If the tops are snipped off, the plants will continue producing for harvest throughout the summer until the first frost. Watercress should not be harvested while the plants are in bloom, because the leaves will have a strong, slightly bitter taste then.

### Winter Squash
Cucurbita

Although they are grown in the summer, these members of the squash family are called winter squash because they store well after the fall harvest and into the winter months.

Winter squash are vining plants. The fruit is eaten when it matures, meaning when the rind or skin becomes hard. Only the flesh is edible. The vine grows to 8 inches high and sprawls along the ground for several feet.

There are several types of winter squash and they are members of different *Cucurbita* species. Acorn and spaghetti squash are *C. pepo*; butternut squash is *C. moschata*; Hubbard and turban squash are *C. maxima*.

Acorn varieties produce dark green, sometimes orange-streaked fruit that is round and deeply ribbed and resembles a large acorn. Butternut varieties are shaped like large pears and have long, thick, cylindrical necks. Hubbard varieties are rounded fruits with ribbed, bumpy skin that is dark green, gold or blue-gray. Turban squash has a flattened shape with a thick, round center resembling a crown or a turban. Spaghetti squash is round or oblong with yellow skin and stringy yellow-orange flesh.

The squash varieties listed below are nonhybrids unless otherwise indicated.

**Acorn varieties.** *'Table Ace,'* 70 days. Semibush plant with black shell and fiberless bright orange flesh. Hybrid.

**Butternut varieties.** *'Butter Boy,'* 80 days. Extra sweet, nutty flavor from reddish orange flesh. Relatively compact plant. Hybrid.

**Hubbard varieties.** *'Blue Hubbard,'* 120 days from seed to ripe fruit. Blue-gray, slightly ridged fruit with fine, sweet, bright yellow-orange flesh.

**Spaghetti varieties.** *'Spaghetti,'* 100 days from seed to ripe fruit. Also called vegetable spaghetti. Flesh looks like light golden spaghetti when cooked and can be used as a substitute for pasta. Fruit is large and oval with a light yellow skin.

**Turban varieties.** *'Turk's Turban,'* 105 days. Bright orange or red fruit with white or green stripes grows to 10 inches across. Fruit is in a flattened, turban-hat shape.

**Growing conditions.** Squash can be started from seeds or from purchased seedlings, but neither should be planted outdoors until all danger of frost has passed and the soil is warm. Seeds sown directly in the soil should be sown ½ inch deep. Seeds can also be started indoors in spring, about three weeks before the last frost date, and then moved into the garden. Germination takes 10 days. The seedlings should be thinned to a spacing of about 4 feet apart.

Soil for squash should be rich, well drained and fertile. Mix 5-10-5 into the soil before planting and fertilize again every three weeks.

Squash plants are susceptible to damage from the squash borer, squash bug, aphid, cucumber beetle, mildew, wilt and damping-off.

**Harvesting.** Winter squash is cut from the vine when the rind becomes hard. Leave a part of the stem on the squash to prevent its rotting during storage.

**Zucchini** see Summer Squash

'BUTTER BOY' BUTTERNUT SQUASH

'BLUE HUBBARD' SQUASH

'TURK'S TURBAN' SQUASH

# 10

# HOUSEPLANTS

*Side by side, two hybrid caladiums of contrasting colors thrive in an ideal indoor environment. Like most houseplants, they benefit from plenty of light, rich soil and the elevated humidity provided by vapor rising from the moistened pebble tray they share.*

Most houseplants are tropical or semitropical in origin, hence their ability to survive warm and stable indoor temperatures. Houseplants fall into two groups: foliage and flowering. Foliage houseplants, which seldom flower, cover a broad range of botanical groupings, not to mention a variety of textures, forms and colors, as shown on pages 531-533. Although most are green, some come in purples, reds and golds. Flowering plants, on the other hand, are the stellar performers among houseplants, commanding attention with showy bursts of color.

Houseplants will thrive indoors, provided that the environment comes close to the conditions the plants enjoyed in nature. Because temperature, humidity, the length of the days and the intensity of the sun's light remain largely constant in the tropics and the subtropics, houseplants are extremely sensitive to changes in their environment. While the temperature in most homes is relatively stable from season to season, other environmental factors—such as humidity and the duration and intensity of light—can change markedly from one season to the next. This can affect the plants' overall health and, for flowering varieties, their propensity to blossom. Refer to page 530 for guidelines on easing a plant's move from garden-supply center to home.

This chapter describes the conditions that houseplants need in order to flourish: proper light, water, humidity and growing medium. A section on light shows where plants should be placed in relation to windows in order to receive the light they need. A section on watering explains when and how to water. Other instructions deal with grooming mature houseplants to keep them tidy and healthy.

# CHAPTER CONTENTS

Given a sunny spot and an occasional watering, many houseplants will remain healthy. But getting them to thrive may require some additional encouragement. Since houseplants spend their lives in containers, the sizes of those containers are important considerations. A section on potting tells when and how to repot plants that have outgrown their pots.

Periodic applications of fertilizer are necessary for healthy houseplants, and this chapter will guide you to the best type and the right amount of fertilizer for the needs of specific plants *(page 538)*. When insects attack, a section on controlling them will prove useful.

Seeing your plants vigorous may make you wish that you had more of them. Reproducing the ones you have may be the most successful, and rewarding, route to increasing your collection of houseplants. Chapter 2 shows in detail several methods for propagating houseplants, including starting seeds indoors, dividing, layering, planting stem and leaf cuttings, and creating your own hybrids.

Keeping your indoor plants healthy demands an awareness of their seasonal needs. For every indoor gardening task, there is a proper season, as described in the Checklist for Houseplants *(pages 546-547)*. In addition, houseplants occasionally demand emergency attention. The Troubleshooting Guide *(pages 548-551)* will help you to diagnose and cure attacks by insects and diseases.

A key to success with houseplants is to evaluate the growing conditions you can provide and to choose your plants accordingly. Among the dozens of plants described and illustrated in the Dictionary at the end of this chapter, you are bound to find many that will grow well in your home—enlivening it with their distinctive colors, forms and textures.

# HOUSEPLANTS
# AND THEIR DIVERSE HABITS

The term "houseplants" covers a wide range of growing things from delicate ferns to spiky cacti, from low-growing succulents to high-spiraling vines. Plants belonging to dozens of botanical families and many thousands of species can be, and are, cultivated indoors. About all they have in common is that they will flourish in the subdued light and year-round warmth of a house.

This great wealth of plant life can nevertheless be divided into six major groupings—as seen on pages 531-533. Only three of the categories found here, the cacti, the bromeliads and the palms, are in fact made up of members of single, distinct botanical families. The other three groupings—the green plants, ferns and succulents—may combine two or more different families.

Still, these broad groupings can be highly useful. Each category is made up of plants that share many physical characteristics. Many originated in similar natural environments. This is vital information for the indoor gardener because species that resemble one another, and derive from the same habitats, will inevitably require the same kind of indoor environment—sunny or shady, warm or cool—as well as similar amounts of water, fertilizer and other sorts of care.

*A corn plant, a Chinese evergreen, a snake plant, a dumbcane, a piggyback plant and a dracaena (clockwise from top left) share the subdued light of a shuttered windowsill. All are members of the diverse group known as green plants, one of the groupings of foliage houseplants.*

## BRINGING A HOUSEPLANT HOME

Most of the houseplants you buy at a store or garden-supply center are recent transfers from the ideal conditions of a commercial greenhouse. These plants will eventually adapt to the lower light levels and lower humidity of the home, and you can help them make the transition.

The best times to bring new plants into the home are in spring and summer, when light levels are higher than in winter. But whatever time of year you bring new plants home, place them where they will receive lots of light. If a plant's permanent location will be in limited light, begin moving the plant away from bright light over a period of days. The gradual move will allow the plant to adjust to the lower light level. Avoid placing plants where they will receive blasts of either cold or hot air, such as from heating vents, air conditioners or doors.

## MOVING WITH HOUSEPLANTS

When you're ready to move into a new home, your houseplants will need to be packed as carefully as your china. Before you move, give your plants a thorough watering; allow excess water to drain off before packing. To prepare small plants for moving, put them into a carton and stuff the area between pots with newspaper to hold them in place. Large plants should be wrapped in sheets of foil or newspaper to help protect the foliage. The potting medium can also be covered to keep it from spilling out of the pot.

Long-distance moves present greater difficulties. Most plants cannot survive a transcontinental trip in a moving van, where they may be subject to darkness and temperature extremes for extended periods. It is safer to transport your plants in a car, so you can make sure they have sufficient water, fresh air and moderate temperatures during the trip.

## GREEN OR FOLIAGE PLANTS

All plants valued especially for their green and often large-leaved foliage, such as the Swiss cheese plant, the grassy-leaved sweet flag and the philodendron shown at left, are often lumped under the heading "green plants" by nursery owners and other horticulturists. Put another way, green plants include almost any decorative varieties that do not belong in the other five categories pictured here and on the following pages. The main ornamental features of green plants are leaf color, texture and shape. Alone, or in combination, green plants can be used to add interest, shade or a soft tone to any room. Mostly originating in subtropical climates, these staples of indoor gardening tolerate a wide range of light and moisture conditions, and will do well in an average home without a lot of special attention.

## FERNS

There are many species of ferns, but generally they divide into two sorts, the epiphytic and the terrestrial. In the wild, the epiphytes grow in the air, or rather, cling in the crevices of trees, drawing nourishment from the rotting vegetation trapped there. Terrestrials normally grow in the soil on the forest floor. Indoors, many epiphytes will grow in pots. Both types, being adapted to shadowy, woodsy environments, grow best in dappled light and humid air, and need soil that is rich in organic matter and kept moist.

## BROMELIADS

These curious plants are related to the pineapple, and the leaves of many of them, like those of a pineapple's top, rise in a rosette pattern from a central base. The leaves are generally stiff and leathery; the flowers spring up from the cup in the middle of the rosette. In their native tropics, many bromeliads are tree-growing epiphytes, living on the rainwater and leafy debris the cups collect. As houseplants, many bromeliads continue to take in moisture through the cuplike formation at the base of their leaves and should be watered accordingly. And being tropical plants, they also need warm temperatures, high humidity and bright light.

## PALMS

The palm family of plants includes more than 200 genera and a staggering 3,000 species. In the wild they have tall, single unbranched trunks topped by fans of usually broad, flat leaves. But grown as houseplants, they rarely reach maturity, and thus remain compact, often with leaves and leafy branches all the way up their trunks, like the parlor palm at right. Coming from warm climates as they do, palms need regular watering, well-drained soil, average warmth and humidity, and bright, but not direct, sunlight.

## CACTI

Most members of the cactus family are native to desert areas and therefore grow best in hot, dry conditions. Their spines are actually leaves—with minimal surface area from which moisture can escape. The bodies of cacti are nothing more than hugely enlarged stems designed by nature to absorb and hold water from infrequent rainfalls. It follows, then, that cacti need generous but infrequent waterings (daily sprinklings only cause rot) and loose, well-drained, sandy soil. They also need warmth and are among the few houseplants that thrive in extended periods of direct sunlight.

## SUCCULENTS

Hundreds of quite disparate-looking species are called succulents. Many not only have thickish, fleshy stems, but also chubby, water-storing leaves like those of the jade plant at right. Others have spiny leaves almost like those on cacti and still others look like (and, in fact, are) small trees. Most originated in arid parts of the world—thus their water-conserving structures. They require infrequent watering, warm temperatures, low humidity and well-drained soil.

# PLACING PLANTS IN THE RIGHT LIGHT

*An arrowhead vine grows green and bushy in its west-facing "summer residence." Sheer curtains on either side diffuse the afternoon sunlight that floods the bay window.*

## AN OUTDOOR VACATION FOR HOUSEPLANTS

Most houseplants—except those with soft, fuzzy leaves, such as purple passion vine—thrive on sunlight, rain and fresh air, and can be moved outdoors, pots and all, as soon as spring has arrived—when night temperatures no longer dip below 50° F. And they can stay out at least until early autumn.

Before they can be planted, indoor plants need to be acclimated to outdoor life. Start by placing pots in a shady, wind-protected corner for two hours each day for a week, then lengthen the time outdoors gradually for a week. Before selecting a planting site, check the sun tolerance of each plant in the Dictionary. Choose a spot that receives the right amount of light, then dig a hole as wide as the pot and about 2 inches deeper *(below)*. Fill the bottom 2 inches of the hole with gravel, then place the pot in the hole. About 1 inch of the pot's rim should be above ground to mark its location. Pour some of the dug-up earth around the pot and firm it with your hands. Spread a mulch in the area to help conserve ground moisture.

Three factors—light, water and nutrients—are vital for thriving plants. Of the three, the most difficult to supply in just the right amount is light. A plant that is starved for light eventually grows weak and spindly; its leaves turn pale and fall off. At the other extreme, too much light causes leaves to wilt and fade, or to be stunted in growth.

Houseplants can tolerate less-than-ideal growing conditions. Yet most prefer lighting that closely approximates their native habitats—dim forest floors, tree-dotted savannas, sun-scorched deserts.

Indoor light is measured in levels of intensity, and falls into three categories: direct light, bright light and limited light. Where you place a plant in your house determines how much light it will receive at a specific time of the year. Rooms that bask in a full day's sun in summer may see only a few hours of winter sunlight. Many houseplants adjust to diminished light by slowing their growth; some even require an annual period of rest. Others benefit greatly if they are moved around the house to "follow the sun."

For a guide to seasonal sunlight, see the opposite page. Each circle is divided into quadrants to represent the points of the compass. The small rectangle in the center of each represents a house. Flowerpots in the quadrants indicate which seasonal exposure will provide one of three light levels. For the preferences of specific plants, consult the Dictionary of Houseplants *(pages 552-575)*.

In locations with little or no natural light, you can raise plants under artificial light, preferably fluorescent bulbs that deliver a kind of imitation sunlight. Leave the bulbs on 12 to 16 hours a day; a timer can be programmed to turn the lights on and off as required. For foliage houseplants, place the bulbs 18 to 24 inches above the plants. For flowering houseplants, install two 40-watt fluorescent bulbs—one a "cool" white bulb that supplies the type of light necessary for foliage development, the other a "warm" white bulb that supplies the type of light necessary for flowers to develop; place the bulbs 6 inches above the plants.

# DIRECT LIGHT

The sun strikes foliage and flowers for at least four hours a day. Direct light is found in summer in unobstructed, uncurtained east-, west- and south-facing windows *(near right)*, but only in south-facing windows in winter *(far right)*. Also found under skylights, direct light is suited to plants of desert origin, but may be too intense for flowering houseplants in summer.

# BRIGHT LIGHT

The sun strikes foliage for less than four hours, but at least one hour a day. Bright light is found in unobstructed, uncurtained north-facing windows in summer *(near right)*; in east- and west-facing windows in winter *(far right)*. Most houseplants do well in this type of light.

# LIMITED LIGHT

The sun rarely strikes foliage directly. Limited light is found in any exposure in summer *(near right)* if you place plants 5 feet from unobstructed windows or hang sheer curtains; in winter *(far right)* it is found on north-facing windowsills. It is suited to plants that grow naturally in jungles and on forest floors, but is insufficient for flowering houseplants to survive. Many plants exposed to only limited light will need artificial light.

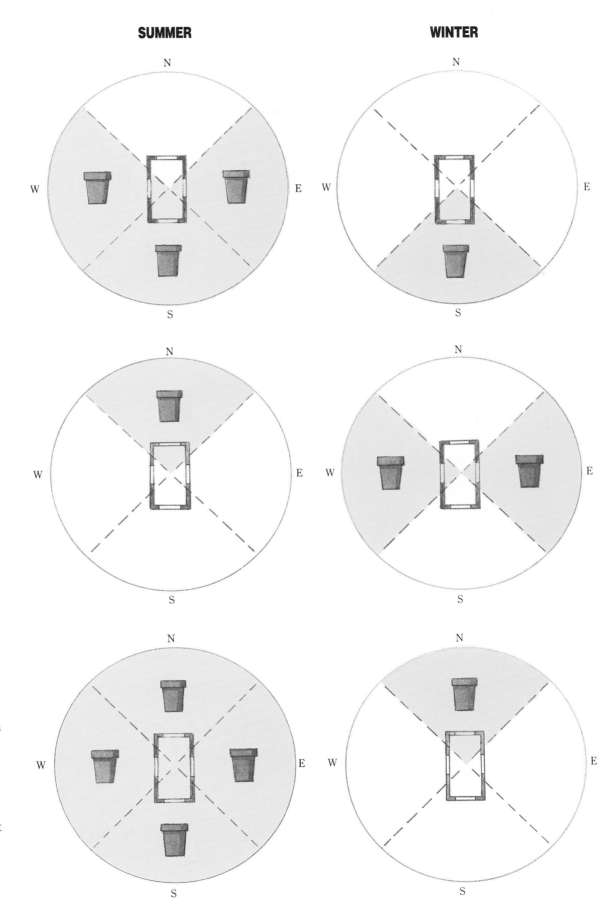

# WATERING HOUSEPLANTS

*The crisp leaves and upright bearing of this 'Silver Queen' Chinese evergreen indicate a well-watered plant. Proper moisture balance is maintained by means of a wick that draws water from a bowl concealed underneath the lower pot into the soil of the upper pot.*

Water is the lifeblood of all plants. It dissolves nutrients and transports them from the soil to the roots and from there to stems, branches and foliage. In addition, internal water pressure helps keep stems and leaves full and firm. A plant that lacks water begins to wilt and eventually dies. For many plants the soil should be kept constantly moist; for others—mainly cacti and succulents—it should dry out between waterings.

There are three ways to water. One is to pour water onto the soil from above until it begins to run out the drainage holes at the bottom of the pot. If you use this method, sprinkle slowly and gently with a watering can. Do not flood the pot with a blast from the water tap; most houseplants die from too much water, not too little. Another method is to set the pot in a pan of water and let the moisture rise into the soil from below. This method is ideal for plants that have dried out. When the soil surface is moist, the plant has had enough and should be removed from the pan. Never let plants sit in water longer than necessary. If the roots become waterlogged, they will eventually rot and the plant will die. A third method of watering, illustrated on the following two pages, is by means of a wick—a length of twine made of cotton or other natural fiber. The wick draws moisture up into the soil slowly and continuously from a reservoir maintained beneath the pot. The method is especially useful if you have to be away from home for a period of time.

Wicking is also an easy way of providing low-maintenance regular care for plants such as ferns and baby's tears, which do best when their soil is kept constantly moist. The method can be used with any plants except cacti and succulents.

Because you will sometimes be combining fertilizing *(page 538)* with watering, no matter which method you use, whitish salts will accumulate on the soil surface and the pot rim from time to time and, if left too long, may burn plant tissues. Whenever you find such a buildup, place your plants under a tap and let water drain through the soil several times.

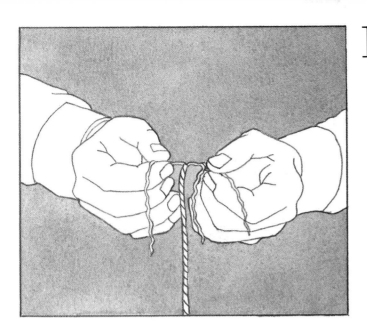

**1** To prepare a wick, take about 2 feet of ordinary cotton or other natural-fiber twine and unravel several inches of one end into separate strands *(left)*. Soak the entire length of twine in water until it is thoroughly wet.

**2** Insert the frayed end of the twine in the drainage hole in the bottom of a flower pot. Pull all of the frayed portion and two inches of the unfrayed portion to the inside of the pot, and leave the remaining portion outside the pot. With one hand take hold of the frayed twine inside the pot; with the other cover the bottom of the pot with at least 2 inches of potting soil—enough to seat the plant you will be placing in the pot. Spread the frayed strands of the twine over the surface of the soil *(left)*.

**3** Pot the plant as you would when repotting it *(page 543, step 4)*. Set a large, empty flower pot upside down on a secure surface and thread the unfrayed end of the twine through the pot's drainage hole. Fill a bowl with tepid, not icy cold, water to serve as a reservoir. Pull the twine from under the large pot and submerge it in the water. Set the potted plant over the large pot so that the twine runs unimpeded through the two drainage holes and into the water *(left)*. Then set the two pots on top of the bowl of water, making sure the twine remains submerged in the water. The wick will draw water up from the reservoir and into the potting soil. Check the soil surface periodically; refill the reservoir when necessary.

Proper watering of a houseplant involves more than just keeping the soil moist. You also have to pay attention to the air around the plant—because in opening its pores to take in carbon dioxide, the plant loses moisture. To slow down this loss, raise the relative humidity. Most houseplants do best at a relative humidity of about 60%; succulents prefer it between 30% and 40%; tropical plants like it at about 80%. To increase humidity around plants, group several of them together; each plant benefits from the moisture evaporating from the others.

---

### ABOUT FERTILIZERS

LIQUID

POWDER

SPIKES

BEADS

From time to time your plants will need fertilizing—not to stimulate growth, but to maintain good condition; they will need nitrogen for healthy foliage, phosphorus for strong roots and potassium for overall vigor. A 1:1:1 or 1:2:1 ratio of those ingredients is best for houseplants. For the fertilizer requirements of many houseplants, check the Dictionary *(pages 552-575)*. Fertilizers come in several forms—liquid, water-soluble powder, timed-release spikes and beads—and the nutrients of all are distributed to plant tissues by means of water. Spikes and beads are inserted in moist soil; the liquids and powders should be mixed with water before being applied.

# GROOMING HOUSEPLANTS

*With its lush green leaves and small white flower buds, a Tahitian bridal veil covers a side table. The plant's dense foliage and compact, mounded shape are the result of regular grooming.*

**M**any maturing houseplants stretch upward too swiftly toward the light—and become overly tall and scraggly with few lower branches and sparse foliage. Or sometimes, branches shoot out too far, throwing the plants out of balance and spoiling their shape. Plants may become caked with dust, or their appearance may be marred by dead or decaying leaves and flowers.

Happily there are several remedies for these developments, as shown below and on the following two pages. Pinching *(page 68)*, edge trimming and pruning will maintain the symmetrical shape of foliage houseplants. The best time of year to pinch, trim or prune them is early spring, when plants have plenty of energy to produce new growth swiftly. Most foliage houseplants respond well to grooming, but some do not. Most of the latter are ones that have a single growing stem—palms, corn plants and Norfolk Island pines, for example. For larger, woody foliage houseplants—such as fig trees or schefflera—controlling their growth can keep them from outgrowing their allotted space.

Bathing foliage, removing spent leaves and deadheading faded blooms will keep all plants, particularly flowering ones, healthy and thriving. For most houseplants, such maintenance should be done once each month or so and more often if you live in a city where grime in the outside air all too readily sifts indoors and into your houseplant garden.

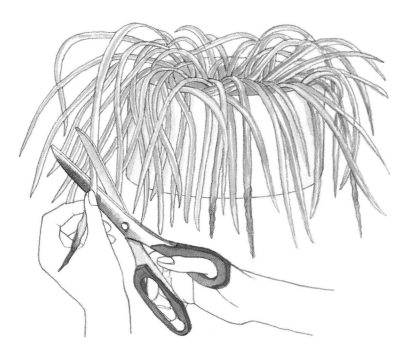

## EDGE TRIMMING

Edge trimming involves removing the leaf tips of houseplants that turn brown, either from a lack of moisture or from excess salts in water and fertilizer. In addition to correcting the problem that caused the leaf tips to turn brown in the first place, you will want to trim off the tips to keep the plant attractive. Use a pair of scissors to trim away the damaged ends. Instead of making a straight cut across the leaf tip, which will mar the plant's appearance, follow the natural contour of the leaf *(left)*. From a distance, you will never notice that the foliage has been trimmed.

## PRUNING

Pruning involves using garden shears or clippers to snip stems and branches too thick or too woody for finger and thumb. The main idea is to reshape a plant that has grown irregularly and make it more symmetrical. But the effect can also help a plant conserve energy, stir dormant buds into life and promote fresh, healthy growth. Shears and clippers, however, can spread plant diseases, so sterilize them between operations by dipping them in a solution of one part bleach and nine parts water. Houseplants that are small trees, such as the jade shown here, can especially benefit from periodic pruning. If a branch sticks out awkwardly, snip it back *(left)*. Also cut off any weak or unhealthy branches in the center of the plant, to open it up to light and air. Cut ½ inch or less above a node—where a leaf or a pair of leaves emerge from the stem.

## CONTROLLING GROWTH

To maintain the health of a small tree, such as the weeping fig shown here, while keeping its growth under control, repot it in its own container. Water the plant, then tip it on its side to ease the root ball out of the pot and onto a sheet of newspaper. If the roots are stubborn and cling to the pot, loosen them by tapping the pot gently using a rubber mallet *(right)*. Use a sharp knife to shave away about 1 inch of soil and roots all the way around the side of the root ball. To repot the plant, gently lower the root ball back into the pot, filling the extra space around it with fresh potting soil. Firm the soil with your hands. Ensure that the plant sits at the same level it did before. Using sterilized clippers, prune some foliage to make up for the root loss. For indoor trees of moderate size, as shown, trim about 10 branches back a few inches as you would any houseplant *(above)*. Then water the plant generously.

## BATHING FOLIAGE

Keeping foliage free of dust is essential because it is through their leaves that plants take in carbon dioxide and give off oxygen. Even a thin layer of house dust may clog a leaf's pores. Worse is the greasy, gritty film left by polluted air. To free foliage of grime and dust, use mild soapy water and a sponge or a soft cloth to gently wipe off the tops and undersides of all leaves. Support the leaves with the fingers of your other hand as you do the wiping so that the leaves do not bend or break *(right)*. Avoid washing houseplants that have hairy, or so-called pubescent, leaves; water may spot them. Rather, use a soft brush to whisk away the dust.

## REMOVING SPENT LEAVES

Foliage that looks withered, rotten, burned or discolored should be removed as soon as you notice it. Besides being unsightly, such foliage depletes a plant's growing energy—and offers targets for insects and diseases. Most leaves will come off if you tug at the base *(left)*. If not, cut them off using scissors, a sharp knife or pruning shears; sterilize the tool with a water and bleach solution between cuts. For a leaf that is only slightly damaged at the tip, trim its edges *(page 539)*. Discard any spent leaves that have fallen onto the soil surface to avoid inviting pests or diseases.

## DEADHEADING FADED BLOOMS

Once a flower wilts or fades, remove it from the plant—for looks and to encourage new buds. But do not just snip off the old blossom; remove its stem as well, cutting where the small stem joins a larger one *(right)*. Discard any faded blooms that have fallen onto the soil surface.

# REPOTTING AN ESTABLISHED PLANT IN A NEW CONTAINER

Well-tended houseplants can grow with surprising speed and therefore need to be replanted in larger pots when they outgrow their old ones. Fortunately for the indoor gardener, a plant that has become pot-bound usually gives off clear signals of distress. The roots may start poking out of the drainage hole in the bottom of the pot, or they may grow upward, becoming visible on the surface of the soil. Or the leaves may yellow, new leaves may be stunted or spread too far apart—or the plant's top growth may suddenly look far too large for the pot underneath.

Whatever the signal, the plant should come out of the pot for a check of its root ball. If the roots turn out to be thickly matted and coiling around the ball, repotting is clearly in order. For the best repotting techniques, see below and opposite.

There are a few general rules to follow. First, a plant should be repotted only when it is growing vigorously—in spring or summer. Second, a plant should not be moved into a new pot that is several sizes larger than the old one. The roots will take so long to stretch into the extra space that water will gather there, and the excess moisture can cause the roots to rot. The best method is to select a new pot that is only 1 to 2 inches wider at the rim than the old one. A pot this size should provide plenty of room for at least one season's new growth.

A last rule: Always replant in a clean container. Even a new pot can benefit from a good rinse. If the chosen pot has been used before, scrub it out with a mild solution of water and bleach to get rid of residual salts and any lingering diseases.

*Three variegated dwarf schleffleras—identical plants, but different in age and size—stand in look-alike pots of staggered sizes, each appropriate to the plant it holds.*

1 Before repotting your plant, moisten the soil. Then place your hand over the soil surface, supporting the stem or stems between your fingers *(right)*. Turn the pot upside down and slide the plant out; if it resists, gently rap the pot. For a large plant, remove it from its pot as you would when controlling its growth *(page 540)*. Because repotting is best done quickly, have the new pot handy.

542

**2** Using both hands, lightly loosen the root ball of the freed plant *(left)*; use a sharp knife to prune out some root tips. This will stimulate new root growth and get rid of some old soil and tired roots. It will also help shake out excess salts that can be left behind by fertilizers or by the saline "hard" water found in many localities.

**3** Fill the bottom of the pot with a 1- to 2-inch layer of clean gravel or pot shards to facilitate drainage and avoid waterlogging the roots. Then drop fresh potting mixture—available at a garden-supply center—by the handful into the new container *(above)* until it is about one-third full. Tamp down the mixture, but do not pack it tightly.

**4** Place the plant in its new, larger pot. It should sit with its soil line an inch or so below the rim of the pot. If it is too low, add more potting mix underneath it. Then fill in around the root ball with additional mix, pressing down lightly. Water well. Should the mix settle too much after watering, add a bit more *(left)*.

# CONTROLLING PESTS INDOORS

Indoor plants are less exposed to health-threatening insects and diseases than outdoor plants. Nevertheless, you should keep a lookout for mealybugs, scales, aphids and spider mites. When buying plants, inspect them carefully to make sure they are pest-free. When replanting, use clean pots and sterile growing medium. Keep plants well groomed *(pages 539-541)*; promptly remove dead or decaying blossoms and foliage, which can provide a breeding ground for pests and diseases.

Regularly examine even healthy-looking plants for insect infestation. Pay special attention to leaf axils, stems and the undersides of leaves. At the first sign of infestation, isolate the plant to keep the trouble from spreading.

The first step to effective treatment is to identify the pest. Mealybugs are small and white, cottonlike in appearance; scales are usually tan, oval-shaped and covered with a hard waxy shell. Both pests weaken plants by sucking sap while excreting a clear sticky substance. To remove mealybugs and scales, rub infested areas with a cotton swab dipped in alcohol or in an insecticidal soap. Repeat until all signs of the pests and their eggs are gone.

Aphids are usually green and oval-shaped insects with long legs that feed on plant sap; they cause leaf malformation, yellowing and wilting and can spread diseases. Spider mites, which are microscopic members of the spider family, are no larger than dust specks; the back sides of infested leaves make a rusty red streak when rubbed on white paper. Spider mites get their name from the webs they spin on the plant. Left untreated, these webs can cover the whole plant, which eventually withers and dies. To remove aphids and spider mites, immerse the entire plant in mild soapy water, then rinse with a spray of fresh water. Repeat several times over a period of weeks until the plant is pest-free.

**Gardener's Tip:** If you opt for a pesticide to control pests, use it safely. Carefully follow the manufacturer's label instructions. When using the pesticide, wear rubber gloves and keep children and pets away from the area.

*With their dark green leaves and shiny pink blossoms, these begonias glow with health. To stay that way, they need to be kept free of aphids, spider mites, mealybugs and other pests that prey on houseplants.*

## KEEPING PETS AWAY FROM PLANTS

Cats and dogs are often attracted to houseplant foliage, which can provide pets with a tasty snack. One way to keep animals away is to grow plants such as cacti and succulents that have their own defense system—sharp teeth or spines. But lush, leafy green plants are defenseless, and need some protection. The answer is to prepare a mist solution with a dash of pepper. Add cayenne pepper to water, strain the mix and then spray the plants. Pets dislike the taste of pepper and should avoid the seasoned foliage.

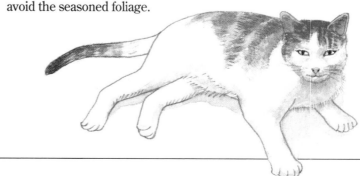

## MEALYBUGS AND SCALES

White, cottony-looking mealybugs, which congregate along leaf axils, and scales, which are usually found on stems and along leaf petioles and ribs, can be removed by swabbing the infested areas with alcohol-soaked cotton *(right)*. Be careful not to use excess alcohol, as it can damage healthy plant tissue. If the infestation persists, repeat the treatment until all pests have been eradicated.

Mealybugs and scales can also be removed by bathing infested foliage with a strong insecticidal soap. To eliminate large infestations of mealybugs, use a pesticide containing natural pyrethrins.

## APHIDS AND SPIDER MITES

Green, oval-shaped aphids, which break the surface of leaves, stems and buds with their beaks and then suck the sap from inside, and spider mites, which betray their presence in the form of fine white webs, can be dislodged from an infested plant by immersing it in a bucket of mild soapy water *(left)*. Agitate the plant gently, then spray it with fresh water to remove the soap. Repeat if pests reappear.

# A CHECKLIST FOR HOUSEPLANTS

### WINTER

- When days are short and light is low, plant growth slows, and the need for moisture and nutrients is reduced. Water your houseplants infrequently and apply little or no fertilizer.

- Cold drafts threaten plants on a windowsill and may cause loss of foliage. For nighttime protection, place a barrier such as a piece of cardboard between the plants and the window.

- Keep windows clean to maximize light penetration.

- Heating systems dry the air. Group your houseplants close together so they share the moisture released from foliage, or use a humidifier.

- Spider mites are especially active in a warm, dry environment. Inspect your houseplants for signs of these and other insects and for diseases.

- Clean empty pots; prepare potting medium for spring planting.

- Order seeds for spring sowing.

- Plant gloriosa lily bulbs and resume normal care.

- Place miniature roses, African violets and geraniums under fluorescent light; they do not need to go dormant in winter and they benefit from supplemental light when days are short. Water and fertilize regularly.

### SPRING

- Now is an ideal time to buy new plants.

- When days lengthen and light levels increase, houseplants resume active growth. Start to water and fertilize your houseplants regularly.

- Now is the time to propagate: sow seeds, take stem and leaf cuttings, layer and divide plants.

- When seedlings become large enough, transplant them to individual containers.

- Check the root systems of all houseplants and repot those that are pot-bound.

- Prune and pinch back leafy green houseplants to encourage full growth.

- Pinch back new growth to keep plants bushy.

- Inspect all plants regularly for insects and diseases.

- Cut back zebra plant and Brazilian plume flower before new growth starts.

- Cut back orchid cactus and azalea after flowers fade.

- Allow cyclamen to go dormant.

## SUMMER

- Now is an ideal time to buy new plants.

- Continue to water and fertilize your houseplants regularly, particularly those in hanging baskets.

- Check houseplants located near windows for signs of sunburn. If the leaves develop tan or brown patches between the veins, move the plants farther away from the source of light or provide shade.

- Check plants that are not growing well to see if they are pot-bound and need to be repotted.

- Houseplants may be moved outdoors for the summer. Check them frequently; once the plants are outdoors, their growth increases, so they require more water and fertilizer.

- Transplant stem and leaf cuttings taken in spring to individual flower pots.

- Inspect all houseplants regularly for insects and diseases. Examine houseplants that you have put outdoors; look for damage done by snails, slugs and other garden pests.

- Protect plants from cold air-conditioner drafts.

- Subject kalanchoe to darkness 14 hours per night for six weeks to force it to bloom.

## FALL

- Prepare to return houseplants indoors. Wash the pots and the foliage to rinse off garden bacteria and insects. Bring the plants indoors as soon as night temperatures drop to 50° F.

- Take stem cuttings of tender perennials such as coleus, geraniums and iresine from the garden to be rooted and grown indoors as houseplants.

- As days shorten, light decreases and plant growth slows, reduce watering and fertilizing.

- As the weather cools and you turn on the heat, make sure your houseplants are grouped close together for adequate humidity; or use a humidifier.

- Watch your houseplants for signs of insects and diseases, especially those that are active in a warm, dry environment.

- Keep windows clean to maximize light penetration.

- Cut back heliotrope, black-eyed Susan vine, lantana and fuchsia after the flowers fade.

- Pot bulbs, such as crocus, hyacinth, iris, lily, grape hyacinth, daffodils, squill and tulips, and store them for forcing. (See Chapter 6.)

- Chill azalea and hydrangea to force them to set flower buds.

# TROUBLESHOOTING GUIDE: HOUSEPLANTS

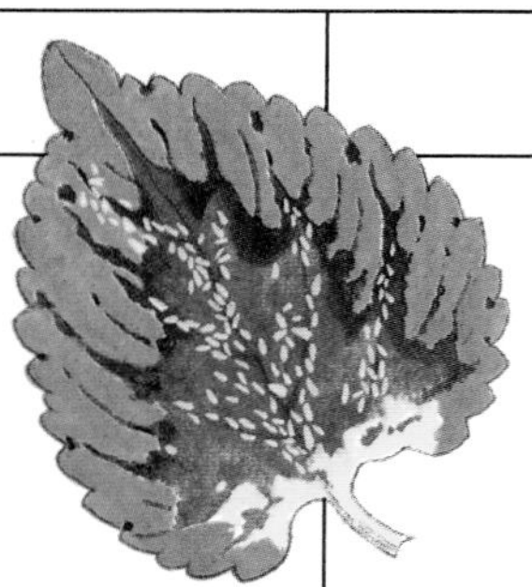

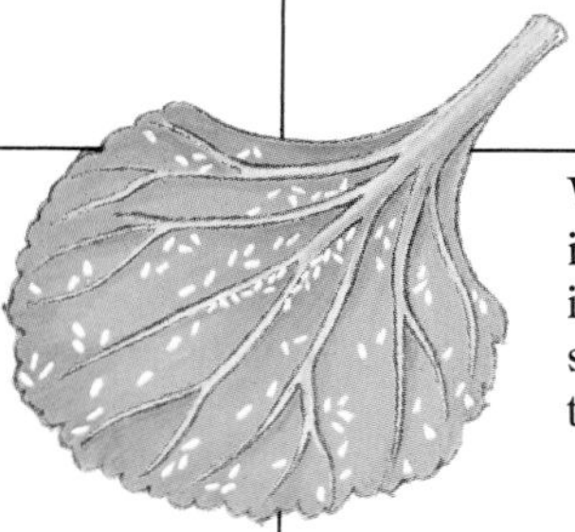

| PROBLEM | CAUSE | SOLUTION |
|---|---|---|
| Leaves lose their color, turn yellow and may curl up. Leaves and stems may be covered with a shiny, sticky substance. Flower buds and flowers become malformed. | Aphids, ⅛-inch semitransparent insects that suck the sap from the foliage. Aphids secrete the sticky substance, which becomes a breeding ground for diseases, such as sooty black fungal disease. | Wipe aphids off the plant with paper toweling and destroy them. Wash the plant with lukewarm, soapy water and rinse well. If the infestation is severe, use an insecticide containing natural pyrethrins. |
| Foliage turns yellow and has a curled or puckered appearance. Brown or silver flecks or streaks may appear along the leaf veins. Flower buds may not open. If they do, the flowers will be distorted and streaked, spotted or edged in white, yellow or brown. | Thrips, 1/16-inch, yellow, green or black insects barely visible to the naked eye. They suck the sap from the foliage. Thrips can also spread virus diseases to plants. | Remove damaged leaves. Treat the plant with an insecticide containing natural pyrethrins. |
| Plants wilt, cease to grow and may die. White, cottonlike masses form at or just below the soil surface. Cacti and succulents are particularly susceptible. | Root mealybugs, 1/16-inch-long insects. Most species feed only on underground roots, but a few also feed on stems. | Dip the entire plant, including the pot, into an insecticide solution. Wash the roots and remove all mealybugs. |
| Plant growth slows or stops. Small, flying insects are evident in the area where plants are grown. | Fungus gnats, black flies up to ⅛ inch long. The flies do not feed on the plants, but they can spread diseases. The larvae, which hatch in the soil, may feed on plant roots or stems below the soil surface. | Drench the soil of infested plants with an insecticide, or dip their roots into an insecticide. Use a household insect spray in the areas around the plants. |
| Plants cease to grow, and foliage turns yellow and then drops. When a plant is shaken or moved, a white cloud of insects appears above the foliage. Coleus, fuchsia and lantana are particularly susceptible. | Whiteflies, 1/16-inch insects that congregate in colonies on the undersides of leaves and suck the sap from the foliage. | Wash the plant with lukewarm, soapy water and rinse well. Repeat in four days to destroy the eggs. If the infestation is severe, use an insecticide. |
| Patches of white, cottonlike growths appear on the undersides of leaves and at the points where the leaves join the stems. Foliage may be coated with a shiny, sticky substance. The plant ceases to grow and may die. | Mealybugs, ¼-inch insects that have soft round bodies covered with fuzzy white filaments. They suck the sap from the foliage and secrete the shiny substance, which becomes a breeding ground for diseases. | Moisten a cotton swab with alcohol and dab it on the mealybugs, which will die and fall off the plant. Then wash the plant in lukewarm, soapy water and rinse well. Alternatively, plunge the plant repeatedly in warm water. If the infestation is severe, use an insecticide. |

| PROBLEM | CAUSE | SOLUTION |
|---|---|---|
| Foliage turns yellow and has a bronzy, dull appearance. Leaves may dry up and fall from the plant. Eventually, webbing will appear on the foliage and around the flower buds and flowers. | Spider mites, nearly microscopic pests that may be red, yellow, green or black. To confirm their presence, gently shake a leafstalk over a piece of paper; tiny, moving, dustlike specks will appear on the paper. | Wash plants regularly with lukewarm water to prevent and control infestation. Maintain high humidity; mites thrive in hot, dry air. If the infestation is severe, use a miticide. |
| Small, irregular holes appear in leaves near the soil. After the plant is watered or moved, masses of small, rapidly moving insects become visible on the soil surface. | Springtails, white or gray wingless insects 1/5 inch long that live in moist soil. Generally, they cause little damage, but when they are present in large numbers, some insects may feed on the foliage. | To prevent infestation, use a sterile medium for potting and allow the medium to dry between waterings. To control springtails, use an insecticide containing natural pyrethrins. |
| Foliage turns yellow and dies back. Rounded or oval bumps that are green, gray or brown appear along the stems and under the leaves. A shiny, sticky substance may cover the leaves. | Scale, a 1/8-inch insect with a round or oval shell-like covering. Scale insects suck the sap from the foliage and secrete the sticky substance, which becomes a breeding ground for diseases. | Repeatedly wash foliage with lukewarm, soapy water and a soft brush to remove scales; then rinse well. Treat severe infestations with an insecticide; root pesticide spikes are effective against scale. Before buying plants, inspect them for scale infestation. |
| Reddish and brown patches appear at the bases of the fronds on bird's nest fern. The patches expand to cover the fronds and eventually the fronds die back. | Foliar nematodes, microscopic worms that bore into the fronds through the surface pores and then feed on the foliage. | Immerse affected plants in hot water for 10 to 15 minutes. Allow the soil to dry between waterings. Do not splash water on the foliage; nematodes are spread by water. Cut off and destroy infested fronds. If damage is extensive, the plant and the potting soil should be discarded, but, to avoid spreading the infestation, not on a compost pile. |
| Plants become leggy and foliage is small and sparse. Leaves that should be variegated or colored red, pink or orange are solid green. Flowers fade and fall prematurely or do not form at all. | If the plant grows toward its light source, the cause is insufficient light. If the plant grows straight, but the leaves lose their variegation, the cause is usually excess fertilizer. The nitrogen in fertilizer speeds the growth of green cells, which overtake the colored cells. | Gradually move the plant into an area that receives more light or add fluorescent light. Keep windows clean to maximize light penetration. Reduce the amount of fertilizer. Cut the foliage back to encourage new growth. |
| Ferns turn yellow, beginning with the fronds in the center of the plant. The tips of the fronds turn brown. Eventually, entire fronds turn brown and die. On flowering houseplants, flowers dry up. Leaves become limp or shrivel up, then turn dry and crisp, and fall from the plant. | Low humidity. | Move plants that require high humidity, such as ferns, to a humid location or place a humidifier nearby. Mist ferns during periods of hot dry weather. Place a flowering plant in a bucket of water if the entire plant displays symptoms. Leave the plant in the water until it revives. Water more frequently, especially in summer. |

| PROBLEM | CAUSE | SOLUTION |
|---|---|---|
| Leaves do not develop to their full size. They have a pale, faded color, and may wilt. Leaf edges become dry and brittle, but do not turn brown. On flowering houseplants, flowers dry up. Leaves become limp or shrivel up, then turn dry and crisp, and fall from the plant. | Insufficient water. | Water plants as soon as symptoms appear. If the soil has completely dried out, soak the pot in water for several hours until the entire root ball is moistened. |
| Leaf edges turn yellow. Yellowing spreads toward the center of leaf until the entire leaf is yellow and drops from the plant. Plant growth may be stunted. | Lack of nitrogen. | Cut the foliage back and begin fertilizing regularly. If symptoms persist, increase the amount of fertilizer. |
| Silvery white, tan or brown areas develop on leaves between the veins. Plant growth is extremely compact. | Excess light. | Remove damaged leaves and move the plant to an area that receives less light or provide shade. |
| Leaves, especially those at the base of the plant, turn light green or yellow and may wilt. Flower buds may not form. If they do, they may rot before they open. Roots become soft, turn brown or black, and may have an unpleasant, sour odor. | Too much water, poor soil drainage or overly compacted soil. | Prune back damaged plants and repot them in a fast-draining medium. Improve soil drainage by adding perlite or vermiculite to the growing medium or by filling the bottom 2 inches of the pot with clean gravel or pot shards. Allow the soil to dry moderately between waterings. |
| Plants fail to grow. Leaves at the base of plants may turn yellow, wilt and die. Stems may be brown at the soil line. Roots are brown and soft. | Crown, root and stem rot caused by fungi that thrive in wet soils. | Allow the soil to dry between waterings. If the soil is heavy, repot the plant in a fast-draining, sterile soil mix. Increase air circulation around plants. Avoid overcrowding plants. |
| Leaves become mottled or streaked with yellow. Plant growth slows. Flowers may be discolored, streaked, malformed or smaller than normal. Stems may turn red. | Viral infection, a condition that may subside on its own. | There are no controls for viral infection, but it can be spread by aphids and other insects, which should be controlled, or by commercial growers propagating infecting plants. Infected plants should be isolated from healthy ones, and if the damage is severe, plants should be discarded. Buy only certified virus-free plants, if possible. Do not propagate plants with virus infection. |

| PROBLEM | CAUSE | SOLUTION |
|---|---|---|
| Leathery brown, rust-colored or black patches appear on cacti. The patches enlarge and the areas eventually shrivel and die. Opuntia is particularly susceptible. | A condition called scab. The cause is unknown, but scab occurs primarily when cacti are kept in areas with high humidity and low light, and it seems to spread from cactus to cactus. | There are no controls. Provide cacti with bright light, dry air and dry soil. Discard infected plants. |
| Soft, sunken, brown or yellow areas appear on stems. Leaves below the diseased area will turn yellow, but will not drop from the plant. Eventually, stems may rot completely and collapse. | Bacterial stem blight, also called soft rot, a disease caused by bacteria that enter the plant through wounds in the stem. | There are no controls. Damaged stems may be removed with a sharp, sterilized knife. If the damage is extensive, the plant should be discarded. Do not buy plants with stem wounds. |
| A fine white powder coats the upper surfaces of leaves and the stems. Foliage may dry out and drop from the plant. | Powdery mildew, a fungus disease. The fungus thrives in a combination of wet soil, high humidity and stagnant air. | Keep houseplants in an area with good air circulation and allow the soil to dry between waterings. Do not allow water to splash on stems or leaves. Wash mildew off plants with lukewarm, soapy water and remove severely damaged foliage. In severe cases, treat the plant with a fungicide. |
| Leaf edges turn brown and brittle. Symptoms appear first on older leaves, which eventually turn yellow and die. White streaks or patches appear on the rims and exteriors of clay pots. Orchids are particularly susceptible. | Salt buildup, caused by an excess of soluble salts in water, fertilizers or soil. | Leach salts that have built up in the soil by flushing the soil with fresh water several times; repeat until the water that drains out is clear. Empty saucers under pots so plants do not stand in drainage water. If damage is severe, repot the plant in a fresh, sterile soil mix. Water plants with demineralized water or rainwater. |
| Brown spots appear on the stems of palm fronds. Eventually, the entire frond turns brown. A pink-brown mold may appear at the base of the stems. | Gliocladium rot, a fungal disease. | Remove any diseased fronds. Avoid splashing water on the fronds; the disease spreads in water. Treat infected palms with a fungicide. |
| Clusters of small green bumps or blisters appear on the surfaces of leaves. Eventually, the blisters turn brown. The leaves may turn yellow and drop. | Edema, a condition that results from excess water in the leaf cells, which causes them to blister. | There are no controls. Grow plants in fast-draining soil, and allow the soil to dry between waterings. Empty saucers under pots so plants do not stand in drainage water. |
| Red, brown or black spots appear on leaves; each spot may be surrounded by a yellow halo. The spots enlarge until they cover the leaves and eventually the leaves die. | Leaf spot disease, caused by bacteria or fungi. | There are no controls. Remove and destroy infected leaves as soon as possible. Do not allow water to splash on the foliage; the disease is spread by water. |

551

ACORUS GRAMINEUS 'VARIEGATUS'

AEONIUM ARBOREUM 'ATROPURPUREUM'

AGLAONEMA COMMUTATUM
'SILVER QUEEN'

ALOCASIA CUPREA

# DICTIONARY OF HOUSEPLANTS

The dictionary that follows describes many houseplants that are amenable to indoor growing. Foliage houseplants are listed on pages 552-567; flowering houseplants follow on pages 568-575.

## Introduction to Foliage Houseplants

Each entry specifies a plant's light, temperature and humidity requirements. In addition, the dictionary specifies the best growing medium for each plant and how often to fertilize, as well as water requirements and repotting and propagating techniques. Plants are listed by their botanical names; common names are cross-referenced.

### Acorus (AK-o-rus)

Moisture-loving, grasslike plant from 6 inches to 2 feet tall. Fan-shaped clumps of flat, sword-shaped foliage, solid green or green with white stripes, emerge from a slender underground stem.

**Selected species and varieties.** *A. gramineus,* grassy-leaved sweet flag, Japanese sweet flag: has green leaves to 6 inches long. 'Variegatus' has white-striped green leaves to 12 inches long.

**Growing conditions.** Give Japanese sweet flag bright light, medium humidity and a cool temperature. Keep the soil evenly moist to wet; dried-out soil can cause the leaf tips to turn brown. Check the soil daily for adequate moisture. Fertilize regularly in spring and summer. Propagate by division and use an all-purpose soil mix for potting. Japanese sweet flag can be damaged by red spider mites, especially if it is grown in a hot, dry environment.

### Aeonium (ee-OH-nee-um)

Green succulent that varies in height from 1 inch to 3 feet, and may form a ground-hugging rosette of fleshy leaves or grow treelike with sparse branches in a loose, open shape. Small, star-shaped flowers are pink, red or yellow and bloom in spring.

**Selected species and varieties.** *A. arboreum:* grows in a treelike form to 3 feet tall. Branch tips produce rosettes of spoon-shaped, glossy green leaves and bear bright yellow flowers. 'Atropurpureum' has green leaves with tinges of purple.

**Growing conditions.** Give aeonium direct light, low humidity, a warm temperature in summer and a cool temperature in winter. Let the soil become dry to the touch between thorough waterings. Fertilize once every six weeks in spring and summer. Propagate from seed or stem cuttings and plant in a cactus mix. Aeonium can be damaged by mealybugs and scale insects. It is susceptible to root and stem rot.

### Aglaonema (ag-lay-o-NEE-ma)
Chinese evergreen

Compact plant, 1 to 3 feet tall, with multiple leafstalks and oval or lance-shaped, patterned green leaves to 12 inches in length.

**Selected species and varieties.** *A. commutatum* 'Silver Queen': has dark green leaves with irregular patches of silver.

**Growing conditions.** Chinese evergreen needs limited light, medium humidity and average temperature. Allow the soil to dry between waterings. Apply fertilizer in spring and summer. Chinese evergreen can be propagated by dividing the plant. An all-purpose soil mix should be used for repotting. Chinese evergreen can be damaged by aphids, mealybugs, scale insects and spider mites. It is susceptible to root rot and stem rot.

### Alocasia (al-o-KAY-zha)
Elephant's ear

Erect, leafy plant that grows from a thick, fleshy underground stem. Leaves are green with silver, white or brownish black markings. They are shaped like an elephant's ear and grow to 2½ feet wide on slender, pencil-shaped stalks.

**Selected species and varieties.** *A. cuprea,* giant caladium: grows to 2 feet tall. Leaves are puckered and metallic green with dark purple undersides. Leaf veins are purplish black.

**Growing conditions.** Provide limited light, a warm temperature and very high humidity. Keep the soil moist. Apply fertilizer in spring and summer. Propagate by division and pot in an all-purpose soil mix. Elephant's ear can be damaged by mealybugs, scale insects, spider mites and whiteflies.

## Aloe (AL-o)

Upright green succulent that can grow to several feet in height. Leaves are dagger-shaped, green, 4 to 30 inches long and may have spines.

**Selected species and varieties.** *A. barbadensis,* also known as *A.vera,* medicine aloe, burn plant: grows to 2 feet tall in stemless clumps. Leaves are fleshy, gray-green, 1 to 2 feet long, 2 to 3 inches wide and have soft teeth along the margins . They contain a jellylike plant tissue that can be used to treat minor skin maladies.

**Growing conditions.** Provide aloe with direct light, average room temperature and low humidity. Keep the soil on the dry side; water infrequently. Fertilize in summer. Propagate from offsets. Repot in a cactus mix. Aloe can be damaged by mealybugs, spider mites and scale insects. It is susceptible to crown rot.

## Ananas (a-NAN-us)

Erect bromeliad that grows in a rosette to a height of 3 feet and produces pineapples. Leaves are green, stiff, sword-shaped and from 1 to 3 feet in length. A flower spike, bearing pink bracts surrounding blue or pink flowers, emerges from the center of the rosette. Eventually, the spike thickens to form a pineapple, which is topped by a cluster of toothed leaves.

**Selected species and varieties.** *A. comosus,* pineapple: has dark green leaves with spiny tips. Fruit can grow to 10 inches long. 'Variegatus,' variegated pineapple, has ivory-colored margins that will turn slightly pink in lavish sunlight.

**Growing conditions.** Pineapple must have direct light to produce its best leaf color. Provide good air circulation, average humidity and a warm temperature. Allow the surface of the soil to dry slightly between thorough waterings. Fertilize once a month during spring and summer. Propagate from offsets. If after three years the plant has not flowered, put it in a plastic bag with an apple and set it in indirect light for four to five days to encourage flowering. Repot in an all-purpose soil mix. Pineapple is susceptible to damage from scale insects.

## Angelwings see *Pilea*

## Aporocactus (a-por-a-KAK-tus)

Spiny desert cactus with trailing, leafless green stems from 3 to 6 feet long and ½ inch wide. Stems have clusters of brownish bristles on small, slightly raised surface pores. Tubular pink, rose or crimson flowers bloom in spring.

**Selected species and varieties.** *A. flagelliformis,* rattail cactus: has bright green stems that can grow to 6 feet long. Bristles are ⅛ inch long. Flowers are crimson-pink and 2 to 3 inches in diameter.

**Growing conditions.** Give rattail cactus direct light; insufficient light will cause spindly, malformed growth. Maintain a warm temperature and low humidity. Allow the soil to dry thoroughly between waterings. Fertilize rattail cactus once a year, in spring. Propagate by taking stem cuttings and pot them in a cactus mix. Rattail cactus can be damaged by aphids, mealybugs, spider mites, scale insects and thrips. It is susceptible to root and stem rot.

## Araucaria (ar-a-KAIR-ee-a)

Evergreen tree to 6 feet tall. Branches are covered with needles that may be stiff or soft, and flat or rounded.

**Selected species and varieties.** *A. heterophylla,* Norfolk Island pine: grows in a symmetrical form with tiers of branches. Needles are bright green, short, soft and rounded.

**Growing conditions.** Norfolk Island pine does best in bright light and average to cool room temperature with good air circulation. It must have medium humidity; low humidity can cause the needles to turn brown. The soil should be watered thoroughly and allowed to dry to the touch before watering again. Fertilizer should be applied in spring and summer. Frequent turning of the pot will maintain even growth. This tree is slow-growing and needs to be repotted only when it grows too big for its container. Because it is such a slow grower, home propagation is not recommended. Norfolk Island pine is susceptible to mealybugs, red spider mites and scale insects.

## Ardisia (ar-DIZ-ee-a)

A broad genus of about 250 species of tropical broad-leaved evergreen shrubs and trees that can grow to 50 feet in their natural habitat. Only one species can be grown indoors.

ALOE BARBADENSIS

ANANAS COMOSUS 'VARIEGATUS'

APOROCACTUS FLAGELLIFORMIS

ARAUCARIA HETEROPHYLLA

ARDISIA CRENATA

ASPARAGUS MYRIOCLADUS

ASPIDISTRA ELATIOR 'VARIEGATA'

ASTROPHYTUM ASTERIAS

BEAUCARNEA RECURVATA

**Selected species and varieties.** *A. crenata,* coralberry: grows to 3 feet tall and can be pruned into a treelike shape. Leaves are shiny, waxy and from 2 to 4 inches long. Small, star-shaped, fragrant white flowers bloom in summer and are followed by clusters of pea-sized red berries. Berries mature in late December.

**Growing conditions.** Coralberry needs bright light in summer and direct light in winter. It does best in cool room temperatures and high humidity. The soil should be kept evenly moist and the plant should be fed regularly in spring and summer; fertilizer will help produce a healthy crop of berries. An all-purpose soil mix can be used for repotting. Home propagation is not recommended. Coralberry is susceptible to damage from scale insects. It can get red spider mites in a hot, dry environment.

**Arrowhead vine** see *Syngonium*
**Artillery plant** see *Pilea*

**Asparagus** (a-SPA-ra-gus)

Feathery-looking green plant that can be erect, climbing or trailing. It resembles, but is not a fern; it is related to the common edible asparagus. Stems may be branched and are covered with delicate, green foliage. Small white flowers bloom at various times of the year and are followed by brightly colored berries.

**Selected species and varieties.** *A. myriocladus,* also called *A. macowanii,* feather plume asparagus fern: grows to 2½ feet with fluffy-looking fronds.

**Growing conditions.** Asparagus fern does best in bright light, average to cool temperature and medium humidity. It can also be grown under fluorescent light. The soil should be kept evenly moist in summer and barely moist in winter; if it is allowed to dry out completely, leaves may turn yellow and drop. Fertilizer can be applied regularly during spring and summer. Asparagus fern can be propagated by division and repotted in an all-purpose soil mix. It is suitable for a hanging basket. Asparagus fern may be damaged by mealybugs, scale insects and spider mites.

**Aspidistra** (as-pi-DIS-tra)

Stemless, upright plant to about 3 feet tall. Narrow, oblong, glossy green leaves grow on long stalks.

**Selected species and varieties.** *A. elatior,* cast-iron plant, barroom plant: has dark green leaves that are 2½ feet long and 4 inches across. 'Variegata' has bright green leaves with white stripes.

**Growing conditions.** Cast-iron plant can survive under adverse conditions. It does best in a cool temperature, medium humidity and bright light, but can adapt to low light. The soil may be kept dry and the plant should be fertilized regularly in spring and summer. Propagate by division and repot in an all-purpose soil mix. Cast-iron plant is susceptible to mites and scale insects.

**Astrophytum** (as-tro-FY-tum)
Star cactus

Squat, rounded, brown or green cactus from 2 to 12 inches tall. The body of the cactus has shallow or deep vertical clefts and may have sharp spines or white hairs. Cup-shaped flowers blossom from the top in spring.

**Selected species and varieties.** *A. asterias,* sand dollar cactus, sea urchin cactus: grows to 2 inches tall and 3 inches wide. Short hairs and dot-like pores cover the gray-green surface. Yellow flowers, sometimes flushed with red, bloom after the cactus is at least three years old.

**Growing conditions.** Star cactus requires direct light, low humidity, a warm temperature in summer and a cool temperature in winter. The soil should be allowed to dry thoroughly between waterings; excessive watering can cause raised, scablike tissue to appear on the cactus. Fertilizer should be applied during the cool-temperature, low-light months of late winter or early spring. The cactus can be propagated by offsets and repotted in a cactus mix. Star cactus can be damaged by aphids, mealybugs, scale insects, spider mites, bacterial soft rot and scab diseases.

**Avocado** see *Persea*
**Baby rubber plant** see *Peperomia*
**Baby's tears** see *Soleirolia*
**Barroom plant** see *Aspidistra*

**Beaucarnea** (bo-KAR-nee-a)
Bottle ponytail

Bottle-shaped succulent from 12 inches to 3 feet tall. A tan, woody stem grows from a swollen base. Long, narrow, straplike green leaves grow from the top of the stem.

**Selected species and varieties.** *B. recurvata,* ponytail or elephant-foot tree: has smooth leaves to 6 feet long.

**Growing conditions.** Provide ponytail with direct light, average temperature and low humidity. Allow the soil to dry out between waterings. Fertilize once a year in spring or summer. Propagate by offsets and repot in a cactus mix. Ponytail is susceptible to damage from mealybugs, scale insects, spider mites and whiteflies.

**Begonia** see Dictionary of Annuals, page 200; Bulbs, page 292
**Belgian evergreen** see *Dracaena*
**Bloodleaf** see Dictionary of Annuals, page 200
**Boston fern** see *Nephrolepis*
**Botanical wonder** see *Fatshedera*

**Brassaia** (BRASS-ee-a)

Tropical shrub that grows from 6 to 10 feet tall and can be trained into a treelike shape. Narrow, long leafstalks produce shiny green compound leaves from 6 to 12 inches long.

**Selected species and varieties.** *B. actinophylla,* also known as *Schefflera actinophylla,* schefflera, Australian umbrella tree, queen's umbrella tree, Queensland umbrella tree: grows to 8 feet in height and has leaflets that radiate from a central point like the spokes on an umbrella.

**Growing conditions.** Schefflera does best in bright light and can adapt to lower light, but too little light can result in legginess. The plant needs a warm temperature and high humidity. The soil should be watered thoroughly, then allowed to dry. Fertilizer can be applied year round. Schefflera can be propagated from seed and repotted in an all-purpose soil mix. Schefflera is very susceptible to spider mites, especially in a hot, dry room. It can also be damaged by mealybugs, scale insects and whiteflies. Schefflera can get bacterial, fungal and viral infections, and crown and stem rot.

**Burn plant** see *Aloe*
**Caladium** see Dictionary of Bulbs, page 292
**Cast-iron plant** see *Aspidistra*

**Cephalocereus** (sef-a-lo-SEER-ee-us)

Hairy cactus to 18 inches tall with a round to columnar leafless stem divided lengthwise into numerous grooved sections. Each stem section is covered with long white or yellow hairs that conceal sharp spines.

**Selected species and varieties.** *C. senilis,* old man cactus: has a stem that grows up to 12 inches tall and is divided into 12 or 15 sections. The stem hairs are 3 to 4 inches long. They are white and turn brown with age. The spines are 1 to 1½ inches long.

**Growing conditions.** Old man cactus requires direct light and a warm temperature. It needs little humidity and little water; the soil should be allowed to dry between waterings. The cactus may be fed just once a year in spring. It can be propagated by offsets or from seeds and repotted in a cactus mix. Old man cactus is susceptible to mealybugs, scale insects and soft rot.

**Chamaedorea** (kam-a-DOR-ee-a)

Slender feathery palm with canelike stems to 3 feet tall. Graceful arching green fronds grow to 18 inches long.

**Selected species and varieties.** *C. elegans,* parlor palm: has broad, sprawling fronds.

**Growing conditions.** Parlor palm needs bright light; it can tolerate lower light, but may become spindly over a period of time. It does best in a warm temperature, high humidity and evenly moist soil. The leaf tips can turn brown as a result of insufficient water and low humidity. Parlor palm should be fertilized regularly in spring and summer. It can be propagated by division of the multiple stems or from offsets and repotted in an all-purpose soil mix. Parlor palm is susceptible to spider mites, especially if the air is dry. It can also attract mealybugs, scale insects and thrips, and can develop Gliocladium rot.

**Chandelier plant** see *Kalanchoe*
**Chinese evergreen** see *Aglaonema*

**Chlorophytum** (klor-o-FY-tum)

Trailing green plant 12 to 15 inches high. Thick, fleshy roots produce narrow, strap-shaped leaves from 6 to 18 inches in length. Leaves can be green, white, yellow or striped. In spring and summer, trailing yellow stems to 2 feet long emerge between the leaves and produce star-shaped white flowers at the ends.

BRASSAIA ACTINOPHYLLA

CEPHALOCEREUS SENILIS

CHAMAEDOREA ELEGANS

CHLOROPHYTUM COMOSUM 'VITTATUM'

CISSUS RHOMBIFOLIA

CITRUS MITIS

CODIAEUM VARIEGATUM PICTUM

**Selected species and varieties.** *C. comosum,* spider plant: has bright green leaves. Spider plant gets its name from its plantlets, which resemble spiders. 'Vittatum' has 6- to 12-inch, medium green leaves, each with a wide white or cream-colored stripe down the center.

**Growing conditions.** Give spider plant bright light throughout the year. Provide average humidity and average room temperature. Allow the soil to dry to the touch between thorough waterings. Apply fertilizer once each season. Propagate by layering or by separating the plantlets that succeed the flowers. Use an all-purpose soil mix for repotting. Spider plant is suitable for a hanging basket. Spider plant is susceptible to damage from scale insects.

**Cholla** see *Opuntia*

**Cissus** (SISS-us)
Grape ivy

Climbing, trailing or vining green plant to 8 feet long. Smooth, velvety or leathery leaves from 2 to 6 inches in length grow from woody stems. Leaves may be solid green or variegated. Most species have curly tendrils that can anchor the plant to a support.

**Selected species and varieties.** *C. rhombifolia,* grape ivy: has glossy dark green leaves with rust-colored hairs on the undersides. Tendrils have forked tips.

**Growing conditions.** Most grape ivies do best in bright light but they can adapt to limited light. They need average room temperature, average humidity and soil kept on the dry side. Grape ivies should be fertilized once in spring and once in summer. The stem tips can be pinched back regularly to keep the plants bushy. They can be propagated from stem cuttings and repotted in an all-purpose soil mix. Grape ivies are suitable for growing in hanging baskets. Grape ivies are vulnerable to damage by mealybugs and spider mites and they also are susceptible to salt buildup.

**Citrus** (SIT-rus)

Broad-leaved evergreen tree that grows to 6 feet tall and produces grapefruit, lemons, limes or oranges. Leafstalks may be flattened and flaring or rounded. Leaves are pointed ovals 3 to 6 inches long and aromatic

when bruised. Fragrant white flowers appear in late spring and are followed in summer by yellow, orange or green fruit. Flowers and fruit may or may not be produced indoors; if they are, the fruit is usually not full-sized.

**Selected species and varieties.** *C. mitis,* Calamondin orange: grows to 3 feet tall and produces miniature oranges. *C.* x *paradisi,* grapefruit: grows to 5 feet. Flattened leafstalks 1 inch long support glossy green leaves 4 inches long. Fruit is yellow, light orange or greenish and has a smooth rind.

**Growing conditions.** Give citrus direct light, average temperature and medium to high humidity. The foliage benefits from a move outdoors in summer into bright light, but not searing sun. Keep the soil moderately moist. Fertilize regularly in spring and summer. Propagate from seeds saved from store-bought fruit and plant them in an all-purpose soil mix. Citrus is susceptible to spider mites, especially if it is grown in dry air; it can also get mealybugs and scale insects. Citrus is vulnerable to scab disease.

**Codiaeum** (ko-dee-EE-um)
Croton

Bushy, tropical shrub that grows to 3 feet high. A single erect stem supports short-stalked, glossy, leathery leaves from 3 to 18 inches long. Leaves are generally narrow and may be linear or twisted, lobed or unlobed, and smooth or crinkled. They are variegated in various patterns with yellow, green, red, pink, orange, brown, cream or a combination of these colors.

**Selected species and varieties.** *C. variegatum pictum:* has shiny green leaves with prominent red or yellow ribs and pink, orange, red or yellow variegation.

**Growing conditions.** To develop its best leaf coloring, croton needs direct light, a warm temperature and medium to high humidity. It thrives in medium-moist soil, but it can tolerate a wide variation in the soil moisture level. Feed regularly from early spring to late summer. Propagate by taking stem cuttings. Repot in standard mix. Croton is vulnerable to attack by mealybugs, scale insects and spider mites.

**Coleus** see Dictionary of Annuals, page 200
**Coralberry** see *Ardisia*

## Cordyline (kor-di-LY-nee)

Shrub or treelike plant that usually has a single erect stem. Leaves are graceful, arching, lance-shaped, and from 1 to 3 feet long and up to 4 inches wide. They may be green, red, copper, cream, pink, bronze or a combination of these colors.

**Selected species and varieties.** *C. terminalis,* ti plant, good luck plant: grows 2 to 6 feet tall and has green leaves variegated in shades of red, pink, cream or copper.

**Growing conditions.** To maintain its best leaf coloring, ti plant needs direct light, average to warm room temperature and high humidity. The soil should be allowed to dry slightly between thorough waterings. Fertilizer should be applied in spring and summer. Ti plant can be propagated from ti logs—short sections of the stem, available at garden-supply centers. An all-purpose soil mix can be used for repotting. The plant is susceptible to damage from aphids, mealybugs, scale insects and spider mites.

**Corn plant** see *Dracaena*

## Crassula (KRASS-yew-la)

Sprawling, bushy or treelike succulent to 3 feet in height. Fleshy stems support green, blue-gray or yellow leaves that can be spoon-shaped, sickle-shaped, rounded, triangular or linear.

**Selected species and varieties.** *C. argentea,* jade plant: grows in a tree-like form with woody branches and rubbery, shiny jade green leaves, sometimes edged in red. Leaves are oblong and 1 to 2 inches long. 'Tricolor' has green leaves tinged with pink.

**Growing conditions.** Jade plant does best in direct light; it can also be grown in fluorescent light. It needs average room temperature and low humidity. Allow the soil to dry between waterings; excess water can cause soft, weak stem growth and root rot. Fertilizer should be applied regularly through spring and summer. Jade plant can be propagated from leaf or stem cuttings and repotted in a cactus mix. Jade plant is subject to attack from aphids, mealybugs, scale insects and spider mites.

**Creeping Charlie** see *Pilea*
**Croton** see *Codiaeum*

## Cryptanthus (krip-TAN-thus)
Earth-star

Low-growing terrestrial bromeliad with star-shaped rosettes of jagged-edged leaves from 3 to 20 inches long.

**Selected species and varieties.** *C. bivittatus:* has wavy, greenish brown or cream-striped leaves with a pink tint. The leaves grow to 4 inches long.

**Growing conditions.** Earth-star adapts to various light conditions, but bright light enhances its leaf color. It requires average room temperature and high humidity. The potting mix should be allowed to dry between waterings, and the plant should be fertilized in spring and summer. Earth-star can be propagated from offsets and repotted in a peat-based soilless mix or in sphagnum moss. Earth-star is vulnerable to damage by scale insects.

**Cyperus** see Dictionary of Grasses and Ground Covers, page 160

## Cyrtomium (sir-TOH-mee-um)

Leathery-leaved fern that grows erect to a height of 3 feet. Furry leafstalks support 2-foot-long fronds. Leaves are green, 4 inches long and grow in pairs.

**Selected species and varieties.** *C. falcatum,* holly fern: has glossy, dark green, jagged-edged leaves that resemble holly leaves.

**Growing conditions.** Holly fern can tolerate low light, dry air and drafts, but it does best in bright light, average to cool temperature and medium humidity. The soil should be allowed to dry between thorough waterings. Holly fern should be fed only occasionally. It can be propagated by division and repotted in a fern mix. Holly fern is susceptible to aphids, mealybugs and scale insects.

**Dallas fern** see *Nephrolepis*
**Date palm** see *Phoenix*
**Desert fan palm** see Dictionary of Trees and Shrubs, page 426
**Devil's ivy** see *Epipremnum*

## Dieffenbachia (deef-en-BOK-ee-a)
Dumbcane

Leafy green plant that grows to 6 feet tall. When young it has a single stout stem; when mature it may have multiple stems. Leaves are variegated and grow to 1½ feet long.

CORDYLINE TERMINALIS

CRASSULA ARGENTEA 'TRICOLOR'

CRYPTANTHUS BIVITTATUS

CYRTOMIUM FALCATUM

DIEFFENBACHIA EXOTICA

DIZYGOTHECA ELEGANTISSIMA

DRACAENA MARGINATA 'TRICOLOR'

EPIPREMNUM AUREUM

**Selected species and varieties.** *D. exotica,* exotic dumbcane: grows in a compact form to 2 feet tall. Leaves are dark green and nearly covered with white or greenish white variegation. *D. maculata,* spotted dumbcane: grows to a height of 4 feet and has dark green leaves with white markings.

**Growing conditions.** Dumbcane can adapt to various growing conditions, but it does best in bright but diffused light, average temperature and medium to high humidity. The soil can be allowed to approach dryness between thorough waterings, but it should not dry out completely. Fertilizer should be applied in spring and in summer. Dumbcane can be propagated from stem cuttings. An all-purpose soil mix can be used for potting. Dumbcane exudes a poisonous sap and should not be grown in a household that has small children. Dumbcane is susceptible to mealybugs and spider mites. It is also subject to bacterial stem blight and stem rot, leaf spot and salt buildup.

**Dizygotheca** (diz-ee-go-THEE-ka)
False aralia

Lacy-looking, treelike plant to 6 feet tall and 20 inches wide. Slender, unbranched stems have long stalks with narrow leaflets arranged in a circle at the tips of the leafstalks.

**Selected species and varieties.** *D. elegantissima:* has jagged leaflets ½ inch wide that are coppery red when young and a dark green when mature.

**Growing conditions.** False aralia needs bright light, warm room temperature and high humidity. The soil should be allowed to dry to the touch between thorough waterings. Fertilizer can be applied once a month in spring and summer. False aralia does not adapt well to being moved or repotted, so it should be repotted only once every few years. An all-purpose soil mix can be used for repotting. False aralia is propagated commercially from seed under special growing conditions, and home propagation is not recommended. False aralia is susceptible to mealybugs, scale insects, spider mites and thrips.

**Dracaena** (dra-SEE-na)

Shrubby or treelike plant from 20 inches to 10 feet tall. Most species have single unbranched stems that may be either succulent or woody. Narrow, arching leaves grow to 2 feet long. They may be solid green or green with stripes or spots.

**Selected species and varieties.** *D. deremensis:* grows to 6 feet tall with shiny green, strap-shaped leaves to 18 inches long. 'Janet Craig' has slightly broader, darker green leaves. 'Warneckii,' striped dracaena, has gray-green leaves about 1 foot long with two narrow white stripes. *D. fragrans massangeana,* corn plant: grows to 5 feet tall on a thick, woody stem. Leaves are bright green with a broad yellow stripe and are about 2 feet long and 4 inches wide. *D. marginata,* red-margined dracaena, dragon tree: grows to 9 feet tall on a straight or curving woody stem. Leaves are sword-shaped, 2 feet long and ½ inch wide, and green with red margins. 'Tricolor' has pink-, cream- and green-striped leaves. *D. sanderana,* Belgian evergreen, ribbon plant: grows to 3 feet tall. Slender, upright stems support narrow, lance-shaped leaves that grow to 9 inches long and are green bordered with white stripes. *D. surculosa,* also called *D. godseffiana,* gold dust plant: looks very different from other dracaenas. It does not grow more than 20 inches tall. Wiry stems support oval, spotted green leaves that are 3 inches long and 1½ inches wide.

**Growing conditions.** All dracaenas thrive in bright light; 'Janet Craig' and 'Warneckii' can gradually adapt to limited light. All need an average to warm temperature and medium to high humidity for new leaf growth, which is inhibited in cool, dry air. The soil should be kept moderately dry and fertilizer should be applied once every three months in spring and summer. Dracaenas can be propagated from stem cuttings and offsets. An all-purpose soil mix can be used for repotting. Most dracaenas are subject to damage from mealybugs, scale insects and spider mites. They are also susceptible to leaf spot disease and salt buildup.

**Dragon tree** see *Dracaena*
**Dumbcane** see *Dieffenbachia*
**Earth-star** see *Cryptanthus*
**Elephant-foot tree** see *Beaucarnea*
**Elephant's ear** see *Alocasia*
**English ivy** see Dictionary of Grasses and Ground Covers, page 160

## Epipremnum (ep-i-PREM-num)
Pothos, devil's ivy

Leafy green plant with multiple stems that grow to 6 feet in length and may be climbing or trailing. Leaves are oval to heart-shaped, 3 to 8 inches long, olive green or medium green with yellow, cream or white markings, and may be glossy or matte.

**Selected species and varieties.** *E. aureum,* formerly *Scindapsus aureus,* golden pothos: has glossy green leaves with irregular yellow markings. 'Marble Queen' has shiny bright green leaves with white swirls and streaks.

**Growing conditions.** Pothos needs bright light, medium humidity and average room temperature. It can also be grown under fluorescent light. The soil can be kept on the dry side. Pothos needs to be fertilized only two or three times during spring and summer. It can be propagated by layering and from stem cuttings and planted in an all-purpose soil mix. It is suitable for a hanging basket and will attach itself to a slab of tree bark or other support. Pothos is generally free from pests and diseases.

**Euonymus** see Dictionary of Grasses and Ground Covers, page 160
**Euphorbia** see Dictionary of Perennials, page 246
**False aralia** see *Dizygotheca*

## x Fatshedera (fats-HED-e-ra)
Botanical wonder

A single-species genus that is a genetic cross of *Fatsia japonica* and *Hedera helix.* It is a large-leaved, rangy plant to 4 feet tall with woody stems that bear long-stalked leaves. The leaves are glossy green, 8 inches wide and have up to five lobes.

**Selected species and varieties.** x *F. lizei:* grows in a shrubby form but with climbing stems. 'Variegata' has green leaves with irregular white patches in the center.

**Growing conditions.** Give botanical wonder bright to direct light or grow it under fluorescent light. Maintain an average room temperature and medium humidity. Let the soil dry slightly between thorough waterings; leaves may drop if the soil is too wet or too dry. Fertilize regularly in spring and summer. Stake botanical wonder plant if the stem needs support and pinch the leaves back to maintain a bushier appearance. Propagate from woody stem cuttings and repot in an all-purpose soil mix. Botanical wonder may be attacked by aphids, mealybugs, scale insects and spider mites.

## Fatsia (FAT-see-a)

Green-leaved shrub to 5 feet tall. A single, woody stem supports long leafstalks and huge leaves from 8 to 18 inches wide. Each leaf is lobed, with up to nine deep clefts.

**Selected species and varieties.** *F. japonica,* Japanese fatsia: has glossy dark green leaves.

**Growing conditions.** Fatsia needs bright to direct light; it can also be grown under fluorescent light. It does best in cool to average room temperature with low to medium humidity. The soil can be kept moderately dry. Fertilizer should be applied regularly during spring and summer. Fatsia can be propagated from seed and from stem cuttings and repotted in an all-purpose soil mix. Care should be taken when handling fatsia. Its new leaves are tender and bruise easily; bruising can permanently mar the appearance of the foliage. Fatsia is vulnerable to attack by aphids, mealybugs, scale insects and spider mites.

**Ficus** see Dictionary of Trees and Shrubs, page 426
**Fig** see Dictionary of Trees and Shrubs, page 426

## Fittonia (fi-TOH-nee-a)

Mounded or creeping plant to 6 inches. Succulent stems bear egg-shaped leaves up to 3 inches long. Green leaves have a network of prominent veins in shades of red, white or silver.

**Selected species and varieties.** *F. verschaffeltii,* red-nerve plant: has olive green leaves with pinkish red veins. *F. verschaffeltii argyroneura,* mosaic plant, silver-nerve plant: has dark green leaves with delicate white or silver veins. 'Minima' has leaves less than 1 inch long.

**Growing conditions.** Give nerve plant limited to bright light or grow it under fluorescent light. Provide medium to high humidity and a warm temperature. Keep the potting mix moderately moist; allow it to dry only slightly

× FATSHEDERA LIZEI 'VARIEGATA'

FATSIA JAPONICA

FITTONIA VERSCHAFFELTII ARGYRONEURA

GIBASIS PELLUCIDA

GYNURA AURANTIACA

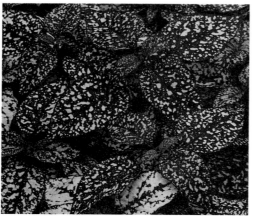
HYPOESTES PHYLLOSTACHYA

KALANCHOE TOMENTOSA

between waterings. Fertilize nerve plant regularly throughout the year. Propagate from stem cuttings and pot in a peat-based soilless mix. Nerve plant is susceptible to damage from mealybugs and mites. It can also get crown rot.

**Freckle-face** see *Hypoestes*
**Geranium** see Dictionary of Annuals, page 200

## Gibasis (ji-BAY-sis)

Leafy, fine-textured trailing plant that grows to 2½ feet long. Slender stems bear delicate green leaves. Dainty white flowers, ¼ inch in size, are produced in profusion.

**Selected species and varieties.** *G. pellucida* (formerly *G. geniculata* and *Tripogandra multiflora*), Tahitian bridal veil: has oval ½-inch leaves with purple undersides.

**Growing conditions.** Tahitian bridal veil does best in bright to direct light; it can also be grown under fluorescent light. It needs an average temperature and medium humidity. The soil should be allowed to dry to the touch between thorough waterings. Fertilizer should be applied regularly throughout the year. Dried leaves can be removed from the plant as they accumulate. The stem tips can be pinched back to encourage bushiness. Tahitian bridal veil can be propagated by division and repotted in an all-purpose soil mix. Tahitian bridal veil can suffer damage from mealybugs, scale insects, spider mites and whiteflies.

**Gold dust plant** see *Dracaena*
**Good luck plant** see *Cordyline; Sansevieria*
**Grape ivy** see *Cissus*
**Grapefruit** see *Citrus*

## Gynura (ji-NEW-ra)

Trailing plant to 6 feet in length. Branching stems support velvety green leaves that are covered on both sides with purple hairs. Pungent, orange-yellow flowers are produced in late spring or early summer.

**Selected species and varieties.** *G. aurantiaca,* purple velvet plant, purple passion vine: grows erect when young and gradually becomes trailing to 3 feet in length as it matures. Leaves are 4 to 8 inches long, 4 inches wide and have jagged edges.

**Growing conditions.** To maintain its coloration, purple velvet plant needs bright light. It needs high humidity and a warm temperature; the foliage can be damaged if the temperature drops below 55° F. The soil should be kept evenly moist. Care should be exercised when watering; splashes of water may leave permanent marks on the leaves. A fertilizer should be applied once a month during spring and summer. Purple velvet plant can be propagated from stem cuttings. An all-purpose soil mix can be used for repotting. Purple velvet plant is susceptible to aphids, mealybugs, scale insects, spider mites, whiteflies and leaf spot.

**Hedera** see Dictionary of Grasses and Ground Covers, page 160
**Heptapleurum** see *Schefflera*
**Holly fern** see *Cyrtomium*

## Hypoestes (hy-po-ES-teez)

Erect, shrubby plant to 3 feet tall. Leaves are oval, 2 inches long, speckled and grow on short leafstalks.

**Selected species and varieties.** *H. phyllostachya,* polka-dot plant, freckle-face: has dark green leaves covered with pink dots.

**Growing conditions.** Polka-dot plant requires bright light to maintain its best leaf coloration. It needs average room temperature and medium humidity. The soil should be allowed to dry slightly between waterings; if the soil becomes too dry, the leaves may wither. Fertilizer should be applied regularly during spring and summer. Polka-dot plant gets leggy with age; it looks best if it is kept pruned to a height of about 2 feet. It can be propagated from seed and from stem cuttings. An all-purpose soil mix can be used for repotting. Polka-dot plant is susceptible to mealybugs, scale insects, spider mites and whiteflies.

**Iresine** see Dictionary of Annuals, page 200
**Ivy** see Dictionary of Grasses and Ground Covers, page 160
**Jade plant** see *Crassula*

## Kalanchoe (kal-an-KO-ee)

Shrubby succulent from 12 inches to 3 feet in height, in low-growing rosettes or on erect stems. Leaves are fleshy and may be oval, rounded or triangular, and green, gray-green or red.

**Selected species and varieties.**
*K. tomentosa,* panda plant: forms ground-hugging rosettes of thick, stubby leaves covered with soft silver hairs. When the plant is young, the leaf margins are tipped with rusty orange hairs; as it matures, the hairs turn chocolate brown.

**Growing conditions.** Kalanchoe needs direct sun, average room temperature and low humidity. The soil can be allowed to dry substantially between waterings. Fertilizer should be applied regularly in spring and summer. Kalanchoe can be propagated from stem and leaf cuttings. A cactus mix should be used for repotting. Kalanchoe can be damaged by aphids, mealybugs, scale insects and spider mites. It is susceptible to powdery mildew.

**Lady palm** see *Rhapis*

**Maranta** (ma-RAN-ta)

A leafy, low-growing green plant to 12 inches tall. Short leafstalks, sheathed at the base, support broad, oval leaves that are 5 inches long and 3 inches wide. Leaves are green with gray or red veins and symmetrical featherlike markings.

**Selected species and varieties.**
*M. leuconeura,* prayer plant: grows to 12 inches in height. Upper leaf surfaces are marked with yellow-green, dark green or brown patches. Undersides may be gray or purple. Leaves fold in the evening in a form that resembles hands in a praying position. *M. leuconeura erythroneura,* red-veined prayer plant: has light green leaves with bright red veins and yellow markings along the center of the leaf. Undersides are reddish purple. *M. Leuconeura kerchoviana,* rabbit's foot, rabbit's tracks, prayer plant: has light green leaves with brown markings resembling a paw print. Undersides of leaves are gray-green.

**Growing conditions.** Prayer plants do best in bright light, average room temperature and medium to high humidity. The soil should be kept evenly moist but not soggy; wet soil can cause root rot. Fertilizer should be applied regularly in spring and summer. Prayer plants can be propagated by division. An all-purpose soil mix can be used for repotting. Prayer plants are subject to attack by aphids, mealybugs, scale insects and spider mites. They are also susceptible to salt buildup and root rot.

**Mimosa** (mi-MO-sa)

Genus of about 500 herbs, shrubs, trees and vines. Only one species is grown as a houseplant.

**Selected species and varieties.**
*M. pudica,* sensitive plant: grows erect and shrublike to 20 inches tall. Prickly stems support long-stalked, light green, ferny-looking foliage. Foliage recoils on contact; the leaves fold inward and the leafstalks droop temporarily.

**Growing conditions.** Sensitive plant requires bright to direct light, warm room temperature and medium to high humidity. The soil should be kept moderately moist and allowed to dry only slightly between waterings. Fertilizer can be applied regularly in spring and summer. Sensitive plant can be propagated from seed or from stem cuttings. It should be repotted when the roots protrude through the drainage hole. Sensitive plant can be damaged by mealybugs and scale insects.

**Monstera** (mon-STAIR-a)

Trailing or climbing vine to 6 feet tall. Aerial roots form on mature plants; some will attach to a nearby support. Long leafstalks bear glossy green leaves that are heart-shaped or rounded.

**Selected species and varieties.**
*M. deliciosa,* split-leaf philodendron (in spite of its common name, it is not a member of the genus *Philodendron*), Swiss cheese plant: has 12-inch leafstalks and broad leaves that may be as much as 18 inches in width. Leaves are heart-shaped. As they grow older, the leaves develop deep clefts and perforations. These perforations are the plant's way of coping with high winds in nature, because they allow air to pass through the leaves without tearing them.

**Growing conditions.** Give splitleaf philodendron bright light in summer and direct sun in winter, or grow it under fluorescent light. Maintain a warm room temperature and medium to high humidity. Water thoroughly and allow the soil to dry before watering again. Fertilize plants regularly from spring until fall. Propagate from stem cuttings or by layering. Pot in an all-purpose soil mix. Provide a tree bark or moss-covered support for the aerial roots to cling to. Split-leaf philodendron can be attacked by aphids, mealybugs, scale insects, spider mites and thrips.

MARANTA LEUCONEURA ERYTHRONEURA

MIMOSA PUDICA

MONSTERA DELICIOSA

NEPHROLEPIS EXALTATA

OPUNTIA MICRODASYS
'ALBISPINA'

PEPEROMIA OBTUSIFOLIA 'VARIEGATA'

**Mosaic plant** see *Fittonia*
**Moses-in-the-cradle** see *Rhoeo*
**Mother-in-law's tongue**
see *Sansevieria*

**Nephrolepis** (ne-FROL-e-pis)
Sword fern

Erect fern to 2 feet in height with arching, compound green fronds from 1 to 6 feet long. Slender, furry runners sprout from rhizomes, or underground stems, and root along the surface of the soil.

**Selected species and varieties.** *N. exaltata:* has feathery, triangular fronds to 6 feet long and 4 inches wide. Fronds are composed of small leaflets with wavy edges. 'Bostoniensis,' Boston fern, has a compact form with bright green fronds that grow to 4 feet in length. 'Dallas' has feathery leaflets on fronds that grow to 2 feet in length. 'Fluffy Ruffles' has stiff, dark green fronds that grow erect to 12 inches in height.

**Growing conditions.** Give sword ferns limited to bright light, average room temperature and high humidity. Keep the soil evenly moist; if the roots dry out, the fronds will turn brown and may die. Fertilize infrequently; once in spring and once in summer is adequate. Propagate by layering or by division. Sword ferns can be damaged by scale insects, thrips and whiteflies.

**Nephthytis** see *Syngonium*
**Norfolk Island pine** see *Araucaria*
**Old man cactus** see *Cephalocereus*

**Opuntia** (oh-PUN-cha)
Cholla, prickly pear cactus

Genus of approximately 300 green cacti, prostrate or erect, several feet tall. The stems are divided into segments that may be flat or cylindrical and that may be covered with spines.

**Selected species and varieties.** *O. microdasys,* rabbit-ears: grows to 3 feet tall in jointed segments of flat, oval pads. The pads are light green and covered with spots of short, bright yellow bristles. 'Albispina' has white bristles. *O. vulgaris:* has oblong, bright green pads covered with short spines that are pink at the base. 'Variegata' has pads mottled with greenish white.

**Growing conditions.** Cholla requires direct light, average to warm room temperature, good air circulation and low humidity. It needs little water.

Fertilizer can be applied once every other month in spring and summer. Cholla is propagated by removing a pad segment from the cactus and planting it in a cactus mix. The pads should be handled with care; their bristles can work their way into the skin and may be difficult to remove. Cholla can be damaged by mealybugs and scale insects.

**Panda plant** see *Kalanchoe*
**Parlor palm** see *Chamaedorea*
**Pelargonium** see Dictionary of Annuals, page 200

**Peperomia** (pep-e-RO-mee-a)

Leafy green plant that grows erect to 12 inches or trailing to several feet in length. Leafstalks are fleshy and from 1 to 10 inches long. Leaves are solid green or variegated, quilted or smooth, heart-shaped, oval, rounded or narrow, and grow to 5 inches long. Flower spikes to 10 inches long are produced throughout the year and may be white, cream or green.

**Selected species and varieties.** *P. argyreia,* watermelon peperomia: grows upright to 12 inches tall. Leaves are 5 inches long and pointed at the tips. They are thick, waxy and dark green with silver lines that resemble the markings on a watermelon rind. Flower spikes are white and about 3 inches long. *P. caperata,* emerald ripple peperomia: grows compact and bushy in a mounded shape to 6 inches high. Leaves are heart-shaped and have a wrinkled texture. They are deep green on the upper surfaces and pale gray-green on the undersides. Flower spikes are white and about 4 inches long.
*P. obtusifolia,* baby rubber plant: grows compact and bushy to 8 inches high and has oval leaves to 3 inches long. Flower spikes are white and about 3 inches long. 'Variegata' has medium green leaves with cream or yellow margins; some leaves are completely yellow. *P. orba,* pixie peperomia: grows in a compact, mounded form on hairy stems to 7 inches long. Leaves are oval and glossy green with faint gray mottling. Undersides are velvety gray-green. The plant sometimes produces creamy white flower spikes up to 6 inches in length. *P. scandens,* philodendron peperomia: grows in a climbing or trailing manner to several feet long. Leaves are light green, heart-shaped and up to 3 inches long. Flowers are rarely produced indoors. 'Variegata' has light green leaves with cream margins.

**Growing conditions.** Variegated peperomias do best in bright light; solid-colored varieties need limited to bright light and protection from the summer sun. Insufficient light can cause stems to become weak and spindly. Peperomias need average to warm room temperature and medium to high humidity. The soil should be allowed to dry between waterings; too much water can cause the leaves to drop. Emerald ripple peperomia is especially sensitive to overwatering and can develop crown or stem rot. Fertilizer should be applied once a month in spring and summer. Peperomias can be propagated from leaf and stem cuttings and by division. An all-purpose soil mix can be used for potting. Peperomia is susceptible to mealybugs, spider mites and whiteflies. It can develop edema and root and stem rot.

### Persea (PUR-see-a)

Genus of about 150 tropical trees that grow to over 60 feet tall in their native habitat. Only one species is grown as a houseplant.

**Selected species and varieties.** *P. americana,* avocado: grows 4 to 6 feet in height on an erect, single stem. Leaves are dark green, leathery, elliptic and grow from 4 to 8 inches in length. Fruit is not produced indoors.

**Growing conditions.** Give avocado direct light; insufficient light will cause spindly growth. Provide a warm temperature and medium humidity. Keep the soil evenly moist but not wet and soggy. Fertilize once a month throughout the year. Propagate from seeds saved from fresh, store-bought avocados. Use an all-purpose soil mix for repotting. Mature plants may require staking. Avocado is vulnerable to aphids, mealybugs, scale insects and thrips.

### Philodendron (fil-o-DEN-dron)

Climbing, trailing or occasionally erect tropical green plant with thick stems to 6 feet in length. Leaves may be green or red, and heart-shaped, fiddle-shaped, sword-shaped, rounded or triangular. They may have smooth edges or deep clefts.

**Selected species and varieties.** *P. bipennifolium,* horsehead philodendron: has deeply cleft, triangular, glossy green leaves approximately 15 inches long. *P.* x 'Burgundy': has narrow, triangular leaves 12 inches long. Leaves are bright red when new and turn green as they mature. The undersides of the leaves remain burgundy. Stems and leafstalks are red. *P. erubescens,* redleaf philodendron: has shiny, dark green, triangular leaves up to 10 inches in length. Undersides of leaves are coppery red. Stems and leafstalks are red.

*P. pinnatilobum* 'Fernleaf,' fernleaf philodendron: has medium green, finely cut leaves that resemble fern fronds. *P. scandens oxycardium,* heart-leaf philodendron: is a trailing vine several feet long with small, heart-shaped leaves to 4 inches in length. Leaves emerge bronze and turn green as they mature. *P. selloum,* tree philodendron: grows erect to 6 feet tall on a trunklike stem. Leaves are glossy green, deeply cleft and 18 inches long.

**Growing conditions.** Philodendron does best in bright light; limited light may cause small leaves and straggly growth. It needs an average to warm temperature and medium humidity. The soil should be allowed to dry to the touch between thorough waterings; overwatering can cause brown spots to form on the leaves and root rot. The leaves can be rinsed or sponged with water often to keep them clean and glossy. Fertilizer should be applied regularly during spring and summer. Climbing philodendrons need a support, such as a piece of bark or a moss-covered pole. Philodendrons can be propagated from stem cuttings and by layering. They can be potted in an all-purpose soil mix. Philodendron is vulnerable to aphids, mealybugs, scale insects and spider mites. It is also susceptible to bacterial leaf spot, root rot and salt buildup.

### Phoenix (FEE-nix)
Date palm

Tropical palm to 6 feet in height. Fronds are compound and grow to 3 feet long from a thick, brown base.

**Selected species and varieties.** *P. roebelenii,* miniature date palm: grows to 4 feet tall and has delicate, arching, dark green fronds.

**Growing conditions.** Date palm can be grown in bright light or under fluorescent light. It needs medium humidity, a warm temperature by day and a slightly cooler temperature at night. The soil should be kept relatively dry. Fertilizer should be applied regularly during spring and summer. Commercially, date palm is propagated from seed under special greenhouse conditions; home propagation

PERSEA AMERICANA

PHILODENDRON SCANDENS OXYCARDIUM

PHOENIX ROEBELENII

PILEA CADIEREI

PLECTRANTHUS AUSTRALIS

RHAPIS EXCELSA

from seed is not recommended. Occasionally, offsets arise from the base of date palms grown indoors; these offsets can be used for propagation. An all-purpose soil mix can be used for potting. Date palm is a slow grower and needs repotting only once every three years or when roots appear along the surface of the soil. Date palm is vulnerable to attack by mealybugs, scale insects and spider mites.

**Piggyback plant** see *Tolmiea*

## Pilea (py-LEE-a)

Compact, bushy green plant that grows erect to 12 inches tall or forms a low mound to 12 inches wide. Stems are fleshy and bear green leaves marked with silver, brown, bronze or red. Leaves may be puckered or smooth and ¼ inch to 3 inches long.

**Selected species and varieties.** *P. acuminata:* has a mounded, compact shape and grows to 8 inches in height. 'Moon Valley' has leaves that are 3 inches long with a quilted texture. Upper surfaces are bright green with brown veins and brown stripes along the center ribs. *P. cadierei,* aluminum plant: grows erect to 12 inches tall. Leaves are 3 inches long and light green with raised silver patches. *P. microphylla,* artillery plant: grows to 10 inches tall in a mounded shape with spreading stems. Tiny leaves about ¼ inch long form in clusters that resemble feathery fern foliage. Artillery plant got its name because it expels its pollen in a strong spray. *P. nummulariifolia,* creeping Charlie: grows in a ground-hugging form and has thin, reddish branches to 10 inches long. Leaves are pale green, rounded, ¾ inch wide and have a quilted surface. *P. spruceana:* grows in either a creeping or an upright form. 'Norfolk,' angelwings, grows in a creeping habit and forms tight rosettes of cross-paired, circular leaves. Leaves are from 1½ to 3 inches wide and bronze with raised silver stripes. 'Silver Tree' grows upright to 10 inches tall and has hairy white leafstalks. Leaves are 3 inches long and greenish bronze with wide silver stripes and silver dots. Undersides are covered with reddish hairs.

**Growing conditions.** Give pileas limited to bright light, warm room temperature and medium to high humidity. Allow the soil to dry to the touch between thorough waterings. Fertilize regularly in spring and summer. Pinch back the mound-forming varieties regularly to maintain full, dense growth. Propagate from stem cuttings and pot in an all-purpose soil mix. Artillery plant, 'Moon Valley' and creeping Charlie are all suitable for hanging baskets. Pileas vulnerable to mealybugs, scale insects and root rot.

**Pineapple** see *Ananas*

## Plectranthus (plek-TRAN-thus)
Swedish ivy

Shrublike or trailing green plant with fleshy, square stems that grow to 3 feet long. Stems bear green leaves that may be heart-shaped, oval or rounded and grow to 2½ inches in length. Leaves emit a distinctive odor when bruised.

**Selected species and varieties.** *P. australis:* trails to 2 feet in length and has shiny, dark green rounded leaves. Small flowers are light blue. *P. coleoides:* trails to 3 feet in length and has furry, heart-shaped gray-green leaves on purple stems. 'Marginatus,' white-edged Swedish ivy, has leaves with white edges.

**Growing conditions.** Swedish ivy does best in bright light, an average temperature and medium humidity. It can also grow in a warm temperature if the humidity is increased. The soil can be allowed to dry moderately between thorough waterings. Fertilizer should be applied regularly in spring and summer. The stems can be pinched back frequently to encourage full, bushy growth. The trailing forms of Swedish ivy are suitable for planting in hanging baskets. Swedish ivy can be propagated from stem cuttings and repotted in an all-purpose soil mix. Swedish ivy can get aphids, mealybugs and whiteflies.

**Podocarpus** see Dictionary of Trees and Shrubs, page 426
**Polka-dot plant** see *Hypoestes*
**Ponytail** see *Beaucarnea*
**Pothos** see *Epipremnum*
**Prayer plant** see *Maranta*
**Prickly pear cactus** see *Opuntia*
**Purple passion vine** see *Gynura*
**Purple velvet plant** see *Gynura*

**Queen's umbrella tree** see *Brassaia*
**Rabbit-ears** see *Opuntia*
**Rattail** see *Aporocactus*
**Red-nerve plant** see *Fittonia*

## Rhapis (RAY-pis)
Lady palm

Reedlike palm that grows to 5 feet in height in clumps of stiff stems. It has fronds that are fan-shaped and divided lengthwise into narrow green leaves that may be blunt-edged or pointed.

**Selected species and varieties.** *R. excelsa,* slender lady palm: has shiny bright green fronds divided into five to eight leaves up to 9 inches long and 2 inches wide.

**Growing conditions.** Give lady palm limited light, average room temperature and low humidity. Allow the potting medium to dry moderately between thorough waterings. Sponge, rinse or shower the foliage regularly to remove dirt and dust. Fertilize once a month during spring and summer. Propagate by division or from offsets and repot in a peat-based soilless mix. Lady palm can be damaged by mealybugs, scale insects and spider mites.

## Rhoeo (REE-o)

Upright green plant that forms rosettes of stiff, dagger-shaped green leaves to 12 inches tall.

**Selected species and varieties.** *R. spathacea,* also known as *R. discolor,* Moses-in-the-cradle: leaves are purple at the base and have purple undersides. Small white flowers bloom inside pink bracts that resemble boats. 'Variegata' has bright yellow vertical stripes.

**Growing conditions.** Moses-in-the-cradle needs bright light, an average temperature and medium to high humidity. The soil should be allowed to dry between waterings. Fertilizer can be applied regularly during spring and summer. Moses-in-the-cradle can be propagated from offsets and repotted in an all-purpose soil mix.

**Rock foil** see *Saxifraga*
**Sand dollar cactus** see *Astrophytum*

## Sansevieria (san-se-VEER-ee-a)
Snake plant, good luck plant

Fleshy, stiff-leaved succulent that may be erect to 3 feet tall or low-growing, in rosettes, to a few inches in height. Leaves can be solid green or variegated.

**Selected species and varieties.** *S. trifasciata:* has narrow, sword-shaped leaves that grow to 3 feet long and are marked with bands of light and dark green. 'Hahnii,' bird's-nest sansevieria, forms squat rosettes of leaves to 6 inches in height. 'Laurentii,' mother-in-law's tongue, has erect, leathery, sword-shaped leaves to 36 inches tall. Leaves may be gray-green or dark green with yellow margins and irregular horizontal bands of silver, light green or black-green. Leaf edges tend to curl.

**Growing conditions.** Snake plant does best in bright to direct light, an average to warm temperature and medium humidity. It can adapt to a wide range of conditions, but limited light and low humidity can slow its growth. The soil should be allowed to dry between waterings; overwatering can foster root rot. It should be fertilized every other month during spring and summer. It can be propagated from offsets, leaf section cuttings and by division of the roots. Snake plant needs repotting only when it outgrows its container. Half cactus mix and half all-purpose mix should be used for repotting. Snake plant can be damaged by mealybugs and scale insects. It is susceptible to leaf and root rot.

## Saxifraga (saks-IF-ra-ga)
Rock foil

Genus of approximately 300 species of low-growing, stemless green plants. Leaves form in rosette-shaped clusters on a central base that grows from underground stems called rhizomes. Only one species is grown as a houseplant.

**Selected species and varieties.** *S. stolonifera,* strawberry begonia: grows to 6 inches tall. Leaves are rounded with scalloped edges. Upper surfaces are olive green streaked with silver; undersides are reddish. Leaves and leafstalks are covered with fine, greenish hairs. Tiny plantlets are produced at the ends of long, trailing stems.

RHOEO SPATHACEA

SANSEVIERIA TRIFASCIATA 'LAURENTII'

SAXIFRAGA STOLONIFERA

SCHEFFLERA ARBORICOLA
'VARIEGATA'

SOLEIROLIA SOLEIROLII

SYNGONIUM PODOPHYLLUM

**Growing conditions.** Give strawberry begonia bright light, average room temperature and medium humidity. Allow the soil to become moderately dry between thorough waterings. Fertilize once a month during spring and summer. Propagate from plantlets and use an all-purpose soil mix for repotting. Strawberry begonia can be attacked by aphids, mealybugs and whiteflies. It is also susceptible to salt buildup.

**Schefflera** see *Brassaia; Schefflera*

**Schefflera** (shef-LEER-a)

Tropical evergreen shrub that grows to 5 feet in height.

**Selected species and varieties.** *S. arboricola,* also known as *Heptapleurum arboricola,* dwarf schefflera: has shiny, leathery green leaves. Each leaf is composed of seven to nine leaflets arranged in a circle on a slender leafstalk. The leaflets are narrow and oval, and grow to 5 inches long. 'Variegata' has pale yellow blotches.

**Growing conditions.** Dwarf schefflera does best in bright light, average room temperature and medium to high humidity. The soil should be allowed to dry to the touch between thorough waterings; wet soil can cause leaves to drop. Fertilize regularly from early spring through late autumn. Dwarf schefflera can be propagated from stem cuttings and repotted in an all-purpose soil mix. Dwarf schefflera is vulnerable to damage by mealybugs, scale insects and whiteflies.

**Sea urchin cactus** see *Astrophytum*
**Sedum** see Dictionary of Perennials, page 246
**Senecio** see Dictionary of Annuals, page 200
**Sensitive plant** see *Mimosa*
**Silver-nerve plant** see *Fittonia*
**Snake plant** see *Sansevieria*

**Soleirolia** (so-le-RO-lee-a)

A mat-forming green plant with creeping, fleshy stems that grow to about 6 inches in length. It has tiny green leaves ¼ inch wide.

**Selected species and varieties.** *S. soleirolii,* baby's tears: has bright green, rounded leaves on short, delicate leafstalks.

**Growing conditions.** Give baby's tears limited light to bright light; direct sun will burn the leaves. Provide an average temperature, high humidity and evenly moist soil or grow it in a terrarium. Fertilize baby's tears regularly during spring and summer. Clip the foliage with scissors to keep it full and compact. Propagate by division and use an all-purpose soil mix for potting. Baby's tears is not generally bothered by insects or diseases.

**Spider plant** see *Chlorophytum*
**Split-leaf philodendron** see *Monstera*
**Star cactus** see *Astrophytum*
**Stonecrop** see Dictionary of Perennials, page 246
**Strawberry begonia** see *Saxifraga*
**Swedish ivy** see *Plectranthus*
**Sweet flag** see *Acorus*
**Swiss cheese plant** see *Monstera*
**Sword fern** see *Nephrolepis*

**Syngonium** (sin-GO-nee-um)

Tropical climbing or trailing vine with fleshy stems that grow to 6 feet in length. Leaves may be green or variegated and from 3 inches to 12 inches long. The leaves change shape as the plant matures; on young plants they are solid and triangular; on older plants they become deeply cleft, forming from three to nine leaflets.

**Selected species and varieties.** *S. podophyllum,* formerly known as *Nephthytis,* arrowhead vine: has lustrous, medium green leaves, often variegated with white or yellow.

**Growing conditions.** Give arrowhead plant bright light, a warm temperature and medium to high humidity. Water moderately and allow the soil to dry between waterings. Fertilize regularly in spring and summer. Propagate from stem cuttings and repot in an all-purpose soil mix. Arrowhead vine is susceptible to mealybugs, spider mites, bacterial leaf spot and root rot.

**Tahitian bridal veil** see *Gibasis*
**Ti plant** see *Cordyline*

## Tolmiea (TOL-mee-a)

One-species genus of compact, mounded green plants to 12 inches tall and 15 inches wide.

**Selected species and varieties.** *T. menziesii,* piggyback plant: has a short stem with 4-inch-long, hairy leafstalks and hairy, heart-shaped, dark green leaves up to 3 inches wide. Young plantlets form at the base of the leaves.

**Growing conditions.** Provide piggyback plant with bright light or grow it under fluorescent light. Maintain cool to average room temperature and medium humidity. Allow the soil to dry between waterings; overwatering can cause leaf tip burn. Fertilize regularly in spring and summer. Propagate from plantlets and pot in an all-purpose soil mix. Piggyback plant can be damaged by mealybugs, spider mites and whiteflies. It is susceptible to powdery mildew and salt buildup.

## Tradescantia (trad-e-SKAN-shi-a)

Trailing green plant with fleshy stems that bear pointed oval leaves from 2 to 4 inches long. Small white or pink flowers bloom in spring.

**Selected species and varieties.** *T. fluminensis,* wandering Jew: grows to 2 feet in length. Upper leaf surfaces are blue-green; undersides are deep purple. Flowers are white. 'Variegata' has leaves with white lengthwise stripes. A few leaves may be solid white or solid green. *T. sillamontana,* white velvet plant: has woolly white hairs on leaves and stems. Leaves are green with purple undersides and grow to 2½ inches long. Flowers are pink-purple.

**Growing conditions.** Wandering Jew and white velvet plant do best in bright light, an average temperature and medium humidity. The soil should be allowed to dry between thorough waterings; overwatering encourages

rot. Fertilizer can be applied regularly from early spring to late fall. Dried leaves should be removed and the stems should be pinched back frequently to encourage full, bushy growth. Both wandering Jew and white velvet plant can be propagated from stem cuttings and repotted in an all-purpose soil mix. Wandering Jew and white velvet plant are susceptible to damage from mealybugs, scale insects, spider mites and whiteflies.

**Tripogandra** see *Gibasis*
**Umbrella tree** see *Brassaia*
**Wandering Jew** see *Tradescantia; Zebrina*
**Washington fan palm** see Dictionary of Trees and Shrubs, page 426
**Watermelon peperomia** see *Peperomia*
**White velvet plant** see *Tradescantia*
**Yucca** see Dictionary of Perennials, page 246

## Zebrina (ze-BRY-na)

Trailing green plant with fleshy stems to 3 feet in length. Leaves are pointed oval and 2 inches long. Small lilac, purple or rose flowers may bloom in spring or summer.

**Selected species and varieties.** *Z. pendula,* wandering Jew: has bright green leaves with broad, silvery lengthwise stripes. Undersides of leaves are flushed with purple. Flowers are deep pink.

**Growing conditions.** Wandering Jew needs bright light to produce its best leaf color. It thrives in average room temperature and medium humidity. The soil should be allowed to dry between waterings; overwatering can foster root rot. Fertilizer can be applied regularly in spring and summer. Dried leaves should be removed and stems should be pinched back to encourage full growth. Wandering Jew can be propagated from stem cuttings and repotted in an all-purpose soil mix. Wandering Jew is susceptible to damage from scale insects, spider mites and whiteflies.

TOLMIEA MENZIESII

TRADESCANTIA SILLAMONTANA

ZEBRINA PENDULA

567

AESCHYNANTHUS PULCHER

ANTHURIUM SCHERZERANUM

APHELANDRA SQUARROSA

## Introduction to Flowering Houseplants

Each dictionary entry will help you achieve healthy plants and, above all, abundant, long-lasting blossoms. The needs of individual plants with regard to growing medium, water and light are described, as are the best means of propagation. Plants are listed by their botanical names; common names are cross-referenced.

**Achimenes** see Dictionary of Bulbs, page 292

**Aeschynanthus** (ess-kuh-NAN-thus) Basket plant

Graceful vining plant with thin, 2- to 3-foot stems, leathery leaves and drooping, tubular, five-lobed flowers at the ends of the stems. The flower buds are long and slender, resemble tubes of lipstick, and bloom in spring.

**Selected species and varieties.** *A. pulcher,* scarlet basket vine, has small, oval, waxy, light green leaves and clusters of showy red, 2-inch flowers that have a yellow throat.

**Growing conditions.** Growing medium should be very rich and evenly moist at all times. Fertilize monthly during spring and summer. After the plant flowers, cut the stems back to 6 inches to encourage new growth. Propagate by stem cuttings taken in spring. Basket plant can attract aphids, mealybugs and spider mites and may develop root rot.

**African violet** see *Saintpaulia*
**Agapanthus** see Dictionary of Bulbs, page 292
**Amaryllis** see *Hippeastrum*

**Anthurium** (an-THUR-ee-um) Tailflower

Tropical plant suitable for growing indoors. Leaves are thick and firm, and have prominent veins. The flowers are tiny, found along a tail-like structure called a spadix, and are surrounded by colorful, shiny, 4- to 12-inch bracts called spathes. Flowers may appear all year and each flower will last for a month or more.

**Selected species and varieties.** *A. scherzeranum,* flamingo flower, has very narrow, lance-shaped leaves on 1- to 2-foot plants. The spathe is shiny and scarlet red; the spadix is orange-red or golden yellow and is often twisted.

**Growing conditions.** Tailflower should be grown where light is limited, air is warm, and humidity is high. If the humidity is too low, the plant will not flower. The growing medium should be rich, fast-draining and constantly wet when the plants are in flower. At other times, keep the medium evenly moist. If aerial roots develop, cover them with moist sphagnum peat moss. Fertilize monthly. Propagate by removing the offshoots at the base of the plant, by division, by stem cuttings, or from seed. Insects do not cause problems; leaf spot may develop.

**Aphelandra** (af-e-LAN-dra)

Tropical plant having large leaves that are topped by 4- to 8-inch spikes of tubular flowers.

**Selected species and varieties.** *A. squarrosa,* zebra plant, has oval, 6-inch leaves that are glossy green with prominent white to silver veins. Pale to golden yellow flowers appear off and on throughout the year. Indoors, plants grow about 12 to 18 inches high.

**Growing conditions.** Zebra plant is easy to grow indoors in an average or warm room with average humidity and bright light. The growing medium should be evenly moist from spring through fall; in winter allow it to dry out slightly between waterings. Fertilize every two weeks from spring through early fall. In early spring, plants may be cut back to encourage compact growth. Propagate by stem cuttings taken in spring, or from seed. Zebra plant can attract mealybugs.

**Atamasco lily** see Dictionary of Bulbs, page 292
**Azalea** see Dictionary of Trees and Shrubs, page 426
**Basket plant** see *Aeschynanthus*
**Begonia** see Dictionary of Annuals, page 200; Bulbs, page 292
**Bellflower** see Dictionary of Perennials, page 246
**Bird-of-paradise** see *Strelitzia*
**Black-eyed Susan vine** see Dictionary of Annuals, page 200
**Brazilian plume flower** see *Justicia*
**Browallia** see Dictionary of Annuals, page 200
**Calendula** see Dictionary of Annuals, page 200
**Calla lily** see *Zantedeschia*
**Campanula** see Dictionary of Perennials, page 246
**Cape primrose** see *Streptocarpus*
**Carpet plant** see *Episcia*

## Cattleya (KAT-lee-a)

Orchid that has thick, leathery foliage and fragrant flowers that appear in sprays. The blooms have three narrow petals, two broader petals, and a large, tubular lip at the bottom front of the flower.

**Selected species and varieties.** There are a large number of *Cattleya* species and hybrids that have large, 5- to 7-inch flowers of white, yellow, pink, blue, green, red, lavender or purple. Plants grow 12 to 18 inches high and, depending on the species and variety, they bloom at different times of year.

**Growing conditions.** To grow cattleya in the house is a challenge even for the experts. If light intensity is too high, the normally yellow-green leaves will turn more yellow and burn; if the plant receives insufficient light, it may not flower. Provide plants with direct light, a warm room and high humidity. Use a growing medium made for orchids, one containing extra fir or redwood bark or osmunda fiber. Fertilize monthly from midfall to midspring, and twice monthly at other times of year, using a complete fertilizer. When plants are in bud or in bloom, they like to be kept evenly moist; at other times, allow the medium to dry slightly between waterings. Stems are long and need to be staked. Cattleya benefits from being placed in a greenhouse when not in bloom, or outdoors in summer and early fall. When dividing the rhizomes for propagation *(see Chapter 5)*, make sure that each division contains three to six pseudobulbs—swellings of stem tissue that stores food and water. Cattleya can also be propagated from seed, but it may take several years for the plants to flower. Scales, mealybugs, spider mites and virus are the major concerns in growing cattleya.

**Chrysanthemum** see Dictionary of Annuals, page 200
**Cigar flower** see Dictionary of Annuals, page 200
**Clivia** see Dictionary of Bulbs, page 292

## Columnea (ko-LUM-nee-a)
Goldfish plant

Tropical plant in the gesneriad family that has trailing branches and is best used in a hanging basket. The flowers, which are 2 to 4 inches long, are tubular, two-lipped, and when fully open look like goldfish. Flowers generally bloom in spring and summer but may appear off and on all year.

**Selected species and varieties.** *C. microphylla* has slender, hairy, reddish brown stems, and hairy, green or red, round, soft leaves up to ½ inch long, much smaller than other members of the genus. Flowers are 2½ inches long, and bright red with a yellow throat and markings at the base of the lower lip.

**Growing conditions.** Goldfish plants do best in warm temperature, high humidity, and bright light. They also grow well under 14 to 16 hours of fluorescent light a day. In winter, they prefer cool temperatures, which aid in setting flower buds. The growing medium should be rich and evenly moist. In the winter, if the plant is not growing or flowering, reduce watering and eliminate the fertilizer. After the plant has flowered, prune it back to encourage fullness and new growth. Pinch the growing tips to keep the plants small and bushy. Propagate from stem cuttings or by division. Mealybugs may attack, but goldfish plant is generally disease-free.

**Convallaria** see Dictionary of Grasses and Ground Covers, page 160
**Crinum** see Dictionary of Bulbs, page 292
**Crocus** see Dictionary of Bulbs, page 292

## Crossandra (kro-SAN-dra)
Firecracker flower

Rounded, shrubby plant that adapts well to indoor growing. It has oval or lance-shaped foliage, and tubular flowers that open into five round lobes. Blooms appear in clusters at the ends of the branches.

**Selected species and varieties.** *C. infundibuliformis* has shiny, wavy-edged, 2- to 5-inch leaves that clothe 12-inch plants. The flowers appear primarily in spring and summer.

**Growing conditions.** Firecracker flower needs bright light, a warm room and high humidity; if humidity is too low, leaves will curl and plants will not flower. The potting medium should be extra rich, and kept evenly moist at all times during the growth and flowering periods. Fertilize every two weeks when the plant is growing or flowering. During fall and winter, allow the medium to dry out slightly between waterings, and do not fertilize. If plants become leggy, the growing tips can be

CATTLEYA HYBRID

COLUMNEA MICROPHYLLA

CROSSANDRA INFUNDIBULIFORMIS

CYCLAMEN PERSICUM

EPIPHYLLUM HYBRID

EPISCIA DIANTHIFLORA

pinched to encourage compactness. Take cuttings to root new plants at any time of year, or start new plants from seed. Spider mites can damage firecracker flower, but few if any diseases attack it.

**Cuphea** see Dictionary of Annuals, page 200

**Cyclamen** (SIK-la-men or SY-kla-men)
Persian violet

Tuberous perennial, one species of which is grown as a houseplant. Leaves form at the base of the plant, are heart-shaped and are marbled in light green, gray or silver on the upper surfaces. The flowers are held high above the foliage.

**Selected species and varieties.** *C. persicum*, florists' cyclamen, generally grows 8 to 10 inches tall, but miniature varieties grow only 4 to 6 inches high. The leaves grow up to 5½ inches across. The flowers are up to 2 inches long and are white, pink, rose, red, magenta, lavender or purple, with a purplish blotch at the base. Some varieties have frilled petals.

**Growing conditions.** Cyclamen needs cool temperature, high humidity and bright light to survive in the house. The potting medium must be very rich and moist at all times. Do not allow water to fall into the crown of the plant during watering, as this may cause crown rot; bottom watering may help prevent this problem. When plants are growing, fertilize once a month; when they are blooming, fertilize every two weeks. After a cyclamen has ceased blooming, gradually withhold water and stop fertilizing. When the foliage has turned yellow, let the plant dry out and store it in its pot in a dark, 45° F area for at least three months. Then bring it back indoors and start watering to encourage new growth. Plants generally flower in winter and spring and rest over the summer when temperatures are high. If the tubers are large, they may be divided in early fall before new growth starts. Cyclamen may also be grown from seed. Botrytis blight, spider and cyclamen mites and thrips may attack cyclamen.

**Daffodil** see Dictionary of Bulbs, page 292

**Epiphyllum** (ep-i-FY-lum)
Orchid cactus

A cactus that is known as jungle cactus because it requires higher humidity, more water and richer soil than desert cactus. The branches are flat, lobed and arching. The flowers are large, tubular and fragrant, and have flaring petals that open into a cup or funnel shape to reveal showy stamens. Some species have flowers that open only at night; others are day-blooming.

**Selected species and varieties.** *Epiphyllum* hybrids have showy flowers of white, yellow, pink, red, blue or purple, many of which bloom in winter; the others, in spring. The flowers are luminescent and may be up to 7 inches long. Because of its arching branches, orchid cactus is suited to a hanging basket.

**Growing conditions.** Grow orchid cactus where temperature and humidity are average and light is bright. Grow in cool temperatures to promote flowering. The potting medium should be slightly rich. In winter, allow the medium to dry slightly between waterings. When flower buds form, increase watering so that the medium is kept evenly moist. If flower buds drop, the plant is not receiving enough water. Avoid moving the plant after flower buds have formed, since any disturbance may cause the buds to drop. After the plant has flowered, pinch it back to keep it compact, and start monthly fertilizing, stopping in fall. The cuttings can be used to root new plants. Orchid cactus may be attacked by spider mites and may develop rot and wilt diseases.

**Episcia** (e-PIS-ee-a)
Carpet plant

Tropical plant in the gesneriad family that adapts to the indoors. The plant has long, slender stems that produce small plantlets at their ends. The leaves are 2 to 5 inches across, oval, and hairy. The flowers are 1 to 1½ inches long, tubular to bell-shaped, five-lobed, and bloom in spring and summer. Because the long stems droop gracefully, carpet plant makes an excellent display in a hanging basket.

**Selected species and varieties.** *E. dianthiflora*, lace flower vine, has soft, hairy, 1½-inch green leaves that are often red-veined, and white flowers.

**Growing conditions.** Grow carpet plant in a warm, humid room where light is bright. The growing medium should be extra rich and evenly moist. Do not allow cold water to touch the leaves, or they may spot. Fertilize monthly during spring and summer. After the plant flowers, cut it back to encourage new growth, and pinch the new growth to encourage fullness. Propagate by rooting the plantlets that form at the ends of the stems, or from stem cuttings. Carpet plant is vulnerable to spider mites, whiteflies, mealybugs and botrytis blight.

**Euphorbia** see Dictionary of Perennials, page 246
**Firecracker flower** see *Crossandra*
**Firecracker plant** see Dictionary of Annuals, page 200
**Flamingo flower** see *Anthurium*
**Four-leaf clover** see *Oxalis*
**Freesia** see Dictionary of Bulbs, page 292
**Fuchsia** see Dictionary of Annuals, page 200
**Gardenia** see Dictionary of Trees and Shrubs, page 426
**Gazania** see Dictionary of Grasses and Ground Covers, page 160
**Geranium** see Dictionary of Annuals, page 200

## Gloriosa (glor-ee-O-sa)
Gloriosa lily

Tuberous, vining perennial. The flowers are yellow, red or purple, and have wavy or crisped margins.

**Selected species and varieties.** *G. superba* has weak stems that grow 3 to 5 feet in height. The leaves are oblong to lance-shaped and 4 to 6 inches long. The flowers are green at first, then yellow with red tips, then change to solid red, and have 3-inch petals. Plants bloom in late summer and fall.

**Growing conditions.** Grow gloriosa lily in warm temperatures, high humidity and direct light. Plant in soilless, well-drained medium, and keep it evenly moist when the plant is growing or flowering. Fertilize every two weeks during the growing and flowering period. Plants should be staked. Plant tubers 3 inches deep in winter for bloom the following summer and fall. After the plants have finished blooming, withhold water and allow them to go dormant. Start watering again the following winter. Propagate gloriosa lily by division of the tubers, by offsets, or from seed. Gloriosa lily is immune to attack by insects and diseases.

**Gloxinia** see *Sinningia*
**Goldfish plant** see *Columnea*

**Grape hyacinth** see Dictionary of Bulbs, page 292
**Heliotrope** see Dictionary of Annuals, page 200
**Heliotropium** see Dictionary of Annuals, page 200
**Hibiscus** see Dictionary of Annuals, page 200

## Hippeastrum (hip-ee-AS-trum)
Amaryllis

Tropical bulb that has narrow to strap-shaped leaves that grow from the base of the plant. Flower clusters have multiple blooms on the tops of stems.

**Selected species and varieties.** *Hippeastrum* hybrids have trumpet-shaped, 4- to 8-inch flowers that range in color from white to pink, orange, yellow and red. Up to four blooms appear on each 18-inch stem. Plants bloom in winter or spring. The leaves may appear with or after the flowers.

**Growing conditions.** Grow amaryllis in a warm room in direct light and high humidity. Plant bulbs half-extending above a rich, well-drained, soilless medium. Plant one bulb per pot, with 1 inch between the pot rim and the bulb. Water the plant after potting, and do not water it again until growth starts. Then keep the medium evenly moist during growth and flowering. Fertilize every two weeks from the time growth starts until midsummer, when the foliage will turn yellow and die down. Keep plants dry and store them in a cool, dark area at 50° F until four to six weeks before flowers are desired. Then the plants should be watered once again and the growth process repeated as above. Propagate by dividing the bulbs or by removing the small bulblets that form at the base of the main bulb *(see Chapter 6)*; plants may be grown from seed but will not come true to variety. Mealybugs, scales and spider mites can attack amaryllis; botrytis blight, leaf spot and virus are common diseases.

## Hoya (HOY-a)
Wax vine

Genus of vining plants, two species of which are grown indoors. The leaves are thick and fleshy or leathery; the flowers are small, waxy and bloom in clusters. Because of its vining habit, wax vine is excellent in a hanging basket.

**Selected species and varieties.** *H. bella,* miniature wax plant, has leaves that are dull green, oval to lance-shaped, and grow to 1¼ inches long.

GLORIOSA SUPERBA

HIPPEASTRUM HYBRID

HOYA BELLA

HYDRANGEA MACROPHYLLA

JASMINUM NITIDUM

JUSTICIA CARNEA

The flowers are ½ inch across, fragrant, and white with a light pink to purple center. Plants at first grow upright to 1 foot high; the branches then droop to form a plant 1½ feet across.

**Growing conditions.** Miniature wax plant should be grown in a room with average to warm temperature, average humidity and direct light. Plant in a soilless medium; keep the medium evenly moist when the plant is in flower, and allow it to dry between waterings at other times. Fertilize every month from spring to early fall. Plants will not flower until they are mature. Flowers are produced repeatedly on leafless spurs which should not be pruned away. The stems can be allowed to trail or trained on a trellis. Propagate by stem cuttings in spring. Wax vine is pestered by mealybugs and aphids, but is generally disease-free.

**Hyacinth** see Dictionary of Bulbs, page 292

**Hydrangea** (hy-DRAN-jee-a)

Deciduous shrub, one species of which can be grown indoors. Plants naturally bloom in spring and summer, but can be purchased in bloom or forced to bloom out of season. Flowers are white, pink or blue.

**Selected species and varieties.** *H. macrophylla,* French hydrangea, has 2- to 6-inch leaves that are shiny, textured, serrated, oval and dark green. The flowers are pink or blue and bloom in dense, rounded clusters. Indoors, hydrangea grows 1½ to 2 feet tall.

**Growing conditions.** Place hydrangea in a room where temperature is average, humidity is average to high, and light is direct. The medium should be soilless and evenly moist at all times. Purchased plants do not need to be fertilized. After the flowers have faded, plants may be moved into the garden. New plants can be propagated by cuttings. To force your own hydrangeas into bloom, plants should be potted in fall and placed outdoors in a dark cold frame for six weeks to induce flower buds before being moved indoors. Temperature must drop below 40° F for flower buds to form. Tall plants may need to be staked. The flower color of hydrangea can be changed by manipulating the pH. Blue flowers require an acidic medium; pink flowers require an alkaline medium. Hydrangea is susceptible to attack from aphids, spider mites, root knot nematodes, mildew, botrytis blight and leaf spot.

**Impatiens** see Dictionary of Annuals, page 200
**Ipomoea** see Dictionary of Annuals, page 200
**Iris** see Dictionary of Perennials, page 246
**Jasmine** see *Jasminum*

**Jasminum** (JAS-mi-num)
Jasmine

Vining tropical plant, with primarily divided leaves and clusters of star-shaped flowers. Most species have fragrant flowers that are used in making perfume.

**Selected species and varieties.** *J. nitidum,* angel-wing jasmine, is a semivining plant that has 3-inch leaves. The flower buds are reddish and open into white, very fragrant, ¾-inch flowers.

**Growing conditions.** Angel-wing jasmine prefers average temperature, direct light and average to high humidity. Grow it in well-drained soilless medium and keep the medium evenly moist during spring and summer. In fall and winter, allow the medium to dry slightly between waterings. Fertilize monthly during spring and summer. After the plant has bloomed, prune it back to 6 inches high. Provide plants with a trellis, a wire hoop or another support. Plants benefit from being placed outdoors in the summer. Propagate from stem cuttings taken in summer. Mealybugs, scales and whiteflies may attack; leaf spot, root rot and virus diseases may also cause problems.

**Justicia** (jus-TIS-ee-a)
Water willow

Tropical shrub, two species of which are grown as houseplants. The leaves are lance-shaped to oval; the flowers are tubular and two-lipped.

**Selected species and varieties.** *J. carnea,* Brazilian plume flower, has oval to oblong 4- to 8-inch leaves with prominent veins. The flowers are rose-pink to purple and bloom throughout the year in spikes at the ends of the stems. Plants may be grown in hanging baskets and are most attractive if kept pruned to 1 to 2 feet in width.

**Growing conditions.** Grow plume flower in a warm room with bright light and high humidity. The growing medium should be rich, soilless, and evenly moist. If a plant ceases to flower in winter, allow the soil to dry slightly between waterings. Fertilize every two weeks in spring and summer. In spring, cut the plant back by half, and occasionally pinch out growing tips to keep the plant compact. Propagate from stem cuttings or from seed. Brazilian plume flower can be attacked by scales and is not generally susceptible to diseases.

**Kafir lily** see Dictionary of Bulbs, page 292

**Kalanchoe** (kal-an-KO-ee)

Genus of succulent plants, several species of which can be grown as houseplants. Some species are grown for their unusual leaves; others for their clusters of bright flowers.

**Selected species and varieties.** *K. blossfeldiana* grows 6 to 12 inches high. The leaves are oval, waxy, thick, 1 to 3 inches long, and dark green edged with red lobes. The flowers are ¼ to ½ inch long, red, orange or yellow, and bloom at the tops of the plants. Flowers naturally bloom in late winter and spring, but can be forced into bloom at other times of year.

**Growing conditions.** Place kalanchoe in a room with average temperature, average humidity, and bright to direct light. To intensify flower color and extend blooming, place plants in a cool room after the flower buds have formed. Grow in well-drained, soilless medium and allow it to dry between waterings. Do not allow water to touch the leaves, which may cause spotting and disease. Fertilize every two weeks when the plants are growing; do not fertilize when they are in flower. To force kalanchoe to bloom in summer, fall and early winter, place it in a totally dark place for 14 hours a night for six weeks. Propagate new plants from stem or leaf cuttings, or from seed. Aphids and spider mites may attack; mildew and root and crown rot are potential diseases.

**Lace flower vine** see *Episcia*
**Lantana** see Dictionary of Grasses and Ground Covers, page 160
**Lilium** see Dictionary of Bulbs, page 292
**Lily** see Dictionary of Bulbs, page 292
**Lycoris** see Dictionary of Bulbs, page 292
**Magic lily** see Dictionary of Bulbs, page 292
**Morning glory** see Dictionary of Annuals, page 200
**Muscari** see Dictionary of Bulbs, page 292
**Narcissus** see Dictionary of Bulbs, page 292

**Nasturtium** see Dictionary of Annuals, page 200
**Nerium** see Dictionary of Trees and Shrubs, page 426
**Oleander** see Dictionary of Trees and Shrubs, page 426
**Orchid cactus** see *Epiphyllum*

**Oxalis** (OK-sal-is)

Genus of annuals and perennials, some of which can be grown as houseplants. Plants grow from bulbs, tubers or rhizomes and have three-part, cloverlike leaves at the base of the plant. Flowers are available in all colors except blue; they are single and five-petaled and bloom indoors from fall through spring. Blooms open only on sunny days and close up at night.

**Selected species and varieties.** *O. deppei*, four-leaf clover, lucky clover, grows to 1¼ feet tall, has four oval leaflets and red flowers.

**Growing conditions.** Grow oxalis in a cool to average room where light is direct and humidity is average. Plant in a well-drained, soilless medium that is allowed to dry out slightly between waterings. Fertilize monthly during the growing and flowering period. After the plant has flowered, the foliage turns brown and dies back. Store the plants in their pots until fall, when they should be returned to the house and the process repeated. Plants can be propagated by division or from seed.

**Peace lily** see *Spathiphyllum*
**Pelargonium** see Dictionary of Annuals, page 200
**Persian violet** see *Cyclamen*
**Pot marigold** see Dictionary of Annuals, page 200
**Rain lily** see Dictionary of Bulbs, page 292
**Rhododendron** see Dictionary of Trees and Shrubs, page 426
**Rose** see Dictionary of Roses, page 360
**Rosemary** see Dictionary of Trees and Shrubs, page 426
**Rosmarinus** see Dictionary of Trees and Shrubs, page 426

**Saintpaulia** (saint-PAUL-ee-a)
African violet

Genus of plants in the gesneriad family, one species of which is grown as a houseplant. Leaves are heart-shaped and hairy, and grow in a basal rosette. The flowers resemble violets and are flat and five-lobed.

KALANCHOE BLOSSFELDIANA

OXALIS DEPPEI

SAINTPAULIA IONANTHA

SINNINGIA SPECIOSA

SPATHIPHYLLUM × HYBRIDUM

**Selected species and varieties.** *S. ionantha* grows 4 to 6 inches high. Some varieties have green leaves; others have bronze or variegated leaves. There are many hybrids that have white, pink, rose, blue, purple or two-toned flowers that are 1 inch across. There are also varieties with ruffled or frilled petals. The hybrids flower freely and will bloom throughout the year if given enough light.

**Growing conditions.** African violet prefers a place where temperature is warm, light is bright and humidity is medium to high. Plant them in a rich, soilless, well-drained growing medium, and keep it evenly moist at all times. Be careful when watering not to drop water on the leaves, or they will spot, and water only with warm water to prevent rings from developing on the leaves. When planting, ensure that the crown of the plant is above the level of the medium. Plants can be grown under fluorescent lights, especially in the winter, to ensure maximum blooming. Fertilize twice a month when the plant is growing and flowering. Leaves that touch the rim of the pot are sometimes killed by contact with the soluble salts that build up on the rim. To prevent this, line the rim with aluminum foil or wax. New plants are propagated from leaf cuttings, by division, or from seed. Insects that may attack are aphids, thrips, mealybugs, root knot nematodes and spider and cyclamen mites. Diseases include botrytis blight, and crown and root rot. Keep the air circulating freely around the plants to reduce the chance of disease.

**Scarlet basket vine**
see *Aeschynanthus*
**Scilla** see Dictionary of
Bulbs, page 292
**Senecio** see Dictionary of
Annuals, page 200

**Sinningia** (si-NIN-jee-a)

Genus of tuberous flowering plants in the gesneriad family. Leaves are basal; flowers are bell-shaped to cylindrical, and open into five lobes.

**Selected species and varieties.** *S. speciosa,* gloxinia, grows up to 12 inches high and has oval to oblong, 8-inch, broad, hairy leaves. The flowers are lavender, rose, pink, red, white or yellow, are often banded or spotted, and bloom mostly in summer. New varieties may bloom at any time of

year. The flowers appear in clusters in the center of the plant, and are trumpet-shaped with frilled edges.

**Growing conditions.** Gloxinia likes warm temperature, bright light and high humidity. Plant the tubers in a rich, soilless medium, and keep it evenly moist while the plant is growing or flowering. Fertilize every month during the growing and flowering period. After the flowers fade, withhold water and allow the foliage to die down. Store the tubers in a dry medium; repot them when new growth appears, in two to four months, and start the process over again. New plants can be grown from division, by leaf cuttings or from seed. Gloxinia can be attacked by aphids, spider mites, thrips, virus, and root, leaf and crown rot.

**Spathe flower** see *Spathiphyllum*

**Spathiphyllum** (spath-i-FIL-um)
Spathe flower, white flag, peace lily

Tropical perennial that can be grown indoors. The leaves are glossy green and oblong. The flowers are white, fragrant, and tiny, and bloom along a tail-like structure called a spadix. The spadix is surrounded by a white or green bract called a spathe. Flowers appear most abundantly in spring and summer.

**Selected species and varieties.** *S.* x *hybridum* is a group of hybrids that have narrow, oblong, 10-inch leaves and grow to 2½ feet high. The spathes are large and white and have green midribs on the undersides.

**Growing conditions.** Grow spathe flower where temperature is warm, light is limited to bright, and humidity is medium to high. Plant in soilless growing medium and keep it evenly moist at all times. Fertilize every two weeks from spring through fall. Dust or wash the foliage frequently. Plants can be divided at any time of year. Spathe flower is not troubled by insects but is susceptible to leaf spot diseases.

**Spider lily** see Dictionary of
Bulbs, page 292
**Spurge** see Dictionary of
Perennials, page 246
**Squill** see Dictionary of
Bulbs, page 292

## Strelitzia (stre-LITS-ee-a)
### Bird-of-paradise

Subtropical perennial that can be grown as a houseplant. The leaves are large, erect and grow in clumps from the base of the plant. The flowers grow from a rigid, green, boatlike bract and resemble the head of an exotic bird.

**Selected species and varieties.** *S. reginae* grows 3 to 6 feet tall. The leaves are 1 to 1½ feet long, stiff, oblong, leathery, pointed, and blue-green with a yellow or red midrib. The flowers have orange or yellow petals and a deep blue tongue that emerges from the bract, which is edged in purple or red.

**Growing conditions.** Place bird-of-paradise in a room where temperature is average, light is direct, and humidity is medium to high. Plants should be grown in soilless, well-drained medium that is allowed to dry out slightly between waterings in winter and kept barely moist the rest of the year. Fertilize every two weeks during spring and summer. Plants may be propagated by division, or from seed, but those grown from seed take several years before they bloom. Bird-of-paradise is susceptible to scales, mealybugs and root rot.

## Streptocarpus (strep-toh-KAR-pus)
### Cape primrose

Large genus of annuals and perennials in the gesneriad family. Flowers are funnel-shaped, five-lobed and bloom throughout the year, but most abundantly in late spring through fall.

**Selected species and varieties.** *S.* x *hybridus* is a large group of hybrids that have 10- to 12-inch oblong, scalloped, wrinkled leaves that grow in a rosette at the base of the plant. The flowers are 2 to 5 inches long, nodding, and may be white, pink, rose, red, blue or purple, often with a throat of a contrasting color. The flowers bloom in small clusters at the top of thin, leafless stems.

**Growing conditions.** *S.* x *hybridus* likes a spot where temperatures are cool in winter and average the rest of the year. The light should be bright; the humidity high. Grow in well-drained, rich, soilless medium and from spring through fall, keep it evenly moist. In winter, water only enough to keep the plant from wilting. Fertilize twice a month during spring and summer. Use a shallow pot to help

reduce the chance of root rot. Grow new plants of *S.* x *hybridus* by division in winter, from leaf cuttings taken in spring or summer, or from seed sown in winter or spring. Aphids, mealybugs and thrips may attack; root rot is the most common disease.

**Tailflower** see *Anthurium*
**Thunbergia** see Dictionary of Annuals, page 200
**Treasure flower** see Dictionary of Grasses and Ground Covers, page 160
**Tropaeolum** see Dictionary of Annuals, page 200
**Tulip** see Dictionary of Bulbs, page 292
**Tulipa** see Dictionary of Bulbs, page 292
**Water willow** see *Justicia*
**Wax plant** see *Hoya*
**Wax vine** see *Hoya*
**White flag** see *Spathiphyllum*

## Zantedeschia (zan-te-DES-kee-a)
### Calla lily

Rhizomatous plant that has arrow-shaped leaves. Flowers are surrounded by a showy, colorful spathe. The spathe flares back at the top, and the edges curl under. The flowers appear from fall through spring.

**Selected species and varieties.** *Z. elliottiana,* golden calla, grows 2 feet high and has 2-foot leaves that are spotted in white. The spathe is 6 inches long, bright yellow on the inside, and greenish yellow on the outside.

**Growing conditions.** Grow calla lily where light is bright and humidity is average. They prefer average temperature. The medium should be soilless, rich, well drained and constantly moist. Fertilize monthly after the flowers appear. After the plant has finished flowering, allow the medium to dry out between waterings for several months to give the plant a rest. Plants may be allowed to go completely dormant in summer; if they are to remain growing, place them in bright light. Propagate new plants by division in late summer or early fall, by removing the offshoots or from seed. Mealybugs, spider mites and root rot may attack.

**Zebra plant** see *Aphelandra*
**Zephyr lily** see Dictionary of Bulbs, page 292
**Zephyranthes** see Dictionary of Bulbs, page 292

STRELITZIA REGINAE

STREPTOCARPUS × HYBRIDUS

ZANTEDESCHIA ELLIOTTIANA

# INDEX

*Numerals in italics indicate illustrations of the subject mentioned. Numerals in bold indicate dictionary descriptions of the subject mentioned.*

# PICTURE CREDITS

**The sources for the illustrations in this book are listed below.**
Watercolor paintings by Nicholas Fasciano and Yin Yi except pages 150-5, 182, 236, 242-5, 290-1, 316-23, 356, 418-22, 466, 470, 502-5, 548: Lorraine Moseley Epstein. 267-9, 284: Catherine Anderson. 462-3, 467: Sanford Kossin. Map page 143, digitized by Richard Furno, inked by John Drummond.

**The sources for the photographs in this book are listed by page and numbered from top to bottom.**
8 Stephen Still • 10 Robert E. Lyons/Color Advantage • 12 Thomas Eltzroth • 18 Horti-cultural Photography, Corvallis, OR • 20 Pamela Harper • 22 Renée Comet • 26 Pamela Zilly • 30 Horticultural Photography, Corvallis, OR • 32, 33 Pamela Zilly • 34 Thomas Eltzroth • 36 Horticultural Photography, Corvallis, OR • 38 Michael Selig • 40 Horticultural Photography, Corvallis, OR • 44 Joanne Pavia • 46 Laurie Black • 48 Thomas Eltzroth • 50 Paul Kingsley • 52 Stephen Still • 54 Ken Druse • 56 Michael Selig • 58, 60 Horti-cultural Photography, Corvallis, OR • 62 Bob Grant • 65 Saxon Holt • 68 Joy Spurr • 70 Renée Comet • 72 Bob Grant • 74 Pamela Harper • 76 Walter Chandoha • 78 Michael Dirr • 80 Horticultural Photography, Corvallis, OR • 82 Bob Grant • 84 Horticultural Photography, Corvallis, OR • 82 Bob Grant • 84 Horticultural Photography, Corvallis, OR • 86 Mike Lowe • 91 Michael Dirr • 94 Thomas Eltzroth • 97, 98 Norm Thomas • 100 Bob Grant • 102 John Colwell/Grant Heilman Photography • 105 Allan Armitage • 113 Bob Grant • 115 Ann Reilly • 118, 120 Horticultural Photography, Corvallis, OR • 124 Jim Strawsen/Grant Heilman Photography • 126 Lefever/Grushow/Grant Heilman Photography • 130 Lou Jacobs, Jr./Grant Heilman Photography • 132 John Colwell/Grant Heilman Photography • 134 Grant Heilman Photography • 136 Jerry Howard/Photo-Nats • 138, 141 Horticultural Photography, Corvallis, OR • 156, 159, 160 Pamela Harper • 161 1- Horticultural Photography, Corvallis, OR, 2- 3- Pamela Harper, 4- Derek Fell • 162 Pamela Harper • 163 1- 2- 4- Pamela Harper, 3- John L. Smith/Photo-Nats • 164 1- Ann Reilly/Photo-Nats, 2- Norm Thomas, 3- Horticultural Photography, Corvallis, OR, 4- Pamela Harper • 165 Pamela Harper • 166 1- Derek Fell, 2- Tony Avent, 3- Susan Roth

• 167 1- Pamela Harper, 2- Ann Reilly/Photo-Nats, 3- Jerry Pavia • 168 1- 4- Pamela Harper, 2- Robert Lyons/Color Advantage, 3- Ann Reilly/Photo-Nats • 169 Pamela Harper • 170 1- 3- Pamela Harper, 2- A. J. Koski • 171 Pamela Harper • 172 1- Pamela Harper, 2- John L. Smith/Photo-Nats, 3- David M. Stone/Photo Nats, 4- Joanne Pavia • 173 Pamela Harper • 174 1- Pamela Harper, 2- Ann Reilly, 3- Joanne Pavia • 175 1- Pamela Harper, 2- 3- Richard Simon • 176 1-3- Pamela Harper, 2- Norm Thomas • 177 1- 2- 3- Pamela Harper, 4- Tony Avent • 178 Saxon Holt • 180 Jerry Pavia • 182 Audrey Gibson • 184 Steven Still • 186 Cole Burrell • 188 Saxon Holt • 190 Pamela Harper • 200 1- Horticultural Photography, Corvallis, OR, 2- 3 Pamela Harper • 201 1- 2- Pamela Harper, 3- William D. Adams • 202 1- Derek Fell, 2- 3- Joanne Pavia • 203 1- Steven Still, 2- Pamela Harper, 3- Michael Dirr • 204 Pamela Harper • 205 1- 2- Pamela Harper, 3- Saxon Holt • 206 1-3- Pamela Harper, 2- Horticultural Photography, Corvallis, OR • 207 1- Pamela Harper, 2- Mike Heger, 3- Robert Lyons/Color Advantage • 208 1- 2- Horticultural Photography, Corvallis, OR, 3- Robert Lyons/Color Advantage • 209 1- William D. Adams, 2- Stephen Still, 3- Pamela Harper • 210 1- Joanne Pavia, 2- Pamela Harper • 211 1- 3- Pamela Harper, 2- Runk/Schoenberger/Grant Heilman Photography • 212 1- Pamela Harper, 2- Robert Lyons/Color Advantage, 3- William D. Adams • 213 1- Steven Still, 2- Pamela Harper, 3- Michael McKinley • 214 1- Saxon Holt, 2- Pamela Harper, 3- Patricia Christopher, 4- Ann Reilly • 215 1- David Scheid, 2- Robert Lyons/Color Advantage, 3- Thomas Eltzroth, 4- Robert Lyons/Color Advantage • 216 1- Karen Bussolini, 2- Maggie Oster, 3- Jerry Pavia, 4- Pamela Harper • 217 1- Joy Spurr, 2- 3- Pamela Harper • 218 1- Hollen Johnson, 2- 3- Pamela Harper • 219 1- Pamela Harper, 2- Michael Dirr, 3- Gary Mottaw • 220 1- 2- Ann Reilly, 3- Saxon Holt • 221 1- Pamela Harper, 2- Jerry Pavia, 3- Robert Lyons/Color Advantage • 222 Derek Fell • 224 Saxon Holt • 226-7 Saxon Holt • 228 Eric L. Heyer/Grant Heilman Photography • 230 Felice Frankel • 231 Andy Alonso • 232 Ann Reilly • 236 Bob Grant • 246-8 Pamela Harper • 249 1- 3- 4- Pamela Harper, 2- Paul Kingsley • 250 1- Cole Burrell, 2- Pamela Harper, 3- 4- Horticultural Photography, Corvallis, OR • 251 Pamela Harper • 252 1- 2- Pamela Harper, 3- Ann Reilly • 253 Pamela Harper • 254 1- 2- Pamela Harper, 3- Grant Heilman Photography • 255 1- 2- Pamela Harper,

3- Saxon Holt • 256 1- Robert E. Lyons/Color Advantage, 2- 3- Pamela Harper • 257 Pamela Harper • 258 1- Steven Still, 2- Pamela Harper, 3- Derek Fell • 259-60 Pamela Harper • 261 1- 2- 3- Pamela Harper, 4- Stephen Still • 262 1- Saxon Holt, 2- 3- Pamela Harper, 4- Steven Still • 263 Pamela Harper • 264 Horticultural Photography, Corvallis, OR • 266 Steven Still • 270 Karen Bussolini • 272 Saxon Holt • 274 Renée Comet • 276 Maggie Oster • 278 Michael Dirr • 280 Derek Fell • 282 Mark Gibson • 284 Horticultural Photography, Corvallis, OR • 292 1- 2- Breck's Dutch Bulbs, Peoria, IL, 3- Thomas Eltzroth • 293 1- Pamela Harper, 2- J. C. Raulston, 3- Saxon Holt • 294 1- Maggie Oster, 2- Pamela Harper, 3- 4- Michael Dirr • 295 1- Horticultural Photography, Corvallis, OR, 2- Saxon Holt, 3- Robert E. Lyons/Color Advantage • 296 1- Emily Johnson/Envision, 2- Pamela Harper, 3- Thomas Eltzroth • 297 1- Anita Sabanese, 2- Robert E. Lyons/Color Advantage, 3- David M. Stone/Photo-Nats • 298 1- Pamela Harper, 2- Steven Still, 3- Gottlieb Hampfler • 299 1- Thomas Eltzroth, 2- Joy Spurr, 3- J. C. Raulston • 300 1- Lefever/Grushow/Grant Heilman Photography, 2- Thomas Eltzroth, 3- Derek Fell • 301 1- 3- Joanne Pavia, 2- Ann Reilly/Photo-Nats • 302 1- Pamela Harper, 2- Breck's Dutch Bulbs, Peoria, IL, 3- Thomas Eltzroth • 303 1- Derek Fell, 2- Maggie Oster, 3- Joanne Pavia • 304 Wanda La Rock/Envision, 2- Joanne Pavia, 3- Pat Toops • 305 1- Thomas Eltzroth, 2- Jerry Pavia, 3- Pamela Harper • 306 1- J. C. Raulston, 2- 3- Robert E. Lyons/Color Advantage • 307 1- Horticultural Photography, Corvallis, OR, 2- Derek Fell, 3- Michael Landis • 308 1- Robert E. Lyons/Color Advantage, 2- 3- Pamela Harper • 309 1- Pamela Harper, 2- Breck's Dutch Bulbs, Peoria, IL, 3- Horticultural Photography, Corvallis, OR • 310 1- Dwight Ellefsen/Envision, 2- Breck's Dutch Bulbs, Peoria, IL, 3- Pamela Harper • 311 1- Derek Fell, 2- Thomas Eltzroth, 3- Derek Fell • 312 1- Horticultural Photography, Corvallis, OR, 2- John J. Smith/Photo-Nats, 3- Walter Chandoha • 313 1- Derek Fell, 2- Steven Still, 3- Lefever/Grushow/Grant Heilman Photography • 314 Robert Lowe • 316 Maggie Oster • 324 Thomas Eltzroth • 328 Pamela Harper • 330 Horticultural Photography, Corvallis, OR • 331 Pamela Zilly • 332 1- Pamela Harper, 2- Selz, Seabolt & Associates, Inc. Chicago, IL • 324 Renée Comet • 336 Saxon Holt • 340 Pamela Harper • 342 Robert Lyons • 344 Mark Gibson • 346 Horticultural Photography, Corvallis, OR • 350 Jack Potter • 360 1- Jack Potter, 2- Pamela Harper, 3- Thomas Eltzroth • 361 1- 3- Thomas Eltzroth, 2- Jack Potter. • 362 1- Jack Potter, 2- Thomas Eltzroth, 3- Bob Grant, 4- Alice Garik • 363 1- Thomas Eltzroth, 2- Saxon Holt, 3- Horticultural Photography, Corvallis, OR, 4- Jack Potter • 364 1- 4- Thomas Eltzroth, 2- 3- Jack Potter • 365 1- 3- 4- Thomas Eltzroth, 2- Jack Potter • 366 1- Robert Lowe, 2- 3- Thomas Eltzroth, 4- Jack Potter • 367 1- Joanne Pavia, 2- 3- Thomas Eltzroth, 4- Pamela Harper • 368 1- Pamela Harper, 2- 3- Jack Potter, 4- Thomas Eltzroth • 369 1- Thomas Eltzroth, 2- Robert Lowe, 3- Bob Grant, 4- Alice Garik • 370 1- Roses of Yesterday and Today, Watsonville, CA, 2- Albert H. Ford, 3- Saxon Holt • 371 1- 4- Jack Potter, 2- 3- Robert Lowe • 372 1- Pamela Harper, 2- 4- Robert Lowe, 3- Jack Potter • 373 1- 3- Thomas Eltzroth, 2- Joanne Pavia, 4- Saxon Holt • 374 1- Pamela Harper, 2- Horticultural Photography, Corvallis, OR, 3- Thomas Eltzroth • 375 1- Alice Garik, 2- Joy Spurr, 3- Robert Alde, 4- Bob Grant • 376 1- Robert Lowe, 2- Jerry Pavia, 3- P. A. Haring, 4- Thomas Eltzroth • 377 1- Thomas Eltzroth, 2- Jack Potter, 3- Robert Lowe, 4- Maggie Oster • 378 1- Thomas Eltzroth, 2-Horticultural Photography, Corvallis, OR, 3- Pamela Harper, 4- Jack Potter • 379 1- Alice Garik, 2- Pamela Harper, 3- Ann Reilly, 4- Jack Potter • 380 Horticultural Photography, Corvallis, OR • 382, 385 Horticultural Photography, Corvallis, OR • 388 Pamela Harper • 390, 394 Horticultural Photography, Corvallis, OR • 396 Elvin McDonald • 398 Horticultural Photography, Corvallis, OR • 400 Pamela Harper • 402 Mark Gibson • 404, 407 Horticultural Photography, Corvallis, OR • 426 1- 1a- Paul Kingsley, 2- 2a- Horticultural Photography, Corvallis, OR, 3- 3a- Michael Dirr • 427 1- 1a- 2- 2a- Pamela Harper, 3- 3a Horticultural Photography, Corvallis, OR • 428 1- Pamela Harper, 1a- 4- 4a- Horticultural Photography, Corvallis, OR, 2- 2a- Bob Grant, 3- 3a- Pamela Harper • 429 1- 1a- 2- 2a- Pamela Harper, 3- 3a Horticultural Photography, Corvallis, OR • 430 1- 1a- Horticultural Photography, Corvallis, OR, 2- 2a- 3- 3a- Pamela Harper, 4- 4a- Michael Dirr • 431 1- 1a- 2- 2a- Michael Dirr, 3- 3a- Horticultural Photography, Corvallis, OR, • 432 1- 1a- 2- 3a- Michael Dirr, 2a- Darrell Apps, 3- Pamela Harper • 433 1- 1a- Pamela Harper, 2- 2a- Renée Comet, 3- John J. Smiths/Photo-Nats, 3a- David Cavagnaro • 434 1- 1a- Horticultural Photography, Corvallis, OR, 2- 2a- John J. Smith/Photo-Nats, 3- Paul Kingsley, 3a- Pamela Harper, 4- 4a- Michael Dirr • 435 1- 1a- 2- 2a- Pamela Harper, 3- 3a- Steven Still, 4- 4a- Michael Dirr • 436 1- 1a- 2- 2a- Pamela Harper, 3- Grant Heilman Photography, 3a- Michael Dirr • 437 1- Derek Fell, 1a- Al Bussewitz/Photo Nats, 2- 2a- 3- 3a- Pamela Harper • 438 1- 1a- 3- 3a- Pamela

Harper, 2- 2a- Horticultural Photography, Corvallis, OR • 439 Pamela Harper • 440 1- 1a- Michael Dirr, 2- 2a- 4- Pamela Harper • 441 1- Al Bussewitz/Photo-Nats, 1a- 2- 2a- Pamela Harper, 3- Steven Still, 3a- Michael Dirr • 442 1- 1a- Pamela Harper, 2- 2a- Horticultural Photography, Corvallis, OR, 3- 3a- Michael Dirr • 443 1- 1a- Grant Heilman Photography, 2- 2a- Pamela Harper, 3- 3a- Horticultural Photography, Corvallis, OR • 444 1- Horticultural Photography, Corvallis, OR, 1a- 2- Pamela Harper, 2a- Michael Dirr, 3- 3a- Bob Grant • 445 1- 1a- 3- 3a- Pamela Harper, 2- 2a- Michael Dirr • 446 1- 1a- Michael Dirr, 2- Stephen Still, 2a- 3- Pamela Harper, 3a- U. S. National Arboretum, 4- 4a- Michael Dirr • 447 1- 1a- 2- 2a- Pamela Harper, 3- 3a- Bob Grant • 448 1- 1a- 2- 2a- 3- 3a- Pamela Harper 4- 4a- Michael Dirr • 449 1- 1a- 2- 2a- Pamela Harper, 3- 3a- Bob Grant, 4- 4a- Thomas Eltzroth • 450 1- 1a- 2- Michael Dirr, 2a- Darrel Apps, 3- 3a- Eugene Memmler, 4- 4a- Horticultural Photography, Corvallis, OR • 451 1- Pamela Harper, 2- 2a- Michael Dirr, 3- 3a- Horticultural Photography, Corvallis, OR • 452 1- 1a- Pamela Harper, 2- 2a- 3- 3a- Horticultural Photography, Corvallis, OR, 4- 4a- Michael Dirr • 453 1- 1a- 2a- Pamela Harper, 2- Stephen Still, 3- 3a- Michael Dirr • 454 1- 2a- 3- Pamela Harper, 2- Michael Dirr, 3a- Horticultural Photography, Corvallis, OR, • 455 1- 1a- 2- 2a- Pamela Harper, 3- 3a- Horticultural Photography, Corvallis, OR • 456 1- 2- 2a- Horticultural Photography, Corvallis, OR, 3- 3a- Pamela Harper • 457 1- 1a- 4- 4a- Pamela Harper, 2- 2a- 3- 3a- Horticultural Photography, Corvallis, OR, 1a- Pamela Harper, 2- 2a- 4a- Saxon Holt, 3- Michael Dirr 4- Robert Fincham/Mitsch Nursery • 459 1- 1a- 3a- 4- 4a- Pamela Harper, 2- 2a- 3- Horticultural Photography, Corvallis, OR • 460 Walter Chandoha • 462 Larry Lefever/Grant Heilman Photography • 464 Walter Chandoha • 466 Walter Chandoha • 468 Walter Chandoha • 470 Derek Fell • 472 Williams D. Adams • 476 Bob Grant • 478 Walter Chandoha • 480 Walter Chandoha • 484 Horticultural Photography, Corvallis, OR • 486 Thomas Eltzroth • 488 Thomas Eltzroth • 496 Runk/Schoenberger/Grant Heilman Photography • 506 1- 2- Thomas Eltzroth • 507 1- Walter Chandoha, 2- Joanne Pavia • 508 1- Joanne Pavia, 2- Derek Fell, 3- Walter Chandoha • 509 1- Derek Fell, 2- 3- Thomas Eltzroth • 510 1- 3- Thomas Eltzroth, 2- Derek Fell • 511 1- Northrup King Co. 1988, 2- Grant Heilman Photography, 3- Ann Reilly • 512 1- William Isom, 2- 3- Walter Chandoha • 513 Derek Fell, 2- Walter Chandoha, 3- Thomas Eltzroth • 514 1- William D. Adams, 2- Walter Chandoha, 3- Derek Fell • 515 1- Ann Reilly, 2- Derek Fell, 3- Walter Chandoha • 516 1- 2- Thomas Eltzroth, 3- Derek Fell • 517 1- Dr. Gilbert McCollum, 2- Walter Chandoha, 3- Ann Reilly • 518 1- 3- Derek Fell, 2- Walter Chandoha, • 519 1- Thomas Eltzroth, 2- Walter Chandoha • 520 1- Thomas Eltzroth, 2- Horticultural Photography, Corvallis, OR, 3- Derek Fell • 521 1- 2- Walter Chandoha, 3- Derek Fell • 522 1- Thomas Eltzroth, 2- 3- Ann Reilly • 523 1- Derek Fell, 2- Ann Reilly, 3- Ivan Massan/Photo-Nats • 524 1- Thomas Eltzroth, 2- Ann Reilly, 3- Derek Fell • 525 1- Derek Fell, 2- Ann Reilly, 3- Walter Chandoha • 526 1- Thomas Eltzroth, 2- Walter Chandoha, 3- Ann Reilly, 4- Derek Fell • 527 1- William D. Adams, 2- John Smith/Photo-Nats, 3- Thomas Eltzroth • 528 Renée Comet • 530 Eric L. Heyer/Grant Heilman • 534, 536, 539, 542 Renée Comet • 544 Thomas Eltzroth • 552 1-2-4- Pamela Zilly, 3- Connie Toops • 553 1- 2- 4- Robert Lyons/Color Advantage, 3- 5- Pamela Zilly 554 1- 2- 3- Pamela Zilly, 4- Robert Lyons/Color Advantage • 555 1- 4- Pamela Zilly, 2- Barry Runk/Grant Heilman Photography, 3- Renée Comet • 556 1- Robert Lyons/Color Advantage, 2- 3- Pamela Zilly • 557 1- 2- 3- Robert Lyons/Color Advantage, 4- Pamela Harper, 5- Connie Toops • 558 1- Robert Lyons/Color Advantage, 2- Pamela Harper, 3- Connie Toops • 559 1- 2- Pamela Harper, 3- Pamela Zilly • 560 1- Pamela Zilly, 2- Robert Lyons/Color Advantage, 3- 4- Connie Toops • 561 1- Robert Lyons/Color Advantage, 2- Runk/Schoenberger, 3- Pamela Zilly • 562 1- Derek Fell, 2- Connie Toops, 3- Pamela Zilly • 563 1- Pamela Zilly, 2- Robert Lyons/Color Advantage, 3- Bob Grant • 564 1- Robert Lyons/Color Advantage, 2- Connie Toops, 3- Pamela Zilly • 565 1- 3- Robert Lyons/Color Advantage, 2- Pamela Zilly • 566 1- 3- Connie Toops, 2- Pamela Zilly • 567 1- Robert Lyons/Color Advantage, 2- Connie Toops, 3- Pamela Zilly • 568 1- Derek Fell, 2- Thomas Eltzroth, 3- Pamela Harper • 569 1- 2- Elvin McDonald, 3- Connie Toops, • 570 1- Harry Smith, 2- Maggie Oster, 3- John A. Lynch/Photo-Nats • 571 1- Olive Adams, 2- Maggie Oster, 3- Harry Smith/Horticultural Photographic Collection • 572 1- Thomas Eltzroth, 2- Elvin McDonald, 3- Olive Adams • 573 1- Thomas Eltzroth, 2- Elvin McDonald, 3- Connie Toops • 574 Lefever/Grushow/Grant Heilman Photography, 2- Maggie Oster • 575 1- Runk/Schoenberger/Grant Heilman Photography, 2- Thomas Eltzroth, 3- Pamela Harper.

# ACKNOWLEDGMENTS

**The editors wish to thank the following:**
All-American Rose Selections, Chicago, Illinois; American Rose Society, Shreveport, LA; Kurt Bluemel and Janet Draper, Kurt Bluemel Inc., Baldwin, MD; Lisa D. Bright, American Society for Horticultural Science, Alexandria, VA; Dr. H. Marc Cathey, Director, U.S. National Arboretum, Washington, DC; Nancy Denig, Denig Design Associates, Vienna, VA; Elizabeth C. Dudley, Ph.D.; Brent Heath, Daffodil Mart, Gloucester, VA; Dr. Charles G. Jeremias, President, American Rose Society, Newberry, SC; Monica Kilby, U.S. Botanic Garden, Washington, DC; National Climatic Data Center, Asheville, NC; Erik Neumann,

Public Information Specialist, U.S. National Arboretum, Washington, DC; Patrick Nutt, Longwood Gardens, Kennett Square, PA; Bill Rooney, American Forestry Association, Washington, DC; United States Department of Agriculture; United States Department of Commerce; Steve VanderMark, Cornell Cooperative Extension, Canton, NY; Kent Whealy, Seed Savers Exchange, Decorah, IA.

**The following persons also assisted in the preparation of this book:**
Solange Laberge, Julie Léger, Nicolas Moumouris, Jacques Proulx, Shirley Sylvain.

# THE FROST-DATE MAP AND PLANTING

Success with an annual bed or a vegetable garden depends on choosing the proper planting date. Timing is critical, because each plant needs the right soil and air temperatures, plus an adequate amount of sunlight each day, to get off to a strong start. To a great extent, those conditions depend on the calendar, on the locality and on the plants themselves.

Annuals are classified as hardy, half-hardy and tender. The hardy ones can withstand light frost and cool soil; they can be planted in early spring, as soon as the soil can be worked, usually four to six weeks before the last frost. Half-hardy annuals are best planted after the last frost, but the plants will survive an unexpected late frost. Tender annuals need warm weather and soil; they cannot be planted outdoors until all danger of frost has passed. Like annuals, some vegetables need cool soil to germinate and must therefore be planted a few weeks before the last spring frost; others need warm soil.

The map at right is a guide to determining planting dates in different regions for annuals and vegetables. It is based on average last frost dates compiled over a 30-year period by the U.S. Department of Commerce, and divides North America into nine regions. Region 1, for example—primarily Canada and the northernmost areas of the United States—has the longest winter and may have frost as late as mid-June. Region 9, which includes the southern areas of California, Florida and Texas, is free of frost as early as January 30—and in fact some parts of the region may never experience frost at all.

The regions on the map, like the frost dates, are to be used only as general guidelines. Within areas, frost-free dates can vary with altitude, and they can vary from year to year when temperatures are higher or lower than normal. For information specific to your area for a particular year, consult a local agricultural extension office or garden-supply center.

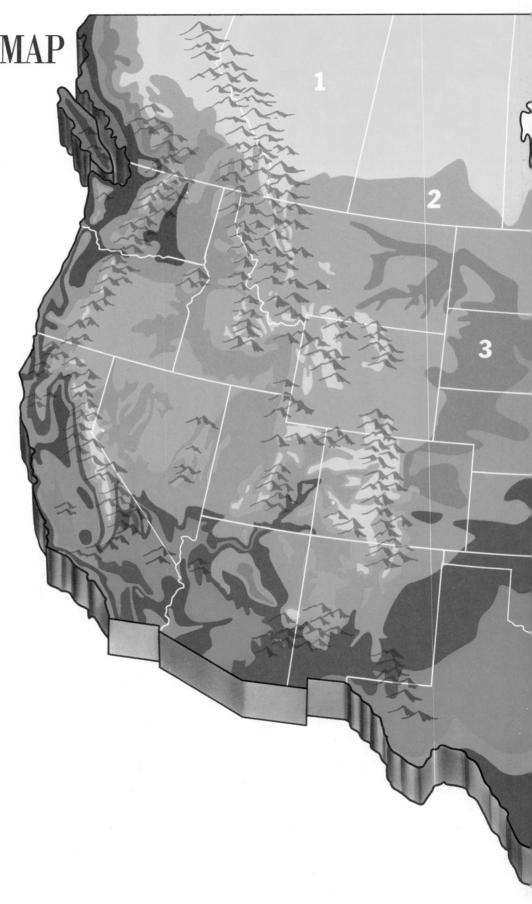